Masterplots

Fourth Edition

Masterplots

Fourth Edition

Volume 7
Madame Bovary—Night Flight

Editor

Laurence W. Mazzeno
Alvernia College

12/10

SALEM PRESS

Pasadena, California   Hackensack, New Jersey

Editor in Chief: Dawn P. Dawson

Editorial Director: Christina J. Moose	*Editorial Assistant:* Brett S. Weisberg
Development Editor: Tracy Irons-Georges	*Research Supervisor:* Jeffry Jensen
Project Editor: Desiree Dreeuws	*Research Assistant:* Keli Trousdale
Manuscript Editors: Constance Pollock,	*Production Editor:* Joyce I. Buchea
Judy Selhorst, Andy Perry	*Design and Graphics:* James Hutson
Acquisitions Editor: Mark Rehn	*Layout:* William Zimmerman

Cover photo: Edna St. Vincent Millay (The Granger Collection, New York)

Library of Congress Cataloging-in-Publication Data

Masterplots / editor, Laurence W. Mazzeno. — 4th ed.
    v. cm.
Includes bibliographical references and indexes.
ISBN 978-1-58765-568-5 (set : alk. paper) — ISBN 978-1-58765-575-3 (v. 7 : alk. paper)
1. Literature—Stories, plots, etc. 2. Literature—History and criticism. I. Mazzeno, Laurence W.
PN44.M33 2010
809—dc22

2010033931

Fourth Edition
First Printing

Contents

Contents

Complete List of Titles

Volume 1

Volume 2

Contents lvii

Complete List of Titles. lxi

Volume 3

Volume 4

Contents cxxxiii

Complete List of Titles cxxxvii

Volume 5

Contents . . . .
Complete List of Titles . . . .

Volume 6

Volume 7

Contents ccxlvii
Complete List of Titles ccli

Volume 8

Volume 9

Contents cccxxiii
Complete List of Titles cccxxvii

Volume 10

Contents ccclxi

Complete List of Titles ccclxv

Volume 11

Volume 12

Contents . . . . cdxxxvii
Complete List of Titles. . . . . cdxxxix

Masterplots

Fourth Edition

Madame Bovary

Author: Gustave Flaubert (1821-1880)
First published: 1857 (English translation, 1886)
Type of work: Novel
Type of plot: Psychological realism
Time of plot: Mid-nineteenth century
Locale: France

Principal characters:
CHARLES BOVARY, a provincial doctor
EMMA BOVARY, his wife
LÉON DUPUIS, a young lawyer
RODOLPHE BOULANGER, a wealthy landowner

The Story:

Charles Bovary is a student of medicine who marries for his own advancement a woman much older than himself. She makes his life miserable with her nagging and groundless suspicions. One day, Charles is called to the bedside of Monsieur Rouault, who has a broken leg, and there he meets the farmer's daughter, Emma, a beautiful but restless young woman whose early education in a French convent has given her an overwhelming thirst for broader experience. Charles finds his patient an excellent excuse to see Emma, whose charm and grace has captivated him.

Charles's whining wife, Héloise, however, soon suspects the true reason for his visits to the Rouault farm. She hears rumors that in spite of Emma's peasant background, the girl conducts herself like a gentlewoman. Angry and tearful, Héloise makes Charles swear that he will not visit the Rouault home again. Unexpectedly, Héloise's fortune is found to be nonexistent. There is a violent quarrel over her deception, followed by a stormy scene between her and Charles's parents, which brings on an attack of an old illness. Héloise dies quickly and quietly.

Charles feels guilty because he has so few regrets at his wife's death. At old Rouault's invitation, he returns once more to the farm and again falls under the spell of Emma's charms. As old Rouault watches Charles fall more deeply in love with his daughter, he decides that the young doctor is dependable and perfectly respectable. He forces the young man's hand, telling Charles he can have Emma in marriage and gives the couple his blessing.

During the first weeks of marriage, Emma occupies herself with changing their new home. She busies herself with every household task she can think of to keep herself from being utterly disillusioned. Emma realizes that even though she thought she was in love with Charles, she does not feel the rapture that should have come with marriage. All the romantic books she has read have led her to expect more from marriage, and the dead calm of her feelings is a bitter disappointment. Indeed, the intimacy of marriage disgusts her. Instead of having a perfumed, handsome lover in velvet and lace, she finds herself tied to a dull-witted husband who reeks of medicines and drugs.

As Emma is about to give up all hope of finding any joy in her new life, a noble patient whom Charles has treated invites them to a ball at his chateau. At the ball, Emma dances with a dozen partners, tastes champagne, and receives compliments on her beauty. The contrast between the life of the Bovarys and that of the nobleman is painfully evident. Emma becomes more and more discontented with Charles. His futile and clumsy efforts to please her only make her despair at his lack of understanding. She sits by her window, dreams of Paris, and then becomes ill.

Hoping a change would improve her condition, Charles takes Emma to Yonville, where he sets up a new practice and Emma prepares for the birth of their child. When their daughter is born, Emma's chief interest in the child is confined to laces and ribbons for her clothes. The child is sent to a wet nurse, where Emma visits her, and where, accidentally, she meets Léon Dupuis, a law clerk bored with the town and seeking diversion. Charmed with the youthful mother, he walks home with her in the twilight, and Emma finds him sympathetic to her romantic ideas about life.

Later, Léon visits the Bovarys in company with Homais, the town chemist. Homais holds little soirees at the local inn, to which he invites the townsfolk. There, Emma's acquaintance with Léon ripens. The townspeople gossip about the couple, but Charles is not acute enough to sense the nature of the interest Emma has in Léon.

Bored with Yonville and tired of loving in vain, Léon goes to Paris to complete his studies. He leaves Emma brokenhearted and deploring her weakness in not having given herself to Léon. She frets in her boredom and once more makes herself ill, but she has no time to become melancholy, for a stranger, Rodolphe Boulanger, has come to town. One day, he brought his farm tenant to Charles for bloodletting. Rodolphe, an accomplished lover, sees in Emma a promise of future pleasure. Emma realizes that if she gives herself to him, her surrender will be immoral. Nevertheless, she rationalizes her doubts by convincing herself that nothing as romantic and beautiful as love can be sinful.

Emma begins to deceive Charles, meeting Rodolphe, riding over the countryside with him, and listening to his urgent avowals of love. Finally, she succumbs to his persuasive appeals. She feels guilty at first but later identifies herself with adulterous heroines of fiction and believes that, like them, she now knows true romance. Sure of her love, Rodolphe no longer finds it necessary to behave like a gentle lover; he stops being punctual for his meetings with Emma, and though he continues to see her, she begins to suspect that his passion is dwindling.

Charles has become involved in Homais's attempt to cure a boy of a clubfoot with a machine Charles designed. Both Homais and Charles are convinced that the success of their operation will raise their future standing in the community. After weeks of torment, however, the boy contracts gangrene, and his leg has to be amputated. Homais's reputation is undamaged, however, for he is by profession a chemist, but Bovary, a doctor, is looked on with suspicion. His medical practice begins to suffer.

Disgusted with Charles's failure, Emma, trying to hold Rodolphe, begins to spend money recklessly on jewelry and clothes, bringing her husband deeply into debt. She finally secures Rodolphe's word that he will take her away, but on the very eve of what was to be her escape, she receives from him a letter in which he hypocritically repents of what he calls their sin. Distraught at the realization that she has lost him, she almost throws herself from the window but is saved when Charles calls to her. She becomes gravely ill with brain fever and lays near death for several months.

Emma's convalescence is slow, but she is finally well enough to go to Rouen to the theater. The tender love scenes behind the footlights make Emma breathless with envy. Once more, she dreams of romance. In Rouen, she meets Léon Dupuis again. This time, Léon is determined to possess Emma. He listens to her complaints with sympathy, soothes her, and takes her driving. Emma, whose thirst for romance still consumes her, yields herself to Léon with regret that she had not done so before.

Charles Bovary grows concerned over his increasing debts. Adding to his own financial worries, the death of his father left his mother in ignorance about the family estate. Emma uses the excuse of procuring a lawyer for her mother-in-law to visit Léon in Rouen, where he has set up a practice. At his suggestion, she secures a power of attorney from Charles, a document that leaves her free to spend his money without his knowing of her purchases.

In despair over his debts, the extent of which Emma has only partly revealed, Charles takes his mother into his confidence and promises to destroy Emma's power of attorney. Deprived of her hold over Charles's finances and unable to repay her debts, Emma throws herself on Léon's mercy with no regard for caution. Her corruption and her addiction to pleasure are now complete, but Emma begins to realize that she has brought her lover down with her. She no longer respects him, and she scorns his faithfulness when he is unable to give her money she needs to pay her bills. When her name is posted publicly for a debt of several thousand francs, the bailiff prepares to sell Charles's property to settle her creditors' claims. Charles is out of town when the debt is posted, and Emma, in one final act of self-abasement, appeals to Rodolphe for help. He, too, refuses to lend her money.

Knowing that the framework of lies with which she had deceived Charles is about to collapse, Emma Bovary resolves to die a heroine's death. She swallows arsenic bought at Homais's shop. Charles, returning from his trip, arrives too late to save her from a slow, painful death.

Pitiful in his grief, Charles can barely endure the sounds of the hammer as her coffin is nailed shut. Later, feeling that his pain over Emma's death has grown less, he opens her desk, to find there the carefully collected love letters of Léon and Rodolphe. Broken with the knowledge of his wife's infidelity, scourged with debt, and helpless in his disillusionment, Charles dies soon after his wife, leaving a legacy of only twelve francs for the support of his orphaned daughter.

Critical Evaluation:

Gustave Flaubert's genius lay in his infinite capacity for taking pains, and *Madame Bovary*—so true in its characterizations, so vivid in its setting, so convincing in its plot—is ample testimony to the realism of his work. This novel was one of the first of its type to come out of France, and its truth shocked contemporary readers. Condemned on one hand for picturing the life of a romantic adulterer, Flaubert was acclaimed on the other hand for the honesty and skill with which he handled his subject. Flaubert does not permit Emma Bovary to escape the tragedy she brings on herself. Emma finds diversion from the monotony of her life, but she finds it at the loss of her own self-respect. The truth of Emma's struggle is universal and challenging.

Since the time of Charles Baudelaire, many critics have noted, either approvingly or disapprovingly, Flaubert's application of an accomplished and beautifully sustained style to a banal subject matter in *Madame Bovary*. In Flaubert's own time, many readers objected to an adulterous heroine not only as banal but also as vulgar. Baudelaire, however, offered the telling defense against this criticism in his acknowledgment that the logic of the work as a whole provides an indictment of the immoral behavior.

Flaubert himself viewed his book as "all cunning and stylistic ruse." His intention was to write "a book about nothing, a book with no exterior attachment . . . a book that would have almost no subject." Flaubert's goals, however, were not as purely aesthetic as they might initially seem, for he did not mean to eschew significance entirely. Rather, he meant that any subject matter, no matter how trivial, could be raised to art by language and pattern. Like Stendhal and Honoré de Balzac, Flaubert believed that quotidian matters could be treated seriously, but he goes further than his predecessors in refusing to provide narrative guidance and interpretation.

Literary critic Erich Auerbach observed that Flaubert seems simply to pick scenes that are significant and endow them with a language that allows them to be interpreted. As a result, many commentators have seen Flaubert as the first modern novelist, even a precursor of the antinovelist, because of his unwillingness to deal with subject matter in the traditional, narrative manner. Certainly, he represents a break with the past, for although he retains the story, he makes the novel, in his own words, into "a coloration, a nuance."

At the heart of the novel is a provincial dreamer, a romantic who distorts her environment and ultimately destroys herself with wish fulfillment born of the desperate boredom of her circumscribed situation. Her romantic illusions are, however, not so much the theme of the novel as they are the prime example of human stupidity, which is reflected by all the characters. Charles is trapped by his complacency as much as Emma is by her vain imaginings. The surrounding figures, more types than fully developed characters, represent contemporary failures—the irresponsible seducer, the usurer, the inadequate priest, the town rationalist. All are isolated from those around them by their personal obsessions or deficiencies, and all contribute to the overwhelming stagnation that smothers Emma.

The novel can be divided into three parts, each of which is controlled by an action and a dominant image. In the first part, Emma marries Charles; here the dominant image is in her visit to Le Vaubyessard. The marriage is the central fact of her discontent, while the visit ostensibly provides her with a view of the opulent life she so desperately craves. In the second part of the novel, where she is seduced by the conscienceless landowner Rodolphe, the dominant image is the Comices Agricoles, the elaborate fair with its rustic and vulgar trappings. To Emma, as she is succumbing to Rodolphe, the Comices Agricoles is the very symbol of the limitations of her life. She is not capable of consciously making such an interpretation. If she were, her perception might save her.

What she does not realize is that her affair is as banal as the fair. The third part of the novel, which describes her seduction by Léon, has as its dominant image the meeting in Rouen Cathedral. The cathedral becomes both church and boudoir, populated not only by images of saints but also by a statue of Diane de Poitiers, a notable adulterer. Once again, Emma reaches out to the grand but is compromised by her own limitations and those of her situation.

The dominant images, which reveal the ambiguity as well as the frustration of Emma's predicament, are reinforced and refined by a series of recurrent, minor images. A striking example is the plaster statue of a curé that deteriorates as Emma is progressively debased. The image is extended by a contrast of the curé's statue with a statue of Cupid: Love and sexuality rise as the holy man disintegrates. Later, the damage to the curé's foot reminds the reader of Charles's peasant boots, which resemble a clubfoot, and of the amputation of Hippolyte's leg as a result of Charles's desperate desire to please Emma. As these complex images recur, they bind together the varieties of stupidity and vanity.

Even more revolutionary than the use of imagery is the point of view, the series of perspectives from which Flaubert narrates the story. He does not assume the stance of the distanced observer but repeatedly shifts the point of view to avail himself of multiple angles of vision. The narrative begins and ends with scenes focused on Charles. Although Flaubert never allows Charles a first-person presentation, readers see the beginning of the novel and, indeed, are introduced to Emma from Charles's perspective. The readers finally return to view the debris of the conclusion from the vantage point of this uncomprehending victim.

Most of the novel is seen from Emma's perspective, but there is such a deft playing off of Emma's perceptions against the narrator's control that the reader is able to analyze her perceptions in a broader context rather than simply accept them as fact. The details of Charles's eating habits, for example, become to Emma and the reader a sign of his bovinity, or dullness, while at the same time, to the reader only, they are a sign of Emma's discontent. Looking out from Emma's or Charles's eyes, interpretations emerge that are beyond the mental capacity of either character. Flaubert presents what they perceive as a means of representing what they fail to perceive. An advantage of this method is that, while the reader becomes aware of Emma's shortcomings, a sympathy develops. The reader recognizes the oppressiveness of Emma's circumstances, the triviality of her evil, and the relative sensitivity of her kind of stupidity.

Apparently subjective presentations, controlled and ordered by Flaubert's selection of image and detail, reveal what the characters themselves do not understand. Emma's romantic idealism is the prime example. If Flaubert cannot make tragedy out of these ingredients, he can quite powerfully describe, in his minuscule characters, personal and social frustration on a grand scale.

"Critical Evaluation" by Edward E. Foster

Further Reading

Bloom, Harold, ed. *Emma Bovary*. New York: Chelsea House, 1994. Includes excerpts from reviews and articles, some contemporaneous with the novel, as well as ten essays that analyze the heroine in light of twentieth century and feminist perspectives and understanding. Extensive bibliography.

_____. *Gustave Flaubert's "Madame Bovary."* New York: Chelsea House, 1988. An excellent and balanced collection of some of the best and most provocative essays published in the last third of the twentieth century. Topics range from thematic to linguistic and from deconstructionist to psychoanalytical analyses.

Curry, Corrada Biazzo. *Description and Meaning in Three Novels by Gustave Flaubert*. New York: Peter Lang, 1997. Focuses on Flaubert's use of imagery in *Madame Bovary, Salammbô*, and *A Sentimental Education*. Demonstrates how his descriptive passages are subject to various possibilities of meaning and nonmeaning.

Fairlie, Alison. *Flaubert: "Madame Bovary."* London: Arnold, 1962. A well-written, sensitive, and insightful interpretation that provides a thorough examination of the themes, characters, narrative structure, style, and importance of the masterpiece.

Gans, Eric. *"Madame Bovary": The End of Romance*. Boston: Twayne, 1989. A brief but very good introduction that covers the work's essential points, influence, and critical reception. Places it in its historical and sociological context.

Giraud, Raymond, ed. *Flaubert: A Collection of Critical Essays*. Englewood Cliffs, N.J.: Prentice-Hall, 1964. Reprints several stimulating pieces on *Madame Bovary* that include a perceptive reading by the poet Charles Baudelaire and thoughtful character analyses by Martin Turnell and Jean Rousset. Includes essays dealing with Flaubert's literary theories and his other works.

Porter, Laurence M., and Eugene F. Gray. *Flaubert's Madame Bovary: A Reference Guide*. Westport, Conn.: Greenwood Press, 2002. Provides information on Flaubert's life and career and discusses the novel's plot, genesis, publication history, social and cultural contexts, and critical reception.

Raitt, A. W. *The Originality of Madame Bovary*. New York: Peter Lang, 2002. Examines the ways in which *Madame Bovary* was a radical departure in the history of the novel, analyzing the book's point of view, dialogue, narrative techniques, use of description, language style, and other characteristics.

Troyat, Henri. *Flaubert*. Translated by Joan Pinkham. New York: Viking Press, 1992. Troyat, an accomplished biographer, provides a thorough, engrossing book that reconstructs Flaubert's life based on the novelist's prodigious correspondence with his family and friends.

Unwin, Timothy, ed. *The Cambridge Companion to Flaubert*. New York: Cambridge University Press, 2004. Collection of essays analyzing all of Flaubert's works and discussing his life, place in literary history, writing process, and other aspects of his fiction. In the final essay, "Flaubert, Our Contemporary," noted novelist Mario Vargas Llosa assesses Flaubert's continued relevance.

Wall, Geoffrey. *Flaubert: A Life*. New York: Farrar, Straus and Giroux, 2002. A critically acclaimed narrative biography. Offers many new details and is a great read.

Williams, Tony, and Mary Orr, eds. *New Approaches in Flaubert Studies*. Lewiston, N.Y.: E. Mellen Press, 1999. The authors of the essays in this collection provide fresh interpretations of Flaubert's works, including discussions of gender roles, flower figures and other imagery, classical influences, and Flaubert and the new technologies.

Mademoiselle de Maupin
A Romance of Love and Passion

Author: Théophile Gautier (1811-1872)
First published: 1835-1836 (English translation, 1887)
Type of work: Novel
Type of plot: Sentimental
Time of plot: Early nineteenth century
Locale: France

Principal characters:
MONSIEUR D'ALBERT, a young aesthete
ROSETTE, his mistress
THÉODORE DE SÉRANNES, in reality MADEMOISELLE
MADELAINE DE MAUPIN

The Story:

D'Albert is a young Frenchman of twenty-two, handsome, artistic, well educated, and well versed in the affairs of the world. He loves beauty, especially female beauty. All his life he has dreamed of women, but he has never met the woman of his dreams, a woman who combines the beauty of a nude painted by Peter Paul Rubens with that of a nude by Titian. It is little wonder that he has not found her.

Another thing lacking in d'Albert's life is a mistress. One day, his friend de C—— offers to take him around the town and discourse on the various ladies of his acquaintance so that d'Albert can make a choice. The expedition is a delightful one, as de C—— seems to have precise and full information not only on the outward circumstances of every beauty but also on the very quality of her mind. After some hesitation, d'Albert finally decides to lay siege to Rosette, a beautiful young woman; he chooses her because he thinks she is the most likely to bring his romantic and poetic mind down to earth.

It does not take d'Albert long to win Rosette's love, and they are soon acknowledged lovers. Rosette is pliable, versatile, and always entertaining. She does not leave d'Albert alone long enough for him to indulge in musing daydreams. Variety is the spice of their love.

For five months they are the happiest of lovers, but then d'Albert begins to tire of Rosette. When she notices that his ardor is cooling, Rosette knows that she must do something different if she wishes to keep his love. If he is growing tired of her in the solitary life they are leading, perhaps he will regain his interest if he sees her among a group of people. For this reason, Rosette takes d'Albert to her country estate for a visit. There she plans parties, dinners, and visits to keep him amused, but he remains bored.

One day, an old friend of Rosette arrives, an extremely handsome young man named Théodore de Sérannes, whose conversation, riding, and swordsmanship all entrance d'Albert. The two men meet every day and go hunting together, and the more d'Albert sees of Théodore, the more fascinated he becomes. Before long, d'Albert realizes that he is in love with Théodore.

He is in love with a man, yet d'Albert always thinks of Théodore as a woman. D'Albert's mind grows sick with the problem of Théodore's true identity. Some days he is sure that Théodore is a woman in disguise. Then, seeing him fencing or jumping his horse, d'Albert is forced to conclude that Théodore is a man. He knows that Rosette is also in love with Théodore, but her infatuation keeps her from noticing d'Albert's interest in the same young man.

One day, d'Albert mentions to a group of friends, including Rosette and Théodore, that his favorite play is William Shakespeare's *As You Like It* (pr. c. 1599-1600, pb. 1623). The rest of the company immediately decide to present the play. At first, Rosette is chosen for the part of Rosalind, the heroine who dresses as a man to escape from her uncle, but when she refuses to wear men's clothes, the part is given to Théodore.

As soon as d'Albert sees Théodore dressed in women's clothes, he guesses rightly that Théodore really is a woman. What he does not know is that Théodore, whose real name is Madelaine de Maupin, has decided that she will have nothing to do with men until she finds a good and noble lover. She knows that as a woman she has no chance to see men as they really are, and so she has devised the scheme of learning about them by dressing as a man. Nevertheless, she has found perfidy and falseness in every man she has met. She has watched with amusement as d'Albert has fallen in love with her, and she has guessed the tortures of his mind at not being able to decide whether she is male or female.

As the rehearsals of the play go on, the parallels between the play and real life become ever more amusing to both d'Albert and Mademoiselle de Maupin. At last, after the play has been presented, d'Albert writes Mademoiselle de Maupin a letter in which he tells her he is sure she is a woman and that he loves her deeply. She takes so long to reply to his letter that d'Albert again becomes afraid that she really is a man. One night, however, as d'Albert stands at a window, a hand gently touches his shoulder from behind. He turns around and beholds Mademoiselle de Maupin dressed in her costume as Rosalind. He is struck dumb with amazement. Mademoiselle de Maupin tells him that since he is the first man who has seen through her disguise, he should be the first to have her as a woman.

That night, d'Albert learns that she is truly the woman of his dreams. In the morning, however, he finds himself alone. Mademoiselle de Maupin has gone, leaving a letter in which she tells d'Albert and Rosette that they will never see her again. She writes separately to d'Albert, telling him that they have known one perfect night. She has answered his dream, and to fulfill a dream once is enough. She ends her letter by telling d'Albert to try to console Rosette for the love she has wasted on the false Théodore and by expressing her hope that the two of them will be very happy for many years to come.

Critical Evaluation:

Théophile Gautier's *Mademoiselle de Maupin* shocked contemporaries with its unrestrained sensuality, but the novel is not concerned primarily with sexual desire; rather, its focus is the quest for an ideal lover. For d'Albert, the pleasures of the spirit hold no appeal. His orientation toward love is aesthetic, just as his evaluations of objects are artistic. The major episodes in the novel are organized around critical moments in d'Albert's quest for ideal beauty. His discouragement initially stems from his failure to find a woman who lives up to his requirements. His affair with Rosette deepens his despair because, even though he finds her sexually exciting, she does not embody ideal beauty. He frequently laments the shortcoming of a world that lacks the embodiment of his conception of perfect beauty. He seeks that beauty in vain until he finds Mademoiselle de Maupin, whom he possesses for only one night. She leaves him because, as she explains, the human tendency to satiety will inevitably cause their happy relationship to deteriorate. The renewal of his relationship with Rosette is a compromise with reality. He rationalizes that his demands may be too extreme and that Rosette can mitigate his suffering.

Like d'Albert, Madelaine seeks the living embodiment of an ideal, but for her it is the character of a loved one that is important. Whereas d'Albert's desires are physical, Madelaine's are ethical. Her demands seem, however, equally extreme, though they are only vaguely described. Rosette's passion for Théodore, the male identity that Madelaine has adopted, demonstrates precisely the kind of love that would bring Madelaine happiness. Rosette's passion for Théodore is so absolute that it requires little requital. Assuming a male disguise, Madelaine discovers that men are fundamentally cynical in their treatment of women. Madelaine wants spiritual love and intense passion, which seem to be precisely what men avoid. At the end of the novel, Madelaine disappears, still hoping to find the ideal lover.

Much of the tension in the novel arises from an emphasis on the ambivalence of human sexuality. The physical duality of Madelaine/Théodore's identity reflects an inner ambiguity of traditional notions of gender. Madelaine's powerful sexual nature and forcefully articulated opinions are traditionally associated with masculinity, but her beauty and emotional sensitivity are portrayed as feminine. Gender confusion extends to the other characters as well. Rosette, who conforms to a traditionally feminine role in her relationship with d'Albert, actively seduces Théodore. D'Albert is told that he dresses in a feminine manner and finds himself looking on Rosette as a platonic friend. Although d'Albert values physical beauty, he finds himself most attracted to Madelaine's keen mind. In fact, Madelaine provides a counterpoint to many of d'Albert's theories. Although d'Albert desires her as a second half, she actually mirrors his own sexual ambivalence.

The triangular relationships in the novel place happiness beyond reach. The dynamics of the triangle depend on tensions and oppositions, attractions and connections. The comic triangle of Shakespeare's *As You Like It*, acted out by Rosette's guests, mirrors and complicates the relationships. Madelaine playing Rosalind is disguised as the youth Ganymede to test her lover Orlando. While disguised as Ganymede, Rosalind attracts the unwelcome attention of Phoebe. This situation mirrors her own: As Théodore she attracts the attention of Rosette, and as Madelaine she appeals to d'Albert. Rosette, as the page Isabel, pursues Ganymede much as she pursues Théodore/Madelaine. D'Albert's confusion mirrors that of Orlando. On seeing Madelaine dressed as Rosalind for the play, both d'Albert and Rosette question her true identity.

The plot traces the protagonists' explorations of their own identities. Since the novel's narrative structure is self-conscious, the explorations of self in the text draw attention to the fiction of fixed identity. D'Albert's identity doubles his own ironic narration. He fantasizes and then critiques his fantasies, and then criticizes that self-reflexive impulse itself. The playacting, both in the characters' rendition of *As You Like It* and in their interactions with one another in the novel, allows the characters to question ambiguities of identity. Gautier frequently resorts to masks and mirrors to express the duality of human existence. Metamorphosis, borrowed from Shakespeare's play as well as from Ovid's *Metamorphoses* (c. 8 C.E.; English translation, 1567), prominently figures as literary allusion and overarching theme.

Mademoiselle de Maupin is not only the most beautifully written of Gautier's novels but also his most sustained profession of his creed. Many of Gautier's theories of art appear in the preface and text, where he derides utility in art and declares that nothing is beautiful unless it is useless. The preface ultimately became the credo of the art-for-art's-sake movement, with its insistence on the sovereignty of art, independent of moral and social conditions. The love of palpable, external beauty is a primary feature of Gautier's work, and the novel reads as a series of vivid visual descriptions. His taste for Greek sculpture and Gothic architecture is apparent, as are rich allusions to literary precursors. A painter's eye for visual form and color contributes to the stylistic beauty of Gautier's prose.

According to Gautier, the artist combines masculine and feminine traits to translate the image of feminine beauty into art. The desire for an androgynous union of male and female surfaces in the novel as well. D'Albert would like to combine the awareness of beauty with the state of being beautiful. The relationship between art and sexuality is a central issue of the novel. D'Albert's quest as both artist and lover reenacts the Romantic quest to overcome the split between self and another. Théodore/Madelaine as a work of art is not so easily appropriated by an observer. There is no simple identity to be unmasked. Constant transformation and veiled appearances dramatize the endless process of aesthetic creativity. The equivocal position of Madelaine, her ability to arouse a double passion, suggests that beauty may be loved independent of sex. Despite his lengthy passages analyzing the Romantic soul, which verge on parody, Gautier emphasizes the confining nature of sexual stereotypes, elaborates the notion of endlessly evolving beauty, and explores the nature of love, pleasure, and desire.

"Critical Evaluation" by Pamela Pavliscak

Further Reading

Barsoum, Marlène. *Théophile Gautier's "Mademoiselle de Maupin": Toward a Definition of the "Androgynous Discourse."* New York: Peter Lang, 2001. Examines Gautier's exploration of language in the novel and asserts that

he uses a mythic androgynous figure to create a theory of perfect expression.

Brians, Paul. "Sexuality and the Opposite Sex: Variations on a Theme by Théophile Gautier and Anaïs Nin." In *The Critical Response to Anaïs Nin*, edited by Philip K. Jason. Westport, Conn.: Greenwood Press, 1996. Compares *Mademoiselle de Maupin* with Nin's novel *A Spy in the House of Love* (1954). Argues that both novels use "similar techniques to allow restless young women to explore the foreign territory of the opposite sex."

Lloyd, Rosemary. "Rereading *Mademoiselle de Maupin*." *Orbis Litterarum: International Review of Literary Studies* 41, no. 1 (1986): 19-32. Provides a valuable overview of previous discussions of the novel, many of which are available only in French. Traces the many literary allusions in the text and places the novel within the larger tradition of explorations of human sexuality.

Richardson, Joanna. *Théophile Gautier, His Life and Times.* London: M. Reinhardt, 1958. One of the most comprehensive biographies of Gautier available in English combines biographical detail with textual evaluation. Proposes that *Mademoiselle de Maupin* is an example of the art-for-art's-sake principle outlined in Gautier's preface to the novel.

Scott, David. *Pictorialist Poetics: Poetry and the Visual Arts in Nineteenth-Century France.* New York: Cambridge University Press, 1988. Argues that the aesthetic theory and literary practice of the nineteenth century combined to produce a new conception of literature's potential. Examines Gautier's preoccupation with the visual arts, as both critic and artist, and its impact on his literary efforts.

Smith, Albert B. *Ideal and Reality in the Fictional Narratives of Théophile Gautier.* Gainesville: University Press of Florida, 1969. Offers a detailed analysis of *Mademoiselle de Maupin* as well as a broad discussion of Gautier's aesthetic philosophy and literary style.

Wing, Nathaniel. "'Vous êtes sans doute très supris, mon cher d'Albert': Improvisation and Gender in Théophile Gautier's *Mademoiselle de Maupin*." In *Between Genders: Narrating Difference in Early French Modernism.* Newark: University of Delaware Press, 2004. Chapter focusing on *Mademoiselle de Maupin* is part of a larger analysis of the forms and themes of five nineteenth century French works in which the authors are preoccupied with gender identity and differentiation.

The Madwoman of Chaillot

Author: Jean Giraudoux (1882-1944)
First produced: La Folle de Chaillot, 1945; first published,
    1945 (English translation, 1947)
Type of work: Drama
Type of plot: Parable
Time of plot: A little before noon in the spring of next
    year
Locale: Chaillot district of Paris

Principal characters:
COUNTESS AURELIA, the Madwoman of Chaillot
MME CONSTANCE, the Madwoman of Passy
MLLE GABRIELLE, the Madwoman of St. Sulpice
MME JOSEPHINE, the Madwoman of La Concorde
THE RAGPICKER
THE PRESIDENT
THE BARON
THE BROKER
THE PROSPECTOR

The Story:

A mighty syndicate of financiers wishes to exploit the untouched deposits of oil under the streets of Paris, and they ignore humanity, beauty, and truth in the process. The free souls of Paris oppose the men and eventually triumph by literally removing the syndicate from the scene.

On one side are the President, the Prospector, the Baron, the Press Agent, the Broker, and the Ladies of the Street. On the other side are the Waiter, the Little Man, the Street Singer, the Flower Girl, the Shoelace Peddler, the Ragpicker, and other folk. In the middle, and significantly devoted to the gentle souls, is the Madwoman of Chaillot, aided by her compatriots, the Madwomen of Passy, St. Sulpice, and La Concorde. The capitalistic forces function as well-oiled machinery; they are devoid of characteristics that set them apart or elicit for them the least bit of empathic reaction. The people of Paris are all recognizable types, but each possesses some quality of individuality.

The Madwoman encounters the President, the Baron, the Prospector, and the Broker at a sidewalk café in the Chaillot district. Her friends are all aware that something terrible is afoot and inform her of the plot to drill for oil beneath the streets. The Prospector sends his agent with a bomb to destroy the city architect, the only obstacle to the drilling. Pierre, the young assassin, is rescued by the Policeman as he is about to throw himself into the river rather than carry out his task. He is revived and convinced by the Madwoman that life is really worth living.

It is apparent to the Madwoman that the only way to combat the materialistic interests is to annihilate them. She and her friends have little chance of opposing them if commonly interpreted methods of justice are used, so she decides upon an infallible plan and sends her confederates scurrying about on errands to help her carry it out.

The Madwoman retires to her quarters in the rue de

Chaillot to receive the delegation of capitalists. They answer her invitation because she has informed them that a large deposit of oil rests under her basement. To prove it, she prepares a sample; a bottle of mixed kerosene and mange cure is waiting for the Prospector, who professes to be able to detect the existence of oil deposits by merely sniffing the air.

Some years before, the Madwoman had rescued a Sewer Man who had promised to show her a secret entrance from her basement into the sewers of Paris. She summons him and he presses the stone concealing the entrance. The other Madwomen, Mme Constance, who takes her invisible lap dog with her everywhere; Mlle Gabrielle, who talks to nonexistent friends; and Mme Josephine, who is an expert at jurisprudence because her brother-in-law is a lawyer, all arrive for a delightful tea scene. They are mad, but that fact in no way prejudices the trial that follows.

Mme Josephine is called upon to conduct a court, for it is only just and proper that the financiers have a fair hearing before they are sent to oblivion. The Ragpicker agrees to speak in their defense, and a damning testimony it is, with money at the root of their materialistic evil. The verdict of the tribunal is unanimous; the accused are guilty on all charges. The Madwoman is authorized to proceed with the extermination.

The guests begin to arrive, and in a wonderful scene of comic irony each group in turn is sent through the door into the sewer. First comes the President, next the Prospector, then the Press Agent, and so on until all, like sheep, have followed the infallible nose of the Prospector down the dark stairway, never to return again.

Immediately, all the wrongs of the world are righted. The pigeons fly again; the air is pure; the sky is clear; grass sprouts on the pavements; complete strangers are shaking hands. Humanity has been saved, and the friends of friendship thank the Madwoman, the triumphant feminine force.

Critical Evaluation:

In *The Madwoman of Chaillot*, Jean Giraudoux orchestrates three of his recurring themes: the inscrutability of woman, the love of humanity, and the abhorrence of materialism. For one who is familiar with all of Giraudoux's plays, the antiwar theme is implied in the latter. Stylistically, Giraudoux employs two of his favorite devices: the fantastic parable and the duality of character. The resulting impact of *The Madwoman of Chaillot* is that it possesses a remarkable unity of form and idea, the unifying theme being the writer's love and faith in the triumph of the human entity in a time of despair. Giraudoux knew something about living in a time of despair.

A very important aspect of *The Madwoman of Chaillot* involves the time of its composition: The play was written by Giraudoux toward the end of the period during which the Germans occupied Paris (from June, 1940, to August, 1944) during World War II. Giraudoux died in the winter of 1943-1944, months before the Allies' invasion of Normandy and the Germans' departure from the city.

Although the play makes no clear mention of the war and there are no direct references to the terrible deprivations suffered by Parisians throughout the Occupation, the play premiered during the first theater season after the liberation of France. Critical responses to this work therefore have frequently been influenced by the knowledge that Giraudoux's attitude toward his own country's defeat and the Occupation was far from positive. For this reason, many have continued to see in the play a commentary on France's ability to resist the fascist oppression of the Nazis. Such an interpretation, which helped make this play a worldwide success, is dependent on an awareness of the period during which the play was written and of the playwright's sympathies, because the script itself seems curiously quiet about such issues.

The Madwoman of Chaillot offers a blend of fantasy and realism in presenting its setting, characters, and story. For example, Chaillot, which is the area located directly across the Seine from the Eiffel Tower, seems, in the play, a timeless place. There are few references to everyday life, and little appears on stage to suggest any specific part of the actual neighborhood. The play lacks any authentic sense of geography: This Chaillot is a charming, bustling neighborhood filled with funny and interesting people who seem to come and go quite freely. Most of the characters are referred to not by name but by who they are or what they do—the Ragpicker, the Baron, and the Policeman, for example. The majority of the more than forty characters who populate *The Madwoman of Chaillot* appear to be self-consciously playing their parts in a highly theatricalized environment. Against the fantasti-

cal backdrop, only a few characters stand out as genuine individuals, notably the Madwomen, who claim particular Paris neighborhoods as their domains: Mme Constance of Passy; Mlle Gabrielle of St. Sulpice; Mme Josephine of La Concorde; and the Countess Aurelia, the Madwoman of Chaillot.

The play's theme is that society is redeemed by those it chooses to label insane. The mad are portrayed in the play as charmingly nonconformist, resistant, and enterprisingly clever. The madness of Countess Aurelia, for example, is liberating in its bold honesty and candor. She is allowed to make whatever remarks she wishes—after all, the woman is crazy—but consistently through the play, her comments, even with all their amusing idiosyncrasies, seem to contain the truth. Eccentric and suspended in a sweeter, happier past, the Madwoman of Chaillot becomes a worthy opponent to those forces who would destroy the beauty of Paris and of the life that may be lived there.

The plot to convert the enchanting city into an oil field is led by a group of highly disagreeable men who lust after money. These characters are painted with broad, often stereotypical strokes: They are quite similar and operate as an effective unit. Opposed to these evil, titled plutocrats and vile money-grubbers are the Waiter, the Ragpicker, the Flower Girl, the Street Singer, the Shoelace Peddler—in other words, the many, varied people who inhabit the play's magical Chaillot. Much of the conflict in the play pits these interesting individuals against the devious, faceless businessmen.

Between these two extremes stands Countess Aurelia, who mediates between the juxtaposed realities of the people and the businessmen. Her attempt to convince Pierre that life is wonderful provides her with her first opportunity to express the play's view of life—that it is worth living. Later, when the trial begins in the Madwoman's basement, she is able to add that what is worth living is worth protecting. The scene in which the enemies of human existence, who wish to turn the city into an ugly, moneymaking machine, are lured into the Paris sewers dramatizes the play's message that if people are willing to fight for what is beautiful, the world will become a better place. No sooner have the villains disappeared than Paris is transfigured.

Although Giraudoux should not be considered a feminist, his play carefully contrasts the materialistic world—led by males—with the sensibilities associated with females. Rather than succumb to the enticements of finances and money, the Madwoman of Chaillot is triumphant in maintaining her values. In this idealized setting, the appreciation of beauty and truth conquers the excesses of capitalism.

As noted above, Giraudoux's fanciful drama scored a major success when it premiered. It was admiringly received by critics and audiences not only in Paris but also in London, New York, and other major theater centers all over the world. Wherever it was produced in the 1950's and 1960's, it enjoyed long runs and revivals. By the 1970's, however, audiences seemed to find *The Madwoman of Chaillot* somewhat dated, even naïve, and literary critics, who had once been interested in Giraudoux, lost interest in him. This play, certainly the dramatist's best-known work, is still produced in France and elsewhere, but it is often regarded as charming but lightweight fare. Perhaps its sense of whimsy and its rather straightforward way of dramatizing how complex problems might be solved seem too simple for modern theatergoers.

"Critical Evaluation" by Kenneth Krauss

Further Reading

Body, Jacques. *Jean Giraudoux: The Legend and the Secret.* Translated by James Norwood. Rutherford, N.J.: Fairleigh Dickinson University Press, 1991. A fascinating series of essays draws important connections between the author's life and his major plays, especially *The Madwoman of Chaillot.* Offers a wealth of facts regarding the play's composition and posthumous production.

Cohen, Robert. *Giraudoux: Three Faces of Destiny.* Chicago: University of Chicago Press, 1970. An excellent analysis of Giraudoux's dramatic works and their philosophical implications. The chapter on *The Madwoman of Chaillot* is especially helpful for its discussion of how the playwright's dramatic style and techniques fit his plays' intellectual and emotional content.

Korzeniowska, Victoria B. *The Heroine as Social Redeemer in the Plays of Jean Giraudoux.* New York: Peter Lang, 2001. Focuses on Giraudoux's female characters, describing the gender politics in his plays and his heroines' roles in both the domestic and public spheres. Places his heroines within the context of the French idealization of women during the interwar years.

Lemaître, Georges Édouard. *Jean Giraudoux: The Writer and His Work.* New York: Ungar, 1971. A good overview of Giraudoux's career. Offers an accurate picture of how the playwright was regarded until the early 1970's.

Raymond, Agnès G. *Jean Giraudoux: The Theatre of Victory and Defeat.* Amherst: University of Massachusetts Press, 1966. Particularly notable for its assessment of the playwright's political ideas and the historical context in which his major works were developed. The chapter on *The Madwoman of Chaillot* examines how the German Occupation affected the writing of the play.

Reilly, John H. *Jean Giraudoux.* Boston: Twayne, 1978. A comprehensive survey of Giraudoux's dramatic works. Reilly sees *The Madwoman of Chaillot* as one of the high points of the playwright's career.

Maggie
A Girl of the Streets

Author: Stephen Crane (1871-1900)
First published: 1893
Type of work: Novel
Type of plot: Naturalism
Time of plot: Late nineteenth century
Locale: New York City

Principal characters:
MAGGIE
JIMMY, her brother
PETE, Jimmy's friend and Maggie's lover
THE MOTHER

The Story:

In the slums of New York City, Maggie and her two brothers grow up in the squalor and corruption, both moral and physical, of that poverty-stricken area. Her father usually comes home from work drunk, and her mother, too, is fond of the bottle. The children are neglected. When the drunken parents rant at each other, the children hide in terror under the table or the bed.

Somehow, Maggie manages to remain untouched by the sordidness. Her younger brother dies. Jimmy, her older brother, goes to work after their father dies. Jimmy fights, drinks, and has many affairs with women. From time to time, he is hounded by some of the women, who demand support for themselves and the illegitimate children he has fathered. Jimmy brushes them aside.

When Jimmy brings his best friend home with him, Maggie falls in love. Pete, a bartender, is handsome, flashy, and exciting. One night, he takes her out to show her the nightlife of the city. Maggie's wonder knows no bounds, for to her the experience is the height of luxury. On the doorstep, she allows Pete to kiss her good-night. Pete is disappointed but not discouraged. He takes Maggie out again. They make love, and Maggie moves in with him.

Pete soon grows tired of Maggie, however, and she is compelled to return home. In furious indignation, her mother orders her out of the house. She has done everything, the mother insists, to bring Maggie up to be a fine, decent girl. She has been an excellent mother and has spared no pains to keep her daughter on the path of virtue. Now her daughter will be dead to her. The neighbors join in, denouncing Maggie. Jimmy, the seducer of other men's sisters, becomes indignant. He and a companion go to the bar where Pete works, intent upon beating him up. When they fail, Jimmy contents himself by shrugging his shoulders and condemning his sister.

Maggie is homeless and penniless. She visits Pete, but he sends her away, irritated and fearful lest he should lose his job. She turns to prostitution, plying her trade by night, but she does not have much luck. One night, she walks forlornly and unsuccessfully in the waterfront district. Resignedly she trudges on, toward the pier and the black, murky depths of the river.

A short time later, Jimmy comes home from one of his prolonged absences. Maggie, the mother wails, is dead. With the neighbors around her, she sobs and moans. What the Lord has given the Lord has taken away, the neighbors tell her. Uncomforted, Maggie's mother shrieks that she forgives her daughter; she forgives Maggie her sins.

Critical Evaluation:

Stephen Crane's *Maggie* reveals a governing social determinism that exonerates the denizens of the Bowery from the hypocritical moral judgments they pronounce on Maggie, and that serves as the basis for an attack on false values. Viewed in this context, *Maggie* conforms to many of the tenets of literary naturalism. When the term "naturalism" is applied to literature, it signifies a philosophical orientation; more specifically, it reflects the presence of a determinism that is either biological or environmental. In other words, the careers of naturalistic protagonists are determined by their inherited traits and by their environments. Caught up in the web of these forces, the protagonists cannot be held responsible for their actions, since they have little, if any, freedom of will. Consequently, the naturalistic work manifests an ethical orientation that is neither moral nor immoral, but amoral. Naturalism is distinguished from realism by several other features as well: a focus on the lower classes, an attack on false values, a reformist agenda, imagery that is either animalistic or mechanistic, and a plot of decline that often leads to catastrophe through a deterministic sequence of causes and effects.

The setting, imagery, and plot of *Maggie* manifest the operation of a governing social determinism that serves as a springboard for Crane's attack on both romantic idealism in works about the slum and on the moral posturing of the church and the Bowery inhabitants. Rum Alley is a sordid, Darwinian landscape of violent people engaged in a brutal struggle for survival. Children are disgorged onto the slum streets from dark doorways where they must fend for themselves. Working conditions in the local factories are bleak. Lacking an education and any positive role models in her life, Maggie turns to the stage melodrama and the popular romance for her values. They give rise to her dream of a perfect lover who will rescue her from the Bowery. They also instill in her the false beliefs that virtue triumphs over vice, and that poverty is ennobling. In the last analysis, Maggie's dream proves as fatal as it is illusory, for in the savage environment of the Bowery, the romantic ideals she inherits from the slum novel and theatrical melodrama have negative survival value.

The bestial, martial, and romantic imagery associated with the principal characters also reflects the social determinism of *Maggie*. Maggie's deluded romanticism is reinforced by the imagery Crane employs to describe her impression of Pete, who appears to her as a glowing sun, a knight in shining armor who has come to her rescue, when, in reality, he is nothing more than a dandified street thug. Similarly, Maggie's fatal incompatibility with her environment is revealed by the images Crane uses to describe her. For example, she is compared to a flower that sprouts from the mud, her soul unstained by the dirt and grime of Rum Alley. By contrast, the images used to describe Pete and Jimmy reflect the extent of their adaptation to their environment. They and their friends fight with the savagery of a pack of dogs. The animalistic imagery is significant, for it reinforces the work's naturalistic orientation; humans are viewed as extensions of the animal kingdom engaged in a Darwinian struggle for survival.

A plot of decline leading to catastrophic closure is further evidence of a governing social determinism in *Maggie*. The initial chapters establish the violent environment of the Bowery. Succeeding chapters contrast Pete's and Jimmy's adaptation to this sordid milieu with Maggie's ardent desire to escape from it. Chapters 6 and 7 chronicle her attempts to realize her dream of escape. Ensuing chapters document the moral backlash and rejection of Maggie by the denizens of the Bowery, and the consequent narrowing of her options, leading to closure and death. First she is rejected by Pete, who claims she is not good enough for him. Forced to pursue a life of prostitution, she is subsequently disowned by her mother, who condemns her thankless disobedience, and shunned by Jimmy for bringing shame upon the family. Turning finally to the church, Maggie is rejected by the priest, who is not willing to risk his respectability to save her soul. The novel assails the hypocrisy of the priest who offers condemnation instead of compassion, who claims to help people, yet disregards their pleas for help, and whose moral posturing encourages others to adopt a similar stance. These characters are not to be blamed for their moral hypocrisy, however, because their harsh environment forces them to act immorally while keeping up moral appearances to survive.

By parodying the sentimental romance, theatrical melodrama, and slum novel to which his audience was addicted, Crane forced his readers to take a closer look at the unsavory conditions of slum life. *Maggie* also exerted an influence on future generations of writers, from Frank Norris and Theodore Dreiser to Dashiell Hammett and Ernest Hemingway, as a result of its many new elements: a focus on the social dregs, the prostitutes, sweat shops, factories, and slums; a terse, laconic style and vernacular dialogue; its subversion of old Victorian sexual taboos and its frank depiction of the sexual needs that drive humans; its portrayal of characters as biological and social pawns with little intellect but great physical attributes; a narrative technique that combined an objective, documentary style with a riot of irony, and that featured an impressionistic approach in which mood and tone were privileged over theme and character. In the final analysis, the novel's impact may be assessed by its publication in 1893, which helped give birth to a new mode of storytelling: American literary naturalism.

"Critical Evaluation" by Stephen G. Brown

Further Reading

Bloom, Harold, ed. *Stephen Crane's "Maggie: A Girl of the Streets."* Philadelphia: Chelsea House, 2005. Designed as a guide for high school and undergraduate students, this book provides a brief biographical sketch of Crane, a list of characters, a plot summary, and essays examining various aspects of the novel. Includes an annotated bibliography.

Crane, Stephen. *Maggie: A Girl of the Streets.* Edited by Kevin J. Hayes. Boston: Bedford/St. Martin's, 1999. Includes numerous documents that place the novel within its social, cultural, and literary contexts. Includes writings by Henry James, William Dean Howells, and Jacob Riis, who describe tenement life, social and cultural life in the Bowery, the conditions of working women, prostitution, the "fallen woman" of slum fiction, realism, and naturalism.

Gandal, Keith. "Crane and Slum Fiction." In *The Virtues of the Vicious: Jacob Riis, Stephen Crane, and the Spectacle of the Slum.* New York: Oxford University Press, 1997. Describes how the American slum in the 1890's became a source of spectacle and a subject for aesthetic, ethnographic, and psychological depiction. Gandal analyzes the representation of the urban slum in two books of the period: *Maggie* and Jacob Riis's *How the Other Half Lives* (1890).

_____. "Stephen Crane's *Maggie* and the Modern Soul." *English Literary History* 60, no. 3 (Fall, 1993): 759-785. Argues that the novel is not about Maggie's moral decline but her loss of self-confidence and self-defensiveness. Asserts that Maggie fails not in trying to redeem her sinful nature—the old story of the fallen woman—but in overcoming self-doubt and cowardice, making it a modern psychological tale.

Irving, Katrina. "Gendered Space, Racialized Space: Nativism, the Immigrant Woman, and Stephen Crane's *Maggie.*" *College Literature* 20, no. 3 (October, 1993): 30-43. Irving asserts that immigrants posed a threat to late nineteenth century American society, especially women prostitutes such as Maggie, who must die before diluting "native" stock.

Monteiro, George, ed. *Stephen Crane: The Contemporary Reviews.* New York: Cambridge University Press, 2009. Presents reviews of Crane's writings, including *Maggie.* Offers "insight into how Crane's reputation was formed and how it changed during his lifetime, ending with the shifts in emphasis upon his early death."

Sorrentino, Paul, ed. *Stephen Crane Remembered.* Tuscaloosa: University of Alabama Press, 2006. Sorrentino brings together nearly one hundred documents from acquaintances of the novelist and poet for a revealing look at Crane the writer and the man.

Sweeney, Gerard M. "The Syphilitic World of Stephen Crane's *Maggie.*" *American Literary Realism* 24, no. 1 (Fall, 1991): 79-85. Discusses how Crane reveals the diseased condition of Maggie's world—including its syphilis and alcoholism. Crane's tough realism suggests Maggie is fortunate to escape through early death.

Wertheim, Stanley. *A Stephen Crane Encyclopedia*. Westport, Conn.: Greenwood Press, 1997. A thorough volume, with entries arranged alphabetically. Features articles about the full range of Crane's work, his family and its influence upon him, the places he lived, his employers, the literary movement with which he is associated, and his characters, among other subjects.

The Magic Mountain

Author: Thomas Mann (1875-1955)
First published: Der Zauberberg, 1924 (English translation, 1927)
Type of work: Novel
Type of plot: Philosophical
Time of plot: 1907-1914
Locale: Davos, Switzerland

Principal characters:
HANS CASTORP, a German engineer
JOACHIM ZIEMSSEN, his cousin
SETTEMBRINI, a patient at Davos-Platz
NAPHTA, Settembrini's friend
CLAVDIA CAUCHAT, Hans's friend
MYNHEER PEEPERKORN, a Dutch planter from Java

The Story:

Hans Castorp is advised by his doctor to go to the mountains for a rest. Accordingly, he decides to visit his cousin, Joachim Ziemssen, a soldier by profession, who is a patient in the International Sanatorium Berghof at Davos-Platz in the mountains of Switzerland. He plans to stay there for three weeks and then return to his home in Hamburg. Hans has just passed his examinations and is now a qualified engineer; he is eager to get started in his career. His cousin's cure at the sanatorium is almost complete. Hans thinks Joachim looks robust and well.

At the sanatorium, Hans soon discovers that the ordinary notions of time do not exist. Day follows day almost unchangingly. He meets the head of the institution, Dr. Behrens, as well as the other patients, who sit in particular groups at dinner. There are two Russian tables, for example, one of which is known to the patients as the bad Russian table. A couple who sits at that table has the room next to Hans. Through the thin partitions, he can hear them—even in the daytime—chase each other around the room. Hans is rather revolted, inasmuch as he can hear every detail of their lovemaking.

One patient interests Hans greatly, a merry Russian woman, supposedly married, named Clavdia Cauchat. Every time she comes into the dining room she bangs the door, which annoys Hans a great deal. Hans also meets the Italian Settembrini, a humanist writer and philosopher. Settembrini introduces him to a Jew, Naphta, who turns out to be a converted Jesuit and a cynical absolutist. Because the two men spend their time in endless discussions, Settembrini finally leaves the sanatorium to take rooms where Naphta lodges in the village.

From the very first day of his arrival, Hans feels feverish and a bit weak. His three weeks are almost up when he decides to take a physical examination, which reveals that he has tuberculosis. So he stays on as a patient. One day, defying orders, he goes out skiing and is caught in a snowstorm. The exposure aggravates his condition.

Hans's interest in Clavdia is heightened when he learns that Dr. Behrens, who likes to dabble in art, has painted her picture. The doctor gives Hans an X-ray plate of Clavdia's skeletal structure. Hans keeps the plate on the bureau in his room. Hans spends most of his free time with Joachim or with Settembrini and Naphta. The Italian and the Jesuit are given to all sorts of ideas, and Hans becomes involved in a multitude of philosophical discussions on the duration of time, God, politics, astronomy, and the nature of reality. Joachim, who is rather humorless and unimaginative, does not enjoy those talks, but Hans, since he himself has become a patient at the sanatorium, feels more at home and is not quite as attached to Joachim as he has been. Besides, it is Clavdia who interests him. On the occasion of a carnival, when some of the restrictions of the sanatorium are lifted, Hans tells her that he loves her. She thinks him foolish and refuses his proposal of marriage. The next day she leaves for Russia. Hans is in despair and becomes listless.

Joachim grows impatient with the progress of his cure when the doctor tells him that he is not yet well and will have to remain on the mountain for six more months. Wanting to rejoin his regiment, Joachim, in defiance of the doctor's injunctions, leaves the sanatorium. The doctor tells Hans that he can leave, too; but Hans knows that the doctor was angry when he said it, and therefore he remains.

Before long Joachim returns, his condition now so serious that his mother is summoned to the sanatorium. He dies shortly afterward. Clavdia also returns. She has been writing to the doctor, and Hans has heard of her from time to time, but she does not return alone. She has found a protector, an old Dutchman named Mynheer Peeperkorn, an earthy, hedonistic planter from Java. Hans gets very friendly with Peeperkorn, who soon learns that the young engineer is in love with Clavdia. The discovery does not affect their friendship at all, and the friendship lasts until the Dutchman dies.

For a time, the guests amuse themselves with spiritualist séances. A young girl, a new arrival at the sanatorium, claims that she can summon anyone from the dead. Hans takes part in one meeting and asks that Joachim be called back from the dead. Dr. Krokowski, the psychologist at the sanatorium, is opposed to the séances and breaks up the sessions. Then Naphta and Settembrini get into an argument. A duel is arranged between the two dialecticians. When the time comes, the Italian says he will fire into the air. When he does so, Naphta becomes more furious than ever. Realizing that Settembrini will not shoot at him, Naphta turns the pistol on himself and pulls the trigger. He falls face downward in the snow and dies.

Hans had come to the sanatorium for a visit of three weeks. His stay lasted more than seven years. During that time he saw many deaths and many changes in the institution. He becomes an old patient, not just a visitor. The sanatorium is another home in the high, thin air of the mountaintop. For him time, as measured by minutes, or even years, no longer exists. Time belongs to the flat, busy world below.

An Austrian archduke is assassinated. Newspapers suddenly bring the world to the International Sanatorium Berghof, with news of war and troop movements. Some of the patients remain in neutral Switzerland. Others pack to return home. When Hans says goodbye to Settembrini, who is his best friend among the old patients, the disillusioned humanist weeps at their parting. Hans is going back to Germany to fight. Time, the tragic hour of his generation, has overtaken him at last, and the sanatorium is no longer his refuge. Dodging bullets and bombs in a frontline trench, he disappears into the smoky mists that hide the future of Europe.

Critical Evaluation:

The Magic Mountain, begun in 1912 but written largely after World War I, was actually planned as a novella, inspired by Thomas Mann's own brief stay at a sanatorium at Davos-Platz, Switzerland. In fact, his early novella *Tristan* (1903) lays much of the groundwork for the later novel, which grew in bulk and complexity to become a veritable mirror of European society in the period leading up to World War I. It comes directly out of the tradition of the German bildungsroman, or novel of development, in which a relatively unformed character is exposed to various aspects of life and a range of influences. In a gradual process, that character achieves form, false goals are cast aside, and the true calling and, even more important, the right relationship to life are discovered.

Hans Castorp is just such a character when he arrives from the flatlands for a brief visit at Berghof. Mann emphasizes his bourgeois background and the lack of firm convictions and direction in his life. For Mann, the North German type—Hans is from Hamburg—always represented the solid, respectable middle-class life. However, Hans is also something of a quester, curious and adventuresome in the spiritual and intellectual realms. He observes the new world of the sanatorium intently and becomes involved with the personalities there, inquiring and holding long conversations. The narrative voice of the novel, as in most of Mann's works, has a certain ironic distance, but the pace of the work is very much tied to Hans's own experience of events and temporal rhythms. The three weeks of his planned visit stretch out to seven years, and the work becomes the record of the growth of his character in a microcosm of European society.

Mann's style developed out of the nineteenth century realist school, and he observes and describes reality with minute care. In his major novels, though, his style becomes increasingly symbolic and the structure increasingly expressive of symbolic values. Thus, the individual character development of Hans reflects the problems of European thought as a whole, and the various ideas to which he is exposed represent various intellectual and spiritual currents of the epoch.

Hans initially falls prey to a fascination with death, a dangerous attraction to the irresponsible freedom of the mountain world, the temptation to turn inward and to fall in love with sickness. He studies the illness whose symptoms he himself soon exhibits. He visits the "moribundi" and has long talks with Behrens and Krokowski, two of the doctors. Here life is seen as a process of decay, and even the intellect and the emotions are reduced to unconscious urges according to the then-new psychology of Sigmund Freud. Hans crystallizes these ideas in his feverish love for Clavdia Cauchat, who represents the Russian temperament—the urge to lose oneself, to give in to the emotions, to live life for the sake of life. She is contrasted to Settembrini, the Italian intellectual, educator, and humanist who is an optimist and believes in the perfectibility of humanity by reason. He opposes the fascination with death that Hans manifests. Settembrini is also contrasted to Naphta, his intellectual opponent, who is an irrationalist, a Jew turned Jesuit, with a highly Nietzschean viewpoint. He is a pessimist, deriding Settembrini's optimism and ridiculing his arguments as inconsistent. In actuality, neither figure means or is meant to convert Hans; their arguments cancel each other, as does so much else in the novel.

Hans finds his own position midway between the various opposing forces. This occurs primarily in the chapter "Snow." If the magic mountain is a timeless realm above the immediate concerns of the world, "now" is a hermetic world within that realm. Hans loses his way in a snowstorm and, exhausted and in danger of death, has a vision in which he sees juxtaposed an idyllic world of tropical paradise, peopled by gentle and happy folk, with a temple in which a terrible ritual of human sacrifice is being performed. This symbolizes the two poles of human life, and Hans's response is clear and decisive: Life is inseparably bound up with death, and the horrible is real and cannot be denied, but for the sake of goodness and love, human beings must not grant death dominion over their thoughts.

It is after this chapter that the figure of Mynheer Peeperkorn for a time dominates the novel, a figure of great vitality, simple in his thoughts, but of powerful personality. He is in love with his life force and terrified of losing it, and therefore he eventually commits suicide rather than face decay. He, like the other figures, represents an aspect of contemporary European thought and attitudes. Indeed, his traits, like those of Settembrini and Naphta, were drawn from life, from figures known to Mann. Thus the novel has something of the autobiographical and represents a stage in Mann's own thought. In the realm he has constructed, all these aspects—fictional bildungsroman, intellectual autobiography, and symbolic portrait of the prewar era—merge. This is made possible in part by the very foundation of the novel, the mountain.

The small community is elevated above the flatlands, in the rarefied Alpine air, remote from the problems of the world and the demands of everyday life. Time is dissolved, the rhythm of the novel moves from sequences of hours to days, weeks, months, and finally years, all rendered indistinguishable by the precise daily routine. In this world outside time, Hans can grow, can hover between conflicting opinions. Here he has freedom, most essentially in the "Snow" chapter, where even space is obliterated. In contrast to the earlier romantic outlook, however, this elevated position of freedom in isolation is not seen as a good thing, for though it provides an aesthetic space in which ideal development can occur, it is divorced from life. Life is the value that Hans's development finally leads him to affirm—life, with its horror as well as its beauty. When the European world saw itself plunged into World War I, Mann saw himself jolted out of his apolitical aesthetic stance. Therefore it is only fitting that Hans, too, must come down from the mountain to the world of time and action, even if only to be lost among the havoc of a world at war.

"Critical Evaluation" by Steven C. Schaber

Further Reading

Duttlinge, Carolin. "Mann, *Der Zauberberg*." In *Landmarks in the German Novel*, edited by Peter Hutchinson. New York: Peter Lang, 2007. An analysis of *The Magic Mountain*, including discussion of the book's significance in the development of the German novel from the eighteenth century through 1959.

Hatfield, Henry. *From "The Magic Mountain": Mann's Later Masterpieces*. Ithaca, N.Y.: Cornell University Press, 1979. The chapter "*The Magic Mountain*" provides a concise and broad introduction to the novel in the context of Mann's other later works; a good place to start for beginners. Includes some discussion of contemporary critical opinion and politics.

Heller, Erich. *Thomas Mann: The Ironic German*. South Bend, Ind.: Regnery/Gateway, 1979. The chapter "Conversation on the Magic Mountain" is a delightfully informative study of the novel in the form of a dialogue. Perhaps Heller's best-known statement on Mann's work, and a key to further study.

Kurzke, Hermann. *Thomas Mann: Life as a Work of Art—A Biography*. Translated by Leslie Willson. Princeton, N.J.: Princeton University Press, 2002. An English translation of a work that was celebrated upon its publication in Germany. Kurzke provides a balanced approach to Mann's life and work, and he addresses Mann's homosexuality and his relationship to Judaism.

Lehnert, Herbert, and Eva Wessell, eds. *A Companion to the Works of Thomas Mann*. Rochester, N.Y.: Camden House, 2004. A collection of essays about the range of Mann's work, including discussions of his late politics and female identities and autobiographical impulses in his writings. Includes "Magic and Reflections: Thomas Mann's *The Magic Mountain* and His War Essays" by Eva Wessell.

Mundt, Hannelore. *Understanding Thomas Mann*. Columbia: University of South Carolina Press, 2004. Mundt discusses the themes, concerns, presentation, and meanings of many of Mann's works, using Mann's later published diaries as one of the sources for her analysis. Chapter 8 is devoted to *The Magic Mountain*.

Ridley, Hugh. *The Problematic Bourgeois: Twentieth-Century Criticism on Thomas Mann's "Buddenbrooks" and "The Magic Mountain."* Columbia, S.C.: Camden House, 1994. A study of the reception of these two major novels in both literary history and political history. Places the works in the contexts of the debate on modernism and of psychological and philosophical criticism.

Robertson, Ritchie, ed. *The Cambridge Companion to Thomas Mann*. New York: Cambridge University Press, 2002. A collection of essays, some analyzing individual works and others discussing Mann's intellectual world, Mann and history, his literary techniques, and his representation of gender and sexuality. *The Magic Mountain* is examined in chapter 9.

Vaget, Hans Rudolf, ed. *Thomas Mann's "The Magic Mountain": A Casebook*. New York: Oxford University Press, 2008. Collection of interpretative essays, some new and others reprinted. Includes discussion of the novel's philosophy of time, Jewish characters, and depictions of medical practice, masculinity, and music.

Weigand, Hermann J. *"The Magic Mountain": A Study of Thomas Mann's Novel "Der Zauberberg."* Chapel Hill: University of North Carolina Press, 1964. Though published first in 1933, this study still offers much to the beginning student of Mann's novel. Provides a close reading with an especially interesting discussion of Germanness in the pre-World War I epoch.

The Magician of Lublin

Author: Isaac Bashevis Singer (1904-1991)
First published: Der Kuntsnmakher fun Lublin, 1959
(English translation, 1960)
Type of work: Novel
Type of plot: Psychological realism
Time of plot: Late nineteenth century
Locale: Poland

Principal characters:
YASHA MAZUR, a magician
ESTHER MAZUR, his wife
MAGDA ZBARSKI, his assistant and mistress
ZEFTEL LEKACH, a deserted wife, also his mistress
EMILIA CHRABOTZKY, a widow whom Yasha loves

The Story:

At his home in Lublin, Yasha Mazur, a magician, gets out of bed and eats the breakfast that his wife, Esther, prepared. Again, he assures her that he has never been unfaithful, even on long trips such as that from which he had just returned. However, while he sits in a tavern drinking beer and discussing women, his thoughts turn to the woman with whom he is presently in love, Emilia Chrabotzky, who wants him to convert to Catholicism, marry her, and move to Italy. Yasha cannot get Emilia out of his mind, but he is reluctant to leave his childless wife, who has made Yasha the center of her life. Moreover, though, unlike his wife, he is careless in religious matters, Yasha is hesitant about rejecting his faith and his people.

Again, Yasha sets off on his travels. Near Piask, he spends the night with the unattractive Magda; her mother, Elzbieta

Zbarski, who treats Yasha like a son-in-law; and Magda's unsavory brother, Bolek, who hates Yasha. The next day, Yasha goes to Piask to visit yet another mistress, Zeftel Lekach, whose husband had disappeared after his escape from prison. Yasha spends the evening with a gang of thieves, his longtime friends, who are awed by his skills, especially his ability to pick locks, and once again urge him to join them and make a fortune.

While Yasha and Magda are on their way to Warsaw, a storm breaks, and they take refuge in a prayer house. Yasha again worries about abandoning his religion. In Warsaw, however, he has to deal with a more urgent matter: his performance schedule. As usual, he learns that he will be working for very low wages. Perhaps, he thinks, Emilia is right in thinking that he should go abroad.

When he sees the beautiful Emilia, Yasha cannot resist agreeing to her terms. He says he will become a Catholic, marry her, and take her to Italy, along with her consumptive daughter Halina and her servant, Yadwiga. Privately, however, he wonders where he will find the money. At a play with Emilia, Yasha becomes so depressed that he considers repenting, but the impulse passes. When Emilia again refuses to allow him into her bed, he becomes even more despondent.

Back at his own apartment, Yasha enjoys being coddled by Magda. Just as he sits down to dinner, however, Zeftel turns up at his door. Although Magda is furious, Yasha leaves to accompany Zeftel to the house where she is staying, fearing that the white slaver who had taken her in would take advantage of her. When he gets there, however, Yasha soon finds himself in a friendly conversation, and he spends most of the night with the white slaver and his female accomplice.

Suddenly recalling that Yadwiga had told him about a rich old man who kept his money in a safe in his apartment, Yasha steals the money he needs. However, he is unable to pick the lock and, when he jumps from the balcony of the apartment, he hurts his foot. Pursued by a watchman, he again takes refuge in a prayer house. This time, he joins in the prayers, convinced that he must return to God and Judaism.

Even though Yasha's foot is now so bad that he fears he will not be able to perform his shows, he refuses to call a doctor. Instead, he limps off to tell Emilia that he has no money for the trip. Then, to Yasha's horror, a police officer stops by to warn Emilia that the thief might have designs on her, since a notebook with her name in it had been left in the old man's apartment. Certain that he will eventually be arrested, Yasha tells Emilia what he had done, but, to his amazement, she responds by rebuking him for bungling the job.

In despair, Yasha wanders into a synagogue where Lithuanian Jews are holding a service. If he were to return to Judaism, Yasha mused, he would not settle for a form so worldly. Only the strictest kind of observance could prevent him from sinning.

Back at his apartment, Yasha discovers that Magda hanged herself, but not before strangling the three animals that he used in his magic act. After Magda's body is removed, Yasha cannot remain in his apartment, and he leaves for a hotel. However, because he did not bring his identification papers, he is turned away. Certainly, he thinks, Zeftel will help him out. At the white slaver's house, however, Yasha receives his second shock of the night. Zeftel and the white slaver are in bed together. Yasha interprets this as a sign: God has left him nowhere to go but to God.

Three years later, Yasha the magician has become Reb Jacob the Penitent. He is back in Lublin, walled up in a tiny cell in the courtyard of his house. His foot has healed, but spiritually he is still in pain, every day remembering yet another sin for which he must be punished. Esther keeps begging him to come out, and strangers break into his meditations to ask for his prayers, to discuss theology, or just to mock him.

One day, an old friend visits with news of the world Yasha had left behind. Elzbieta is dead, Bolek is in prison, and Zeftel is married to the white slaver and running a brothel in Argentina. Irrationally, Yasha feels responsible for all of these disasters. In a long letter to him, however, Emilia says that she, not he, is to blame for their affair and assures him that she and her daughter are both well and happy. Although Emilia has remarried, she counts her days with Yasha as the happiest in her life. She insists that Yasha is basically a good, kind man and urges him not to be so hard on himself. Finally, Emilia says that she, her daughter, and even the professor think of Yasha with affection, and that, in Warsaw, he is widely admired once again.

Critical Evaluation:

Writing in Yiddish about Yiddish-speaking Jewish communities in Poland, Isaac Bashevis Singer established the reputation that in 1978 won for him the Nobel Prize in Literature. Although later works about Holocaust survivors in the United States have won high praise, *The Magician of Lublin*, in setting, plot, and characterization, is typical of the fiction that brought Singer his initial fame and ensured his lasting popularity.

The plot of *The Magician of Lublin* is not as simple as it seems. It begins as a picaresque novel; Singer establishes an interesting character and then follows him on his travels, pointing out how, through trickery, his protagonist manages to survive, though not always unharmed. However, there is a second story line in the novel, a second journey involving the same character. Even while he pursues fame, fortune, and Emilia, without realizing it, Yasha is traveling in quest of God.

The historical setting of the novel also involves a duality of perspective. The villages Singer describes appear to be self-sufficient, insulated from the outside world. Within them, the characters may quarrel and reconcile, suffer and survive, but actually their lives move in a pattern as inevitable as the seasons, as old as their religious heritage. Even a rebel like Yasha knows this; he counts time not only by the coming of spring but also by the coming of Shabuoth.

However, *The Magician of Lublin* contains reminders that this apparent permanence is an illusion. When the villagers talk about the power of czarist Russia, they are not aware of what Singer's readers know: that, within a few decades, there will be no czar in Russia. When they arrange marriages and plan the futures of their children, they have no way of knowing that a half century later, a set of conscienceless criminals will murder Jews by the millions, wipe out their villages, and destroy their way of life. One's knowledge of this historical fact, in particular, contributes to the poignancy of novels that, on the surface, are comic or perhaps tragicomic in tone.

Singer's characterization, too, is more complex than one might think. Yasha's women, for example, are initially presented almost as stereotypes: Esther, the devout and devoted wife; Magda, the girl so unattractive that she cannot catch a husband; Zeftel, the vulnerable, deserted wife; Emilia, the widow who, though desperately in love, is virtuous. In the course of the novel, however, Emilia and Zeftel prove to be more practical than sentimental, Magda reveals a capacity for tragic intensity, and Esther discards her dignity in a vain attempt to get Yasha back into her bed.

Yasha, too, begins as a stereotype, in his case as a folk hero. There is nothing he cannot do, no feat of magic he cannot perform, no lock he cannot pick, no acrobatic stunt that is too much for him, no woman who does not adore him, no role he cannot play. Later, however, Yasha is perceived as less perfect than his admirers thought him to be. In one way or another, all of his mistresses desert him, and when he attempts burglary, he fails to pick a simple lock and also falls and injures his foot. It can be argued, of course, that it is not a matter of Yasha's having been overrated; it is that God chose to humble him to bring Yasha back to God.

Clearly, it is the meaning of this change in Yasha that is crucial to any interpretation of *The Magician of Lublin*. It has been suggested that Reb Jacob the Penitent is as foolish as the original Yasha, for surely, as the rabbi suggests, a sensible man would search for a mean between two extremes. However, it seems more likely that, instead of rebuking his ascetic protagonist, Singer understands his need to retreat from the world. By nature, Yasha is not moderate; his imagination is as excessive as his appetites. It is not surprising then that, for him, there is no middle way, such as that represented by the practical Catholic, Emilia, or the worldly Lithuanian Jews. For Yasha, there are only two possibilities: the street or the synagogue. His God is uncompromising. Singer may be suggesting that, unpalatable as the idea may be to modern minds, this is the very nature of God.

Rosemary M. Canfield Reisman

Further Reading

Alexander, Edward. *Isaac Bashevis Singer: A Study of the Short Fiction*. Boston: Twayne, 1980. Considers *The Magician of Lublin* as a novel marking a new direction for Singer. Instead of the Jewish community, his subject is the individual, in this case the artist, as he vacillates between freedom and faith.

Friedman, Lawrence S. *Understanding Isaac Bashevis Singer*. Columbia: University of South Carolina Press, 1988. Discusses the theme of identity in *The Magician of Lublin*. A good starting point for the study of Singer.

Hadda, Janet. *Isaac Bashevis Singer: A Life*. New York: Oxford University Press, 1997. Focusing on both the forces of family and the social environment that influenced Singer, Hadda uncovers the public persona to reveal a more complex person than previously understood.

Lee, Grace Farrell. *From Exile to Redemption: The Fiction of Isaac Bashevis Singer*. Carbondale: Southern Illinois University Press, 1987. A chronological study of Singer's works, intended to show how his views altered with the years. A perceptive section on *The Magician of Lublin* focuses on symbolism in the novel.

Malin, Irving, ed. *Critical Views of Isaac Bashevis Singer*. New York: New York University Press, 1969. Collection of essays offering numerous interpretations of Singer's work. J. S. Wolkenfeld's "Isaac Bashevis Singer: The Faith of His Devils and Magicians" compares the moral choices of several major characters, including Yasha, in *The Magician of Lublin*.

Noiville, Florence. *Isaac B. Singer: A Life*. Translated by Catherine Temerson. New York: Farrar, Straus and Giroux, 2006. An informative biography written in concise, easy-to-read language. Noiville gleans information from interviews with Singer's wife, son, friends, and colleagues, as well as his autobiography, *In My Father's Court*. She focuses on Singer's life struggles, his relationships with others, and the adversities he faced as a Jewish writer.

Qiao, Guo Qiang. *The Jewishness of Isaac Bashevis Singer*. New York: Peter Lang, 2003. Analyzes the theme of Jewishness in Singer's work, finding a unique place for the writer within American Jewish literature. Focuses on his depiction of Jewish assimilation in both Poland and the United States, examines his narrative strategies, and compares Jewish identity and historical consciousness in works by Singer, Saul Bellow, Bernard Malamud, and Philip Roth.

Ran-Moseley, Faye. "The Ethnic Fool and the Mad Magician: Isaac Bashevis Singer's *The Magician of Lublin*." In *The Tragicomic Passion: A History and Analysis of Tragicomedy and Tragicomic Characterization in Drama, Film, and Literature*. New York: Peter Lang, 1994. Focuses on the character of the fool in Singer's novel and other works of twentieth century literature, film, and drama, analyzing how the fool reflects the tragicomic nature of these works.

Wolitz, Seth L., ed. *The Hidden Isaac Bashevis Singer.* Austin: University of Texas Press, 2001. A collection of es-says, including discussions of Singer's use of the Yiddish language and cultural experience, themes that persist throughout his writing, his interface with other times and cultures, his autobiographical work, and a translation of a previously unpublished "gangster" novel.

Magnalia Christi Americana
Or, The Ecclesiastical History of New-England

Author: Cotton Mather (1663-1728)
First published: 1702
Type of work: History

The Puritans of the Massachusetts Bay Colony in and around Boston believed they had been called to the New World to fulfill God's Providence. They were part of the Protestant Reformation, which they considered the most significant period of history since Christ himself walked the earth and one that would hasten the millennium.

For some twenty-five years before the publication of Cotton Mather's *Magnalia Christi Americana*, there had been, according to Kenneth Silverman, calls for someone to document the history of the New England colony. Many felt that Mather's father, Increase, was in the best position to write such a magisterial work. Thus, Cotton, being not only Increase's son but also the grandson of two other essential contributors to the Puritan settlement of America—John Cotton and Richard Mather—felt it his familial duty to take responsibility for this monumental ecclesiastical history.

In the estimation of Silverman, the book was begun in 1693 and was compiled from diaries, Increase's correspondence, and manuscript histories of New England by William Bradford and William Hubbard. Mather and his father also were acquainted with survivors of the first generation of settlers, or their families. Although Mather had interviewed many of them, he wanted even more information. In 1700, the manuscript of the book was sent to England for publication. After many delays and discouragements, Mather learned that it had been published in 1702. He was dismayed, however, to find that the publisher had made some three hundred typographical errors in the text.

According to Perry Miller and Thomas H. Johnson, the book's Latin title means "great achievements of Christ in America." The phrase originates from a Latin translation from the Greek of the book of Acts 2:11 that uses the phrase "magnalia dei," or "wonderful works of God." The title also might have derived from *Magnalia Dei Anglicana* by John Vicar, published in London in 1646. In any event, Mather's title reflects the purpose of the book, which is to celebrate the marvelous works of Christ in the New World, particularly the rise of a Reformed Evangelical Church forced to leave a flawed Old World to practice Christianity as it was intended, and a church intended to serve as "a city on a hill," in John Winthrop's words, for the rest of the world to emulate. More immediately, Mather hoped to reinvigorate what he perceived as a flagging enthusiasm in his—the third—generation of New Englanders by citing the pure beliefs and heroic actions of the Puritan ancestors.

The collection of historical sketches and documents, including sermons, biographies, and historical narratives, spans eight hundred folio pages in double columns. Babette M. Levy points out that Mather includes seventeen of his previously published works, including a long biographical sketch of Sir William Phips, one of the later governors of Massachusetts. This sketch is out of proportion to the other biographies (including those of more significant people) in book 2. Such additions give the sense of a miscellany of history rather than a seamless historical narrative.

Critics have complained that the book is sprawling, heavily allusive, and pedantic. Mather's writing style has been called artificial, turgid, fantastic, and overloaded, full of dense jungles of quotation, analogy, and other embellishments. The word "baroque" best describes an artistry that is highly ornamental, elaborate in verbal usages, and crowded with figures of speech. Many of the devices Mather employs, such as repetition, puns, paradoxes, anagrams, and other wordplay, are probably ones he found effective in the pulpit.

Although Mather was attacked as ostentatious, idiosyncratic, extravagant, and intemperate, scholars such as Barrett Wendell and Lyman Kittredge note his veracity and ability to capture the spirit of his times. He was certainly quite conversant with the languages of the age. Kenneth B. Murdock notes four languages in particular that he masters in the work: the language of the English Renaissance, shown especially in his allusions in their original Latin and Greek to works of classical antiquity; the Old Testament jeremiad, in which he, like the prophets of old, warns that sinful behavior will be punished; typology, in which Old Testament events and persons prefigure New Testament ones; and a rich exegetical dialogue about the book with which he was most familiar, the Bible.

The central theme of Mather's masterwork concerns divine Providence: the belief that events happen when they do, persons rise to occasions in the manner that they do, and enemies fall as they do because an omnipotent and deeply interested God designed the universe for his own purposes. Puritan historiography is providential, each anecdote illuminating some aspect of God's eternal will. No incident happens by chance or luck.

Magnalia Christi Americana consists of seven books and a general introduction. The latter imitates the opening of Vergil's epic *Aeneid* (c. 29-19 B.C.E.; English translation, 1553), which indicates Mather's desire to stress the heroism of the Puritans' errand into the wilderness and to place his story in the literature of the world. His stated intention is to describe the wonders of Christ as revealed in America in the community of a small, chosen band of Puritan wanderers who had left England to settle in the Massachusetts Bay region of America in the seventeenth century. It is a history of evangelical Protestants driven away from the Church of England by powerful, but mistaken, brothers in the faith who departed from a course of reformation meant to restore the church to its original form at the time of Christ and his apostles. To the Puritans of New England, that reformation had not yet been completed. Mather expects his work to be criticized by those who disagree with the Puritan view, but he cheerfully takes on the task as an act of service to Christ's kingdom.

The first of the seven books treats what Mather calls antiquities. He gives an account of the discovery of America by European explorers, thus providing a context for the eventual settling of Massachusetts and Connecticut by the pilgrims and the Puritans. Book 2 traces the lives of the first governors of these colonies, emphasizing the importance of William Bradford of Plymouth and John Winthrop of Massachusetts Bay but also mentioning other governors, such as Edward Winslow, Simon Bradstreet, and Edward Hopkins. Appended to this section is a long, previously published account of "The Life of Phips," the most recent governor of Massachusetts Bay and a parishioner of Cotton and Increase Mather in their Boston church.

Book 3 focuses on the ministers who guided the faith of the New Englanders. According to Levy, some seventy-seven of these divines were graduates of Cambridge and Oxford and were practicing in England before coming to America. Dozens followed them. The measure that Mather uses for these ministers' greatness is ethical significance. As with the governors, these pastors follow a similar pattern of sainthood, according to David Levin. Although they struggled with doubt and uncertainty, all glorified God and instructed posterity by their example.

Book 4 notes the early and essential role Harvard College played in developing new spiritual leaders in the colonies. Mather's father was president of the college, and several of his commencement addresses (in Latin) are included in the *Magnalia Christi Americana*. Later in his life, Mather would be disappointed that he himself was not to be appointed to the college's presidency. He did attend the school, however, beginning at the age of twelve. This book sketches nine ministers' lives, all earning Harvard degrees. Book 5 is a discussion of the congregational churches in New England and the synods in which representatives of individual congregations agreed on organizational structure, membership requirements, and other matters of the church polity.

Book 6 concerns what Mather calls wonderful providences that illustrate God's hand at work in New England. Among the examples cited are rewards of the worthy and punishments of the sinful. Some examples recount deliverance from storms at sea, a frequent source of anxiety for the colonists who depended on ships to bring their loved ones and supplies; other examples involve remarkable conversions, including those of Native Americans. Mather also cites instances of witchcraft and demon possession. All these events have a supernatural aura that challenges the rationality and skepticism of the times.

The final book of the *Magnalia Christi Americana* describes various tribulations, from Indian wars to heretics in the church to political problems with England's governance of the colony. Each problem, to Mather's way of thinking, is ultimately the result of sinfulness among the colonists themselves, which causes God to punish them. He includes his own jeremiad on the subject, which warns of further retribution if the colony does not reform itself.

Sacvan Bercovitch argues that the apocalyptic nature of the *Magnalia Christi Americana* establishes very early on in American history a corporate American identity. It is one of the first prophetic books in American literature, and may be less significant as history than as myth and archetype. Mather's treating America as exceptional in both its creation and central role in world history has greatly influenced American thought, including the ideas of such literary figures as Benjamin Franklin, Ralph Waldo Emerson, Henry Wadsworth Longfellow, Harriet Beecher Stowe, and Nathaniel Hawthorne. The *Magnalia Christi Americana* set an important standard by which Americans came to identify themselves.

William L. Howard

Further Reading

Baker, Dorothy Z. *America's Gothic Fiction: The Legacy of "Magnalia Christi Americana."* Columbus: Ohio State University Press, 2007. In this study, Baker examines how nineteenth-century writers Edgar Allan Poe, Harriet Beecher Stowe, and Nathaniel Hawthorne, among others, turned to Mather's *Magnalia Christi Americana* to "refashion his historical accounts as gothic fiction."

Bercovitch, Sacvan. "Cotton Mather." In *Major Writers of Early American Literature*, edited by Everett Emerson. Madison: University of Wisconsin Press, 1972. Answers charges that Mather was egotistical and ostentatious by demonstrating his moral idealism, his subordination of self to Christ, and his belief in the unity of all knowledge.

Levin, David. *Cotton Mather: The Young Life of the Lord's Remembrancer, 1663-1703*. Cambridge, Mass.: Harvard University Press, 1978. Chronicles the first forty years

of Mather's life. Includes discussions of the *Magnalia Christi Americana*, its structure, and its biographical pattern of finding variety in one essential paradigm of good individuals.

Levy, Babette M. *Cotton Mather.* 1979. Reprint. New York: G. K. Hall, 1999. A basic study covering the life and works of Mather with a chronology, notes, and a bibliography. Includes a full chapter on the *Magnalia Christi Americana.*

Miller, Perry, and Thomas H. Johnson, eds. *The Puritans: A Sourcebook of Their Writings.* 1963. Reprint. Mineola, N.Y.: Dover, 2001. An anthology of Puritan writings. An excellent introduction places the Puritans in their historical context, corrects popular misconceptions of them, and explains their beliefs.

Murdock, Kenneth B., ed. *Selections from Cotton Mather.* 1926. Reprint. New York: Hafner, 1973. Murdock's introduction sketches Mather's precocious childhood and remarkable career as scholar, writer, minister, and scientist. Critiques his historical method and writing style and traces his influence on American writers and thinkers.

Silverman, Kenneth. *The Life and Times of Cotton Mather.* 1984. Reprint. New York: Welcome Rain, 2002. A thorough biography that includes an analysis of the *Magnalia Christi Americana*'s sources, structure, publication history, and significance.

Wendell, Barrett. *Cotton Mather: The Puritan Priest.* New York: Harcourt, Brace and World, 1963. First published in 1891, this biography reopened serious discussion of Mather, telling his story largely in his own words. Relies on diaries, letters, and published works.

The Magnificent Ambersons

Author: Booth Tarkington (1869-1946)
First published: 1918
Type of work: Novel
Type of plot: Social realism
Time of plot: 1873-early twentieth century
Locale: A city in the Midwest

The Story:

Major Amberson creates the family fortune in the 1870's. When Isabel, his daughter, is about twenty years old, she is courted by two men: Wilbur Minafer, a quiet businessman,

Principal characters:
GEORGE AMBERSON MINAFER, the protagonist
ISABEL AMBERSON MINAFER, his mother
GEORGE AMBERSON, his uncle
FANNY MINAFER, his aunt
EUGENE MORGAN, a prosperous industrialist
LUCY MORGAN, his daughter

and Eugene Morgan, a debt-ridden lawyer. Morgan destroys his chances in a drinking incident on the Amberson estate. Isabel marries Wilbur, and their only child is George

Amberson Minafer. Isabel spoils her wild boy. George treats others with contempt and was once expelled from a prep school for his bad behavior. The townspeople hope to see George get his comeuppance.

When George is an eighteen-year-old college student, a ball is held in his honor at the Amberson mansion. Here George meets Eugene Morgan, his mother's former suitor, and falls in love with his nineteen-year-old daughter, Lucy. Eugene had left town at the time Isabel dismissed him, become an inventor, and returned to town twenty years later to manufacture horseless carriages.

George informs Lucy that he has no career plans. During their sleigh ride the next day, George attempts to embarrass the inventor by racing his sleigh past Morgan's inoperative horseless carriage. George's sleigh crashes, and he and Lucy have to hitch a ride back into town on the new vehicle. After George returns home for summer vacation, he renews his relationship with Lucy. When she and her father attend one of the Major's weekly Sunday dinners, the latter reveals that Isabel and Eugene had once been engaged. On the night before George returns to college, Isabel tells him of Wilbur's declining health. His father is deeply worried because he and George's uncle, George Amberson, have tied up much of the family's assets in a company owned by their friends, an investment that is turning sour.

During the following summer, George proposes to Lucy when he hears a false rumor that she is engaged to Fred Kinney. Though she declines to say either yes or no at that time, she promises to settle the matter before he returns to school. On George's final night before returning to college, Lucy still leaves their relationship unsettled. She tells him that they are "almost" engaged. While back at college, Isabel writes George that she has gotten the ailing Wilbur to take a vacation and that his uncle, Sydney Amberson, and his wife have taken their one-third share of the Amberson fortune. Then Wilbur dies, and his business failure leaves Uncle George and Fanny broke. George Minafer gives his father's insurance money to Fanny as compensation.

After George's graduation from college, he is horrified to see five new houses on the family estate—the Major's attempt to recoup the family fortune. George becomes increasingly hostile to both Eugene Morgan and his automobiles. Lucy refuses to go beyond their "almost" engagement because George, unlike her father, refuses to pursue a career. George then insults Eugene Morgan during a Sunday dinner. Angered by his differences with Lucy and by a rumor that Isabel had always been in love with Eugene, George confronts the rumormonger, Mrs. Johnson, and then bars the industrialist from his house. George then tells Isabel that he has

to protect the Amberson name from scandal, and bullies her into ceasing all contact with Eugene Morgan. George subsequently tells Lucy that he and Isabel are to leave the country indefinitely.

Then the Amberson holdings fall into decay, the Major's new houses prove a failure, and Uncle George and Fanny invest heavily in an ill-fated headlight invention. Against Uncle George's advice, Fanny secretly stakes all of her money on the scheme. After several years abroad, George brings his mother back when she is gravely ill. As she lay dying, George refuses to let Eugene see his old flame one last time. Isabel later tells her son that she wants to see Morgan once more. With Isabel's demise, the Major loses all interest in business. When Fanny tells George that the gossip died out soon after his departure, George then fears that his interference had been a grave error. Then the headlight scheme collapses, and Uncle George reveals that Isabel had never received a deed for her house.

When Major Amberson dies, the Amberson estate goes bankrupt, and Sydney and Amelia, having taken the best part of it, refuse to help. Uncle George is awarded a consulship in another city, while George is to room with Fanny and study law. When Fanny confesses that she is destitute, George has to accept a dangerous job involving explosives to support her. The growing city quickly effaces all traces of the Ambersons, and George feels the humiliation the townspeople had long ago desired. George is then seriously injured by an automobile. When Eugene is away on business, he discovers that both he and Lucy have a vision of Isabel. His subsequent visit to a psychic and a second vision of Isabel suggests to him that she wants him to help George. Upon returning home, Eugene rushes to George's hospital room and finds Lucy and Fanny already there. George begs his forgiveness, and Eugene realizes that he can regain his connection with Isabel by helping her son.

Critical Evaluation:

Perhaps more than any other American writer of the twentieth century, Booth Tarkington demonstrates the insecure position of an author in relation to his critics. Born into an upper-middle-class Indianapolis family and educated at Purdue and Princeton universities, Tarkington went on to become one of the most popular and critically acclaimed writers of the early twentieth century. During this period, he readily produced his plays and regularly published his short stories and novels. Critical reception was no less favorable, with the novels *The Magnificent Ambersons* and *Alice Adams* (1921) both receiving Pulitzer Prizes. Although postwar critics have virtually ignored Tarkington, his well-wrought tales are important examples of social realism. They chart the development of an industrial giant, the United States.

Tarkington is primarily a regional writer, his major works depicting the social upheaval of industrialism and its effects upon Midwest locales and their inhabitants in the industrial era. *The Magnificent Ambersons* is no exception. Initially published in 1918, Tarkington reissued the novel in the 1920's as part of the Growth trilogy, which also includes *The Turmoil* (1915) and *The Midlander* (1923). Like the other realist writers of his time, Tarkington effectively employs physical detail to depict a palpable and often gritty reality. In *The Magnificent Ambersons*, much of the story takes place in the early years of the twentieth century. Tarkington recreates the immediate past for the readers of 1918 by opening the novel with a lengthy discussion of the changing fashions—from clothing fads to the particular jargon of George Minafer's social stratum. The most striking example of Tarkington's brand of realism is the smoke created by the burning of soft coal. Though little more than a nuisance at the beginning of the novel, it obscures and eventually engulfs the Amberson estate when the latter goes bankrupt, casting a pall on the once mighty family. In Tarkington's skillful hands, a seemingly minor detail comes to symbolize for the Ambersons a dark future they can neither recognize nor accept.

Told in a conventional third-person narration, Tarkington's tale charts the transition of a large Midwestern town (presumably Indianapolis, although it is never stated) into a modern city. Specifically, the novel deals with characters who are wedded to the past (the Ambersons) and those who look forward to the future (the Morgans). George Amberson Minafer, the protagonist and Major Amberson's only grandchild, is clearly linked to an earlier age in the novel. As a nine-year-old child, George reigns like a feudal lord over the growing town, rebelling against any kind of authority and thrashing his perceived enemies. Indeed, the "F.O.T.A." clubroom contains a representation of a shield and battle axes. His chivalric tendencies are also reflected in his ultimately disastrous efforts to protect his mother's reputation. Calling those who are not of his own class "riffraff," Tarkington's protagonist fully embodies an aristocratic old order, one who prefers a horse to the horseless carriage. Significantly, George wins Lucy only when he sheds this veneer of nobility and adopts her father's work ethic. Clearly, Tarkington rejects an American aristocracy.

In its broadest terms, *The Magnificent Ambersons* depicts the rags-to-riches-to-rags scenario that is the dark side of the American success story. The novel's central theme is the necessity of adapting to change in a time of transition. Simply put, Major Amberson's empire crumbles because he and his family fail to accommodate change. In contrast to the old guard, Eugene Morgan heralds change and is its most visible exponent. Indeed, he nurtures its most potent symbol, the automobile. Irony is the means by which Tarkington explores this theme. This is evident in specific incidents, but irony is also a factor in the larger structure of the book. When George attempts to show his bravado by racing past Eugene Morgan's machine, the destruction of the sleigh ironically leaves the former little choice but to ride in the horseless carriage he sought to mock. The irony is compounded when this scene is compared with George's more successful stunts as a child. In addition to demonstrating George's lack of growth, Tarkington increases the irony by having his protagonist defeated by the embodiment of the future in the book, Eugene Morgan. Even more ironic is the automobile accident that lands George in the hospital. From the "princely terror" who whipped the hardware man in the third chapter, George has now become the hapless victim in chapter 34—felled by the very riffraff he so vigorously disdained. Most ironic of all is the economic context of the Ambersons' rise and fall: They build their empire in a time of great hardship and lose it in a period of booming prosperity.

Critics have faulted the novel for what they regard as its sentimental and overly optimistic ending, but Tarkington's conclusion serves two important purposes. First, it brings to a close the moral education of George Minafer. Having lost his aristocratic status and having received his deserved punishment, he is ready to adopt the American work ethic. Second, Tarkington's adept engineering of the final reconciliation brings about a merging of the old and the new.

Cliff Prewencki

Further Reading

Fennimore, Keith J. *Booth Tarkington*. New York: Twayne, 1974. One of the best books on Tarkington for the general reader, offering a good overview of the author and his novels, a useful chronology, and an excellent annotated bibliography. Emphasizes the interaction between the aristocrats and the upstarts in *The Magnificent Ambersons*.

Gray, Donald J. Introduction to *The Magnificent Ambersons*, by Booth Tarkington. Bloomington: Indiana University Press, 1989. Provides valuable overviews of both the novel and Tarkington's prolific career. Claims that Tarkington is less concerned with psychological realism than with social realism.

LeGates, Charlotte. "The Family in Booth Tarkington's *Growth* Trilogy." *Midamerica* 6 (1979): 88-99. The family occupies the center of Tarkington's world, and LeGates's discussion of it in *The Magnificent Ambersons* and the other novels in the trilogy is exemplary.

Mallon, Thomas. "Hoosiers." *Atlantic Monthly*, May, 2004. Takes a close look at Tarkington's oeuvre, finding that his few good works have been "suffocated" by the majority of the mediocre ones. Asks how the once ubiquitous Tarkington could "disappear so completely."

Mayberry, Susanah. *My Amiable Uncle: Recollections About Booth Tarkington*. West Lafayette, Ind.: Purdue University Press, 1983. Tarkington's niece recollects her personal experiences with the writer, providing an important contribution to Tarkington's biography. Includes family photographs.

Noe, Marcia. "Failure and the American Mythos: Tarkington's *The Magnificent Ambersons*." *Midamerica* 15 (1988): 11-18. Contends that failure is a prominent theme in American literature and that this novel is Tarkington's most thorough treatment of that theme. Holds that George's failure as an aristocrat is an essential element in the novel in that it paves the way for his moral growth.

Woodress, James Leslie. *Booth Tarkington: Gentleman from Indiana*. Philadelphia: J. B. Lippincott, 1955. An old but valuable biography that includes insightful analyses of Tarkington's plays and novels. Highlights the importance of work as the foundation of Tarkington's moral vision and the purifying power of a woman's love in *The Magnificent Ambersons*.

Magnificent Obsession

Author: Lloyd C. Douglas (1877-1951)
First published: 1929
Type of work: Novel
Type of plot: Domestic realism
Time of plot: Early twentieth century
Locale: Detroit, Michigan; Europe

Principal characters:
DR. WAYNE HUDSON, a famous brain surgeon
HELEN BRENT HUDSON, the doctor's second wife
JOYCE HUDSON, the doctor's daughter and Helen's school friend
ROBERT MERRICK, a physician
NANCY ASHFORD, the superintendent at the Hudson Clinic

The Story:

The staff at the Hudson Clinic is worried about the head of the hospital, Dr. Wayne Hudson. The doctor has suddenly become nervous and haggard, a bad condition for an eminent practicing surgeon, and his staff tries to advise the doctor to take six months away from his work. The doctor himself surprises his staff by announcing that he is about to marry his daughter's school friend, Miss Helen Brent. The couple are married within a short time and live at the doctor's lakeside cottage. Soon afterward, a shocking tragedy occurs at the lake. Dr. Hudson drowns because the inhalator that might have saved his life had been dispatched across the lake to resuscitate a wealthy young playboy, Robert Merrick.

While he is recuperating, young Merrick believes that the doctors and nurses at the Hudson Clinic resent him. He does not yet know that he is alive at the expense of the life of the hospital's chief surgeon. He questions the superintendent of the clinic, Nancy Ashford, who had been in love with her chief, Dr. Hudson, but Ashford does not give him a satisfac-

tory answer. Later, overhearing a conversation, Merrick discovers why the people at the hospital seem to despise him. He talks again to Ashford, who tells him the only way he can ever make amends would be to take Dr. Hudson's place in life by becoming a great surgeon.

After weeks of pondering on the idea of going to medical school, Merrick decides that he will try to fill Dr. Hudson's place. When he tells Ashford of his plans, she tells him the story of the doctor's many philanthropies. She also gives him a book the doctor had written in code. After many days and nights of perseverance, the young man manages to break the cipher. When he has done so, it seems to him that the doctor, whom he has come to look upon as an ideal, had been a lunatic, for the book is a strange, mystic tract about doing good. From Ashford, he learns that the deceased doctor had been a great mystic, believing that his gift as a surgeon came to him from what he called the Major Personality. That power was earned by doing good unknown to others, philanthropy that would aid the recipient in leading a valuable life of service.

During the next few years, Merrick attends the state medical school. One night, as he sits studying, he suddenly feels a call to go to a nightclub where he knows Joyce Hudson, the doctor's daughter, is to be. After rescuing her from a drunken scene, he takes her home. There he meets the doctor's widow, Helen Hudson.

That semester, Merrick almost fails at medical school. Discouraged with his own efforts, he decides to experiment with the knowledge he gained from the dead surgeon's manuscript. He aides a fellow student, Dawson, who is about to leave school because he lacks funds. Immediately, he feels renewed hope and plunges into his work with enthusiasm.

Helen Hudson leaves for Europe, where she remains for three years. Near the end of that time, she discovers that the cousin who is handling her affairs has been dishonest. Needing funds, she writes to Ashford to ask if her stock in the Hudson Clinic can be sold. Ashford tells Merrick, now a doctor at the clinic, about Helen's letter. He sends Helen twenty-five thousand dollars and sells some of the stock for her.

Toward the end of her stay in Europe, Helen meets Mrs. Dawson, wife of the medical student whom Merrick had helped through medical school. Merrick had asked Mrs. Dawson to learn something of Helen's financial losses so that he might put her affairs in order. After telling Mrs. Dawson her troubles, Helen discovers an envelope Mrs. Dawson addressed to Merrick. Helen promptly disappears.

Merrick visits the cousin who is managing Helen's financial affairs. The man has stolen from Helen about $100,000. Merrick makes good the loss and sends the man out of the country, bringing no charges against him because he is related to Helen. Before the cousin leaves, he learns Merrick's theory of personality projection and makes up his mind to lead an honest life.

Tired from overwork, Merrick vacations in the country for several weeks. Then he returns to his laboratory and begins a program of hard work. His meals are returned to the kitchen almost untouched. His labors are at last successful, for he perfected a scalpel that automatically cauterizes by means of electricity. The device opens a new field of brain surgery because it prevents hemorrhage as it cuts into the tissue.

About Christmastime, Helen returns to the United States. In Detroit, she goes to her trust company and asks to see the shares of stock that they hold in her name. As she suspects, they had been transferred from Merrick. When she leaves the bank, she does not know whether to feel thankful or insulted. Helen goes next to the Hudson Clinic, where she asks to see

Merrick immediately. Her confusion is even greater when he tells her he cannot take back the money. He tries to explain the transfer of her stock, but she is in no mood for explanations. As he takes her to the door, they meet her stepdaughter. Joyce complicates the tense situation by proposing a theater party for the next day. To not create gossip, both Helen and Merrick agree to go to dinner and the theater afterward. As he helps Helen into the taxi, Merrick murmurs that he loves her.

The next evening at dinner, Merrick asks Helen not to tell about all that had been done for a needy Italian family at Assisi. He adds that the philanthropy would lose its value if the story were told.

The following summer, Merrick travels to Europe to visit eminent surgeons in Vienna and to demonstrate his cauterizing scalpel to them. While he is in Paris, he hears that Helen has been injured in a train wreck near Rome. Hurrying to Rome, he operates on the injured woman and saves her life. Then, in quixotic fashion, he leaves Rome before anyone can tell her who had performed the delicate operation. Helen guesses Merrick's identity, however, from the few words he had mumbled in her presence. Weeks later, when she discovers that he was planning to visit her, Helen, ashamed of her previous attitude toward his interest in her affairs, arranges to leave for the United States. However, Merrick flies to Le Havre ahead of her, arranges for their marriage, and meets her on the dock. When she sees him waiting, she walks into his arms. She does not have to be told why he had come.

Critical Evaluation:

Critics never understood the popularity of Lloyd C. Douglas's novels, condemning them for trite language, superficial characterization, and thin ideas. By Douglas's death in 1951, more than seven million copies of his books had been sold. Of those, one and a half million were of his first novel, *Magnificent Obsession*. He was the highest-selling author in American publishing history in his time. As late as the close of the twentieth century, he lacked entries in standard dictionaries of literary biography. What made him such a popular novelist for the two decades in which he wrote?

For almost three decades before publishing *Magnificent Obsession*, Douglas was a minister in several Lutheran and Congregational pulpits. As he moved from pulpit to pulpit, from Washington, D.C., to Ann Arbor to Akron to Los Angeles, his theology became increasingly liberal but his rhetoric stayed the same. His vivid narratives held crowds spellbound, and he achieved some fame in religious circles for his lectures, essays, and sermons. Before beginning his writing career, he often commented that he would like to try his hand at a novel. To Douglas, the novel-reading public constituted "a larger parish" with which to share the joys of Christian living.

Magnificent Obsession had its beginnings in two sources. One was a newspaper story reporting the death of a Detroit doctor who could have been saved had his respirator not been used to rescue a young man across the lake. The second was a series of sermons Douglas had preached in Los Angeles on the secrets of exultant living. According to his biographer daughter, he had been trying to convince people that their religion could have a practical dynamic effect in their lives if only they would put Jesus' words about secret altruism—let not your left hand know what your right hand is doing—into practice. When his wife remarked that for the first time she understood what he was saying, he admitted that it was his most important message. Then his daughter, Betty, asked why he did not include that message in his novel. So *Magnificent Obsession* came to be, although its early days were not secure. It had originally been sent to *Harper's* magazine as the manuscript "Salvage." It was rejected, revised as *Magnificent Obsession*, and again rejected by *Harper's* and several others before being published by a small religious house in Chicago in 1929. Within eighteen months, however, it was on best-seller lists, seemingly having hit a nerve of many people whose lives were being buffeted by economic forces beyond their control.

Theme was all-important to Douglas. He considered his novels to be "purpose novels." In a letter, Douglas stated the thesis of *Magnificent Obsession* as "how to get what you want and be what you would like to be through a practice of a Galilean principle of secret philanthropy." To demonstrate such a principle of living, Douglas fleshed it out in the lives of characters, who either act on the principle or who provide a contrast by refraining from acting on the principle. Robert Merrick, the playboy whose life is saved by Dr. Wayne Hudson's secret philanthropy, is skeptical for a long while, even after he reluctantly goes to medical school so that he may take Dr. Hudson's place at the Hudson Clinic. Merrick is skeptical even after he begins to decipher the journal that contains Hudson's philanthropic activities and beliefs. When Hudson's administrative assistant claims that "It's all true, Bobby. You do get what you want that way, if what you want contributes to the larger expression of yourself in constructive service," he could only think that it sounded foolish. Nevertheless, just having helped a fellow medical student out of his financial predicament, and beginning to read the New Testament accounts of how Christ had quietly helped people, Merrick mystically encounters a power that can change lives, thus launching his successful career as a brain surgeon, medical inventor, and philanthropist. Eventually, Merrick does get his heart's desire, Dr. Hudson's young widow as his own wife.

It is no accident that the central figures in this novel are physicians. For Douglas, a doctor rather than a minister is in a better position in society to help people. Doctors are practical, scientific, and compassionate, embodying all the characteristics Douglas admired most. Merrick himself convinces a popular preacher that the purely intellectual, critical approach to religion that the preacher has been preaching to large crowds each Sunday is bankrupt compared to Merrick's own scientific appropriation of the power of his Major Personality. That power has proved practical in Merrick's own life. He uses it not only to heal the sick but also to invent better ways to do brain surgery and—eventually—to gain his own love's reward.

Although Douglas cloaks his ideas in character and action, his style is not symbolic. Rather, it is direct and vivid, filled with action verbs and many descriptive words and phrases. There is much dialogue, yet little preaching. It is this nonliterary style that riled the literary establishment but attracted a huge reading audience. A direct, accessible style accounts for much of the popularity of Douglas's fiction, along with the appeal of his message to a nation undergoing a spiritual crisis fostered by the economic depression. Carl Bode, a critic writing in the 1950's, claimed that Douglas was the most popular religious writer of the century because he understood America and its religious needs so well.

"Critical Evaluation" by Barbara J. Hampton

Further Reading

Becnel, Kim. *The Rise of Corporate Publishing and Its Effects on Authorship in Early Twentieth-Century America.* New York: Routledge, 2008. Examines how the work of Douglas and other authors writing in the 1930's were affected by changes in the book publishing business, the result of new marketing ideas, new ideas of the audience, and new models of the author-publisher relationship.

Bode, Carl. *The Half-World of American Culture: A Miscellany.* Carbondale: Southern Illinois University Press, 1965. Bode concludes that Douglas is important not for his literary contributions but rather as a link to the American literary and religious arenas. Includes a preface by C. P. Snow.

_____. "Lloyd Douglas—Loud Voice in the Wilderness." *American Quarterly* 2 (Winter, 1950): 340-352. Bode argues that "to know Douglas's novels is to understand" the United States "at least a little better."

Dawson, Virginia Douglas, and Betty Douglas Wilson. *The*

Shape of Sunday: An Intimate Biography of Lloyd C. Douglas. Boston: Houghton Mifflin, 1952. This biography of Douglas by his daughters gives many anecdotes of his life. Provides the personal background to the writing and reception of *Magnificent Obsession.*

Hale, Frederick. "Evolving Attitudes Towards Thaumaturgy in the Works of Lloyd C. Douglas." *Religion and Theology* 14, nos. 3/4 (2007): 310-329. An analysis of *Magnificent Obsession* and some of Douglas's other works, focusing on his treatment of miracles.

The Magus

Author: John Fowles (1926-2005)
First published: 1965; revised, 1977
Type of work: Novel
Type of plot: Psychological realism
Time of plot: 1953
Locale: England and Greece

Principal characters:
NICHOLAS URFE, a twenty-six-year-old English teacher
ALISON KELLY, his lover
MAURICE CONCHIS, a wealthy English-born Greek philosopher
JULIE HOLMES, an actor
LILY DE SEITAS, a friend of Conchis and Julie's mother
JOJO, a young Scottish woman

The Story:

Nicholas Urfe, a twenty-six-year-old Englishman looking for something to do with his life, takes a teaching job on the Greek island of Phraxos. He had previously met and romanced an Australian woman, Alison Kelly, and abandoned her at a party in London, and he has little direction or meaning ahead of him.

Discussions with his British predecessor at the Greek school lead Urfe to make the acquaintance of Maurice Conchis, a wealthy man who owns an estate near the school. Conchis tells Urfe something of his past, and what develops over time is a strange mixture of past and present as characters from Conchis's life appear during Urfe's visits to the man's villa. One of these is Lily, Conchis's former sweetheart, who, in reality, is Julie Holmes, a British actor. Urfe falls in love with Lily/Julie. Later, Urfe is reunited with Alison in Athens, but after he tells her of his love for Julie, Alison apparently kills herself. Urfe is shaken by the suicide, but he begins to pursue Julie.

Events take a strange turn when Urfe is drugged, taken into a subterranean prison on Phraxos, and forced to judge the people who have appeared in his episodes with Conchis. He is offered the opportunity to punish Julie by whipping her, but he refuses. Then Urfe is bound and forced to watch a pornographic film that stars Julie and Joe Harrison, another actor in Conchis's bizarre orchestration of events. Following the film, Julie and Joe appear and consummate their sexual relationship in front of Urfe.

Urfe is enraged by what has been inflicted on him. When he is released from his imprisonment, he finds that he has been fired from his teaching job, and he returns to Athens. He discovers that the news of Alison's suicide had been false. He then goes to London in search of Julie and meets her mother, Lily de Seitas, a woman who cooperated with Conchis in Urfe's deception. Lily explains to Urfe that what Conchis and the others did to him was for his own good, to make him a better person. She insists that he wait for Alison to reappear.

Meanwhile, Urfe meets Jojo, an earthy young Scottish woman, at a theater. She falls in love with him, and, try as he might, he is unable to keep from hurting her. Despairing of the pain that he has caused Jojo, Urfe meets Alison in a park, and the story ends as he and she negotiate a resumption of their relationship.

Critical Evaluation:

The Magus is a very involved, appropriately controversial, and mystifying novel, made even more so by a revised version that John Fowles published in 1977. The story's fundamental thrust seems to be the moral rehabilitation of its hero/antihero, Nicholas Urfe. At the story's outset, Urfe is a disaffected, rather self-absorbed young man who is unable to find much of value in life. His relationship with a young Australian woman, Alison Kelly, is primarily sexual; she, on the other hand, wants a commitment from him that he is not willing to make. Ultimately, the reader is asked to accept the fact that a good deal of time, effort, and expense are devoted to making Urfe see how cruel he has been to Alison and how important it is to treat other people responsibly.

As the reader finds at the end of the story, the wealthy thinker Maurice Conchis has made something of a career of punishing and enlightening wrongdoers such as Urfe. After Urfe's arrival at Conchis's villa on the Greek island of Phraxos, Conchis orchestrates multilevel real-life theater designed primarily to manipulate and humiliate Urfe and, finally, encourage him to come to grips with ethical behavior in a world where God's presence is obscured at best.

While Urfe is in Conchis's thrall on Phraxos, he is made to fall in love with a British actor named Julie Holmes and, eventually, to be made a fool of because of this. In a particularly crucial part of the story, Urfe is drugged and held prisoner underground. He sees a number of the characters in the real-life play Conchis has directed and is asked to judge them for what they have done to him. Indeed, he is given a whip and is placed before the naked Julie; those who watch wait to see if he will punish her.

He chooses not to whip the woman who has so humiliated him, and, in so doing, quickly understands what freedom is. Urfe sees that Conchis has given him the responsibility to exercise a moral option. The young man has evidently realized that what he does in life is entirely his responsibility. Conchis has taught him that in a world where humanity is the source of moral evil, where all things are permitted and anything might happen, each person is nevertheless able to create his or her own values and thereby salvage personal worth and identity.

Conchis has already explained his idea of freedom to Urfe in one of their many conversations. Conchis tells the story of his own choice when, during the Nazi occupation of Phraxos, when he was mayor of the village, the Germans ordered him to execute a group of Greek partisans. In an epiphany, Conchis recalls, he understood that freedom is an absolute, that all are free to commit the most heinous crimes—and to choose to refrain from them.

The basic philosophical focus of the story is reflected in the novel's four epigraphs, a passage from a book on the tarot and three quotations from a 1787 novel by the Marquis de Sade. Fowles's epigraphs relate to Conchis as a magus— that is, a seer, magician, or juggler—and to Nicholas's passage from irresponsible, reprehensible reprobate to participant in dark affairs to philosophically informed survivor of Conchis's machinations.

The novel's epigraphs constitute only one small dimension of its allusions, symbolism, and cultural resonance. The protagonist's last name, Urfe, is a reference to a seventeenth-century French pastoral novel, *L'Astrée* (1607-1628; *Astrea*, 1657-1658), written by Honoré d'Urfé, which suggests that Fowles's young, naïve hero is a suitable target for disillusionment. *The Magus* is full of allusions to the occult, classical mythology, French existentialism, cinema, and twentieth century history. Suitably enough, as the story develops, Urfe is compared to such mythological heroes as Orpheus, Ulysses, and Theseus, all characters who were changed in some ways by extraordinary journeys.

The literary and cultural baggage of the work shows that *The Magus* can be approached on at least two levels: as little more than a long but interesting thriller and as a complex philosophical novel. As the novel ends, Urfe has evidently learned that one cannot treat other people selfishly and narcissistically as objects for one's own pleasure. He also sees the difference between love and sexual attraction, and he has acquired a sense of guilt for the wrongs he has perpetrated in the past and a resolve to act otherwise in the future.

The Magus is a surprisingly conservative novel from a moral perspective. Its lesson that human beings can fulfill themselves and be happy only if they are kind to one another is a direct reaction to the atmosphere of moral permissiveness that certain popular schools of thought expressed in the 1960's. Likewise, where Urfe only plays at being a self-conscious existentialist before he meets Conchis, by the end of the novel he has learned some of the basic lessons one learns from reading such writers and philosophers as Jean-Paul Sartre and Albert Camus. Both Sartre and Camus are preoccupied with how one should conduct oneself in the absence of God and with impressing humanity with its burden of freedom. While Fowles does not deal in *The Magus* explicitly and extensively with humanity's relationship to God or even with God's existence, he stresses the practical nature of intelligent moral choices, as do Sartre and Camus.

Gordon Walters

Further Reading

Acheson, James. *John Fowles*. New York: St. Martin's Press, 1998. Provides an excellent introduction to Fowles's life and works. Traces the development of his novels, with a chapter devoted to each major work of long fiction. Chapter 3 focuses on *The Magus*.

Butler, Lance St. John. "John Fowles and the Fiction of Freedom." In *The British and Irish Novel Since 1960*, edited by James Acheson. New York: St. Martin's Press, 1991. Addresses the centrality of the concept of freedom in Fowles's fiction and discusses the author's coming to terms with freedom in his fiction in an existential sense.

Argues that Fowles's development as a writer followed the same course as that of existentialism.

Foster, Thomas C. *Understanding John Fowles*. Columbia: University of South Carolina Press, 1994. Provides an accessible critical introduction to Fowles's principal works, including *The Magus* and *The French Lieutenant's Woman* (1969).

Huffaker, Robert. *John Fowles*. Boston: Twayne, 1980. Provides biographical information as well as an introductory overview of Fowles's work.

Lenz, Brooke. *John Fowles: Visionary and Voyeur*. New York: Rodopi, 2008. Presents a feminist analysis of Fowles's work. Argues that Fowles progressively creates female characters who subvert male voyeurism and invent alternative narratives. Chapter 2 focuses on *The Magus*.

Reynolds, Margaret, and Jonathan Noakes. *John Fowles: The Essential Guide*. London: Vintage, 2003. Resource designed for students, teachers, and general readers contains an interview with Fowles as well as reading guides and reading activities for three novels: *The Collector* (1963), *The Magus*, and *The French Lieutenant's Woman*. Includes a glossary.

Rommerskirchen, Barbara. *Constructing Reality: Constructivism and Narration in John Fowles's "The Magus."* New York: Peter Lang, 1999. Offers a constructionist interpretation of the novel, focusing on how the construction of reality is a central concept in the work.

Warburton, Eileen. *John Fowles: A Life in Two Worlds*. New York: Viking Press, 2004. Thorough, entertaining, and well-reviewed biography provides insight into Fowles's fiction. Drawing on full access to Fowles's journals and personal papers, Warburton presents many previously untold details of his life, most notably concerning his thirty-seven-year love affair with his wife.

Wolfe, Peter. *John Fowles: Magus and Moralist*. 2d ed. Lewisburg, Pa.: Bucknell University Press, 1979. Examination of Fowles's novels focuses on the concepts of magic and ethical behavior, two concerns of *The Magus*.

The Mahabharata

Author: Unknown

First transcribed: c. 400 B.C.E.-200 C.E. (English translation, 1834)

Type of work: Poetry

Type of plot: Epic

Time of plot: Antiquity

Locale: India

Principal characters:

KING DHRITARASHTRA, the father of the Kauravas

KING PANDU, his brother and father of the Pandavas

YUDHISHTHIRA,

BHIMA,

ARJUNA,

NAKULA, and

SAHADEVA, the five sons of King Pandu

DRAUPADI, the Pandavas's wife

DURYODHANA, the oldest son of Dhritarashtra

The Poem:

Among the descendants of King Bharata (after whose name India was called Bharata-varsha, land of the Bharatas) there are two successors to the throne of Hastinapura. Of these, the elder, Dhritarashtra, is blind and gives over the reins of government to his younger brother, Pandu. Pandu grows weary of his duties and retires to hunt and enjoy himself. Again, Dhritarashtra takes control, aided by the advice and example of his wise old uncle, Bhishma. Upon Pandu's death, his five sons are put under the care of his younger brother, who has one hundred sons of his own.

At first the king's household is peaceful and free from strife, but gradually it becomes apparent that Pandu's sons are far more capable of ruling than any of Dhritarashtra's heirs. Of the Pandavas, the name given to the five descendants of Pandu, all are remarkably able, but the oldest, Yudhishthira, is judged most promising and therefore is chosen heir-apparent to the throne of the old blind king. To this selection of their cousin as the future king, the king's own sons take violent exception. Accordingly, they persuade their father to allow the Pandavas to leave the court and live by themselves. From a trap set by the unscrupulous Duryodhana, leader of the king's sons, the five brothers escape to the forest with their mother. There they spend some time in rustic exile.

In the meantime, King Drupada has announced that the hand of his daughter, Princess Draupadi, will be given to the hero surpassing all others in a feat of strength and skill, and he has invited throngs of noblemen to compete for his daughter's hand. In disguise, the Pandavas set out for King Drupada's court.

More than two weeks are spent in celebrating the approaching nuptials of the princess before the trial of strength that will reveal the man worthy of taking the lovely princess as his wife. The test is to grasp a mighty bow, fit an arrow, bend the bow, and hit a metal target with the arrow. Contestant after contestant fails in the effort to bend the huge bow. Finally, Arjuna, third of the sons of Pandu, comes forward and performs the feat with little effort to win the hand of the princess. In curious fashion, Princess Draupadi becomes the wife of all five of the brothers. At this time, also, the Pandavas meet their cousin on their mother's side, Krishna of Dvaraka. This renowned Yadava nobleman they accept as their special counselor and friend, and to him they owe much of their future success and power.

Hoping to avert dissension after his death, King Dhritarashtra decides to divide his kingdom into two parts, giving his hundred sons, the Kauravas, one portion and the Pandavas the other. Thus, Dhritarashtra's sons rule in Hastinapur and the five sons of Pandu in Indraprastha. The dying king's attempt to settle affairs of government amicably results in peace and prosperity for a brief period. Then the wily Duryodhana, leader of the Kauravas, sets another trap for the Pandavas. On this occasion he entices Yudhishthira, the oldest of the brothers, into a game of skill at dice. When the latter loses, the penalty is that the five brothers are to leave the court and spend the next twelve years in the forest. At the end of that time they are to have their kingdom and holdings once again if they can pass another year in disguise, without having anyone recognize them.

The twelve-year period of rustication is one of many romantic and heroic adventures. All five brothers are concerned in stirring events; Arjuna, in particular, travels far and long, visits the sacred stream of the Ganges, is courted by several noble ladies, and finally marries Subhadra, sister of Krishna.

When the long time of exile is over, the Pandavas and Kauravas engage in a war of heroes. Great armies are assembled; mountains of supplies are brought together. Just before the fighting begins, Krishna steps forth and sings the divine song, the *Bhagavad Gita*, in which he sets forth such theological truths as the indestructibility of the soul, the necessity to defend the faith, and other fundamental precepts of the theology of Brahma. By means of this song Arjuna is relieved of his doubts concerning the need to make his trial by battle.

The war lasts for some eighteen consecutive days, each day marked by fierce battles, single combats, and bloody attacks. Death and destruction are everywhere—the battlefields are strewn with broken bodies and ruined weapons and chariots. The outcome is the annihilation of all the pretensions of the Kauravas and their allies to rule over the kingdom. Finally, Yudhishthira ascends the throne amid great celebrations, the payment of rich tribute, and the ceremonial horse sacrifice.

Later, the death of their spiritual and military counselor, Krishna, leads the five brothers to realize their weariness with earthly pomp and striving. Accordingly, Yudhishthira gives up his duties as ruler. The five brothers then band together, clothe themselves as hermits, and set out for Mount Meru, the dwelling place of the gods on high. They are accompanied by their wife, Draupadi, and a dog that joins them on their journey. As they proceed, one after the other drops by the way and perishes. At last only Yudhishthira and the faithful dog remain to reach the portals of heaven. When the dog is refused admission to that holy place, Yudhishthira declines to enter without his canine companion. Then the truth is revealed—the dog is in reality the god of justice himself, sent to test Yudhishthira's constancy.

Yudhishthira is not content in heaven, for he soon realizes that his brothers and Draupadi have been required to descend to the lower regions and there expiate their mortal sins. Lonely and disconsolate, he decides to join them until all can be united in heaven. After he spends some time in that realm of suffering and torture, the gods take pity on him. Along with his brothers and Draupadi, he is transported back to heaven, where all dwell in perpetual happiness.

Critical Evaluation:

In its present form in Sanskrit, *The Mahabharata* runs to some 200,000 verses in couplets (*slokas*), in eighteen sections or books, although there is credible evidence to assume that earlier versions were considerably less extensive. About one-third to one-quarter of the whole relates to the central story, that of a civil war between two great royal houses of India. *The Mahabharata* is a massive collection of fascinating heroic and mythological legends, sermonlike essays, worldly and spiritual advice, material constituting codes of law, popular apothegms and proverbs, and moral tales for the edification of its audience. *The Mahabharata* is a history of prehistoric times and a compendium of materials that throw light on the religious, social, political, ethical, and moral ideals and practices of the people of ancient India.

Western readers who pick up *The Mahabharata* for the first time are often puzzled by the seemingly amorphous nature of this collection. Unlike Homer's *Iliad* (c. 800 B.C.E.) or Vergil's *Aeneid* (c. 29-19 B.C.E.), which have a clear narrative focus, *The Mahabharata* is a rambling account of a war between two factions of Indians, interspersed among a number of treatises that seem only tangentially related to the story. While plot features parallel Western epics and world folk literature (the reluctant warrior, the descent into the underworld, the battles in which gods take part), Western readers may sense that this work is essentially different from those to which they may be more accustomed.

The Western reader may find it helpful to note analogues between *The Mahabharata* and Western literature to compare cultural concepts and assumptions. *The Mahabharata* and the Bible share a similar format. The story of Savitri and the story of Ruth have much in common. The polyandry of Princess Draupadi with the Pandavas is reflected in some of the marriages of the Old Testament. The richest source of analogues to *The Mahabharata* is found in Greek mythology. The bow-and-arrow feat of strength for the hand of Princess Draupadi is mirrored in the test of Penelope's suitors. The twelve-year exile and wandering of the Pandavas has its parallel in the *Odyssey*, just as the battle between the Pandavas and the Kauravas is echoed in the *Iliad*.

The Mahabharata is classified as a heroic epic to distinguish it from the literary epic and the mock epic. In some formal respects, it does not follow the pattern of the Western epic. Whereas the Greek heroic epic contains twenty-four books and the English literary epic has twelve, *The Mahabharata* consists of eighteen books. The number eighteen does not appear to be arbitrary. The *Bhagavad Gita* section of *The Mahabharata*, for example, is a microcosm of the greater work, and is divided into eighteen chapters. Additionally, the war in which Duryodhana and his forces are defeated lasts eighteen days. Also, while most Western heroic epics are nationalistic, *The Mahabharata* is concerned with a story of conflict primarily for high moral purpose, a struggle between good and evil.

The Mahabharata is an accretion of texts from different periods by different hands, assembled perhaps by the person known as Vyasa ("the arranger"). While it lacks the relatively concise plotting one finds in works by Homer and Vergil, *The Mahabharata* is nevertheless carefully constructed to move readers from one point of understanding about human nature to another. There is coherence, too, in the general movement in the poem from an emphasis on action toward a celebration of the principle of *Samkhya*, or renunciation of materialism in favor of a higher spiritual dimension, the attainment of which may provide humans eternal peace.

The Mahabharata is a frame story in which various narrators or characters within narratives relate additional stories or discourse on topics such as the proper role of people in society, right behavior for those in authority, or the best course for one to follow in leading a fulfilling life. While they may be read simply as accounts of heroic actions by larger-than-life characters from a bygone era, the individual episodes have long been considered fables intended to vivify for readers a number of important moral, philosophical, and religious doctrines. For example, the war between the Pandavas and the Kauravas may be taken as an allegory of the eternal struggle between good and evil. The struggles of the warrior Arjuna (who shares some affinities with his Western cousin Achilles) can be interpreted as an example of the trials people must go through to discern their proper social and political roles. The adventures of Yudhishthira, whose story concludes the epic, are intended to illustrate the virtues of justice and renunciation of material values.

The frame story is probably based upon a historical event: a war between two neighboring peoples, the Kurus and the Panchalas, who inhabited the west and east points of the Madhyadesa (the "middle land" between the Ganges and the Jumna) respectively, with the war ending in the overthrow of the Kuru Dynasty. *The Mahabharata*, however, is best construed on more than one level. For example, the *Bhagavad Gita* is, in one sense, simply a dialogue between Arjuna and Krishna. The circumstances and setting—the impending battle, Arjuna's ethical reservations, and the question-answer format—are devices to dramatize Krishna's ethical and metaphysical sermon. On another, allegorical level of interpretation, the *Bhagavad Gita* is about good striving for supremacy over evil: Arjuna is the individual soul, and Krishna is the eternal Supreme Spirit that resides in each heart. Arjuna's chariot stands for the mortal body. King Dhritarashtra's blindness represents ignorance, and his hundred sons are the evil tendencies of humankind. The battle, then, becomes a perennial one between the power of good and the power of evil, and the warrior who heeds the advice of the Supreme Spirit speaking from within will succeed physically in battle and spiritually in attaining the highest good.

While the aggregated collection may seem only loosely tied together, individual sections of *The Mahabharata* are often quite carefully structured and contain some of the most inspiring passages in all of literature. Certainly in Western countries the most widely read section of the poem has been the *Bhagavad Gita*, a treatise on Eastern religious theory and practice presented in the form of a dialogue between the warrior Arjuna and his charioteer, Krishna. The circumstances under which this dialogue takes place are relevant to the story of the war between the Kauravas and the Pandavas. The aim of the discussion is to persuade a despondent Arjuna to take up arms for his people. Since God is doing the persuading, Arjuna listens. The context is often forgotten, however, by readers who become fascinated with the philosophical and religious dimensions of this important section. In the course of this conversation, Arjuna is asked to confront significant moral questions: Should one take up arms in a bloody war even for a just cause? To what end is this action, or any action, justified? The answers are designed to raise the warrior's level of consciousness so that he becomes aware of the limited vision of life possessed by any individual. His mystical experience, told in highly charged poetic language that suggests the possibility of attaining a more profound understanding of human nature than most people reach, has attracted Western readers for over two centuries.

The Mahabharata contains many popular tales; one is that of Savitri, whose love for her husband and devotion to her father-in-law triumph over Yama, the god of death. In this legend, a woman has a prominent role as a heroine. This tale gives evidence of the high place women held in ancient Indian culture. *The Mahabharata* also provides ethical guidance and in time became an authoritative treatise on dharma (truth, duty, righteousness), teaching of the divine origin of Brahman institutions, including the caste system.

In an appendix to *The Mahabharata*, called the *Harivamsa*, there is a genealogy of the god Hari (Vishnu), of whom Krishna was the eighth avatar. If considered as an anthology, *The Mahabharata* is structurally comparable to the Bible. Although there is no Bible, as such, in Hinduism, there is still a great quantity of sacred literature, including *The Mahabharata* and the *Vedas* (c. 1000-500 B.C.E.), the *Upanishads* (c. 900 B.C.E.), and the *Ramayana* (c. 500 B.C.E.). To the pious Hindu, the most familiar is the *Bhagavad Gita*.

The *Bhagavad Gita* is what is most familiar to Western literature as well. From the earliest English translations in the eighteenth century, the work has exerted strong influence on diverse figures, including Johann Wolfgang von Goethe (who was also enamored with the section of *The Mahabharata* dealing with the exploits of Sakuntala), Ralph Waldo Emerson, and Matthew Arnold.

The *Bhagavad Gita* is, however, only a part of a work whose impact on Eastern literatures has been great. Buddhist and Sanskrit writings, as well as works in Asian countries outside India, have also been influenced by the stories and the philosophy contained in *The Mahabharata*. Two philosophical principles that emerge from the story have universal applicability. First, the work dramatizes the notion that human existence in its material form seems confining, and that a spiritual dimension exists, imprisoned in one's body, waiting for the liberating effect that can come only when one reaches a higher state of consciousness—and eventually through what humankind usually calls death. Second, and equally important, is the lesson that one achieves dignity, power, and esteem only through suffering. This concept, vividly dramatized in the story of the heroes and heroines in this Indian epic and so closely akin to the philosophy that informs Western tragedy, links *The Mahabharata* with great works of world literature.

"Critical Evaluation" by Joanne G. Kashdan;
revised by Laurence W. Mazzeno

Further Reading

Badrinath, Chaturvedi. *The Mahabharata: An Inquiry in the Human Condition.* New Delhi: Orient Longman, 2006. A scholarly study of the Hindu philosophy expressed in *The Mahabharata*. Badrinath maintains the epic is a systematic inquiry into the human condition, concerned with individual liberty, knowledge, equality, love, friendship, and other issues of everyday life.

Brodbeck, Simon, and Brian Black, eds. *Gender and Narrative in "The Mahabharata."* New York: Routledge, 2007. A collection of essays analyzing the treatment of gender, paternity, marriage, and ethics in *The Mahabharata*.

Dhand, Arti. *Woman as Fire, Woman as Sage: Sexual Ideology in "The Mahabharata."* Albany: State University of New York Press, 2008. Dhand demonstrates how *The Mahabharata* expresses Hindu ideas regarding sexuality and women.

Goldman, Robert P. *Gods, Priests, and Warriors: The Bhrgus of "The Mahabharata."* New York: Columbia University Press, 1977. An analysis of the literary and mythic significance of the tales of the priestly clan known as the Bhrgus, of Bhargavas, whose exploits make up a substantial portion of the text of *The Mahabharata*. Explores the relationship of the epic to events that may have inspired it.

Hiltebeitel, Alf. *Rethinking "The Mahabharata": A Reader's Guide to the Education of the Dharma King.* Chicago: University of Chicago Press, 2001. A rereading of the epic, focusing on Yudhishthira, also known as the Dharma King; Hiltebeitel demonstrates how Yudhishthira's relationships to other characters, especially his author-grandfather, Vyasa, and his wife, Draupadi, are threaded throughout the epic's confusing array of frames and stories within stories. Hiltebeitel also proposes a revisionist theory about the dating and creation of the original text.

_____. *The Ritual of Battle: Krishna in "The Mahabharata."* Ithaca, N.Y.: Cornell University Press, 1976. Focuses on the role of the Indian god Krishna in the epic. Hiltebeitel explains the structure of the work and describes its relationship to Indian myth and history.

McGrath, Kevin. *The Sanskrit Hero: Karna in Epic Mahabharata.* Boston: Brill, 2004. McGrath focuses on the character of Karna to describe the nature and function of the hero and of "heroic religion" in epic Indic poetry.

Narasimhan, Chakravarthi V. Introduction to *The Mahabharata.* New York: Columbia University Press, 1965. Narasimhan outlines the plot of this complex, rambling work. He highlights the human qualities of the epic heroes and notes the underlying emphasis on the necessity for peace to bring about happiness.

Van Nooten, Barend A. *The Mahabharata.* New York: Twayne, 1971. An excellent guidebook to the epic. Includes a detailed summary of the story; explains its mythology, and examines the literary history of the work. Assesses the impact of *The Mahabharata* on modern India and on the West.

The Maid of Honour

Author: Philip Massinger (1583-1640)
First produced: c. 1621; first published, 1632
Type of work: Drama
Type of plot: Tragicomedy
Time of plot: Renaissance
Locale: Palermo and Siena, Italy

Principal characters:
ROBERTO, king of Sicily
FERDINAND, duke of Urbin
BERTOLDO, a natural brother of Roberto and a Knight of Malta
GONZAGA, a Knight of Malta, general to the duchess of Siena
ASTUTIO, a counselor of state to the king of Sicily
FULGENTIO, the favorite of King Roberto
ADORNI, a Sicilian gentleman, in love with Camiola
AURELIA, duchess of Siena
CAMIOLA, the Maid of Honour

The Story:

At the court of Roberto, king of Sicily, at Palermo, where the arrival of an ambassador from the duke of Urbin is momentarily expected, the conversation of those waiting has turned to discussion of the sinister influence of Fulgentio, the king's unworthy favorite, and of the soldierly qualities of Bertoldo, the king's illegitimate half brother. Upon the arrival of the ambassador, the political situation is explained: The duke of Urbin, in love with the duchess of Siena but rejected by her, has attacked her territories. On the verge of defeat at the hands of the Sienese, he is appealing to Sicily for aid on the basis of a treaty of mutual assistance. King Roberto, however, maintains that the treaty has been rendered void by the aggressive action of the duke and that Sicily is not obligated to come to the rescue. This pacifistic attitude is abhorrent to the king's half brother, Bertoldo, who in a fiery speech accuses the king of cowardice, claims that Sic-

ily's honor demands intervention, and urges the nobles to follow him to the relief of the duke. The king, angered by the speech, replies that any might volunteer who wishes, but that they will then cease to be his subjects and can expect no protection from him if fortune goes against them.

On that same day, at the house of Camiola, the maid is being plagued by the suit of one Sylli, a man of almost unbelievable conceit. He, however, leaves upon the arrival of Bertoldo, who has come to say farewell and to declare his own love. In spite of Camiola's evident love for Bertoldo, she rejects his suit because, as a Knight of Malta, he is vowed to celibacy, nor can she be moved by his suggestion that a dispensation can be obtained. He leaves for the war with the determination to have honor as his only mistress.

The next day King Roberto learns of Bertoldo's departure with his volunteers and is displeased at the news. Fulgentio, however, is delighted, for with Bertoldo gone he can pursue his own wooing of Camiola. On his arrival at her house he behaves in an overbearing manner toward all present, particularly her other suitors, Sylli and Adorni. Sylli faints, but Adorni is prepared to fight until restrained by Camiola. In a series of frank and witty speeches, Camiola tells Fulgentio exactly what she thinks of him and outlines his despicable character. He leaves, vowing to avenge himself by ruining her reputation by spreading scandal about her.

Meanwhile, in the territories of Siena, the forces of the duke of Urbin are still faring badly. Bertoldo and his Sicilian volunteers have arrived, but they cannot change the fortunes of war. In the ensuing battle they are captured. When Gonzaga, the Sienese general, recognizes Bertoldo as a Knight of Malta, he tears the cross from his prisoner's cloak, for Bertoldo has broken the vows of the order by attacking the duchess in an unjust war. Further, when Astutio arrives as ambassador from King Roberto to disclaim his sovereign's part in the attack, Gonzaga agrees to accept the usual ransom for all the Sicilian nobles except Bertoldo, for whom he demands fifty thousand crowns. Astutio bears the news that the king will pay nothing for his half brother and has, in fact, confiscated the unfortunate man's estates. Unable to pay the ransom, Bertoldo faces a lifetime of imprisonment.

In Sicily, Adorni challenges Fulgentio for his treatment of Camiola, but the cowardly favorite declines the challenge. On Camiola's birthday, in the middle of the celebration, Adorni enters bleeding. He has been wounded in the fight that he finally forced upon Fulgentio, but he has compelled the latter to sign a paper repudiating the slanders he has been spreading about Camiola. Adorni then confesses his love for Camiola, but she rejects him with the admonition that he must not aspire so high. When, through the agency of the ransomed Sicilian noblemen, she learns of Bertoldo's plight, she is ready enough, however, to send Adorni with the fifty thousand crowns to ransom the man she loves. Adorni promises to execute the commission faithfully, although he feels that he will not survive for long, and departs for Siena to bring happiness to his rival. Bertoldo, in ecstasies at the goodness of Camiola, gladly agrees to sign the contract of betrothal that she has demanded. It is his tragedy, however, to be sent for by the victorious duchess of Siena, who has heard of his martial prowess. Almost instantly she falls violently in love with him, and he, after a short struggle against the sin of ingratitude, falls equally in love with her and promises to marry her.

While this surprising event is in progress at Siena, an equally unexpected change of fortune is taking place in Sicily. The king and his favorite arrive at Camiola's house;

the former, with seeming sternness, rebukes her for disobedience in refusing Fulgentio's suit and for urging Adorni to attack him. Camiola defends her conduct and accuses Fulgentio of having slandered her. King Roberto then orders Fulgentio out of his sight, threatens him with death, and praises the behavior of Camiola. Thus the villain is discomfited.

Camiola, informed by the faithful Adorni of Bertoldo's perfidy, makes plans accordingly. At a reunion in the palace at Palermo, the king forgives his half brother and consents to his marriage to the duchess of Siena. Camiola enters and, after promising Fulgentio to try to secure his peace with the king, asks the monarch for justice on Bertoldo. Producing the contract of betrothal that he has signed, she makes such a noble plea for her rights that even the love-smitten duchess acknowledges her superiority and yields Bertoldo to her, while he admits his falseness and confesses himself branded with disloyalty and ingratitude. Camiola forgives him and announces her approaching marriage.

The entrance of a group of friars provides another surprise for the gathering. Camiola announces that she has determined to become the bride of the Church; by entering a religious order she is to become, in another sense, a maid of honor. As her last act, she gives Adorni one-third of her estate and returns to Bertoldo the cross of the Knights of Malta, bidding him to redeem his honor by fighting against the enemies of the faith. As she departs for the convent, King Roberto states admiringly that she well deserves her title of Maid of Honor.

Critical Evaluation:

While it is generally accepted that Philip Massinger's *The Maid of Honour* was performed before Henrietta Maria, queen of Charles I of England, in 1630, the precise date of the play's composition is unknown. Some scholars have dated its writing to around 1621 and others to as late as 1630. The earlier date would make it one of Massinger's first independent plays; the latter date would place it during his mature period of authorship. External evidence provides information about the play's performance and publication but gives little or no indication of when it was written. Internal evidence, largely in the form of topical allusions to intrigues at the English court, is subject to various interpretations. What is clear is that the play, whenever it was written, comments upon issues facing English society and politics during the period. The play also transcends these topical issues to touch on enduring themes such as honor, loyalty, and courage.

Massinger, the only son of a family moderately prominent in the cultural and political life of the times, attended

Oxford but left without receiving his degree and soon after entered a long and productive life in the theater. His extensive experience included collaboration with many distinguished playwrights, including John Fletcher and Thomas Dekker. He also wrote a number of dramas by himself, and became known as one of the finest of contemporary writers for the stage. In 1620, John Taylor's poem "The Praise of Hemp-Seed" listed Massinger as one of England's premier dramatists, along with notable authors such as John Drayton, Ben Jonson, George Chapman, John Marston, John Middleton, and Thomas Heywood.

The Maid of Honour clearly shows why Massinger was accorded such praise, for it is an excellent display piece for Massinger's talents. It has a clear and fluent style, a deeply felt sense of morality, and a keen appreciation of individual character and motivation, which is seen most clearly in Camiola's renunciation of the world and her fiancé at the moment when she appears to have won both.

The central themes of *The Maid of Honour* are money; the morality involved in the activities of royalty, especially marriages and foreign alliances; and the concept of just versus unjust war. All of these are folded into one overriding theme: the conflict between virtue and expediency. Massinger's play explores this theme in three fashions: through reference to English political life; by correspondences to earlier plays, in particular dramas by William Shakespeare; and in its own original way.

In political terms, *The Maid of Honour* examines certain general moral and philosophical issues, such as the concept of a just war and the virtue of neutrality during armed conflict, both issues that were of immediate concern at the time and that evoked spirited debate among intellectuals and statesmen. Not infrequently, such debates found expression on the popular stage. The underlying thematic concerns that the play addresses are the role of justice and virtue in political affairs, and how much morality a nation can afford in its relationships with other kingdoms.

In exploring this theme, *The Maid of Honour* echoes specific events of English political life, particularly those during the reign of King James I (r. 1603-1625). A number of critics have commented on the close correspondence between the events in the play and those during the latter years of the reign of James I, in particular his son-in-law's abortive invasion of Bohemia. So close are the parallels between the play's Roberto, king of Sicily, and his favorite, Fulgentio, and history's James I and the duke of Buckingham, that some scholars have expressed surprise that the drama was ever authorized for performance and publication.

The Maid of Honour also includes a number of correspondences to other dramas of its own and earlier periods, in particular Shakespeare's *All's Well That Ends Well* (pr. c. 1602-1603, pb. 1623). Some critics go so far as to see *The Maid of Honour* as a mirror image of Shakespeare's play, with the ending reversed. In *All's Well That Ends Well*, the heroine Helena leaves a life of seclusion to marry her beloved, Bertram. In *the Maid of Honour*, Camiola leaves her fiancé to enter a convent. There are numerous other parallels between the two dramas in setting, scenes, and even dialogue. Massinger, who was well-versed in the drama of his own and earlier times, is clearly conducting a dialogue with his great predecessor.

Finally, *The Maid of Honour* is an impressive drama in its own right. Although it works within an established pattern—that of the "testing" play, in which the heroine must prove her loyalty and fidelity—it expands beyond the confines of the genre, becoming a meditation on power and statecraft. Its characters, especially Camiola, the maid of honor, are presented as a mix; they are particular individuals and types. They present general and specific truths about human nature.

Massinger's style has been criticized by numerous scholars as lacking in vigor and as not sufficiently poetical. T. S. Eliot, for example, has said that the playwright's verse "without being exactly corrupt, suffers from cerebral anaemia." If such criticisms are just, and there is ample room to dispute the matter, *The Maid of Honour* is an outstanding exception to such charges. In this play, Massinger's use of language is supple and flexible, deploying a blank verse that expresses its meaning clearly yet carries a level of allusion and symbolism that adds to the depth and richness of the play.

"Critical Evaluation" by Michael Witkoski

Further Reading

Adler, Doris. *Philip Massinger*. Boston: Twayne, 1987. A brief but thorough overview of Massinger's life and career. Traces his relationships and collaborations with other playwrights of his times. A good introductory volume.

Cruickshank, A. H. *Philip Massinger*. 1920. Reprint. New York: Russell & Russell, 1971. Although dated, Cruickshank's book remains one of the scholarly foundations for any study of Massinger and his work. Brief in terms of Massinger's biography, it is much fuller in its assessment of his writings, especially their relationship to the literature of the period.

Edwards, Philip. "Massinger's Men and Women." In *Philip Massinger: A Critical Reassessment*, edited by Douglas

Howard. New York: Cambridge University Press, 1985. Contains a perceptive and revealing study of Camiola, placing her in the context of the drama of the period.

Eliot, T. S. *The "Waste Land," and Other Writings.* New York: Modern Library, 2001. Includes Eliot's influential 1920 essay, "Philip Massinger," a thought-provoking commentary on Massinger, especially his artistic and rhetorical abilities. Indispensable reading.

McDonald, Russ. "High Seriousness and Popular Form: The Case of *The Maid of Honour.*" In *Philip Massinger: A Critical Reassessment*, edited by Douglas Howard. New York: Cambridge University Press, 1985. A thorough and precise consideration of the drama, displaying clearly how Massinger uses the form of the testing play to present serious ethical and political ideas.

Sanders, Julie. *Caroline Drama: The Plays of Massinger, Ford, Shirley, and Brome.* Plymouth, England: Northcote House/British Council, 1999. Analyzes plays written between 1625 and 1642 by Massinger and three other dramatists, focusing on these plays' concerns with issues of community and hierarchy.

Zucker, Adam, and Alan B. Farmer, eds. *Localizing Caroline Drama: Politics and Economics of the Early Modern Stage, 1625-1642.* New York: Palgrave Macmillan, 2006. Collection of essays about Caroline drama, including the work of Massinger. The numerous references to the playwright, and the references to *The Maid of Honour*, are listed in the index. In addition, one of the essays provides an analysis of Massinger's play *The Renegado*.

The Maids

Author: Jean Genet (1910-1986)
First published: Les Bonnes, 1948 (English translation, 1954)
Type of work: Drama
Type of plot: Surrealism
Time of plot: Indeterminate
Locale: An elegant feminine bedroom

Principal characters:
SOLANGE, a maid approximately thirty-five years of age
CLAIRE, a maid, Solange's younger sister
MADAME, their mistress, approximately twenty-five years of age

The Story:

Two women are in a bedroom. One is playing with her rubber gloves, alternately fanning her arms and folding them again. This greatly irritates the other woman, who finally yells, in an exaggerated fashion, "Those gloves! Those eternal gloves!" She continues yelling at her maid, insulting her, accusing her of trying to seduce the milkman. She tells her maid to take the gloves and leave them in the kitchen, which the maid does.

The younger woman—Madame—sits at the dressing table, calling for the maid—Claire—to lay out her clothes and jewels. Madame again taunts Claire about the milkman. When Claire spits on the shoes to polish them, Madame expresses her disapproval and remarks that Claire hates her, that Claire is smothering her with attention and flowers.

Madame then drops her overexaggerated tragic tone and briefly speaks to Claire as an equal about the milkman, who despises them. Just as quickly, she recovers her tone, demanding her white dress. Claire refuses and explains why. In her explanation, she mentions Monsieur, who is Madame's lover, and widowhood. This brings up the fact that Madame has denounced Monsieur in a letter to the police, although he is only imprisoned, not dead. She declares her devotion to him, swearing that she will follow him even to Devil's Island, and therefore she should wear white, to mourn like a queen.

As Claire helps Madame into her dress, Madame complains that Claire smells like the servants' quarters. Madame says that it is more difficult to be a mistress, because she has to be both a mistress and a servant, containing all the hatred of a servant and her own beauty.

Claire, inspired by Madame's confession, begins raving and tells Madame how much she hates her. During her tirade, she spits on Madame's dress and accuses her of wanting to steal the milkman. Madame loses control, and Claire slaps her face to prove they are on the same level. Her talk becomes more and more ominous, as she speaks of rebellion and hatred that emanates from the maids' quarters, from the kitchen.

Suddenly, an alarm clock rings, and the two women grasp each other. The woman who is impersonating Madame starts removing her dress. She complains that the woman who is impersonating Claire does not finish. The real Claire puts on her maid's outfit. The two begin straightening up the room and waiting for the real Madame to return. That night is special, since Claire actually has written the letter leading to Monsieur's arrest.

Solange, Claire's older sister, begins taunting Claire about her dressing up at night and pretending to be a queen. Claire counters that Solange is scared of having put Monsieur in jail. Solange declares that no one loves them, but Claire disagrees. She says Madame loves them. Solange says Madame loves them "like her bidet," and that they, the maids, can love no one because filth cannot love filth. She calls her spit her spray of diamonds.

Claire wants to talk of Madame's kindness. Solange points out how easy it is to be kind if you are beautiful and rich. Otherwise, you have to act like Claire, dressing up in Madame's clothes and parading around the bedroom. Claire points out that it is Solange who is so taken with the idea of following her lover to Devil's Island when it is her turn to play Madame. Claire tells Solange that she will not disturb her fantasy; she hates her for other reasons. Claire tells Solange that she knows her sister tried to kill Madame, but symbolically it is Claire she is trying to kill. Solange admits to the attempt, but claims she did it to free Claire from Madame's bittersweet kindness, even though she knows Claire will denounce her. When Solange sees the figure of Madame, however, she is unable to carry through with her plot. She compares her own dignity to Madame's, and remarks how Madame is transfigured by grief.

The phone rings; it is Monsieur calling to say he has been released on bail. Solange blames Claire for the failure of their plan, but Claire retorts that it is Solange who has failed to kill Madame earlier, thus forcing Claire to try the letter. Claire calls Solange weak and says she would have been able to kill Madame in her sleep. She claims that where Solange has bungled, she, Claire, will succeed.

Claire compares the act of killing Madame to stories in history of women guided by visions and religion to kill. She will be supported, she says, by her milkman, and they will be saved. The two begin to formulate a new plan to kill Madame when she returns home. Solange tries to comfort her, but Madame declares that she will follow Monsieur to Devil's Island if necessary.

Madame starts planning her mourning when Claire comes in with the drugged tea. Madame pulls the red dress out of the closet and gives it to her as a gift. She gives Solange her fur stole. She is about to go to bed when she notices the phone is off the hook. When she asks why, Claire and Solange mention that Monsieur is out on bail and waiting for Madame. She orders Solange to get a taxi. While she is waiting, Claire offers to heat up the tea, but Madame is not interested. When Solange finally returns with the taxi, Claire makes one final effort to get Madame to drink the tea, but fails.

After Madame leaves, Solange reprimands Claire for failing. She warns that Madame and Monsieur will find out that Claire has written the letters. She is sick that Madame's joy comes from the maids' shame. Solange decides it is time for the two to flee, but Claire is exhausted and thinks it is too risky. They already lost control of so much, the slightest mistake would show their guilt. They recommence their game. Solange tells Claire to skip the preliminaries and go straight to the transformation. In Madame's white dress, Claire begins insulting the maid right away, comparing maids to grave diggers, scavengers, and police, calling them the distorting mirrors of respectable society.

After more of the bizarre game, during which Solange makes "Madame" crawl and whip her, Claire becomes sick, and Solange takes her to the kitchen. Solange returns to the bedroom alone, speaking to invisible people. She says Madame is dead, strangled by the rubber gloves. She imitates Madame and speaks to an imaginary detective and to Madame and Monsieur. She speaks of the dignity of servants, which she says the police, as outcasts themselves, would understand but Madame and Monsieur never would. Claire reenters the room as Madame and asks for her tea. She clearly understands what she is doing, as does Solange, who refuses. Finally, she relents, and Claire drinks the tea while Solange sees in it Madame's death and the maids' assumption.

Critical Evaluation:

Jean Genet, who spent most of his early life in prison, is considered one of the most important French writers of the twentieth century. His writing centers on the themes of illusion versus reality, freedom versus slavery, and the ultimate similarity of good and evil. Throughout his writing, Genet expresses his philosophies: that there can be no evil in evil, since the double negative would make a positive, thus good; that the police and criminals are both outcasts from society and, therefore, equals; and that fiction was too often confused with reality and must be separated. His writings are mostly concerned with criminals, prostitutes, and servants. In *The Maids*, Genet expresses these concepts primarily through the characters of the maids, who begin and end the play pretending to be mistress and servant.

Genet was bothered by the concept of suspension of disbelief upon which most plays and films rely. In his instructions for producing *The Maids*, Genet originally stated that he wanted men to play the roles. His intent, according to his greatest patron, Jean-Paul Sartre, was to show the artificiality of the play and the players. If a woman played the role of Claire, she would have to play only a maid and a maid playing her mistress; a man, however, would have to play not only the maid and the maid playing her mistress but also the woman, thus bringing one more level of artifice to the play.

The falseness of the play is further revealed through the maids' game. They take turns pretending to be the mistress, imitating her. The play has several levels: men playing women, women playing maids, maids playing the mistress, and men playing women playing maids playing the mistress playing a maid. It is when there is a slip in the action, an unexpected intrusion or word, that the levels become confused, such as the time Claire comments on the milkman. The complex circularity of the play goes further, however, when Genet introduces the concept of love. The maids talk about how they love Madame, but, as Solange says, filth cannot love, which must mean they hate Madame—not because she is mean or cruel to them, but because she is good and therefore she can love. It is impossible for her to love, however, because her lover is in prison. In fact, he is the only one of the four characters who never appears. He is also the only man. The circle is completed by the fact that the maids, being outcasts like criminals and the police, were responsible for Monsieur's imprisonment in the first place, thus bringing him to their level and (in Genet's philosophy) making him an outcast, depriving him of the ability to love.

The maids, being outcasts, society's "distorting mirrors," have two ways of becoming a society of their own: through imitating Madame's gestures and words or through her death. Madame is a fake, however, so the maids are doomed to failure. This is why the maids never succeed in killing Madame, and why Claire ends up killing herself while playing Madame—it is the closest she will ever get to becoming the mistress. Solange also knows this and believes that through her sister's-mistress's death, she will be elevated to a higher level, while she only ends up being a criminal and her dead sister a mere servant suicide—in dramatic contrast to Solange's last words: "We are beautiful, joyous, drunk, and free!"

Gregory Harris

Further Reading

Barber, Stephen. *Jean Genet.* London: Reaktion Books, 2004. Concise biography of Genet. Barber provides information about the events of Genet's life, his thoughts, and the recurrent themes in his work.

Jones, David Andrew. *Blurring Categories of Identity in Contemporary French Literature: Jean Genet's Subversive Discourse.* Lewiston, N.Y.: Edwin Mellen Press, 2007. Analyzes how Genet's work destroys binary oppositions by integrating opposing character traits, such as homosexuality and heterosexuality, blackness and whiteness, and masculine and feminine. Focuses on Genet's use of language, interpreting it from the perspectives of deconstruction, feminist theory, queer theory, and postcolonialism. For advanced students or readers with a prior knowledge of Genet's works.

Knapp, Bettina L. *Jean Genet.* Rev. ed. Boston: Twayne, 1989. Analytical look at Genet, geared toward giving readers a concise understanding of the French author's work. Part of Twayne's World Authors series.

Read, Barbara, and Ian Birchall, eds. *Flowers and Revolution: A Collection of Writings on Jean Genet.* London: Middlesex University Press, 1997. The essays discuss many aspects of Genet's works, analyzing how they challenge conventional ways of understanding society and personal experience and how they influence writers and pop-culture figures such as David Bowie and Patti Smith.

Reed, Jeremy. *Jean Genet: Born to Lose.* London: Creation Books, 2005. A brief biography, with many illustrations, in which Reed recounts the details of Genet's life and work, including his writing, criminal activities, sexual relationships, friendships, and obsession with death.

Sartre, Jean-Paul. *Saint Genet: Actor and Martyr.* Translated by Bernard Frechtman. New ed. New York: Pantheon Books, 1993. This volume of description and philosophy addresses Genet's life and work, including a long section on *The Maids.* Central to an understanding of the author.

White, Edmund. *Genet: A Biography.* New York: Alfred A. Knopf, 1993. Definitive English-language biography discusses the chronology behind *The Maids,* as well as Genet's reactions to the play.

_____. *The Selected Writings of Jean Genet.* Hopewell, N.J.: Ecco Press, 1993. Includes excerpts from Genet's works, including *The Maids,* as well as a short synopsis of the play and a discussion of its place in the Genet oeuvre.

The Maid's Tragedy

Authors: Francis Beaumont (c. 1584-1616) and John
  Fletcher (1579-1625)
First produced: c. 1611; first published, 1619
Type of work: Drama
Type of plot: Tragedy
Time of plot: Antiquity
Locale: Rhodes

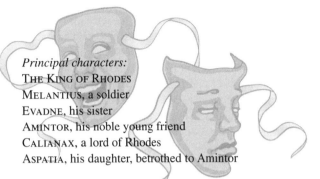

Principal characters:
THE KING OF RHODES
MELANTIUS, a soldier
EVADNE, his sister
AMINTOR, his noble young friend
CALIANAX, a lord of Rhodes
ASPATIA, his daughter, betrothed to Amintor

The Story:

Melantius, a military hero, returns to Rhodes from the wars. There he finds himself involved in a difficult situation. The king, ostensibly to show his gratitude, has given the hand of Evadne, Melantius's sister, to Amintor, a young courtier and a dear friend of Melantius. The difficulty lay in Amintor's having already promised himself to Aspatia, daughter of Calianax, an old lord.

Preparations are being made for elaborate nuptial festivities. Aspatia grieves. In the royal banqueting hall, just before the presentation of the marriage masque, Melantius encounters Calianax, who insults him. The king's entrance checks animosities. A masque follows, after which the king, wishing the wedded couple goodnight, asks Amintor to father a boy who will grow up to defend the kingdom.

As Evadne prepares to retire, Aspatia, who is present, cannot share the general enthusiastic anticipation of the marriage night, and she expresses her belief that she will soon be dead of a broken heart. Amintor, coming into the apartment, receives a kiss from Aspatia before she departs. He suffers momentary misgivings for having forsaken her, but he forgets her when he sees Evadne. His bride, as he soon discovers, does not appear to be interested in the consummation of their marriage. In fact, she tells Amintor that she hates him and will never share his bed. Threatened by Amintor, she finally confesses that she has already given herself to the king. Amintor is deeply injured when she reveals to him that the marriage is merely a means to make legitimate any children born of that affair. Determined to make the marriage seem normal, however, he sleeps in her bedchamber, on the floor.

Aspatia, meanwhile, returns to her home, where she warns her maids never to trust their hearts to men and recounts classical stories of women who, much to their distress, gave their hearts away. Old Calianax, always a coward at heart, vows to be valiant in avenging the slight to his daughter. The next morning Amintor, emerging from the

bedchamber, encounters Melantius, whom he puzzles with ambiguous remarks about the virtues of the soldier's family. Later, Amintor's assumed manner arouses the king's suspicions; in private he accuses Evadne of faithlessness. To prove her steadfastness to the king, Evadne provokes Amintor into revealing that the marriage has not been consummated. Amintor is overcome by the enormity of the way he has been treated, but he refuses to draw his sword on the king. Still, he vows to avenge the insult somehow.

Melantius, meanwhile, ponders Amintor's peculiar behavior. Dismissing a foolish challenge from Calianax, he encounters Amintor, whom he persuades to unburden his heart of its troubles. When Amintor reveals that Evadne is the king's mistress, Melantius, incapable of believing Amintor's story, draws his sword and threatens to kill his friend. When Amintor seems to welcome death, Melantius, convinced, sheathes his sword and swears to avenge his sister's disgrace. Amintor, who feels that it is he who should do the avenging, challenges Melantius to fight. Melantius refuses, calms the youth, and promises that the two could effect a scheme to right the wrongs done them.

Melantius directs his brother, Diphilus, to prepare his armor for battle. He also asks Calianax, the castellan of Rhodes, to deliver the garrison to him. The old man, promising permission within the hour, hastens to report the rebellion to the king.

Melantius confronts Evadne with his knowledge of her transgression. Upon asking her to name her seducer, she pretends to be insulted and suggests that he tend to his military affairs. When Melantius threatens to kill her, she confesses the truth. Then, realizing the extent of her disgrace, she promises Melantius that she will kill the king. She also expresses her remorse to Amintor and begs him for forgiveness. Amintor kisses her and cautions her never to sin again.

Meanwhile, at a dinner in the palace, Calianax tells the king of Melantius's scheme to kill him and to escape to the fortress of Rhodes. The king, doubting, calls Amintor into the dining chamber, where with leading questions he tests Amintor and Evadne, as well as Melantius, who accompanies them. Melantius maintains his poise. When the king discloses his knowledge of the plot, Melantius continues to dissemble and states that Calianax is an irresponsible, foolish old man. The king is convinced that Melantius is innocent. When Melantius, in asides, importunes Calianax about the fortress, the old man tries to convince the king that Melantius is making overtures under his very eyes, but the ruler suggests that someone put the weak-minded old man to bed. The thoroughly confounded lord submits reluctantly to Melantius's demands for the fortress.

On the night for revenge, Diphilus takes command of the fortress. Amintor, encountering Melantius, asks his assistance in killing the king. Melantius, fearful lest his plans fail, reminds Amintor that the king's person is sacred.

Evadne, going to the king's bedchamber, ties the sleeping monarch to the bed. Awakening, the king thinks at first that his bondage is a pretty joke of Evadne, but he is filled with apprehension when he sees her draw a knife. Reciting his villainy toward her, she stabs him to death; then she forgives him.

Soon afterward, the death of the king having been discovered, the king's brother Lysippus and his followers go to the citadel, where Melantius and his people are in control. Melantius affirms his loyalty to Rhodes, but declares that if he is not given amnesty he could very easily destroy the city. Lysippus and Melantius agree to a general amnesty.

Meanwhile, Aspatia, disguised as a man, enters Amintor's apartment, where she tells Amintor that she is Aspatia's long-lost brother, returned to avenge his sister. In her disguise, Aspatia challenges Amintor to a duel. When he refuses, she strikes him. Goaded to action, Amintor draws and wounds Aspatia.

Evadne, bloody dagger in hand, enters and tells Amintor that she has killed the king. When she asks Amintor to recognize her as his wife, he, appalled, refuses and leaves her. Evadne stabs herself to death. Aspatia, meanwhile, has revived long enough to reveal her true identity to Amintor, who declares his unworthiness and his shame for the way that he has treated her. When Aspatia dies, Amintor, having nothing more to live for and wishing to be with his true love, stabs himself.

Melantius, entering, is so overcome by the sight of his dead sister and his dying friend that he attempts to take his own life. Calianax, upon recognizing his daughter, the dead Aspatia, is reconciled to Melantius. Lysippus, the new ruler, looks upon the scene as an object lesson to kings to be chaste.

Critical Evaluation:

Francis Beaumont and John Fletcher's *The Maid's Tragedy* is a typical example of the kind of play written and produced in the Jacobean period (the reign of King James I, 1603-1625), which also encompasses the later plays of William Shakespeare and the work of Ben Jonson. Although there were very few theaters at that time, audiences constantly demanded new plays, and there was opportunity for many playwrights to try their hands.

The plays of the Jacobean era are, in the main, very similar and use ideas, motifs, and characters that were interesting to the audiences of the time but are somewhat lacking to a contemporary reader. This is one of the reasons why Jacobean dramas are rarely produced even in Great Britain, where only Shakespeare and, to a lesser extent, Jonson are regularly presented.

Most Jacobean plays have all the trappings of a Shakespearean play, but little of the content. This play, in which the grandeur of court life and the disastrous, bloody fate of several characters, including a king, are explored, is a rather thin story of the secret love affair of the king of Rhodes and the sister of his greatest general. There is some lack of credibility immediately apparent in his insistence on marrying her to one of his nobles, Amintor, despite Amintor's betrothal to another noblewoman, Aspatia. The king must marry her off to avoid scandal if she becomes pregnant, but why he marries her off to Amintor, who is engaged, is something of a mystery. One of the marks of a second-rate drama is a tendency to pay little attention to credibility. The audiences of the time liked odd conduct, and they seemed quite prepared to accept arbitrary actions, particularly from monarchs. The historical ironies are clear; the literary legacy is clouded. The higher the rank, the less dependable the characters or their actions.

The characters in the plays also expect questionable conduct from their rulers, and the king of Rhodes is typical. Equally Jacobean is the way in which problems are solved, usually, by violent action. The revenge theme, in which personal or family affronts are not so much solved as aggravated by further affront, in the form of payback, is played out in *The Maid's Tragedy* with some considerable style. Part of the revenge motif is its getting out of hand, often causing the death of those who do not deserve to die. In this play, the king gets what he deserves, but the play does not stop there; instead, it manages to draw in Evadne, who is less guilty than her lover, and Aspatia and Amintor, who are entirely innocent. This element of the play is typical of Jacobean drama.

Beaumont and Fletcher tend to put emphasis upon a love affair as a central theme for their dramas, and they take some care to allow for the poetic expression of amorous feeling. It is generally assumed that Beaumont probably wrote the more lyric passages, and that Fletcher, who is assumed to have had a temperament somewhat less romantic than that of Beaumont, is responsible for the sharper, conversational, sometimes comic material. This play is less comic than others, but the exchanges between Melantius and Calianax, however serious the context, display the kind of smart, combative dialogue enjoyed by the Jacobean audience. Calianax is a typical comic figure, the old man who is the butt of all jokes, however cruel they may be, simply because of his age.

What makes the play difficult for a contemporary reader is its seeming lack of serious substance. It is hardly a tragedy, since the matter at hand is relatively unimportant. The issue has no great import to anyone except for the small handful of intimates, although it does eventually cause the death of a monarch, who is quickly replaced. The matter, however, is somewhat more exclusively personal than is usually the case in tragedy. Certainly in comparison to the psychological, social, and political densities of Shakespeare, the play seems less formidable.

The play is certainly less than consequential in its quick changes of mind. Evadne, seemingly besotted with the king and emotionally committed to deception, needs very little persuasion to reject her lover and to sink immediately into the despair that turns her into a killer. No attempt is made to use her dilemma as an opportunity for extended soliloquy in the Shakespearean style. There are several quick reversals in the play that bother a contemporary reader but that were accepted as part of the convention for this kind of romantic tragedy, which has a ludic aspect to it, since so many of the plays of the time were variations on the pattern. Credibility was unimportant for an audience with a taste for watching the aristocracy, usually in a foreign land, acting arbitrarily, unfairly, and eventually murderously. Characters who are shallow were expected to use language extravagantly and well.

In short, what the Jacobean audience came to see was another version of the old tale of foreign folk of aristocratic power living lives of wild extravagance, lashing about politically, socially, and personally in ways beyond the abilities of the commoners. In this respect, Jacobean plays are not unlike the violent fantasy of late twentieth century adventure films. The obvious difference is the language, which is always intelligent, sophisticated, and often touching.

"Critical Evaluation" by Charles Pullen

Further Reading

Appleton, William W. *Beaumont and Fletcher: A Critical Study.* Winchester, Mass.: Allen & Unwin, 1956. A short examination of the collaboration, with discussion of *The Maid's Tragedy* in the context of the canon. Appleton also considers the playwrights' influence on Restoration drama.

Bliss, Lee. *Francis Beaumont.* Boston: Twayne, 1987. An introductory overview of Beaumont's life and work. Bliss maintains that one of the problems in studying Beaumont and John Fletcher lies in the difficulty of distinguishing their respective contributions to their plays. He also discusses their influences.

Bradbrook, M. C. *Themes and Conventions in Elizabethan Tragedy.* 2d ed. New York: Cambridge University Press, 1994. A good source for understanding the peculiar dependence of Elizabethan and Jacobean drama on the repetition of certain themes, conventions, and motifs.

Braunmuller, A. R., and Michael Hattaway, eds. *The Cambridge Companion to English Renaissance Drama.* 2d ed. New York: Cambridge University Press, 2003. This collection of essays discussing various aspects of English Renaissance drama includes numerous references to Beaumont and Fletcher and examines *The Maid's Tragedy.*

Clark, Sandra. *Renaissance Drama.* Malden, Mass.: Polity Press, 2007. This accessible overview of Renaissance drama places the plays of Beaumont and Fletcher, including *The Maid's Tragedy,* within their broader literary context.

Ellis-Fermor, Una. *The Jacobean Drama: An Interpretation.* 1958. Reprint. London: Methuen, 1973. Another seminal text with an overall view of Jacobean drama. Chapter 2 deals with Beaumont and Fletcher, providing some discussion of their use of romance and their approach to character and plot.

Fletcher, Ian. *Beaumont and Fletcher.* London: Longmans, Green, 1967. A short work, but a good starting point for further study, touching on all the problems involved in understanding the collaborations between Beaumont and Fletcher.

Gayley, Charles Mill. *Beaumont: The Dramatist.* 1914. Reprint. Eastbourne, England: Gardners Books, 2007. The first half of this classic work is a standard critical biography; the second half deals with specific critical questions, including versification, diction, and critical approaches. Part of the Legacy Reprint series.

Main Currents in American Thought
An Interpretation of American Literature from the Beginnings to 1920

Author: Vernon Louis Parrington (1871-1929)
First published: 1927-1930
Type of work: History

Vernon Louis Parrington's three-volume *Main Currents in American Thought* is generally considered monumental for two reasons. First, the detailed tables of contents show an awesome knowledge of literary and political history and the ability to place the major and minor American writers from 1620 to 1900; second, the guide to this imposition of order is a passionate belief in Jeffersonian democracy as the essential philosophy of the United States. Parrington's work had the revolutionary effect of giving American writers a social dimension never seen in histories of English literature or English thought. This dimension made meaningful and, in turn, greatly accelerated the study of American literature in schools and colleges, as did the work of Frederick Jackson Turner stimulate the study of American history in terms of the United States.

For Parrington, two currents affected the American mind, Romanticism and realism, with the division between the two coming at 1860. His first problem, however, was to establish the growth and actual existence of the American mind itself; this task is accomplished in the historical survey of the first volume, *The Colonial Mind, 1620-1800*, where colonial conditions formed a certain way of thinking, a way of thinking that changed during the Revolutionary War into the American mind. Parrington then studies the national temper in the two succeeding volumes, dealing with Romanticism and realism.

The first volume contains three books. The first book, "Liberalism and Puritanism," covers the first century of American history, 1620-1720, in which conflict appears between Carolinian liberalism and Puritanism; the new environment comes into play and strengthens the latter so that the first part of this book records the triumph of theocratic oligarchy in Massachusetts up to 1660. The ground for this triumph is prepared for in the growing rigidity of Puritan thought and practice as a result of transplanting European ideas, but Parrington's sympathy is with the independents, especially Roger Williams, who excites some of his loftiest prose. That triumph led to the twilight of the oligarchy after 1660; Increase Mather is attacked as intolerant and dictatorial, and Cotton Mather is analyzed pitilessly; the fall of Mas-

sachusetts is symbolized in the witch trials of Salem and caused by increasing rigidity of thought in the face of growing economic pressure for changes in the social system.

The second book, "The Colonial Mind," is also divided into two parts: the making of the colonial mind and the awakening of the American mind, with the division at 1763. The colonial mind, having lost the Puritan systemization, is at first at the greater mercy of the environment: The eighteenth century influx of Scotch-Irish and Germans—the latter settling mostly in Pennsylvania—develops a consciousness of the hinterland that veers between adulation, in Michel-Guillaume Jean de Crèvecœur, and contempt, in Mme Knight, with William Byrd in between. Jonathan Edwards is pushed offstage along with the Great Awakening, and the spotlight given to Benjamin Franklin, the heir to French Physiocratic views and the first American with a truly American mind. The second part is largely political, outlining the mind of the American Tory, Thomas Hutchinson; the American Whig, John Dickinson; and the American Democrat, Samuel Adams. At the conclusion of this part, American literature makes its first appearance as "literary echoes" in the form of Whig and Tory satires.

Literature is better represented in the third part of book 3, "Liberalism and the Constitution," which covers the last seventeen years of the eighteenth century and introduces at its close the first novelist, Hugh Henry Brackenridge, and the poets Philip Freneau and Joel Barlow, whom Parrington approves of for their republicanism. He does not think much of the Hartford Wits, whom he labels with his worst stigma, "arch conservatives." The literature in these stirring years takes second place to politics, in which the clash is between the transplanted English ideas of laissez faire and the agrarianism that is, for Parrington, the soundest basis for his cherished liberalism. Agrarianism was defeated in the years between 1783 and 1787, according to Parrington, in spite of Thomas Jefferson, the towering figure who dominates all of Parrington's work and brings the first two centuries of American thought to a fitting close. Jefferson was able to rethink transplanted ideas into an American context and thus establish the American mind as an independent and vital entity.

In the next two volumes, Parrington sets out to trace the fortunes of currents of this mind through the nineteenth century up to 1920. He traces an even break between them at 1860.

New England comes into its own again in the second volume, *The Romantic Revolution in America, 1800-1860*. This preeminence is not surprising, for the period covered is the first half of the nineteenth century, the decades of the Transcendentalists. Three "minds" are established as well, those of the American Middle East, the South, and New England. The first is treated comparatively briefly under three headings in book 2 of this volume: writers of Philadelphia, such as Charles Brockden Brown; those of New York, the new literary capital; and those who came to New York from New England, William Cullen Bryant, Horace Greeley, and Herman Melville; the treatment of Melville is simply headed "Pessimist" and shows at its worst Parrington's inability to analyze literature that does not contain his ideas. Much more sympathetic is his study of James Fenimore Cooper, largely because of the social criticism Parrington discerned in his work. In the New Yorker school, Parrington subdivided Washington Irving and James Kirke Paulding as Knickerbocker Romantics, and preferred the latter on equally bad grounds, labeling Irving an idle man-about-town.

The strength of the second volume is its three parts devoted to "The Mind of the South," with which the volume opens. Howard Mumford Jones has testified, in *The Theory of American Literature* (1948), to the astonishment of young scholars at Parrington's recovery of writers who had gradually been forgotten under the New England ascendancy of the post-American Civil War years. The best example is the fourth chapter of part 2, devoted chiefly to the achievements of Charleston as a literary center, best represented by William Gilmore Simms. Perhaps equally surprising is the title of part 1: "The Virginia Renaissance." Although this section begins with the tradition of agrarianism, it passes on to literary matters in the eleven pages devoted to John Pendleton Kennedy and concludes with three on Edgar Allan Poe; literary radicalism (and perhaps insensitivity) could scarcely go further.

Parrington is at his best, however, in his scrupulously fair analysis of the Southern defense of slavery, but it must have been with some relief that he concluded the first book with a summary of the positions of Andrew Jackson and Abraham Lincoln as symbols of the West. Parrington also concludes with a summary of the first example of Western literature, Augustus Baldwin Longstreet's *Georgia Scenes* (1835 and 1840). He prefers the realism of the former to the myth of Davy Crockett—"a wastrel."

The third book of the second volume is divided into four parts on the New England mind. The first two parts have remained valuable as summaries of the political and social thought of New England. These two parts include sections on Brook Farm, John Greenleaf Whittier, and Harriet Beecher Stowe, which are largely economic or environmental studies. Literature occupies the third and fourth parts and is somewhat loosely organized as the Transcendental and "other" aspects of the New England mind, the latter including Nathaniel Hawthorne, Oliver Wendell Holmes, and James Russell Lowell, with a brief mention of Henry Wadsworth Longfellow. The "other" writers suffer the stigma of being "genteel," which is interpreted as "unrealistic." This idea allows Parrington to demonstrate the necessary decline in the Romantic movement with which the whole volume is supposed to be concerned, but which is largely evidenced in Henry David Thoreau and Ralph Waldo Emerson. Discussion of the decline closes the volume and prepares the way for the celebration of realism in the third.

The third volume, *The Beginnings of Critical Realism in America, 1860-1920*, was published after Parrington's death. Of the three books to this volume, the first is almost complete and the second is almost half complete. Book 1 takes the story of United States' thought through two decades after the Civil War, but the press of economic and political analysis is so great that the writers tend to be sandwiched into the second chapter of part 1—Walt Whitman, Mark Twain, and the local colorists—and the concluding chapter of part 2—Henry James and William Dean Howells. The social and mental background is still Parrington's forte, and the information in book 1 and the first half of book 2 is valuable, but it is regrettable that Parrington was unable to complement his accompanying studies of Hamlin Garland and Edward Bellamy with those of other naturalists, such as Frank Norris and Stephen Crane, and the frontier writers. All that remains of the third volume are the addenda of scattered notes on writers, the plan, and an unfinished introduction. Perhaps death preserved Parrington from the increasing difficulties of applying his method and purpose to a much greater volume of literature, but one would like to have seen the attempt to fit writers such as Edith Wharton and F. Scott Fitzgerald into his grand design.

Further Reading

Cowley, Malcolm, and Bernard Smith, eds. *Books That Changed Our Minds*. 1939. Reprint. Freeport, N.Y.: Books for Libraries Press, 1970. Claims Parrington's history was well received by conservatives as well as liberals; maintains that the influence exerted by this work places

Parrington on par with Oswald Spengler, Alfred North Whitehead, and Vladimir Ilich Lenin.

Gabriel, Ralph W. "Vernon Louis Parrington." In *Pastmasters: Some Essays on American Historians*, edited by Marcus Cunliffe and Robin W. Winks. 1969. Reprint. Westport, Conn.: Greenwood Press, 1979. Discusses the publication history of *Main Currents in American Thought* and examines the personal quality of Parrington's approach to history. Reviews the contemporaneous reception of the work and surveys its influence on later historians.

Hall, H. Lark. *V. L. Parrington: Through the Avenue of Art.* Kent, Ohio: Kent State University Press, 1994. Comprehensive biography tracing Parrington's intellectual development. Hall argues that Parrington was in search of a personal myth, and *Main Currents in American Thought* marked the culmination of that search.

Hofstadter, Richard. *The Progressive Historians: Turner, Beard, Parrington.* 1968. Reprint. Chicago: University of Chicago Press, 1979. Links Parrington with other histori-ans who engaged in their profession as a means of influencing contemporary politics. Asserts that *Main Currents in American Thought* helps explain the nature of the American liberal mind.

Noble, David Watson. *Historians Against History: The Frontier Thesis and the National Covenant in American Historical Writing Since 1830.* Minneapolis: University of Minnesota Press, 1965. Describes *Main Currents in American Thought* as "the single most important book written by a historian of the frontier tradition," synthesizing work by earlier historians and paying tribute to a way of life that disappeared in the decades that followed its publication.

Skotheim, Robert Allen. *American Intellectual Histories and Historians.* 1966. Reprint. Westport, Conn.: Greenwood Press, 1978. Claims that *Main Currents in American Thought* is the first work to offer a systematic view of American intellectual history. Highlights the contrast of progress and reaction that characterizes Parrington's methodology.

Main Street
The Story of Carol Kennicott

Author: Sinclair Lewis (1885-1951)
First published: 1920
Type of work: Novel
Type of plot: Social satire
Time of plot: c. 1910-1920
Locale: A small midwestern town

Principal characters:
CAROL KENNICOTT, an idealist
DR. WILL KENNICOTT, her husband

The Story:

When Carol Milford graduates from Blodgett College in Minnesota, she thinks she can conquer the world. Interested in sociology, and village improvement in particular, she often longs to set out on her own crusade to transform dingy prairie towns into thriving, beautiful communities. When she meets Will Kennicott, a doctor from Gopher Prairie, and listens to his praise of his hometown, she agrees to marry him. He convinces Carol that Gopher Prairie needs her.

Carol is an idealist. On the train, going to her new home, she deplores the rundown condition of the countryside and wonders whether the northern Midwest has a future. Will tells her that the people are happy. As they travel through town after town, Carol notices with a sinking heart the shapeless mass of hideous buildings, the dirty depots, the flat wastes of prairie surrounding everything. She knows that Gopher Prairie will be no different from the rest, and she is right. The people are as drab as their houses and as flat as their fields. A welcoming committee meets the newlyweds at the train. To Carol, all the men are alike in their colorless clothes and in their overfriendly, overenthusiastic manner. The Kennicott house is a Victorian horror, but Will says he likes it.

At a party held in her honor, Carol hears the men talk of motorcars, train schedules, and "furriners" while they praise Gopher Prairie as God's own country. The women are interested in gossip, sewing, and cooking, and most of them belong to the two women's clubs, the Jolly Seventeen and the Thanatopsis Club. At the first meeting of the Jolly Seventeen,

Carol dismays everyone when she says that the duty of a librarian is to get people to read. The town librarian staunchly asserts that her primary trust is to preserve the books.

Carol is unconventional from the start. She hires a maid and pays her the overgenerous sum of six dollars per week. She gives a party with an Asian motif. She occasionally kicks off a slipper under the table, revealing her arches. Worse, she redecorates the old Kennicott house and gets rid of the mildew, the ancient bric-a-brac, and the dark wallpaper. Will protests against her desire to change things.

Carol joins the Thanatopsis Club, hoping to use the club as a means of awakening interest in social reform, but the women of Gopher Prairie, while professing charitable intentions, have no idea of improving social conditions. When Carol mentions that something should be done about the poor people of the town, everyone firmly states that there is no real poverty in Gopher Prairie. Carol also attempts to raise funds for a new city hall, but no one thinks the ugly old building needs to be replaced. The town votes against appropriating the necessary funds.

Will buys a summer cottage on Lake Minniemashie. There, Carol enjoys outdoor life, and during the summer months she almost loses her desire for reform. When September comes, however, she hates the thought of returning to Gopher Prairie.

Carol resolves to study her husband. He is well regarded in the town, and she romanticizes herself as the wife of a hardworking, courageous country doctor. She falls in love with Will again on the night she watches him perform a bloody but successful operation on a poor farmer. Carol's praise of her husband, however, has little effect. Will does not fit into any romantic conception. He accepts his duties as a necessary chore, and the thought that he saved the life of a human being does not occur to him. His interest in medicine is identical to his interest in motorcars. Carol turns her attention to Gopher Prairie.

Carol, trying to interest the Thanatopsis Club in literature and art, finally persuades the members to put on an amateur theatrical; but everyone's enthusiasm soon wanes. Carol's choice of a play, George Bernard Shaw's *Androcles and the Lion*, is vetoed and replaced with something less known. Carol considers even that choice too subtle for Gopher Prairie, but at least it revives the town's interest in theater.

After three years of marriage, Carol discovers that she is pregnant. When her son is born, she resolves that some day she will send little Hugh away from Gopher Prairie, to Harvard, Yale, or Oxford. With her new status of motherhood, Carol finds herself more accepted in the town, but because she devotes nine-tenths of her attention to Hugh she has little

time to criticize the town. She wants a new house, but she and Will cannot agree on the type of building. He is satisfied with a square frame house. Carol has visions of a Georgian mansion, with stately columns and wide lawns, or a white cottage like those at Cape Cod.

Carol meets a tailor in town, an artistic, twenty-five-year-old aesthete with whom she eventually imagines herself in love. She often drops by his shop to see him, and one day, Will warns her that the gossip in town is growing. Ashamed, Carol promises she will not see him again. The tailor leaves for Minneapolis.

Carol and Will decide to take a long trip to California. When they return three months later, Carol realizes that her attempt to escape Gopher Prairie has not been a success. For one thing, Will was with her on the trip, but what she needs is to get away from her husband. After a long argument with Will, Carol takes little Hugh and goes to Washington, D.C., where she plans to do war work. However, hers is an empty kind of freedom. She finds the people in Washington an accumulation of the population of thousands of Gopher Prairies all over the nation. Main Street has been transplanted to the larger city. Though she is disheartened by her discovery, Carol has too much pride to return home.

After thirteen months, Will goes to Washington to find Carol and Hugh. He misses her terribly, he says, and begs her to come back. Hugh is overjoyed to see his father, and Carol realizes that she has to return to Gopher Prairie. Home once more, Carol finds that her furious hatred for Gopher Prairie has burned itself out. She makes friends with the club women and promises herself not to be snobbish in the future. She will go on asking questions—she can never stop herself from doing that—but her questions now will be asked with sympathy rather than with sarcasm. For the first time, she feels serene. In Gopher Prairie, she at last feels that she is wanted. Her neighbors had missed her. For the first time, Carol feels that Gopher Prairie is her home.

Critical Evaluation:

Sinclair Lewis frequently had difficulty in determining in his own mind whether his works were meant as bitterly comic satires of American life and values or whether they were planned as complex novels centering on the lives of the characters he made famous. One of the difficulties of reading Lewis is that these two conflicting sorts of writing are both present in many of his works, and frequently at odds with each other. This is demonstrably true of *Main Street*. For all his satire of small-town attitudes and values, Lewis is not unequivocal in his attack. He finds a great many things of value in the best *Main Street* has to offer, and he seems to see Carol

Kennicott's reconciliation with the town at the end of the novel as a triumph rather than a failure on her part. Though *Main Street* is, as it has been frequently called, a revolt against the village, it is a revolt marked by the complexity of Lewis's attitude toward Gopher Prairie and toward its real-life counterpart, Sauk Center, Minnesota, where Lewis spent his early years.

Lewis's characters, particularly Will and Carol Kennicott, are other complicating factors in this novel that prevent its being simply a satire. Unlike the one-dimensional figures typical of satire, the Kennicotts develop into real people who demand the reader's attention and sympathy. Carol in particular is developed more novelistically than satirically, as Lewis traces her development from a naïve and foolishly idealistic young women into a more tolerant and understanding human being. Readers who accept only the critical and satiric portrait of the small town that lies at the surface of *Main Street* would be embracing the same overly simplistic attitudes that characterized Carol at the beginning of the novel.

During the early part of the century, Americans tended to accept on faith the premise that all that was best in life was epitomized by the small-town environment. Though by no means the first author to attack this premise, Lewis with *Main Street* achieved the widespread popularity that gave new prominence to this revolt against the small town. Lewis, himself a small-town boy, knew well the discrepancy between the vision of the village as utopia and the actuality of its bleak cultural and moral atmosphere. As Lewis makes clear in his prologue, *Main Street* represents all such towns, and by his treatment of Gopher Prairie, Lewis sought to strike a satiric blow at the very heartland of America. Rather than utopia, Lewis discovers in the provincial mentality of the small town a surfeit of hypocrisy, bigotry, ignorance, cruelty, and, perhaps most damning of all, a crippling dullness and conformity that is essentially hostile to any possibility of intellectual or emotional life. Yet, even while ruthlessly exposing these negative qualities of the small town, Lewis finds, particularly in the matter-of-fact courage and determination of Will Kennicott, some of the very qualities that initially gave the small town its reputation as the strength of America. Lewis himself was ambivalent in his attitude toward the village, and this indecisiveness creeps into the novel to mitigate his criticism.

The action of the novel centers on Carol's discovery of the nature of life and society in Gopher Prairie and culminates in her eventual compromise with the town. Carol's growth as a human being is an excellent device through which to expose the bleak heart of the midwestern town, and Lewis does so by contrasting the town's qualities and values with Carol's own. Young, educated, intelligent, and idealistic, Carol can cause Gopher Prairie to see what it lacks. Yet her idealism is accompanied by a naïveté and intolerance, which are poor qualifications for accomplishing the reforms she advocates. She can only hope to change Gopher Prairie by becoming part of it. In losing her naïveté, Carol gains a capacity to confront reality and even to change it over time.

Actually, most of Carol's reforms are too superficial to cure what Lewis called the "village virus." Carol's concern is more with manners than values, and she would only substitute the slick sophistication of the city for the provincial dullness she finds so intolerable. The perfect foil to her is Will, who, while epitomizing all the worst of the town's boorishness, goes about his daily medical practice with quiet efficiency, determination, and even courage, which Lewis clearly admires. Ultimately, it is Gopher Prairie that triumphs when Carol reconciles herself to its full reality.

"Critical Evaluation" by William E. Grant

Further Reading

Bucco, Martin. *Main Street: The Revolt of Carol Kennicott.* New York: Twayne, 1993. Focuses on Lewis's development of his *Main Street* heroine, especially her unconscious self-perceptions as prairie princess, Carol D'Arc, Lady Bountiful, Mater Dolorosa, Village Intellectual, American Bovary, and Passionate Pilgrim.

Davenport, Garvin F. "Gopher-Prairie-Lake-Wobegon: The Midwest as Mythical Space." In *Sinclair Lewis at One Hundred.* St. Cloud, Minn.: St. Cloud State University Press, 1985. Creates a connection between fictional places and their residents, relating them to humanist geographer Yi-Fu Tuan's theories about the duality of the fear and possibility of space and the familiarity, comfort, and constriction of place.

Grebstein, Sheldon Norman. *Sinclair Lewis.* New York: Twayne, 1962. A comparison of Lewis's works. Concludes that *Main Street* critiques the falseness and shallowness of American life, unlike some of Lewis's other novels that defend it.

Hutchisson, James M. *The Rise of Sinclair Lewis, 1920-1930.* University Park: Pennsylvania State University Press, 1996. Focuses on Lewis's career in the 1920's, when he wrote *Main Street* and the other novels that earned him the Nobel Prize in Literature. Hutchisson examines the techniques Lewis used to create his novels, devoting this book's first chapter to an analysis of *Main Street.*

_____, ed. *Sinclair Lewis: New Essays in Criticism*. Troy, N.Y.: Whitston, 1997. Includes three essays about *Main Street*: "Return to *Main Street*: Sinclair Lewis and the Politics of Literary Reputation," "'Extremely Married': Marriage as Experience and Institution in *The Job*, *Main Street*, and *Babbitt*," and "'Scarlet Tanager on an Ice-Floe': Women, Men, and History on *Main Street*."

Light, Martin. *The Quixotic Vision of Sinclair Lewis*. West Lafayette, Ind.: Purdue University Press, 1975. Demonstrates Lewis's pattern, especially obvious in *Main Street*, of sending his heroes into the world motivated by heroic chivalry, which results in not only foolish beliefs and behavior but also kindness, generosity, sympathy, and idealism.

Lingeman, Richard R. *Sinclair Lewis: Rebel from Main Street*. New York: Random House, 2002. A critical biography that includes analysis of Lewis's novels. Lingeman provides a detailed description of Lewis's unhappy life.

Main-Travelled Roads
Six Mississippi Valley Stories

Author: Hamlin Garland (1860-1940)
First published: 1891
Type of work: Short fiction
Type of plot: Social realism
Time of plot: Late nineteenth century

In 1887, Hamlin Garland traveled from Boston to South Dakota to visit his mother and father, whom he had not seen in six years. According to his own account, the trip through farming country was a revelation. Although he had been brought up on a farm, he had never realized how wretched farmers' lives were. The farther west he traveled, the more oppressive it became for him to see the bleakness of the landscape and the poverty of its people. When he reached his parents' farm and found his mother living in hopeless misery, Garland's depression turned to bitterness, and in this mood he wrote *Main-Travelled Roads*, a series of short stories about farm life in the Midwest.

In one of these stories, "Up the Coolly," Garland recreates the mood of his trip under somewhat similar circumstances. Howard McLane, after years spent traveling with his own theatrical troupe, returns to the West for a surprise visit with his mother and brother. He finds them living in poverty on a small, unproductive farm, the family property having been sold to pay off a mortgage. Although his mother and his sister-in-law greet him warmly, Grant, his brother, makes it plain that he blames Howard for the loss of the farm that, had he shared his wealth, could have been saved. Howard's attempt to win his brother's friendship results only in alienation until Howard finally admits his selfishness and neglect and offers to buy the farm back. The brothers are reconciled, but the story ends bleakly with Grant's refusal to accept any assistance.

Not many of Garland's stories end on so despondent a note; most of them end hopefully and some even happily. Garland spares none of his principal characters a bitter sense of failure, but most of them manage to overcome it. Thus, in "A 'Good Fellow's' Wife," Jim Sanford loses the savings of all the farmers who had invested in his bank. In "A Branch Road," Will Hannon loses the beautiful girl he loves and only regains her when she becomes prematurely old and wasted. In "Under the Lion's Paw," Tim Haskins is forced to pay twice the former price of a farm whose value he himself has doubled by hard work.

Even in the stories that are lighter in tone, the characters taste the bitterness of life. In "The Creamery Man," which is about a young man's carefree courtship, Claude Williams wins not Lucindy Kennedy, the lovely daughter of a prominent farmer, but Nina Haldeman, the unrefined daughter of an immigrant. In "Mrs. Ripley's Trip," Gran'ma Ripley makes a journey back east, where she had been born, but not without a sense of guilt for leaving her husband, even for so short a time.

Beyond reflecting the bitterness that Garland himself felt, many of his stories set forth a disillusioning contrast between the farm life he remembered and the reality he found when he returned after a long absence. "The Return of a Private," for instance, depicts the return of an American Civil War soldier to his farm. Expecting the farm to be as prosperous as when he had left it, Private Smith finds it "weedy and encumbered, a rascally renter had run away with his machinery . . . his children needed clothing, the years were coming upon him, he was sick and emaciated." In "God's Ravens," Robert Bloom, who had moved to the country because he felt stifled by city life, goes through an apprenticeship of misery before the country people finally accept him and make him feel at home.

Garland's disillusionment should not be overemphasized; practically all the stories in *Main-Travelled Roads* have a hopeful ending in that love for and trust in the land are ultimately shown to be justified. It is clear that with hard work Private Smith will restore his farm to its former prosperity. Robert Bloom discovers that the cause of his discontent is within himself, not in the hearts of his farmer neighbors. Tim Haskins, robbed by one man, is set on his feet by another. Garland's realistic portrayal of hardship and poverty did much to shatter romantic illusions about an American pastoral idyll, but the book's somber tone was not enough to discredit the traditional view of the farmer as a doughty, virtuous frontiersman. Rather, it was Garland's accomplishment to expose the pathos, in some cases even tragedy, of people who felt the futility and injustice of farm life but were unable to change that life and so accepted it with fortitude and resignation.

Main-Travelled Roads is more than a social document. The respected author William Dean Howells recognized that it was important in the development of a new American literature. In an essay that was reprinted as an introduction to later editions of *Main-Travelled Roads*, Howells commended Garland for the social significance of his work and went on to praise his "fine courage to leave a fact with the reader, ungarnished and unvarnished, which is almost the rarest trait in an Anglo-Saxon writer, so infantile and feeble is the custom of our art." Singled out for special praise was the ending of "A Branch Road," in which Will Hannon persuades Agnes Dingman to leave her husband and the farm to lead a life of comfort and ease. Such an ending Howells deemed immoral but justifiable, since for these characters it was probable and realistic. Howells's judgment was sound. It is because of Garland's contribution to the rise of American literary real-

ism as well as for his social commentary that his works are still read.

Further Reading

Fiske, Horace S. *Provincial Types in American Fiction*. Port Washington, N.Y.: Kennikat Press, 1968. Includes a detailed critical analysis of Garland's short stories, explaining their realistic style and intent.

Foote, Stephanie. "The Region of the Repressed and the Return of the Region: Hamlin Garland and Harold Frederic." In *Regional Fictions: Culture and Identity in Nineteenth-Century American Literature*. Madison: University of Wisconsin Press, 2001. This chapter includes a lengthy analysis of *Main-Travelled Roads*, comparing it to other works of American regionalism. Foote argues that Americans' conceptions of local identity originated with Garland and other regional fiction writers of the late nineteenth and early twentieth centuries.

Howells, William Dean. "Editor's Study." In *Critical Essays on Hamlin Garland*, compiled by James Nagel. Boston: G. K. Hall, 1982. Discusses style and themes in the stories "Among the Corn Rows," "A Branch Road," "Mrs. Ripley's Trip," "Up the Coolly," and "Return of a Private."

Knight, Grant C. *American Literature and Culture*. New York: Cooper Square Press, 1972. Includes a discussion of Garland's collection of short stories as they relate to a literary portrayal of rural culture in America. Knight looks specifically at the themes and realistic style in "Up the Coolly" and "Return of a Private."

Newlin, Keith. *Hamlin Garland: A Life*. Lincoln: University of Nebraska Press, 2008. Newlin's biography of Garland, the first to be published in more than forty years, is based in part on newly available letters, manuscripts, and family memoirs. Discusses Garland's contributions to literature and places Garland's work within the artistic context of its time. Chapter 8 focuses on *Main-Travelled Roads*.

Parrington, Vernon L. *The Beginnings of Critical Realism in America, 1860-1920*. Vol. 3 in *Main Currents in American Thought*. New York: Harcourt, Brace & World, 1958. This authoritative classic source discusses the factual elements in Garland's stories as well as the kinds of plots and characterizations he used. Explains some of the ways in which Garland's stories compare with other realistic fictional portrayals of American rural life.

Major Barbara

Author: George Bernard Shaw (1856-1950)
First produced: 1905; first published, 1907
Type of work: Drama
Type of plot: Play of ideas
Time of plot: January, 1906
Locale: London and Middlesex, England

Principal characters:
SIR ANDREW UNDERSHAFT, a munitions manufacturer
LADY BRITOMART, his wife
BARBARA, their daughter and a major in the Salvation Army
ADOLPHUS CUSINS, Barbara's fiancé and a professor of Greek

The Story:

Lady Britomart Undershaft summons her children to her house in the fashionable London suburb of Wilton Crescent. Stephen, the first to arrive, greets his mother in the library. Lady Britomart, a formidable woman fifty years of age, intends to discuss the family's finances. She reminds Stephen that his sister Sarah's fiancé, Charles Lomax, whose inheritance is still ten years off, is too brainless to support a wife. She objects less to Adolphus Cusins, a professor of Greek, who is engaged to her daughter, Barbara, a major in the Salvation Army.

Stephen timidly mentions the name of his father, Andrew Undershaft, a wealthy munitions manufacturer who is estranged from his family. Lady Britomart admits that she had invited Andrew that night to solicit financial help from him. Stephen disdains the tainted Undershaft capital, but his mother informs him that their present income comes not from her own father, whose only legacy to his family is an aristocratic name, but from Andrew. She also explains that her separation from Andrew comes from her objections to the longstanding Undershaft tradition of turning over the munitions operations to a talented foundling. Seven generations of foundlings have taken the name Andrew Undershaft and run the business, but she objects against Andrew's disinheriting Stephen.

The girls and their fiancés arrived shortly before Andrew, who, having been away for twenty years, does not recognize his own children. Barbara's conspicuous Salvation Army uniform turns the conversation to a discussion of personal morality. Andrew's motto, he explains, is "unashamed," and he candidly admits that he reaps handsome profits from "mutilation and murder." He and Barbara challenge one another to a sort of conversion contest. Andrew agrees to visit Barbara's shelter in the slums if she will visit his weapons factory in Middlesex.

At the squalid Salvation Army post in West Ham a few days later, two poor Cockneys, Snobby Price and Rummy Mitchens, huddle for shelter from the January cold. In low voices they discuss how they routinely make up dramatic public confessions of sins to get free meals. Jenny Hill, a worker for the army, brings in Peter Shirley, who recently lost his job. Unlike Rummy and Snobby, Shirley balks over accepting charity. A loud bully named Bill Walker swaggers in looking for his girlfriend, who recently converted. When he recognizes Jenny as the Salvationist who had helped reform his girlfriend, he angrily wrenches her arm, pulls her hair, and hits her in the face with his fist. Jenny tearfully asks God for strength and runs off.

When Barbara arrives to deal with Bill Walker, her father follows and observes. She awakens Walker's conscience in part by mentioning Todger Fairmile, a former wrestler who is now a sergeant at the army's Canning Town barracks. Walker offers a sovereign to ease his shame, but Barbara says that she and the army cannot be bought off and will accept nothing less than Walker's repentant soul.

Mrs. Baines, the commissioner, comes in to report that the prospect of having to close several shelters because of a lack of money, has receded again after a sizable donation from Lord Saxmundham. Barbara is dismayed when Andrew explains that this donor is really Horace Bodger, the whiskey tycoon, whose product had ruined so many of the West Ham destitute. Andrew calls Bodger's donation mere conscience money and, not wanting to be outdone, offers to match it with an equal gift of his own. Barbara knows that neither Bodger nor her father has reformed. She is aghast to see Mrs. Baines accept the tainted money. She slowly removes her Salvation Army badge as Undershaft, Cusins, and Mrs. Baines march off to celebrate. Bill Walker, having observed the transaction, taunts a disillusioned Barbara by saying, "What price salvation?"

The next day, in Lady Britomart's library, Cusins reports to the family about the fiery religious meeting the day before. Amid music and hysteria, Mrs. Baines had announced the donations and the army had recorded 117 conversions. Lady Britomart settles the earlier financial question by persuading

Andrew to provide support for Charles Lomax and Sarah. Andrew is resolute, however, about upholding the Undershaft tradition and disinheriting Stephen in favor of a foundling. Having seen Stephen's lack of curiosity and intelligence, he suggests a career in politics or journalism for his son.

The entire family later travels to Andrew's factory in Middlesex, a place that shocked them for being so clean and respectable. They marvel at the nursing home, town hall, libraries, and schools. Peter Shirley, they discover, has been given a job as a gatekeeper. Andrew proudly brags that the profits from the bloody business of warfare has eliminated from his community the worst crime of all: poverty. Its by-products of misery, crime, and hunger are also unknown. Cusins then startles everyone by explaining that technically he himself is a foundling since his Australian parents were not legally married in England. Andrew happily offers him the position of Andrew Undershaft VIII, which he accepts.

Attention returns to Barbara. Andrew invites her to bring her gift for saving souls to his community, telling her that unlike the poor in West Ham the souls of his workers are hungry because their stomachs are full. After considering, Barbara accepts. She announces that she is over the bribe of bread and that "the way of life lies through the factory of death."

Critical Evaluation:

Major Barbara is one of George Bernard Shaw's most stimulating plays. In the early and middle years of his career, he used wit and realism as weapons in his attempt to bestir a complacent society. His iconoclastic nature delighted in overturning accepted morality; one of his famous aphorisms is "all great truths begin as blasphemies." In his second play, *Mrs. Warren's Profession* (1893), he blames prostitution on the men who have no convictions rather than on the poor women without chastity; in *Arms and the Man* (1894), he mocks romantic views of love and war; and in *Candida: A Mystery* (1897), he boldly reversed the emphasis of Henrik Ibsen's *Et dukkehjem* (pr., pb. 1879; *A Doll's House*, 1880) by showing that behind the stereotype of the strong male provider lay crippling insecurities and the inability to love. Although *Major Barbara* was written and performed in 1905, Shaw coyly set it in January, 1906—slightly ahead of his time—as if to dramatize an imminent time when his thesis about poverty being the root of all evil could be heard.

Shaw's technique in this play is to use the first act to dramatize the comforts of capitalism and the second to expose its cruelties. In affluent Wilton Crescent, Lady Britomart comically reduces all questions of morality to matters of good and bad taste. To her, polite hypocrisy is a necessary social lubricant. She explains that what infuriated her about Andrew was not that he did wrong things (which he did not) but that he delighted in saying and thinking wrong things and had a type of "religion of wrongness." She scolds Barbara for speaking about religion as if it were something pleasant and not the social drudgery that she knows it to be. Barbara's strong will asserts itself in her language of inversion and paradox. She proves to be a match for her father in their early encounters, showing that she resembles him in being a larger-than-life presence. In the second act, the drawing-room comedy gives way to the realism of the slums.

Many Shavian dramas present mentor-pupil relationships in which a pupil, who starts by believing a set of traditional values, goes through a process of disillusionment and maturation until freed from the artificial trappings of societal values and ready to learn genuine strength. Act 2 of *Major Barbara* may be Shaw's most compelling example of this formula. Here, the pupil Barbara proves equal to her mentor father. Shaw pivots their clash of values around the soul of Bill Walker, and at first it almost seems as if Barbara may win. When she learns about Horace Bodger's donation, however, and sees Snobby Price sneak off with Bill Walker's unclaimed sovereign, she realizes that Snobby's confessions were manufactured for free meals and that her own work has been futile. The Salvation Army accommodates poverty by merely treating its symptoms and accepting the social status quo. Although the offstage conversions of Todger Fairmile and Walker's girlfriend are presented in earnest, even Snobby Price recognizes that the army makes more good citizens than true believers: "It combs our air and makes us good little blokes to be robbed and put upon." The army perpetuates a cycle in which poverty will always have a place. Barbara's disillusionment is genuine and moving.

Its strengths notwithstanding, the play's third act is commonly regarded as flawed. (Shaw himself was still rethinking his ending some thirty-five years later when *Major Barbara* was filmed.) To friends to whom he read his first version of the play, Shaw lamented, "I don't know how to end the thing." In his revision, he sought to balance some of the initial one-sidedness. In the version that now exists, Barbara's disillusionment at the end of act 2 is followed by a second conversion in which she sees that "turning our backs on Bodger and Undershaft is turning our backs on life." In Shaw's final design, Barbara, Cusins, and Undershaft form a trinity of sorts in which Undershaft's power is matched by Cusins's intelligence and Barbara's spirituality. Shaw's creative evolution thus becomes the utopian fantasy that concludes his drama.

Neat symmetries notwithstanding, the play loses some of its emotional appeal in this improved last act. The concluding Shavian discussion excites the mind more than the emotions, and the fine balance of thought and feeling that Shaw achieved in acts 1 and 2 is dissipated in act 3. The earlier vivid image of Barbara's shattered faith when Mrs. Baines accepts the money of the whiskey king threatens to overshadow her later change of heart. Moreover, details about Barbara's new mission to the workers at Perivale St. Andrews are vague.

All weaknesses aside, *Major Barbara* is a rich and rewarding comedy of ideas. Its insistent realities remain compelling: that all social institutions, even churches, are owned by the captains of industry; that the more destructive war becomes, the more fascinating it is to people; and that any system of morality must fit the facts of life or be scrapped as worthless.

Glenn Hopp

Further Reading

Bentley, Eric. *Bernard Shaw.* 1947. Reprint. Milwaukee, Wis.: Applause Theater & Cinema Books, 2002. A renowned writer on modern drama, Bentley sets forth ideas about Shaw that place later critics in his debt. His study is one of the first important books on Shaw.

Dukore, Bernard F. *Shaw's Theater.* Gainesville: University Press of Florida, 2000. Focuses on the performance of Shaw's plays and how *Major Barbara* and other plays call attention to elements of the theater, such as the audience, characters directing other characters, and plays within plays. Includes the section "Bernard Shaw, Director."

Holroyd, Michael. *Bernard Shaw: The One-Volume Definitive Edition.* 1997. New ed. New York: W. W. Norton, 2006. This indispensable biography by Holroyd is an authoritative, superbly written, and richly detailed model of the biographer's art. Gives particular attention to the troublesome third act of *Major Barbara* and its ambiguities.

Innes, Christopher, ed. *The Cambridge Companion to George Bernard Shaw.* New York: Cambridge University Press, 1998. Collection of scholarly essays examining Shaw's work, including discussions of Shaw's feminism, Shavian comedy and the shadow of Oscar Wilde, Shaw's "discussion plays," and his influence on modern theater. References to *Major Barbara* are indexed.

Pagliaro, Harold E. *Relations Between the Sexes in the Plays of George Bernard Shaw.* Lewiston, N.Y.: Edwin Mellen Press, 2004. Demonstrates how the relationship between men and women is a key element in Shaw's plays. Notes a pattern in how Shaw depicts these relationships, including lovers destined by the "life force" to procreate; relations between fathers and daughters and mothers and sons; and the sexuality of politically, intellectually, and emotionally strong men.

Shaw, George Bernard. *The Collected Screenplays of Bernard Shaw.* Edited by Bernard F. Dukore. London: George Prior, 1980. In his introduction, Dukore devotes twenty-eight pages to a thorough analysis of Shaw's script for the 1941 film version of *Major Barbara* and an informative comparison of that version with the stage play.

_____. *George Bernard Shaw's Plays: "Mrs. Warren's Profession," "Pygmalion," "Man and Superman," "Major Barbara"—Contexts and Criticism.* 2d ed. Edited by Sandie Byrne. New York: W. W. Norton, 2002. In addition to an annotated text of *Major Barbara,* this volume contains critical essays, excerpts from books, and reviews discussing Shaw's work generally and *Major Barbara* specifically.

Zimbardo, Rose, ed. *Twentieth Century Interpretations of "Major Barbara."* Englewood Cliffs, N.J.: Prentice-Hall, 1970. Six complete essays and portions of five others offer differing approaches to the play. Zimbardo's remarks on the play's conformity to the comic paradigm, Joseph Frank's essay on the play's movement toward a Shavian salvation, and Anthony S. Abbott's comments on realism are insightful and accessible.

The Making of Americans
Being a History of a Family's Progress

Author: Gertrude Stein (1874-1946)
First published: 1925; abridged, 1934
Type of work: Novel
Type of plot: Psychological realism
Time of plot: Probably late nineteenth and early twentieth centuries
Locale: Bridgepoint, Maryland; Gossols, California

Principal characters:
HENRY DEHNING, a wealthy man
MRS. DEHNING, his wife
JULIA DEHNING, their eldest daughter, who marries Alfred Hersland
DAVID HERSLAND, an immigrant
DAVID HERSLAND, his son, a rich businessman
FANNY HISSEN HERSLAND, his ailing, unhappy wife
MARTHA HERSLAND, the eldest of the Herslands' three children
ALFRED HERSLAND, their son, a lawyer, who marries Julia Dehning
DAVID HERSLAND, the youngest son, who dies before middle age
PHILLIP REDFERN, an intellectual, who marries Martha Hersland
MADELEINE WYMAN, one of the Hersland children's governesses

The Story:

The Dehning and Hersland families' American history begins with their immigrant grandparents' separate journeys to America. Both families settle in Bridgepoint. Years later, the two families come together when Julia Dehning, who is connected with the old world because she is named for her grandmother, wants to marry Alfred Hersland. Her father cautions her not to encourage Alfred's advances. Although Julia quietly feels a vague dread about Alfred's plans for her father's money, she resists Henry Dehning's hesitation and he slowly begins to accept their wedding plans. Finally, Julia and Alfred are married after a year's engagement.

A long time before the Dehnings came to know the Hersland family, David Hersland's grandparents sell all of their possessions and travel to America to strike it rich. David's grandfather does not want to leave his home. As the family departs for America, David's grandfather keeps returning to take a last look at his old home. Still, he knows that he must begin again in the New World.

David's father makes a similar trip a generation later when he moves his family, including his well-to-do wife, Fanny, from Bridgeport to Gossols. Fanny Hissen has been raised by her religious father and dreary mother to feel important in Bridgepoint society. In Bridgepoint, David's sister, Martha, arranges her brother's marriage, and the family

moves west to Gossols. The Hersland house in Gossols sits on ten acres in the country, away from the other rich people in town. Although the children feel divided between city living and country living, they identify with the poor country people living around them more than with their own parents. After the Hersland family becomes established in Gossols, Fanny Hersland, cut off from Bridgepoint society and ignored by her husband and her children, loses all of her feeling of importance at being rich.

At this time, Madeleine Wyman, the Hersland family governess, has little to do with the children. Instead, she listens to Fanny's stories of her early life in Bridgepoint. This attention makes Mrs. Hersland feel important. When Madeleine is pressured by her family to marry a rich man, Mrs. Hersland attempts to persuade her to stay with the family. Fanny commissions her best dressmakers to make a dress for the governess. Madeleine finally marries the rich man, and she realizes why Fanny's early life had made her feel important.

Martha Hersland, the eldest child, leads a particularly uninteresting life until she witnesses a man beating a woman with an umbrella in a city street. This incident prompts her to leave Gossols to pursue her college education. At college, Martha meets the young intellectual Phillip Redfern, a student of philosophy, who becomes her close friend. They marry three years later. The women's college at Farnham invites Phillip to chair the philosophy department. The Redferns accept; however, Phillip and Martha are not a happy couple. In their marriage, Phillip's elaborate chivalry clashes with his wife's crude intelligence. In spite of compelling evidence, Martha cannot admit her husband's marital infidelities or understand why their marriage has failed. They leave Farnham around the time of Alfred and Julia's wedding, and never live together again. Martha believes that she is unworthy of Phillip's love, but she studies and travels to prepare herself for the time when they might be together again. After Phillip's death, Martha returns to Gossols to stay with her father.

Alfred Hersland's happy childhood is marred only by his confusion about being the eldest son, but the middle child. Alfred thinks he is superior to Martha because she is female. Many times he tries to get her into trouble. He spends his days playing in the orchard with the poor people who live nearby, until he is old enough to go to Bridgepoint for college. There, he meets his Hissen relatives, and with the characteristic Hersland impatience, he develops the urge to marry many years before he knows Julia Dehning.

Like Phillip and Martha's marriage, Alfred and Julia's marriage is unsuccessful. When Alfred faces trouble in his business, Julia's father, Henry, gives him a large loan, even though he knows Alfred to be dishonest. Julia's dread regarding her husband grows, and eventually Alfred and Julia come to love other people. Alfred marries Minnie Mason, an acquaintance of his younger brother, and Julia falls in love with a sick man named William Beckling. She never marries him.

The youngest Hersland son, David, is obsessed with his own mortality, and he dies before he reaches middle age. When, like his siblings before him, he had arrived in Bridgepoint for his college education, David was introduced to Alfred's friends. He was a remarkably clear thinker and began to advise Julia about his brother. David was the child who offered the most hope for the progress of his family.

The Hersland and Dehning families, like all families, contain a range of human nature, which reflects all possibilities and potentialities. Family living continues to exist, because all individuals possess something of their ancestors. Thus, the dead family members continue to exist in the living ones.

Critical Evaluation:

In the United States, Gertrude Stein is perhaps better known for her eccentric personality and her artistic relationships with Pablo Picasso, Sherwood Anderson, and Ernest Hemingway than for her own literary compositions. Stein's

encyclopedic novel, *The Making of Americans*, warrants, however, comparison with other modernist masterworks, such as Marcel Proust's *Remembrance of Things Past* (1913-1927), James Joyce's *Ulysses* (1922), and John Dos Passos's *U.S.A.* (1938). In *Everybody's Autobiography* (1937), Stein herself recognizes the significance of *The Making of Americans* and insists that "everybody ought to be reading at it or it."

The Making of Americans has had a tortuous publishing history. Although Stein's ambitious project was written and revised sporadically from 1903 to 1911, it was not published until 1924, when about 150 pages of it appeared in serial form in Ford Madox Ford's *Transatlantic Review*. An abridged edition of 416 pages was published in 1934 and republished in 1966. Stein cited this abridged text during her tour of the American lecture circuits, and it offers the most readable text for students.

Those who have read *The Making of Americans* can understand an editor's trepidation when confronted with Stein's excessive book. Its tortuous publishing history is understandable. Its length aside, *The Making of Americans* does not progress according to a plot, but develops laterally by rhythm and repetition. The initial section of the story focuses on the Dehnings and the Herslands, but Stein quickly abandons the Dehnings to concentrate on the Hersland family. Stein deliberately withholds "important" plot information, including the names of several minor characters and the subject of Alfred's dishonesty, to investigate the psychology of her characters. Many characters have the same names, signifying the passing on of "bottom natures" from one generation to the next. Some critics even suggest that the novel is flawed because Stein became bored with the exhaustive process of outlining the countless permutations of the book's personality types. Stein unravels these variations in long, twisted sentences that stretch the limits of language. The difficulties a reader faces in *The Making of Americans* contribute, however, to Stein's attempt to write "a history of every one and every kind of one and all the nature in every one and all the ways it comes out of them."

The novel's subtitle, *Being a History of a Family's Progress*, discloses Stein's intention to make Americans out of a generation of immigrants. On the novel's opening page, she writes,

It has always seemed to me a rare privilege, this, of being an American, a real American, one whose tradition it has taken scarcely sixty years to create. We need only realise our parents, remember our grandparents and know ourselves and our history is complete.

The Making of Americans goes beyond its autobiographical roots in Stein's family (Martha Hersland is Gertrude) to strive toward a comprehensive, subjective history of Americans.

Stein's family chronicle signals that Victorian ideas of linear, objective history and progress are, as she writes in *Wars I Have Seen* (1945), "dead dead dead." Her interest in describing all personality types requires repetition to establish "kinds" or "types." This shifts the focus away from individual events, which might be organized into a plot sequence, and toward the system she is creating and her psychological creation of her world. Stein's focus simultaneously deconstructs linear history and dismantles the notion of humanity's evolutionary progression. Successive generations of the Hersland and Dehning families in *The Making of Americans* are often more degenerate, more confused, and more dysfunctional than those of their parents, in part because the parents have passed on the worst part of their "bottom nature" to their children.

The final section of the novel, an abstract coda of twenty pages without events or characters, moves completely into the dense, unfolding narrative consciousness that is one of Stein's most significant achievements. Stein's making of Americans through this consciousness creates a philosophically complex world, one that challenges her readers to reexamine how they are connected with history. *The Making of Americans* is Stein's most ambitious novel.

Trey Strecker

Further Reading

Bowers, Jane Palatini. *Gertrude Stein*. New York: St. Martin's Press, 1993. A succinct, feminist-oriented introduction to Stein, with separate chapters on her novels as well as her short fiction and plays. Includes notes and a bibliography.

Curnutt, Kirk, ed. *The Critical Response to Gertrude Stein*. Westport, Conn.: Greenwood Press, 2000. A collection of contemporary and modern reviews and essays about Stein's works and persona. Accompanying quintessential pieces on Stein by Carl Van Vechten, William Carlos Williams, and Katherine Anne Porter are works by H. L. Mencken, Mina Loy, and Conrad Aiken.

Dearborn, Mary. "*The Making of Americans* as an Ethnic Text." In *Pocahontas's Daughters: Gender and Ethnicity in American Culture*. New York: Oxford University Press, 1986. Provides a thematic reading of Stein's novel, concentrating on its depictions of the interlocking experiences of ethnicity and gender in American culture.

Detloff, Madelyn. "Stein's Shame." In *The Persistence of Modernism: Loss and Mourning in the Twentieth Century*. New York: Cambridge University Press, 2009. Analyzes the works of Stein and other writers to explain the endurance of modernism in literature. Argues that modernism continues to offer relevant narratives of memory, nation, loss, and recovery. The numerous references to *The Making of Americans* are listed in the index.

Doane, Janice L. "Beginning and Beginning Again: The Discomposing Composition of *The Making of Americans*." In *Silence and Narrative: The Early Novels of Gertrude Stein*. Westport, Conn.: Greenwood Press, 1986. Details how Stein's novel records her first serious struggle with artistic composition, authorship, origins, and identity. Contains significant biographical material.

Frieling, Kenneth. "The Becoming of Gertrude Stein's *The Making of Americans*." In *The Twenties: Fiction, Poetry, Drama*, edited by Warren French. Deland, Fla.: Everett/Edwards, 1975. Asserts that Stein overcomes the vision of America as a wasteland in *The Making of Americans* through a unifying consciousness that engulfs her characters' lives in the stream of a continuous present tense.

Katz, Leon. "Weininger and *The Making of Americans*." In *Critical Essays on Gertrude Stein*, edited by Michael J. Hoffman. Boston: G. K. Hall, 1986. Describes the development of Stein's understanding of personality types as influenced by her reading of psychologist Otto Weininger's *Sex and Character* (1903), which theorizes psychological differences between males and females.

Kellner, Bruce, ed. *A Gertrude Stein Companion: Content with the Example*. New York: Greenwood Press, 1988. In addition to characterizing its general form, Kellner's entry on *The Making of Americans* supplies some useful facts concerning the text's history and its adaptation to play and opera libretto forms by scholar Leon Katz in 1973.

Knapp, Bettina L. *Gertrude Stein*. New York: Continuum, 1990. References to *The Making of Americans* characterize the text as a tapestry of its author's theories of psychology, aesthetics, economics, and sexuality. Knapp also terms it an "antinovel" in its tendency to dispense with novelistic conventions.

Moore, George B. *Gertrude Stein's "The Making of Americans": Repetition and the Emergence of Modernism*. New York: Peter Lang, 1998. Analyzes the use of repetition in the novel, Stein's theories of art and human character, and her changing relationship to writing. Places the novel, which Stein considered her masterpiece, within the context of her development of a modernist aesthetic.

Walker, Jayne L. "History as Repetition: *The Making of Americans*." In *The Making of a Modernist: Gertrude Stein from "Three Lives" to "Tender Buttons."* Amherst: University of Massachusetts Press, 1984. Demonstrates

how Stein's rejection of linear plot in *The Making of Americans* reinforces her commitment to repetition as the source of historical knowledge. Traces how her desire for complete understanding reveals the pitfalls of totalizing systems.

The Malcontent

Author: John Marston (1576-1634)
First produced: 1604; first published, 1604
Type of work: Drama
Type of plot: Tragicomedy
Time of plot: Thirteenth century
Locale: Genoa, Italy

Principal characters:

GIOVANNI ALTOFRONTO, the Malcontent, at one time the duke of Genoa but now disguised as Malevole
PIETRO JACOMO, the duke of Genoa
MENDOZA, a court minion
FERNEZE, a young courtier
AURELIA, Pietro Jacomo's wife
MARIA, Altofronto's wife
BILIOSO, an old marshal
MAQUERELLE, an old woman and panderer
CELSO, a friend of Altofronto
EMILIA and BIANCHA, Aurelia's attendants
PASSARELLO, Bilioso's fool

The Story:

Duke Altofronto has been banished from Genoa. A political coup staged by Mendoza with the help of the Florentines brings the weak Pietro Jacomo to power through his marriage to Aurelia, the daughter of a powerful Florentine leader. Altofronto, disguised as Malevole, prepares to bide his time until the state wearies of the new duke. Altofronto's devoted duchess, Maria, waits faithfully in prison for his return, and Celso acts as his secret informant on matters of state.

Altofronto, as the Malcontent, is described as a likable person of marked intelligence and straightforward honesty. He refuses to flatter as others do. On the negative side, however, he is described as more monster than man, more discontented than Lucifer in his fall, a man living on the vexations of others and at variance with his own soul. It is a mixture that makes him seem unpredictable and serves Altofronto well in plotting against his adversaries. This description of him comes from Pietro, who is strangely attracted to the erratic individual known as the Malcontent. It is Altofronto, disguised as Malevole, who tells Pietro that he is being cuckolded by Mendoza. This condition, Malevole declares, is

most unnatural, for a cuckold is a creation of woman and not of God. In this way, Altofronto torments Pietro and inflames him against Mendoza.

Incensed by the thought of a relationship between Mendoza and Aurelia, Pietro confronts the minion with accusations and threats to kill him, but Mendoza placates the duke with disparagement of women and their habits, absolving himself of Pietro's accusations by telling him that Ferneze is the offender against the duke's marital rights. To prove his point, he suggests that Pietro break into Aurelia's room that night; should Ferneze try to escape, Mendoza will kill him. The situation occurs as Mendoza had planned: Ferneze is discovered in Aurelia's room and is, the minion believes, killed in his attempt to flee.

Later, when Mendoza and Aurelia are alone, they plan Pietro's murder. Aurelia promises to use her influence to have Mendoza made duke of Genoa. Unbeknownst to them, however, Ferneze has not been killed. Wounded, he attracts the attention of Altofronto, who revives and hides the young courtier.

Knowing that Pietro is hunting, Mendoza hires the Malcontent to pursue and murder the duke. Taken in by Altofronto's apparent willingness to aid him in his villainy, Mendoza outlines the remaining steps to his ultimate goal. With Pietro removed and his alliance with Aurelia established, he will be ready to make his bid for power. The banishment of Aurelia will be an easy step because he will publicize her infidelity to the Florentines. Then he intends to marry Maria, Altofronto's imprisoned wife, whose friends will strengthen Mendoza and his faction.

Reassured by Mendoza's admission that he does not love Maria, that she too is only a pawn to him, Altofronto takes heart in his assurance that Maria is still true to him, as Celso has reported. Altofronto suggests to Mendoza that they hire a wretch or holy man to report that he has seen Pietro, bereft of reason because of his wife's infidelity, throw himself into the sea. He also offers to act as Mendoza's emissary in winning Maria's favor.

Instead of murdering Pietro, Altofronto divulges to him the plot against his life and provides him with the disguise of the hermit who is to report his suicide. Pietro, in disguise, gives a vivid description of his own anguished demise while lamenting Aurelia's unfaithfulness. Mendoza immediately banishes Aurelia. He then instructs Altofronto to negotiate with Maria.

Duped by the supposed hermit, Mendoza sends him after Altofronto, with orders to poison the Malcontent at supper. When Altofronto returns for a letter that will admit him to Maria's quarters in the citadel, he receives Mendoza's instructions to poison the hermit.

Altofronto and Pietro encounter the banished Aurelia in abject grief because of her indiscretions and her love for Pietro. Altofronto eases Pietro's hurt by reminding him that many great men have had unfaithful wives, among them Agamemnon, King Arthur, and Hercules. Maria's faithfulness to Altofronto is proved beyond doubt when Maquerelle and the disguised Altofronto wait on her to deliver Mendoza's offer of marriage. In answer to their proposal and the promise of great riches if she will accept Mendoza, she announces that she already has a husband. Banished or in power, present or absent, Altofronto remains her true lord.

Mendoza's only remaining threat to power is Altofronto, who in the disguise of the Malcontent knows too much of the usurper's malice. To be rid of him, Mendoza plans to use the fumes of one of the two boxes that had been given him by his intended victim. According to the giver, the fumes of one box will put the person who breathes them to sleep for twelve hours; the fumes of the other box will kill him immediately. Unhesitatingly, Mendoza opens what he supposes is the lethal box under Altofronto's nose. The box is, in fact, empty,

but Altofronto feigns death. Later, he appears at a masked ball given by Mendoza to celebrate the deaths he had planned. In the meantime, spurned by Maria, Mendoza accuses her of murdering the hermit—the disguised Pietro—whom Altofronto has reported dead. The faithful wife welcomes death as a fate better than that of being married to the usurper.

At the ball, Altofronto chooses Maria as his partner. Revealing his identity, he asks her to remain composed so that others will not recognize him. Pietro dances with Aurelia, who repents of her past deeds and vows her undying devotion to him. At a prearranged signal, Mendoza's three supposed victims—Altofronto, Pietro, and Ferneze—reveal themselves, to the consternation of Mendoza and the joy of the assemblage. Altofronto is immediately restored to his rightful place as duke of Genoa.

Mendoza pleads for his life, but he is summarily ejected from the court. Aurelia and Pietro are given the blessing of the court. Maquerelle is allowed to carry on her pandering in the suburbs. Bilioso, a sycophant who chose to stand with the wrong rather than fall with the right, is summarily dismissed from any further court favor. Altofronto and Maria are joyously reunited.

Critical Evaluation:

The Malcontent was written during a period of melancholic disillusionment that spanned the turn of the century. This fin de siècle mood was similarly expressed in William Shakespeare's *Hamlet, Prince of Denmark* (pr. c. 1600-1601, pb. 1603) and John Donne's poems *An Anatomy of the World: The First Anniversary* (1611) and *Of the Progress of the Soule: The Second Anniversary* (1612). In the drama of the period, two of the characters "allowed" to express such disillusionment were the fool and the melancholic, or malcontent. Both are to be found in plays as diverse as *Hamlet*, a tragedy, and *As You Like It* (pr. c. 1599-1600, pb. 1623), a comedy. *The Malcontent* takes up a middle ground between tragedy and comedy. In the figure of Hamlet, the melancholic becomes the hero. His role is therefore not that of satiric spectator, as is Jaques in *As You Like It*, but he is as active an instrument in restoring justice. The way offered him, though he struggles with it, is revenge. As a Christian response, *Hamlet* is tragic because the revenge ethic is necessarily tragic, doubly so when seen as inauthentic.

Two years after *Hamlet*, John Marston reworked a similar theme quite differently. Retaining the tone of satiric disillusion, though it is possibly closer to Shakespeare's *Timon of Athens* (pr. c. 1607-1608, pb. 1623), Marston reworked the melancholic as a specific role and as a specific disguise.

Hamlet's disguise of madness was haphazard and probably more an expression of mental disorder than anything deliberately assumed. There are elements of this in Marston's play, too. It is difficult to see Malevole as a mere mask for Altofronto, for there is a genuine expression of personality, an alter ego, expressed in powerful language coming from the heart. Yet Altofronto is clearly in control of his disguise, and he possesses an ability to manipulate events to his advantage that is totally lacking in Hamlet's character.

Marston gives the play an Italian setting, as is very typical of other Jacobean dramatists, such as Cyril Tourneur, John Webster, and Thomas Middleton. The Italian influence is also seen in the genre of tragicomedy, which was new to English theater but common in the Italian, and in the language. Whole speeches are taken from Giambattista Guarini's *Il Pastor Fido*, which had been translated into English in 1602. Perhaps even more important, the figure of Mendoza is based on what the English saw as a typical Italian villain, Niccolò Machiavelli's prince. The Machiavellian villain became typified as a schemer who has no time for conventional morality or religion, is power-hungry, and considers the ends always to justify the means.

Marston created a dramatically well-balanced drama between the two schemers: the deposed duke, who seeks to regain his rightful authority through disguise, and the would-be duke, who seeks power through deceit and violence. In the middle stands the actual duke, Pietro, a weak-willed man and a puppet of the Florentines. Yet, as with much Jacobean drama and unlike Shakespearean tragedy, the plot, such as it is, is motivated, not by political moves but by sexual passion. Sexual imagery merges with political imagery to give a picture of total immorality and degradation. Maquarelle is the key female character because she plays out the moves of the brothel as the moves of the court. The images are reinforced in the language used by Altofronto in his role as Malevole, Passarello the fool, and in a different way, Bilioso, the biggest panderer of all.

The use of the tragicomic genre is a significant shift away from the more typical Jacobean revenge tragedy. In this genre, the moral conflicts and tensions could be resolved without losing the satiric worldview. Shakespeare likewise experimented with this alternative in *Measure for Measure* (pr. c. 1604, pb. 1623), which, like *The Malcontent*, has a supposedly absent duke who watches over the events, and in *The Tempest* (pr. 1611, pb. 1623), where another deposed duke regains power, but this time by magic. Although *Measure for Measure* is usually not classed as a tragicomedy (the term "problem play" is sometimes used), *The Tempest* can rightfully be seen as one. All of these plays reject the revenge ethic. Marston's solution must be seen as predominantly successful. Evil overreaches itself and in becoming too confident, becomes too naïve; at the same time, the good learn to become "as wise as a serpent," accept the corrupting nature of power, and seek to bring about repentance and change of heart.

It is in the interpretation of such moral patterning that ambiguity is revealed. Such patterning can be interpreted to be Stoic, representing the return to political and moral equilibrium, the restoration of true authority, and the rejection of extremes of naïveté (folly) and Machiavellianism. It can also be interpreted to be Christian, in which patterns of sin, repentance, restoration, and forgiveness are dominant. Other critical interpretations have suggested that Marston's attacks on the Church in the play give rise to the more pessimistic moral that hypocrisy and deceit are everywhere. Altofronto himself is a mask, and his forgiveness of Mendoza will only set the cycle of evil going again. Yet other interpretations, which emphasize the absurd "pretence" motifs and the nature of the play's language, interpret the play in terms of twentieth century absurdism.

Certainly the language of the play has been a source of critical contention. Although the play is dedicated to Ben Jonson, the style bears little resemblance to the controlled, ironic language of Jonsonian drama. In fact, Jonson made fun of Marston's apparently uncontrolled satiric style. Earlier commentators corroborated the Jonsonian censure and pointed to the amount Marston borrowed from other plays. Later critics, however, see energy and creativeness in the "free play" of Marston's language and in its breaking down of the borders of poetry and prose. *The Malcontent* is a play that will continue to attract critical interest and controversy.

"Critical Evaluation" by David Barratt

Further Reading

Cathcart, Charles. *Marston, Rivalry, Rapprochement, and Jonson*. Burlington, Vt.: Ashgate, 2008. Chronicles Marston's literary rivalry with his contemporary, Ben Jonson.

Finkelpearl, Philip. *John Marston of the Middle Temple: An Elizabethan Dramatist in His Social Setting*. Cambridge, Mass.: Harvard University Press, 1969. Covers Marston's biographical and social background and seeks to relate the plays to that background. Includes a bibliography and an index.

Geckle, George L. *John Marston's Drama: Themes, Images, Sources*. Rutherford, N.J.: Fairleigh Dickinson University Press, 1980. Chapter 7 discusses *The Malcontent*, dealing in particular with the theme of fortune. Geckle argues that the dominant motif is not disguise but rather the wheel of fortune, and he points to the themes that are related to this symbol. He agrees that the play is a tragicomedy, but he stresses the tragic aspects of the wheel motif. Includes an index.

Huebert, Ronald. "The Adverse Body: John Marston." In *The Performance of Pleasure in English Renaissance Drama*. New York: Palgrave Macmillan, 2003. Examines how English Renaissance dramatists, including Marston, pursue and create pleasure, both the erotic pleasure presented onstage and the aesthetic pleasure experienced by readers and theatergoers.

Scott, Michael. *John Marston's Plays: Theme, Structure, and Performance*. London: Macmillan, 1978. The plays are not dealt with separately, but under a variety of subject headings. Scott tries to read Marston as an absurdist and

looks to typical twentieth century categories. Offers some discussion of performance tradition. Includes an index.

Tucker, Kenneth. *John Marston: A Reference Guide*. Boston: G. K. Hall, 1985. Follows the standard format and sequencing of the Reference Guide to Literature series. Includes a bibliography and an index.

Wharton, T. F. *The Critical Fall and Rise of John Marston*. Columbia, S.C.: Camden House, 1994. Focuses on the critical debates on Marston and his works. Takes note, among much else, of T. S. Eliot's notable essay on Marston, which sparked twentieth century critical concern. Includes an index.

_____, ed. *The Drama of John Marston: Critical Revisions*. New York: Cambridge University Press, 2000. Collection of critical essays about Marston's plays including "*The Malcontent*: Hunting the Letter" and "Sexual Politics in Marston's *The Malcontent*."

Malone Dies

Author: Samuel Beckett (1906-1989)
First published: Malone meurt, 1951 (English translation, 1956)
Type of work: Novel
Type of plot: Absurdist
Time of plot: 1940's
Locale: A hospital

Principal characters:
MALONE, a dying old man
SAPOSCAT/MACMANN, the protagonist of a story Malone tells
MOLL and LEMUEL, other characters in Malone's story

The Story:

Malone, an old man, is sitting in a hospital bed and is writing. He hears the sounds of other men coming and going. He then recalls having been brought to the hospital in an ambulance. He is bedridden, almost incapable of movement. His memory is unreliable; he does not know whether he is recalling memories or inventing them. Then, abruptly, he begins to write a story about a man named Saposcat. "I wonder if I am not talking yet again about myself," he muses. A page later, however, Malone notes, "Nothing is less like me than this patient, reasonable child."

A family, the Lamberts, have befriended Saposcat, who lives on a farm. Saposcat, known by the nickname of Sapo, helps Mr. Lambert bury a mule. Incest, according to Malone, is in the air in the Lambert home. The Lambert children, a girl and a boy, share a bedroom and masturbate in each other's presence.

Malone drops his pencil, and it takes him forty-eight

hours to recover it. He says he has spent two unforgettable days of which nothing will ever be known. The pencil is described at some length. It is getting shorter all the time and soon will vanish from wear and tear. Malone is not worried, for he remembers that somewhere in his bed he has another pencil, scarcely used.

Encountering again the protagonist of his story, Malone changes the name from Saposcat to Macmann. Macmann, caught in a rainstorm, decides to lie flat on the ground, so that at least some portion of himself will stay dry. As the rain continues with unabated violence, Macmann rolls over and over, until he begins to dream of becoming a cylinder and never having to walk upright again.

Malone then interrupts himself to begin an inventory of his possessions. He speaks of the pleasure he used to take in putting his hands deep into his pockets and fingering the "hard shapely" objects that were there and how he loved to fall asleep holding a stone, a horse chestnut, or a cone in his hand.

He interrupts himself once more—or is interrupted by memory—with the thought of Macmann, and Malone says that it looks like he will never finish anything "except perhaps breathing." Malone wonders whether he has died already. No doubt feeling that they will constitute a proof of his continued existence, he imagines taking all of his possessions into the bed with him—his photograph, his stone, his hat, and his buttons.

Malone then wonders if he is hungry. He writes, "I would gladly eat a little soup, if there was any left. No, even if there was some left I would not eat it." He gives no reason for this change of heart.

Having previously lost (and then painstakingly retrieved) his exercise book and his pencil, Malone now loses his stick. Only now does he realize how much it means to him. Rapidly, however, his thoughts return to food. He wonders if the hospital workers feed him while he sleeps, or if they withhold soup from him to help him die more quickly. He thinks that it would have been quicker to poison him and wonders if they fear an autopsy. He then recalls that he has some pills, but he is not sure what they are for. They are either sedatives or laxatives. It would be annoying, he says, to turn to them for calm and to get diarrhea instead. He admits he could be calmer, but adds "enough about me."

One day, much later, Macmann awakes in an asylum, the House of Saint John of God. The person who tells him this is a Christlike figure, who hands Macmann the stump of a pencil, requesting that Macmann sign himself into the hospital. He and his attendants leave, and a small, ugly old woman called Moll takes a chair by his bed. For earrings she wears two long ivory crucifixes. She turns out to be the person charged with his care. She keeps bringing him food, emptying his chamberpot, and helping him wash himself. When Macmann one day notices his clothes are gone, Moll calms him.

Macmann and Moll become lovers. Moll writes him love letters. In return, Macmann writes little love poems, "remarkable for their exaltation of love regarded as a kind of lethal glue." Another kind of writing is done by Lemuel, an attendant, who dutifully notes Macmann's questions in a thick book but does not return with answers.

Malone interrupts himself to report on a visit from a person unknown to him, who had hit him on the head and subsequently scattered his things. This person is malevolent, a characteristic later attributed to Lemuel. He supposes this visitor might be a mourner or a mortician, and himself dead already. Malone makes a list of things to say to him. He is cut

short by violent symptoms, perhaps fatal ones. His account becomes even more confused.

The story of Macmann is then resumed with much coherence. The story of his attempted escapes is recounted; he is always thwarted because he hides in the same place each time. From one of these escapades, he fetches back a stick. When Lemuel finds it, he has him beaten with it.

Malone concludes with an account of an excursion from the asylum on which Macmann is taken, along with fellow inmates. The account, however, fails to conclude, presumably because of the death of its creator, Malone.

Critical Evaluation:

This novel is simultaneously a last will and testament of an old man who knows he is soon to die and a moment-by-moment record of his feelings and impressions as he awaits death. He is talking to himself and writing things while sitting in a bed in some public building. One can deduce from this that he is in a hospital. Samuel Beckett's narrative unfolds phenomenologically; the reader is given bits and pieces, glimpses, details from which he or she can derive the bigger picture or watch as Malone derives it.

Malone is indeed writing at least some of these words, because he says at one point, "I fear I must have fallen asleep again. In vain I grope, I cannot find my exercise book. But I still have the pencil in my hand." His musings—typical of this narrative—raise one question while answering another: Where has he written those words?

Such teasing fills this novel. Beckett toys with the frame, always reminding his readers that they are reading words and not seeing through them to an objective reality solidly anchored in some real world. Yet the realities of life and death are ever present. These are not so much called into question as is the ability of words to be their equal, to cope with the facts of mortality and temporality.

Malone "speaks" in the first person. He says, "I, Malone," and whenever he says this, he is also saying, "I'm alone." All Beckett's works, be they drama, poem, or novel, are powered by this single phrase. Such punning is second nature with Beckett, whose works, like those of his mentor and fellow Irishman James Joyce, are strewn with homonyms both comic and telling.

Absurdly thrown into a universe without appeal, Beckett's characters, often suffering from mental and physical diseases, often maimed or physically trapped, keep reminding us of our own humiliating and disgusting limitations, our own failures to realize our potential, our own approaching unceremonious end. Yet Beckett manages to get readers to sit through such unremitting reminders through the use of contradictions and puns. This technique actually appears between, rather than in, each sentence. Nearly every sentence contradicts, qualifies, or undermines the previous sentence. The effect is to keep readers on the edge of their seats and to call the authority of the narrator into question. The embodiment of a mind changing itself before one's very eyes lends authenticity to the book. This impression can be sustained even when Beckett portrays Malone as developmentally challenged to the point of farce.

Malone Dies is an extremely funny book despite its horribly depressing subject matter: disintegration, disease, and death. The way Beckett views human limitations, the human tendency to self-mutilate and self-destruct, can be as humorous as any satire since Jonathan Swift's. Consider Lemuel in this passage:

> One day rolling up the leg of his trousers, he showed Macmann his shin covered with bruises, scars and abrasions. Then producing smartly a hammer from an inner pocket he dealt himself, right in the middle of his ancient wounds, so violent a blow that he fell down backwards, or perhaps I should say forwards. But the part he struck most readily, with his hammer, was the head, and that is understandable, for it too is a bony part, and sensitive, and difficult to miss, and the seat of all the shit and misery, so you rain blows upon it.

Beckett shares with Swift a fascinated disgust with bodily functions, and this disgust frequently drives his sense of humor, as in the description of Macmann and Moll attempting sexual intercourse: "The spectacle was then offered of Macmann trying to bundle his sex into his partner's like a pillow into a pillow-slip." There are also strikingly lyrical passages, as when Malone describes the sensations he has when he is dying.

The entire work is moving, all the more so because Beckett is so unsentimental. He refuses to intervene between the reader and the sufferings of his characters by framing their misery in the way that Charles Dickens would. Eventually, the life that springs up in each of Beckett's sentences triumphs over the death of Malone. After all, once dead, Malone can no longer say "I, Malone." He has been taken back into the company of the universe; all of his isolating thinking has been canceled.

David Bromige

Further Reading

Binns, Ronald. "Beckett, Lowry, and the Anti-Novel." In *The Contemporary English Novel*, edited by John Russell Brown and Bernard Harris. London: Edward Arnold, 1979. Binns finds that the center of attention is the narrator himself, a garrulous confabulator who undermines confidence in the reality of any world offered by such writing, suggesting that all writing has credibility problems.

Kenner, Hugh. *Samuel Beckett: A Critical Study.* New ed. Berkeley: University of California Press, 1973. The definitive work on Beckett. Kenner reads a text like a detective, uncovering not so much clues as a network of references, literary, historical, and personal. He also provides useful figures to help readers imagine what Beckett's concerns and intentions might be. He places Beckett in relation to James Joyce and Marcel Proust.

Kern, Edith. "Black Humor: The Pockets of Lemuel Gulliver and Samuel Beckett." In *Samuel Beckett Now*, edited by Melvin J. Friedman. 2d ed. Chicago: University of Chicago Press, 1975. Kern ties together a number of Beckett's works by tracing the theme of pockets and the objects they contain. She helps clarify passages in *Malone Dies* by evoking similar passages in Beckett's *Waiting for Godot* and *How It Is, Molloy*. She also suggests precedents for Beckett's satirical vision in Jonathan Swift's *Gulliver's Travels* (1726).

Knowlson, James. *Damned to Fame: The Life of Samuel Beckett.* New York: Simon & Schuster, 1996. Knowlson, Beckett's chosen biographer, provides a meticulously detailed book, containing much new material, as well as detailed notes and a bibliography.

McDonald, Rónán. *The Cambridge Introduction to Samuel Beckett.* New York: Cambridge University Press, 2006. Chapter 4 of this concise overview of Beckett's life and work includes a discussion of *Malone Dies*.

Pultar, Gönül. *Technique and Tradition in Beckett's Trilogy of Novels.* Lanham, Md.: University Press of America, 1996. Analyzes Beckett's three novels in the order of publication, devoting a chapter to each. The chapter on *Malone Dies* emphasizes its form of narration and the philosophical underpinnings of the narrative. Other chapters compare the three novels to other works of European literature and philosophy.

The Maltese Falcon

Author: Dashiell Hammett (1894-1961)
First published: 1930
Type of work: Novel
Type of plot: Detective and mystery
Time of plot: 1928
Locale: San Francisco

Principal characters:
SAM SPADE, a private detective
EFFIE PERINE, his secretary
BRIGID O'SHAUGHNESSY, his client
CASPER GUTMAN, her employer
WILMER COOK, Gutman's bodyguard
JOEL CAIRO, Gutman's onetime agent
SERGEANT TOM POLHAUS, a police detective
LIEUTENANT DUNDY, a police detective

The Story:

Brigid O'Shaughnessy visits Sam Spade and Miles Archer, detectives, to ask them to trail Floyd Thursby. Archer, who takes the job, is murdered. Later that same night, Thursby is shot down in front of his hotel. The police suspect Spade of killing Thursby to avenge Archer's murder. Brigid leaves word at Spade's office that she wants to see him. She moves out of her hotel because she is afraid. At her new apartment, she says she cannot divulge the whole story, but she does tell Spade that she had met Thursby in Asia. They had arrived in San Francisco the week before. She assumes Thursby killed Archer but does not know who killed Thursby.

When Spade returns to his office, Joel Cairo is waiting. He offers Spade five thousand dollars for the recovery of a statuette of a black bird. That night, Spade is trailed by a small young man in a gray overcoat. Spade eludes him long enough to slip into Brigid's apartment building. There, he learns that Brigid is connected in some way with a mysterious black bird, a replica of a falcon. Later they go to Spade's apartment to meet Cairo. She tells Cairo she does not have the falcon. He will have to wait, possibly a week, before she can sell it to him.

The police learn that Spade is having an illicit affair with Iva Archer and begin to suspect Spade might have killed Archer so he could marry his partner's wife. When the police arrive to question Spade about their new line of inquiry, they discover Cairo and Brigid in a squabble. Spade introduces Brigid as an operator in his employ and says they are questioning Cairo about the two murders. After Cairo and the police officer leave, Brigid tells Sam she does not know what makes the falcon important. She had been hired to steal it from a Russian named Kemidov in Constantinople, Turkey.

Next morning, before Brigid awakens, Spade gets groceries and then incidentally searches her apartment for the falcon, which he fails to find. He is certain Brigid knows where it is. Brigid is afraid of what Cairo might do, however, and Spade arranges for her to stay at the home of his secretary.

In explaining to Cairo how Thursby was killed, Brigid outlined the letter "G" in the air; Spade knows that special significance is attached to that letter. He confronts the youth who is trailing him and says that "G" will have to deal with him. Shortly after, a Mr. Gutman calls, inviting Spade to his hotel suite. Spade tells him that Cairo offered ten thousand dollars, not five, for the falcon. Gutman laughs derisively; the statuette is obviously worth a fortune. Pretending to be furious because Gutman will reveal no more, Spade storms out, saying he will give Gutman until 5:30 that evening to talk.

From a taxi driver, Spade learns that instead of going to Effie's house, Brigid had hurried to the waterfront after buying a newspaper. When Gutman summons him back to his hotel suite, Spade learns that the falcon is an ancient ornament, made in Malta, encrusted with precious gems and later in its bloody history covered with black enamel to conceal its value. Gutman traced it to the Constantinople home of Kemidov, where Gutman's agents had stolen it but had run off with it.

Next day, Spade searches Cairo's hotel room and finds that something had been torn out of Cairo's newspaper the day before. He buys another copy of that paper and sees that the section Cairo had torn out reports the arrival of the ship *La Paloma* from Hong Kong. Remembering that Brigid mentioned Asia, he associates her impromptu waterfront errand with the ship's arrival. Later, he learns that Cairo has checked out of his hotel. Meanwhile, Spade boards *La Paloma* and learns that Gutman, Cairo, the strange young man, and Brigid had held a long conference with Jacobi, the captain.

While Spade is later relating his discoveries to his secretary, a man bursts in, holds out a bundle, and drops dead. Spade opens the bundle and discovers the falcon. Spade is sure that the dead man is Captain Jacobi. He has his secretary call the police while he checks the falcon at a nearby bus terminal and mails the receipt to his own post-office box. He then answers a distress call from Brigid, who claims she is being forcibly held at Gutman's hotel suite. She is not there. Instead, Spade finds Gutman's daughter, who sends him on a wild-goose chase. When he returns to his apartment, he meets Brigid waiting outside, obviously terrified. Opening the door, he finds Gutman, the young man, and Cairo waiting with drawn guns.

Spade realizes that his wild-goose chase had been designed to get him out of the way long enough to give these people time to find Jacobi before he returned. Spade says he will relinquish the falcon for ten thousand dollars and someone on whom to blame the murders. He suggests the young man, Wilmer Cook, as the fall guy. Spade explains that if Wilmer were hanged for Thursby's murder, the district attorney would drop the case, taking it for granted that Jacobi had been killed by the same person. Gutman, sure that Thursby had killed Archer, finally consents to make his young bodyguard the scapegoat.

Gutman produces ten one-thousand-dollar bills. Spade calls Effie and asks her to get the claim check from the post office and redeem the falcon. After she delivers the package, Gutman unties it and finds a lead imitation. Kemidov had tricked him. Spade gives back nine thousand dollars and the men leave in haste, after discovering that Wilmer has slipped away unnoticed. Then Spade calls the police and tells them that Wilmer had killed Jacobi and Thursby and that Gutman and Cairo are accessories.

Knowing that Gutman will implicate him and Brigid in the affair, Spade makes Brigid confess that she had lured Archer into an alley that first night and had shot him with Thursby's revolver. He tells Brigid he intends to turn her over to the police. He has to clear himself of suspicion of killing his partner and will not let a woman stand in his way.

Critical Evaluation:

Dashiell Hammett was the leading writer of what came to be called the hard-boiled school of American mystery writers. Hard-boiled crime fiction began with the pulp magazines, which were exceedingly popular before the then-new entertainment medium of television began to undermine them in the late 1940's. The magazines, printed on cheap paper, sold for ten or fifteen cents a piece. There were many different kinds of pulp magazines, including true crime, mysteries, romances, Westerns, and science fiction. Being directed to a mass audience, they were written in simple English and emphasized action and dialogue. Many of the writers were hacks who were paid a penny a word and did not have the talent or motivation to produce quality literature. From the beginning of his career, Hammett distinguished himself as an exception.

One reason for Hammett's distinction as a mystery writer was that he had actually been a private detective himself for many years. He knew what he was talking and writing about. His early writing career was linked with the legendary *Black Mask*, a pulp magazine featuring male-oriented action and adventure. Hammett also was a gifted writer, although he did not have a great deal of formal education. His practical knowledge, his care and concern about his craft, and his sheer talent made him the leader in his field. *The Maltese Falcon* was originally published as a serial in *Black Mask* and then published in hard cover. It is Hammett's best novel.

One outstanding stylistic feature of the novel is that is was written in a totally objective manner. The author describes a setting and then tells only what the characters say and do. He never attempts to go into any character's mind and explain what he or she is thinking. The story is told entirely from Spade's point of view. The author does not indicate that Spade actually observes everything, but Spade is always present. Nothing happens that he could not have observed.

Hammett deliberately maintains a very fast pace. This was something he learned to do as a *Black Mask* writer. One of the ways he maintains this pace is by crowding several different events into the same chapter. A scene that begins in one chapter often ends in the next, while a new scene begins before that chapter ends. The reader is given the impression that Spade is constantly on the move, conducting his investigation while trying to cope with problems others are creating for him.

Hammett was famous for his ability to write dialogue. Good dialogue sounds realistic and conveys information without doing so conspicuously. It also characterizes the speaker. Because *The Maltese Falcon* is written in an entirely objective manner and is full of good dialogue, it could easily be turned into a stage play—and Hammett indicated to his publisher that he would like to see such a play produced.

It was obvious that the novel would also make a good motion picture; indeed, it has been adapted to film several times. The most famous version is *The Maltese Falcon* (1941), directed by John Huston and starring Humphrey Bogart as Sam Spade, the role that made him a superstar.

In addition to writing outstanding dialogue, Hammett wrote clean, straightforward, graphic prose that differed radically from the convoluted, affected prose to be found in many of the classic English mystery novels, as well as in much of the other English and Anglophilic literature produced before writers such as Sherwood Anderson, Ernest Hemingway, and Hammett began writing in the language used by ordinary Americans.

The theme of *The Maltese Falcon* can be summed up in a

familiar quotation from the Bible: "The love of money is the root of all evil." A reviewer wrote that Hammett, who had strong socialist sympathies and who admired Karl Marx, "regarded moral evil as economically determined." According to character Gutman, the real falcon had a history of bloodshed from its creation in Malta in the sixteenth century. Greed brings out the worst in Gutman, Cairo, and Brigid; it leads directly or indirectly to the deaths of Archer, Thursby, Jacobi, and Gutman. Wilmer will be executed for three murders. Brigid will spend at least twenty years in prison if she avoids execution. The falcon might have led to Spade's own downfall if he had not been shrewd enough to circumvent the traps that everyone, including the police, set for him. When the falcon turns out to be a fake, it symbolizes the futility of materialistic values.

Hammett was responsible for the creation of a distinctively American type of hard-boiled mystery. He influenced, because of his talent, craftsmanship, and seriousness of purpose, crime writers around the world. Critics in the United States, England, France, and Germany acknowledge that Hammett elevated the mystery genre to the rank of quality literature. His influence can be seen in mainstream fiction as well as in genre fiction.

Films based on Hammett's novels influenced filmmakers worldwide. Conversely, the films influenced novelists because few novelists do not dream of selling a book to Hollywood. Hollywood made Hammett rich and famous, but its easy money and notoriously loose living undermined him physically and mentally. His heavy drinking ruined his career and hastened his death. He died a pauper, leaving nothing to posterity but his unique literary creations and his personal legend as a proud, independent individual with a strict code of integrity, one not unlike that of his most famous character, Sam Spade.

"Critical Evaluation" by Bill Delaney

Further Reading

Bruccoli, Matthew J., and Richard Layman. *Hardboiled Mystery Writers: Raymond Chandler, Dashiell Hammett, Ross Macdonald—A Literary Reference*. New York: Carroll & Graf, 2002. A handy supplemental reference guide that includes interviews, letters, and previously published studies. Also includes illustrations.

Chandler, Raymond. *Chandler: Later Novels and Other Writings*. New York: Library of America, 1995. This collection of Raymond Chandler's works includes his essay "The Simple Art of Murder." Chandler, a renowned American writer of hard-boiled mysteries, discusses the shortcomings of the traditional British mystery novel and the advances in the genre inspired by Hammett.

Gale, Robert L. *A Dashiell Hammett Companion*. Westport, Conn.: Greenwood Press, 2000. An encyclopedic collection devoted to Hammett, featuring a chronology of the major events in his life and alphabetically arranged entries about his works, characters, family, and acquaintances. Includes bibliographical references and an index.

Layman, Richard. *Shadow Man: The Life of Dashiell Hammett*. New York: Harcourt Brace Jovanovich, 1981. One of the best available biographies of Hammett, who led a colorful life and resembled Sam Spade in his moral code and unsentimental view of human nature. Discusses in detail the genesis of *The Maltese Falcon*, Hammett's most acclaimed novel.

_____, ed. *Discovering "The Maltese Falcon" and Sam Spade: The Evolution of Dashiell Hammett's Masterpiece, Including John Huston's Movie with Humphrey Bogart*. Rev. ed. San Francisco: Vince Emery, 2005. A collection of memorabilia about Hammett, his novel, and the film adaptation of *The Maltese Falcon*. Examines Hammett's detective career, his life and publications, and the sources and notes he used to create *The Maltese Falcon*.

Marling, William. *The American Roman Noir: Hammett, Cain, and Chandler*. Athens: University of Georgia Press, 1995. Links the hard-boiled detective writing of Hammett, James M. Cain, and Raymond Chandler to contemporary economic and technological changes. Marling sees these writers as pioneers of an aesthetic for the postindustrial age. Includes a twenty-two-page analysis of *The Maltese Falcon*.

_____. *Dashiell Hammett*. Boston: Twayne, 1983. Contains a thorough discussion of Hammett's life and art, with considerable attention to *The Maltese Falcon*. Includes excellent reference notes and a selected bibliography.

Nolan, William F. *Dashiell Hammett: A Casebook*. Santa Barbara, Calif.: McNally & Loftin, 1969. A book about Hammett's life and writing by an authority on American crime fiction in general and on Hammett in particular. Discusses *The Maltese Falcon* thoroughly.

Wolfe, Peter. *Beams Falling: The Art of Dashiell Hammett*. Bowling Green, Ohio: Bowling Green State University Popular Press, 1980. Wolfe, a specialist in the study of writers of hard-boiled crime fiction, presents full-length analyses of Hammett's stories and novels. "Beams Falling" alludes to the much-debated "Flitcraft Episode" in *The Maltese Falcon*.

The Mambo Kings Play Songs of Love

Author: Oscar Hijuelos (1951-   )
First published: 1989
Type of work: Novel
Type of plot: Social realism
Time of plot: 1930's-1980's
Locale: Cuba and the United States

Principal characters:
CESAR CASTILLO, an immigrant musician from Cuba, living in New York
NESTOR CASTILLO, his younger brother, also a musician
DELORES CASTILLO, Nestor's wife
EUGENIO and LETICIA, Nestor's children

The Story:

Cesar, Nestor, and their three brothers grow up in the sugar-mill town of Las Piñas, in Oriente Province, Cuba. The family moves from the mill to a livestock farm where the father, Pedro Castillo, slaughters animals; he is proud of his physical strength and demands respect from his frightened sons with cruel beatings. The powerless mother, Maria, attributes his violent behavior to his hard life since childhood.

As a child, listening to a music box, Cesar learns to dance, and he enjoys orchestra performances. After he hears Eusebio Stevenson playing background music for Hollywood silent films in a movie theater, he requests lessons. Pucho, a mulatto, or person of mixed-race, teaches him music and magic African chants. Cesar challenges paternal authority when he decides to become a musician.

In 1937, at the age of nineteen, Cesar starts his singing career in Santiago de Cuba, invited by the well-known band leader Julián García. Nestor, also musically talented, joins the orchestra. Cesar marries the shy schoolteacher Luisa García, Julián's niece; they live happily until Cesar starts drinking, shouting, and cheating on his wife. He loves Luisa and their daughter, Mariela, but his macho temperament leads him to fear the loss of freedom symbolized by married life. After they are divorced, Luisa marries a schoolteacher and has another child.

In Havana, as instrumentalists, composers, and singers, Cesar and Nestor struggle to earn a living at a time when American big brass jazz bands are in vogue. They had met Desi Arnaz in Santiago de Cuba and knew about his fame in the United States. Inspired by stories about Cubans who, since the 1930's, had gotten rich making films in Hollywood or playing in New York, they daydream of achieving the same success.

The brothers arrive as immigrants in New York in early 1949, the beginning of the mambo boom. Sponsored by their cousin, Pablo, they get a job in a meat-packing plant. At night, playing in clubs and dance halls, they become performing stars, the Mambo Kings, with their own Latin dance band. They live with Pablo's family near Harlem; his kind-hearted wife, Miriam, provides warmth and Cuban home cooking.

Cesar remembers Cuba and misses his daughter, but he likes to look forward to a better future. Nestor thinks constantly about the past, tortured by memories of Maria Rivera, a beautiful mulatto dancer in Havana who had abandoned him after a passionate affair and married somebody else. He wants to believe that she still loves him and, hoping that a song will bring her back, he writes twenty-two different versions. The mournful tune of "Beautiful Maria of My Soul" catches the attention of Desi Arnaz, who invites the brothers to appear on his television show, *I Love Lucy*, performing the song that will make them famous.

The gregarious Cesar enjoys music, food, friendship, and women, while the somber Nestor writes songs expressing torment and sorrow. When Nestor meets Delores Fuentes, who cleans houses and hopes to be a teacher, she represents the prospect of a new love lifting him out of his melancholia. They are married and have two children, Eugenio and Leticia. Nestor feels unprepared for fatherhood; worried about his children's physical health, he relives his own childhood of illness and near-death experiences.

Nestor's wife arrives from Havana with her father, Daniel, in 1942, at the age of thirteen. Her mother remains in Cuba with the older sister, Ana Maria. The father's unhappiness increases with the years. When he dies on the job, in 1949, Ana Maria comes to live with her sister, trying to make her go out instead of staying home, reading books. Delores marries Nestor, and her purpose in life is to make him happy. She later notices his growing distance from her and realizes that he can never forget Maria.

One winter night, after a performance, Nestor is driving Cesar's car while Cesar is in the back seat with his girlfriend, Vanna. The car slides over a patch of ice and crashes into a tree, killing Nestor. Cesar is unable to recover from the loss of his beloved brother; tormented by memories and ghosts, he leaves his band. In 1958, he visits his daughter, who later becomes a ballet dancer; he sees his relatives for the last time in Cuba. After the Cuban Revolution, two of his brothers, Eduardo and Miguel, settle with their families as exiles in Miami, Florida.

Cesar tries to change his life by joining the Merchant Marine; upon his return, he holds several jobs until his landlady, Mrs. Shannon, offers him the job of superintendent, and free rent. He becomes a musician again, and owns a nightclub until the business fails and his health deteriorates. He searches for lost youth in affairs with younger women; Lydia Santos is his last love. Eugenio, Nestor's son, takes care of him at home and in hospitals.

In 1980, Cesar prepares for death at the Hotel Splendour, where he had enjoyed happier times with women. He dies drinking, in the company of old letters, photographs, and records, listening to Nestor's song. A year later, Eugenio visits Desi Arnaz and watches the old show's rerun, seeing the Mambo Kings alive again; he re-creates the family saga with his own memories of them.

Critical Evaluation:

A native New Yorker of Cuban parentage, Oscar Hijuelos graduated from the City College of New York. His first novel, *Our House in the Last World*, was published in 1983. *The Mambo Kings Play Songs of Love*, winner of a 1990 Pulitzer Prize, became a major motion picture. *The Fourteen Sisters of Emilio Montez O'Brien* appeared in 1993. The three novels illustrate immigrant life in the United States, with remembrance and nostalgia serving as sources of narrative imagination.

The family saga of *The Mambo Kings Play Songs of Love* is narrated in the first and third person, shifting from one character's story to the next, from one recollection to another, moving back and forth in time, with flashbacks within flashbacks, and foreshadowing the future. The disjointed narrative, with extensive footnotes and inventory-like descriptions, enlivened with monologues and dialogues, finds a focus in the musical career and romantic adventures of Cesar and Nestor Castillo, the Mambo Kings.

The novel is divided into five sections; the first and last, the shortest and untitled, are narrated by Eugenio, who provides his own memories of events. The second and third sections, entitled "Side A" and "Side B," respectively, refer in their subtitles to a night in 1980, at the Hotel Splendour, where Cesar spends his last hours, listening to the 1956 record album "The Mambo Kings Play Songs of Love." The fourth section, "Toward the End, While Listening to the Wistful 'Beautiful María of My Soul,'" includes a Spanish version of the song, handwritten by Cesar, and found next to him after his death.

Hijuelos presents the 1930's and 1940's music scene in Cuba, and then captures the times and spirit of the 1940's and 1950's in New York, when Latin music influenced American jazz and dancing required expertise in the arts of the mambo, rumba, and cha-cha. The "cu-bop" exemplified the cross-cultural fusion of the Afro-Cuban music and hot bebop Harlem jazz. Sociocultural dualism is depicted in the novel with the fluid transition from English to Spanish, including expressions and titles in both languages and a bilingual version of the bolero "Beautiful María of My Soul," or "Bellísima María de mi alma."

Music is the driving force in the lives of the Mambo Kings. It gives them courage to disobey their father and leave their homeland in search of fame and the American Dream. After rising to stardom with their band in New York, they tour the United States. The performance on television with Desi Arnaz and Lucille Ball represents the climax of their career. The American Dream of immigrants is often based on Hollywood films and television shows. As with music and literature, miracles are possible on screen; Cesar and Eugenio see the Mambo Kings resurrected and preserved on the rerun of the *I Love Lucy* show. Arnaz and Ball appear as characters in the novel's fictional world.

At the best and worst times, musical creation allows the expression of feelings and spiritual survival. An epigraph at the beginning of the novel states that music transforms fiction into reality and "will make it all possible." Nestor expresses pure love and desire in his song, hoping that Maria, possessed magically by it, will return to him. At the end, music brings memories of Cuba to Cesar, and as he listens to the notes, bouncing back and forth in time and place and "swirling inside him like youth," he feels pain and death taken away.

In the novel, lives are re-created, most of all, through the willful exercise of memory and imagination. In the Hotel Splendour, Cesar relives the glories of the past and the complex relationships with family, friends, women, and age. His encounters with ghosts after Nestor's death provide touches of Magical Realism, denoting the Afro-Cuban influence in his childhood. Sad memories of his abusive father are compensated with images of the loving, religious mother and the caring black women involved with magic. The novel depicts discrimination evident in both Cuba and the United States. The prejudiced father is proud to be a white "gallego" from Spain. In the United States, although the brothers have light skin, their "Latin look" and Spanish language make them "spics," and black musicians are segregated.

Cesar inherits his father's machismo and his sexist attitude toward women, acting like a stereotypical, flamboyant

Latin lover, ending up with regrets and fears of lifelong loneliness without love. Nestor fears that he can never be a "real macho in the kingdom of machos" and yet, while he adores the mythic Maria, he mistreats his wife, Delores, trying to stop her from going to college. Eugenio inherits his family's melancholia; finally, remembering his father and uncle, he dreams of hearts liberated from pain, reaching "toward the sky, floating away."

Hijuelos's novel represents Cuban American literary expression. Cuba is experienced through the nostalgic remembrance of immigrants from the island nation. The younger generation, born in the United States, re-creates the memories, depicting Cuban culture and its influence in the United States.

Ludmila Kapschutschenko-Schmitt

Further Reading

Foster, David William, comp. *Handbook of Latin American Literature*. 2d ed. New York: Garland, 1992. The section on Cuban Americans discusses Hijuelos's novel as a text inspired and guided by music, which becomes "the center of the narrative," recalling influential times in Latin music. Considers the dynamics of the exile experience as a major aspect of the work.

Kevane, Bridget A. "The Fiction of Oscar Hijuelos: *The Mambo Kings Play Songs of Love*." In *Latino Literature in America*. Westport, Conn.: Greenwood Press, 2003. An overview of Hijuelos's publishing career and an examination of his novel.

Luis, William. "Master Codes of Cuban and Cuban-American Culture: Oscar Hijuelos's *The Mambo Kings Play Songs of Love* and Cristina Garcia's *Dreaming in Cuban*." In *Dance Between Two Cultures: Latino Caribbean Literature Written in the United States*. Nashville, Tenn.: Vanderbilt University Press, 1997. Luis describes how Hijuelos and other Latino-Caribbean writers living in the United States are engaged in a "metaphorical dance" between the culture of their homeland and the dominant Anglo-American culture.

Patteson, Richard F. "Oscar Hijuelos: 'Eternal Homesickness' and the Music of Memory." *Critique* 44, no. 1 (Fall, 2002): 38-48. Compares the novel to the work of Marcel Proust because it "engages in a process of remembering and imagining" Cuba as an "essential element in the composition of an evolving, present-day, and very American reality."

Perez Firmat, Gustavo. *Life on the Hyphen: The Cuban-American Way*. Austin: University of Texas Press, 1994. A scholarly volume of criticism focusing on selected Cuban cultural figures, such as Desi Arnaz and his television show *I Love Lucy*. Hijuelos and his Pulitzer Prize-winning novel also are discussed.

Shorris, Earl. *Latinos: A Biography of the People*. New York: W. W. Norton, 1992. The chapter "Neither Here nor There" examines the commercial and critical success of Hijuelos's novel and discusses death as a major theme in the story.

Stavans, Ilan. "Words and Music: Oscar Hijuelos." In *Conversations with Ilan Stavans*. Tucson: University of Arizona Press, 2005. Reprints literary critic Stavans's interviews with Hijuelos and other Hispanics.

Man and Superman
A Comedy and a Philosophy

Author: George Bernard Shaw (1856-1950)
First produced: 1905; first published, 1903
Type of work: Drama
Type of plot: Play of ideas
Time of plot: c. 1900
Locale: England and Spain

Principal characters:
JACK TANNER, an eloquent anarchist and social philosopher
ANN WHITEFIELD, an attractive young woman whose father has just died
ROEBUCK RAMSDEN, her guardian
OCTAVIUS ROBINSON, her suitor
VIOLET ROBINSON, Octavius's sister
HECTOR MALONE, her husband
HENRY STRAKER, Jack's chauffeur
MENDOZA, a bandit
DON JUAN
DOÑA ANA DE ULLOA, a Spanish noblewoman
DON GONZALO, her father
THE DEVIL

The Story:

Act 1. Ramsden and Octavius discuss Ann, whom Octavius wants to marry, and John Tanner, Octavius's friend and the author of *The Revolutionist's Handbook.* Tanner enters, protesting that he and Ramsden had been named Ann's guardians in her father's will. Ramsden does not wish to serve with Tanner and Tanner does not wish to serve at all, but Ann, entering with her mother, refuses to dispense with either guardian. Tanner states that Ann will do what she likes in any case. When they are left alone, Tanner and Octavius discuss Ann; Tanner predicts that she will eventually marry Octavius. Ann and Ramsden return with the news that Octavius's unmarried sister, Violet, is pregnant. Ramsden and Octavius leave, and Tanner and Ann engage in a long discussion about their relations when younger. Tanner asserts that he has grown up and no longer plays romantic games; now he is concerned to break creeds and demolish ideals. When Violet comes in, Tanner approves of her conduct, but Violet says that she is, in fact, married, but she refuses to name the man.

Act 2. While Henry Straker, the chauffeur, is working on Tanner's car, Octavius announces that he has proposed to Ann and has been put off. Ann comes in and discusses why she has forbidden her sister to take a drive with Tanner. Tanner says he is off on a trip to Algiers and jestingly asks Ann if she wishes to accompany him. To his horror, she accepts. Ramsden, Octavius, Mrs. Whitefield, and Hector Malone, a rich young American, enter, and Hector says that he will take Violet in his car. All except Hector leave for a walk, where-

upon Violet returns and kisses Hector. They have been keeping their marriage secret because Hector's rich father wants him to marry a British aristocrat. After they leave, Straker and Tanner come back discussing Ann; Straker insists that it is Tanner whom Ann is pursuing. At that, Tanner panics and orders Straker to get ready to set off on a trip to North Africa.

Act 3. In the Sierra Nevada of southern Spain, a group of brigands led by Mendoza captures Straker and Tanner for ransom. Mendoza reveals that he is a former waiter at the Savoy Hotel and hopelessly in love with Louisa, who turns out to be Straker's sister. Tanner tries to talk Mendoza out of his obsession with Louisa. While they sleep, Don Juan and the Old Woman appear in Hell. The woman, who has just died and protests that she does not belong there, turns into a young Doña Ana, a former beloved of Don Juan. She looks much like Ann Whitefield. The commander, Doña Ana's father, who had once been slain by Don Juan, appears on a visit from Heaven, after which the Devil appears. The commander, who resembles Roebuck Ramsden, wants to live in Hell because Heaven is so dull. The Devil, the commander, and Don Juan explain at length to Doña Ana the true nature of Heaven and Hell. Hell is the home of the unreal and of the seekers for happiness, a place of playing and pretending; Heaven is a place of contemplation, where live the masters of reality, helping the struggle of the Life Force upward. Then follows a long discussion of the Life Force and of its sidetracks in life on Earth.

Don Juan leaves for Heaven. The commander leaves with the Devil and mentions Friedrich Nietzsche's Superman. Doña Ana asks where she can find the Superman; the Devil says he has not yet been created. Doña Ana is left on a darkening stage, crying out for a father for the Superman. As the scene returns to the Sierra, Ann, Hector, Ramsden, Violet, and Octavius appear, accompanied by soldiers; the brigands are captured but Tanner saves them from arrest by claiming that they are his escorts.

Act 4. In the garden of a villa in Granada, Violet and Hector's father, who has intercepted a note from Violet to Hector, discusses Hector; Malone threatens to disinherit Hector if he marries Violet, and when Hector enters, they quarrel. When it becomes known that Violet and Hector are already married, Hector's father capitulates. Ann tells Octavius that she cannot live up to his ideal of her and that her mother wants her to marry Tanner. Mrs. Whitefield tells Tanner that she has not influenced Ann but does think it would be a good idea because Tanner could handle Ann. When Tanner and Ann are left alone, Tanner protests that he does not want to marry Ann but that everyone else seems to take it for granted that he will. The Life Force urges Tanner on, and he takes Ann, who fainted, in his arms. Everyone returns to find that Tanner has yielded.

"The Story" by Gordon N. Bergquist

Critical Evaluation:

Frequently the subtitles of George Bernard Shaw's plays are just as informative and clever as the prefaces. Certainly they are always more to the point. Such is the case with *Heartbreak House* (1913-1919), which is subtitled *A Fantasia in the Russian Manner on English Themes*; *Fanny's First Play, an Easy Play for a Little Theatre* (1911), and *In Good King Charles's Golden Days, A True History That Never Happened* (1939). So, too, with *Man and Superman*, which is subtitled simply but significantly, *A Comedy and a Philosophy*. For *Man and Superman*, though it was written early in Shaw's career, represents the culmination of Shaw's theory that the drama is but a device for getting the public to listen to philosophy—social, political, economic, or Shavian. With the possible exception of *Back to Methuselah* (1921), *Man and Superman* is Shaw's most philosophical play.

In its simplest terms, the philosophical meaning of the play is that in the war between the genders, Woman always emerges conqueror (even if Man, her antagonist, is a Superman) and that in a battle between instinct and intelligence, instinct always wins. To develop this theme, Shaw claimed to have written a philosophical interpretation of the Don Juan

story, which means that Don Juan is reincarnated as a Shavian hero in England at the turn of the century. The closest resemblance between Shaw's hero and the libertine celebrated in music and literature lies in their names: John Tanner, Don Juan Tenorio. Any other similarity is purely coincidental, for Shaw transformed literature's most notorious libertine into a man of moral passion, a Nietzschean Superman who lives a life of pure reason in defiance of the traditions of organized society.

As a Shavian hero, Tanner is impeccably moral, even chaste. The philosophical meaning of the play arises from the fact that Tanner, representing the good man, is unsuccessful in defending his chastity. Pitted against a scheming woman who embodies the sexual, maternal drive, Tanner is forced to surrender his control of sexual instinct. He capitulates and marries. In effect, he commits moral suicide by succumbing to conventionality.

On one level, this theme is worked out in a contrived, almost trivial but nevertheless hilarious plot. On another, more esoteric, level, the philosophical implications of the theme are developed. Tanner has a dream—a play within the play—which turns out to be no less than a Platonic dialogue: "Don Juan in Hell." In this scene, four of the principals are reembodied as historical or mythical personages and are universalized as moral forces. Tanner appears as Don Juan, the man of moral passion; Ann as Doña Ana de Ulloa, the eternal maternal female; Ramsden as Don Gonzalo, the man of pleasure; and Mendoza (leader of the bandits) as the Devil. These four engage in a debate that Don Juan, speaking for Shaw, monopolizes with a series of lengthy monologues. Herein the theme of the play is recapitulated in abstract but certain terms. The subject is Man.

The end of Man, Don Juan argues, is the cultivation of intellect, for only by exercising it dispassionately can Man discover his purpose, and discovering it, fulfill it. Therefore, the good Man, the Man of moral passion, will eschew anything that subverts the life of reason. Woman, however, will not be eschewed, and it is Woman, with her relentless desire to propagate, and marriage, the instrument by which she domesticates, that undermine Man. If Man surrenders to Woman, he is doomed.

The conclusion of the play is in that sense a gloomy one. By marrying Ann, Tanner admits that Woman, bolstered by the "Life Force," is bound to triumph; that Man, even Superman, is bound to abandon the pursuit of his own goal to serve Woman in her goal of perpetuating the race. Despite the ending and the verbose dream play, the prevailing tone of the play is comic and light. Above all, the drama, despite its philosophy, is eminently playable, principally because Shaw succeeded in making his characters gloriously human and therefore funny. Tanner, for example, is intensely moral, but he is fallible, even a bit ridiculous, and Ann delights in puncturing his eloquent utterances with the charge of political aspiration. Ann herself is as engaging a heroine as any in Shaw's plays. An incorrigible liar, an inveterate hypocrite, she is nevertheless thoroughly charming.

The minor characters were invented to fit into the thematic framework of the drama, but they, too, contribute to the fun. Both Ramsden and Mrs. Whitefield represent the authority of the old order that Tanner is trying to overthrow; both, however, have distinctly comic personalities. Octavius, who believes that a man's duty lies in protecting the so-called weaker sex, serves primarily as a foil to Tanner and provides many laughs as a lovesick youth. Mendoza, the bandit, Straker, the impudent chauffeur, and Malone, the senile American millionaire, figure in Shaw's design and provide a balance to the underlying seriousness of that design.

Considered as a whole, with the "Epistle Dedicatory," which serves as a preface, and "The Revolutionary's Handbook," which is an appendix of sorts, *Man and Superman* is one of Shaw's most important plays. It is neither Shaw's masterpiece nor his best play, being too obviously a piece of propaganda, but it is central to Shaw's philosophy, and philosophy is always central to Shaw's plays.

Further Reading

Crompton, Louis. "*Man and Superman.*" In *Shaw the Dramatist.* 1969. Reprint. Ann Arbor, Mich.: UMI Research Press, 1994. Discusses the play's social, philosophical, and historical background. Offers a clear presentation of Shaw's ideas and their sources in the nineteenth century intellectual tradition.

Dukore, Bernard F. *Shaw's Theater.* Gainesville: University Press of Florida, 2000. Focuses on the performance of Shaw's plays and how his plays call attention to elements of the theater, such as the audience, characters directing other characters, and plays within plays. Includes a section on "Bernard Shaw, Director."

Holroyd, Michael. *Bernard Shaw: The One-Volume Definitive Edition.* 1997. New ed. New York: W. W. Norton, 2006. In this indispensable biography, Holroyd emphasizes Shaw's musical structure in *Man and Superman* and

shows how Shaw inverts popular conventions as part of his attack on conventional morals.

Innes, Christopher, ed. *The Cambridge Companion to George Bernard Shaw.* New York: Cambridge University Press, 1998. Collection of scholarly essays examining Shaw's work, including discussions of Shaw's feminism, Shavian comedy and the shadow of Oscar Wilde, Shaw's "discussion plays," and his influence on modern theater. References to *Man and Superman* are indexed.

Nethercot, Arthur H. *Men and Supermen: The Shavian Portrait Gallery.* 2d ed., corr. New York: Benjamin Blom, 1966. Elaborate treatment of Shaw's ideas on the Superman. Discusses *Man and Superman* and its underlying philosophy and relates the work to a number of other plays.

Pagliaro, Harold E. *Relations Between the Sexes in the Plays of George Bernard Shaw.* Lewiston, N.Y.: Edwin Mellen Press, 2004. Demonstrates how the relationship between men and women is a key element in Shaw's plays. Notes a pattern in how Shaw depicts these relationships, including lovers destined by the "life force" to procreate; relations between fathers and daughters, and mothers and sons; and the sexuality of politically, intellectually, and emotionally strong men.

Shaw, George Bernard. *George Bernard Shaw's Plays: "Mrs. Warren's Profession," "Pygmalion," "Man and Superman," "Major Barbara"—Contexts and Criticism.* 2d ed. Edited by Sandie Byrne. New York: W. W. Norton, 2002. In addition to an annotated text of *Man and Superman,* this volume contains critical essays, excerpts from books, and reviews discussing Shaw's work generally and *Man and Superman* specifically.

Silver, Arnold. "*Man and Superman:* Erecting a Creed." In *Bernard Shaw: The Darker Side.* Stanford, Calif.: Stanford University Press, 1982. Starts with the premise that the play is a fairly standard romantic comedy and relates it to Shaw's courtship of Charlotte Payne-Townshend at the time he was writing the play.

Wisenthal, J. L. "*Man and Superman.*" In *The Marriage of Contraries: Bernard Shaw's Middle Plays.* Cambridge, Mass.: Harvard University Press, 1974. Discusses how Shaw presents and ultimately unifies the varying views and philosophies represented by the play's characters.

A Man for All Seasons

Author: Robert Bolt (1924-1995)
First produced: 1954, radio play; 1960, full-length play;
first published, 1960
Type of work: Drama
Type of plot: Historical
Time of plot: 1530-1535
Locale: London and environs

Principal characters:
THE COMMON MAN, part narrator, part character in the
play
THOMAS MORE, a scholar and statesman
LADY ALICE MORE, his wife
MARGARET MORE, Sir Thomas's daughter
RICHARD RICH, an ambitious young man and an
acquaintance of More
DUKE OF NORFOLK, a friend of More
CARDINAL WOLSEY, Lord Chancellor of England
THOMAS CROMWELL, Wolsey's unscrupulous secretary
SIGNOR CHAPUYS, the Spanish ambassador
HENRY VIII, the king of England

The Story:

Richard Rich, eager to find employment at court, arrives at the manor of his acquaintance, Thomas More, to request aid. When Sir Thomas warns Rich of the bribes and other temptations of court, and offers to help Rich find a position as a teacher, Rich is deeply disappointed. More gives Rich a silver cup that had been sent to More as an attempted bribe. As they are talking, the duke of Norfolk enters with Lady Alice and Lady Margaret More, and the duke surprises the gathering by announcing that Thomas Cromwell has become secretary to Cardinal Wolsey. At that moment, a message arrives from the cardinal, summoning More to him, although it is late at night.

When More arrives at the cardinal's chambers, Wolsey rebukes him for having opposed him in council that day. The two men then discuss the dynastic situation. King Henry desperately desires a son to continue the Tudor line, but his wife, Catherine, cannot get pregnant, and the pope refuses to grant a dispensation so that Henry can divorce Catherine to marry again. More is dismissed by the cardinal to return home by boat after they take opposing views about what Henry VIII should do.

When More returns, he finds William Roper has arrived early in the morning to visit Margaret and ask Sir Thomas for his daughter's hand in marriage. Sir Thomas replies that the answer will be no so long as Roper remains a heretic—that is, a Lutheran. After Roper leaves, Sir Thomas refuses to discuss the political situation with his wife and daughter, except to warn them that times are dangerous and that they should be careful.

The Common Man informs the audience that, upon Wolsey's death, Thomas More had been appointed Lord Chan-

cellor. The Spanish ambassador and Cromwell try to obtain information from Sir Thomas's steward; the man takes their bribes, but he evades giving them any real information.

The king visits Sir Thomas's house and, drawing Thomas aside, asks for his help in securing the divorce from Catherine. The king is reproachful when Thomas says that he cannot renounce his obligations to the Church. Although Henry expresses his respect for Sir Thomas's conscience, he is clearly disappointed. After the king's departure, William Roper and Richard Rich enter; Roper has returned to belief in the Catholic Church and expresses some potentially dangerous opinions regarding the divorce. Rich informs More that Cromwell and others had been after Rich for incriminating evidence against Sir Thomas.

Cromwell and Rich meet at a room in a pub, and Cromwell offers Rich the position of collector of revenues for York in return for help in proving a case of bribery against More. Rich responds by giving information about the cup More had presented him earlier. After the Common Man notes that some two years have passed, More and Roper discuss the momentous changes that have taken place. The king has been declared supreme head of the Church of England, but Sir Thomas has found a legal loophole that allows him safety. More is interrogated by Signor Chapuys, the Spanish ambassador, as to what More will do if the king forces a more definite break with the Catholic Church. Roper and the duke of Norfolk enter with word that the break has indeed taken place. More, with the help of his daughter, Margaret, removes the chain of office and hands it to Norfolk. When Norfolk leaves, More tries to explain to his wife and daughter that his continued silence on the issue is their only hope of safety. Norfolk and Cromwell discuss the situation, and Cromwell explains to the duke that because of More's reputation for honesty and intelligence, it is necessary that he openly declare his support of the break with Rome. Cromwell announces that he has proof that More has accepted bribes and that this pressure can be used against him. Rich and the woman who had tried to bribe More enter and Norfolk, contemptuous, dismisses the evidence. Cromwell and Rich conclude they must have better evidence against Sir Thomas.

Chapuys visits More with a secret letter from the king of Spain, expressing admiration for the stand More has taken on the matter of the divorce. Sir Thomas points out that he has taken no stand and refuses to take the letter. After Chapuys leaves, More again explains to his wife and daughter that in his silence lies their only security.

Cromwell has More brought before him, with Rich as a secretary to record their meeting. Cromwell tries to trip up More on several points, including that More had written a book in defense of Catholic doctrine now repudiated by the king. When More disproves this point and still refuses to yield, Cromwell reads a short note from the king accusing More of ingratitude and being traitorous as a subject. Then, More is dismissed. On his way home, More encounters Norfolk and deliberately provokes a quarrel to protect his friend.

When More refuses to swear the oath to the Act of Succession passed by Parliament, he is imprisoned, where he is questioned under difficult conditions repeatedly. He is visited by his wife and daughter and learns that Margaret has promised to try to convince him to take the oath. He refuses and his wife tells him of the hard times the household is suffering, but still More holds fast.

More is brought to trial on the charge of high treason. Through wit and logic, he refutes the charges made against him by Cromwell. Rich perjures himself by claiming that More has denied Parliament's authority to declare the king to be the head of the Church. More realizes his ordeal is over, his battle lost, and he finally breaks his silence and affirms his belief that the laws of humanity cannot supersede the law of God. Found guilty of treason, he is beheaded.

Critical Evaluation:

A Man for All Seasons (first presented as a stage play in 1960) functions on three separate, related levels. It is first a historical drama that follows, rather closely, the story of Thomas More's fatal collision of wills with his monarch, Henry VIII of England. The piece is also a representation, almost an allegory, of a struggle between two ways of looking at the world, between a secular and a religious view of life.

Finally, it is a play about itself: The Common Man frequently comments, analyzes, and considers the actions that have taken place and that are about to occur; his musings become a play within a play.

Historically, the play remains fairly scrupulously within the boundaries of known facts. The characters, with the exception of the Common Man and a few minor figures, are taken from the historical record. Their actions, and even many of their words, have been adapted by Robert Bolt from contemporary accounts of the period. Where Bolt invents dialogue—as, for example, in conversations between More and his wife or daughter—Bolt has taken special care to maintain the sprightly, witty, yet serious tone unique to the England of the period. England at that time was poised between the Middle Ages and the Renaissance.

The tension between the two periods is revealed within the characters themselves. More, for example, is a man of learning, representative of the rebirth of classical letters and the birth of experimental science. At the same time, he is a profoundly pious and quite orthodox Catholic, unwilling and perhaps unable to surrender or even compromise his beliefs, even to save his own life. He is easily the most complex and intricate figure in the play, and the character created by Bolt in his drama is one of the most finely drawn and fascinating in English theater.

More is not alone in his vivid complexity. The king (Henry VIII, although he is never referred to by that name in the play) is tugged in conflicting directions. Unlike More, however, the king is a more ambiguous figure. He may or may not be devout and religious, convinced that the pope is no more than the bishop of Rome and hence not the supreme ruler of the Church. He is willing to grasp this thorny theological problem only when the pope does not grant a divorce. Henry may be read two ways, as principled or as unprincipled.

The conflicts in the play are acted out most strongly in the relationship between More and his monarch. Sir Thomas and the king clearly have an affinity and a bond between them, and the rupture caused by the divorce and the king's remarriage clearly pains both men. This seems historically plausible. Bolt skillfully develops the relationship between the two characters.

This relationship also supports a symbolic interpretation. Sir Thomas and the king, while they represent actual historical figures, are also metaphors. One is the loyal but independent subject and the other is the sometimes gracious but ultimately overbearing monarch. Their clash is not only one of wills but also of two differing political and moral views of the world. Is a citizen free to think as he or she will, or must a citizen follow the dictates of the state? Such a question is not restricted to monarchies; it is fully applicable in the modern world as well.

Other characters and relationships also are universal. The duke of Norfolk, More's superior in feudal rank but his inferior in intellect and faith, bends to the king's will and is ready to sign an oath of allegiance that he freely, even cheerfully, admits, contains elements that he does not fully understand. Norfolk, a friend of More—first presented in More's house, enjoying the conversation and company—is willing to adapt his conscience and actions to what he sees as political realities. Although the duke is highly unlikely to have read Niccolò Machiavelli, he clearly understands the Florentine's precepts.

The relationship between More and his wife, Lady Alice, is a representation of an actual marriage and a symbolic presentation of such a relationship. Lady Alice, who remains loyal to More to the end, is furious that he throws away all that makes life dear: his position, his income, and, finally, even his family for an ideal. In a sense, she is an innocent bystander caught in a deadly game. She cannot fathom it, so she must make simple fidelity her guide.

Finally, there is the element of the play within the play. *A Man for All Seasons* is, in many ways, about itself. The Common Man, who takes a succession of roles, is both a narrator and a guide for the audience. He sets the stage and provides rapid exposition of unfolding events and transposition between scenes. His comments to the audience concern both the actions on the stage and their larger, more philosophical meaning. Shrewd, skeptical, yet sympathetic, the Common Man is in many ways the most modern of the play's characters. He is respectful but largely indifferent to the religious concerns that obsess More, and his reaction to figures such as the powerful Thomas Cromwell is one of overt politeness that masks a practical realism. These three strands of narrative realism, symbolic representation, and self-conscious

presentation, together with the vivid portrayal of character and the brilliant, sparkling use of language, combine to make *A Man for All Seasons* a complex and insightful examination of an eternal human situation.

Michael Witkoski

Further Reading

Kirkpatrick, D. L., and James Vinson, eds. *Contemporary Dramatists*. 4th ed. Chicago: St. James Press, 1988. Includes a helpful discussion about *A Man for All Seasons* that places the drama within the scope of Bolt's career.

Nightingale, Benedict. *A Reader's Guide to Fifty Modern British Plays*. New York: Barnes & Noble, 1982. A brief but informative view of the play, providing an excellent starting point for beginning students and general readers.

O'Connell, Marvin. "*A Man for all Seasons*: An Historian's Demur." *Catholic Dossier* 8, no. 2 (March-April, 2002): 16-19. Critically examines Bolt's play for its reputation as the definitive popular account of Thomas More's life and deeds.

Prüfer, Sabine. *The Individual at the Crossroads: The Works of Robert Bolt, Novelist, Dramatist, Screenwriter*. New York: Peter Lang, 1998. Prüfer analyzes Bolt's stage plays, screenplays, and novels, pointing out his general themes of selfhood and individual integrity.

Turner, Adrian. *Robert Bolt: Scenes from Two Lives*. London: Hutchinson, 1998. Turner recounts the events of Bolt's life, including his 1979 stroke, which left him paralyzed, and chronicles his screenwriting career.

Tynan, Kenneth. *A View of the English Stage, 1944-1965*. New ed. London: Methuen, 1984. A highly personal, even idiosyncratic view of the play. Since the bulk of the essays in this volume were originally reviews, they provide a clue about how the play was received during its debut. Includes an index.

The Man of Feeling

Author: Henry Mackenzie (1745-1831)
First published: 1771
Type of work: Novel
Type of plot: Sentimental
Time of plot: Mid-eighteenth century
Locale: England

Principal characters:
MR. HARLEY, a sensitive young Englishman
MISS WALTON, a wealthy heiress
OLD EDWARDS, a farmer befriended by Harley
MISS ATKINS, a prostitute befriended by Harley
BEN SILTON, a friendly old man
HARLEY'S AUNT

The Story:

One day in early September, a rural clergyman takes a friend from town hunting with him. When they stop to rest, the friend finds some indecipherable initials carved on the bark of a tree. The curate says they are probably the work of a young man named Harley, a former resident of the parish. The clergyman adds that he has a manuscript in his possession that tells the greater part of Harley's story. The manuscript was found among the possessions of a former parishioner, Harley's friend. The curate thought the work of no great value and has used the papers for wadding in his gun. Upon request, however, the clergyman gives the bundle of disconnected papers to his friend, who returns to town and pieces together the melancholy story they contain.

Mr. Harley, an orphan reared by a maiden aunt, is descended from a good family among the country gentry in England. The passing years have decreased the family's fortunes, and by the time he reaches manhood he has only a very modest income from the remaining small estate. The young man, who is extremely virtuous, does not feel that he needs any more money, but his friends insist that with very little trouble he can secure the use of some adjoining lands belonging to the Crown. At his friends' insistence and because he is very much in love with Miss Walton, an heiress, Harley sets out for London to attempt to obtain a lease to the lands. The lease would handsomely increase his fortunes in return for a low rental fee. He undertakes this mission with reluctance, though, because he is uneasy with the idea of striving for financial gain.

Once in London, Harley has several amazing adventures, partly because he is willing to believe all people are good until he finds them to be bad and partly because he wishes to help anyone who needs aid. These adventures take place over several weeks, for Harley finds that the baronet who is to help him in his suit for the lease is not an easy man to see. On the occasion of one visit to see the baronet, Harley meets someone pretending to be a man about town. Harley wishes to know more about London and spends the evening with the young man, only to learn that the fellow is a former footman who serves as a procurer for wealthy men.

A short time later, an unnamed friend invites Harley to accompany a party to the asylum at Bedlam. There, Harley is much affected by the insane, particularly by a young woman who went mad after her lover's death; she touches Harley's heart when she cries out that he resembles her dead lover. As the party leaves the young lady, a gentleman offers to tell Harley about some of the inmates. Harley assents, only to find within a few minutes that his guide is himself a madman who imagines himself to be an Asian potentate.

A few evenings later, Harley goes for a walk through the park. While there, he meets an elderly gentleman who invites him to partake of a glass of cider at a nearby pub. Impressed by the gentleman's attitude of benevolence to a nearby beggar, Harley agrees. Once in the house, Harley is invited to play a hand in a friendly card game, during which the old gentleman and an accomplice swindle the good-hearted Harley out of a substantial sum of money. Leaving the pub and still unaware that he has been swindled, Harley is accosted by a prostitute who begs him for something to eat and drink. Harley hates to see another human in distress and leaves himself open to severe criticism by taking the girl, a Miss Atkins, to a brothel where she can get some food. When she pours out a tale of seduction to him, he agrees to help her if he can and promises to see her the following day.

The next morning, Harley goes to see Miss Atkins. She tells him she wants only to return to her father, a retired army officer. Just as she has finished telling her story, her father appears. He misjudges the scene and almost becomes violent toward Harley and his daughter. A fainting spell on the part of Miss Atkins gives Harley a chance to explain everything her father, who then forgives his daughter and takes her back.

Harley's London adventures are cut short by a notice from the baronet that someone else has been granted the Crown lands sought by Harley. The successful petitioner turns out to be the pander whom Harley met at the baronet's house. Discouraged, Harley takes a coach to return home.

The coach takes Harley to within a day's walk of his home. From there, the young man sets out for his house on foot rather than wait for a public conveyance. On the way, he meets Ben Silton, a garrulous and wise elderly gentleman, as well as an elderly soldier. The soldier turns out to be a farmer named Old Edwards, whom Harley knew when he was a child. Edwards tells several lengthy stories of his life, conveying experiences that, while utterly alien to the relatively sheltered Harley, nonetheless manifest the virtue of feeling that Harley and Edwards share. Edwards explains to Harley why he is attired as he is: The Enclosure Acts passed by Parliament gave Edwards's landlord an excuse to move the farmer and his family from a good farm to a poor one. Bad crops further decreased the man's ability to make a livelihood, and eventually he and his married son were forced to become tenants on a tiny, depleted bit of ground. A press gang seized Edwards's son as well. The only way to secure the young man's release had been for Edwards himself, a man of advanced years, to enter the service in his son's place, after buying off the relevant officials with the little money he had left.

While a soldier in the East Indies, Edwards befriended an aged Hindu, who made him a present of gold. Upon his release from the service, Edwards returned to England, and he is now on his way to visit his son. When he and Harley arrive in Edwards's old neighborhood, they find that Edwards's run of disastrous luck has not ended: His son and daughter-in-law have died, leaving two small children. Harley promises the old man a farm on his own estates, and, taking the two orphans with them, Harley and Edwards continue their journey.

Home once more, Harley sees Edwards comfortably established on a small farm. Unhappiness, however, soon overtakes Harley, despite all his accumulation of good deeds. Miss Walton is affianced by her father to a rich man. Although he has never declared his love to Miss Walton or anyone else, Harley is heartbroken. He takes to his bed with a severe, undiagnosed, and inexplicable illness. After many weeks of continued illness, Harley's doctors and friends fear for his life. Miss Walton hears of his illness and comes to visit him, hoping to cheer up the young man for whom she has a great deal of esteem—more, indeed, than anyone has ever guessed.

A tearful and touching scene occurs when Miss Walton appears at Harley's sickbed. Harley realizes that he is near death and tells Miss Walton of his love for her. Although she is promised to another, she tells Harley of her own love for him. Then, she faints, and he dies. He is buried near his mother, as he once told his aunt he wished to be. Miss Walton remains single, preferring not to marry after Harley's death. For many years, she is often seen walking or reading near the place where Harley's house once stood.

Critical Evaluation:

The Scottish Enlightenment of the late eighteenth century represented a remarkable efflorescence of cultural activity. Among its prominent contributors were the chemist Joseph Black; his close friend, the geologist James Hutton; Hutton's followers, John Playfair and James Hall; the economist Adam Smith; the historian William Robertson; the philosopher Adam Ferguson; and the portrait painter who preserved likenesses of them all, Henry Raeburn. However, for all this talent in other disciplines, imaginative writers were slow to appear on the Scottish scene. The few notable exceptions included the forger of the Osian poems, James Macpherson, as well as the rhetorical critic Hugh Blair. Another great exception was Tobias Smollett, but he made his career largely in England.

Philosophers, a term that then included scientists, tended to find more ready access to print culture than did literary practitioners, but by the later eighteenth century these philosophers had been followed by a remarkable group of literary lawyers, who brought to writing the same critical skills that their profession required. Henry Mackenzie was one such lawyer. Through most of his life, Mackenzie was the most prominent arbiter of literary opinion in Edinburgh. He championed the dialect poetry of Robert Burns, for example, and he strongly encouraged the early literary efforts of Sir Walter Scott, also a lawyer, who dedicated his first novel, *Waverley: Or, 'Tis Sixty Years Since* (1814), to Mackenzie. Highly regarded as a critic, editor, poet, and playwright, Mackenzie wrote many essays for literary periodicals, was active in the Highland Society, and oversaw the multidisciplinary *Transactions of the Royal Society of Edinburgh* when they appeared in 1785. A hardheaded, practical opportunist, he had nothing in common with the hero of his most famous book.

The Man of Feeling, a short and fragmentary novel of fewer than one hundred pages, is the work for which Mackenzie is best remembered. Though often cited as the quintessential sentimental novel, and seemingly a reflection of its times, *The Man of Feeling* remained in manuscript for several years. When it was finally published, it became extremely popular. Mackenzie went on to write two more novels. Of these, *The Man of the World* (1773) was intended to be a contrastive sequel to *The Man of Feeling*. Its title character, appropriately named Sindall, was as iniquitous as Harley was good. Mackenzie's third novel, *Julia de Roubigné* (1777), was strongly influenced by Mackenzie's theatrical aspirations. In it, he attempted to move from melodrama into genuine tragedy. Though little known by modern readers, *Julia de Roubigné* is often considered Mackenzie's best work. It is indebted to a novel with a similar title, *Julie: Ou, La Nouvelle Héloïse* (1761; *Eloise: Or, A Series of Original Letters*, 1761; also as *Julie: Or, The New Eloise*, 1968; better known as *The New Héloïse*), by Jean-Jacques Rousseau.

As a novelist, Mackenzie belongs to an intermediate period in the history of the form. His three works came after the contributions of Samuel Richardson, Henry Fielding, and Smollett earlier in the eighteenth century but before the advent of Jane Austen and Sir Walter Scott early in the nineteenth century. He may be a lesser figure than any of these, but he is significant nevertheless. Mackenzie's experimentation with the form of the novel owed something to Lawrence Sterne's *The Life and Opinions of Tristram Shandy, Gent.* (1759-1767; commonly known as *Tristram Shandy*), which is, in addition to its other qualities, an outrageous parody of the structural perfection achieved by Fielding. The tone of *The Man of Feeling*, however, was different from those of the works of either Sterne or Fielding, both of whom believed in ironic detachment. Sterne also favored a playfulness, and sometimes a naughtiness, entirely foreign to Mackenzie.

Mackenzie's book was arguably the work of literature that most embodied the idea of sentimentality in literature, and it was an important bridge to the novel that would represent the virtual apotheosis of that idea, Johann Wolfgang von Goethe's *Die Leiden des jungen Werthers* (1774; *The Sorrows of Young Werther*, 1779). Mackenzie's ideas about sentiment were influenced in part by Richardson's emphasis on inner feeling, by Fielding's celebration of the variety of human nature, and by Rousseau's emphasis on the natural goodness of humans and the depravity of society, which inverted normative Christian assumptions. Rousseau in particular emphasized the virtue of feeling and denigrated the stoic restraint that, in the past, had often been premised on an awareness of either Christian Original Sin or human weakness and vulnerability generally. Mackenzie's novel paints a portrait of a man who, even at great cost to himself, offers a great depth of sentiment to a world that does not understand it. It thus partakes in the Christian sense of benevolence but adds to it a sense of innate human goodness.

It would be a mistake to assimilate Mackenzie totally to a proto-Romantic paradigm, as there were important differences between *The Man of Feeling* and the emphasis on expressiveness and authenticity that would mark the Romantics of the generation after Mackenzie. Without accusing Harley of insincerity or imposture, the character evinces a certain performative quality, a manifest demonstrativeness that sees feeling as a trait to be exhibited. This exhibition stands in contrast to the Romantic vision of an innate human tendency that pours out from a sort of hydraulic reserve no matter what the conscious will would have. Readers are meant to admire Harley's overflow of feeling, to perhaps take aspects of it into their lives, and to be aware of the need to show they are doing things for others. They are not, however, meant to imitate it wholesale. Harley's life, after all, ends tragically, and even though this is because he is too good for the world of the novel, that world is meant to stand for the same world that the book's readers must inhabit.

Harley is not, in contemporary parlance, a "role model," and this fact demonstrates the limits to the reach of his sentimentality. Furthermore, that sentimentality dovetails with eighteenth century ideals of politeness and gentlemanliness. Those ideals are to some extent incompatible with Romanticism's emphasis on the wild and the uncultivated. For instance, Harley—the man of sentiment—cannot be anything other than upper class, and this is true despite the novel's considerable critique of inequality.

That critique of inequality is itself quite significant. Most of the figures of the Scottish Enlightenment were, in their various ways, rather hard-headed, and they were generally proponents of nascent capitalism, even if out of a sense of a general benevolence rather than a crudely defined self-interest. However, the same economic forces that Adam Smith saw as ultimately benign were sharply critiqued by Mackenzie. Harley falls victim to the selfishness of others and their indifference to his message of compassion and sympathy, but he also struggles against the looming capitalist tide: He preaches altruism to a society whose growing taste for the pursuit of self-interest is evident even among the friends who urge Harley to go to London in the first place. Harley is a profoundly contradictory figure, in that his reluctant pursuit of self-interest at the behest of others launches him on a doomed career of feeling and caring for others rather than accomplishing anything for himself. The contradiction between self-interest and accomplishing good things, the novel argues, is hardly limited to the experience of its protagonist. Thus, while Mackenzie's novel is a portrait of an exquisitely sensitive man, it is also a form of social critique.

"Critical Evaluation" by Dennis R. Dean;
revised by Nicholas Birns

Further Reading

Ahern, Stephen. "'Eloquent Beyond the Power of Language': Staging Sentimental Communion in Mackenzie's *The Man of Feeling*." In *Affected Sensibilities: Romantic Excess and the Genealogy of the Novel, 1680-1810*. New York: AMS Press, 2007. This examination of Mackenzie's book places it within the broader context of the early British novel. Ahern traces the British novel's development from the seventeenth century Restoration era to the culture of sentimentality and the beginnings of Romanticism in the eighteenth and early nineteenth centuries.

Crane, R. S. "Suggestions Toward a Genealogy of *The Man of Feeling*." In *Backgrounds to Eighteenth-Century Literature*, edited by Kathleen Williams. Scranton, Pa.: Chandler, 1971. This famous essay by the Chicago-based leading neo-Aristotelian critic of the mid-twentieth century, first published in *English Literary History* 1, no. 3 (1934) and often reprinted, explains the intellectual origins of the eighteenth century belief in the "moral sense."

Gerard, William Blake. "The Ethics of Vision: Sentimentalism in Contemporary Illustration of *A Sentimental Journey* and *The Man of Feeling*." In *Laurence Sterne and the Visual Imagination*. Burlington, Vt.: Ashgate, 2006. Examines the illustrations that accompanied Sterne's fiction; compares the "didactic sentimentalism" of the artwork for *The Man of Feeling* with that for Sterne's *A Sentimental Journey Through France and Italy* (1768).

Harkin, Maureen. "Mackenzie's *Man of Feeling*: Embalming Sexuality." *ELH* 61, no. 2 (Summer, 1994): 317-340. Feminist analysis that asserts that Mackenzie's foregrounding of feeling and emotion also served to repress and normalize representations of sexuality. Harkin, who later edited *The Man of Feeling* for Broadview Press, sees tensions in the novel's effort to establish community by means of feeling and suggests that Mackenzie's vantage point serves to recoup some aspects of solidarity at the expense of others, repressing the class tensions concomitant with growing divisions in wealth stemming from a nascent capitalist economy.

Lilley, James D. "Henry Mackenzie's Ruined Feelings: Romance, Race, and the Afterlife of Sentimental Exchange." *New Literary History* 48, no. 4 (Autumn, 2007): 649-666. Concentrates on the prologue (the frame story) and its evocation of a ruined castle. Lilley differs from Harkin in seeing community as more-or-less successfully established in the book, but he argues that there is a deeply elegiac strain in the author's implied attitude toward this community: Community, for Mackenzie, entails a loss of privacy and subjectivity that will ultimately place the integrity of feelings such as those manifested by Harley in peril. Argues that the man of feeling is a socially recognized, acculturated, and urbane figure, even as he draws upon a reservoir of profoundly internal emotion; this negotiation can flourish momentarily but is in the end overwhelmed by the cultural contradictions of capitalism.

Thompson, Harold W. *A Scottish Man of Feeling*. London: Oxford University Press, 1931. The standard biography of Mackenzie. Presents reliable information about his life, but should be supplemented by Mackenzie's *Letters to Elizabeth Ross of Kilravock* (1967), as well as later biographical studies.

Van Sant, Ann Jessie. *Eighteenth-Century Sensibility and the Novel: The Senses in Social Context*. New York: Cambridge University Press, 1993. Mackenzie and *The Man of Feeling* are discussed in this thorough and diligent survey of the eighteenth century novel. Focuses on the depiction of suffering and responses to suffering, relating them to the social conduct and scientific ideas prevalent at the time. The best place for the beginning student to start.

Walker, Marshall. "Henry Mackenzie's *The Man of Feeling*." In *Scottish Literature Since 1707*. London: Longman, 1996. Discusses Mackenzie's novel and places it within the context of Scottish literature.

The Man of Mode
Or, Sir Fopling Flutter

Author: Sir George Etherege (c. 1635-1691)
First produced: 1676; first published, 1676
Type of work: Drama
Type of plot: Comedy of manners
Time of plot: 1670's
Locale: London

Principal characters:
DORIMANT, a young man about town
LADY LOVEIT, Dorimant's mistress
BELLINDA, a young woman in love with Dorimant
YOUNG BELLAIR, Dorimant's friend
OLD BELLAIR, young Bellair's father
EMILIA, a young woman in love with young Bellair
HARRIET WOODVILL, a young countrywoman who loves Dorimant
SIR FOPLING FLUTTER, a dandy

The Story:

One morning, Dorimant is lounging in his room when an orange-woman appears. In the course of buying some fruit, Dorimant, who has a remarkable reputation as a lover, hears that a young woman of quality and fortune from the country had fallen in love with him at sight, despite her mother's attempts to keep her daughter away from thoughts of loving any heartless man of the fashionable world. Although he is in the process of ending an affair with Lady Loveit and beginning a new one with Bellinda, Dorimant is interested. Shortly afterward he receives his friend Bellair, a fop who is very much in love with a young woman named Emilia and wishes to marry her instead of the wealthy bride his father has picked out for him. The father's choice is Harriet, the young woman who was so taken with Dorimant.

To complicate matters for young Bellair, his father arrives in town to hasten the marriage. Lodging in the same house with Emilia and unaware of his son's affection for her, the old gentleman has fallen in love with her and wishes to make her his own bride. Young Bellair, with the help of his aunt, Lady Townley, hopes to win his father's consent to marrying Emilia.

Meanwhile, Lady Loveit is beside herself at the neglect she suffers at the hands of her lover. She complains bitterly to Bellinda, not knowing that it is Bellinda who has won the recent attentions of Dorimant and is about to become his mistress. True to his promise to Bellinda, Dorimant visits that afternoon and notifies Lady Loveit that he is finished with her. His action frightens Bellinda, although the deed was done at her request.

At Lady Woodvill's lodgings that day, the lady herself is preparing Harriet to meet young Bellair, for Harriet's mother is as anxious for the match as is his father. That Harriet does not wish to marry him makes little difference to the mother. When the two young people meet, they quickly confide their dislike of the match to each other. Then they proceed to play a mock love scene for the benefit of the parents, to throw them off the track.

That same afternoon, Bellinda and Dorimant meet at the home of Lady Townley. Dorimant makes Bellinda promise to have Lady Loveit walk on the Mall that evening so that Dorimant can confront her with Sir Fopling Flutter, a fool of a fop, and accuse her of being unfaithful. As they speak, Sir Fopling Flutter enters the company and then demonstrates what a fool he is by the oddities and fooleries of his dress, deportment, and speech.

That evening, young Bellair and Harriet go for a walk on the Mall. There they meet Dorimant, who is forced to leave when Harriet's mother appears. Lady Loveit tries to make Dorimant jealous by flirting, but only succeeds in bringing Dorimant's reproaches on her head.

Later that same night there is a party at Lady Townley's house. Dorimant is one of the group, under the alias of Courtage, so that Harriet's mother will not realize that he is the gallant who is trying to woo her daughter. Under his false name, Dorimant succeeds in ingratiating himself with the mother. Harriet, trying to hide her love and admiration from him, shows that her wit is as sharp as that of Dorimant. Sir Fopling Flutter joins the party late and shows himself to be even more of a fool.

By the time the party breaks up, it is five o'clock in the morning. Dorimant has to hurry home to keep a rendezvous he had made with Bellinda, who had promised to spend part of the night with him in his rooms. In the morning, as she is ready to leave, she is almost discovered there by several of Dorimant's friends. Bellinda escapes by going down the back stairs and stepping into a sedan chair. Her danger is not past, however, for the carriers, accustomed to taking Lady Loveit from Dorimant's house, take Bellinda to the former's lodging. Lady Loveit, still awake, sees Bellinda step from the chair. Only quick wit on the part of Bellinda, who tells the men to say they had picked her up elsewhere, prevents her assignation with Dorimant from being known to Lady Loveit, who does not suspect that Bellinda is her rival.

A few minutes afterward, Dorimant arrives. He begins berating Lady Loveit in a high-handed fashion, only to be embarrassed when Bellinda appears from an adjoining room. He is so discomfited that he can only mutter excuses and leave the house.

Early that morning, at Lady Townley's house, young Bellair and Emilia are married, the bridegroom taking that drastic step before his father could force him to marry Harriet. As the ceremony is ending, Lady Woodvill, Harriet, old Bellair, and an attorney arrive. They had come to meet with young Bellair and to sign the marriage contract between the two families. Not knowing what to do, Lady Townley temporarily hides the clergyman in a closet. In the confusion of the moment, Emilia asks Harriet if she is in love with Dorimant. Harriet refuses still to admit that she is, saying that she only hates to think of leaving the pleasures of the town to be made a prisoner in the country. At that point, while the others are off in another room to go over the terms of the marriage contract, Dorimant himself arrives. When he confesses his love to Harriet, she admits that she is in love with him.

The others then return. Old Bellair, eager to have the marriage celebrated, calls for a parson. The clergyman, released from the closet, declares that he had already performed one ceremony when he married young Bellair to Emilia. Old Bellair is thunderstruck. Just then Lady Loveit and Bellinda arrive in pursuit of Dorimant. He makes his excuses to Lady Loveit by telling her that he intends to marry Harriet and thus improve his fortunes. Lady Loveit, who knows the value of money, admits that under the circumstances she can only wish him well. Bellinda is grateful because his excuse conceals her affair with him and keeps her honor intact. Lady Woodvill, overhearing the conversation, is furious with Dorimant for capturing Harriet's heart, but when she learns that his intentions were honorable and that he is the same Courtage whom she had admired the evening before, she is mollified to the extent of inviting him to visit the Woodvill estate in Hampshire.

Old Bellair, not to be outdone in graciousness, gives his blessing to his son, who had gone against his will in marrying Emilia. The only person completely dismayed is Lady Loveit, who vows that she will never again trust a man or go out in society.

Critical Evaluation:

The Man of Mode is, along with William Wycherley's *The Country Wife* (1675) and William Congreve's *The Way of the World* (1700), one of the finest comedies of Restoration theater. It owes its critical acclaim to its etched-in-acid portrait of love rituals in contemporary London high society, the brilliance of its dialogue, and—surprisingly enough—the humanity of its characters.

All of the character types in Sir George's Etherege's last play are the stock-in-trade of Restoration comedy. Dorimant is the fashionably witty rake who enjoys juggling two or three affairs at the same time. In one of the running metaphors of the play, he holds passion in love to be merely a disease, fortunately only a temporary one. "Constancy at my years?" he asks Mrs. Loveit, "you might as well expect the fruit of autumn ripens I' the spring." The heroine is, of course, beautiful, but more important, fully a match in wit for Dorimant. Her ability to discomfit him in their verbal battles is the main reason for his conceding to her the victory over his bachelorhood. Harriet has no intention of becoming one more in the long line of Dorimant's mistresses. Other conventional types include the Frenchified Sir Fopling Flutter, the standard by which all later stage fops were to be judged; the cast-off mistress, the hero's confidant, a couple of foolish older people, and a pair of lovers in the "high" plot, who set off, through their idealized love, the more earthbound love of Dorimant and Harriet. Basing their relationship on a compromise between passion and social forms, Harriet tells Dorimant, "Though I wish you devout, I would not have you turn fanatic."

Earlier critics of Restoration comedy lamented the pernicious morality of such plays as *The Man of Mode*, which appeared to sanction, or at least accept, libertinism. More recent critics have seen such dramatists as Etherege striving to present an acceptable mean of behavior in matters of love. Dorimant, for instance, is neither as boorishly crude as the country gentleman old Bellair nor as excessively fastidious about his dress and grooming as Sir Fopling, who finds entertainment in front of a mirror. Harriet, who maintains that "women ought to be no more fond of dressing than fools should be of talking," is similar to Dorimant in this respect.

Both hero and heroine prefer to make do with a minimum of affectation and pretense, though complete honesty in love is seen to be either unrealistic in the case of young Bellair and Emilia, or unwise, in the case of Mrs. Loveit, who wears her anguished heart on her passionate sleeve. The audience may be apprehensive that Dorimant's love for Harriet may be no more permanent than any of his previous inamorata—and indeed, it may not be. What gives their future relationship at least a reasonable chance is their similarity in temperament and wit. Only with Harriet, a woman whose insight into his true nature is penetrating, does Dorimant speak with utter sincerity and feeling.

Audiences like the characters not because they recognize them as types, but because they recognize them as human beings. Dorimant, by all accounts, should be an unsympathetic character: He is callous and cynical in his treatment of people, and his wit may seem inadequate compensation for his larger defects of character. As Bellinda realizes, there is a point beyond which his brutal treatment of women stops being amusing and becomes ugly, even to those who profit by it. Dorimant is, however, just as vulnerable as his victims: His humiliations in the Mall and later, before his former and present mistresses, as well as his awkwardness before the incisive Harriet, reveal a vain man almost pathetically in need of "reputation"; that is, the reputation of being a dispassionate and consummate rake.

Etherege's treatment of Mrs. Loveit is also multifaceted. On one hand, the extravagance and violence of her passion make her a figure to be ridiculed. On the other hand, she is a figure of pathos. Her only crime, after all, is in having loved Dorimant too much. A careful reading of the play will reveal her not as a caricature but as a woman treated by the playwright with understanding, sympathy, and even dignity: "I would die to satisfy [your love!]" she tells Dorimant, "I will not, to save you from a thousand racks, do a shameless thing to please your vanity." Such probing treatment of personal and social behavior, in a genre almost rigidly standardized in its conventions, is a major reason for the continued fascination exerted by the play.

Further Reading

Holland, Norman N. *The First Modern Comedies: The Significance of Etherege, Wycherley, and Congreve*. Cambridge, Mass.: Harvard University Press, 1967. This masterful collection of essays underscores the conflict in *The Man of Mode* between personal fulfillment and social expectations. Holland contends that Etherege exposed false sentiments and pretentiousness as agents of hypocrisy.

Huseboe, Arthur R. *Sir George Etherege*. New York: Macmillan, 1987. Even though this is a literary biography, the author devotes nineteen pages and many more cross-references to *The Man of Mode*. Discusses character types and frames the discussion in the context of aristocratic manners and mores as defined by the court of Charles II. Carefully examines Etherege's use of heroic couplets, blank verse, and prose.

Kachur, B. A. *Etherege and Wycherley*. New York: Palgrave Macmillan, 2004. Analyzes the two playwrights' work within the context of the cultural and historical changes that took place during the early years of Charles II's reign. Provides performance histories for the plays. Chapter 5 focuses on *The Man of Mode*.

Markley, Robert. "'Still on the Criminal's Side, Against the Innocent': Etherege, Wycherley, and the Ironies of Wit." In *A Companion to Restoration Drama*, edited by Susan J. Owen. Malden, Mass.: Blackwell, 2001. Markley examines *The Man of Mode* and other plays by Etherege. There are other references to this play, and to Etherege, throughout this collection of essays on Restoration drama. References are listed in the index.

Powell, Jocelyn. "George Etherege and the Form of Comedy." In *Restoration Dramatists: A Collection of Critical Essays*, edited by Earl Miner. Englewood Cliffs, N.J.: Prentice-Hall, 1966. This wide-ranging essay links Etherege's realism to the physical action and narrative promise in Anton Chekhov's plays. Emphasizes dramatic technique and the naturalism of details.

Rosenfeld, Nancy. "The Mode of Man: *The Man of Mode*." In *The Human Satan in Seventeenth-Century English Literature: From Milton to Rochester*. Burlington, Vt.: Ashgate, 2008. A study of the development of the Satanic character in English literature, describing how writers successively humanized these characters. The chapter on *The Man of Mode* focuses on Etherege's treatment of Dorimant.

Underwood, Dale. *Etherege and the Seventeenth-Century Comedy of Manners*. New Haven, Conn.: Yale University Press, 1957. Underwood justifies the critical and historical importance of *The Man of Mode* as a masterpiece of English comedy. Highlights Etherege's distinction between nature and reason in terms of pre-Enlightenment idealism. Discusses the "comedy of values" motifs.

The Man Who Came to Dinner

Authors: George S. Kaufman (1889-1961) and Moss Hart (1904-1961)
First produced: 1939; first published, 1939
Type of work: Drama
Type of plot: Comedy
Time of plot: Christmas season, late 1930's
Locale: Mesalia, Ohio

Principal characters:
SHERIDAN WHITESIDE, a radio pundit and bon vivant
MAGGIE CUTLER, his secretary
MISS PREEN, his nurse
DR. BRADLEY, his local physician
BERT JEFFERSON, a newspaper reporter
ERNEST W. STANLEY, Whiteside's reluctant host
DAISY STANLEY, his wife
RICHARD, their son
JUNE, their daughter
LORRAINE SHELDON, an actor
BEVERLY CARLTON, an actor
BANJO, a comic actor

The Story:

Just before a Christmas in the late 1930's, Sheridan Whiteside, a noted radio personality, is invited to dinner at the home of Ernest W. and Daisy Stanley in Mesalia, Ohio. After slipping on ice and claiming to have dislocated his hip, he becomes an intrusive and outrageously demanding houseguest. Since he must use a wheelchair for mobility, he immediately banishes his hosts to the second floor and turns the first-floor living room and library into his personal rooms, threatening the none-too-gracious Mr. Stanley with a lawsuit to intimidate him.

An egotistical tyrant, Whiteside browbeats and manipulates everyone who comes in range. He treats his nurse, Miss

Preen, with caustic insult; on others, like Dr. Bradley, he uses self-serving and dissembling flattery. Utterly selfish and shameless, he shows no concern for the feelings of others or any sense of the disruption he causes. At first, it does not seem as if his behavior can have any long-term consequences. Although he is rude to the Stanleys and their neighbors, his demands are manageable: that the Stanleys live on the second floor, keep the mornings quiet, and avoid using the telephone. The Stanleys feel they can put up with the crate of penguins, the cockroach city, and various other oddities delivered to Whiteside at their house. They can even tolerate the steady stream of his outlandish guests, which include inmates from Whiteside's favorite charity, the Crockfield Home, a halfway house for convicts.

As Christmas approaches, however, Whiteside begins to interfere in the personal lives of the others. Whether his motives in doing so are selfish or merely thoughtless, his interference can have serious and hurtful consequences. One of the first schemes he puts in motion is an effort to seduce the Stanleys' servants, John and Sarah, into his service. A gourmand, Whiteside appreciates Sarah's cooking and thinks that John, her husband, might be an acceptable butler. He ignores their loyalty to the Stanleys and cajoles and flatters them without a thought of his hosts. He also begins to give pseudopaternal advice to the Stanleys' older children, Richard and June. He encourages young Richard to follow his dream of becoming a professional photojournalist by just hopping on a boat and steaming off to foreign ports. To June he suggests that she elope with her boyfriend, Sandy, an employee and labor organizer at her father's factory and a young man whom Mr. Stanley intensely dislikes and had tried to fire.

Whiteside's assistant, Maggie Cutler, falls in love with Bert Jefferson, a local newspaper reporter and aspiring playwright. Whiteside, unwilling to give Maggie up to anyone, selfishly plots to undermine her plans. At first, he tries to convince Maggie that the affair is ridiculous, but when she proves stubborn, he resorts to a deceitful scheme. Feigning interest in a new play Jefferson has written, he calls the actor and notorious vamp Lorraine Sheldon, who is en route to America on the liner *Normandie* and asks her to come directly to Ohio. Whiteside wants to distract Jefferson by introducing him to Miss Sheldon as a collaborator and leading lady. Maggie soon realizes Whiteside's true intention.

After Lorraine arrives, Maggie arranges for Beverly Carlton, an actor and skilled mimic, to call Lorraine pretending to be Lord Botomley (the English peer whom Lorraine had been hoping to ensnare as a husband) and propose marriage. Unfortunately for Maggie, Whiteside discovers the deception and convinces Lorraine that she has been duped.

Whiteside's scheme threatens to come apart from other complications, however. Dr. Bradley informs him that there is actually nothing wrong with him and that his X ray was mixed up with that of another patient. Since disclosure of that fact would have proved inconvenient, Whiteside claims to be fascinated with the doctor's work-in-progress. Dr. Bradley is easily hoodwinked and enters a conspiracy of silence, bribed by Whiteside's insincere promise to work with him on his manuscript. Mr. Stanley, however, is more intractable. Increasingly outraged by Whiteside's interference in his family's affairs, Mr. Stanley threatens to evict Whiteside, lawsuit or no lawsuit, and obtains a warrant and the service of two sheriff's deputies. At the last minute, Whiteside saves himself by using his knowledge that Stanley's mysterious sister is none other than Harriet Sedley, a woman who had murdered her parents with an ax.

On Christmas Day, having finally realized how serious are Maggie's feelings for Jefferson, and prompted by his zany friend Banjo, Whiteside allows the more generous part of his character to triumph over his selfishness. He and Banjo conspire to get rid of Maggie's competition by trapping Lorraine inside one of Whiteside's bizarre gifts—an Egyptian mummy case. Banjo, assisted by the two deputies, then takes her to an airplane bound for Nova Scotia. That solves Maggie's problem. The Stanleys think their problems are over, too, as Whiteside is in the process of leaving, but just as Whiteside steps on the porch, he falls on the ice again and has to be carried back inside. He immediately bellows for Miss Preen and threatens the Stanleys with a new lawsuit. Mr. Stanley throws his hands up in despair, and his wife sinks to the floor in a dead faint.

Critical Evaluation:

George Kaufman and Moss Hart dedicated *The Man Who Came to Dinner* to their friend, the renowned drama critic and radio personality Alexander Woollcott, after whom they modeled the character of Sheridan Whiteside. He is a delightfully outrageous character, a comic parody of Woollcott's traits, especially his notorious gormandizing, cruel wit, and graceless behavior as a houseguest. With the exception of Maggie Cutler, Whiteside dominates everyone around him, using acerbic wit, saccharine cajolery, or threats as the situation seems to call for it. Since he is a massive egotist, he is so caught up in his own conceit as to be completely blind to the harm he can and does do.

The plot of the play is a well-worn one, that of the unwanted intruder who disrupts the normal life and peaceful equanimity of a household. The premise presents a tense situation fraught with comic possibilities that can be mined as long as the intruder remains the play's central figure and driver of the plot. Whiteside is the master of comic bluster and an outrageous manipulator who has no qualms about riding roughshod over anyone who stands in his way.

It is hard to sympathize with Whiteside's victims, for the comedy is nonsensical farce, and most of his targets deserve at least some of the comic derision to which they are subjected. Mr. Stanley, for example, is so staid and proper that he is easily intimidated by legal threats. Daisy Stanley, his wife, is one of those society matrons who patronize the arts to bolster their own esteem and be able to crow over their friends. Dr. Bradley and Lorraine Sheldon deserve their treatment because they have an inflated sense of their own talents, Bradley as a writer and Sheldon as a serious actor.

The rapid pace of the play and the stream of oddball characters who flit on and off stage serve to mitigate any real concern the audience might feel for the victims. Only Maggie and Bert Jefferson, who refuse to be cowed or cajoled by Whiteside, can command much respect. Maggie deftly penetrates Whiteside's bluster, and she is, as he knows, his match. Paradoxically, this is the reason he values her. She is like a daughter to him, and even when he addresses her in insulting terms such as "repulsive" and "sex-ridden hag," his affection for her shapes the insults' subtext.

Most other people are mere toys to Whiteside, and many of them, like Banjo and Beverly Carlton, he values simply because they delight him by being unpredictable or clever. The impression of Whiteside as a rich, willful, spoiled child is reinforced by the physical debris that accumulates during the play as the Stanleys' first floor is turned into Whiteside's personal romper room. Throughout the comedy, gifts for Whiteside pour in from scores of real and fictitious celebrities. By the beginning of the second act, piles of gifts collect under an imposing Christmas tree, put there for Whiteside's exclusive amusement. In the last act, the comic proliferation of things and people includes a radio production crew that turns the Stanleys' living room into Whiteside's private broadcast studio.

Because the play is rich with topical materials and allusions, it has gradually become a bit dated. Whiteside talks to or about real personalities of his day, from the great actor Katharine Cornell to the early master of science fiction, H. G. Wells. The frenetic name-dropping is part of the fun, and some of the play's characters are even based on well-known celebrities of the day—Banjo, for example, was inspired by Harpo Marx, Lorraine Sheldon by Gertrude Lawrence, and Beverly Carlton by Noël Coward. As pure entertainment, however, *The Man Who Came to Dinner* is hard to fault. It is one of those sparkling, witty, Depression-era comedies that seemed designed to make audiences forget their troubles.

John W. Fiero

Further Reading

Bach, Steven. *Dazzler: The Life and Times of Moss Hart*. New York: Alfred A. Knopf, 2001. Examines the creative origins of *The Man Who Came to Dinner* and other details of Hart and Kaufman's dramatic collaboration.

Brown, Jared. *Moss Hart: A Prince of the Theatre*. New York: Back Stage Books, 2006. Comprehensive biography devotes two chapters to Hart's collaboration with Kaufman, with chapter 6 examining *The Man Who Came to Dinner* in most detail.

Goldstein, Malcolm. *George S. Kaufman: His Life, His Theater*. New York: Oxford University Press, 1979. Excellent critical biography of Kaufman with insightful discussions of his plays.

_____. *The Political Stage: American Drama and Theater of the Great Depression*. New York: Oxford University Press, 1974. Important study of the theater in the United States in the Kaufman-Hart era. Helpful for understanding the political, social, and artistic context of their work.

Mason, Jeffrey D. *Wisecracks: The Farces of George S. Kaufman*. Ann Arbor, Mich.: UMI Research Press, 1988. Most helpful monograph on the comedies of Kaufman as farce, including those written with Hart. Apt discussion of Whiteside as "clown" and "master of the revels."

Pollack, Rhoda-Gale. *George S. Kaufman*. Boston: Twayne, 1988. A critical biography with a chronology and select bibliography. Gives helpful background information on allusions to Woollcott and others in *The Man Who Came to Dinner*.

Teichmann, Howard. *Smart Aleck: The Wit, World, and Life of Alexander Woollcott*. New York: William Morrow, 1976. Intimate biography of the real person behind Sheridan Whiteside, with a significant chapter on *The Man Who Came to Dinner*.

The Man Who Loved Children

Author: Christina Stead (1902-1983)
First Published: 1940; revised, 1965
Type of work: Novel
Type of plot: Impressionistic realism
Time of plot: 1936-1940
Locale: Washington, D.C.; Baltimore and Eastport,
   Maryland

Principal characters:
SAMUEL CLEMENS POLLIT, a government anthropologist
HENRIETTA "HENNY" POLLIT, his wife
LOUISA, Sam's daughter with his first wife, Rachel
ERNEST and TOMMY, Sam and Henny's sons
EVELYN, their daughter
SAUL and SAM, their twin boys
CHARLES-FRANKLIN, their newborn son
BONNIE POLLIT, Sam's sister
JOSEPHINE "JO" POLLIT, Sam's older sister, a
   schoolteacher
BERT ANDERSON, Henny's lover
HESSIE COLLYER, Henny's sister, who owns a fish market
MISS AIDEN, a schoolteacher adored by Louisa

The Story:

Ongoing tension defines the relationship between Henny and Sam Pollit. They do not speak to each other except to argue violently. Sam expends enormous energy on his children, getting their help with projects around Tohoga House in Washington, D.C., a rambling rundown property they rent cheaply from Henny's father. Sam speaks various forms of partly made-up speech with the children and calls them by numerous pet names. He has high praise for them at one moment and then turns on them, sometimes physically.

Sam's relationship with his daughter Louisa is particularly problematic, as he has high hopes for her but is disappointed by her fat awkward body and her tendency toward romantic literature. Sunday-Funday is Sam's day at home with the children.

Henny, who feels herself ruined after her ten-year marriage to Sam and after raising their five children, goes into town the next day to see Bert Anderson, who is her friend and presumably her lover, as they retire to his place after lunch. Then Aunt Jo visits the Pollits to complain that her sister, Bonnie, who works at Tohoga House, is carrying on with a married man and ruining Jo's reputation as well as her own.

Back at Tohoga, the battles between Sam and Henny continue over such issues as a servant for Henny (who does not like Sam's sister, Bonnie) and over Henny's stepdaughter, Louisa, whom Henny neither likes nor feels she can manage. Sam tries to talk to Louisa about the problems. They discuss, among other things, the possibility that murder might be for the good of the many at the cost of the victim. Henny, meanwhile, is in bed, worrying about all the debts she is secretly running up, vaguely hoping that her sister Hessie Collyer or

her father will help her, and focusing on how idiotic she finds Sam with his dreams for the future of humanity and for his wild domestic schemes.

Sam, who is an anthropologist employed by the federal government, tells Henny that he is going to Malaya on a Smithsonian expedition for six to eight months and that he will send her money. She threatens to take the children and move back to her father's house. Sam explodes at the idea that the family would be broken up. Finally, he hits her, and she responds by slashing him several times with a bread knife. After the violence they come to an uneasy truce, and Sam reminisces about the early betrayal of his marriage, when Henny flirted seriously with Mark Colfax.

Louisa visits for the summer with her dead mother's family along the Shenandoah. The family has a long and twisted history stretching back to the American Revolution. She stays with Rachel's sister and meets all the family, including Grandfather Issac. Henny and the children go to Monocacy, where they meet Old Ellen Collyer, Henny's mother, but do not see Henny's father, David. Louisa does see the debauched, sleeping Barry, Henny's brother, a drinker and fornicator.

The children write letters to their father in Malaya, while Sam sends five hundred dollars to Henny. Henny is now pregnant. In Malaya, Sam voices his love of all humankind. He also runs seriously afoul of Colonel Willard Willets, the expedition leader. Sam also loses his chief clerk, Lai Wan Hoe, who has to flee his creditors, leaving Sam to complete his own report. Sam later receives an invitation to become a professor in China but deduces that this is an indirect indication that Wan Hoe has escaped safely.

On Sam's joyful return, all of his extended family celebrate. Sam loses his temper when he discovers that alcoholic punch is being served, which was Bonnie's idea. Henny breaks out in fierce anger over her marriage and pregnancy, and before Sam can open all the boxes of wonders he has brought from Singapore, he receives a telegram saying that Henny's father has died. Before he can tell Henny, she goes into labor, and Sam and the children await the birth through the night. They take turns going to see mother and baby.

Sam is pushed out of his job by his enemies, including Colonel Willets, who bring him down. Sam refuses to fight, assuming that right will win out. It soon emerges that Old David Collyer's estate is worth much less than expected, so Tohunga House has to be sold, forcing the Pollits to move to the rundown Spa House on the Baltimore shoreline at Eastport. The family gets poorer, but Sam is expecting to get work as a biologist. Also, Henny is starting to get tiny sporadic payments from her father's estate.

Louisa goes to Annapolis High School, where she becomes more and more influenced by romantic literature. She makes a new friend, Clare—whose home life is even poorer than hers—and develops a deep crush on Miss Aiden, her teacher, for whom she writes a cycle of poems. Miss Aiden visits the family for dinner and sees their poverty firsthand. She also is unpleasantly overwhelmed by Sam's chatter and ideas.

Sam works around the house with the children as their poverty becomes worse. Henny and Sam's marriage further deteriorates. Sam embarrasses Louisa horribly when he finds and reads aloud her poems. Louisa is shamed more and more by her father and stepmother. However, it is Henny who attempts to escape the family. She leaves for Washington, D.C., but the trip ends in the collapse of her affair with Bert. She flees to her sister Hessie for several days.

Jo comes to Spa House to complain that Bonnie has had a child out of wedlock at Jo's house and that this has ruined Jo's reputation. Then, Sam superintends a disastrous experiment of boiling down a marlin (sent by a friend) for its oil, causing a permanent stink to pervade the whole house. Henny has a physical quarrel with her son Ernie, whose small savings she has stolen.

Louisa, torn by her romantic notions, the overwhelming presence of her father's alternating love and anger, and the domestic struggle between her father and stepmother, decides she can save her siblings by murdering her parents with the cyanide from Sam's darkroom. The plan goes partly awry, as only Henny drinks the poison and dies. (There is some indication that she did so willingly.)

Finally, after a coroner's inquest and revelations of Henny's extensive hidden debts leads to a finding of suicide, the house settles. Bonnie arrives with her baby to live at the house. Louisa packs her few possessions and runs for her freedom, away from her father, but not before she fails to convince him that she was the one who poisoned Henny.

Critical Evaluation:

Christina Stead's novel *The Man Who Loved Children* buries a series of the most painful of human relationships under a welter of humor, silliness, visionary ideas, satire, and comic action and through a vivid depiction of a time, place, and social reality in the vein of Tennessee Williams. Stead has faced head on how truly awful family members can be to one another, where character is formed and distorted by relationships. She solves the problem without losing her readers. This is a novel of excess: excessive talk, excessive and often trivial action made exciting, excessive domestic tension that often leads to violence or fainting or people hiding from others in their rooms. Its excesses, however, arise from the natures of its central characters and from the style of the whole, which has been described as domestic gothic.

All of the excesses begin with Sam Pollit, who characterizes himself as Sam-the-Bold and is a bubbling amalgam of the American dreamer, at once an ideal yet awful father, a truly horrible husband, and a person happy to be driven by his obsessions. Sam is selfish, exercising his wild imagination with almost no care for others. He ruins his career and takes the family into poverty all the while babbling in made-up languages to the children and running about his houses fixing and experimenting, and spouting vague internationalist ideas and scientific predictions of the future. He is still a child in his thirties, and at the close of the book he remains unchanged, seemingly unaware that he has done such harm to his wife, his family, and particularly to his daughter Louisa.

Stead picked up on many aspects of American life in her years in the United States: Sam's rambling, his decaying houses, and his decaying sisters, father, and cousins; and the genteel poverty of Henny's "old" Baltimore family waiting for its patriarch to die.

Randall Jarrell, the American critic who revived this novel in 1965, speaks of Henny as "a violent, defeated process leading to a violent end." Her decaying gentility, her revulsion at her situation, and her own self-made trap of debt and marriage leave her almost nothing but bursts of violent language, brooding, and futile attempts to escape her doomed life. The pace of her suffering and desperation finally accelerates to the point where she drinks the poison. She steals and borrows partly to save her family, but in the end, her life is one of self-pity turned into bitter anger.

Stead partly modeled Sam on her Australian father, a biologist, conservationist, and Marxist. To some extent, she based the novel on her family experiences, but the amazing excesses of language, incident, and detail transmute those aspects of autobiography into a moving story, at times irritating and wildly willful. As read, the novel is often a comic romp rich in eccentricity. As analyzed, the novel is a powerful early document in women's writing that raises the most essential questions about marriage and family.

Peter Brigg

Further Reading

Brydon, Diana. *Christina Stead.* New York: Macmillan, 1987. A thorough examination of all of Stead's novels. Discusses the critical reception of Stead's fiction. While admitting that she presents Stead's work from an essentially feminist perspective, Brydon qualifies this stance by examining Stead's fiction as about both genders in varied social relationships.

Harris, Margaret, ed. *The Magic Phrase: Critical Essays on Christina Stead.* St. Lucia: University of Queensland Press, 2000. Collection of sixteen essays that includes some that review Stead's entire career and others that concentrate on individual works. Among the novels discussed is *The Man Who Loved Children.*

Jarrell, Randall. "An Unread Book." Introduction to *The Man Who Loved Children,* by Christina Stead. New York: Holt, Rinehart and Winston, 1965. Randall, an American poet, provides the first serious and thorough critical examination of Stead's work, incorporating many of the themes on which subsequent critics would enlarge.

Lidoff, Joan. *Christina Stead.* New York: Frederick Ungar, 1992. A biography of Stead that opens up the idea of her work as domestic gothic. Deals also with the quality of excess in Stead's writings.

Pender, Anne. *Christina Stead: Satirist.* Altona, Vic.: Common Ground, 2002. Focuses on Stead's satirical attacks on the social and political realities of her times.

Petersen, Teresa. *The Enigmatic Christina Stead: A Provocative Rereading.* Melbourne, Vic.: Melbourne University Press, 2001. Closely examines five novels and a collection of short stories to argue that Stead's work contains a subtext of lesbian sexuality and male homosexuality.

Rowley, Hazel. *Christina Stead: A Biography.* Melbourne, Vic.: Heineman, 1993. Reprint. Melbourne: Miegunyah Press, 2007. A comprehensive, integrated, biographical account and reading of Stead's life and works.

The Man Who Was Thursday
A Nightmare

Author: G. K. Chesterton (1874-1936)
First published: 1908
Type of work: Novel
Type of plot: Allegory
Time of plot: Early twentieth century
Locale: London

Principal characters:
LUCIAN GREGORY, an anarchic poet
GABRIEL SYME, a poet and police detective
THE SECRETARY, Monday in the council
GOGOL, Tuesday
MARQUIS DE ST. EUSTACHE, Wednesday
PROFESSOR DE WORMS, Friday
DR. BULL, Saturday
SUNDAY

The Story:

Lucian Gregory is in the habit of declaiming his anarchistic views to anyone who will listen. He strikes others, particularly women, as a thrilling poet, and surely his anarchism is only a pose. By chance, Gabriel Syme happens along and disagrees thoroughly with Gregory. In Syme's view, the real wonder lay in order; anarchists hope only to shock others and deceive themselves by their nihilistic views.

The dispute grows so intense that Gregory invites Syme to see for himself that there are real anarchists intent on destroying the world. However, Syme has to swear never to tell the authorities what Gregory will reveal.

The two take a cab to a restaurant in a poorer part of town. There, Syme is surprised to be served an excellent dinner. Then Gregory takes him down a subterranean passage lined with firearms to a council room filled with bombs. This room is the meeting place of the group of anarchists to which Gregory belongs. There is to be an election that night, and Gregory confides that he is confident that he will be elected to the post of Thursday on the Central Anarchist Council, the inner ring presided over by the redoubtable Sunday. Before the meeting convenes, Syme swears Gregory to silence and confides that he is really a police detective. Gregory is filled with confusion and makes a poor speech to the assembly. The members grow suspicious of Gregory's private convictions and elect Syme to act as Thursday on the Council.

Syme had become a detective in an unusual way. One day, he met a police officer who had gone to school at Harrow. The officer said that he was one of the new force recruited to combat intellectuals who were out to destroy law and order. Syme, interested in joining the new force, was taken to a pitch-dark room in Scotland Yard, where a man he could not see gave him a job.

Now, as an elected member of the inner council of the anarchists, he is taken down the Thames River on a tug to a landing, where the Secretary greets him and takes him to the meeting, which is being held on a balcony in open view. Huge, menacing Sunday is presiding at the banquet table. As Syme surveys the other members, he is struck by how normal they look.

The business at hand is the assassination of the czar of Russia and the president of France. The bombing is to be done by the dapper Marquis de St. Eustache, called Wednesday. Suddenly, Sunday shuts off debate and announces that there is a spy present. He appoints Bull to finalize the plans and then unmasks Gogol as a police spy. Gogol leaves hurriedly.

As Syme leaves the meeting, he is shadowed by the aged, decrepit-seeming Professor de Worms. Despite Syme's best efforts to elude him, he is unable to shake de Worms, and they go on an absurd chase all over London. Finally, in a tavern, de Worms tells Syme that he is really a young actor disguised as an old professor, another police spy.

Syme and de Worms resolve to visit Bull, since he is the one planning the assassination. When the conversation with Bull seems to be leading nowhere, Syme suddenly has a brilliant idea and persuades him to take off his dark spectacles. Seeing the young man's kindly eyes, Syme declares that he cannot really be an anarchist, and Bull confesses that he, too, is a police spy.

The three Scotland Yard men follow St. Eustache to the Continent to try to stop him from bombing the czar and the president. They come upon St. Eustache in a café in Calais. Syme decides that his best chance to delay the Frenchman is to provoke him to a duel by trying to pull his nose. His challenge

is accepted, and it is arranged that the duel be fought near a railroad station. Syme thinks the place has been chosen so that St. Eustache can board a Paris train immediately afterward. Syme does his best to prolong the duel so that St. Eustache will miss the train, but the Frenchman suddenly offers to end the duel by letting Syme pull his nose. As the train comes into the station, St. Eustache pulls off his own nose; he also pulls off his wig and various bits of padding and disguise, revealing that he, too, is a police spy. Led by the Secretary, a menacing-looking masked mob gets off the train and marches toward the men from Scotland Yard. The four confessed spies run.

The chase is a mad one. The pursued use horses and a car to seek safety with the police, but the alarmingly well-disciplined mob keeps up with them. At last, the spies find themselves crowded together on a pier. Arrayed against them is the mob, firing rifles and pistols. To their horror, they see that the police, too, have joined their enemies. As it turns out, however, it is all a misunderstanding, for the Secretary is yet another Scotland Yard man, and he has been attempting to capture the others so as to thwart the bombing. The five detectives return to London, where they pick up Gogol. They are determined to confront Sunday.

When they find him, Sunday begins to run with surprising speed and grace. He uses several hansom cabs and a fire engine in his flight, and he even commandeers an elephant from the zoo. On the outskirts of London, he jumps into the basket of a balloon and floats out of their reach.

The six spies pursue Sunday in spite of the rough countryside. When his balloon comes to earth, they think they have overtaken him at last. A servant meets them, however, and shows them to a carriage. They are taken to a nearby castle and royally received. A valet has laid out costumes for them that symbolize the days of the week and reflect their personalities. Syme is given a gown embellished with a sun and a moon; for according to Genesis, the Lord created the sun and the moon on Thursday.

They learn that Sunday is the Scotland Yard official who had initially employed them all. That evening there is a festive gathering in the garden, with the councilors seated on thrones. Sunday is gowned in pure white, symbolizing the sanctity of the Sabbath. He lectures them on the Sabbath as a holy day; they should use it to gather strength and comfort for the week's work. When Gregory arrives at the party, he, the intellectual anarchist, is denounced as the real enemy.

Critical Evaluation:

One possible clue to the many ambiguities and levels of meaning in *The Man Who Was Thursday* is in the novel's subtitle, *A Nightmare*, which implies that after debating poetry and anarchy with his friend, Lucian Gregory, Gabriel Syme falls into a reverie in which symbolic events occur and then, the adventure completed, returns to reality. Once this dream structure is accepted, the apparently illogical and progressively symbolic narrative creates no insurmountable difficulties. Nevertheless, it is unlikely that any two readers will arrive at precisely the same interpretation of the meaning behind Syme's adventures and his encounter with the enigmatic Sunday.

G. K. Chesterton states in his *Autobiography* that *The Man Who Was Thursday* was the product of his intellectually and spiritually unsettled youth: "The whole story is a nightmare of things, not as they are, but as they seemed to the young half-pessimist of the 1890's." Initially, the major targets of the satire are the negative philosophies that seemed to him to dominate the intellectual atmosphere of the late Victorian period. As Chesterton suggested in his poetic dedication to E. C. Bentley, "Science announced nonentity and art admired decay."

Each of the anarchists embodies one possible perversion of intellect: Gogol (Tuesday) is the stereotypical gruff, bearded anarchist; Professor de Worms (Friday) is the perverted scholarly intelligence; Dr. Bull (Saturday) represents cold, scientific rationalism, whereas Marquis de St. Eustache (Wednesday) represents decadent aristocracy and death worship; and the Secretary (Monday) embodies political fanaticism and power madness. This political satire, however, changes into something quite different as each of the supposed anarchists is, in turn, exposed as an upholder of the moral order. "I thought it would be fun," Chesterton commented in an interview, "to make the tearing away of menacing masks reveal benevolence."

Syme prefers the old world of clearly defined good and evil. However disruptive evil may be, it is preferable to moral and spiritual ambiguity. As he runs from a mob that he believes to be in the service of Sunday (they turn out to be good citizens who believe him to be an anarchist), Syme speculates on his new view of reality:

Was not everything, after all, like this bewildering woodland, this dance of dark and light? Everything only a glimpse, the glimpse always unforeseen, and always forgotten. . . . He had found the thing which the modern people call Impressionism, which is another name for that final skepticism which can find no floor to the universe.

Thus, Syme's nightmare turns from a crusade against tangible evil to a search for reality itself, and that reality—or the absence of it—seems to be embodied in Sunday.

Following a wildly comic chase after Sunday, the search for reality ends in the fantastic, symbolic final scene of the book, where Sunday reveals his identity, only to leave the meaning of the novel more ambiguous than ever. With all the detectives dressed in elaborate costumes that suggest their days in Genesis, Sunday identifies himself. "I am the Sabbath. I am the peace of God." The detectives challenge him to explain and justify his behavior, but the skepticism of the believers is submerged by the negations of the true denier, Lucian Gregory, who presents himself as the authentic anarchist: "I am the destroyer. I would destroy the world if I could."

Gregory issues two challenges that bring the book to its ideological climax. He demands that the five detectives—representatives of human moral order—justify themselves in the light of the fact that they have never suffered. Syme, speaking for Chesterton and humanity, denies the anarchist's charge: "We have been broken upon the wheel," he retorts, "we have descended into Hell!" When the challenge is put directly to Sunday—"Have you ever suffered?"—Sunday responds with a question of his own and ends the dream fantasy: "Can ye drink of the cup that I drink of?"

Once when he was questioned about Sunday's identity, Chesterton said,

I think you can take him to stand for Nature as distinguished from God. Huge, boisterous, full of vitality, dancing with a hundred legs, bright with the glare of the sun, and at first sight, somewhat regardless of us and our desires.

When asked about Sunday's final question, however, Chesterton admitted that it "seems to mean that Sunday is God. That is the only serious note in the book. The face of Sunday changes, you tear off the mask of Nature and you find God."

The story Chesterton began as a comic parody of the intrigue-adventure novel ends as a speculation on divine ambiguity. Chesterton suggests that the pessimism of the anarchist is wrong, but the optimism of the pantheist is inadequate. What remains can only be the god behind nature, who embraces both limited views and demands a faith and commitment beyond rationalization and speculation.

Further Reading

Chesterton, G. K. *The Annotated Thursday: G. K. Chesterton's Masterpiece, "The Man Who Was Thursday."* Annotated by Martin Gardner. San Francisco: Ignatius Press, 1999. In addition to the text of the novel, Gardner provides extensive footnotes to explicate the work and an introductory essay about the novel's allegorical meaning.

Also includes illustrations and a bibliography listing earlier editions and stage adaptations of the novel.

Clipper, Lawrence J. *G. K. Chesterton*. New York: Twayne, 1974. A useful survey of Chesterton's sources of inspiration, works, and themes. Clipper sees *The Man Who Was Thursday* and *Orthodoxy* (both written in 1908) as Chesterton's open declaration of commitment to Christianity as a cure for the problems of twentieth century society. Includes a chronology, a list of works by Chesterton, and a bibliography of critiques.

Coates, John D. *G. K. Chesterton as Controversialist, Essayist, Novelist, and Critic*. Lewiston, N.Y.: Edwin Mellen Press, 2002. Coates refutes Chesterton's reputation as a minor writer, maintaining that his detective novels remain important and relevant works. He places Chesterton's fiction within the context of modernism and the Edwardian novel of ideas.

Conlon, D. J., ed. *G. K. Chesterton: A Half Century of Views*. New York: Oxford University Press, 1987. A strong collection of critical essays on Chesterton's work by many of the finest critics writing between 1936 and 1985, including Graham Greene, C. S. Lewis, George Orwell, and Dorothy Sayers. Includes two selections specifically discussing *The Man Who Was Thursday*.

Ffinch, Michael. *G. K. Chesterton: A Biography*. San Francisco: Harper & Row, 1986. A lively and lucid biography examining Chesterton's life and literary achievements.

Probably the most informative work of its kind since Chesterton's 1936 *Autobiography*. Gives a concise discussion of *The Man Who Was Thursday* as a nightmarish work resembling works of Franz Kafka.

Hollis, Christopher. *The Mind of Chesterton*. London: Hollis & Carter, 1970. A wide-ranging critique of Chesterton's literary accomplishments. Includes a discussion and many references to *The Man Who Was Thursday*.

Kestner, Joseph A. *The Edwardian Detective, 1901-1915*. Brookfield, Vt.: Ashgate, 2000. Assesses *The Man Who Was Thursday* and other early twentieth century British detective novels as works of cultural history, reflecting contemporary ideas about legal reform, marital relations, surveillance, international diplomacy, and other subjects.

Pearce, Joseph. *Wisdom and Innocence: A Life of G. K. Chesterton*. San Francisco: Ignatius Press, 1996. A scholarly and well-written biography of Chesterton. Contains many quotations from and a good analysis of his works, as well as useful data on his family and friends.

Worthington, Heather. "Identifying Anarchy in G. K. Chesterton's *The Man Who Was Thursday*." In *To Hell with Culture: Anarchism and Twentieth-Century British Literature*, edited by H. Gustav Klaus and Stephen Knight. Cardiff: University of Wales Press, 2005. Reviews the impact of anarchism and anarcho-syndicalism on Chesterton's novel and other works of twentieth century British literature.

The Man with the Golden Arm

Author: Nelson Algren (1909-1981)
First published: 1949
Type of work: Novel
Type of plot: Social realism
Time of plot: Late 1940's
Locale: Chicago

Principal characters:
FRANCIS MAJCINEK, war veteran, drug addict, and card dealer
SOPHIE, his wife
MOLLY NOVOTNY, his mistress
DRUNKIE JOHN, Molly's former boyfriend
SPARROW SALTSKIN, a gambling room steerer
LOUIE FOMOROWSKY, a drug dealer
STASH KOSKOSKA, an icehouse worker
VIOLET, Stash's wife
ZERO SCHWIEFKA, a gambling room owner

The Story:

Twenty-nine-year-old Francis Majcinek, known as Frankie Machine because of his skill in dealing cards, is wounded in World War II, deployed to a hospital with shrapnel in his liver, and sent home for discharge. During his hospitalization, large doses of morphine control his pain. He becomes hooked on drugs, which he has to take regularly to function.

Frankie's relationship to his wife, Sophie, has never been

a healthy one. While dating her, he had told her that he needed his freedom. To keep him, Sophie had lied that she was pregnant. A guilt-ridden Frankie, nineteen years of age at the time, married her. The marriage deteriorated dramatically when Sophie incurred injuries in an accident caused by Frankie's drunk driving.

Sophie is permanently disabled, suffering from paralysis that her doctors say has no physical basis. Frankie, again guilt-ridden, is trapped in a loveless relationship. Seeing no way out, he endures a life of futility, scrounging for drug money and dealing cards at Zero Schwiefka's establishment, where, before his military service, he had gained a reputation as a top dealer.

Sparrow Saltskin, who steers gamblers to Frankie's table, has great admiration for his deftness with cards and, during Frankie's absence in the service, longed for his return. He did not know, when Frankie came home, that Frankie was addicted to drugs, that he had a "monkey on his back," as members of the drug culture say.

Frankie's drug supplier, Nifty Louie Fomorowsky, is dedicated to helping Frankie's monkey grow. Nifty Louie uses every possible ploy to feed the monkey. He helps Frankie graduate from morphine to a broader panoply of drugs. Frankie's frustration and the guilt that defines his relationship to his wife make him an apt candidate for a huge monkey.

Among those occupying Frankie's world are Stash Koskoska and his wife, Violet, or Vi, a sexy woman considerably younger than her husband. Stash labors in an icehouse so he can bring Vi bread and sausages that are on sale. While Stash is working, Vi stuffs these goodies into Sparrow, with whom she is having an affair. Vi also attends to Sophie, cleaning her apartment for her and taking her on outings to double features at the motion-picture theater.

Among the neighborhood bars is the Tug and Maul, a gathering place for a variety of motley characters. Across the street from the Tug and Maul is the Safari, a sleazy club with an upstairs room in which Nifty Louie gives the community junkies their fixes, regularly adjusting the dosage to keep the addicts coming, and paying, for ever-increasing hits.

Molly Novotny, approximately twenty years of age, is the nubile girlfriend of Drunkie John, a never-sober habitué of the Tug and Maul, until he dumps her. She then falls into the welcoming arms of Frankie Machine, with whom she forms a continuing relationship. It takes a quarter-grain fix to feed Frankie's monkey at this time.

The Sparrow-Stash-Violet love triangle grows increasingly complicated. Sparrow spends as much time jailed for petty crimes as he spends free. Frankie's life takes an ugly turn when he catches Louie cheating in a card game with the

Umbrella Man, a Tug and Maul fixture. He exposes Louie, who retaliates by upping the price of the drugs Frankie needs to stay steady enough to deal.

The bad feelings between the two grow until, in a back alley, Frankie, badly in need of a fix, interlocks the fingers of his hands to control their shaking and, in an impassioned moment, brings them down on Louie's neck while he is bending over to pick up Frankie's lucky silver dollar, which Sparrow had dropped deliberately. Louie dies instantly.

Frankie and Sparrow concoct an alibi that shifts suspicion from them. Others in the neighborhood fall under suspicion when they show unexpected signs of affluence. Then Frankie and Sparrow steal some electric irons from a department store. Sparrow flees, but Frankie is caught and imprisoned for the theft.

While Frankie is incarcerated, a feisty prison doctor gets him off drugs, helping him to make the long trip "from monkey to zero" as Frankie calls it. When he returns to the street, however, he reverts to his old ways, even though Molly Novotny, to whom he has confessed murdering Louie, intermittently helps him to control his drug habit. He needs drugs to give him the steady hands dealers require.

Police captain Bednar is setting up a sting operation in which Sparrow will sell drugs to Frankie while hidden police officers watch. When the drugs are passed, both men are arrested. Frankie, as a user rather than a pusher, is released. Sparrow is detained.

Frankie hides out for three weeks with Molly, whom Drunkie John has been blackmailing. When John comes to the apartment, an angry Frankie orders him to leave. An equally angry John calls the police, who shoot Frankie's heel as he flees to a flophouse where, cornered by the police and realizing the futility of running, he hangs himself. Molly Novotny, Antek Witwicki, and the investigating officer offer the final report on Frankie's life and death, presented as a witness sheet of the State of Illinois in a question-answer format. The book's epitaph is the poem "The Man with the Golden Arm."

Critical Evaluation:

The Man with the Golden Arm, written during Nelson Algren's two years on stipends from the Newberry Library and the American Academy of Arts and with a sixty-dollar-a-week advance from his publisher, is the first novel in the United States to explore fully the drug culture. The novel was an immediate success: In 1950, it was the first book to receive the newly instituted National Book Award. Otto Preminger optioned the book's film rights and eventually produced the first feature-length commercial film to deal openly with drug addiction.

The great difference between the book and the film, released in 1956, is that the book deals respectfully and compassionately with its characters and presents its information factually, bereft of editorializing, whereas the film degenerates into a sensationalized presentation of drug addiction and of the triumph of the forces of right.

Algren's special magic in this landmark novel rests in the fact that he has constructed a sound, viable novel that accommodates what he wanted to say about the drug culture and about the entire culture surrounding West Division Street. Just as John Steinbeck in *Tortilla Flat* (1935) presents Danny and his friends with respect and even affection, consistently allowing them their personal dignity, Algren deals respectfully and affectionately with his characters in *The Man with the Golden Arm*, a book that grew out of his close association through many years with the sort of people about whom he was writing. His room on Chicago's Wabansia Street was in the middle of the kind of environment about which he writes in this book.

One of the themes Algren explores fully in this novel is guilt, both as it is personified by Frankie and, in a more general sense, as it exists in society. The second part of the novel, beginning with Frankie's imprisonment, is entitled "Act of Contrition," clearly suggesting this theme. Algren's characters are the dispossessed; as such, they experience guilt at being propertyless in a society that values individual progress and possession while providing the means for the ambitious to succeed. These ambitious, successful, up-by-the-bootstrap Americans, however, are not those about whom Algren chooses to write. He focuses on the down-and-outers, whom he understands.

For Frankie, exchanging marriage vows with Sophie when he was nineteen did not really marry the two. The real marriage, the marriage in which Frankie would remain forever trapped, occurred when, through his negligence, Sophie became disabled. Now he had to endure her endless complaining for the rest of his life because of the special burden of guilt her condition placed upon him.

The value system among Algren's characters has a great deal to do with their continual hustling, their ongoing efforts to turn everything they can to their personal advantage. Sparrow lets Frankie take the rap in the theft of the electric irons. Violet makes her husband a cuckold without a second thought, taking Sparrow into her orb when it suits her but dropping him with equal alacrity when she realizes she can better her lot by giving her sexual favors to the landlord rather than to the hapless, lying Sparrow.

Frankie feels little remorse at killing Louie, nor are readers likely to think ill of Frankie for his lack of remorse. The murder was unpremeditated, a sudden act of passion brought on by drug withdrawal. It is ironic that Frankie is jailed for another crime and, during that incarceration, gets the monkey off his back. Any glimmer of hope that his temporary rehabilitation might suggest is dashed when he returns to Sophie's nagging and belittling and realizes that he cannot do the only job he can do well unless his nerves are soothed by the drugs that Louie can provide.

In *The Man with the Golden Arm*, Algren produces some of his finest female characters, particularly in Molly Novotny and Violet, both multifaceted women caught in the kinds of naturalistic dilemmas that recall the writing of Theodore Dreiser and Frank Norris. Algren's characters emerge, however, as considerably more fulfilled than those earlier heroines and are imbued with comic characteristics that Dreiser's and Norris's women lack.

R. Baird Shuman

Further Reading

Algren, Nelson. *The Man with the Golden Arm*. Edited by William J. Savage, Jr., and Daniel Simon. New York: Seven Stories Press, 1999. In addition to the text of the novel, this fiftieth anniversary edition features essays about Algren and his work, as well as a letter in which Algren describes the genesis of the novel. Some of the essays are previously published remembrances of Algren and analyses of his work that appeared in the 1950's. Some of the other essays about Algren's work were commissioned for this book, as was a photo essay on Algren.

Beauvoir, Simone de. *America Day by Day*. Translated by Patrick Dudley [pseud.]. London: Duckworth, 1952. This book, which displeased Algren, contains considerable detail about the genesis of *The Man with the Golden Arm*, which Algren had nearly completed when he went on an extended trip with Beauvoir to New Orleans, Mexico, and Guatemala.

Cox, Martha Heasley, and Wayne Chatterton. *Nelson Algren*. Boston: Twayne, 1975. Based on material from Algren's letters to and interviews with the authors, who did exhaustive research for this book. Covers Algren's career to 1970. Accurate, well written, and thorough.

Donohue, H. E. F. *Conversations with Nelson Algren*. New York: Hill & Wang, 1964. Extensive interviews from 1962 and 1963 provide detailed information about Algren's background, childhood, and early years. Valuable discussion of Algren's wanderings after his graduation from the University of Illinois in 1931.

Drew, Bettina. *Nelson Algren*. New York: G. P. Putnam's

Sons, 1989. Detailed, authoritative critical biography of Algren, covering his life up to his death in 1981. Much of the book is based on the extensive collection of Algren's papers at Ohio State University, to which Drew had full access.

Giles, James. "The Harsh Compassion of Nelson Algren." Introduction to *The Man with the Golden Arm*, by Nelson Algren. New York: Four Walls Eight Windows Press, 1990. Provides valuable insights into the pervasive comic element in Algren's writing.

Horvath, Brooke. *Understanding Nelson Algren*. Columbia: University of South Carolina Press, 2005. Features a brief introduction to Algren's life and work, as well as a detailed analysis of *The Man with the Golden Arm*. Horvath examines Algren's literary style, including his lyricism and humor, as well as the social and political concerns expressed in his work.

Ward, Robert, ed. *Nelson Algren: A Collection of Critical Essays*. Madison, N.J.: Fairleigh Dickinson University Press, 2007. Two of the essays focus on the novel: "Making Nakedness Visible: Narrative Perspective in Nelson Algren's *The Man with the Golden Arm*" and "Textual Outlaws: The Colonized Underclass in Nelson Algren's *The Man with the Golden Arm*."

The Man Without a Country

Author: Edward Everett Hale (1822-1909)
First published: 1863
Type of work: Short fiction
Type of plot: Historical
Time of plot: Nineteenth century
Locale: United States and the high seas

Principal character:
PHILIP NOLAN, a man convicted of treason and sentenced to a life of exile

The Story:

Few people notice in the newspaper columns of 1863 the report of the death of Philip Nolan. Few people would have recognized his name, in fact, for since 1817, Nolan's name had never been mentioned in public by any naval officer, and the records concerning his case had been destroyed by fire years before his death.

As a young officer in Texas, Nolan meets Aaron Burr and becomes involved in Burr's infamous plot against the United States government. When Burr's treason is revealed and the rebels are brought to trial, Nolan is indicted along with some of the lesser figures of the plot. Asked at his trial whether he had any statement to make concerning his loyalty to the United States, Nolan, in a frenzy, curses the name of his country. Shocked, Colonel Morgan, who is conducting the court-martial, sentences Nolan never again to hear the name of his native land.

The secretary of the U.S. Navy is requested to place the prisoner aboard a naval ship with a letter to the captain explaining Nolan's peculiar punishment. For the remainder of his life, Nolan and this letter go from one ship to another, Nolan traveling alone, speaking only to officers who guard their country's name from his ears. None of the officers want to have him around because his presence prevents any talk of home or of politics. Once in a while, he is invited to the officers' mess, but most of the time, he eats alone under guard. Because he wears a U.S. Army uniform with perfectly plain buttons, he becomes known as Plain Buttons.

The periodicals and books he reads have been edited to delete any naming of or allusion to the United States. One incident is marked well by those who witnessed it. Some officers had been gathered on deck one day reading aloud to one another Sir Walter Scott's *Lay of the Last Minstrel*. When it came his turn, Nolan took up the poem at the section that contained the lines, "This is my own, my native land!" He colored, choked, and threw the book into the water as he ran to his room. He did not emerge for two months.

Nolan alters considerably as time passes, and he loses the bragging air of unconcern he had assumed at first. After the incident of the poem, he becomes shy and retiring, conversing with few people and staying in his quarters most of the time. He is transferred from ship to ship, never coming closer than one hundred miles to the land whose name he was forbidden to hear. Nolan once comes close to gaining his freedom from this bondage of silence. It happened during a naval battle with a British ship. A good shot from the enemy strikes one of the ship's guns, killing the officer in charge and scattering the men. Unexpectedly, Nolan appears to take command of the gun, heroically ignoring his own safety and aiding in the defeat of the English ship. He is highly praised by the captain, who promises to mention him in his naval report. Nolan's case had been so forgotten in Washington, D.C., that there seem to be no orders concerning him. His punishment is being carried on simply by repetitive habit and naval form.

During his extensive studies, Nolan keeps scholarly notebooks. For diversion, he begins a collection of organic specimens of wildlife, which are brought to him by ship's men from ashore. He never gets ill, and often he nurses those who are. So the expatriate passes his years—nameless, friendless, loveless. If there are any records of him in Washington, no evidence of such papers is ever uncovered. So far as the government is concerned, Nolan does not exist. Stories about the lonely man circulate through mess halls, but many of the stories are untrue.

During the last fifteen years of his life, Nolan ages rapidly. The men whom he had known when he first began his endless journey in 1807 have retired, and younger men have taken their places on the ships. Nolan becomes more reserved than ever, but he is always well regarded by those who know him. It is said that young boys idolize him for his advice and for his interest in them.

Constantly, the men are on guard never to reveal to their prisoner any news about the United States. This secrecy is often difficult to maintain, for the nation is growing rapidly. With the annexation of Texas, there arose a strained incident. The officers puzzle over the removal of that state from Nolan's maps, but they decide that the change will give him a hint of westward expansion. There are other inconvenient taboos. When the states on the West Coast join the Union, the ships that carry Nolan have to avoid customary landings there. Although Nolan suspects the reason for this change in his habitual itinerary, he keeps silent.

Nolan lays dying, and the captain of the ship comes to see him. He finds that Nolan has draped the stars and stripes around a picture of George Washington. On one bulkhead hangs the painting of an eagle grasping the entire globe in its claws; at the foot of the bed is a map of the United States that Nolan had drawn from memory. When Nolan asks for news from home, the captain, who likes and pities Nolan, tells him about the progress of the United States during the more than fifty years of Nolan's exile. Seeing Nolan's joy at the news of his country, the captain cannot bring himself to tell the dying man that the United States is engaged in a civil war. Nolan dies in 1863. His last request had been that he be buried at sea, his only home.

Critical Evaluation:

Although Edward Everett Hale lived a long, vigorous, colorful life as a journalist, novelist, editor, historian, reformer, and Christian minister (including a stint as U.S. Senate chaplain), his fame rests almost entirely on his first well-known publication, the short story "The Man Without a Country."

Hale was a young man when he first determined to write a work of fiction about an exile who longs for home, but it took the national trauma of the American Civil War and, in particular, the 1863 Ohio gubernatorial campaign to crystallize his idea into "The Man Without a Country." When one candidate proclaimed that he did not want to live in a country led by Abraham Lincoln, Hale became enraged and wrote his short, patriotic fiction as a political polemic. Ironically, Hale's effort had no effect whatsoever on the specific election, since its first publication in the *Atlantic* magazine was delayed until well after the event (the pro-Southern candidate was trounced anyway). Instead, it caught the public fancy and quickly became the great and popular artistic embodiment of American patriotic sentiment.

The factors behind the story's immediate impact are not hard to understand—the trauma of the Civil War, a roused and committed public opinion, the atmosphere for fervent nationalism and jingoism—but the reasons for its continued popularity are somewhat more difficult to pinpoint. It is easy enough to fault the story for thin characterization, vague scenes, sentimentality, and blatant didacticism, but such a judgment misses the nature and intention of the work. "The Man Without a Country" is a secular parable. It is not a realistic story that is spoiled by too much rhetoric; it is a didactic story—even a sermon—that is given color and vigor through the use of realistic narrative devices. In the final analysis, the greatness of "The Man Without a Country" lies in its perfect blending of rhetoric and storytelling.

Once the reader accepts Philip Nolan's unlikely sentence as fact, the rest of the story follows believably. The realism of the tale is enhanced by Hale's quasi-documentary approach. In the best nineteenth century tradition, the reality of the tale is certified by the manner of its telling. The narrator of the story claims to be an old naval officer recounting his experiences with Nolan. These experiences are given plausibility through the use of specific details: ships, places, historical events, and naval procedures. Hale is especially skillful in fitting Nolan's fictional story into the real events surrounding the downfall of Aaron Burr. The narrator's reasonable explanation for the "suppression" of Nolan's story, coupled with the fact that Hale originally published the story anonymously, convinced nineteenth century readers that Nolan was a real person; for years, even after Hale acknowledged the piece as his own fiction, the Navy received protests and inquiries on the matter. The device may have long ago been exposed as fictional, but it still gives the story a strong sense of reality and immediacy.

The action of the tale moves swiftly and easily. In each scene, Nolan emerges from his mysterious cabin to confront another reminder of his exile—the reading of Scott's poem on patriotism, a shipboard dance with an old female acquaintance, combat with a British ship, and contact with a slave ship. The climax of the tale occurs when, as Nolan lies dying, the reader is finally admitted to his cabin and encounters a miniature America made out of bits and pieces. Admittedly, the emotions evoked are sentimental and pathetic, rather than tragic, but as a distillation of nationalistic attitudes and evocation of patriotic emotions, "The Man Without a Country" unquestionably realizes the author's stated intention to create a "sensation story with a national moral" directed "towards the formation of a sentiment of love for the nation."

Further Reading

Adams, John R. *Edward Everett Hale.* Boston: Twayne, 1977. Includes a chapter devoted to *The Man Without a Country.* Discusses the work's analogues and sources—mainly the pro-Confederacy pronouncements of Ohio politician Clement Laird Vallandigham made early in the Civil War—and its factual background, narrative core, and popularity. Discusses Hale's sequel, *Philip Nolan's Friends* (1876).

Bronstein, Lynne. "A New Look at 'The Man Without a Country.'" *Humanist* 62, no. 2 (March/April, 2002). According to Bronstein, the lesson of Hale's work is that patriotism and loyalty should not be interpreted by outward displays, nor should people be condemned as traitors for expressing unpopular opinions.

Brooks, Van Wyck. Introduction to *The Man Without a Country,* by Edward Everett Hale. New York: Franklin Watts, 1960. Succinctly presents a biography of the versatile, conservative, patriotic Hale, and briefly discusses the political inspiration for the story.

Lawson, Melinda. "'A Profound National Devotion': The Civil War Union Leagues and the Construction of a New National Patriotism." *Civil War History* 48, no. 4 (December, 2002): 338-362. Describes how the message of patriotism in Hale's story was part of the larger mission of Union Leagues in Boston, New York, and Philadelphia to rally support for the Union. Includes a perceptive discussion of the story, a description of the leagues' goals, and a discussion of Hale's membership in the Union League of Boston.

Oxley, Beatrice. "The Man Who Wasn't There." *English Journal* 38 (September, 1949): 396-397. Explains the care with which Hale provided pseudofactual details and data concerning the life and background of his fictional character Philip Nolan. Dated but still relevant.

Thomas, Brook. "*The Man Without a Country*: The Patriotic Citizen, Lincoln, and Civil Liberties." In *Civic Myths: A Law-and-Literature Approach to Citizenship.* Chapel Hill: University of North Carolina Press, 2007. Brook analyzes four works of literature that express various views of U.S. citizenship, demonstrating how *The Man Without a Country* presents a "patriotic citizen." Also discusses Hale's views of government.

Van Doren, Carl. Introduction to *The Man Without a Country,* by Edward Everett Hale. New York: Heritage Press, 1936. Defines Hale's motive for writing his unrealistic story as fervent patriotism in the face of the jeopardy in which the United States existed at the time of the work's composition. Dated but still relevant.

The Man Without Qualities

Author: Robert Musil (1880-1942)
First published: Der Mann ohne Eigenschaften, 1930-1943, 3 volumes (English translation, 1953-1960, 3 volumes; 1995, 2 volumes)
Type of work: Novel
Type of plot: Philosophical
Time of plot: 1913
Locale: Vienna

Principal characters:
ULRICH, a mathematician
WALTER and CLARISSE, Ulrich's childhood friends
MOOSBRUGGER, a simple carpenter
AGATHE, Ulrich's sister
DIOTIMA, Ulrich's cousin

The Story:

In August, 1913—just one year before the assassination of Austrian archduke Francis Ferdinand, which prompts the beginning of World War I—thirty-two-year-old Ulrich, exhausted by the seeming meaningless that underlies most of his life, chooses to take a yearlong sabbatical from his everyday life. He wants to search for the emotional intensity and spiritual depth that he knows must lie beneath the quotidian. As a mathematician, he has sought much of the order of life in rigorous formulas that defy easy reduction to the vagaries of spirituality and mysticism.

Ulrich has been reflecting for some time on society's negative view of mathematics and science. He observes that many people continue to testify that the soul has been destroyed by mathematics. However, he believes that mathematics and science can change people's lives for the better, that mathematics can turn the world around. His youthful ardor for science remains with him even as he trudges through his military and political careers. Still, Ulrich is ultimately uncertain that mathematics and science represent the only way to discover deep meaning in the world. The stability that other people demonstrate because of their deeply held political or religious positions eludes Ulrich, for his lack of qualities makes him uncertain about holding any position dogmatically.

Ulrich's father as well as his cousin Diotima suggest another method for finding meaning and order in life; they recommend that Ulrich become the secretary of Parallel Action, a group of intelligent and patriotic minds, which is charged with planning and organizing the celebration, in December, 1918, of the seventieth anniversary of the reign of Austrian emperor Francis Joseph I. (Such efforts become futile, however, because the emperor dies in 1916 and the Habsburg Empire collapses in 1918.) Diotima's salon becomes the gathering place for supporters of the Parallel Campaign, and at the salon Ulrich encounters everyone from diplomats and generals to novelists, poets, and scientists who support this campaign. The Parallel Action, however, embodies just the sort of empty, sterile, and superficial approach to life that Ulrich finds lacking in meaning and spiritual intensity.

In a separate series of events, a day laborer-carpenter named Moosbrugger kills a prostitute, and Ulrich follows his trial, as do many of Ulrich's friends, with curiosity and horrified fascination. Taught as a child that women want nothing but sex, Moosbrugger pathologically avoids them, thinking that any contact with them will taint his soul. When a young prostitute begins to follow him, mainly for protection, he viciously kills her. A number of questions arise. Is Moosbrugger guilty of murder, or is he insane? Should he be executed if he is convicted? Can Moosbrugger, in his madness, grasp the precision of the soul for which Ulrich is searching? In one of his delirious states, Moosbrugger senses the oneness of the external world and the internal world; he becomes one with all the objects around him. This state of madness is a manifestation of the order that Moosbrugger tries to impose on reality.

Ulrich's childhood friends, Walter and Clarisse, also follow Moosbrugger's trial with fascination. These friends, now married, possess their own manner of establishing meaning in life. An accomplished pianist, Walter finds that he is suddenly blocked creatively, and that he lacks the inspiration to compose as he did before he married Clarisse. Clarisse, who believes fervently in Walter's artistic genius, decides to withhold sex from him until he regains his artistic vision and composes his masterpiece. An artist herself, Clarisse calls Walter her prince of light who brings her a new gospel of the power of art. Clarisse's fantasies of Walter's artistic powers, and her fantasies about her own attempts to will genius into her life through her own art, bear a strong resemblance to Ulrich's desires for a mystical union with the world. The two characters who are most able to discover some measure of spiritual intensity are Moosbrugger and Clarisse, and Ulrich uncomfortably recognizes these individuals' abilities to transcend their respective cultures to find the spiritual order that lies beyond those cultures.

After his father's death, Ulrich withdraws from the world almost completely. During this period, he meets his sister, Agathe, as if for the first time, as they are settling their father's estate. Their spiritual and physical attraction to each other is so great that she divorces her husband, and the two siblings withdraw from society and live together. The two achieve a kind of mystical union that allows them to understand the secret of living in this world differently. It appears that Ulrich finally has found a way to balance scientific rigor with spiritual intensity and has discovered meaning and order in the world. As with Ulrich's other attempts to find spiritual meaning, however, no one knows if this mystical union with his sister will succeed as hoped.

Critical Evaluation:

Robert Musil's *The Man Without Qualities* defies easy summary, for it is not a novel in the realist tradition, with a clear beginning, middle, and end. In addition, Musil had written and published the novel in pieces over several years, and he left the novel unfinished at his death in 1942. In 1938, Musil had withdrawn at minimum twenty chapters from the galleys of the second volume, and those chapters, in addition to more than three hundred pages of notes, character sketches, and narrative drafts, were published posthumously, in 1943.

Much like Marcel Proust's *À la recherche du temps perdu* (1913-1927; *Remembrance of Things Past*, 1922-1931, 1981) and James Joyce's *Ulysses* (1922), Musil's novel plays loosely with conventional literary structure. *The Man Without Qualities* eschews plot and action in favor of an essayistic structure in which the central characters dart in and out of various situations set in Vienna, Austria, against the backdrop of the year just before the outbreak of World War I. Musil's approach to the novel as a kind of experiment in which no characters can be fixed in their identities and no story can be reduced to a formula also makes easy summary of the story difficult. Some have even described Musil's novel as a set of events in search of a plot and in terms of a destiny without a destiny— it meanders over much territory without a specific end in sight, though with one large historical ending (the fall of the Habsburg Empire) in mind.

Like *Remembrance of Things Past*, *The Man Without Qualities* captures the tortured consciousness of a protagonist who must reconcile the vagaries of time and space with the slow demise of a social world on the brink of destruction. Like *Ulysses*, Musil's novel tests the boundaries of realistic fiction, creating its own rules for tracing the jerky movements of its protagonist through daily life. More than either of these modernist classics, however, Musil's novel resembles Hermann Hesse's *Das Glasperlenspiel* (1943; *The Glass Bead Game*, 1969), with its focus on the desire for mystical spiritual union, and, above all, Franz Kafka's parables of bureaucracy gone mad in *Der Prozess* (1925; *The Trial*, 1937) and *Das Schloss* (1926; *The Castle*, 1930). Like Joseph K. in *The Trial*, Ulrich discovers that he is caught in a social world where no discernible meaning exists. Caught in the labyrinthine justice system filled with dead ends and no endings, Joseph K. fruitlessly strives to find the right life (*das rechte Leben*). In the same way, Ulrich fruitlessly strives to find the right life, only to be frustrated, or at least to come up empty-handed, in his search. Ironically, both *The Trial* and *The Man Without Qualities* were unfinished at the time of their respective authors' deaths.

Musil's novel also shares similarities with Thomas Mann's *Der Zauberberg* (1924; *The Magic Mountain*, 1927), for Ulrich, much like Hans Castorp, withdraws completely from society in his quest for some kind of mystical and spiritual understanding of the world. *The Man Without Qualities*, too, anticipates W. G. Sebald's meandering novels of spiritual malaise, lost worlds, and postponed endings.

Musil was not a novelist by profession; he was a scientist who had written one of the most respected treatises on the theories of the Austrian philosopher-physicist Ernst Mach. When Musil wrote *The Man Without Qualities*, he brought to the story his own scientific sensibilities. As a scientist, he strived for the greatest precision in representing the novel's characters and their views. The novel contains every imaginable dialect, and Musil presents people of various professions—scientists, philosophers, poets, politicians—and social classes speaking in their own vocabularies. As a scientist, Musil was searching for a single language in which all these speakers could communicate; thus, one of the reasons that Ulrich fails to embrace any other character's position is that he cannot objectively understand the other's position.

As many critics have pointed out, Musil strives through this novel to present experience in all of its complexity by gathering data much as he would gather data for a scientific experiment. The novel then becomes a laboratory—much like it had been for Émile Zola—in which the knowledge of reality grows through a meticulous and demanding process of experimentation. As Ulrich demonstrates in *The Man Without Qualities*, such experimentation leads to a greater and more sophisticated knowledge of morality. Only by experimenting with various methods of achieving meaning, order, and spiritual intensity does Ulrich come close to reaching, with his sister, Agathe, the kind of moral order for which he is searching.

The Man Without Qualities resembles a collection of essays more than it does a novel, in part because of Musil's obsession with precision in capturing the ideas and attitudes of a particular society. Musil had coined his own word, "essayismus," to describe his writing style. In a long reflection on the nature of essayismus, he observes that an essay is the unique and unalterable form assumed by a person's inner life in a decisive thought. In Musil's definition, an essayist is not a writer like Samuel Johnson or Charles Lamb but a master of the "hovering life" because his (or her) realm lies between various areas: religion and knowledge, example and doctrine, love of the intellect and poetry. Ulrich is the essayistic man because he hovers between the world of science and the world of aesthetics, the world of order and the world of disorder, the world of spirit and the world of matter, the world of love and the world of loss, and the world of morality and the world of metaphysics. Given this definition, Musil's novel is a series of extended essays on the search for order and the experiments that Ulrich carries out so that he can achieve with precision the moral meanings for which he continues to search.

In his diaries, Musil writes that a work is well written if, after a period of time, it strikes one as alien, as if one would be incapable of writing that same work a second time. *The*

Man Without Qualities demonstrates the force of Musil's reflection, and readers cannot imagine how Musil's precision in writing the novel could be repeated a second time.

Henry L. Carrigan, Jr.

Further Reading

Bartram, Graham, and Philip Payne. "Apocalypse and Utopia in the Austrian Novel of the 1930's: Hermann Broch and Robert Musil." In *The Cambridge Companion to the Modern German Novel*, edited by Graham Bartram. New York: Cambridge University Press, 2004. An excellent exploration of the themes of inner harmony and social utopia in a world coming to its end. Part of a collection of essays on the modern German novel, with many references to Musil's writings.

Bernstein, Michael André. "Robert Musil: Precision and Soul." In *Five Portraits: Modernity and the Imagination in Twentieth-Century German Writing*. Evanston, Ill.: Northwestern University Press, 2000. Essay expresses great admiration for the novelist's narrative abilities. Part of a larger examination of the work of five modernist German writers—Musil, poets Rainer Maria Rilke and Paul Celan, philosopher Martin Heidegger, and literary and cultural theorist Walter Benjamin. Also examines Musil's concept of "essayismus," or the essayistic writing style.

Bloom, Harold, ed. *Robert Musil's "The Man Without Qualities."* Philadelphia: Chelsea House, 2005. An uneven collection of critical essays on the novel that explores topics as diverse as chance and narrative in Musil, Austrian history, and experimental utopias.

Jonsson, Stefan. *Subject Without Nation: Robert Musil and the History of Modern Identity.* Durham, N.C.: Duke University Press, 2000. Analyzes *The Man Without Qualities*, demonstrating how Musil's novel expresses a new concept of identity in Western culture. Maintains that the novel's protagonist is a "new human being" who refuses to become part of Austria's imperialism, nationalism, and fascism.

McBride, Patrizia C. *The Void of Ethics: Robert Musil and the Experience of Modernity.* Evanston, Ill.: Northwestern University Press, 2006. McBride examines Musil's fiction, essays, plays, and notebooks as she explores the manner in which Musil searches for an ethics in a pluralistic society that lacks absolute standards of judgment.

Payne, Philip. *Robert Musil's "The Man Without Qualities": A Critical Study.* 1988. Reprint. New York: Cambridge University Press, 2009. A thorough and helpful critical introduction to the content, structure, and themes of Musil's novel.

Payne, Philip, Graham Bartram, and Galin Tihanov, eds. *A Companion to the Works of Robert Musil.* Rochester, N.Y.: Camden House, 2007. Collection of essays includes several on *The Man Without Qualities*. Others examine Musil's life, his position as an intellectual, and his politics. Includes a biographical chronology, a bibliography, and an index.

Rogowski, Christian. *Distinguished Outsider: Robert Musil and His Critics.* Columbia, S.C.: Camden House, 1994. Chronicles the scholarly reception of Musil's works, describing how critics both during and after his lifetime viewed Musil's writings from a multitude of different perspectives. Includes a bibliography and an index.

Manette Salomon

Authors: Edmond de Goncourt (1822-1896) and Jules de Goncourt (1830-1870)
First published: 1867
Type of work: Novel
Type of plot: Naturalism
Time of plot: Nineteenth century
Locale: Paris

Principal characters:
NAZ DE CORIOLIS, a young painter
ANATOLE BAZOCHE, his close friend and a painter
MANETTE SALOMON, a model and Coriolis's mistress
GARNOTELLE, a painter of the classical school
CHASSAGNOL, a painter of the modern school

The Story:

Visitors to the Paris zoo are startled one day by a young man, who seems to be a guide, pointing out landmarks in the magnificent view of the city below in terms that might be used to describe the zoo itself. The young man, Anatole Bazoche, delights in such pranks; he is studying art at Langibout's studio and keeps everyone there in a constant uproar. The son of a stolid bourgeois widow, he has become an artist over her protests; although he has talent, he is content to dissipate it in bright, superficial paintings. His gift for farce symbolizes the age, which, disillusioned and effete, laughs at everything. Art has become restless eclecticism, turning increasingly to a romanticism that is essentially literary.

In the same art studio as Anatole are Chassagnol, a compulsive talker who hopes for a new vision; Garnotelle, a quiet little peasant who tries earnestly to follow rules for good painting; and Naz de Coriolis. Of Italian and Creole descent, Coriolis is feared for his temper and pride and envied for his money. Caring for nothing but his painting, he remains aloof from all but Anatole.

Coriolis becomes dissatisfied with the bohemian world in which he is living, filled as it is with talk and pranks, and he decides to travel in the Near East for a time. As he and Anatole sit talking before his departure, a woman brings her little girl to his door and asks if he needs a model. Captivated by the child's extraordinary beauty, he catches her up in his arms. As he swings her down again, she pulls his gold watch and chain to the floor. Laughing, he lets her keep them.

Garnotelle, who has left the studio, wins the Prix de Rome for his careful, if mediocre, academic art. Cut off from funds by his mother, Anatole experiences a series of ups and downs; he takes on any hack jobs that come his way until his uncle invites him to accompany him to Marseilles and from there to Constantinople. Unfortunately, the uncle becomes jealous of Anatole's charm and leaves him in Marseilles. After helping care for the sick during a cholera epidemic, Anatole joins a circus. He meets Coriolis, who has inherited great wealth; Coriolis is now on his way back to Paris, and he generously invites Anatole to share a studio with him. Once settled in Paris, the two begin painting. Coriolis has vowed never to marry; he feels that marriage and fatherhood destroy an artist because they attach creativity to a lower order of things. He knows, too, that he needs even more discipline than most, owing to his lazy Creole temperament.

Coriolis's first paintings, fruits of his travels, are not favorably received. Volatile and filled with light, they do not conform to the fashionable critical notions of Near Eastern landscapes. Naïvely astonished, Coriolis discovers that the critics and the public prefer Garnotelle's sterile work. Determined to prove that he is more than an exotic colorist, he begins painting nudes.

During his search for a model, Coriolis sees a young Jewish woman, Manette Salomon, and, through Anatole, arranges for her services. Manette is absolute perfection; her body has a pliant beauty that seems the quintessence of the feminine. They become lovers, and Coriolis, obsessed by her beauty, wants to keep her all to himself; Manette, however, is a true Parisian bohemian and wants only to be free. Her frankness and ignorance delight him; her serenity gives him peace. Once, in his jealousy, he follows her, but she goes only to the synagogue. This experience makes him suddenly aware of her Jewishness—a strange, foreign element akin to something he found in his travels. One day, he recognizes a watch chain that Manette has, and he realizes that she is the child he admired so long ago. She too remembers her benefactor, and she vows tenderly never to leave him.

Coriolis's painting of Manette, which captures her glorious flesh tones, is a huge success, and its purchase by a museum restores his faith in himself. Feeling that she too is now famous, Manette begins to change: The praise of the picture Coriolis has painted of her raises a feeling of pride in her that is almost love, whereas Coriolis, like most artists, thinks of his mistress as a charming, necessary little animal.

Soon afterward, when he falls ill, Manette nurses him back to strength, never leaving his side. To speed his convalescence, Coriolis goes with Manette and Anatole to a little inn in the country near Fontainebleau. Manette, completely city bred, is delighted by the strange new world and plunges into it eagerly. Coriolis finds nature soothing and inspiring for a time, but he grows bored and misses the comforts of his studio. Anatole luxuriates in the freshness of the countryside and falls under its spell, but he enlivens his stay by tricking, mocking, and entertaining the other guests at the inn.

Manette, accepted by this bourgeois group as Coriolis's wife, finds her new status attractive, and in her ignorance she believes this bourgeois world worth entering. Then a new arrival who senses her true relationship to Coriolis snubs her. Hurt and resentful, Manette wants to leave the inn. The three move to a small house near that of the landscapist Crescent and his wife, an ample, friendly woman who takes Manette to her heart. The two young artists learn from the old peasant Crescent, but Madame Crescent cools toward Manette after finding out that she is Jewish; Madame Crescent also senses (partly through peasant superstition, partly through a kind of animal instinct) something hidden, profound, and destructive in the young woman's nature. Shortly thereafter, Coriolis, who cannot agree with the moralistic basis of Crescent's art, decides to return to Paris.

After their return to Paris, Manette becomes pregnant, and her body takes on new languor. When Coriolis's son is born, Manette acquires a new outlook on life. The carefree bohemian has become a mother, and her stubborn pride and greed for success come to the fore.

Coriolis begins to work on a new kind of painting, an attempt to create art through the truth of life. He does not intend to imitate photography but rather to make of the harmonies available in painting a re-creation unfolding the inner realities of contemporary life. The two paintings he creates, particularly one that depicts a wedding, arouse derision, and Manette, seeing his failure, cools toward him.

Coriolis dotes on his son, watches him play, and sketches him. As time passes, however, he becomes unable to work and sinks into inactivity and despair. He cannot understand a world that neglects him in favor of Garnotelle, who is now supremely fashionable with his superficial, heartless paintings.

Manette decides that for the sake of their child and her own growing desire for respectability, Coriolis should rid himself of such bohemian friends as Anatole and Chassagnol and model himself on Garnotelle. She sets about arousing Coriolis's suspicions concerning Anatole and herself. She then persuades Coriolis to go to the country as treatment for his lingering cough, and to take along the child and some new servants, who are her relatives. There is no room at the country house for Anatole. Coriolis has grown increasingly dependent on Manette to run his home, tend his wants, and make his decisions; he is too weak to refuse her suggestions.

Left alone, Anatole becomes a true bohemian, living from day to day on handouts and forgetting his art entirely. On Coriolis's return, Manette sets about alienating his friends in earnest. They cease to visit him, cutting him off from valid artistic communication. Though Manette understands the artist's life and has been able to adapt herself to it, she is fundamentally ignorant. Her ambitions are for money and success. To her, art is a business, whereas to Coriolis it is a religion. He does not oppose her, however. Her mother comes to live with them, and feminine domination begins to affect his health; as his psychosomatic illness increases, so does his dependence on Manette. He paints as she wants him to and becomes filled with self-loathing. Always eager for more money, she persuades him to sell some of his "failures." Surprisingly, a connoisseur recognizes their true artistic merit and purchases them at a fantastically high price. Again Coriolis becomes successful.

In despair, Coriolis turns on Manette, accuses her of destroying a number of his canvases, and orders her out of the house. She calmly goes about her business as though she has not heard him. She has beaten him. A broken man, he is still strong enough in his belief to refuse a medal he has won for a wedding picture because he feels unworthy of the award. Manette scornfully removes herself still further from him, but he cannot leave her.

Some years later, Anatole hears that Garnotelle has married a princess, and that Coriolis was the best man. He sees Coriolis from afar, with Manette and several dreadful bourgeois types following him. Though love has long since waned between Manette and Coriolis, they are married and her ambitions are fulfilled. Coriolis paints almost nothing and becomes increasingly ill. Anatole, visiting the zoo again, watches the lions in their cages. He lazes on the grass, feeling himself a part of all nature and completely free.

Critical Evaluation:

Manette Salomon portrays the world of art in Paris during the middle of the nineteenth century. Like most of the novels written by the brothers Edmond and Jules de Goncourt, this work emerged out of their personal experiences. In addition to writing extensive reviews of art exhibitions and salons, both the Goncourts were practicing artists themselves and were acquainted with many of the most famous artists of their time. The relationships between artists in *Manette Salomon* reflect the dynamics of the art world the authors knew.

The main characters represent certain types of artists. Langibout represents the older generation of artist nurtured on officially sponsored schools, and he provides training for younger artists. His stature contrasts with that of the budding artists under his tutelage. Garnotelle is a parody of the classical academic artist. He compensates for his humble background and lack of training by painting in a formulaic manner. Garnotelle enjoys success as a fashionable society portrait painter, and he becomes overbearing and pompous.

Anatole Bazoche represents an artist who may have talent but is more attracted to the life of an artist than to art itself. He attempts to paint a serious work of art but instead creates a horrendous allegorical tableau of democracy and progress with Christ at its center. In the end, he is haunted by the figure of Pierrot, in whom he sees himself. His alter ego, his pet monkey Vermilion, wears the same mask of levity and even tries painting and fails. When Vermilion dies, Anatole buries his playfulness and abandons both art and the bohemian life to become an assistant zookeeper.

Crescent represents the successful artist, someone with talent and a stable personality. He has somehow avoided the corrupting influence of civilization. His wife, unlike Manette, helps to further his career. She takes care of the farm and finances while he works. They have no children, so she does not undergo the same unhealthy transformation as Manette. While the Goncourts show Crescent integrating personal and artistic goals, they, like Coriolis, advocated celibacy as the ideal state for an artist.

The principal character is the artist Coriolis, and his developmental struggle is the focus of the novel. Coriolis not only has real talent but also has the capacity for hard work. While traveling the Continent, he discovers a new approach to painting that resembles Impressionist technique. The method is based on the observation of nature in the open air, using detached bits of colors and lighting effects. Coriolis truly comes to life when he strains to achieve absolute beauty in art. The Goncourts themselves keenly sympathized with the quest for the ideal, and they were able to translate vividly the emotional effort and urgency involved in painting, in attempting to capture the ideal. They describe the play of light and color in Coriolis's canvases as appealing more to the senses than to the intellect.

Manette Salomon opens with a detailed depiction of the artist's world in Paris, after which the Goncourts finally introduce Coriolis and attempt to reconcile the broad social canvas with their protagonist's individual psychology. The love between Coriolis and Manette rapidly disintegrates. At first, Manette does not endanger Coriolis's career, for she is a professional artist's model dedicated to her own art and seems to Coriolis the incarnation of Beauty. Even when she becomes his mistress, the relationship does not seem serious on either side. Only after Manette appears as an Eastern dancing girl at Coriolis's costume ball does he become infatuated with the illusion.

Coriolis has resolved never to marry because he believes that the pleasures of family will ruin him as an artist. When Manette becomes a mother however, he yields. Once married, Manette changes entirely. She becomes very greedy for money, which the Goncourts associate with her Jewishness. Her Jewish relatives are caricatures of grasping materialism, and her son is depicted as a monster who is alienated from his father. The Goncourts imply that the true identity of Manette is revealed after marriage and motherhood, and that her character is determined by biological imperative, but the layers of illusion that initially mask her character seem too complex for such a simple conclusion.

Manette, by debasing Coriolis's art and his character, convinces him to pursue money and official honors rather than pure art. As a result, he finally loses his artistic impulse. The novel dramatizes the clash between two impulses toward creation: man's drive toward artistic creation and woman's drive for maternity. The woman emerges the winner in this struggle because of man's sexual desire and woman's acceptance of lust. Coriolis's suffering, and the accompanying decadent motifs of disintegration and fragmentation, portend the end of a neurotic civilization. Images of winter and nightfall dominate the final chapters, in which Coriolis longs for death. His predicament encapsulates the vain attempt to grasp the ideal. The Goncourts suggest that eternal beauty is masked by the vagaries of popular taste. The theme of the illusive external world opposed to reality extends beyond the question of identity to the nature of art. Not only is true beauty veiled by illusory beauty, but also any explanation of beauty is an illusion, even though beauty itself is real.

The Goncourts' style transposes painting into literature in a style resembling that of the Impressionists, with its attention to nuance of tone. They succeed in creating a picture of an artist's life in mid-nineteenth century Paris and in depicting the conflict between the "Ingrists," etchers who emphasized line, and the colorists. As champions of antiacademic art, the Goncourts thought that the glory of French painting lay in the return to nature. The brothers' styles mesh in *Manette Salomon*. Whereas Jules de Goncourt inclined toward broadly comical sketches and picturesque comparisons, Edmond de Goncourt showed sensitivity toward nuance and was more methodical and pedantic. Their collaborative novel caricatures the Jewish race and indicts women for their pernicious influence over men, but, much more important, *Manette Salomon* depicts in vivid detail the artistic trends of the time and the individual artist's struggle to create pure art.

"Critical Evaluation" by Pamela Pavliscak

Further Reading

Armstrong, Carol M. "*Manette Salomon*: Another View of Modern Painting." In *Manet Manette*. New Haven, Conn.: Yale University Press, 2002. Armstrong's study of painter Edouard Manet discusses several literary works of Manet's era, including *Manette Salomon*, which explores issues of artistic identity, modernity, painting, and femininity.

Ashley, Katherine. *Edmond de Goncourt and the Novel: Naturalism and Decadence*. New York: Rodopi, 2005. Analyzes the four novels that Edmond de Goncourt wrote without the collaboration of his brother and argues that these books deviate from the strict naturalistic style that characterizes the novels the brothers wrote together. Places Edmond's work within the larger context of late nineteenth century fin de siècle literature.

Baldick, Robert. *The Goncourts*. London: Bowes, 1960. Brief but excellent volume provides a survey of the Goncourts' novels. Concentrates on biographical background to the brothers' work, but also explores major themes and aspects of their literary style. Chronicles their pursuit of an accurate documentary basis for their novels and their ties to the art world.

Billy, Andre. *The Goncourt Brothers*. Translated by Margaret Shaw. New York: Horizon Press, 1960. Considered the standard biography of the Goncourts. Elucidates events in the lives of the brothers that became incorporated in the novels and also discusses the contemporary reception of their fiction.

Grant, Richard B. *The Goncourt Brothers*. New York: Twayne, 1972. Solid survey examines the life and works of Jules and Edmond de Goncourt. Integrates information on the lives of the authors with detailed stylistic and thematic analyses of their novels. The chapter on *Manette Salomon* elaborates their involvement in contemporary art and its effect on the novel.

Scott, David. *Pictorialist Poetics: Poetry and the Visual Arts in Nineteenth-Century France*. 1988. Reprint. New York: Cambridge University Press, 2009. Argues that aesthetic theory and literary practice of the nineteenth century combined to produce a new conception of literature's potential. Discusses the visual sources that influenced the Goncourts' literary efforts.

Silverman, Deborah. *Art Nouveau in Fin de Siècle France: Politics, Psychology, and Style*. Berkeley: University of California Press, 1989. Focuses primarily on the collecting habits and art criticism of the Goncourt brothers, but provides some valuable insights into their fictional works from a feminist perspective.

Manfred

Author: Lord Byron (1788-1824)
First published: 1817; first produced, 1834
Type of work: Drama
Type of plot: Poetic
Time of plot: Indeterminate
Locale: The Alps

Principal characters:
MANFRED, a lonely, guilt-haunted magician
A CHAMOIS HUNTER
THE ABBOT OF ST. MAURICE

The Story:

At midnight, alone in a Gothic gallery, Manfred is meditating about his life. He has undergone many experiences, but only one has profoundly affected him. When he calls on the spirits of the universe to appear before him, none come. He summons them three times, and the third time voices of the seven spirits are heard, invoking a mysterious curse on Manfred's soul. The first voice is that of the Spirit of Air. It is followed by the voices of the spirits of the mountains, ocean, earth, winds, night, and Manfred's guiding star. They agree to do his bidding and ask what he would have them do.

Manfred replies that he desires forgetfulness. When the Spirit of Air seeks further explanation, Manfred does not reveal what he wishes to forget. Surely, he insists, spirits that control earth, sky, water, mountains, winds, night, and destiny can bring the oblivion he seeks. The spirits reply, however, that they have no powers beyond their own realms. When Manfred, failing in his hopes, asks the spirits to take bodily forms, the seventh spirit, the star of his destiny, takes the shape of a beautiful woman. At the sight of her, Manfred, hinting at a former love, attempts to hold her, but she vanishes, leaving him senseless. An unidentified voice then utters a lengthy incantation, in which Manfred is cursed and

seemingly condemned to wander the earth forever with his spiritual agony unassuaged.

The next morning, alone on a cliff of the Jungfrau in the Bernese Alps, Manfred resolves to forego all superhuman aid. He praises the beauty of nature around him, but he also recognizes his alienation from it. While Manfred is musing on the relative merits of life and death, a chamois hunter approaches unobserved, just in time to restrain Manfred from flinging himself over the cliff. Together, they descend the rocky trail.

In his cottage, the hunter urges Manfred to rest a while before journeying on. Manfred refuses guidance and declares that he will go on alone. When the hunter offers Manfred his best wine, Manfred exclaims in horror that he sees blood, a symbolic transformation in which Manfred turns communion into guilt. The hunter, thinking Manfred mad, suggests that the wretched man seek comfort in contemplation and in the Church. Manfred spurns the suggestion, saying that he wishes he were mad, for then his mind would be tortured by unrealities instead of the truths that now beset him. He envies the hunter's simple life, but when the hunter, noting Manfred's high-born appearance, wonderingly asks if his guest wishes to change stations in life, Manfred replies that he would not wish any human to suffer his own wretchedness. To this, the hunter remarks that surely a man capable of such tenderness cannot harbor a soul belabored by evil. Manfred, departing, protests that the evil is not within himself; he has destroyed those he loved.

Again on the Alps, in a lower valley, Manfred summons the Witch of the Alps to share the loveliness of nature with him. To her, he describes his past spiritual life, when he lived among men but not with them: Preferring solitude, he studied ancient mysteries, and he loved—and destroyed with love— a woman said to resemble him. The witch promises to aid him if he swears obedience to her, but he refuses her offer, and she leaves.

The three Destinies and Nemesis gather for a festival in the Hall of Arimanes, spirit of evil and prince of earth and air. Manfred, daring to approach, is recognized as a magician. He tells them he has come in quest of Astarte, the symbol of his sin. When she is summoned from her tomb, Manfred asks for forgiveness, but she only says that the next day will end his despair.

Back in his castle, Manfred feels a sublime calm. The abbot of St. Maurice, having heard that Manfred has practiced witchcraft, arrives to save his soul. To Manfred's bitter assurance that his sins lie between heaven and himself, the abbot urges that Manfred turn to the Church for help. Manfred explains that he has always lived alone and will remain alone. The abbot mourns that he cannot help such a noble man.

While his servants gossip about their master's strange behavior, Manfred stands alone in his tower. There, the abbot comes once more in a last vain attempt to save Manfred. Warned that a dangerous spirit is approaching, the abbot insists that he will confront the spirit, who has come to summon Manfred. Manfred, however, defies the summons; he is willing to die but not to join the spirits of hell, to whom he owes nothing. As the demon disappears, Manfred dies, still lonely but unconquerable to all but death itself.

Critical Evaluation:

When *Manfred* was published in 1817, Lord Byron was both the most famous and the most notorious man of letters in Europe. His fame derived primarily from cantos 1 and 2 (pb. 1812) of *Childe Harold's Pilgrimage* (complete work pb. 1819), whose contemporary attitudes, daringness, and originality had made Byron the dominant literary figure of his time. By the spring of 1816, however, a series of well-publicized liaisons with highly placed women and his openly expressed affection for his own half sister, Augusta Leigh, had led to scandal. With his reputation and his marriage to Anne

Isabella Milbanke destroyed, Byron left England and lived the remainder of his short life abroad.

In many ways, *Manfred* embodies the concerns of the Romantic poets. Bryon, as is typical of Romantic poets, wished to try new forms of writing. *Manfred* is his first dramatic work. It comprises three acts, a number of characters, and a central conflict, but it is a closet drama—a play meant to be read rather than staged. However, since *Manfred* was published, it has been staged and also set to music. Byron intended *Manfred*, as indicated by the subtitle, *A Dramatic Poem*, to be just that. It is a hybrid, combining drama and lyric. The lyric "Incantation" (1816), in act 1, was published as a separate poem six months before *Manfred*. Dramatic conflicts within the poem occur between Manfred and values represented by other characters, such as the chamois hunter and the abbot, as well as between Manfred's own contradictory desires.

Byron assigns to nature an importance characteristic of Romantic poetry, but nature functions more as a setting than as a force in *Manfred*: Byron's interest lies more with his hero than with the landscape. The poem is set in the Alps; Manfred reflects on the beauty of nature, but—unlike William Wordsworth's characters, for instance—he can find no solace in nature. Nor does he empower nature with the ability to provide a haven for the soul. *Manfred* differs from the works of Wordsworth and Percy Bysshe Shelley in that natural beauty and sublimity cannot detract from the hero's self-absorption. In act 1, Manfred invokes spirits that symbolize aspects of nature: Air, Mountain, Ocean, Earth, Winds, Night, and Manfred's own guiding star. As a powerful philosopher-magician, he exercises control over them. Much as in the poetry of Shelley, the spirits represent the "spirit of the place," but they are not able to supply what Manfred wants: oblivion.

In scene 2, Manfred relocates to the Jungfrau and looks around him and down on the earth, yet he cannot see the beauty of nature or love it. He sees the peril of nature but does not fear it, fearing living more. Unlike in other Romantic poetry, nature does not provide tranquility, or even escape. The shepherd's pipe makes Manfred wish he could be a part of the harmony of nature, but that is not to be.

Byron does create a man who is in harmony with the natural world, the chamois hunter, who is similar to Wordsworth's leech gatherer. The hunter saves Manfred from leaping off the mountain because such an act would have polluted the natural world with Manfred's "guilty blood." He is represented as a "peasant of the Alps," characterized by his dignity and self-respect. The chamois hunter can be contrasted to Manfred. The hunter lives a simple, poor, innocent life, at one with nature. He exemplifies ordinary humanity. Manfred, however, is apart from nature; he is complex, wealthy, and laden with guilt. In his courage and daring, Manfred resembles Prometheus, the Titan of Greek myth who created humans out of clay and stole fire from the gods for the benefit of his creation. Manfred's turning away from society echoes the acts of the rebel Prometheus.

The character of Manfred is the embodiment of the Romantic hero, an individual who takes responsibility for his own choices and who rejects society's restraints and institutions. Byron's particular deployment of this figure has come to be known as the Byronic hero. Typically, he is a man carrying unbearable guilt, full of remorse for an unspeakable act, and doomed to search for oblivion or forgiveness. Much like Samuel Taylor Coleridge's title character in *The Rime of the Ancient Mariner* (1798), Manfred has committed an act against nature. Manfred's crime is incest, loving his sister, who is portrayed as Astarte. His sister is like him; his love for her is a form of excessive self-love, and he destroys her.

The theme of incest was used in other Romantic and Gothic writing, such as Matthew Gregory Lewis's *The Monk: A Romance* (1796; also known as *Ambrosio: Or, The Monk*). Incest is another act of self-assertion, a way for an individual to break the bonds established by society. The heroic quest for forgiveness and death is in the tradition of the Wandering Jew, Ahasuerus, who is doomed to roam the earth, unable to die. Whereas Coleridge's mariner must continually travel and find a listener for his tale, Manfred only tells of his "crime" to the Witch of the Alps. He tells her of his attempts to forget, but he seems destined to live forever. The Witch offers to help him, but for a price: to "swear obedience" to her will. Manfred refuses and continues on his quest for oblivion through death.

Unlike Coleridge's mariner, Manfred has power over the spirits. In act 2, scene 4, he fearlessly confronts the Destinies and Nemesis. They order him, a mere mortal, to bow to them, but he will not. The refusal to bow to anyone or any spirit carries over to Manfred's rejection of salvation by the Church, reflecting the skepticism exhibited by the Romantic poets, Blake and Shelley particularly, toward established systems of belief. In act 3, the abbot offers Manfred a change for penitence and pity if he will be reconciled to the Church. In an earlier version of the poem, Bryon's abbot was a self-serving meddler, but in the final version he is kind, caring, and brave, ready to combat the demons for Manfred's soul. He offers absolution as well, knowing Manfred will die. Manfred says it is too late; he takes responsibility for his acts and vows to die as he has lived, alone.

Some critics have stated that Manfred is too derivative of the character of Faust in Christopher Marlowe's *Doctor Faustus* (pr. c. 1588, pb. 1604) and Johann Wolfgang von Goethe's *Faust: Ein Fragment* (pb. 1790; *Faust: A Fragment*, 1980). Byron, however, claimed no knowledge of the Marlowe play and did not read German; he had heard the story of Faust only as told by Lewis. What differentiates Manfred from Faust is that Faust bargains with Satan for knowledge and power and surrenders his soul. Manfred, who has knowledge and power and wishes for forgetfulness, does not bargain with anyone, much less Arimanes, who represents darkness and evil. The magician surrenders only his life, not his soul, when he dies, and his death has been long sought.

Manfred's final words are that it is "not difficult to die." When this line was dropped in the printing of the first edition of *Manfred*, Byron was angry with the publisher and pointed out that the line was critical to the moral of the poem. Manfred struggles with guilt throughout the poem; he continually looks for forgiveness and for death, but he refuses to bargain for either. He finally triumphs by embracing his death. *Manfred*, in true Romantic fashion, demonstrates the power of individuals to choose their own destiny.

"Critical Evaluation" by Dennis R. Dean;
revised by Marcia B. Dinneen

Further Reading

Butler, E. M. *The Fortunes of Faust*. New York: Cambridge University Press, 1952. Traces the Faust theme from its first appearance in 1587 to the present. Includes discussion of *Manfred* and compares Byron's work with that of Johann Wolfgang von Goethe.

Crane, David. *The Kindness of Sisters*. New York: Alfred A. Knopf, 2003. A study of Byron's reputation after death, exploring bitter and conflicting accounts by the wife he divorced and the sister he seduced.

Evans, Bertrand. *Gothic Drama from Walpole to Shelley*. Berkeley: University of California Press, 1947. One of the few studies, and certainly one of the best, on the topic of gothic drama.

Franklin, Caroline. *Byron*. New York: Routledge, 2007. Part of the Routledge Guides to Literature series, this study includes an overview of *Manfred*, with reference to specific critical viewpoints. Includes an annotated list of further references, as well as helpful material on closet drama.

Marchand, Leslie. *Byron: A Biography*. 3 vols. London: John Murray, 1957. It is almost impossible to discuss *Manfred* apart from the unconventional life of its author, particularly because the setting, the hinted-at theme of incest, and the ambiguous treatment of remorse are so central to its meaning. Marchand's book is the standard biography of Byron. The author's twelve-volume edition of Byron's letters is equally admirable and should be consulted (volume 5 for *Manfred*), in part because Byron was an extremely interesting letter writer.

Richardson, Alan. "Byron and the Theatre." In *The Cambridge Companion to Byron*, edited by Drummond Bone. New York: Cambridge University Press, 2004. Provides an overview of Byron's plays, including *Manfred*. This play is also discussed in another one of the book's essays, "*Childe Harold III* and *Manfred*," by Alan Rawes.

Simpson, Michael. *Closet Performances: Political Exhibition and Prohibition in the Dramas of Byron and Shelley*. Stanford, Calif.: Stanford University Press, 1998. Examines the closet dramas that Byron and Shelley wrote between 1816 and 1823, when they were both living in Italy.

Manfred and the writers' other political plays are discussed in chapter 3.

Stabler, Jane, ed. *Palgrave Advances in Byron Studies*. New York: Palgrave Macmillan, 2007. Contains twelve scholarly essays interpreting Byron's work, including "Byron's *Manfred* and Eco-Criticism" by Tim Morton. Other essays discuss Byron in terms of homosexuality, gender, history, popular culture, war, and psychoanalytic criticism.

Thorslev, Peter L., Jr. *The Byronic Hero: Types and Prototypes*. Minneapolis: University of Minnesota Press, 1962. One of the most helpful books for a beginning student of British Romantic literature. Describes the period as the last great age of heroes. Enumerates seven types of Romantic heroes, as well as the specific heroes that appear in Byron's major works. *Manfred* and *Cain: A Mystery* (pb. 1821) are analyzed together in chapter 11 as "metaphysical dramas" dealing with the supernatural.

Manhattan Transfer

Author: John Dos Passos (1896-1970)
First published: 1925
Type of work: Novel
Type of plot: Impressionistic realism
Time of plot: 1920's
Locale: New York City

Principal characters:
ELLEN THATCHER, an actor
CONGO, a French sailor who later becomes a wealthy bootlegger
GUS MCNIEL, a milkman who later becomes an assemblyman
JIMMY HERF, a newspaper reporter
GEORGE BALDWIN, a lawyer
JOE HARLAND, a drunk
JOE O'KEEFE, a young labor organizer
STAN EMERY, the beloved of Ellen

The Story:

New York City, perhaps the novel's main protagonist, is cruel and indifferent to individuals and their hopes. The city is improbably generous to a few, but above all exciting and glamorous.

Ed and Susie Thatcher have their first child, a girl they name Ellen. After the birth of the child, Susie becomes deeply depressed and wants to die. Congo and Emile, two French boys, had come to New York to make their fortunes. Emile marries a widowed Frenchwoman who owns a delicatessen. Congo does not like New York and returns to sea.

Gus McNiel, a milkman, is run over by a train. George

Baldwin, a young lawyer, takes Gus's case against the railroad and obtains a settlement for the injured man. While Gus is in the hospital recovering from the accident, George has an affair with Gus's wife, Nellie.

Jimmy Herf arrives from Europe with his widowed mother, who is in delicate health. One evening, she has a heart attack; not long afterward, she dies. Jimmy's rich uncle, Jeff, and aunt, Emily Merivale, become his legal guardians. One evening at their house, Jimmy meets Joe Harland, the drunken black sheep of the family, who had won and lost several fortunes on Wall Street.

Susie Thatcher dies, and Ed works hard for little Ellen. He stays at the office until late each evening, working and dreaming of all the fine things he will do for his daughter some day. Ellen grows up, works on the stage, and marries John Oglethorpe, a competent but lazy actor. Ellen's married life becomes unhappy when she discovers that her husband is gay.

Jimmy Herf's Uncle Jeff tries to get him interested in business, but Jimmy will have none of it. He gets a job as a reporter and becomes acquainted with Ruth Prynne, a young actor who lives in the boardinghouse where Ellen and John Oglethorpe stay.

George Baldwin forgets Nellie McNiel and is now interested in Ellen. One afternoon, as he and Ellen sit together at tea, a drunken college student stops at their table. George introduces him to Ellen as Stan Emery. Ellen and Stan fall in love. She is miserable with John. Ellen decides that she and John can no longer live together. She packs her belongings and moves to a hotel. Stan goes on a long drunken spree after being expelled from college. He goes to Jimmy Herf's room. Later in the day, they meet John and Ellen drinking tea together. Stan leaves, but Jimmy stays to talk with Ellen. Ellen moves from her hotel to an apartment. She is supporting herself well now, for she has become a success on Broadway.

George Baldwin sits at breakfast with his wife, Cecily, whom he had married for social position. They are not happy, and Cecily knows of his affairs with other women. George does all he can to keep her from leaving him because a scandal would ruin him in the business world.

Joe Harland is now forty-five years old and almost broke. He spends his last bits of money on a few shots of whiskey to bring back memories of the old prosperous days on Wall Street. He finally gets a job as a night watchman. One evening, he is visited by a young labor organizer, Joe O'Keefe. The older man warns him against getting mixed up in labor troubles, but O'Keefe says that Gus McNiel, now an assemblyman, is on the side of labor.

Harry Goldweiser, a rich Broadway producer, falls in love with Ellen and asks her to marry him. She refuses, but in a friendly way, for her career depends upon him.

Gus retains George Baldwin as his lawyer throughout his rise to political power. George warns him against getting mixed up with labor because, as a member of a conservative law firm, George will not be able to help Gus with labor troubles.

Ellen wants Stan to stop drinking so much, but he refuses. Drink is the only means by which he can adjust himself to the world. One evening, Ellen goes to dinner with George Bald-

win. Everyone is excited about the beginning of the war. George, however, can think only of Ellen, and in a fit of rage, he threatens her with a gun. Gus, who is nearby, takes away the gun and hushes up the incident. Jimmy Herf, who had been talking to the bartender, Congo, takes Ellen outside and sends her home in a taxi.

Ellen finally obtains a divorce from John, and Goldweiser renews his attentions. One evening, Ellen and Harry meet Stan dancing with a girl named Pearline. Stan reveals that he and Pearline are now married. Later, Stan comes home drunk, disgusted with his life and with Pearline. He pours kerosene around the apartment and sets fire to it. Pearline returns just in time to see the firefighters carry Stan from the burning building.

Ellen is crushed by Stan's death, for he was the only man she had really loved. Being with Jimmy gives her some comfort because he had been Stan's friend. Jimmy still loves her, however, and he wants to be more than a friend. She tells him that she is going to have Stan's baby and that she wants to leave show business and rear the child; instead, she has an abortion. Ellen and Jimmy go to Europe to do Red Cross work during the war. They marry and return from France with their baby.

Joe O'Keefe comes back from the war with a chip on his shoulder. He feels veterans deserve a bonus because they have lost out on the big money at home. His other reason for feeling bitter is that he caught syphilis somewhere overseas.

George Baldwin's home life was still troubled. Having postwar political ambitions, he turns against his old friend, Gus McNiel, and runs for mayor on a reform ticket. Meanwhile, Jimmy and Ellen drift apart. Jimmy becomes despondent and quits his job. George finally gets a divorce. He proposes to Ellen. Too weary of her muddled life to resist him, she accepts his proposal.

One night, Jimmy is walking the streets when a car pulls up beside him and stops. In it is the Frenchman, Congo, now a wealthy bootlegger. He takes Jimmy home with him and tries to cheer him up. Late one evening after a party, Jimmy wanders down by the river. As he waits for a ferry to take him from Manhattan, he realizes that he feels happy for the first time in many months. Morning finds him walking along a concrete highway, penniless but still happy. He does not know where he is going; he knows only that it will be a long way.

Critical Evaluation:

It was with *Manhattan Transfer*, his third published novel, that John Dos Passos made his first experiments in attempting in a novel to depict an entire society, that of a city that for him embodied the best and worst of American culture. The techniques he began using in this work came to fruition in the trilogy entitled *U.S.A.* (1937). Both *Manhattan Transfer* and *U.S.A.* use the same stripped, staccato style in their narrative passages, and the earlier work foreshadows the later trilogy in its rapid, abrupt shifts among a large and varied cast of characters. The speed of modern life is reflected not only in the style but also in those shifts, and the vividly colorful imagery adds to the effect.

Manhattan Transfer also prefigures *U.S.A.* in telling the stories of many characters while lacking a central plot. Such characters as Ellen Thatcher, Jimmy Herf, and George Baldwin receive more attention than others, but the novel can hardly be said to have a main protagonist. In fact, the central character is New York City. When Jimmy Herf escapes the clutches of the city at the end, he presumably saves his soul by heading for the hinterlands, but he leaves behind forever the city that made his life worth living.

Like other novels that intend to portray entire societies, *Manhattan Transfer* contains characters from many different economic and social levels (although it reflects the time of its creation in failing to include any African Americans among its major figures). The family that adopts Jimmy Herf is distinctly rich and upper class, and Herf's uncle, Jeff Merivale, and other members of that family are very disappointed when as a young man he adopts the profession of newspaper reporter, a line of work much less prestigious than banking or law. It is even worse that Jimmy socializes with theater people and such "riffraff" and with Joe Harland, whom the Merivales no longer acknowledge as a relation.

In the story of Gus and Nellie McNiel, Dos Passos focuses attention on the laboring class and the political life of the city. The railroad accident that the lawyer George Baldwin turns into a modest fortune for Gus enables the onetime milkman to become a minor elected official and to set himself up as a friend of working men and women. Joe O'Keefe, the union organizer, provides another point of view on the struggles between labor and management.

The strongest thread holding the novel together is the story of Ellen Thatcher. Her birth is the focus of the early part of the novel, and her romances and marriages link such diverse characters as Jimmy Herf, the wealthy theatrical backer Harry Goldweiser, her first husband John Oglethorpe, and the lawyer George Baldwin. In his portrayal of Ellen and her activities, Dos Passos is also able to show the realities of the supposedly glamorous world of the theater. When after a series of ill-fated marriages and romances Ellen marries Jimmy Herf in Europe and returns to this country with him and their baby, Dos Passos is able to repudiate the conventional fictional happy ending. For this marriage is no more successful than the preceding ones, and when Jimmy leaves for the hinterlands, he leaves behind his wife and child as well as his career.

Another important aspect of life during the Roaring Twenties is conveyed by the activities of the French sailor named Congo. He jumps ship in New York with a friend and stays in the city, eventually contracting a marriage of convenience with a woman who owns a restaurant where he is working. Congo eventually becomes a wealthy bootlegger, and in narrating his life, Dos Passos depicts the world of the speakeasies. He also includes an episode in which Congo and the men who work for him engage in an exciting battle with the U.S. Coast Guard, which is trying to stop a shipment of illegal liquor.

Manhattan Transfer is in many ways the most successful novel of Dos Passos's long and productive career, and it conveys as well as any novel of the time the frenetic pace of life in New York City during the 1920's. While its scope is narrower than that of the trilogy *U.S.A.*, this fact allows Dos Passos to avoid the sprawling structure of the later work and to provide a tighter focus on the cast of characters. It also was easier for him to convey the sense of life in a single city— even one as large and diverse as New York—than, as he later tried, the sense of life in an entire nation.

Perhaps most important, *Manhattan Transfer* does not carry the strong political message that marks *U.S.A.* The earlier novel makes it clear that Dos Passos's sympathies are with working people rather than with their employers, with those driven to break the law rather than with those who enforce the law, and with outcasts rather than with pillars of the community. His views, however, are not yet informed by a specific doctrine as they were in later years. For its style, its depiction of city life, and its vigor, *Manhattan Transfer* remains one of the genuine classics of the twentieth century novel.

"Critical Evaluation" by John M. Muste

Further Reading

Casey, Janet Galligani. *Dos Passos and the Ideology of the Feminine.* New York: Cambridge University Press, 1998. Discusses Dos Passos's female characters, placing them within the context of ideas about gender that were prevalent in the 1920's and 1930's. Chapter 3 is devoted to an analysis of *Manhattan Transfer.*

Clark, Michael. *Dos Passos's Early Fiction, 1912-1938.* Selinsgrove, Pa.: Susquehanna University Press, 1987. A detailed examination of the works leading up to and including *U.S.A.*, with emphasis on *Manhattan Transfer* as the most significant of Dos Passos's early works.

Harding, Desmond. "*Ulysses* and *Manhattan Transfer*: A Poetics of Transatlantic Literary Modernism." In *Writing the City: Urban Visions and Literary Modernism*. New York: Routledge, 2003. Although the book focuses on James Joyce's depiction of Dublin, this chapter also discusses Dos Passos, comparing how he and Joyce envisioned the city in their novels *Manhattan Transfer* and *Ulysses*, respectively.

Ludington, Townsend. *John Dos Passos: A Twentieth Century Odyssey*. Rev. ed. New York: Carroll & Graf, 1998. A standard biography first published in 1980. The revised edition contains a new introduction. Ludington compre-

hensively chronicles Dos Passos's artistic endeavors and political leanings, and he analyzes *Manhattan Transfer* and the writer's other novels.

Nanney, Lisa. *John Dos Passos Revisited*. New York: Twayne, 1998. An excellent introductory study of Dos Passos's life and works. Nanney draws on previously untapped sources to describe how Dos Passos's own paintings, his interest in the visual arts, and his friendship with artists affected his development as a modernist.

Wagner, Linda. *Dos Passos: Artist as American*. Austin: University of Texas Press, 1979. A good biography emphasizing Dos Passos's deliberate artistry and showing how his aims, as in the later novels, shaped the structure of *Manhattan Transfer*.

Manifesto of Surrealism

Author: André Breton (1896-1966)
First published: Manifeste du surréalisme, 1924
    (English translation, 1969)
Type of work: Essay

The main goal of André Breton's *Manifesto of Surrealism* is to free one's mind from the past and from everyday reality to arrive at truths one has never known. By the time Breton wrote his manifesto, French poets—including Breton himself—and artists had already demonstrated Surrealist techniques in their work. In this sense, Breton was intent on explaining what painters and poets such as Giorgio de Chirico, Joan Miró, Robert Desnos, Max Ernst, and Breton himself had already achieved.

As a medical student in Nantes, France, before World War I, Breton became interested in the theories of Austrian neurologist Sigmund Freud, now known as the founder of psychoanalysis. Later, during the war, Breton was an ambulance driver in the French army and found Freud's ideas useful in helping to treat the wounded. Eventually, Breton and his literary and artistic colleagues contributed to the acceptance in France of Freud and his theories of psychoanalysis, even though Freud's written work itself would not be translated into French until the late 1930's.

In his manifesto, Breton alludes to Freud's ideas about the meaning and significance of dreams and what Freud called the "psychopathology of everyday life," those apparently inadvertent slips of the tongue and other behavioral "mistakes"

that can be traced to states of the subconscious mind. Freud's theories interested Breton largely because they refer to a subconscious life that, Breton believed, constitutes a resource rich in visual and intellectual stimulation.

In Breton's view, one can learn to ascend to perception of a higher reality (the surreal), or more reality, if one can manage to liberate one's psyche from traditional education, the drudgery of work, and the dullness of what is only useful in modern bourgeois culture. To achieve the heightened consciousness to which Breton wants humanity to aspire, those interested can also look to the example set by children, poets, and to a lesser extent, insane persons.

Children, Breton suggests, have not yet learned to stifle their imaginations as most adults have, and successful poets have, similarly, been able to break down the barriers of reason and tradition and have achieved ways of seeing, understanding, and creating that resemble the free, spontaneous imaginative play of children. On the other hand, as one grows up, one's imagination is dulled by the need to make a living and by concern for practical matters. Hence, in the manifesto's opening paragraphs, Breton calls for a return to the freedom of childhood. Furthermore, if the "insane" are, as Breton suggests, victims of their imaginations, one can learn from the mentally ill that hallucinations and illusions are often sources of considerable pleasure and creativity.

Because of Freud, Breton says, human beings can be imagined as heroic explorers who are able to push their investigations beyond the mere facts of reality and the conscious mind and seize dormant strengths buried in the subconscious. Freud's work on the significance of dreams, Breton says, has been particularly crucial in this regard, and the manifesto contains a four-part defense of dreams.

Breton believes that Freud has shown that dreams must be respected as coherent sources of truth and of practical assistance in life. Indeed, despite what is often believed, it may be reality that interferes with dreams rather than the reverse. Hence, Breton recommends that one give oneself up to one's dreams, allowing oneself to be satisfied by what is received from dream states instead of applying the criteria of reason to dreams. Here, Breton's analysis takes on the language of religious fervor when he insists that if one reconciles dreams and reality, one will attain an absolute reality: surreality.

It is important to note, however, that the "surrealist consciousness" about which Breton writes is not uniquely the tool of artists. He believes, to the contrary, that ordinary people will be happier and will be able to solve heretofore difficult problems once they have regained what he sees as a psychic wholeness.

At this point, Breton's manifesto divides itself broadly into two general elements: the development of theory and the accounts of practice, or how theory can be used. One way Surrealist theories can be put into practice is by means of what Breton calls "automatic writing." This process is actually similar to activities of free association or, in the practice of psychology, tests such as the well-known Rorschach test, in which the person being tested is shown various inkblot designs and asked to name objects that he or she thinks those shapes resemble.

As Breton and his friend, poet Robert Desnos, practiced automatic writing, the activity involved writing as quickly as one could whatever came into one's mind, without regard for constraints such as punctuation. The point is to bypass the restrictions of the analytical reasoning processes that one has learned and to which one has grown accustomed. As Breton says, the results of the automatic writing exercise include a new awareness of the relationships between things, words, and images. Automatic writing, which Breton calls "spoken thought," therefore stimulates the creative process by allowing one to create new relationships between things, relationships that one never would have seen by means of the customary ways of thinking.

In a section of the manifesto called "Secrets of the Magic Surrealist Art," Breton offers details of how one might participate in the Surrealist experience of automatic writing. One should make oneself as passive and receptive as possible and avoid thinking about literary criteria or items that others have written. Automatic writing must avoid any preconceived subject matter, and one should give oneself up to what Breton calls the "inexhaustible flow" of one's inner voice.

Out of this experience come Surrealist images, which Breton likens to images that come from drug-induced mental states. Surrealist images result from the fortuitous juxtaposition of two disparate elements, such as "stream" and "song," "daylight" and "white napkin," or "the world" and "a purse." Such juxtapositions, it is to be noted, have nothing to do with reason, which, Breton says, is limited in this process to observing and appreciating the work of the subconscious. Eventually, according to Breton, with the help of automatic writing, one arrives at an ideal realm, a "supreme reality," where even one's reason will recognize that one's knowledge has been extended greatly, opposites have been reconciled, and the mind as a whole has made extraordinary advances.

The tangible results of this automatic writing led to Breton and poet Philippe Soupault's idea of Surrealism. In the manifesto, Breton defines Surrealism as pure psychic automatism that allows one to express—either verbally, in writing, or in some other fashion—the true functioning of thought without regard to any concern for morality or aesthetics.

Breton argues that imaginative literature, such as the novels of British writer Matthew Lewis, is superior to realistic literature, in which the author carefully details physical description and, in effect, tells too much. Breton thinks that poetry and imaginative literature are worthy means of escape from the chores of daily reality. In fact, Breton says, the poet is like God, proposing and disposing of his or her own spiritual life and achieving a sense of fulfillment that reality steals from most people. He offers a list of writers, past and present, who have represented or represent Surrealist ideals: Jonathan Swift, the Marquis de Sade, Victor Hugo, and Arthur Rimbaud, as well as Victor Jarry, Leon Fargue, and Pierre Reverdy, among others. In art, Breton points to such painters as Pablo Picasso, Henri Matisse, Gustave Moreau, Georges Seurat, and Marcel Duchamp as major figures in the development of visual Surrealism. Dozens of women, too, were part of its early development, and most have been left out of the histories of Surrealism. Women active in Surrealism in the 1920's include Denise Lévy, Simone Kahn Breton, Nadja, Fanny Beznos, Suzanne Muzard, and Valentine Penrose. Breton believed, however, that Desnos was the ideal Surrealist artist, submitting to numerous experiments and perfecting the ability to follow his train of thought orally, to "speak Surrealist."

While stopping short of recommending the application of the free-association spontaneity of automatic writing to action, Breton nevertheless emphasizes that the great discoveries of science, for example, will be made by truly independent minds, those persons who have transcended the past by means other than what he calls the "roads of reason." Here, Breton deals with genius, as embodied by those scholars and scientists who work, he suggests, without a clear plan of exploration, striking out instead into the unknown. As for crime, where individuals might plead a kind of Surrealist lack of responsibility for what they have done, Breton does imply that a new moral order may one day replace the present ideas of right and wrong. This might happen, he suggests, once Surrealist methods gain widespread favor outside science and the arts.

Ultimately, Breton's *Manifesto of Surrealism* has perhaps had less influence, especially in the United States, than Surrealism's expressions in the visual arts. Spanish painter Salvador Dalí came to best represent Surrealism in the popular imagination in the second half of the twentieth century. Dalí's strange paintings, such as the famous *The Persistence of Memory*, feature mirage-like landscapes in which the painter placed, as Breton had suggested, objects that ordinarily have nothing to do with one another or that exhibit bizarre properties. Oddly enough, Dalí's melting watches, dead trees, and insects piqued the imagination of a large group of art lovers, and he became an international celebrity. Breton did not, however, approve of Dalí's courting of public favor in such a theatrical way, and Breton eventually expressed his disdain of Dalí's work and public image. Nevertheless, Dalí's painting and his escapades must surely account in large part for the popular currency of the term "Surrealist," which entered the everyday vocabulary of most Americans as synonymous with the extraordinarily unexpected or shocking in a dreamlike or nightmarish way.

Gordon Walters

Further Reading

Alquié, Ferdinand. *The Philosophy of Surrealism.* Translated by Bernard Waldrop. 1965. Reprint. Ann Arbor: University of Michigan Press, 1969. Alquié examines the ideological origins and content of Breton's ideas and those of other Surrealist writers. Chapters 3 and 4 deal in great part with Breton's manifestos and how their ideas relate particularly to poetry.

Balakian, Anna. *André Breton: Magus of Surrealism.* New York: Oxford University Press, 1971. Balakian's biography devotes a long section to Breton's two Surrealist manifestos. Equally thorough studies of Breton's other writings are here as well, along with an entire chapter on Surrealism and painting.

_____. *Surrealism: The Road to the Absolute.* 3d ed. Chicago: University of Chicago Press, 1986. Balakian traces the development of Surrealism and considers its application to the visual arts. Even more interesting perhaps is that the author sees a relationship between Surrealism and the hypotheses of nuclear physics. Includes an updated introduction.

Caws, Mary Ann. *André Breton.* New York: Twayne, 1996. In this updated edition, originally published in 1974, Caws focuses on newer aspects of Breton's work and adopts another point of view. Focuses on Breton's texts, including his manifestos, and not on his life or the history of Surrealism, although it includes a brief introduction to the basic tenets of Surrealism.

Charvet, P. E., ed. *The Twentieth Century, 1870-1940.* Vol. 5 in *A Literary History of France.* New York: Barnes & Noble, 1967. Part 2, chapter 10 of this history focuses on Surrealism and poetry, beginning with the transition from Dada to Surrealism and Breton's manifesto of 1924. This section includes a brief but pointed reference to Sigmund Freud and Surrealism.

Cruickshank, John, ed. *The Twentieth Century.* Vol. 6 in *French Literature and Its Background.* New York: Oxford University Press, 1970. Includes a chapter on Surrealism by R. Short, which is especially good on the historical and literary background of the movement. The volume also includes an extensive bibliography on Breton and Surrealism.

Durozoi, Gérard. *History of the Surrealist Movement.* Translated by Alison Anderson. Chicago: University of Chicago Press, 2002. Durozoi, a French philosopher and art critic, provides a voluminous history of Surrealist art and literature, heavily illustrated and spanning the movement's global reach. The book looks at Breton's life and his participation in and influence on the movement. Chapter 2 focuses on the publication and contents of the *Manifesto of Surrealism.*

Manon Lescaut

Author: Abbé Prévost (1697-1763)
First published: 1731, as *Histoire du chevalier des*
  Grieux et de Manon Lescaut (English translation,
  1734); revised, 1753 (English translation, 1786)
Type of work: Novel
Type of plot: Sentimental
Time of plot: 1700
Locale: France; New Orleans, Louisiana

Principal characters:
MANON LESCAUT, a courtesan
THE CHEVALIER DES GRIEUX, her lover
TIBERGE, his friend
MONSIEUR DE G—— M——, a wealthy nobleman
MONSIEUR LESCAUT, Manon's brother

The Story:

The young Chevalier des Grieux, a student of philosophy in Amiens, becomes friendly with a fellow student named Tiberge. One day, he stands idly with his friend and watches the arrival of the Arras coach. Among the passengers is a beautiful young woman, who attracts the chevalier's attention. Politely introducing himself, he learns that her name is Manon Lescaut and that she has come to Amiens under the protection of an elderly man. Against her will, she is to enter a convent. She accepts the chevalier's offer to set her free from that fate, and after skillfully and untruthfully disposing of her escort, she accompanies the young student to an inn. They plan to flee to Paris the next day. Tiberge argues with his friend against this folly, but the chevalier is hopelessly infatuated. In Paris, he and Manon take a furnished apartment, where for three weeks they are absorbed in each other.

The idyll ends when the young lover discovers that his mistress has also bestowed her affections on Monsieur de B——. The chevalier's love for Manon is so great, however, that he forgives her. Then three lackeys, sent by the chevalier's father, come to the apartment and take the young man home. There his father tries in vain to persuade him that Manon has behaved treacherously. Finally, the father locks his son in his room for six weeks. During this time, Tiberge visits him, bringing him news that Manon is being kept at the expense of Monsieur de B——. Tiberge persuades the young man to enroll at the Seminary of Saint-Supplice as a student of theology. With his father's permission, he enters the school and becomes an outstanding student. Manon is present to hear his declamation at the public disputation at the Sorbonne, and after the ceremonies she visits him. A single passionate embrace makes him forget his future in the Church. The chevalier escapes from his school without money, and Manon furnishes the funds for them to set up quarters at Chaillot, outside Paris.

Then begins a life of extravagance and riotous living far beyond their slender means. In Paris, they meet Manon's brother, Monsieur Lescaut, of the Royal Guards, who does not scruple to install himself in their house. When a fire destroys all of their money and possessions, the brother suggests that Manon sell her charms to some freehanded nobleman. The chevalier rejects this proposal but consents to become a professional gambler to support Manon. He borrows enough money from Tiberge to begin his career as a card cheat. For a time his luck holds, but their period of prosperity ends when a maid and a valet flee with all the valuable possessions of the new household. Urged by her brother, Manon consents to become the mistress of the old and wealthy Monsieur de G—— M——, who had promised her a house, servants, and a large sum of money.

The young couple decide to play on Manon's protector by introducing the chevalier into the household as her brother. Having duped the man to make his settlement on Manon, they run away with the jewels and money he had given her. They are followed by the police, apprehended, and imprisoned, Manon at the Hôpital Général and the chevalier at Saint-Lazare.

Once lodged at Saint-Lazare, the chevalier begins to plan his escape. He cultivates his superiors and makes a show of reading theology. M. de G—— M——, hearing of the chevalier's studious habits, visits him; but when the young man hears, for the first time, that Manon also is imprisoned, he seizes the old man by the throat. The monks stop the fight and save the old man's life.

The chevalier now writes to Tiberge, asking his old friend to visit Saint-Lazare. He entrusts to Tiberge a note addressed to M. Lescaut. Using a pistol that Manon's brother brought him soon afterward, the chevalier escapes, killing a turnkey in his flight. Later, by bribing the attendants at the hospital, he arranges for Manon's escape. Wearing men's clothing, Manon is safely conveyed to her brother's house, but just as the happy pair descend from the carriage, M. Lescaut is shot by a man whose fortune the guardsman had won at cards. Manon and the chevalier flee to the inn at Chaillot to escape apprehension for the murder.

In Paris the next day the chevalier borrows a hundred pistoles from Tiberge. He also meets M. de T——, a friend, whom he invites to Chaillot for supper. During the meal the son of old M. de G—— M—— arrives at the inn. The impetuous young chevalier wants to kill him at once to get revenge on the father, but M. de T—— persuades him rather to meet young de G—— M—— in a friendly manner over the supper table. The young man is charmed with Manon; like his father, he offers to maintain her handsomely. Manon accepts his rich presents, but she and her lover plan to deceive the gullible young man and avenge themselves on his father. The chevalier plans to have street ruffians capture and hold the infatuated young man while Manon and the chevalier enjoy the supper and the bed de G—— M—— has arranged for himself and his mistress. The young man's father learns of the scheme, however, and Manon and the chevalier are surprised by the police, who hurry them off to the Chatelet.

The young chevalier now appeals to his father, whose influence is great enough to secure his son's release. He refuses to interest himself in Manon, however, and she is sentenced to exile on the next shipload of convicts to be sent to the penal colony in Louisiana. After a bungled attempt to rescue her from the prison guards, the chevalier accompanies his mistress on the trip from the prison to Havre-de-Grace. He also gains permission to accompany her on the voyage to America. On board ship and on their arrival in New Orleans, they pass as husband and wife.

In New Orleans, they settle in a rude shelter. After the chevalier secures honorable employment, Manon desires above all things that they become legally husband and wife. The chevalier appeals to the governor for permission to marry and admits his earlier deceit. The governor refuses, for his nephew, M. Synnelet, has fallen in love with Manon. As a result, the chevalier fights a duel with Synnelet. Thinking that he has killed his opponent, he and Manon leave the colony, but on the journey Manon, ill from fatigue, dies in the middle of a vast plain. The chevalier is heartbroken. Tiberge, who followed his friend to America, persuades him to return to France. There the chevalier resolves to turn to God in penance.

Critical Evaluation:

Most critics agree that the mercurial life of Abbé Prévost contributed to the creation of *Manon Lescaut*. After vacillating between the priesthood and the military and being satisfied with neither, he launched in the 1720's one of the most prolific careers of the century as novelist, editor, translator, journalist, and chronicler of travel accounts.

After completing four volumes of *Le Philosophe anglais: Ou, Les Mémoires de Cleveland* (1732-1739; *The Life and Entertaining Adventures of Mr. Cleveland, Natural Son of Oliver Cromwell*, 1734, 1753), Prévost began to travel between England and Holland. Apparently he was in debt in each country, possibly as the result of an uncertain relationship with a reputed Madame Lenki. In 1734, he was absolved of all clerical transgressions and received a sinecure at Evreux, which he used as a point of departure for Paris and Holland. In 1740, he traveled, again under mysterious circumstances, to Belgium and Germany. In 1746, he settled at Chaillot and continued his remarkable productivity. Church authorities rewarded his efforts by adding to his endowment.

In addition to *Manon Lescaut*, two other works by Prévost—*The Story of a Modern Greek* (1740) and *The Journal of an Honest Man* (1745)—belong in the genre of the sentimental French novel. Two themes in these novels, which are also present in the English literature that Prévost translated by such writers as Samuel Richardson, Frances Sheridan, and John Dryden, are passionate, tragic love and redemption through suffering.

Manon Lescaut was published in 1731 as the seventh volume of *Mémoires et aventures d'un homme de qualité, qui s'est retiré du monde* (1728-1731; *Memoirs of a Man of Quality After His Retirement from the World*, 1738), a rambling collection of quixotic tales and personal adventures narrated by the Marquis de Renoncour. The commonly used abridged title tends to give Manon an importance she was probably not meant to have. Renoncour introduces the Chevalier des Grieux, the protagonist of the story, but he himself does not participate in the events and he merely acts as an impartial observer of the various picaresque adventures—storms at sea, abductions, chance encounters and recognitions, and tranquil moments shattered by action and suspense. All of this is revealed from the marquis' point of view, and it is therefore difficult to ascertain Manon's response to her situation.

Prévost combines realism—his use of the social types, names of places, and the importance of money—with pre-Romantic sentimentality. This combination allows the novel to operate on several levels. Even though Manon is at times promiscuous and des Grieux is an impetuous social deviant, they live without shame in naïve defiance of aristocratic conventions. The spirit of the novel is defined by sensuality, emphasis on living in the present, and restless frivolity. Manon and des Grieux play the following psychological roles: jilted lover, faithful husband, provider, brother and sister, mistress-mother, and abandoned child.

Perhaps this explains the magnetism of *Manon Lescaut* to each new generation of readers. Manon was the adopted heroine of the nineteenth century; she was rhapsodized as an image of enigmatic femininity. The idealistic reader might argue that Manon's originally pure love for des Grieux was corrupted by the harmful influence of civilization. Love is dependent on economics in the capitalist marketplace. Manon is not heartless or predatory, but she is mostly interested in maintaining a certain way of life. Perhaps the need for emotional security represents her deepest impulse. She certainly takes enormous risks to attain it. The prison scenes, the deportation of prostitutes, and the gambling dens remind the reader that a heavy penalty awaited those who failed to bargain successfully with fate.

For this reason, *Manon Lescaut* has continued to receive praise from influential writers, and it has inspired a sequel, several dramatic versions, and three famous operas—Daniel-François-Esprit Auber's *Manon Lescaut* (1856), Jules Massenet's *Manon* (1884), and Giacomo Puccini's *Manon Lescaut* (1893). This cluster of interpretations has crystallized into a composite image of des Grieux and Manon as archetypal lovers.

It is equally instructive to regard *Manon Lescaut* as a product of its times. The age of uncertainty produced by the regency of Louis XV, the South Sea bankruptcy scam in England, and the breakdown of the French economy under John Law had literary repercussions. *Manon Lescaut* promotes love as an innocent passion in a reckless moral climate in which ethical judgment has become dependent on situation. Des Grieux, a second son, is relegated to a choice between the Knights of Malta or the seminary. Manon, not commanding a dowry, is sent to a convent. Des Grieux's infatuation for her leads to criminality, yet his own and Manon's delinquency seems beyond his comprehension. This psychotic indifference to his past is contrasted with Tiberge's personality—the Christian alter ego—and by disastrous interventions through the heavy hand of parental or legal authority.

Prévost's style depends largely on the presentation of contrasting moods and images. The peaceful and retired life is juxtaposed with the Parisian demimonde. Des Grieux's fervor is counterbalanced by Tiberge's spiritual calm. The courtesan and her paramour see their love extinguished in a stark, indeterminate setting, geographically different but emotionally identical to their origins. Prévost develops the timeless motifs of pleasure, luxury, amusement, loss, bereavement, and obsession with economy of language, unaffected lyricism, and classical reserve. These qualities are even more evident in the 1953 revision of the first edition, which eliminated superfluous language and softened the emotional effect.

French historian Jules Michelet claimed that *Manon Lescaut* evokes a nostalgia for the manners and mores of the ancien régime. In that context, Manon and des Grieux resemble figures in a painting in which the richly polished, cinematic interior scenes are set against the turbulent background of eighteenth century life in Europe and the New World. Whether Manon is viewed as siren or saint, des Grieux as hero or misfit, their literary reputation as quasi-mythical, amoral lovers continues to be affirmed.

"Critical Evaluation" by Robert J. Frail

Further Reading

Auerbach, Erich. *Mimesis: The Representation of Reality in Western Literature*. Translated by W. R. Trask. New ed. Princeton, N.J.: Princeton University Press, 2003. A legendary study of Prévost's artistic technique, originally published in 1953. Auerbach uses *Manon Lescaut* as an intellectual springboard to evaluate a wide range of Enlightenment configurations. A vigorous, thought-provoking analysis of erotic sentimentality in literature. The 2003 edition includes a new introduction.

Coleman, Patrick. *Reparative Realism: Mourning and Modernity in the French Novel, 1730-1830*. Geneva: Librairie Droz, 1998. Coleman examines *Manon Lescaut* and novels by Jean-Jacques Rousseau, Benjamin Constant, Madame de Staël, and Honoré de Balzac to describe how grief and bereavement were handled in eighteenth and nineteenth century French fiction.

Gilroy, James P. *The Romantic Manon and Des Grieux: Images of Prévost's Heroine and Hero in Nineteenth-Century French Literature*. Sherbrooke, Que.: Éditions Naaman, 1980. A compelling and evocative study that celebrates Manon's status as the enigmatic darling of French literature. Traces the universality of Manon and des Grieux as archetypal lovers who transcend barriers of time and place.

Harkness, Nigel. "Negotiating Masculinity: Nineteenth-Century Re-interpretations of *Manon Lescaut*." In *Depicting Desire: Gender, Sexuality, and the Family in Nineteenth Century Europe—Literary and Artistic Perspectives*, edited by Rachel Langford. New York: Peter Lang, 2005. Harkness's study, originally presented at a conference in 2001, reassesses the depiction of gender, sexuality, and family in Prévost's novel.

Kory, Odile A. *Subjectivity and Sensitivity in the Novels of the Abbé Prévost.* Montreal: Didier, 1972. Somewhat rambling and discursive, but points out the importance of *Manon Lescaut* as an arranging element in eighteenth century French fiction. Discusses the timeless dimensions of morality, psychology, and the quest for identity in the novel.

Mander, Jenny. *Circles of Learning: Narratology and the Eighteenth Century French Novel.* Oxford, England: Voltaire Foundation, 1999. Mander's study of narration and autobiography in the eighteenth century French novel focuses on works by Abbé Prévost and Marivaux. Includes bibliographical references and an index.

Rabine, Leslie W. *Reading the Romantic Heroine: Text, History, Ideology.* Ann Arbor, Mich.: UMI Research Press, 1995. A lively and engaging study that emphasizes the pivotal importance of *Manon Lescaut* in pre-Romantic fiction.

Segal, Naomi. *The Unintended Reader: Feminism and "Manon Lescaut."* New York: Cambridge University Press, 1986. A review of critical reactions to *Manon Lescaut* over a two-hundred-year period, with an emphasis on the phenomenon of seduction by language. Segal attempts to apply Freudian Oedipal analogies to issues of female autonomy, identity, and self-esteem.

Man's Fate

Author: André Malraux (1901-1976)
First published: La Condition humaine, 1933 (English translation, 1934)
Type of work: Novel
Type of plot: Social realism
Time of plot: 1927
Locale: Shanghai, China

Principal characters:
CH'EN, a Chinese terrorist
KYO, a Communist organizer of French and Japanese parentage
GISORS, Kyo's father
MAY, Kyo's German wife
BARON DE CLAPPIQUE, a French adventurer
KATOV, a Russian revolutionist
HEMMELRICH, a German revolutionist
FERRAL, a French businessman
KONIG, the chief of Chiang Kai-shek's police

The Story:

The Reds, a revolutionary group with a nucleus of Moscow agents, have made a temporary alliance with Chiang Kai-shek, their immediate object being to control Shanghai with the help of the Kuomintang. The alliance, however, is an uneasy one, for neither side trusts the other. The Reds had completed their plans to seize Shanghai, ostensibly as part of Chiang Kai-shek's campaign, but they intend to put a Communist in control before the Blue army arrives. On their part, the Blues hope to use the Communists to seize the city and afterward disperse the revolutionaries.

Ch'en, the terrorist, stands ready to strike through the mosquito netting and kill the sleeper in the bed. Nerving himself for his first murder, he plunges his dagger into the man's heart. Quickly from the dead man he takes a paper that will authorize the delivery of arms now aboard the *Shantung*, at anchor in the harbor. The Reds count on these arms to seize control of the city before government troops arrive.

Ch'en takes the document to Hemmelrich's phonograph shop, where Kyo is waiting. There they all congratulate him—Kyo, Katov, and Hemmelrich. Kyo and Katov test their new code of paralleled phonograph records. One record gives an innocent language lesson, the other a loud hiss that covers all but the key words on the first record. Satisfied with their work, they plan a final check of their revolutionary cells. Hemmelrich refuses to go with them; his wife and child are sick.

Kyo and Katov visit their two hundred units. A general strike at noon will paralyze the city. At the same time, saboteurs will wreck the railway so that the government cannot send reinforcements from the battlefront. Other groups will take over police stations and army posts and seize all firearms. With the grenades already on hand, they will be equipped to resist even tanks.

Kyo goes to the Black Cat, a nightclub where he knows he

will find de Clappique. The Frenchman is drunk, but he has to be trusted. De Clappique is commissioned to take a forged order to the *Shantung*, directing the ship to shift anchorage. Tired and tense, Kyo goes home. Gisors, his father, is still awake, and Kyo tells him a few details of the plan. Then May, Kyo's wife, comes home exhausted from her hospital work. She is one of the few women doctors in all Shanghai, a woman with advanced views on marriage relationships. She and Kyo quarrel because of her affair with another doctor. During the quarrel, de Clappique visits to report that the *Shantung* has moved. A messenger recalls Kyo to headquarters.

Dressed as government soldiers, Kyo and Katov, with ten others, board the *Shantung* and get the arms, but only after seizing the captain and holding him prisoner. Now the revolutionaries can plan with confidence. Meanwhile Ferral, head of the French Chamber of Commerce, decides to throw his support to Chiang Kai-shek. After giving orders to send funds to the Blues, he returns with his mistress, Valerie. It is arranged that she will see him the following night at her hotel. He is to bring her a pet bird in a cage. At the appointed time Ferral asks for Valerie at the hotel desk. To his surprise, she is out. A young Englishman is also waiting for her with a caged bird. As revenge, Ferral buys the entire stock of a pet store—forty birds and a kangaroo—and sets it loose in Valerie's room.

The uprising takes place as planned. Ch'en seizes one police station with ease and arms his small band. The second station is better defended, and grenades fail to dislodge officers barricaded on the top floor. Ch'en sets fire to the building, killing the resisters as well as his own wounded comrades.

The feeble central government cannot fight both Chiang and the Reds at the same time. While the government forces are occupied with the Blues, the Reds easily take control of the city. Two days later, the Blues, under Chiang, approach Shanghai. The general had been shrewd enough to send his first division, composed largely of Communists, to another front; consequently, the Communists find themselves confronting an unsympathetic Blue army, which in turn takes over the city. Many of the Communists are arrested. When Moscow orders all armed Communists to surrender their weapons to Chiang's police, dissension breaks out among the Reds. Many of the Chinese desert the Moscow party and embark on a terroristic campaign of their own.

Ch'en conceives the idea that he must kill Chiang to free China. He lays in wait with two companions to throw a bomb into the general's car. His first attempt having failed, Ch'en goes to Hemmelrich's shop. Hemmelrich refuses to shelter

him. In a second attempt, Ch'en throws himself with his bomb under the automobile. The car is wrecked and Ch'en is killed, but Chiang is not in the car.

Chiang's police destroy Hemmelrich's shop, accidentally killing his wife and baby. Believing his cowardice is the cause of Ch'en's action and the subsequent riot, Hemmelrich seizes some grenades and joins the rioters. All are killed except Hemmelrich, who escapes by murdering an officer and fleeing in his uniform.

Now in complete control, Chiang's police chief, Konig, rounds up the Communists, and Katov is among them. When the word goes out that Kyo is to be arrested, Gisors begs de Clappique to intervene because the baron is Konig's good friend. Instead of warning Kyo, de Clappique lingers in a gambling house until after Kyo has been arrested. Later, de Clappique goes to Konig to ask for Kyo's release. The Frenchman is given only forty-eight hours to leave China. In prison, Katov and Kyo each have cyanide tablets. Kyo poisons himself, but Katov gives half his tablet to each of two panic-stricken prisoners and goes to his execution with his revolutionary group.

Each of the survivors seeks safety in his own way. Gisors returns to Japan to teach painting. May goes to Moscow to practice medicine. By disguising himself, de Clappique gets aboard the same French liner that is taking Ferral back to France. So the Communists and their sympathizers are destroyed by relentless Chiang and the vacillating policy of Moscow. Yet there is good news from China for the survivors; the quiet work of revolution has already started again.

Critical Evaluation:

In this novel, depicting the aborted Communist Revolution in China in 1927, André Malraux presents three types of revolutionaries. Each is attracted to the revolution for different reasons and reacts to the events in a distinctive manner. Ch'en, the terrorist, is shown in the opening scene of the novel in the process of committing his first murder. This experience is so intense that he feels himself separated from those who have been killed. His sense of isolation leads him to believe that individual acts of terrorism are superior to any other form of revolutionary action. He ultimately comes to the conclusion that the only way to have the revolution is to kill Chiang. He initially attempts to perform this act with the aid of two comrades, but the attempt fails. He then decides to perform the deed alone. Ironically, he is killed while throwing himself with a grenade on a car he believes to be occupied by Chiang. Although Chiang is not in the car, Ch'en has died a death consistent with his beliefs, a death that has given his life meaning.

Kyo is the theorist who finds it difficult to reconcile his belief in Marxist theory with the realities of the revolution. For example, although he theoretically believes that no person can be the property of another and that love is free, he is jealous when his wife, May, tells him that she has slept with another man. Kyo is drawn to the revolution because of his belief in the need for human dignity. He loses faith in Communist theory when he finds out (during a trip to Hankow) that the leaders of the party are willing to betray the people on orders from Moscow. Kyo believes that Communist theory is only of value if it helps the masses to live a more dignified life; he cannot reconcile his beliefs with the political machinations that confront him. During a brief stay in jail, he sees human beings submitted to degrading humiliation. When offered a choice of life or death, he chooses death with dignity (suicide by taking cyanide) rather than life with humiliation. His death, although very different from that of Ch'en, is consistent with his life.

Katov is the most experienced of the three, for he fought in the Russian Revolution. Unlike Ch'en, who cherished his solitude, Katov cherishes his solidarity with his comrades. Like the others, his death is consistent with his life. Although he, like Kyo, has a cyanide pill, Katov chooses to share his pill with two young frightened comrades. Since there is only enough cyanide to kill two men, his gift of the capsule is the supreme sacrifice, for Katov faces death by being thrown alive into the boiler of a train engine. He believes that his sacrifice gives his life meaning, for through his sacrifice he achieves the fraternity for which he fought in the revolution.

Although these three men are very different, they are similar in their desire to join the revolution as a way to give meaning to their lives. Each man acts as a revolutionary and dies as a revolutionary in a manner consistent with his beliefs.

Further Reading

Bloom, Harold, ed. *André Malraux's "Man's Fate."* New York: Chelsea House, 1988. Collection of critical essays about the novel arranged in chronological order of their publication.

Boak, Denis. *"La Condition humaine."* In *André Malraux.* Oxford, England: Clarendon Press, 1968. A judicious consideration of the novel within the perspective of Malraux's development as a writer. Emphasizes its metaphysical rather than political aspects. Provides detailed consideration of imagery and characterization.

Frohock, W. M. *André Malraux and the Tragic Imagination.* Stanford, Calif.: Stanford University Press, 1952. Classic consideration of Malraux's fictional canon. The chapter on *Man's Fate* analyzes Malraux's style, the rhythm and pattern of the novel's action, its characterization, and the thematic and aesthetic effects of the characters' fates.

Harris, Geoffrey. *André Malraux: A Reassessment.* New York: St. Martin's Press, 1996. An updated, balanced look at Malraux's works. Harris argues that Malraux's writings are "nonideological," express an "elitist humanism," and strive to transform mundane human activity into something more sublime. Includes bibliographical references and an index.

Hiddleston, J. A. *Malraux: "La Condition humaine."* London: Edward Arnold, 1973. Useful but somewhat critical of Malraux. Focuses on Malraux's concern with the individual's ability to question the world, which leads to his characters' recurrent dilemma of whether to be or to do. Organized into two sections, the first dealing with characters and themes, the second with thought and form.

Lyotard, Jean François. *Signed, Malraux.* Translated by Robert Harvey. Minneapolis: University of Minnesota Press, 1999. A complex, intellectual, and unconventional biography by an important French critic. Lyotard attempts to deconstruct Malraux's life by demythologizing his image, and he describes the contrasts between Malraux's life and work.

Shorley, Christopher. *"La Condition humaine": Malraux.* London: Grant & Cutler, 2003. This work provides a summary of critical literature about *Man's Fate.*

Todd, Olivier. *Malraux: A Life.* Translated by Joseph West. New York: Knopf, 2005. Originally published in French in 2001, this biography is a critical analysis of the writer's life and work. Todd is especially good at describing Malraux's charismatic personality and his confused relationships with women.

Mansfield Park

Author: Jane Austen (1775-1817)
First published: 1814
Type of work: Novel
Type of plot: Domestic realism
Time of plot: Early nineteenth century
Locale: Northamptonshire, England

Principal characters:
FANNY PRICE, a poor relation at Mansfield Park
SIR THOMAS BERTRAM, the owner of Mansfield Park
LADY BERTRAM, his wife
TOM,
EDMUND,
MARIA, and
JULIA BERTRAM, Fanny's cousins
MRS. NORRIS, a busybody aunt
HENRY CRAWFORD, a self-centered young gentleman
MARY CRAWFORD, his sister
MR. RUSHWORTH, Maria Bertram's suitor
MR. YATES, a young man of fashion

The Story:

The three Ward sisters have each fared differently in marriage. One married a wealthy baronet, one married a poor lieutenant of the marines, and the last married a clergyman. The wealthiest of the sisters, Lady Bertram, agrees at the instigation of her clerical sister, Mrs. Norris, to care for one of the unfortunate sister's nine children. Accordingly, a shy, sensitive, ten-year-old Fanny Price comes to make her home at Mansfield Park. Among her four Bertram cousins Tom, Edmund, Maria, and Julia—Fanny finds a real friend only in Edmund. The others usually ignore her except when she can be of use to them, but Edmund comforts and advises her. He alone seems to recognize that she possesses cleverness, grace, and a pleasant disposition. Besides Edmund's attentions, Fanny receives some of a very different kind from her selfish and hypocritical Aunt Norris, who constantly calls unnecessary attention to Fanny's dependent position.

When Fanny is fifteen years old, Sir Thomas Bertram goes to Antigua to look after some business affairs. His oldest son, who is inclined to extravagance and dissipation, goes with him, and the family is left to Edmund's and Lady Bertram's care. During Sir Thomas's absence, his older daughter, Maria, becomes engaged to Mr. Rushworth, a young man who is rich and well-connected but extremely stupid.

Another event of importance is the arrival in the village of Mary and Henry Crawford, the sister and brother of Mrs. Grant, whose husband has become the rector after the death of Mr. Norris. Both the Bertram girls like Henry immensely; since Maria is engaged, however, he rightfully "belongs" to Julia. They also become close friends with Mary Crawford,

who in turn attracts both Tom, now returned from abroad, and Edmund.

Fanny regrets the Crawfords' arrival, for she sees that Edmund, whom she herself loves, was falling in love with the shallow, worldly Mary, and that her cousin, Maria, is carrying on a most unseemly flirtation with Henry. The less observant, like Mrs. Norris, see only what they wish to see and insist that Henry is paying particular attention to Julia.

At the suggestion of Mr. Yates, a pleasure-loving friend of Tom, the young people decide to put on some private theatricals; they choose for their entertainment the sentimental play *Lovers' Vows* (1798) by Elizabeth Inchbald. Fanny opposes the scheme from the start, for she knows Sir Thomas would have disapproved. Edmund tries to dissuade the others but finally lets himself be talked into taking a part because there are not enough men for all the roles. Rehearsals and preparations go forward, and the plan grows more elaborate as it progresses. The unexpected return of Sir Thomas, however, puts an end to the rehearsals. The house is soon cleared of all signs of theatrical activity, and of Mr. Yates, whose trifling, affected ways Sir Thomas dislikes immediately.

Maria, who is willing to break her engagement to Mr. Rushworth, had hoped her father's return would bring a declaration from Henry. Instead of declaring himself, however, he announces his departure for a stay in Bath. Maria's pride is hurt, but she resolves that Henry Crawford should never know she had taken their flirtation seriously. She is duly married to Mr. Rushworth.

Julia goes to Brighton with the Rushworths. With both the Bertram sisters gone, Henry begins an idle flirtation with Fanny, which ends with his falling in love with her. Her beloved brother, William, has just visited her at Mansfield Park. One of Henry's plans for winning Fanny's favor is a scheme for getting a promotion for William in the navy. Although Fanny is grateful for this favor, she promptly refuses him when he proposes. In doing so, she incurs the serious displeasure of her uncle, Sir Thomas, who regards the sentiments that made her turn down such an advantageous match as sheer perversity. Even Edmund encourages her to change her mind, for he is too preoccupied with his attachment to Mary Crawford to guess that Fanny has more than a cousinly regard for him. Edmund has just been ordained as a clergyman, a step that Mary Crawford ridicules, and he is not sure she will accept him as a husband. He persists in believing, however, that her frivolous dislike of the clergy is only a trait she acquired from her worldly friends; he believes that he can bring about a change in Mary's opinion.

About this time, Fanny is sent to Portsmouth to visit her family and to be reminded of what poverty is like. The stay is a depressing one, for she finds her family, with the exception of William, disorderly and ill-bred by the standards of Mansfield Park. In addition, several catastrophes occur at Mansfield Park to make her wish she could be of help there. Tom, the oldest son, has such a serious illness that his recovery is uncertain; Maria, now Mrs. Rushworth, has run away with Henry, who forgot his love for Fanny long enough to commit this irrevocable mistake; and Julia elopes with Mr. Yates. Only now, crushed under this series of blows, does the Bertram family at last realize Fanny's value and dearness to them. She is welcomed back to Mansfield Park with a tenderness that touches her deeply.

Mrs. Norris, as spiteful as ever, says that if Fanny had accepted Henry Crawford as she should have, he would never have run away with Maria. Sir Thomas, however, gives Fanny credit for seeing Henry's character more clearly than he had, and he forgives her for having refused Henry. He blames himself for Maria's downfall, for he realizes he had never taken the trouble to know his children well.

Nevertheless, good comes from all this evil. Tom's illness sobers him, and he proves a better son thereafter. Although not a great match for Julia, Mr. Yates has more income and fewer debts than Sir Thomas had anticipated, and he seems inclined to settle down to quiet domesticity. Henry and Maria separate after spending a few unhappy months together. Sir Thomas refuses to receive her at Mansfield Park but provides a home for her in another part of the country. Mrs. Norris lives with her favorite niece, to the great relief of everyone at Mansfield Park.

Edmund finally realizes Mary Crawford's frivolous and worldly nature when he sees how lightly she treats the affair of his sister and her brother. Her levity shocks him and makes it easier for him to give up thoughts of such an unsuitable marriage. Eventually, he falls in love with the cousin who had loved him for so long a time. Fanny and he are married and move to the parsonage near Mansfield Park.

Critical Evaluation:

Jane Austen's *Mansfield Park* explores important moral themes woven into a seeming Cinderella story of a poor girl taken in and then neglected by proud, wealthy relatives. Fanny Price is slighted by three of her four confident, energetic cousins. While they pursue their favorite activities, she is required to run endless errands and perform tedious tasks for her aunts. Having little share in the friendships of her cousins, she is happiest alone in her room, a cold, cheerless place furnished with old, cast-off things. Small, timid, and seemingly docile, Fanny does not seem to fit the image of the romantic heroine, but she grows in strength of body and mind as the novel progresses. By the end of the story, her strength of character and unshakable moral convictions win for her the praise, love, and social position she desires.

When the story opens, the unfortunate young cousin from a large, poor family is terrified by the grandeur of Mansfield Park. After she becomes accustomed to life there, she enjoys staying in the background, assisting her aunts and meekly accepting her inferior position in a luxurious household. She feels content with her place in the world. While most of her relatives think her boring and stupid, cousin Edmund, who seeks out her friendship, grows to respect and care for her. With his kind support, she overcomes her timidity to ride horseback for outdoor exercise and to speak up for herself. These instances show that Fanny is capable of a more active life when encouraged.

In fact, Fanny is the only one at Mansfield Park with convictions and character strong enough to refuse to act in the amateur play production, an activity Sir Thomas has forbidden. Her relatives, when tempted by the chance to impress or placate someone they admire, turn away from what they have been taught to believe right and thus betray the values of the family. Fanny alone remains faithful to the routines and rules of the household. Her cousins are amazed by her courage, and Aunt Norris calls her refusal to oblige the others positively wicked.

Later, Fanny is pressured by relatives and friends to accept the marriage proposal of the wealthy, charming Henry Crawford. She again shows surprising strength of character by refusing to follow the wishes of others when they go against her own values. Sir Thomas finds her decision "offensive, and disgusting beyond all common offense." Nevertheless, Fanny prefers staying at Mansfield Park as almost an unpaid servant to marrying someone she does not care for and respect, though by marrying she could have gained approval, security, and social position. Fanny, who is usually obedient and cooperative, proves to be a strongly independent character in matters of importance.

In contrast with Fanny, her Bertram cousins, who at first appear decisive and confident, are swept along in circumstances that bring them shame and disappointment. Tom gambles until he has amassed staggering debts and becomes seriously ill. Maria ruins her marriage and reputation by eloping with Henry Crawford after she has married foolish Rushworth out of spite. Julia, because she is bored, marries a careless, frivolous friend of her brother. Thus, the seemingly fortunate cousins spoil their lives by impulsive and thoughtless actions.

Henry and Mary Crawford, the worldly London brother and sister visiting in the neighborhood, are the most intelligent, talented, and attractive characters of the novel. They glow with life and sparkle with wit, making Fanny and her cousins look dull by comparison. The Crawfords, too, understand the true worth of human goodness. Henry so fully recognizes and admires Fanny's purity of heart and inner beauty that he wishes to marry her. Mary begins to fall in love with sincere, good Edmund and to imagine herself as his wife.

The Crawfords bewitch everyone by their charm except Fanny, who finds them dangerous. She envies the attraction the glamorous Mary exerts on Edmund, and she distrusts Henry's flirtatious ways with her female cousins. Even more, she distrusts their opportunistic and scheming ways: Henry callously flirts with both Maria and Julia merely to discover whether he can make them fall in love with him; Mary lies to help her brother have his way and casually overlooks his seducing and ruining of Maria. Flawed as they are, Austen has sketched the Crawfords so brilliantly that they sometimes seem to dominate the story. Some readers have wondered whether Fanny and Henry would not have been excellent marriage partners, each complementing the other's abilities. Some wonder whether Edmund would not have been made happier by vivacious Mary than by his quiet, tender cousin, Fanny.

Austen's style and tone in this novel are generally serious and thoughtful. The themes of right conduct and integrity of personal values influence the tone of conversations as well as the delineation of the characters. Lighthearted moments often express frivolous or insincere feelings and thoughts rather than simple enjoyment. When Mary Crawford observes about a career in the navy during wartime, "The profession is well enough under two circumstances; if it make

the fortune, and there be discretion in spending it," her sentiment mocks the heroic efforts of sailors fighting against Napoleon.

The role of parents in caring for their children is of particular interest in Mansfield Park. Fanny moves from her parents' chaotic, poverty-stricken home to the well-organized, luxurious home of the Bertrams. There Sir Thomas rigidly oversees the children's upbringing while his agreeable wife, Lady Bertram, sits nodding on the sofa, petting her lap dog, Pug. Family life continues smoothly enough until Sir Thomas is called away on business. Left alone and neglected by their incapable mother, the children rebel against family rules in various ways that lead to pain and misfortune. Sir Thomas returns in time to witness but too late to prevent the disaster. Only Fanny is spared disaster.

"Critical Evaluation" by Patricia H. Fulbright

Further Reading

Armstrong, Isobel. *Jane Austen: "Mansfield Park."* New York: Penguin Books, 1988. A short but perceptive feminist examination of *Mansfield Park* with excerpts from contemporary influences, such as Mary Wollstonecraft, John Locke, and Elizabeth Inchbald. Includes a select bibliography.

Austen, Jane. *Mansfield Park: Authoritative Text, Contexts, Criticism.* Edited by Claudia L. Johnson. New York: W. W. Norton, 1998. In addition to the annotated text, this volume includes contemporary materials about religion, the slave trade, and the conduct of women in Austen's time and essays analyzing the novel. Includes a chronology and a selected bibliography.

Butler, Marilyn. *Jane Austen and the War of Ideas.* New York: Oxford University Press, 1987. Explores Austen's conservative attitudes toward female education by contrasting Fanny, the "perfect" Christian heroine, with the other female characters. Argues that Fanny is a paradoxical and appealing mixture of feeble passivity and quiet endurance.

Copeland, Edward, and Juliet McMaster, eds. *The Cambridge Companion to Jane Austen.* New York: Cambridge University Press, 1997. One of the thirteen essays focuses on an analysis of *Mansfield Park*, *Emma*, and *Persuasion*, while other essays deal with broad issues, such as class consciousness, religion, and domestic economy in Austen's work. This excellent overview includes a chronology and concludes with an assessment of late twentieth century developments in Austen scholarship.

Fleishman, Avrom. *A Reading of "Mansfield Park": An Es-*

say in *Critical Synthesis*. Minneapolis: University of Minnesota Press, 1967. A detailed discussion of the novel from many perspectives. Places the novel in its historical context, examines the psychological realism of Austen's characters, and analyzes the novel's mythical structure. Also contains a helpful bibliography.

Lambdin, Laura Cooner, and Robert Thomas Lambdin, eds. *A Companion to Jane Austen Studies*. New York: Greenwood Press, 2000. A collection of essays interpreting Austen's works. Two of the essays deal with *Mansfield Park*: "Fanny Price's 'Customary' Subjectivity: Rereading the Individual in *Mansfield Park*" and "The Critical History of *Mansfield Park*."

MacDonagh, Oliver. *Jane Austen: Real and Imagined Worlds*. New Haven, Conn.: Yale University Press, 1991. An illuminating contextual study by a historian who reads *Mansfield Park* in contemporary religious terms.

Mooneyham, Laura G. *Romance, Language, and Education in Jane Austen's Novels*. New York: St. Martin's Press, 1988. Interprets the central issue of *Mansfield Park* as the heroine's education. Sees this, however, as Fanny's progress from the negative—because incomplete—virtues of duty and patience to the positive, active, virtues of judging and directing.

Morgan, Susan. *In the Meantime: Character and Perception in Jane Austen's Fiction*. Chicago: University of Chicago Press, 1980. A thoughtful analysis of Fanny as a developing character.

Todd, Janet M. *The Cambridge Introduction to Jane Austen*. New York: Cambridge University Press, 2006. Todd, an Austen scholar, provides an overview of Austen's life, novels, context, and reception. Includes a detailed discussion about each novel and provides a good starting point for the study of her major works.

The Mansion

Author: William Faulkner (1897-1962)
First published: 1959
Type of work: Novel
Type of plot: Social realism
Time of plot: 1908-1948
Locale: Mississippi

Principal characters:
MINK SNOPES, the protagonist
LINDA SNOPES KOHL, Eula Snopes's daughter
FLEM SNOPES, Linda's "public" father
GAVIN STEVENS, an attorney and Linda's friend
V. K. RATLIFF, Gavin's friend

The Story:

Mink Snopes, convicted of Jack Houston's murder, receives a life sentence. Mink killed Houston over a one-dollar pound fee. He learns parole is possible if he behaves and does not attempt escape. Mink accepts this, planning to return in twenty years to murder Flem. Being close kin and powerful, Flem, Mink thinks, should have helped him.

After seventeen years, through Flem's manipulations, Montgomery Ward Snopes is imprisoned at Parchman prison for possession of bootleg whiskey. Flem tells Montgomery to set Mink up to escape and be caught. Montgomery tells Mink that Flem wants him to wear a girl's dress for the escape. Mink, caught and sentenced to twenty additional years, does not fault Flem for tricking him but sends word that "he hadn't ought to used that dress." Two years before Mink's release date, Linda Snopes Kohl initiates a petition, securing his release. With $13.85, he leaves Parchman and hitchhikes to Memphis.

V. K. Ratliff reviews the history of Eula, Flem, Manfred de Spain, and himself, interpreting aspects of the story. Eula, de Spain's mistress, stays with Flem to give Linda respectability, and Flem secures the bank presidency from de Spain after Linda, who, for the chance to get away from the town of Jefferson, has signed over to Flem her part of her maternal grandfather's wealth. Flem goes to Will Varner, offering to exchange the paper for the bank presidency. Will's resulting confrontation with de Spain forces Eula to decide between Linda's living as the daughter of a suicide or of a whore; she chooses suicide.

Linda leaves for Greenwich Village, begins an affair with a communist—Barton Kohl—marries him, and together they go to fight in Spain. Gavin and Ratliff, recently returned to Jefferson from Linda and Barton's wedding, receive word that Barton's plane is shot down. Linda, an ambulance driver on the front lines, remains in Spain until a bomb explodes near her, deafening her. Linda returns to Jefferson. Gavin helps her improve her "dead-duck" voice, pleads with her to quit trying to educate black students, shields her from the Federal Bureau of Investigation (which had learned she was a card-carrying communist), and gets her a job as a riveter with the Pascagoula Shipyards. He marries a former sweetheart to please Linda.

After delaying adventures, Mink reaches Memphis, haggles at a pawn shop for an old pistol and three rounds, and hitchhikes toward Jefferson. Linda, back in Jefferson, drinks bootlegged whiskey and walks incessantly. She has Gavin initiate a petition to release Mink. Gavin, certain Mink will murder Flem, tries to dissuade her without telling her his fears. He believes her innocent of any conspiracy, but wants to avoid complicity in the murder. He has the warden offer Mink the pardon if Mink takes $250 (with the promise of $250 quarterly) and never return to Mississippi. Mink goes along with the plan but gives the money to a trustee to give back to the warden, and then he leaves.

Ratliff goes to Parchman, misses Mink, and calls Gavin to report. Gavin warns Flem, who seems undisturbed, and alerts the Memphis police. The police discover the pawn shop and report to Gavin that the gun is useless. Mink reaches the mansion while Flem is unguarded, enters the house (passing by an open door by which Linda sits), and goes into Flem's room. Flem swivels around and watches Mink fumble until the gun fires, killing Flem. Flem and the chair fall, Mink runs toward a closed door, and Linda speaks behind him. He throws the gun at her; she tells him to take it and leave.

The day of Flem's funeral, Gavin learns that Linda had ordered a Jaguar after Mink's pardon was assured. Gavin confronts her, aware, then, that she had maneuvered Flem's murder, making Gavin an accomplice. She agrees, and, perhaps not as contrite as she could have been, assigns Gavin three more tasks: put a monument on Flem's grave, give the deed to the de Spain mansion to the two surviving de Spains, and give Mink $1,000.

Sickened, Gavin leaves the mansion, not seeing Linda again. Ratliff and Gavin go to Frenchman's Bend, find Mink, and give him $250. Gavin says he will send him money quarterly. Ratliff and Gavin leave. Mink, feeling equal to any and all, stretches himself peaceably upon the ground.

Critical Evaluation:

Criticism often faults *The Mansion* for contradictions and discrepancies, hinting that William Faulkner's talent was waning when he wrote the novel. Faulkner, who said his fiction was only about the "human heart in conflict with itself," wrote that the discrepancies and contradictions resulted from his knowing the characters better, after living with them for thirty-four years. Critics are taking a closer look at Faulk-

ner's later works, seeing them afresh and discovering significant insights overlooked before. This novel shows society its own ugly warts.

The Mansion focuses on the plight of the downtrodden in the hands of the powerful; Faulkner depicts that society artfully. Far from being a faulty work by the Nobel Prize winner, *The Mansion* magnifies what Faulkner meant when he said, in his address to the Nobel academy, "I believe that man will not merely endure, he will prevail." In this last novel of the Snopes trilogy, the reader learns, among much else, what Faulkner had learned about his most interesting "prevailer," Mink Snopes.

The Mansion is divided into three sections: on Mink, Linda, and Flem. The book's main character is Mink. The Linda section foreshadows her as a threat to Gavin, in some way Ratliff cannot fathom, and makes it believable in the end that she, not Mink, is the one who manipulates Flem's murder. The section on Flem makes him a flat character who simply waits on Mink to shoot him. The novel debunks Gavin Stevens, the character critics have often championed as Faulkner's most promising creation, exposing him as a willing pawn, manipulated (in ways Mink would never be) by Linda. He is also a self-confessed coward. From the first sentence to the last, *The Mansion* is Faulkner's monument to Mink.

Physically, Mink, murderer of two, is "small, almost childlike." Neither his physical appearance nor his physical actions endear him to anyone, but he is thoroughly complex in action, thought, and sentiment. While Flem is impotent, Mink is Faulkner's most sexually potent male. The reader learns this in the first novel of the trilogy, and it resonates in the last when, in prison, Mink, thinking of the hardness of the land, recalls the "amazement . . . reverence . . . and incredulous excitement" he felt when he touched his bride, Yettie, on their wedding night. In the same moment, he regrets how their subsistence lifestyle, warring with earth, wore Yettie to "leather-toughness" and himself to "exhaustion." Mink voices the regret he had when, looking at their two little girls, he saw "what was ahead of that tender and elfin innocence."

In spite of physical smallness, Mink could do hard labor twenty-four hours a day: He paid off his fine to Houston by digging post holes and putting up a fence, simultaneously plowing and planting his own crops far into the night. At Parchman, the warden says Mink worked the cotton "unflaggingly," harder than any man "of his stamp and kind" worked his own crop.

Philosophically, Mink is a self-contained man who lives by a personalized value system. He believes in an indefinite "them" and "they." Life is a test by "them." "They" make him account for any lie he tells, so he counts each lie, keeping rules and accounts carefully. He expects to beat "them." To illustrate, Mink accepts an extra twenty-year prison term without complaint, because he had been warned not to attempt escape.

In prison, he merges "they" and "them" with "Old Moster." He gains first a kind of bravado, then a tenacious faith that Old Moster plays fair with him. Mixed in with Mink's philosophy is his relationship to the land. He expresses the Edenic view that sin makes humans earn their food by the sweat of their brows as they war with earth. He says the land "owned" the sharecroppers, passing "their doomed indigence and poverty from holding to holding."

Mink lives tenaciously on the edges of life, a human being who prevails by remaining true to his inner voice in the face of whatever life deals him. His thoughts are often poetry; he holds to his rules religiously. He also abuses his wife and children verbally and emotionally (although Faulkner makes his heart belie these actions), and he breaks the most serious of laws—committing murder twice.

At each blow from life, Mink is forced to choose between his values and society's values. From infancy he was on his own, developing his own hard-bought, self-examined, inner light. That evolving light was Mink; to hold to it was to hold to himself. Murder is indefensible, but it came after a lifetime of indefensible treatment perpetrated on those such as Mink by an indefensible society of Flems and Houstons, a society whose wealth is sustained by the Minks of the world. Two men take more than Mink can give and keep his own soul. The first is Jack Houston, the second Flem Snopes.

Houston took too much when, after Mink had worked off his debt to Houston, Houston tacked on a one-dollar pound fee (equal to two days of labor) because Mink figured a day from sunup to sunup (and so left his cow one night more at Houston's) and the law figured it from sundown to sundown, making the pound fee legal. Mink paid the fee off, but for the shame of it, he killed Houston. Legally, he paid twice for that murder.

Not much was required of Flem, under Mink's value system, but Montgomery allowed Mink to think that Flem decreed that Mink wear a girl's dress in his attempted escape, and it was for that dress, more than anything else, that Flem is killed. Significantly, Faulkner's ending of book and trilogy exonerates the Minks of the world, leaving them pardoned and peaceful. Near the end of his canon, Faulkner chose Mink as prevailer, because Faulkner had no illusions about human perfectibility. In their complexity, all his characters are wicked and wonderful. Faulkner obviously learned that "damned little murdering bastard," Mink, was both.

The Mansion is not the work of a failing writer. Its complexity invites serious study; if it is a study that horrifies or causes critics to shake their heads at its implications, all the more reason to plumb its depths. If Faulkner ever presented any character who exemplified "the human heart in conflict with itself," that character is Mink Snopes.

Jo Culbertson Davis

Further Reading

Donaldson, Susan V. *"Faulkner's Snopes Trilogy and Cold War Masculinity."* In *White Masculinity in the Recent South*, edited by Trent Watts. Baton Rouge: Louisiana State University Press, 2008. Donaldson's essay examining the depiction of the male characters in *The Mansion*, *The Hamlet*, and *The Town* is included in this study of the representation of white southern manhood since World War II.

Gwynn, Frederick L., and Joseph L. Blotner, eds. *Faulkner in the University: Class Conference at University of Virginia, 1957-1958*. Charlottesville: University of Virginia Press, 1959. Faulkner responds to questions about his work, presenting his view of the novel and its characters. Index provides easy access to pertinent points in *The Mansion* and to its key characters.

Kirk, Robert W., with Marvin Klotz. *Faulkner's People: A Complete Guide and Index to Characters in the Fiction of William Faulkner*. Berkeley: University of California Press, 1963. This well-indexed source provides a description of all Faulkner's characters, with specific reference to pages on which they appear in his works. Faulkner's many characters are classified and cross-referenced.

Millgate, Michael. *The Achievement of William Faulkner*. New York: Random House, 1966. Millgate presents a compelling view of Mink Snopes, *The Mansion*'s primary figure, counteracting the view that Gavin is the central figure in the Snopes trilogy, of which *The Mansion* is part.

Polk, Noel. "Water, Wanderers, and Snopes Trilogy." In *Faulkner and Welty and the Southern Literary Tradition*. Jackson: University Press of Mississippi, 2008. An analysis of *The Mansion*, *The Hamlet*, and *The Town* by a preeminent scholar of southern literature.

Towner, Theresa M. *The Cambridge Introduction to William Faulkner*. New York: Cambridge University Press, 2008. An accessible book aimed at students and general readers. Focusing on Faulkner's work, the book provides detailed analyses of his nineteen novels, discussion of his other works, and information about the critical reception of his fiction.

Marat/Sade

Author: Peter Weiss (1916-1982)

First produced: Die Verfolgung und Ermordung Jean-Paul Marats, dargestellt durch die Schauspielgruppe des Hospizes zu Charenton unter der Anleitung des Herrn de Sade, 1964 (*The Persecution and Assassination of Jean-Paul Marat as Performed by the Inmates of the Asylum of Charenton Under the Direction of the Marquis de Sade*, 1965); first published, 1964

Type of work: Drama

Type of plot: Social morality

Time of plot: 1808

Locale: Near Paris

Principal characters:

MARQUIS DE SADE, a self-centered individualist

JEAN-PAUL MARAT, a revolutionary

CHARLOTTE CORDAY, Marat's assassin

DUPERRET, a Girondist deputy

JACQUES ROUX, a former priest and radical socialist

THE HERALD, the stage manager

COULMIER, the director of the asylum

The Story:

This two-act play is divided into thirty-three scenes, with the first few setting the stage for the play and the play-within-the-play. At the Charenton clinic, Sade signs to the Herald for the play to begin. Coulmier explains to the audience, seated on the side and consisting of himself, his wife, and his daughter, that Sade has written this historical play portraying the assassination of Marat by Charlotte Corday on July 13, 1793. The performance has two purposes: entertainment for the visitors and therapy for the inmates. The performance is July 13, 1808, exactly fifteen years after the assassination. The Herald then introduces those inmates playing major roles, apologizing for their lack of skill. Sade plays himself. Marat is played by a paranoiac. The Marat, in the play, as in life, has a skin disease that necessitates his remaining constantly in a warm bath. Charlotte Corday is played by a woman suffering from sleeping sickness and melancholia.

The play-within-the-play begins with the "Homage to Marat" sung by four balladeers: Kokol, Polpoch, Cucurucu, and Rossignol, who represent the attitudes and grievances of the masses. For them, Marat is the only revolutionary, and they want to be assured that he will never give up their fight. When Roux elevates their cries for bread and freedom, Coulmier demands that Sade keep the performers to the approved script so as not to confuse and unsettle the patients.

Next, Charlotte Corday is introduced as both a character in the play and a historical personage. Corday believes Marat has become the evil genius of France and gains an audience with him through deceit, promising to betray the Girondists of her hometown, Caen. Marat is preparing his "fourteenth of July call/ to the people of France." On the street, Corday has

witnessed the crowd performing a dance of death as they march to the guillotine. A pantomime, narrated by Marat, portrays a history of past executions.

Sade and Marat discuss the meaning of life and death. Sade compares death to the indifference he observes in nature. For him, life and death are purely a matter of the survival of the fittest, without human compassion. Marat, on the other hand, maintains that it is absolutely essential to intervene whenever injustice occurs, especially when perpetrated in society by the Church and the state. When Coulmier objects to this characterization of society, the Herald sarcastically suggests that everything is different now and the comments serve only to provide a historical context within the play. Sade expresses his ambivalence about humanity's ability to improve its lot through revolution, while Marat maintains that the time has come to put the writings of the "Declaration of the Rights of Man" into action. The masses, however, demand an immediate revolution.

Corday continues to believe in her mission, yet now she describes Marat, in her somnambulism, as the image of Napoleon. Duperret attempts to dissuade her, believing that Marat and his revolution will soon be conquered and freedom restored. Sade has lost faith in the idealism of the revolution, while Marat believes in it all the more, a viewpoint vigorously supported by Roux and the masses. They sing, "We want our rights and we don't care how/ We want our Revolution now."

Corday and Duperret believe the long-awaited freedom promised by the revolution will soon be realized. Marat, however, delivers a litany exposing those beliefs as lies and attempts to warn the masses against deception. Sade suggests that they are only interested in profiting from the revolution. Sade's views are substantiated when Corday visits Marat a second time and gives him a letter in which she says, "I am unhappy/ and therefore have a right to his aid."

The first act concludes with the scene in which Marat's life is mocked and ridiculed by characters representing his youth, science, the army, the Church, the nouveaux riches, and even Voltaire and Antoine-Laurent Lavoisier. Roux again comes to his defense, asserting that only Marat realizes the need for a fundamental change in society.

The second act begins with Marat's imaginary speech to the National Assembly attempting to rally the people to continue and conclude the revolution in accordance with his views. Sade, in his haughty and scornful manner, ridicules Marat's idealism, proposing that he give up since all his writings and speeches have been futile.

Corday, who dreams she is saving a corrupt world, approaches Marat for the third time that day, to assassinate him. Sade makes a final attempt to dissuade Marat from his revolutionary ideas, suggesting the masses will fight only if they perceive a direct and personal reward. Their new cry is now, "And what's the point of a revolution/ without general copulation." The murder is interrupted momentarily by a musical history of the revolution, highlighting political events between Marat's assassination in 1793 and the time of the play in 1808. In the epilogue, Coulmier and the masses sing the glories of their day, with Napoleon ruling the nation as emperor. The final lines, however, are spoken by Roux, admonishing everyone, "When will you learn to see/ When will you learn to take sides."

Critical Evaluation:

With *Marat/Sade*, Peter Weiss became an internationally acclaimed and highly respected dramatist. Prior to writing plays in the 1960's, Weiss had spent many years as a painter, novelist, filmmaker, and translator. Born in Germany, he lived most of his adult life in Sweden, making only short visits to Germany—then both East and West—to lecture, read, and participate in the production of his plays.

Weiss began *Marat/Sade* in 1963 and prepared at least five versions before the play premiered on April 29, 1964, in West Berlin. The East German premiere was on March 26, 1965, in Rostock. In the fall of 1964, Peter Brook produced *Marat/Sade* for the Royal Shakespeare Company in London, making the play an international success in the English-speaking world. Brook also produced the film version in 1966. An operatic version of *Marat/Sade* premiered in 1984 in Kassel, Germany.

There are many highly complex dramatic devices in the play. Whereas the early German stagings tended to rely on Bertolt Brecht's epic theater of alienation for their overall structure, Brook and many English productions were influenced by Antonin Artaud's concept of the theater of cruelty. Both approaches must deal with the difficulties of presenting a multilayered play and a play-within-a-play, unpunctuated language ranging from doggerel and popular balladry to sophisticated free verse, song, dance, and pantomime, and scenes that are tragic, comical, melodramatic, and highly lyrical.

As Weiss indicated in his "Note on the Historical Background to the Play," certain parts of the drama are based on actual events. The record shows that Sade, now known primarily as the author of erotic novels, was imprisoned at the Charenton asylum from 1801 until his death in 1814. While Sade did write many plays, some performed by the inmates of Charenton, he never wrote a play about Marat. Another historical fact, in no way associated with Sade, is Charlotte Corday's assassination of Marat. Although not a radical agitator, she sympathized with the Girondists in the French Revolution. Corday felt that Marat, as a supporter of the more extremist views of the Jacobins and their waging a deadly war on the Girondists, had become the evil dictator of France. She resolved to emulate the biblical Judith and went to Paris, where she assassinated Marat on July 13, 1793. She was sent to the guillotine shortly thereafter.

With these basic historic facts at hand and a thorough understanding of Marat's and Sade's philosophical viewpoints, Weiss wrote this play. As the title states, the outer framework is a play about Marat's assassination written by Sade and performed by the inmates of Charenton. This dramatic activity becomes the play-within-the-play. Of course, there is a third level to this play, namely the contemporary audience. Thus, three real times are presented: 1793 and the assassination of Marat, 1808 with the presentation of Sade's play, and the present.

The actors represent these various time periods. For the present time audience, all actors on the stage play specific roles. Those who play the parts of Coulmier and his family represent France in 1808 as well as in the present time. The actor in the role of Sade is more complex. He plays the historical Sade as playwright and director of this play, and the philosophical sparring partner with the character playing the historical or real Marat. The role of Marat is likewise manifold. The actor must play the role of a paranoiac, play the historical person of Marat, and, occasionally, he must engage the real Sade in philosophical discourse. The other actors each have two roles to perform: the inmates and the historical roles that have been assigned to them.

It is not difficult to understand those aspects of the play that deal with the historical events of either 1793 or 1808. It can be difficult, however, for the present time audience to always know exactly what role the performers playing Marat and Sade are presenting, but that is basically Weiss's intent. One major purpose in this play is to examine the aims and goals of the French Revolution and why the movement failed despite its noble "Declaration of the Rights of Man" and its advocacy of "Liberty, Equality, Fraternity!"

The battle cry of the masses—"Revolution Revolution, Copulation Copulation"—epitomizes the conflict and confusion that prevailed after the storming of the Bastille on July 14, 1798, which marked the outbreak of the French Revolution. Neither Marat nor Sade, however, articulated decisive plans that would lead to a successful revolution. Marat, in his idealism, advocated action that was unreasonable for the masses since their most basic needs remained unfulfilled, proclaiming, "The important thing/ is to pull yourself up by your own hair." Sade, on the other hand, believed that humans are by nature incapable of acting beyond themselves. Both stressed an ideological point of view: Marat believed in the perfectibility of society; Sade was convinced that humanity was impossible to perfect. This is the philosophical dilemma that Weiss presents to the audience. Ultimately, he gives the last word to Roux, the most politically aware among the masses, refusing to accept defeat and attempting to continue Marat's revolution.

Weiss's intention in *Marat/Sade* was to provoke and engage the audience in discussion, not to make statements or present answers. His main question centered on the failure of revolutions: the French Revolution, other liberation movements in nineteenth century Germany, the great October Revolution (1917) in Russia, and revolutions and national liberation movements in various developing world nations. In *Marat/Sade*, Weiss investigated the potentiality of establishing a more humane society, a possibility he regarded as feasible in an ideal socialist world.

Thomas H. Falk

Further Reading

Berwald, Olaf. "Staging Writers as Outcasts: *Marat/Sade, Trotzki im Exil, Hölderlin, Der Prozess,* and *Der neue Prozess.*" In *An Introduction to the Works of Peter Weiss.* Rochester, N.Y.: Camden House, 2003. A detailed examination of Weiss's plays. Includes an introductory chapter discussing Weiss's life and his work in exile.

Cohen, Robert. *Understanding Peter Weiss.* Columbia: University of South Carolina Press, 1993. A well-balanced introduction to Weiss's life and works, recommended as a beginner's source.

Cooper, Pamela. "'World of Bodies': Performing Flesh in *Marat/Sade.*" In *Captive Audience: Prison and Captivity in Contemporary Theater,* edited by Thomas Fahy and Kimball King. New York: Routledge, 2003. Focuses on the "converging of contrasts" in the play, arguing that "*Marat/Sade* relies upon a constant and irresolute rhythm of opposites simultaneously asserted and denied."

Ellis, Roger. *Peter Weiss in Exile: A Critical Study of His Works.* Ann Arbor, Mich.: UMI Research Press, 1987. A comprehensive study of Weiss's dramas, with special emphasis on *Marat/Sade.*

Hilton, Ian. *Peter Weiss: A Search for Affinities.* London: Oswald Wolff, 1970. A brief discussion of Weiss's earlier life and works. Includes selected translations from essays, novels, and dramas.

Ramanathan, Geetha. "The Erotic Female Body: Weiss's *Marat/Sade.*" In *Sexual Politics and the Male Playwright: The Portrayal of Women in Ten Contemporary Plays.* Jefferson, N.C.: McFarland, 1996. A feminist interpretation of Weiss's play and its representation of women, women's bodies, and eroticism.

Rokem, Freddie. "Peter Brook, *Marat/Sade.*" In *Performing History: Theatrical Representations of the Past in Contemporary Theatre.* Iowa City: University of Iowa Press, 2000. Analyzes three post-World War II dramas that depict the French Revolution, including *Marat/Sade.* Describes how the plays unite the historical past with the theatrical present.

Sontag, Susan. "Marat/Sade/Artaud." In *Against Interpretation.* New York: Farrar, Straus & Giroux, 1966. Reprint. New York: Picador, 2007. An influential discussion of the reception and performances of *Marat/Sade* in the United States. Examines how Betrolt Brecht's and Antonin Artaud's dramatic theories can be used in producing this play.

White, John. "History and Cruelty in Peter Weiss's *Marat/Sade.*" *Modern Language Review* 63 (1968): 437-448. Outlines Weiss's use of historical materials in *Marat/Sade,* illustrating how facts and documents of the French Revolution are integrated to reveal later periods in history. Discusses how Antonin Artaud's concept of the theater of cruelty was adapted in Peter Brook's first London production of Weiss's play.

The Marble Faun
Or, The Romance of Monte Beni

Author: Nathaniel Hawthorne (1804-1864)
First published: 1860
Type of work: Novel
Type of plot: Psychological realism
Time of plot: Mid-nineteenth century
Locale: Rome

Principal characters:
MIRIAM, an artist
HILDA, an artist and a friend of Miriam
KENYON, an American sculptor
DONATELLO, a young Italian

The Story:

Nothing at all is known about Miriam. In the artistic world of Rome, she lives without revealing anything about herself and without arousing the curiosity or suspicion of those living around her. She enjoys friendships with Hilda, a young woman from New England, and Kenyon, a sculptor, that her mysterious origin does not shadow, so complete is their understanding and trust of one another.

One day, the three friends, accompanied by Donatello, a young Italian, see the statue known as the Faun by Praxiteles. Struck by Donatello's resemblance to the statue, they ask jokingly to see whether the Italian also has pointed ears under his golden locks. Indeed, Donatello is very much like a faun in his character. He has great agility, cheerfulness, and a sunny nature unclouded by melancholy or care. He is deeply in love with Miriam.

On another occasion, the friends go to visit the catacombs. While there, Miriam disappears for a moment and then returns with a strange man whom she has met inside one of the tombs. After that, the man follows Miriam wherever she goes. No one knows anything about him. He and Miriam have conversations together, and he speaks of the hold he has on her and of their life together in a mysterious past. Miriam becomes more and more unhappy. She tells Donatello, who is ever ready to defend her, that he should go away before she brings doom and destruction down on him. Donatello stays, however.

One day, Miriam visits Hilda and leaves a packet with her that Hilda is to deliver on a certain date to the address written on the packet. Shortly afterward, the friends go out one night and climb the Tarpeian Rock, over which the old Romans used to throw criminals. As they are getting ready to return home, Miriam's persecutor appears. Miriam goes with him, followed by Donatello, who attacks the man. Grasping the tormentor securely, Donatello looks at Miriam. Her eyes give him his answer, and he throws the man off a cliff to his death.

United by their crime, Miriam and Donatello also become united in love. They do not know, however, that Hilda has

witnessed the murder and is suffering because of it. They have all agreed to visit the Church of the Capuchins the following afternoon to see a painting that supposedly bears a resemblance to Miriam's tormentor, but Hilda does not keep the appointment. The others go to the church, and there they find a mass for Miriam's persecutor in progress. Later, when Miriam goes to see Hilda, Hilda tells her that their friendship is over. Donatello, too, has changed. He is no longer the unworried faun; he has become a person with a guilty conscience. He begins to avoid Miriam, even to hate her. He leaves Rome and goes back to his ancestral home. Kenyon visits him there, but Hilda stays in Rome by herself, lonely and distraught.

At Donatello's country home, Kenyon learns the local legend about his friend's family—that Donatello is, in fact, reputed to be descended from a race of fauns who inhabited the countryside in remote times. He learns, too, of Donatello's feelings of guilt but, unaware of the murder, does not know the reason for Donatello's changed spirit. When Miriam tries to see Donatello at his home, he will not see her. Kenyon tells her that Donatello still loves her, and she agrees to meet both of them later on. When they meet in the city square, Miriam stands quietly, waiting for Donatello to speak. When at last he speaks her name, she goes to him and they are united once more, but their union continues to be haunted by their sin.

Hilda has in the meantime delivered the packet that Miriam earlier left in her keeping. The address was that of a person high in the affairs of the government. After Kenyon returns to Rome, he looks for Hilda everywhere. He has come to realize that he is in love with her, and he is worried about her disappearance. During the carnival season, he meets Donatello and Miriam, and finally, on the day the carnival is at its height and the streets are filled with a merrymaking throng, he sees Hilda again. She tells him that her knowledge of the crime had weighed so heavily on her that at last she had gone to confession and poured out the tale to a listening priest. When she delivered the packet, as Miriam had requested, she was detained in a convent until the authorities were satisfied that she had taken no part in the murder on the Tarpeian Rock. She has just been released from her captivity. While they stand talking, there is a commotion in the crowd nearby; the police have seized Donatello and are taking him to jail.

Donatello is tried and sentenced to prison for the murder, but Miriam is not brought to trial, because her only crime was the look in her eyes telling Donatello to murder her persecutor. Miriam's history, however, is finally revealed. Although she herself was innocent, her family had been involved in a crime that had made the family name infamous. She had traveled to Rome in an attempt to escape the past, but evil had continued to haunt her; the past had reappeared in the form of the persecutor, who had threatened to make her identity known to the world.

After Kenyon and Hilda are married, they see Miriam once more, kneeling in the Pantheon before the tomb of Raphael. As they pass, she stretches out her hands to them in a gesture that both blesses and repulses them. They leave her to her expiation and her grief.

Critical Evaluation:

Throughout his writing career, Nathaniel Hawthorne was preoccupied with the theme of humanity's fall into sin and mortality. Symbolic representations of Adam and the Garden of Eden underlie much of his best work. Hawthorne turns to this theme again in *The Marble Faun*, his last major romance; however, he deploys the idea less skillfully in this work than in some of his earlier stories. His usually subtle symbolic method here becomes a somewhat heavy-handed allegory, and the rather slight, simple story is weighted down with descriptions of Rome and Roman art. These descriptive passages—which Hawthorne frequently lifted with little alteration straight from his notebooks—have almost no organic relationship to the novel's theme. While *The Marble Faun* may be considered one of Hawthorne's weaker romances, however, both the faults and the virtues of the work, as in most of his writing, reveal his view of the world. The work features several of the character types on which Hawthorne drew most often and whose interactions he typically used to dramatize the themes that most preoccupied him.

The theme of the story, as the title indicates, centers most particularly on Donatello, the contemporary counterpart of the Faun of Praxiteles. For Hawthorne, Donatello's faunlike qualities are associated with the innocence and animalistic nature of humans before the Fall brought the knowledge of sin and death. Donatello's country estate is a counterpart to

Eden and suggests a pagan and pre-Christian paradise, bypassed by time, in which primordial innocence has been retained. Though touching in its childlike qualities, Donatello's innocence is not one of which Hawthorne can approve. Because it lacks the knowledge of sin that is part of humankind's humanity, Hawthorne considers it subhuman and incapable of understanding the real nature of the world. Salvation is a direct result of sin, and therefore Donatello, existing outside the world of sin and death, is not a candidate for God's greatest gift to humanity until Miriam, acting the part of an Eve figure, tempts him to murder. She thus becomes the instrument that brings about his fall into humanity. The irony of Hawthorne's scheme is obvious, as the "fall" is in fact a rise from the subhuman condition. Hawthorne is a proponent of the idea of the "fortunate fall" that proves necessary for humans to achieve salvation. The price Donatello is called on to pay in guilt, suffering, and shame is no more than the price of his initiation into the human race, with its potential blessing of salvation.

The two women in *The Marble Faun* represent the two extremes of Hawthorne's fictional women: Miriam, the mysterious, dark woman and Hilda, whose innocence and religious faith are everywhere manifest. Both become salvation figures, however, by becoming instruments for humanizing men. Miriam's tempting of Donatello and her own ambiguous past, with its suggestions of sin and guilt, define her as an Eve figure who tempts the man to the sin that will humanize him. Hilda, described in almost unreal terms of innocence and virtue, is a different sort of salvation figure. She brings Kenyon out of his cold isolation by awakening his ability to love. Ironically, by giving Miriam multilayered complexity of character, Hawthorne makes her more interesting than Hilda, whom Hawthorne depicts as an incorruptible symbol of Christian goodness. It is clearly Hilda, however, who represents for Hawthorne the moral standard the novel is meant to affirm.

The character in the novel closest to Hawthorne himself is the sculptor, Kenyon. Hawthorne refers to him at one point as "a man of marble," implying that such a description fits his moral nature as well as his profession. Like the light and dark women and the prelapsarian Adamic figure represented by Donatello, Kenyon is a recurrent type in Hawthorne's work. For Hawthorne, the artist and the scientist by their very nature tend to isolate themselves from humanity and to become cold observers who, without emotion of their own, exploit the lives of others for their own ends. In his artist's isolation, Kenyon suppresses what is human in himself for his art until he, in effect, loses his soul to it. Though his moral condition does not exactly parallel Donatello's, Kenyon is equally outside the human community and he, too, needs salvation. Hilda saves Kenyon not through a dramatic temptation to sin but through awakening what is most human in his own heart.

While the flaws of *The Marble Faun* are obvious, the novel's total effect is strengthened by the fact that the characters are among the most important of Hawthorne's creations, and the dual themes of the "fortunate fall" and crime and punishment give the work an honored place within the long tradition of Western literature. Moreover, the novel's setting in Rome anticipated the European novels of Henry James and the literary genre of the international novel that he popularized. For all these reasons, *The Marble Faun* is a significant work of American literature.

William E. Grant

Further Reading

Bell, Millicent, ed. *Hawthorne and the Real: Bicentennial Essays*. Columbus: Ohio State University Press, 2005. Collection of essays, published in commemoration of the bicentennial of Hawthorne's birth, explores his connection to the "real" world and how he expresses this relationship in his writing. Offers discussion of Hawthorne and politics as well as examinations of his treatments of slavery, feminism, and moral responsibility. Includes the essay "Working Women and Creative Doubles: Getting to *The Marble Faun.*"

Carton, Evan. *"The Marble Faun": Hawthorne's Transformations*. Boston: Twayne, 1992. Discusses biographical details that relate to *The Marble Faun*, indicates the importance of the admittedly flawed novel, and surveys the major literature that deals with the novel.

Herbert, T. Walter, Jr. "The Erotics of Purity: *The Marble Faun* and the Victorian Construction of Sexuality." *Representations* 33 (Fall, 1991): 114-132. Asserts that purity is sometimes not admirable, as when Hilda arouses but frustrates Kenyon, is shocked by Miriam's sensuality, and ignores the representative human being who is stained by knowledge.

Idol, John L. "'A Linked Circle of Three' Plus One: Nonverbal Communication in *The Marble Faun.*" *Studies in the Novel* 23 (April, 1991): 139-151. Analyzes the interactions among Hawthorne's characters through their body movements, facial expressions, and physical distances from one another. Examples presented include Hilda's avoidance of Miriam's embrace, Miriam's ocular order to Donatello to commit murder, and Kenyon's sculpting of Donatello's sin-altered face.

Millington, Richard H. *The Cambridge Companion to Nathaniel Hawthorne*. New York: Cambridge University Press, 2004. Collection of essays presents analyses of various aspects of Hawthorne's work, covering topics such as his depictions of American masculinity and his female characters. Includes the essay "Perplexity, Sympathy, and the Question of the Human: A Reading of *The Marble Faun*," by Emily Miller Budick.

Pennell, Melissa McFarland. *Student Companion to Nathaniel Hawthorne*. Westport, Conn.: Greenwood Press, 1999. Offers an introductory overview of Hawthorne's life and work designed for students and general readers. Includes a discussion of Hawthorne's contribution to American literature and analyses of his four major novels.

Person, Leland S. *The Cambridge Introduction to Nathaniel Hawthorne*. New York: Cambridge University Press, 2007. Provides an accessible introduction to the author's life and works. Includes analyses of all Hawthorne's novels, with a chapter devoted to *The Marble Faun*.

Stern, Milton R. *Contexts for Hawthorne: "The Marble Faun" and the Politics of Openness and Closure in American Literature*. Urbana: University of Illinois Press, 1991. Analyzes Hawthorne's pull toward closure, as seen in his classical conservatism, preference for past and present, and aesthetic control and unity, and his push toward openness, as reflected by his romanticism, revolutionary tendencies, repudiation of the past, and preference for future expansionism.

Weldon, Roberta. *Hawthorne, Gender, and Death: Christianity and Its Discontents*. New York: Palgrave Macmillan, 2008. Examines how Hawthorne depicts dying and his characters' reactions to death in *The Marble Faun* and other fictional works. Supplemented with bibliography and index.

Wineapple, Brenda. *Hawthorne: A Life*. New York: Alfred A. Knopf, 2003. Presents a meticulously researched, evenhanded analysis of Hawthorne's often contradictory life and proposes that much of his fiction was autobiographical. Includes extensive supporting notes, bibliography, and index.

March

Author: Geraldine Brooks (1955-   )
First published: 2005
Type of work: Novel
Type of plot: Historical
Time of plot: 1861-1862
Locale: Concord, Massachusetts; Washington, D.C.;
    Virginia

Principal characters:
JOHN MARCH, a chaplain of the Union army
MARGARET "MARMEE" MARCH, his wife
MEG,
JO,
BETH, and
AMY, their daughters
GRACE CLEMENT, a nurse and former slave
AUGUSTUS CLEMENT, a plantation owner
MRS. CLEMENT, his wife
ETHAN CANNING, a plantation manager

The Story:

After the Battle of Ball's Bluff, John March, chaplain of the Union army, writes a letter from the battlefield to his wife, Margaret "Marmee," and their daughters Meg, Jo, Beth, and Amy. The family lives in Concord, Massachusetts. Because of the atrocities March has witnessed, he exerts a certain self-censorship on his letters home. The brutality of war, including vultures eating the flesh of corpses and the horrors of the field hospital, are too brutal to be conveyed in letters read aloud to his innocent daughters. March had been in this part of the United States before, and he tells the following story.

It is twenty years earlier, and eighteen-year-old March is visiting Virginia as a peddler. For a while, he is a guest of a plantation owner, Augustus Clement. March meets Grace, an African American slave who nurses senile Mrs. Clement. March feels attracted to Grace, and with her help, he begins teaching a little slave girl to write, even though the law forbids teaching slaves to read and write. Soon, his teaching becomes known, and he is expelled from the plantation, but not before he witnesses Grace being brutally whipped.

After being expelled from the Clement plantation, young March makes a fortune as a peddler. Wealthy, he sells out his business and goes back home. He next becomes a preacher. When the Reverend Day invites him to go to Concord to preach, he meets the reverend's sister, Margaret, or Marmee, a young woman with ideas of her own about women's education.

Grace turns down the opportunity to leave the plantation to join the Union army as a nurse, unwilling to leave the dying Mr. Clement. March tries to persuade Grace, but she reveals to him that she is Mr. Clement's daughter by a slave woman and feels morally obliged to stay and care for him until he dies. Though Clement had offers for selling her, he

chose not to sell her to a brothel. The scars from the whippings made her undesirable for the brothel owners. Grace and March embrace passionately.

March is given a new destination in charge of organizing the freed slaves who have joined the Union army and are considered contraband goods. March learns that the real reason behind his dismissal is that someone accused him of having an affair with Grace. Though he regrets their embrace, nothing had happened between them. Ashamed and unable to tell his wife the truth, he writes to her that he is going to preach to the former slaves.

A young, enamored March decides to move to Concord to be closer to Marmee. He finds a job with a pencil-maker, whose son, Henry David Thoreau, reluctantly works while he dreams of leaving for the woods. March soon becomes friends with other local residents, including the Emersons. He discovers that Marmee is a strong abolitionist with a fierce temper and that she is involved in the Underground Railroad. One night, March meets Marmee in the woods, and they make love. They are quickly married a few weeks later. Their first daughter, Meg, is born nine months later.

March writes home again, describing his new post in a plantation run by Union forces and worked by free African Americans, whom he is to teach to write and read. Right after arriving, he discovers that although blacks are now free and free from beatings, they still are brutally punished. The plantation manager, Ethan Canning, imposes strict discipline on his workers, who complain that they had received better treatment in their old age and during their sicknesses from their old master.

The newlywed Marches lead a comfortable life in Concord, their happiness augmented by the birth of Jo. They are also active in the Underground Railroad, building a station in their own basement. Soon after, Beth is born. After attending a lecture by political agitator John Brown and seeing Marmee's enthusiasm, March decides to invest heavily in Brown's experiment, which leads March to bankruptcy by the time their fourth child, Amy, is born. They are forced to sell their house and move into a smaller one. Meg begins working as a governess, and Jo accepts a job as a paid companion to Aunt March.

March begins teaching his eager students, but he is appalled by the cruelty of the Union soldiers. As news reaches them that the army is withdrawing from the area, his students warn him to run off, but he decides to stay. The guerrillas appear at the plantation and shoot and maim Canning; then they come looking for March. March hides, and a man is killed in retaliation, leaving March guilty and remorseful. When the guerrillas begin to viciously attack the workers, March shows up. He and Canning are shot.

Marmee, accompanied by John Brooke, their neighbor's tutor, goes to Washington, D.C., to nurse her convalescent husband, whom she finds almost unrecognizable and drifting in and out of consciousness. Marmee discovers Grace caressing her husband and jumps to the conclusion that Grace and her husband are lovers. Marmee confronts Grace, who tells her the whole story. Marmee is outraged that her husband did not tell her the true reasons for his new post.

When he regains consciousness, March does not want to be discharged on account of his poor health. On the contrary, he wants to go back to the battlefield and seek redemption. Beth becomes ill with scarlet fever, and Marmee goes back home. March feels guilty for having survived and thinks he does not deserve to return to his family. Grace urges him to go home and write sermons advocating for equality.

March gets home in time for Christmas. He knows he is not the same man he used to be, and he is haunted by memories of the dead. He realizes that he can learn to live with his memories.

Critical Evaluation:

In *March*, a sequel to Louisa May Alcott's *Little Women* (1868), Geraldine Brooks provides life to the largely absent and unknown John March, the father of the four March girls. Alcott's novel says little about Mr. March, who, as her novel begins, is away in his capacity as a Union army chaplain during the American Civil War. After his return home, he has a tendency to hide from his family in his library, making him an absent father, a typical figure in nineteenth century novels.

If Alcott based the four March sisters on herself and her three sisters, Brooks perused Mr. March's journals for her own depiction. The fictional figure Mr. March rehabilitates

the historical figure A. Bronson Alcott, Louisa May Alcott's own father, with whom she had a complex relationship. Mr. Alcott is often remembered as an ineffectual parent whose inability to financially provide for his family prompted his second daughter to attempt publishing to support the family. He now has become a footnote in most history textbooks, which ignore his significant contributions to pedagogy and his defense of causes such as abolitionism or vegetarianism. His philosophy has been overshadowed by his better-known neighbors and close family friends, Henry David Thoreau and Ralph Waldo Emerson, who appear as friends of Mr. March in *March*. Mr. Alcott's advanced views on teaching were misunderstood in his time, and he was accused of corrupting children's innate innocence with his Socratic methods. A strong advocate of abolitionism, he enrolled an African American student in his school, leading his other students to drop out and forcing the school's closure.

About *March*, which was awarded the 2006 Pulitzer Prize for fiction, Brooks has claimed that

> I made a fast rule for myself that I would only go where Louisa May Alcott had chosen not to go . . . and simply tried to add some darker adult resonances in the voids of her sparkling children's tale.

Alcott had included as one of her favorite books *Uncle Tom's Cabin: Or, Life Among the Lowly* (1851-1852, serial; 1852, book) by Harriet Beecher Stowe, a book known for its strong endorsement of the abolitionist cause. However, the topics of abolitionism and African American rights are conspicuously absent from *Little Women*, despite being set during the Civil War. The advocacy of abolitionism is more evident in *March*. As the cover of the paperback edition of *March* proclaims, the novel is a story of "a good man caught between love and guilt, courage and fear." *March* deals with issues such as the moral dilemmas posed by the war. It also shows that wars are complex and ideologies are sometimes blurred, with not everybody on one side endorsing fully that side's values, as March realizes, much to his dismay, when some of his fellow Union soldiers treat African Americans mercilessly. Idealism and practical sense are confronted in the course of war, and March concludes that there are no noble ideals in war, that there is no justice to be found on the battlefield.

The novel also presents some scarcely known realities of the Civil War, such as how freed slaves were regarded as contraband by Union troops. Also, Southern plantations were leased to Union sympathizers to run for their own profit. The novel also explores a number of reform movements such as vegetarianism and women's education and roles in society.

Though a supporter of woman suffrage herself, Alcott did not discuss it in *Little Women*. Brooks, however, has Marmee voice strong opinions about women's education and roles.

M. Carmen Gomez-Galisteo

Further Reading

Alcott, Louisa May. *Louisa May Alcott: Her Life, Letters, and Journals*. Ann Arbor: University of Michigan Library, 2009. Originally published in the nineteenth century, this reprint of Alcott's letters and journals provides deeper insight into the personality of Alcott, whose *Little Women* serves as the starting point for Brooks's novel *March*.

Brooks, Geraldine. *March*. New York: Perennial, 2006. This edition of the novel includes interviews with the author, informational features, and an article by Brooks titled "Little Facts."

_____. "Orpheus at the Plough: The Father of *Little Women*." *The New Yorker*, January, 2005. Offers a biographical study of A. Bronson Alcott, the father of Louisa May Alcott and the father figure who inspired Brooks to create the story of Mr. March.

Hubbard, Stacy Carson. "The Understory of *Little Women*." *Michigan Quarterly Review* 45, no. 4 (October, 2006): 722-726. An analysis of Brooks's book in the light of *Little Women*, highlighting the two main sources of conflict in the original novel and how Brooks resolves these conflicts.

Mardi, and a Voyage Thither

Author: Herman Melville (1819-1891)
First published: 1849
Type of work: Novel
Type of plot: Allegory
Time of plot: Mid-nineteenth century
Locale: Islands of the Western Pacific

Principal characters:
THE NARRATOR, later called Taji, a young American sailor mistaken for a god by the islanders
YILLAH, a blonde native, beloved of Taji, and symbolizing Good
HAUTIA, a dark native queen, in love with Taji, and symbolizing Evil
JARL, Taji's sailor companion
SAMOA, a native companion
MEDIA, a native king
YOOMY, Media's minstrel
BABBALANJA, Media's court philosopher

The Story:

The narrator of the story, a young American sailor, is picked up at Ravavai, a Pacific island, by a whaling vessel, the *Arcturion*. The voyage of the *Arcturion* is not a successful one, and when the ship begins to head for the cold climate of the Bay of Kamchatka, the young narrator and his special friend in the forecastle, Jarl, decide to leave the ship. Knowing the captain will not land them anywhere, they provision a small boat and in it escape from the ship under cover of darkness.

Heading westward, the two men hope to reach some hospitable islands. After sailing for many days, they come upon a drifting ship that seems to be a derelict. Finding it in fairly seaworthy condition, they board it. The following morning, a native man and woman are found in the rigging, where they had hidden from the narrator and Jarl. With the help of the natives, who had escaped with the ship from an unfriendly tribe of islanders after the latter had killed the ship's crew, the narrator and Jarl continue their voyage in search of land.

After many days of voyaging, the vessel is becalmed. In the storm that follows, the vessel is wrecked. Jarl and the narrator, with the native man, Samoa, set out in a little whaleboat. The native woman is killed during the storm. Many days later, they see a sail in the distance. Taking up their oars to aid the force of the sail, they slowly close in on the craft they had spotted. As they draw close, they see it is a strange arrangement of two native canoes with a platform built over them. After some discussion between the native priest in charge of the craft and the narrator, the sailor and Samoa board the native vessel. Once aboard the craft, they discover a beautiful blonde girl, but they have to force a passage through the natives to regain the whaleboat. In the scuffle, they take two of the natives prisoners. From the natives, they learn that the blonde girl is the priest's prisoner. Going back aboard the native craft, the sailor and Samoa rescue the girl and escape with her from the natives.

The girl, whose name is Yillah, wishes to return to her native islands. The narrator soon falls in love with her, and the girl, in native fashion, returns his affection. The narrator then decides that he will remain with her on her island home. Sighting a group of islands at last, the party heads for the nearest beach. Before they reach the shore, however, natives swim out to the whaleboat and give them an excited welcome. Towing the boat into shallow water, the natives pick it up and carry it ashore on their shoulders. The visitors are completely puzzled by their reception until they learn that the narrator has been mistaken for the natives' god, Taji, who, according to an ancient prophecy, would one day revisit them in human form. The natives also think that the other three occupants of the whaleboat are deities whom Taji has brought from another world for companionship.

Media, king of the atoll, makes the guests welcome, and Taji, as the narrator is now called, decides to make the best of his position, as long as his godhood put him under no particular constraints. He and Yillah, housed in a splendid grass house, live a life of tranquil happiness, doing no more than the islanders, who in their turn have little to do to make life comfortable. Then, suddenly, unhappiness strikes the island and Taji. He awakes one morning to find Yillah gone without a trace. Within a few days of Yillah's disappearance, Taji receives a visit from a portentously disguised messenger, who gives the young sailor a set of flower symbols from Queen Hautia, the dark queen of a group of distant islands.

The natives interpret the flower symbols from Hautia to mean that the Queen loves Taji, wishes his presence, and bode him not look for Yillah, his lost love. Not to be dissuaded, however, Taji, accompanied by King Media and a party of his courtiers, including Yoomy the poet-singer and Babbalanja the philosopher, sets sail in a huge, ornate native canoe in search of Yillah. Before the voyagers journeyed far on the ocean, they meet a black canoe containing more emissaries sent to Taji from Queen Hautia. The messengers, again using flower symbols interpreted by Yoomy, bode Taji forget his quest of the fair love and turn his canoe toward the kingdom of Hautia. Taji refuses and continues on his quest.

Taji's first stop is on the island of Juam, where Taji makes

a friend of King Donjalolo, a monarch who tries to escape reality by moving from one bower to another in his island kingdom and by taking no heed of anyone's happiness but his own and that of people who are in his company. Donjalolo aides Taji in his quest by sending messages around his island kingdom to ask for news of Yillah. After the petty princes come to Donjalolo's court to report that they know nothing of the girl, Taji decides to set out once more in the canoe, in the company of Media and his courtiers, to continue his search for his lost love. Again, this time in a more menacing fashion, he is accosted at sea by a canoe load of emissaries from Queen Hautia, who demand that he go to her immediately. Again, Taji refuses.

After many days and nights, during which Taji and his companions have lengthy conversations on many branches of knowledge and philosophy, they touch at an island where they visit the temple of Oro and learn of the Polynesian prophet, Alma, who had many years before, according to legend, brought peace, serenity, and love to the islands. Continuing their voyage through the archipelago of Mardi, representing the world and all its ideas, Taji and his party visit Vivenza, modeled on the United States, pass the Cape of Capes, see many other islands, regale one another with many philosophical conversations during the long hours at sea, and are finally becalmed. After the calm, a death cloud passes them. Following that adventure, they land at Serenia, a land that proves too quiet and too good for them.

At last, the only place left to look for Yillah, who has not been found on any one of the many atolls Taji and his companions have visited, is the bower of Queen Hautia herself. Babbalanja the philosopher, who remains in Serenia, tells Taji he will never find the unattainable Yillah, but Taji continues until three emissaries from Queen Hautia meet him and guide him to her land. Taji finds himself entranced by Hautia, who seems in some strange way connected with Yillah, though she invites him to sin; but still he asks in vain for word of Yillah. He is left in that land by the companions of his travels.

Critical Evaluation:

Perhaps no book by Herman Melville has been the subject of as much negative criticism as *Mardi, and a Voyage Thither.* Having written two books based on his actual experiences in the South Seas—*Typee* (1846) and *Omoo* (1847)—Melville wished in this, his third book, to abandon the travel narrative form for the imaginative freedom of the novel. *Mardi* imagines a map of islands unknown not only to its American narrator but also to the companion islanders who join him in a search for his beloved Yillah throughout the archipelago.

Somewhat in the manner of Jonathan Swift's *Gulliver's Travels* (1726), these islands are each allegories of different conditions of humanity. Some, like Dominora (England) and Vivenza (the United States), even represent actual nations. Many critics have objected to the confusion of the numerous symbols in this journey; the hodgepodge of different styles employed by Melville in the book; the weak main character, Taji; and the frequent passages of philosophical dialogue between Taji's companions, a Mardian king, philosopher, historian, and poet.

On the other hand, *Mardi* in many ways anticipates the concerns of Melville's later masterpiece, *Moby Dick* (1851). It has begun to be seen as a great work in its own right, although not without its challenges for the reader. Following Ralph Waldo Emerson's call for an authentic and original American literature, *Mardi*'s display of literary invention was fueled by Melville's ambition to be the author of the great work America awaited. This ambition led to a supremely self-conscious novel in which literary improvisation plays a large role.

Several different allegories are at work at once in this complex novel. Alongside Taji's search for Yillah, an embodiment of beauty, is the Mardian philosopher Babbalanja's search for the perfect society. In the meantime, the party flees Hautia, a lustful native queen, who represents possession of the narrator and an end to the quests of all involved. Frequent reflections of the process of writing itself indicate that the novel is first and foremost an allegory about literature and the novelist's attempt to create something new. Tension arises between the knowledge that one learns how to live from the past and the knowledge that one must break with this past if one is to make works that are original and worthwhile. As is true with Ishmael, the narrator of *Moby Dick*, Taji describes the writing of the work as if he were the author himself. Unlike Ishmael (and Melville), however, Taji understands that his book is not fully realized. Nonetheless, he is proud of having risked catastrophe, a possibility only when one has been ambitious enough to risk originality. "Give me, ye gods," he says late in the novel, "an utter wreck, if wreck I do." The reader's ultimate opinion of the novel will rest on whether he or she admires the degree to which Melville chanced something new, or, on the other hand, insists on a more polished finished product.

Even for readers who do not ultimately feel the novel is successful, Melville's brilliance as a novelist and thinker comes through: for instance, in his satirical edge in depicting Vivenza, an allegory of the United States. The natives of Vivenza are loud and jingoistic, braggarts with a high-flown rhetoric of freedom and selective historical memory who ignore the oppression of slaves and the poor, excusing all of their own faults through the singular merit of being without kings. This criticism is half-retracted as the party leaves the island, noting that Vivenza's democratic government may prove a light to the rest of the archipelago in the future, but Melville's points are clear. The United States in the 1840's was a confident nation, growing and pushing ever westward. Melville cautions Americans not to be blind to the national shame of slavery (still an institution when he wrote the novel), nor to trust that a rhetoric of freedom can replace its actual practice. What is called freedom may only be a disguise for misuse of individual authority and responsibility.

During the tour of islands, Melville increasingly uses the Mardian philosopher Babbalanja as a didactic mouthpiece, often very effectively. First, Babbalanja often cites the Mardian epic, *Koztanza*, by Lombardo, composed in much the same improvisational fashion as Melville's own work. Babbalanja's own quest also becomes important, linked with Taji's. His quest is not so much for truth as for peace of mind: a society where he can pursue spirituality with a conscience untroubled by the misery of others. Everywhere else in the archipelago, there is a dark underside to the locals' claims of utopia and right worship of Alma, the Mardian Christ figure. Often, injustice is economic in nature. The Mardian currency is human teeth; thus, the wealth of the rich is often directly composed of the misery of the poor. When the party reaches Serenia, where Alma is worshiped and all goods are shared (a suggestion of the incompatibility of Christianity and free-market capitalism), Babbalanja stays, calling his search complete.

Babbalanja here instructs Taji to give up his own quest, warning him that desire cannot be appeased. Life in Serenia is perfect for one who wishes to give up worldly concerns, but it is unsuitable to those who still want to pursue their desires. Taji's quest has been made problematic by his refusal to see his platonic companionship with Yillah as having any link to the sinful lust expressed by Hautia. Critics have suggested that Melville, recently married as he wrote the novel, projected his own puritanical sexual repression onto Taji in this allegory. Taji is surprised when he discovers, visiting Hautia's bower, that she and Yillah are linked. This means that desire for beauty (humanity's highest pursuit) and sexual expression (humanity's basest instinct) are linked. Taji cannot accept this association between his beloved and the power that he flees. The book ends with Taji still pursued by Hautia and her companions, as much Taji's personal demons as an objective embodiment of evil.

"Critical Evaluation" by Ted Pelton

Further Reading

Davis, Merrell. *Melville's "Mardi": A Chartless Voyage.* New Haven, Conn.: Yale University Press, 1952. The first book-length study of *Mardi.* Demonstrates Melville's ambition through analysis of letters to publisher John Murray. Asserts that the novel is an important harbinger of *Moby Dick* but in itself a failure.

Delbanco, Andrew. *Melville: His World and Work.* New York: Knopf, 2005. Delbanco's critically acclaimed biography places Melville in his time, with discussion about the debate over slavery and details of life in 1840's New York. Delbanco also discusses the significance of Melville's works at the time they were published and their reception into the twenty-first century.

Kelley, Wyn. "'A Regular Story Founded on Striking Incidents': *Mardi, Redburn,* and *White-Jacket.*" In *Herman Melville: An Introduction.* Malden, Mass.: Blackwell, 2008. Chronicles Melville's development as a writer, providing analyses of his works.

_____, ed. *A Companion to Herman Melville.* Malden, Mass.: Blackwell, 2006. Collection of thirty-five original essays aimed at twenty-first century readers of Melville's works. Includes discussions of Melville's travels; Melville and religion, slavery, and gender; and the Melville revival. Also includes the essay "The Motive for Metaphor: *Typee, Omoo,* and *Mardi.*"

Pullin, Faith, ed. *New Perspectives on Melville.* Kent, Ohio: Kent State University Press, 1978. Excellent collection of essays on Melville, including the essay "*Mardi:* Creating the Creative," a strong reply to Davis's thesis (above).

Rogin, Michael Paul. *Subversive Geneologies: The Politics and Art of Herman Melville.* Berkeley: University of California Press, 1979. Incisive psychological and Marxist reading of Melville's life and work, arguing that Melville was one of the leading thinkers of his age. The book's reading of Melville's family's place in the historical context of the 1840's is unparalleled.

Rollyson, Carl E., and Lisa Paddock. *Herman Melville A to Z: The Essential Reference to His Life and Work.* New York: Checkmark Books, 2001. Comprehensive coverage of Melville's life, works, and times. The 675 entries provide information on the characters, settings, allusions, and references in his fiction, his friends and associates, and the critics and scholars who have studied his work.

Maria Magdalena

Author: Friedrich Hebbel (1813-1863)
First produced: 1846; first published, 1844 (English translation, 1935)
Type of work: Drama
Type of plot: Domestic realism
Time of plot: Nineteenth century
Locale: Germany

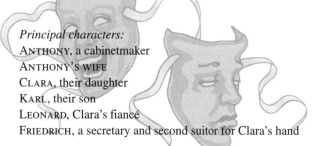

Principal characters:
ANTHONY, a cabinetmaker
ANTHONY'S WIFE
CLARA, their daughter
KARL, their son
LEONARD, Clara's fiancé
FRIEDRICH, a secretary and second suitor for Clara's hand

The Story:

After a long illness, from which she was not expected to recover, Anthony's wife, a woman in her fifties, feels that she has been given another chance to make herself worthy of heaven. To show her gratitude for this second chance, she dresses herself in her wedding gown, which is also to be her shroud, and goes to church the first Sunday morning she is able. Before she goes, she and her daughter Clara have a heart-to-heart talk, during which the mother discloses her fears about her son, Karl, who spends too much time drinking and playing and not enough time working steadily. The mother feels that his attitudes and his conduct are her fault, but still she refuses to believe he is really a bad young man.

The mother also raises the subject of Leonard, a poor young clerk who has visited Clara regularly but has not been seen for a while. Shortly after Clara's mother leaves for church, Leonard comes to see Clara and explains that he has not seen her for two weeks for a particular reason. During that time he has been attentive to the mayor's daughter in an effort to get himself a job as clerk for the city. Leonard also accuses her of being in love with another man even though, a very short time before, Clara had given herself to Leonard to prove her love. After they have straightened out the situation, Leonard tells Clara he has come to ask her father for her hand in marriage. Clara assures him that they must soon be married, lest her sin is to show. Even so, she has some misgivings about him when she learns of the chicanery he has executed in securing his position as town clerk.

Clara's father, when he learns of the proposed marriage and Leonard's prospects, seems agreeable to the marriage. Then the young man, knowing that old Anthony has loaned out a large sum of money, brings up the question of a dowry. He is surprised to learn, however, that Anthony has called in his money and has used it to help an old man who had befriended him in his youth. When the man had died, Anthony had refused to collect from the widow and had put the dead man's note in his casket. Leonard begins to think that, pregnancy or no, Clara is not a desirable wife for him.

At that time, the mother comes home from church and tells of having seen a newly prepared grave at the churchyard, a grave the sexton dug as an extra, in case it is needed while he is on a holiday. Anthony views it as an evil omen. Then the talk turns to a jewel robbery at the home of a rich merchant in town. Anthony recalls that his worthless son, Karl, has done some work at the house on the day of the robbery. Bailiffs knock at the door and demand permission to search the house for the stolen goods. The shock is so great that the mother swoons and dies. Leonard, who is already none too eager to marry Clara, seizes upon the charge as an excuse to break his betrothal to the girl.

As the days pass, Anthony's house is a place of wretchedness. All evidence seems to point to Karl's guilt in the matter of the theft, even though the jewels are not discovered in the house. Anthony also begins to suspect that Clara has strayed from the paths of virtue. He tells her that if she also brings shame on the family, he will cut his own throat with a razor. Clara, not wanting to be the cause of her father's death, decides that she must commit suicide before her father could do away with himself. One day, while Anthony is away visiting a deaf old woodcutter who has not heard of his family's disgrace, the rich merchant appears at the house with word that Karl is not guilty, that the jewels have been discovered in his own home, where the merchant's own mad wife had hidden them.

Clara, pleased to learn that Karl had been exonerated, believes that something will occur to make her life right again. Her belief seems to come true when Friedrich, a childhood sweetheart, calls to tell her that he still loves her and wishes to marry her. Even after Clara tells him of her fall from virtue, he says he loves her and will make her his wife. He also swears that he will arrange a duel with Leonard

and seek to kill the man who had seduced her. Since Friedrich has a good job as a secretary, Clara knows that her father will be glad to see her married to him. After the secretary leaves, however, all Clara's doubts again assail her, and she once more begins to think of suicide.

At last, Clara decides to see Leonard, whom she finds planning to fulfill his ambitions by marrying the mayor's daughter. Clara confronts him with the letter he had written her on the day of her mother's death, a letter telling her that he found it impossible to unite himself with the sister of a thief. Even though her brother has been cleared of the charges, Leonard still does not want to marry her, for he knows that a marriage with the mayor's daughter holds greater prospects for him. When Clara tells him of her father's plans for suicide, Leonard says the old man thinks too well of life to take his own. Even though Clara tells him she herself contemplated death, he shrugs off her threat, telling her she is not the first woman to be faced with the prospect of producing an illegitimate child. After Leonard again refuses to marry her, Clara leaves.

Shortly after her departure, the secretary appears with a pair of pistols and forces Leonard to leave with him. As they leave to fight a duel, Clara, at home, meets her brother, who tells her of his plans to go to sea. He asks Clara to get him something to eat. She complies and then goes to the well, ostensibly to get some fresh water, but actually to drown herself. While she is gone, Anthony returns from his visit with the woodcutter. Soon afterward the secretary, mortally wounded from the duel, staggers to the door. He tells how Leonard has been killed and asks old Anthony to forgive the girl. Just as Anthony begins to realize Clara's predicament, Karl runs in with the news that she has killed herself by jumping into the well. Friedrich points out to Anthony that his own weakness and pride caused him to talk of suicide and thus send his daughter to her death, lest her sin be a reflection on her father. All Anthony can say is that he no longer understands the world.

Critical Evaluation:

Maria Magdalena was the first bourgeois tragedy in German literature in which all the characters belonged to the lower middle class. Previous bourgeois tragedies had derived their momentum from conflict between the upper and lower classes. For example, a lower-class girl might be seduced and then abandoned by an upper-class lover. Friedrich Hebbel, however, has shown that "one need only be human to have a fate and in certain circumstances a terrible fate."

Written in prose instead of verse, *Maria Magdalena* is the germinal point in the emergence of modern realist drama. As

Hebbel points out in his preface, previous authors made mistakes in writing the dialogue of the common people, either giving them beautiful speeches that made them appear as "bewitched princes and princesses" or making them appear so woodenly stupid that it was surprising they could manage to say anything. Hebbel avoids both extremes and lets his characters speak naturally and convincingly.

While introducing the realist style, Hebbel still observed the three unities required by classical drama: the unities of time, place, and action. *Maria Magdalena* takes place within a few days, the encounters are mainly in Anthony's house, and the action centers on Clara's dilemma.

Clara is the main tragic figure in the play. Under duress, she submits to the sexual demands of Leonard, a member of her own class, but is subsequently jilted by him. Rather than bring shame on the family by having an illegitimate child, she commits suicide. The real tragedy, though, lies in the narrow bourgeois mentality that permits no exception to its notion of correctness.

Clara has reached an age where it is no longer acceptable for her to be single. The pressure on her to marry is made evident at the beginning of the drama in her mother's conversation and costume. In a masterful dramatic touch, Hebbel has the mother ask Clara pointedly about Leonard while wearing her own wedding dress. The theme of marriage is presented with strong visual reinforcement.

Significantly, Clara's thoughts are not so much of marriage as of self-sacrifice. Her ideal church scene, described in her closing monologue of act 1, scene 3, was enacted by a little Roman Catholic girl who had been given the first cherries of the year. Rather than eating them, she carried them to the altar as an offering. This vivid image of the cherries that are not eaten foreshadows the drastic fate of Clara and her child. She sacrifices herself to make sure that her family will not be disgraced.

Hebbel's economy of style ensures that every image enhances a major theme. Marriage is suggested by the wedding dress; self-sacrifice, by the cherries. Likewise, death is suggested by the grave digger. In an uncanny touch, the grave he is digging turns out to be for Clara's mother. Her death in turn foreshadows the trio of deaths at the end of the drama: Leonard, Friedrich, and Clara all meet violent ends. Repeated mention of wells and water creates a resonance of expectation in the audience for the circumstances of Clara's death.

The most widely used image in *Maria Magdalena* is the snake, which connotes deception and evil. Leonard is generally perceived as a snake because of his duplicity. He readily reveals his machinations and actually uses the snake image to describe himself. He says to Clara, "You be harmless as a dove, my sweet, and I'll be sly as a snake." Clara later uses the image in a way that stresses Leonard's predatory nature: "I thank you as I would a serpent that had wound itself about me and then suddenly let me go to prey on something else." Leonard, however, is not the only snake in the drama. Hebbel expands his application of the image to include the malicious gossips so dreaded by Anthony. In Friedrich's dying speech he says, "All you thought about was the tongues that would hiss—but not about the worthless snakes they belonged to."

Like Friedrich, many critics place the blame entirely on Anthony, the illiterate, self-righteous father who could tolerate anything but shame. It was his petty bourgeois values and threat of suicide that drove Clara to despair. However, in addition to depicting the destructive side of those values, Hebbel suggests by omission that the reaction Anthony anticipated on the part of the neighbors was grossly exaggerated. Society is not as much to blame as one might think. The neighbors, in fact, say nothing. They are conspicuously absent from the drama. Any influence they exert on Anthony's family is purely in Anthony's imagination; he is concerned with the insubstantial. The pastor tells Anthony that he is accountable for no one but himself and that it is "unchristian pride" that makes him want to accept responsibility for his adult son. Yet Anthony persists in his authoritarian and judgmental approach to his own children. Only in the title of the drama does Hebbel suggest the truly Christian alternative of forgiveness. The biblical reference in the title to Mary Magdalen, the fallen woman in need of forgiveness, exemplifies Hebbel's technique of influencing the audience directly without working through the medium of the players.

While it is tempting to follow Friedrich's lead and blame Anthony, one cannot ignore the complexity of the characters and oversimplify the action. Friedrich himself is not guiltless. Although loving Clara since childhood, he did not stay in touch with her during his student years, and, at the crucial moment, gave priority to dueling with Leonard rather than to comforting Clara. Leonard, the supposed blackguard, is also not completely guilty. Seen in his own right, he did have cause to be jealous and to be unenthusiastic about Clara's joyless description of married life. He was also properly disappointed that her dowry had disappeared and wary of the scandal surrounding her brother. As in real life, the distinctions are blurred between good and bad, right and wrong.

For such a short drama, *Maria Magdalena* has a tremendous impact. It is thought-provoking and masterfully written, with every detail essential to the whole. Hebbel introduced realism with consummate artistry.

"Critical Evaluation" by Jean M. Snook

Further Reading

Flygt, Sten G. *Friedrich Hebbel*. New York: Twayne, 1968. A useful plot summary of the play with interpretive observations. Discusses *Maria Magdalena* as Hebbel's first masterpiece; all characters belong to the lower middle class, which is presented as being ripe for change.

Glenn, Jerry H. "The Title of Hebbel's *Maria Magdalena*." *Papers on Language and Literature* 3, no. 2 (Spring, 1967): 122-133. An excellent analysis of the entire play. Like the Pharisees in the Bible, the members of Hebbel's bourgeois society are quick to condemn. The title suggests the Christian message of love and forgiveness that is so conspicuously absent in the play.

Hart, Gail K. "Sara and Klara: The Anachronistic Agonies of Hebbel's *Maria Magdalena* and the Italian Aftermath." In *Tragedy in Paradise: Family and Gender Politics in German Bourgeois Tragedy, 1750-1850*. Columbia, S.C.: Camden House, 1996. Examines *Maria Magdalena* and other German bourgeois family tragedies in which female characters threaten the stability of the domestic order by challenging male authority.

Menhennet, Alan. "Non-Austrian Historical Drama: C. F. Hebbel." In *The Historical Experience in German Drama: From Gryphius to Brecht*. Rochester, N.Y.: Camden House, 2003. A study of German dramas that convey an experience of history. Places these plays within the broader context of German history and literature.

Walsøe-Engel, Ingrid. *Fathers and Daughters: Patterns of Seduction in Tragedies by Gryphius, Lessing, Hebbel, and Kroetz*. Columbia, S.C.: Camden House, 1993. Devotes a chapter to an analysis of *Maria Magdalena*. Walsøe-Engel focuses on the father-daughter relationship in this and other German plays, and how that relationship is threatened when another man finds the daughter sexually alluring.

Weiss, Hermann F. "Animal and Nature References in F. Hebbel's *Maria Magdalena*." *Seminar* 7, no. 3 (October, 1971): 191-200. Anthony is associated with a hedgehog since he maintains a defensive position; Leonard, the villain of the play, is seen as a snake. The negative animal imagery emphasizes the inhumanity of society's moral standards.

Wells, G. A. "Hebbel's *Maria Magdalena* and Its Critics Past and Present." *Quinquereme* 6, no. 2 (1983): 141-154. Good formal and stylistic analysis of the play, with a critical overview of its reception. The characters Anthony, Leonard, and Friedrich are fatally flawed by their concern with "what people will say," making the play a tragedy of narrow-mindedness.

Marius the Epicurean
His Sensations and Ideas

Author: Walter Pater (1839-1894)
First published: 1885
Type of work: Novel
Type of plot: Philosophical
Time of plot: Second century
Locale: Roman Empire

Principal characters:
MARIUS, a young Roman of pagan tradition
FLAVIAN, a close friend of Marius at school
CORNELIUS, a Roman army officer and friend of Marius
MARCUS AURELIUS, philosopher-emperor of Rome
CECILIA, a friend of Cornelius and a Christian leader

The Story:

Marius is a young Roman whose family has for many years lived on Whitenights, an estate in northern Italy. On that estate, Marius had grown to adolescence in an atmosphere of pagan piety and rural simplicity. The family leads a relatively simple life because Marius's grandfather had squandered much of the family fortune. In the atmosphere of his childhood, Marius finds a great joy in worshiping the household gods and in overseeing the work on the estate. His life is one of contemplation rather than one of activity, and his idealism and religiosity are almost morbid in their extreme.

While still in his teens, young Marius is taken to a temple of Aesculapius in the Etrurian hills for the cure of a childhood disease. There the quiet, fresh atmosphere of the place, as well as the teachings of Galen, the great Roman physician, give him a new outlook on life. Upon his return home, Marius finds his mother's health failing. She dies shortly afterward, and the effect of her death on Marius is to turn him into a skeptic, a young man who questions all aspects of life as they present themselves to him.

Soon afterward, relatives send young Marius to Pisa, where he attends school. While there, he conceives the idea of becoming a poet of the intellectual school. His inclination in that direction is stimulated by his friendship with Flavian, a schoolmate. Flavian is three years older than Marius and has great influence over the younger boy. The two read all the literature and philosophy they find. Among the works they pore over is the *Metamorphoses* of Apuleius; its ornate style is a source of great joy to Marius.

The studies in literature and philosophy that the two young men plan, however, are short-lived. Flavian gets sick after an excursion with Marius, and he dies soon after of a plague brought back to Italy by the armies of Marcus Aurelius, who had just returned from a campaign into the eastern reaches of the Roman Empire. After Flavian's death, Marius needs an intellectual crutch to carry him through the agony of seeing his young friend die, and he becomes attracted to the study of mysticism. At last, he puts aside the desire to look to Asian mystic lore and turns to early Greek philosophers to find some answer to his problems in their writings and thought.

One of the first writers he studies is Heraclitus, who teaches him to limit his labors so that he will not lose everything by trying to master all knowledge at once. From Heraclitus, he turns to the teachings of Aristippus of Cyrene, founder of the Epicurean school. From his study of Cyrenaic philosophy, Marius concludes that knowledge is limited to experiences received through the senses, and he thinks that he owes it to himself to have many sensuous experiences to reach the highest possible point of wisdom.

The idea appeals to Marius because of the immensely practical ethics that the whole concept implies. Life as the primary end of life is the code that Marius finds himself professing; it is, of course, an antimetaphysical metaphysic. Through it, Marius hopes to find, by means of cultural knowledge, the secret of the present in the changing universe; he wants to discover all the subtle realizations implied in each moment of life. Like Epicureans of that time and since, Marius finds there are those who misinterpret his credo and believe that he seeks pleasure as an end in itself; yet hedonism, the search for pleasure as the purpose of life, is farthest from his mind. Such a life would have been too gross for one of Marius's pietistic background. During his search for an answer to life, Marius turns from poetry to prose, which he feels better fits his nature and his studies.

About the time that his Epicureanism became crystallized in his mind, Marius feels some pangs of regret that his emotional life seems to have become stunted. He wonders why it is that he feels more inclined to research of the mind than to normal human emotions. He cannot feel the necessity of pursuing feminine company and does not regret that he has not found it a matter of urgency that he acquire a wife. Love, in the ordinary sense of the word, does not seem to be a part of his makeup.

At a time when this problem is disturbing him, he has a summons to Rome that interrupts his worries. He is called to become secretary and editor to Emperor Marcus Aurelius, a prolific writer and a patron of the arts and philosophy. Marcus Aurelius has been working for some time on a memoir and a series of disconnected meditations that he wished someone to put into edited form. That task was assigned to Marius.

On the way to Rome, Marius meets a young officer of the army named Cornelius, an officer of the famed Twelfth Legion, who is returning to Rome after service in the farther reaches of northern Europe. Under the tutelage of Cornelius, Marius quickly makes himself at home in the city. Fortunately, Marius's family has a house in Rome, although it has not been used in many years. To the young Epicurean, Rome is a wonderful place in which to live; for several years, Marius is happy there. Experiences of the richest nature are his; thanks to his family background and the emperor's patronage, he moves in the best of circles.

There is, however, something that Marius cannot fathom. His friend, Cornelius, seems much happier than he. Since Cornelius is not a simple materialistic person, Marius cannot understand why his friend is so much happier. One day as they are returning from a trip away from Rome, Cornelius takes Marius into a rich home on the Appian Way. It is the residence of the widow of Cecilius. Cecilia, the home's mistress, is a Christian, as is Cornelius. From that moment, Marius begins to comprehend something of the new religion that is making converts in the empire. He finds a strange kind of happiness in attending mass in the home of Cecilia, and he also feels a strange attraction to Cecilia herself.

Some months later, when Cornelius and Marius are once again away from Rome, the small town in which they have stopped was shaken by an earthquake. After the first tremors of the quake pass, Cornelius, accompanied by Marius, joins a group of Christians who are publicly thanking the Deity for their escape from death. Fearing that the Christians caused the earthquake, the pagans of the town assault them. Marius and Cornelius are arrested because of their rank and sent to Rome. On the way, their captors learn that one of them is not a Christian. To save his friend, Marius says that the non-Christian is Cornelius, who is then set free. Marius himself becomes violently ill before he and his guards reach Rome. He is left behind to die, but some villagers, who are also Christians, find him and nurse him. He dies with Christian prayers in his ears.

Critical Evaluation:

Walter Pater's novel was an answer to those who had misunderstood his views on art and philosophy. The novel is, in great part, a fictional rendering of Pater's own struggle for a philosophical position, and the personality of Marius is a reflection of the author himself. The volume is also an appreciation of the culture of the second century of the Christian era in Roman Italy. Although sharply criticized by historians of fact, Pater's careful study of the environment has caught the spirit of the times and the people. No one who has not some familiarity with the writers of the time, and before, can read with signal success the intellectual adventures and development of the young Roman who is the central figure of the book; the work is, to some extent, a veritable patchwork of ideas and even quotations from the classical authors who would be the basis of knowledge for a young Roman studying seriously during the reign of Marcus Aurelius.

In his portrayal of Marius the Epicurean, Pater shows what might have happened to a young man of Marius's sort during Marcus Aurelius's reign. With precision and accuracy, he also unconsciously delineates the nature of a middle-aged, middle-class bachelor-scholar of about the year 1880. Pater thought that the purpose of higher education was to teach art and poetry, so he incorporates this philosophy into Marius's development. Perhaps this is the reason that *Marius the Epicurean* contains more poetry—not from books and pictures, but from life as Pater saw it—than any of Pater's other works.

The setting of Marius's spiritual journey is chiefly Rome. It is in this, "the most religious city of the world," that readers are given glimpses of many various religions: the religion of Numa, the religion of Isis, the medical cult of Aesculapius, and the new Christianity. It is by mentioning these religions and having Marius influenced by them that Pater is, from the beginning, able to present a deeply serious tone to the work.

Having chosen the appropriate setting, Pater selected characters that best suited his purpose from the history, philosophy, art, and literature of the age. Such characters as Lucius, Apuleius, Cornelius, Fronto, Marcus Aurelius, and Lucien are leading figures in the Latin literature of Marius's day. The Greek physician Galen is also introduced, and also

presented is the future patron saint of Christian music, Cecilia. Ideas of Pliny, Tibullus, Lucretius, Horace, and Vergil are sprinkled throughout the book and add to the philosophical and literary atmosphere. With the imaginary life of Marius as his framework, Pater is able to present what is to him the most important and impressive ideas of the period.

Marius the Epicurean is not easily classified. From its opening pages, one is aware of an unusual reading experience. Pater's writing is often obscure, but is often leisurely and poetic. Interested readers should consult Pater's *Appreciation with an Essay on Style* (1889) for his views on style. Whereas many great Victorian literary artists tend to argue their various doctrines with heavy-handed urgency, Pater whispers and murmurs to his audience, usually in a calm, almost somber tone. It is because each phrase is intricately fashioned that *Marius the Epicurean* is often referred to not only as a philosophical romance (rather than a novel) but also as a prose poem. The many details of the story are easily forgotten, but the overall tonal effect of the work lingers in the mind. It is not the figures, lingering in misty shadows, that capture the attention; the philosophy, aesthetics, and religious doctrines are not easily associated with any concrete individual or personality. The characters serve mainly as vehicles through which Pater can fulfill his major purpose—exposing his listener to the intellectual and philosophical timbre of ancient Rome.

Further Reading

Bloom, Harold, ed. *Walter Pater.* New York: Chelsea House, 1985. Includes considerable evaluation of *Marius the Epicurean.* Ranges from detailed stylistic analysis to questions of genre. Pater's work is also evaluated as an inspiration to writers of the early twentieth century.

Brake, Laurel, Lesley Higgins, and Carolyn Williams, eds. *Walter Pater: Transparencies of Desire.* Greensboro, N.C.: ELT Press, 2002. Collection of essays, including discussions of *Marius the Epicurean*, Pater and modernism, and Pater's reception outside England. Contains a bibliography and an index.

Crinkley, Richmond. *Walter Pater: Humanist.* Lexington: University Press of Kentucky, 1970. In the chapter analyzing *Marius the Epicurean*, the circular structure of the text and the diminished presence of the author is considered. Also delineates the decorative elements in Pater's prose.

Daley, Kenneth. *The Rescue of Romanticism: Walter Pater and John Ruskin.* Athens: Ohio University Press, 2001. Daley examines the relationship of the two prominent Victorian art critics, focusing on their different theories of

Romanticism. He demonstrates how Pater's theory was a response to John Ruskin, whom Pater considered a conservative thinker.

Donoghue, Denis. *Walter Pater: Lover of Strange Souls.* New York: Knopf, 1995. An exceptional biographical and critical source. Donoghue defines Pater as a precursor of modernism who influenced the later works of James Joyce, T. S. Eliot, Virginia Woolf, and others.

Iser, Wolfgang. *Walter Pater: The Aesthetic Moment.* Translated by David H. Wilson. New York: Cambridge University Press, 1987. Examines the narrative structure of Pater's portraits. Finds that significant narrative inconsistencies create a state of flux between past and present. Considers Pater's theories on memory and history.

Monsman, Gerald. *Walter Pater.* Boston: Twayne, 1977. Combines a broad overview of Pater's work with a more focused critique of the novels. The chapter on *Marius the Epicurean* points out the emphasis on inward vision rather than outward events.

Shuter, William. *Rereading Walter Pater.* New ed. New York: Cambridge University Press, 2005. A reevaluation of Pater's writings. Shuter initially provides a conventional account of the texts in the order in which they were written; he then returns to the earlier books, demonstrating how the later work, paradoxically, offers an introduction to the earlier.

Ward, Anthony. *Walter Pater: The Idea in Nature.* London: Macgibbon & Kee, 1966. Traces Pater's explorations of a literary style that expresses the complexity of experience and the inconstancy of meaning. Also examines the recurrent quest for beauty in Pater's fictional and nonfictional works.

Marmion
A Tale of Flodden Field

Author: Sir Walter Scott (1771-1832)
First published: 1808
Type of work: Poetry
Type of plot: Historical
Time of plot: Early sixteenth century
Locale: Scottish border

Principal characters:
LORD MARMION, an English knight
RALPH DE WILTON, wronged by Marmion, disguised as a palmer
CLARE FITZ-CLARE, loved by de Wilton
CONSTANCE DE BEVERLEY, betrayed by Marmion
ARCHIBALD DOUGLAS, earl of Angus

The Poem:

Wherever Lord Marmion goes, he is welcomed and honored as a brave and valiant knight. The English king has sent him to the Scottish court to try to persuade that country's king to end armed raids in the Border country. Marmion asks a Scottish lord to furnish him a guide, someone of peaceful appearance, and since no one else is available the lord sends a palmer, a holy man who had made many pilgrimages to religious shrines.

At the same time, an abbess, accompanied by several nuns, is making a sea voyage to Cuthbert Isle to hold an inquisition over two prisoners of the Church. One of the young nuns aboard, still a novice, is Clare Fitz-Clare, a lovely young woman who had entered the abbey after her lover, dishonored, had, it was believed, died. One of the accused is Constance de Beverley, a nun who has broken her vows and run away from the convent. Before she is put to death, Constance tells the abbess and her other accusers the story of her fall from grace.

Constance's betrayer is Lord Marmion. Believing his protestations of love for her, she escapes from the convent and follows him for three years as his page. Then Marmion meets lovely Clare Fitz-Clare, and, because she is an heir of great wealth, he abandons Constance to seek Clare for his bride. The king promises him that he should have Clare, but she loves another knight, Ralph de Wilton.

Marmion forges papers that offer false proof that Wilton is not true to the king. The two knights fight a duel, and de Wilton is left for dead. Constance, soon to die, gives the papers proving the forgery to the abbess and implores her to get the papers to the king to save Clare from a hateful marriage. Although the woman has entered a convent rather than marry Marmion, the king will force the marriage if Clare is found, for Marmion is a great favorite at court. Although her judges pity her, Constance is put to a horrible death after she tells her story.

Marmion continues on his way to the court. Guilty thoughts of Constance worry him; he had been responsible for her capture by the Church. He soothes his conscience with the belief that she will not be severely punished. One night as they stay at an inn a young boy sings a ballad about the soul's disquiet of every man who would betray a maid. At the end of the song Marmion thinks he hears the tolling of a death bell. When the knight mentions the tolling sound he hears, the palmer speaks his first words, saying that it is the toll of death for a friend. That night Marmion, unable to sleep, goes out into the dark to ride. There he is attacked by what seems a devil, for the man has the face of de Wilton, long dead. The strangest part is that Marmion's mysterious adversary could have killed him, but instead sheathes his sword and rides off into the night.

As Marmion and his men ride through the Border country, they notice everywhere huge numbers of armed clansmen readying for battle. On their arrival at the Scottish court, Marmion cannot persuade King James to halt preparations for battle. The Scots, claiming that the English wronged them, demand vengeance. Courtesy requires that Marmion be given safe conduct during his mission, however, and so the king puts him in the care of Archibald Douglas, one of the most powerful of all the lords of Scotland. Douglas also is charged with the care of the abbess and her nuns, who are to be returned safely to their convent but who have been taken captive, it being time of war, by the Scots. The abbess fears for Clare's safety if Marmion should learn that she is among the party of nuns. To save Clare from a forced and hated union, the holy woman gives the papers proving Marmion's forgery to the palmer and begs him to deliver them to the English king.

Marmion, learning the woman's identity, secures an order directing him to take Clare to her home, with Douglas for an escort. Separated from the abbess, Clare fears for her safety with Marmion, but he plans not to press his suit until she has been returned to her kinsmen, who will be dominated by the king. Marmion and Clare are quartered in Tantallon Castle, owned by Archibald Douglas, earl of Angus, to await the impending battle between English and Scottish troops.

Clare, lonely and afraid, walks out onto the battlements of the castle. There she meets a young knight who proves to be de Wilton. Clare hears his story. He had not been mortally wounded in his combat with Marmion, but had been healed and cared for by one of his servants. The loyal servant asks one boon for saving his life, that should de Wilton's deadliest enemy fall beneath his sword that enemy should be spared. The young knight wanders far, his name scorned by all who once loved him because he is now branded as a traitor. At last he disguises himself so well that no one recognizes in the lowly palmer the once-proud knight. It is de Wilton who had so frightened Marmion during his midnight ride, but he had kept his promise to his old servant and spared the life of the man who had ruined him. The young man told Douglas his story, which was confirmed by the papers given him by the abbess. That night Douglas restores to de Wilton his knightly honors, and the next day de Wilton joins the English troops.

Marmion, unable to resist the spectacle of troops drawn up for battle, defies Douglas and rides off to join the fight. Having learned from one of his company the palmer's true identity and fearing that he will lose Clare, he takes her to a place of safety behind the English lines. When the battle begins, Marmion is mortally wounded. Clare, pitying the man she hates, tended him gently. Before he dies, Marmion learns of the death of Constance and repents all his sins.

The English defeat the Scots in a bloody battle on Flodden Field. De Wilton is everywhere in the thick of the fighting. After the battle, his lands and his titles are returned to him, and Clare is given to him with the king's blessing. The proud name of de Wilton is known again through the land. Marmion, as he deserved, lay in an unmarked grave.

Critical Evaluation:

In 1488, a group of Scottish nobles rebelled against their king, James III, and defeated him in battle. Following their murder of the monarch, James III was succeeded on the throne by his fifteen-year-old son, James IV, who unified Scotland and led it to new prosperity. During the twenty-five years of James IV's eventful reign, the Spanish Inquisition would establish a well-deserved reputation for intolerance and cruelty, the Star Chamber of England's Henry VII would deprive his subjects of their civil rights, a fanatic Florentine monk named Girolamo Savonarola would preach against the supposed sinfulness of some of the world's greatest art, and Christopher Columbus would land in the Americas. As subsequent explorations revealed hitherto unknown lands in the Americas and Africa and new trade routes to Asia, European powers struggled to adjust.

The opportunities offered by political instability and expanded geographical horizons tempted many to enhance their fortunes through military conquests of various kinds, not only in the New World but also in Europe. Anxious to gain influence over his southern neighbor, for example, James IV of Scotland expanded his army and navy, actively supported a young pretender to the English throne named

Perkin Warbeck, and threatened to invade England. Scotland had allied itself with France against England, but England defeated them both. James IV's attempt to take England by force came to an abrupt halt September 9, 1513, just south of the border between the two countries. In the Battle of Flodden Field, an army sent from London defeated that of the Scots, killing James IV and most of his nobles. This is also the conflict that climaxes Sir Walter Scott's *Marmion*.

In *Marmion*, Scott makes no attempt to depict the broader aspects of early sixteenth century history, exciting and significant as they certainly were. The world of *Marmion* comprises the English, the Scots, and the Church, with the latter represented ambiguously by both the Inquisition and various nuns. As was usual in Scott's work, Marmion himself (supposedly the protagonist or hero) is mostly a spectator to the great historical events of which he is accidentally a part. What was not usual is that he also appears as something of a villain, having forged an important letter dishonoring the real hero of the poem, de Wilton. In the end, he dies and deserves to. If Marmion is compared with any of the characters in Scott's previous long poem, *The Lay of the Last Minstrel* (1805), it is apparent that, unlike them, Marmion embodies complexities, contradictions, and internal torment. Although still somewhat crude, Marmion is the most sophisticated character yet created by Scott.

In some respects, *Marmion* is also a better-written poem than its predecessor. Although *Marmion* makes use of several different stanzaic forms, there is less experimentation overall. Interpolated songs and tales are less frequent and generally longer, as with the Host's Tale in canto 3, stanzas 19 to 25. The narrator also emerges as a separate voice in canto 3, stanza 12, but he remains unidentified and has disappeared by the end of the poem. The epigrammatic wisdom of which he is sometimes master emerges most memorably in canto 6, stanza 17 ("Oh! what a tangled web we weave/ When first we practice to deceive," a reference to Marmion's forgery of the letter). The lines in stanza 30 are also famous. Notable, too, is the incisive portrait of James IV in canto 5, stanzas 8 and 9. "Lochinvar," the famous interpolated song, is at canto 5, stanza 12, but is irrelevant to the plot.

Each of the poem's six cantos is preceded by an introduction. These introductions (some of which originated as separate poems before *Marmion* was begun) are verse epistles, or letters, to individuals then living, all of them friends of Scott. Personal, confessional, and often charming, Scott's introductions are more in accord with modern taste than are the cantos they introduce; one can only regret that Scott did not choose to write more often about himself and those he knew at first hand.

In the introduction to canto 1, Scott abandons his usual reticence on contemporary matters to praise the recently deceased English statesmen William Pitt and Charles Fox. He also recalls the grand poetic tradition of England, including the sixteenth and seventeenth century writers Edmund Spenser, John Milton, and John Dryden, who, although they may have themes in common, are to be contrasted with the "dwindled sons of little men" writing at that time. The introduction to canto 4 similarly recalls William Shakespeare and the eighteenth century poet Thomas Gray. Imitating the latter's artificial diction, Scott humorously refers to his own, less carefully crafted verse as "this rambling strain." The youthful, aspiring poet Lord Byron would fully agree with Scott's self-deprecation and promptly satirized *Marmion* in "English Bards and Scotch Reviewers" (1809). The general strength of canto 6, including the delightful invocations of Christmas now and then, de Wilton's history (stanzas 6-10), the death of Marmion (31-32), and the elegiac regard for defeated Scotland (34-35), set a standard that Byron then could not have met.

"Critical Evaluation" by Dennis R. Dean

Further Reading

Alexander, J. H., and David Hewett, eds. *Scott and His Influence.* Aberdeen: Association for Scottish Literary Studies, 1983. Collection of scholarly papers on a variety of Scott topics, including a discussion of *Marmion*.

Cockshut, A. O. J. *The Achievement of Walter Scott.* London: Collins, 1969. A reasonable, centrist, and widely available introduction to Scott and his work. Chapters on Scott's major poems precede those dealing with his novels and other works.

Felluga, Dino Franco. *The Perversity of Poetry: Romantic Ideology and the Popular Male Poet of Genius.* Albany: State University of New York Press, 2005. An examination of the nineteenth century reception for Romantic poetry, focusing on the work of Scott and Lord Byron. Demonstrates how Scott's poetry was represented as a panacea for the era's utilitarianism, capitalism, industrialism, and democracy.

Gamer, Michael. "'To Foist Thy Stale Romance': Scott, Antiquarianism, and Authorship." In *Romanticism and the Gothic: Genre, Reception, and Canon Formation.* New York: Cambridge University Press, 2000. Gamer analyzes Scott's poetry and works by other Romantic writers to demonstrate how these authors were influenced by many of the conventions of earlier gothic literature.

Goslee, Nancy Moore. *Scott the Rhymer.* Lexington: University Press of Kentucky, 1988. Includes separate chapters on *Marmion, The Lay of the Last Minstrel*, and *The Lady of the Lake* (1810). One of the few serious critiques of Scott's long poems since modern techniques of analysis were developed.

Johnson, Edgar. *Sir Walter Scott: The Great Unknown.* 2 vols. New York: Macmillan, 1970. Johnson's critical biography is one of the most important modern books on Scott. Contains unsurpassed discussions of his major poems, including *Marmion, The Lay of the Last Minstrel*, and *The Lady of the Lake.* Commemorates the two hundredth anniversary of Scott's birth.

Lincoln, Andrew. "Towards the Modern Nation: *The Lay of the Last Minstrel, Marmion, The Lady of the Lake,* and *Waverly.*" In *Walter Scott and Modernity.* Edinburgh: Edinburgh University Press, 2007. In his examination of Scott's novels and poems, Lincoln argues that these are not works of nostalgia; instead, Scott used the past as a means of exploring modernist moral, political, and social issues.

The Marquise of O——

Author: Heinrich von Kleist (1777-1811)
First published: 1808 (English translation, 1960)
Type of work: Novella
Type of plot: Symbolic realism
Time of plot: Early nineteenth century
Locale: Northern Italy

Principal characters:
GIULIETTA, the MARQUISE OF O——, a young widow with two children
LORENZO G——, her father, a colonel
HER MOTHER,
COUNT F——, a Russian lieutenant colonel

The Story:

A young widow, Giulietta, the marquise of O——, has placed a notice in the newspaper announcing that she is pregnant and does not know how she came to be pregnant. The notice says that she will marry the man who presents himself as the father of her child. The marquise already has children and enjoys the respect of her family and community. Her father is a colonel and in command of a fortress, and her late husband, the marquis, had died on a business trip to Paris. After his death, she was urged home by her mother, and she has been living with her parents quietly, pursuing her own education and that of her children while caring for her parents.

War breaks out, disturbing the marquise's tranquil retreat. Before she and her mother can leave the fort, Russian troops storm in. The wing of the house where the women have taken shelter catches fire, and the marquise flees, separated from her mother and exposed to the invading soldiers. A group of sharpshooters attacks her with the intention of raping her. Russian count F—— comes to her rescue. He fights her attackers, gives her his arm with a polite address in French, and guides her to safety in the other wing of the palace. She perceives her rescuer as an angel. The marquise's women servants arrive, and the count leaves to return to the fight.

Colonel Lorenzo G——, Giulietta's father, has been awaiting an opportunity to surrender to the proper authority, and when the count appears he hands over his weapon and asks to see his family. He learns of the attack on his daughter and tells the Russian general who comes to take charge of the fort about the disgraceful behavior of his troops. The count, meanwhile, has been working feverishly to put out the fire in the palace, and when his general asks him to identify the men who insulted the marquise, he says that he was unable to see their faces. The general orders summary execution of the men after finding one wounded participant in the attack who names his partners in crime. The Russian troops, including Count F——, vacate the fort. The marquise tries to contact her hero, but he sends his apologies and does not see her again.

While the family is trying to find a way to thank the count, news arrives that he has been fatally shot in battle, a shot witnessed by the bearer of the message himself. The count's dying words indicate that the shot is his just punishment for a crime he has committed against a woman named Giulietta. The marquise, hearing this, is amazed that he has been intimate with a woman who shares her first name.

The colonel and his family turn the fort over to the Russian victors and move into a house in the nearby town, where they resume their quiet and ordered life. The daily routine is disrupted when the marquise begins to have symptoms that, in any other woman, she would identify with pregnancy. They all laugh about this impossibility.

The count shocks the family by appearing at their new home. He looks pale, and before they can ask any questions, he inquires about the health of the marquise. She answers that she has been a little ill. He unexpectedly asks her to marry him. The whole family feels astonishment, and they deflect the proposal with questions about his own miraculous recovery from the purportedly fatal bullet wound. He replies that he was on the verge of death and thought only of the marquise. After returning to the army, he reports, he began to write many times, but since he is now en route to deliver messages to Naples, he had decided to come in person. He thinks he will be sent on a longer journey to Saint Petersburg, so he urges an immediate answer to his suit, puzzling the family even more. When he insists on staying with the marquise until she makes a decision—placing him in peril of a court martial—the family decides together that the marquise will wait for him to complete his duty to the army and will then consent, provided the investigation into his lineage and character reveal no obstacles to the match.

The count leaves, and the inquiries proceed with good results. The marquise begins to feel ill again and calls in the family doctor, who states unequivocally that she is pregnant. Greatly distressed, the marquise asks for a midwife, and after an examination, the midwife confirms the pregnancy. The marquise cannot understand her own condition, and her father finds her protested innocence incredible. The colonel dictates a letter to his daughter through his wife, and Giulietta's tearful mother delivers the verdict that her daughter must leave the house. Giulietta pleads with her father in person. He reaches for his pistol, accidentally firing it into the ceiling. The marquise prepares to leave, and when her father sends for the children, she refuses to part with them.

Strengthened by the knowledge that she is innocent and by her ability to act on her own resolve, she returns to her former husband's estate to live a cloistered existence. She decides to place a notice in the newspaper, asking for the hand of the father of her child.

The count returns after his longer-than-expected journey and learns that the family has disowned Giulietta because of her pregnancy. He rides at once to find her and discovers her working in the garden of her house. His appearance surprises the marquise. He embraces her and assures her that he fully believes her claim that she is innocent and does not know the father of her child. He reiterates his desire to marry and then kisses her, but she refuses to listen to the secret he wants to whisper—she leaves him. When he returns to the inn where he is staying, he is shown the notice placed by the marquise in the newspaper and recognizes this new opportunity to approach her.

A responding notice appears in the paper requiring the marquise to meet the father of her child at the home of her parents. She contacts her father for permission to meet the unknown man at his house. The colonel suspects a ruse on his daughter's part, but her mother develops a test of her daughter's innocence and her father allows her to carry out the plan. The marquise's mother goes to her daughter with the news that a penniless groom had fathered the child as she slept. Giulietta readily accepts this fiction, proving her purity. Father and daughter are reconciled, though mother insists that the colonel humble himself and ask his daughter's forgiveness. He does so, and he and the marquise spend hours in his study in a rapt embrace before mother returns and calls them to a joyful dinner.

On the morning when the father of the child is to present himself, the household vibrates with tension. The count appears, wholly unexpected. Although the family is inclined to be relieved that he is the prospective husband and the father, Giulietta refuses to speak with him and storms out of the room. Because of her pregnancy, the marriage continues as planned, and the two are united in a cold, formal ceremony at the church. The count withdraws, and the marquise proceeds with life as if she had no husband.

The child is born and the count has been living in town for some time without attempting to contact or disturb his wife or child in any way. His consistent respect for her wishes finally wins her over. The marquise says that she could only see him as a demon—until now—because she had first seen him as her savior.

Critical Evaluation:

Heinrich von Kleist's *The Marquise of O——* plays an important role in genre studies of the novella, a form closely associated with the Romantic period of literature in Germany. The novella occupies a place between the short story and the novel and usually involves a framing device of some kind and often a central symbol. Though Kleist characterized this work as a tale (*Erzählung*), critics have assimilated it to the novellas contemporary to it because of its substantial length and the framing device in which the narrator claims to be telling a true story.

The work also allows significant character development, as it spans the time from the first encounter between Giulietta and Count F—— to the birth of their child and subsequent reconciliation. The narrator frames the story as if it were factual by claiming to have changed the setting from southern to northern Italy and by suppressing the names of the characters.

The central symbol of the novella can be seen in the

count's memory of throwing mud at a white swan as a child on his father's estate. As the count recovers from a bullet wound, he recounts this vision to the marquise, explaining that her face became interchangeable with the figure of the swan in his fevered mind.

The Marquise of O—— supports powerful psychological readings of family relationships, both between the parents and their daughter and between the lover-rapist Count F—— and his beloved-victim Giulietta. The powerful bond between the marquise and her parents grows even stronger when she moves back in with them as a widow. Her status as widow leaves her open to both a return to the status of a minor under her father's protection and to the ambiguous status of unmarried daughter. A widow can no longer prove her virginity in the face of public slander, and a daughter cannot rely on the protection of a husband in the face of a father's wrath.

Within the erotic economy of the story, the reconciliation between Giulietta and Lorenzo G——, her father, who are the only two named characters in the story, is depicted in startling romantic fashion that parallels the scene in which the count enters the garden and embraces Giulietta. The initial meeting between Giulietta and Count F—— places him in the role of rescuer and opportunistic rapist, a paradox that drives the action toward a forced resolution.

Amee Carmines

Further Reading

Fischer, Bernd, ed. *A Companion to the Works of Heinrich von Kleist*. Rochester, N.Y.: Camden House, 2003. This useful overview places Kleist in the history of the novella and offers a fine general reading of this particular story. It includes chapters on theme as well as chapters centered on specific works.

Gelus, Marjorie. "Patriarchy's Fragile Boundaries Under Siege: Three Stories of Heinrich von Kleist." *Women in German Yearbook: Feminist Studies in German Literature and Culture* 10 (1995): 59-82. Gelus offers a balanced feminist approach to *The Marquise of O——* with special attention to the symbolic nature of the count's dream about the white swan.

McAllister, Grant Profant, Jr. *Kleist's Female Leading Characters and the Subversion of Idealist Discourse*. New York: Peter Lang, 2005. This book approaches Kleist from a philosophical perspective and reads female characters such as the marquise in terms of their power to contest the dominant ideological frame of the works in which they appear.

McGlathery, James M. *Desire's Sway: The Plays and Stories of Heinrich von Kleist*. Detroit, Mich.: Wayne State University Press, 1983. McGlathery offers a compelling reading of the centrality of human desire—which may issue in love or death—in Kleist's novellas and plays.

Weineck, Silke-Maria. "Kleist and the Resurrection of the Father." *Eighteenth Century Studies* 37, no. 1 (Fall, 2003): 69-89. This article carries out a nuanced psychoanalytical reading of *The Marquise of O——* in relation to other works by Kleist that treat the role of the father figure.

Winnett, Susan. "The Marquise's 'O' and the Mad Dash of Narrative." In *Rape and Representation*, edited by Lynn A. Higgins and Brenda R. Silver. New York: Columbia University Press, 1991. Winnett offers a feminist reading of the novella replete with the most current theoretical thinking, in particular that of critic-novelist Monique Wittig. Winnett's reading helps explain the ongoing interest in this early nineteenth century tale.

Marriage à la Mode

Author: John Dryden (1631-1700)
First produced: 1672; first published, 1673
Type of work: Drama
Type of plot: Comedy of manners
Time of plot: Seventeenth century
Locale: Sicily

Principal characters:
RHODOPHIL, a captain of the king's guards
DORALICE, his wife
PALAMEDE, a courtier
MELANTHA, his betrothed
POLYDAMAS, king of Sicily
PALMYRA, his daughter
LEONIDAS, the true prince

The Story:

Palamede, a courtier who has just returned to Sicily after an absence of five years, overhears Doralice singing a song justifying inconstancy in marriage. Smitten by her great beauty, Palamede promptly declares his love. The information that Doralice is married does not abate his ardor; instead, he confesses that he himself is to be married in three days. The two resolve to meet again. Having been informed that Rhodophil, her husband, is approaching, Doralice abruptly departs.

Rhodophil welcomes Palamede back to court. He sympathizes with him over his approaching marriage, complaining that he himself has found no joy in marriage after the first six months. Palamede advises him to take a mistress, a remedy that Rhodophil says he was already trying to effect. He has found a woman whom he desires, but her obsession with court society has prevented her from keeping her assignations. The conversation ends with the approach of Argaleon, the king's favorite, who brings a message summoning Rhodophil to the king.

Amalthea, sister to Argaleon, discusses with a court lady the reason for the king's visit to so remote a section of Sicily. King Polydamas is searching for his son. Many years before, when Polydamas had usurped the throne, the wife of the former king had fled with an infant son. To Polydamas's amazement, his pregnant wife, Eudoxia, fled with the queen. No news had been heard of them until recently, when Polydamas was led to believe that his wife had died but that their child still lives.

Polydamas orders brought before him a fisherman in company with a youth and a maid whom the fisherman claims were his children but who look too noble to be a peasant's offspring. The fisherman turns out to be Hermogenes, who had fled with Eudoxia and the queen. Under threat of torture, Hermogenes asserts that the queen, her son, and Eudoxia had died, but that Polydamas's son is alive and is, in fact, Leonidas, the youth who accompanies him. Hermogenes insists, however, that the girl Palmyra is his own daughter. The king accepts Leonidas as his son and decrees that Palmyra shall live at court so as not to be separated from her foster brother.

Later, Palamede presents himself to Melantha, the woman his father has ordered him to marry. Much to his regret, he finds Melantha to be just such an affected lady as Rhodophil has described his mistress to be. Indeed, Palamede soon learns that Melantha is Rhodophil's mistress—at least in name—and that Doralice is Rhodophil's wife. The confusion is compounded when Rhodophil learns that his mistress is to be Palamede's wife.

Royal affairs also are entangled. Polydamas orders Leonidas to marry Amalthea. When Leonidas refuses, Polydamas threatens banishment but is dissuaded by Amalthea from carrying out the threat. Leonidas swears to Palmyra that he will wed none but her. When spies inform the king that Leonidas loves a commoner, Polydamas orders Palmyra to be set adrift in a boat. Hermogenes saves her from this fate by producing evidence that she, not Leonidas, is the king's child. Although Polydamas offers to confer nobility on Leonidas, the youth chooses to live in poverty with Hermogenes.

Palamede has arranged to meet Doralice, and Rhodophil to meet Melantha; both assignations are for the same time and the same place. At the tryst, when the couples converge, all four individuals fabricate excuses that the others pretend to believe. Palamede then leaves with his intended, and Rhodophil with his wife.

Amalthea informs Leonidas that her brother, Argaleon, has arranged to marry Palmyra and to have Leonidas banished. Although Amalthea loves Leonidas, she agrees to help him see Palmyra by taking him to the masquerade that evening. There Leonidas arranges an assignation with Palmyra at Hermogenes' house, not, however, before being recognized by Argaleon.

Both Doralice and Melantha plan to attend a masquerade dressed as boys, but they get only as far as an eating house where they exchange insults, much to the delight of their lovers, who hug and kiss them at each unflattering remark. The game is ended by a message summoning Rhodophil to the king. The two "boys" are left to fend for themselves.

At Hermogenes' house, Eubulus, a former governor who had helped Eudoxia in her escape, informs Palmyra that Leonidas is in reality Theagenes, the son of the late king. Leonidas tells Palmyra of a plan to unseat the king, her father, and make her a prisoner when she opposes the plan. Before the conspiracy can be carried out, however, Polydamas arrives with his guards and seizes the rebels.

When Palamede is informed that his father expects him to marry Melantha at once, he solicits the advice of Philotis, her maid, about how best to woo the lady. Philotis supplies him with a list of French words, of which the lady is inordinately fond. Won by these words, Melantha accepts Palamede as her suitor and they agree to marry. Following this development, Palamede and Rhodophil pledge to respect each other's wives, and Rhodophil and Doralice are reconciled.

Affairs in the royal household end just as happily for most of those concerned. Suspecting that Leonidas is the true heir to the throne, Argaleon advises the young man's immediate execution, advice that Polydamas decides to follow in spite of Palmyra's pleas for mercy. The sentence would have been carried out had not Amalthea revealed Leonidas's true identity, whereupon Rhodophil and Palamede fight successfully to free the prince. The new king forgives Polydamas and asks for Palmyra's hand in marriage, a request gratefully granted. Having rejected Leonidas's offer of clemency, Argaleon is sentenced to life imprisonment. Amalthea, still in love with Leonidas, declares her intention to spend her life in prayer and mourning.

Critical Evaluation:

John Dryden's *Marriage à la Mode* is a curious mixture of heroic tragedy and comedy of manners. One plot concerns the playful seventeenth century attitude toward married love, another concerns court intrigue. Skillful characterization, especially in the comic plot, has assured a continuing place for the play. In that plot, Dryden illustrates the view of life prevalent in Restoration drama, which sees humans as creatures of appetite constantly searching for new sensations and always battling to steal or conquer the property of others. In both of the play's two plots, the characters play out this view of life through their actions, but in the end, Dryden leads them to a very different conclusion from the one no doubt expected by a Restoration audience.

All the partners in the romantic plot share the belief that a desired love conquest loses its attractiveness the moment it is possessed. In their pursuit of women, Rhodophil and Palamede are like sated, jaded gourmets in frantic search of new delicacies to intrigue their palates. They are caught in a dilemma that seems to have no solution: If love depends on desire, how can love remain after desire has once been satisfied? Unable to solve this riddle, the characters have accepted the proposition that extramarital affairs are necessary. The opening song in the play states the premise that no one should feel bound to a silly marriage vow once passion has cooled. Operating on this assumption, the characters hopelessly entangle themselves in a confusion of affairs: Palamede, engaged to Melantha, tries to seduce Rhodophil's wife, Doralice, while Rhodophil is trying to secure Melantha as his mistress. Their exploits are described in a series of images relating sex to appetite, sport, war, and stolen property, as they fight to conquer someone else's partner while safeguarding their own from like treatment.

The plot dealing with court politics is pervaded with the same belief in the attraction of the forbidden and in the need to dominate. Melantha understands the social hierarchy within which she is battling to ascend, and she knows that manners and dress are the signs by which different classes or castes are identified. Thus she constantly assimilates the ever-changing modes of dress and behavior currently in vogue; she wears the latest fashion as faithfully as she parrots the newest gossip or adheres to the most recent opinion of Leonidas. When she feels discouraged in the daily battle for popularity at court, she can always comfort herself with her vast moral superiority to those lowly creatures not connected with the palace—the women who live in the city, or worse, in the country.

By the end of *Marriage à la Mode*, Dryden has come full circle from the proposal stated in the opening song, by showing that a life of indulged appetites can only lead to satiety and discomfort. Miserable and at the point of fighting, Palamede and Rhodophil agree to halt competition and abide by rules of mutual respect for each other's "property." The message of the play is that marital love and peace are possible if humans can curb their greed for greener pastures and enjoy the estate at home.

Further Reading

Eliot, T. S. *John Dryden: The Poet, the Dramatist, the Critic.* 1932. Reprint. New York: Haskell House, 1966. This classic discussion by a writer who helped introduce Dryden to twentieth century readers serves as a standard reference. Explains why Dryden's drama continues to interest critics and students.

Hammond, Paul, and David Hopkins, eds. *John Dryden: Tercentenary Essays.* New York: Oxford University Press, 2000. This collection, published during the tercentenary of Dryden's death, examines some of Dryden's individual works, as well as more general characteristics of his writing. Some of the essays question if Dryden is a classic, explore the "staging of popular politics," and describe the dissolution evident in his later writing.

Hopkins, David. *John Dryden.* New York: Cambridge University Press, 1986. An introduction to Dryden and a contextual study of his place among English writers. Hopkins includes a plot summary of *Marriage à la Mode* and discusses marriage and gender relationships in the play.

_____. *John Dryden.* Tavistock, England: Northcote House/British Council, 2004. Concise overview of Dryden's life and work. Hopkins demonstrates that Dryden not only was a man of his times; his ideas are relevant to twenty-first century audiences as well.

Lewis, Jayne, and Maximillian E. Novak, eds. *Enchanted Ground: Reimagining John Dryden.* Buffalo, N.Y.: University of Toronto Press, 2004. Collection of essays that apply modern critical perspectives to Dryden's work. The first section focuses on Dryden's role as a public poet and the voice of the Stuart court during Restoration; the second explores his relationship to drama and music.

Loftis, John. "Chapter Two: Dryden's Comedies." In *Writers and Their Background: John Dryden*, edited by Earl Miner. Athens: Ohio University Press, 1972. Carefully differentiating between the play's comic and serious plots, this discussion calls attention to the sexual play, the witty speeches, and the social distinctions operating in Dryden's most famous comedy.

Rawson, Claude, and Aaron Santesso, eds. *John Dryden, 1631-1700: His Politics, His Plays, and His Poets*. Newark: University of Delaware Press, 2004. Contains papers presented at a Yale University conference held in 2000 to commemorate the tercentenary of Dryden's death. The essays focus on the politics of Dryden's plays and how his poetry was poised between ancient and modern influences.

Wasserman, George R. *John Dryden*. New York: Twayne, 1964. This study covers Dryden's career as well as the political, philosophical, and literary background of his plays for the general reader. The discussion of *Marriage à la Mode* highlights structural problems not developed elsewhere.

Zwicker, Steven N., ed. *The Cambridge Companion to John Dryden*. New York: Cambridge University Press, 2004. Among these seventeen essays are discussions of Dryden and the theatrical imagination, the invention of Augustan culture, and patronage, and Dryden's London and the "passion of politics" in his theater.

The Marriage of Figaro

Author: Pierre-Augustin Caron de Beaumarchais (1732-1799)

First produced: La Folle Journée: Ou, Le Mariage de Figaro, 1784; first published, 1785 (English translation, 1784)

Type of work: Drama
Type of plot: Comedy
Time of plot: Eighteenth century
Locale: Spain

Principal characters:
FIGARO, a clever barber and the bridegroom-to-be
COUNT ALMAVIVA, his lord
COUNTESS ALMAVIVA, wife of the count
SUZANNE, Figaro's fiancé and maid to the countess
MARCELINE, the housekeeper
DR. BARTHOLO, the former guardian of the countess
CHÉRUBIN, a page

The Story:

Three years after Figaro, the clever barber, had helped Count Almaviva steal his beloved Rosine from her guardian, Dr. Bartholo, the count has become tired of his wife and has begun to pursue other attractive women, particularly Suzanne, his wife's maid, who is betrothed to Figaro. Suzanne informs Figaro of the count's interest, including his plan to send Figaro on a mission to England so that he can pursue Suzanne undisturbed. Figaro vows to prevent this.

Figaro also has trouble from another source. Marceline, the count's housekeeper, has Figaro's note for a sum of money she had lent him; if he does not repay the money he will have to marry her. Marceline wants to marry someone, and Figaro, despite the disparity in their ages, seems the likeliest prospect. Bartholo is helping her, mostly to revenge himself on Figaro for having outwitted him.

The count's young page, Chérubin, is fascinated by all women, especially the countess. When the count learns of this infatuation, he banishes the page from the castle and orders him to join the count's regiment. Figaro has other ideas. He plans to dress Chérubin in Suzanne's clothing and send him to keep a rendezvous with the count. Figaro hopes that the count will feel so embarrassed and appear so ridiculous when the trick is exposed that he will stop pursuing Suzanne. Figaro also sends the count an anonymous letter hinting that the countess has a lover. When the count bursts into his wife's chambers in search of this lover, he finds no one but Suzanne, for Chérubin, who had been there moments earlier, had jumped out of a window. After fabricating several stories to account for strange coincidences, Figaro is delighted when the count has to beg his wife's forgiveness for his unfounded suspicions.

Figaro does not have the chance to send Chérubin to keep the tryst with the count because the countess and Suzanne are also plotting to foil the count's plan. After the count tells Suzanne that he will not allow her to marry Figaro unless she meets him at a pavilion that night, she and the countess concoct a plan to defeat him.

Marceline takes her case against Figaro to court. Since he wants to place obstacles in the way of Figaro's wedding, the count himself presides at the hearing; he rules that Figaro must either repay the money to Marceline or marry her immediately. The sentence has scarcely been pronounced, however, when Marceline discovers that Figaro is her long-lost illegitimate son by Bartholo. She says the relationship explains the love that had made her want to marry him. Marceline and Bartholo finally agree to marry, though Bartholo is unhappy that his worst enemy has turned out to be his son. During the dancing to celebrate Suzanne's and Figaro's wedding, Suzanne passes a note to the count to set up their rendezvous. Figaro sees it and is devastated.

That night in the garden, Suzanne and the countess, dressed in one another's clothing, prepare to spring the trap on the count. Figaro, who does not know of the women's plan, has hidden himself in a pavilion to observe Suzanne's treachery; Bartholo and Marceline accompany him, and he broods at length about his topsy-turvy destiny and the general injustice of society. The countess, disguised as Suzanne, meets the count and permits him to woo her, accepting money and gifts from him. The count protests his love for her and compares her favorably with his wife. Enraged at Suzanne's apparent duplicity, Figaro approaches the supposed countess (Suzanne in disguise) and begs her favor; when he recognizes his beloved's voice, he decides to turn her trick around and began to woo her. Suzanne slaps him soundly for his apparent duplicity. Figaro is delighted to learn that Suzanne has not played him false and that the count is actually trying to seduce his own wife.

After much confusion, during which the count discovers that everyone has observed his folly, the situation is untangled. The countess fondly forgives her husband, and the count consents to the marriages of Suzanne and Figaro, Marceline and Bartholo, and Chérubin and the gardener's daughter. Both the count and countess give a large dowry to Suzanne, and Figaro at last has parents, a fortune, and a beautiful wife. Everyone joins in rejoicing that wit and intelligence can even the social odds.

Critical Evaluation:

In *The Marriage of Figaro*, Pierre-Augustin Caron de Beaumarchais takes Figaro through more intrigues and adventures. Again the shrewd barber matches wits with those who would oppress him, again young lovers must overcome obstacles planted by their more powerful enemies, and the high good humor and clever wit of Figaro triumph. Critics have interpreted *The Marriage of Figaro* as everything from a giddy sensual romp to the first rumblings of the French Revolution. Certainly aspects of this delightful play can be used to support a number of interpretations. Beaumarchais claimed about this work, as he did about all his writings, that it was his intention both to entertain and to reform society.

Although Beaumarchais's comic style was often copied by other writers of his day, it was never surpassed. With charm and gaiety, *The Marriage of Figaro* examines love in its many forms and the mad things people do in pursuit of love. Nevertheless, Beaumarchais allows everything to come right in the end: In spite of the lustful lord and predatory spinster, Suzanne and Figaro let nothing keep them from their love match; the estranged count and countess rediscover what had first drawn them together and reconcile under the moonlit chestnut trees; Marceline, who seemed ridiculous in her pursuit of the unwilling Figaro, blooms when she learns she can now love him as her long-lost son—she even gets Bartholo to marry her, albeit thirty years late.

Beaumarchais's meticulous stage directions contribute to the breathless fun. The play teems with examples of the split-second timing and mistaken identities that are so necessary to farce: Chérubin slips behind and then into a chair, only to be discovered as the count mimes finding him; Suzanne and Chérubin switch places in the countess's dressing room; Suzanne loses her composure when she sees Figaro kissing Marceline. The continuing small confusions climax in the total confusion of the last act.

The play revels in a sunny sensuality. Much of the action involves the trappings of feminine apparel; Suzanne and the countess take delight in exchanging clothes and in dressing Chérubin up as a girl (especially droll since Chérubin is usually played by a woman). The dialogue repeatedly refers to soft fabrics, flowers, ribbons, and smooth skin, a subtle reminder that virtually all the characters are thinking about sex.

The play also deals with the social tensions and injustices that would soon destroy the ancien régime, particularly in Figaro's long tirade in act 5. He rhetorically asks the absent count, "What have you done to deserve so much? You took the trouble to be born, and nothing more." He describes the struggles of his own early life—his poverty, his imprisonment for political "crimes," and controversies with censors. At every step, Figaro learned that society is rigged against men who are intelligent but have no status.

In the character of the count, the play implicitly criticizes those who have and abuse power. The count, the passionate lover in *Le Barbier de Séville: Ou, La Précaution inutile* (pr., pb. 1775; *The Barber of Seville: Or, The Useless Precaution*,

1776), is in this work a bored husband who misuses his power as an aristocrat, especially toward the women in his domain. He and Figaro, formerly allies against the pompous Bartholo, now oppose each other as the count seeks to reclaim the *droit du seigneur* (the right of a lord to take the virginity of a peasant bride on her wedding night). Figaro twice forces him to renounce this right publicly, but even so the count intends to enjoy Suzanne, if necessary by extortion in withholding the dowry needed to pay Figaro's debt to Marceline. The count abuses his power in other ways, too. He feels justified in jealously bullying his wife when he mistakenly suspects her of being as unfaithful as himself. He sends Chérubin off to the army because Chérubin pursues the same women he does. He has the final say in judicial proceedings and, purely out of spite, does his best to force Figaro to marry Marceline.

These actions seem humorous because they all fail, thanks to the efforts of the women and Figaro. Yet the potential for real damage remains, as becomes clear in Beaumarchais's little-known sequel to *The Marriage of Figaro, L'Autre Tartuffe: Ou, La Mère Coupable* (pr. 1792, pb. 1797; *Frailty and Hypocrisy,* 1804). Here, soon after the reconciliation, the count resumes his habits of unfaithfulness and leaves the unhappy countess to seek consolation in the arms of Chérubin; that liaison results in a child, as does one of the count's liaisons, and the romantic involvement of those half-siblings twenty years later gives a blackmailing lawyer his opening. When the ashamed Chérubin had learned of the countess's pregnancy with his child, he had let himself be killed in battle. Had the count remained a faithful, loving husband, the countess would not have had an affair, and the charming Chérubin might not have died so young. Though Figaro again manages to foil the count and young love triumphs here, too, this play shows even more clearly than the first two what harm unthinking abuses of power can cause.

Although he roundly criticized the social system of his time, Beaumarchais was, however, not advocating revolutionary change. He strongly supported the American Revolution, contributing generously to the cause and persuading the French government to do the same, but he had too much at stake in the French monarchy and aristocracy to want their downfall. Beaumarchais enjoyed life in the highest circles of French society and even added the title "de Beaumarchais" to his name after marrying a wealthy widow. Like Figaro, he had tried his hand at a wide variety of careers, among them watchmaker, musician, financier, pamphleteer, diplomat, gunrunner, and spy. Also like his creation, he wound up hitching his fortunes to those of the rich and well born. Beaumarchais wrote as an insider who saw the flaws of the

system and sought to reform it, not as a radical seeking to destroy it.

"Critical Evaluation" by Susan Wladaver-Morgan

Further Reading

Brown, Gregory S. *Literary Sociability and Literary Property in France, 1775-1793.* Burlington, Vt.: Ashgate, 2006. A history of the Société des Auteurs Dramatiques, the first professional association for creative writers in Europe. The organization was founded by Beaumarchais in 1777, and its members were the playwrights most closely associated with the Comédie-Française. Brown traces the group's conception, founding, eventual demise, and its efforts to acquire increased remuneration and societal prestige for its members.

Cox, Cynthia. *The Real Figaro: The Extraordinary Career of Caron de Beaumarchais.* London: Longmans, 1962. Focuses primarily on Beaumarchais's many activities other than writing. In her discussion of his ventures into diplomacy, Cox notes Beaumarchais's success as an intriguer and interprets the character of Figaro as a self-portrait. Includes illustrations and a good bibliography.

Grendel, Frédéric. *Beaumarchais: The Man Who Was Figaro.* Translated by Roger Greaves. London: MacDonald and Jane's, 1977. Interprets Figaro as Beaumarchais's alter ego and *The Marriage of Figaro* as the pinnacle of his career. Believes Beaumarchais was a reformer, not a revolutionary, and traces his chameleonlike adaptability to the fact that he was secretly a Protestant in Catholic France. Includes illustrations and a selected bibliography.

Howarth, William. D. *Beaumarchais and the Theatre.* New York: Routledge, 1995. A critical biography. After recounting the events of Beaumarchais's life and career, Howarth places his work within the broader context of dramatic writing and the theater in the eighteenth century and within the culture of theatergoing in prerevolutionary France. Chapter 13 provides an analysis of *The Marriage of Figaro,* its critical reception, influence on contemporary drama, and the operatic adaption by Wolfgang Amadeus Mozart.

Lever, Maurice. *Beaumarchais: A Biography.* Translated by Susan Emanuel. New York: Farrar, Straus and Giroux, 2008. Instead of a strict chronological biography, Lever provides an entertaining and detailed account of the many fascinating episodes in Beaumarchais's life. Describes his many occupations, including espionage, watchmaking, pamphleteering, and international trade, as well as his support of the American Revolution.

Ratermanis, J. B., and W. R. Irwin. *The Comic Style of Beaumarchais*. Seattle: University of Washington Press, 1961. Interesting scene-by-scene analysis of *The Marriage of Figaro*, analyzing what makes the comedy work on stage, especially in the context of the decline of comic dramatic writing in eighteenth century France. Uses theories of Henri Bergson and others on the nature of humor to interpret the works.

Sungolowsky, Joseph. *Beaumarchais*. New York: Twayne, 1974. Concise biographical treatment, with a useful chronology, notes, selected bibliography, and detailed analysis of all the plays.

Wood, John. Introduction to *"The Barber of Seville"* and *"The Marriage of Figaro,"* translated by John Wood. Baltimore: Penguin Books, 1964. Excellent concise discussion of the plays and their social context. The edition also includes Beaumarchais's own notes on the characters and their costumes.

The Martian Chronicles

Author: Ray Bradbury (1920-   )
First published: 1950; revised, 1997
Type of work: Short fiction
Type of plot: Science fiction
Time of plot: 1999-2026
Locale: United States and Mars

Principal characters:
YLLA K., a Martian
YLL K., her husband
CAPTAIN JONATHAN WILLIAMS, leader of an Earth expedition to Mars
CAPTAIN WILDER, another Earth expedition leader
JEFF SPENDER, a member of his crew
HATHAWAY, another member of Wilder's crew
SAM PARKHILL, a human hot-dog vendor on Mars

The Story:

"Rocket Summer" takes place in January, 1999. It is winter in Ohio, where the first rocket to Mars turns the cold into a summer-like warmth. "Ylla" takes place in February, 1999, on Mars. Through a telepathic connection, Ylla K. dreams of the captain of the first rocket, Nathaniel York, arriving on Mars. Out of jealousy, her husband Yll K. kills him. "The Summer Night" takes place in August, 1999. Their growing telepathic connection with Earth manifests when Martians sing songs in English.

In "The Earth Men," which is set in August, 1999, Captain Jonathan Williams and his crew are perceived on Mars as insane Martians. Their appearance and rocket ship are believed to be telepathic manifestations of their madness. Diagnosed as incurable, they are shot by their Martian doctor. After they are dead, the "illusions" remain. The doctor, thinking he must have become infected with the madness, kills himself.

"Taxpayer" takes place in March, 2000. Fearing an atomic war, Pritchard, an ordinary citizen, wants to be a part of the third expedition to Mars, but he is turned away. "The Third Expedition" is set in April, 2000. The titular expedition reaches Mars. The Martians use the illusion of a small Midwestern town, populated with deceased relatives of the expedition's crew members, to lure them into a deadly trap.

In "—and the Moon Be Still as Bright," which takes place in June, 2001, the fourth Earth expedition to Mars finds that the remaining members of the already-dying Martian civilization have been killed by chicken pox, which was brought to the planet by one of the earlier expeditions. Jeff Spender tries to defend the ancient Martian civilization, killing several members of the expedition before he is finally killed by Captain Wilder.

"The Settlers" takes place in August, 2001, when the first colonists (as opposed to explorers) arrive on Mars. In "The Green Morning," set in December, 2001, Benjamin Driscoll acts as a latter-day Johnny Appleseed, seeding and magically transforming Mars. "The Locusts" takes place in February, 2002, as more colonists arrive on Mars, further terraforming the planet.

"Night Meeting," set in August, 2002, describes a chance meeting of human worker Tomas Gomez and Martian Muhe Ca. They are from different times, and each questions the other's reality before finally accepting it.

In "The Shore," which takes place in October, 2002, further colonists arrive, all of them American, as the rest of Earth is either at war or thinking about going to war. "Interim" is set in February, 2003, as an American town is built on Mars. In "The Musicians," which occurs in April, 2003, groups of boys play with the remains of dead Martians in their old town before the remains are burned.

"Way in the Middle of the Air" is set in June, 2003. A mass exodus of African Americans from the American South to Mars occurs. Samuel Teece is the representative of a group of white supremacists trying to stop this exodus. In "The Naming of Names," which spans 2004-2005, places on Mars get human names. Many are named after the first humans who landed there. With the naming also come the rules and regulations of Earth.

"Usher II" takes place in April, 2005. In order to take revenge upon a bureaucratic government that has burned all fantastic literature and art, William Stendahl builds an exact copy of the titular mansion of Edgar Allan Poe's "The Fall of the House of Usher" (1839). Stendahl populates the mansion with a robotic army of fantastic characters. There, he kills the prominent people responsible for the destruction of fantasy, finally destroying the house just as is described in Poe's original text.

"The Old Ones" is set in August, 2005. Scores of elderly people arrive on Mars. "The Martian" takes place in September, 2005. One of the last Martians comes to the Lafarge couple in the guise of their son, as he reacts to the needs of humans around him, becoming what they are searching for. On a trip to town, the Martian gets lost as he is drawn to the needs of other people. Finally, he dies surrounded by the townspeople, who all see someone different in him.

"The Luggage Store" is set in November, 2005. Martian colonists receive news of war on Earth. It seems unreal to them because of the great distance between the planets, but nevertheless they start preparing to return to Earth.

"The Off Season" takes place in November, 2005. Sam Parkhill, owner of a hot-dog stand on Mars, is one day approached by a Martian whom he mistakenly kills. He flees from more approaching Martians, who only want to give him the rights to half of Mars. However, the gift turns out to be meaningless, as Earth is devastated in an atomic war the same night. "The Watchers" is also set in November, 2005. Humans watching the destruction of Earth receive signals urging them to come home. On the following morning, they begin a mass remigration to Earth.

"The Silent Towns" takes place in December, 2005. One of last humans remaining on Mars, Walter Gripp, desperately tries to find another human being. When he finally finds a female companion, she turns out to be utterly unattractive. Fleeing from her, he decides to live alone after all.

"The Long Years" is set in April, 2026. Two members of the fourth Earth expedition to Mars meet again on Mars after years apart. Hathaway has remained on Mars, while Captain Wilder flew to the outer planets and has returned. Mars is now almost lifeless. To survive the loneliness after his family died, Hathaway has built robot replacements for them. Hathaway dies, and Captain Wilder leaves Mars to the robot family, who will live there for a long time.

"There Will Come Soft Rains" takes place in August, 2026. After an atomic strike in California, a lone standing house controlled by robots continues its daily routine, unable to understand that there is no one left to take care of. Finally, the house is destroyed in a fire.

"The Million-Year Picnic" is set in October, 2026. William Thomas and his family travel to Mars before Earth is finally destroyed. Together with other possible survivors, they are about to start a new life on Mars, effectively becoming Martians themselves.

Critical Evaluation:

The Martian Chronicles was published in 1950, bringing together a selection of earlier short stories that Ray Bradbury rewrote for the publication, as well as new texts written for the volume. At the suggestion of his publisher, Bradbury added bridging stories to connect the various tales in a more coherent fashion. In 1997, a revised edition was published adding two stories while dropping one. The dates of the individual stories were also advanced by thirty-one years to keep them in the future.

Along with *Fahrenheit 451* (1953), *The Martian Chronicles* continues to be one of Bradbury's most influential works. It has never been out of print, selling more than four million copies and being translated into twenty-seven languages. The book was adapted into a television miniseries in 1979. It has also been adapted to radio, for the stage, and into a computer game. After receiving a favorable review by literary critic Christopher Isherwood, the text entered the literary mainstream.

Although it is a collection of short texts, *The Martian Chronicles* can be classified as a novel because of its thematic unity and the composite chronicle style in which it is written. However, the twenty-six different stories belong to different subgenres, including parody, mystery, horror, adventure, and dystopian fiction. They also incorporate a variety of themes and discourses such as race, gender, and colonialism, all against the background of Bradbury's rather unscientific and highly poetic Martian scenery.

Bradbury himself is generally perceived as a science-fiction writer despite the fact that he has written texts in many other genres. Those of his texts that are labeled as science fiction do not concern themselves overly with technical details, as does hard science fiction. Instead, they rely on human characters and a sense of magic, so they are generally described as science fantasy. One could even call *The Martian Chronicles* a science or space fairytale, reflecting Bradbury's childhood in small-town midwestern Waukegan, Illinois. Bradbury himself has cited Sherwood Anderson's *Winesburg, Ohio: A Group of Tales of Ohio Small Town Life* (1919) and John Steinbeck's *The Grapes of Wrath* (1939) as major influences. Another major influence on the tales was the pulp magazines of the early twentieth century, chiefly Edgar Rice Burroughs's *John Carter of Mars* series (1912-1943).

The central theme of the colonization of Mars critically reflects on the colonization of America, with the Martians in the role of the Native Americans, being wiped out by the colonizers. However, this central theme also reflects on the frontier myth as a major element in American history, making the colonization of Mars and the destruction of its culture inevitable.

Stefan Buchenberger

Further Reading

Eller, Jonathan. "The Body Eclectic: Sources of Ray Bradbury's *Martian Chronicles.*" *University of Mississippi Studies in English* 11/12 (1993): 376-410. Study of all of Bradbury's Martian stories; argues for the classification of *The Martian Chronicles* as a novel.

Eller, Jonathan R., and William F. Touponce. *Ray Bradbury: The Life of Fiction.* Kent, Ohio: Kent State University Press, 2002. An extensive study of sixty years of Bradbury's writing.

Gallagher, Edward J. "The Thematic Structure of *The Martian Chronicles.*" In *Ray Bradbury*, edited by Joseph D. Olander and Martin Harry Greenberg. New York: Taplinger, 1980. Analysis and interpretation of the structural unity of *The Martian Chronicles*, connecting the stories into one novel.

Mengeling, Melvin E. *Red Planet, Flaming Phoenix, Green Town: Some Early Bradbury Revisited.* Bloomington, Ind.: First Books Library, 2002. Analysis of Bradbury's early writing, including *The Martian Chronicles*, based on his biography.

Rabkin, Eric S. "To Fairyland by Rocket: Bradbury's *The Martian Chronicles.*" In *Ray Bradbury*, edited by Joseph D. Olander and Martin Harry Greenberg. New York: Taplinger, 1980. Reading of *The Martian Chronicles* as a fairytale.

Reid, Robin Anne. *Ray Bradbury: A Critical Companion.* Westport, Conn.: Greenwood Press, 2000. Study of Bradbury's major works, including a chapter on *The Martian Chronicles*; includes much bibliographical information and an overview of the research on Bradbury.

Wolfe, Gary K. "The Frontier Myth in Ray Bradbury." In *Ray Bradbury*, edited by Joseph D. Olander and Martin Harry Greenberg. New York: Taplinger, 1980. Interpretation of *The Martian Chronicles* using the so-called Turner thesis, which postulates the frontier myth as the central motif in the development of American society.

Martin Chuzzlewit

Author: Charles Dickens (1812-1870)
First published: 1843-1844, serial; 1844, book
Type of work: Novel
Type of plot: Social realism
Time of plot: Nineteenth century
Locale: England and the United States

Principal characters:
OLD MARTIN CHUZZLEWIT, a selfish old man
MARTIN CHUZZLEWIT, his grandson
MARY GRAHAM, old Martin's ward
ANTHONY CHUZZLEWIT, old Martin's brother
JONAS CHUZZLEWIT, his son
MR. PECKSNIFF, a hypocrite
CHARITY and MERCY, his daughters
TOM PINCH, young Martin Chuzzlewit's friend
RUTH PINCH, his sister
MARK TAPLEY, another friend of young Martin
MRS. SARAH GAMP, a bibulous Cockney

The Story:

Selfishness is a strong family trait in Martin and Anthony Chuzzlewit, two aged brothers. From his cradle, Anthony's son, Jonas, has been taught to think only of money and gain; in his eagerness to possess his father's wealth, he often grows impatient for the old man to die. Old Martin Chuzzlewit suspects the world of having designs on his fortune; his distrust and lack of generosity have turned his grandson, his namesake, into a model of selfishness and obstinacy. The old man's heart is not as hard as it seems, for he has taken into his house as his companion and ward an orphan named Mary Graham. He tells her that she will have a comfortable home as long as he lives but that she should expect nothing at his death. His secret wish is that love might grow between her and his grandson, but when young Martin tells him that he has chosen Mary for his own, old Martin is displeased, afraid that the young couple are acting in their own interests. A disagreement follows, and the old man turns his grandson out of his house.

Thrown on his own resources, young Martin decides to become an architect. He arranges to study with Mr. Pecksniff, an architect and land surveyor, who lives in a little Wiltshire village not far from Salisbury. Mr. Pecksniff agrees to train two or three pupils in return for a large premium and exorbitant charges for board and lodging. He thinks highly of himself as a moral man, and he has a copybook maxim to quote for every occasion. He and old Martin Chuzzlewit are cousins, but even though there has been bad feeling between them in the past, Mr. Pecksniff sees in young Martin a possible suitor for one of his daughters, and he accepts him as a student without requiring the customary fee.

Mr. Pecksniff has never been known to build anything, a fact that takes nothing away from his reputation. With him live his two affected daughters, Charity and Mercy, both as hypocritical and mean-spirited as their father. His assistant is a former pupil named Tom Pinch, a meek, prematurely aged draftsman who looks upon Mr. Pecksniff as a tower of knowledge.

Young Martin arrives in Wiltshire and takes the place of John Westlock in Mr. Pecksniff's establishment. Westlock was never a favorite in the household, his contempt for Mr. Pecksniff having been as great as his regard for the honest, loyal Tom Pinch. At first, Martin treats Tom in a patronizing manner. Tom, accustomed to the snubs and ridicule of Charity and Mercy, returns Martin's slights with simple goodwill; before long, the two become friends.

One day, Mr. Pecksniff and his daughters depart suddenly for London, summoned there by old Martin Chuzzlewit. The old man calls on them at Mrs. Todgers's shabbily genteel rooming house and accuses his grandson of having deceived the worthy man who shelters him. Mr. Pecksniff pretends to be pained and shocked to learn that Mr. Chuzzlewit has disowned his grandson. When the visitor hints at future goodwill and expectations if the architect will send the young man away at once, Mr. Pecksniff—even though the old man's proposal is treacherous and his language insulting—agrees eagerly. Returning to Wiltshire, he puts on a virtuous appearance as he announces that young Martin has ill treated the best and noblest of men and has taken advantage of his own unsuspecting nature. His humble roof, Mr. Pecksniff declares, can never shelter so base an ingrate and impostor.

Homeless once more, Martin makes his way to London in the hope of finding employment. As the weeks pass, his small store of money dwindles steadily. At last, when he has nothing left to pawn, he decides to try his fortunes in America. A twenty-pound note in a letter from an unknown sender gives him the wherewithal for his passage. Mark Tapley, the hostler of the Blue Dragon Inn in Wiltshire, accompanies him on his adventure. Mark is a jolly fellow with a desire to see the world. Martin cannot leave London, however, without seeing Mary Graham. He reads her a letter he has written to Tom Pinch, in which he asks his friend to show her kindness if the two should ever meet. Martin also arranges to write to Mary in care of Tom.

As steerage passengers, Martin and Mark have a miserable voyage to New York. Martin is not fond of the bumptious, tobacco-chewing Americans he meets, but he is excited by accounts of the fortunes to be made out West. Taken in by a group of land promoters, he writes to Mary, telling her of his bright prospects.

Meanwhile, old Anthony Chuzzlewit dies suddenly in the presence of his son, Mr. Pecksniff, and a faithful clerk, Chuffey. Sarah Gamp is called in to prepare the body for burial. She is a fat, middle-aged Cockney with a fondness for the bottle and a habit of quoting endlessly from the sayings of Mrs. Harris, a friend whom none of her acquaintances has ever seen.

After the burial, Jonas Chuzzlewit goes with Mr. Pecksniff to Wiltshire, for his cautious inquiries have revealed that Mr. Pecksniff is prepared to make a handsome settlement on his daughters, and Jonas is ready to court one or the other. A short time later, old Martin Chuzzlewit and Mary Graham arrive to take rooms at the Blue Dragon Inn in the village. There Tom Pinch meets Mary and, in his humble manner, falls deeply in love with her. Only his friendship with Martin keeps him from declaring his love to her.

Mr. Pecksniff had hoped that Jonas would marry Charity, his elder daughter, but Mercy is the suitor's choice, much to her sister's chagrin. After the wedding ceremony, Mr. and Mrs. Jonas Chuzzlewit return to London, and before long Jonas begins to treat his bride with ill humor and brutality. Having some business to transact at the office of the Anglo-Bengalee Disinterested Loan and Life Insurance Company, Jonas discovers that Mr. Montague, the president, is in reality Montague Tigg, a flashy speculator whom Jonas had previously known as an associate of his rascally cousin Chevy Slyme. Lured by the promise of huge profits, Jonas is persuaded to invest in the company and become a director. Tigg, however, has little trust for his new partner, and he tells Nadgett, his investigator, to learn whatever he can about Jonas.

Jonas has a guilty secret. Before his father's death, he obtained poison from a debt-ridden young doctor and mixed it with old Anthony's medicine. Actually, his father did not take the dose, but the circumstances, of which Chuffey, the clerk, is also aware, would be incriminating if they were to become known. Nadgett uncovers this secret, and the information gives Tigg a hold over his partner.

In Wiltshire, old Martin Chuzzlewit's condition appears to be deteriorating. When his mind seems to fail, Mr. Pecksniff sees an opportunity to get control of his kinsman's fortune. He hopes to make his position doubly secure by marrying Mary Graham, but Mary finds his wooing distasteful. When she tells Tom Pinch about his employer's unwelcome attentions, Tom, for the first time, realizes that Mr. Pecksniff is a hypocrite and a villain. Having overheard the conversation between Mary and Tom, Mr. Pecksniff discharges Tom after telling Mr. Chuzzlewit that the young man has made advances to Mary. Tom then goes to London to see his sister Ruth. Finding her unhappily employed as a governess, he takes her with him to hired lodgings and asks John Westlock, his old friend, to help him in finding work. Before Westlock can provide him any assistance, however, an unknown patron hires Tom to catalog a library.

In America, young Martin and Mark fare badly. They thought they had bought land in Eden, but on their arrival, they find nothing more than a huddle of rude cabins in a swamp. Martin falls ill with fever, and when he recovers, Mark becomes sick. While he nurses his friend, Martin has time to realize the faults of his character and the true reason for the failure of his hopes. More than a year passes before the travelers are able to return to England.

John Westlock, having become interested in Jonas Chuzzlewit, befriends Lewsome, the young doctor from whom Jonas had secured poison. From Mrs. Gamp, who has nursed the physician through an illness, he learns additional details that make him suspect the son's guilt in old Anthony's death.

Old Martin seems to be in his dotage when his grandson and Mark arrive to see him at Mr. Pecksniff's house, where he has been living. Martin attempts to reconcile with his grandfather and to end the misunderstanding between them, but Mr. Pecksniff breaks in to say that the old man knows the young man for a villain and a deceiver, and that he, Mr. Pecksniff, would give his life to protect the sick old man. Old Martin says nothing. Young Martin and Mark then travel to London, where they find Tom Pinch and Ruth. They also hear from John Westlock his suspicions regarding Jonas Chuzzlewit.

Jonas becomes desperate when Tigg forces him into a scheme to defraud Mr. Pecksniff. On their journey into Wiltshire, Jonas makes plans to dispose of Tigg, whom he hates and fears. After Mr. Pecksniff has agreed to invest his money in their company, Jonas returns to London and leaves Tigg to handle the transfer of securities. That night, disguised as a workman, he returns secretly to the village and attacks and kills Tigg as he is walking to his room at the inn. Leaving the body in the woods, Jonas takes a coach to London and arrives there at daybreak. Nadgett, ever watchful, has seen Jonas leave and return, and he follows the murderer when he tries to dispose of the clothing he had worn on his journey.

Old Martin Chuzzlewit, miraculously restored in body and mind, arrives unexpectedly in London for the purpose of righting many wrongs and turning the tables on the hypocritical Mr. Pecksniff. Having heard Westlock's story, old Martin goes with him to confront Jonas with their suspicions. A few minutes later, police officers, led by Nadgett, appear to arrest Jonas for Tigg's murder. The wretched man realizes that he is trapped and takes the rest of the poison he had obtained from Lewsome. The next day, old Martin meets with all concerned. It was he who hired Tom Pinch, and he now confesses that he has tested his grandson and Mary and found them worthy. When Mr. Pecksniff enters and attempts to shake the hand of his venerable friend, the stern old man strikes him to the floor with a cane.

The passing years bring happiness to the deserving. Young Martin and Mary are married, followed a short time later by Westlock and Ruth Pinch. Mark Tapley wins the mistress of the Blue Dragon Inn. Old Martin, out of pity, befriends Mercy Chuzzlewit. He himself rejoices in the happiness of his faithful friends, but there is no joy for Mr. Pecksniff. When news of Tigg's murder reached the city, another partner in the shady enterprise ran away with the company funds, and Mr. Pecksniff was ruined. He has become a drunken old man who writes begging letters to Martin and Tom and who has little comfort from Charity, the shrewish companion of his later years.

Critical Evaluation:

Charles Dickens completed *Martin Chuzzlewit* immediately upon his return from a trip to the United States in 1842, and the novel reflects some of the same concerns as his nonfiction work *American Notes* (1842). Although the novel lagged disappointingly in sales—a situation that ultimately led Dickens to sever his connection with the publisher Chapman and Hall—he felt himself at the top of his creative powers and believed the book to be his best work yet.

Both in structure and in vividness of character portrayal, *Martin Chuzzlewit* does reveal Dickens at the height of his creative power, and it marks a transition from his rather loosely organized earlier novels to the more structured later works. Yet, while not an absolute failure with the public, it met with perhaps the poorest reception of any of his novels. A number of theories have been forwarded to explain why Dickens's audience did not respond to the book, among them the fact that in this work Dickens treats his characters and themes rather harshly and with less of his previous tongue-in-cheek manner. *Martin Chuzzlewit* has little of the genial warmth and affectionate comedy that mellows even the bitterest of Dickens's earlier satire.

Another reason put forth for the novel's disappointing initial performance is its biting satire on America and Americans in those portions of the novel in which young Martin seeks his fortune in the United States. In his earlier *American Notes*, Dickens had been careful to balance his criticisms with observations on the many virtues he found in the young nation; the American press nevertheless reacted to his polite criticism with hot anger, and Dickens felt obliged to pull out all the stops the next time. Indeed, his own enjoyment in creating a scathing portrait of America may perhaps have led him to indulge it to a greater extent than was warranted by the structural importance of the American episodes. The American scenes are an important part of the overall story, if only because Martin's sufferings in Eden and his grateful appreciation of Mark Tapley are needed to drive home his awareness of his own selfishness. Throughout a large part of the young men's American adventures, however, the focus is less on Mark and Martin than on America itself.

In all fairness, Dickens saves an even fiercer scorn for the evils at home. He shows nothing in America to equal the whining insolence of a Chevy Slyme or the greedy meanness of the whole Chuzzlewit family. No American impostor comes close to the insincerity of the hypocritical Pecksniff. The Eden Land Corporation is no more disreputable a swindle than the Anglo-Bengalee Disinterested Loan and Life Insurance Company. It is this deeper inwardness of vision that distinguishes Dickens's handling of evil in his native land from his pictures of trickery and folly in America.

Despite the extraordinary vividness with which he exposes a wide range of American types and their mannerisms, and despite his wit in parodying their methods of speaking, Dickens never gets inside these characters. The British characters, in contrast, even when they are melodramatically lurid or outrageously satirized, are seen to some degree from within as well as from without, which endows them with an imaginative sympathy lacking for the American portraits. Dickens has no love for Jonas or Montague, but he knows their thoughts, just as he knows Pecksniff, too, to his very depths. It is this difference that makes the hilarious satire of the American scenes appear more sharply hostile than the far deeper condemnation with which Dickens surveys corruption at home.

Perhaps the supreme achievement of the novel is in the characters of Mrs. Gamp and Mr. Pecksniff. Mrs. Gamp, with her imaginary friend Mrs. Harris, represents such an almost transcendent vision of character that she threatens to overwhelm the rest of the novel. She has been hailed as one of the greatest comic creations in English literature, an adept in the use of language who would not be surpassed in literature until James Joyce's creation of Molly Bloom. Perhaps even greater is Dickens's achievement with the character of Pecksniff, who has been hailed as a prodigious achievement of imaginative energy, likened to a Tartuffe despoiled of his terrifying and satanic power and an embodiment of all the bourgeois hypocrisy of Victorian England. Dickens constructs this character with great elaborateness and illustrates him from a thousand angles.

Critical response to *Martin Chuzzlewit* changed significantly after the initial aloofness with which the book was received, and it became recognized as perhaps second only to *Pickwick Papers* (1836-1837, serial; 1837, book) in the degree of its comic achievement. The work also came to be seen to mark an important stage in Dickens's development as a novelist; his subsequent works became increasingly panoramic, striving toward a coherent overview and sense of totality. Dickens wrote *Martin Chuzzlewit* out of the whole available literary tradition as it bore on his chosen subject, and it was in this work that he began to discover the subjects and technique that he eventually made wholly his own.

"Critical Evaluation" by Craig A. Larson

Further Reading

Adrian, Arthur A. "The Heir of My Bringing-Up." In *Dickens and the Parent-Child Relationship*. Athens: Ohio University Press, 1984. Presents an informative study of the parent-child relationship in *Martin Chuzzlewit*, using the example of Anthony and Jonas Chuzzlewit. Argues that the novel explores the harm done by parents in shaping their children's futures.

Cain, Lynn. *Dickens, Family, Authorship: Psychoanalytic Perspectives on Kinship and Creativity*. Burlington, Vt.: Ashgate, 2008. Focuses on *Martin Chuzzlewit* and three other novels that Dickens wrote during the decade beginning in 1843, a period of feverish personal and professional activity. Asserts that the representation of the family in these novels is a paradigm for Dickens's development as an author.

Gilmour, Robin. *The Novel in the Victorian Age: A Modern Introduction*. London: Edward Arnold, 1986. Includes a good discussion of *Martin Chuzzlewit* as a transitional novel in Dickens's oeuvre, one that possesses both the strengths and the weaknesses of his earlier novels at the same time that it anticipates the more complex social vision of his later novels.

Hardy, Barbara. *Dickens and Creativity*. London: Continuum, 2008. Focuses on the workings of Dickens's creativity and imagination, arguing that these are at the heart of his self-awareness, subject matter, and narrative. *Martin Chuzzlewit* is discussed in chapter 5, "Talkative Men and Women in *Pickwick Papers, Nicholas Nickleby, Martin Chuzzlewit*, and *Little Dorrit*."

Jordan, John O., ed. *The Cambridge Companion to Charles Dickens*. New York: Cambridge University Press, 2001. Collection of essays includes information about Dickens's life and times, analyses of his novels, and discussions of topics such as Dickens's use of language and his depictions of family and domestic life.

Metz, Nancy Aycock. *The Companion to "Martin Chuzzlewit."* Westport, Conn.: Greenwood Press, 2001. Contains extensive annotations that provide information about the novel's historical and literary contexts and its topical allusions.

Miller, J. Hillis. "*Martin Chuzzlewit*." In *Charles Dickens: The World of His Novels*. Cambridge, Mass.: Harvard University Press, 1958. Classic work remains one of the most important essays on this novel. Argues that the central problem facing the characters in *Martin Chuzzlewit* is "how to achieve an authentic self, a self which, while resting solidly on something outside of itself, does not simply submit to a definition imposed from without."

Paroissien, David, ed. *A Companion to Charles Dickens*. Malden, Mass.: Blackwell, 2008. Collection of essays provides information about Dickens's life and work. Topics addressed include Dickens as a reformer, Christian, and journalist as well as his treatments of gender, technology, and America. An essay by Goldie Morgentaler is devoted to *Martin Chuzzlewit*.

Mary Barton
A Tale of Manchester Life

Author: Elizabeth Gaskell (1810-1865)
First published: 1848
Type of work: Novel
Type of plot: Social realism
Time of plot: First half of the nineteenth century
Locale: Manchester, England

Principal characters:
MARY BARTON, a young working-class woman
JOHN BARTON, her father, a mill worker
JEM WILSON, the son of John's closest friend
JANE WILSON, Jem's mother
ALICE WILSON, Jem's aunt
MARGARET JENNINGS, a friend of Mary
JOB LEGH, Margaret's grandfather
MR. CARSON, a mill owner
HARRY CARSON, his son

The Story:

John Barton, his pregnant wife, Mary, and their thirteen-year-old daughter, "little" Mary, are on a spring outing with their friends George and Jane Wilson and the Wilsons' twin babies and son Jem. Mary is extremely worried because her sister Esther has disappeared, probably with a lover. When the group returns to the Barton home for tea, George's sister

Alice joins them. Later that night, Mary goes into labor; there are complications, and the doctor is unable to save her life. John blames Esther for his wife's death.

The next year, young Mary becomes an apprentice to a dressmaker. Through Alice Wilson, she meets Margaret Jennings, a poor girl blessed with a beautiful voice, and Margaret's self-educated grandfather, Job Legh. Margaret tells Mary that she is going blind. Since she will no longer be able to do needlework, her only hope is to earn a living by singing.

When the mill catches fire, Jem Wilson saves both his father and another mill worker from the flames, becoming a hero. The owners of the mill, including Mr. Carson, think the fire was a godsend, for with the insurance money they will be able to replace outdated equipment. Their former employees, however, out of work because the mill is not operating, face starvation. When an epidemic rages among the weakened workers, the Wilson twins, always delicate, become ill and die.

Although Mary has strong feelings for Jem, she is surreptitiously seeing Harry Carson, encouraged in this by Sally Leadbitter, another apprentice. When George Wilson dies suddenly Mary is shaken, but she does not pay a visit of condolence because she cannot face Jem. Margaret's future looks brighter after she finds work as a singer.

John Barton's situation, on the other hand, is grim. He had quit his job and gone to London with a group of mill workers to petition Parliament, but the petition was rejected, and no one will hire a Chartist and a union man. He and Mary have to pawn their possessions in order to live. Angry and frustrated, John begins taking opium. One night Mary's aunt, Esther, now a prostitute, comes to warn John about his daughter's involvement with Harry, but, still holding Esther responsible for his wife's death, John refuses to listen.

Mary, however, finally realizes that all she likes about Harry is his wealth. It is Jem she loves, but some time earlier she firmly rejected Jem's proposal of marriage. At Margaret's suggestion, Mary calls on Jem's mother. There she sees Jem's sister Alice, now deaf and blind, and meets Alice's foster son, Will Wilson, a fine young sailor, who becomes Margaret's suitor.

Esther tells Jem about Mary's involvement with Harry, and shortly thereafter, Jem seeks out his rival. Carson strikes Jem with his cane, and Jem knocks him down. At a trade union meeting, the members draw lots to decide which of them will attack one of the mill owners; John is chosen. Soon after, Harry Carson is shot and killed. Jem is arrested for the crime, as his gun is identified as the weapon used, and his feelings for Mary suggest a motive.

After Esther brings Mary a piece of paper she found at the scene of the crime, Mary realizes that her father is the murderer. Margaret remembers that Jem had walked to Liverpool with Will on the night that Harry was shot. Job, Jem, and Mary all set out for Liverpool, where Jem is to be tried. Mary needs to find Will, who can establish an alibi for Jem. After taking a boat out to Will's ship and obtaining his promise to appear in court, Mary returns to testify. She publicly admits her love for Jem and manages not to collapse until Will turns up, along with a pilot who can corroborate his story. Jem is acquitted.

Having been dismissed from his job, Jem begins making plans to emigrate to Canada with his mother and Mary. John knows now that he is dying. Calling for Mr. Carson, he confesses to the killing of Harry and begs the bereaved father's forgiveness. At first, Carson refuses, but after seeing the charitable behavior of a little girl, he returns to the Barton house, where John dies in his arms. Carson thereafter becomes a guiding spirit in improving working conditions in Manchester.

Just before Jem, Mary, and Jane are to leave England, Esther comes home to die. In a final scene set in Toronto, Jane is playing with her little grandson when Jem brings home good news: After surgery, Margaret has recovered her sight; she and Will are soon to be married, and when Will makes his next voyage, Margaret and Job intend to accompany him and visit their friends.

Critical Evaluation:

In *Chartism* (1839) and *Past and Present* (1843), the great British intellectual Thomas Carlyle voiced his concerns about the condition of his country. It was becoming increasingly divided, he said, into two classes, one of which lived in luxury while the other suffered, starved, and died unheeded. Carlyle's works were at least partially responsible for inspiring the novels of social and political criticism that appeared in the 1840's, among them those written by Benjamin Disraeli, who was later to be the British prime minister, and by Elizabeth Gaskell.

Whereas Carlyle and Disraeli viewed the situation from a comfortable distance, however, Elizabeth Gaskell, though not a member of the working class, lived with the problems about which she was writing. As the wife of a Unitarian minister in Manchester, one of the industrial capitals of England, she knew the wealthy leaders of her fashionable church, but she also knew the poor. She saw how hard most of them worked, how easily their lives were shattered, and how desperate many of them had become. In *Mary Barton*, her first novel, Gaskell hoped to persuade her readers that working-class men and women were not automatons but real people deserving of respect, sympathy, and consideration.

Gaskell makes her argument compelling by creating individuals for her novel, not types, and by doing so with marvelous skill. John Barton, for example, is a thoughtful man, an idealist who does not easily accept the difference between the way things are and the way they should be. He seeks for the causes of misfortunes. Essentially, he is a good man, but when Parliament refuses to accept his union's petition for redress, John's heart hardens. His compassion for others turns into anger toward those who are causing the suffering, and he becomes a killer. His repentance is in character, based as it is on his compassion for the father of his victim—indeed, on his identification with him, since John, too, knows what it is to lose a son.

Gaskell's other working-class characters also challenge her readers' presuppositions. Job Legh, for example, has the mind of a scientist. Jem is not just a stalwart hero but also a brilliant inventor. The quiet Margaret Jennings turns out to have considerable initiative; instead of just bemoaning her blindness, she breaks into a new field. There is no dullness of mind or lack of ambition in such characters, no justification for their being oppressed and ignored.

Cleverly, Gaskell uses her characters' very imperfections to prove that they are just as human as their supposed betters. Mary is not immune to materialism; when she thinks of Harry, she thinks of his luxurious lifestyle. In the hands of a more sentimental writer, Jane Wilson might have been a pathetic creature, a woman who has lost her twins and her husband and now is facing the loss of her beloved son. Gaskell shows her as a spirited woman who insists on going to her son's trial. She is also a sharp-tongued and jealous woman who has to learn to forgive Mary for taking Jem away from her.

Although characterization is probably Gaskell's most effective means for achieving her purpose, she also incorporates a good many practical observations into her book, primarily through dialogue. She reveals, for example, that most industrial accidents occur in the final hours of a too-long workday, and she notes the ironic truth about the new child labor laws, which, because they did not provide funds to allow poor children to attend school, merely put them out on the street while reducing the incomes of their families.

Gaskell was well aware that the conditions she pointed out and dramatized provided a fertile field for revolution. She stopped short, however, of advocating radical political reforms. Instead, she pinned her hopes on personal goodwill. When John sees in Mr. Carson not an oppressor but a bereaved father, and when Mr. Carson, remembering that he is a Christian, manages to forgive his son's murderer, Gaskell implies that the gap between rich and poor has been bridged. As a result of one influential man's new understanding, improvements begin to be made.

The social changes mentioned in such vague terms do not affect the principal characters in the novel. John Barton, Alice Wilson, and the unhappy Esther escape from misery by dying; Mary, Jem, and Jane, by emigrating to Canada. Even Job and Margaret loosen their ties to England when they become dependent on Will, a sailor who can live wherever he likes.

In retrospect, given the rift between rich and poor so graphically described in *Mary Barton*, it is amazing that, unlike France, England was never torn apart by revolution. Historians suggest many reasons that such an event did not occur. Certainly, the emigration of people such as Jem was one of the most important releases of tension. As long as there were alternatives elsewhere, people saw no need to stay and fight. Ultimately they helped create new countries with the energy and beliefs that had been rejected by the old one.

Rosemary M. Canfield Reisman

Further Reading

Bonaparte, Felicia. *The Gypsy-Bachelor of Manchester: The Life of Mrs. Gaskell's Demon.* Charlottesville: University Press of Virginia, 1992. Presents a sensitive reading of Gaskell's life and fiction. Innovative approach treats the writer's life, letters, and works as a single "poetic text."

Brodetsky, Tessa. *Elizabeth Gaskell.* Leamington, England: Berg, 1986. Includes a chapter on *Mary Barton* that places the novel within the historic, economic, and social events leading up to the Chartist movement and British trade unionism. Also examines the theme of miscommunication in the novel and gives an extended analysis of the characters.

Easson, Angus. *Elizabeth Gaskell.* London: Routledge & Kegan Paul, 1979. Biographical work includes analysis of Gaskell's novels. Discussion of *Mary Barton* points out the contradiction between Gaskell's organic and Christian view of society and her representation of the social deprivation of the poor and also briefly describes some of the contemporary reactions to the novel.

Foster, Shirley. *Elizabeth Gaskell: A Literary Life.* New York: Palgrave, 2002. Offers an accessible introduction to the author's work, relying on the best available biographies. Presents interesting comparisons of Gaskell's novels with others of the period and emphasizes women's issues as addressed by Gaskell.

Hughes, Linda K., and Michael Lund. *Victorian Publishing and Mrs. Gaskell's Work.* Charlottesville: University Press of Virginia, 1999. Places Gaskell's writing in the context of the Victorian era, noting that Gaskell negotiated her way through the publishing world by producing work that was commercially successful even though it defied the conventions of her times. *Mary Burton* is discussed in chapter 2.

Nash, Julie. *Servants and Paternalism in the Works of Maria Edgeworth and Elizabeth Gaskell.* Burlington, Vt.: Ashgate, 2007. Examines the servant characters in Gaskell's stories and novels, including *Mary Barton*, to show how her nostalgia for a traditional ruling class conflicted with her interest in radical new ideas about social equality.

Schor, Hilary M. *Scheherezade in the Marketplace: Elizabeth Gaskell and the Victorian Novel.* New York: Oxford University Press, 1992. Discusses Gaskell as a woman writer in Victorian England. Includes analysis of *Mary Barton* that explores Gaskell's use of a romantic plot and a marriage-bound heroine to critique an authoritarian political and social structure.

Spencer, Jane. *Elizabeth Gaskell.* New York: St. Martin's Press, 1993. Provides a good overview of the writer and her works. Points out that Gaskell's intention in *Mary Barton* was to provide a voice for the working class and that she was addressing her own group, the largely Unitarian Manchester establishment.

Stoneman, Patsy. *Elizabeth Gaskell.* 2d ed. New York: Manchester University Press, 2006. Notes that in *Mary Barton* the author opposes a working class with feminine, nurturing virtues to a middle class characterized by masculine vices. This anticipates later books that deal specifically with issues of gender.

Wheeler, Michael. *The Art of Allusion in Victorian Fiction.* New York: Barnes & Noble, 1979. Includes a chapter on *Mary Barton* that explains the significance of many of Gaskell's references in the work. Notes that the structure of the novel, which is often criticized, is justified by the fact that Gaskell based her work on the biblical Dives-Lazarus story.

The Masque of the Red Death

Author: Edgar Allan Poe (1809-1849)
First published: 1842
Type of work: Short fiction
Type of plot: Gothic
Time of plot: Middle Ages
Locale: Europe

Principal characters:
PRINCE PROSPERO, the ruler of a petty nation
THE RED DEATH, the personification of a fatal disease

The Story:

The Red Death, a bloodier version of the Black Death, ravages Europe in the early fourteenth century. In response, the feudal overlord Prince Prospero selects a thousand congenial individuals from the upper ranks of the society he rules and isolates them within a lavishly furnished and securely sealed, fortified abbey. There, they plan to enjoy themselves to their hearts' content while the plague runs its deadly course outside.

After several months of seclusion, the courtiers' entertainments climax in a munificent masked ball held in a mazy complex of seven rooms, each one decorated in a different color and equipped with apposite stained-glass windows, all illuminated by a single central fire. The terminal chamber is decorated in black, and its windows are blood red, producing such a terrible effect that hardly anyone dares venture into the room. The ebony clock in the chamber strikes exceedingly peculiar notes when it chimes, inevitably causing the ball's musicians to pause. The exotic costumes worn by the masqueraders follow exemplars provided by the Prince himself, many of them being described as "dreams."

As the masquerade reaches the height of its excitement at the approach of midnight, the revelers notice the presence among them of a red-clad figure whose mask simulates the symptoms of the final phase of the Red Death. The appearance of this intruder angers the prince, who considers it a calculated mockery of his stratagem. He commands that the individual should be seized, unmasked, and hanged from the battlements at dawn, but no one dares lay a hand on the mysterious figure as he retreats through the sequence of colored rooms. Eventually, the enraged Prospero rushes after his disrespectful guest himself, pursuing him all the way to the black room—where he is revealed to be a literal personification of the Red Death, come to extend his dominion to the last refuge of the arrogant and mighty.

Critical Evaluation:

The imagery of "The Masque of the Red Death"—which was initially published as "The Mask of the Red Death" in *Graham's Magazine*, probably because the periodical's editor thought the word "masque" was too exotic—has been echoed many times since, in all manner of literary and cinematic works. It is perhaps most familiar to twenty-first century readers from film adaptations of Gaston Leroux's novel *Le Fantôme de l'Opéra* (serial 1909-1910, book 1910; *The Phantom of the Opera*, 1911) and stage and film versions of the musical by Andrew Lloyd Webber also based on that novel. Contemporary audiences may also know Roger Corman's relatively lavish film version—which also takes in the Edgar Allan Poe story "Hop-Frog: Or, The Eight Chained Ourangoutangs" (1849), the climax of which is similarly set at a decadent masquerade.

Within the story itself, the costumes adopted in the masked ball are likened to those featured in Victor Hugo's verse drama *Hernani* (pr., pb. 1830; English translation, 1830), whose sensational premiere at the Comédie-Française in February, 1830, was elevated to legendary status by Théophile Gautier's *Histoire du romantisme* (1872; history of Romanticism). Gautier lavishly described and celebrated a pitched battle allegedly fought at the premiere between the playwright's supporters and outraged defenders of Classicist tradition. The imagery of this description was, however, effectively effaced by Poe's own description, the gaudiness of which became an ideal of exotic decadence to which all actual masked balls aspired in vain.

The apocalyptic flamboyance of the story constitutes pure Gothic imagery: The Gothic novel, as it was called in England, had long been established as prose fiction's principal contribution to the Romantic rebellion against Classicist ideals of artistic form and decorum. The story also marked the beginning of a new tendency in nineteenth century literature. The literary method of Victor Hugo, who was thought of as the figurehead of the French Romantic movement, had been described by the Classicist critic Desiré Nisard as "decadent," and, although Hugo himself rejected that descriptive term vehemently, some of his more disillusioned contemporaries were only too enthusiastic to embrace it and glory in it. Principal among these self-described decadents was Poe's French translator, Charles Baudelaire.

In Poe, Baudelaire thought he had found a twin soul, one who had given voice in prose to the dark sentiments Baudelaire routinely expressed in his poetry. "The Masque of the Red Death" was one of the works the French poet held up as a central exemplar of a decadent sensibility and a decadent style. When Joris-Karl Huysmans provided the ultimate celebration of decadent ideas and ideals in his lifestyle fantasy novel *À rebours* (1884; *Against the Grain*, 1922), its narrator argued that the prose poem was the ideal form for the exercise of decadent style, and "The Masque of the Red Death" then became one of the type specimens to which all decadent prose ought to aspire. Its ornate manner and nihilistic trajectory were widely imitated, but there remained a sense in which they remained unsurpassable, having already sounded the extremes of potential.

The style of "The Masque of the Red Death" is deliberately artificial, its narrative viewpoint is calculatedly distant, and it only contains one item of speech. In all these respects, it runs counter to the dominant trend in the development of nineteenth century prose fiction, which was to import the elements of novelistic narrative realism into the short story, converting its key exemplars into delicate "slices of life." Perhaps, therefore, Poe's piece should not be regarded as a "story" at all, but rather as a "tale" akin to and derived from the tradition of oral narration rather than affiliated with the evolution of written texts. Like many folkloristic tales—but not the literary adaptations of such tales for the moral instruction of children—"The Masque of the Red Death" is unremittingly bleak in its outlook. It is also curiously triumphant in its echoing of the grim consolation of the medieval *danse macabre*, an image often found on church walls and intended to remind rich and poor alike that Death—characteristically personified as a hooded skeletal figure—will, in the end, lead everyone away in an endless procession. Actual quasi-orgiastic masques had long been associated with the carnival (literally "farewell to meat") of Mardi Gras, the day before the beginning of the forty-day Lenten fast whose climax was the Easter celebration of the crucifixion and resurrection of Christ. Thus, masques had always had the kind of climactic and valetudinarian aspect that Poe exaggerates to its limit in his short story.

"The Masque of the Red Death" was only one of a host of groundbreaking works that Poe produced, the sum of which established him as one of the most innovative writers of all time. No other American writer has proved as influential, and there is a tragic irony in the fact that Poe was so completely unappreciated in his own time that he virtually starved to death, leaving behind a highly misleading reputation as a drink-addled maniac. One of Poe's early twentieth century biographers, J. A. T. Lloyd, titled his outraged account of the poet's sad fate *The Murder of Edgar Allan Poe* (1931) and identified the depraved indifference of Poe's eventual literary executor, Rufus W. Griswold, as the criminal act in question. It is highly probable that the incipient despair of Poe's actual existence is reflected in his story, although its composition long antedates the death of his child-bride Virginia, not only in its compensatory image of sumptuous existence but also in the refined savagery with which it destroys everything contained in and represented by that image.

Like many of Poe's works, "The Masque of the Read Death" has been subjected to various processes of speculative psychoanalysis. The Freudian critic Marie Bonaparte argues that the Red Death is symbolic of a father returning to punish a son for his Oedipal desires, while Richard Wilbur suggests that the Red Death symbolizes the disease of rationalism and that Prospero's attempt to seclude himself from it is a representation of the flight of the poetic imagination from worldly consciousness into dreams. There are, however, numerous critics who insist that no such secondary elaboration is necessary and that the story is exactly what it seems to be on the surface: a calculatedly gaudy but essentially straightforward recognition of the inevitability of death.

The gaudiness of the story's imagery adds an extra dimension to its reiteration of the moral lesson of the *danse macabre*; it panders unrepentantly to the universality of resentful envy, as it invites readers to rejoice in the annihilation of Prospero and everything for which he stands. That appeal to meanspiritedness does not, however, reduce the work to the status of a mere revenge fantasy, because the narration maintains a grandeur and magnificence of its own while it recounts the devastation of the grandeur and magnificence it describes. Poe's prose has an irreducible elegance not merely of style but of content as well. The symbolism of its garishly colored rooms, incarnate dreams, and ebony-cased timepiece had already been echoed and imitated so many times by the time Poe wrote the story as to seem hackneyed, and such apparatus was already standard in the Gothic fiction produced at the end of the eighteenth century. Poe, however, distilled and purified this symbolism with a rare economy and an unprecedented intensity of focus, forging a veritable masterpiece.

Brian Stableford

Further Reading

Buranelli, Vincent. *Edgar Allan Poe*. 2d ed. Boston: Twayne, 1977. Provides a good synoptic introduction to Poe's life and works and includes a good selected bibliography with brief annotations, updated for the new edition.

Hyneman, Esther F. *Edgar Allan Poe: An Annotated Bibliography, 1827-1972*. Boston: G. K. Hall, 1974. Represents a heroic attempt to provide a guide to the vast secondary literature devoted to Poe. The literature continues to grow apace, but annual summaries supplementing Hyneman's foundation work are provided by the journal *Poe Studies*, published by the College of Liberal Arts at Washington State University.

Maul, Kristen. *About Edgar Allan Poe's "The Masque of the Red Death."* Munich: GRIN, 2007. Fifty-six-page academic essay focusing closely on the story, with particular reference to its symbolism and to the possible identity of its narrator (which may be problematic, because all the witnesses to the catastrophe perish).

Quinn, Arthur Hobson, and Shawn Rosenheim. *Edgar Allan Poe: A Critical Biography*. Baltimore: Johns Hopkins University Press, 1998. The most comprehensive of the recent biographies, capitalizing on previous research and providing a useful selected bibliography in addition to twelve documentary appendices. "The Masque of the Red Death" is discussed as one of Poe's "arabesque" tales, attempting to draw terror from the symbolism of color.

Silverman, Kenneth. *Edgar A. Poe: Mournful and Never-Ending Remembrance*. London: Weidenfeld, 1993. One of the more scrupulously detailed Poe biographies, useful for its extensive, detailed notes and references.

Symons, Julian. *The Tell-Tale Heart: The Life and Works of Edgar Allan Poe*. London: Faber & Faber, 1978. One of the most succinct and readable of many Poe biographies; pays more attention than most to his writings and defends "The Masque of the Red Death" cogently against some of its more exotic critical reinterpretations.

Werner, James V. *American Flaneur: The Cosmic Physiognomy of Edgar Allan Poe*. New York: Routledge, 2004. Links Poe's life and works to contemporary French exercises in lifestyle, including the theory of "dandyism," and to contemporary pseudoscientific interests; "The Masque of the Red Death" is discussed in a chapter on physiognomic revelation.

Zimmerman, Brett. *Edgar Allan Poe: Rhetoric and Style*. Montreal: McGill-Queen's University Press, 2005. An intense theoretical study, which includes one of the most extensive essays focused on "The Masque of the Red Death" in its fifty-five-page second chapter: "Allegorica, Chronographia, and Clock Architecture in *The Masque of the Red Death*."

The Master and Margarita

Author: Mikhail Bulgakov (1891-1940)
First published: Master i Margarita, 1966-1967
   (English translation, 1967)
Type of work: Novel
Type of plot: Satire
Time of plot: 30 C.E. and 1920
Locale: Jerusalem and Moscow

Principal characters:
WOLAND THE DEVIL, who arrives in Moscow as a foreign
   expert in theater
BERLIOZ, a high-ranking member of the literary elite
IVAN BEZDOMNY, a poet
THE MASTER, a Soviet writer who has written a novel
   about Jesus and Pontius Pilate
MARGARITA, the Master's beloved and the wife of a
   successful Soviet scientist
PONTIUS PILATE, the Roman procurator of Judaea
YESHUA HA-NOTSRI, an accused rabble-rouser from Galilee

The Story:

On a warm spring afternoon, two Russian writers meet in a Moscow park. One of them, Berlioz, is the editor of a leading literary journal; the other is a poet named Ivan Bezdomny, who has been reviled for writing a poem about Jesus that depicts him as if he had really existed. The two writers are discussing atheism, the official Soviet policy, when they are joined by a strange, foreign-looking person who asks them provocative questions and gives even more provocative answers to their questions. He even prophesies about their immediate future, telling them, for example, that Berlioz will die before the day is over. In the ensuing philosophical debate, he tells them the story of Pontius Pilate. By the end of the afternoon, Berlioz has been decapitated by a streetcar. Bezdomny ends up in a mental hospital because no one would believe his story about the strange visitor.

The visitor, who has the German-sounding name Woland, professes to be a professor of black magic. He is actually an incarnation of the Devil, and he is accompanied by a black cat named Behemoth, a naked maid, a disreputable clown, and an evil trickster. Woland and his minions proceed to play tricks on the Soviet literary and theatrical establishments and on the ordinary people of Moscow. Various people are packed off to places thousands of miles away, their vices dramatized, their moribund consciences awakened or called to answer, and their philistine natures exposed.

The unnamed Master, an aspiring writer, has written a novel about Pontius Pilate. When he tries to get the novel published, he is unsuccessful. In fact, the book is criticized severely and the author himself subjected to various forms of persecution from both the literary and the political powers in Moscow. As a result, the author burns his manuscript, resolves never to write again, and then, confirming the judgment of his critics that he is mentally ill, turns himself in at the insane asylum. He is placed in the same ward where Bezdomny is languishing.

The Master's lover, Margarita, is frantic when her lover disappears. Hoping to find him, she makes a Faustian pact with Woland and agrees to preside as queen over the annual Satan's ball, which is to take place in the tiny apartment of the deceased Berlioz. At the ball, Woland demonstrates his links with the supernatural world by producing a copy of the Master's burned manuscript. The Devil knows its contents and declares that he has talked to Pilate himself. In the Master's novel, the New Testament account of the Passion of Jesus, or Yeshua, is retold in fresh terms. Yeshua has been betrayed by Judas. Pilate, while acting as Roman procurator and responding to the political pressure, tries to keep Yeshua from incriminating himself. Yeshua is not eager to suffer or to die, but he refuses to admit that any temporal power has jurisdiction over him. As a result, the procurator is unable to release him, and Yeshua is executed. Matthew arrives too late to relieve his pain, just as Margarita has come too late to keep the Master from burning his manuscript.

While presiding over the ball, Margarita observes a parade of human vices and follies as hundreds of dead are brought back to life to answer once more for their deeds. When Margarita shows compassion for a grief-stricken woman who has choked her baby to death, Woland grants her wish for the Master's return and leaves the lovers in a peaceful life together in death. Soviet agencies find rational explanations for all the irrational events.

Critical Evaluation:

The Master and Margarita was Mikhail Bulgakov's crowning achievement. He had previously written other acclaimed novels, short stories, and plays, but this novel established him as a major writer of the twentieth century. Despite Bulgakov's politically enforced silence in the early 1930's and his debilitating illness and premature death, his work had a significant impact on Russian as well as world literature.

Many of Bulgakov's previous writings anticipate features of *The Master and Margarita*. His telling but nonaggressive satire and a sophisticated humor are evident in his short stories; a flair for dramatics enlivens his plays; and philosophical connotations can be found in almost all his works.

The entire action in *The Master and Margarita* takes place on four days, from Wednesday to Sunday of the Holy Week, a significant choice of days. In addition to being a satire on Soviet life in the late 1920's and the early 1930's and a love story, this "tale of two cities" is also laden with philosophical overtones. This tone is struck at the very outset by Bulgakov's use of a motto borrowed from Johann Wolfgang von Goethe's *Faust*, part one (1808): "Say at last—who art thou?"/ "That power I serve/ Which wills forever evil/ Yet does forever good." The motto relates to the Devil, commonly recognized as the source of all evil, and to Woland who, together with his retinue, commits acts of violence and vengeance but also reunites the Master and Margarita and forces the Muscovites to face up to their shortcomings and sins. The basic ethical question of good and evil thus becomes the focal point of the novel, with a Manichaean twist of equality between good and evil. By painting the Devil in colors other than black, and by using Jesus Christ's ethnic name, Yeshua, and making alterations in his age and the account of his crucifixion, Bulgakov urges his readers to abandon the customary, dogmatic, and political way of thinking.

Bulgakov raises another philosophical question, posed by Pontius Pilate to Jesus: What is truth? Without presuming to answer this age-old question, Bulgakov is here addressing the Soviet's usurped monopoly on the truth and their brutality to those who question that truth. To underscore the fact that there is no one truth, Bulgakov tells the Crucifixion story in three narratives—Woland's, the Master's, and Bezdomny's. He shows that everything has more than one side to it, and that looking from only one angle leads to atrophy and death.

Bulgakov poses yet another important question, that of reality, by allowing Woland and his retinue to perform supernatural acts that undermine the Soviet axiom of materialistic reality as the only permissible one. The meaning of the supernatural happenings in the novel lies not in their logical explanation, however, but in the allowance that some other reality—supernatural, spiritual, irrational, or mystical—also exists. To this end, Bulgakov tells the Jerusalem story in a straightforward, realistic manner, without mythical or supernatural elements, whereas the Moscow story is replete with unreal and supernatural details. Bulgakov seems to ask, If today's reality cannot be explained without resorting to the supernatural, although the events of two thousand years ago are crystal clear, how valid is a reliance on reason and facts? In fact, Bulgakov uses the Jerusalem angle not to give yet another account of the Crucifixion but to entice the reader to abandon dogmatic thinking of any kind.

In this novel, Bulgakov is engaged in an ongoing argument with the Soviet rulers. Nowhere is this clearer than in the statement, repeated in several passages, that cowardice is the greatest sin. This sin lies at the core of Pilate's behavior (hence the emphasis on him, and not on Christ), it figures in the betrayal of Jesus by Matthew, and it constitutes the chief failure of the Master. The author's own stakes in this altercation are obvious from his biography. His longstanding battle with the Soviet bureaucracy and his resignation to his fate lead to a conclusion that Bulgakov was trying to assuage his own guilty feelings for having been bullied into at least superficial submission to the authorities. *The Master and Margarita* was written during the final and most painful period of Bulgakov's life, while he was enduring internal exile. Indeed, at least some aspects of *The Master and Margarita* are based on personal experiences. Like the Master, Bulgakov was hounded into intellectual obscurity by literary and political dogmatists. Margarita is modeled after his second wife, who encouraged him to persevere and did much of the copying work after Bulgakov lost his eyesight in the last years of his life. Just as the Master's novel was rescued from the fire, Bulgakov's novel was preserved after his death by his wife. Both Bulgakov and his character the Master had to rely on faith in basic goodness.

This complex novel has given rise to many equally complex interpretations. Andrew Barratt, for example, has promulgated the theory that the novel's main postulates are based on the Gnostic philosophy of the second century, a precursor of the third century Manichaean movement. According to this philosophy, a supernatural being periodically comes to Earth bearing a message that, if properly deciphered, promises the possibility of divine illumination. The message is recognized by only a small number of people in whom the divine spark has not been totally extinguished by the conditions of earthly existence. According to this interpretation, Woland can be regarded as an emissary. His messages are that life is imperfect and must be accepted as such; that good and evil will coexist forever and that evil exists to help human beings recognize what good is; that human striving toward the good leads to suffering and death, but ultimately to life, the only life worth living; and, finally, that cowardice is the greatest sin.

No one interpretation answers all the questions posed by the work, a riddle-novel as the author himself called it. Bulgakov died before giving it its final form, but even as it stands, *The Master and Margarita* remains one of the most thought-provoking, intriguing, and amusing novels in world literature.

Vasa D. Mihailovich

Further Reading

Barratt, Andrew. *Between Two Worlds: A Critical Introduction to "The Master and Margarita."* New York: Oxford University Press, 1987. One of the most astute treatments of the novel, examining many interpretations of it, including that of the Gnostic message and the messenger in the person of Woland. A challenging study.

Curtis, J. A. E. *Bulgakov's Last Decade: The Writer as Hero.* New York: Cambridge University Press, 1987. A thoughtful study of Bulgakov's literary profile that includes comparisons with Molière, Alexander Pushkin, and Nikolai Gogol. *The Master and Margarita* is discussed in detail on pages 129 to 187.

Drawicz, Andrzej. *The Master and the Devil: A Study of Mikhail Bulgakov.* Translated by Kevin Windle. Lewiston, N.Y.: Edwin Mellen Press, 2001. Drawicz analyzes all of Bulgakov's works, placing them within the context of the author's life and times. The initial chapters focus on his life, providing new biographical information, while subsequent chapters concentrate on his novels and other writings.

Haber, Edythe C. *Mikhail Bulgakov: The Early Years.* Cambridge, Mass.: Harvard University Press, 1998. Discusses Bulgakov's early life and career, describing how his novels and other works arose from his experiences during the Russian Revolution, civil war, and early years of communism. Traces the themes and characters of his early works and demonstrates how he perfected these fictional elements in *The Master and Margarita.*

Milne, Leslie, ed. *Bulgakov: The Novelist-Playwright.* New York: Routledge, 1996. Twenty-one essays survey Bulgakov's works from a wide variety of perspectives. Several essays examine *The Master and Margarita*, including one comparing the novel to Salman Rushdie's *The Satanic Verses.* Includes an index of Bulgakov's works.

Proffer, Ellendea. *Bulgakov: Life and Work.* Ann Arbor, Mich.: Ardis, 1984. One of the best book-length studies of Bulgakov, discussing both his life and his works in scholarly detail. *The Master and Margarita* is examined at length on pages 525 to 566.

Weeks, Laura D., ed. *"The Master and Margarita": A Critical Companion.* Evanston, Ill.: Northwestern University Press, American Association of Teachers of Slavic and East European Languages, 1996. Collection of essays discussing various aspects of the novel, genre and motif, mythic structure, political structure, the apocalyptic horse and rider, and the book's connection to Johann Wolfgang van Goethe.

Weir, Justin. *The Author as Hero: Self and Tradition in Bulgakov, Pasternak, and Nabokov.* Evanston, Ill.: Northwestern University Press, 2002. Weir analyzes novels by three Russian authors—Bulgakov's *The Master and Margarita*, Boris Pasternak's *Dr. Zhivago*, and Vladimir Nabokov's *The Gift*—to describe how these authors reveal themselves through their writing, transforming the traditional author into the hero of their novels.

Wright, Anthony Colin. *Mikhail Bulgakov: Life and Interpretations.* Buffalo, N.Y.: University of Toronto Press, 1978. Includes a solid treatment of *The Master and Margarita.* Good select bibliography.

The Master Builder

Author: Henrik Ibsen (1828-1906)
First produced: Bygmester Solness, 1893; first published,
    1892 (English translation, 1893)
Type of work: Drama
Type of plot: Psychological realism
Time of plot: Nineteenth century
Locale: Norway

Principal characters:
HALVARD SOLNESS, the master builder
ALINE SOLNESS, his wife
DOCTOR HERDAL, his physician
KNUT BROVIK, in Solness's employ
RAGNAR BROVIK, Knut's son
KAIA FOSLI, Solness's bookkeeper
HILDA WANGEL, Solness's inspiration

The Story:

Halvard Solness rose to his high position as a master builder because of a fire that had destroyed the ancestral estate of his wife's family. On the site he built new homes that won him fame and assured success in his profession. The fire gave him his chance, but he made his own opportunities, too, by crushing all who got in his way.

Knut Brovik, employed by Solness, had once been a successful architect, but Solness had crushed him, too, and then used him as he had many others. Ragnar, Brovik's son, is a draftsman in Solness's office, and it is Brovik's only wish that before his own death his son should have a chance to design something of lasting value. Although Ragnar has drawn plans for a villa that Solness does not wish to bother with, the builder will not give him permission to take the assignment. Ragnar is engaged to Kaia Fosli, Solness's bookkeeper, and he cannot marry her until he has established himself. Ragnar does not know that Kaia has come under the spell of the master, as had so many other young women. Solness pretends to Kaia that he cannot help Ragnar because to do so would mean losing her; in reality, he needs Ragnar's brain and talent and cannot risk having the young man as a competitor.

Solness's physician, Doctor Herdal, and his wife fear that the builder is going mad. He spends much time in retrospection and also seems to have morbid fears that the younger generation is going to ruin him. Not all of the younger generation frightens Solness. When Hilda Wangel appears at his home, he is at once drawn to her. He had met Hilda ten years before when he hung the traditional wreath atop the weather vane on a church he built. She was a child at the time. Now she tells him that he had called her his princess and had promised to come for her in ten years and carry her off to build her a kingdom. Because he has not kept his promise, she has come to him. Solness, who cannot remember the incident, decides that he must have wished it to happen and thus made it come to pass. This, he believes, is another example of his power over people, and it frightens him.

When Hilda asks to see all he has built, especially the high church towers, he tells her that he no longer builds churches and will never build one again. Now he builds homes for mothers and fathers and children. He is building a home for himself and his wife, and on it he is building a high tower. He does not know why he is putting the high tower on the house, but something seems to be forcing him. Hilda insists that he complete the tower, for it seems to her that the tower will have great meaning for her and for him.

Hilda tells Solness that his need of her is the kingdom he has promised her and that she will stay near him. She wants to know why he builds nothing but homes, and he tells her of the fire that had given him his chance. At the time of the fire, he and his wife had twin baby boys. Although all had been saved from the fire, the babies died soon afterward from the effects of the fevered milk of their mother. Solness knows that his position and his fame are based on the tragedy of the fire and on his wife's heartrending loss, but he believes also that he had willed the fire to have his chance. Whatever he wills happened, and afterward he has to pay somehow the horrible price for his almost unconscious desires. So he builds homes for others, never able to have a real home himself. He is near madness because his success is based on his and his wife's sorrow.

Solness seems to have power over human beings as well as events. Brovik is one man who serves him, his son Ragnar another. Solness, afraid of Ragnar's younger generation, believes that it will crush him as he has crushed others.

Hilda, begging him to give Ragnar and the other young people a chance, says that he will not be crushed if he himself opens the door to them. She tells him that his near-madness is caused by a feeble conscience, that he must overcome this weakness and make his conscience robust, as is hers. She persuades him to give Ragnar the assignment the young man wants. She wishes Solness to stand completely alone and yet be the master. As final proof of his greatness, she begs

Solness to lay the traditional wreath on the high tower of his new home, and she scoffs at a builder who cannot climb as high as he can build.

Hilda alone wants Solness to climb the tower, and only she believes that he will do so. She once had seen him standing on a church tower, and his magnificence had thrilled her. She wants the thrill again. On that other day she heard a song in the sky as the master builder shouted into the heavens, but it is not until now that she learns what he had shouted. He tells her that as he had stood at the top of the church he had known why God made the fire that destroyed his wife's estate. It was to make Solness a great builder, a true artist building more and more churches to honor God. God wanted him to have no children, no real home, so that he could give all his time to building churches. Solness, however, had defied God that day. He had shouted his decision to build no more churches, only homes for mothers and fathers and their children.

God had taken his revenge. There is little happiness in the homes Solness builds. From now on he will build only castles in the air, with Hilda to help him. He asks Hilda to believe in him, to have faith in him. Hilda, however, demands proof. She must see him standing again, clear and free, on the top of the tower. Then his conscience will be freed, and he will remain the master builder. He will give her the kingdom he promised.

Even though his wife and others plead with him not to make the ascent, Solness is guided by Hilda's desire. As he climbs higher and higher, she hears a song in the air and thrills to its crashing music. When he reaches the top of the tower, he seems to be struggling with an invisible being. He topples and falls to the ground, lifeless. Then Hilda hears music in the sky. Her master builder has given her her kingdom.

Critical Evaluation:

The Master Builder belongs to a series of dramas that depart from the earlier types written by Henrik Ibsen. In this play the bitter satire of the social dramas is not present; instead, the play is mysterious, symbolic, lyrical. Ibsen here deals with the human soul and its struggle to rise above its own desires. The idea had been in Ibsen's mind for many years before he actually wrote the play, which is one of the most original of his works.

Ibsen completed *The Master Builder* in 1892, two years after the stormy but mostly favorable reception of *Hedda Gabler* (pb. 1890, pr. 1891; English translation, 1891). Whereas he had labored slowly and revised with care the earlier play, his work on *The Master Builder* proceeded smoothly, requiring few major changes from the first draft to the finished manuscript. One year before, Ibsen had left Munich to return to Norway, where he resided in Oslo until his death in 1906. His return to his native land, an event marked by great professional success and personal satisfaction, corresponded with a significant change in his dramatic style. His early romantic plays in verse are generally lofty, treating historical or epical subjects. The second period of his creative work, including *Et dukkehjem* (pr., pb. 1879; *A Doll's House*, 1880), consists of social dramas, written in conversational, realistic prose. The last period, beginning with *The Master Builder* and including *Naar vi døde vaagner* (pb. 1899, pr. 1900; *When We Dead Awaken*, 1900), is noted for qualities often described as metaphysical or spiritual. Confessional plays with a clear autobiographical impulse and written in a style that moves easily from prose to prose-poetry, they break new ground in the history of the late nineteenth century European theater.

Although Ibsen never denied the subjective character of *The Master Builder*, the play should not be studied merely as a symbolic summary of the writer's life. Instead, it is a great work of dramatic art and, judged solely on the basis of its structural values, one of Ibsen's most finely crafted pieces. Nevertheless, as a confessional drama, *The Master Builder* certainly presents some of Ibsen's important ideas and obsessions. For example, like Halvard Solness, Ibsen was impressed with (although not neurotically dismayed by) the success of younger writers. Ibsen himself wrote of Camilla Collett that "A new generation is now ready to welcome and understand you." Also like Solness, Ibsen was attracted to youthful women. Critics generally believe that Hilda Wangel is modeled upon Emilie Bardach, who was also a part-prototype for Hedda Gabler. At any rate, shortly after the production of *The Master Builder*, Emilie sent the author a photograph signed "Princess of Orangia," which apparently annoyed him. If Emilie was not the single inspiration for Hilda, then surely another of Ibsen's young friends might have been part of the composite picture, beginning with Engelcke Friis and continuing with Helene Raff, Hilda Andersen, or the youngest, Edith Brandes.

In many other ways, the career of the Master Builder parallels Ibsen's own. Solness began by building churches. Later he decided to design "only houses for people to live in." Finally, to please himself and reassert his will to achieve the impossible, he designed a splendid house with a tower, fanciful as a "castle-in-the-air." Ibsen's experience with the theater similarly consisted of three stages: Romantic poetic drama, social drama intended to reform outworn traditions, and personal drama with a special concern for a philosophy of life and death. There are other parallels as well. The high point of Solness's art as a Master Builder was the time he climbed a church tower and, as was the custom among Norwegian builders at that time (much like the christening of a ship), hung a garland at the topmost spire. Hilda had seen the triumph of her hero and remembered the precise date. "It was ten years ago," she said, "on the nineteenth of September." It was on September 20, 1889, that Ibsen wrote on the visitor's ledger at Gossensass, "The great, painful joy of striving for the unattainable." Also, like Solness, Ibsen was troubled by great heights. When he was a youth, he attempted to scale a mountain in Italy but discontinued his ascent in fear, lying flat to the ground clutching a boulder. Finally, like the Master Builder, he was deeply interested in the power of thought transference, and Ibsen was an avid follower of studies on hypnotism and spiritualism.

However interesting are the similarities between the author's life and parallel themes of the play, *The Master Builder* is best enjoyed as theater rather than autobiography. The sharply defined conflicts of the play are resolved only at the conclusion. For this reason, the play performs especially well, although it has never been quite so popular as *Hedda Gabler* or *A Doll's House*. The central conflict is that between high aspiration—romantic dreams to attain the impossible—and the limitations of reality. As Master Builder, Solness has achieved a measure of financial success and even fame, but, as he discloses to Doctor Herdal and later, more completely, to Hilda, he considers himself a mere shell, a failure. Having defied God at the church tower, he has since feared that he will be cursed for his presumptuousness. At first he believes that the younger generation will be the agent of his destruction. Later, as he allies himself with the idealism of Hilda, he fears that his downfall will come not so much from rivals like Ragnar Brovik but from the failure of his own will. All his life he has depended upon "Helpers and Servers" to advance his career. Although a genius in his own right, he has nevertheless had to fight the world. His powerful will, like the nearly hypnotic force that controls the affections of Kaia Fosli, has directed the helpers and servers to perform his wishes. Without assistance, however, he loses confidence in his art.

Finally, however, Solness understands that the enemy to his peace lies not outside himself but within. He really has no need to fear the young, and he does not require the blind obedience of servitors. His failings are those of conscience. He believes that he is going insane. So terrible is his sense of guilt—guilt because of his conduct toward his wife; guilt because he has abandoned the dreams of creating great edifices, churches; guilt because he has defied God—that he becomes increasingly isolated, almost paranoid. When Hilda encour-

ages him to perform the impossible, to prove to the world that only he should be allowed to build, his inner conflict breaks. He determines to hazard everything, even his life, to satisfy his princess and provide her with her promised kingdom—to top a wreath on the tower of the new house.

At this point in the drama, the center of conflict shifts from Solness—now that he has made his idealistic decision—to Hilda. Will she allow the Master Builder to risk his life simply to satisfy her own iron will (or from another viewpoint, the passions of a spoiled child)? She knows that Solness experiences giddiness when he is climbing. Ragnar tells her that the Master Builder has always been afraid to place the wreath on the topmost place, that other workmen perform the task. Yet she steadfastly demands her castle-in-the-air. In a romantic bond with the artist, she has identified her passion with his. Like the Viking women of old, with whom she has declared her kinship, she disdains a bourgeois conscience. For in her sprightly way she, too, is a warrior, and with a robust conscience she demands of her hero a sacrifice to prove his manhood.

A modern audience may perhaps judge Hilda more harshly than would Ibsen. As a character of social realism, she is idealistic to the point of folly. Careless, selfish, and willful, she contrasts with the sober, self-sacrificing, dutiful Aline Solness, the Master Builder's wife. Yet when the audience comes to understand Mrs. Solness better, it sees that she has lived too narrow a life, devoid of romantic risks and heroism. She has never dared to confide to her husband the secret of her own guilt—that after the fire that destroyed her ancestral house, she lamented the loss of her nine dolls more grievously than that of her twin sons, who died shortly afterward. While the audience sympathizes with her human frailty (for she is not to be condemned for grasping firmly to such symbols of the past), it also sees in a contrasted light the heroic striving of Hilda. The trolls (hobgoblins that are symbols both of destructive and creative forces) that guide her life are still strong, not diminished by civilization. At the end of the play—when she shrieks with wild intensity, "My—my Master Builder!"—she identifies his romantic achievement with her own. She has willed his triumph. To Ibsen, the death of a mere man, even a genius, is an insignificant price for such a triumph. In his visionary play, the Master Builder lives on in his work and in Hilda.

"Critical Evaluation" by Leslie B. Mittleman

Further Reading

Binding, Paul. *With Vine-Leaves in His Hair: The Role of the Artist in Ibsen's Plays*. Norwich, England: Norvik Press,

2006. Examines the character of the artist-rebel in *The Master Builder* and four other Ibsen plays. Binding demonstrates how this character represents the tensions of contemporary society.

Clurman, Harold. "Fears and Flights." In *Ibsen*. New York: Collier Books, 1977. A discussion of Ibsen's last four plays, in which he abandons social polemics to probe his own failures as a man and an artist. Clurman points out biographical parallels in Ibsen's life and the character of Solness.

Goldman, Michael. *Ibsen: The Dramaturgy of Fear*. New York: Columbia University Press, 1999. Analyzes dialogue, plot, and other elements of Ibsen's plays to demonstrate how he challenges his audience's opinions and expectations. Includes a discussion of *The Master Builder*.

Knight, G. Wilson. "The Ascent." In *Henrik Ibsen*. New York: Grove Press, 1962. Knight describes the central symbolic action of *The Master Builder* as the climbing of a tower—to live one's art. The play coalesces an external event with spiritual meaning.

McFarlane, James, ed. *The Cambridge Companion to Ibsen*. New York: Cambridge University Press, 1994. Collection of essays, including discussions of Ibsen's dramatic apprenticeship, historical drama, comedy, realistic problem drama, and working methods. References to *The Master Builder* are indexed.

Meyer, Michael. "The Master Builder." In *Ibsen: A Biogra-phy*. Garden City, N.Y.: Doubleday, 1971. Discusses the inception and writing of the play, its reception by critics, Ibsen's deliberate self-portrayal, and its theme of an old man's fear of and longing for youth.

Muir, Kenneth. "Ibsen." In *Last Periods of Shakespeare, Racine, Ibsen*. Detroit, Mich.: Wayne State University Press, 1961. Discusses how Ibsen's last four plays are linked in theme; each protagonist is a genius facing conflicting claims of vocation and personal life, each is compelled to recognize his guilt, and each expresses Ibsen's own personal conflicts.

Robinson, Michael, ed. *Turning the Century: Centennial Essays on Ibsen*. Norwich, England: Norvik Press, 2006. Collection of essays published in the journal *Scandinavica*, including discussions of Ibsen's style, language, and the reception of his plays in England. One essay analyzes *The Master Builder*.

Shaw, Bernard. "The Master Builder." In *The Quintessence of Ibsenism*. New York: Hill & Wang, 1957. Shaw's classic introduction to Ibsen remains invaluable. Shaw concludes that old gentlemen and poetic young women are apt to build castles in the air.

Templeton, Joan. *Ibsen's Women*. New York: Cambridge University Press, 1997. Templeton examines the women characters in Ibsen's plays and their relationship to the women in the playwright's life and career. Chapter 10 includes an analysis of *The Master Builder*.

"MASTER HAROLD" . . . and the Boys

Author: Athol Fugard (1932-   )
First produced: 1982; first published, 1982
Type of work: Drama
Type of plot: Political realism
Time of plot: 1950
Locale: Port Elizabeth, South Africa

Principal characters:
WILLIE MALOPO, a restaurant floor washer
SAM SEMELA, a waiter
HALLY, a student and the son of the restaurant owner

The Story:

Willie Malopo and Sam Semela are forty-five-year-old black men who work at St. George's Park Tea Room, a restaurant owned by a white family. The restaurant is empty because of heavy rains, so Willie practices his dance steps, coached by Sam. Willie had entered a dance contest, and he needs some advice from Sam, the more experienced dancer.

Sam, who is more educated than Willie, learns that Willie, who has a history of beating women, has hit his dance partner, Hilda Samuels. Sam encourages Willie to apologize to Hilda, but Willie does not feel he should have to apologize to a woman.

Hally, a seventeen-year-old student whose parents own the restaurant, comes into the Tea Room with a school bag and a wet coat as Sam is demonstrating his dancing ability.

Hally learns from Sam that the hospital called and that Hally's mother has gone there to pick up his disabled, alcoholic father. Hally tries to deny that his father is returning home. Later, Hally tries to convince Sam that he has not heard his mother's message correctly.

While Sam calls the owner's son "Hally," Willie calls Hally "Master Harold." Hally treats Sam as if he were a fellow pupil, and they discuss topics such as corporal punishment, social reform, and powerful historical people. Hally shares his problems from school as well as his dreams for writing books, short stories, and novels. Sam, who has created a competition between Hally and himself that helps Hally get better grades, tells Hally that he had gone from a fourth-grade to a ninth-grade education because of Hally.

Before they bought the restaurant, Hally's parents had owned the old Jubilee Boarding House. Sam and Willie, then thirty-eight years old, had been tenants there, but they were called "boys" by Hally's mother. Hally recalls his experiences visiting in Sam's room at his parents' boardinghouse. The best memory for Hally is the day Sam created a kite from brown paper, tomato-box wood, glue made from flour and water, and a tail made from Hally's mother's old stockings. Hally is embarrassed about the appearance of the kite, but he loves its flying ability.

Sam explains that the dance is the most important event of the year in New Brighton. Hally becomes interested in the event as a possible topic for his essay assignment. Hally knows that his English teacher does not like "natives," or blacks, but Hally plans to point out that in "anthropological terms the culture of a primitive black society [included] its dancing and singing." Sam helps Hally with the facts concerning the ballroom dancing contest. When Hally wants to know more about the dance scoring, Sam compares ballroom dancing to everyday collisions and world politics.

Just when Hally feels a bit optimistic about the future, his mother calls with news that his father is coming home. Sam listens to the conversation and tells Hally that his conversation with his mother "sounded like a bad bump." Hally gets angry at Sam for interfering and realizes that there can be no world without collisions. Sam scolds Hally for calling his father a "cripple" and blaming the collisions in his life on his father. Hally's shame toward his father turns to rage against Sam, and he demands that Sam, like Willie, call him "Master Harold." Hally tells Sam an antiblack joke related to the definition of "fair" that he says he "learned from [his] father." As a reaction to the punch line in the joke, Sam responds literally and pulls down his pants to show Hally his Basuto buttocks. Hally retaliates by spitting in Sam's face, to which Sam responds by calling him Master Harold.

Sam tells Harold that he has made him feel dirtier than he has ever felt in his life because he is not sure how to wash off Harold's and his father's filth. Sam reminds Harold of the time they had to fetch Harold's drunken father from the floor of the Central Hotel Bar. Harold had to go into the bar and ask permission for Sam, a black man, to go into the white bar. People crowded around to watch a black man carrying his drunken master on his back. Sam says that Hally had walked with downcast eyes and a heart filled with shame as he carried his father's crutches. Hally had walked behind Sam as he carried his drunken father down the center of the town's main street. Everyone in town watched the strange spectacle of a black servant carrying a drunk master.

Sam retells the story of making the kite because he wants Hally to look up and stop walking around with his eyes cast on the ground. Sam tells him that there is a twist to the short story: The bench to which Sam tied the kite is a whites-only bench, and only Hally can sit there.

Sam goes back to calling Harold "Hally" and tries to reconcile the differences with Hally, but he is unsuccessful. Hally leaves Sam and Willie alone in the restaurant to close up. Willie tries to lift Sam's spirits by promising that he will find Hilda and tell her he is sorry. Willie uses his bus money to play "Little Man You're Crying" in the jukebox so that he can dance with Sam.

Critical Evaluation:

Athol Fugard's *"MASTER HAROLD" . . . and the Boys* is a tightly woven one-act play that examines the author's personal experience as a white South African in troubled times. The play won international acclaim but was considered revolutionary in South Africa because there were black and white actors on the same stage. One of Fugard's close associates was Zakes Mokae, a black actor who studied at Yale University and created the role of Sam in the first performance of the play at the Yale Repertory Theatre.

In this perfectly choreographed drama, Fugard illustrates the duplicity in the friendship between the seventeen-year-old white "Master Harold" and the black forty-five-year-old "boys," Sam and Willie, who work for his family. The relationship between Sam and Hally and the interaction between Sam and Willie create a pulsing rhythm of personal conflicts within the play. Hally had taught Sam everything that he himself learned in school, thus creating a verbal sparring partner who could argue with him about topics related to history, literature, and tolerance. To the throbbing beat of historic names from Hally's teachers, texts, and home, Sam offers ideas based on his limited textbook knowledge and his life experience. Willie, who is not as educated, has neither Sam's book knowledge nor his rhythm, but he provides a perfect counterpoint to the beat of the discussion in the Tea Room. Sam's relationship with Hally is intellectual and fatherly, his relationship with Willie is racial and brotherly.

A conflict within one person is Hally's frustration with the dichotomy between the teaching of his prejudiced and "crippled" drunken father and Sam's sensible, more educated nonprejudiced teaching. Hally dislikes his father, but he becomes angry when Sam scolds Harold for talking badly about his father. At that point, Sam crosses the fine line of master/servant relationships. While Harold was trying to bring Sam closer to an understanding of the white world, Sam tried to impose a rule of parental respect. This results in the climax of the play, where Hally demands that Sam call him "Master Harold." Hally attributes his superior attitude to his mother, who has said that Sam is only a servant and should not "get too familiar" with the white proprietor. This confrontation illustrates a person versus society conflict.

Several themes create cohesiveness in the play, among them that of the multiple shades of love and hate. Hally loves Sam for his guidance and companionship, yet despises him because he represents the culture he was raised to consider inferior. Male/female relationships are another theme. The relationship between an overbearing male and a submissive female is represented by Hally's father and mother as well as by Willie and Hilda, showing the strong parallel of noncommunication in different cultures. Another theme relates to family and generations. Hally's parents would like him to continue as a biased white person, but his interaction with Sam has caused a split in that prejudiced thinking because Hally sees Sam display an intelligence and insight that Hally had been told blacks did not possess.

Fugard makes use of several symbols in the play. The bench in the park is first mentioned as a starting point from which to fly a kite. New hope of racial cooperation is symbolized by Sam's and Hally's makeshift kite. Only much later in the play is it revealed that the bench was for whites only. At the end of the play, the bench becomes a symbol to discard old prejudices when Sam advises Hally to "stand up and walk away from it." Another symbol is the dancing that flows through the play. Dancing is the symbol of the smooth interaction of people or nations in which no one "bumps" into anyone. Sam, the expert dancer, had integrated white education and black knowledge. Willie was trying to learn to dance to avoid bumps, but Hally refused to learn to dance. The implication is that Sam and Willie are closer to moving toward harmony than Hally and his parents, who would continue to "bump," or fight.

Hally experiences a rite of passage from innocence to experience. All through the play, his immaturity is clear. Once at the beginning, when Sam teases Willie about a "leg trouble" that has a sexual innuendo, Hally takes the remark literally. Earlier, Sam had created the kite to help Hally forget the shame of having seen his drunken father carried through the town streets. While Hally was old enough to appreciate the kite flying, he was not mature enough to understand the implications of the need to distract his sadness, nor did he understand the implications of the whites-only bench. Finally, Hally did not fully understand his father's joke, which concerned white skin versus black skin, until Sam demonstrated the literal and social implications of "fairness" by showing Hally the blackness of his buttocks.

"MASTER HAROLD" . . . and the Boys illustrates that race has no bearing on intelligence or common sense and that prejudice creates conflicts that education can help to alleviate. Fugard weaves a rich dialogue that illustrates the conflicts between the black and white communities and shows the possibilities of harmony in a vision of the world as a politically smooth ballroom dance.

Annette M. Magid

Further Reading

Benson, Mary. *Athol Fugard and Barney Simon: Bare Stage, a Few Props, Great Theatre.* Randburg, South Africa: Ravan Press, 1997. Benson recounts her friendships with Fugard and Barney Simon, a South African theater producer and playwright, describing how they create their plays and productions.

Crow, Brian, with Chris Banfield. "Athol Fugard and the South African 'Workshop' Play." In *An Introduction to Post-Colonial Theatre.* New York: Cambridge University Press, 1996. A postcolonial interpretation of the work of Fugard and six other playwrights from the developing world, Europe, and the United States.

Durbach, Errol. "'MASTER HAROLD' . . . and the Boys': Athol Fugard and the Psychopathology of Apartheid." *Modern Drama* 30 (December, 1987): 505-513. A thorough analysis of the political atmosphere of black/white relationships as portrayed by Fugard in comparison with the realities of apartheid in South Africa.

Fugard, Athol. "Vividly South African: An Interview with Athol Fugard." Interview by Lynn Freed. *Southwest Review* 78 (Summer, 1993): 296-307. A detailed account of apartheid and the interpersonal repercussions it caused. Discusses Fugard's impact as a playwright as well as his antiapartheid themes.

Post, Robert. "Victims in the Writing of Athol Fugard." *Ariel* 16 (July, 1985): 3-17. Well-written essay that includes a comprehensive interview with the playwright regarding the characters in his work. Excellent analysis of the black "boys" of *"MASTER HAROLD" . . . and the Boys*. Post also analyzes whites as victims of a society poisoned with prejudice and misinformation.

Richards, Lloyd. "The Art of Theater VIII: Athol Fugard." *Paris Review* 31 (Summer, 1989): 129-151. Provides a discussion of the playwright's background and analyzes Fugard's talent for character and conflict development.

Sarinjeive, Devi. "Athol Fugard's Dramatic Representations and Gender Politics." In *Pre-Colonial and Post-Colonial Drama and Theatre in Africa*, edited by Lokangaka Losambe and Devi Sarinjeive. Trenton, N.J.: Africa World Press, 2001. Examines African playwrights of the 1980's and 1990's, describing how their work links African literary tradition with contemporary theater technique.

Walder, Dennis. *Athol Fugard*. Tavistock, England: Northcote House/British Council, 2003. Concise account of Fugard's career and the themes of his plays. Walder demonstrates how Fugard's work seeks to bring reconciliation and harmony to South Africa.

Wertheim, Albert. *The Dramatic Art of Athol Fugard: From South Africa to the World*. Bloomington: Indiana University Press, 2000. Analyzes the content and form of Fugard's plays, examining how they express concerns about South Africa, as well as universal issues of human relationships, racism, and the power to create change. References to *"MASTER HAROLD"* are listed in the index.

The Masters

Author: C. P. Snow (1905-1980)
First published: 1951
Type of work: Novel
Type of plot: Psychological realism
Time of plot: Mid-twentieth century
Locale: Cambridge, England

Principal characters:
ELIOT,
BROWN,
CALVERT,
GAY,
NIGHTINGALE,
WINSLOW,
JAGO, and
CHRYSTAL, faculty members at a college of Cambridge University
ALICE JAGO, Jago's wife

The Story:

Eliot, a young tutor at a college of Cambridge University, is informed by Jago, a senior tutor, that the master of the college, Vernon Royce, has been diagnosed with terminal cancer. Jago goes on to tell him that a new master will have to be elected within a few months. Jago himself desires the position. Soon after, Eliot is invited to meet with two other fellows of the college, Chrystal and Brown, about influencing a wealthy London businessman, Sir Horace Timberlake, to make a large contribution to the college. The subject of Jago's bid to be master comes up, and both Brown and Chrystal agree that he will make a good candidate. Others, too, agree, and it seems that Jago might be elected with a clear majority.

When the faculty of the college is told of Brown's plan to support Jago, a second faction forms, in support of Crawford, a senior physicist. The announcement of opposition to Jago's candidacy leads to a bitter argument between Eliot and Getliff, one of Crawford's supporters, and the college becomes divided between the two factions, with each trying to win converts from the other side. Although he is somewhat confident of victory for the party supporting Jago, Brown warns that they consist mainly of junior, not senior, faculty members.

During the waiting period, a series of political maneuvering takes place. Jago's party hopes that securing the large grant from Timberlake might give more clout to their side.

Internal problems soon begin to take their toll. One of the junior tutors, Nightingale, begins to use his support of Jago as a lever to advance himself at Eliot's expense. Later, Nightingale switches his allegiance to Crawford's party. Brown's attempts to win him back are to no avail. With Nightingale's defection, Jago's supporters no longer hold a clear majority. Jago contemplates withdrawing his name, but the others advise against it.

As the master of the college wastes away, the contest between Crawford and Jago becomes increasingly bitter. Insults and insinuations circulate about Jago and his wife, and tension grows. Jago and Crawford agree that it would be proper if they themselves do not cast votes in the contest. Nightingale threatens Luke, a younger faculty member, with loss of position if he does not change sides. Luke dismisses the threat as insubstantial, but both he and Eliot lament the situation.

The conflict permeates all aspects of college life. When Winslow's son does poorly on his university examinations, Calvert behaves rudely to him. When Eliot visits his old friends, Getliff and his wife, Katherine, their dinner is spoiled by a bitter argument over Jago's fitness for the position of master.

The stalemate threatens to result in a possibility none of the faculty relishes, that the decision will revert to the local bishop, who might even appoint an outsider as master. Calvert suggests that all involved in the election sign a petition instructing Jago and Crawford to vote for themselves to bring about a clear majority for one of them and to prevent the appointment of an outsider; if they fail to do this, all the faculty will switch their votes to favor one of the two. Jago and Crawford are upset by this move, which they consider disrespectful to their rank as senior members. Calvert secretly hopes it will strengthen Jago's position.

When the master of the college dies, Gay, an old, eccentric, and sightly senile faculty member, takes charge of the election. Brown and his friends learn that they have secured the large grant from Timberlake. Winslow, who is college bursar, resigns because he feels incompetent; he did nothing to gain the grant and does not feel qualified to manage it.

Though the grant appears to have strengthened Jago's position, his election is suddenly placed in jeopardy when Pilbrow announces that he cannot vote for him. Jago's party is disheartened by this shift and decides to try to persuade Gay to support their side. Before they can do so, a new problem arises. Jago's wife, Alice, is greatly affected by a flyer Nightingale has written and circulated that attacks her character and abilities. She is so upset that Brown and Eliot put off their plans to visit Gay while they comfort her, and Jago again thinks of backing out. At dinner that night, Jago re-

bukes Crawford for letting his supporters resort to such tactics. At first, Crawford does not acknowledge his responsibility in the matter, but later he agrees to talk to Nightingale about his behavior.

When Brown and Eliot visit Gay, they secure a reasonable assurance that he will vote for Jago. At a final meeting of both parties, Chrystal surprises his friends by announcing that he is satisfied with neither of the two candidates and wishes to choose a new one. The group debates his suggestion, then rejects it. At the last minute, Chrystal throws his support to Crawford. This decides the outcome of the election, since, even with Gay's support, Jago could no longer win. Election day comes. Brown, Crawford, Calvert, Gay, Eliot, and Luke vote for Jago; Chrystal, Desperd-Smith, Getliff, Jago, Nightingale, Pilbrow, and Winslow vote for Crawford, who thus won the election with a clear majority.

Afterward, Eliot's party is glum and wonders how Jago will react. At dinner that night, Jago asks Crawford to be his guest for dinner on the following day, and he participates in a toast to the new master.

Critical Evaluation:

C. P. Snow began his academic career not as a novelist but as a scientist. Unable to gain financial assistance for a university education other than on a scientific scholarship, he earned a doctorate in physics. Initially, he worked as a researcher, then as a government official overseeing the hiring of scientists for the British government. His first love, however, was writing, and throughout his life he produced novels, plays, essays, and lectures. His three areas of expertise—science, government, and literature—gave him much of the thematic material for his literary works.

Snow's familiarity with the world of the humanities and of science provided the background of his most famous and controversial work, *The Two Cultures and the Scientific Revolution* (1959). In this work, Snow argued that scientists and other educated individuals are out of touch with one another and tend to regard the endeavors of others with suspicion. Snow feared that this condition was resulting in a fragmenting culture that would eventually be disastrous for society. He recommended remedial education—more math and science in the lower grades and more humanities in the upper grades. Snow was also concerned with the technological gap between the developed and developing countries of the world and thought that the more industrialized nations should assist the nonindustrial nations.

In his fictional works, Snow examined the arrangements upon which societies are founded. *The Masters* is one of a series of eight novels, to which he gave the title *Strangers and*

Brothers (1940-1970), that trace the life of Lewis Eliot, the narrator of *The Masters*. The book deals with social change, relationships, the nature of power, and the dynamic of human personality. Eliot's life is outlined in these books by the use of two different narrative techniques, one presenting "direct experience," the other "observed experience." The stories are told from Eliot's perspective, but in the works using "observed experience," including *The Masters*, Eliot is principally a reporter who observes and reports the actions of those around him. In other books of the series, Eliot relates his experiences directly.

Strangers and Brothers explores the nature of humanity, recognizing that humans live in relative isolation and loneliness but that they are also joined by the sorrows and joys of life that they all experience. This theme is central to *The Masters*. To a large extent, each of the main characters is alone in his private world. They have their own areas of research and their private lives, personal agendas, and hidden aspirations are separate from those of their colleagues. Each of them secretly pursues his goals in isolation. On the other side, they are all members of the same college and function together as a community, forming friendships and allegiances to achieve goals or out of mutual admiration or need.

The Masters examines the dynamic of interpersonal relationships especially as they relate to power, position, and the workings of institutional politics. It is an important psychological portrait of the ways in which individuals evaluate one another and the ways in which the private worlds of personal endeavor—the "stranger" aspects of life—come to bear on the public realm, where the "brother" aspect becomes most apparent.

This conjoining of private and public is seen in the lives of all the main characters. Jago, who makes the unsuccessful bid for master, is recognized by Eliot and others as a good man who is humane and accepting. His lack of substantial scholarship, his marriage to a woman who is somewhat emotionally unstable, and his own quick temper and erratic shifts of personality gradually surface and change the opinion of some of his supporters. Nightingale, who shifts his allegiance from Jago to Crawford, is a failure in his academic endeavors and personal relationships; his bitterness and mean spirit result from the disillusionment he feels in his private world. For all the characters, the hidden worlds of their private lives inevitably touch on the public world.

Despite some pessimistic turns, *The Masters*, like Snow's other novels, tends to reflect optimism about the ability of people to get along. The political conflict in the college is resolved and, with the exception of Nightingale, all the faculty members manage to stay on socially acceptable terms. Snow was deeply concerned about the divisions within society, but he believed in the possibility of reconciliation.

David W. Landrum

Further Reading

Cooper, William. *C. P. Snow*. Rev. ed. London: Longman, 1971. Part of the Writers and Their Work series, this booklet provides valuable information on Snow, especially on the unifying themes found in his literature.

Eriksson, Bo H. T. *The "Structuring Forces" of Detection: The Cases of C. P. Snow and John Fowles*. Uppsala, Sweden: Uppsala University, 1995. Analyzes the novels in the Strangers and Brothers series as mystery and detective fiction.

Green, Martin Burgess. *Science and the Shabby Curate of Poetry: Essays About the Two Cultures*. New York: W. W. Norton, 1965. A variety of scholars respond to Snow's theory that separate scientific and literary cultures exist in Europe and around the world.

Heptonstall, Geoffrey. "Venturing the Real: The Significance of C. P. Snow." *Contemporary Review* 290 (Summer, 2008): 224-232. Offers a brief overview of Snow's life and literary career. Critiques some of his novels and defines his style as a combination of scientific realism and the description of sensory experience that is typical of modernist literature.

Karl, Frederick Robert. *C. P. Snow: The Politics of Conscience*. Carbondale: Southern Illinois University Press, 1965. Deals with the themes in Snow's novel, particularly his concerns over class struggle and division in the English society he knew and in society worldwide.

Shusterman, David. *C. P. Snow*. Rev. ed. Boston: Twayne, 1991. A good starting point for the study of Snow. Three chapters are devoted to the Strangers and Brothers series. Contains biographical information, including a chronology, extensive notes and references, and a select bibliography, with annotations for secondary sources.

Maud
And Other Poems

Author: Alfred, Lord Tennyson (1809-1892)
First published: 1855
Type of work: Poetry
Type of plot: Melodrama
Time of plot: Early nineteenth century
Locale: England

Principal characters:
THE PROTAGONIST, a young man
MAUD, the young woman he loves

The Poem:

Thinking in recollection, the protagonist reminisces about many things, including his despair in the red-ribbed hollow where his father had died, his rapture in Maud's high Hall-garden, his ostracism from the grand political dinner and dance because of the opposition of Maud's brother, his killing Maud's brother in a duel, his exile on the Breton Coast, his madness in the London asylum, and finally, his pursuit of the blood-red blossom of war aboard a British troop ship on its way to the Black Sea.

The protagonist, an angry twenty-five-year-old, angrily laments the death of his father and the failure of his intimate relationship with the sixteen-year-old Maud, whose own father's treachery in a business transaction caused the demise of the protagonist's father. The grief-stricken young man reacts to his father's death with a savage denunciation of the self-serving greed of the age—which he regards as wreaking havoc on the lives of the poor and which had caused his own family's downfall. Confident that his morbid mood mirrors the moral rot of society, the protagonist is convinced that fighting in a just war is preferable to the implicit acquisition of peace.

The hero emerges from his depression through a growing involvement with Maud, the neighboring squire's daughter, who has returned home with her brother to the family's country estate after having been abroad. By chance, the protagonist sees Maud in a passing carriage and later meets and falls deeply in love with the girl, whom he remembers from childhood. Having won her love, the hero kills her interfering brother in a duel and is forced to retreat into exile.

The protagonist lives his exile in Brittany, where he learns that Maud has died. Later, he suffers successive phases of insanity and remorse, is confined to a London madhouse, and is haunted by hallucinations of Maud. The speaker's nightmare finally yields to a dream in which Maud is no longer a threatening ghost but rather an angel coming to him with a message of hope. "Sane but shattered," he expiates his crime by joining a noble cause, England's involvement in the Crimean War.

"The Story" by James Norman O'Neill

Critical Evaluation:

Maud is a tour de force, a work of considerable complexity and originality in form and content. For its time, it had been a strikingly original internal monologue, unlike any of Alfred, Lord Tennyson's other poems and anticipating by more than half a century the poetic technique of T. S. Eliot in his "The Love Song of J. Alfred Prufrock" (1915). Although most contemporary critics disparaged *Maud*, Robert Browning proclaimed it a great poem and is reputed to have read it many times.

The hallmark of Tennyson's poem is ambiguity, and questions abound. For example, is the protagonist speaking or thinking? How long ago did his father die? How did Maud die? Are her postmortem visitations supernatural phenomena or hallucinations? Did Tennyson incorporate specific autobiographical elements into the poem, as some have maintained? These ambiguities are further complicated by the poem's narrative technique. Eschewing the linear narration that he later employed in *Enoch Arden, and Other Poems* (1864), Tennyson chose to tell his story in the manner of such near-contemporary verse novels as George Meredith's *Modern Love, and Poems of the English Roadside* (1862) and Robert Browning's *The Ring and the Book* (1868-1869; 4 vols.). *Maud* is a story related by implication with unclear time intervals, unspecified scenes, and abrupt transitions.

When *Maud* was published in 1855, it was met by a barrage of hostile reviews. Critics castigated the poem for its obscurity, its dark melancholy, and the protagonist's support of the Crimean War, used in the poem as a palliative for a depraved materialism. Always hypersensitive to criticism, Tennyson was devastated. He made revisions to moderate the more bellicose content and then turned from writing about contemporary society to the medieval world. The first four books of *Idylls of the King* (1859-1885) was his subsequent undertaking.

Maud is divided into three parts of widely different lengths. Each part is divided into units, or snapshots into the protagonist's mind, varying in length from two to thirty-five lines. In part one, the units are sometimes further divided into subunits, making for a complex and, for some, a bewildering organization. Part one of this interior monologue takes the listener/reader into the mind of an extremely egocentric misanthrope, haunted by his father's suicide and his mother's "shrill-edged shriek."

The protagonist rages continually against the heartless materialism of his age, a world in which "chalk and alum and plaster are sold to the poor for bread/ And the spirit of murder works in the very means of life." The mind of the protagonist is a welter of heightened thoughts and emotions, sparked by his hatred of the aristocracy as embodied by Maud's father and brother; his belittlement of organized religion, science, and poetry; his praise of war as a cleansing agent of a corrupt society; his feelings of complete self-abasement and nihilism; and his alienation, paranoia, and suicidal fancies. In the course of this longest section of the poem the protagonist falls desperately in love with Maud to the point of apotheosizing her, proclaiming that "Queen Maud" descended directly from "the snow-limb'd Eve" before the Fall. He proclaims that her gentle will has changed his fate and made his "life a perfumed altar-flame." Part one ends with the often anthologized lyric "Come into the garden, Maud" on a note of high drama.

Part two opens with the protagonist's remorse for having killed Maud's brother in the "red-ribb'd hollow behind the wood," ironically the very spot where his own father's body had been found after his fatal fall. The protagonist is beset by a flitting shadow, either of Maud or "a juggle born of the brain." Ever introspective, the protagonist thinks how the mind when overwrought with passion can fix its attention on an object otherwise unnoticed; he remembers a ring on the finger of Maud's dying brother that he thought was his mother's hair. Haunted by nightmares and the "abiding phantom" of Maud, the protagonist descends into madness. He thinks he is buried in a too-shallow grave, "Only a yard beneath the street," and the horses' hooves beat into his brain. Part two ends with the protagonist avowing to cry out for somebody to bury him deeper, "ever so little deeper."

In part three, which consists of only fifty-nine lines, the protagonist has emerged from madness, transformed by a dream vision of *Maud*, who "seem'd to divide in a dream from a band of the blest/ And spoke of a hope for the world in the coming wars." The pathological misanthropy and delusions of the protagonist have given way to a resolute determination "to fight for the good [rather] than to rail at the ill." The poem ends somewhat summarily with the protagonist on board a warship in the Crimean War.

The unnamed protagonist is one of the more memorable characters of Victorian poetry, as much so as the characters of Tennyson's more traditional dramatic monologues, such as "Ulysses" (1842), "Tithonus" (1860), and "Lucretius" (1868). In psychopathology, Tennyson's protagonist is in the company of Robert Browning's hateful monk ("Soliloquy of a Spanish Cloister," 1842), sociopathic lover ("Porphyria's Lover" 1836), and psychopathic nobleman ("My Last Duchess" 1842). Furthermore, Tennyson called *Maud* a "little Hamlet." While the protagonist shares Hamlet's introspection and emotional instability, he is but a shadow of William Shakespeare's prince of Denmark, of necessity lacking Hamlet's complexity and nobility of character as well as his incisive insights into human nature.

Considerable criticism has explored the biographical content of *Maud*, much of it speculative and hypothetical. Tennyson was the victim of a tainted heredity. He had a melancholy cast of mind and was subject to bouts of debilitating depression, particularly after the death of poet and close friend Arthur Henry Hallam in 1833. These psychological characteristics are reflected in *Maud*, as they are in many of his poems.

It has been suggested that *Maud* is a didactic poem used by Tennyson at the height of his powers to influence public opinion in favor of the Crimean War. However, such a suggestion seems unlikely in view of the pathological state of the protagonist. A number of elements in *Maud* recur in the body of Tennyson's work: mental breakdown, including hallucinations; violence; death and a desire to communicate with the dead; criticism of established religion; interest in the cosmos and humankind's place in it; the struggle for survival in nature; censure of the nouveau riche as greedy, calloused, and inane; and use of landscape to reflect psychological states.

The language of *Maud* is more in the tradition of William Wordsworth than in the neoclassical tradition. The clear, unadorned diction of the poem's first line is characteristic of the whole: "I hate the dreadful hollow behind the little wood." Tennyson uses image clusters to indicate the protagonist's thoughts and moods, and he uses a wide variety of meters—trimeter, tetrameter, pentameter, hexameter—to avoid monotony and to indicate the protagonist's shifting nature of thought. Maud is often associated with light and flowers, while her brother, the "Sultan of brutes," is associated with images of darkness and disease. Maud's "dark father" is a "gray old wolf."

"Critical Evaluation" by Robert G. Blake

Further Reading

Barton, Anna. *Tennyson's Name: Identity and Responsibility in the Poetry of Alfred, Lord Tennyson.* Burlington, Vt.: Ashgate, 2008. Traces the development of Tennyson's poetry, focusing on his reaction to the increasing importance of "brand names" in Victorian culture. Argues that Tennyson had a strong sense of his professional identity and the ethics of literature, which led him to establish a "responsible" poetry.

Buckley, Jerome Hamilton. *Tennyson: The Growth of a Poet.* Boston: Houghton Mifflin, 1960. Buckley's critical biography, a standard reference, contains an excellent commentary on Tennyson's emotional and intellectual development. Includes a brief but perceptive discussion of *Maud.*

Drew, Philip. "Tennyson and the Dramatic Monologue: A Study of *Maud.*" In *Tennyson*, edited by D. J. Palmer. Athens: Ohio University Press, 1973. A collection of essays about the poems of Tennyson in their intellectual, social, and artistic contexts. Contains an excellent article on *Maud* in addition to a reader's guide to Tennyson, a chronological table, and a bibliography.

Glanville, Priscilla J. *Tennyson's "Maud" and Its Critical, Cultural, and Literary Contexts.* Lewiston, N.Y. Edwin Mellen Press, 2002. Examines the major artistic and cultural influences on the poem, most notably William Shakespeare's *Hamlet*, as well as Pre-Raphaelitism and previous closet dramas.

Hood, James W. *Divining Desire: Tennyson and the Poetics of Transcendence.* Brookfield, Vt.: Ashgate, 2000. An analysis of Tennyson's poetry, focusing on his attempt to depict desire in a divine fashion. Argues that "Tennyson's poems, his characters, and his speakers employ erotic devotion and artistic creation as the means by which to approximate the transcendence that constitutes their ultimate goal." Chapter 5 is devoted to an examination of *Maud.*

Lovelace, J. Timothy. *The Artistry and Tradition of Tennyson's Battle Poetry.* New York: Routledge, 2003. A close reading of *Maud* and *Idylls of the King*, demonstrating how these works were influenced by the *Iliad* and *Aeneid.* Describes how Tennyson uses image patterns and other elements of these classical works to adapt the heroic epic for his own time.

Mazzeno, Laurence W. *Alfred Tennyson: The Critical Legacy.* Rochester, N.Y.: Camden House, 2004. Traces the critical reception of Tennyson's work, from the opinions of his contemporaries to those from the end of the twentieth century. Charts how his work has been both reviled and revived since his death, discusses his reputation among the poststructuralists, and provides a twenty-first century prospectus.

O'Neill, James Norman. "Anthem for a Doomed Youth: An Interdisciplinary Study of Tennyson's *Maud* and the Crimean War." *Tennyson Research Bulletin* 5, no. 4 (November, 1990). A thorough treatment of the continuing debate over Tennyson's advocacy of the Crimean War in part 3 of *Maud.* Contains a close reading of the poem's conclusion and includes historical information about the start of the war, the sudden change of public opinion, and the military blunders that occurred.

Ricks, Christopher. *Tennyson.* New York: Macmillan, 1972. A standard reference, this study contains close textual analyses of Tennyson's best-known poems. A major Tennyson scholar and the editor of *The Poems of Tennyson*, Ricks provides lucid explanations of Tennyson's central themes and preoccupations.

Maud Martha

Author: Gwendolyn Brooks (1917-2000)
First published: 1953
Type of work: Novel
Type of plot: Autobiographical and bildungsroman
Time of plot: c. 1924-1945
Locale: Chicago

Principal characters:

MAUD MARTHA BROWN, an African American girl who comes of age
BELVA BROWN, her mother
HELEN, her sister
HARRY, her brother
PAUL PHILLIPS, her husband
PAULETTE BROWN, her daughter
ERNESTINE BROWN, her grandmother
RUSSELL, her first boyfriend
DAVID MCKEMSTER, her second boyfriend
SONIA JOHNSON, the owner of a beauty shop
MISS INGRAM, a white woman who sells cosmetics
THE HAT WOMAN, a salesperson in a hat store
MRS. BURNS-COOPER, a woman who hires Maud as a domestic worker
SANTA CLAUS, an employee at a department store

The Story:

Sensitive, intelligent, and discerning, Maud Martha Brown is a member of a solid family, but she competes with her sister Helen, who is prettier and more attractive than Maud, according to the standards of their family and of society. Maud is African American, and in Chicago she discovers the complexities and cruelties of racism in not only her relationships with whites but also her connections with other blacks.

Maud has dark skin, and African Americans who are lighter-skinned receive preferential treatment from others, even though Maud's loyalty and intelligence deserve recognition as well. Maud's central philosophy is that the common and ordinary features of daily life are beautiful, too, and should be cherished. The dandelion, for example, is common and simple, but it is also radiant and beautiful.

For the young and observant Maud, death and the responses of people to illness and death are impressive. Maud and her siblings visit their grandmother, Ernestine Brown, in the hospital, and to Maud, Grandmother Brown, whose bed is equipped with sideboards to prevent her from falling out of bed, seems to be lying in a coffin. People who visit her ask foolish and predictable questions, and she can only gasp in response. The children return home. Their father receives a phone call, informing him of grandmother's death.

Later, Maud's uncle Tim dies, leading Maud to recall his daily personal habits and some memorable moments. Seeing her uncle in the coffin, Maud vainly thinks of her own death and how she wants to be laid in her coffin to reveal her most favorable profile. This silly vanity is counterbalanced by Maud's observation that life is like a book in the hands of Jesus, but before death, people fail to see that the answers to life's questions are all listed at the back of the book.

As Maud matures, courtship becomes an important part of her life. Her first boyfriend, Russell, is attractive but insubstantial. David McKemster, her second boyfriend, is dedicated to the styles of the university. Though he is from a modest home and does menial jobs to make his way, he longs for refinement, education, and tasteful possessions.

Maud's third boyfriend is Paul Phillips. She is thoroughly attracted to him and aims to marry him, but she has some doubts about his full attraction to her—perhaps he would prefer a woman of lighter complexion. Their courtship becomes serious, and they make plans for an apartment and decide on furnishings. Though both would like to have a fine apartment, their limited resources permit them to get only a kitchenette apartment, one with roaches, thin walls that allow the sounds of neighbors to be heard, and prevailing odors of sweat and the result of bodily functions. Despite these shortcomings, the apartment becomes their home.

Like all young couples, Maud and Paul have their moments of pleasure and frustration. One night, they go to the World Playhouse and enjoy a film, feeling conspicuous as the only African Americans in the theater. Paul later accepts an invitation from the Foxy Cats Club to attend a ball, and Paul and Maud attend in high dress. Maud enjoys the gala event, but when Paul dances with another woman, Maud becomes decidedly jealous.

Despite these difficulties, Paul and Maud conceive a child, and Maud gives birth in the apartment. Paul frantically tries to get a doctor, but events proceed too quickly, and Maud, with the help of her neighbors, gives birth. When the doctor arrives and affirms that the newborn girl is in good health, Maud's mother and Paul are bewildered. Maud feels fine and is thankful for her kind neighbors.

Maud's neighbors at Gappington Arms, the apartment building, reveal all the strengths and weaknesses of humans in general. Oberto, a grocer, loves Marie, his sensuous but not always dutiful wife. Eugena Banks, a white woman married to a black man, seeks advice from Maud on pleasing a black man because Eugena fears her judgment in marrying a black man might have been faulty. Particularly inspiring among Maud's neighbors is Clement Lewy, the second grader who maintains a high spirit and responsible behavior even as his mother works twelve hours as a housemaid. When she comes home, Clement greets her with enthusiasm. In contrast to Clement's mother, Richard, a truck driver, finally decides to stop coming home. With his wages declining and his tiny apartment offering more disorder than satisfaction, Richard leaves his wife and three children to fend for themselves.

Maud and Paul live in an apartment slightly larger than that of Richard. One day, Maud receives a visit from Binnie, an unpredictable young man who roams the halls. Binnie enters Maud's apartment and puts his hands on everything, creating a tense mood. Maud is thankful when he leaves. Much more delightful than Binnie are the Whitestripes, whose simple one-room apartment does not limit their affection and concern for each other. Rounding out the list of Maud's neighbors are Maryginia Washington, a white-haired woman who claims she is a descendant of George Washington, and Josephine Alberta Snow, a graduate of Fisk University, who takes pride in her refinement and has little patience with people who do not share her ideas. In all, the people at Gappington Arms reveal hardships and difficulties in the community, but they also demonstrate resilience, resourcefulness, and intelligence.

Social situations test Maud and reveal her attitudes. In one encounter, Maud meets David, her old boyfriend, and David, though obliged to be courteous, seems to look for a way to make their contact brief. David has two white friends, and he engages them in a conversation loaded with academic references and name dropping. Maud notices every nuance of their adopted style.

Maud visits Sonia Johnson's beauty shop, where Miss Ingram, a white cosmetics salesperson, utters a racial epithet that startles Maud but draws no reaction from Sonia. After Miss Ingram leaves, Sonia explains to Maud that the racial epithet is taken too seriously by blacks, but Maud, still stunned, cannot comprehend her point.

Paul feels that the people at the club have an authentic style—an appropriate sense of taste—but Maud observes Paul and knowingly thinks to herself that dreams of sophistication are fulfilled for few. The real rule of life, she believes, is that most lives come to nothing at all.

Maud visits a hat shop, where a salesperson tries to conceal her racist attitudes about blacks to make a sale. The woman presumes that blacks have oily, greasy hair, and that they might damage merchandise if they tried on the hats; still, she is ready to offer a discount to complete a sale. Maud, however, senses the undertones of racism and walks out of the shop.

Down to her last scraps of food, Maud accepts a job as a maid for Mrs. Burns-Cooper, but the woman proves to be a harsh taskmaster with an air of arrogant superiority. The woman's mother-in-law intensifies the supervision of Maud. At the end of the day, Maud walks out, confident that she will not return. Maud's life is humble, but she is a human being with a husband and child. She does not have to bow down to anyone.

Maud's own mother, Belva Brown, comes for a visit. At her own apartment, Maud must endure her mother's inspection. Maud serves gingerbread, and her mother likes it, despite a need for additional cinnamon. Belva chides Maud, reminding her that Paul should do better and provide more than a kitchenette apartment. When Maud learns that Helen, her sister, might marry the family doctor, who is much older than Helen, Maud hears no disapproval from her mother. The conversation is a trial for Maud, but she endures.

Maud soon experiences sharper humiliation. At a department store at Christmastime, Maud urges her shy daughter Paulette to talk to Santa Claus, but Santa, apparently a racist, refuses to show enthusiasm. Maud tries to soothe her child's feelings and avoid an experience of racial hatred, but Maud, on the inside, is furious about Santa's failure to embrace her child.

The war is over, and Maud's brother, Harry, is safely home. Maud is pregnant again. The world seems to renew itself despite the forces of destruction.

Critical Evaluation:

The autobiographical novel *Maud Martha* describes the experiences of a young woman named Maud Martha Brown, following her growth from the age of seven through courtship, marriage, and motherhood. The novel deftly blends aspects of the story and poetry. As a whole, the thirty-four segments reveal Maud's coming of age. The language in each segment is often poetic, and Gwendolyn Brooks takes some poetic license with punctuation, sentence structure, and vocabulary. Many of the segments could be free-standing stories, but the focus on Maud in each episode links the stories to create a novel. The overall narrative of Maud's growth is clear, but Brooks places more emphasis on the sensitivity of Maud and her responses to those around her.

A central theme is the dismantling of preconceptions of African Americans, especially as such preconceptions existed among readers in 1953. Maud surprises with her refinement and perceptiveness, but she also connects well to readers because, like them, she wants the satisfaction of home and family. As a family, the Browns have small problems, but on the whole, they are loyal to each other, hard working, and stable. This depiction of an African American family does not conform to stereotype. The members of Maud's community also exemplify lively diversity. Just as Geoffrey Chaucer in his prologue to *The Canterbury Tales* (1387-1400) reveals the full range of human integrity and frailty, Brooks, in segments such as "kitchenette folks," "a self-solace," and "an encounter," reveals the range of strengths and weaknesses among African American neighbors and community members.

A second theme is the challenge to the definition of beauty. Why, in both the white and black worlds, is lightness of color more beautiful than darkness? In judging beauty, why do people overlook the characteristics of inner beauty, such as compassion and intelligence, and focus instead on the texture of hair and the creaminess of complexion?

Some readers question the positive ending of the novel, charging that Maud's optimism does not follow from her negative experiences. This view fails to recognize the consistent development of Maud's optimism. From the beginning she finds beauty in daily life, and she strives to develop her goodness, even as she finds a mouse in a trap, prepares a chicken for cooking, or considers the kindness of her neighbors after her daughter is born. Maud's optimism reveals her

success in becoming a good person in spite of the hypocrisy around her.

An important dimension of *Maud Martha* is its connection to other works by Brooks. *Annie Allen* (1949) earned the Pulitzer Prize in fiction, but that autobiographical text was poetry—sometimes rather difficult poetry. Like *Annie Allen*, *Maud Martha* covers the life experiences of a sensitive African American woman, but the prose is accessible, illuminating some aspects of the character Annie Allen. Supplementing both *Annie Allen* and *Maud Martha* is *Report from Part One* (1972), an autobiography, complete with photographs.

William T. Lawlor

Further Reading

Bryant, Jacqueline K., ed. *Gwendolyn Brooks' "Maud Martha": A Critical Collection*. Chicago: Third World Press, 2002. Bryant's collection of critical essays on *Maud Martha* offers diverse views of the novel.

Frazier, Valerie. "Domestic Epic Warfare in *Maud Martha*." *African American Review* 39, nos. 1-3 (Spring/Summer, 2005): 133-141. Frazier sees Maud as a woman who is judicious about battling for what she deserves.

Lattin, Patricia H., and Vernon Lattin. "Dual Vision in Gwendolyn Brooks's *Maud Martha*." *Critique: Studies in Contemporary Fiction* 25, no. 4 (Summer, 1984): 180-188. Compares *Maud Martha* to Ralph Ellison's *Invisible Man* and Richard Wright's *Native Son* and finds that Brooks's account is more delicate and restrained, but still forceful.

Shaw, Harry B. "The War with Beauty." In *A Life Distilled: Gwendolyn Brooks, Her Poetry and Fiction*, edited by Maria Mootry and Gary Smith. Urbana: University of Illinois Press, 1987. Shaw analyzes Maud's examinations of conventional standards of beauty, as detailed in her novels and poetry.

Washington, Mary Helen. "Taming All That Anger Down: Rage and Silence in Gwendolyn Brooks's *Maud Martha*." *Massachusetts Review* 24, no. 2 (1983): 453-466. Washington unfolds the underlying rage in the seemingly serene personality of Maud Martha.

Maurice

Author: E. M. Forster (1879-1970)
First published: 1971
Type of work: Novel
Type of plot: Bildungsroman
Time of plot: 1903-1913
Locale: Cambridge and London, England

Principal characters:
MAURICE HALL, the protagonist
CLIVE DURHAM, Maurice's Cambridge schoolmate
ALEC SCUDDER, Durham's gamekeeper at Penge

The Story:

At the age of fourteen, Maurice (pronounced like "Morris") Hall is sent to the same mediocre public school his dead father had attended. Maurice is not a remarkable student, though he is proficient at his lessons and is athletic and handsome. Mr. Ducie, a schoolmaster, is aware that Maurice has no proper male role model and takes it upon himself to instruct Maurice in sexual matters during a walk on the beach. Maurice realizes that Ducie's explanation does not explain Maurice's own sexual urges. Maurice is perplexed by his schoolmates' mixture of rude and cruel behavior tempered by tenderness, especially concerning their sexual roles.

When Maurice arrives at one of the less prestigious colleges at Cambridge, he comes to understand his sexual inclinations and finds them both disgusting and confusing. At Cambridge, Maurice falls under the influence of Greek culture and thought, whose ideals are sexual freedom and tolerance, when he is introduced to Plato's *Symposium* by Clive Durham, a tutor with whom he falls in love and who persuades Maurice to abandon his conventional religious ideas. A year older than Maurice, Clive becomes Maurice's first love. Rejecting Christianity and understanding the stirring of his heart, Maurice begins to think about the nature of his identity.

Clive loves Maurice, but in a romantic way that idealizes homosexuality. Clive is guilt-ridden by his desires, but liberated by Plato's writings. He derives a freedom to idealize homosexual love from Plato's *Phaedrus*, but not the license to act on his sexual desires. Maurice, taller and more athletic than Clive, desires physical fulfillment of their love. Despite their contrary philosophies, an idyll begins between the two. The pair travel to Italy. After graduation from Cambridge, Maurice and Clive settle in London to fulfill their families' expectations. Maurice is accepted into his father's brokerage firm; Clive studies law in preparation for a career in politics. For two years, the two men spend every Wednesday night and weekend together; however, their relationship remains strictly platonic.

When Maurice refuses to accompany Clive on a trip to Greece, their relationship is forever altered. Alone in Greece,

Clive concludes that he is mistaken about homosexuality and decides he loves women. Clive returns to London and, wrapped in bandages by Maurice's mother and sisters (who were in training as World War I nurses), sees Maurice again. Clive confesses his choice of a heterosexual identity to Maurice and an argument ensues, causing a rift between the men. Clive marries for socioeconomic reasons after Risley, Clive and Maurice's Cambridge friend, has his life ruined after arrest on a morals charge. A rising barrister, Clive rejects Risley's plea for help and warns Maurice that they must forget the past and respect the boundaries of friendship.

Maurice, twenty-three years old, plunges into a deep depression. He experiences guilt over his homosexuality after being rejected by Clive. Desperate and self-loathing, Maurice considers suicide because death seems preferable to self-denial or the scandal associated with homosexuality. With the distraction of his grandfather's death, Maurice comes out of his depression to an extent, but still wants to be normal. Maurice spends some time with Clive and his wife. Maurice consults a quack hypnotist who has supposedly helped other men overcome their homosexuality. Science, however—as religion had before—proves what Maurice intuitively knew: He cannot change who he is.

A year later, Maurice accepts his sexual identity when he meets Alec Scudder, the gamekeeper of Clive's estate, Penge. Alec's profession keeps him outdoors, attuned to nature, in sharp contrast to the indoor world of Maurice and his friends. Maurice breaks down class barriers when he enters into a relationship with Alec after a day of playing cricket. Maurice is still conflicted, however, about his homosexuality. Clive believes Maurice's secret trysts are with a girlfriend about whom Maurice has not told Clive. As his relationship with Alec deepens, Maurice becomes concerned about their class differences and the possibility that Alec might blackmail him. When Clive discovers that Maurice's lover is a man, he is appalled—especially by Alec's working-class background—and more than a little jealous.

Alec tries to reconcile with Maurice, but to no avail. Alec

decides to emigrate. At the last moment, he decides to stay in England and goes to his and Maurice's usual trysting place, where Maurice and a new life together await him. Maurice rejects society's standards and accepts his love for another man wholeheartedly. He finally feels as if he were a fully integrated personality. At peace with himself, Maurice convinces Alec to share a life together—a man loving a man, both intellectually and physically. While there is no promise of permanence in Maurice and Alec's relationship, Maurice speaks to Clive one last time with unprecedented eloquence. Maurice tells Clive that he, Maurice, loves Alec, that Clive had trapped himself into a dull marriage, and that Maurice is bidding farewell to the life and society in which he had been born and raised. In the manner of earlier bands of English outlaws—those who were alienated from society—Maurice and Alec withdraw to live in the greenwoods where they can find the freedom and happiness necessary to preserve their love. At the age of twenty-four, Maurice's inner journey to find himself seem complete.

Critical Evaluation:

During his long life, E. M. Forster distinguished himself with six novels. Two, *Where Angels Fear to Tread* (1905) and *A Room with a View* (1908), are known as the Italian novels because they are set in Italy and because they share certain qualities, themes, characterizations, and tone. *Maurice* was first written between September, 1913, and July, 1914. Because of its gay-themed content and the tenor of the times, the novel was not published in Forster's lifetime. Forster published three other major novels in his lifetime, *The Longest Journey* (1907), *Howards End* (1910), and *A Passage to India* (1924).

During the next fifty years, Forster reworked *Maurice*, and as late as 1960 made substantial revisions, adding a "Terminal Note." This note describes the novel's origins, which can be traced to Forster's visit with the writer Edward Carpenter, who has been called the first modern writer on sex in England. Carpenter heavily influenced D. H. Lawrence but is now virtually forgotten as a significant writer. Carpenter's lover, George Merrill, had touched Forster at one time, a touch and "sensation," Forster later said, that "was unusual." He added, "and I still remember it." Forster soon began to write *Maurice*, a novel that is part autobiography disguised as novel and part novel as wish fulfillment. In *Maurice*, Forster utilizes the epigrammatic theme from *Howards End*: "Only connect." In doing so, he writes a novel of a young man's inner journey toward understanding the nature of his sexual identity.

The genius of Forster's novel lies in his creation of Maurice Hall, an Everyman who is "someone handsome, healthy, bodily attractive, mentally torpid, not a bad businessman and rather a snob." Maurice's homosexuality is the "ingredient" that brings Maurice to life: It puzzles him, awakens him, torments him, and finally saves him. In Maurice's efforts to connect, he first meets Clive, whose Hellenic values attract Maurice and awaken his sexual identity. When Maurice determines that he and Clive will never connect physically, only mentally, he is again tormented. When Maurice connects with Alec Scudder, the gamekeeper on Clive's estate, Maurice saves himself by rejecting the conventions of the society in which he was reared.

The character of Alec is loosely based on Stephen Wonham, a man of working-class origins with whom Forster had a relationship. To say, however, that the thematic focus of *Maurice* is finding love despite class hierarchy distinctions would be inaccurate. The theme of *Maurice* is the search for self-fulfillment through realization of sexual and self-identity as well as the place of gays in society. Forster thought, by 1960, that the book was dated because it belonged to an era when it was still possible to escape to "the greenwood" and get "lost." This is still possible but unnecessary for gays, given the changing mores that include a greater acceptance of gay and lesbian sexuality. The theme of connection in *Maurice* is still relevant to any confused young man who may be uncertain of his sexual identity and who is experiencing the puzzlement such a discovery brings about.

Change, discovery, and connection are all very much part of *Maurice*. Maurice discovers that his options in life are not limited to those of his deceased father. He does not make this discovery on his own. When Clive speaks openly about his own feelings and platonic ideals, Maurice awakens to the possibility that what had puzzled him about sexuality since his walk on the beach with Mr. Ducie and their discussion of the birds and the bees was the existence of an "other" sexuality. Maurice makes discoveries only when challenged by others; he is as much an Everyman as a hero.

Alec is crucial to the novel. He represents nature—a vital life force—feeling free to roam and to satisfy his sexual urges without guilt or shame. In keeping with the tradition of English literature, Forster makes Alec an archetypal dweller in the greenwoods, the places untouched by the corrupt and corrupting values of society, religion, and other institutions. Alec and Maurice move into a darkness that symbolizes fecund nature and the mysteries of love. Alec's presence is—if anything—primal at its best. In a scene in which Maurice moves to the open window at Penge, he knows there is someone or something waiting for him in the darkness to be discovered. Maurice cries out into the night, "Come!," consciously unaware that anyone might hear him, and intuitively aware that someone will. When Alec appears from the darkness, he brings light into Maurice's life—the light of an older, more primitive enlightenment than the so-called enlightened society in which they live.

This concern for the instinct and the subconscious self is one that Forster shared with Lawrence. By giving Alec primal qualities—like the wild, shining brown eyes of an animal—Forster's sexual theme is linked with Lawrence's sexual themes. (Lawrence used some of the same symbolism in *Lady Chatterley's Lover*, 1928.) Historically, *Maurice* is important because it establishes a voice contemporaneous with Lawrence that uses an honest, open approach to the body and homosexuality. *Maurice* might provoke less tolerant members of society to question their personal attitudes toward homosexuality. As Forster wrote in the "Terminal Note," "We had not realized that what the public really loathes in homosexuality is not the thing itself but having to think about it." A faithful film adaptation of the novel, directed by James Ivory and produced by Ismail Merchant, was made in 1987.

Thomas D. Petitjean, Jr.

Further Reading

Bradshaw, David, ed. *The Cambridge Companion to E. M. Forster.* New York: Cambridge University Press, 2007. Collection of essays analyzing various aspects of Forster's life and work, including discussions of Forster and the novel, women, and England, Forsterian sexuality, and postcolonial Forster. "*Maurice*" by Howard J. Booth focuses on this novel.

Colmer, John E. *E. M. Forster: The Personal Voice.* 1975. Reprint. New York: Routledge, 1983. A full, balanced account of Forster's life and critical assessment of Forster's major works.

Curr, Matthew. "Recuperating E. M. Forster's *Maurice.*" *Modern Language Quarterly* 62, no. 1 (March, 2001): 53-70. A reevaluation of the novel. Curr describes how the book was criticized for its weaknesses after it appeared in 1971, and he takes exception to some of these remarks.

Gardner, Philip, ed. *E. M. Forster: The Critical Heritage.* 1973. Reprint. New York: Routledge, 1999. Dealing with contemporaneous views of Forster and his works, this work's critical assessment of *Maurice* is balanced and judicious and includes autobiographical details.

Keeling, Bret L. "'No Trace of Presence': Tchaikovsky and the Sixth in Forster's *Maurice.*" *Mosaic* 36, no. 1 (March, 2003): 85-102. Examines the function of Peter Ilich Tchaikovsky's *Sixth Symphony* in the novel. Keeling argues that Tchaikovsky's symphony offers a strategy of disclosure for Clive Durham in his relationship with Maurice Hall.

Page, Norman. *E. M. Forster.* New York: St. Martin's Press, 1987. This compact resource charts the life and career of Forster. Page ranks *Maurice* among Forster's minor fiction and is critical of the work, regarding it as an "experiment that misfired," too subtle in its handling of homosexuality.

Max Havelaar

Author: Multatuli (1820-1887)
First published: 1860 (English translation, 1868)
Type of work: Novel
Type of plot: Satire
Time of plot: 1857
Locale: Java, Dutch East Indies

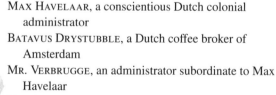

Principal characters:
MAX HAVELAAR, a conscientious Dutch colonial administrator
BATAVUS DRYSTUBBLE, a Dutch coffee broker of Amsterdam
MR. VERBRUGGE, an administrator subordinate to Max Havelaar
THE ADHIPATTI, the native regent of Lebak, Havelaar's district
SAIDYAH, the son of a Javanese rice farmer
THE SHAWLMAN, a schoolmate of Batavus Drystubble and a writer
MR. SLIMERING, Havelaar's superior officer

The Story:

Batavus Drystubble, a self-satisfied coffee broker in Amsterdam, is accosted one day on the street by a former schoolmate who has obviously fallen on bad times. The Shawlman, as Drystubble calls him, pressed his prosperous former schoolfellow to look over a bundle of manuscripts, in the hope that Drystubble might be willing to help him have some of them published. Drystubble, thinking he might have a book written about the coffee trade, turns over the manuscripts to a clerk in his firm to edit. The clerk agrees to make a book of the materials, after securing a promise from his employer not to censor the results before publication. Out of the bundle of manuscripts comes the story of Max Havelaar, a Dutch administrator in Java, in the Dutch East Indies (now Indonesia).

Havelaar is an idealist who believes in justice for everyone, even the poor Javanese who labor in the fields. When he arrives at Rangkas-Betoong to take over the post of assistant resident of Lebak, a section of the residency of Bantam, in Java, he finds the situation much worse than anticipated, for the Dutch administrators, despite their oath to protect the poor and lowly, have acquiesced in the robbery and mistreatment of the native Javanese by the Javanese nobility, through whom the Dutch ruled the island. The Adhipatti of Lebak is a relatively poor man because his region does not produce many of the exports wanted by the Dutch. To keep up appearances befitting his rank and to support a large and rapacious family, the Adhipatti extorts goods, materials, and services from the people, who feel helpless because of the treatment they will suffer from the native chief if they complain to Dutch officials.

Havelaar, a man who loves a good fight for justice's sake, is glad he has been assigned to Lebak. In his opening speech to the Adhipatti and the lesser chiefs, he declares that justice must be done, and he begins trying to influence the Adhipatti by advancing him tax money in the hope that the chief will be less exacting on his people. Suggestions and help are of little use, however, for the same evil practices continue. The people, learning that Havelaar wishes to see justice done, steals to his home under cover of darkness to lodge their complaints and give the assistant resident information. Havelaar rides many miles to redress complaints. He also gives an example to the chiefs by refusing to use more native labor than the law allows, even to letting the grounds of the residency go largely untended and revert to jungle. He realizes what he is fighting against, for he is in his middle thirties and has spent seventeen years in the Dutch colonial service.

Havelaar's faithful adherent in his battle against injustice is his wife, Tine, who is devoted to her husband and knows he is in the right. Of less help is Mr. Verbrugge, the controller serving under Havelaar. He knows the Javanese are being exploited, but he hates to risk his job and security by fighting against the tide of complacency of Dutch officialdom. Mr. Verbrugge realizes that Havelaar's superiors are interested only in keeping peace, in submitting reports that bespeak prosperity, and in providing wealth for the homeland—regardless of what happens to the Javanese.

One example is the story of Saidyah, the son of a Javanese rice farmer. One by one Saidyah's father's possessions are taken from him by extortion, even the buffalo that had faced a tiger to save the boy's life. Finally, Saidyah's father runs away to escape punishment for failing to pay his taxes, and Saidyah himself leaves his home village to seek work in Batavia, vowing to his beloved that he will return in three years' time to marry her. When he returns, however, he finds that she and her family had been forced to flee and have joined rebellious Javanese on another island. Saidyah finally finds his beloved, but only after she had been killed and mutilated by Dutch troops. Overcome with grief, Saidyah rushes upon the troops and is impaled on their bayonets.

As time passes, Havelaar realizes he can expect little help from Mr. Slimering, the resident of Bantam and his immediate superior. Yet Havelaar hopes optimistically that some support will be forthcoming from that quarter. Havelaar learns that his predecessor has probably been poisoned because he sought to stop the exploitation of the population by the native chiefs. Havelaar learns this from his predecessor's native wife, who still lives at the official residence.

Having finally gained what he deemed sufficient information against the Adhipatti, Havelaar lodges an official protest with Mr. Slimering. He requests that the Adhipatti and his subordinate chiefs be taken into custody and removed from Rangkas-Betoong, lest their presence intimidate the people and prevent their giving testimony of the abuses. Instead of acceding to any part of the request, Mr. Slimering comes to Havelaar's district, denounces Havelaar's actions, and even gives money to the Adhipatti. Havelaar, hoping to find support higher up in the administration, appeals to the governor-general, saying that unless he receives some support to eradicate the injustices he will have to resign after seventeen years of faithful service to the colonial administration.

At this point in the manuscript a section is inserted, supposedly written by Batavus Drystubble, who expresses the views of a complacent Dutch businessman in the homeland. Drystubble says that he has been royally entertained by retired colonial officials who assured him that the charges made in Shawlman's manuscripts are groundless. Drystubble adds that as a religious man, he feels that the heathen Javanese are being given their just deserts for not being Christians and that the Dutch are profiting at the expense of the Javanese because the former are decent, God-fearing, and obedient Christian people who deserve divine favor.

After waiting a month, Havelaar learns that he has been relieved of his post in Lebak; he is ordered to another part of Java. He cannot accept this official action, knowing that he will have the same fight all over again, a losing battle, in a new assignment. He leaves Lebak after his successor arrives and goes to Batavia to present his case personally before the governor-general. That worthy man, too busy to see him, puts off Havelaar with one pretext after another. On the eve of the governor-general's departure for Holland, Havelaar writes an angry letter as a last hope. That stinging letter does no good; the governor-general sails for home, leaving Havelaar poor and forsaken.

At the end of the novel, Multatuli steps in to break off the story and speak in his own voice, dismissing Shawlman and the clerk from Drystubble's office, who as fictional characters have been writing the novel. Multatuli, after expressing his loathing of the hypocritical, money-grabbing Drystubble, says that he wishes to leave an heirloom for Havelaar's children and to bring his appeals to the public. The author says that he knows his book is not well written, but all that matters is that people learn how the Javanese are being mistreated, thirty million of them, in the name of King William of the Netherlands.

Critical Evaluation:

Max Havelaar is considered the greatest Dutch literary achievement of the latter half of the nineteenth century. This era was a time of literary awakening in many smaller Northern European countries. For example, Norway saw the drama of Henrik Ibsen and Sweden saw that of August Strindberg. These writers, although working in languages spoken by a small minority of the world's population, created works that spoke to the world. The works of Eduard Douwes Dekker, known as Multatuli, are Dutch literature's nearest equivalent to those of Strindberg and of Ibsen. As did the beliefs of Strindberg and Ibsen, Multatuli's liberalism, skepticism, and feminism startled the reading public of his nation. Multatuli's work, however, did not have the impact of the two Scandinavian dramatists. Multatuli wrote comparatively little, in contrast to the voluminous composition of Strindberg and Ibsen. Multatuli's work is also very complex and multilayered, and it deals with specifically Dutch experiences; these factors may well make *Max Havelaar* opaque to the foreign reader.

Max Havelaar's appeal to the reader is, most likely, not its representation of Dutch national literature, although this is still an important concern. *Max Havelaar* is engaging as literature. It is not simply a cultural artifact. *Max Havelaar* seems ahead of its time in terms of formal awareness and self-consciousness. The shifts in levels of reality that the reader encounters in the narrative unsettle conventional expectations. Another element that gives the book a contemporary feel is its portrayal of the colonial experience, specifically the Dutch colonial presence in Java. It is often forgotten that the Dutch maintained a considerable colonial empire of their own in the East Indies and in the West Indies, including Suriname. Also, until the British seized South Africa in the Napoleonic Wars, the Dutch controlled that region.

Multatuli's portrait of the Dutch East Indies in *Max Havelaar* can fruitfully be compared to the portrait of Borneo in Joseph Conrad's novel *Lord Jim* (1900), but the books are also different because the Dutch and British colonial experiences were different. Whereas the British had always claimed to be acting in the name of progress and good government, the motives of the Dutch were frankly economic. The portrait of the Lebak coffee plantation in *Max Havelaar* shows the greed and brutality associated with the Dutch colonization of Indonesia. The title character, Max Havelaar, struggles to define himself and to adhere to ideals of honor and right conduct amid the squalor he encounters in Java. When Havelaar arrives, virtually the only person of good will he meets is Mr. Verbrugge. Verbrugge is clearly a well-intentioned man who is nonetheless ineffectual and powerless in the face of the cold indifference of the governor-general and the scheming malevolence of Slimering. It is the native Javanese (exemplified in the story of Saidyah) who suffer above all, and this is the lesson the book brings home to its reader.

Multatuli's account of Java is searing. The novel is filled with bitterness and pain on personal and political levels, making the author's pseudonym (which means "I have suffered much" in Latin) no accident. Most of the material is based on Dekker's own experiences in Java, and the polemical nature of the Javanese passages has led critics to compare the novel to Harriet Beecher Stowe's antislavery work, *Uncle Tom's Cabin* (1851-1852). *Max Havelaar*'s polemicism is modified by its ironic narrative structure. The novel is narrated (in a way also reminiscent of the works of Conrad) not by the protagonist, Havelaar, but by Drystubble, who frames Havelaar's story in a web of garrulous deception and self-promotion. A further level of intricacy intrudes when it is hinted that Drystubble is "mirrored" in the colonial world of Lebak by Slimering, while Shawlman is, most probably, Havelaar himself, thus solving the mystery of how the

Havelaar manuscript came into his hands. Furthermore, Multatuli comes onstage at the end, proclaiming that Drystubble's illusion-making is but an inadequate reflection of Multatuli's own authorial reality. It is left uncertain how authoritatively the reader is to take this last intervention.

Max Havelaar seems a forerunner of modernist self-conscious text, of a kind of fiction more concerned with the ironies and processes of storytelling than in conveying an external reality. Yet the novel's greatest force comes in its realistic portrait of colonial Java. Furthermore, whatever the games played by Multatuli in the novel, the reader's moral sympathies are meant to lie with Havelaar. The reader's empathy with him is only occasionally made questionable.

Part of the contradiction involved in the use of polemical and self-conscious text in one work may be explained by the history of Dutch literature, in which, unlike that of most European countries, Romanticism and realism began more or less at the same time. In other literatures, such as English or German (the two languages closest to Dutch, and the two cultures most influential upon Dutch culture), Romanticism flourished in the early nineteenth century and was largely associated with poetry, whereas realism flourished in the later nineteenth century and was largely associated with fiction. In Dutch literature, however, Romanticism began only in the nineteenth century, with the group of poets known as the Tachtigers, or "men of the eighties." *Max Havelaar* was published in 1860, and it is apparent that in Dutch literature the two movements are far more conflated in time than readers may expect. This fact might help to explain what seem to be the many contradictions in the book. *Max Havelaar*, whatever its idiosyncrasies, is a significant contribution to world literature.

"Critical Evaluation" by Nicholas Birns

Further Reading

Beekman, E. M. "Dekker/Multatuli, 1820-1887: The Dialogic Truth from the Tropics." In *Troubled Pleasures: Dutch Colonial Literature from the East Indies, 1600-1950*. New York: Oxford University Press, 1996. Describes *Max Havelaar* as the first modern Dutch novel, using Mikhail Bakhtin's theories about dialogic discourse to analyze the book. Beekman maintains the novel moved Dutch literature "from the moribund orthodoxy of the nineteenth century to the 'expressive capacities' of the modern prose text."

Feenberg, Anne-Marie. "*Max Havelaar*: An Anti-Imperialist Novel." *Modern Language Notes* 112, no. 5 (1997): 817-835. A detailed analysis of the novel, focusing on Multatuli's message of anti-imperialism.

King, Peter. *Multatuli*. New York: Twayne, 1972. A comprehensive study of Multatuli. Gives an overview of *Max Havelaar*'s complexity, as well as its relation to its author's life. An excellent starting place.

_____. "Multatuli: Some Reflections on Perk, Kloos, and Boon." In *European Context: Studies in the History and Literature of the Netherlands*, edited by P. K. King and P. F. Vincent. Cambridge, England: Modern Humanities Research Association, 1971. Examines Multatuli's relationship to the Dutch Romantic writers, known as Tachtigers, who wrote in his shadow.

Schreurs, Peter. "Multatuli, a Soul-Brother of Rizal." *Philippine Quarterly of Culture and Society* 14, no. 3 (September, 1986): 189-195. Explores Multatuli's similarities with nineteenth century Filipino poet José Rizal, examining the relevance of *Max Havelaar* to discussions of the colonial and the postcolonial condition in the Philippines and in Indonesia (formerly the Dutch East Indies).

Van den Berg, H. "Multatuli and Romantic Indecision." *Canadian Journal of Netherlandic Studies* 5, no. 2 (Fall, 1984): 36-47. Discusses the curious mixture of Romanticism and realism in *Max Havelaar* and explores the novel's roots in Dutch literature.

_____. "Multatuli as a Writer of Letters." *Canadian Journal of Netherlandic Studies* 13, no. 2 (Fall, 1992): 17-22. Examines how the "private man" of Multatuli's letters reveals himself in the writer's fiction.

Zook, Darren C. "Searching for *Max Havelaar*: Multatuli, Colonial History, and the Confusion of Empire." *MLN* 121, no. 5 (December, 2006): 169-189. Examines Multatuli's writings, discussing his significance in Dutch literary history and his influence on Dutch culture.

The Maxims

Author: François de La Rochefoucauld (1613-1680)
First published: Maximes, 1665-1678 (English
   translation, 1706)
Type of work: Philosophy

François de La Rochefoucauld describes his *Maxims* as a "portrait of the human heart." He writes in the preface to the first edition that these reflections on human conduct will probably offend many persons because the aphorisms are full of truths that are unacceptable to human pride. He suggests that the reader suppose him- or herself to be the sole exception to the truth revealed and should avoid the tendency to have his or her opinion influenced by *amour-propre*, or self-love, as that would prejudice his or her mind against the maxims.

The reference to self-love, the basic concern for the self by which the value of any action, person, or thing is presumed to be judged, is characteristic of La Rochefoucauld. Critics generally describe this great French writer as a cynic and take as evidence his maxims, in which he attributes to self-love the central role in human conduct. Yet a mere cynic is one who hopes for a better world than the present one; a cynic constantly compares what could be and what ought to be with what is, responding to the disparity with bitterness. Consequently, everything that cynics say is the truth as they see it; as they see it, it is worthy only of a sneer. La Rochefoucauld, on the other hand, takes self-love to be an undeniable fact of human existence and does not hope for anything better. Consequently, his view of the world is that of a person amused to see the difference between what people conceive themselves to be and what they are; his or her delight is in a witty revelation of the facts of life. Throughout *The Maxims*, as in the refreshing self-portrait with which the collection begins, La Rochefoucauld reveals an intelligent sense of humor that takes the sneer out of what he says.

"My normal expression is somewhat bitter and haughty," he writes in his initial self-portrait, and "makes most people think me supercilious, though I am not the least so really." He goes on to describe himself as "inclined to melancholy" but not from temperament alone: "It is due to . . . many other causes." He calls himself an intellectual who delights in the conversation of cultured persons, in reading, in virtue, and in friendship. His passions are moderate and under control. He is neither ambitious nor afraid of death. He has given up "light amours" and wonders why so many people waste their time paying "pretty compliments." The portrait concludes with the assurance that were he ever to love, he would love with the strong passion that is a sign of noble character; however, he doubts that his knowledge of the value of strong passion will ever "quit my head to find a dwelling in my heart."

The first maxim is important as a summary statement of La Rochefoucauld's central conviction.

So-called virtue is often merely a compound of varied activities and interests, which good fortune or our own assiduity enables us to display to advantage; so it is not always courage that makes the hero, nor modesty the chaste woman.

With the second maxim, the author names the concern that is essential to the human heart: "Amour-propre is the archflatterer."

In many of the maxims, La Rochefoucauld expresses his conviction that virtue is the accidental result of an exercise of the passions; acts undertaken passionately to satisfy the demands of a pervasive self-concern are interpreted in other ways, as signs of nobility of character. In maxim 7, for example, he declares that "Illustrious deeds, of dazzling brilliance, are represented by politicians as the outcome of great aims, whereas they are usually the result of caprice or passion." Similarly, "The clemency of princes is often nothing more than a political artifice designed to secure the goodwill of their subjects" (maxim 15). "Such clemency, though hailed as a virtue, is the product sometimes of vanity, sometimes of indolence, not infrequently of timidity, and generally of all three combined" (maxim 16).

One way of summarizing La Rochefoucauld's philosophy is to point out that, to him, virtue is usually passion misunderstood. People do something because their own irresistible self-love drives them to it; the world observes the power of the act and mistakes it for the grandeur of courageous virtue. Not all of the maxims develop this theme, however. Many of the comments are both wry and true, and the effect is heightened all the more by their pithiness. Examples of this include "The desire to appear clever often prevents our being so" (maxim 199), "We all have enough strength to bear the misfortunes of others" (maxim 19), "Flattery would do us no harm if we did not flatter ourselves" (maxim 152), and "There is no fool so troublesome as a fool with brains" (maxim 451).

Some of the maxims have a positive note, an appeal to the honesty by which people may lessen the damage caused by their self-love. La Rochefoucauld implies that there is hope for those who find it possible to recognize the worth of others and to do so sincerely, for those who know their own limitations and acknowledge them, and for those who admit that their show of virtue is often an empty show. The author respects such honesty, and it is apparent that *The Maxims* are confessional as well as didactic.

La Rochefoucauld found through his own experience certain truths that writers of all ages have expressed in various ways and that gain power through repetition. In several maxims, he develops the idea that it is doing people an injury to be so much concerned with their welfare as to burden them with the necessity of being grateful. He recognizes that people tend to be free with advice to others but not eager to accept it for themselves. People admit such shortcomings as a poor memory to hide something like the lack of intelligence.

La Rochefoucauld's psychology is that of the sophisticated courtier. He was too much aware of his own disguises ever to have acquired the knowledge that would have led to a more objective and more scientific psychology. His psychology, like his philosophy, while not that of the person in the street, is certainly that of the person at court—clever enough to see behind the masks of those who travel in high society but not tolerant enough of possibilities to be willing to admit that those whom he calls honest people are more common than he supposes. When his psychology has the strong ring of truth, it is more by accident than discernment; and when it is false, he seems embittered to distortion—hence the charge of cynicism.

Nevertheless, some of his maxims do define something of the human character: "To disclaim admiration is to desire it in double measure" (maxim 149), "We easily forget our faults when they are known only to ourselves" (maxim 196), "Excessive eagerness to discharge an obligation is a form of ingratitude" (maxim 226), and "If we were faultless ourselves, we should take less pleasure in commenting on the faults of others" (maxim 31).

Behind the revealing wit of La Rochefoucauld there is the murmur of an injured man. No one can discern the falsity of others better than a timid man who believes himself betrayed, longs for recognition and gratitude, and feels he does not receive enough of either. La Rochefoucauld reveals himself when he reveals the desperate *amour-propre* that moves all human beings.

Further Reading

Culpin, D. J. *La Rochefoucauld: Maximes*. London: Grant & Cutler, 1995. Concise introductory overview and interpretation of *The Maxims*, including information about the context of the work and La Rochefoucauld's ideas about virtue and human nature.

Hodgson, Richard G. *Falsehood Disguised: Unmasking the Truth in La Rochefoucauld*. West Lafayette, Ind.: Purdue University Press, 1995. Examines La Rochefoucauld's ideas about truth and falsehood within the context of his views on self-love, the passions, vice, and virtue. Explains how his ideas emerged from seventeenth century Baroque culture and other moralists, and assesses his impact on later philosophers.

Hope, Quentin M. "Humor in the *Maximes* of La Rochefoucauld." *Dalhousie French Studies* 58 (Spring, 2002): 3-9. Examines La Rochefoucauld's literary interest in "humor," namely teasing, laughter, and making fun. Hope claims that many of the maxims should be understood as jokes.

Lewis, Philip E. *La Rochefoucauld: The Art of Abstraction*. Ithaca, N.Y.: Cornell University Press, 1977. Describes the problematic nature of La Rochefoucauld's abstract reflections on the conflict between self-love and love for others. Discusses the psychological and ethical dimensions of *The Maxims*.

Moore, Will G. *La Rochefoucauld: His Mind and Art*. Oxford, England: Clarendon Press, 1969. A clear introduction to the many levels of meaning in La Rochefoucauld's pithy and marvelously ambiguous moral maxims. Discusses the political, social, and religious implications of *The Maxims*.

Mourgues, Odette de. *Two French Moralists: La Rochefoucauld and La Bruyère*. New York: Cambridge University Press, 1978. A thoughtful comparison of La Rochefoucauld and Jean de La Bruyère, two eminent French moralists. Explores La Rochefoucauld's reflections on subjectivity, and contains an excellent bibliography of major critical studies on these two thinkers.

Thweatt, Vivien. *La Rochefoucauld and the Seventeenth-Century Concept of the Self*. Geneva: Droz, 1980. Discusses the influence of St. Augustine and neo-Stoicism on La Rochefoucauld. Examines his reflections on people's efforts to maintain their individuality in a society that favors and rewards conformity.

Zeller, Mary Francine. *New Aspects of Style in "The Maxims" of La Rochefoucauld*. 1954. New ed. New York: AMS Press, 1969. Explains clearly why La Rochefoucauld's *The Maxims* permits a wide variety of interpretations. Discusses the refined rhythms and complex structures in many maxims.

The Maximus Poems

Author: Charles Olson (1910-1970)
First published: 1960, 1968, 1975, 1983
Type of work: Poetry

The Maximus Poems is Charles Olson's most significant work. Sections of *The Maximus Poems*, begun in 1950, were published as Olson produced complete parts. The first volume of the book, called simply *The Maximus Poems*, was published in 1960. A second volume, titled *Maximus Poems IV, V, VI*, was published in 1968. *The Maximus Poems, Volume Three* was published in 1975. Charles Boer, Olson's executor, had the job of emending the text at the University of Connecticut, producing the final volume, published in 1983 by the University of California, Berkeley.

Only a half dozen or so legitimate long poems were published in the United States during the twentieth century, and Olson's is certainly one of the more important. Some of the reason for this has to do with the poet, and some has to do with his teaching at Black Mountain College in North Carolina and his other writing, in particular *Mayan Letters* (1953) and his famous essay "Projective Verse." Both of these relate to the business of *The Maximus Poems.*

Olson was born near Gloucester, Massachusetts, the town he adopted as his through *The Maximus Poems*. He was an imposing figure, standing six feet, ten inches tall, with penetrating eyes and, during the last twenty years of his life, long white hair. He spent time in Washington, D.C., visiting Ezra Pound at St. Elizabeths Hospital; time in the Yucatán Peninsula; and time at Harvard University, where he wrote a work on Herman Melville titled *Call Me Ishmael: A Study of Melville* (1947). Many of his ideas and discoveries are found in the correspondence he conducted with American poet Robert Creeley. The letters in *Mayan Letters* were all written to Creeley. Later, Olson became provost of the experimental Black Mountain College, offering his own classes in poetics, in which *The Maximus Poems* and their theories weighed heavily.

Olson conceived of the idea of writing a long poem with a central, larger-than-life figure at its center, a person to be called Maximus. The Maximus of the poems may have been meant to resemble Olson himself, being larger than life and living in Gloucester. Many of the poems are interpretations of events that occurred in Gloucester, from simple daily events, such as the fishing boats going out, to a murder that was never solved. The geography of the town was also important to Olson, as were even the smallest details of the

place. Many of the poems discuss "the cut," which is a channel between the fishing boats and an inland waterway. A movable bridge was built where Olson's cut used to be.

A fair proportion of the population of Gloucester in Olson's time consisted of Portuguese immigrant fishermen and their families. They are referred to in the poems, as are surrounding villages. This area, close to Cape Cod, later became very popular with tourists, but it was not so when Olson lived in a tiny apartment overlooking the ocean, an apartment crammed with books and his typing materials. He used to walk the streets at night, in the manner of Edgar Allan Poe, absorbing sounds and smells that would become part of his epic book.

What was Olson about with this book, with which he expressed dissatisfaction near his death? There is no easy answer, but clues can be gleaned from his other writing. In "Projective Verse," he writes of a kind of poetry that would live on the page, that would be kinetic, that would utilize the entire page and whatever other materials the poet felt called upon to utilize. The result in his own poetry, including hundreds of pages of *The Maximus Poems*, is a poetry that looks chaotic on the page but that follows his own prescripts in his essay. Many of the poems are spread out across the page in what Olson referred to as "the field of the page," utilizing open parentheticals, sometimes a complete lack of punctuation, and often decisions of how to read the poem that can be answered only by a reader.

Olson was also a student of history, back to the Greeks. One defining element in *The Maximus Poems* is the notion that a human being can be a *polis*, or a city, that an individual may have the ability to contain knowledge, power, and influence. Olson tried to present his Maximus figure as just such a *polis*. At other times in the poems, Olson seems to acknowledge that a person—most people, anyway—will be incapable of such a feat; then, a literal city, such as Gloucester, becomes *polis*. The best place to see this in action is in the collection *Maximus to Gloucester: The Letters and Poems of Charles Olson to the Editor of the "Gloucester Daily Times," 1962-1969* (1992). During the period covered in this text, Olson lived in Gloucester only part of the time, but he kept up his subscription to the town's newspaper. Olson was not deferential about sending his poems, often poems that became part of *The Maximus Poems*, to the newspaper's editor as commentary on thing he read in the paper. His overall interest in the Gloucester newspaper reflects his interest in *polis* and his belief that the body politic is of utmost importance.

Another issue receiving attention in *The Maximus Poems* is Olson's "discovery" in the Yucatán Peninsula. Olson thought that he had come upon the descendants of the people of the area who, very unlike Americans or Europeans, were capable of wearing their insides on their outsides. His poem "A Moebius Strip" uses a mathematical phenomenon to illustrate what he means. He saw these people as being utterly disingenuous, without pretense: You got what you saw, both inside and outside.

Parts of *The Maximus Poems* do not so much attempt to find or construct such a model as meditate upon it. Stylistically, a good portion of *The Maximus Poems* is rather dry and abstract. Other sections are very difficult to follow, and anyone trying to read and understand all of *The Maximus Poems* at once is taking on a daunting challenge. Olson did not feel a particular debt to his reader; he felt a debt to his muse. Some poems sound like essays, and others have allusive qualities that make them very difficult.

Anyone attempting to decipher *The Maximus Poems* would be aided by a good working knowledge of Greek mythology. The work contains a number of references to Aphrodite and Demeter, as sexual goddess and earth mother, respectively. It takes some interpreting to develop these ideas. Persephone is in the curl of a wave, and the imagery sounds sexual with proper study. Without some kind of guidance, however, a reader is likely to glean only ocean references.

References to Gloucester politics and history emerge in poems such as the famous "The Librarian," in which Olson asks the open question at the end of the poem, "Who lies behind/ Lufkin's Diner?" Presumably, all references in the work would be clear to someone who lived in Gloucester at the time these lines were written, but they pose challenges to anyone reading these poems after Olson's death in 1970.

A reader may also get the impression of speed while reading *The Maximus Poems*, a sense that one cannot let up. That response may come from Olson's dictum, stated in "Projective Verse," that "one perception must immediately and directly lead to a further perception." Such was his theory for poetry as a whole, with which many of his poet friends disagreed. In fact, the writing of *The Maximus Poems* probably at times was a lonely enterprise. Some of Olson's peers appear to have viewed the project as overly ambitious. Olson wanted to write a poem that would include it all and do it all; that may have struck some as being overly ambitious, to put it mildly.

Reading *The Maximus Poems*, one learns about the Native Americans who inhabited the area in the seventeenth century, about the "settling" of the area, and why Gloucester became a fishing village, with very little other trade important to the village. All one need do is glance through George Butterick's *A Guide to "The Maximus Poems" of Charles Olson* (1978) to see the depth and breadth of Olson's knowledge and research.

Another way to view these poems is to see them as mythmaking in the raw, using at their central core the changed figure of Olson himself, Olson become Maximus. If most myth is, as theory has it, based on reality and history and on stories, then Olson brought into the twentieth century the materials of that construction, or what he calls "the materials of the weight,/ of pain," perhaps a reference to what such an enterprise took from him in its twenty years of development.

The evidence is that although Olson was preparing to write a very long poem around 1950, he had already written several poems with the name Maximus within them. He seemed ready to start a long poem with a poem titled "Bigmans I," obviously close in statement to "Maximus." He had a corpus of work at hand, and he added "I, Maximus," drawing even tighter his own personal hold on the concept of this long poem that he knew would be based in Gloucester, though Cape Ann figures prominently in the poems. A guiding principle to Olson was John Keats's line, "A man's life of any worth is a continuous allegory," a statement that is in evidence throughout *The Maximus Poems*.

Clearly, Olson had been impressed by his visits with Ezra Pound, and while in the midst of *The Maximus Poems*, Olson visited Pound in seclusion in Italy. Olson had also used Pound's *Cantos* as a text at Black Mountain College. His reverence for the long poem had been long established. Olson's "Projective Verse" ends on a note calling for epic and long poems. Early in February of 1950, Olson rejected the long poems of T. S. Eliot, William Carlos Williams, and even Pound, and began on *The Maximus Poems*, a poem that would attempt to fit it all in, a long poem for the twentieth century in all of its complexity and mythmaking.

John Jacob

Further Reading

Bollobas, Eniko. *Charles Olson*. New York: Twayne, 1992. Focuses on Olson's poetic decisions, the most important of which is *The Maximus Poems*, in relation to the events of his life.
Butterick, George F. *A Guide to "The Maximus Poems" of Charles Olson*. Berkeley: University of California Press,

1978. Indispensable resource for anyone seeking to understand the allusions and references in Olson's long poem. Many of the annotations, which took ten years to write, include arcane material, but they give a view into Olson's mind.

Fredman, Stephen. *The Grounding of American Poetry: Charles Olson and the Emersonian Tradition.* New York: Cambridge University Press, 1993. Analyzes Olson's focus on the intellect and on thought processes in his poetry, as opposed to the American tradition of emotional and responsive poetry. Discussion of *The Maximus Poems* describes it as an abstract, highly intellectual text.

Kim, Joon-Hwan. *Out of the "Western Box": Towards a Multicultural Poetics in the Poetry of Ezra Pound and Charles Olson.* New York: Peter Lang, 2003. Describes how Olson's poetry explores diverse cultures, anticipating the future rise of multicultural and deconstructive criticism.

Maud, Ralph. *Charles Olson at the Harbor.* Vancouver, B.C.: Talonbooks, 2008. Critical biography demonstrates how Olson's essay "Projective Verse" created a significant and enduring change in poetic thought.

Olson, Charles. *Maximus to Gloucester: The Letters and Poems of Charles Olson to the Editor of the "Gloucester Daily Times," 1962-1969.* Edited by Peter Anastas. Gloucester, Mass.: Ten Pound Island, 1992. Letters and poems show how the local was important to Olson, particularly the local as applied to Gloucester politics and day-to-day life.

Von Hallberg, Robert. *Charles Olson: The Scholar's Art.* Cambridge, Mass.: Harvard University Press, 1978. Provides a good introduction to the complexity of Olson's poetry. Points out Olson's use of myth and other original contributions to *The Maximus Poems* and also notes the importance of thought to Olson's poetics.

The Mayor of Casterbridge
The Life and Death of a Man of Character

Author: Thomas Hardy (1840-1928)
First published: 1886
Type of work: Novel
Type of plot: Psychological realism
Time of plot: Nineteenth century
Locale: Wessex, England

Principal characters:
MICHAEL HENCHARD, the mayor of Casterbridge
SUSAN HENCHARD-NEWSON, his abandoned wife
ELIZABETH-JANE NEWSON, his stepdaughter
RICHARD NEWSON, a sailor
DONALD FARFRAE, a grain merchant
LUCETTA LE SUEUR, Henchard's beloved and later Farfrae's wife

The Story:

On a late summer afternoon in the early nineteenth century, a young farm couple with their baby arrives on foot at the village of Weydon-Priors. A fair is in progress. The couple, tired and dusty, enters a refreshment tent where the husband proceeds to get so drunk that he offers his wife and child for sale. A sailor, a stranger in the village, buys the wife, Susan, and the child, Elizabeth-Jane, for five guineas. The young woman tears off her wedding ring and throws it in her drunken husband's face; then, carrying her child, she follows the sailor out of the tent.

When he awakes sober the next morning, Michael Henchard, the young farmer, realizes what he has done. After taking an oath not to touch liquor for twenty years, he searches many months for his wife and child. In a western seaport, he is told that three persons answering his description emigrated a short time before. He gives up his search and wanders on until he comes to the town of Casterbridge. There, he decides to seek his fortune.

The sailor, Richard Newson, convinces Susan Henchard that she has no moral obligations to the husband who sold her and her child. He marries her and moves with his new family to Canada. Later, they return to England. Eventually, Susan learns that her marriage to Newson is illegal, but before she can remedy the situation Newson is lost at sea. Susan and her attractive eighteen-year-old daughter, Elizabeth-Jane, return to Weydon-Priors. There, they hear that Henchard has gone to Casterbridge.

Henchard has become a prosperous grain merchant and the mayor of Casterbridge. When Susan and her daughter arrive in the town, they hear that Henchard has sold some bad grain to bakers and that restitution is expected. Donald Farfrae, a young Scots corn expert who is passing through Casterbridge, hears of Henchard's predicament and tells him a method for partially restoring the grain. Farfrae so impresses Henchard and the people of the town that they prevail on him to remain. Farfrae becomes Henchard's manager.

When Susan and Henchard meet, they decide that Susan and Elizabeth-Jane should take lodgings and that Henchard will begin to pay court to Susan. Henchard admits to young Farfrae that he has been philandering with a young woman from Jersey named Lucetta le Sueur. He asks Farfrae to meet Lucetta and prevent her from coming to Casterbridge.

Henchard and Susan are married. Elizabeth-Jane develops into a beautiful young woman for whom Donald Farfrae feels a growing attraction. Henchard wants Elizabeth-Jane to take his name, but Susan refuses his request, much to his mystification. He notices that Elizabeth-Jane does not possess any of his personal traits.

Henchard and Farfrae fall out over Henchard's harsh treatment of a simpleminded employee. Farfrae has surpassed Henchard in popularity in Casterbridge. The break between the two men becomes complete when a country dance sponsored by Farfrae draws all the town's populace, leaving Henchard's competing dance unattended. Anticipating his dismissal, Farfrae sets up his own establishment but refuses to take any of Henchard's business away from him. Henchard refuses to allow Elizabeth-Jane and Farfrae to see each other.

Henchard receives a letter from Lucetta saying she plans to pass through Casterbridge to pick up her love letters. When Lucetta fails to keep the appointment, Henchard puts the letters in his safe. Susan falls sick and writes a letter for Henchard, to be opened on the day that Elizabeth-Jane is married. Soon afterward, she dies, and Henchard tells the girl that he is her real father. Looking for some documents to corroborate his story, he finds the letter his wife had left in his keeping for Elizabeth-Jane. Unable to resist, Henchard reads Susan's letter; he learns that Elizabeth-Jane is really the daughter of Newson and Susan and that his own daughter died in infancy. His wife's reluctance to have the girl take his name is explained, and Henchard's attitude toward Elizabeth-Jane becomes distant and cold.

One day, Elizabeth-Jane meets a strange woman at the village graveyard. The woman is Lucetta Templeman, formerly Lucetta le Sueur, who has inherited property in Casterbridge from a rich aunt named Templeman. She employs Elizabeth-Jane to make it convenient for Henchard, her old lover, to call on her.

Young Farfrae comes to see Elizabeth-Jane, who is away at the time. He and Miss Templeman are immediately attracted to each other, and Lucetta refuses to see Henchard any more. Elizabeth-Jane overhears Henchard berate Lucetta under his breath for refusing to admit him to her house; she becomes even more uncomfortable when she sees that Farfrae has succumbed to Lucetta's charms.

Henchard is now determined to ruin Farfrae. Advised by a weather prophet that the weather will be bad during the harvest, he buys grain heavily. When the weather stays fair, Henchard is almost ruined by low grain prices. Farfrae is able to buy grain cheap, and, when the weather turns bad late in the harvest and prices go up, Farfrae becomes wealthy.

In the meantime, Farfrae has continued his courtship of Lucetta. When Henchard threatens to expose Lucetta's past unless she marries him, Lucetta agrees to his demand. However, an old woman discloses to the village that Henchard is the man who years earlier sold his wife and child. Lucetta is ashamed and leaves town. On the day of her return, Henchard rescues her and Elizabeth-Jane from an enraged bull. He asks Lucetta to give evidence of their engagement to a creditor. Lucetta confesses that in her absence she and Farfrae have been married. Utterly frustrated, Henchard again threatens to expose her. When Elizabeth-Jane learns of the marriage, she leaves Lucetta's service.

The news that Henchard once sold his wife and child to a sailor spreads through the village. Henchard's creditors close in, and he becomes a recluse. Henchard and Elizabeth-Jane are reconciled during his illness. Upon his recovery, he hires out to Farfrae as a common laborer.

Henchard's oath expires, and he begins to drink heavily. Farfrae plans to set up Henchard and Elizabeth-Jane in a small seed shop, but the project does not materialize because of a misunderstanding. Despite Lucetta's desire to leave the village, Farfrae becomes mayor of Casterbridge.

Jopp, a former employee of Henchard, knows of Lucetta's past, because he lived in Jersey before coming to Casterbridge. He uses this information to blackmail his way into Farfrae's employ. Henchard finally takes pity on Lucetta and gives Jopp the love letters to return to her. Before delivering them, Jopp reads the letters aloud in an inn.

When royalty visits Casterbridge, Henchard wishes to regain his old stature in the village and forces himself among the receiving dignitaries. Farfrae pushes him aside. Later, during a fight in a warehouse loft, Henchard has Farfrae at his mercy, but the younger man shames Henchard by telling him to go ahead and kill him.

The townspeople are excited over the letters they have heard read and devise a mummery employing effigies of Henchard and Lucetta riding back to back on a donkey. Farfrae's friends arrange for him to be absent from the village during the mummers' parade, but Lucetta sees it and is horrified. She dies of a miscarriage that night.

Richard Newson turns out not to have been lost after all. He comes to Casterbridge in search of Susan and Elizabeth-Jane. There, he meets Henchard, who sends him away, telling him that both Susan and Elizabeth-Jane are dead.

Elizabeth-Jane joins Henchard in his poverty. They open a seed shop and begin to prosper again in a modest way. Farfrae, to Henchard's dismay, begins to pay court to Elizabeth-Jane again, and they plan to marry soon. Newson returns, having realized that he was duped. Henchard leaves town but returns for the marriage festivities, bringing with him a goldfinch as a wedding present. When he sees that Newson has completely replaced him as Elizabeth-Jane's father, he sadly goes away. Newson is restless and departs for the sea again after Farfrae and his daughter are settled. Henchard pines away and dies, ironically, in the secret care of the simpleminded old man whom he once mistreated.

Critical Evaluation:

The decline of Michael Henchard, which comprises the primary action in Thomas Hardy's *The Mayor of Casterbridge*, is enacted against the backdrop of the agricultural and manufacturing upheavals of the Industrial Revolution. Henchard is committed to preindustrial methods and attempts to hold back the town's modernization. He insists upon using old agricultural methods, for example, and his trust of a "weather prophet" to predict harvest conditions results in a ruined grain crop that threatens the town's survival. Living in an area of southwest England that is littered with decaying artifacts of Roman power, Henchard ironically finds himself struggling to assert himself in a town destined for change beyond its own choosing. Henchard meets defeat in every encounter with newer ideas and procedures; his failure to understand and his lack of moderation in his desires incite him to brutal aggression followed by pain and regret, as he becomes more and more isolated from humanity.

The extreme guilt Henchard endures for years after selling his wife and infant daughter seems indicative of the intense emotions with which he responds to circumstances. As his status grows in Casterbridge, so does the importance to him of his own good name and character. Remarrying Susan

soon after she and Elizabeth-Jane appear in town is not only a means of making amends but also an ill-advised attempt to protect his reputation. Henchard loses the esteem and respect of the town's citizens because of his crop blunder, initiating and shaping his tragic relationship with Farfrae: The young man's ability to repair damaged wheat benefits the town, but it causes him to usurp rather than repair the popularity that Henchard desperately wants to preserve. The fortunes of Farfrae, the novel's representative of new methods in agriculture, rise, while those of Henchard tumble.

Like many of Hardy's novels, *The Mayor of Casterbridge* prominently features elements of coincidence and chance, as each chapter introduces unlikely events and the timely appearances of major and minor characters. In fact, many scenes in each chapter are exquisitely crafted, incorporating coincidence into the narrative action and characterization with such skill that each scene seems a miniature of the entire novel. Hardy believed that chance was a force governing things over which people have no control. However, this force operates without conscious design, and, although it represents the will of the universe, it seems to produce consequences more malign than benign. Although Hardy received much criticism for his pessimism, he referred to himself as a "meliorist," or one who sees the world improving with human aid. The reappearance of Susan and Elizabeth-Jane forms the coil necessary to Henchard's decline, as Susan's death and the knowledge that Elizabeth-Jane is Newson's daughter and not his own prompts his estrangement from Elizabeth-Jane and a feeling of being deceived by Susan.

Henchard, who ends his relationship with Lucetta when Susan arrives in town, attempts, after Susan's death, to resume it. Lucetta, put off by Henchard's manner, refuses and marries Farfrae instead. Henchard's sense of betrayal by women increases dramatically when the "furmity woman," arrested and brought before Henchard as judge, relates the story of Henchard's sale of his wife and daughter nearly two decades earlier. Strangely, Henchard admits the deed and ruins his reputation. The event brings to light Henchard's continuing feelings of shame at the deed, which coincide with Henchard's socioeconomic failure to hasten his end.

Numerous critics have found elements of Greek tragedy in *The Mayor of Casterbridge*. Reflecting Hardy's own tragic view of life and partially refuting Victorian optimism and sentimentality, the novel seems to represent a reinvention of ancient tragedy for the nineteenth century. As Greek tragedy emphasized the connection between character and fate, so Hardy's novel focuses upon character and fate; Henchard experiences conflicts with the town and with himself. Henchard's passionate, turbulent character directly affects his rise and fall within Casterbridge, as well as his inability to find any respite from shame and guilt. Much as in Sophocles' *Oidipous Tyrannos* (c. 429 B.C.E.; *Oedipus Tyrannus*, 1715), Henchard's initial error occurs prior to the time depicted in the novel proper. Oedipus unwittingly slays his own father, Laius, twenty years before the main events of Sophocles' play, in which he suffers the consequences of his action. Henchard's betrayal of his family similarly recedes to the background of his life, only to reappear eighteen years later, driving the events depicted in the novel. Hardy's rustics, or inhabitants of Casterbridge, function similarly to a Greek chorus, voicing traditional wisdom and reflecting the social changes occurring in the town.

Hardy's subtitle for this book, *The Life and Death of a Man of Character*, suggests his admiration for Henchard, who is the center of interest in the book. Despite his misdeeds early in the story, Henchard exhibits virtues that, in comparison with the traits of the novel's other characters, are exceptional. Henchard's rise to prominence in Casterbridge accentuates his authority in accordance with the strength and vitality he gains by becoming the town's leading businessman. Henchard's reliance on preindustrial agriculture, however, endangers the town's welfare and paves the way for its acceptance of Farfrae's new agricultural procedures and its eventual preference of Farfrae over Henchard to be mayor.

Next to the passionate Henchard, Farfrae seems mechanical and knowledgeable—a paler specimen of humanity. In the tests of strength between Henchard and Farfrae, Henchard proves the stronger when he beats Farfrae in a physical confrontation. By contrast, Farfrae's agricultural skills consistently prove superior to Henchard's, as do his interpersonal skills with townspeople and with women.

Henchard's actions—resulting from his own difficult temperament—have created the world he inhabits. In suffering from ill-advised actions and then defiantly standing up to forces arrayed against him, Henchard appears larger than life. He finally retreats, however, from his attempts to impose his will upon a world he has created but in which he no longer has a place. This retreat signals that he accepts his doom. Hardy's novel demonstrates that life can destroy essentially good individuals as well as bad.

"Critical Evaluation" by Mary Hurd

Further Reading

Berger, Sheila. *Thomas Hardy and Visual Structures: Framing, Disruption, Process*. New York: New York University Press, 1991. Berger analyzes the narrative style of Hardy's novels, focusing on acts of storytelling, subjective points of view, and the construction of the omniscient narrator.

Daleski, H. M. *Thomas Hardy and Paradoxes of Love*. Columbia: University of Missouri Press, 1997. Reevaluates the treatment of gender in Hardy's novels, defending the author from charges of sexism and maintaining that some of Hardy's female characters are depicted sympathetically. Argues that Hardy is the premodern precursor of later depictions of sexual failures and catastrophic ends.

Enstice, Andrew. *Thomas Hardy: Landscapes of the Mind*. London: Macmillan, 1979. A good historical analysis of the novel; provides a thorough discussion of nineteenth century Dorset and its economic circumstances, using the town's history to interpret Hardy's rendition of Casterbridge.

Kramer, Dale, ed. *The Cambridge Companion to Thomas Hardy*. New York: Cambridge University Press, 1999. Combines an introduction and general overview of all of Hardy's work with specific demonstrations of Hardy's ideas and literary skills. Individual essays explore Hardy's biography; his aesthetics; and the impact on his work of developments in science, religion, and philosophy in the late nineteenth century. Also contains a detailed chronology of Hardy's life and Jakob Lothe's essay "Variants on Genre: *The Return of the Native, The Mayor of Casterbridge, The Hand of Ethelberta*."

Mallett, Phillip, ed. *The Achievement of Thomas Hardy*. New York: St. Martin's Press, 2000. A collection of essays that analyze Hardy's representations of nature and of poets, the architecture of his work, and other topics. Includes bibliography and index.

Page, Norman, ed. *Oxford Reader's Companion to Hardy*. New York: Oxford University Press, 2000. An encyclopedia containing three hundred alphabetically arranged entries that examine Hardy's work and discuss his family and friends, important places in his life and work, his influences, critical approaches to his writings, and a history of his works' publication. Also includes a chronology of his life, lists of places and characters in his fiction, a glossary, and a bibliography.

Tomalin, Claire. *Thomas Hardy*. New York: Penguin, 2007. This thorough and finely written biography by a respected Hardy scholar illuminates the novelist's efforts to indict the malice, neglect, and ignorance of his fellow human beings. Also discusses aspects of his life that are apparent in his literary works.

Widdowson, Peter. *Hardy in History: A Study in Literary Sociology*. New York: Routledge, 1989. An interesting analysis of traditional readings of Hardy's novels; argues that Hardy has been produced as a rural novelist in the literary imagination but that, in reality, his writing deploys an urban vision of Wessex. Lends a new perspective to the relationships of Casterbridge to the countryside and to London, relationships central to Michael Henchard's fate.

Williams, Raymond. *The Country and the City.* New York: Oxford University Press, 1973. A seminal book on the class relations and rural-urban dislocations that underlie Hardy's representation of Wessex and the lives and fortunes of his "rural" characters.

Wolfreys, Julian, ed. *"The Mayor of Casterbridge": Thomas Hardy.* Houndmills, England: Macmillan, 2000. Collection of essays analyzing the novel, including the fate of Michael Henchard's character, sexuality in the novel, and the novel as a bourgeois tragedy.

The Mayor of Zalamea

Author: Pedro Calderón de la Barca (1600-1681)
First produced: El alcalde de Zalamea, 1643; first published, 1651 (English translation, 1853)
Type of work: Drama
Type of plot: Tragedy
Time of plot: Sixteenth century
Locale: Zalamea, Spain

Principal characters:
PHILIP II, the king of Spain
DON LOPE DE FIGUEROA, the commander of a Spanish regiment
DON ALVARO DE ATAIDE, a captain
PEDRO CRESPO, a farmer of Zalamea
JUAN, his son
ISABEL, Pedro's daughter
REBOLLEDO, a soldier
CHISPA, his mistress

The Story:

As the troops of Don Lope de Figueroa approach the village of Zalamea, old campaigner Rebolledo grumbles in true veteran fashion about the hardships of the march. Quite ready to stop and relax in the village, Rebolledo predicts that the mayor of the village will bribe the officers to march the regiment through and beyond the little community. When he is taken to task by his fellows for this unsoldierly talk, Rebolledo declares that he is mainly concerned for the welfare of his mistress, Chispa, who accompanied the troops. Chispa retorts that, although she is a woman, she can endure the march as well as any man. To cheer up the men, she sings a marching song.

Chispa's song is barely finished when the column reaches Zalamea. It is announced that the troops will be billeted in the village to await the imminent arrival of their commander, Don Lope. The captain of the column is pleased to learn that he will be billeted in the home of a proud farmer whose daughter is reputed to be the beauty of the neighborhood.

At the same time that the troops enter Zalamea, an impoverished squire, Don Mendo, accompanied by his servant, Nuno—the pair bore a marked resemblance to Don Quixote and Sancho Panza—arrives in the village also. Don Mendo seeks the favors of Isabel, the daughter of the proud farmer,

Pedro Crespo. Isabel bangs together the shutters of her window when Don Mendo greets her in foolishly extravagant terms. Crespo and his son Juan find the presence of Don Mendo highly objectionable.

When the sergeant announces to Crespo that the captain, Don Alvaro de Ataide, will be quartered in Crespo's house, the farmer graciously accepts this imposition; Juan, however, is displeased and suggests to his father that he purchase a patent of gentility so that he might avoid having to billet troops in his home. Crespo declares that as long as he is not of gentle blood he can see no point, even though he is rich, in assuming gentility.

Isabel and her cousin, Inés, having learned of the presence of the troops, go to the attic of the house, where they will remain as long as the soldiers are in the town. On the captain's arrival, the sergeant searches the house but is unable to find Isabel. He reports, however, that a servant tells him the woman is in the attic and will stay there until the troops depart. The captain plans to win Isabel by any means.

Rebolledo asks the captain for the privilege of officially conducting gambling among the soldiers. The captain grants the privilege in return for Rebolledo's help in his plan to discover Isabel. The captain and Rebolledo then pretend to fight; Rebolledo, feigning great fright, flees, followed by the captain, up the stairs to the attic. Isabel admits him to her retreat and, in pleading to the captain for his life, she presents such a charming aspect to the young officer that he is completely smitten.

The clamor of the pretend fight draws Crespo home. He and Juan, with swords drawn, race upstairs to the attic. Juan senses the trick and hints as much, but Crespo, impressed by the captain's courtesy, is duped. Insulted by Juan's innuendoes, the captain is about to come to blows with Juan when Don Lope, the regimental commander, enters. When he demands an explanation of the scene, the captain says that Rebolledo's insubordination had been the cause. Rebolledo, in denial, explains that the disturbance was intended to discover Crespo's daughter. Don Lope orders the captain to change his quarters and the troops to remain in their billets; he himself chooses to stay in Crespo's house.

Crespo, jealous of his honor, declares that he will give up all of his worldly goods in submission to the will of the king, but that he will destroy the man who would jeopardize his good name. The captain, stricken with desire for Isabel, courts her under her window; she remains disdainful. Don Mendo, hearing what has happened, arms himself and sets out to meet the captain on the field of honor. Meanwhile, the captain prevails upon Rebolledo to assist him further in his suit. Rebolledo, reconciled, suggests that Isabel can be overcome with song.

At Crespo's, the proud farmer, mollified by Don Lope's seeming gentility, invites the commander to sup in the garden. Don Lope, wounded in the leg in the Flemish wars, so that he is in constant pain, plays upon his infirmity to arouse Crespo's pity. When he requests the company of Isabel at supper, Crespo readily assents, assuring Don Lope that he will be proud to have his daughter wait on such a fine gentleman. After Isabel joins Don Lope, a guitar and a vocal serenade can be heard from the street. Those in the garden are so disturbed by the serenade that the supper abruptly ends.

Outside, an armed, skinny Don Mendo says he can barely refrain from attacking the captain and his followers, but as long as Isabel does not appear in her window he will not attack. As Chispa sings a particularly vulgar song, Crespo and Don Lope, swords drawn, fall upon the serenaders and scatter them. In the fray, Don Lope belabors Don Mendo, who has somehow become involved. A short time later the captain reappears with soldiers in an official capacity to maintain the peace. Don Lope commends the captain and assures him that the trouble is of no importance. Because dawn is approaching, Don Lope tells the captain to order the regiment out of Zalamea.

The next day, the troops having left, the captain expresses his determination to stay and make a last attempt to enjoy Isabel's favors. Further encouraged by the news that Juan has decided to become a soldier and that he will leave that day with Don Lope, he orders Rebolledo to accompany him and the sergeant on his mission. Chispa declares that she will go along, disguised as a man.

Toward sundown, Don Lope says his farewell to Crespo and gives Isabel a diamond brooch. Crespo gives fatherly advice to Juan. As father and daughter watch Don Lope and Juan gallop away, Isabel observes that it is the day for the election of municipal officers. Suddenly the captain and his followers come upon them. The captain seizes Isabel; the sergeant and Rebolledo seize Crespo.

Later that night, in the forest near Zalamea, a distracted Isabel comes upon her father tied to a tree. She tells how Juan had come upon the scene of her rape and had fought the captain. Frightened, she had run away from the fight. Crespo, comforting Isabel, vows revenge. As the old man and his daughter start for home, they encounter the town notary, who announces that Crespo has been elected mayor. He adds that the wounded captain is in the village.

In Zalamea, Crespo confronts the captain in private. He suggests that the captain, having disgraced the family honor, take Isabel as his wife, but the captain, not fearing a provincial mayor, scoffs at Crespo's request. Crespo then orders his officers to place the captain and his followers in jail to await the judgment of the king, who is approaching Zalamea.

Returning to his house, Crespo finds Juan prepared to take Isabel's life, to wipe out the disgrace she has innocently brought on her family. Crespo, sternly just, orders his officers to take Juan to jail for having fought his superior officer, the captain. Don Lope, on the highway, is informed that the captain has been jailed by the mayor of Zalamea. He returns to the village, goes to Crespo, and, unaware that Crespo has been elected mayor, declares that he will thrash the town official for arresting one of the king's officers. Crespo reveals that he is the mayor and that he fully intends to see the captain hanged. Don Lope orders the regiment to return to the public square of Zalamea.

The soldiers having returned, a pitched battle between them and the townspeople of Zalamea seems imminent when King Philip II enters the village with his entourage. Don Lope explains the situation to the king, and Crespo shows his majesty depositions taken from the captain's associates. The king agrees that the captain's crime is vile; he declares, however, that Crespo has authority neither to judge nor to punish an officer of the king. When Crespo reveals that the captain has already been garroted in his cell and that no one knows who strangled him, the king, unable to deny that Zalamea had meted out true justice upon the captain, appoints Crespo perpetual mayor of the village. Crespo, after declaring that Isabel will take the veil of a nun, releases Rebolledo, Chispa, and Juan from jail, and returns Juan to the charge of his military mentor, Don Lope.

Critical Evaluation:

The Mayor of Zalamea is Pedro Calderón de la Barca's reworking of a play by his illustrious predecessor, Lope de Vega Carpio. Calderón, who was himself a soldier, delineates in this play the military life of seventeenth century Spain. He also portrays with sympathy the proud and independent farmer of the provinces. In the tradition of Spanish theater, the play blends comedy and tragedy; the jokes and song at the beginning of the play yield to the terrible crime and punishment at the end. A point of comparison is William Shakespeare's *Romeo and Juliet* (pr. c. 1595-1596, pb. 1597), which, one may argue, begins as a comedy and ends as a tragedy. *The Mayor of Zalamea* has achieved a place in the first rank of the world's dramatic masterpieces.

The play displays a perfect harmony and unity of thought and style. The work, generally assigned to the category of costumbristic drama—that is, drama based partly on history or popular tradition—has become, however, one of Calderón's most popular plays. The theme of *The Mayor of Zalamea* is honor, particularly in the first two acts where it is sharply contrasted with dishonor, as personified in the deeds of Captain Alvaro. The principal cause of the conflicts that drive the plot is the lodging of troops in a house where there is an unmarried woman, Isabel, and the captain's curiosity concerning a beauty he is forbidden to see. The effects of these situations are predictable, and the resultant action is fast moving, with an abduction, a rape, a garroting, and a jurisdictional battle that is resolved by the king. The incidents are structured on a ladder arrangement in that each one develops from the preceding one both logically and psychologically, which escalates into a tide of mounting tension by the end of each act. The play is perfectly constructed.

The conflict is depicted on two levels, exterior and interior. Each level involves a question of jurisdiction. The exterior conflict revolves around the clash between Crespo and Lope over the question of whether the king's justice is to be administered by the military or the civilian authorities. The external conflicts are set forth as debates or arguments and encompass the theme of honor. It may be difficult for the reader to comprehend the importance that honor had in Spain in the seventeenth century. One may find it simply abhorrent and incomprehensible, for example, that a brother may intend to kill his sister, after she has been raped, to preserve the family's honor. Honor as a theme in Calderón's work has manifold faces—honor ranges from a matter of the highest religious principle to a parody of social convention. One should read the play, therefore, with attention toward the importance that honor has in the play, from the first moments (when a starving gentleman discusses the proper way to woo a rich peasant) to the last (when the king decides whether Crespo and the other villagers, whose lives are at stake, have acted honorably).

The interior conflict also evolves from the concept of honor. The internal problem centers on the decision Crespo must make as to whether he should act in his capacity as a father or as the newly elected mayor of Zalamea. He finally chooses the latter because it embraces a broader sphere of justice than does the personal. The author's style, like the action, is simple and direct. The argumentative aspects of the style are borne out in the aforementioned debates over the concept of honor, but the quaint patter of the lower characters reveals an aspect of Calderón's style that adds a high degree of realism and naturalness to the dialogue. If the debates on honor seem artificial to today's reader, the oaths of Rebolledo, a raw recruit, who curses the officer who forces the troops to march without rest, are timeless bits of dialogue.

Like the style, the characterizations are significant for their attention to variety and detail. A case in point is Crespo, who represents justice and prudence but, at the same time, while being symbolic of virtue, is very much a flesh-and-blood character, with human defects. The soldiers think of him as vain, pompous, and presumptuous. He is proud of his lineage, and he has a sense of honor and personal dignity. Calderón's technique of revealing aspects of one character through the eyes of another is a strong factor in making the character more human and balanced in the eyes of the reader.

The Mayor of Zalamea is an allegory: The Spanish king, as representative of God, finally recalls all of the players to their fixed and rightful positions within the social order. Thus, while Crespo, for example, has an identity as a human being, on another level he is representative of the abstract virtue of justice, while Captain Alvaro is the embodiment of several dishonorable traits.

The Mayor of Zalamea is Calderón's most popular drama. In critical discussions of this work, it is common to read that it is unlike any of the author's other works. Some critics call it a revolutionary play, while others refer to it as a social drama, or Calderón's only drama of character. In truth, the play does not necessarily occupy an exceptional place in the playwright's canon. It is Calderón's usual kind of play, and it is unusual only in that the protagonist is a common man. Calderón was primarily a man of the theater, and the most significant argument in his selection of material was that of its applicability to the stage. *The Mayor of Zalamea*'s plot is perfectly suited to dramatic presentation. Since its first performance in the seventeenth century, it has perhaps never been out of production.

"Critical Evaluation" by Stephen Hanson

Further Reading

Benabu, Isaac. *Reading for the Stage: Calderón and His Contemporaries*. Rochester, N.Y.: Tamesis, 2003. Analyzes play texts for works by Calderón and contemporary playwrights. A play text is usually read by the theater company at the beginning of a play's production and provides the playwright's directions for staging his or her work. Benabu's examination of play texts discusses the religiosity of Spanish theater in the Golden Age, Calderón's devotional comedies, and the character of Pedro Crespo in *The Mayor of Zalamea*.

Calderón de la Barca, Pedro. *Calderón de la Barca: Four Plays*. Translated and introduction by Edwin Honig. New York: Hill and Wang, 1961. Honig's introduction and Norman MacColl's appendix provide illuminating context for understanding Spanish drama of the period.

Gerstinger, Heinz. *Pedro Calderón de la Barca*. Translated by Diana Stone Peters. New York: Frederick Ungar, 1973. Discusses another of the play's central themes: order and disorder, and how order is needed to limit human passions. Argues against the play's being unique among Calderón's works. Includes a bibliography.

Heigl, Michaela. *Theorizing Gender, Sexuality, and the Body in Calderonian Theater*. New Orleans, La.: University Press of the South, 2001. Focuses on the transvestites, scolds, sodomites, monsters, and other "deviant" characters in Calderón's plays, demonstrating how they embody the idea of excess and subvert the boundaries between genders and between different social classes. Heigl maintains that these characters represent the inherent corruption and perversion in society.

Hesse, Everett W. *Calderón de la Barca*. New York: Twayne, 1967. Describes *The Mayor of Zalamea* in terms of genre (it is a costumbristic play) and theme (honor). A good starting place for the study of Calderón. Includes a bibliography.

Maraniss, James E. *On Calderón*. Columbia: University of Missouri Press, 1978. Stressing Calderón's sense of "order triumphant," Maraniss moves through the canon, examining the structural integrity of each play, the symmetry of the plots, and the repeated ideas of social order.

Parker, Alexander A. *The Mind and Art of Calderón: Essays on the Comedias*. Edited by Deborah Kong. New York: Cambridge University Press, 1988. Discusses historical allusions in the play. Includes notes and an index.

Rodríguez Cuadros, Evangelina. "Pedro Calderón de la Barca." In *The Cambridge History of Spanish Literature*, edited by David T. Gies. New York: Cambridge University Press, 2004. An overview of Calderón's life and work, placing it within the broader context of Spanish literature.

Thacker, Jonathan. *A Companion to Golden Age Theatre*. Rochester, N.Y.: Tamesis, 2007. An introductory overview of Spanish Golden Age theater. In addition to a chapter on Calderón, the book examines the work of other playwrights, describes the different types of plays produced in this era, and traces the growth and maturation of Spanish theater.

Measure for Measure

Author: William Shakespeare (1564-1616)
First produced: c. 1604; first published, 1623
Type of work: Drama
Type of plot: Tragicomedy
Time of plot: Sixteenth century
Locale: Vienna

Principal characters:
VINCENTIO, the duke of Vienna
ANGELO, the lord deputy
ESCALUS, an ancient counselor
CLAUDIO, a young gentleman
LUCIO, his friend
ISABELLA, Claudio's sister
MARIANA, Angelo's former sweetheart
JULIET, Claudio's fiancé

The Story:

The growing political and moral corruption of Vienna is a great worry to its kindly, temperate ruler, Duke Vincentio. Knowing that he himself is as much to blame for the troubles as anyone because he has been lax in the enforcement of existing laws, the duke tries to devise a scheme to revive the old discipline of civic authority.

Fearing that reforms instituted by himself might seem too harsh for his people to accept without protest, he decides to appoint a deputy governor and to leave the country for a while. Angelo, a respected and intelligent city official, seems just the man for the job. The duke turns over the affairs of Vienna to Angelo for a certain length of time and appoints Escalus, a trustworthy old official, to be second in command. The duke then pretends to leave for Poland. In reality, he disguises himself as a friar and returns to the city to watch the outcome of Angelo's reforms.

Angelo's first act is to imprison Claudio, a young nobleman who got his betrothed, Juliet, pregnant. Under an old statute, now revived, Claudio's offense is punishable by death. After being paraded through the streets in disgrace, the young man is sent to prison. He asks his rakish friend, Lucio, to go to the nunnery where Claudio's sister, Isabella, is a young novice about to take her vows and to ask her to plead with the new governor for his release. At the same time, Escalus, who has known Claudio's father well, begs Angelo not to execute the young man. The new deputy remains firm, however, in carrying out the duties of his office, and Claudio's well-wishers are given no reason to hope for their friend's release.

The duke, disguised as a friar, visits Juliet and learns that the young couple had been very much in love and had, in fact, been formally engaged; they would have been married but for the fact that Juliet's dowry had become a matter of legal dispute. There is no question of heartless seduction in the case at all.

Isabella, going before Angelo to plead her brother's cause, meets with little success at first, even though she has been thoroughly coached by the wily Lucio. Nevertheless, Angelo's cold heart is somewhat touched by Isabella's beauty. By the second interview, he has become so passionately aroused as to forget his reputation for saintly behavior. He tells Isabella frankly that she can obtain her brother's release only by yielding herself to his lustful desires, otherwise Claudio will die. Isabella is shocked at these words from the deputy, but when she asserts that she will expose him in public, Angelo, amused, asks who will believe her story. At her wit's end, Isabella rushes to the prison where she tells Claudio of Angelo's disgraceful proposition. When he first

hears the deputy's proposal, Claudio is outraged, but the thought of death so terrifies him that he finally begs Isabella to placate Angelo and give herself to him. Isabella, horrified by her brother's cowardly attitude, lashes out at him with a scornful speech, but she is interrupted by the disguised duke, who has overheard much of the conversation. He draws Isabella aside from her brother and tells her that she will be able to save Claudio without shaming herself.

The friar tells Isabella that five years earlier, Angelo had been betrothed to a high-born lady named Mariana. The marriage did not take place, however. After Mariana's brother had been lost at sea with her dowry, Angelo broke the engagement, hinting at supposed dishonor in the young woman. The friar suggests that Isabella plan a rendezvous with Angelo in a dark, quiet place and then let Mariana act as her substitute. Angelo will be satisfied, Claudio released, Isabella still chaste, and Mariana provided with the means to force Angelo to marry her.

Everything goes as arranged, with Mariana taking Isabella's place at the assignation. Cowardly Angelo, however, fearing public exposure, breaks his promise to release Claudio and instead orders the young man's execution. Once again the good friar intervenes. He persuades the provost to hide Claudio and then to announce his death by sending Angelo the head of another prisoner who has died of natural causes.

On the day before the execution, a crowd gathers outside the prison. One of the group is Lucio, who accosts the disguised duke as he wanders down the street. Furtively, Lucio tells the friar that nothing like Claudio's execution would take place if the duke had been ruler. Lucio confidentially says that the duke cares as much for the ladies as any other man and also drinks in private. In fact, says Lucio, the duke beds about as much as any man in Vienna. Amused, the friar protests against this gossip, but Lucio angrily asserts that every word is true.

To arouse Isabella to accuse Angelo publicly of wrongdoing, the duke allows her to believe that Claudio is dead. Then the duke sends letters to the deputy informing him that the royal party will arrive on the following day at the gates of Vienna and will expect to be welcomed. The command also orders that anyone who has grievances against the government while the duke is absent should be allowed to make public pronouncement of them at that time and place.

Angelo grows nervous upon receipt of these papers from the duke. The next day, however, he organizes a great crowd and a celebration of welcome at the gates of the city. At the prearranged time, Isabella and Mariana, heavily veiled, step forward to denounce Angelo. Isabella calls him a traitor and violator of virgins; Mariana claims that he will not admit her as his wife. The duke, pretending to be angry at these tirades against his deputy, orders the women to prison and asks that someone apprehend the rascally friar who has often been seen in their company.

Then the duke goes to his palace and quickly assumes his disguise as a friar. Appearing before the crowd at the gates, he criticizes the government of Vienna severely. Escalus, horrified at the fanatical comments of the friar, orders his arrest, seconded by Lucio, who maintains that the friar had told him only the day before that the duke is a drunkard and a frequenter of bawdy houses. At last, to display his own bravado, Lucio tears away the friar's hood. When the friar stands revealed as Duke Vincentio, the crowd falls back in amazement.

Angelo realizes that his crimes will now be exposed, and he asks simply to be put to death without trial. The duke orders him to marry Mariana first, and he tells Mariana that Angelo's goods, once they are legally hers, will secure her a better husband. The duke is surprised when she begs for Angelo's pardon, in which entreaties she is joined by Isabella, but he relents. He does, however, send Lucio to prison. Claudio is released and married to Juliet. The duke himself asks Isabella for her hand.

Critical Evaluation:

Measure for Measure is one of those troubled plays, like *All's Well That Ends Well* (pr. c. 1602-1603, pb. 1623) and *Troilus and Cressida* (pr. 1601-1602, pb. 1609), that William Shakespeare composed during the same years he was writing his greatest tragedies. Though they are dark and often bitter, however, they are not straightforward tragedy or history or comedy; they have instead frequently been described as problem plays, which generally refers to plays that examine a thesis. The main concern in *Measure for Measure* is a rather grim consideration of the nature of justice and morality in both civic and psychological contexts.

The tone of this play, and of the other problem plays, is so gloomy and pessimistic that critics have tended to try to find biographical or historical causes for their bleakness. Some have argued that they reflect a period of personal disillusionment for the playwright, but there is no external evidence of this. Others have laid the blame on the decadence of the Jacobean period. Although such dramatists as John Marston and Thomas Dekker did write similar plays around the same time, the historical evidence suggests that the period was, on the contrary, rather optimistic. What is clear is that Shakespeare has created a world as rotten as Denmark but without a tragic figure sufficient to purge and redeem it. The result is

a threatened world, supported by comic remedies rather than purified by tragic suffering. Consequently, *Measure for Measure* remains a shadowy, ambiguous, and disquieting world even though it ends with political and personal resolutions.

The immediate source of the play seems to be George Whetstone's *History of Promos and Cassandra* (1578), which is based on a narrative and a dramatic version of the tale in Giambattista Giraldi Cinthio's *Hecatommithi* (1527), from whom Shakespeare also derived the plot of *Othello, the Moor of Venice* (pr. 1604, pb. 1622). However, *Measure for Measure* is such an eclectic amalgamation of items from a wide variety of literary and historical loci that a precise identification of sources is impossible. Indeed, the plot is essentially a conflation of three ancient folktales, which J. W. Lever has identified as the Corrupt Magistrate, the Disguised Ruler, and the Substituted Bedmate. Shakespeare integrates these with disparate other materials into a disturbing, indeterminate analysis of justice, morality, and integrity.

The title of the play comes from the scriptural text: "With what measure ye mete, it shall be measured to you again." As the play develops and expands on this quotation, it becomes clear that a simple but generous resolution "to do unto others what you would have them do unto you" will not suffice to resolve the situation. The play pursues its text so relentlessly that any easy confidence in poetic justice is undermined. In the final analysis, the action tends to support an admonition to "Judge not that ye be not judged," which can be either Christian charity or cynical irresponsibility.

The play, however, takes place in a world in which the civil authorities must judge others. Indeed, that is where the play begins. Vienna, as the duke himself realizes, is a moral morass, and bawdry and licentiousness of all sorts are rampant. The duke accepts responsibility for having been lax in enforcing the law. Corruption seethes throughout society from the nobility down to the base characters who are engaged less in a comic subplot than in a series of vulgar exemplifications of the pervasive moral decay.

The chilling paradox is that when Angelo, renowned for his probity and puritanical stringency, is made responsible for setting things right, he almost immediately falls victim to the sexual license he is supposed to eliminate. Claudio, whom Angelo condemns for making Juliet pregnant, had at least acted out of love and with a full intention to marry. Things do not turn out to be as they seemed. He who is responsible for justice yields to temptation while someone apparently guilty of vice is extenuated by circumstances.

Isabella, called on to intercede for her brother, is faced with an especially nasty dilemma, since her choice is between her honor and her brother's life. Neither is a noble alternative, and Claudio is not strong enough to offer himself up for her and turn the play into a tragedy. Unfortunately, when Claudio shows his reluctance, she behaves petulantly rather than graciously. True, her position is intolerable, but she spends more time speaking in defense of her virtue than in acting virtuously. For all her religious aspirations, which are eventually abandoned, she is not large enough to ennoble her moral context.

Always lurking in the background is the duke, who watches developments and stands ready to intervene to avoid disaster. He seems slow to step in, but then if he had intervened earlier, or had never left in the first place, there would not have been a play that examines the ambiguities of guilt and extenuation, justice and mercy. The duke and Shakespeare allow the characters to act out the complex patterns of moral responsibility that are the heart of the play. When Angelo, thinking he is with Isabella, is in fact with Mariana, his act is objectively less evil than he thinks because he is really with the woman to whom he had earlier plighted his troth. Yet in intention he is more culpable than Claudio, whom he had imprisoned. Such are the intricate complications of behavior in the flawed world of *Measure for Measure.*

The justice that the duke finally administers brings about a comic resolution. Pardons and marriages unravel the complications that varying degrees of evil had occasioned, but no one in the play escapes untainted. The duke, after a period of moral spectatorship that borders on irresponsibility, restores order. Angelo loses his virtue and reputation but gains a wife. Isabella abandons her religious commitment but learns to be more human, for which she is rewarded with a marriage proposal. Everything works out, and justice, tempered with mercy, prevails. The audience is left, however, with an unsettled feeling that tendencies toward corruption and excess may be inextricably blended with what is best and most noble.

"Critical Evaluation" by Edward E. Foster

Further Reading

Bennett, Josephine Waters. *"Measure for Measure" as Royal Entertainment.* New York: Columbia University Press, 1966. Comprehensive discussion of the play, centering on how it would have appeared to contemporary audiences. Rejects earlier criticisms of the work as "dark comedy," and considers instead that in its historical context, it would have been viewed as high entertainment.

Clark, Ira. *Rhetorical Readings, Dark Comedies, and Shakespeare's Problem Plays.* Gainesville: University Press of Florida, 2007. Examines *Measure for Measure* and two other "problem plays," those plays that do not fit the usual mold of Elizabethan comedy. Analyzes the most prominent rhetorical features of these plays, including rhetorical devices that were commonly used in Elizabethan literature.

Lloyd Evans, Gareth. *The Upstart Crow: An Introduction to Shakespeare's Plays.* London: J. M. Dent and Sons, 1982. A comprehensive discussion of Shakespeare's dramatic works, including information on the plays' critical reviews and sources, as well as on the circumstances surrounding their gestation.

Marsh, Nicholas. *Shakespeare: Three Problem Plays.* New York: Palgrave Macmillan, 2003. Examines the unresolved issues in *Measure for Measure* and two other plays by analyzing excerpts from their texts, pointing out the multiple interpretations of young men, women, politics and society, and fools. Places the plays in relation to Shakespeare's life and oeuvre, providing historical and cultural context and analyses by five literary critics.

Shakespeare, William. *Measure for Measure.* Edited by J. W. Lever. London: Methuen, 1965. In addition to the text of the play, this edition contains more than ninety pages of introductory material about the play's sources and a critical evaluation of the work. Includes appendixes with the original texts of Shakespeare's sources.

Shuger, Debora Kuller. *Political Theologies in Shakespeare's England: The Sacred and the State in "Measure for Measure."* New York: Palgrave, 2001. Analyzes political thought in post-Reformation England, focusing on the relationship between the government and religion, and demonstrates how this thinking is reflected in *Measure for Measure.* Discusses the play's depiction of the legislation of morals, competing claims of law and equity, Christian justice, and the power of the monarchy.

Wheeler, Richard P., ed. *Critical Essays on Shakespeare's "Measure for Measure."* New York: G. K. Hall, 1999. Includes discussions of the play's depiction of sexuality, life and death, marriage, transgression and surveillance, and the power of Christianity.

Medea

Author: Euripides (c. 485-406 B.C.E.)
First produced: *Mēdeia*, 431 B.C.E. (English translation, 1781)
Type of work: Drama
Type of plot: Tragedy
Time of plot: Antiquity
Locale: Corinth

Principal characters:
MEDEA, a sorcerer
JASON, her lover
CREON, the king of Corinth
GLAUCE, the daughter of Creon
AEGEUS, the king of Athens

The Story:

When Medea discovers that Jason has deserted her and married Glauce, the daughter of Creon, she vows a terrible vengeance. Her nurse, although she loves Medea, recognizes that a frightful threat now hangs over Corinth, for she knows that Medea will not let the insult pass without some dreadful revenge. She fears especially for Medea's two sons, since the sorcerer includes her children in the hatred she now feels for their father.

Medea's resentment increases still further when Creon, hearing of her vow, orders her and her children to be banished from Corinth. Slyly, with a plan already in mind, Medea persuades him to allow her just one day longer to prepare herself and her children for the journey. She already has decided the nature of her revenge; the one problem that remains is a place of refuge afterward.

Then Aegeus, the king of Athens and a longtime friend of Medea, appears in Corinth on his way home from a journey. Sympathetic with her because of Jason's brutal desertion, he offers her a place of refuge from her enemies in his own kingdom. In this manner Medea assures herself of a refuge, even after Aegeus learns of the deeds she will soon commit in Corinth.

When the Corinthian women visit her, Medea tells them of her plan, but only after swearing them to absolute secrecy. At first she considers killing Jason, his princess, and Creon, and then fleeing with her own children. After she thinks about it, however, she feels that revenge will be sweeter with Jason living to suffer long afterward. Nothing is more painful than to grow old without a lover, without children, and without friends, and so Medea plans to kill the king, his daughter, and her own children.

She calls Jason to her and pretends that she forgives him for what he had done, recognizing at last the justice and foresight he had shown in marrying Glauce. She begs his forgiveness for her earlier rage, and asks that she be allowed to send her children with gifts for the new bride, as a sign of her repentance. Jason is completely deceived by her supposed change of heart, and expresses his pleasure at the belated wisdom she is showing.

Medea draws out a magnificent robe and a fillet of gold, presents of her grandfather, Helios, the sun god, but before she entrusts them to her children she smears them with a deadly drug. Shortly afterward, a messenger comes to Medea and tells her to flee. One part of her plan has succeeded. After Jason and the children leave, Glauce dresses herself in her wonderful robe and walks through the palace. As the warmth and moisture of her body come in contact with the drug, the fillet and gown cling to her body and sear her flesh. She tries frantically to tear them from her, but the garments only wrap more tightly around her, and she dies in a screaming agony of flames. When Creon rushes in and sees his daughter writhing on the floor, he attempts to lift her, but is himself contaminated by the poison. His death is as agonizing as hers had been.

Meanwhile. the children have returned to Medea. As she looks at them and feels their arms around her, she is torn between her love for them and her hatred of Jason, between her desire for revenge and the commands of her maternal instinct. The barbarous part of her nature—Medea being not a Greek, but a barbarian from Colchis—triumphs. After reveling in the messenger's account of the deaths of Creon and his daughter, she enters her house with the children and bars the door. While the Corinthian women stand helplessly outside, they listen to the shrieks of the children as Medea kills them with a sword. Jason appears, frantically eager to take his children away lest they be killed by Creon's followers for having brought the dreadful gifts. When he learns Medea had killed his children, he is almost insane with grief. As he hammers furiously on the barred doors of the house, Medea suddenly appears above, holding the bodies of her dead children, and drawn in a chariot that Helios, the sun god, had sent her. Jason alternately curses her and pleads with her for one last sight of his children as Medea taunts him with the loneliness and grief to which he is doomed. She tells him that her own sorrow will be great, but it is mitigated by the sweetness of her revenge.

The chariot, drawn by winged dragons, carries Medea first to the mountain of the goddess Hera. There she buries her children. Then she journeys to Athens, where she will spend the remainder of her days feeding on the gall and wormwood of her terrible grief and revenge.

Critical Evaluation:

Commonly regarded as Euripides' greatest work, *Medea* is a powerful study of impassioned love turned into furious hatred. As a tragedy, this play is completely unlike the Aristotelian concept of tragedy, but it has a nerve-jarring impact. It also reveals the extent to which Euripides diverges from his fellow tragedians, Aeschylus and Sophocles, in his depiction of human pain. With *Medea* there is no comforting philosophy to put the tragic agony at a safe psychological distance. Instead, Euripides tries to make Medea as close to an actual woman as possible, and to show her fiery lust for vengeance in naked action with nothing to mitigate its effect. The audience is witness to a hideous passion and cannot be certain whether Euripides approves of it or condemns it. He simply presents it objectively so that we understand Medea, but he leaves it to his audience to determine his meaning.

Euripides was probably in his fifties when this play was first produced in 431 B.C.E., an age when a sensitive person is fully aware of the agony that life can inflict on a person. What struck him most was the universality of suffering. Confronted with pain, every other human reality seemed to dissolve. In the face of Medea's consuming hatred, kingship, laws, culture, self-esteem, and even motherly love have become meaningless. In *Medea*, Euripides portrays a very important aspect of terrible suffering, namely, the desire of the sufferer to create the identical agony in the person who caused it. The dramatist recognized the crucial link between anguish and hate. Reports of Euripides say that he was a bookish recluse, but it is understandable that a man as vulnerable to human misery as he was should shut himself off from people.

Euripides turned to the old legend of Jason and the Golden Fleece to illustrate his preoccupation. He takes up the story after all of Jason's successes have been accomplished with Medea's help. Jason has deserted Medea to marry the Greek princess, Glauce, leaving Medea with two small sons. As the nurse remarks in her opening monologue, Medea is not one to take such a betrayal lightly. Although Medea is prostrate with bitter grief and hoping to die as the play begins, the nurse knows how murderous her mistress really is, and she fears for the safety of Medea's sons. A common technique of Euripides is to use the opening speech or section to explain the background of the action and to suggest the climactic development.

Medea is a barbarian princess and sorcerer who is accustomed to having her own way in everything. Furthermore, as a barbarian she has none of the restraints that civilization imposes. Jason is a Greek, subject to law, rationality, and practical calculation. As a result, he seems cold and indifferent beside Medea, who is a creature of passion. However, this is merely a surface appearance. Euripides exposes the inner layers of their psyches with unflinching honesty in the course of the play.

As a woman of passion, Medea is wholly committed to Jason as the object of her emotional life, whether in love or hate. When she loved Jason she did not hesitate to kill her brother, betray her father and country, or instigate Pelias's murder for Jason's sake. She is equally amoral in her hatred. The drama consists of the unfolding of her plans for revenge and their ultimate execution. When Medea first appears on stage before a chorus of sympathetic women, she is the image of the wronged woman, and one feels pity for her. At the end of the play, however, after a bloodbath of four persons that includes her sons and that leaves Jason's life a total desolation, one feels only horror.

These murders are as coldly calculated as any in classical tragedy, and Medea feels no penitence at all. It is precisely the icy manner in which she goes about the killings that inspires dread. She caters to Creon to gain time to kill him and his daughter, Glauce. Medea plans to kill Jason, too, but when she sees Aegeus heartsick at being childless, she determines to render Jason childless, wifeless, and friendless. Medea pretends a reconciliation with Jason to slay Creon and Glauce in a loathsome fashion. Then, after hesitating to kill her sons because of temporary softness, she butchers them without mercy. Medea is a practitioner of black magic, a cold-blooded murderer, and a total monster; but under Euripides' spell the audience understands her.

The passion by which Medea lives makes her both subhuman and superhuman. When Euripides finally has her escape in a dragon-drawn chariot through the air, one comes to realize that Medea is a piece of raw nature—barbaric, violent, destructive, inhumanly powerful, and beyond all moral standards. Jason becomes entangled with a force that crushes his dignity and detachment, that tears his successes to tatters. At the end, he is in exactly the same position as Medea. Both are bereaved of mate, children, and friends. Both are free to grow old without comfort. Both are utterly empty inside, except that Jason is now filled with the same burning hatred that possessed Medea.

This play operates on several levels. The antagonism between Jason and Medea can be read as the enmity between man and woman, between intelligence and passion, between civilization and barbarism, or between humanity and nature. In each instance, the woman, the passions, the barbarian, the forces of nature—all embodied in Medea—have the power to turn and reduce the masculine elements to nothing. *Medea* is a strong, depressing, fearsome drama in which Euripides presents his stark vision of life.

"Critical Evaluation" by James Weigel, Jr.

Further Reading

Allan, William. *Euripides: "Medea."* London: Duckworth, 2002. This companion to the play analyzes the myth of Medea before Euripides and how he treated this myth in his play. Places the play within the context of gender politics in ancient Athens. Allan also discusses how Medea was viewed as a barbarian, examines the moral and emotional impact of her revenge, and traces the play's reception over the years.

Bloom, Harold, ed. *Euripides: Comprehensive Research and Study Guide.* Philadelphia: Chelsea House, 2003. Includes a biography of Euripides and a plot summary, a list of characters, and seven critical essays providing various interpretations of *Medea.*

Luschnig, C. A. E. *Granddaughter of the Sun: A Study of Euripides' "Medea."* Boston: Brill, 2007. Demonstrates the many facets of Medea's personality by focusing on the positive aspects of her character, such as her intellect, successful relationships with other characters, and her roles as wife, mother, and political hero.

McDermott, Emily A. *Euripides' "Medea": The Incarnation of Disorder.* University Park: Pennsylvania State University Press, 1989. McDermott presents Medea as heroic, sympathetic, morally repugnant, and the incarnation of disorder because of her repeated assaults on family stability and her lack of adherence to the expectations of the parent-child relationship.

Morwood, James. *The Plays of Euripides.* Bristol, England: Bristol Classical, 2002. Morwood provides a concise overview of all of Euripides' plays, devoting a separate chapter to each one. He demonstrates how Euripides was constantly reinventing himself in his work.

Mossman, Judith, ed. *Euripides.* New York: Oxford University Press, 2003. Collection of essays, some providing a general overview of Euripidean drama and others focusing on specific plays. Includes the essay "The Infanticide in Euripides' *Medea.*"

Ohlander, Stephen. *Dramatic Suspense in Euripides' and Seneca's "Medea."* New York: Peter Lang, 1989. Scene by scene, Ohlander explores Euripides' sense of dramatic suspense, examining how motifs from mythic tradition are handled and how Euripides manufactures new ones.

Pucci, Pietro. *The Violence of Pity in Euripides' "Medea."* Ithaca, N.Y.: Cornell University Press, 1980. Pucci examines the painful experience audience members suffer when exposed to the play's violence and the ways Euripides' language moves them from dread to contemplation of the peacefulness of their own existence.

Rabinowitz, Nancy Sorkin. *Anxiety Veiled: Euripides and the Traffic in Women.* Ithaca, N.Y.: Cornell University Press, 1993. Focusing on women in Athens and in tragedy, Rabinowitz explores female desire as a threat to family and the Athenian polis, interpreting Medea as a victim who, though initially sympathetic to the audience, forfeits that sympathy by indulging in a vengeance made excessive—an act for which she pays no price.

Meditations

Author: Marcus Aurelius (121-180)
First transcribed: Tōn eis heauton, c. 171-180 C.E. (English translation, 1634)
Type of work: Philosophy

Although the Greek philosopher Zeno is generally given the credit for creating the school of philosophy called Stoicism, its greatest fame arises from the popularity and widespread influence of the utterances of two later figures: Epictetus, a slave, and Marcus Aurelius, emperor of Rome. Of the two, Marcus, born four years before the death of Epictetus in 125, has probably achieved the greater fame; and this fame results almost entirely from his *Meditations*, one of the most famous philosophical books ever conceived.

For the average reader, however, there is a disturbing characteristic in the work, which is obscure and often seemingly unrelated; there are passages that suggest that the book has traveled through time in a disorganized, even careless, form. One widely accepted suggestion to account for this difficulty is the possibility that Marcus intended his writings to be read by no one else, that he recorded his thoughts only for himself. It is certain that the *Meditations* was written during the period between Marcus's accession to the imperial rank in 161 and his death in 180; it is equally certain that the various books were composed during rigorous military campaigns and trying political crises. Although these facts explain in part the irregularity of the book, other scholars feel that there is clear evidence of the emperor's design to publish at least parts of the work.

If this is so, and if Marcus did not merely keep a private journal, then the reason for the present form of the *Meditations* probably lies in errors and misunderstandings by copyists and later editors of the text. In either event, the book contains two generally different styles side by side: a nearly casual, sometimes aphoristic, way of writing, and a more literary, more carefully planned, technique. Throughout the twelve books that make up the whole, there are passages that read like admonitions addressed by the author to himself; in contrast to these are sections that sound as if Marcus were offering philosophical advice to the Romans or to humanity in general. Despite these irregularities, and in spite of the absence of an organized system of thought, a careful reading reveals that the emperor presents to the world some of the wisest suggestions for leading the good life and some of the most effective expressions of the tenets of later Stoicism to be found anywhere.

To say, however, that Marcus can be given credit for profound original thinking is going too far. *Meditations* was not written in a vacuum. It rephrases and reinterprets much of that which is usually considered the best of ancient Greek and Roman philosophy. The author acknowledges his debt to his teachers and his wise forbears; his quotations from, and references to, the leading thinkers of his and earlier times prove his wide reading and careful study, which colors his injunction to throw aside one's books and to live one's philosophy.

Perhaps the fact that Marcus did live by his philosophy, one that was tested by almost continually difficult circumstances, is one of the chief charms of his book. There is very little in the *Meditations* that the emperor probably did not find occasion to think of in relation to his own life. Much of practical philosophic value can be found here. His advice at the opening of book 2, for example, to begin each day with the thought that one will meet during that day men (and women) who are arrogant, envious, and deceitful, but to remember that these men are so because of their ignorance of the good and the right, is surely a sound practical application of the Platonic idea that evil is only the absence of knowledge.

Many readers have found the *Meditations* their surest guide to living by Stoic principles. Although happiness must surely come by the pursuit of Stoic virtue, duty is the greatest good in the Stoic view. The word "duty" appears rarely in the book, but the emperor's conviction that a person must face squarely his or her responsibilities is implicit in almost every paragraph. Often a note of Roman sternness appears, as in the beginning of paragraph 5 of book 2:

Every moment think steadily as a Roman and a man to do what thou hast in hand with perfect and simple dignity, and feeling of affection, and freedom, and justice; and to give thyself relief from all other thoughts.

To achieve true virtue, the emperor says, one must live in accord with both kinds of nature: the nature of humankind and the nature of the universe. The book departs from a commonly held view of the philosopher as an isolated dreamer in its insistence that one must live wisely with one's fellows. One should not be a hermit. Since each individual partakes of the same divinity that informs all people, each must live and work with others; certainly such is the divine intention, and this, then, is one's social duty. The duty one has to the universe is to perceive the informing intelligence that pervades and guides it. Here Marcus is close to pantheism.

With this foundation in mind, the reader can understand the emperor's notion of evil as something that cannot harm or disturb the great plan of the universe; it is simply ignorance and harms only the doer. Thus, no one can be harmed by a force from the outside. Injury comes from within. The advice of the *Meditations*, along with that of other Stoic writings, is to accept calmly what cannot be avoided and to perform to the best of one's ability the duties of a human being in a world of humans. Since one cannot understand the workings of the great force that rules the universe, one must do what can be done in his or her own sphere.

Although he believes the world to be divinely guided, Marcus has no illusions about life; therefore, he scorns fears of death. Life is full of trouble and hardship, and no one should be sorry to leave it. In paragraph 14 of book 2, the author says that however long or short a person's life, a person loses at death only the present moment. No one possesses the past or the future; furthermore, since the progress of time is simply a revolution, and all things have been and will be the same, one loses nothing by an early death. This passage displays something of the occasional coldness of the emperor's thought, but it is one of many sections devoted to the consolation for the hard facts of existence.

Regardless of the varied character of the writing and the thinking in these paragraphs, it is clear that a reasonably consistent philosophy inspired them. The statement that one rarely comes to grief from not knowing what is in another's soul, that true misery results from not understanding what lies within oneself, is of a piece with the rest of the book.

Some readers have found in Marcus a basically Christian spirit and believe that, in many passages, the *Meditations* somewhat foreshadows later religious writings. Considerable doubt exists as to his feeling about the Christians or the extent of his responsibility for their persecution during his reign, but there is little question that a great deal of his thinking is closely allied with that of later spiritual leaders. The readership and influence of *Meditations*, written by perhaps the greatest pagan ruler who ever lived, is as wide as those of other works of its kind, and far greater than those of most.

Further Reading

Arnold, E. Vernon. *Roman Stoicism*. Reprint. London: Routledge & Kegan Paul, 1958. A series of easy-to-follow lectures by a classical scholar. Four chapters discuss the thought of Marcus Aurelius.

Birley, Anthony. *Marcus Aurelius: A Biography*. London: Eyre and Spottiswoode, 1966. Rev. ed. New York: Routledge, 2006. In this well-researched study, Birley aims to disinfect the image of Marcus of numerous historical fictions. Includes an illuminating profile of the philosopher-ruler's early education as revealed through correspondence with his tutor, Fronto.

Farquharson, A. S. L. *Marcus Aurelius: His Life and His World*. Edited by D. A. Rees. 2d ed. London: Basil Blackwell, 1952. A fine biography, especially with regard to Marcus's birth, childhood, and education. Contains one of the few discussions of his home life. Situates the *Meditations* within Stoic philosophy and the literature of the age.

Forstater, Mark. *The Spiritual Teachings of Marcus Aurelius*. London: Hodder & Stoughton, 2000. Compendium of the spiritual insights contained in the *Meditations* and a consideration of their continued relevance in the twenty-first century.

Hadot, Pierre. *The Inner Citadel: The Meditations of Marcus Aurelius*. Translated by Michael Chase. Cambridge, Mass.: Harvard University Press, 1998. This eminent scholar discerns the *Meditations* as spiritual exercises practiced in accordance with the Stoic method, particularly as espoused by Epictetus. Engaging, clear, and accessible to the general reader, the book includes a fascinating concordance of the quotations and literary allusions in the *Meditations*.

Marcus Aurelius. "The *Meditations* of Marcus Aurelius." Translated and edited by George Long. In *Plato, Epictetus, Marcus Aurelius*, edited by Charles W. Eliot. 2d ed. New York: P. F. Collier and Sons, 1937. Long's translation of Marcus's work is accompanied by his brief and interesting life of the author. His companion essay, "The Philosophy of Antoninus," includes a useful explanation of Stoicism and traces its progress and decline in the Roman world.

Rutherford, R. B. *The "Meditations" of Marcus Aurelius: A Study*. New York: Oxford University Press, 1989. Rutherford aims to make the *Meditations* accessible to the general reader. He places the work within its historical and philosophical context and examines Marcus's ideas and writing style.

Stedall, Alan. *Marcus Aurelius: The Dialogues*. London: Shepheard-Walwyn, 2005. Concise description of the philosophical ideas contained in the *Meditations*. Stedall re-creates a meeting that actually occurred between Marcus and four other historical figures of classical antiquity; during the meeting, Marcus discusses and defends his beliefs, providing readers with an accessible description of his philosophy.

Meditations on First Philosophy

Author: René Descartes (1596-1650)
First published: Meditationes de prima philosophia,
    1641 (English translation, 1680)
Type of work: Philosophy

The appearance of *Meditations on First Philosophy* in 1641 marked a dramatic turning point in the history of Western thought. Born in France in 1596, René Descartes was sent to a Jesuit school as a young man and in 1616 obtained a law degree. He spent much of his youth traveling. Like many young Frenchmen of the time, he enlisted as a gentleman volunteer in the army of Prince Maurice of Nassau in Holland during the Thirty Years' War. In November, 1619, when the onset of winter had slowed the fighting, Descartes retired to the village of Ulm on the Danube River to devote himself to study and contemplation. He wrote that one day, while trying to escape the cold in a heated room, he had three visions or dreams in which he saw flashes of light and heard thunder. He said it seemed to him that some spirit was revealing a new philosophy to him. He interpreted these visions as a divine sign that it was his destiny to place all of human thought on the firm foundation of mathematics.

In 1637, Descartes had published *Discours de la méthode* (*Discourse on Method*, 1649), which roughly outlined that new philosophy. Both *Discourse on Method* and *Meditations on First Philosophy* were written in French rather than Latin, the usual language of scholarly works. Like Galileo before him, who wrote in Italian, Descartes intended to reach beyond the university to a larger educated audience.

The great intellectual tension of Descartes's time was that between belief in traditional Christianity and belief in the potential of the new physical and mathematical sciences. Philosophers before Descartes used a philosophical method called Scholasticism, which was entirely based on comparing and contrasting the views of recognized authorities, especially Aristotle. Since Scholastic philosophy was built on the opinions of many thinkers, it could not provide much in the way of certainty on any given subject.

Instead of accepting the traditional views, Descartes believed that people must instead study from "the great book of the world." To know the opinions of others, he said, is history, not science; people should do their own thinking, and the clear and simple process of mathematics would provide the clue for how to proceed on the path to certain knowledge. Descartes turned all questions of human knowledge inward by first thinking about the process of thinking itself, examin-

ing the method of knowing as a prerequisite for assuming that certain knowledge has been attained. Descartes was trying to find a body of irrefutable and self-evident truths that every person of common sense and reason could accept. If truths could be established in philosophy as they had been in mathematics, this would end the debates about the existence of God, the immortality of the soul, and the reality of the external world.

In the first meditation, Descartes begins by doubting all knowledge that he has previously accepted as true. Up to the present time, he says, he has accepted the knowledge acquired through sensory experience as the truest and the most certain knowledge; yet sense perceptions may be illusions, the products of dreams or hallucinations, or the products of an all-powerful being causing these sensations or ideas to form. Individuals could be existing in a prolonged "dream state" that seems quite real while there is no way to prove that they are awake. These facts led Descartes to doubt the certainty of everything. The only thing he could not doubt was that he existed.

In the second meditation, Descartes declares that this universal doubt makes him feel like a swimmer who is suddenly plunged into deep water. Unable to touch bottom or see the surface, he cannot find a fixed reference point from which to begin. He therefore must assume that everything is false and that he has no memory, no senses, and no body. Even what he perceives as "reality" could possibly be a deception. Even if, however, he is in a state of universal doubt—even if he is being deceived—he remains a thinking being. He can therefore at least assert that he is "a thing which thinks." At this point he has found the first of what he calls "clear and distinct ideas," ideas so certain that they cannot possibly be denied.

Descartes can now proceed to the more difficult task of proving the existence of the material world. For this purpose, he introduces the famous "wax argument": A piece of wax fresh from the beehive can be seen to have color, size, and smell that present themselves to human senses, but if the wax is placed near a fire it melts and those qualities disappear. Where did they go? Descartes's answer is that there had only been the assumption that the qualities existed in the object, while in fact they were merely intuitions of the mind. The best that humans can do at this point is to speculate that there are material objects outside themselves that cause sensations in the mind.

Descartes's third meditation is devoted to a proof of God's existence, which is also intended to show that the world perceived through the senses is not a deception. Since the existence of the outside world is still in doubt, Descartes begins by examining the ideas present in his mind. He notices that some ideas seem to be "born" with him, while others seem to come from outside; he observes that things seem to be happening around him and independently of his will. For example, as he sits by the fire he feels heat and is persuaded that the heat does not originate from within him; similarly, he has a concept of God, which also does not seem to have come from within him. He asks himself how, given that he himself is not an infinite, all-knowing, all-powerful being, he could produce the idea of a God with these attributes. Because he does not possess these qualities, Descartes argues, they could not have originated within him, and since God is perfect, he could not be a deceiver. Therefore, the world he perceives through his senses must have been created by a being greater than himself, and if God is not a deceiver, the world he perceives must be the "real" world and not an illusion. Thus, in establishing the existence of God, Descartes established the foundation of all knowledge.

In the fourth meditation, Descartes points out that even though ideas such as the self and God are perceived clearly and distinctly, humans make errors in their thinking because their intellects are finite and they possess free will. This is not an imperfection on God's part but merely a sign of the imperfection of human beings. Since he is not himself the Supreme Being, he says, he should not be surprised that he occasionally falls into error. The power of free will received from God is perfect, but sometimes the will surpasses the understanding, which causes error.

In the fifth meditation, Descartes discusses the essence of material things. To determine further whether anything certain can be known about material things, he presents a second argument for God's existence, which states that just as within the idea of a triangle is contained the concept of "three angles," the idea of "existence" is necessarily contained within the concept of "God." To speak of a "nonexistent God," he says, would be a contradiction, because the property of existence is a part of God's essence. The logical certainty of God's existence means that all things depend upon God for their existence and that God, being perfect, could not be deceiving humans about the external world. Thus, Descartes feels assured that the certainty of the existence of the material world is guaranteed by the certainty of God's existence.

In the sixth and final meditation, Descartes completes his argument as to whether material things exist. He begins by differentiating between "extended things" out in the world, and "thinking things" in his mind. Descartes believes that it is certain that material things exist, and the fact that they can be described with the clear and distinct ideas of mathematics supports the certainty that there is an objective reality independent of the human mind. In addition, because God is not a deceiver, Descartes has no reason to believe that what he himself perceives as the material world is not really there.

What Descartes has established with this line of thinking is that there are actually two realities: mind and matter. In terms of Descartes's own existence, his mind is distinct from his body; but if the human body is a material machine, how can the immaterial mind act upon it? Descartes simply answers that it does, like a captain who lives inside his ship. Perhaps, he suggests, God arranges the interaction of mind and body in mysterious ways, beyond finite understanding.

Descartes was one of the most original thinkers of his time. By using mathematics as his model of certain knowledge, he believed that he had placed all of human knowledge on a firm foundation. Philosophy, he believed, like mathematics, must start with clear and simple truths and then advance toward more complex truths. By showing with absolute certainty that he exists—"I think, therefore I am"—and that God exists, he proceeded to show that the external world exists as well, even though humans may err in their perceptions about the world.

The English philosopher John Locke challenged Descartes's notion of innate ideas, believing instead that at birth human beings' minds are a tabula rasa, or "blank slate"—devoid of any ideas of self or God. The German philosopher Immanuel Kant disputed Descartes's proofs for God's existence, especially the proof contained in the fifth meditation. It certainly does not follow, Kant claimed, that something can be asserted to exist merely because it can be conceived.

Descartes acknowledged his critics through his friend and fellow mathematician Marin Mersenne, who sent copies of Descartes's manuscript to contemporary philosophers and theologians. When their criticisms were returned to him, Descartes in turn commented on them and published the entire discussion along with *Meditations on First Philosophy*.

In breaking with Scholasticism, a mode of philosophical thinking that had lasted for almost four hundred years, Descartes was a major influence on every philosopher who came after him. By making a clean sweep of the philosophical landscape and attempting to build it from the foundation up,

Cartesian philosophy raised many new difficulties and provoked a host of questions that have continued to challenge philosophers.

Raymond Frey

Further Reading

Chappell, Vere, ed. *Descartes's "Meditations": Critical Essays*. Lanham, Md.: Rowman & Littlefield, 1997. A collection of important essays by scholars who carefully assess the perspectives and problems in the *Meditations*, one of Western philosophy's most significant and far-reaching works.

Cottingham, John. *Descartes*. New York: Routledge, 1999. An excellent biographical introduction to the thoughts of the philosopher, clearly presented and requiring no special background. Includes a bibliography.

_____, ed. *The Cambridge Companion to Descartes*. New York: Cambridge University Press, 1999. A helpful collection of essays focusing on a variety of topics in Cartesian philosophy. Includes an essay on Scholastic philosophy as "intellectual background" to Descartes's thought.

Gaukroger, Stephen. *Descartes: An Intellectual Biography*. New York: Oxford University Press, 1995. A veteran interpreter of Descartes offers an important account of the philosopher's intellectual development and the times and places in which it took place.

_____, ed. *The Blackwell Guide to Descartes' "Meditations."* Malden, Mass. Blackwell, 2006. Collection of essays analyzing various aspects of Descartes's philosophy as expressed in the *Meditations*, including skepticism, the nature of the mind, the doctrine of substance, and seventeenth century responses to the *Meditations*.

Rorty, Amélie Oksenberg, ed. *Essays on Descartes' "Meditations."* Berkeley: University of California Press, 1986. Prominent philosophers, representing different perspectives, offer well-crafted studies of Descartes's best-known work. Part of the Major Thinkers series.

Rubin, Ronald. *Silencing the Demon's Advocate: The Strategy of Descartes' "Meditations."* Stanford, Calif.: Stanford University Press, 2008. Rubin interprets the *Meditations*, focusing on Descartes's thoughts on the cogito, mind and body, God's essence and existence, and the other ideas.

Strathern, Paul. *Descartes in Ninety Minutes*. Chicago: Ivan Dee, 1996. A quick but helpful introductory overview of key points in Cartesian philosophy.

Vinci, Thomas C. *Cartesian Truth*. New York: Oxford University Press, 1998. An evaluation of the strengths, weaknesses, and implications of Cartesian approaches to questions about knowledge and truth.

Williams, Bernard. *Descartes: The Project of Pure Enquiry*. 1978. Reprint. New York: Routledge, 2005. A detailed dissection of the careful structure of Descartes's significant philosophical arguments.

Yolton, John W. *Perception and Reality: A History from Descartes to Kant*. Ithaca, N.Y.: Cornell University Press, 1996. Yolton appraises the significance of Descartes's attempts to show how it is possible for human beings to obtain knowledge in spite of skepticism.

Mein Kampf

Author: Adolf Hitler (1889-1945)
First published: 1925, volume 1; 1926, volume 2
   (English translation, 1930)
Type of work: Politics, history, and autobiography

In 1924, Adolf Hitler dictated *Mein Kampf* ("my struggle") to political associates while he was serving a short prison term for having attempted to overthrow the regional government of Bavaria. The two-volume work constitutes a potpourri of autobiographical anecdotes and reflections about German history and politics. Hitler published the work with the goal of advancing his career and political agenda. Initially, he had planned to utilize the title "Four and a Half Years of Struggle Against Lies, Stupidity, and Cowardice," but his publisher, Max Amann, adopted the simpler title.

The first volume includes a combination of autobiographical anecdotes and reflections about the deplorable conditions in Germany and the establishment of the National Socialist German Workers Party (abbreviated the Nazi Party). Volume 2 goes into more detail about the party's ideology and domestic agenda. Produced hurriedly in a tone of anger and bitterness, both volumes are frequently repetitive, and almost all scholars agree that they are of limited literary or philosophical quality. Except for the author's historical significance, they would not be worthy of serious consideration.

Although *Mein Kampf* is only partly autobiographical, a large portion of the first volume is devoted to selective and impressionistic episodes from Hitler's life experiences. In summarizing his early years in northern Austria, he praises his father's character and patriotism, but he expresses strong resentment toward his father's attempts to convince him to pursue a career in the civil service. He writes that during his youth he became a "fanatical German Nationalist," enthusiastically singing the anthem, "Deutschland über Alles" (Germany above all) and despising the "conglomeration of races" in the Habsburg Empire. While living in the capital city of Vienna between 1907 and 1912, he spent much time observing the proceedings of the Austrian parliament, which he found appalling because of its chaotic "huckstering and bargaining" and the deputies' use of Slavic dialects. Having always spoken the German dialect of lower Bavaria, Hitler found it relatively easy before World War I to move to the Bavarian capital of Munich, where he succeeded in earning a modest living as an artist. This prewar period is described as "the happiest and by far the most contented" of his life.

Soon after the outbreak of World War I, Hitler obtained permission to join the Bavarian army. When accepted, he fell to his knees and "thanked heaven" for the opportunity to fight for the fatherland. Like countless other frontline soldiers, Hitler experienced Germany's surrender in 1918, which he dubbed "the November crime," as a traumatic shock. Attributing defeat to a "stab in the back," he believed that the guilty persons were a combination of pacifists, Marxists, Jews, and politicians. He despised this "whole gang of miserable party scoundrels and betrayers of the people," and observed that all of them were "ripe for hanging." Like the vast majority of Germans, he bitterly resented the harsh Treaty of Versailles (1919), which he characterized as "an act of highway robbery against our people."

Mein Kampf places a great deal of emphasis on Hitler's weltanschauung (worldview), which is defined as his "structure of personal thought or outlook on life." This worldview is based on militaristic values, focusing on the necessity and benefits of conflict and warfare. Hitler's experiences in the war reinforced and helped develop this value system. Directly or indirectly, moreover, his biases were reinforced by the philosophy of social Darwinism, which viewed human history from the evolutionary perspective of "survival of the fittest." In contrast to Marxist socialists, who believed that human history was based on struggle among social classes,

Hitler believed that human evolution was the result of struggle among competing races and that the most fundamental law of nature was that the most powerful humans are the only ones who have a right to survive. Time and again he emphasized that "those who do not want to fight in this world of eternal struggle do not deserve to live." Pacifists and others who disagreed with such a viewpoint were ridiculed as "dreamers" who ignored "reality."

Hitler asserts in *Mein Kampf* that humans are divided into genetically discrete races, and he asserted that racial conflict provides "the key not only to world history but to all human culture." Viewing races as equivalent to fundamentally different species, he draws a parallel with the animal world: "Each animal mates only with one of its own species. The titmouse cohabits only with the titmouse, the finch with the finch." Racial purity is of primary importance, because "blood mixture and the resultant drop in the racial level" has been the cause for the decline of nations and empires. Germany, therefore, must not follow the example of the French, whose social and colonial policies are likely "to remove all traces of French blood" and result in a primitive "Euro-African Mulatto State." Moreover, in Hitler's eyes, Aryans have been responsible for all achievements of high culture, and the primary reason has been their noble "instinct of self preservation, as manifested in their willingness to subordinate their individual egos in service to the community."

Declaring that Jews constitute a race and not a religion, Hitler refers to the Jewish race as a "noxious bacillus" that threatens Aryan purity, and he warns: "With satanic joy in his face the black haired Jewish youth lurks in wait for the unsuspecting girl whom he defiles with his blood, thus stealing her from her people." As proof that Jews are attempting to take over the world, he points to a document purported to be a secret Jewish plan to do just that: *Protocoly sionskikh mudretsov* (pb. c. 1903; *The Red Bible*, 1919; better known as *The Protocols of the Wise Men of Zion*, 1920). Observing that liberal newspapers have insisted that this document is a hoax, he simply answers that such allegations by the Jewish-controlled media constitute "the best proof" that it is authentic. Questionable logic of this kind occurs frequently in *Mein Kampf*.

Insisting that individuals must be willing to sacrifice their selfish interests for the benefit of a larger society, Hitler defines true idealism as "the subordination of the interests and life of the individual to the community." He applies this principle to a program of eugenics, which he sees as necessary for the development of a superior race. Because the most "humane act of mankind" is to prevent "defective" people "from propagating equally defective offspring," the state must take the necessary steps to prevent the continuing propagation of persons who have inherited diseases or physical defects. Hitler also makes it clear that he despises the practice of democracy and that he favors government in the hands of a firm, authoritarian leader (or *führer*), one man with wisdom, fortitude, and moral strength.

Hitler provides a number of hints about the foreign policies that he plans to pursue if he is able to take control of the German government. Comparing the size of German territory with those of Russia, China, and the United States, he makes no secret of his desire for a war of conquest. Observing that eighty million Germans are scattered throughout Europe, he envisions a united and prosperous nation of over three times that number within a century. The annexation (*anschluss*) of Austria to Greater Germany, he says, is "a task to which we should devote our lives." Openly declaring that additional living space (*lebensraum*) will be needed to accommodate population growth, he writes that the only real option is to annex portions of "Russia and her vassal border states." Adding that the goal of Germanization applies only to territory and not to teaching people to speak German, he writes that "nationality or rather race does not happen to lie in language but in the blood." Since he clearly asserts that the Slavic peoples of the east are genetically unacceptable, the implication is that they will have to be driven out of the conquered lands and replaced by persons of pure Germanic blood.

When *Mein Kampf* appeared, enough people bought copies to provide Hitler with a stable income. Most twenty-first century readers find it difficult to understand why the work became so popular and influential. In explaining its appeal, historians emphasize that the majority of Germans shared Hitler's anger and frustrations over the outcome of World War I, and the outbreak of the Great Depression in 1929 further increased the number of persons prepared to accept the book's message. In addition, its various themes—including nationalism, anti-Semitism, eugenics, and dissatisfaction with the government—appeared to be relatively widespread and to resonate with the political culture of the period.

Thomas Tandy Lewis

Further Reading

Barnes, James J., and Patience P. Barnes. *Hitler's "Mein Kampf" in Britain and America: A Publishing History, 1930-39.* New York: Cambridge University Press, 1980. In addition to translations and publishing, the two authors discuss the diverse reactions to Hitler's ideas in Britain and America.

Burk, Kenneth. "The Rhetoric of Hitler's Battle." *Philosophy of Literary Form.* 3d ed. Berkeley: University of California Press, 1973. First published in 1941, Burk's classic article emphasizes rhetorical devices, such as constant repetition of simple concepts, and observes that fear of a "common enemy" often unites people.

Burleigh, Michael. *The Third Reich: A New History.* New York: Hill & Wang, 2000. Includes a succinct analysis of *Mein Kampf* within its historical context, emphasizing Hitler's "new philosophy of life," including his ideas on race, social Darwinism, eugenics, and the values of warfare.

Carr, Robert. "*Mein Kampf*: The Text, Its Themes, and Hitler's Vision." *History Today* 57 (March, 2007): 30-35. A dependable summary, especially helpful for readers with limited historical background.

Dawidowicz, Lucy. *The War Against the Jews.* New York: Bantam Books, 1975. Emphasizes *Mein Kampf*'s virulent anti-Semitism; argues that the book reveals intentions to wage a war of aggression and eradicate Jews from German territory.

Evans, Richard J. *The Coming of the Third Reich.* New York: Penguin Press, 2004. Denies that *Mein Kampf* provided a blueprint for Hitler's later actions and calls it a "confused *mélange* of autobiographical reminiscences and garbled political declamations."

Jäckel, Eberhard. *Hitler's Weltanschauung: A Blueprint for Power.* Middletown, Conn.: Wesleyan University Press, 1972. A succinct work arguing that *Mein Kampf* expressed a coherent worldview that was consistent with Hitler's later racist and expansionist policies.

Maser, Werner. *Hitler's "Mein Kampf": An Analysis.* Translated by R. H. Barry. London: Faber, 1970. An eminent German historian's analysis of the book within its historical context.

Rash, Felicity. *The Language of Violence: Adolf Hitler's "Mein Kampf."* New York: Peter Lang, 2006. A linguistic analysis that emphasizes Hitler's rhetorical devices, particularly his use of conventional and well-worn metaphors. Provides references to other linguistic and rhetorical studies.

Melmoth the Wanderer

Author: Charles Robert Maturin (1780-1824)
First published: 1820
Type of work: Novel
Type of plot: Gothic
Time of plot: Early nineteenth century
Locale: Ireland

Principal characters:
JOHN MELMOTH, a young Irishman
MELMOTH THE WANDERER, young Melmoth's ill-starred ancestor
ALONZO MONCADA, a Spaniard shipwrecked in Ireland
YOUNG MELMOTH'S UNCLE

The Story:

In the autumn of 1816, John Melmoth, a student at Trinity College, Dublin, leaves his school to visit an uncle, his only surviving relative, who is dying. Melmoth's uncle is particularly glad to see his young nephew, for the old man is fearfully afraid of something that he has not revealed to anyone else. The uncle dies and leaves all of his money and property to the young Melmoth. A note at the end of the will tells Melmoth to destroy the hidden portrait of an earlier John Melmoth, a painting dated 1646, and also a packet of letters to be found in a secret drawer.

The day after his uncle's death, young Melmoth makes inquiries to learn whether his uncle had been a man of superstitious nature. He is told that the uncle was not superstitious, but that in recent months, he had insisted that a strange man had appeared and disappeared around the manor house.

Young Melmoth destroys the portrait as the will requested, but he opens the packet of manuscript, which contains a strange story about the man whose portrait he destroyed. The document tells how the original John Melmoth had been seen many times after his reported death in Germany and had been written of by an Englishman named Stanton, who had met Melmoth the Wanderer in Spain. The Wanderer, apparently angered by Stanton's curiosity, had prophesied that Stanton would be confined in Bedlam, although he is sane. The prediction having come true, the Wanderer appeared to Stanton in his misery and promised the miserable man his freedom if he would sell his soul to the devil. Stanton refused, and the Wanderer disappeared. Stanton wrote down his experiences and left the manuscript with the Melmoth family when he visited Ireland to discover more about the man who had tempted him.

After reading the manuscript, young Melmoth goes to bed. That night he also sees the Wanderer. His strange ancestor pays the young man a visit and, as proof of his appearance, leaves a bruise on young Melmoth's wrist. The next night, a ship is wrecked on the Irish coast not far from the Melmoth estate. When young Melmoth and his retainers leave to help rescue the sailors, Melmoth sees the Wanderer high on a rock overlooking the ruined ship and hears him laugh derisively. Young Melmoth tries to ascend the rock but falls into the sea, from which he is rescued by Alonzo Moncada, a Spaniard who had escaped from the doomed ship. Young Melmoth and the Spaniard return to the manor house. A few days later, the Spaniard discloses that he, too, knew the Wanderer.

Moncada tells young Melmoth a series of stories about the activities of the Wanderer in Spain. The first story is about the Spaniard himself, who is an exile from his country, although he is descended from a noble family. Moncada had been born out of wedlock and thus cannot inherit the ducal title of his ancestors. As a means of getting him out of the way so that his presence will not tarnish the proud name of his house, his family destined him for a monastery. Moncada does not want to be a monk, but his wishes in the matter are ignored by his family, including his own mother.

After a few years, Moncada's brother has a change of heart; he tries to secure the monk's release from his vows and thereby calls down the hatred of the Church upon both Alonzo and himself. Failing to secure a release legally, the brother then arranges for Moncada's escape. Monastery officials learn of the scheme, have the brother killed, and denounce Moncada to the Inquisition. While he lays in prison, Moncada is visited by Melmoth the Wanderer, who tempts him to secure release by selling his soul to Satan. Moncada refuses; he escapes later when the prison of the Inquisition burns.

Moncada finds refuge with an old Jewish doctor interested in the history of the Wanderer. From the doctor, Moncada learns the story of still another person whom the Wanderer has tempted. The doctor tells how Don Francisco di Aliaga, a Spanish nobleman, had lost his daughter in a shipwreck while she was still a baby. The child and her nurse, Moncada relates, were cast upon an unknown and uninhabited island. The nurse dies, but the baby grows up alone on the island to become a beautiful young woman. The Wanderer appears to her on several occasions, each time tempting her to sell her soul to Satan to gain knowledge of the world.

Strangely enough, the young woman and the Wanderer fall in love. She refuses to marry him, however, under any auspices but those of the Church.

Soon afterward, the young woman is found and returned to her family in Spain. There the Wanderer sees her again. Their love is still great and, unknown to anyone, they are married in a Satanic ceremony. Meanwhile, the Wanderer is conscience-stricken by fears that he will bring sorrow to the one he loves; he appears to Don Aliaga and warns him, by stories of the Wanderer's Satanic activities, of dangers surrounding the woman.

The Wanderer tells Don Aliaga of the temptation of a father whose children are starving, and of a young woman, during the reign of Charles II of England, who has been tempted to have the man she loves. In both cases, however, those tempted refused to pay the price of damnation in return for earthly happiness. Don Aliaga recognizes the meaning of these tales, but pressing business affairs keep him from acting at once.

When Don Aliaga finally returns to his home, he brings with him the young man he has selected to be his daughter's husband. Unknown to her father, however, the woman is about to give birth to a child by the Wanderer. When the Wanderer appears to claim her at a masked ball, her connection with the accursed guest is revealed, and she is turned over to the Inquisition. She dies shortly after giving birth to her child, and her dying words are the wish that she and the Wanderer will enter Heaven.

Such is the tale the Jewish doctor tells to Moncada, who is escaping from Spain when he is shipwrecked on the Irish coast. The tale ends, and the Wanderer suddenly appears in the room with them. He tells his horrified listeners that he has returned to his ancestral home to end his earthly wanderings. His fate had been to roam the earth for 150 years after his death under a terrible command to win souls for the devil. Everyone he had tempted, however, had refused to exchange earthly happiness for eternal damnation.

The Wanderer then asks that he be left alone to meet his destiny. A short time later, young Melmoth and the Spaniard hear strange voices and horrible noises in the room where they left the Wanderer. The next morning, the room is empty. The only sign of the Wanderer is a scarf caught on a bush at the place where he had plunged or had been thrown into the sea.

Critical Evaluation:

Charles Robert Maturin's novel has been called by many literary scholars the greatest of the novels of terror that were so popular in English fiction during the early years of the

nineteenth century. Other writers have admired and have been influenced by *Melmoth the Wanderer*, partly because of the striking qualities of the plot and partly because of the theme of the never-ending life that it describes. Among the admirers of the novel were Edgar Allan Poe, Dante Gabriel Rossetti, and Charles Baudelaire. Oscar Wilde, after being disgraced in the 1890's, took for himself the name of Sebastian Melmoth, which combined the idea of the wanderer with that of the arrow-pierced saint.

Maturin said in the book's preface that he was ashamed of appearing as a novelist, but that his profession as a clergyman did not pay him enough to avoid such shameful activities as writing novels. Although Maturin lamented the fact that he was forced to write *Melmoth the Wanderer* out of economic necessity (he was out of favor with the Church hierarchy, deeply in debt, and the sole support of eleven people), it will be a mistake to regard *Melmoth the Wanderer* simply as a potboiler written only for money. Even in the "unseemly character as a writer of romances," Maturin remained the preacher, and this novel stands as a profound social, moral, and religious statement—perhaps even a fictionalized sermon.

Structurally, it is the most complex of the important gothic novels. It is actually a series of stories set one into another like a nest of Chinese boxes. In the frame story, young John Melmoth visits his dying uncle and inherits, among other things, a vague story about a demoniac ancestor, also named John Melmoth; a picture of the man; and a manuscript, "The Tale of Stanton," which is the first of the novel's stories. Then he takes in a shipwrecked Spaniard, Alonzo Moncada, who tells his story, "The Tale of the Spaniard," in the center of which "The Tale of the Parricide" occurs. After recounting his own story, Moncada then retells "The Tale of the Indians," a story given to him for translation by an old Jew. Two additional narratives, "The Tale of Guzman's Family" and "The Tale of the Lover" are inserted within "The Tale of the Indians." These finished, Melmoth himself then returns to conclude the novel by paying his debt to the power of darkness.

Although different in substance, each narrative contains similar thematic elements; each tale, except "The Tale of the Parricide," climaxes at the point at which Melmoth intrudes upon the suffering victim and makes his diabolical offer. Maturin presents an elaborate theme and variation structure that continually develops and reinforces his ideas while tantalizing the reader with new and different shocks, torments, and sensations. The brooding presence of Melmoth is always in the background, moving in and out of the narratives; his story and fate are revealed in bits and pieces as the novel progresses.

The overriding thematic motif of the novel concerns the ways in which one's greatest natural inclinations—to worship God and to love—are perverted and distorted by individual weaknesses and institutional corruption. Several other notions reinforce these major ideas: the effects of an unchecked thirst for knowledge, the nature of madness and its relationship to fanaticism, the saving power of love, the family as a moral unit, the line between love and hate, human isolation and alienation, and the relationship between money and happiness.

In "The Tale of Stanton," Maturin introduces a number of these themes. Stanton is made vulnerable to Melmoth's appeal because he, too, has an insatiable curiosity about the forbidden. Fortunately for his soul, he rejects this side of himself when put to the test. As a result of his erratic behavior, Stanton also is made the victim of a familial betrayal when an unscrupulous relative has him committed to Bedlam—the first in a series of such betrayals. All of the stories involve either the destructive cruelties present in a bad family or the positive strengths of a good one.

In the madhouse scenes, Maturin begins his exploration of the moral and psychological nature of insanity that continues throughout the book. Although some of the inmates of the asylum are pure victims, most are fanatics who have simply pushed their religious or political proclivities to their logical conclusions. Maturin shows little sympathy for such madmen, although he recognizes that they differ from the rest of society only in being socially inconvenient; when madness is brought into socially acceptable institutions, Maturin suggests, it becomes not only tolerable but also dominant.

Maturin's analysis of the perversion of the religious impulse and the corruption of institutionalized religion—especially Roman Catholicism in Spain—is developed most completely in "The Tale of the Spaniard." Although anti-Catholicism, especially antimonasticism, had been a staple element of the gothic novel since Matthew Lewis's *The Monk* (1796), Maturin's treatment of the subject is probably the most intense and convincing, because he concentrates on the psychological damage of such institutional confinement rather than the more lurid and sensational accounts rendered by his contemporaries.

Under the rigid, arbitrary, artificial authority of such a life, all natural human capacities are stifled, the firmest faith is dissipated, the kindliest nature is thwarted, and the keenest intellect is stultified. The endlessly repetitive and absurd routine creates an ennui that is poisonous. Petty spite, gossip, and cruelty become the way of life. The smallest infractions of the silliest rules are treated as major crimes, and any person who exhibits the slightest trace of individualism becomes the monastery scapegoat.

The most blatant example of this institutional corruption can be seen in the parricide who is taken into the monastery in spite of, or because of, his criminal nature, and who works out his salvation by instigating the damnation of others. As a parricide, he represents the ultimate betrayal of the familial relationship; because, unlike Melmoth, he enjoys his deeds, he is the most extreme example of human evil. His sadism is the inevitable product of the social system he represents.

The extent of his diabolism and the most gothic scene in the novel is seen in the climax to his story. As he and Moncada wait huddled in the underground tunnel, he gleefully tells how he lured an errant couple into the same subterranean vault, nailed them in, and listened as, without food or water, their love turned to hate.

> It was on the fourth night that I heard the shriek of the wretched female—her lover, in the agony of hunger, had fastened his teeth in her shoulder—that bosom on which he had so often luxuriated, became a meal to him now.

Nowhere is Maturin's theme of the perversion of the natural into the destructive presented with more gruesome clarity.

Although some of the individual scenes may be impressive, it is the central character of Melmoth that makes the novel memorable. He is, in many ways, the supreme gothic hero-villain. Melmoth is damned but, like Faustus, his damnation is not the product of an evil nature but of a questing spirit that simply cannot accept human limitations.

In "The Tale of the Indians," Melmoth's character is most clearly presented. The last two stories in the novel, "The Tale of Guzman's Family" and "The Tale of the Lover," add little to Melmoth's saga and are the least gothic, most sentimental, and dramatically weakest in the book. In "The Tale of the Indians," however, Melmoth himself assumes an active role and reveals truly human emotions. It is in this love affair between Melmoth and the native girl, Immalee, which resembles Goethe's "Faust-Margaret" story, that Melmoth's fate is actually decided: only the power of innocent love can save him from his chosen damnation—if he has the strength to accept it.

Since Immalee has grown up in an idyllic state of nature, she is ignorant of society's corrupting influences. It is Melmoth who introduces her to human decadence, although he is ambivalent in his feelings toward her from the beginning. He is reluctant to tempt her consciously, and his teachings are more of a response to her eagerness than an attempt to ensnare her. For her part, Immalee's spontaneous love for him causes her to desire further information about his world, even though this new knowledge proves painful. Therefore, Melmoth becomes the tormented lover as well as the Satanic tempter. He will love her, but he fears that such love will damn her also. So he alternately woos her and thrusts her away; he entices her and warns her against himself. In the end, he succumbs to his role as tempter, but not before he has struggled desperately with a soul that he no longer believes he possesses. When Melmoth makes his awful proposal to her, he is damned; because Immalee refuses, she is saved.

The central irony is that her love could have saved them both. There is no bargain with the devil that cannot be abrogated by love. Melmoth's damnation comes, finally, not from his formal contract with Satan but from his disbelief in the power of the human spirit. Accepting the corruption he describes as the whole truth, he does not see the evidences of human worth around him: the love exhibited by the Walbergs in "The Tale of Guzman's Family," by Elinor Mortimer in "The Tale of the Lover," and most of all, by Immalee.

As a result of his embracing evil, Melmoth's condemnation is inevitable; but, because of his lost potential, it is tragic. Therefore, for all the sensationalism and crudity characteristic of the gothic novel, it contains the elements of classical tragedy. No writer of gothic romances came closer to realizing that possibility than Maturin in *Melmoth the Wanderer*.

Keith Neilson

Further Reading

Coughlan, Patricia. "The Recycling of *Melmoth*: A Very German Story." In *Literary Interrelations: Ireland, England, and the World*, edited by Wolfgang Zach and Heinz Kosok. Vol. 2. Tübingen, Germany: Narr, 1987. Demonstrates the imaginative impact of *Melmoth the Wanderer* on contemporary authors. Versions of the story by Honoré de Balzac and James Clarence Mangan are given a detailed analysis. Highlights some of the novel's social and political implications.

Fowler, Kathleen. "Hieroglyphics in Fire: *Melmoth the Wanderer*." *Studies in Romanticism* 25, no. 4 (Winter, 1986): 521-539. Focuses on the novel's artistic methods and the relation between these methods and the novel's religious preoccupations. Discusses the use of the book of Job in the novel.

Johnson, Anthony. "Gaps and Gothic Sensibility: Walpole, Lewis, Mary Shelley, and Maturin." In *Exhibited by Candlelight: Sources and Developments in the Gothic Tradition*, edited by Valeria Tinkler-Villani, Peter Davidson, and Jane Stevenson. New York: Rodopi, 1995. This study of gothic literature includes Johnson's learned and clear discussion of how Maturin handles the gaps in reality that are exploited in gothic fiction.

Kiely, Robert. *The Romantic Novel in England*. Cambridge, Mass.: Harvard University Press, 1979. A significant contribution to the study of the romantic novel. Includes a chapter on *Melmoth the Wanderer*, emphasizing its religious and political elements. The novel's psychological interest and cultural implications also are assessed.

Kramer, Dale. *Charles Robert Maturin*. New York: Twayne, 1973. Succinct account of Maturin's life and career, and an extended consideration of *Melmoth the Wanderer*. Discusses the novel's folkloric dimension and the organizational principles governing the cohesiveness of the various tales.

Moynahan, Julian. "The Politics of Anglo-Irish Gothic: Charles Robert Maturin, Joseph Sheridan Le Fanu, and the Return of the Repressed." In *Anglo-Irish: The Literary Imagination in a Hyphenated Culture*. Princeton, N.J.: Princeton University Press, 1995. Moynahan's analysis of gothic literature by the two authors is included in his study of literary works written by Anglo-Irish authors during the nineteenth century.

Norton, Rictor, ed. *Gothic Readings: The First Wave, 1764-1840*. London: Leicester University Press, 2000. This study of gothic literature includes an excerpt from *Melmoth the Wanderer*, which is defined as belonging to "the German school of horror," and two contemporary reviews of the novel, including one by Sir Walter Scott. Useful for placing Maturin within the larger context of the gothic and Romantic novel.

The Member of the Wedding

Author: Carson McCullers (1917-1967)
First published: 1946
Type of work: Novel
Type of plot: Impressionistic realism
Time of plot: 1945
Locale: Georgia

Principal characters:
BERENICE SADIE BROWN, the black cook in the Addams household
FRANKIE ADDAMS, a twelve-year-old girl
MR. ADDAMS, her father
JARVIS, her brother and a U.S. Army corporal
JOHN HENRY WEST, her cousin
JANICE EVANS, Jarvis's fiancé
HONEY CAMDEN BROWN, Berenice's foster brother
A SOLDIER

The Story:

In the summer of her twelfth year, Frankie Addams feels isolated and disconnected. She is a lanky girl with a crew haircut and skinned elbows. Some of the older girls she has played with the year before have a neighborhood club, and there are parties with boys on Saturday nights, but Frankie is not a participant. That summer, she gets herself into so much trouble that at last she just stays home with John Henry West, her little cousin, and Berenice Sadie Brown, the Addams's cook. Through long, hot afternoons, they sit in the dingy, sad Addams kitchen and play cards or talk until their words sound strange, with little meaning.

Berenice Sadie Brown is short and black and the only mother Frankie has ever known, her own mother having died when she was born. The cook has been married four times, and during one of her marriages, she lost an eye while fighting with a worthless husband. Now she owns a blue glass eye that always interests John Henry West. He is six years old and wears gold-rimmed glasses. Sometimes Frankie grows tired of him and sends him home. Sometimes she begs him to stay all night. Everything seems so mixed up that she seldom knows what she wants.

Then, on the last Friday in August, something happens that makes life wonderful once more. Frankie's brother, Jarvis, a soldier home from Alaska, has come to dinner with Janice Evans, a girl who lives at Winter Hill. They are to be married there on Sunday, and Frankie and her father are going to the wedding. After dinner, Janice and Jarvis return to Winter Hill. Mr. Addams goes downtown to his jewelry store. Later, while she sits playing cards with Berenice and John Henry, Frankie thinks of her brother and his bride. Winter Hill becomes all mixed up in her mind with snow and icy glaciers in Alaska.

Jarvis and Janice bring Frankie a doll, but she has no time for dolls anymore. John Henry could have it. She wishes her hair were not so short; she looks like one of the freaks from the Chattahoochee Exposition. Suddenly angry, she chases John Henry home. When Berenice teases her, saying that Frankie is jealous of the wedding, Frankie declares that she is going to Winter Hill and never coming back. For a minute, she wants to throw a kitchen knife at the black cook. Instead, she hurls it at the stairway door. Berenice goes out with Honey Camden Brown, her foster brother, and T. T. Williams, her beau. Honey is not quite right in the head, and Berenice is always trying to keep him out of trouble. T. T. owns a black restaurant. Frankie does not realize that the cook's pity for the unhappy, motherless girl keeps her from marrying T. T.

Left alone, Frankie wanders around the block to the house where John Henry lives with Aunt Pet and Uncle Eustace. Somewhere close by, a horn begins to play a blues tune. Frankie feels so sad and lonely that she wants to do something she has never done before. She thinks again of Jarvis and Janice. She is going to be a member of the wedding; after the ceremony, the three of them will go away together. She is not plain Frankie Addams any longer. She will call herself F. Jasmine Addams, and she will never feel lonely or afraid again.

The next morning, with Mr. Addams's grunted permission, Frankie goes downtown to buy a new dress and shoes. On the way, she finds herself telling everyone she meets about the wedding. That is how she happens to go into the Blue Moon, a cheap café where she knows children are not allowed. F. Jasmine Addams, however, is no longer a child, and so she goes in to tell the Portuguese proprietor about the wedding. The only other person in the café is a red-headed soldier from a nearby U.S. Army post. Frankie scarcely notices him at the time, but she remembers him later when she sees him on the street. By that time, he is drunk and trying to buy an organ-grinder's monkey. The soldier buys Frankie a beer and asks her to meet him that night at the Blue Moon.

When Frankie finally arrives home, she learns that Berenice and John Henry are also to attend the wedding. An aged kinsman of the Wests has died, and Aunt Pet and Uncle Eustace are going to the funeral at Opelika. Berenice, dismayed when she sees the orange silk evening dress, the silver hair ribbon, and the silver slippers Frankie bought to wear at the wedding, tries, without much success, to alter the dress for the gawky young girl. Afterward, they begin to talk about the dead people they had known. Berenice tells about Ludie Freeman, the first husband she truly loved. The story of Ludie and the three other husbands make them all feel lonesome and sad. Berenice holds the two children on her knees as she tries to explain to them the simple wisdom life had taught her. They begin to sing spirituals in the half-dark of the dingy kitchen.

Frankie does meet the soldier that night. First, she goes with John Henry to Big Mama's house and has her palm read. Afterward, she tells John Henry to go home; she does not want him to know she is meeting someone at the Blue Moon. The soldier buys two drinks, but Frankie is afraid to taste hers. He asks her to go up to his room. Frightened when he tries to pull her down beside him on the bed, she picks up a glass pitcher and hits him over the head. Then she climbs down the fire escape and runs home. She is glad to get into bed with no one but John Henry by her side.

The wedding day turns into a nightmare for Frankie. Everything is lovely until the time comes for the bride and groom to leave. When they carry their bags to the car, she runs to get her own suitcase. Then they tell her, as kindly as possible, that they are going away alone. She grasps the steering wheel and weeps until someone drags her away. Riding home on the bus, she cries all the way. Berenice promises her a bridge party with grown-up refreshments as soon as school opens, but Frankie knows that she will never be happy again. That night, she tries to run away. Not knowing where else to go, she goes to the Blue Moon. A police officer finds her there and sends for her father.

By November, however, Frankie has almost forgotten the wedding. Other things have happened. John Henry died of meningitis. Honey Camden Brown, drug-crazed, had tried to hold up a drugstore and is now in jail. Mary Littlejohn became her best, real friend. She and her father were leaving the old house and going to live with Aunt Pet and Uncle Eustace in a new suburb. Berenice, waiting to see the last of the furniture taken away, is sad, for she knows that Frankie will depend on her no longer. Frankie—she wants to be called Frances—is now thirteen years old.

Critical Evaluation:

All of Carson McCullers's fiction turns on the theme of loneliness and longing as the inescapable condition of humanity. In *The Member of the Wedding*, the issues of the larger world are reflected in the experiences of the twelve-year-old girl trapped in the confusion of her own adolescence. The novel tells the story of several decisive days in the life of Frankie Addams, and much of the meaning of her plight is made clear in her random talk with Berenice Sadie Brown and John Henry West as the three sit around the table in the kitchen of the Addams house. Frankie seizes upon her soldier brother's approaching wedding to will herself into the social community, only to discover that the bride and groom must by necessity reject her and that she must learn to fend for herself.

In the story of Frankie, the writer has reduced the total idea of moral isolation to a fable of simple outlines and a few eloquently dramatic scenes, set against a background of adolescent mood and discovery familiar to everyone. It is easy enough to understand why this novel has also been a success in dramatic form. The play of the same name, written by McCullers, is a sympathetic study of inward conflicts. It received two Donaldson Awards and the New York Drama Critics Circle Award in 1950.

Throughout her career as a novelist, short-story writer, and playwright, McCullers explored the human condition from several perspectives, but all with the common focus of loneliness and dissatisfaction. *The Heart Is a Lonely Hunter* (1940) reveals the isolation of a "deaf-mute" in a southern town, and it draws parallels to the phenomenon of fascism. *Reflections in a Golden Eye* (1941) also takes place in the South, but *The Member of the Wedding* explores anxieties in finer detail. *The Ballad of the Sad Café, and Collected Short Stories* (1952) includes the famous novella of the title, which was dramatized by Edward Albee in 1963, twenty years after it was first published. McCullers's last two works were *The Square Root of Wonderful* (1957), a play, and *Clock Without Hands* (1961), a novel. McCullers's unpublished works, including some early poetry, appeared posthumously in 1971 under the title *The Mortgaged Heart*.

Although *The Member of the Wedding* certainly deals with themes of loneliness and dissatisfaction, the story is quite interesting as a discussion of the means through which a particular individual attempts to escape these isolating emotions. This psychological novel is enhanced by McCullers's masterful handling of language and point of view. Although the narrative is not in the first person, the language makes it clear that Frankie's viewpoint is of primary concern. The result is that one is able both to observe Frankie objectively and at the same time to appreciate her emotions immediately. Frankie's feelings are, in addition, juxtaposed with the intrusion of adult observation (most often from Berenice and Mr. Addams) so that the reader has a realistic synthesis of information. The structural result is triangular. The adult view cannot comprehend the adolescent because it has grown beyond that stage. The adolescent view, in turn, cannot yet encompass the adult. The reader completes the triangle, gaining the adolescent view through Frankie, and adding the adult view through appreciating the irony of Frankie's observations of adults.

Frankie, Berenice, and John Henry, despite apparent enmities, form a tribunal, sharing experiences and opinions and evaluating them both literally and symbolically, and each is essential in his or her role in the tribunal. Frankie, literally, is the causing factor of the group's existence: Berenice is hired to care for her, and John Henry is present because Frankie wants juvenile companionship to counter that of Berenice. Although she realizes that she is not yet capable of understanding the activities of the adult world, however, Frankie, aided by John Henry, symbolizes the almost divine nature often assigned to the child. Frankie knows certain truths, as Berenice occasionally confirms in bewilderment, because the girl's mind has not yet been spoiled by the mundane concerns that obscure those truths. Her almost innate, although selective, knowledge is part of a literary and philosophical ideology most clearly typified by the Wordsworthian view of children. Yet Frankie's strongest understanding is also the most ironic: She realizes that she is incomplete and is terrified by reminders of that fact. In her earnest efforts to belong, to be completed, she is driving herself toward adulthood, in which one loses the innate knowledge she possesses.

Berenice, one of McCullers's most interesting characters, serves multiple functions. Just as she is employed to care for Frankie in many ways, she is also the pivotal character upon whom the novel depends on several levels of development. In simple terms, she is a counterexample of Frankie's search to belong and to love. Although McCullers's familiar theme of such unending search persists in Berenice, she illustrates that love, even when directed toward a vague objective, has the eventual effect of grace. In addition, she is a surrogate mother upon whom Frankie depends, made more credible by being representative of the black parent figure of many southern novels. Frankie is locked into dependence upon Berenice, but it is dependence from a distance; although she longs to be independent of Berenice and all other authority figures, Frankie knows intuitively that she is not old enough to ignore Berenice. She knows the woman has a function in her life, has necessary information to which she has not yet been exposed. She does not want to block Berenice out entirely (while the servant speaks to her, Frankie puts her fingers in her ears, but not enough to prevent Berenice's voice from reaching her) since if Frankie did so she would have to confront life later as an adult without sufficient data.

Frankie knows instinctively that ignoring Berenice is only self-defeating. Berenice is, therefore, like an oracle; and she comes from the ancient literary tradition of the blind or one-eyed person who speaks the truth clearly because of missing vision. Berenice has a glass eye ("glass" and "truth" are related etymologically in Latin); so Berenice sees truth through her glass eye, not through her physically functioning one. McCullers is thus able to elevate the group in the kitchen to mythic dimensions: Berenice is the oracle, John Henry is her acolyte, and Frankie is the pilgrim-initiate.

By emphasizing Frankie's progressive learning and by concentrating primarily on the emotions and experiences of only three days in Frankie's life, McCullers achieves the effect of gradually increasing the reader's expectations. By the end of *The Member of the Wedding*, the reader has been led to believe that the day before the wedding is Frankie's "last afternoon" in town—if not literally, then at least figuratively. This increasing momentum, however, is not followed by a fulfillment of expectation; Frankie is essentially unchanged by the trauma of disappointment. It is suddenly apparent that the initiation of youth into adulthood through artificial, specific rites is a myth. The search for belonging is an unending one; it is simply one's orientation toward that search that can change by the natural process of maturing. In fact, as Berenice's life illustrates, the childlike element of selectively believing in salvation can be concomitantly protective, making both life and the search for social identity not only possible but also bearable.

"Critical Evaluation" by Bonnie Fraser

Further Reading

Bloom, Harold, ed. *Carson McCullers*. New York: Chelsea House, 1986. Barbara A. White's essay "Loss of Self in *The Member of the Wedding*" interprets Frankie as a tomboy neither wanting to remain a child nor to become a young woman. An excellent source for discussion of the novella.

Carr, Virginia Spencer. *Understanding Carson McCullers*. 1990. New ed. Columbia: University of South Carolina Press, 2005. A thoughtful guide to McCullers's works, with separate chapters analyzing *The Member of the Wedding*, *The Heart Is a Lonely Hunter*, *Reflections in a Golden Eye*, and *The Ballad of the Sad Café*. This edition of the book includes post-1990 scholarship about Mc-Cullers.

Clark, Beverly Lyon, and Melvin J. Friedman, eds. *Critical Essays on Carson McCullers*. New York: G. K. Hall, 1996. A collection of essays ranging from reviews of McCullers's major works to tributes by such writers as Tennessee Williams and Kay Boyle and to critical analyses from a variety of perspectives.

Cook, Richard M. *Carson McCullers*. New York: Frederick Ungar, 1975. A biography containing a twenty-two-page chapter on *The Member of the Wedding*, along with a helpful chronology and index. Defends McCullers's concerns with human isolation and loneliness.

Gleeson-White, Sarah. *Strange Bodies: Gender and Identity in the Novels of Carson McCullers*. Tuscaloosa: University of Alabama Press, 2003. Gleeson-White analyzes McCullers's major novels, including *The Member of the Wedding*, examining how their "grotesque" depictions of gender roles and sexuality provide the possibility of freedom and redemption for her characters.

Graver, Lawrence. *Carson McCullers*. Minneapolis: University of Minnesota Press, 1969. Helpfully condensed discussion of the author's life and work. Views *The Member of the Wedding* as a journey of adolescent initiation, combining early dissatisfaction with jubilant hope and disillusionment with wisdom about life's limits.

Jenkins, McKay. *The South in Black and White: Race, Sex, and Literature in the 1940's*. Chapel Hill: University of North Carolina Press, 1999. Covers McCullers along with several other writers in a consideration of the role of race and sex in southern literature.

McCullers, Carson. *The Mortgaged Heart*. Edited by Margarita G. Smith. Boston: Houghton Mifflin, 1971. This collection of short stories and personal essays by McCullers is an important primary source about her life and her motives and practices in writing.

McDowell, Margaret B. *Carson McCullers*. Boston: Twayne, 1980. Insightful discussion of *The Member of the Wedding* that stresses the novelist's thematic concerns with time as it relates to life's stages, and isolation and the fear of independence applied to the novella's three major characters.

Savigneau, Josyane. *Carson McCullers: A Life*. Translated by Joan E. Howard. Boston: Houghton Mifflin, 2001. The McCullers estate granted Savigneau access to McCullers's unpublished papers, enabling her to obtain new, revealing details about her subject's life.

Westling, Louise. *Sacred Groves and Ravaged Gardens: The Fiction of Eudora Welty, Carson McCullers, and Flannery O'Connor*. Athens: University of Georgia Press, 1985. In this study, important comparisons are made between these three major southern writers. While Westling is not the first to use a feminist approach with McCullers, the book offers useful insight concerning the portrayal of the female characters and the issue of androgyny in McCullers's fiction. Includes useful endnotes and a bibliography.

Whitt, Jan, ed. *Reflections in a Critical Eye: Essays on Carson McCullers*. Lanham, Md.: University Press of America, 2008. A collection of critical essays on McCullers, including "The Daughter as Outlaw in *The Heart Is a Lonely Hunter* and *The Member of the Wedding*," and discussions of lesbian desire in her novels.

Memed, My Hawk

Author: Yashar Kemal (1923-   )
First published: *İnce Memed*, 1955 (English translation, 1961)
Type of work: Novel
Type of plot: Folklore
Time of plot: Early twentieth century
Locale: Turkey

Principal characters:
SLIM MEMED, a brigand
ABDI AGHA, a cruel landowner
JABBAR, Memed's comrade
LAME ALI, a skillful tracker
HATCHE, Memed's fiancé
IRAZ, Hatche's cell mate
SERGEANT ASIM, the police chief

The Story:

In a village called Deyirmenoluk, located in the Taurus Mountains of Turkey, Slim Memed and his mother, Deuneh, live at the mercy of their cruel landlord, Abdi Agha, who terrizes them and takes two-thirds of their crops annually. Unable to endure the *agha*'s beatings, Memed flees from his village, escaping over the mountains to the ranch of Old

Süleyman. For several weeks, he lives as Süleyman's adopted son, herding goats and enjoying himself. One day, however, he drives the goats too far and encounters a man from his village. News soon spreads that Memed is alive, and Abdi Agha goes to Süleyman's ranch and forces the boy to return. As punishment for Memed's disobedience, his family has to forfeit three-fourths of their crops, and they nearly starve that winter.

Several years pass, and the oppression continues. As he matures into manhood, Memed grows bitter and callous under the *agha*'s reign of terror. Only fifteen-year-old Hatche, the most beautiful girl in the village, can inspire tenderness in the young man. Soon after Abdi Agha announces the girl's engagement to his nephew, Memed and Hatche elope. They make love in the hollow of a rock during a rainstorm.

Furious at Memed's disobedience, the *agha* enlists Lame Ali, a skillful tracker, to find the couple. In a violent encounter in the forest, Memed wounds Abdi Agha and kills his nephew, then flees from the scene. Hatche returns to the village, only to be arrested by the authorities for the nephew's murder. She is taken to the nearest town and imprisoned.

Memed makes his way to Süleyman's ranch, where he receives a warm welcome from his old friend. Advised by Süleyman to hide in the mountains, Memed joins Mad Durdu's band of mountain brigands. Durdu is notorious for stopping travelers on the road, ordering them to strip naked, and stealing their money and underclothing. Although Memed does not approve of these tactics, he obeys his leader. As Durdu grows more reckless, however, Memed begins to worry. In one bloody exchange with the police, several of Durdu's men are killed or wounded, and Memed barely escapes. When Durdu later tries to rob Kerimoghlu, the proud leader of a group of nomads, Memed intervenes, and Durdu vows to avenge the insult.

Accompanied by two comrades, Jabbar and Sergeant Rejep, Memed embarks upon a career as an independent brigand, but he does not have the heart to rob groveling travelers. He decides to return to Deyirmenoluk and punish Abdi Agha. From his mother's friend in the village, Memed learns that the *agha* has killed his mother and arranged for Hatche's imprisonment. Memed and his comrades storm the *agha*'s house but find only the *agha*'s two wives and children at home. Sergeant Rejep kills one of the wives and is going to kill the children, but Memed stops him, preferring to exact revenge on Abdi Agha himself. By sparing the children's lives, Memed earns the respect of the villagers.

Memed then summons Lame Ali and orders him to track down Abdi Agha, who went into hiding after he learned that Memed had become a brigand. Feeling guilty for betraying Memed and Hatche, Lame Ali leads Memed and his comrades to Abdi Agha's hiding place in a distant village. In an attempt to burn the *agha* out of his hiding place, the three brigands set fire to the entire village, destroying it. The villagers pursue them into the mountains, where Sergeant Rejep dies from a neck wound that he had received earlier. After returning to Deyirmenoluk to resume his life, Memed learns that Abdi Agha is still alive. He and Jabbar return to the mountains for their safety.

In the village of Vayvay, Abdi Agha has sought refuge with another powerful *agha*, Ali Safa Bey, who controls a band of mountain brigands led by Kalayji. Ali Safa has promised to use Kalayji to destroy Memed. Kalayji sends Horali, who had been a member of Durdu's gang, to lead the unsuspecting Memed into a trap. Discerning the ploy, however, Memed and Jabbar kill Horali and Kalayji. Across the countryside the news spreads that Memed has defeated Ali Safa's man. In the countless retellings of the feat, Memed grows larger than life, until he is a legend. Big Osman from Vayvay starts referring to Memed as "my hawk." He collects a large sum of money from his fellow villagers, who are tired of being oppressed by Ali Safa, and delivers it to Memed and Jabbar on their mountaintop.

Jabbar and Memed part company when Memed decides to visit Hatche in prison. Later, as the police are transporting Hatche to another prison, Memed ambushes them and single-handedly frees his fiancé and her friend Iraz. The three fugitives retreat to a cave on top of Mount Alidagh, where they receive supplies periodically from Lame Ali and Kerimoghlu. At Abdi Agha's prodding, the government sends a former brigand, Black Ibrahim, and a police officer, Sergeant Asim, to arrest Memed. During a shootout on Alidagh, Hatche gives birth to a son; Memed then surrenders to Sergeant Asim, who takes pity on the new father and allows him to escape.

Abdi Agha is furious and frightened. He writes letters to the government, which then sends Captain Faruk after Memed. In yet another shootout, Faruk kills Hatche. Memed, who manages to escape, leaves his son with Iraz and ensures Hatche's proper burial. He then finds Lame Ali and learns about Abdi Agha's hiding place. Despite a general amnesty granted to criminals by the Turkish government, Memed goes to the town where Abdi Agha is hiding and kills him. A fugitive once more, Memed returns to the mountains, never to be seen again.

Critical Evaluation:

Memed, My Hawk, a translation of the first part of *İnce Memed* (which means "Slim" or "Thin" Memed), is important as one of the few Turkish novels to attract attention in Europe and the United States. In this folktale, Yashar Kemal depicts a lowborn man with compassion and respect. His protagonist, Memed, a larger-than-life folk hero, has been likened to Robin Hood because he steals from the rich and gives to the poor. Like a majestic hawk, Memed swoops down on the cruel *aghas* (lords), frustrating their greed. He is able to evade capture because he has the support of the village people. Unlike the other brigands, who rob and humiliate indiscriminately, Memed punishes selectively, never forgetting his roots in the village.

Kemal's novel often reads like a courtesy book for brigands. Through example and contrast, and sometimes even dialogue, the reader is shown the proper way to resist institutionalized corruption and oppression. One should not follow the example of the brigand Durdu, who terrorizes not only government officials and powerful landowners but also farmers, women, and children. He robs his victims of their honor as well as their purses, sending men home naked to their families and kidnapping and raping village women. Kalayji, another brigand, sells himself as a hired gun to a wealthy *agha*, in effect becoming an instrument of oppression. Memed, in contrast, engages in moral terrorism, never robbing for fun or mere profit, always championing the rights of the poor.

The close association between the people and the land is an important theme in *Memed, My Hawk*. Most of the characters are tenant farmers whose survival depends on the fickle weather, the quality of the land, and the caprices of the landowners. The farmers are slaves to the *aghas* who own the land. Only by owning the land can the farmers free themselves. Freedom, then, is integrally related to property. Early in the novel, the author proclaims that people, like trees, require rich soil in which to grow strong and tall. The Taurus Mountains consist of dry, rocky soil, covered with thistles, and yield only stunted trees with gnarled branches. The same can be said of Memed, whose growth has been stunted by his meager diet, the constant toil of plowing, and the *agha's* physical abuse. Only in rebellion against Abdi Agha does he grow "as tall as a poplar." The harsh terrain of the Taurus Mountains symbolizes the *agha's* oppressive rule over the villagers. It is significant that when the *agha* dies, the villagers take his property and burn the thistles to make the land more suitable for cultivation.

Western readers may have difficulty understanding the behaviors and motivations of the characters in *Memed, My Hawk*, who are products of a different culture. In many Western societies, premarital sex is less uncommon than it is in Turkish society, particularly Turkish rural communities.

When Hatche runs away with Memed and yields to him sexually in the woods, her behavior is atypical and extremely courageous, indicating that she must love Memed very much. The concepts of honor and hospitality are also different in Turkey. By forcing his male victims to give him their underpants and sending them home naked, Durdu is not merely embarrassing them but also impinging upon their honor. It is for this reason that the nomad leader, Kerimoghlu, refuses to strip in front of his family, although he knows that Durdu may kill him. Throughout the novel, Memed encounters strangers who welcome him as if he were a family member. They offer him food and a place to sleep, and they become offended if he declines their hospitality. This behavior may be alien to readers who are not accustomed to being treated so warmly by strangers or who are unfamiliar with the role that food plays in Turkish hospitality.

Other cultural differences may prevent Western readers from appreciating the narrator's irony and various nuances in meaning. For example, when Kalayji kills his cousin Bekir during his wedding celebration, "the bride's hands were red with henna, the marriage not yet consummated." It is customary in Turkey for the bride to paint her hands red with henna before her marriage as a sign of her happiness. In this context, however, the red hands ironically become associated with her husband's blood and the tragedy of his death. Later, the old woman Hürü dyes her hair red with henna in celebration of the *agha's* death. This, too, is ironic.

Edward A. Malone

Further Reading

Darnton, John. "Istanbul Journal: A Prophet Tests the Honor of His Own Country." *The New York Times*, March 14, 1995. Profile of Kemal describes him as "Turkey's best-known and best-loved novelist." Recounts Kemal's battles with Turkish authorities over what Kemal claims is the government's racism against Kurds and other minorities.

Edebiyat: A Journal of Comparative and Middle Eastern Literatures 5, nos. 1/2 (1980). Special issue, edited by Ahmet Ö. Evin, is devoted to Kemal and his work. Four articles discuss *Memed, My Hawk* in detail.

Kemal, Yashar, with Alain Bosquet. *Yaşar Kemal on His Life and Art*. Translated by Eugene Lyons Hébert and Barry Tharaud. Syracuse, N.Y.: Syracuse University Press, 1999. Bosquet, a French writer, poses a series of questions to Kemal, enabling the Turkish writer to discuss his life, political opinions, the development of his writing, and the influence of both Turkish and Kurdish epic literature on his work.

Prokosch, Frederic. "Robin Hood in Anatolia." *Saturday Review* 44, no. 3 (August 19, 1961): 19, 55. Argues that *Memed, My Hawk* fails as social criticism but succeeds as myth.

Rau, Santha Rama. "Robin Hood of the Taurus Mountains." *The New York Times Book Review*, June 11, 1961. Praises the novel for its romantic and epic qualities.

Theroux, Paul. "Turkish Delight." *The New York Times Book Review*, July 10, 1977. In a review of *İnce Memed II* (1969; *They Burn the Thistles*, 1973), which is a sequel to *Memed, My Hawk*, Theroux compares Kemal to William Faulkner and laments the Turkish author's relatively small audience in the United States compared to his audiences in Turkey and Europe.

"Turkish Robin Hood." *Time*, June 16, 1961. A representative review of the novel when it was first published in the United States. Touts Memed as a latter-day Robin Hood and speculates about the influence of the author's life on the narrative.

Memento Mori

Author: Muriel Spark (1918-2006)
First published: 1959
Type of work: Novel
Type of plot: Psychological realism, mystery and detective, satire
Time of plot: 1950's
Locale: London

Principal characters:
DAME LETTIE COLSTON, a pioneer penal reformer
GODFREY COLSTON, her brother
CHARMIAN COLSTON, Godfrey's wife
JEAN TAYLOR, a resident in a nursing home
MABEL PETTIGREW, Godfrey's housekeeper
ALEC WARNER, a retired sociologist
GUY LEET, a poet
PERCY MANNERING, a poet
OLIVE MANNERING, his granddaughter
HENRY MORTIMER, a retired police inspector

The Story:

Each time Dame Lettie Colston answers the telephone, the anonymous caller announces "Remember, you must die." Unnerved by the calls, the old woman contacts the police, but they cannot identify the caller. Lettie's brother, Godfrey, is too preoccupied with his own problems to be sympathetic. He is exasperated by the mental deterioration his wife, Charmian, has suffered after her stroke.

Miss Jean Taylor, a resident in a nursing home, reflects upon the many years of her work as companion for Charmian, the famous novelist. Now she is trapped in a ward where the other women exhibit signs of memory loss, the staff patronizes the residents, and the head nurse brutalizes and demoralizes the residents.

Godfrey and Dame Lettie attend a memorial service for Lisa Brooke, who has died after suffering a stroke. Godfrey had an affair with Lisa many years before. At the service is an old acquaintance, Guy Leet, whom he is surprised to see. Guy is now an old man severely afflicted with arthritis.

Mrs. Pettigrew, Lisa's housekeeper, has been named beneficiary of Lisa's estate. No one knows that Mrs. Pettigrew had blackmailed Lisa for many years because of Lisa's affair with Godfrey.

Alec Warner, a retired sociologist, is fascinated with the problems of old age. When he turns seventy years old, he begins the immense project of compiling records of old people's physical condition, routines, attitudes, and tastes. Many years earlier he had loved Jean Taylor, but when he was advised to marry someone of his own class, he ended his relationship with her.

Dame Lettie hires Mrs. Pettigrew to help take care of Charmian. Mrs. Pettigrew planned to blackmail Godfrey just as she had blackmailed Lisa. She is frustrated when she finds out that Leet, who had secretly married Lisa many years ago, will inherit Lisa's estate.

Jean faces a new challenge in the nursing home. Although the malicious head nurse has been released, her successor admits eight severely demented residents to the ward. Their wails and bizarre behaviors upset Jean and the other longtime residents.

About six months later, Godfrey Colston receives one of

the anonymous calls. Godfrey often visits Olive Mannering, a young woman, to satisfy his sexual longings; he pays her for raising her skirt and allowing him to gaze upon her thigh. Godfrey is preoccupied by the threat of Mrs. Pettigrew's blackmail, and he tells Olive about it.

Charmian, whose memory had begun to improve over the winter, announces that she wishes to move to a nursing home outside London. When she receives the anonymous caller's message, "Remember, you must die," she responds cheerfully, saying that she often thinks of her death.

Olive Mannering tells Alec Warner about Mrs. Pettigrew's plot. When he returns home, Alec becomes the third person to receive the anonymous telephone message that day. He immediately makes notes in his file cards about the event.

Retired chief inspector Henry Mortimer welcomes those who had received the telephone calls to his home to review the evidence. He notes that each person who had received a call attributes different characteristics to the caller. Mortimer believes the caller was "death" himself, but he does not reveal this opinion to his guests. Instead, he advises them to make up their own minds as to the identity of the culprit.

Mrs. Pettigrew discovers a newspaper item reporting that Olive Mannering is to marry an old widower, Lisa's brother-in-law. Mrs. Pettigrew, realizing that Godfrey has been visiting Olive on his mysterious outings, blackmails him. Feeling helpless, Godfrey allows her to drag him to his lawyer's office to make changes in his will. Jean Taylor wants to free Godfrey from Mrs. Pettigrew's domination, so she tells Alec Warner to tell Godfrey that Charmian had had an affair with Guy Leet for many years. Alec does so, and Godfrey dismisses Mrs. Pettigrew.

Dame Lettie becomes increasingly fearful about the intentions of the anonymous caller and shuts herself up in her house. One night, she surprises a burglar and is bludgeoned to death. Her body is not discovered for four days.

Guy visits Charmian in the nursing home outside London. He still expects to inherit Lisa's estate. When he returns home, Percy Mannering is waiting for him. The two men begin to argue about poetry. The telephone rings and the caller asks for Percy, telling him "Remember, you must die." The two men stop bickering and spend the evening together. Percy is inspired to write a sonnet on mortality.

During the investigation of Dame Lettie's murder, the police, with the help of Henry Mortimer, discover that Lisa had already been married when she married Guy. Her real husband, who had been a patient in a mental hospital for forty years, becomes the benefactor of Lisa's estate.

Alec Warner, who had visited patients in that hospital as part of his gerontological research, loses all of his geronto-

logical files when his apartment catches fire. Four months later, he visits Taylor, who encourages him to begin his research anew. He feels unable to do so. He tells Jean that Lisa's mentally ill husband has died. Now Mrs. Pettigrew will inherit Lisa's fortune.

Critical Evaluation:

Although Muriel Spark's novel about a stern and unyielding schoolteacher, *The Prime of Miss Jean Brodie* (1961), is her most popular and well-known work, many critics consider *Memento Mori* to be her greatest achievement. In this novel, Spark creates a diverse cast of characters, almost all of whom are more than seventy years old, and examines the way these individuals face their own mortality. Unlike other novels that treat the experience of aging—among them John Updike's *The Poorhouse Fair* (1959), William Trevor's *The Old Boys* (1964), and Kingsley Amis's *Ending Up* (1974)—Spark's novel creates a community of older adults who are unified in their response to a particular crisis. Most of the characters have received one or more telephone calls from an anonymous person who says simply, "Remember, you must die."

Spark uses the conventions of the detective story to generate mystery and suspense. Most of the characters think of themselves as targets of harassment. They become uneasy and fearful, and some turn to the police to solve the mystery. Dame Lettie, for instance, is sure the caller is a threat to her safety, and she is overcome by terror as the calls continue. Her outcry and the concern the others feel lead to a police investigation, but Chief Inspector Mortimer is unable to solve the case. In fact, he believes the caller to be death himself and that the purpose of the calls is to remind people to lead a rich, full life while they are alive.

The detective story mystery is the structural underpinning of the novel, but the identity of the anonymous caller is never revealed. Spark is more interested in the moral and ethical dilemmas that face human beings. In the ways her characters respond to the anonymous message, Spark reveals their attitudes toward aging and life in general; she also reveals such human attributes as vanity, piety, mean-spiritedness, self-absorption, loneliness, hardihood, and rebellion. Dame Lettie and Godfrey fail to reflect on their own mortality and ignore reminders of their finiteness. They prefer to continue their own comfortable existence without inconvenience or interruption. Mrs. Pettigrew is so self-centered and so intent on manipulating others that she succeeds in denying she ever received one of the calls. Percy Mannering responds to his call with intellectual detachment, viewing the message as an opportunity for poetic inspiration and writing a sonnet on mortality. These responses reveal the extent to which some people are unable to face the implications of their mortality.

An important stylistic device in the novel is Spark's use of satire in describing the pompous self-absorption of those characters who take their lives and their old age far too seriously. Alec Warner is an amateur gerontologist, obsessed with recording details of temperature, pulse, and behaviors in old age. Dame Lettie devotes her time to revising her will to punish her relatives for lapses of affection. The two old poets, Guy Leet and Mannering, harbor grudges against each other. The housekeeper, Mrs. Pettigrew, is determined to make her fortune—by whatever means necessary—before she retires. Godfrey pursues sexual fantasies. Spark deflates these characters' egos by poking fun at their idiosyncrasies, foibles, failings, pettiness, fears, insecurities, and manipulative ways.

Religion plays an important role in the novel, too, though most of the characters in *Memento Mori* lack a specific connection to religious faith. Most of them are officially members of the Anglican faith, but their lives are dominated by secular priorities—making money, finding fame, getting even, seeking comfort and security, and enjoying their leisure. Religious and spiritual concerns are not a part of their daily lives. Two of the characters, Charmian Piper and Jean Taylor, are Roman Catholic—in fact, Jean had converted to Catholicism during the time she was a lady's companion to Charmian—and, unlike the other characters, these two women derive comfort and security from their faith. When Charmian receives her telephone call, she admits to the caller that she thinks often of death and is unafraid. Taylor never receives one of the anonymous calls, probably because she is depicted as a woman who does not need a reminder of her mortality. Although she suffers from arthritis and often experiences loneliness as a resident of a nursing home, she does not despair. She tolerates her difficult situation and views the senile old woman in the nursing home as her personal "memento mori."

Charmian and Taylor, along with Chief Inspector Mortimer, are the moral centers of the novel. When Charmian gradually recovers her mental powers and decides to move to a nursing home rather than remain with her husband, she expresses both her acceptance of the limitations of old age and her freedom to make decisions about her own welfare. Taylor, too, accepts her fate. She even feels a contentment and appreciation for her life in the nursing home, where she feels a part of a community. Her understanding of the anonymous caller is similar to Mortimer's understanding: He believes that the message is an exhortation to self-enrichment and equanimity in the face of impending mortality.

Robert E. Yahnke

Further Reading

Apostolou, Fotini E. *Seduction and Death in Muriel Spark's Fiction*. Westport, Conn.: Greenwood Press, 2001. A postmodernist and poststructuralist analysis of Spark's fiction. Argues that Spark's work often considers the seductive and destructive power of education, religion, and other social structures.

Cheyette, Bryan. *Muriel Spark*. Tavistock, England: Northcote House/British Council, 2000. Examines common elements in all of Spark's novels, including *Memento Mori*. Argues that Spark should not be categorized as a Catholic writer; her hybrid background—part English, Scottish, Protestant, and Jewish—makes her a "diasporic writer with a fluid sense of self" and a limitless imagination.

Hynes, Joseph. *The Art of the Real: Muriel Spark's Novels*. Cranbury, N.J.: Associated University Presses, 1988. Examines *Memento Mori*'s satirical portrayal of old age and the relationships between humor and religious themes.

Kemp, Peter. *Muriel Spark*. London: Paul Elek, 1974. A thorough treatment of the novel's characters and themes. Analyzes the responses of the major characters to the anonymous telephone caller's message and examines the subtlety of the author's depiction of old age.

McQuillan, Martin, ed. *Theorizing Muriel Spark: Gender, Race, Deconstruction*. New York: Palgrave, 2002. Collection of essays analyzing Spark's work from numerous perspectives, including feminism, queer theory, psychoanalysis, postcolonialism, and deconstructionism. Includes an interview with Spark and Nicholas Royle's examination of *Memento Mori*.

Page, Norman. *Muriel Spark*. New York: St. Martin's Press, 1990. An excellent overview of *Memento Mori*'s characters, plot, and themes. Compares the novel to others that have treated themes of aging. Considers the novel a parody of the conventional detective story.

Richmond, Velma Bourgeois. *Muriel Spark*. New York: Frederick Ungar, 1984. Analyzes characters and their relationships. Considers the conflicts of characters as part of the tension between the earthly and the eternal, between human desires and God's will. Provides a historical perspective on the remembrance of death since the Middle Ages.

Whittaker, Ruth. *The Faith and Fiction of Muriel Spark*. New York: St. Martin's Press, 1982. A concise survey. Examines the theme of religious faith and the supernatural. Considers *Memento Mori* a pessimistic treatment of human failings that shows the redemptive power of faith in helping some of the characters find meaning in their lives.

Memoirs of a Physician

Authors: Alexandre Dumas, *père* (1802-1870), and
   Auguste Maquet (1813-1888)
First published: Mémoires d'un médecin, 1846-1848
   (English translation, 1846)
Type of work: Novel
Type of plot: Historical
Time of plot: Eighteenth century
Locale: Paris and environs

Principal characters:
BARON DE TAVERNEY
PHILIPPE, his son
ANDRÉE, his daughter
GILBERT, in love with Andrée
LOUIS XV, king of France
MONSIEUR DE CHOISEUL, the king's minister
MADAME JEANNE DU BARRY, the king's favorite
ARMAND DE RICHELIEU, a political opportunist
JOSEPH BALSAMO, also known as COUNT DE FENIX, a
   sorcerer and revolutionary
LORENZA FELICIANI, his wife
ALTHOTAS, his instructor in magic
MONSIEUR DE SARTINES, a police lieutenant
JEAN-JACQUES ROUSSEAU, the philosopher

The Story:

At the court of Louis XV of France, Armand de Richelieu plots with Madame Jeanne du Barry, the king's favorite, to replace Monsieur de Choiseul as the king's minister. They consult Count de Fenix, who turns out to be the reputed sorcerer Joseph Balsamo; ten years earlier the necromancer had predicted that Madame du Barry would one day be queen of France.

Balsamo uses his wife, Lorenza Feliciani, as an unwilling medium for his sorcery. Through her he gives Richelieu and Madame du Barry compromising information contained in a letter sent by the duchess of Grammont to her brother, de Choiseul, showing that the minister is encouraging the revolt of parliament against the king and attempting to bring about war with England. Fortified with this information, Richelieu forces the king to dismiss his minister.

The philosopher Jean-Jacques Rousseau, standing in the crowd gathered outside the palace after the king at a "bed of justice" had defied parliament, is urged to attend a secret meeting at which he will be initiated into the mystic order of Freemasonry. Rousseau declares he could do more for the world by not joining the order. The chief of the council, who is Balsamo, reads a communication from Swedenborg that warns them of a traitor among them.

To demonstrate to the surgeon Marat, a member of the secret fraternity, that body and soul can be separated and then reunited and that the soul has a greater knowledge than the body, Balsamo hypnotizes one of Marat's patients. As the patient's crushed leg is amputated, Balsamo makes the patient sing. He also hypnotizes Marat's maid, draws from her an ad-

mission of the theft of her master's watch, and, still in the condition of sleep, makes her repeat the contents of a letter she could not read while awake.

Andrée, daughter of the impoverished Baron de Taverney, has recently been saved from the violence of a mob by Gilbert, a son of the people, but she is ignorant of this circumstance because Balsamo brings her home in his carriage. After the woman has been settled at the Trianon through the request of the dauphiness, her beauty charms the king completely, and he commissions Richelieu to present her with a necklace worth several million livres, but she declines the gift. Richelieu, escorting de Taverney through the gardens after they had supped with the king, is heard by Gilbert, hidden in a dense thicket, advising the baron to send his daughter to a convent. Philippe, Andrée's brother, who holds a commission in the royal army, pays a farewell visit to his sister; she confides to him her fears and forebodings. After his departure, Andrée weeps. Gilbert approaches and declares his love for her, but Andrée rebuffs him.

In his mansion, Balsamo is summoned to Lorenza's room, where she begs him to release her so that she can retire to a convent. When he refuses, she plunges a dagger into her breast. After commanding Lorenza to sleep, Balsamo ascends to the chamber of the alchemist Althotas, who reminds him that in a week the aged man will be one hundred years old, by which time he must have the last three drops of blood of a child or a young female to complete the elixir that will preserve him for another half century. Balsamo, having promised his help, is returning to the sleeping Lorenza when he is interrupted by the arrival of Richelieu, who has come for a special sleeping draught for Andrée. Richelieu has already left instructions that a love potion be given to the king that will cause him to fall in love with the first woman he sees upon waking.

Gilbert overhears Nicole, Andrée's maid, tell her lover that Richelieu arranged for them to escape together after first drugging Andrée and leaving her door unlocked; later he sees them ride off. Andrée, plunged into a hypnotic sleep by the drink, descends the stairs of her apartment in a trance and passes the astounded Gilbert. A flash of lightning discloses the concealed figure of Balsamo, who orders Andrée to tell what has happened at his house in Paris after Lorenza had tried to kill herself and he put her to sleep. Andrée, describing Lorenza's flight, tells how she has taken with her a box of papers and, on reaching the street, has inquired the address of the police lieutenant, Monsieur de Sartines. At this news, Balsamo leaps to his horse and without releasing Andrée from her trance, dashes off for Paris.

Andrée, left alone, sinks to the ground. Gilbert, a witness of this scene at a distance, rushes toward her, lifts her up, and carries her back to her chamber. As he places her on the couch, he hears a step. He hastily blows out the candle. Realizing that the visitor is the king, Gilbert flees. King Louis, seeing Andrée lying pale and immobile and thinking her dead, also flees in panic.

Balsamo, riding toward Paris, knows that his only hope of preventing Lorenza from revealing his secrets to the police lies in his magic power over her. Abruptly he reins in his horse and with all the force at his command wills Lorenza to fall asleep wherever she is. From Sevres, he sends a hasty note to Madame du Barry in Paris. Meanwhile, Lorenza arrives at the office of the police, but before she can give them Balsamo's address, she falls to the floor, overcome by a strange dizziness. A valet carries her into an adjoining room. Monsieur de Sartines bursts open the coffer, however, and a clerk deciphers the secret papers, which implicate Balsamo in plans affecting the king and the government.

At that moment, Balsamo, under the name of Count de Fenix, is announced. Seeing that the coffer has been opened, he threatens to shoot Monsieur de Sartines. Madame du Barry, acting quickly on receipt of Balsamo's letter, arrives at that moment, and Monsieur de Sartines surrenders the coffer to her. She, in turn, hands it to Balsamo with all the papers intact.

On his return to his chambers, Balsamo finds Lorenza there in convulsions. His determination to kill her ebbs as he gazes on her beauty, and an overpowering love for her sweeps his being and causes him to feel that if he surrenders his control over her he might still earn some heavenly recompense. For three days the very thought plunges him into a happiness he had never before experienced, while in her trance Lorenza dreams aloud her own mysterious love. On the third day after she had asked him to test if her ability still remains to see through space despite intervening material obstacles, Balsamo wills her to report what Madame du Barry is doing. Lorenza reports that the king's favorite is on her way to see him.

Balsamo puts Lorenza into a still deeper sleep. As he is leaving her, he thinks he hears a creak. Looking back, he sees only her sleeping form. In her sleep, Lorenza thinks she sees part of the ceiling of her room descend and from this moving trap a Caliban-shaped creature creep toward her. Powerless to escape, she feels him place her on the circular trap, which then ascends slowly toward the ceiling.

Madame du Barry, worried because she has been followed, tells Balsamo that she saved him from arrest when Monsieur de Sartines had handed the king the deciphered names from the coffer. In appreciation, Balsamo presents her with a vial containing a draught that will ensure her twenty years of additional youth. After her departure, Balsamo returns to Lorenza's couch, only to find her gone. He ascends to his instructor's room and there discovers the body of Lorenza. To his horror he realizes that Althotas has drained from her the blood needed for his elixir.

Cursing his master, from whose hands the vial with the precious liquid slips and breaks, Balsamo falls unconscious on the lifeless body of his wife. He stirs only when notified by his servant that "the five masters" are waiting to see him. They had come from the secret fraternity to pronounce sentence on him as a traitor. Having watched his movements, they had seen Lorenza leave his home with a coffer containing secret names in cipher. Later, he himself arrived at the police office, and Lorenza had departed alone; he had left with Madame du Barry, whom he had summoned there to receive the secret information for which he was paid. The paper that revealed their secrets had been left with the police, they charged, but Balsamo had removed the coffer to avoid implication. As a result of this betrayal, five of their prominent agents were arrested. Balsamo does not defend himself. When he asks only for a few minutes to bring proof that will speak for him, they let him go. He returns, bearing the body of Lorenza, which he lets slip from his arms to fall at their feet. In consternation, his judges flee.

Althotas, enraged at his pupil and fearing death for himself, sets fire to his precious manuscripts and perishes in the flames. All night the fire roars in the rooms above, while Balsamo, stretched beside Lorenza's body, never moves. The vaulted walls are thick, however, and the fire finally burns itself out.

Andrée recovers from her prostration and retires to a convent. Baron de Taverney, repudiated by the king and Richelieu, slinks back to his impoverished estate. Philippe sails for America, and Gilbert follows. Balsamo vegetates in his mansion, from which he is supposed to have reappeared during the violence of the French Revolution. On May 9, 1774, the king's physician says the king is suffering from smallpox. The king's daughter, Madame Louise of France, leaves her convent cell to attend him, and he is given extreme unction. Madame du Barry is sent to the château of the duchess d'Aiguillon. The king dies the next day, and Louis XVI ascends to a throne about to be engulfed in the flames of rebellion and anarchy.

Critical Evaluation:

Memoirs of a Physician is an intricate plot of court intrigue in the closing days of the reign of Louis XV, with dramatis personae as diverse as the scheming Duc de Richelieu, the philosopher Jean-Jacques Rousseau, and the favorite-dominated king. Manipulating all these by means of his magical control of natural forces and the power invested in him as a representative of the secret brotherhood of Freemasonry is the mysterious figure of Joseph Balsamo. The climax is as lurid as any modern thriller.

For its full historical value this volume should be read as one of a series of five, all concerned with the court life of France at the time of Louis XV and XVI. Called the Marie Antoinette romances, the five novels are *Memoirs of a Physician*, *Le Chevalier de Maison-Rouge* (1846, with Auguste Maquet; *Marie Antoinette: Or, The Chevalier of the Red House*, 1846; also known as *The Chevalier de Maison-Rouge*, 1893), *Le Collier de la reine* (1849-1850, with Maquet; *The Queen's Necklace*, 1855), *Ange Pitou* (1851; *Six Years Later*, 1851), and *La Comtesse de Charny* (1853-1855; *The Countess de Charny*, 1858).

Without doubt the most fascinating character in the *Memoirs of a Physician* is that remarkable impostor, Balsamo. From his first introduction, he is seen as a powerful and contradictory figure with great resources and unscrupulous ambitions. His passion for the unnatural and unexplainable adds to the fascination his personality holds for the reader. The phenomena of occultism had long fascinated Alexandre Dumas, *père*, and it was inevitable that he should work it into one of his novels. The manner in which he used his interest in the *Memoirs of a Physician*, however, is a spectacular success, one of the most remarkable examples of his genius. Dumas dabbled, at different times, in palmistry, phrenology,

clairvoyance, and spiritualism. To test the reality of this power, he made several experiments at the time when he was writing the Balsamo sequences of the novel, apparently with considerable success. In this novel, the possibilities of this and other unusual or unexplainable phenomena were stretched to the furthest demands of his fiction. Dumas's skill, however, was such that the reader willingly suspends disbelief and is drawn into the spell cast by the writer and his sorcerer character.

The arch-quack Balsamo is presented with all of his quackeries, his schemes and ploys, and his ruthless use of his supernatural powers to exploit the innocent and further his own ends. He believes, however, in himself and in his mission to re-create humanity by destroying the existing order; as the head of a society of nihilists, whose motto is L.P.D. (*lilia pedibus destrus*), he directs the undermining of society's foundations. He loves nothing so much as pulling the strings by which the puppets are made to dance. Balsamo, or Count de Fenix, as he is also known, is a unique and remarkable character, and he holds the reader's interest even after the virtuous characters are forgotten.

Many famous people appear in the pages of this long novel, some more successfully than others. Rousseau is probably the most illustrious member of the cast, but his portrait does not quite come off; one suspects that Dumas held Rousseau in such high esteem that he could not entirely relax while drawing his portrait. Marat, the young surgeon who continually urges prompt and violent methods to cleanse society of its corruption, while less admirable, is realized more successfully than the old philosopher. He pulsates with a vitality and drive almost equal to that which infuses Balsamo with such remarkable life. In some respects, Madame du Barry, with all of her intrigues to keep her position, is a triumph of characterization. Whatever the real du Barry was like, the reader feels that she ought to have been as Dumas describes her. The eminent churchman, Cardinal de Rohan, shines in that wonderful scene in which he is dazzled by the sight of the alchemist Balsamo "making gold."

With great skill, Dumas weaves into his story the social conditions prevalent in Paris and the country at the time, the conditions that must inevitably lead to revolution. The brilliant opening scene of the families searching for the dead and injured after a great riot quickly sets the tone of the novel. The division of the citizens of France into the revolutionaries and reactionaries is seen to be developing, and the tragic consequences are vividly foreshadowed. While the book is far from a social tract, Dumas seems to take delight in presenting the corruption of the court and the vices of the rich, and, above all, the exploitation of the poor by the powerful.

Dumas was always fascinated by power and its various permutations. He explored in novel after novel the schemes and actions of the lovers of power and their ruthless natures. In this novel of intrigue and incipient revolution, Dumas allows himself plenty of room to analyze his favorite subject.

The plot is as complicated and convoluted as most of the plots of Dumas's other novels, but the action moves swiftly, and Dumas's narrative skill keeps the threads traceable; the story is seldom incomprehensible. Even when the plot seems most tangled, the vivid characterizations hold the reader's interest. Perhaps more than many of Dumas's novels, *Memoirs of a Physician* presents some acute character analyses. The principal characters reveal themselves through their actions, as well as through their self-evaluations. The minor characters in the book and the young and idealistic lovers, however, are much less successfully realized and are inclined to be pawns of the plot.

The style of the writing, while vigorous, is not subtle. The dialogue is often completely unrealistic, the characters speaking to inform the reader, rather than one another, of their intentions. The melodrama of the plot carries over into the prose, and many chapters end with cliff-hanging episodes that are lushly overwritten. These scenes are frequently implausible, and the violence of the emotions and the posturing of the characters is sometimes laughable.

Despite these flaws, which are, after all, as much the fault of the era of the author as they are of the author's craft, the novel remains a masterpiece. Dumas never tried to write like Gustave Flaubert and was not interested in realism, yet he managed to create a "real" world with his pen. The Paris and France of *Memoirs of a Physician* is as vivid to the reader as the provincial towns of Flaubert's masterpieces, and the breathless narrative drive, for which Dumas is so justly famous, continually holds the reader's attention. The style is consistent throughout, and the prose retains the vigor that characterizes the author's earlier books.

"Critical Evaluation" by Bruce D. Reeves

Further Reading

Bell, A. Craig. *Alexandre Dumas: A Biography and Study*. London: Cassell, 1950. Still one of the better studies of the works of Dumas, this book places some emphasis on *The Memoirs of a Physician*. The biography chronicles Dumas's social circle.

Davidson, Arthur F. *Alexandre Dumas (père): His Life and Works*. Honolulu, Hawaii: University Press of the Pacific, 2002. Originally published in 1902, this classic biography of Dumas is an excellent starting point for all readers. Includes illustrations.

Dumas, Alexandre, *père. The Road to Monte Cristo: A Condensation from "The Memoirs of Alexandre Dumas."* Translated by Jules Eckert Goodman. New York: Charles Scribner's Sons, 1956. An excellent, abridged translation of Dumas's memoirs that relate to his source material for his novels, including *The Memoirs of a Physician*.

Maurois, André. *The Titans, a Three-Generation Biography of the Dumas*. Translated by Gerard Hopkins. 1957. Reprint. Westport, Conn.: Greenwood Press, 1971. Considered the authoritative biography of Dumas, *père*, and his father and son. Includes an excellent bibliography. Discusses *The Memoirs of a Physician* in a cursory fashion.

Schopp, Claude. *Alexandre Dumas: Genius of Life*. Translated by A. J. Koch. New York: Franklin Watts, 1988. A biographical and critical approach to the life and works of Alexandre Dumas, *père*. Contains a discussion on Dumas's problems with the serialization of *The Memoirs of a Physician*.

Stowe, Richard S. *Alexandre Dumas (père)*. Boston: Twayne, 1976. An excellent starting point for an analysis of the life and works of Alexandre Dumas, *père*, and one of the best sources in English. *The Memoirs of a Physician* is analyzed in the chapter "The Marie-Antoinette Romances," of which the novel is the first of five installments.

Memoirs of Hadrian

Author: Marguerite Yourcenar (1903-1987)
First published: Mémoires d'Hadrien, 1951 (English
    translation, 1954)
Type of work: Novel
Type of plot: Historical realism
Time of plot: Second century C.E.
Locale: Rome and the Roman Empire

Principal characters:
HADRIAN, the Roman emperor
ANTINOUS, a Bythinian youth
TRAJAN, the previous Roman emperor
PLOTINA, Trajan's wife and friend of Hadrian
ANTONINUS, a virtuous senator and public servant
SABINA, Hadrian's wife

The Story:

In a book-length letter addressed to Marcus Aurelius, his adopted grandson and heir, the sixty-year-old Emperor Hadrian tells of his impending death and meditates upon his life to instruct his heir through his accumulated experience, knowledge, and wisdom. The descendant of wealthy aristocratic administrators, Hadrian had been born in Spain. After his father's death, the twelve-year-old boy went to Rome to complete his education, which included science, mathematics, art, literature, and Greek, and to begin his military training. Following his studies, he was named to a series of judgeships, which taught him about human motives and how to listen carefully and organize his time.

Hadrian had been promoted to junior officer rank in the army and stationed in Central Europe, where he was exposed to new experiences and ideas. There, he learned that Emperor Nerva had died and that his cousin, Trajan, had ascended the throne. Although such a family connection, coupled with his own ability and courage, offered new opportunities, advancement was not smooth, for the new emperor and Hadrian often clashed on private and public affairs. Since Trajan wanted to consolidate and increase Roman conquests, he embarked on many campaigns. As a result, Hadrian saw service all over Europe. He acquitted himself daringly and brilliantly and gained both a solid reputation among his colleagues on the battlefield and popularity in Rome. The emperor was so pleased with Hadrian's contribution that he gave him a ring symbolic of imperial favor.

Increasingly influential in the emperor's circle, partly because of Trajan's wife, who shared many of his beliefs, Hadrian performs a variety of administrative functions as well as writing and delivering the emperor's speeches. Gradually, however, this relationship, further strengthened by Hadrian's marriage to Trajan's grandniece, Sabina, begins to arouse irritation and jealousy in the old sovereign, who resents the successes of his subordinate.

Renewed conflicts in the empire make it necessary that Hadrian visit various fronts to impose discipline on the troops. Several bold strokes on his part defeat Rome's enemies but not without diminishing his humanity and aging him prematurely. With Plotina's help, he continues to rise in the ranks of the administration and army, becoming first a consul, then governor and military legate in Syria. When the emperor wants to wage war again and conquer Asia, Hadrian advises him instead to sign advantageous commercial treaties with communities along the Silk Road, for he realizes that Asia, despite some early Roman victories, would be difficult, perhaps impossible, to defeat.

Given his age and illness, Trajan should officially designate Hadrian as his heir, yet he hesitates. Plotina works hard to foster his candidacy, however, and shortly before the emperor dies, he names Hadrian his successor in his will. In 117 C.E., at the age of forty, Hadrian becomes ruler. More interested in the betterment of humankind than in the trappings of power, he immediately resolves to seek peace abroad and compromise with senators at home. He institutes reforms to improve life in the empire, ranging from innovative social programs to the granting of new individual freedoms; underlying his reforms is his intent to increase human happiness. To ensure the permanence of Roman peace he encourages commerce, literature, and the arts and fosters the building of new cities all over the Mediterranean basin. In addition, he civilizes Britain and the German plain and continues to experience everything in life to the fullest.

During one of his travels, Hadrian becomes infatuated with a handsome Greek adolescent named Antinous, who begins to accompany him everywhere and with whom he shares an unequaled intimacy. This is the beginning of fabulous years. For Hadrian, there is no activity too demanding, no gift too wonderful, as his passion turned into blissful, though not exclusive, adoration. Out of his own overwhelming love for the emperor, Antinous decides, when just short of his twentieth birthday, to commit suicide so that his unlived years can be added to those of Hadrian. Numb with sorrow and guilt, Hadrian, upon his return to Italy, devotes time to literary and scientific pursuits while he works on modifying laws and constitutions so that they will respect local customs and national character. He also continues to build and to improve city services.

The only serious flaw in Hadrian's otherwise excellent rule concerns the Jews in Judea who, unlike his other non-Roman subjects, attack Rome for its occupation of their land and its intolerance toward their religious rituals and ways of considering God. Unable and unwilling to accommodate an alternate point of view, Hadrian sends in well-equipped, well-trained troops to crush Simon Bar-Kochba's guerrilla army. The campaign takes more than four years and results in the resisters' mass suicide.

Suffering from increasingly ill health and wishing to avoid Trajan's imprudent delaying, Hadrian names Antoninus, an honest and virtuous man, to be his successor under the condition that he will agree to adopt Hadrian's grandson, the philosopher Marcus Aurelius. Having settled all public and private affairs, and surrounded by close friends, Hadrian waits peacefully for death.

Critical Evaluation:

When Marguerite Yourcenar in 1948 began to think of Hadrian, she had already developed her literary gifts in her previous works of fiction. She understood well the first-person narrative form; she had previously evolved themes both human and universal; she was interested in historical research as an aid to conveying eternal ideas; and she had developed an acute understanding of human frailty. In *Memoirs of Hadrian*, her first recognized masterpiece, Yourcenar makes full use of her talents, skills, and knowledge.

The work is divided into six parts, each having a Latin title taken from Hadrian's poetry, philosophical ideas, or coins minted during his reign. Each title describes, and each part is devoted to, different phases of the emperor's life. Each section's title and subject correspond to the development of aspects of Hadrian's power and personality. The first part gives an account of the progress of his illness and his renunciation of many activities as his soul prepares to leave his body. The second describes the variety and complexity of his character, followed by a section dealing with "the stabilized earth." Part 4 equates the golden age with Hadrian, since that age represents the period when his life reached its apogee, a moment when nothing seemed impossible and when all was easy. There follows a section entitled "the August but humane discipline," which is Hadrian's contemplation of life from a different point of view, and the book concludes with a meditation on death.

Yourcenar intends to portray a great historical personage who, thanks to his broad humanist culture and inquiring intelligence, was able, without illusions and with remarkable objectivity and lucidity, to analyze his life and times. Hadrian is at once an aesthete, art lover, poet, tireless traveler, general, economist, master builder, and political scientist: In other words, he is deeply interested in everything.

Yourcenar's book is, however, far more than the autobiography of Emperor Hadrian. It has also been called a learning "manual for princes" that explains how human knowledge and consciousness can be united with imperial knowledge and consciousness to create a better ruler. In his all-encompassing outlook on the world in which he lives, Hadrian is a kind of unique Everyman, a representative of the people without elements of demagoguery, who at the same time stands apart from the people and thus allows his rare genius full play in all areas of human endeavor.

Hadrian is sufficiently practical and pragmatic that in appreciating the beauty of such treatises as Plato's *Republic* (third century B.C.E.) he is able to take such daring views further and to implement many of them in his rule. Thus, he restructures the state to be both less intrusive and more responsive to its citizens and he codifies better, because simpler, laws. His generous nature leads him to improve the status of slaves through proper regulation; he works to modify the ambiguous legal condition of women who "are at one and the same time subjugated and protected, weak and powerful, too much despised and too much respected." Of course, despite his otherwise forward-looking liberalism, he does remain a man of his century, as is evident, for example, in his lack of understanding for women as individual and equal human beings.

Hadrian's attitude toward his job and position is based on an honest regard for all the people in his care and exemplified by the statement "We emperors are not Caesars; we are functionaries of the State." All of his life he had wanted to better the lot of the people by the wise application of three basic concepts—humanity, happiness, and liberty—tempered by discipline and patience, and he vehemently refused to believe that the masses are unworthy of such treatment or that such treatment could make them corrupt and complacent.

Memoirs of Hadrian has often been called a historical novel, but it lacks many of the customary attributes of the genre, such as descriptions of local color, period dress, and quaint customs. The Emperor Hadrian characterizes himself partly through accounts of his actions, more often through perspicacious analyses of his thoughts and feelings. If, at times, the book deviates from the recorded truth, it is only because Yourcenar is not presenting the picture of an epoch or an emperor in time, but presenting a human being out of time and with that collective sensibility or consciousness that had taken this particular and very special Roman for its spokesman.

The style of *Memoirs of Hadrian*, in which the narrator speaks in the first person, is not an interior monologue in the usual sense of the word but rather what has been described as the interior discourse. Through Hadrian's retelling, Yourcenar has exposed universal truths and explored archetypes that have their origins in Western culture. She has demonstrated that her Roman emperor not only incarnates the serene Roman patience but also represents the fears and aspirations of thinking readers everywhere.

Pierre L. Horn

Further Reading

Armbrecht, Thomas J. D. *At the Periphery of the Center: Sexuality and Literary Genre in the Works of Marguerite Yourcenar and Julien Green*. New York: Rodopi, 2007. A comparative study of the two twentieth century writers, focusing on the depiction of homosexuality in their novels and plays.

Farrell, C. Frederick, Jr., and Edith R. Farrell. *Marguerite Yourcenar in Counterpoint*. Lanham, Md.: University Press of America, 1983. A collection of essays, written between 1978 and 1982, interpreting a variety of Yourcenar's works. Includes a substantial essay on *Memoirs of Hadrian* that concentrates on the image of Hadrian as a "good prince" and the significance of the novel in postwar Europe. Another essay looks at the role of women in Yourcenar's work, acknowledging that they are rarely central characters but defending their influence and depiction.

Horn, Pierre. *Marguerite Yourcenar*. Boston: Twayne, 1985. A good overview of Yourcenar's work, discussing the plots and characters of her major works. Horn notes that Yourcenar refused to be characterized as a "women's writer" and resisted "ghettoization." Although Horn acknowledges that Yourcenar does emphasize male homosexuality as a theme, sometimes coupled with sadistic actions toward women, he argues that she does so because she portrays characters in revolt against arbitrary moral and political restrictions. He defends her use of female characters in "important" supporting roles, if not as central characters, and points out that her central concern is the liberation of humanity as a whole.

Howard, Joan E. *From Violence to Vision: Sacrifice in the Works of Marguerite Yourcenar*. Carbondale: Southern Illinois University Press, 1992. A scholarly and well-informed study of the role played first by myth and then by sacrificial situations in seven illustrative works, including *Memoirs of Hadrian*.

Rousseau, George. *Yourcenar*. London: Haus, 2004. A biography of Yourcenar, who led what Rousseau describes as "a life of contradictions," including that she was a lesbian who wrote primarily in the voice of a gay man; the epilogue examines the question "Is Yourcenar a Gay Writer?" Includes a chronology, a list of Yourcenar's works, and a secondary bibliography.

Saint, Nigel. *Marguerite Yourcenar: Reading the Visual*. Oxford, England: Legenda, 2000. Examines Yourcenar's historical novels, including *Memoirs of Hadrian*, and her lesser-known essays from the perspectives of art history and critical theory. Includes a bibliography and an index.

Sarnecki, Judith Holland, and Ingebory Majer O'Sickey, eds. *Subversive Subjects: Reading Marguerite Yourcenar*. Madison, N.J.: Fairleigh Dickinson University Press, 2004. Collection of essays examining the issues of self, desire, and "the other" in Yourcenar's work. One essay analyzes *Memories of Hadrian*.

Savigneau, Josyane. *Marguerite Yourcenar: Inventing a Life*. Translated by Joan E. Howard. Chicago: University of Chicago Press, 1993. A highly personal biography examining the life, friendships, and personality of Yourcenar, without offering literary analysis of her work. Savigneau does, however, consider Yourcenar's attitude toward feminism, most particularly in relation to her election to the French Academy. She delves deeply into Yourcenar's longtime love relationship with her American translator, Grace Frick, and offers valuable insights into the humanist studies from which the *Memoirs of Hadrian* grew. Annotated by both author and translator.

Men and Women

Author: Robert Browning (1812-1889)
First published: 1855
Type of work: Poetry

Men and Women is Robert Browning's only significant publication during the period of his marriage to poet Elizabeth Barrett. These were the years when Browning made Italy his home and when his output of poetry was markedly curtailed by a number of other interests: his family, his dabbling in painting and sculpture, and his study of Italian Renaissance art. The quality of his poetry, however, had never been higher than in the poems produced during this period. It was in the original 1855 edition of *Men and Women*, above all, that he brought the dramatic monologue to perfection. Indeed, his reputation is largely due to his mastery of the dramatic monologue.

The title *Men and Women* first was appended to two volumes of poems containing fifty-one of Browning's most celebrated works. Beginning with the collected edition of 1863, the number of poems appearing under this title is thirteen, only eight of which had been in the 1855 edition of *Men and Women*. Of the other forty-three poems, thirty are grouped by Browning as dramatic lyrics (the most famous of these being "Love Among the Ruins," "A Toccata of Galuppi's," "Saul," "'De Gustibus—,'" and "Two in the Campagna"). Twelve poems are grouped as dramatic romances (including "'Childe Roland to the Dark Tower Came,'" "The Statue and the Bust," "The Last Ride Together," and "A Grammarian's Funeral"). The poem "In a Balcony" eventually was listed separately, under its own title. The poems that remain include several of Browning's greatest dramatic monologues: "Fra Lippo Lippi," "An Epistle Containing the Strange Medical Experience of Karshish, the Arab Physician," "Bishop Blougram's Apology," "The Bishop Orders His Tomb at Saint Praxed's Church," "Andrea del Sarto," and "Cleon."

Life in Italy suited Browning, and the atmosphere of that land permeates many of the poems in this collection. Some are Italian simply in landscape, such as the humorous "Up at a Villa—Down in the City." In other poems, such as "A Serenade at the Villa," "By the Fire-Side," and "Two in the Campagna," it is apparent that Browning's primary interest is in examining human relationships that could take place anywhere; the setting is Italy, but it is incidentally so. Other poems, however, owe more to their Italian sources, including curious customs ("Holy-Cross Day") and local legends ("The Statue and the Bust"). In later years, Browning would

often say that "Italy was my university"; what he had studied at that university was Italian art. "Old Pictures in Florence" reflects his interest in that art, as do "Fra Lippo Lippi" and "Andrea del Sarto," both of which are imaginary character studies of real Renaissance painters. "The Guardian-Angel: A Picture at Fano" is based on an actual painting. "'De Gustibus—'" contains the clearest statement of Browning's love for Italy: "Open my heart and you will see/ Graved inside of it, 'Italy.'"

The Italian element is, however, less important than another personal influence, that of the poet's marriage to Barrett. Although the love poems in *Men and Women* are not necessarily autobiographical, they do reflect, at least indirectly, the relationship between Barrett and Browning. In "By the Fire-Side," communication is complete; love is serene. In "The Last Ride Together," "Andrea del Sarto," "Love in a Life," "Life in a Love," and "Any Wife to Any Husband," communication breaks down and love fails. "Two in the Campagna" deals with "Infinite passion and the pain/ Of finite hearts that yearn." Thus, Browning indicates the gap between love in dreams and love in reality. Most of these poems dramatize a love situation and are content to evoke it without commenting on it. "The Statue and the Bust," however, includes a flatly stated moral: "Let a man contend to the uttermost/ For his life's set prize," and never miss that prize because of wasted opportunities.

Some have suggested that in examining the vicissitudes of love Browning was revealing flaws in his own marriage. "A Lover's Quarrel," for example, does involve disagreement over two subjects about which he and his wife differed: spiritualism (she believed in it; he scoffed at it) and Napoleon III, emperor of France (she was an admirer; he was not). The evidence is by no means conclusive, however, and the one poem in *Men and Women* that is openly autobiographical, "One Word More: To E. B. B.," is Browning's dedication—both his and that of the book—to Barrett.

Many of Browning's favorite themes are broached in the poems of *Men and Women*. The idea that the course of one's life may turn upon a moment's decision is expressed in "The Statue and the Bust." The idea that "A man's reach should exceed his grasp" is the subject of "Andrea del Sarto," as well as "Old Pictures in Florence" and "A Grammarian's Funeral."

Browning's attitudes toward religion and religious belief are presented in "Saul," "Cleon," "An Epistle Containing the Strange Medical Experience of Karshish, the Arab Physician," and "Bishop Blougram's Apology."

"Memorabilia," a slight poem, is chiefly remembered because it alludes to Percy Bysshe Shelley, one of Browning's early enthusiasms and the subject of Browning's only important prose essay. "Popularity" is a tribute to another of Browning's favorite poets, John Keats. In this poem there is further allusion to Browning's belief that the poet's role is somehow linked with the divine mission. One of Browning's most explicit statements about what poetry should aim to be is found in "'Transcendentalism': A Poem in Twelve Books." In this work he makes clear his preference for Keatsian or Shelleyan "song" to the overlabored, earnest "thought" that characterizes so much bad Victorian poetry. One poet, speaking to another, says, "'Tis you speak, that's your error. Song's our art:/ Whereas you please to speak these naked thoughts/ Instead of draping them in sights and sounds." Browning has no objection to thought in poetry, but it should not be presented baldly, for its own sake. Rather, it should be draped "in sights and sounds."

"I only knew one poet in my life," says the speaker in "How It Strikes a Contemporary," and the poem itself is in many ways Browning's own description of what a poet should be. The poet, first of all, looks the world full in the face; the poet is no idle dreamer. The poet sees life and sees it whole, taking "such cognizance of men and things" that the poet can truthfully be called "a recording chief-inquisitor." This poem can be seen as a veiled defense of Browning's own tendency to write about characters and events that, to one who thinks poetry must be about pretty things, might not be sufficiently "poetic." If, in Browning's view, the poet's proper sphere is life as it really is, the poet's function is nonetheless an exalted one: The poet writes in the service of God. In "How It Strikes a Contemporary," the poet "walked about and took account/ Of all thought, said and acted, then went home,/ And wrote it fully to our Lord the King."

In the two dramatic monologues that are generally acknowledged to be the finest poems in *Men and Women*, "Fra Lippo Lippi" and "Andrea del Sarto," Browning gives further insights into his theories of art. It is obvious that, in bringing these two Renaissance painters to life, his own sympathies as an artist lie completely with Lippo Lippi and not at all with Andrea del Sarto. He depicts the latter as a skilled craftsperson whose hand and eye are deft, but who has only "something of a heart." His paintings are accomplished, but cold-blooded and uninspired. In the poem del Sarto comes to realize that he has failed to infuse into his work the quality of

a great soul. An artist's success, Browning is saying, resides not merely in technical perfection but also in the ability to give sufficiently of oneself to make the work burn with the true "light of God." Besides this self-revelation, del Sarto speaks of his troubled marriage, in that his wife desires the high life and living well beyond her means. Del Sarto is forced to compromise to gain sufficient commissions to keep up with her ambition, rather than his own.

In seeing the creation of a work of art as a moral act Browning is not advocating the kind of art that merely moralizes, although Browning's own late poems, in the years after *The Ring and the Book* (1868-1869; 4 volumes), frequently do exactly that. Lippo Lippi's monastic superiors have forced him to paint pious pictures that will "say to folk—remember matins,/ Or, mind you fast next Friday." They have told him that his purpose is not to depict the world but to "forget there's such a thing as flesh" and "to paint the souls of men." Lippi himself, however, is too honest an artist, and too fully a man, to be content with their dictates: "zooks, sir, flesh and blood,/ That's all I'm made of!" Lippi loves the things of the world, but not merely in and for themselves. He sees the beauty of the world as God's creation and therefore not to be despised. The artist, he believes (and Browning with him), by portraying finite beauty, comes closest to portraying infinite beauty as well. "I never saw," says Lippi, "beauty with no soul at all." In his characterization of this Italian monk Browning has given readers, at a distance, a veritable portrait of himself as an artist.

Three poems in *Men and Women* are about artists. Three are about churchmen, two of which, "The Bishop Orders His Tomb at St. Praxed's Church" and "Bishop Blougram's Apology," have been reckoned on an almost equal par with the two painterly monologues. All four poems delve into the respective speaker's character and motivations; all four reveal Browning's rich psychological insights as well as his ability to create the exact tones of the speaking voice as it reflects quickly changing states of mind.

"The Bishop Orders His Tomb" has a somewhat ambiguous title: Is the bishop putting his tomb in order or is he asking for it to be made in a certain way? Once again, Browning sets us in the High Renaissance, this time with "Rome, 15—," a strange mixture of faith, worldliness, ambition, and cultured learning. The bishop's rambling dying thoughts reveal his character and his values. Browning brilliantly reconstructs the obsessive nature of the bishop's motives through constant repetitions and circular arguments. The obsessions form a judgment on the bishop as a person. After all, these are his dying concerns: not heavenly at all, or asking of forgiveness, but ones concerned that some material memorial be left to him that should signify his victory over his deadly rival, Gandolf. He has already beaten Gandolf in love, having kept the beautiful mistress who is the mother of the children now greedily clustering round his deathbed. He now wants to make sure his tomb outshines that of Gandolf.

The tension in the bishop's ramblings is that the illegitimate children will not pay out the expenses for his grandiose order. He fears that the huge lump of lapis lazuli will not be placed in the tomb with him, and that the marble will not be of a fine enough quality. Even though he is bequeathing his children a fine villa, they may in their greed want more. Likewise, he fears the Latin of his epitaph will not be in a high enough style. He imagines himself lying in eternity in this tomb. There are no thoughts at all of being in Heaven. His is a purely material faith. Thus, Browning comments too on the quality of the Catholicism he sees typifying the Renaissance.

By contrast, "Bishop Blougram's Apology" is set in contemporary England. The context is the reinstatement of the Roman Catholic hierarchy in Great Britain under Cardinal Wiseman, recently appointed archbishop of Westminster, the senior Catholic in the country. The reinstatement had produced an enormous outcry in a very Protestant era, when anti-Catholic sentiments were running high, some of which Browning shared. Browning admitted that his portrayal of Blougram was based on the brilliant Wiseman.

It has often been supposed, therefore, that Browning's poem is a satire, exposing the bishop's worldliness as being of the same sort as in the previous poem. At one level, it is. The bishop is talking to a second-rate journalist, probably modeled on a friend of Browning, Alfred Domett. The journalist has written something deprecatory on Blougram; in response, Blougram invites him to dinner, and the monologue takes place over glasses of wine after the meal is over. Blougram all the time stresses how materially advantageous his life of faith is, compared to Gigadibs' life of meager earnings, derived from his unbelief.

Thus, Blougram's defense of faith seems as materialistic as that of the other bishop, and as worthless. However, Blougram is shown to have a quick and self-aware mind, as well as a keen enjoyment in sophistry, that is, constructing clever, even shocking arguments for the sheer sake of argumentation. So the reader never quite knows whether Blougram actually believes anything he is arguing. At the end, Browning, unusually, writes an epigraph that suggests that Blougram's real, gut beliefs have remained unspoken. Browning has been criticized for needing the epigraph, in which he also states that after the interview, Gigadibs had given up journalism and emigrated, just as Domett had done.

It may well be that Browning found himself warming to the rogue bishop and actually giving him sentiments that he, too, had believed—such as, for example, the fight of faith and the test of character such a struggle brings. Blougram takes over some of philosopher-theologian Blaise Pascal's arguments about the divine wager, but mixes them provocatively with the idea of accommodation. The memorable image he uses is indeed about cabin accommodation on board ship, and the analogy works brilliantly.

When readers have sifted Browning's poems for their ideas, even those about art, they have done him less than justice as a poet. His greatness is, ultimately, located in his creation of memorable characters: the Chaucerian Fra Lippo Lippi, the self-pitying Andrea del Sarto, the wily Bishop Blougram, the Greek Cleon, the Arab Karshish, the dying bishop concerned about his tomb, and a whole gallery of lovers in a splendid variety of moods. Browning's early failures as a writer for the stage taught him a valuable lesson: His abilities were best suited for the delineation of "Action in Character, rather than Character in Action." His psychological studies of action within his justly famous characters, particularly in the dramatic monologues, are the main basis for his great reputation.

It is interesting to note that, during his lifetime, Browning's fame came slowly. The sale of so great a collection of poems as *Men and Women* was disappointingly small, and no second edition was ever called for. It was not until the publication of *Dramatis Personae*, in 1864, that Browning began to receive the recognition he deserved.

Revised by David Barratt

Further Reading

Browning, Robert. *Robert Browning's Poetry: Authoritative Texts, Criticism.* Selected and edited by James F. Loucks and Andrew M. Stauffer. 2d ed. New York: W. W. Norton, 2007. In addition to a selection of Browning's poetry, this volume contains essays about his work written by nineteenth and twentieth century poets, writers, and critics. Includes novelist George Eliot's piece about *Men and Women.*

Erickson, Lee. "The Self and Others in Browning's *Men and Women.*" *Victorian Poetry* 21, no. 1 (Spring, 1983): 43-64. Browning exemplified Georg Wilhelm Friedrich Hegel's pattern for romantic art, creating monologists who gained true self-consciousness by interacting with another; frequently, this other is God.

Haigwood, Laura E. "Gender-to-Gender Anxiety and Influence in Robert Browning's *Men and Women.*" *Browning*

Institute Studies: An Annual Review of Victorian Literary and Cultural History 14 (1986): 97-118. To break ten years of silence and to write in a new style, Browning needed to distance himself from his wife, Elizabeth Barrett Browning, who was a more successful and more popular poet. Suggests that Browning may have respected her editorial judgment too highly.

Hawlin, Stefan. *The Complete Critical Guide to Robert Browning*. New York: Routledge, 2002. This student sourcebook contains information about Browning's life and times, as well as discussion and criticism of his work. Devotes a chapter to *Men and Women* and *Dramatis Personae*, focusing on the poems about art, religion, and love.

Jack, Ian. *Browning's Major Poetry*. Oxford, England: Clarendon Press, 1973. One of the best introductions to Browning's poetry. Chapter 12 deals with the final collection of *Men and Women*.

Kennedy, Richard S., and Donald S. Hair. *The Dramatic Imagination of Robert Browning: A Literary Life*. Columbia: University of Missouri Press, 2007. A literary biography, recounting the events of Browning's life and placing his life within the context of its times. Offers critical commentary on his poetry. *Men and Women* is discussed in chapter 25.

Willy, Margaret. *A Critical Commentary on Browning's "Men and Women."* New York: Macmillan, 1968. An excellent introduction to *Men and Women*. Defines the dramatic monologue, summarizes Browning's philosophy and style, describes his modernity, and offers analyses of various poems.

Woolford, John. *Robert Browning*. Tavistock, England: Northcote House/British Council, 2007. In his time, Browning was called a grotesque poet. Woolford examines the meaning of this term and how it defines Browning's poetry.

The Menaechmi

Author: Plautus (c. 254-184 B.C.E.)

First produced: Second century B.C.E. (English translation, 1595)

Type of work: Drama

Type of plot: Farce

Time of plot: Third century B.C.E.

Locale: Epidamnum, a city of Macedonia

Principal characters:

MENAECHMUS OF EPIDAMNUM

MENAECHMUS SOSICLES, his twin brother

MESSENIO, Menaechmus Sosicles' servant

WIFE OF MENAECHMUS OF EPIDAMNUM

EROTIUM, a courtesan, Menaechmus of Epidamnum's mistress

PENICULUS, a parasite, hanger-on to Menaechmus of Epidamnum

The Story:

When the two Menaechmi are seven years old, one, later to become Menaechmus of Epidamnum, accompanies his merchant father from their home in Syracuse to Tarentum. There, fascinated by the confused activity, the boy wanders away, becomes lost, and is finally picked up by another merchant who takes him to the merchant's own home in Epidamnum and adopts him. The boy's family is so grief-stricken at his loss that his name is given to the remaining son. This boy, Menaechmus Sosicles, grows up, and when he comes of age and inherits his father's property, he goes out on a quest for his brother.

Menaechmus of Epidamnum by this time has inherited his foster father's wealth, married a somewhat shrewish woman, and acquired a mistress. On the day Menaechmus Sosicles arrives in Epidamnum on his undirected search, Menaechmus of Epidamnum quarrels with his suspicious wife and parts from her, secretly bearing one of her robes as a gift to Erotium, his mistress. Delivering the robe, he instructs Erotium to prepare an elaborate meal for their evening's entertainment; then he leaves to attend to some business at the Forum.

Shortly afterward, Menaechmus Sosicles happens to arrive before Erotium's house and, much to his dismay, is addressed familiarly, first by one of her servants and then by Erotium herself. Confusion follows, but Menaechmus Sosicles finally decides that this is merely Erotium's way of trying to seduce him; so he gives his servant Messenio his wallet for safekeeping and accompanies the courtesan into the house.

When he comes out later, having consumed the food that Menaechmus of Epidamnum ordered for himself and his parasite, Erotium gives him the robe so that he can have it altered for her. As he walks away, intent on selling the robe for his own gain, he is accosted by Peniculus, Menaechmus of Epidamnum's parasite, indignant at having missed a banquet to which he was invited only a short time before and convinced that he was purposely affronted. Menaechmus Sosicles finally dismisses Peniculus with an insult, and the latter, believing himself grievously treated by his erstwhile benefactor, goes to Menaechmus of Epidamnum's wife and reveals to her that her husband is not only keeping another woman but also gave his mistress his wife's robe. When Peniculus finishes, Menaechmus of Epidamnum comes by on his way from the Forum to Erotium's house, and, in concealment, the two overhear him soliloquizing in a way that substantiates Peniculus's whole story. Satisfied with what she hears, the wife steps forward and accosts her husband. There follows a confused argument in which Menaechmus of Epidamnum alternates between dissembled ignorance regarding the theft of the robe and genuine dismay regarding his assumed presence at the banquet Erotium gave. At last, seeing that Peniculus revealed all, he agrees to get the robe and return it. When he goes to Erotium and, unaware that Menaechmus Sosicles already took the robe, tries to explain his dilemma, she assumes he is trying to defraud her, grows angry, and slams her door in his face.

Meanwhile, Menaechmus Sosicles, still carrying the robe, meets the angry wife, who assumes that he is Menaechmus of Epidamnum returning the robe as he promised. While the whole situation is still in confusion, the wife's father arrives to take her part. Menaechmus Sosicles decides to feign madness to get rid of the two and is so successful in his attempt that they go off in search of a physician and men to restrain him.

When these people are assembled, they meet Menaechmus of Epidamnum instead of his brother. They are about to carry him off when Messenio happens along and, mistaking Menaechmus of Epidamnum for his brother, beats off the assailants. When the others flee, Messenio asks for his freedom in return for saving his "master's" life; his request is granted by the amazed Menaechmus of Epidamnum, and Messenio goes off to collect his master's belongings and to return them.

On the way, however, he meets Menaechmus Sosicles. Gradually the nature of the confusion comes to light. The two brothers finally confront each other and exchange their stories. Menaechmus of Epidamnum decides to sell his property and return to Syracuse with his brother. Messenio is freed again, this time by his own master, and is made auctioneer for the sale of the property. Everything is to be converted into cash, including Menaechmus of Epidamnum's wife.

Critical Evaluation:

The Menaechmi can be counted as one of Plautus's most enduring successes. As is often noted, there is a more-or-less direct line of descent from his story of separated twins, almost certainly taken from a Greek play, to William Shakespeare's *The Comedy of Errors* (pr. c. 1592-1594, pb. 1623), a Renaissance farce of two sets of separated twins; to the twentieth century American Broadway musical *The Boys from Syracuse* (1938) by Richard Rodgers and Lorenz Hart. The borrowing may not be over yet.

The history of this mistaken-identity plot goes back to the ancient Greeks and most probably to the source of many Latin plays, the Greek New Comedy. It was customary for the Roman playwrights to base their plays on the Greek originals. The plays of Plautus, however, like those of his contemporaries, reflect the Roman society of his day rather than depicting the lives of the ancient Greeks. The illusion of another time and place supplied by the Greek dress employed on the Roman stage merely enabled playwrights to poke fun at Roman ways under the guise of attacking the Greeks.

Since very few Greek originals have been recovered, it is not easy to evaluate Plautus's originality. Moreover, it is also thought that Latin playwrights combined the Greek New Comedy with the earlier dramatic forms of Italy, which were farcical and included much song and dance. However much he owed to his sources, Plautus is appreciated for his ultimate products, which had a great influence on Western drama.

Three of the achievements that make his plays living theater are Plautus's gift with the Latin language, his memorable characters, and his humor. His language, though certainly hard to appreciate in translation, is well regarded by Latin scholars for being both colloquial and wonderfully fluent: The idiomatic Latin is lively and vulgar, yet the metrics are supple. The vulgarity caused Plautus to fall into disfavor in certain periods, such as the Middle Ages in Europe. Since the rediscovery and reappreciation of all things classical during the Renaissance, Plautus has entertained all those who appreciate Latin.

Equally, in the theater, his gift for farcical situations and his use of song and dance have produced entertaining plays. Whether his plays have a social message remains a matter of debate. Plautus is held in low regard by some critics because his plays seem merely to be wildly amusing. Others, perhaps in response, have found some social commentary in the plays. A third group finds meaning in the social function of plays, whether or not the plays themselves hold any deep meaning.

The Menaechmi is in several respects illustrative of the best Plautine elements of comedy. It is generally admired for its exquisitely balanced and neat construction. Given the basic improbability of the situation, which is that the visiting brother who sets out to find his missing brother with the same name is being mistaken for someone else and yet does not understand his predicament, the swift pace of the play and Plautus's lively language and songs and dance keep it entertaining for the audience.

Beyond its excellence as farce, *The Menaechmi* may be interpreted as a comic wish-fulfillment of its original Roman, mostly male, audiences. As the scholar Erich Segal notes, what Menaechmus Sosicles experiences is, though confusing, a male dream fulfilled: money, sex, and food for nothing. The confusion adds to the dreamlike, fantasy state. A comparison of the dietary restrictions of the times with the food described for the feasts in the play, Segal also notes, is another example of defying social conventions.

Although Plautus's comedies, along with other Latin comedies, have long and often been credited—or perhaps accused—with setting the example for the clichéd, romantic comedy with a happy ending, *The Menaechmi* shows the great range and variety to be found in his works. This range of tone indicates that Plautus is not responsible for the sentimentality of later playwrights. The clearest example of the antiromantic, unsentimental tone in this particular play is the cynical treatment of love. The married brother has a shrewish wife. Part of the plot complication is that he has a mistress to whom he gives what he steals from his wife. Menaechmus of Epidamnum is already bouncing back and forth between duty to a wife he does not love and pleasure with a courtesan when his brother further complicates his life. Furthermore, neither woman is portrayed in an attractive light. The wife is a nag and Erotium is greedy and grasping. The ending, in which the brothers go off with each other and leave everyone else behind, is somewhat startling to anyone used to a more conventional happy ending. The rightness of a traditional family at the end of a comedy is generally reinforced by having errors cleared up. In this play, the brothers decide that the situation is hopeless and simply leave.

On the other hand, some scholars would argue, this ending is also appropriate if one considers the social function of comedy. Comedy often endorses the overturning of too-rigid social customs and the momentary release of inhibitions.

Plautus uses the common stock of comedies to win the approval of audiences seeking a momentary change in their ordinary lives.

That *The Menaechmi* survived so long is a testament to Plautus's great skill in constructing a swiftly moving plot, amusing characters, and entertaining language. Whether he intends social commentary as well is a matter of interpretation. In using much of the local color of his day—the Roman references to places, customs, sayings—he leaves a stamp of his culture on a durable plot of mistaken identity.

"Critical Evaluation" by Shakuntala Jayaswal

Further Reading

Beare, William. *The Roman Stage*. 1965. Reprint. London: Methuen, 1977. This introduction to the history of Latin drama has three chapters on Plautus. Provides a quick overview of his life and work. Useful as background.

Candido, Joseph. "Dining Out in Ephesus: Food in *The Comedy of Errors*." *Studies in English Literature* 30, no. 2 (Spring, 1990): 217-241. Focused on the Shakespeare play based on *The Menaechmi*, this article explains the significance of food in both plays and sheds light on Plautus's play.

Duckworth, George. *The Nature of Roman Comedy: A Study in Popular Entertainment*. 2d ed. Norman: University of Oklahoma Press, 1994. The classic study of Roman comedy. Provides a comprehensive introduction to Latin playwrights, including Plautus.

Fraenkel, Eduard. *Plautine Elements in Plautus*. Translated by Tomas Drevikovsky and Frances Muecke. New York: Oxford University Press, 2007. This is the first English translation of a German study initially published in 1922. Fraenkel, an influential twentieth century classicist, provides an analytical overview of Plautus's plays, including their motifs of transformation and identification, mythological material, dialogue, and the predominance of the slave's role.

Leigh, Matthew. *Comedy and the Rise of Rome*. New York: Oxford University Press, 2004. Analyzes the comedies of Plautus and Terence, placing them within the context of political and economic conditions in Rome during the third and second centuries B.C.E. Discusses how audiences of that time responded to these comedies.

McCarthy, Kathleen. *Slaves, Masters, and the Art of Authority in Plautine Comedy*. Princeton, N.J.: Princeton University Press, 2000. Analyzes four of Plautus's plays, including *The Menaechmi*, focusing on audience reactions to the heroic trickster characters. McCarthy maintains that the plays derive their comedy from the conflict between their naturalistic and farcical elements.

Plautus. *Menaechmi*. Introduction by A. S. Gratwick. New York: Cambridge University Press, 1993. The English-language introduction to the Latin-language play is comprehensive, containing information on Plautus, the play, and how to scan Latin verse.

Segal, Erich. *Roman Laughter: The Comedy of Plautus*. Cambridge, Mass.: Harvard University Press, 1968. Organized by topics. Argues that all of Plautus's comedies

were meant to make the Romans laugh by reversing Roman values on stage. This study is often quoted in articles about Plautus.

_____, ed. *Oxford Readings in Menander, Plautus, and Terence*. New York: Oxford University Press, 2001. Includes essays on Plautus and the public stage, the response of Plautus's audience, and traditions, theatrical improvisation, and mastery of comic language in his plays. Erich Segal's essay, "*Menaechmi*: Roman Comedy of Errors," analyzes this play.

The Merchant of Venice

Author: William Shakespeare (1564-1616)
First produced: c. 1596-1597; first published, 1600
Type of work: Drama
Type of plot: Tragicomedy
Time of plot: Sixteenth century
Locale: Venice

Principal characters:
SHYLOCK, a Jewish moneylender
PORTIA, a wealthy young woman
ANTONIO, an impoverished merchant, Shylock's enemy, who is championed by Portia
BASSANIO, Portia's husband and Antonio's friend
NERISSA, Portia's waiting-woman
GRATIANO, Nerissa's husband and Bassanio's friend
JESSICA, Shylock's daughter
LORENZO, Jessica's husband

The Story:

Bassanio, meeting his wealthy friend Antonio, reveals that he has a plan for restoring the fortune he carelessly spent and for paying the debts he incurred. In the town of Belmont, not far from Venice, there lives a wealthy young woman named Portia, who is famous for her beauty. If he can secure some money, Bassanio declares, he is sure he can win her as his wife. Antonio replies that he has no funds at hand with which to supply his friend, as they are all invested in the ships he has at sea, but that he will attempt to borrow money for him in Venice.

Portia has many suitors for her hand. According to the strange conditions of her father's will, however, anyone who wishes her for his wife has to choose correctly among three caskets of silver, gold, and lead the casket that contains the message that Portia is his. In case of failure, the suitors are compelled to swear never to reveal which casket they chose and never to woo another woman. Four of her suitors, seeing they cannot win her except under the conditions of the will, depart. A fifth, a Moor, decides to take his chances. The unfortunate man chooses the golden casket, which contains a

skull and a mocking message. The prince of Arragon is the next suitor to try his luck. He chooses the silver casket, only to learn from the note it holds that he is a fool.

True to his promise to Bassanio, Antonio arranges to borrow three thousand ducats from Shylock, a wealthy Jew. Antonio is to have the use of the money for three months. If he finds himself unable to return the loan at the end of that time, Shylock is given the right to cut a pound of flesh from any part of Antonio's body. Despite Bassanio's objections, Antonio insists on accepting the terms, for he is sure his ships will return a month before the payment is due. He is confident that he will never fall into the power of the Jew, who hates Antonio because he often lends money to others without charging the interest Shylock demands.

That night, Bassanio plans a feast and a masque. In conspiracy with his friend, Lorenzo, he invites Shylock to be his guest. Lorenzo, taking advantage of her father's absence, runs off with the Jew's daughter, Jessica, who takes part of Shylock's fortune with her. Shylock is cheated not only of his daughter and his ducats but also of his entertainment, for the wind suddenly changes and Bassanio sets sail for Belmont.

As the days pass, the Jew begins to hear news of mingled good and bad fortune. In Genoa, Jessica and Lorenzo are lavishly spending the money she took with her. The miser flinches at the reports of his daughter's extravagance, but for compensation he has the news that Antonio's ships, on which his continuing fortune depends, were wrecked at sea.

Portia, much taken with Bassanio when he comes to woo her, will have him wait before he tries to pick the right casket. Sure that he will fail as the others did, she hopes to have his company a little while longer. Bassanio, however, is impatient to try his luck. Not deceived by the ornateness of the gold and silver caskets, and philosophizing that true virtue is inward virtue, he chooses the lead box. In it is a portrait of Portia. He chose correctly. To seal their engagement, Portia gives Bassanio a ring. She declares he must never part with it, for if he does, it will signify the end of their love.

Gratiano, a friend who accompanied Bassanio to Belmont, speaks up. He is in love with Portia's waiting-woman, Nerissa. With Portia's delighted approval, Gratiano plans that both couples should be married at the same time.

Bassanio's joy at his good fortune is soon blighted. Antonio writes that he is ruined, all his ships failing to return. The time for payment of the loan past due, Shylock demands his pound of flesh. In closing, Antonio declares that he clears Bassanio of his debt to him. He wishes only to see his friend once more before his death. Portia declares that the double wedding should take place at once. Then her husband will be able to set out for Venice in an attempt to buy off the Jew with her dowry of six thousand ducats.

After Bassanio and Gratiano depart, Portia declares to Lorenzo and Jessica, who had come to Belmont, that she and Nerissa are going to a nunnery, where they will live in seclusion until their husbands return. She commits the charge of her house and servants to Jessica and Lorenzo.

Instead of taking the course she described, however, Portia sets about executing other plans. She gives her servant, Balthasar, orders to take a note to her cousin, Doctor Bellario, a famous lawyer of Padua, in order to secure a message and some clothes from him. She explains to Nerissa that they will go to Venice disguised as men.

The duke of Venice, before whom Antonio's case is tried, is reluctant to exact the penalty in Shylock's contract. When his appeals to the Jew's better feelings go unheeded, he can see no course before him but to allow the moneylender his due. Bassanio tries to make Shylock relent by offering him the six thousand ducats, but, like the duke, he meets only a firm refusal.

Portia, dressed as a lawyer, and Nerissa, disguised as her clerk, appear in the court. Nerissa offers the duke a letter from Doctor Bellario, in which the doctor explains that he is very ill, but that Balthasar, his young representative, will present his opinion in the dispute.

When Portia appeals to the Jew's mercy, Shylock merely demands the penalty. Portia then declares that the Jew, under the letter of the contract, cannot be offered money in exchange for Antonio's release. The only alternative is for the merchant to forfeit his flesh.

Antonio prepares his bosom for the knife, for Shylock is determined to take his portion as close to his enemy's heart as he can cut. Before the operation can begin, however, Portia, examining the contract, declares that it contains no clause stating that Shylock can have any blood with the flesh. The Jew, realizing that he is defeated, offers at once to accept the six thousand ducats, but Portia declares that he is not entitled to the money he already refused. She states also that Shylock, an alien, threatened the life of a Venetian citizen. For that crime Antonio has the right to seize half of his property and the state the remainder.

Antonio refuses that penalty, but it is agreed that one-half of Shylock's fortune should go at once to Jessica and Lorenzo. Shylock is to keep the remainder, but it is to be willed to the couple after his death. In addition, Shylock is to undergo conversion. The defeated man has no choice but to agree to the terms.

Pressed to accept a reward, Portia takes only a pair of Antonio's gloves and the ring that she herself gave Bassanio. Nerissa, likewise, manages to secure Gratiano's ring. Then Portia and Nerissa start back for Belmont, to be there when their husbands return. They arrive home shortly before Bassanio and Gratiano appear in company with Antonio. Pretending to discover that their husbands' rings are missing, Portia and Nerissa at first accuse Bassanio and Gratiano of unfaithfulness. At last, to the surprise of all, they reveal their secret, which is vouched for by a letter from Doctor Bellario. For Jessica and Lorenzo, they have the good news of their future inheritance, and for Antonio a letter, secured by chance, announcing that some of his ships arrived safely in port after all.

Critical Evaluation:

Through the years, *The Merchant of Venice* has been one of William Shakespeare's most popular and most frequently performed plays. The work has an interesting and fast-moving plot, and it evokes an idyllic, uncorrupted world reminiscent of folktale and romance. From the opening description of Antonio's nameless sadness, the world is bathed in light and music. The insistently improbable plot is complicated only by the evil influence of Shylock, and he is disposed of by the end of act 4. However, Shakespeare uses this fragile vehicle to make significant points about justice, mercy, and friendship, three typical Renaissance virtues. Although some critics suggest that the play contains all of the elements of tragedy only to be rescued by a comic resolution, the tone of the whole play creates a benevolent world in which, despite some opposition, things will always work out for the best.

The story, based on ancient tales that could have been drawn from many sources, is actually two stories in one—the casket plot, involving the choice by the suitor and his reward with Portia, and the bond plot, involving the loan and the attempt to exact a pound of flesh. Shakespeare's genius is revealed in the way he combines the two. Although they intersect from the start in the character of Bassanio, who occasions Antonio's debt and is a suitor, they fully coalesce when Portia comes to Venice in disguise to make her plea and judgment for Antonio. At that point, the bond plot is unraveled by the casket heroine, after which the fifth act brings the celebratory conclusion and joy.

The most fascinating character to both audiences and critics always has been Shylock, the outsider, the anomaly in this felicitous world. Controversy rages over just what kind of villain Shylock is and just how villainous Shakespeare intended him to be. The matter is complicated by the desire to absolve Shakespeare of the common medieval and Renaissance vice of anti-Semitism. Some commentators argued that in Shylock Shakespeare takes the stock character of the Jew—as personified in Christopher Marlowe's Barabas in his *The Jew of Malta* (1589)—and fleshes him out with complicating human characteristics. Some went so far as to argue that, even in his villainy, Shylock is presented as a victim of the Christian society, the grotesque product of hatred and ostracism. Regardless of Shakespeare's personal views, the fact remains that, in his treatment, Shylock becomes much more than a stock villain.

The more significant dramatic question is just what sort of character Shylock is and what sort of role he is being called upon to play. Certainly he is an outsider in both appearance and action, a stranger to the light and gracious world of Venice and Belmont. His language is full of stridency and materialism, which isolates him from the other characters. He has no part in the network of beautiful friendships that unites the others. He is not wholly a comic character, for despite often appearing ridiculous, he poses too much of a threat to be dismissed lightly. However, he is too ineffectual and grotesque to be a villain as cold and terrifying as Iago or Edmund, or one as engaging as Richard III. He is a

malevolent force, who is finally overcome by the more generous world in which he lives. That he is treated so harshly by the Christians is the kind of irony that ultimately protects Shakespeare from charges of mindless anti-Semitism. Still, on the level of the romantic plot, he is also the serpent in the garden, deserving summary expulsion and the forced conversion that is both a punishment and a charity.

The rest of the major characters have much more in common with each other as sharers in the common civilization of Venice. As they come into conflict with Shylock and form relationships with one another, they act out the ideals and commonplaces of high Renaissance culture. Antonio, in his small but pivotal role, is afflicted with a fashionable melancholy and a gift for friendship. It is his casually generous act of friendship that sets the bond plot in motion. Bassanio frequently comments on friendship and knows how to accept generosity gracefully, but Bassanio is not only a model Renaissance friend but also a model Renaissance lover. He is quite frankly as interested in Portia's money as in her wit and beauty; he unself-consciously represents a cultural integration of love and gain quite different from Shylock's materialism. When he chooses the leaden casket, he does so for precisely the right traditional reason—a distrust of appearances, a recognition that the reality does not always correspond. Of course, his success as suitor is never really in doubt but is choreographed like a ballet. In any case, it is always the third suitor who is the successful one in folktales. What the ballet provides is another opportunity for the expression of the culturally correct sentiments.

Portia, too, is a heroine of her culture. She is not only an object of love but also a witty and an intelligent woman whose ingenuity resolves the central dilemma. That she, too, is not what she seems to be in the trial scene is another example of the dichotomy between familiar appearance and reality. More important, she has the opportunity to discourse on the nature of mercy as opposed to strict justice and to give an object lesson that he who lives by the letter of the law will perish by it.

With Shylock safely, if a bit harshly, out of the way, the last act is an amusing festival of vindication of cultural values. The characters have had their opportunity to comment on the proper issues—love, friendship, justice, and the disparity between appearances and reality. Now all receive their appropriate reward in marriages and reunions or, in the case of Antonio, with the pleasantly gratuitous recovery of his fortune. There is no more trouble in paradise among the people of grace.

"Critical Evaluation" by Edward E. Foster

Further Reading

Adelman, Janet. *Blood Relations: Christian and Jew in "The Merchant of Venice."* Chicago: University of Chicago Press, 2008. Argues that the play's depiction of the uneasy relationship between Christians and Jews reflects Christians' anxiety and guilt about their simultaneous dependence on and disavowal of Judaism.

Bulman, James. *Shakespeare in Performance: The Merchant of Venice.* New York: St. Martin's Press, 1992. Provides a survey of nineteenth century productions and a critique of several major twentieth century productions, including a comparison of Jonathan Miller's stage version, featuring Laurence Olivier as Shylock, with the British Broadcasting Corporation television version he produced ten years later.

Danson, Lawrence. *The Harmonies of "The Merchant of Venice."* New Haven, Conn.: Yale University Press, 1978. An excellent full-length study of the play that treats everything from "The Problem of Shylock" to law and language, miracle and myth, love and friendship, and the "quality of mercy."

Gross, John. *Shylock: Four Hundred Years in the Life of a Legend.* London: Chatto & Windus, 1992. Examines *The Merchant of Venice* and the character of Shylock within the context of the history of anti-Semitism in the Western world. Discusses the stage history of the play, including several adaptations.

Gross, Kenneth. *Shylock Is Shakespeare.* Chicago: University of Chicago Press, 2006. Argues that Shylock is the voice of Shakespeare himself, a "mask for Shakespeare's own need, rage, vulnerability and generosity." Maintains *The Merchant of Venice* is a dramatic breakthrough, in which Shakespeare realizes his power to create characters that are larger than the plays in which they appear.

Hamilton, Sharon. "Daughters Who Act in Their Fathers' Stead: Portia (*The Merchant of Venice*), Viola (*Twelfth Night*), and Rosalind (*As You Like It*)." In *Shakespeare's Daughters.* Jefferson, N.C.: McFarland, 2003. Analyzes the relationship of Portia and her father.

Janie, Vicki K. *"The Merchant of Venice": A Guide to the Play.* Westport, Conn.: Greenwood Press, 2003. Introductory overview describing the play's themes, contexts, critical reception, and performance history.

Levin, Richard A. *Love and Society in Shakespearean Comedy.* Newark: University of Delaware Press, 1985. Devotes one chapter to *The Merchant of Venice* and focuses on one of the play's central problems: the ambiguity of Shylock's conflicting motives in the third scene of act 1. The bond proposed may have been "a vicious and deceptive offer," or it may have been an incentive for better treatment from Antonio and others.

Macon, John W., and Ellen Macleod Macon, eds. *"The Merchant of Venice": New Critical Essays.* New York: Routledge, 2002. John W. Macon's lengthy essay, "The Fortunes of *The Merchant of Venice* from 1596 to 2001," provides a valuable introduction to the major issues in the play. Some of the other essays discuss the depiction of the Jewish daughter in Elizabethan literature, the characters of Shylock, Portia, and Jessica, and the play in performance.

Rabkin, Norman. *Shakespeare and the Problem of Meaning.* Chicago: University of Chicago Press, 1981. In a superb essay on *The Merchant of Venice*, Rabkin notes the many significant inconsistencies and contradictions in the play and shows the impossibility of imposing an easy, reductivist interpretation on it.

Meridian

Author: Alice Walker (1944-   )
First published: 1976
Type of work: Novel
Type of plot: Social realism
Time of plot: 1950-1970's
Locale: Georgia, Mississippi, and New York City

Principal characters:
MERIDIAN HILL, a civil rights worker and college student
TRUMAN HELD, a civil rights worker, college student, and Meridian's lover
LYNNE RABINOWITZ, Meridian's friend, and a volunteer
GERTRUDE HILL, Meridian's mother
EDDIE, Meridian's husband
THE WILD CHILD, a pregnant orphan

The Story:

Truman Held returns to Chickokema, Georgia, to find his former lover Meridian Hill. He stops to ask directions and witnesses Meridian confronting an old military tank, originally purchased by the town during the 1960's and now functioning as an amusement for poor kids. Truman then goes to Meridian's stark house, where he and Meridian eventually have a discussion that hints at their past history, both as lovers and as participants in the Civil Rights movement.

Meridian remembers her time as a student at Saxon College, and her story is as follows: Meridian is involved with the Wild Child, an orphaned pregnant girl to whom she shows compassion. Meridian brings the child to her room at college, bathes her, and feeds her. The next morning, the Wild Child runs out of the house and is hit by a car as she crosses the street. College officials refuse to allow a funeral for the Wild Child, so Meridian and her friends riot, in the process chopping down The Sojourner, a symbolic, historical tree central to the campus.

Meridian's mother and father are religiously legalistic. Her father owns a piece of land with a unique mound called Serpent's Tail. He deeds the land back to a Cherokee Indian because the Cherokee once owned the land. Eventually, the land is made into a historical site, but is closed to African Americans.

Meridian lacks preparation for love; she is socially ignorant and has no knowledge of sex or sexuality. She eventually becomes pregnant, then marries her boyfriend, Eddie. Given its awkward beginning, her love for Eddie does not last. She also is becoming more keenly aware of social and political tensions. When she unexpectedly gets a scholarship for college, she gives up Eddie and her child for the chance to attend, against the wishes of her mother, Gertrude Hill. Meridian is followed by guilt, but continues to involve herself in political issues. Meridian's desire for equality is contrasted with the relatively resigned life of her mother.

Meridian falls ill. She collapses and is bed-ridden for a month. She battles this condition for some time, as the illness comes to affect her mood and her energy.

Back in school, Meridian meets Truman, and they become lovers. They spend much of their time and energy registering blacks to vote. Meridian also meets Lynne Rabinowitz, who has come to the South from New York to participate in the Civil Rights movement. Lynne will soon become entangled with Truman, further complicating Meridian's attempts to find peace and purpose. Lynne is often ignored by the black rights-workers, or is simply taken for granted; she often turns to Meridian for consolation. Later, Lynne is raped by one of Truman's friends. Truman, meanwhile,

moves on to other lovers. He eventually reunites with Meridian, but she refuses his sexual advances.

The Reverend Martin Luther King, Jr., is assassinated, leading Meridian to reflect on the Civil Rights movement in general and on her personal involvement in the movement and her growth in particular. She remains friends with Truman and seems free from sexual and other kinds of entanglements.

Years later, in the early 1970's, Meridian is still actively involved in voter registration, political activism, and civil rights organization. She continues working, as the work for social justice continues.

Critical Evaluation:

Alice Walker, the Pulitzer Prize-winning author of the novel *The Color Purple* (1982), draws on some of her own personal experiences, such as registering black voters, to create a realistic and heartrending account of the subtle but intense layers of social hierarchies of the American South during the years of the Civil Rights movement. The novel's gritty scenes and dialogues confront readers with the physical and psychological effects resulting from the intense social changes of the time.

One primary theme of the novel is how the fight for social justice takes its toll on those working toward that end. It becomes clear in the novel that although a character may participate in a struggle for equality, this overarching, idealistic goal does not preclude selfish and chaotic behavior on the part of individuals working in the struggle.

Meridian is a character-driven novel, rather than one driven by plot, highlighting the feelings of fear and failure of its principal characters. The novel is structured into three main parts that roughly follow Meridian's experiences from college to her independent but isolated self as a caring person who is unattached and free to love without the burdens of sex, abuse, and institutional baggage. Structurally, it is possible to regard Meridian's development, her movement from naïveté to understanding, as an innovation of the classic bildungsroman.

The novel contains many historical references, realistically conveying the context of the American Civil Rights movement. Walker alludes to figures such as activist Medgar Evers and murdered student activists. A chapter describing the funeral of the assassinated Reverend Martin Luther King, Jr., is also prominent.

The novel is more than a factual account of history, however. Walker imagines a tender, big-souled, albeit initially naïve protagonist whose name suggests the bloody division between the Old South and the potential for a new day. Meridian is an uncertain protagonist who grows toward self-confidence. She also symbolizes qualities beyond her individual character. It is possible to see her as a symbolic embodiment of the Civil Rights movement itself, young and growing, uncertain but idealistic. In the face of human failure along the way, she eventually is successful because of her sheer determination.

The cause that demanded equality for African Americans was greater than any individual. Through Walker's vision of Meridian and the others in the novel, readers gain entrance into the particular, intense, and unpleasant intimacy of the people involved in that greater cause—one whose full fruition was probably beyond what even they could imagine. This novel is marked by the day-to-day working out of love and lust, hope and despair, and purpose and apathy within entangled human relationships.

Another critical theme in the novel is that of opposites working together. The truth of any situation is found not in the extremes but rather in the elastic interchange between polar opposites. To help the reader visualize the nuances of human behavior and motivation, Walker uses pairings in herstory: black/white, male/female, educated/uneducated, southern/northern, idealism/reality, capitalism/socialism, justice/injustice, violence/compassion, sacrifice/self-preservation, arrogance/humility, and aggressiveness/complacency. Walker establishes these opposing forces to engage her readers in the complexities of human behavior, especially as it affects personal motivation.

Perhaps Walker's most developed pairing concerns gender. In several respects, *Meridian* is a feminist novel, in which girls and women face abusive, no-win situations with men and boys. In contrast, men and boys, despite their involvement in a just cause, are self-centered and directed by sexual urges, even rape. Walker powerfully leads readers to consider the psychological pain her female characters endure simply by being taken for granted, ignored, or misunderstood. Walker's female characters, however, also demonstrate a confusing, sometimes ignorant, desperation. The chaos of the personal relationships between women and men cannot simply be blamed on male sexual aggression and sexism. Nevertheless, Walker's storytelling suggests a simultaneous, complex view of human entanglements that persist despite high ideals.

Kenneth E. Hada

Further Reading

Barnett, Pamela E. "'Miscegenation,' Rape, and 'Race' in Alice Walker's *Meridian*." *Southern Quarterly* 39, no. 3 (2001): 65-81. This article focuses on *Meridian*'s interracial rape scene and its implications for the novel. Readers are torn between "repulsion and sympathy," as the article tries to locate where a feminist, antiracist reader would comfortably "align" herself or himself.

Brown, Joseph A. "'All Saints Should Walk Away': The Mystical Pilgrimage of *Meridian*." *Callaloo* 39 (Spring, 1989): 310-320. This article discusses a "mystical journey" within the larger "Afro-American religious tradition" that details and makes possible the personal growth of the main character in *Meridian*.

Collins, Janelle. "'Like a Collage': Personal and Political Subjectivity in Alice Walker's *Meridian*." *CLA Journal* 44, no. 2 (December, 2000): 161-188. This article recognizes the nonlinear structure of the novel and argues that Walker refuses to "privilege one discourse" over another. The competing discourses are necessary to understand the novel's message. Also examines the unique quality of the Civil Rights movement as experienced by young black women.

Danielson, Susan. "Alice Walker's *Meridian*, Feminism, and the 'Movement.'" *Women's Studies* 16, nos. 3/4 (1989): 317-330. This article notes the relationship between personal growth and the larger Civil Rights movement. Establishes a feminist lens for reading the novel, suggesting that feminism helps one to understand change and cultural vitality.

Dixon, Henry O. *Male Protagonists in Four Novels of Alice Walker: Destruction and Development in Interpersonal Relationships*. Lewiston, N.Y.: Edwin Mellen Press, 2007. Examines the roles that male characters play in four of Walker's early novels, including *Meridian* and *The Color Purple*.

Lauret, Maria. *Alice Walker*. New York: St. Martin's Press, 2000. Offers provocative discussion of Walker's ideas on politics, race, feminism, and literary theory. Of special interest is the exploration of Walker's literary debt to Zora Neale Hurston, Virginia Woolf, and even blues singer Bessie Smith.

Pifer, Lynn. "Coming to Voice in Alice Walker's *Meridian*: Speaking Out for the Revolution." *African American Review* 26, no. 1 (Spring, 1992): 77-88. Argues that Meridian's individuality has been repressed by patriarchal institutions. Meridian's newfound understanding of her cultural history frees her to speak confidently rather than live on the margins at the mercy of other repressive voices.

White, Evelyn C. *Alice Walker: A Life*. New York: W. W. Norton, 2004. A full-length biography of Walker that recognizes the interdependence between Walker's activism and her art. Includes many references to *Meridian*. Also includes a list of publications, source notes, and an index.

Yoon, Seongho. "Gendering the Movement: Black Womanhood, SNCC, and Post-Civil Rights Anxieties in Alice Walker's *Meridian*." *Feminist Studies in English Litera-*

ture 14, no. 2 (Winter, 2006): 179-207. Examines the historical problem of seeing civil rights only in terms of a black/white binary. Also analyzes the role of women, black women in particular, whose understated leadership roles are often unappreciated.

The Merry Wives of Windsor

Author: William Shakespeare (1564-1616)
First produced: 1597; first published, 1602
Type of work: Drama
Type of plot: Comedy
Time of plot: Sixteenth century
Locale: England

Principal characters:
SIR JOHN FALSTAFF, a rogue
FENTON, a young gentleman
SLENDER, a foolish gentleman
FORD and PAGE, two gentlemen living at Windsor
DOCTOR CAIUS, a French physician
MISTRESS FORD, Ford's wife
MISTRESS PAGE, Page's wife
ANNE PAGE, the daughter of the Pages
MISTRESS QUICKLY, a servant of Doctor Caius

The Story:

Sir John Falstaff is, without doubt, a rogue. True, he is fat, jolly, and in a way lovable, but he is still a rogue. His men rob and plunder the citizens of Windsor, but he himself is seldom taken or convicted for his crimes. His fortunes at low ebb, he hits upon a plan to remedy that situation. He meets Mistress Ford and Mistress Page, two good ladies who hold the purse strings in their respective houses. Falstaff writes identical letters to the two good ladies, letters protesting undying love for each of them.

The daughter of one of the ladies, Anne Page, is the center of a love triangle. Her father wishes her to marry Slender, a foolish gentleman who does not love her or anyone else, but who will marry any girl recommended to him by his cousin, the justice. Mistress Page, on the other hand, wants her daughter married to Doctor Caius, a French physician then in Windsor. Anne herself loves Fenton, a fine young gentleman deeply in love with her. All three lovers pay the doctor's housekeeper, Mistress Quickly, to plead their cause with Anne, for Mistress Quickly convinces each that she alone can persuade Anne to answer yes to a proposal. Mistress Quickly is, in fact, second only to Falstaff in her plotting and her trickery.

Unknown to poor Falstaff, Mistress Ford and Mistress Page compare the letters received from him, alike except for the lady's name. They decide to cure him of his knavery once

and for all. Mistress Ford arranges to have him come to her house that night when her husband will not be there. Mistress Page writes that she will meet him as soon as she can cautiously arrange it. In the meantime, two former followers of Falstaff tell the two husbands of that knave's designs on their wives. Page refuses to believe his wife unfaithful, but Ford becomes jealous and plans to spy on his wife. Disguising himself as Mr. Brook, he calls on Falstaff. His story is that he loves Mistress Ford but cannot win her love, and he comes to pay Falstaff to court her for him. His stratagem is successful; he learns from Falstaff that the knight already has a rendezvous with the lady that very night.

At the appointed time, previously arranging to have several servants assist in the plot, the two ladies are ready for Falstaff. While Falstaff is trying to make love to Mistress Ford, Mistress Page rushes in and says that Ford is on his way home. Quickly the ladies put Falstaff in a clothes basket and have him carried out by the servants, to be dumped into the Thames. Ford does arrive, of course, for, unknown to his wife, he knows Falstaff is to be there. After looking high and low without finding the rogue, he apologizes to his wife for his suspicions. Mistress Ford does not know which was the most sport, having Falstaff dumped into the river or listening to her husband's discomfited apologies.

The ladies have so much fun over their first joke played on

Falstaff that they decide to try another. Mistress Ford then sends him another message, this one saying that her husband will be gone all of the following morning, and she asks Falstaff to call on her at that time so that she can make amends for the previous affair of the basket. Again Ford, disguised as Brook, calls on Falstaff, and again he learns of the proposed assignation. He learns also of the method of Falstaff's previous escape and vows the old roisterer should not again slip through his fingers.

When Mistress Ford hears from Mistress Page that Ford is returning unexpectedly, the ladies dress Falstaff in the clothes of a fat woman whom Ford hates. Ford, finding the supposed woman in his house, drubs the disguised knight soundly and chases him from the house. Again Ford searches everywhere for Falstaff, and again he is forced to apologize to his wife in the presence of the friends he brought with him to witness her disgrace. The two ladies think his discomfiture the funniest part of their joke.

Once more the wives plan to plague poor Falstaff, but this time they take their husbands into their confidence. When Mistress Page and Mistress Ford tell about the letters they received from Falstaff and explain the details of the two previous adventures, Ford feels very contrite over his former suspicions of his wife. Eagerly, the husbands join their wives in a final scheme intended to bring Falstaff to public shame. The ladies persuade Falstaff to meet them in the park at midnight. Falstaff is to be disguised as Herne the Hunter, a horned legendary huntsman said to roam the wintry woods each midnight. There he will be surrounded by Anne and others dressed as fairies and elves. After he is frightened half to death, the husbands will accost him and publicly display his knavery.

A quite different event was planned for that night. Page plots to have Slender seize Anne in her disguise as the fairy queen and carry her away to marry her. At the same time, Mistress Page arranges to have Doctor Caius find Anne and take her away to be married. Anne, however, has other plans. She and Fenton agree to meet in the park and under cover of the dark and confusion flee her parents and her two unwelcome suitors.

All plans are put into effect. Falstaff, after telling the supposed Brook that on this night he will for a certainty win Mistress Ford for him, dons the horns of a stag and meets the two ladies at the appointed place. Quickly the fairies and witches surround him, and the women run to join their husbands and watch the fun. Poor Falstaff tries to pretend that he is asleep or dead, but the merry revelers burn his fingers with tapers they carry and pinch him unmercifully. When Falstaff throws off his disguise, Ford and Page and their wives lay hold of

him and soundly scold him for his silly gallantry and bombast. The wives ridicule his ungainly body and swear that none will ever have such a fool for a lover. Such is Falstaff's nature, however, that no one can hate him for long. After he admits his guilt and his stupidity, they all forgive him.

While all this merriment is going on, Anne and Fenton steal away to be married. They return while the rest are busy with Falstaff. Page and his wife are in such good humor over all that occurs that they forgive the young lovers and bestow their blessing on them. Then the whole company, Falstaff included, retires to Page's house to laugh again over the happenings of that night.

Critical Evaluation:

Under public pressure to bring back Sir John Falstaff after Prince Hal's arrogant dismissal of his boyhood friend in *Henry IV, Part II* (pr. 1598, pb. 1600) and *Henry V* (pr. c. 1598-1599, pb. 1600), William Shakespeare reintroduces the fat knight in a slapstick romp, *The Merry Wives of Windsor*. On one hand, the farce can be viewed as a ridiculous satire of the London burghers, the Fords and the Pages, who successfully outwit the not-so-sly fox of an aristocrat, Falstaff, who is trying in his usual way to disrupt the pleasures and the comforts of the conventional.

Another way of approaching the play is by viewing it as a comic resolve of a story similar in some incidents to Shakespeare's earlier play, *Romeo and Juliet* (pr. c. 1595-1596, pb. 1597). Unwittingly, Falstaff, in his buffoonery, performs the role of diverting the Pages from the elopement of their daughter, Anne, and Fenton, the comic Romeo. A potential tragedy thus averted, love is allowed to flourish. Falstaff plays the same role that Shakespeare assigned to him in the histories. As opposed to the deliberate Hal, who orders everything in his life, even his leisure with his cronies, Falstaff devotes his whole life to play, the gratification of the instincts, and the preservation of the self. His dalliance with the Mistresses Page and Ford may be a mockery of good burgher virtue, but he also pursues it with a good deal of pleasure, pleasure for its own sake. Everyone wins in the process. Anne is married to the man she loves, and the Pages, the Fords, and Sir John all have a thoroughly fine time in the romp. The only loser is respectability, which takes a back seat to the loud, vulgar guffaws of "Fat Jack" Falstaff.

Further Reading

Barton, Ann. "Falstaff and the Comic Community." In *Shakespeare's "Rough Magic": Renaissance Essays in Honor of C. L. Barber*, edited by Peter Erickson and Coppélia Kahn. Newark: University of Delaware Press, 1985. An excellent study of Falstaff, the most controversial character in the play. Shows that Shakespeare was consciously trying to exclude such self-seeking epicureans from his plays; Falstaff in *The Merry Wives of Windsor* was the last time such a character received such prominence.

Green, William. *Shakespeare's "Merry Wives of Windsor."* Princeton, N.J.: Princeton University Press, 1962. Chronicles the history of the play, from its composition to its first performance and audience.

Hunt, Maurice. "'Gentleness' and Social Class in *The Merry Wives of Windsor*." *Comparative Drama* 42, no. 4 (December, 2008): 409-432. Examines the use of the word "gentle," as well as the variations "gentleman" and "gentlewoman," in the play, analyzing what these words mean within the overall context of the comedy. Argues that the play might be concerned with "authentic gentleness."

Leggatt, Alexander, ed. *The Cambridge Companion to Shakespearean Comedy*. New York: Cambridge University Press, 2002. Although none of the essays is specifically about *The Merry Wives of Windsor*, there are numerous references to this play that are listed in the index.

Edward Berry's essay, "Laughing at 'Others,'" is particularly useful.

Roberts, Jeanne Addison. *Shakespeare's English Comedy: "The Merry Wives of Windsor" in Context*. Lincoln: University of Nebraska Press, 1979. Places *The Merry Wives of Windsor* within the context of the development of Shakespeare's career, arguing that the play provided his transition from writing histories to writing tragedies. Includes chapters on the text, date, sources, and genre.

Wells, Stanley, ed. *The Cambridge Companion to Shakespeare Studies*. New York: Cambridge University Press, 1986. This is where all studies of Shakespeare should begin. It includes excellent chapters introducing the poet's biography, conventions and beliefs of Elizabethan England, and reviews of scholarship in the field.

White, R. S. *The Merry Wives of Windsor*. Boston: Twayne, 1991. Critical interpretation of the play, focusing on the character of Falstaff. Argues that Falstaff reflects the acquisitiveness, misogyny, and other aspects of provincial society. Examines Shakespeare's use of plot, character, and language in the play.

Metamorphoses

Author: Ovid (43 B.C.E.-17 C.E.)
First transcribed: c. 8 C.E. (English translation, 1567)
Type of work: Poetry

Metamorphoses is generally conceded to be Ovid's finest work. In this collection of poems, Ovid manages to draw together artistically most of the stories of Greek and Roman legend. He renders more than two hundred of the myths of the ancient world into an organic work whose unifying theme is that of transformation. Thus Jove changes himself into a swan, Narcissus is transformed into a flower, Tereus is turned into a bird, and Midas is given the ears of an ass. Ovid arranges these stories into fifteen books, containing in the original Latin version almost twelve thousand lines of sweetly flowing verse in the dactylic hexameter common in classical poetry. The poems were written when Ovid was a mature man of perhaps fifty, shortly before Augustus Caesar banished him far from the city he loved to the little town of Tomi on the shores of the Black Sea. Ovid wrote that he destroyed his own copy of *Metamorphoses*, apparently because he

was dissatisfied with his performance, but he nevertheless seemed to feel that the work would live after him. In his epilogue to *Metamorphoses*, he wrote,

> Now I have done my work. It will endure,
> I trust, beyond Jove's anger, fire, and sword,
> Beyond Time's hunger. The day will come, I know,
> So let it come, that day which has no power
> Save over my body, to end my span of life
> Whatever it may be. Still, part of me,
> The better part, immortal, will be borne
> Above the stars; my name will be remembered
> Wherever Roman power rules conquered lands,
> I shall be read, and through all centuries,
> If prophecies of bards are ever truthful,
> I shall be living, always.

As if it were necessary for a work of literary art to have some edifying or moral purpose, the poems are sometimes regarded primarily as a useful handbook on Greek and Roman mythology. Certainly the work does contain a wealth of the ancient legends, and many later writers have become famous in part because they were able to build on the materials Ovid placed at their disposal. However, *Metamorphoses* is a work of art in its own right.

In later times, stories about the gods of the pagan Pantheon have been viewed in a different light from that in which Ovid's contemporaries regarded them. Where readers in later times could smile, Ovid's light, even facetious, tone is regarded by serious Romans as having more than a little touch of blasphemy. Perhaps his irreverent attitudes were even a partial cause for his exile, for Augustus Caesar was at the time attempting moral reforms. Moreover, after dealing good-humoredly with various gods, Ovid turned at the end of *Metamorphoses* to describe the transformation of Julius Caesar into a god. How seriously he meant this to be taken is not clear from the tone of the poem.

Ovid begins his collection with a description of how the universe comes into being with the metamorphosis of Chaos, the unshaped stuff, into Cosmos, the ordered universe. Describing how the Lord of Creation, "Whatever god it was," established order in the universe, Ovid gives a picture of the four ages. He starts his account with the Golden Age, when justice and right exist everywhere, and when law and punishment are absent because they are unnecessary. When Saturn is sent to the land of shadowy death, writes Ovid, and Jove becomes chief of the gods, then comes the Age of Silver, when human beings first build houses to guard themselves against the seasons and plant fields to provide themselves with a harvest. Next comes the Age of Bronze, when warlike instincts and aggression come into being, to be succeeded in its turn by the Iron Age, when modesty, truth, and righteousness are displaced by trickery, violence, and swindling. This age is so bad that Jove strikes down the living and nature brings forth a new race of human beings who are, as Ovid puts it, "men of blood." Of this race, all except Deucalion and Pyrrha, a righteous man and woman, are wiped from the face of the earth by Jove, who with Neptune's aid causes a flood to cover the globe. Ovid's stories of the Creation and the Flood, told in a pagan environment, are strikingly similar to the stories of the same phenomena told in the Old Testament.

Much of Ovid's poetry in *Metamorphoses* deals with love. It is not romanticized, sentimentalized love, however, for the poet recognizes the physical reality that men and women represent to one another, and his gods and goddesses exhibit human passions. In love, as Ovid describes it, there is

often a strain of cruelty and brutality; the veneer of civilization is thin enough to let his readers sense the savagery of violence, revenge, and cruelty underlying human nature. In this connection, Ovid recalls Lycaon boiling and broiling the flesh of a human hostage before the altar of Jove; Tereus raping Philomela and then cutting out her tongue to keep the deed a secret; a satyr being flayed alive by Apollo, the son of Latona, for trying to surpass him at playing the flute; sixteen-year-old Athis having his face battered to mere splinters of bone by Perseus; and Pelias's daughters' letting their father's blood at the behest of Medea. In these stories gory details are described in the account of each brutal act; brains, blood, broken bones, and screams of agony and hate fill the lines. Love and hate, both powerful, basic human emotions, are close in Ovid's *Metamorphoses*.

Mere enumeration does not do Ovid's collection the justice it deserves. Practically every phase of the Greco-Roman mythology is at least represented in the fifteen divisions of the work. The stories are drawn together with consummate skill. However, the noteworthy fact in assessing Ovid's mastery of his materials and craft is that he himself was a skeptic who did not believe in these stories as having actually happened. Without the sincerity of belief, he nevertheless writes in such a way as to induce in the reader the mood that Samuel Taylor Coleridge, almost two thousand years later, described as the "willing suspension of disbelief."

Ovid places believable personalities in his pages. His men and women and his gods and goddesses hate and love as human beings always did. Later readers always recognize in themselves the same surges and flows of emotion they find in Ovid's poetry. In this way, later times, despite technological advances, are little different from the Roman empire of Ovid and Augustus.

Ovid's style also includes a large amount of specific detail with which he creates a vivid picture of people or actions. Particularly vital moments include that when Myrrha, in "Cinyras and Myrrha," flings herself, face down, to cry into her pillow; when Pygmalion lavishes gifts of pet birds, seashells, lilies, and lumps of precious amber on his beloved statue; and when Dorylas, in "The Battle of the Centaurs," is wounded by Peleus and dies trailing his entrails, treading and tangling them with his centaur's hoofs. These details are a reminder that Ovid's Rome was a culture that included not only greatness in art but also the grim and bloody scenes of death by violence within the arena at the Colosseum.

Further Reading

Brown, Sarah Annes. *Ovid: Myth and Metamorphosis*. London: Bristol Classical Press, 2005. An introduction to the poem in which Brown examines how it has influenced both high and popular culture. She focuses on five of its stories—those involving Daphne, Actaeon, Philomela, Arachne, and Pygmalion—to describe how these tales have been adapted by writers, filmmakers, and others.

Hardie, Philip. *The Cambridge Companion to Ovid*. New York: Cambridge University Press, 2002. Collection of essays examining the historical contexts of Ovid's works, their reception, and the themes and literary techniques of his poetry. The numerous references to *Metamorphoses* are listed in the index.

Innes, Mary M. Introduction to *Metamorphoses of Ovid*. Translated by Mary M. Innes. 1955. Reprint. New York: Penguin Books, 1975. Includes sections on Ovid's life and works, a commentary on *Metamorphoses*, a discussion of its influence on later European literature, and a note on Innes's translation.

Johnson, Patricia J. *Ovid Before Exile: Art and Punishment in the "Metamorphoses."* Madison: University of Wisconsin Press, 2008. Johnson argues that Ovid wrote *Metamorphoses* in an atmosphere of artistic censorship that culminated in his exile from Rome, and she describes how the poem reflects this atmosphere. The poem depicts the danger of artistic creation and shows how artists who appease powerful audiences succeed, while defiant or subversive artists are destroyed.

Knox, Peter E., ed. *Oxford Readings in Ovid*. New York: Oxford University Press, 2006. Collection of twenty influential scholarly essays published since the mid-1970's that provide a range of interpretations of Ovid's poetry. Includes three essays about *Metamorphoses*: "Voices and Narrative 'Instances' in the Metamorphoses" by Alessandro Barchiesi, "Pyramus and Thisbe in Cyprus" by Peter E. Knox, and "Form in Motion: Weaving the Text in the *Metamorphoses*" by Gianpiero Rosati.

Mack, Sara. "*Metamorphoses*." In *Ovid*. New Haven, Conn.: Yale University Press, 1988. Contains chapters on the reception of Ovid in his own time and later, on his love poetry, on *Metamorphoses*, and on Ovid the poet. The chapter on *Metamorphoses* focuses on such difficult aspects of the poem as its structure, transitions, and the inclusion of less-appealing tales.

Otis, Brooks. *Ovid as an Epic Poet*. New York: Cambridge University Press, 1966. Describes the plan and structure of the poem. Finds the unity of the poem in its order or succession of episodes, motifs, and ideas. Argues that this unity is marred by disharmony between the poem's Roman-Augustan element and its amatory element.

Rand, Edward Kennard. "Poet of Transformations." In *Ovid and His Influence*. New York: Cooper Square, 1963. Devotes a chapter to each of Ovid's major works; analyzes Ovid's influence on medieval and Renaissance authors.

The Metamorphosis

Author: Franz Kafka (1883-1924)
First published: Die Verwandlung, 1915 (English translation, 1936)
Type of work: Novella
Type of plot: Allegory
Time of plot: Early twentieth century
Locale: Prague

Principal characters:
GREGOR SAMSA, a man who wakes up as a giant insect
GRETE SAMSA, his sister
MR. SAMSA, his father
MRS. SAMSA, his mother
THE CHIEF CLERK, his boss

The Story:

Gregor Samsa wakes one morning from uneasy dreams to find that he has been transformed during the night into a gigantic insect. At first, he tries to remain calm and go back to sleep. His transformed body, however, prevents him from getting comfortable. Regardless of the changes in him, Gregor's thoughts turn to the job he hates, and, as he looks at the clock, he fears being late at the office. Through the locked door to his room, his mother reminds him of the time, and he notices the change in his voice when he replies. His response alerts the rest of his family that he is still at home, which is unexpected at this time of day.

Still attempting to maintain some semblance of normality, Gregor tries to get out of bed, but it requires an unusual effort, rocking back and forth, before he finally falls out of bed onto the floor. When the chief clerk from his office arrives to check on Gregor's whereabouts, he doubles his efforts to return to normal. Gregor's father calls to him to allow the clerk to enter his room, but Gregor refuses because he is afraid that his job will be jeopardized if the chief clerk discovers his transformation. He is convinced that he can explain his rudeness later, after he has recovered. The clerk threatens him, and Gregor hears the clerk comment about how inhuman his voice sounds. Gregor finally wedges himself against the door and opens the lock with his jaws, but, as he appears in the doorway, his altered appearance frightens the clerk, who flees the apartment. Gregor's family stares at him, amazed at the metamorphosis he has undergone. Finally, his father forces him back into his room and shuts the door.

The next morning, Gregor's sister leaves him food on the floor of his room, but Gregor remains hidden underneath the sofa while she is in the room, lest he should frighten her. For the next two days, he overhears his family discussing what they should do about him and the changes they will have to make in their lives, since he has supplied their only source of income. Gregor worries about his family and mulls over the guilt he feels for losing his job and his place as breadwinner of the household. Night after night, he huddles in the dark and thinks about his predicament.

For the first fortnight, Gregor's parents cannot bear to enter his room, but Grete removes his furniture piece by piece, claiming that he will be more comfortable if he can move around unencumbered by things that are no longer useful to him. His mother argues with her about leaving the room alone, hoping that he will recover from his illness, but his father has lost hope and insists that he will never recover.

One day, Gregor's mother enters his room and sees him clinging to the wall by the sticky feet of his many legs. The shock at seeing him behaving like an insect shatters her attachment to him and destroys forever any hope she has for his eventual recovery. Despite his changed appearance, Gregor remains lonely for the company of his family and, one night, in a desperate attempt to join his family, ventures out of his room once more. However, his father, angry at Gregor's intrusion into the family's quarters, yells at him and pelts him with apples, wounding him in the back before forcing Gregor to return to the solitude of his room.

Gregor's movements are hindered by his injury. He observes, through his door, which is inexplicably left open every evening, the changes his family experiences during his absence. Even though his father has returned to work and

they had to dismiss the maid, his parents are strained economically, physically exhausted, and increasingly despondent. They largely neglect Gregor and leave him alone in his room. He seldom sleeps and is increasingly haunted by the thought that he will one day recover and once again provide for his family.

To increase their income, the family takes in three lodgers, and one evening they request that Grete play her violin. Attracted by the music, which reminds him of the way his life used to be, Gregor leaves his room once again, seeking the warmth and companionship of the others. The lodgers, who do not know of his existence, are outraged by his appearance and threaten to leave. For the first time, Gregor hears Grete demand that something be done about him. She calls him a creature and denies that he is still her brother. In his weakened condition, it is difficult for him to return for the final time to his room. Once back inside, though, Gregor realizes that he, too, feels the same despair his sister does and longs for death. During the night, he loses consciousness. The next morning, the charwoman finds the husk of Gregor's dead body in the room and sweeps him up with the trash.

Gregor's family seems little surprised by his death. They all leave the apartment the same day for the first time in months, going into the country to discuss their prospects for the future. They decide to move to a smaller and more convenient apartment. Observing the vivacious change in their daughter, brought about by Gregor's death, her parents realize that it is time to find her a husband.

Critical Evaluation:

Franz Kafka began writing in his early twenties while studying law at the University of Prague from 1901 to 1906. In 1908, he began publishing extracts from his novel, *Amerika* (1927; *America*, 1938; better known as *Amerika*, 1946), and *The Metamorphosis* was written in late 1912, appearing in print in 1915. His working career spans only sixteen years, and, when he died in 1924 at the age of forty-one, many of his major novels had not been published; his work was little known beyond avant-garde German literary circles.

Kafka is now regarded as a central figure in twentieth century literature. The commentary on his writings and his life is extremely large, including scores of books and hundreds of articles. Of all his publications, *The Metamorphosis* is undoubtedly his most famous. The novella has been widely anthologized and is available in several single-volume editions; in addition, the number of articles and portions of books about the story make it the most heavily analyzed of all Kafka's works.

Because the work has been so frequently discussed from so many different perspectives—psychological, sociological, political, philosophical, linguistic, and religious—it is difficult to summarize the responses to *The Metamorphosis*. Marxists, psychoanalysts, postmodernists, feminists, Zionists, structuralists, and poststructuralists have all interpreted the story in different ways. However, there is some general agreement that such overall themes as guilt, judgment, retribution, alienation, and the place of the artist in society are contained in the core of the narrative.

Kafka's writings largely originated from the conflicted relationship he experienced with his family, especially his father. This biographical connection has been much discussed, and it is easily perceived in Gregor Samsa's reaction to his family. Although constrained by his obligations to support his father, mother, and sister, Gregor nevertheless seeks throughout the tale to be reintegrated into the family circle. Made aware of his alienation from them by his transformation, he vainly attempts to ignore the change at first and to maintain a semblance of normality, until he is finally abandoned by his sister, with whom he had had a close relationship. It is her firm rejection of him as a person that ultimately causes him to surrender his own sense of self, precipitating his death.

The Metamorphosis is constructed in three acts, each involving an escape by Gregor from his room and a return to it. With each retreat, Gregor becomes noticeably less human and more accepting of his transformative state. With each act, Gregor also becomes physically weaker. As his family abandons its denial of his insectlike appearance and their hope for his full recovery to a normal human condition, they gradually become indifferent to his fate and recognize their need to pursue their lives without him. His father returns to work, his mother learns to operate the house without the help of a maid, even adding the burden of taking in boarders, and his sister assumes the responsibilities of adulthood. Where once he was the center of their lives, he now becomes an unnecessary burden and an embarrassment.

The horror of a tale about a man who transforms into an insect is heightened by Kafka's literary style: a matter-of-fact tone laced with mordant humor. The fact that Gregor initially greets his metamorphosis with a chilling calm suggests that he previously saw himself as verminlike, as somebody who was already less than human. This internal lack of self-esteem and the insecurities it produces are heightened by the change in his body. One of the major problems to reading *The Metamorphosis* is accepting Gregor's transformation as literal and not merely symbolic; he has really turned into an insect. The strangeness of this fact, along with his and his fam-

ily's reactions to it, is what makes the narrative so fascinating and rich in interpretative possibilities.

The power of Kafka's fiction relies primarily on the uncanny ways he captures the alienation of twentieth century life. Denied the saving grace of religious belief, skeptical of the achievements of modern science, and leery of the significance of art, Kafka's characters are left adrift in a world of their own making over which they seem to have little control. *The Metamorphosis* captures all of the fear and doubt with which human beings face their future.

Charles L. P. Silet

Further Reading

Bloom, Harold, ed. *Franz Kafka's "The Metamorphosis."* New ed. New York: Bloom's Literary Criticism, 2008. Collection of essays interpreting *The Metamorphosis*, including discussions of the liberation of Gregor, competing theories of identity in the work, and *The Metamorphosis* and the search for meaning in twentieth century German literature.

Boa, Elizabeth. *Kafka: Gender, Class, and Race in the Letters and Fictions*. New York: Oxford University Press, 1996. An excellent study focusing on the representation of gender in Kafka's works, including *The Metamorphosis*. Boa also examines Kafka's letters to his fiancé and to a Czech female journalist to understand his views of women.

Eggenschwiler, David. "*The Metamorphosis*, Freud, and the Chains of Odyseus." In *Modern Critical Views: Franz Kafka*, edited by Harold Bloom. New York: Chelsea House, 1986. The author traces the psychological origins of the story in Kafka's life and encourages a recognition of the tension between parable and interpretation.

Gray, Richard T., Ruth V. Gross, Rolf J. Goebel, and Clayton Koelb. *A Franz Kafka Encyclopedia*. Westport, Conn.: Greenwood Press, 2005. A comprehensive volume that contains alphabetized entries that discuss all aspects of Kafka's life and work, including the characters, places, and events in his writings.

Gray, Ronald. *Franz Kafka*. New York: Cambridge University Press, 1973. This is one of the best and most accessible short analyses of Kafka's work, and it furnishes a literary context for the tale.

Hayman, Ronald. *K: A Biography of Kafka*. New ed. London: Phoenix, 2001. Presents a solid and readable account of Kafka's life, intended for beginning students and general readers. Includes a chronology and an extensive bibliography. First published in 1981.

Karl, Frederick. *Franz Kafka: Representative Man—Prague, Germans, Jews, and the Crisis of Modernism.* New York: Ticknor & Fields, 1991. A massive study, perhaps the most comprehensive attempt to place Kafka within the context of his own time and to study his writings as central to the modernist movement in twentieth century literature.

Preece, Julian, ed. *The Cambridge Companion to Kafka.* New York: Cambridge University Press, 2002. Collection of essays about Kafka. Although none of the essays focuses on *The Metamorphosis*, the work is discussed throughout the book. References to the novella are listed in the index.

Metamorphosis

Author: Edith Sitwell (1887-1964)
First published: 1929, in *Gold Coast Customs*; revised 1946
Type of work: Poetry

The writings of Dame Edith Sitwell sparked both friendly and hostile responses from twentieth century critics. Poets William Butler Yeats and Stephen Spender praised her work, but other critics denounced her work as unpoetic. Sitwell's sharp criticism of those, such as poet Ezra Pound, who did not like her work, led to strongly partisan views of her poetry, with few critics taking time to evaluate the content and genius of her poetry. In the tradition of T. S. Eliot and other symbolist poets, Sitwell enjoyed using sharply contrasting images to evoke emotions in the reader.

Metamorphosis, both in its original version and even more so in its 1946 revision, represents a transition from Sitwell's earlier, more self-conscious work to her more cohesive, thematically consistent poetry of later years. This poem also appeared in the book *Five Variations on a Theme* (1933), where it is grouped with four other poems, including "Elegy on Dead Fashion" (1926), "Two Songs" ("Come, My Arabia," and "My desert has a noble sun for heart"—both left out of Sitwell's *Collected Poems* of 1954), and "Romance" (1933). As with many of Sitwell's other poetry, this set of poems shares several themes, especially that of death overcoming the destructive forces of time and leading to the brightness of eternity. In developing these themes she repeats imagery such as green grass and shadows and shade, along with longer passages of imagery, to emphasize the poems' interrelatedness.

Even in this set of five poems, *Metamorphosis* stands as a transitional work, revealing as it does her growing openness to a Christian resolution. By the time she arranged her *Collected Poems* in their 1954 version, Sitwell could declare in the preface to that work, "My poems are hymns of praise to the glory of Life." *Metamorphosis* clearly represents a step in this direction.

One of the major debates about the work concerns which version should be considered authoritative or most representative of Sitwell's intentions. In the preface to her *Collected Poems*, Sitwell refuses to choose between the two versions, simply declaring them both internally consistent with her intended expression of feeling and therefore both satisfactory, though quite different. Consequently, she there presents the two versions side by side without further comment.

The 1946 version of *Metamorphosis* is far more precise in expression and has fewer loose ends than does the 1929 version, but even more significant are the differences in tone between the two versions. The earlier poem is decidedly more melancholy than the later one. The 1929 version begins with a comparison of the snow to the Parthenon as a symbol for the ravages of time, after which the poet introduces the rose as beauty's daughter growing dark with time. Through various images, such as that of the darkening rose, the poem goes on to lament the cruelty of time in contrast to death, which offers a release from suffering and anxiety. As the poem declares, "Death has never worm for heart and brain/ Like that which Time conceives to fill his grave." Sitwell presents death as variously as the climate for living and travel, or as the sun to illumine "our old Dim-Jewelled bones," the topaz, sapphires, and diamonds hidden in the bones. These images of death are woven with images of integration and relating, including the portrayal of the persona's soul as Lazarus come back from the dead, or as the grass growing from the bones of the deceased.

One of Sitwell's favorite refrains is that all people are Ethiopian shades of death, or are burned away by the sun's heat, which represents death. In this apparently grim discussion of death, the poem's emphasis falls on unity achieved through death. As the poet notes near the end of the poem, "Since all things have beginnings; the bright plume/ Was once thin grass in shady winter's gloom,/ And the furred fire is barking for the shape/ Of hoarse-voiced animals." As this compact section of the poem illustrates, all creation is united in the cycle of life, and each aspect of creation reflects the rest of the created order, even in its mortality.

The conclusion of the poem introduces one more actor, Christ, or Heavenly Love, which like the sun will melt the "eternal ice/ Of Death, and crumble the thick centuries." Not only do blades of grass die and become plumes, not only is time overwhelmed by death, at last even death itself will be metamorphosed and life will remain. As the title of the poem implies, metamorphosis is built into creation in such a way as to foreshadow the greater metamorphoses yet to come.

Metamorphosis is rich with allusions from Greco-Roman, Judeo-Christian, and pagan antiquity, as is exemplified by allusions to nymphs, Saturn, Panope, Hector, Parthenon, Jove, Gehenna, and Lazarus. Sitwell thus underscores the universality of the ravages of time that she decries. Although the basic movement of the 1929 version of *Metamorphosis* is fairly consistent and many of the images are striking and intriguing, several of the images seem facile, inappropriate, or racially slighting. Turkeys are, for example, compared to sultans wearing turbans, an unflattering comparison in which neither image promotes the basic themes of the poem, and in several places people are identified as being as black as Ethiopia or as being like a small Negro page. Such images might be seen as evidence of the nature of metamorphosis, as unlike things are being compared, but the assumptions behind the images are unflattering at best and insensitive at worst. Eliot had similar problems with his caustic treatment of Jewish people as examples of rootless and unprincipled people in his *The Waste Land* (1922). Such aspects, while reflecting the perceptions current during the author's age, undercut the poem's movement toward unity of humanity and all creation.

By the time of the 1946 version of *Metamorphosis*, with its 132 lines less than half the length of the 1929 version, which has 288 lines, the number of racial references has been reduced, and they are usually couched in ambiguous or ironic contexts. For example, shortly after referring to how "Death

is the Sun's heat making all men black!," the poet declares again "All men are Ethiopian shades of thee [Death]"; two lines later, there is a reference to the rich and thick Ethiopian herds. In this context the references to Ethiopia are more positive and universal than before. The most significant change between the 1929 and 1946 versions is evident in the way the poet clarifies the essential tension between time and death and more overtly states her Christian resolution to this tension. Whereas this version of the poem still includes allusions to Greek and pagan myths, the allusions to Christian beliefs have been heightened. By stanza 9, the author has already introduced two Judeo-Christian images, the rainbow as a symbol of God's light and promises of mercy, and the dark rose as a symbol of God's love as shown through Christ, the rose of Sharon.

These Christian images of hope and love are linked with the sun, a seventeenth century pun for son or the Son of God, a connection clarified in the closing stanza of this poem. This sun comes to overcome both time and death with the bright hope of eternity expressed through scarlet colored clothing, symbolizing the blood of martyrdom and the flaming blooms of spring. Christ thus comes as a symbol of redemption and resurrection.

The closing two stanzas of the poem are powerful not only for their complex and multifaceted images that encompass the suffering of all time but also for their intriguing metrical variety. Both the 1929 and 1946 versions of this poem make heavy use of iambic pentameter with rhymed couplets, iambic being the natural walking meter in English and rhymed couplets being the easiest to organize. However, all of these conventions are transformed in the closing stanzas, as if a metamorphosis has taken place that could be described only in a new mode. Here the work reveals some of the rhythmic variety and intensity of contrasting images often found in the writings of Gerard Manley Hopkins, whom Sitwell had admired. The penultimate stanza illustrates this pattern well:

> So, out of the dark, see our great Spring begins—
> Our Christ, the new Song, breaking out in
>   the fields and hedgerows,
> The heart of Man! O, the new temper of Christ,
>   in veins and branches.

Here it can be noted how the standard iambic pentameter has been translated into a form of sprung rhythm or accentual verse, verse that depends on a set number of accented syllables and any given number of unaccented syllables between them.

Metamorphosis, especially in its 1946 version, represents

a major shift in Sitwell's poetic career. Her early poetic career is characterized by an exacting exploration of human suffering and pain, often in language that seems somewhat posed and artificial, although certainly learned. Her later poetry, including the superb poem "Still Falls the Rain" (1942), demonstrates a profound sense of balance between her awareness of the suffering of all humanity and her understanding of Christ's sacrifice to bring healing into the world. Her acceptance of the Christian sense of resolution is all the more profound because of her honest acknowledgment of the pervasiveness of suffering in the world.

At her best, Sitwell's use of contrasting imagery and lyrical rhythms is as skillful as that of Dylan Thomas. Both poets understood well how truth is born in paradox. Sitwell's sense of suffering as a unifying factor in creation is in her later work carefully balanced with her recognition that divine love is finally greater than suffering and hate and evil. Like poet Dante Alighieri, Sitwell brought her work not to the easy resolutions of humanists' praise of the capacity of humankind to endure hardships but to the recognition that all live under the sentence of suffering and death from which only divine love as expressed through Christ's redemptive work can free them. Although some may reject Sitwell's Christian conclusions, her work follows the same line as that of Eliot, especially in his *Four Quartets* (1943), which Sitwell also had admired.

Metamorphosis demonstrates growth toward a vision of life large enough to swallow all its pain and lead it to the hope of eternal love. Poetically, this work demonstrates considerable maturity in Sitwell's artistic and theological development.

Daven M. Kari

Further Reading

Brophy, James D. *Edith Sitwell: The Symbolist Order.* Carbondale: Southern Illinois University Press, 1968. A detailed and skillful analysis of Sitwell's full range of literary achievement. Places *Metamorphosis* in the context of *Five Variations on a Theme*, which deals with the defeat of time.

Cevasco, G. A. *The Sitwells: Edith, Osbert, and Sacheverell.* Boston: Twayne, 1987. Reviews the lives and literary achievements of the three Sitwell siblings. A very useful beginning source on Edith Sitwell, although *Metamorphosis* is discussed only briefly. Includes a chronology and an annotated bibliography.

Dowson, Jane, and Alice Entwistle. "Modernism, Memory, and Masking: Mina Loy and Edith Sitwell." In *A History of Twentieth-Century British Women's Poetry.* New York: Cambridge University Press, 2005. Analyzes the poets' modernist works from the mid-1920's, when they "aimed to enlarge their readers' consciousness by defamiliarisation."

Mills, Ralph J., Jr. *Edith Sitwell: A Critical Essay.* Grand Rapids, Mich.: William B. Eerdmans, 1966. A short and concise treatment of Christian themes in Sitwell's poems, especially as they began to develop in *Metamorphosis* and later blossomed in her poetry of the 1940's.

_____. "The Poetic Roles of Edith Sitwell." In *Essays on Poetry.* Normal, Ill.: Dalkey Archive Press, 2003. Describes how Sitwell uses several forms of expression and technique in her poetry that correspond to various stages in the development of her thoughts and experiences.

Sitwell, Edith. *Taken Care Of: The Autobiography of Edith Sitwell.* New York: Atheneum, 1965. An intensely personal and at times painful revelation of the feelings and driving forces behind the poet's work. She has harsh criticism of many of her contemporaries and critics, especially of her parents, who scorned her appearance.

Villa, Jose Garcia, ed. *A Celebration for Edith Sitwell.* 1948. Reprint. Freeport, N.Y.: Books for Libraries Press, 1972. A collection of seventeen essays and other observations by such prominent critics as Stephen Spender, John Piper, Gertrude Stein, and John Russell. Includes Kenneth Clark's insightful discussion of both versions of *Metamorphosis*, which he claims present clues to the poet's growing artistic achievements.

Metaphysics

Author: Aristotle (384-322 B.C.E.)
First transcribed: c. 335-323 B.C.E., as *Ta meta ta physika* (English translation, 1812)
Type of work: Philosophy

Metaphysics as a branch of philosophy—concerning the most fundamental level of reality—originated with Aristotle, who produced a work that is known as the *Metaphysics*. However, Aristotle coined neither the title nor the term. Apparently, Aristotle bequeathed his writings and lectures upon his death to a person or persons who willed them forward twice more, and the philosopher's work was eventually discovered and purchased by Apellicon of Teos, a scholar of the first century. Apellicon collected these manuscripts and organized them into the treatises that survive today and that are credited to Aristotle.

The work known as the *Metaphyics* is a compendium of fourteen books in the tradition of an Aristotelian metaphysics defined by wisdom, science, and theology—a form of philosophy that was barely two hundred years old at the time of its compilation. The work is arranged to present the principles and causes of the nature of being in general. In particular, the subject matter concerns cause, being, substance, and the nature of God as they are beyond or after physics.

Scholars tend to approach the work from two different interpretive positions. One position holds that the *Metaphysics* moves forward primarily by way of the science of "being *qua* being." This interpretation focuses on the portion of book 1 in which Aristotle introduces a science of the first principle or causes of things, as well as passages in books 4, 6, and 11 that mention "being *qua* being." In these passages, Aristotle is said to be offering a singular study of a singular subject. He investigates being (that is, existence) in the context of that singular existing thing alone. In this interpretation, *qua* is taken to mean "by way of," or "whereby." It is a term pointing to a study of an existing thing in terms only of itself, its own characteristics of beingness, and not any other characteristics or qualities.

The second interpretive position is arguably more generous in giving Aristotle credit for expansive thought. This position holds that three dynamics are at work in the *Metaphysics*: First, Aristotle is considered as investigating the subject of being, regarding being as being in and of itself, and regarding that act of regarding being. That is, this second approach sees Aristotle as delivering the very definition of metaphysics—in the sense that he is investigating not only a subject of study but also a way of investigating that subject. Aristotle is moving beyond physics to metaphysics by studying the study of being; he is moving beyond analysis to meta-analysis by thinking about the act of thinking about something—in this case, being.

This threefold purpose is demonstrated from the start of the *Metaphysics*, as Aristotle introduces the human desire for and degrees of knowledge. The degrees of knowledge are part of the initial inquiry into cause, and they are treated according to principles of reasoning, experience, memory, sensation, and perception. It is also in book 1 that one of Aristotle's traditional strategies is begun: This strategy, which continues through the next seven books, involves Aristotle considering the thought of other philosophers who have come before him on the same subject and then refuting those previous philosophers' ideas. The inclusion of the thought of prior philosophers leads to a historical survey of sorts, and Aristotle moves to emphasize the methodology of scientific inquiry in book 2 by discussing science as a means to consider specific truths—which means that it is difficult to use it to investigate the nature of truth as such. Aristotle dismisses early errors and recommends a less futile methodology, although he never specifically outlines this methodology.

In subsequent books of the *Metaphysics*, Aristotle presents his thought in a form that has frustrated many thinkers who came after him, a form that has come to be thought of as distinctively Aristotelian: The rubric of questions in the *Metaphysics* is presented to reflect Aristotle's inquiry into the problems of defining being, cause, and substance. Those questions shape the work in a way that reiterates the difficulties involved in inquiry itself. That is, the *Metaphysics* poses questions with puzzling subtleties, dubious nuances, and no actual answers. Thus, preliminary questions about the nature of a thing or of being, such as those regarding cause, become a yet greater question. It is typical of Aristotle that straightforward questions such as "What is this object's shape?" "What is it made of?" and "Who made it?" become a much more metaphysical question: "Is the fundamental nature of a thing to be found in its matter or its form?"

Such questions prompt book 4, wherein being *qua* being is broached as an intended subject, as the object of the work.

These questions also lead to book 5, which Aristotle uses as a sort of lexicon, wherein the being discussed in book 4 is explained in terms of analogies not only to causes but also to properties and principles. In book 6, Aristotle reiterates that his objective is to understand being *qua* being, and he discusses being as it is distinguished by mobility or motion. Then, he returns to a discussion of science in general and particular sciences. This discussion informs his ongoing contemplation of truth, and Aristotle takes the opportunity afforded by it to further distinguish between authentic and inauthentic forms of being.

As they have been in the making throughout the first six treatises, books 7, 8, and 9 devote attention to substance as it is characterized by cause (especially formal cause), as it relates to motion (specifically change), and as it informs Aristotle's contemplation of ontological potentiality and actuality. He again considers each of these topics in the context of the categorical considerations of substance by previous thinkers. Books 7, 8, and 9—like books 4 and 5—contain a subscript that Aristotle offers on the actual manner, or means, of conveying truth. He emphasizes that the truth of being can only be conveyed in words and that it is said in many ways. In this respect, others do not broach the subject of truth itself during their inquiry into the truth of being. Nevertheless, Aristotle does not come to any clear resolution, though his argument on potentiality versus actuality—one of the more renowned of Aristotle's proposals—does come close to answering such questions of being as it exists in (and as a certain condition of) potency. This is the only kind of being that preexists another kind of being, being in act.

In book 10, Aristotle returns to what he asserted earlier (in books 3 and 4) as the primary principle of being: being's identity of unity, or oneness. It is here that the philosopher insinuates a continued inquiry into the puzzle of being and of substance, asking a seemingly tautological question by challenging whether unity and being are a thing's substance or whether the substance of being makes for an inherent characteristic of a thing. The definitive answer is not to be had in the subsequent books. Instead, in book 11 Aristotle not only offers a summative review of earlier *Metaphysics* principles, especially those from books 4, 5, and 6, but also hearkens further back to the work preceding the *Metaphysics*, now titled *Physica* (n.d.; *Physics*, 1812). Likewise, in book 12, Aristotle revisits the primary principles of being and furthers his account of theological notions of substance. He also discusses the attributes of motion that lend themselves to the supreme beings Aristotle maintains are the "unmoved movers" of the universe. Books 13 and 14 do not necessarily conclude *Metaphysics* but rather introduce the science of mathematics in an ontological context, returning Aristotle to his general consideration of mathematics as studying being *qua* quantitativeness, of natural science as studying being *qua* motility, and of metaphysics as studying being *qua* being.

Roxanne McDonald

Further Reading

De Rijk, L. M. *Aristotle: Semantics and Ontology.* Vol. 2. Boston: Brill, 2002. A complex application of scientific inquiry with an eye toward specific Aristotelian principles involving unity, conversion, and categorization, among others.

Halper, Edward C. *One and Many in Aristotle's "Metaphysics."* Las Vegas, Nev.: Parmenides, 2005. Close and scrutinizing scholarship examining the four causes and processes of being by way of reconstructing Aristotle's arguments.

Politis, Vasilis. *Routledge Philosophy Guidebook to Aristotle and the "Metaphysics."* New York: Routledge, 2004. A systematic guide to the major premises of the arguments in the *Metaphysics*.

Scotus, John Duns. *Questions on the "Metaphysics" of Aristotle.* Vol. 2. Translated by Girard J. Etzkorn and Allan B. Wolter. St. Bonaventure, N.Y.: Franciscan Institute, 1998. Critical investigation into the *Metaphysics* by the thirteenth century academician known as the Subtle Doctor for his scrutinizing analysis of philosophical principles.

Suárez, Francisco. *A Commentary on Aristotle's "Metaphysics": A Most Ample Index to the "Metaphysics" of Aristotle.* Translated by John P. Doyle. Milwaukee, Wis.: Marquette University Press, 2004. A rigorous study of Aristotle's principles of metaphysics as they inform theology.

Michael Kohlhaas

Author: Heinrich von Kleist (1777-1811)
First published: 1810 (English translation, 1844)
Type of work: Novella
Type of plot: Historical realism
Time of plot: Sixteenth century
Locale: Germany

Principal characters:
MICHAEL KOHLHAAS, a horse dealer
LISBETH, his wife
HERSE, his groom
WENZEL VON TRONKA, a knight
MARTIN LUTHER
ELECTOR OF BRANDENBURG, ruler of a German state
ELECTOR OF SAXONY, ruler of a German state
JOHANNES NAGELSCHMIDT, an outlaw
A GYPSY WOMAN

The Story:

Michael Kohlhaas, a horse dealer from Brandenburg, is on his way to sell some of his fine horses when he is stopped at Tronka castle in the neighboring state of Saxony. He is asked to pay a toll and show a pass before proceeding—a requirement he has not had to satisfy on seventeen previous trips. Leaving his groom Herse and two horses as security, Kohlhaas goes to Dresden, capital of Saxony, where he is given a pass, though no pass is required. He returns to the castle to find his horses emaciated, and he learns that his groom has been beaten and chased away. Determined to find justice for himself and other travelers, he rides home to question his groom; if the groom was at fault, he is prepared to forfeit the horses.

Kohlhaas finds that Herse has been badly injured and his horses were mistreated. He returns to Dresden to file suit against the castle owner, Wenzel von Tronka, asking that the knight be punished, that the horses be restored to health, and that he be compensated for damages done to him and his groom. The suit is dismissed because two relatives of Tronka have influence at court. Kohlhaas is advised to negotiate with Tronka for return of the horses without seeking further legal action.

Kohlhaas decides to sell his properties as he plans his next course of action. He tells his anxious wife Lisbeth that he will present his complaint to the Saxon ruler in person, but he accepts her offer to hand his petition to the elector of Brandenburg, his sovereign. Lisbeth is badly injured by an aggressive guard and dies shortly thereafter. Before she dies, she shows Kohlhaas a passage in the Bible urging forgiveness for one's enemies. At her funeral, he receives the elector's reply to his petition: He is to pick up his horses at Tronka castle and pursue the matter no further; otherwise, he risks a jail sentence.

Planning his revenge, Kohlhaas issues a decree ordering Tronka to return the horses and fatten them in Kohlhaas's own stables. When his order is not obeyed, Kohlhaas sends his children away, arms seven grooms, and leaves for Tronka castle. He sets the castle on fire and kills a relative of the knight, as well as the castle warden, steward, and their families, but Tronka escapes.

Kohlhaas arms additional men and is about to attack a convent where Tronka is thought to be hiding when a mighty lightning stroke stays his hand. Told that Tronka is in Wittenberg, Kohlhaas sets out for that city with ten men. Calling himself "a free man of the Empire and the world who was subject only to God," he sets Wittenberg on fire on the evening before Pentecost—and twice more thereafter. With a band of 109 men, Kohlhaas defeats the Saxon forces and sets fire to the city of Leipzig. Claiming to be an emissary of the Archangel Michael sent to punish the world's deceit, Kohlhaas calls on the people to create a better order in the name of his provisional world government.

At this point, Martin Luther, the Reformer, addresses a stern appeal to Kohlhaas. Writing in Wittenberg, Luther calls Kohlhaas a godless sinner who has not tried hard enough to find justice, a robber and murderer who has broken into a peaceful community like a wolf. He says that only God can judge a ruler whose civil servants suppress lawsuits behind his back. Kohlhaas, who admires Luther greatly, goes to see him and offers to present his complaint in Dresden if given safe conduct. Because Kohlhaas refuses to forgive Tronka, as Luther suggests, the Reformer will not give him communion but agrees to ask the elector of Saxony for safe conduct. Criticizing the elector's staff for not acting on Kohlhaas's complaint, Luther urges the elector to grant amnesty to Kohlhaas to press his case. The elector grants safe conduct to Kohlhaas on the condition that he disarm in three days. Kohlhaas disarms his men, returns his booty and goes to Dresden to plead his case.

Accompanied by three guards and a large crowd, Kohlhaas appears at court, and Tronka is summoned to Dresden to answer Kohlhaas's suit. The case is complicated by a member of Kohlhaas's band, Johannes Nagelschmidt, who is marauding in Saxony with his own band of outlaws. Kohlhaas condemns Nagelschmidt's violence but agrees to lead his band temporarily while asking Nagelschmidt to help him escape from Dresden, where Kohlhaas is under guard. Kohlhaas plans to go overseas to escape from his legal entanglements, but when his letters to Nagelschmidt are intercepted Kohlhaas is arrested and sentenced to be drawn and quartered.

The elector of Brandenburg has Kohlhaas extradited from Saxony so he can be tried under Brandenburg law. The elector of Saxony asks the emperor in Vienna, who is not bound by Kohlhaas's amnesty, to prosecute him in Berlin for his breach of the peace. Kohlhaas wears a capsule containing a sealed paper given to him by a gypsy woman who resembled his late wife. The paper contains vital information about the elector of Saxony, but Kohlhaas refuses to give it up, even though it might save his life. The gypsy woman prophesies a long reign for the elector of Brandenburg but not for the Saxon elector.

In Berlin, Kohlhaas is charged with breach of the peace. After being informed that he will get full satisfaction from Tronka, Kohlhaas is sentenced to death for his crimes. An emissary of Luther administers communion to him, and his two sons are knighted. Before he is executed, two well-fed horses are returned to him, and Herse's medical expenses are paid in full. Mounting the scaffold before a large public crowd, Kohlhaas swallows the sealed paper in view of the Saxon elector, who returns home a broken man. After his death, descendants of Kohlhaas continue to be active.

Critical Evaluation:

Michael Kohlhaas is described as "one of the most righteous and also one of the most terrible men of his time" (*einer der rechtschaffensten zugleich und entsetzlichsten Menschen seiner Zeit*). A model citizen until he is thirty, he becomes a robber and murderer when his sense of justice turns into a need for revenge. The novella's complex plot deals with a quest for justice in a disordered world—an abiding concern of troubled young writer Heinrich von Kleist. Kleist was the son of a distinguished military family, raised in the Prussian tradition of loyalty, obedience, duty, and service, but, as a committed writer, he could not conform to this tradition. Living at a time of political turmoil when his country was invaded by Napoleon, unrecognized for his singular literary

work and rejected by his family, he committed suicide at the age of thirty-four.

Kohlhaas seeks absolute justice, not realizing that justice is subject to the whims of those who administer it. In his effort to recover his two horses, he engages in violence that is out of proportion to the original offense. Though he is aware that the world is in a fragile state (*der gebrechlichen Einrichtung der Welt*), his need for revenge—a flaw in his character—moves him to take the law into his own hands. He acts as if the injustice committed against him entitles him to proclaim himself an avenging angel who will punish the unjust with fire and sword. Kohlhaas is constitutionally unable to assess the result of his actions; he acts without considering the consequences. There is a strong element of immaturity in his headlong rush to act out his compulsions. Indeed, the narrator suggests a strain of mental instability and even pathology in Kohlhaas's decrees.

Kohlhaas's encounter with Martin Luther demonstrates the pitfalls of the horse dealer's black-and-white view. Luther informs him that the Saxon elector did not know of Tronka's offense and Kohlhaas's complaint because the relevant documents had been side-tracked by Tronka's relatives at court. A similar situation occurs at the court of Brandenburg. Kohlhaas thus acts prematurely, but the handling of his case reveals corruption at both courts. The question then arises whether Kohlhaas is acting against a corrupt system and whether, given the corruption, his actions are excessive. Luther responds ambiguously: He condemns Kohlhaas's violence but concedes that the horse dealer has a valid case. Ambiguous, too, is Luther's confusion of safe conduct and amnesty in his appeal to the Saxon elector, as well as the Reformer's warning that the elector should consider Kohlhaas's armed band a danger to the state—an argument that undermines Kohlhaas's suit.

Such inconsistencies occur not infrequently in Kleist's writings. This story contains a few examples of explanations withheld for no stated reason, such as the reference to a conflict between Poland and Saxony. Some questions remain unresolved at the end of the book: Why does the elector of Brandenburg seek to try Kohlhaas under Brandenburg law, only to see him judged by the emperor? Why is the rejection of Kohlhaas's petition to the elector of Brandenburg, which Lisbeth tried to deliver, brought to him at the very time of his wife's funeral? Why is a letter to Kohlhaas from Luther's envoy lost? Why are only two of his children mentioned by name when he actually has five children? These are psychic quirks in Kleist's writing that show his awareness of life's absurdities or perhaps a certain distractedness inherent in his precipitous narration. It seems at times as if the writer is too burdened or too contrary to be fully in control of the material.

His writing is dramatic, lacking reflection, repose, and description.

It is characteristic of Kleist that he begins his tale with an opening paragraph of four fact-filled sentences that contain a characterization of Kohlhaas and a foreshadowing of the plot. It has been suggested that Tronka and the elector of Saxony are unworthy adversaries of Kohlhaas's campaign. Tronka enjoys carousing with his companions, and he does not have the courage to confront Kohlhaas or to control the actions of his subordinates. The elector of Saxony is a weak ruler who does not make decisions easily, does not choose advisers wisely, and finally leaves it to the emperor to deal with Kohlhaas. These antagonists are arbitrary and feckless but not evil, hardly appropriate targets of a crusader. Nor does the novella portray a case of class warfare: Kohlhaas is conducting a personal vendetta, not an attempt to change the system. The social turmoil in the story reflects the upheaval in Germany at the height of the Reformation.

Just before his execution, Kohlhaas has a chance to save his life, but he prefers to die rather than help the Saxon elector. He disregards the advice of the gypsy, an apparition of his late wife, to reveal the secret paper's message to the elector, and he dies happy to have harmed the elector. Kohlhaas's glee at frustrating the elector contrasts sharply with his death sentence. The story ends with a kind of poetic justice: Kohlhaas has to die for his violent acts, but his two sons are knighted and his descendants live on, while the Saxon elector and his dynasty fade away. *Michael Kohlhaas* is a striking account of what can happen when bad means are used toward a good end.

Henry A. Lea

Further Reading

Ellis, John M. *Heinrich von Kleist: Studies in the Character and Meaning of His Writings.* Chapel Hill: University of North Carolina Press, 1979. Contains a detailed analysis of *Michael Kohlhaas* that assumes a close knowledge of the text.

Gailus, Andreas. *Passions of the Sign: Revolution and Language in Kant, Goethe, and Kleist.* Baltimore: Johns Hopkins University Press, 2006. Explores the influence of the French Revolution upon Kleist and two other major German Enlightenment thinkers. Reads both *Michael Kohlhaas* and a critical essay by Kleist to argue that the author puts forward an energetic and unstable model of language and human subjectivity that reveals the precarious nature of society and of social institutions.

Greenberg, Martin. Introduction to *The Marquise of O——, and Other Stories*, by Heinrich von Kleist. New York: Criterion Books, 1960. A brief assessment of Kleist's career and his approach to the novella.

Hamburger, Michael. *Contraries: Studies in German Literature.* New York: Dutton, 1970. Includes a chapter on Kleist that discusses specific aspects of Kleist's writings and worldview. Draws on a thorough knowledge of Kleist's life and texts to provide a sophisticated overview of his work.

Helbling, Robert E. *The Major Works of Heinrich von Kleist.* New York: New Directions, 1975. Offers general observations about Kleist's literary practice and brief comments about *Michael Kohlhaas*.

Mann, Thomas. "Kleist and His Stories." Preface to *The Marquise of O——, and Other Stories*, by Heinrich von Kleist. Translated by Francis Golffing. New York: Criterion Books, 1960. A psychological profile of Kleist, followed by an essayistic discussion of his stories.

Silz, Walter. *Heinrich von Kleist: Studies in His Works and Literary Character.* Philadelphia: University of Pennsylvania Press, 1961. Contains a detailed and informed discussion of themes in *Michael Kohlhaas*.

Simonsen, Karen-Margrethe. "Evilness and Law in Heinrich von Kleist's Story *Michael Kohlhaas*." In *Understanding Evil: An Interdisciplinary Approach*, edited by Margaret Sönser Breen. New York: Rodopi, 2003. Explores the relationship between legal and moral discourses within Kleist's novella.

Midaq Alley

Author: Naguib Mahfouz (1911-2006)
First published: Zuqaq al-Midaqq, 1947 (English
   translation, 1966, 1975)
Type of work: Novel
Type of plot: Historical realism
Time of plot: World War II
Locale: Cairo

Principal characters:
UNCLE KAMIL, a confectioner
ABBAS HILU, a barber
SALIM ALWAN, the owner of a large retail store
SHEIKH DARWISH, a "holy man"
"DR." BUSHI, a quack dentist
KIRSHA, a coffeehouse owner
HUSAIN KIRSHA, his son
RADWAN HUSAINI, a devout Muslim
HAMIDA, a prostitute
UMM HAMIDA, her foster mother
IBRAHIM FARAJ, a pimp

The Story:

Night falls on Midaq Alley, a small dead-end street in the ancient Gamaliyya section of Cairo. The entrance to this alley was established by two typical shops: on one side a sweets shop operated by Uncle Kamil and across the street a barbershop run by Abbas. The men represent the traditional slow and never-changing life of this lower middle-class society at a time when the outside world and wartime are threatening to overwhelm them. Uncle Kamil is an old, lethargic man who spends most of his days asleep on a chair in front of his shop. He is now awakened by Abbas, reminding him that it is time to close. Abbas, although young and energetic, is satisfied with operating his shop and observing the social and religious customs that his society always practiced.

The two men join others from the alley for an evening at Kirsha's coffeehouse, a typical male gathering place; the men discuss an old man who served as the poet in this café for several decades. Times changed, and customers now prefer the radio to recitations of classical Arabic poetry. Two men come to the aid of this public performer, although neither is able to save his job; the two men are Sheikh Darwish, a "holy man" who makes generally incomprehensible pronouncements in English to the group, and Radwan Husaini, the spiritual leader of Midaq Alley.

Umm Hamida is a matchmaker. Her foster daughter is named Hamida. Hamida prepares herself for her customary afternoon walk outside Midaq Alley, a place she loathes and whose people she hates. Much to her dismay, however, she does not have a new dress with which to exhibit her beauty.

Husain Kirsha also feels real repugnance toward the alley and its people. Rather than remain in Midaq Alley, Husain goes to work at a British army camp, where he earns much money. He supplements his income by selling stolen goods.

With these ill-gotten funds, Husain buys fancy foods, wine, and hashish, all of which are forbidden by the Muslim religion. He persuades his childhood friend, Abbas Hilu, to leave the barbershop and work for the British.

Whenever Hamida leaves the alley, she is carefully watched, particularly by Salim Alwan and Abbas, both of whom covet her. One day, Abbas decides to follow her, to speak to her, and to tell her of his love, a rather bold move for the normally shy and reticent barber. Hamida does not reject her suitor outright, because she believes that he is the only eligible bachelor in Midaq Alley. Abbas interprets her response as the first sign of love, and he is exhilarated. After many more meetings, Abbas finally asks Hamida to become his wife. He knows of her strong yearning for money and material objects, so he tells her that he will work for the British in another town, save his earnings, and give her everything she wants. The greedy Hamida accepts his proposal and sets the traditional engagement procedures into motion: "Dr." Bushi goes on Abbas's behalf to ask Umm Hamida for her daughter's hand in marriage. Uncle Kamil brings sweets for a celebration. Finally, the couple read the appropriate verse from the Qur'ān validating their intention to marry. The evening before he leaves, Abbas and Hamida seal their vows with their first kiss.

The first problem arises shortly after Abbas's departure. Salim Alwan, the wealthy and sexually frustrated middle-aged owner of the retail store in Midaq Alley, decides to divorce his wife and marry the young and beautiful Hamida. Umm Hamida and her daughter see this as an opportunity to acquire great wealth. There is, however, the problem that Hamida is already engaged. Umm seeks advice from Radwan Husaini, the most knowledgeable and devout Muslim in the alley. Husaini speaks against the marriage to Salim Alwan, but Husaini's counsel is rejected, and wedding plans are made. That same night, Salim Alwan's scheme is foiled when he has a severe heart attack; the attack devastates Hamida and her mother. Their plot to gain riches is thwarted.

A short time later, another opportunity arises when Ibrahim Faraj begins to pursue Hamida. A stranger to Midaq Alley, Faraj wears European clothes and seems to have considerable wealth; he is the type of man whom Hamida dreams of marrying. Hamida runs away with him; she believes that he loves her and that they will soon marry. Faraj's elegant apartment, however, actually serves as his "school" for prostitutes, and his intent is to put Hamida to work for him. Her beauty makes her a successful and wealthy prostitute, especially among British and American soldiers.

After quite some time, Abbas returns to Cairo. He has worked hard, saved money, and now wants to marry Hamida, but she is gone. Neither he nor most others in Midaq Alley know about Hamida's life as a prostitute. With his friend, Husain Kirsha, Abbas finds consolation visiting bars and drinking wine; Abbas previously never did this. One day, Abbas recognizes Hamida as she rides through the streets in an elegant carriage. He pursues her and calls out her name, but she is reluctant to acknowledge his presence. He tells no one in Midaq Alley about this meeting. People advise him to return to his job and to forget Hamida.

Hamida's life changes greatly during the period she works for her pimp, Ibrahim. She resents the power that he has over her, and she is searching for a way to escape from this enslavement. Now that Abbas returns and expresses a willingness to help her, she resolves to have Abbas kill Ibrahim the following Sunday. Husain convinces Abbas that Abbas has to avenge the insult Ibrahim brought on Abbas's honor. The two men go to a bar where the murder is to take place; they find Hamida surrounded by a group of soldiers. Enraged, Abbas calls out to Hamida; however, she rejects him. He hurls a beer glass at her and cuts her beautiful face. The angry soldiers attack Abbas and kill him, while Husain stands by and watches.

The following morning, the news of Abbas's death reaches Midaq Alley. There is general mourning; Uncle Kamil weeps. After a short while, the crisis subsides, and life in the alley returns to its tradition-bound, established way of life.

Critical Evaluation:

In 1988, Naguib Mahfouz became the first Arabic-language author to win the Nobel Prize in Literature, for with his "works rich in nuance—now clear-sightedly realistic, now evocatively ambiguous—he has formed an Arabic narrative that applies to all mankind."

Mahfouz has been a prolific writer. In addition, he worked for thirty-five years as a full-time civil servant in numerous government ministries until his retirement in 1971. For many years, he also regularly contributed articles on a host of topics to Cairo newspapers.

A man of habit and great discipline, Mahfouz is seen as Egypt's finest writer, and he is credited with making the novel and short story popular in Arabic literature, where poetry was the preferred genre for centuries. His work has been favorably compared to such Western European novelists as Honoré de Balzac, Charles Dickens, Thomas Mann, and John Galsworthy. He became well-known in his native Egypt with the Cairo trilogy (1956-1957), which traces the lives of three generations of a middle-class family between 1917 and 1944, a period of convulsive change in Egyptian society.

Mahfouz established his reputation in the English-speaking world with the translation of *Midaq Alley*, whose characters resemble people he met in the coffeehouses he frequented in the neighborhood of his birth. Consequently, his novels portray a realistic world; at the same time, the novels represent a universal social landscape. The novel is divided into thirty-five chapters and includes more than fifty named characters, of which a dozen play major roles. The real character however, is Midaq Alley; the people represent the personalities that make up the life of Midaq Alley. Beyond the main story are numerous parallel and subplots that add seriousness and complexity.

Midaq Alley pictures life in two different worlds—in the alley and away from there—and at two different times: the old time that stands still, and the new time of changes. Each major character is confronted by these conflicts between the old and the new, the here and the there, and each character comes to realize that for survival, life demands a commitment to one or to the other.

It is clear that Hamida chooses a new life away from Midaq Alley, and it is clear that she will survive. Her primary goal in life is to acquire material luxuries that the poverty of the alley is unable to provide. Since she is not bound by a traditional ethical code, becoming a prostitute presents no moral conflict for her, especially since she gains the personal power over others that she seeks.

Abbas, however, is a victim of this changing world. His love for Hamida forces him to leave the alley in order to earn money to provide a life for Hamida outside the only environment in which he can survive. When he finally returns, Hamida rejects him, and she uses him, once more, to fulfill her personal search for power.

Like Abbas, other characters find that they cannot exist in the duality. Salim Alwan is unable to fulfill the sexual fantasies of an elderly man longing for a young and beautiful wife. Umm Hamida has probably lost the riches that her foster daughter could have provided. Husain Kirsha finds his progress toward a life of ease halted when the British no longer employ him as the war comes to an end. Sheikh Darwish and Radwan Husaini become irrelevant in the alley. Although they attempt to represent positive moral forces, no one accepts their counsel.

Uncle Kamil, the opposite of the character of Hamida, is a survivor because he makes no effort to change his place in Midaq Alley, and he is not affected by the changing times. Hamida willingly prostitutes herself in the new world, and Uncle Kamil is always asleep.

Other characters, although important to the story, do not portray full lives either inside or outside Midaq Alley. Their purpose is to enhance and complete the mosaic of a complex society in a critical period of transition.

Thomas H. Falk

Further Reading

Allegretto-Diiulio, Pamela. *Naguib Mahfouz: A Western and Eastern Cage of Female Entrapment*. Youngstown, N.Y.: Cambria Press, 2007. Feminist analysis of Mahfouz's major novels, including a chapter on *Midaq Alley*. Describes how Mahfouz used the elements of daily life in Cairo to depict the city's culture and life during the British occupation of Egypt.

El-Enany, Rasheed. *Naguib Mahfouz: His Life and Times*. Cairo: American University in Cairo Press, 2007. Comprehensive account of Mahfouz's life and work, with an assessment of his ouevre.

_____. *Naguib Mahfouz: The Pursuit of Meaning*. New York: Routledge, Chapman & Hall, 1993. Major study concentrating on the themes and issues in Mahfouz's novels. Includes a carefully articulated examination of *Midaq Alley*.

Kilpatrick, Hilary. "The Egyptian Novel from *Zaynab* to 1980." In *Modern Arabic Literature*, edited by M. M. Badawi. New York: Cambridge University Press, 1992. An important, in-depth examination of contemporary Egyptian literature, with special reference to Mahfouz. Positions him as a significant author of twentieth century prose.

Le Gassick, Trevor, ed. *Critical Perspectives on Naguib Mahfouz*. Washington, D.C.: Three Continents Press, 1991. A collection of essays published between 1971 and 1989 in various journals. Articles range from discussions to commentaries on specific works, including a sociocultural analysis of *Midaq Alley*. Le Gassick translates some essays from Arabic.

Milson, Menahem. *Najib Mahfuz: The Novelist-Philosopher of Cairo*. New York: St. Martin's Press, 1998. Insightful account of Mahfouz's life and literary career. Milson describes how Mahfouz became both "Egypt's most popular writer" and "the literary conscience of his country."

Moosa, Matti. *The Early Novels of Naguib Mahfouz: Images of Modern Egypt*. Gainesville: University Press of Florida, 1994. Concentrates on Mahfouz's work from the formative years in the 1930's, his historical novels, and the novels dealing with contemporary Egypt up to 1959. Includes a detailed analysis of the Cairo trilogy and a thorough examination of *Midaq Alley*.

Somekh, Sasson. *The Changing Rhythm: A Study of Najib Mahfuz's Novels*. Leiden, the Netherlands: E. J. Brill, 1973. This examination, considered by many scholars to be a classic study, remains an important and valuable assessment of Mahfouz's writings, especially his earlier prose works. Includes a useful survey of the development of the Egyptian novel as an emerging literary form in the twentieth century.

Mid-Channel

Author: Arthur Wing Pinero (1855-1934)
First produced: 1909; first published, 1910
Type of work: Drama
Type of plot: Psychological realism
Time of plot: Early twentieth century
Locale: London

Principal characters:
ZOE BLUNDELL, an attractive, intelligent woman
THEODORE BLUNDELL, husband of Zoe
HONORABLE PETER MOTTRAM, a friend of the Blundells
LEONARD FERRIS, Zoe's lover
ETHEL PIERPOINT, fiancé of Leonard
MRS. PIERPOINT, Ethel's mother
ALICE ANNERLY, Theodore's lover

The Story:

Mrs. Pierpoint and her daughter, Ethel, visit Zoe Blundell to inquire about the possibility of Leonard Ferris as a suitor for Ethel. Mrs. Pierpoint wants Zoe's opinion because Leonard is one of Zoe's tame robins, a group of male friends and admirers who gathers around Zoe. Unknown to the Pierpoints, Zoe's marriage is breaking up and Leonard is sexually attracted to Zoe. Zoe at first believes her relationship with Leonard is harmless because she feels much, much older than he. Leonard is thirty-two years old, five years younger than Zoe, but he is a "fresh, boyish young man" and Zoe is a "mature woman." Zoe's husband, Theodore, is forty-six years old.

Zoe's perspective reflects society's double standard that an older man may be interested in a younger woman but an older woman should not be interested in a younger man. After the Pierpoints leave, Leonard arrives to see Zoe and confesses he does not want to marry anyone, although he is attracted to Ethel because she reminds him of Zoe.

Leonard leaves and the Honorable Peter Mottram arrives to discuss Zoe's marriage problems. Peter, a friend of Zoe and Theodore who also functions as an informal marriage counselor between the Blundells, tells Zoe that her marriage is like some trophies on a shelf. The trophies themselves are not valuable so much as the struggle to win them. Zoe, he thinks, has to keep the trophies—like her marriage—new and fresh. Then Theodore arrives, and Peter tries to talk Theodore into mending the marriage. Peter gives another analogy: He describes a body of water between Folkestone and Boulogne in which there is a midchannel, a shoal that causes the passengers of a boat to experience rough travel. Peter says, "Everythin's looked as enticin' as could be; but as we've neared the Ridge—mid-channel—I've begun to feel fidgety, restless, out o' sorts—hatin' myself and hatin' the man who's been sharin' my cabin with me." He tells the Blundells the crisis will end if they can wait. After Peter leaves, the Blundells do not heed his advice. Instead, they fight, and Theodore walks out on Zoe.

Some time later, Leonard and Zoe return from a tour of Italy. They had a brief affair in Perugia and should have been more discreet. Claud Lowenstein saw them together at the Brufani Hotel. Upon returning to London, Leonard and Zoe learn that Theodore has been dating Alice Annerly, a thirty-year-old divorcé. Zoe has a fever, a physical reflection of her declining moral state. Peter reappears and tries to get Zoe and Theodore to mend their marriage. He again uses an analogy. This time it concerns two cracked Ming vases. Would it not, he ask, be better to repair the broken vases than to throw them away? After Peter leaves, Ethel arrives to discuss her relationship with Leonard. She tells Zoe that Leonard has come close to proposing marriage, but that he has changed since Italy and she fears he looks different, as if he has gotten "mixed up with some woman of the wrong sort." Leonard's guilt, like Zoe's, is also having a physical effect on him. Ethel innocently asks Zoe's help in saving him. Zoe says she will. Ethel leaves, and Leonard returns.

Zoe confronts Leonard about his relationship with Ethel, and he admits he has been close to proposing marriage. Zoe says they should break up so that he can return to Ethel. Instead, Leonard confesses his love for Zoe and asks her to marry him. Zoe first responds with laughter, then anger. She calls him a coward and tells him she never wants to see him again. He leaves furious.

Theodore and Alice Annerly discuss Theodore's relationship with Zoe. Theodore has discovered that he is still fond of his wife and unhappy with Alice. He tells Alice their relationship has ended. Alice tells him she feels compromised; Theodore writes Alice a check for fifteen hundred dollars. Alice leaves and Peter comes back, telling Theodore that Zoe wants to reunite. Theodore has been miserable without her and is anxious to be with her again. Zoe enters at this point, and Theodore asks her if she can forgive him for Alice. Zoe says she will. Encouraged by Theodore's confessions, she asks him to forgive her for the affair she had with Leonard. Theodore is outraged. He says he wants a divorce if Leonard will agree to marry Zoe.

Zoe and Theodore have a showdown. Leonard tells Zoe he plans to return to Ethel. Zoe approaches him thinking he will still marry her. Leonard returns from the meeting with Zoe in which he had proposed to her and rips apart her pictures. He then goes back with Ethel. Talking with Leonard in his room, Zoe finds that the pictures of her are no longer there; she is out of his life. When Theodore arrives to ask if Leonard will marry Zoe, she leaves the room thinking that Leonard belongs with Ethel, and she has no one. Leonard tells Theodore, however, that he will still marry Zoe. While the two men converse, Zoe kills herself by jumping off the balcony.

Critical Evaluation:

Arthur Wing Pinero was one of the pioneers of psychological realism. He addressed the plight of women in unhappy marriages. His best-known play, *The Second Mrs. Tanqueray* (1893), preceded *Mid-Channel* by sixteen years and made Pinero's reputation as a serious playwright. Both plays are examples of the idea play, which centers on a societal issue.

The Second Mrs. Tanqueray deals with a frustrated marriage and ends in the suicide of Paula Tanqueray. The two plays have much in common, especially in their treatment of women. Both plays address the problems women encounter in marriage, but the solution to their problems leaves much to be desired: They both escape the marriage through suicide. This reflects the limited choices of women in England at the time. In *Mid-Channel*, Zoe Blundell has sinned and therefore must die. This illustrates the double standard; Theodore Blundell and Leonard Ferris have also sinned but they are able to redeem themselves. The blame for the unhappy marriage is placed upon Zoe although Theodore walks out on her. Zoe feels that she should have children, and many critics during the first run of the play said this was the primary reason for the Blundells' disastrous marriage. A marriage without children, after all, cannot be happy. The fact that the Blundells had no children was actually Theodore's fault because he told Zoe he did not want any children. Now that the Blundells are comfortable and their struggles are over, they find they cannot rest. They have hit middle age and feel they had accomplished nothing.

Zoe is an intelligent, perceptive woman. The men surrounding her—Theodore and Leonard—both love but fail to understand her. Peter is the only one who shows insight into Zoe's predicament, but he does not predict her suicide. Peter is a catalyst, one who causes changes but remains unchanged himself. Had Peter not arranged the reconciliation of the Blundells, the other events would probably never have happened. Ironically, therefore, Peter's meddling indirectly brings about Zoe's suicide.

Much of the action takes place outside the play—often between acts. The audience learns of events through conversations. At the beginning of the twentieth century, a play about divorce and suicide was daring and shocking; it is not surprising, therefore, that much of the play's action takes place off stage. Pinero was not the only writer of the period to show suicide as the only alternative to an unhappy marriage. The heroines in Henrik Ibsen's *Hedda Gabler* (1890) and Kate Chopin's *The Awakening* (1899) take their own lives rather than stay married and miserable.

Mary C. Bagley

Further Reading

Cunliffe, John W. *Modern English Playwrights: A Short History of the English Drama from 1825.* 1927. Reprint. Port Washington, N.Y.: Kennikat Press, 1969. Shows how *Mid-Channel* was received in the United States and Great Britain. Claims, however, that the play is overrated by American critics.

Dawick, John. *Pinero: A Theatrical Life.* Niwot: University Press of Colorado, 1993. Comprehensive account of Pinero's personal and professional life, based in part on the writer's correspondence and unpublished materials from his literary estate. Discusses Pinero's plays and other writings within their theatrical and social contexts, particularly the Victorian concern about respectability.

Nicoll, Allardyce. *British Drama: An Historical Survey from the Beginnings to the Present Time.* 5th rev. ed. London: Harrap, 1978. Discusses Pinero's treatment of theme, the lack of sentiment, and cynical point of view. Describes Pinero's views of human weakness and how he acquired the reputation of one of London's master playwrights.

Powell, Kerry, ed. *The Cambridge Companion to Victorian and Edwardian Theatre.* New York: Cambridge University Press, 2004. Although no essay in this book focuses on Pinero, the index lists numerous references. Helps place Pinero's work within the larger context of Victorian- and Edwardian-era theater.

Roy, Emil. *British Drama Since Shaw.* Carbondale: Southern Illinois University Press, 1972. Claims Pinero needed to be more rebellious in his dramatic works. Argues that his drama functioned as middle-class escapist theater.

Middle Passage

Author: Charles Johnson (1948-   )
First published: 1990
Type of work: Novel
Type of plot: Bildungsroman, historical, and adventure
Time of plot: 1830
Locale: New Orleans, Louisiana; at sea

Principal characters:
RUTHERFORD CALHOUN, a freed slave
ISADORA BAILEY, a teacher
PAPA ZERINGUE, a gangster
EBENEZER FALCON, ship captain
NGONYAMA, an Allmuseri tribesman
BALEKA, a slave child
JOSIAH SQUIBB, ship's cook
PETER CRINGLE, ship first-mate

The Story:

Rutherford Calhoun, twenty-two years old and newly freed from slavery by an Illinois farmer on his deathbed, is enjoying life in the wicked city of New Orleans, Louisiana. His former master had educated young Rutherford in the classics and the Bible. However, for Calhoun, freedom means living the dissolute life of a petty thief, gambler, and womanizer. He has run up a debt of fifty thousand francs, owed to a black gangster, Papa Zeringue.

Calhoun has been keeping company with Isadora Bailey, a free black schoolteacher with impeccable morals and ambitions to reform him. She loves him; but he does not have marriage in mind. Zeringue, acting as Isadora's protector, has agreed to forgive Calhoun's debts if he will marry her.

The night before the wedding, Calhoun, after an orgy of drinking in a seaside tavern, steals the identity papers of drunken sailor Josiah Squibb, a cook on the ship *Republic*, and sneaks aboard as a stowaway. When he awakes with a hangover, he discovers that the ship, a wreck constantly needing repair, has a crew of malformed, incompetent misfits. An exception is Peter Cringle, the first mate, who is a New England gentleman. Captain Ebenezer Falcon is a pederast who rapes young Tom, the cabin boy. Squibb is permanently drunk, and Calhoun must take over the galley. He soon confirms his suspicion that the ship is a slaver, bound for Guinea to pick up forty Allmuseri, members of a tribe of mysterious wizards. With the slaves aboard, the *Republic* begins its homeward journey, the Middle Passage of slaves from Africa to the United States.

Calhoun is highly educated, with a knowledge of Latin, Greek mythology, and philosophers such as Immanuel Kant, Georg Wilhelm Friedrich Hegel, and Saint Thomas Aquinas. He is something of a mystic—homeless and on a quest to discover the truth of his identity. When the ship reaches Africa, he scavenges the cabin of Captain Falcon while the crew is ashore, stealing some money. He is discovered by Falcon but, instead of being punished, is taken into Falcon's confidence and agrees to spy on the crew. The captain's cabin is filled with illegal plunder from his other voyages. His latest acquisition is a huge, mysterious crate, installed in the ship's hold; it terrifies the crew.

As he observes the brutal treatment of the slaves, Calhoun begins to move beyond his self-concern to develop compassion for their plight. He seeks the company of the mysterious Ngonyama, one of the Allmuseri, whom the captain has assigned to oversee the slaves. Ngonyama is silent and cunning, with strange powers such as the ability to carve a roast pig without touching bone, as if he could see the invisible parts of the animal. Calhoun begins to teach him English; he in turn begins to learn the Allmuseri language. Calhoun also becomes the protector of the eight-year-old slave child Baleka, with whom he shares his food.

In a fierce storm, several sailors and slaves are swept away to their deaths. Ngonyama appears on deck, entirely dry, and the storm ceases. Fearful that Captain Falcon is leading them to certain death at sea, the crew, led by Cringle, plans a mutiny. Calhoun, acting in his own best interests, changes loyalties several times. He admires Cringle's stern New England morality, agrees to support the rebels, and breaks into the captain's cabin to disarm his weapons. When Falcon discovers him, however, Calhoun reveals the plans for mutiny. Falcon agrees to be merciful to the rebellious crew and promises to double Calhoun's share of the profit from the voyage, thus making him complicit in the transport and sale of the slaves.

Falcon, a mad genius as well as a criminal, tells Calhoun that the mysterious crate contains the god of the Allmuseri, a creature without a name or image. Like the god of the Old Testament, it converses with humans, including Falcon himself. This god has solved the classic philosophical paradox about the omniscience of a deity: making a stone so heavy but unable to lift it.

Calhoun reveals to Squibb the story of his former master, the Reverend Chandler, who on his deathbed made Calhoun and his brother Jackson his heirs. Jackson generously divided the property in a massive act of reparation for all slaves. Rutherford inherited forty dollars, a Bible, a bedpan, and an unforgiving rage at his brother for depriving him of his inheritance.

Life on the *Republic*, Calhoun learns, has strange powers to transform its passengers. The slaves seem caught between two worlds—no longer entirely African, but not yet American. Calhoun himself undergoes a powerful change of heart and acknowledges the evil deeds he has committed. In yet another reversal of his loyalties, he steals the key to the slaves' chains and gives it to Ngonyama, enabling the Africans to take over the ship. Only fifteen Africans survive the takeover; they kill all but four of the crew. Rutherford convinces Ngonyama to treat Falcon as a slave and to spare Cringle's life because only he can navigate the ship, which the Allmuseri intend to sail back to Africa.

Rutherford now begins to identify with the humane spirituality of the Allmuseri, who, as believers in the unity of all beings, see the killing of the crew as an evil that must be expiated by the ritual cleansing of the ship, lest they be haunted by sins that will become a part of their nature. He meets the Allmuseri god, a shape-shifter who takes the form of Calhoun's father. Calhoun, who had blamed his father for abandoning him, learns the truth: His father was killed by white men during an escape attempt.

The *Republic*, circling aimlessly in the Atlantic, headed neither for Africa nor America, descends into chaos. The remaining crew and slaves undergo a period of trial, with horrifying illnesses, an instance of cannibalism, and the suicide of Captain Falcon. Only Calhoun remains healthy and devotes himself to caring for the others. In a fortuitous coincidence, the survivors of the *Republic* are rescued by the ship *Juno*. Squibb, Calhoun, and three Allmuseri children survive, including Baleka, who sees Calhoun as a father figure.

Aboard the rescue ship are Papa Zeringue and Isadora, who are about to be married. Calhoun, now transformed, confronts Zeringue, threatening him with blackmail for illegally transporting slaves. With his new spiritual insight, Calhoun realizes that he loves Isadora, who has become a beauty. Calhoun and Isadora reconcile in a final scene in which they discover a spiritual love that transcends sexual desire. They will care for the three surviving Allmuseri children and return to Illinois to reunite with Calhoun's brother, Jackson. Calhoun's voyage into chaos, his symbolic "middle passage," has convinced him of the connectedness of all human life and has given him the promise of a true home.

Critical Evaluation:

Middle Passage works effectively as an exciting adventure of a calamitous sea voyage, but the author, Charles Johnson, introduces much deeper philosophical questions about the nature of reality. Rutherford Calhoun, the narrator who speaks in a multiplicity of voices ranging wildly from philosophical argument to twentieth century black English, writes the ship's log. The story becomes his own postmodernist revision of history. Calhoun, like the African trickster of folklore, transforms his tale into a masterpiece of sly humor, parody, and allusions to other literary works that invite the complicity of the reader.

The characters, although fully developed with psychological motives and realistic physical attributes, represent far more than this. Johnson, a lifelong student of philosophy, has immersed himself in the history of slavery and narratives of the sea. Most obvious is his debt to Herman Melville's *Moby Dick* (1851) and its narrator, Ishmael. The story also calls up the historic 1839 takeover of the slave ship *Amistad*, the only instance of African slaves succeeding in a mutiny on the high seas.

The classic slave story *Narrative of the Life of Frederick Douglass, an American Slave* (1845) could serve as a model for *Middle Passage*, but Johnson references the work for his own purposes. Frederick Douglass, the protagonist of the traditional slave narrative, journeys from mental and physical slavery to freedom and a new life in the North. The fictional Calhoun, however, is legally free but enslaved by his physical appetites. Douglass taught himself to read and write so that he could report his own story. Calhoun, given the task of writing the ship's log, assumes the authority to create not just his own journey but the symbolic record of the Middle Passage of the *Republic*.

Johnson's manipulation of the various styles of language and his use of anachronisms provide much of the dark humor in the story. Juxtaposed against the often outrageous dialogue and comic allusions, the author recounts the horrors of slavery and the misery of life aboard a nineteenth century sailing ship. He is unsparing in describing the cruel separation of slave families and the brutal overcrowding of the starving human cargo in the hold of the ship. Some readers may find this conflation of comedy and tragedy unconvincing. Critics such as Henry Louis Gates, Jr., and Nellie Y. McKay, however, praise Johnson's innovative vision as introducing philosophical exploration into traditional African

American literature. According to critic Francine Dempsey, Calhoun's first-person narration, expressed in wildly varying, but ultimately convincing, voices, effectively holds the narrative together.

In his preface, Johnson acknowledges the sources for his knowledge of the sea, African history, and different cultures and speech patterns. His epigraphs include quotations from Aquinas, Robert Hayden's poem "Middle Passage," and the Upanishad, a disparate collection of references that attests to his breadth of scholarship and his dedication to philosophy. Johnson has said in several interviews that his writing is inseparable also from his Buddhist beliefs. He believes that slavery, like all evil, is rooted in the perception that all matter is duality, or opposition. The wise, mysterious Allmuseri, who appear in several of the author's writings, are peace-loving beings, uncorrupted by the desire for material wealth and who believe in the unity of all matter.

The "middle passage" of the title is for Calhoun the transformation from an unprincipled reprobate into a compassionate man who values all life and finds redemption through spiritual love. The narrative transcends Calhoun's personal redemption, however. The aptly named *Republic*, a physical and moral wreck that ultimately sinks under the weight of the evil it has borne, suggests the worst attributes of American society. However, hope for the redemption of the ship is voiced in Calhoun's revelation.

If this weird, upside-down caricature of a country called America, if this land of refugees and former indentured servants, religious heretics and half-breeds, whoresons and fugitives—this cauldron of mongrels from all the points of the compass—was all I could rightly call *home*, then aye: I was of it.

Johnson's work in both fiction and nonfiction has been widely praised by critics. *Middle Passage* won the National Book Award in 1990. Among his other accolades are a MacArthur genius award in 1998 and the American Academy of Arts and Letters Award for Literature in 2002. Through his writings, Johnson proposes a new vision that combines Western and Eastern philosophies, a new vision that, he believes, is missing in traditional African American literature.

Marjorie Podolsky

Further Reading

Byrd, Rudolph P. *Charles Johnson's Novels: Writing the American Palimpsest*. Bloomington: Indiana University Press, 2005. Provides a helpful guide for new readers of Johnson's work, offering insights into his novels, including *Middle Passage*.

"Charles Johnson." In *The Norton Anthology of African American Literature*, edited by Henry Louis Gates, Jr., and Nellie Y. McKay. New York: W. W. Norton, 1997. An authoritative overview of Johnson's work as a new and distinctive voice in African American literature. Part of a collection edited by respected scholars of African American and black studies.

Conner, Marc C., and William R. Nash, eds. *Charles Johnson: The Novelist as Philosopher*. Jackson: University Press of Mississippi, 2007. Collection of essays examines Johnson's fictional and philosophical writings and discusses how they are connected. Includes bibliographic references and an index.

Dempsey, Francine. "*Middle Passage*." In *Masterpieces of African American Literature*, edited by Frank N. Magill. New York: HarperCollins, 1992. A comprehensive analysis of *Middle Passage*, with emphasis on its philosophical, literary, and historical allusions.

Flick, Arend. "Stowaway on a Slave Ship to Africa." *Los Angeles Times Book Review*, June 24, 1990. Discusses *Middle Passage* as representing a philosophical split between Western and Asian thought. Praises its attributes both as a story and as an intellectual experience.

Johnson, Charles. "An Interview with Charles Johnson." Interview by Michael Boccia. *African American Review* 30, no. 4 (Winter, 1996): 611-618. Johnson traces the writers and the philosophical ideas that have influenced his fiction. He states his intention to write black philosophical fiction and notes the influence of Buddhism on his life and writings.

Nash, William R. *Charles Johnson's Fiction*. Chicago: University of Illinois Press, 2003. Focuses on the evolution of Johnson's literary aesthetic in terms of his "hybrid philosophy of Buddhism and phenomenology" and his rejection of racialist thinking in favor of a larger, more universal concept of identity and possibility.

Storhoff, Gary. *Understanding Charles Johnson*. Columbia: University of South Carolina Press, 2004. Provides an introduction to Johnson's work for students and general readers, with a brief biographical section and chapters devoted to all of his novels.

Thaden, Barbara Z. "Charles Johnson's *Middle Passage* as Historiographic Metafiction." *College English* 59, no. 7 (November, 1997): 753-766. A theoretical approach to the novel, especially useful for instructors who want creative ideas for teaching *Middle Passage*.

Middlemarch
A Study of Provincial Life

Author: George Eliot (1819-1880)
First published: 1871-1872
Type of work: Novel
Type of plot: Psychological realism
Time of plot: Nineteenth century
Locale: England

Principal characters:
DOROTHEA BROOKE, an idealistic young woman
EDWARD CASAUBON, her scholarly husband
WILL LADISLAW, Casaubon's cousin
TERTIUS LYDGATE, a doctor
ROSAMOND VINCY, the woman Lydgate married
CELIA, Dorothea's sister
SIR JAMES CHETTAM, Celia's husband

The Story:

Dorothea Brooke and her younger sister, Celia, are young women of good birth who live with their bachelor uncle at Tipton Grange near the town of Middlemarch. So serious is Dorothea's cast of mind that she is reluctant to keep jewelry she had inherited from her dead mother, and she gives all of it to her sister except a ring and a bracelet.

At a dinner party where the middle-aged scholar Edward Casaubon and Sir James Chettam both vie for her attention, she is much more attracted to the serious-minded Casaubon. Casaubon must have had an inkling that his chances with Dorothea were good; for he seeks her out the next morning. Celia, who does not like his complexion or his moles, escapes to other interests.

That afternoon, Dorothea considers the scholar's wisdom. While she is out walking, she encounters Sir James by chance; he tells her that he is in love with her and, mistaking her silence for agreement, assumes that she loves him in return. When Casaubon makes his proposal of marriage by letter, Dorothea accepts him at once. Mr. Brooke, her uncle, thinks Sir James a much better match; Dorothea's decision merely confirms his bachelor views that women are difficult to understand. He decides not to interfere in her plans, but Celia feels that the event will be more like a funeral than a marriage and frankly says so.

Casaubon takes Dorothea, Celia, and Mr. Brooke to see his home so that Dorothea might order any necessary changes. Dorothea intends to defer to Casaubon's tastes in all things and says she will make no changes in the house. During the visit, Dorothea meets Will Ladislaw, Casaubon's second cousin, who does not seem in sympathy with his elderly cousin's marriage plans.

While Dorothea and her new husband are traveling in Italy, Tertius Lydgate, an ambitious but poor young doctor, is meeting pretty Rosamond Vincy, to whom he is much at-

tracted. Fred Vincy, Rosamond's brother, has indicated that he expects to receive a fine inheritance when his uncle, Mr. Featherstone, dies. Meanwhile, Vincy is pressed by a debt he is unable to pay.

Lydgate becomes involved in petty local politics. When the time comes to choose a chaplain for the new hospital of which Lydgate is the head, the young doctor realizes that it is in his best interest to vote in accordance with the wishes of Nicholas Bulstrode, an influential banker and founder of the hospital. A clergyman named Tyke receives the office.

In Rome, Ladislaw encounters Dorothea and her husband. Dorothea has begun to realize how pompous and incompatible she finds Casaubon. Seeing her unhappiness, Ladislaw first pities and then falls in love with his cousin's wife. Unwilling to live any longer on Casaubon's charity, Ladislaw announces his intention of returning to England and finding some kind of gainful occupation.

When Fred Vincy's note comes due, he tries to sell a horse at a profit, but the animal turns out to be vicious. Because of Fred's inability to raise the money, Caleb Garth, who had signed his note, now stands to lose one hundred and ten pounds. Fred falls ill, and Lydgate is summoned to attend him. Lydgate uses his professional calls to further his suit with Rosamond.

Dorothea and her husband return from Rome in time to hear of Celia's engagement to Sir James. Will Ladislaw includes a note to Dorothea in a letter he writes to Casaubon. This attention precipitates a quarrel that is followed by Casaubon's serious illness. Lydgate, who attends him, urges him to give up his studies for the present time. Lydgate confides to Dorothea that Casaubon has a weak heart and must be guarded from all excitement.

Meanwhile, all the relatives of old Mr. Featherstone are waiting impatiently for his death. He hopes to circumvent their desires by giving his fortune to Mary Garth, daughter of the man who had signed Fred Vincy's note. When she refuses the money, he falls into a rage and dies soon afterward. Upon the reading of his will, everyone learns that he left nothing to his relatives; most of his money is to go to Joshua Riggs, who is to take the name of Featherstone, and a part of his fortune is to endow the Featherstone Almshouses for old men.

Plans are made for Rosamond's marriage with Lydgate. Fred Vincy is ordered to prepare himself finally for the ministry, since he is to have no inheritance from his uncle. Mr. Brooke has gone into politics; he now enlists the help of Ladislaw in publishing a liberal paper. Mr. Casaubon now dislikes his cousin intensely after he rejected further financial assistance, and he has forbidden Ladislaw from entering his house.

After Casaubon dies suddenly, a codicil to his will gives Dorothea all of his property as long as she does not marry Ladislaw. This strange provision causes Dorothea's friends and relatives some concern because, if publicly revealed, it will appear that Dorothea and Ladislaw had been indiscreet.

On the advice of his Tory friends, Mr. Brooke gives up his liberal newspaper and cuts off his connection with Ladislaw. Ladislaw realizes that Dorothea's family is in some way trying to separate him from Dorothea, but he refuses to be disconcerted about the matter. He resolves to stay on in Middlemarch until he is ready to leave. When he hears of the codicil to Casaubon's will, he is more than ever determined to remain so that he can eventually disprove the suspicions of the village concerning him and Dorothea.

Meanwhile, Lydgate and Rosamond have married, and the doctor has gone deeply in debt to furnish his house. When he finds that his income does not meet his wife's spendthrift habits, he asks her to help him economize. They begin to quarrel, and both his practice and his popularity decrease.

A disreputable man named Raffles appears in Middlemarch. Raffles knows that Ladislaw's grandfather had amassed a fortune as a receiver of stolen goods and that Nicholas Bulstrode, the highly respected banker, had once been the confidential clerk of Ladislaw's ancestor. Moreover, Bulstrode's first wife had been his employer's widow. Bulstrode built his fortune with money inherited from her, money that should have gone to Ladislaw's mother.

Bulstrode had been blackmailed by Raffles earlier, and he reasons now that the scoundrel will tell Ladislaw the whole story. To forestall trouble, he sends for Ladislaw and offers him an annuity of five hundred pounds and liberal provision in his will. Ladislaw, feeling that his relatives have already tainted his honor, refuses; he is unwilling to be associated in

any way with the unsavory business and decides to leave Middlemarch for London, even though he has no assurance that Dorothea loves him.

Lydgate drifts more deeply into debt. When he wishes to sell what he can and take cheaper lodgings, Rosamond manages to persuade him to continue keeping up the pretense of prosperity a little longer. When Bulstrode gives up his interest in the new hospital and withdraws his financial support, the situation grows even worse. Faced at last with the seizure of his goods, Lydgate goes to Bulstrode and asks for a loan. The banker advises him to seek aid from Dorothea and abruptly ends the conversation. When Raffles, in the last stages of alcoholism, returns to Middlemarch and Lydgate is called in to attend him, Bulstrode, afraid the doctor will learn the banker's secret from Raffles's drunken ravings, changes his mind and gives Lydgate a check for one thousand pounds. The loan comes in time to save Lydgate's goods and reputation. When Raffles dies, Bulstrode feels at peace at last. Nevertheless, it soon becomes common gossip that Bulstrode had given money to Lydgate and that Lydgate had attended Raffles in his final illness. Bulstrode and Lydgate are publicly accused of malpractice in Raffles's death. Only Dorothea takes up Lydgate's defense. The rest of the town is busy with gossip over the affair. Rosamond is anxious to leave Middlemarch to avoid public disgrace. Bulstrode, too, is anxious to leave town, because Raffles had told his secret while drunk in a neighboring village; Bulstrode becomes ill, however, and his doctors will not permit him to leave his bed.

Feeling sympathy for Lydgate, Dorothea is determined to give her support to the hospital and to try to convince Rosamond that the only way Lydgate could recover his honor is by remaining in Middlemarch. Unfortunately, she comes upon Rosamond pouring out her grief to Will Ladislaw. Dorothea, suspecting that Rosamond is involved with Ladislaw, leaves abruptly. Angered at the false position Rosamond had put him in, Ladislaw tells her that he has always loved Dorothea from a distance. When Dorothea forces herself to return to Lydgate's house the following morning, Rosamond tells her of Ladislaw's declaration. Dorothea realizes she is willing to give up Casaubon's fortune for Ladislaw's affection.

Despite the protests of her family and friends, they are married several weeks later and leave Middlemarch to live in London. Lydgate and Rosamond live together with better understanding and prospects of a happier future. Fred Vincy becomes engaged to Mary Garth, with whom he has long been in love. For a time, Dorothea's family ignores her, but they are finally reconciled after Dorothea's son is born and Ladislaw is elected to Parliament.

Critical Evaluation:

Modestly subtitled "A Study of Provincial Life," George Eliot's *Middlemarch* has long been recognized as a work of great psychological and moral penetration. Indeed, the novel has been compared with Leo Tolstoy's *Voyna I mir* (1865-1869; *War and Peace*, 1886) and William Makepeace Thackeray's *Vanity Fair* (1847-1848, serial; 1848, book) for its almost epic sweep and its perspective of early nineteenth century history. These comparisons, however, are partly faulty.

Unlike *War and Peace*, *Middlemarch* lacks a philosophical bias, a grand Weltanschauung that encompasses the destinies of nations and generations. Unlike *Vanity Fair*, Eliot's novel is not neatly moralistic. In fact, much of *Middlemarch* is morally ambiguous in the twentieth century sense of the term. Eliot's concept of plot and character derives from psychological rather than philosophical or social necessity. This is to say that *Middlemarch*, despite its Victorian trappings of complicated plot and subplot, slow development of character, accumulated detail concerning time and place, and social density, in many respects resembles the twentieth century novel that disturbs as well as entertains.

Eliot published *Middlemarch* in eight books between December, 1871, and December, 1872, eight years before her death. She was at the height of her powers and had already achieved a major reputation with *Adam Bede* (1859), *The Mill on the Floss* (1860), and *Silas Marner* (1861). Nevertheless, her most recent fiction, *Felix Holt, the Radical* (1866) and the dramatic poem *The Spanish Gypsy* (1868), had been considered inferior to her best writing and had disappointed her readers. *Middlemarch* was, however, received with considerable excitement and critical acclaim. Eliot's publisher, Blackwood, was so caught up with the narrative as he received chapters of her novel by mail that he wrote back to her asking questions about the fates of the characters as though they were real people with real histories.

Eliot did scrupulous research for the material of her novel. Her discussion of the social climate in rural England directly preceding passage of the Reform Bill of 1832 is convincingly detailed; she accurately describes the state of medical knowledge during Lydgate's time; and she treats the dress, habits, and speech of Middlemarch impeccably, creating the metaphor of a complete world, a piece of provincial England that is a microcosm of the greater world beyond.

The theme of the novel itself, however, revolves around the slenderest of threads: the mating of "unimportant" people. This theme, which engages the talents of such other great writers as Jane Austen, Thomas Hardy, Henry James, and D. H. Lawrence, allows Eliot the scope to examine the whole range of human nature. She is concerned with the mating of lovers because people in love are most vulnerable and most easily the victims of romantic illusions. Each of the three sets of lovers in *Middlemarch*—Dorothea Brooke, Edward Casaubon, and Will Ladislaw; Rosamond Vincy and Tertius Lydgate; and Mary Garth and Fred Vincy—mistake illusion for reality. Eventually, whether or not they become completely reconciled with their mates, all come to understand themselves better. Each undergoes a sentimental education, a discipline of the spirit that teaches the heart its limitations.

Paradoxically, the greater capacity Eliot's characters have for romantic self-deception, the greater their suffering and subsequent tempering of spirit. Mary Garth—plain, witty, honest—is too sensible to arouse psychological curiosity to the same degree as does proud Dorothea, rash Ladislaw, pathetic Casaubon, ambitious Lydgate, or pampered Rosamond. Mary loves simply, directly. Fred, her childhood sweetheart, is basically a good lad who must learn the lessons of thrift and perseverance from his own misfortunes. He "falls" in class, from that of an idle landowner to one of a decent but socially inferior manager of property. In truth, what he seems to lose in social prominence he more than recovers in the development of his moral character. Moreover, he wins as a mate the industrious Mary, who will strengthen his resolve and make of him an admirable provider like her father Caleb.

Dorothea, on the other hand, more idealistic and noble-hearted than Mary, chooses the worst possible mate as her first husband. Edward Casaubon, thirty years her senior, is a dull pedant, cold, hopelessly ineffectual as a scholar, absurd as a lover. Despite his intellectual pretensions, he is too timid, fussy, and dispirited ever to complete his masterwork, "A Key to All Mythologies." Even the title of his project is an absurdity. He conceals as long as possible his "key" from Dorothea, fearing that she will expose him as a sham. Nevertheless, it is possible that she might have endured the disgrace of her misplaced affection were Casaubon only more tender, reciprocating her own tenderness and self-sacrifice; but Casaubon, despotic to the last, tries to blight her spirit when he is alive and, through his will, to restrict her freedom when he is dead.

Dorothea's second choice of a mate, Will Ladislaw, is very nearly the opposite of Casaubon. A rash, sometimes hypersensitive lover, he is capable of intense affection, above all of self-sacrifice. He is a worthy suitor for Dorothea, who finds greatness in his ardor if not his accomplishments; yet Will, allowing for his greater vitality, is after all a logical successor to Casaubon. Dorothea had favored the elderly scholar because he was unworldly, despised by the common herd. In her imagination, he seemed a saint of intellect. In time, she comes to favor Will because he is also despised by most of the petty-minded bigots of Middlemarch, because he has suffered from injustice, and because he seems to her a saint of integrity. A Victorian St. Theresa, Dorothea is passive, great in aspiration rather than deed. Psychologically, she requires a great object for her own self-sacrifice and therefore chooses a destiny that will allow her the fullest measure of heroism.

Tertius Lydgate is, by contrast, a calculating, vigorous, and ambitious young physician who attempts to bend others to his own iron will. His aggressive energy contrasts with Dorothea's passiveness. Like her, however, he is a victim of romantic illusion. He believes that he can master, through his intelligence and determination, those who possess power. Nevertheless, his choice of a mate, Rosamond Vincy, is a disastrous miscalculation. Rosamond's fragile beauty conceals a petulant, selfish will equal to his own. She dominates him through her weakness. Insensitive except to her own needs, she offers no scope for Lydgate's sensitive intelligence. In his frustration, he can battle only with himself. He comes to realize that he is defeated not only in his dreams of domestic happiness but also in his essential judgment of the uses of power.

For Eliot, moral choice does not exist in a sanctified vacuum; it requires an encounter with power. To even the least sophisticated dwellers in Middlemarch, power is represented by wealth and status. As the widow Mrs. Casaubon, Dorothea's social prestige rests on her personal and inherited fortune. When she casts aside her estate under Casaubon's will to marry Ladislaw, she also loses a great measure of status. At the same time, she acquires moral integrity, a superior virtue for Eliot. Similarly, when Mary Garth rejects Mr. Featherstone's dying proposition to seize his wealth before his relatives make a shambles of his will, she chooses morally, justly, and comes to deserve the happiness she eventually wins. Lydgate, whose moral choices are most ambiguous, returns Bulstrode's bribe to save himself from a social embarrassment, but his guilt runs deeper than mere miscalculation. He has associated himself, first through choosing Tyke instead of the worthier Farebrother as vicar, with Bulstrode's manipulation of power. Lydgate's moral defeat is partial, for at least he understands the extent of his compromise with integrity. Bulstrode's defeat is total, for he loses both wealth and social standing.

As for Middlemarch, that community of souls is a small world, populated with people of good will and bad, mean spirits and fine, and is the collective agent of moral will. Af-

ter all, it is the town that endures, the final arbiter of moral judgment in a less than perfect world.

"Critical Evaluation" by Leslie B. Mittleman

Further Reading

Anderson, Quentin. "George Eliot in *Middlemarch*." In *George Eliot: A Collection of Critical Essays*, edited by George R. Creeger. Englewood Cliffs, N.J.: Prentice-Hall, 1970. A thorough discussion of Eliot's background and preparation of the novel, the provincial panorama she creates, and the plot development that proceeds in an interplay between public opinion and self-regard. Also includes a bibliography.

Armstrong, Heather V. *Character and Ethical Development in Three Novels of George Eliot: "Middlemarch," "Romola," "Daniel Deronda."* Lewiston, N.Y.: Edwin Mellen Press, 2001. Focuses on the encounters between characters in the three novels, applying philosophical concepts to an analysis of these works. Examines Eliot's ideas about morality, duty, sympathy, and imagination.

Billington, Josie. *Eliot's "Middlemarch."* London: Continuum, 2008. A study guide to the novel, examining its historical, intellectual, and cultural contexts, and its language, style, genre, critical reception, publication history, and literary influences.

Chase, Karen, ed. *Middlemarch in the Twenty-first Century.* New York: Oxford University Press, 2006. Collection of essays reappraising Eliot's narrative ambitions, including discussions of Dorothea's lost dog, the novel's conclusion, and space, movement, and sexual feeling in *Middlemarch*.

Hardy, Barbara. *George Eliot: A Critic's Biography.* London: Continuum, 2006. An examination of Eliot's life combined with an analysis of her works, which will prove useful to readers with some prior knowledge of her writings. Includes an outline of her works and the events in her life.

_____. "The Woman at the Window in *Middlemarch*." In *Dorothea's Window: The Individual and Community in George Eliot*, edited by Patricia Gately, Dennis Leavens, and Cole Woodcox. Kirksville, Mo.: Thomas Jefferson Press, 1994. This essay shows how the recurrent window image in the novel first isolates Dorothea, then unites her with the world of useful work.

_____, ed. *Critical Essays on George Eliot.* New York: Barnes & Noble, 1970. This collection, edited by a pioneer in Eliot studies, helped interest critics in feminist analyses of her work. One of the essays is devoted to an analysis of *Middlemarch*.

Nuttall, A. D. "Mr. Casaubon in *Middlemarch*." In *Dead from the Waist Down: Scholars and Scholarship in Literature and the Popular Imagination*. New Haven, Conn.: Yale University Press, 2003. Examines the public's concepts of scholars and scholarship by focusing on three figures: Issac Casaubon, a classical scholar who lived from 1559 to 1664; Mr. Casaubon, a character in *Middlemarch*; and Mark Pattison, a nineteenth century rector at Oxford, who many believe was Eliot's model for the Casuabon character.

Paris, Bernard J. *Rereading George Eliot: Changing Responses to Her Experiments in Life*. Albany: State University of New York Press, 2003. Paris reconsiders Eliot's fiction and argues that her greatest strength lies in the "psychological intuition" that is evident in her portrayal of characters and relationships. Demonstrates her skill by closely analyzing the major characters in *Middlemarch*.

Stiritz, Susan. "An Enigma Solved: The 'Theresa' Metaphor." In *Dorothea's Window: The Individual and Community in George Eliot*, edited by Patricia Gately, Dennis Leavens, and Cole Woodcox. Kirksville, Mo.: Thomas Jefferson Press, 1994. This chapter explains Eliot's comparison of Dorothea to St. Theresa of Avila, with reference particularly to a woman's discovery and acceptance of her sexuality.

Uglow, Jennifer. *George Eliot*. New York: Pantheon Books, 1987. Shows Eliot in her fiction demolishing gender stereotypes and the illusion of norms, replacing these with insistence on individuality. Analyzes Ladislaw as a figure of light and change who, as the awakener of Dorothea's senses, is an appropriate husband for her.

Midnight's Children

Author: Salman Rushdie (1947-   )
First published: 1981
Type of work: Novel
Type of plot: Magical Realism
Time of plot: 1915-1977
Locale: India, including Kashmir, Amritsar, Agra, Delhi, Bombay, and the Sunderbans; Rawalpindi and Karachi, Pakistan; Dacca, Bangladesh

Principal characters:
SALEEM SINAI, the narrator, who was born at midnight on August 15, 1947—the moment India achieved independence
PADMA, Saleem's audience and coworker in a pickle factory
JAMILA SINGER (THE BRASS MONKEY), Saleem's sister
SHIVA, another child of midnight and the biological father of Aadam Sinai
PARVATI (LAYLAH SINAI), a child of midnight who later becomes Shiva's lover and Saleem's wife
DR. AADAM AZIZ, Saleem's grandfather
NASEEM (REVEREND MOTHER), Saleem's grandmother
MUMTAZ (AMINA SINAI), Saleem's mother
AHMED SINAI, Saleem's father
AADAM SINAI, Saleem's son

The Story:

In the early spring of 1915 in Kashmir, Dr. Aadam Aziz meets his future wife, Naseem, through a perforated sheet. After their marriage in 1919, they travel to Amritsar just in time to witness Mahatma Gandhi's hartal on April 7 and the Jallianwala Bagh massacre on April 13. They then move to Agra, where they have five children: Alia, Mumtaz, Hanif, Mustapha, and Emerald. In 1942, the second annual assembly of the Free Islam Convocation led by Mian Abdullah (the Hummingbird) is held in Agra; Mian Abdullah is assassinated. His secretary, Nadir Khan, flees and hides in the Aziz household. In 1943, Nadir Khan becomes Mumtaz's first husband. In 1945, Major Zulfikar (who subsequently marries Mumtaz's youngest sister, Emerald) attempts to arrest Nadir Khan. Before fleeing, Nadir Khan divorces Mumtaz, allowing her to marry Ahmed Sinai the following year. She changes her name to Amina Sinai. The Sinais move to Delhi, where

Amina receives a prophecy about Saleem, and then to Bombay (Mumbai) in 1947, where they purchase a piece of William Methwold's estate. The estate is handed over to them exactly at midnight on August 15—the date of India's independence from the British. They live there with the Catracks, Ibrahims, Dubashes, Dr. Narlikar (a gynecologist who delivers Saleem), and the Sabarmatis.

Also at the stroke of midnight on August 15, 1947, two children are born, one to a poor couple, Wee Willie Winkie and Vanita, and the other to Ahmed and Amina Sinai. The father of Vanita's son is actually William Methwold, who had an affair with Vanita. A nurse at the hospital, Mary Pereira, intentionally switches the two babies in an act of socialist resistance; the biological son of Methwold and Vanita grows up as Saleem Sinai, while the biological son of Ahmed and Amina grows up as Shiva. Pereira later becomes Saleem's nanny.

A little over a year later, on September 1, 1948, Saleem's sister, the Brass Monkey, is born. In the summer of 1956, Saleem learns about his mother's first love, Nadir Khan (who is now called Qasim Khan and is a member of the Communist Party of India), while hidden in a washing chest. He thus discovers that he has the ability to hear voices in his head. These voices include the thoughts both of the people immediately around him and of those from other parts of India. In 1957, as a result of a bicycle accident, Saleem manages to use his miraculous ability to convene the voices of all the children born during the first hour of India's independence from the British. These children all have miraculous powers. Saleem names these children (including himself) the Midnight Children's Conference (M.C.C.). Through the M.C.C., Saleem reconnects with Shiva, who has become a gangster, and meets Parvati, another child of midnight.

Saleem, who already possesses a big nose, is mutilated twice in 1958. A schoolteacher, Emil Zagallo, mutilates his hair, leaving him with a monk's tonsure, and a group of school bullies chases him and slams his finger in a door. While in the hospital after the second mutilation, Saleem discovers via a blood test that he is not the biological son of his parents. Consequently, his horrified parents condemn him to his first exile at his Uncle Hanif and Aunty Pia's apartment. A few months after Saleem's return from exile, Mary Pereira finally confesses to switching the babies.

The M.C.C. disintegrates. At the same time, Saleem instigates the Sabarmati affair by delivering an anonymous note to Commander Sabarmati about his wife Lila's affair with Homi Catrack. The end result is that Commander Sabarmati shoots and kills Homi, as well as shooting and injuring his wife, before turning himself in. Side consequences to the

Sabarmati affair are that Amina stops meeting Qasim Khan in secret and that all the part owners of the Methwold estate other than the Sinais sell their portions.

Near the end of 1958, because of his father's alcoholic raging and his inability to accept a child that is not his by birth, Saleem (with his mother and sister) begins his second exile to his Uncle Zulfikar and Aunt Emerald's house in Rawalpindi, Pakistan. While in Rawalpindi, Saleem assists in General Ayub's military coup. Four years later, on the Brass Monkey's fourteenth birthday in 1962, she becomes Jamila Singer, intending to become a singing star. Before she hits popular stardom, however, Amina, Saleem, and Jamila are called home because Ahmed is ill. Once home in Bombay, Saleem attempts to reconvene the M.C.C. but leaves out Shiva; however, the other midnight's children ultimately flee him. On November 21, 1962, Saleem is taken to a clinic to have his inflamed sinuses drained. That surgical draining also removes all his telepathic powers, but it provides Saleem with a superhuman sense of smell.

In 1963, the Sinais finally sell their piece of Methwold's estate and move to Karachi, Pakistan, where Jamila launches her singing career. At the age of sixteen, Saleem discovers his love for Jamila, but she rejects him. In 1964, Aadam Aziz and Nehru die. Naseem moves to Rawalpindi with the widowed Pia (Hanif having committed suicide in 1958). In 1965, Amina becomes pregnant again. Saleem attributes her deteriorating health and his father's failing towel factory business to the vengeful machinations of his jealous Aunt Alia. Also in 1965, Saleem's cousin, Lieutenant Zafar Zulfikar, encounters smugglers in the Rann who work for his father. Because of the smuggling operation and his childhood humiliations (one of which turns out to be enuresis even in adulthood), Zafar kills his father and is imprisoned for murder.

The Indo-Pakistani war breaks out, annihilating—and, in his opinion, purifying—Saleem's family. Falling bombs kill Naseem, Pia, Emerald, Zafar, Alia, Amina, and Ahmed. Jamila Singer and Saleem survive. Although the war ends in a ceasefire, it lasts only six years: Another war begins in 1971, when Pakistan invades Bangladesh. In that war, Saleem (now known as the buddha), abandoned by Jamila Singer and newly made a citizen of Pakistan, works as a tracker in the Canine Unit for Tracking and Intelligence Activities (CUTIA). His sense of smell is more powerful than that of any dog. During the war, Saleem and his handlers flee into the jungle of the surreal Sundarbans for seven months. After leaving the Sundarbans, Saleem goes to Dacca, where he meets his dying childhood friends Sonny Ibrahim, Hairoil Sabarmati, and Eyeslice Sabarmati, who are now enemy soldiers on a battlefield. Saleem also reunites with Parvati, who is part of an entertainers' troop, and returns with her to the magicians' ghetto in Delhi.

Saleem moves from the magicians' ghetto to his uncle Mustapha's home, also in Delhi, and stays there for 420 days before returning to the magicians' ghetto on February 23, 1973. Exactly two years later, he marries Parvati (who becomes Laylah Sinai after her conversion to Islam), although he first rejects her and causes her to turn to his nemesis Shiva (now known as Major Shiva). She gives birth to Aadam Sinai (biologically Shiva's son) at midnight on June 25, 1975. At the same time, Indira Gandhi (the Widow) imposes a state of emergency on India. In 1976, during that emergency, Parvati dies in the razing of the magicians' ghetto, and Saleem is arrested by Major Shiva. Saleem is forced to reveal the names of all the previous M.C.C. members. The entire M.C.C. undergoes forced vasectomies (except for Major Shiva, who cooperates voluntarily). At the end of the emergency in 1977, Saleem is released. He finds Aadam looked after by friends from the magicians' ghetto. He and Aadam follow a friend and father-figure, Picture Singh, to Bombay, where Saleem reunites with Mary Pereira and gets a job in her pickle factory.

Critical Evaluation:

Salman Rushdie was knighted in 2007 for his literary accomplishments. His writing career was launched based on the merit of *Midnight's Children* (his second novel), which won the Booker Prize and the Booker of Bookers (best Booker prizewinner in a twenty-five-year period). *Midnight's Children* was groundbreaking in its treatment of history, memory, and fantasy. Rushdie used all three avenues in a compendious effort to grapple with the history of India just before and thirty years after it gained independence from the British.

Rushdie's narrator, Saleem Sinai, is born in Bombay at the same moment that the independent nation of India is born. Rushdie was born in Bombay in 1947 as well, but about two months before Saleem. Saleem very quickly establishes himself as an unreliable first-person narrator; he makes factual errors and tells lies. However, he is a very engaging and endearing storyteller because of his humour, his sense of foreshadowing, and his fallibility. He is also very self-centered and self-conscious; he sees himself as an important player in the unfolding of historical events, and he pays great attention to his storytelling and to the responses of his audience, Padma the pickle-factory worker.

In Saleem's narrative, history, memory, and fantasy are represented by three powerful metaphors: pickling, a perfo-

rated sheet, and a silver spittoon inlaid with lapis lazuli. These metaphors permeate the story. Rushdie highlights, both literally and metaphorically, the fallibility of perception and memory in Saleem's attempt to recount historical events. The narrative incorporates several verifiable historical dates, times, and places, but it also incorporates elements of Magical Realism that test a reader's sense of believability, emphasize Saleem's subjectivity, and question the production and authority of history. Magical Realism also functions within both postcolonial and postmodern endeavors to produce alternative versions of reality as opposed to one authoritative version of history.

Although the story is told in one voice, Rushdie's novel includes strong characters that represent both genders, various religious backgrounds, diverse ethnic groups, different social classes, and varying political bents. The story contains clear allusions to Hindu mythology, although Saleem (like Rushdie) comes from a middle-class Indian Muslim background. Saleem's life parallels India's in its first thirty years of independence; like India, his many fathers (William Methwold, Wee Willie Winkie, Ahmed, Nadir Khan, Hanif, Major Zulfikar, Dr. Schaapsteker, and Picture Singh) and mothers (Vanita, Amina, Mary Pereira, Pia, Reverend Mother, Indira Gandhi, and Mother India) reflect his varied and complicated origins and trajectory. Although Saleem's narrative tone is jaunty, he constantly talks about dying and falling apart. Consequently, *Midnight's Children* is not only a tribute to India's teeming milieu and multitudinous perspectives but also a lament at its state of corruption and lack of civil liberties.

Lydia Forssander-Song

Further Reading

Booker, M. Keith, ed. *Critical Essays on Salman Rushdie.* New York: G. K. Hall, 1999. At least half of the essays in this collection deal with *Midnight's Children.*

Herwitz, Daniel, and Ashutosh Varshney, eds. *Midnight's Diaspora: Critical Encounters with Salman Rushdie.* Ann Arbor: University of Michigan Press, 2008. A collection of essays on Rushdie, including two interviews with the author and a response by him.

Mukherjee, Meenakshi, ed. *Rushdie's "Midnight's Children": A Book of Readings.* Delhi: Pencraft International, 1999. A collection of essays on *Midnight's Children* including an interview with Rushdie and a chapter from Neil Ten Kortenaar's book on *Midnight's Children.*

Rushdie, Salman. *Conversations with Salman Rushdie.* Edited by Michale R. Reder. Jackson: University Press of Mississippi, 2000. Contains twenty interviews with Rushdie conducted by scholars, journalists, and other writers.

_____. *Imaginary Homelands: Essays and Criticism, 1981-1991.* London: Granta Books, 1991. Includes several essays by Rushdie, most notably the title essay and

"'Errata': Or, Unreliable Narration in *Midnight's Children.*"

Ten Kortenaar, Neil. *Self, Nation, Text in Salman Rushdie's "Midnight's Children."* Montreal: McGill-Queen's University Press, 2004. One of the few books solely dedicated to an analysis of *Midnight's Children.*

A Midsummer Night's Dream

Author: William Shakespeare (1564-1616)
First produced: c. 1595-1596; first published, 1600
Type of work: Drama
Type of plot: Comedy
Time of plot: Antiquity
Locale: Athens

Principal characters:
THESEUS, duke of Athens
LYSANDER and DEMETRIUS, in love with Hermia
BOTTOM, a weaver
HIPPOLYTA, queen of the Amazons, fiancé of Theseus
HERMIA, in love with Lysander
HELENA, in love with Demetrius
OBERON, king of the fairies
TITANIA, queen of the fairies
PUCK, fairy page to Oberon

The Story:

Theseus, the duke of Athens, is to be married in four days to Hippolyta, queen of the Amazons, and he orders his master of the revels to prepare suitable entertainment for the nuptials. Other lovers of ancient Athens, however, are not so happy as their ruler. Hermia, in love with Lysander, is loved also by Demetrius, who has her father's permission to marry her. When she refuses his suit, Demetrius takes his case to Theseus and demands that the law be invoked. Theseus upholds the father; by Athenian law, Hermia either must marry Demetrius, be placed in a nunnery, or be put to death. Hermia swears that she will enter a convent before she will consent to become Demetrius's bride.

Faced with this awful choice, Lysander plots with Hermia to leave Athens. He will take her to the home of his aunt and there marry her. They are to meet the following night in a wood outside the city. Hermia confides the plan to her good friend, Helena. Demetrius had formerly been betrothed to Helena, and although he had switched his love to Hermia he is still desperately loved by the scorned Helena. Helena, willing to do anything to gain even a smile from Demetrius, tells him of his rival's plan to elope with Hermia.

Unknown to any of the four young people, there are to be others in that same woods on the appointed night, midsummer eve. A group of Athenian laborers is to meet there to practice a play the members hope to present in honor of

Theseus and Hippolyta's wedding. The fairies also hold their midnight revels in the woods. Oberon, king of the fairies, desires for his page a little Indian foundling, but Oberon's queen, Titania, has the boy. Loving him like a son, she refuses to give him up to her husband. To force Titania to do his bidding, Oberon orders his mischievous page, called Puck or Robin Goodfellow, to secure the juice of a purple flower once hit by Cupid's dart. This juice, when placed in the eyes of anyone sleeping, causes that person to fall in love with the first creature seen on awakening. Oberon plans to drop some of the juice in Titania's eyes and then refuse to lift the charm until she gives him the boy.

While Puck is on his errand, Demetrius and Helena enter the woods. Making himself invisible, Oberon hears Helena plead her love for Demetrius and hears the young man scorn and berate her. Demetrius has come to the woods to find the fleeing lovers, Lysander and Hermia, and Helena is following Demetrius. Oberon, pitying Helena, determines to aid her. When Puck returns with the juice, Oberon orders him to find the Athenian and place some of the juice in his eyes so that he will love the woman who dotes on him.

Puck does as he is ordered, while Oberon squeezes the juice of the flower into the eyes of Titania as she sleeps. Puck, coming upon Lysander and Hermia as they sleep in the woods, mistakes Lysander's Athenian dress for that of

Demetrius and pours the charmed juice into Lysander's eyes. Lysander is awakened by Helena, who has been abandoned deep in the woods by Demetrius. The charm works, although not as intended; Lysander falls in love with Helena. That poor woman, thinking that he is mocking her with his ardent protestations of love, begs him to stop his teasing and return to the sleeping Hermia. Lysander, pursuing Helena, who is running away from him, leaves Hermia alone in the forest. When she awakens she fears that Lysander has been killed, since she believes that he would never have deserted her otherwise.

Titania, in the meantime, awakens to a strange sight. The laborers, practicing for their play, had paused not far from the sleeping fairy queen. Bottom, the comical but stupid weaver who is to play the leading role, becomes the butt of another of Puck's jokes. The prankster claps an ass's head over Bottom's own foolish pate and leads the poor fool on a merry chase until the weaver is at the spot where Titania lays sleeping. Thus, when she awakens she looks at Bottom, still with the head of an ass. She falls instantly in love with him and orders the fairies to tend to his every want. This turn pleases Oberon mightily. When he learns of the mistake Puck had made in placing the juice in Lysander's eyes, however, he tries to right the wrong by placing love juice also in Demetrius's eyes, and he orders Puck to have Helena close by when Demetrius awakens. His act makes both women unhappy and forlorn. When Demetrius, who she knows hates her, also begins to protest his ardent love to her, Helena thinks that both men are taunting and ridiculing her. Poor Hermia, encountering Lysander, cannot understand why he tries to drive her away, all the time protesting that he loves only Helena.

Again, Oberon tries to set matters straight. He orders Puck to lead the two men in circles until weariness forces them to lie down and go to sleep. Then a potion to remove the charm and make the whole affair seem like a dream is to be placed in Lysander's eyes. Afterward he will again love Hermia, and all the young people will be united in proper pairs. Titania, too, is to have the charm removed, for Oberon taunts her about loving an ass until she gives up the prince to him. Puck obeys the orders and places the potion in Lysander's eyes.

The four lovers are awakened by Theseus, Hippolyta, and Hermia's father, who had gone into the woods to watch Theseus's hounds perform. Lysander again loves Hermia and Demetrius still loves Helena, for the love juice remains in his eyes. Hermia's father persists in his demand that his daughter marry Demetrius, but since that young man no longer wants her and all four are happy with their partners, he ceases to oppose Lysander's suit. Theseus gives them permission to marry on the day set for his own wedding to Hippolyta.

Titania also awakens and, like the others, thinks that she has been dreaming. Puck removes the ass's head from Bottom and the bewildered weaver makes his way back to Athens, reaching there just in time to save the play, since he is to play Pyramus, the hero. The master of the revels tries to dissuade Theseus from choosing the laborer's play for the wedding night. Theseus, however, is intrigued by a play that is announced as tedious, brief, merry, and tragic. So Bottom and his troupe present an entertainingly awful *Pyramus and Thisbe*, much to the merriment of all the guests. After the play all the bridal couples retire to their suites, and Oberon and Titania sing a fairy song over them, promising that they and all of their children will be blessed.

Critical Evaluation:

A Midsummer Night's Dream marks the maturation of William Shakespeare's comic form beyond situation and young romantic love. One plot focuses on finding young love and on overcoming obstacles to that love. Shakespeare adds to the richness of comic structure by interweaving the love plot with a cast of rustic guildsmen, who are out of their element as they strive to entertain the ruler with a classic play of their own. The play also features a substructure of fairy forces, whose unseen antics influence the world of humans. With this invisible substructure of dream and chaos, *A Midsummer Night's Dream* not only explores the capriciousness and changeability of love (as the young men switch their affections from woman to woman in the blinking of an eye) but also introduces the question of the psychology of the subconscious.

Tradition held that on midsummer night, people would dream of the person they would marry. As the lovers enter the chaotic world of the forest, they are allowed, with hilarious results, to experience harmlessly the options of their subconscious desires. By focusing in the last act on the play presented by the rustic guildsmen, Shakespeare links the imaginative world of art with the capacity for change and growth within humanity. This capacity is most laughingly realized in the play by the transformation of the enthusiastic actor, Bottom, into half-man, half-ass, an alteration that continues to delight audiences.

The play was originally performed at a marriage ceremony, and the plot is framed by the four-day suspension of ordinary life in Athens in expectation of the nuptial celebration of Theseus and his queen, Hippolyta. Both characters invoke the moon as they anticipate their union. The lunar spirit of nebulousness, changeability, and lunacy dominates much of the play's action.

A Midsummer Night's Dream is remarkable for its blending of diverse personages into an eventually unified whole.

In addition to Theseus and Hippolyta, the cast includes three other categories of society, each distinguished by its own mode of discourse. Theseus and Hippolyta speak high blank verse, filled with leisurely confidence and classical allusion. The four young and mixed-up lovers—Hermia and Lysander, Helena and Demetrius—can also muster blank verse but are typified by rhyming iambic lines that indicate the unoriginal speech of those who woo. The rustic guildsmen are characterized by their prose speech, full of halts and stops, confusions, and malapropisms. The fairies for the most part speak a light rhymed tetrameter, filled with references to nature. Oberon and Titania, as king and queen of the fairies, speak a regal verse similar to that of Theseus and Hippolyta. The roles of the two kings and the two queens are often played by the same actors, since the characters are not on stage at the same time.

In the background of all the love matches is a hint of violence or separation. Theseus conquers Hippolyta. Oberon and Titania feud over a changeling boy. Pyramus and Thisbe, the lovers in the rustics' play, are kept apart by a wall. Demetrius stops loving Helena for no apparent reason and switches his affections to Hermia, who dotes on Lysander. The father of Hermia, supported by Theseus and Athenian law, would keep his daughter from marrying the man of her choosing and instead doom her to death or life in a nunnery.

When Puck addresses the audience in the play's epilogue, he points to a major theme of the badly acted play-within-a-play: Art requires an act of imaginative engagement on the part of those who experience it. Art can reveal alternatives, horrible or wonderful turns that life may take. Art's power to transform is only as effective as the audience's capacity to distinguish illusion from reality and to bring the possible into being.

"Critical Evaluation" by Sandra K. Fischer

Further Reading

Arthos, John. "The Spirit of the Occasion." In *Shakespeare's Use of Dream and Vision*. Totowa, N.J.: Rowman & Littlefield, 1977. Describes how Shakespeare connects nature with the dream world and its dual potential of horror and bliss. Dreams stem from and inform the psyche, and they share a cognitive function with the world of art.

Blits, Jan H. *The Soul of Athens: Shakespeare's "A Midsummer Night's Dream."* Lanham, Md.: Lexington Books, 2003. A line-by-line analysis of the play, discussing its plot, characters, language, allusions, and other literary devices. Argues that the play examines the duality of the human soul.

Buccola, Regina, ed. *"A Midsummer Night's Dream": A Critical Guide*. New York: Continuum, 2010. A comprehensive introduction to the play's performance history, including stage productions and versions for television, film, opera, and ballet. Also examines modern criticism and research trends.

Calderwood, James L. *"A Midsummer Night's Dream."* New York: Twayne, 1992. Drawing on the different theoretical approaches to literary interpretation, Calderwood organizes the experience of the play around topics such as patriarchal law, desire and voyeurism, marginality, the power of naming, and the illusion of conciliation and unity. An excellent critical introduction to the play and to the state of reading Shakespeare.

Halio, Jay L. *"A Midsummer Night's Dream": A Guide to the Play*. Westport, Conn.: Greenwood Press, 2003. Introductory overview discussing the play's textual history, contexts, sources, dramatic structure, and themes. Summarizes critical approaches to the play and describes the play in performance on stage and on film.

Nostbakken, Faith. *Understanding "A Midsummer Night's Dream": A Student Casebook to Issues, Sources, and Historical Documents*. Westport, Conn.: Greenwood Press, 2003. Provides an overview of the dramatic and literary concerns of the play. Includes primary source documents on gender relations, social distinctions, popular culture, and the imaginary world of dreams and fairies in Shakespeare's time. Traces the evolution of the play's popularity and perspectives over more than four hundred years.

Patterson, Annabel. "Bottom's Up: Festive Theory." In *Shakespeare and the Popular Voice*. New York: Blackwell, 1989. Reads the play's representation of the lower classes in political terms. Argues that Bottom's malapropisms represent a suppression of voice and class, yet his creative use of language points toward a more synthetic utopian society.

Pennington, Michael. *"A Midsummer Night's Dream": A User's Guide*. London: Nick Hern, 2005. Pennington, an actor and director, provides a scene-by-scene analysis of the play's workings on stage. Discusses the choices for actors performing the play and the impact of these choices.

Turner, Henry S. *Shakespeare's Double Helix*. New York: Continuum, 2007. Analyzes how Shakespeare in *A Midsummer Night's Dream* comes to terms with new fields of knowledge, such as magic, astrology, alchemy, and mechanics, which raised unsettling questions about the natural world.

The Mighty and Their Fall

Author: Ivy Compton-Burnett (1884-1969)
First published: 1961
Type of work: Novel
Type of plot: Domestic realism
Time of plot: Mid-twentieth century
Locale: Unnamed town in England

Principal characters:
NINIAN MIDDLETON, a widower and father
LAVINIA, his oldest daughter
RANSOM, his brother
HUGO, his adopted brother
SELINA, his mother
TERESA CHILTON, Ninian's second wife
AINGER and COOK, servants in the house

The Story:

To this polished, stodgy, upper-class British family replete with house servants and a governess, Ninian Middleton, the father, who is a widower, announces that he is engaged to marry Teresa Chilton. The news is ill-received by all, because the forthcoming event requires redefining family roles and relationships.

Teresa visits the family and conversation turns to such trivial matters as what the children should call their new stepmother. She is made to feel uncomfortable and unwanted by the family. After her visit, she writes a letter to Ninian saying that if he wants out of the engagement all he needs to do is ignore the letter; that is, not reply to it. Lavinia, in a misguided attempt to protect Ninian, hides the letter (not yet read by Ninian), which is not discovered for some ten days after Teresa's appointed deadline. Ninian contacts Teresa and the two are married, but it remains a mystery as to which family member had hidden the letter. Eventually, it is revealed that Lavinia is the culprit. Ninian and other family members are ostensibly forgiving, but in truth they are not—Lavinia is to be made to live in her family as a sinner.

Ransom, Ninian's younger brother, arrives home and reveals that he is terminally ill. Dying, he has taken a flat near Ninian's house; he wants one of the children to come and live with him during his last days. He chooses Lavinia, because the two of them are the family's appointed reprobates. Before dying, Ransom devises a trick on Ninian that is designed to reveal Ninian's honesty—or lack thereof. Ransom writes two wills, one in which Ninian is named chief benefactor and the other naming Lavinia. Ransom asks Ninian to burn the will that lists Ninian as chief inheritor of Ransom's estate. Ninian fails the moral test. Ransom reveals all to the family. Thus, it is proved that the father is as morally reprehensible as both Ransom and Lavinia.

Ransom dies, leaving his wealth to Lavinia. Lavinia and Hugo, Ninian's adopted brother and Lavinia's uncle, are to be married. All are in a state of shock, although it is well established that the two are not blood kin. Selina, mother to Ninian and Hugo, then claims that Hugo is a family member by blood. Specifically, that the dead father had brought Hugo home as a bastard son and that Ninian and Hugo are half-brothers. Hugo, professing his love for the now-rich Lavinia, insists that the story is not true. He departs to investigate. Shortly, he returns with proof that Selina is lying and that he is not a blood member of the family. Thus, all is cleared for the wedding.

Selina devises her own plan to control the event from beyond the grave. She, too, has become sick to the point of death; she writes a will in which she makes Hugo her chief benefactor. Upon her death, Hugo succeeds to great sums of money. He decides that he does not want to marry, after all, because he likes his life of debauchery and bachelorhood too much. Lavinia is then welcomed back into the family, since it is agreed that her own treachery in hiding the letter is certainly no greater than her father's in burning the will, in Selina's for telling the lie about Hugo's birth, or in Hugo's for being so quickly and manifestly bought off from love with money. All of the mighty family members are fallen, a fact commented upon by the servants in the kitchen.

Critical Evaluation:

Written in the later years of Ivy Compton-Burnett's career and a few years before her death, *The Mighty and Their Fall* has never been considered a work of literature of first quality. The faults are too numerous and too glaring for such ranking. *The Mighty and Their Fall* does succeed within what may be called the genre of drawing-room novel—one written more for diversion and entertainment than for great and involved meaning.

The most noticeable element of Compton-Burnett's style is her use of conversation. Some 90 percent of the work is given in dialogue: short, terse, clipped sentences exchanged between characters with little or no attached explanations to alert the reader about how the utterances are made, what context they have, or even who the speakers are. It is rather as if one were reading the script of a play with little or no stage directions. Experimental, or at least unique, in this respect, *The Mighty and Their Fall* proceeds with little in common with what is usually identifiable as elements of the novel.

At the same time, the work is structured around moral tension, dilemma, and resolution. In fact, a whole series of such patterns occur, with certain common elements. Lavinia decides to hide her father's letter from his fiancé as a way to protect him from himself, but her hiding the letter also is an act of selfishness. She fully believes it would be better for her father if he did not remarry; at the same time, she fully believes that her own lot in life, and that of other family members, will also be better if he does not remarry. She performs the act of treachery and is caught.

The pattern is repeated by her own father. Ninian burns the wrong will not so much because he wants the major portion of Ransom's inheritance upon his death but because, so he reasons, his family will be in better circumstances if Lavinia does not receive the whole lot herself. He, too, is caught and exposed, and therefore must acknowledge his own moral kinship to his daughter, Lavinia.

Upon Lavinia and Hugo's announcement that they are engaged to be married, Selina, the matriarch of the family, falls into the same trap. She tells lies about Hugo's parentage to prevent the marriage. In claiming that Hugo is actually a biological, illegitimate son to her long-dead husband, Selina, like Lavinia and Ninian, maneuvers to protect others from themselves. At the same time, she does so for selfish reasons, despite being at the point of death. When Hugo exposes his mother's lie, all three family members are now in the same category of moral depravity.

Hugo is bought off from the marriage. Given financial independence, he, too, is shown to be morally defunct. As his mother understands the situation, Hugo does not marry Lavinia because his real motivation is for money and not for love. Four of the family members have all lied, cheated, and been immoral, and all have been caught and revealed.

The novel's comment about human nature is centered on that of familial relationships. Those in power abuse those who are dependent upon them. In particular, Ninian and Selina act to repress their children and grandchildren to control them, acting in what Ninian and Selina believe is their descendants' best interests. The pattern is reversed when the children (Lavinia and Hugo) respond in a like manner toward the superiors in their family. The author's moral is clear: People have no right to condemn others until they have experienced similar temptations and resisted them. In this case, all four main characters fail the test of morality put before them. Thus, not one is morally superior to the others.

Against the main action of the work is the conversation of the servants in the kitchen. Ainger and Cook, so it would seem, are happy that the affairs of the family are going as they are. It provides them with amusement and a subject for conversation. There is no difference between the morality of the servants and that of the upper-class family. Indeed, the kitchen help is not given to the same whims and silliness as the family. Consequently and fortunately, they do not find themselves given to such moral perplexities.

The Mighty and Their Fall, then, is something of a social satire upon the English upper classes. Their concerns are trivial and petty, their actions are inconsequential (whether they make the correct moral choices or not), their relationships are all shallow and pointless, and the servants are better off, morally. All of the main characters are revealed to act primarily out of selfishness and not from the desire to protect others, as each claims.

Finally, the "mighty" fall, but they are none the worse for it. Their lives will continue more or less the same regardless of who marries (or does not marry) whom and regardless of who does or does not inherit money from Ransom and Selina. The upper crust of this society survives because of its determination to protect its own regardless of morality or other considerations.

Carl Singleton

Further Reading

Baldanza, Frank. *Ivy Compton-Burnett*. New York: Twayne, 1964. Set in the context of the author's biography and career, *The Mighty and Their Fall* is discussed in terms of characters, plot, and theme.

Cavaliero, Glen. "Family Fortunes: Ivy Compton-Burnett." In *The Alchemy of Laughter: Comedy in English Fiction*. New York: St. Martin's Press, 2000. Cavaliero includes works by Compton-Burnett in his examination of comedy in English novels, in which he discusses the elements of parody, irony, satire, and other types of humor in these books.

Gentile, Kathy Justice. *Ivy Compton-Burnett*. New York: St. Martin's Press, 1991. Establishes Compton-Burnett as a feminist and adds new and important perspectives to her work, including feminist analyses of all the writer's novels. Includes an excellent bibliography

Ingman, Heather. "Ivy Compton-Burnett: Tyrants, Victims, and Camp." In *Women's Fiction Between the Wars: Mothers, Daughters, and Writing*. New York: St. Martin's

Press, 1998. Explores how Compton-Burnett and five other authors depict the mother-daughter relationship in their work. Ingman argues that Compton-Burnett's novels "provide a devastating insight into the psychopathology of Victorian family life and a critique of the patriarchal power structures underpinning it."

Karl, Frederick R. *The Contemporary English Novel*. New York: Farrar, Straus & Giroux, 1962. Contains a chapter that delineates the important characteristics of Compton-Burnett's novels: problems of Victorian and post-Victorian families, moral choices that involve material values, familial attachments and relationships, drawing-room ethics, the roles of governesses and servants, and tragic and semitragic events.

Kiernan, Robert F. *Frivolity Unbound: Six Masters of the Camp Novel*. New York: Continuum, 1990. One of the masters of the "camp novel" is Compton-Burnett. Kiernan examines the ironically formulaic banality of her work.

Ross, Marlon B. "Contented Spinsters: Governessing and the Limits of Discursive Desire in the Fiction of Ivy Compton-Burnett." In *Old Maids to Radical Spinsters: Unmarried Women in the Twentieth-Century Novel*, edited by Laura L. Doan. Champaign: University of Illinois Press, 1991. Discusses the role of the spinster or "old maid" in the novels of Compton-Burnett. Miss Starkie, the children's governess, and Selina Middleton, family matriarch, fill the role in *The Mighty and Their Fall*.

The Mikado
Or, The Town of Titipu

Author: W. S. Gilbert (1836-1911)
First produced: 1885; first published, 1885
Type of work: Drama
Type of plot: Satire
Time of plot: Middle Ages
Locale: Titipu, Japan

Principal characters:
THE MIKADO OF JAPAN
NANKI-POO, his son, disguised as a minstrel
KO-KO, Lord High Executioner of Titipu
POOH-BAH, Lord High Everything Else
YUM-YUM,
PITTI-SING, and
PEEP-BO, wards of Ko-Ko
KATISHA, an elderly lady in love with Nanki-Poo
PISH-TUSH, a noble lord

The Story:

Ko-Ko is now the Lord High Executioner in the town of Titipu in old Japan, and to his courtyard come many knights and lords to flatter and cajole the holder of so dread and august an office. One day a stranger appears at Ko-Ko's palace, a wandering minstrel who carries his guitar on his back and a sheaf of ballads in his hand. The Japanese lords are curious about his presence there, for he is obviously not of noble birth and therefore can expect no favors from powerful Ko-Ko. At last, Pish-Tush questions him about his business with Ko-Ko. Introducing himself as Nanki-Poo, the minstrel announces that he seeks Yum-Yum, the beautiful ward of Ko-Ko, with whom he had fallen in love while playing the second trombone in the Titipu town band a year before. He heard that Ko-Ko is to be executed for flirting, a capital offense in the land of the Mikado, and since

Ko-Ko is to die, he hopes that Yum-Yum will be free to marry him.

Pish-Tush corrects the rash young man, telling him that the Mikado had revoked the death sentence of Ko-Ko and raised him at the same time to the great and noble rank of the Lord High Executioner of Titipu. Nanki-Poo is crestfallen, for he realizes that the ward of an official so important would never be allowed to marry a lowly minstrel. Pooh-Bah, another nobleman, secretly resents that he, a man of ancient lineage, has to hold minor office under a man like Ko-Ko, previously a mere tailor. Pooh-Bah, however, is interested in any opportunity for graft; he is even willing to betray the so-called state secret of Ko-Ko's intention to wed his beautiful ward. Pooh-Bah advises Nanki-Poo to leave Titipu and by all means to stay away from Yum-Yum.

Meanwhile, Ko-Ko has been preparing a list of the types of criminals he intends to execute—autograph hunters, people who insist upon spoiling a tête-à-tête, people who eat peppermint and breathe in another's face, the man who praises every country but his own, and apologetic statesmen. Uncertain of the privileges of his new office, the Lord High Executioner consults the Lord High Everything Else about the money to be spent on his impending marriage. Pooh-Bah advises him, first as private secretary, and gives one opinion; then as Chancellor of the Exchequer he expresses a contrary point of view. He has a different opinion for every one of his many offices and official titles. They are interrupted, however, by the appearance of Yum-Yum and her sisters Peep-Bo and Pitti-Sing. Ko-Ko attempts to kiss his bride-to-be, but she openly expresses her reluctance and distaste.

When the three sisters see Nanki-Poo loitering nearby, they rush to greet him, astonished to find him in Titipu. Ko-Ko, baffled and displeased by their schoolgirl mirth, demands an introduction to the stranger. When Yum-Yum and Nanki-Poo have a few moments alone with each other, the minstrel reveals his true identity as the son of the Mikado and confesses the reasons for his flight from court. Katisha, a middle-aged woman in the court, had misunderstood acts of Nanki-Poo as overtures of romance. She mentioned them to the Mikado. He in turn misunderstood his son's conduct and requested that Nanki-Poo marry Katisha. Nanki-Poo, already in love with Yum-Yum, fled the court in the disguise of a minstrel and went to Titipu.

That same day, Ko-Ko receives from the Mikado a communication that instructs him to execute somebody within a month. Otherwise the office of Lord High Executioner will be abolished; Ko-Ko would be beheaded for neglecting his duties, and the city of Titipu would be ranked as only a village. Perplexed by this sudden and unhappy news, Ko-Ko sees no solution until he discovers Nanki-Poo carrying a rope with which to hang himself. Seeing a way of escape, Ko-Ko bargains with Nanki-Poo, promising him a luxuriant life for thirty days, if at the end of that time the minstrel would allow himself to be executed officially. Nanki-Poo agrees on the condition that he be allowed to marry Yum-Yum at once.

This acceptable solution is upset, however, by the arrival of Katisha, who recognizes Nanki-Poo and tries to claim him for her husband. When she learns that he is to marry Yum-Yum, she attempts to reveal his true identity, but her voice is not heard above the singing and shouting instigated by Yum-Yum. Hearing of the proposed marriage of Yum-Yum and Nanki-Poo, Pooh-Bah informs Ko-Ko that the wife of a beheaded man must be buried alive, a law that would mean Yum-Yum's death if Nanki-Poo were executed. Again lost as

to a way out of his problem, Ko-Ko is spurred to action by the unexpected arrival of the Mikado himself. Desperate, he conceals Nanki-Poo and shows the Mikado a forged certificate of Nanki-Poo's execution.

When the Mikado reads the name of the victim, he announces that the heir-apparent has been executed. According to law, Ko-Ko's life has to be forfeited. Luckily for Ko-Ko, Nanki-Poo and Yum-Yum appear at that moment. Husband and wife at last, they are ready to start on their honeymoon. Seeing his son happily married and not dead as he had supposed, the Mikado forgives everyone concerned in Ko-Ko's plot—the unfortunate Lord High Executioner, however, only after he has wed the jilted Katisha.

Critical Evaluation:

The Mikado is the work of the most famous collaborators of light opera, W. S. Gilbert and Arthur Sullivan (1842-1900). For about twenty years, they produced many of the most enduring and charming operettas the world has ever known, with Gilbert as librettist and Sullivan as composer. The two began collaborating in 1869, but it was not until they met Richard D'Oyly Carte in 1874 that they started to achieve the fame that continues today. D'Oyly Carte leased an old opera building for their productions and, in 1881, he built the Savoy Theatre especially for the D'Oyly Carte company to produce Gilbert and Sullivan's comic operas.

Gilbert suggested to Sullivan the subject of *The Mikado* in 1884. The British fashion for things Japanese was at its height as the result of a Japanese village exhibition in the London borough of Kensington. (Knightsbridge, in the Kensington area, is mentioned in the dialogue as the place where Nanki-Poo was to have fled.) The opening of Japan to the West, spurred by U.S. naval officer Commodore Matthew Perry in 1853, created a Victorian fascination for Japanese art and architecture, and wealthier homes displayed expensive Japanese vases, decorated screens and fans, and colorful marionettes, items mentioned in the introductory chorus of nobles. In music, composers experimented with Japanese five-tone scales, rhythmic drums, and the exotic sounds of instruments such as the koto and gongs. The culmination of this musical fascination was Gilbert and Sullivan's *The Mikado*, which ran for more than six hundred nights after it was first presented at the Savoy on March 14, 1885, and Giacomo Puccini's popular Italian opera *Madam Butterfly*, first performed in Milan on February 17, 1904.

The Mikado is not really about Japan. It is about late nineteenth century England, and Japanese kimonos cloak characters whom most Victorian theatergoers would have easily recognized. The Mikado, for instance, is a paternalistic, self-important parliamentarian out to punish "all prosy dull society sinners," a type of politician who remains common. The "criminals" for whom he plans punishment include advertising quacks, music-hall singers, billiard hustlers, and defacers of the windows of railway carriages. Like a true politician, the Mikado labors to make the punishment fit the crime: The billiard sharp is doomed to play with a twisted cue and elliptical billiard balls, the quack is condemned to have all his teeth extracted by amateur dentists, and shrill tenors must exhibit their vocal powers to an audience of wax dummies at Madame Tussaud's museum.

In the same way, others are recognizable Victorian types. Ko-Ko, Lord High Executioner, and Pooh-Bah, Lord High Everything Else, are deferential small-town English civil servants who would willingly eradicate almost anyone. In act 1, part 2, Ko-Ko's hate list includes autograph seekers, children who memorize historical dates, people with flabby handshakes, those with peppermint on their breath, cross-dressers, and women novelists. None of them would be missed, he assures us.

The young lovers, Nanki-Poo and Yum-Yum, are faced, as were many Victorian youths, with a father who forbids flirting and courtship, in this case under penalty of death. Katisha, an aging spinster spurned in love by youthful Nanki-Poo, is a vengeful old maid of Victorian melodrama, albeit a comic one. In the end, she marries Ko-Ko, who takes the lady to prevent himself from being plunged into boiling oil or molten lead, and only after proper assurance that Katisha is old enough to marry—"sufficiently decayed," as Ko-Ko puts it. All of these characters, with names derived from the Victorian nanny-talk of nurseries, were readily identified by Savoy audiences. (Ko-Ko means "pickles" in Japanese.)

The essence of *The Mikado*, however, is neither topical nor geographical; it is universal. Gilbert and Sullivan's operas, after all, are enjoyed the world over not because audiences are interested in Victorian England but because they are willing to laugh at themselves and their fellow human beings. The characters and situations, no matter how exotic the setting, are universal types and patterns found throughout literature. The plot of a prince disguised to escape undesirable consequences recalls similar incidents in many plays, as do the marriage of an unwilling young woman to a villainous suitor and the mistaken identities. The comic songs contain much literary parody, from Nanki-Poo's "The flowers that bloom in the spring" (a parody of sentimental Victorian nature verse) and the song of the three little maids from school (a parody of Victorian notions of the innocence of young girlhood) to Ko-Ko's uncharacteristic song to the titwillow, whose sad warbling is the result of either a weak intellect or

an undigested worm. Gilbert glories in comic words in the same way that film actor W. C. Fields did later. The mere name "titwillow" elicits a smile, more so than, say, the word "sparrow."

Gilbert is also fond of coupling the serious with the ridiculous, and a sense of fun pervades the entire opera. Ko-Ko's comprehensive hate list, for instance, recalls the hit list of many a tyrant, but it includes such a ludicrous array of offenders that it is impossible to take it seriously. In the same way, the Mikado's insistence upon his humane philanthropy is undermined by his ridiculous opinion of wrongdoers, from mystical Germans who preach too much to ladies who dye their hair yellow and puce. Much of Gilbert's comedy also comes from his comic rhymes: "struggled" and "guggled," for example, or "if they do" and "Titipu." Some of Sullivan's tunes, in turn, parody some genuine Japanese music, including the War Song of the Imperial Army. (*The Mikado* was banned in England in 1907 for fear it might offend visiting Japanese dignitaries.) Finally, the play parodies the romantic theme of the young lover willing to die rather than live without his beloved and the fact that the couple lives happily ever after is the standard stuff of comedies. Put all this together and one has in *The Mikado* one of the all-time comic masterpieces of the musical stage.

"Critical Evaluation" by Kenneth Seib

Further Reading

Ainger, Michael. *Gilbert and Sullivan: A Dual Biography.* New York: Oxford University Press, 2002. Chronicles the lives and working partnership of Gilbert and his collaborator, describing how their different personalities spurred them to produce their best work.

Ayre, Leslie. *The Gilbert and Sullivan Companion.* 1972. Reprint. London: Papermac, 1987. A reference book, containing anecdotes, details about each opera, and a listing of famous artists who have played leading roles. Includes a foreword by D'Oyly Carte star Martyn Green.

Baily, Leslie. *Gilbert and Sullivan: Their Lives and Times.* 1974. Reprint. New York: Penguin Books, 1979. Lively biography that puts the two collaborators and their operas in the context of Victorian times. Contains many illustrations and photographs.

Crowther, Andrew. *Contradiction Contradicted: The Plays of W. S. Gilbert.* Cranbury, N.J.: Associated University Presses, 2000. An examination of all of Gilbert's plays, including his collaborations with Sullivan. Crowther compares previous critiques of the plays with the plays themselves.

Fischler, Alan. *Modified Rapture: Comedy in W. S. Gilbert's Savoy Operas.* Charlottesville: University Press of Virginia, 1991. Brief but informative analysis of Gilbert's comedic techniques and their appeal to the "bourgeois prejudices" of Victorian audiences.

Sullivan, Arthur. *The Complete Plays of Gilbert and Sullivan.* Illustrated by W. S. Gilbert. New York: W. W. Norton, 1976. Contains all of Gilbert's libretti, as well as more than seventy amusing illustrations that accompany his songs. Contains a brief chronology of Gilbert and Sullivan's collaborative career.

Sutton, Max Keith. *W. S. Gilbert.* Boston: Twayne, 1975. Good single-volume introduction to Gilbert's life and works. Sees *The Mikado* as a "ritual" drama, with its emphasis on human sacrifice and absolute law.

Wilson, Robin, and Frederick Lloyd. *Gilbert and Sullivan: The Official D'Oyly Carte Picture History.* New York: Alfred A. Knopf, 1984. One-hundred-year history of the D'Oyly Carte company, with dozens of color illustrations, photographs, drawings, reproductions of paintings, posters, cartoons, and memorabilia.

Wren, Gayden. *A Most Ingenious Paradox: The Art of Gilbert and Sullivan.* New York: Oxford University Press, 2001. An analysis of the operettas in which Wren explores the reasons for the continued popularity of these works. Chapter 11 is devoted to an examination of *The Mikado.*

The Mill on the Floss

Author: George Eliot (1819-1880)
First published: 1860
Type of work: Novel
Type of plot: Domestic realism
Time of plot: Nineteenth century
Locale: England

Principal characters:
MR. TULLIVER, the owner of the mill on the Floss
MRS. TULLIVER, his wife
TOM TULLIVER, their son
MAGGIE TULLIVER, their daughter
AUNT GLEGG and AUNT PULLET, the sisters of Mrs. Tulliver
PHILIP WAKEM, Maggie's suitor
LUCY DEANE, the cousin of Tom and Maggie
STEPHEN GUEST, Lucy's fiancé

The Story:

Dorlcote Mill stands on the banks of the River Floss near the village of St. Ogg's. Owned by the ambitious Mr. Tulliver, the mill provides a good living for the Tulliver family, but Mr. Tulliver dreams of the day when his son Tom will achieve a higher station in life. Mrs. Tulliver's sisters, who had married well, criticize Mr. Tulliver's unseemly ambition and openly predict the day when his air castles will bring himself and his family to ruin. Aunt Glegg is the richest of the sisters and holds a note on his property. After he quarrels with her over his plans for Tom's education, Mr. Tulliver determines to borrow the money and repay her.

Tom has inherited the placid arrogance of his mother's relatives; for him, life is not difficult. He is resolved to be fair in all of his dealings and to deliver punishment to whomever deserves it. His sister Maggie grows up with an imagination that surpasses her understanding. Her aunts predict she will come to a bad end because she is tomboyish, dark-skinned, dreamy, and indifferent to their commands. Frightened by her lack of success in attempting to please her brother Tom, her cousin Lucy, and her mother and aunts, Maggie runs away, determined to live with the gypsies, but she is glad enough to return. Her father scolds her mother and Tom for abusing her. Her mother is sure Maggie will come to a bad end because of the way Mr. Tulliver humors her.

Tom's troubles begin when his father sends him to study at Mr. Stelling's school. Having little interest in spelling, grammar, or Latin, Tom wishes he were back at the mill, where he can dream of someday riding a horse like his father's and giving orders to people around him. Mr. Stelling is convinced that Tom is not just obstinate but stupid. Returning home for the Christmas holidays, Tom learns that Philip Wakem, son of a lawyer who is his father's enemy, is also to enter Mr. Stelling's school.

Philip is disabled; Tom, therefore, cannot beat him up. Philip can draw, and he knows Latin and Greek. After they overcome their initial reserve, the two boys become useful to each other. Philip admires Tom's arrogance and self-possession, and Tom needs Philip to help him in his studies, but their fathers' quarrel keeps a gulf between them.

When Maggie visits Tom, she meets Philip, and the two become close friends. After Maggie is sent away to school with her cousin, Lucy, Mr. Tulliver becomes involved in a lawsuit. Because Mr. Wakem defends the opposition, Mr. Tulliver says his children should have as little as possible to do with Philip. Mr. Tulliver loses his suit and stands to lose all of his property as well. To pay off Aunt Glegg, he borrowed money on his household furnishings. Now he hopes Aunt Pullet will lend him the money to pay the debt against which those furnishings stand forfeit. He can no longer afford to keep Maggie and Tom in school. When he learns that Mr. Wakem had bought up his debts, the discovery brings on a stroke. Tom makes Maggie promise never to speak to Philip Wakem again. Mrs. Tulliver weeps because her household possessions are to be put up for sale at auction. In the ruin that follows, Tom and Maggie reject the scornful offers of help from their aunts.

Bob Jakin, a country brute with whom Tom had fought as a boy, turns up to offer Tom partnership with him in a venture where Tom's education will help Bob's native business shrewdness. Because both of them are without capital, Tom takes a job in a warehouse for the time being and studies bookkeeping at night.

Mr. Wakem buys the mill but permits Mr. Tulliver to act as its manager for wages. It is Wakem's plan eventually to turn the mill over to his son. Not knowing what else to do, Tulliver stays on as an employee of his enemy, but he asks Tom to sign a statement in the Bible that he will wish the Wakems evil as long as he lives. Against Maggie's entreaties, Tom signs his name. Finally, Aunt Glegg gives Tom money, which he invests with Bob Jakin. Slowly, Tom begins to accumulate funds to pay off his father's debts.

Meanwhile, Maggie and Philip have been meeting secretly in the glades near the mill. One day, he asks her if she loves him. She puts him off. Later, at a family gathering, she shows feeling for Philip in a manner that arouses Tom's suspicions. He makes her swear on the Bible not to have anything more to do with Philip, and then he looks for Philip and orders him to stay away from his sister. Shortly afterward, Tom shows his father his profits. The next day, Mr. Tulliver thrashes Mr. Wakem and then suffers another stroke, from which he never recovers.

Two years later, Maggie, now a teacher, visits her cousin, Lucy Deane, who is also entertaining young Stephen Guest in her home. One difficulty Lucy foresees is that Philip, who is friendly with both her and Stephen, might leave during Maggie's visit. Stephen had already decided that Lucy is to be his choice for a wife, but he and Maggie are attracted to each other at first sight. Blind to what is happening, Lucy is pleased that her cousin Maggie and her friend Stephen are becoming good friends.

Maggie asks Tom's permission to see Philip at a party that Lucy is giving. Tom replies that if Maggie should ever consider Philip as a lover, she must expect never to see her brother again. Tom stands by his oath to his father. He feels his dignity as a Tulliver, and he believes that Maggie is apt to follow the inclination of the moment without giving consideration to the outcome. He is right. Lacking the iron will that characterizes so many of her relatives, Maggie loves easily and without restraint.

When Philip learns that Lucy's father has promised to try to buy back the mill for Tom, he hopes to persuade his father to sell the mill. Philip is sure that in return Tom will forget his old hatred.

Stephen Guest tries to kiss Maggie at a dance. She evades him, and the next day avoids Philip as well. She feels she owes it to Lucy not to allow Stephen to fall in love with her, and she feels that she owes it to her brother not to marry Philip. She lets herself be carried along by the tide. Her relatives will not let her go back to teaching, for Tom's good luck continues and he has repossessed his father's mill. Both Stephen and Philip want her to marry them, neither knowing about the other's suit. Certainly, Lucy does not suspect Stephen's growing indifference to her.

One day, Stephen takes Maggie boating and tries to convince her to run away with him and be married. She refuses. Then the tide carries them beyond the reach of shore, and they are forced to spend the night in the boat.

Maggie dares the wrath and judgment of her relatives when she returns and attempts to explain to Lucy and the others what had happened. They refuse to listen to her. Tom turns her away from the mill house, with the word that he will send her money but that he never wishes to see her again. Mrs. Tulliver resolves to go with Maggie, and Bob Jakin takes them in. One by one, people desert Maggie, and she slowly begins to realize the meaning of ostracism. Only Aunt Glegg and Lucy offer sympathy. Stephen writes to her in agony of spirit, as does Philip. Maggie wants to be by herself. She wonders if there could be love for her without pain for others.

That autumn a terrible flood ravages St. Ogg's. Maggie knows that Tom is at the mill, and she attempts to reach him in a boat. The two are reunited, and Tom takes over the rowing of the boat. The full force of the flood, however, overwhelms them and they drown, together at the end as they had been when they were children.

Critical Evaluation:

Shortly after George Eliot published *Adam Bede* in 1858, she began to work on a new novel under the tentative title "Sister Maggie." As the book took shape, she considered other possible titles—"The House of Tulliver," "The Tulliver Family," "The Tullivers"—before her editor suggested *The Mill on the Floss*, a title she approved with some reservations. She objected, initially, to the title because the "mill is not strictly on the Floss, being on its small tributary" and because the title "is of rather laborious utterance." Having voiced her usual concern for precise details and delicacy of style, she agreed that the new title was "the only alternate so far as we can see." On March 21, 1860, she completed the book then vacationed in Rome with her husband, George Henry Lewes, and awaited the news of the book's reception, which proved to be almost wholly favorable. Eliot reported with satisfaction, "From all we can gather, the votes are rather on the side of 'The Mill' as a better book than 'Adam.'"

The Mill on the Floss is certainly the more poignant novel of the two. Although both fictions have as their setting the Warwickshire background that Eliot remembered from her childhood, *The Mill on the Floss* is less genially picturesque and more concerned with psychological truth. *Adam Bede* concludes with a happy marriage for Adam and Dinah, probably contrary to the author's best artistic judgment. Tom and Maggie Tulliver, however, die in the flood, their fate unmitigated by sentimentality. Indeed, much of the novel's power derives from the consistent play of tragic forces that appear early and unify the whole work.

As a boy, Tom entrusts his pet rabbits to his sister Maggie's care. She is preoccupied and allows the creatures to die. Despite her tearful protestations, Tom upbraids her bitterly but finally forgives her. This childhood pattern of close sibling affection, deep hurt and estrangement, and reconciliation determines the structural pattern of the novel. Although Henry James admired the design of *The Mill on the Floss*, he criticized the conclusion for its melodrama. As a matter of fact, the conclusion is implicit in the story from the beginning. The flood that carries the brother and sister to their doom is not an accidental catastrophe. Rather, it is symbolic of the tide that sweeps away two passionate souls divided in conflict yet united by the closest bonds of affection.

Tom Tulliver, like his father, has a tenacious will that is not always under control of his reason. Even as a child, he is fiercely although honorably competitive. He is slow to forgive injury. Robust and vigorous, he despises weakness in others. As a youth, he insults Philip Wakem by drawing attention to the boy's physical disability. When Maggie demeans, as Tom mistakenly believes, the good name of the

Tulliver family through her foreshortened "elopement" with Stephen Guest, he scorns her as a pariah. Nevertheless, his tempestuous nature is also capable of generosity. To redeem his father's good name and restore Dorlcote Mill to the family, he disciplines himself to work purposefully. To this end, he sacrifices his high spirits and love of strenuous excitement, indeed any opportunities for courtship and marriage. He dies as he had lived and labored, the provider of the Tulliver family.

Maggie, many of whose sprightly qualities are drawn from Eliot's memories of her own childhood, is psychologically the more complex character. Whereas Tom is sturdily masculine, Maggie is sensitive, introspective, and tenderly feminine. Quick to tears—to the modern reader perhaps too effusive in her emotions—she cannot control her sensibilities, just as her brother cannot keep his temper. As a youngster, she has the qualities of a tomboy. She is energetic and, unlike the typical Victorian girl, fights for her place in the world. Intelligent, diligent, earnest, she would have made better use of Mr. Stelling's classical schooling than her brother, but girls of her time rarely had the opportunity to advance in education. Therefore, she must content herself, although secretively restive, with the narrow place Victorian society allows for girls of her class. Like Dorothea Brooke in *Middlemarch* (1871-1872), she is attracted to a scholarly but fragile lover, Philip. Her sympathetic nature completes what is lacking in the young man's disposition—courage and self-esteem—and he, in turn, offers her a sense of artistic dedication for which she yearns.

Some astute critics of *The Mill on the Floss* have objected to Maggie's other suitor, Stephen Guest, who is Lucy Deane's fiancé. The impetuous Stephen would have been a satisfactory mate for Lucy, a more typical Victorian heroine, sweet but passive. According to Sir Leslie Stephen, Maggie, in her passion for Lucy's betrothed, throws herself away upon a "low creature." His daughter, Virginia Woolf, repeated Sir Leslie's judgment in describing Stephen's "coarseness." Later views of the character did not support such hostile interpretations, considering Stephen neither low nor coarse but instead an ardent lover who rouses a sexual response in Maggie that she does not feel for Philip. Maggie's torment is to be torn between her promises to Philip (who certainly loves and needs her) and her deeper feelings for Stephen. She senses the call of duty and propriety but also feels the sweep of wild emotion. When she masters her feelings and returns to Philip, she betrays her needs as a woman.

For the same reason that some critics refuse to accept Maggie as a mature woman with normal sexual responses, some readers are troubled by the apparent change in her character as she grows from child to adult. The portrait of Maggie the girl is so vital, charming, and convincing that readers may wish to cherish her youthful image, but Maggie the woman does not really change. Within the prudish conventions of the Victorian novel, Eliot can only suggest her heroine's psychological and moral development. Nevertheless, she conveys a sense of Maggie's greater sexual vulnerability with the description of her "highly strung, hungry nature." When Maggie renounces Stephen, she renounces her own happiness. From that point, her tragedy is inevitable. Her mother, Lucy, and Philip have faith in her to the last, but the provincial gossips of St. Ogg's cast her off, and her beloved brother rejects her. Nevertheless, Maggie characteristically determines, "I must not, cannot seek my own happiness by sacrificing others." The floodwaters that carry Maggie and her brother downstream cleanse their guilt and unite them as when they were innocent children. Finally, Eliot tells us, they are "not divided."

"Critical Evaluation" by Leslie B. Mittleman

Further Reading

Ashton, Rosemary. *"The Mill on the Floss": A Natural History.* Boston: Twayne, 1990. A book-length study useful to beginners. Discusses the novel in relation to Eliot's life, the historical context, natural history, and literary influences. Includes an annotated bibliography.

Barrett, Dorothea. "Demonism, Feminism, and Incest in *The Mill on the Floss.*" In *Vocation and Desire: George Eliot's Heroines.* New York: Routledge, 1989. Argues that three elements discussed separately by previous critics work together in *The Mill on the Floss.* Emphasizes a positive view of the novel's "passionate idealism."

Beer, Gillian. *George Eliot.* Bloomington: Indiana University Press, 1986. A reassessment of Eliot's fiction that refutes other feminist criticisms. Asserts that Maggie Tulliver's passion represents her desire for knowledge and freedom as well as sexual love, and that Eliot challenged the boundaries of women's roles in Victorian society. Contains an extensive bibliography.

Carroll, David. "*The Mill on the Floss*: Growing Up in St. Ogg's." In *George Eliot and the Conflict of Interpretations: A Reading of the Novels.* New York: Cambridge University Press, 1992. Considers the problem of reading the novel as two kinds of narrative: a realistic fiction containing anthropological treatment of the lives of Maggie's relatives and a legend of a unified pastoral world of childhood.

Creeger, George R., ed. *George Eliot: A Collection of Critical Essays.* Englewood Cliffs, N.J.: Prentice-Hall, 1970. An important collection of scholarly essays on Eliot's novels, including an essay on *The Mill on the Floss* that explores the novel's philosophical underpinnings. Includes a chronology of Eliot's publications and a short bibliography.

Draper, R. P., ed. *George Eliot: "The Mill on the Floss" and "Silas Marner."* London: Macmillan, 1977. A collection of extracts from Eliot's journals, letters, and essays concerning such issues as realism and "the Woman Question," early reviews of *Silas Marner* and *The Mill on the Floss*, comments on these novels by other famous authors, and critical studies of such issues as sociology, morality, and unity of form in these novels.

Ermarth, Elizabeth Deeds. *George Eliot.* Boston: Twayne, 1985. An excellent introductory study of Eliot's work, including a biographical chapter and a brief study of her intellectual concerns. The chapter on *The Mill on the Floss* emphasizes the cultural rifts the novel explores at a time when society was rapidly changing. Includes a thorough chronology of Eliot's life, an annotated bibliography, and an index.

Hardy, Barbara. *George Eliot: A Critic's Biography.* London: Continuum, 2006. An examination of Eliot's life combined with an analysis of her work, which will prove useful to readers with some prior knowledge of her writings. Includes an outline of her works and the events in her life.

_____, ed. *Critical Essays on George Eliot.* New York: Barnes & Noble, 1970. This collection, edited by a pioneer in Eliot studies, helped interest critics in feminist analyses of her work. One of the essays is devoted to an analysis of *The Mill on the Floss.*

Levine, George, ed. *The Cambridge Companion to George Eliot.* New York: Cambridge University Press, 2001. Collection of essays analyzing Eliot's work from various perspectives, including discussions of her early and late novels and of Eliot and realism, philosophy, science, politics, religion, and gender.

Newton, K. M., ed. *George Eliot.* London: Longman, 1991. An important collection of some of the best essays on Eliot's works by current Eliot scholars, including works written from feminist and social perspectives. Includes an introductory explanation of these various critical perspectives, a bibliography, and an index.

Yousaf, Nahem, and Andrew Maunder, eds. *"The Mill on the Floss" and "Silas Marner": George Eliot.* New York: Palgrave, 2002. Collection of essays, including "*The Mill on the Floss*, the Critics, and the Bildungsroman" by Susan Fraiman, "Narcissistic Rage in *The Mill on the Floss*" by Peggy R. F. Johnstone, and "Men of Maxims in *The Mill on the Floss*" by Mary Jacobus.

The Mill on the Po

Author: Riccardo Bacchelli (1891-1985)
First published: Il mulino del Po, 1938-1940, three
   parts (English translation, 1950, parts 1 and 2; 1955,
   part 3)
Type of work: Novel
Type of plot: Historical
Time of plot: 1812-1918
Locale: Po River region, near Ferrara, Italy

Principal characters:
LAZZARO SCACERNI, a miller
DOSOLINA, his wife
GIUSEPPE, his son
CECILIA, his daughter-in-law
LAZZARINO, his grandson

The Story:

In 1817, a new water mill appears on the Po River, near the city of Ferrara. Its owner is young Lazzaro Scacerni, who has mysteriously become the miller. He is, however, no stranger to the river—his father was a ferryman at Ariano and died in the peasant uprising of 1807. Shortly afterward, the young Lazzaro was sent, along with other orphans, to serve as a cabin boy in the navy. When older, he became an army engineer who built pontoon bridges. Now, in 1812, he finds himself a part of Napoleon Bonaparte's ill-fated Russian campaign.

During the terrible 1812 retreat, a dying captain gives Lazzaro a mysterious receipt, which the illiterate young man cannot read. He guards it closely, however, as he straggles homeward from a debacle in which fourteen out of every fifteen Italian soldiers perish. Finally returning to the neighborhood of Ferrara, Lazzaro leads a life of struggle while waiting for a chance to make use of his one mysterious asset. He learns to read well enough to decipher the name and address attached to the receipt. His search leads him to a Jewish man in Ferrara's ghetto. The receipt is for jewels, plundered from Spanish churches by Lazzaro's benefactor. His windfall assured, Lazzaro cannily ponders how to apply it. Millers, he decides, are least affected by times of adversity, so he has a friendly old shipwright build him a floating mill. In due time it is finished and put into operation.

As the years pass, the miller prospers. As his trade grows, Lazzaro hires three boys as helpers. His success inspires more envy than affection among his neighbors, and a few wives and daughters succumb to his dashing gallantries. Nearly forty years old and wearying of bachelorhood, Lazzaro falls in love with Dosolina, poor but delicately beautiful and twenty years his junior. Lazzaro buys a house, marries Dosolina, and settles down to enjoy his prosperity.

Fate, however, does not always smile on Lazzaro and his mill. Floods come, the bane of the Po River millers. Smugglers, crossing between the Papal State and occupied Austria north of the River Po, insolently use his mill for a rendezvous. On the birth night of his son, Giuseppe, Lazzaro's troubles reach a climax. While Dosolina is writhing in difficult labor, the desperate Lazzaro fights to save his mill from the swollen menace of the Po. Slipping on the wet deck, he breaks a leg but continues to direct his laborers, two of whom are strong workers. The third, Beffa, is malformed and secretly hates his master; he also has become a tool of the smugglers. Shedding all restraint, Beffa openly exults over his master's plight and scornfully asserts that the miller has been cuckolded. Lazzaro, using his muscular arms, reaches out, seizes Beffa, and hurls him into the river.

Dosolina recovers, and the mill is saved, but Beffa's dismissal causes Lazzaro to receive disturbing threats from Raguseo, leader of the smugglers. Soon afterward, however, a feud breaks out among the outlaws that disposes of Raguseo, after which Lazzaro breathes more easily. Some dangers are over, but others soon come. Intermittent floods continue to threaten the mill. One day a large mill washes ashore near Lazzaro's own, its only occupant a girl named Cecilia, orphaned by the flood. To Cecilia, her mill had meant home. She is very happy when the Scacernis befriend her and reestablish her mill alongside theirs. From that time on Lazzaro regards the girl almost as his own daughter.

Lazzaro is much less pleased, however, with the character and disposition of his own son. Bandy-legged, crafty, and cowardly, Giuseppe cares nothing about his father's trade except its profit. Early on, he had shown considerable skill, as well as great avarice, in business dealings of various kinds, but now, he is held in contempt by all, except by his mother.

During the late 1840's, Lazzaro begins a successful traffic in grain with the hated Austrians. The same years bring new distress to Lazzaro's family. Roving bands of partisans, Italians or Austrian mercenaries, infest the countryside and disturb the peace and security of the Scacernis. Finally, both mills are commandeered by the Austrians, and Lazzaro and

Cecilia are required to transfer the mills to the opposite side of the river.

After a few months, the mills are allowed to be returned to the Italian side of the river, but the political atmosphere is still cloudy and confused among the rival claims and interests of the Papacy, the Italian nationalistic movement, and Austria. Lazzaro, who is growing old and querulous, finds much to complain about. Only at the mills, in the company of his helpers and Cecilia, does he feel comfortable. Even there, he sometimes rails at the smuggling, which carries scarce grain across the river to Austria. He is outraged when he learns that Giuseppe has taken a leading role in the transactions.

A problem in the family suddenly arises, causing distress to both Scacerni parents. Giuseppe, apparently inattentive to women, has long slyly coveted Cecilia for his wife, in spite of her clear indifference to him. Not daring to risk her mockery by a proposal, he goes about winning her by characteristic trickery. Meanly playing on her fondness for his father, Giuseppe blandly announces that Lazzaro has broken a law by possessing concealed firearms. His son tells Cecilia that he could exert influence to head off his father's arrest and punishment, but only for a price: Cecilia's consent to marry him. Taken by surprise, Cecilia is confused, angry, and ignorantly fearful. Her devotion to Lazzaro, however, is greater than her repugnance for his son, and in the end, Giuseppe has his way.

Lazzaro, unaware of Cecilia's sacrifice, is baffled and feels hurt by what he considers her poor judgment. In turn, Dosolina regards her new daughter-in-law as little better than a river gypsy and quite unworthy of her son. Neither of the parents, however, have long to lament the marriage. In 1855, Dosolina is the victim of a wave of cholera that sweeps all Europe. The next morning, Lazzaro is found dead beside her.

The structure of Italy is changing: Time is bringing defeat to Austria, the end of papal rule, and the dawn of a united nation. These things, of course, mean little to Cecilia Scacerni, but the warmth of her nature at last finds a rewarding outlet. Her firstborn and favorite, Lazzarino, is vigorous and intelligent, a reminder of his grandfather in more than name. Even his grasping, mean-natured father openly adores his son.

Lazzarino is not destined to match his grandfather in years, however. Miserable at the general mockery of his father's cowardice, he runs off to join Garibaldi's volunteers. News of his death staggers Cecilia; its effect on Giuseppe is catastrophic. Grief gnaws at his reason, and the destruction of his house and crops by flood completes his downfall. Howling obscenely, he is carted off to an asylum.

Left alone, Cecilia survives with calm courage. There is work to do, and she will see that it is done. With her seven children, she succeeds in rebuilding the mills in these, the early years of the Italian unification. The taxes on mill owners are enormous, causing Cecilia to cheat on the unfair taxes by fixing the counting mechanism to show lower activity. A tax inspector experiences a tragic accident during an inspection of the mills that results in a long prison sentence for one of Cecilia's sons. A series of economic problems ensue and befall the Scacerni family so that, at Cecilia's death, only one son, named Lazzarino, after his grandfather, is left. Reversals of the family's fortune cause him to join the Italian army during World War I. He is killed while trying to erect a pontoon bridge over the River Piave.

The Scacerni family has passed from the Italian scene, and the Po continues its eternal flow. The family has been conquered by nature and by their own tragic conduct.

Critical Evaluation:

Riccardo Bacchelli's *The Mill on the Po* is divided into three parts, or volumes, all of which were published individually in their original Italian and then published in English in 1950 (parts 1 and 2, *God Save You* and *Trouble Travels by Water*) and in 1955 (part 3, *Nothing New Under the Sun*, only). The 1975 reprint of *The Mill on the Po* suggests that the first two parts of Bacchelli's novel have had more readers than the final part.

Bacchelli's writing style and the mood of his story change from section to section, but changes in history in contrast with the unchanging River Po provide pivotal points for the novel on which to progress. Readers with the patience for a trilogy that takes place in a part of the world and at historical moments that are unfamiliar to most Anglophones should nevertheless derive rewards from sections of Bacchelli's novel.

Bacchelli applies features of literary modernism to all three volumes of the trilogy, but with *The Mill on the Po* as a whole, Bacchelli has produced a work that deliberately swims against the stream of modernism. The trilogy form permitted Bacchelli to tell his epic tale of four-and-a-half generations of one Italian family during a decisive historical period for Italy, from the end of the Napoleonic era in the early nineteenth century to World War I.

Although it plays a role in the novel, the unification of Italy is not its main theme; it is not the factor that provides the thrust of Bacchelli's trilogy. His principal theme is one family's struggle for economic and personal survival in the face of natural, political, and sociological vicissitudes. He notes signal events, such as the public guillotining of a protesting prisoner, and notes signal objects, such as the appearance and sound of the first mechanical thresher on the banks of the Po. He depicts factors and occurrences that will change Italian life. He dwells on the decline of an enervated nobility and other postfeudal powers, soon to be replaced by a segment of the peasantry that is ascending and will become the new middle class.

However, Bacchelli is much more interested in the human nucleus that Italians consider the essential guarantor of their survival: the family. Wives and daughters-in-law in Bacchelli's novel, however, do not see eye-to-eye; sons are not improved exemplars of their fathers. The tragedy of this trilogy is that the Scacerni family loses its struggle to survive in the new Italy and perishes in the end.

Bacchelli was one of the few authors of the time whose novels did not incur Fascist censure, in part because he returned to the literary past, both in content and in style. He opted not to follow the lead of the modernist Italo Svevo and not to write like the neorealists Elio Vittorini or Carlo Levi, whose novels, published after Benito Mussolini's dictatorship, proved groundbreaking. However, Bacchelli did enjoy post-World War II success when *The Mill on the Po* was adapted into a highly popular miniseries on Italian television in 1963. His social stature increased as well when he was awarded the Italian Grand Cross in 1971.

Although the popularity of *The Mill on the Po* has declined since the 1970's, it can still be rewarding reading for those who enjoy historical fiction and the romance and adventures it offers. In retrospect, the weakest point of the novel is the characterization. Although well drawn, the characters are more stereotypes than individuals. The problems the characters face are so severe that readers may remember the adventures more easily than the details of an individual character's development, or lack thereof.

"Critical Evaluation" by Patricia Ann King;
revised by Robert B. Youngblood

Further Reading

Bartolini, Paolo. "Riccardo Bacchelli." In *The Oxford Companion to Italian Literature*, edited by Peter Hainsworth and David Robey. New York: Oxford University Press, 2002. A brief but useful biocritical introduction to Bacchelli and his writings.

Licastro, Emanuele. "Riccardo Bacchelli." In *Italian Prose Writers: 1900-1945*, edited by Luca Somigli and Rocco Capozzi. Detroit, Mich.; Thomson Gale, 2002. A ten-page biographical essay examining Bacchelli's life and work.

Milton

Author: William Blake (1757-1827)
First published: 1804-1808
Type of work: Poetry

William Blake composed this brief epic poem to explain Christianity to a troubled England. Geoffrey Chaucer, Edmund Spenser, and John Milton before him wrote on that theme, but Blake created a far more personal and highly original myth. As he saw it, England's Christianity traded supernatural spirituality for scientific rationality. Blake thought scientific rationality, or what he called natural religion, would lead to commercial imperialism, dehumanizing mechanization of work, and worldwide wars. One may say that he was right. He blamed natural religion on John Milton's Puritanism with its orthodoxy, dualism, hypocritical moral virtue, militancy, and bondage to law.

Blake wrote *Milton* to correct the errors of this religion, which overvalued reason, undervalued love, and lacked any

concept of the Holy Spirit. In his domestic life, Milton was tormented by the sinister aspects of female will. In *Paradise Lost* (1667, 1674) he blamed the Fall on Adam's adoration of Eve and depicted their love as dangerous and lustful. Milton's Messiah reminded Blake of Job's Satan, and Blake thought Milton was "of the Devil's party without knowing it." Milton saw man after the Fall struggling under law in fear of punishment until the Last Judgment. Blake's epic follows that cycle of fall, struggle, redemption, and apocalypse. For Blake, the Fall was caused by an usurpation of reason by emotion, and redemption liberates man from laws of moral virtue.

Blake's epic is almost without a plot. Milton finds himself unhappy in heaven. A bard's song moves him to return to earth, where he is reincarnated in Blake. Through mighty struggles with symbolical characters, he purges himself of intellectual error and unites with his female counterpart, Ololon.

Action is spare in this epic because its meanings are revealed not in events but in various unfolding perspectives of characters on those events as Blake presents them throughout the poem. The readers' experience is unlike anything else in literature. Blake puts readers through mental contortions designed to reveal new modes of perception. They must enter Blake's mythical cosmos with the characters interpreting revelations as they happen.

The epic action is actually a single flash of inspiration, and the narrative relates events that are virtually simultaneous. Perspectives shift without warning. Characters are not only personalities but also places, states of mind, systems of thought, and historical epochs. They multiply and divide, travel through time as well as space, and merge with one another to make points about ideas they symbolize. Milton can be discussing philosophy in Beulah at the same time he is falling to earth, struggling with Urizen by the river, and entering Blake. The poet's objective is to take readers' minds completely out of the ordinary, beyond the confines of familiar time and space, in order to comprehend humankind's past and future as a single mental form, eternally human and divine. *Milton* is a poem about how a poet envisions eternal truth with the fourfold power of imagination.

Some background in Blake's cosmic mythology is helpful. Before the fall, Albion (fourfold man) was united with his bride Jerusalem (heaven), and the Four Zoas (aspects of man) presided over their respective realms. The realms are Tharmas (body), Urizen (reason), Luvah (emotion), and Urthona (imagination). When Luvah encroaches on Urizen, however, all fall and split asunder. Luvah is divorced from Vala (nature) and turns into Orc (revolt). Urizen casts off his Emanation, Ahania (pleasure). Tharmas becomes Enion (lust), and Urthona divides into Los (time) and Enitharmon (space). All howl in discord, each claiming to be God. They exist within Albion's bosom and throughout the cosmic vastness beyond the Mundane Shell that encloses earth, where Los labors in Golgonooza, giving form to uncreated things. His four-dimensional gates open onto Eden, Beulah, Generation, and Ulro, places like Milton's heaven, Eden, earth, and hell.

Interestingly, Blake's myth foresees modern psychology, for he portrays fallen man with a split personality: a masculine, reasoning, ravenous, selfish Spectre, and a feminine Emanation, an elusive shadow representing all the Spectre desires. Originally man had fourfold vision, sensory powers

that were infinitely expansive and lucid. The fall drops him through successive states of error until he reaches the merciful limits of contraction (Adam) and opacity (Satan). So, symbolically, Milton falls through Luvah, Urizen, and the Mundane Shell, into Albion's bosom, all the way to the limits of contraction (Adam) and opacity for his final confrontation with Satan.

For six thousand years, fallen man tries to regain the fourfold vision, through seven epochs, each called an Eye of God. First comes Lucifer, whose error is egotism. Then comes three phases of infernal justice: Molech (execution), Elohim (judgment), and Shaddai (accusation). Next comes Pahad, a reign of terror after justice fails, followed by two attempts at order: Jehovah (law) and Jesus (forgiveness). Blake further subdivides history into twenty-seven churches (systems of religious thought) in three groups: from Adam to Lamech, from Noah to Terah, and from Abraham to Luther. Blake sees Milton as the eighth Eye or twenty-eighth church, a new concept of religion without hierarchy, orthodoxy, and other Satanic perversions of faith. Thus, Blake's epic announces a new phase of Christianity liberated from dogma and law.

The personages and machinery of Blake's myth are revealed to characters in the poem through visions that are also witnessed and overheard by readers. Book 1 opens with a bard's song that tells a parable of Satan's fall and the creation of the three classes of men in a story about Los's sons. There is Palamabron, an honest farmer and prophet; Rintrah, an angry prophet; and Satan, the miller, a mild-mannered, respectable prince of this world. They swap places for a day, with catastrophic results. Trying to drive the harrow in pity's path, Satan drives the horses and servants mad. Meanwhile Palamabron revels in wine, song, and dance with workers in the Satanic mills. Satan blames Palamabron, who demands a trial before the Eternals. Rintrah testifies for Palamabron, saying Satan did wrong because "pity divides the soul/ And man unmans." The Eternals refuse to impute guilt to pity, and their judgment falls on Rintrah for his wrath. Enraged, Satan accuses Palamabron of malice and ingratitude. Exiled to Ulro, Satan declares himself God and is worshiped in churches. His daughter Leutha tries but fails to reverse Satan's condemnation by taking the blame on herself. The Eternals rule that Satan must endure among the Elect, unredeemed, until someone dies for him. They create two other classes of men: the Reprobate, like Rintrah, who transgress the law but keeps the faith; and the Redeemed, like Palamabron, who labor productively despite being tormented by the Elect.

Milton realizes that the bard's song is about himself. "I in my Selfhood am that Satan," he declares, vowing to descend through a vortex into Ulro, where he can annihilate his Spectre and reunite with his Emanation. Like a falling star, Milton travels to earth and is reincarnated in the poet Blake, entering through his left foot. The fallen Zoas dread Milton's approach. Urizen does battle with him, turning the ground beneath his feet to marble and pouring icy water on his brain. Milton molds red clay around Urizen's feet to give him new flesh and a human form. Rahab sends her daughters to entice Milton with lust, but he pays no heed and strives onward to Golgonooza.

As Albion stirs in his sleep, Blake starts, noticing something strange on his left foot in the form of a sandal. Though not yet realizing that Milton has come to him, Blake straps on the sandal to stride through Eternity. Los appears and helps him with his sandals, becoming one man with Blake too. At Golgonooza the poet-prophet meets Rintrah and Palamabron, who ask whether Milton comes to let Satan loose, unchain Orc, and raise up Mystery, the Virgin Harlot Mother of War. They see revolution in America and the Covering Cherub advancing from the East. The Covering Cherub represents false dogmas of religion consolidated in the warring churches of Paul, Constantine, Charlemagne, and Luther. Los urges his sons not to flee in fear, for he knows Milton's arrival signals the Last Judgment. Book 1 ends with a glorious account of the redemptive labors of Los in Golgonooza, where material nature and the mental abstractions of Ulro are transformed by imaginative vision and given particularly human forms.

Book 2 opens in Beulah, a dreamy place of respite from the fury of poetic inspiration in Eden. All Beulah laments, for Ololon vows to follow Milton into Ulro. Milton's immortal part converses with the angels, explaining the doctrine of States. According to this doctrine, individual identities never change, but they pass through States that do. Satan, reason, and memory are States to be annihilated; and Milton is about to become a State called Annihilation, where the living go to defeat Death.

Then everything suddenly culminates in a moment of inspiration. Ololon arrives at Blake's garden, and so does Milton. Standing on the sea not far away, Satan thunders. Blake enters Satan's bosom to behold its formless desolation. Milton condemns Satan and his priests for, with their laws and terrors, making men fear death. Satan replies that he is judge of all, God himself in holiness (not mercy). With that, the garden path erupts in flame and the Starry Seven blow trumpets to awaken Albion and the Four Zoas from their slumber of six thousand years. Satan withdraws and Rahab appears, bearing the name of Moral Virtue and revealing herself to be Religion hid in War.

Ololon and Milton discuss times past. They reach the realization that they are contraries who can be reconciled once their inhibiting selfhoods are expunged. Ololon thereupon sheds her formidable female will, which sinks into the sea with Milton's spectral shadow. Purged, the two are reunited. Milton declares:

> I come in Self-annihilation & the grandeur
>   of Inspiration,
> To cast off Rational Demonstration by Faith
>   in the Saviour,
> To cast off the rotten rags of Memory
>   by Inspiration,
> To cast off Bacon, Locke & Newton from
>   Albion's covering,
> To take off his filthy garments & clothe him
>   with Imagination,
> To cast aside from Poetry all that is
>   not Inspiration.

Clothed in a garment dipped in blood and inscribed with words of divine revelation, Jesus appears and enters into Albion's bosom. God unites with man. Terror-struck, Blake collapses on the path and is revived by his wife. The lark is heard on high, and all go forth to the Last Judgment.

John L. McLean

Further Reading

Bentley, G. E., Jr. *The Stranger from Paradise: A Biography of William Blake*. New Haven, Conn.: Published for the Paul Mellon Centre for Studies in British Art by Yale University Press, 2001. Bentley, a veteran Blake scholar, has compiled a meticulously researched and comprehensive account of Blake's life and work, illustrated with 170 black and white and color reproductions of Blake's art work.

Bloom, Harold. *Blake's Apocalypse: A Study in Poetic Argument*. Garden City, N.Y.: Doubleday, 1963. A comprehensive, line-by-line exposition of Blake's prophetic poems. Bloom sensitively explains the intricate subtleties of Blake's myth and traces its connections to biblical and other literary traditions.

Damon, S. Foster. *A Blake Dictionary: The Ideas and Symbols of William Blake*. Providence, R.I.: Brown University Press, 1965. This handy glossary collects and interprets clues to Blake's terminology, which is scattered through all of his works. There are entries for each character, work, symbol, and geographical or historical reference. Includes maps, illustrations, and diagrams of difficult concepts, such as Golgonooza.

Eaves, Morris, ed. *The Cambridge Companion to William Blake.* New York: Cambridge University Press, 2003. Collection of essays that cover the entire range of Blake's works, including "*Milton* and Its Contexts, 1800-1810" by Mary Lynn Johnson. The book also features a chronology, a guide to further reading, and a glossary of Blake's terminology.

Fox, Susan. *Poetic Form in Blake's "Milton."* Princeton, N.J.: Princeton University Press, 1976. Fox patiently establishes the structural principle of parallelism beneath the seeming chaos of the poem. Explores the echoes, paired passages, cyclical patterns, and thematic symmetries.

Frye, Northrop. *Fearful Symmetry: A Study of William Blake.* Princeton, N.J.: Princeton University Press, 1947. A brilliant and influential critical analysis of Blake's poetry and thought. Chapter 10 examines *Milton*.

Howard, John. *Blake's Milton: A Study in the Selfhood.* Madison, N.J.: Fairleigh Dickinson University Press, 1976. A psychological analysis that credits Blake for anticipating twentieth century psychological theories. Focuses on Milton's descent as a journey within the psyche and analyzes Blake's Spectres as models of self-paralyzing inhibition.

Williams, Nicholas M., ed. *Palgrave Advances in William Blake Studies.* New York: Palgrave Macmillan, 2006. Collection of essays that apply modern critical perspectives to analyze Blake's works. Includes discussions of Blake and language, gender studies, the Bible, psychology, the communist tradition, and postmodernism.

The Minister's Black Veil
A Parable

Author: Nathaniel Hawthorne (1804-1864)
First published: 1836
Type of work: Short fiction
Type of plot: Gothic
Time of plot: Early eighteenth century
Locale: Milford, Massachusetts

Principal characters:
THE REVEREND MR. HOOPER, pastor of Milford
ELIZABETH, his fiancé
THE REVEREND MR. CLARK, pastor of Westbury

The Story:

A church sexton is ringing a bell, summoning people of the village to church. He customarily stops ringing when he sees Reverend Mr. Hooper leave his house, but this Sabbath morning the sexton is astonished at the sight of the minister. A thirty-year-old bachelor, Parson Hooper is wearing a black veil made of two folds of crape that conceal all features except his mouth and chin. He can see through the veil, but it darkens everything he sees.

The people murmur about Hooper's dreadfully changed appearance, questioning if it is truly his face behind the veil or if he has lost his sanity. When Hooper walks to the pulpit, all eyes fixate on the black veil. His sermon topic concerns the secret sins that people hide from their closest associations, even from their own consciousness, forgetting that God is omniscient. The melancholy black veil makes his sermon seem more powerful, much more so than his normally mild, calm preaching style.

Isolation is immediate. No one walks by the reverend's side; even old Squire Saunders, who generally invites Hooper to his table each Sunday, fails to do so today. The pastor smiles sadly at the thought that two small pieces of material produce such negative reactions. One woman, thinking the veil has transformed him into a ghost, tells her husband she would not be alone with Hooper for any price; she surmises he is probably afraid to be alone.

In the afternoon, a funeral for a young woman initiates the rumor that Hooper is wearing the veil because of his own secret sin, one he had committed with the young woman. A superstitious old woman attending the funeral thinks the corpse shudders when the minister is near. Another woman imagines the minister and the spirit of the young woman walking together, holding hands in the funeral procession and, thus, linked in secret sin. At a wedding this evening, the minister's veil, which had fit in well with the funeral's mourning, casts an evil pall over the festivities.

In the ensuing days, the veil's influence becomes evident. One mischievous child mimics the pastor, covering his face with an old black handkerchief, frightening both himself and his playmates. People who had previously advised the pastor try to persuade him to take off the veil, but in the presence of the intimidating veil, their words cease.

One person, however, is brave enough to speak with the pastor—his fiancé, Elizabeth. She had asked him to remove the veil earlier, but he had answered that he must wear it until eternity, when all people will remove their veils. She now asks him to explain his motives and his mysterious veiled words. She inquires if some deep sorrow or grief causes him to darken his eyes forever. She begs him to take off the black veil, thereby removing the rumors of scandal that are circulating about his ministry.

After periods of pleading, silence, and then crying, Elizabeth experiences for herself the terror of the black veil and begins to tremble. In desperation, Hooper pleads with her not to leave him, telling her that the veil is mortal; in eternity there will be no veil on his face, or separation between their souls. After he shares how lonely he feels behind the black veil, Elizabeth asks him to lift it just once. When he refuses, she leaves. Even in his sorrow, the sad smile again appears as he wonders how a small physical symbol could separate two who love each other.

From this day forward, no one attempts to have Hooper remove the veil. Because most people shrink away and avoid him out of fear, he cannot walk the streets or take his habitual walk to the cemetery. His own antipathy to the veil is so intense that he avoids mirrors or other reflecting surfaces. He becomes completely isolated. Still known as a gentle and loving man, he is not loved in return, only feared. During times of joy, he is not welcome.

At times when sinners are dying, they still cry for Hooper, refusing to yield in death until he comes to them. The veil has a deep influence on tormented souls, who feel the pastor can better sympathize with them. As the years pass, Hooper's long life, blameless and above reproach, earns for him a new title—Father Hooper. He outlives many of his parishioners, many of whom are now buried in the graveyard.

Father Hooper is dying. Surrounding him are deacons; a zealous young reverend named Clark, who is from a neighboring village; and his nurse, who is none other than Hooper's own beloved Elizabeth, who has never married.

When the Reverend Clark asks Father Hooper if he is ready to lift the veil that separates time from eternity, he agrees, with faint words. Then the young minister asks to remove the black veil so Hooper's reputation as a godly man will have no shadow on its memory. The dying minister follows with a sudden surge of energy. Moving his hands from under the blankets and pressing the veil to his face, he says it will never be removed while he is on this earth. In horror, Clark questions what unconfessed crime Hooper is taking with him into eternity to face judgment.

With the death rattle in his throat and the black veil on his face, Reverend Hooper smiles that same faint, sad smile. He then tells the people encircling his bed that this black veil, which has caused terror in men, women, and children, is not present on his face alone. He sees every face wearing a black veil.

Hooper's corpse is brought to its grave. Many years pass, and grass covers his grave and moss covers the stone. A dreadful thought remains: his face turned to dust under the black veil.

Critical Evaluation:

Nathaniel Hawthorne is considered by many a towering figure of American literary history. His works include children's stories, nonfiction sketches, a presidential campaign biography of Franklin Pierce, four major novels, and essays. Isolation is a central theme in his works, perhaps because he was a solitary child of a widowed recluse. After college, he was alone again for twelve years before he married. It was during this time that he wrote "The Minister's Black Veil."

Unlike his contemporaries, such as writer-philosopher Ralph Waldo Emerson, a romantic Transcendentalist, Hawthorne believed that sin and evil are palpable and real and present in humans. Herman Melville, author of *Moby Dick* (1851), said this "power of blackness" in Hawthorne comes from "that Calvinistic sense of Innate Depravity and Original Sin, from whose visitations, in some shape or other, no deeply thinking mind is always and wholly free."

Hawthorne explores the presence of sin through several works. "Young Goodman Brown" (1835), which was followed by "The Minister's Black Veil," observes the nature of temptation and its aftermath of isolation. Then came Hawthorne's classic masterpiece, *The Scarlet Letter* (1850), which explores the effects of sin on four individuals. In "Ethan Brand" (1851), he examines unpardonable sin.

Hawthorne, an allegorical writer on a quest for spiritual meaning, models his writing after John Bunyan and Edmund Spenser. He identifies "The Minister's Black Veil" as a parable, a genre often defined as a short story with moral intent. The overt moral to the story is that the Reverend Hooper thinks that every human has a secret sin, which is veiled from all except God. Only on Judgment Day, in the "sunshine of eternity," will a person's veil be removed. Accompanying the story is a note by Hawthorne about an actual minister who had lived in eighteenth century York, Maine. This minister, as a youth, had accidentally killed a close friend. From that day until his death, he had hidden his face with a veil.

The center of this story is the effect of the veil. Hooper tells Elizabeth it is a symbol, but he does not interpret it. The veil, a common part of clothing in weddings and funerals, is a gothic element, producing an uncanny, unsettling effect that makes the familiar strange. Because weddings and funerals are social gatherings, Hooper's veil creates a sense of alienation, even in a crowd. Although present at these events, Hooper is alone. At his deathbed is Elizabeth, as his nurse but not his wife. The veil "had separated him from cheerful brotherhood and woman's love, and kept him in that saddest of all prisons, his own heart."

One feature of Hawthorne's emblematic writing is its ambiguity; it provides enough evidence to support more than one view but never completely resolves the mystery. The motive for Hooper's wearing of the veil is ambiguous. Hooper tells his fiancé, Elizabeth (the name of both Hawthorne's mother and sister), "If I hide my face for sorrow, there is cause enough . . . and if I cover it for secret sin, what mortal might not do the same?"

Perhaps the Reverend Hooper is really a hypocrite, pretending to be holy while his veil hides his true identity and character, or perhaps he is pure, a spiritual guide choosing to visually teach a moral precept to his community, even at the cost of personal sacrifice. His ensuing path of loneliness and sorrow follows the footsteps of Old Testament prophets, such as Jeremiah and Ezekiel, who are known for their visual object-lessons. Hooper prays at the young woman's funeral, saying that every living mortal will be ready "for the dreadful hour that should snatch the veil from their faces." The young reverend, Mr. Clark, initially remarks that Hooper is one who is "holy in deed and thought."

Further clues to the mystery of the veil appear at the end of the story. Reverend Hooper's final words emphasize the moral meaning of the veil. In his view, all individuals are incarcerated in the shadows of their own black veil, unable to show their true faces. He believes the veil causes terror not because of its literal appearance but because of the truth it represents: Secret sin is universal—"I look around me, and, lo! on every visage a Black Veil!"

Hawthorne concludes with the thought that Hooper's veil lives on, although buried in the grave. Hawthorne's story, too, lives on, attracting readers attempting to resolve the ambiguous mystery that remains veiled.

Amy Alexander

Further Reading

Fogle, Richard Harter. *Hawthorne's Fiction: The Light and the Dark*. Rev. ed. Norman: University of Oklahoma Press, 1964. A classic analysis of the antitheses in Hawthorne, such as light and darkness, clarity and ambiguity, and appearance and reality. Discusses his complexity and the need to reconcile opposites for unity and understanding. "The Minister's Black Veil" is discussed in chapter 3.

Idol, John L., and Melinda M. Ponder, eds. *Hawthorne and Women: Engendering and Expanding the Hawthorne Tradition*. Amherst: University of Massachusetts Press, 1999. Thorough and informative, this work examines the influence of women on Hawthorne, his frequent inclusion of the female perspective, the contemporary women who reviewed his works, and Hawthorne's continuing influence on women authors, past and present. "The Minister's Black Veil" is discussed in the essay "Stowe and Hawthorne."

Leone, Bruno, ed. *The Greenhaven Press Literary Companion to American Authors: Readings on Nathaniel Hawthorne*. San Diego, Calif.: Greenhaven Press, 1996. A collection of critical essays that provides a good beginning study of Hawthorne and his historical and philosophical contexts. Includes essays by Hawthorne's contemporaries.

Millington, Richard H. *The Cambridge Companion to Nathaniel Hawthorne*. New York: Cambridge University Press, 2004. Essays analyze various aspects of Hawthorne's work, including Hawthorne and American masculinity, and the question of women. Discusses his major novels.

Person, Leland S. *The Cambridge Introduction to Nathaniel Hawthorne*. New York: Cambridge University Press, 2007. An accessible introduction to the author's life and works designed for students and general readers. Includes analysis of Hawthorne's fiction, a brief survey of Hawthorne scholarship, and a bibliography.

Waggoner, Hyatt H. *Hawthorne: A Critical Study*. Rev. ed. Cambridge, Mass.: Belknap Press, 1963. A foundational comprehensive work on Hawthorne as an artist and as a man. Examines his fiction to distinguish between two types of meaning, one that originates from the conscious mind, the other from the haunted subconscious mind. Also discusses his alternation between traditional allegory and modern symbolism.

Wineapple, Brenda. *Hawthorne: A Life*. New York: Alfred A. Knopf, 2003. A meticulously researched, even-handed analysis of Hawthorne's often contradictory life that proposes that much of Hawthorne's fiction was autobiographical. Includes more than one hundred pages of notes, a bibliography, and an index.

The Ministry of Fear
An Entertainment

Author: Graham Greene (1904-1991)
First published: 1943
Type of work: Novel
Type of plot: Psychological realism
Time of plot: World War II
Locale: London and environs

Principal characters:
ARTHUR ROWE, a middle-aged Englishman who kills his wife
ANNA HILFE, an Austrian refugee
WILLI HILFE, Anna's brother and a fifth-column leader
DR. FORESTER, English dupe of Willi Hilfe

The Story:

Arthur Rowe, a middle-aged Englishman, happens one day onto a fete in blitz-torn London. In an effort to recapture some spirit of the brighter past, he enters the grounds. While there, he has his fortune told, and the seer tells him the weight of a cake that is to go to the person who guesses the weight correctly. Rowe wins the cake and starts to leave, but the clergyman in charge of the affair tries to get the cake back. Rowe is angered and donates a pound note to the cause and leaves.

Just before the German bombers fly up the Thames to terrorize the city that same night, Rowe has his first visitor in months, a man who rents a room in the same house. The visitor behaves very oddly. When given a piece of cake by Rowe, he crumbles it as if looking for something. Then, while Rowe is out of the room, the man slips something into Rowe's tea. Rowe returns and smells the peculiar odor of the tea, but before he can say or do anything, a bomb falls, wrecking the house. He regains consciousness to find the house demolished.

Because he has few friends to whom he can turn since he killed his wife in a mercy killing, the worried Rowe goes to a detective agency the next day, where he hires a man named Jones to watch after him and discover why someone wishes to take his life. Rowe then goes to the relief office, which was in charge of the fete at which he won the cake. There he finds a young woman, Anna Hilfe, and her brother Willi in charge of the office. The two say they are Austrian refugees. Willi goes with Rowe to the home of the fortune-teller in an effort to uncover the reason for the attempt on Rowe's life.

At the fortune-teller's home, the two men are invited to stay for a séance. During the séance, the man sitting next to Rowe is murdered with Rowe's knife. With Willi's aid, Rowe escapes from the house before the police arrive. He goes to an air-raid shelter and there remains through the night. He writes a letter to the police, but before he posts it, he calls Anna, who tells him that "they" are still after him. "They" are supposed to be Nazi agents. Rowe still cannot understand why he is a marked man. Anna agrees to aid Rowe and tells him to send an address where he can be reached.

After talking to her, Rowe calls the detective agency. He then learns that Jones, the man he hired, disappeared and that the head of the agency called the police in on the case. Rowe wanders aimlessly about the city until the afternoon, when he meets a man who asks him to take a valise full of books to a Mr. Travers at a hotel. When Rowe arrives at the hotel, he is escorted to Travers's room. There he finds Anna waiting for him. In fear of their lives, the two wait for the air raids to begin. They believe that Nazi agents will kill them during the noise and confusion of the raids. Then a bomb falls on the hotel. Rowe awakens in a private nursing home without memories beyond his eighteenth year.

Anna visits him several times in the nursing home, and Rowe falls in love with her during the visits. She will not tell him of his past and claims that the head of the institution, Dr. Forester, wants the recovery to be slow enough to avoid shock. One day, a military officer being treated in the home confides that he saw someone digging on the island in a pond on the grounds. The officer is immediately put into a straitjacket, and Rowe is confined to his room without newspapers or his clothes on the pretext that he suffered a mild relapse.

Convinced that some evil is afoot, Rowe escapes from the room and visits the officer. His visit with the officer confirms his suspicions. Within a few hours, the doctor returns and, extremely angry at Rowe, threatens him, too, with a straitjacket. With the help of an attendant, Rowe escapes and goes to Scotland Yard. He turns himself in as the murderer of the victim at the séance; to his surprise, however, he is told that no one was murdered there. The police turn him over to a counterintelligence agent, who tells Rowe that the murder was a fraud to drive him into hiding and that the nursing home is actually a front for fifth-column activities.

The agent, Rowe, and a man from the hotel where Rowe was injured go to the tailor shop run by the man who supposedly was murdered. During the interview, the tailor places a phone call. After the call is completed, he kills himself. Angry at losing the man before learning any information, the agent tells Rowe that he inadvertently was given a cake containing secret film that was taken by Nazi agents from British documents.

Rowe and the agent then go to the home of the fortune-teller. They fail to find the film there, and they get no information. The last stop of the trip is at the nursing home. There they find the military officer dead, killed by Dr. Forester, who, as Rowe now remembers, was at the fortune-teller's home on the night of the supposed murder. The doctor is also dead; he was killed by the attendant who helped Rowe to escape.

Without telling the counterintelligence agent, Rowe calls the number he saw the tailor dial. When the call is answered, he finds Anna at the other end. Going to her apartment, Rowe discovers that it is her brother Willi who is the head of the fifth-column ring. With Anna's help, Rowe almost gets the film. Anna, torn between love for her brother and love for Rowe, allows Willi to escape. Rowe, whose memory is almost complete, follows Willi and regains the film at the railroad station. He returns Willi's gun to him but with only one bullet in it. Willi then goes to the washroom and kills himself, but not before he reveals the last piece of information that Rowe failed to remember: the fact that Rowe killed his first wife to put her out of pain. Rowe is ready to give the film in his possession to the police. He returns to Anna's apartment to tell her of her brother's death and to declare his love to her. Although Rowe drove her brother to his death, Anna pledges her love for him.

Critical Evaluation:

With the publication of *Brighton Rock* in 1938, Graham Greene began to categorize his works as either "novels" or "entertainments," with the latter term suggesting a work of somehow lesser stature. The distinguishing factor between the two appears to be the way in which religion is treated; the novels are set apart by a more serious consideration of religious and ethical problems, while the entertainments focus more on plot, action, and melodrama, with religious problems as secondary concerns.

Nevertheless, despite their overall lack of seriousness, the entertainments often show Greene at his best, committed to keeping his readers in suspense and making the action exciting, with the goal of telling the best story possible. In some cases, the entertainments even appear to serve as preliminary sketches for the more elaborate treatment of similar themes in the novels that follow them.

This might be argued in the case of *The Ministry of Fear*, the most ambitious, arguably the best, of Greene's entertainments. In its focus on how the emotion of pity can destroy those in which it is overdeveloped, the book is also an obvious precursor to one of Greene's finest achievements, the novel *The Heart of the Matter* (1948).

Moved by an almost corrupting sense of pity, Arthur Rowe, the book's protagonist, kills his wife, who is suffering from an incurable illness. His sense of pity is corrupting, because it is really a disguised form of contempt for others. To pity other people is to regard them as inferior.

Whether he does it to end her suffering or to free himself from having to watch her endure, he cannot be certain. If he kills her quickly by poison because he cannot stand to watch her die slowly from cancer, then his mercy killing springs from selfishness. This "mercy killing," of which the court acquits him, has an echo in a childhood memory. As a boy, Rowe happened upon a struggling rat with a broken back and ended its suffering, an experience that appears to define his character.

Rowe is obviously a precursor to Major Scobie, the main character in *The Heart of the Matter*. Like Rowe, Scobie is defined by his pity. Like Rowe's, Scobie's sense of responsibility for his fellow human beings and his concern with their unhappiness imply a lack of trust, a lack of faith in God. It is the treatment of this theme that most separates the two works, as the entertainment chooses to leave it unexplored, whereas the novel treats this lack of trust as one of its primary themes.

In Rowe, pity is overdeveloped to an extreme. In the person of the book's antagonist, the Nazi sympathizer Willi Hilfe, Greene delves into the other extreme: underdeveloped pity or pitilessness. Hilfe is a monstrous villain, an utterly selfish, amoral criminal who loses the sense of worth of human life.

Rowe's overwhelming sense of pity makes him capable of bearing pain but equally incapable of causing pain to others. As he unwittingly becomes involved with the activities of an undercover Nazi organization in war-torn London during the air raids of World War II, Rowe ironically becomes the spokesman of humanity as he must face down Hilfe and the threat his group poses. This involvement with Hilfe and his group, however, is necessary for Rowe to achieve self-actualization. To overcome the hurdles that block his rebirth, Rowe must give up both his private life and his safety to help the common cause and rid his country of the threat Hilfe embodies.

The book's structure is notable. *The Ministry of Fear* is divided into four parts. The first, "The Unhappy Man," deals with Rowe, describing the experiences that combine to create him. As a result of the mercy killing, Rowe becomes a solitary man, unable to find a job and without friends. The fact that the murder is a mercy killing does not soften anybody's harsh opinion of Rowe—even Rowe's opinion of himself. He stands condemned just as deeply in his own eyes as in those of others.

Because the story is set during World War II, Rowe is all the more alone because he is cut off from the sense of community engendered by wartime experience. This section sets the stage for the action, portraying the fete at which Rowe wins, ironically, the cake in which the undercover organization places a microfilm of secret naval plans.

The second section, "The Happy Man," deals with a Rowe who, as a result of a bomb blast, loses the memory of his past, along with the sense of pity that propels him. Rowe becomes Richard Digby and is in a countryside nursing home under the care of the famous Dr. Forester. Rowe is at peace, at least as much as it is possible for him to experience peace. His amnesia allows him to rest and rejuvenate, which eventually leads to thoughts of escape.

In the third section, "Bits and Pieces," Rowe slowly begins his reorientation as he rediscovers his beliefs and convictions. Since he did not yet redevelop his overdeveloped sense of pity, he is still essentially happy. The fourth section, "The Whole Man," presents Rowe's public and private reintegration as a complete knowledge of his past returns to him.

This structure, which involves Rowe losing touch with himself, only gradually to relearn the painful facts of life, connects *The Ministry of Fear* with the idea of "the divided man," "the man within" of Greene's earlier novels. Were it not for this "man within," an ideal, imagined fantasy self, the ordinary, instinctive man would find it easier to come to terms with actuality.

However, surprisingly, Rowe does not entirely lose touch with his sense of pity at the book's end. He comes full circle to a new life with Anna Hilfe but is still so obsessed with his sense of pity at the idea of human suffering that he is willing, at the story's end, to enter into this new relationship with Anna without being completely honest. Rowe's pity will cause the relationship to be one based in fear and dishonesty, as he attempts to spare her the knowledge that he remembers killing his wife.

Easily one of the strongest of the entertainments, *The Ministry of Fear* falls short of Greene's criteria for his novels only because of the lighter treatment of religious themes. A strong thriller narrative, combined with numerous artistic and thematic complexities, makes *The Ministry of Fear* one of Greene's best works.

"Critical Evaluation" by Craig A. Larson

Further Reading

Allott, Kenneth, and Miriam Farris. *The Art of Graham Greene*. New York: Russell, 1963. One of the first book-length studies of Greene and still one of the best. Views *The Ministry of Fear* in terms of Greene's obsessions with "the divided mind" or "the fallen world."

Bergonzi, Bernard. *A Study in Greene: Graham Greene and the Art of the Novel*. New York: Oxford University Press, 2006. Bergonzi examines all of Greene's novels, analyzing their language, structure, and recurring motifs. He argues that Greene's earliest work was his best, *Brighton Rock* was his masterpiece, and his novels published after the 1950's showed a marked decline in his abilities. Chapter 3 includes a discussion of *The Ministry of Fear*, and other references to the novel are listed in the index.

Boardman, Gwenn R. *Graham Greene: The Aesthetics of Exploration*. Gainesville: University Press of Florida, 1971. Boardman maintains the novel is "an ingenious parable on the nature of love." She sees the book as a commentary on the state of the world and "the mess that Western civilization" was in at the time.

Bosco, Mark. *Graham Greene's Catholic Imagination*. New York: Oxford University Press, 2005. Focuses on the elements of Catholic doctrine in Greene's novels. Bosco contradicts many critics, who maintain these elements are present only in Greene's early novels, demonstrating how the writer's religious faith is a pervasive aspect in all of his work.

Cuoto, Maria. *Graham Greene: On the Frontier*. New York: St. Martin's Press, 1988. An excellent discussion of the book's complexities. Cuoto maintains that Greene's "artistry lies in breaking the mold of the thriller to integrate tragic and spiritual concerns."

DeVitis, A. A. *Graham Greene*. Rev. ed. Edited by Kinley E. Roby. Boston: Twayne, 1986. An excellent starting point for a consideration of Greene's work. Insightful chapter on the "entertainments" as opposed to the "novels."

Land, Stephen K. *The Human Imperative: A Study of the Novels of Graham Greene*. New York: AMS Press, 2008. A chronological consideration of all of Greene's work, demonstrating the common themes and character types in his novels and other fiction. Charts Greene's development as a writer.

Malmet, Elliott. *The World Remade: Graham Greene and*

the *Art of Detection*. New York: Peter Lang, 1998. Focuses on Greene's genre fiction, analyzing the narrative strategies, themes, motifs, and philosophical and theosophical meanings in the author's thrillers and detective novels. Includes bibliography and index.

Wolfe, Peter. *Graham Greene the Entertainer*. Carbondale: Southern Illinois University Press, 1972. Essential book-length study that chiefly addresses those works classified as "entertainments." Devotes an entire chapter to *The Ministry of Fear*.

The Miracle Worker

Author: William Gibson (1914-2008)
First produced: 1957, teleplay (first published, 1957); 1959, stage play (first published, 1959)
Type of work: Drama
Type of plot: Psychological realism
Time of plot: 1880's
Locale: Tuscumbia, Alabama; Boston

Principal characters:
ANNIE SULLIVAN, an obstinate, once-blind teacher
CAPTAIN ARTHUR KELLER, a Southern gentleman
KATE, his second wife
HELEN, their deaf, blind daughter
JAMES, the Captain's indolent son

The Story:

One-and-a-half-year-old Helen Keller is sick with acute congestion and a high fever. She makes it through the ordeal, but after the doctor leaves, her parents, Captain Arthur and Kate Keller, are horrified to discover that the illness left Helen deaf and blind. Five years pass and the Keller family is unable to find any doctor, teacher, or quack who can do anything to help Helen. The undisciplined, groping, curious girl is left to her own devices, grabbing toys from other children, knocking papers off desks, and eating off other people's plates. When she overturns the cradle, tumbling the baby, Mildred, onto the floor, the Captain agrees to write to yet another rumored specialist in the hope that someone might be able to train Helen.

The Captain's letter eventually finds its way to Boston and the Perkins Institute for the Blind, where a governess is found for Helen. Twenty-year-old Annie Sullivan just completed her own education at Perkins. She was an abandoned child, left to care for her sickly brother, Jimmie, who died in the state almshouse. Now, after nine eye operations and a turbulent education, Annie is being sent to try to teach Helen. Her teacher, Mr. Anagnos, warns her not to expect miracles.

The Keller family is shocked by Annie's youth and inexperience. It is especially difficult for the Captain's indolent son, James, to see a woman no older than himself given this responsibility. When Annie announces that she intends to teach Helen language, Kate laments that they were not even able to teach her to sit still. From the moment of her arrival, Annie begins to fingerspell into Helen's hands. The first attempt to impose some structure onto Helen erupts the mo-

ment the child does not get her own way. Helen hits Annie in the face with a doll, knocking out a tooth. Helen then locks Annie in Helen's room and gropes her way out to the pump in the yard. When James smugly informs the Captain of Annie's plight, the Captain angrily has a ladder fetched and carries the humiliated Annie to the ground. Annie watches the family go in to eat dinner and turns to Helen, who, believing she is alone, gleefully drops Annie's room key down the well.

The next morning James and the Captain are arguing again, resulting in James comparing Annie to General Grant at the Battle of Vicksburg. At breakfast, when Helen gropes her way around the table, Annie refuses to allow Helen to eat off her plate. A battle of wills follows, with Annie expelling the family from the dining room and physically forcing Helen to sit down and eat properly. The siege lasts all morning, leaving the room a disaster, but Helen eats breakfast with her own spoon and folds her napkin. Exhausted and discouraged, Annie goes upstairs to pack. In the meantime, the Captain informs Kate that the insolent teacher must be fired. Instead of giving up, Annie develops a plan. She convinces the Kellers that in order to succeed, she must have control of every aspect of Helen's life. The Kellers reluctantly agree to set Annie up in their garden house and leave her in complete charge of Helen for two weeks. After disorienting Helen by driving her around in a wagon, she is delivered into Annie's care. At first Helen refuses to have anything to do with the unyielding teacher who demands personal discipline. Annie finally gets Helen to cooperate by fingerspelling into the hand of another child. Helen's jealousy overcomes her and she forces herself onto the teacher.

At the end of the two weeks, the wild beast that was Helen seems to be tamed. Annie spells thousands of words into her hands. Helen learns eighteen nouns and three verbs. It is all just a finger game, however; Helen does not connect the fingerspelling to the concept of language. Annie begs for more time but is denied, even though the Kellers are overwhelmed with what she accomplished. The Captain agrees, at the very least, to maintain the self-control that was instilled in Helen. The family sits down to eat a celebratory meal, but back in her old environment, Helen immediately tries to revert to her undisciplined ways. When Annie does not tolerate it, Helen throws a tantrum and dumps the water pitcher onto Annie. Ignoring the protests of the Captain, Annie pulls Helen into the yard and forces her to refill the pitcher at the pump. Then the miracle happens. As Annie spells W-A-T-E-R into her hand, Helen makes the connection that the finger game spells a word that means the thing. Helen rushes around grasping everything in reach while Annie spells its name into her hand. She finds and hugs her mother, and then turns to find her teacher, whom she embraces and pulls into the house to join the Kellers at the table.

Critical Evaluation:

William Gibson is generally credited with pioneering the modern biographical drama. He did not invent the biographical play; the lives of real people have always supplied playwrights with material. It is how Gibson combined biography with literary and dramatic techniques in *The Miracle Worker* that gives him the distinction of creating the model for biographical drama of the twentieth century. After winning six Tony Awards in 1960, the play has continued as one of the most popular and best-known American plays of the mid-twentieth century. This success is partially the result of the compelling nature of its characters. There is a dramatically rich conflict between a deaf, blind child who, for pity's sake, has been allowed to behave as an animal, and an obstinate, once-blind teacher with a fierce Irish temper. Its success is also attributable to the literary qualities that give the play value as literature as well as theater.

Gibson achieved early recognition as a poet and novelist before writing the first version of *The Miracle Worker* for television. Each facet of his career influenced the play. As a poet, he developed a command of language and imagery. As a novelist, he developed skill in storytelling and theme development. As a writer for television, he developed facility in handling the rigors of succinct dramatic construction, character development, and theatricality. These overlapped as he

discovered techniques to develop themes and to explore the thoughts of a character on stage. The end result was the creation of a language for *The Miracle Worker* that is almost without equal in the modern theater, at once literate and dramatic but that does not call undue attention to itself. The script, for example, is replete with religious imagery and metaphor, from the title through James Keller's comparing Annie to the angel who wrestled Jacob, providing a great blessing after causing great pain.

In his book *Shakespeare's Game* (1978), Gibson develops a theory of drama that was greatly influenced by his wife, Margaret Brenman, a psychoanalyst. *The Miracle Worker* is a prime example of Gibson's theory that the roots of dramatic conflict lie in cognitive psychology, specifically examining the struggles of the individual against social and psychological isolation. Helen Keller is isolated by her deafness, her blindness, and her family's inability to discipline her. Discipline would include her in everyday family life. Annie Sullivan is isolated psychologically when the death of her brother, Jimmie, leaves her spiritually dead, looking for a "resurrection"; she is isolated physically as the intruder facing the almost insurmountable obstacle of breaking into Helen's world. Annie also must fight for the right to wage the battle to educate Helen. Annie's chief weapon is language, another recurring theme in Gibson's collective works. For Gibson, language has the power to illuminate the mind even more than eyes illuminate the world. Through Annie, he preaches language, theorizes language, and practices language at every opportunity. Even in the midst of their most physical battles, Annie never stops fingerspelling words, language, into the hands of Helen. At the climax of the play, it is language that bubbles up and out of Helen's mind just as the underground water bubbles up and out of the downstage pump, the play's omnipresent symbol of Helen's miracle. The social and psychological isolation of both teacher and student are resolved through language, and both receive the new life Annie had been seeking.

Each of Gibson's themes is reinforced via a parallel conflict between the Captain and his son, James. The Captain wants desperately to teach James to stand up to the world, but James, who wants to be accepted as a man, fights like a child, wounding with words, throwing a quick barb and retreating. The Captain uses the very techniques on James that he cannot abide to see Annie use on Helen. When the Captain and James debate the Confederate Army's eventual defeat in the Battle for Vicksburg, their own conflict is developed while their argument becomes a metaphor for the teaching of Helen. The Southern General Pemberton represents the Kellers, Vicksburg becomes Helen, and the stubborn General

Grant is Annie. Grant won because, despite his lack of training, he never gave up, foreshadowing Annie's eventual victory in the battle to teach Helen. In the end, James also learns to use language to stand up to the Captain and end his own psychological isolation.

The play's climax is both exhilarating and wrenching. *The Miracle Worker* successfully illuminates the human condition while avoiding most of the pitfalls of sentimentality. In the end, it is not the pathos of the characters that wrings emotion from the audience but the triumph of the human spirit.

Gerald S. Argetsinger

Further Reading

Brustein, Robert. "Two for the Miracle." *The New Republic*, November 9, 1959. Argues that Gibson is a gifted writer, with literary and dramatic skills, but that *The Miracle Worker* is merely an essay on interpersonal relations and that Gibson's weakness for the inspirational dooms him to the second rank.

Carr, David. "William Gibson, Playwright, Dies at Ninety-four." *The New York Times*, November 28, 2008. An obituary reviewing Gibson's career.

Geller, Conrad. "A Battle to Free a Human Soul." *Writing* 24, no. 5 (February/March, 2002): 14. Analyzes the conflict between characters in *The Miracle Worker*, quoting excerpts of the play's dialogue. Describes why this conflict is significant to the play's success and discusses the humor within the conflict.

Hayes, Richard. "Images." *Commonwealth* 71, no. 10 (December 4, 1959): 289. Argues that *The Miracle Worker*'s message of goodness is aesthetically irrelevant.

Kerr, Walter. "*The Miracle Worker*." In *The Theater in Spite of Itself*. New York: Simon & Schuster, 1963. Discusses how *The Miracle Worker* succeeds in spite of some weaknesses.

Klages, Mary. "Redefining Disability and Sentimentality: *The Miracle Worker*." In *Woeful Afflictions: Disability and Sentimentality in Victorian America*. Philadelphia: University of Pennsylvania Press, 1999. This examination of how disabled persons were portrayed sentimentally in the nineteenth century includes a chapter on the twentieth century depiction of disability in *The Miracle Worker*. Klages states that "The play currently exists as the most prevalent text defining contemporary cultural meanings of disability."

Tynan, Kenneth. "Ireland Unvanquished." *The New Yorker*, October 31, 1959. Describes Gibson's juxtaposition of laughter, combat, and pathos. Argues that the play affirms the dignity of the species.

"Who Is Stanislavsky?" *Time*, December 21, 1959. Discusses the theatrical qualities of *The Miracle Worker*, especially the fight sequences, and examines the development of Annie Sullivan and Helen Keller as characters in the play.

The Misanthrope

Author: Molière (1622-1673)
First produced: Le Misanthrope, 1666; first published, 1667 (English translation, 1709)
Type of work: Drama
Type of plot: Comedy of manners
Time of plot: Seventeenth century
Locale: Paris

Principal characters:
ALCESTE, in love with Célimène
PHILINTE, friend of Alceste
ORONTE, in love with Célimène
CÉLIMÈNE, a young widow
ÉLIANTE, cousin of Célimène
ARSINOÉ, a self-righteous prude

The Story:

Alceste has been called a misanthrope by many of his friends, and he takes a rather obstinate delight in the name. This characteristic leads him to quarrel heatedly with his good friend, Philinte, who accepts uncritically the frivolous manners of the day. When Philinte warmly embraces a chance acquaintance, as is customary, Alceste maintains that such behavior is hypocritical, especially since Philinte hardly knows him.

Philinte reminds Alceste that his lawsuit is nearly ready for trial, and that he will do well to moderate his attitude toward people in general. His opponents in the suit are doing everything possible to curry favor, but Alceste insults everyone he meets and makes no effort to win over the judges. Philinte also taunts Alceste on his love for Célimène, who, as a leader in society, is hypocritical most of the time. Alceste has to admit that his love cannot be explained rationally.

Oronte interrupts the quarrel by coming to visit Alceste, who is puzzled by a visit from suave and elegant Oronte. Oronte asks permission to read a sonnet he had lately composed, as he is anxious to have Alceste's judgment of its literary merit. After affecting hesitation, Oronte reads his mediocre poem. Alceste at first hedges but then, too honest to give false praise, condemns the verses and even satirizes the poor quality of the writing. Oronte takes instant offense at this criticism, and a quarrel breaks out between them. Although the argument is indecisive, there are hints of a possible duel.

Alceste then calls on Célimène. As soon as he sees her, he begins perversely to upbraid her for her frivolous conduct and her hypocritical attitude toward other people. He points out that although Célimène could slander and ridicule with a keen wit and a barbed tongue while a person is absent, she is all flattery and attention when talking with that person. This attitude displeases Alceste.

The servant announces several callers, including Éliante. To Alceste's dismay, they all sit down for an interminable conversation. The men take great delight in naming all their mutual acquaintances, for as each name is mentioned, Célimène makes unkind remarks. The only gentle person in the room is Éliante, whose good sense and kind heart are in striking contrast with Célimène's caustic wit. Éliante is overshadowed, however, by the more brilliant Célimène. The men all declare they have nothing to do all day and each swears to outstay the other so as to remain longer with Célimène. Alceste determines to be the last to leave.

A guard appears, however, to summon Alceste before the tribunal. Astonished, Alceste learns that news of his quarrel with Oronte had reached the authorities, who intend to prevent a possible duel. Loudly protesting that except for an order direct from the king nothing can make him praise the poetry of Oronte, Alceste is led away.

Arsinoé, an austere woman who makes a pretense of great virtue, calls on Célimène, taking the opportunity to warn Célimène that her conduct is creating a scandal and that her many suitors and her sharp tongue are hurting her reputation. Célimène speaks bitingly of Arsinoé's strait-laced character. Arsinoé thereupon decides to talk privately with Alceste, with whom she is half in love. She comforts him as best she can for being so unfortunate as to love Célimène, and compliments him on his plain dealings and forthright character.

Carried away by the intimacy of her talk, Arsinoé offers to do much for Alceste by speaking in his favor at court, but the two conclude that Alceste's love for Célimène, though unsuitable from almost every point of view, is a fast tie.

Éliante and Philinte are in the meantime discussing Alceste and his habit of antagonizing his friends with his frankness. Philinte tells her of Alceste's hearing before the tribunal, in which he had insisted that Oronte's verses are bad but that he had nothing more to say. Éliante and Philinte begin to discover a mutual liking. If Éliante ever loses her fondness for Alceste, Philinte intends to offer himself as her lover.

Alceste receives an unflattering letter, purporting to come from Célimène, which describes him in malicious terms. After much coy hesitation, Célimène admits that she had sent the letter and expressed surprise at Alceste's indignation. Other suitors appear, all much upset and each holding a letter. On comparing notes, they find that they have all been ridiculed and insulted.

Alceste has meanwhile made up his mind to ask Éliante to marry him, but reconsiders when he realizes that his proposal will seem to spring from a desire to avenge himself on Célimène. To the misanthrope there seems to be no solution except to go into exile and live a hermit's life.

When Célimène's suitors clamor for an explanation, she tells them that she had written the letters because she is tired of the niceties of polite conversation. For once she had decided to say what she really thought. This confession is shocking to the suitors, who consider frankness and rudeness unpardonable crimes. Hypocrisy, flattery, cajolery, extravagances—these are the marks of a gentle lady. Protesting and disdainful, they leave together, never to return.

Only Alceste remains, whereupon even the coquettish and malicious heart of Célimène is touched. When Alceste repeats his vows of fidelity and asks her once more to marry him, she almost consents. When, however, Alceste reveals that he wants them to go into exile and lead quiet, simple lives, she refuses. Célimène could never leave the false, frivolous society she loves.

Now completely the misanthrope, Alceste stalks away with the firm resolve to quit society forever and to become a hermit, far removed from the artificial sham of preciosity. Philinte and Éliante, more moderate in their views, decide that they will marry.

"The Story" by Phyllis Mael

Critical Evaluation:

Although Molière in *The Misanthrope* humorously depicts a frivolous and hypocritical society, Alceste's misperceptions about himself provide the play's most biting humor. Alceste sees himself as the only honest person in his social circle, although he, too, tries to be tactful sometimes, as when he repeatedly tells Oronte that he had not criticized Oronte's poem when he had so indirectly until disgust and frustration got the better of him. Even more strikingly, Alceste almost begs Célimène to tell him comforting lies rather than unpleasant truths. Arsinoé and Célimène, however, reveal with vicious honesty what they truly think of one another, even though each wraps her nastiness in assurances that she is criticizing only to help the other. By contrast, Alceste's more moderate friends, Philinte and Éliante, converse frankly, and in the process each finds a loving and trustworthy mate. Molière makes is clear that Alceste cannot recognize honesty when he sees it.

Moreover, for all his much-vaunted independence, Alceste does not take responsibility for his fate or even his day-to-day actions. He has no trouble describing what he dislikes, but he seems hard-pressed to define what would make him happy, much less do it for himself. He says and probably believes that Célimène's exclusive love, far away from the corrupt court, alone with him in his self-imposed exile, would satisfy him. He thus places responsibility for his happiness in the hands of another. In fact, he tends to react to external events instead of consciously choosing his own way. For these reasons, he sees himself as a victim of circumstances. In his view, everything that occurs—losing his lawsuit, antagonizing Oronte, bullying and alienating the woman he loves—happens to him and is the fault of someone else.

Finally, Alceste also considers himself a highly intelligent and astute critic and a perceptive observer. Certainly he can see the faults of everyone around him and, in truth, this society does deserve criticism. Nevertheless, he errs on two counts, the first being that he allows his emotions to precede his reasoned reaction (he feels, he speaks, then only does he, perhaps, think), and the second that his extremism blinds him to the value of good things right in front of him. While he believes he is offering clear-eyed criticism to a world desperately in need of reform, he is actually merely reacting emotionally to everything around him. His feelings lie so close to the surface that he cannot tell a trivial slight from a serious injury, so he responds with the same vehemence to both.

This last misperception provides the key to the play's power. The eighteenth century English writer Horace Walpole remarked that "This world is a comedy to those that think, a tragedy to those that feel." The clever Célimène basks in the admiration of her many suitors but seems not to care deeply about any of them. Philinte, a moderate, reasonable man, can see the attraction and humor in his society's artificiality and hypocritical flattery. He understands the spiteful wordplay as simply a game of wits; people who play by the rules do not get seriously hurt.

Although Alceste's mistaken perception of himself makes him a fool and a figure of fun to others, his pain is undeniably real. Even when he finally recognizes that his extreme views have forced him to abandon human society, he cannot change. In this, Alceste resembles some of Molière's other great characters, such as Harpagon in *The Miser* (1668). When the miser loses his treasure, he grieves for his "poor money" and weeps as others would for a dead child. His wildly excessive reaction strikes the audience as ridiculous, but he feels his loss as a tragedy. Such characters as Alceste and Harpagon experience the world at the level of pure feeling, which is what most people do when it comes to deeply cherished beliefs. At the same time that audiences laugh at the ludicrous excesses of the characters on stage, they recognize that those poor fools represent painful truths about themselves.

Many comedies aim simply to divert. By contrast, *The Misanthrope*, perhaps because it reflects Molière's own situation so closely, touches a raw nerve. By the time he wrote the play in 1666, he had seen his *Tartuffe* (1664) banned for its supposed attack on religion and *Don Juan* (1665) suddenly withdrawn from production; he himself was virtually excommunicated by the Church. Moreover, he and his friend, Jean Racine, the great playwright whose earliest works Molière himself had produced, had quarreled bitterly, never to be reconciled. His increasingly frequent work for King Louis XIV had allowed him to observe and experience firsthand the supercilious manners of the court. Perhaps most crucially, the middle-aged Molière and his beautiful young wife, actor Armande Béjart, had just separated, mostly because of her involvement with several young noblemen. Armande both acted the part and provided the model for the casually cruel Célimène, opposite a Molière playing Alceste. At the time Molière was writing the play, he and his wife saw each other only on stage.

Aspects of all these events and circumstances found their way into *The Misanthrope*. Like Molière, Alceste gets into serious legal, economic, and social trouble for speaking the truth as he sees it. He feels betrayed by old friends, beset by two-faced courtiers, and tormented by a frivolous woman he cannot help but love. Yet, miraculously, Molière was able to make his alter ego, Alceste, not a pitiful victim but a believable human being with a full complement of human faults and virtues. Even through his pain, Molière could see a man so like himself as both a hero and a fool. That clear vision makes *The Misanthrope* a comedy of manners that transcends its original time and place, for characters like Alceste remain timeless.

"Critical Evaluation" by Susan Wladaver-Morgan

Further Reading

Bloom, Harold, ed. *Molière*. Philadelphia: Chelsea House, 2002. Collection of critical essays, including two pieces examining the philosophical implications and the legal elements in *The Misanthrope*.

Gossman, Lionel. *Men and Masks: A Study of Molière*. Baltimore: Johns Hopkins University Press, 1963. Divides Molière's plays into two groups: those, like *The Misanthrope*, that reach a social stalemate and those, like *Les Fourberies de Scapin* (1671), that transcend that apparent dead end. Includes an entire chapter on *The Misanthrope*.

Guicharnaud, Jacques. *Molière: A Collection of Critical Essays*. Englewood Cliffs, N.J.: Prentice-Hall, 1964. Very useful collection that treats *The Misanthrope* in the context of Molière's other plays, of other theatrical and comedic traditions (including those of Charles Chaplin), and as a supremely experimental work.

Hawcroft, Michael. *Molière: Reasoning with Fools*. New York: Oxford University Press, 2007. Examines the characters in Molière's plays whom Hawcroft calls *raisonneurs*—the thoughtful, witty, and resourceful friends of the foolish protagonists. Analyzes the *raisonneur*'s role as friend and rival in *The Misanthrope*.

Knutson, Harold C. *The Triumph of Wit: Molière and Restoration Comedy*. Columbus: Ohio State University Press, 1988. Considers Molière's influence on Restoration comedy in England and concludes that, rather than excessive English borrowing from Molière, both sorts of comedy sprang from similar social circumstances.

McCarthy, Gerry. *The Theatres of Molière*. New York: Routledge, 2002. Places Molière's life and work within the context of the French theater of his time. Discusses the productions of some of his plays, including their actors, scenes, and costumes.

Mander, Gertrud. *Molière*. Translated by Diana Stone Peters. New York: Frederick Ungar, 1973. Includes descriptions and analyses of fourteen plays and a usefully detailed chronology of Molière's life.

Polsky, Zachary. *The Comic Machine, the Narrative Machine, and the Political Machine in the Works of Molière*. Lewiston, N.Y.: E. Mellen Press, 2003. Examines the nature of seventeenth century French comedy by analyzing the works of Molière. Discusses the moralism and political context of Molière's plays and describes the use of speech, voice, and body in their performance. Detailed analysis of *The Misanthrope*.

Scott, Virginia. *Molière: A Theatrical Life*. New York: Cambridge University Press, 2000. Chronicles Molière's life and provides an overview of his plays, placing them within the context of seventeenth century French theater.

Miscellanies

Author: Abraham Cowley (1618-1667)
First published: 1656; also published as *Poems*
Type of work: Poetry

The reputation of Abraham Cowley has been affected more than that of many other English poets by the vicissitudes of literary taste. His contemporaries considered him one of their most distinguished poets. John Milton ranked him with William Shakespeare and Edmund Spenser. John Dryden considered him a model, following Cowley's example in writing Pindaric odes. By the end of the eighteenth century, however, Cowley had fallen from favor, largely through the influential judgments rendered against him by Samuel Johnson in *The Lives of the Poets* (1779-1781).

The first poet to be immortalized in Johnson's collection, Cowley is considered too irregular and "specific" a poet to be ranked among the greatest practitioners of the genre. Johnson found Cowley's penchant for irregular versification and his tendency to reach for extraordinary and unusual comparisons disturbing. Johnson described the approach taken by Cowley—and his contemporaries John Donne, Andrew Marvell, Richard Crashaw, and George Herbert—in the term that became a touchstone for classifying many poets of the early seventeenth century: metaphysical. To Johnson, and to many readers of the eighteenth and nineteenth centuries, Cowley's verse displayed more virtuoso learning than it did deep appreciation for that which is important to all humankind.

The charges against Cowley may be accurate in fact, but perhaps erroneous in implication. The verse forms Cowley uses, modeled on Greek writers such as Anacreon and Pindar, are not those that readers in the eighteenth century valued; individual poems contain within them lines of various lengths, irregular rhyme schemes, and varied stanzaic patterns. In addition, Cowley was intensely interested in capturing some of the new learning—scientific discoveries—in his work, and many of his unorthodox comparisons are attempts to integrate scientific learning into his art.

Tastes change, however, and by the middle of the nineteenth century, poets were returning to the practice of irregular versification and stanza patterns; by the twentieth century, the introduction of free verse and other forms of poetry expanded the boundaries of the definition of the genre so that Cowley's works no longer seem so unusual. Readers who take the time to peruse the *Miscellanies* may discover that Cowley displays in his poetry the qualities of seriousness, learning, and imagination that characterize the best of the metaphysical poets.

Miscellanies is representative of Cowley's work. The volume was published shortly after the poet's return to England from France. Cowley, dispossessed of his fellowship at Cambridge University, had joined friends among the followers of Charles I at Oxford during the early years of the civil war. When many of the Royalists fled to France, Cowley was among them. In exile, he assisted the English queen in her correspondence with the king in England.

Miscellanies, according to Cowley's preface, represents his attempt to preserve in print all of his poetry that he considered worth keeping for posterity. His avowed motivation was that he intended to write no more verse, and he wished to publish his own edition, so that an edition containing spurious or inferior writings would not be published after his death, as had already happened in the cases of Shakespeare and Ben Jonson.

The *Miscellanies* consists of four parts. The first is a collection of poems on a variety of themes, some written when Cowley was quite young. The second section includes the poems Cowley had published in 1647 as *The Mistress: Or, Several Copies of Love Verses*, a series dealing with love in various aspects. The third part, which he labeled "Pindarique Odes," includes translations from Pindar and free imitations in English of that poet's work. The final portion of the volume contains the four books of the *Davideis* (1656), an unfinished epic poem, which Cowley completed.

In the first section, there are odes on wit, on the king's return from Scotland, on Prometheus, on the pleasures of wine over the pangs of love, and on friendship; there are also imitations, in English, of both Horace and Martial. A light but pleasant poem is "The Chronicle," an example of *vers de société* dealing with the experiences of a young man in love with a long series of young women. Of note also is a poem celebrating the publication of the first two books of Sir William Davenant's *Gondibert* (1651, unfinished). The best, certainly the sincerest, poems of the *Miscellanies* are those written on the deaths of persons the poet had known and respected in life. The most outstanding of these is "On the Death of Mr. William Hervey." Although the poem may seem to the twenty-first century reader extravagant in its tone, diction, and imagery, it compares favorably with the best elegiac poetry of the time. Other elegiac poems in the collection are those on Sir Henry Wotton; Mr. Jordan, a master at Westminster School; Sir Anthony Van Dyck, the painter; and Crashaw, the poet. Of little interest, other than for historical purposes, are some English paraphrases of the Greek lyric poet Anacreon.

Most critics have been less inclined to favor *The Mistress*. Like much of the love poetry of the earlier part of the seventeenth century, *The Mistress* is bound too closely by conventions in many respects. It supposedly deals with a courtship and the lady's reception of the suit over a period of three years. That Cowley actually loved a woman of higher social rank and courted her with this poetry is doubtful, for the suffering lover, the standoffish lady of higher degree, and extravagant protestations of love are typical of the love poetry of the time—usually mere convention. Cowley's unusual figures of speech, apparently influenced by Donne, were the target of critics through the late twentieth century. With the revived interest and renewed sympathy for the metaphysical poets and their techniques, however, Cowley's exercise of his exceptionally learned and fertile fancy was viewed less stringently. In this section, the poem "The Spring" represents Cowley at his best, while "Written in Juice of Lemmon" shows him at a poorer level of performance.

For approximately one century, the ode—particularly the Pindaric ode as it was established by Cowley—was a favorite verse form among English poets and their imitators. In the eighteenth century, however, Johnson, literary arbiter of the era, pronounced against it. Undoubtedly the freedom of meter introduced by Cowley and exercised in his "Pindarique Odes" was a decisive factor in the popularity of the form, for, as they were written by Cowley, the odes appear deceptively easy. Modern literary opinion has been negative toward Cowley's odes, declaring them too flat and imitative.

The last portion of the *Miscellanies* is taken up with the unfinished *Davideis*, four of the twelve books originally planned on the model of Vergil's *Aeneid* (c. 29-19 B.C.E.; English translation, 1553). Cowley's strong religious convictions led him to choose the figure of David, traditional ancestor of Jesus, as the hero for an epic poem. In these four books, he incorporated much of his learning, often in wide and only loosely connected digressions. Critics have argued the fitness of the subject; Cowley himself seems to have changed his mind about its suitability, since he left the work unfinished. What is more, as announced in the preface to the *Miscellanies*, Cowley wrote almost no poetry after publication of this volume.

Further Reading

Burrow, Colin, ed. *Metaphysical Poetry.* New York: Penguin, 2006. This anthology of metaphysical poetry, including selections from Cowley, features a brief but informative introduction that examines and defines "metaphysical poetry" for readers new to the style.

Cowley, Abraham. *Selected Poems.* Edited with an introduction and notes by David Hopkins and Tom Mason. Man-

chester, England: Carcanet Press, 1994. The critical introduction and annotations in this edition of Cowley's poems enhances the understanding of the poet's work.

Taaffe, James G. *Abraham Cowley.* New York: Twayne, 1972. A useful survey of Cowley's poetic career. Analyzes and evaluates his major works, including the *Miscellanies*. Includes helpful notes and an annotated bibliography.

Williamson, George. *Six Metaphysical Poets: A Reader's Guide.* New York: Farrar, Straus & Giroux, 1967. Reprint. Syracuse, N.Y.: Syracuse University Press, 2001. Offers a detailed examination of a number of Cowley's poems from the 1656 collection as expressions of Metaphysical wit, a concept that Williamson uses to connect Cowley's poetry to that of John Donne and other major poets active between the Renaissance and the neoclassical period.

Zwicker, Steven N., ed. *The Cambridge Companion to English Literature, 1650-1740.* New York: Cambridge University Press, 1998. Cowley's work is discussed in two of this book's essays: "Lyric Forms" by Joshua Scodel and "Classical Texts: Translations and Transformations" by Paul Hammond.

The Miser

Author: Molière (1622-1673)
First produced: L'Avare, 1668; first published, 1669 (English translation, 1672)
Type of work: Drama
Type of plot: Comedy
Time of plot: Seventeenth century
Locale: Paris

Principal characters:
HARPAGON, a miser
CLÉANTE, his son
ÉLISE, his daughter
VALÈRE, Élise's lover
MARIANE, a young woman loved by Cléante and Harpagon
ANSELME, the father of Valère and Mariane

The Story:

Valère, the steward of Harpagon's house, is in love with his employer's daughter, Élise. Valère is sure that he is of a good family, but until he can find his relatives he has little hope that Harpagon will give his consent to a marriage between his daughter and his steward. Harpagon is a miser of such great avarice and stinginess that he loves nothing but money. He lives in constant fear that someone will rob him of the large sum he has buried in his garden. Valère knows that his only hope lies in gaining Harpagon's affection by flattering the old man shamelessly.

Harpagon's son, Cléante, is also in love. The object of his love is Mariane, a poor girl who lives with her wid-

owed mother. Cléante's love is as hopeless as that between his sister, Élise, and Valère. Since Mariane has no money, Harpagon will not consent to a marriage, and Cléante keeps his love for the girl from his father. What he does not know is that his father has seen Mariane and wants her for himself. He has been a widower for many years, and the young girl's beauty makes him desire her. He must first, however, secure a dowry for her; his miserliness is stronger than his love.

Élise learns from her father that, against her wishes, she is to be married to Anselme, a wealthy man fifty years old. The fact that Anselme will take his daughter without a dowry is too good a proposition for Harpagon to miss. Élise appeals to

Valère for help. The clever lad pretends to agree with her father while he whispers to her to take heart and trust him to prevent the marriage. If all else fails, he and Élise will flee from the house and be married without her father's consent.

Cléante is so determined to marry Mariane that he arranges through an agent to borrow from a moneylender. Never is a higher rate of interest demanded. Cléante is to pay twenty-five percent interest and to take part of the loan in goods which he must sell. With no choice but to agree, he meets the moneylender. He is horrified to find that the moneylender is his own father. Harpagon is equally angry that his son should be such a spendthrift that he must borrow money at such high rates. The two part without completing the loan, Cléante to try to arrange a loan elsewhere and Harpagon to try to secure a dowry for Mariane.

Harpagon arranges a party in honor of Mariane, whom he has not as yet met. He cautions the servants to be very sparing with the food and drink, as it is an injustice to one's guests to stuff them full. Although Mariane finds Harpagon repulsive, she is bound by her poor mother's wish that she take a rich husband. When Mariane learns that Harpagon is the father of her beloved Cléante, she detests him more than ever. Cléante gets a small measure of revenge on his father by taking a huge diamond ring from his father's finger and presenting it to Mariane after telling her that Harpagon wants her to have it. The miser is helpless; he cannot get it back unless he admits his stinginess to the girl he wishes to marry.

After Harpagon tricks Cléante into admitting his love for Mariane, the old man vows more than ever to have her for himself. Cléante curses his father and swears that the old miser will never have the girl, and Harpagon disinherits his son. Then a servant rushes in with the news that Harpagon has been robbed of his buried money. All else is forgotten by the miser as he cries out for help. He suspects everyone of stealing the money, even himself. He will have the whole household hanged, and if the money is not found he will hang himself.

A jealous servant tells Harpagon that Valère took the money. Harpagon orders the magistrate to arrest the steward, even though there is no true evidence against him. Anselme arrives in time to hear Valère shouting to Harpagon that he will marry Élise in spite of the miser's objections. Anselme says that he will bow out of the courtship, for he has no desire to take the girl against her wishes. Harpagon is furious. Where else can he find a wealthy son-in-law, particularly one who will demand no dowry? He presses the magistrate to arrest Valère, but that young man stops the official with the announcement that he is the son of Don Thomas d'Alburci, a nobleman of Naples who was forced to flee his native city.

Valère says that he and a manservant survived a shipwreck and made their way to Paris. He produced the family seals to prove his identity. Then Mariane rushes to him and tells him that she is his sister, that she and her mother had also been saved from the wreck and had thought the rest of the family dead. There is more joy to come for the reunited brother and sister. Anselme is their father, the former Don Thomas d'Alburci, who had also been saved. Thinking his loved ones dead, he had settled in Paris under the name of Anselme.

These revelations make no difference to Harpagon. He still insists that Valère return his money. While he is ranting, Cléante enters the room and says that he has found the money and will return it to his father as soon as his father gives him permission to marry Mariane. This is no hard choice for Harpagon to make. He will gladly exchange Mariane, even his own children, for his money. Anselme also gives his consent to the marriage. Harpagon insists that Anselme pay for both weddings. Anselme is willing to do this, and the happy couples and Anselme leave to find Mariane and Valère's mother. Harpagon has an errand of his own. He goes to examine his cashbox, the true love of his mean and stingy nature.

Critical Evaluation:

Unlike his two greatest contemporaries Pierre Corneille and Jean Racine, who wrote everything from tragedies based on Greek and Roman history to scathing contemporary satires, Molière concentrated primarily on comedies of manners, particularly those dealing with the urban middle class. The scene is frequently a comfortable bourgeois home, and the plot usually revolves around tensions between husbands and wives or parents and children—tensions that arise because at least one member of the family has developed some sort of obsession that disturbs family harmony. It was Molière's genius to weave dark threads of tragedy into his comic vision of this comfortable life, and he never did so more effectively than in *The Miser* and in *The Misanthrope* (1666).

Like *The Misanthrope*, *The Miser* focuses on a monomaniac, but while Alceste the misanthrope directs all his attention outward onto the faults of the courtly society that surrounds him, Harpagon the miser could probably live with no social contact, as long as he has his treasure to console him. Though he seeks a new young wife, his motives for doing so remain vague. He definitely hopes to secure a dowry from her family, but he probably wishes to acquire cheap domestic labor; he may also want to beget a new heir, the better to disinherit his two existing children whom he holds in contempt. After all, he curses his only son, and he tells his daughter he would not care if she had drowned. By contrast, he constantly breaks off conversations to go and check his beloved money, and, when it is stolen, he becomes so distraught that he stands ready to kill himself.

Harpagon's monomania affects everyone around him, for, unlike Alceste, he holds considerable power as a father and as a wealthy man. This combination of obsession and power makes Harpagon an irrational tyrant, who can do real damage to the lives of those who should be dearest to him. His single-minded focus on money and his unwillingness to hear any opinion that contradicts his own distort every social interaction in which he participates. His children have no choice but to rebel against him, unless they want to be treated as possessions, not as people. Moreover, as Valère notes early on, the only way to approach Harpagon is through flattery and indirection; other characters, including Frosine and Cléante, soon follow suit. In the presence of such an egocentric fanatic, nearly all the characters have to speak in code, with one message for Harpagon and another hidden message for each other. When Harpagon's faithful old servant dares to tell the truth, he is beaten for his effort. Simply to have the chance to communicate with Harpagon, everyone else must become something of a liar. Harpagon's obsession thus forces hypocrisy on those around him, and even vows of love may become suspect.

Structurally, *The Miser* derives from a classical model, *The Pot of Gold* (c. 195), a farce by the Roman playwright Plautus. That work focused on a poor man who receives a pot of money and becomes terrified of losing it; he finally gives it away so he no longer has to think about it. Molière clearly took this theme in a different direction. Like most farces, however, Molière's work revels in exaggeration, mistaken identities (Valère and Mariane are actually brother and sister, and Anselme, the rival for Élise's hand, is their long-lost father), coincidences (Harpagon is unwittingly the usurious lender to his desperate son), and a massively improbable ending that reunites all the lovers with their loves, including Harpagon with his money box. Molière heightens the contrasts by neatly pairing and balancing all the characters: fathers (one stingy, one munificent), brothers and sisters (extravagant Cléante and cautious Valère, feisty Élise and timid Mariane), and servants and go-betweens. Perhaps to emphasize the relationship between love and money, he cleverly uses economic words in the context of personal and romantic relationships. Love and money may appear to be opposites, he implies, but people need a modicum of both for a happy life, and all the characters except Harpagon realize it.

Molière also experiments with comedy as a form. For instance, at a time when most five-act comedies were written in verse, he wrote *The Miser* in prose. Most strikingly, he flouts the conventions of the theater by having Harpagon break through "the fourth wall" in his great tirade in the fourth act. Harpagon virtually explodes beyond the stage in his anguish, searching the whole audience for the thief and reacting frantically to the spectators' mocking laughter. He weeps for his "poor money," as if it were a living being. In this way, he directly confronts the audience with an appalling vision of unmitigated obsession. Though the audience members laugh at his extreme ideas, they also recognize a man beside himself with grief and panic, a man who cannot tell where he himself ends and his possessions begin. In other words, they see a portrait of madness.

At that point, the play comes close to veering into tragedy, which it would become were the audience to regard events from Harpagon's point of view. After all, from his perspective, he is an old man whose ungrateful children defy him at every turn, whose only security and joy consist of gold that unscrupulous people are forever trying to steal. In his own eyes, he might as well be King Lear. That is why Molière instead concludes the play with a family reunited, lovers requited, and a generous and grateful father lavishing money to obtain happiness for everyone. In spite of the sugar coating, however, a serious, even bitter message remains at the heart of the play: Harpagon has learned nothing from his experiences. He still cares for no one and nothing except his money. The distorting evils of greed and obsession remain alive and well, in the world as in the play. Thus, although *The Miser* works as a cheerful comedy, this brilliant creation never loses its disturbing power.

"Critical Evaluation" by Susan Wladaver-Morgan

Further Reading

Bermel, Albert. *Molière's Theatrical Bounty: A New View of the Plays*. Carbondale: Southern Illinois University Press, 1990. Provides original interpretations of the plays, partly designed to help actors think about the characters' motivations, such as why Harpagon seeks a new wife. Considers *The Miser* a rich and complicated work.

Hall, H. Gaston. *Comedy in Context: Essays on Molière*. Jackson: University Press of Mississippi, 1984. Analyzes Molière's work thematically. Sees Molière's use of comic images as implying both laughter and moral judgment, using the example of Harpagon's soliloquy in act 4 of *The Miser*.

Koppisch, Michael S. *Rivalry and the Disruption of Order in Molière's Theater*. Madison, N.J.: Fairleigh Dickinson University Press, 2004. Argues that Molière's plays involve rivalries that eventually collapse the characters' differences. Chapter 7 analyzes love, greed, and rivalry in *The Miser.*

McCarthy, Gerry. *The Theatres of Molière.* New York: Routledge, 2002. Places Molière's life and work within the context of the French theater of his time. Discusses the productions of some of his plays, including their actors, scenes, and costumes.

Mander, Gertrud. *Molière.* Translated by Diana Stone Peters. New York: Frederick Ungar, 1973. Discusses *The Miser,* particularly in terms of its focus on bourgeois family life, seeing the conflicts there as the most bitter in Molière's works. Sets forth the opinion that Harpagon's avarice makes him a monster, forcing others into unnatural or uncharacteristic actions, but he is not a tragic figure.

Polsky, Zachary. *The Comic Machine, the Narrative Machine, and the Political Machine in the Works of Molière.* Lewiston, N.Y.: E. Mellen Press, 2003. Examines the nature of seventeenth century French comedy by analyzing the works of Molière. Discusses the moralism and political context of Molière's plays and describes the use of speech, voice, and body in their performance.

Scott, Virginia. *Molière: A Theatrical Life.* New York: Cambridge University Press, 2000. Chronicles Molière's life and provides an overview of his plays, placing them within the context of seventeenth century French theater.

Miss Julie

Author: August Strindberg (1849-1912)
First produced: Fröken Julie, 1889; first published, 1888 (English translation, 1912)
Type of work: Drama
Type of plot: Naturalism
Time of plot: Nineteenth century
Locale: A country estate in Sweden

Principal characters:
MISS JULIE, a headstrong young woman
JEAN, Miss Julie's lover and her father's valet
CHRISTINE, a cook and Jean's fiancé

The Story:

Miss Julie's broken engagement to the county attorney was quite a scandal to the servants in the house. Miss Julie, the twenty-five-year-old daughter of a count, had made her fiancé actually jump over her horsewhip several times, giving him a cut with the whip each time. He finally put an end to such conduct and the engagement by snatching the whip, breaking it, and striding away from the manor.

A few weeks later, on Midsummer Eve, a great holiday observed throughout the Swedish countryside, Miss Julie enters into the festivities and dances with the servants. She dares to do so because her father has gone to the city and is not expected to return. Although the servants dislike her joining in their fun, they are powerless to stop her or to let her know of their dislike, for she is their mistress. Her father's valet, Jean, leaves the festivities after dancing once with Miss Julie. He retreats to the kitchen, where his fiancé, Christine the cook, gives him a little supper.

Miss Julie gives Jean no peace, however. She comes into the kitchen and drags him out to dance with her again, even though she knows that he had promised to dance with Christine. After dancing once more with Miss Julie, Jean again escapes to the kitchen. He is afraid that Christine will be angry, but she assures him that she does not blame him for what has happened. Just then, Miss Julie returns to the kitchen and demands that Jean change from his livery into a tailcoat and dance with her again. While he is changing, Christine falls asleep in a chair. When he returns, Miss Julie asks him to get her something to drink. Jean gets a bottle of beer for her and another for himself.

After finishing the beer, Miss Julie teases Christine by trying to wake her up. Christine, moving as if asleep, goes to her own room. After she leaves, Miss Julie begins to ogle Jean, who warns his mistress that it is dangerous to flirt with a man as young as he. Miss Julie pays no attention to him. Jean, falling in with her mood, tells about his early life as a cotter's child and how, even as a small child, he had been in love with his young mistress. They talk until the other servants come to look for Jean. Rather than expose themselves to the comments and the scandal of having drunk together in the kitchen, Jean and Miss Julie go into Jean's room. They are there a long time, for the servants stay in the kitchen and dance and sing. During that time Miss Julie gives herself to Jean.

After the servants leave, neither Jean nor Miss Julie knows just what to do. They agree only that it is best for them to leave the country. Jean suggests that they go to Como, Italy, to open a hotel. Miss Julie asks Jean to take her in his arms again. He refuses, saying that he cannot make love to her a second time in her father's house, where she is the mistress and he the servant. When she reminds him of the extravagant language he used a little while before, he tells her the time has come to be practical.

To comfort her, Jean offers Miss Julie a drink of wine from a bottle he had taken from the count's cellar. She sees whose it is and accuses him of stealing. An argument follows, with bitter words on both sides. When they had both calmed a little, Miss Julie tries to tell Jean how she had come to be who she is. She says that she had been brought up to do a man's work by her mother, who hated to be a slave to men. She tells also how her mother had revenged herself on Miss Julie's father by taking a brick manufacturer as her lover and how her mother's lover had stolen great sums of money from the count. From her mother, says Miss Julie, she had learned to hate men and to wish to make them her slaves. He understands then why she had treated her fiancé as she had. Miss Julie ends her recital with the recommendation that she and Jean go abroad at once. To her suggestion that when they cease enjoying one another they should commit suicide, Jean, far more practical, advises her to go away by herself. Miss Julie, helpless in the urgency of the situation, does as Jean suggests and prepares to leave.

While Miss Julie is upstairs dressing, Christine comes into the kitchen. Seeing the glasses on the table, she knows that Miss Julie and Jean had been drinking together. She guesses the rest, and Jean admits what had happened. Christine tells Jean that fine people do not behave that way with their servants. Christine urges him to go away with her as soon as possible. She loves him and does not intend to lose him to her mistress.

Christine persuades Jean to get ready to go to church with her, for it is Sunday morning. When they are both dressed, Miss Julie and Jean meet in the kitchen. Julie carries a bird cage. When Jean says she cannot take her pet finch with her, she orders him to kill it. While watching her bird die, Miss Julie's love turns to hate. She despises Jean for killing in cold blood the pet she has loved so much, and she rages at him and tells him that her father would soon return. She would tell him what had happened. Miss Julie declares that she now wishes to die.

When Christine appears, ready for church, she tells Miss Julie bluntly that she will not allow her mistress to run off with the man who has promised to become her husband. Miss Julie tries to persuade Christine to go with them to Como. While the two women talk, Jean leaves the room. He returns a few moments later with his razor. Christine, refusing to join in the flight, leaves for church after saying that she has spoken to the men at the stables about not letting anyone have horses until the count's return.

After Christine departs, Miss Julie asks Jean what he would do if he were in her position. He indicates the razor in his hand. At that moment the valet's bell rings. The count has returned. Jean, answering the bell, receives instructions to have boots and coffee ready in half an hour. His master's voice reduces Jean once again to the mental attitude of a servant. Miss Julie, almost in a state of trance, is filled with ecstasy at the thought of freeing herself by committing suicide. She takes the razor Jean had given her and leaves the kitchen with it in her hand.

Critical Evaluation:

August Strindberg wrote the naturalistic tragedy *Miss Julie*, which is recognized as one of the playwright's greatest, for André Antoine's avant-garde Theatre Libre in Paris. Strindberg's power, complexity, and originality of technique and vision have led such later writers as Eugene O'Neill to consider him the most progressive and influential playwright of his time.

Strindberg's achievements are all the more remarkable in view of the squalor of his upbringing. Born in Stockholm into a bankrupt family, one of twelve children, Strindberg was neglected even by his own mother. After her death when he was thirteen years old, his new stepmother added harshness to neglect. This early experience developed in him a strong, lifelong dislike of conventional authority figures. In his writing this is evident in his rejection of traditional stage techniques and traditional societal beliefs and conventions.

Strindberg's private life was equally unconventional. Each of his three marriages was characterized by an intense component of love-hate dichotomy. Strindberg was prosecuted for blasphemy upon the publication of his collection of short stories *Giftas II* (1886; *Married*, 1913). The combination of these personal and public tensions led to an unstable psychological state marked by spells of insanity and delusions of persecution. Between the years 1894 and 1896, the increasing violence of his hallucinations led to the crisis known as his Inferno period. His inner torment during this crisis gave rise to a shift in technique from the psychological naturalism of *Fadren* (pr., pb. 1887; *The Father*, 1899) and *Miss Julie* to symbolist and expressionist departures from external reality in the imaginative brilliance of dramas such as *Ett drömspel* (pb. 1902, pr. 1907; *A Dream Play*, 1912) and *Spöksonaten* (pb. 1907, pr. 1908; *The Ghost Sonata*, 1916).

While in Paris in 1883, Strindberg became familiar with the doctrine of literary naturalism espoused by Émile Zola, and he successfully applied this approach to drama. He even sent a copy of his first naturalistic play to Zola for comments. In a long foreword to *Miss Julie*, Strindberg explains his use of naturalistic doctrine in the play, but his definitive formulation of dramatic naturalism is found in an 1889 essay, in which he suggests that the true essence of naturalism is a presentation of the polarization of the basic conflicts of life—love and hate, life and death—through the Darwinian principle of survival of the fittest found in both personal relationships and class conflicts. Strindberg's knowledge of psychology contributes to the creation of his powerful authentic dramas, which remain as moving today as when they first appeared.

Strindberg introduced a number of important innovations in writing and production in which he was ahead of his time. His dialogue, like that of Anton Chekhov, is meant to reproduce the pauses, wanderings, and flatness of everyday speech. *Miss Julie* is cast in one uninterrupted act so as to capitalize on the emotional involvement of the audience. Strindberg also calls for music, mime, ballet, and improvisation to make use of the full range of actors' talents. He calls for new lighting techniques to illuminate faces better, allowing them to use less makeup and to appear more natural. Finally, he asks for a return to a smaller theater for a more intimate relationship between the stage and the audience.

Julie's complex motivations are ample evidence of Strindberg's art. She is presented as a product of both heredity and environment. Her mother was born into a lower-class family, and she despised conventional social roles for women. She reared Julie as a boy, creating in her a fascination with animals and a loathing for the opposite gender that leads to self-disgust when she becomes sexually attracted to men. Her mother suffered from strange attacks of mental instability that seem to have been passed on to Julie. There is also the strong element of chance: Julie's father's absence frees Julie and Jean from customary restraints. It is chance that leads the couple into the locked room. The sensual excitement of the Midsummer's Eve celebration contributes to the seduction and to Julie's final tragedy.

Jean's motivation, although less complex than Julie's, is also conditioned by his environment, his biological drives, his psychological desires, and his social aspirations. At the same time that he can despise the weaknesses of the old aristocrats, he finds himself unable to break his social conditioning. Only in the count's absence could Jean have brought himself to seduce Julie.

An added complication is the class conflict in which the decaying aristocracy, which Julie represents, must, by law of nature, be destroyed to make way for a stronger lower class that is more fit for the new world. Some things of value, such as aesthetic sensitivity and a sense of personal honor, are lost; these are the qualities that break Julie and her father, whereas brutality and lack of scruples ensure Jean's final triumph. He survives because of his animal virility, his keen physical senses, and his strength of purpose. Religion has been discarded by the aristocracy as meaningless, and it is used by the working class to ensure their innocence. Love is seen as no more than a romantic illusion created by the aristocracy to be used, as Julie uses it, to explain animal instincts in an acceptable manner. Jean, the pragmatic realist from the lower class, has no such need for excuses for sexual release.

To underline his themes and characterizations, Strindberg uses recurring animal imagery that links human beings with their animal nature, a technique that may be seen in the dreams of Julie and Jean, the foreshadowing effect of Julie's mother, Julie's attitude toward her dog, and the brutal death of Julie's beautiful caged bird.

Miss Julie is a naturalistic tragedy that follows the Aristotelian concepts of pity, fear, and catharsis. Pity is aroused in the viewer by the characters' inherent weaknesses and the social class structure they inhabit; fear is aroused when they realize that the same fate could overcome any of them; catharsis results when they realize that the old, decaying order must give way to the newer and stronger order if life is to continue.

"Critical Evaluation" by Ann E. Reynolds

Further Reading

House, Poul, Sven Hakon Rossel, and Göran Stockenström, eds. *August Strindberg and the Other: New Critical Approaches*. New York: Rodopi, 2002. Collection of papers delivered at a 2000 conference, "Strindberg at the Millennium—Strindberg and the Other," interpreting the motifs of the other and otherness in Strindberg's work.

Johnson, Walter. "Master Dramatist." In *August Strindberg*. Boston: Twayne, 1976. Discusses the plays Strindberg wrote from 1882 to 1894. Asserts that in *Miss Julie*, Strindberg achieves the goals of naturalistic drama that he outlined in the play's preface.

Robinson, Michael, ed. *The Cambridge Companion to August Strindberg*. New York: Cambridge University Press,

2009. Essays analyze Strindberg's work, placing it within the context of his life and times. Ross Shideler's essay "*Miss Julie*, Naturalism, the Battle of the Brains, and Sexual Desire" is a helpful discussion of *Miss Julie*. Includes a bibliography and an index.

Shideler, Ross. "Strindberg's Struggle." In *Questioning the Father: From Darwin to Zola, Ibsen, Strindberg, and Hardy*. Stanford, Calif.: Stanford University Press, 1999. Examines how Strindberg adapted late nineteenth century Darwinian ideas and the ideas of the women's rights movement to create family dramas and novels in which he questions the role of the father. Argues *Miss Julie* is one of three Strindberg plays that best exemplify the confrontation between a Darwinian centered "bioworld" and the Scandinavian patriarchal family.

Sprinchorn, Evert. *Strindberg as Dramatist*. New Haven, Conn.: Yale University Press, 1982. Puts Strindberg's drama within the context of his life, psychology, and the dramaturgy of his time. Argues that *Miss Julie* and *The Father* move beyond naturalism into tragedy; compares *Miss Julie* with Jean Genet's *The Maids* (1947).

Törnqvist, Egil. "Speech Situations in *Fröken Julie/Miss Julie*." In *Strindbergian Drama: Themes and Structure*. Atlantic Highlands, N.J.: Humanities Press, 1982. Analyzes the dialogue in the play, dividing it into duologues, triologues, and monologues, and pointing out the significance of each.

Valency, Maurice. "Strindberg." In *The Flower and the Castle: An Introduction to Modern Drama*. 1963. Reprint. New York: Schocken Books, 1982. Sees in Strindberg's works a continuous spiritual autobiography styled in the art of the unbalanced and the excessive. In *Miss Julie*, Strindberg identifies himself with Jean and characterizes Julie as an iconic femme fatale.

Miss Lonelyhearts

Author: Nathanael West (1903-1940)
First published: 1933
Type of work: Novel
Type of plot: Social satire
Time of plot: Late 1920's
Locale: New York City

Principal characters:
MISS LONELYHEARTS, an advice-to-the-lovelorn columnist
BETTY, his girlfriend
WILLIE SHRIKE, his boss, the paper's features editor
MARY SHRIKE, the boss's wife
PETER DOYLE, a "cripple"
FAY DOYLE, his wife

The Story:

Miss Lonelyhearts finds it difficult to write his agony column for the *New York Post-Dispatch*: The letters are not funny, and there is no humor in desperate people begging for help. "Sick-of-it-all," for example, with seven children in twelve years, is pregnant again and ill, but being a Catholic, she cannot consider an abortion and her husband will not leave her alone. "Desperate," a sixteen-year-old girl, a good dancer with a good figure and pretty clothes, would like boyfriends, but cries all day at the big hole in the middle of her face. She has no nose; should she commit suicide? "Harold S.," fifteen years old, writes that his sister, Gracie, age thirteen and deaf, unable to speak, and not very smart, had something dirty done to her by a man, but Harold cannot tell their mother that Gracie is going to have a baby because her mother would beat her up. Willie Shrike, the paper's features editor and Miss Lonelyhearts's tormentor, is no help at all: Instead of the same old stuff, he says, Miss Lonelyhearts ought to give his readers something new and hopeful.

At Delehanty's speakeasy, where Miss Lonelyhearts goes to escape his problems, his boss still belabors him about brooding and tells him to forget the Crucifixion and remember the Renaissance. Meanwhile, Shrike is trying to seduce Miss Farkis, a long-legged woman with a childish face. He also taunts the columnist by talking of a Western sect that prays for a condemned slayer with an adding machine, numbers being their idea of the universal language.

Miss Lonelyhearts's bedroom walls are bare except for an ivory Christ nailed with large spikes, and the religious figure combines in a dream with a snake whose scales are tiny mirrors in which the dead world takes on a semblance of life. First, he is a magician who cannot move his audience by tricks or prayer; then he is on a drunken college spree with two friends. Their attempt to sacrifice a lamb before barbecuing it, with Miss Lonelyhearts chanting the name of Christ, miscarries when the blade breaks on the altar, and the lamb slips out of their bloodied hands. When the others refuse to go back to put the lamb out of its misery, Miss Lonelyhearts returns and crushes its head with a stone.

One day, as he tries to put things in order, everything goes against him; pencils break, buttons roll under the bed, shades refuse to stay down, and instead of order, he finds chaos. Miss Lonelyhearts remembers Betty, who could bring order into his world, and he goes to her apartment. Yet he realizes that her world is not the world of, and could never include, the readers of his column; his confusion is significant, and her order is not. Irritated and fidgety, he can neither talk to her nor caress her, although two months before she had agreed to marry him. When she asks if he is sick, he can only shout at her; when she says she loves him, he can only reply that he loves her and her smiling through tears. Sobbing that she was feeling swell before he came over and now feels lousy, she asks him to go away.

At Delehanty's, he listens to talk of raping a woman writer, and as he gets drunker, he hears friends mock Shrike kidding him; but whiskey makes him feel good and dreams of childhood make the world dance. Stepping back from the bar, he collides with a man holding a beer. The man punches him in the mouth. With a lump on his head, a loose tooth, and a cut lip, Miss Lonelyhearts walks in the fresh air with Ned Gates.

In a comfort station, they meet an old man with a terrible cough and no overcoat, who carries a cane and wears gloves because he detests red hands. They force him to go to an Italian wine cellar. There they tell him they are sex researchers Havelock Ellis and Richard von Krafft-Ebing and insultingly mock him with taunts of homosexuality. When Miss Lonelyhearts twists his arm—imagining it is the arm of Desperate, Broken-hearted, or Sick-of-it-all—the old man screams, and someone hits the columnist with a chair.

Instead of going to the office after Shrike phones him, Miss Lonelyhearts goes to the speakeasy; he knows Shrike finds him too perfect a target for his jokes to fire him. Needing a woman, Miss Lonelyhearts phones Mary, Shrike's wife, whom he has never seduced. Mary hates her husband and uses Miss Lonelyhearts to arouse Shrike. At a nightclub, in a cab, and at Mary's apartment door, Miss Lonelyhearts tries to talk Mary into sleeping with him; Shrike opens the door, however, ending that scheme.

The next day, Miss Lonelyhearts receives a letter from Fay Doyle, unhappily married to a "cripple," asking for an appointment. Although Miss Lonelyhearts first throws the letter away, he retrieves it, phones her to meet him in the park,

and takes her to his apartment. In the intervals of making love, she tells of her married life and her child Lucy, whose father is not her husband, Peter Doyle.

Physically sick and exhausted in his room for three days, he is comforted by Betty, who tries to get him to quit his Lonelyhearts job. He says he had taken the job as a joke, but after several months, the joke escaped him. Pleas for help had made him examine his own values, and he became the victim of the joke. While Betty suggests that he go to the country with her, Shrike breaks into the room and taunts him to escape to the South Seas or with hedonism, art, suicide, or drugs. Shrike ends by dictating an imaginary letter from the columnist to Christ.

After he has been ill for a week, Betty finally persuades Miss Lonelyhearts to go with her to her aunt's Connecticut farm. They camp in the kitchen, sit near a pond to watch frogs and deer, and sleep on a mattress on the floor. They walk in the woods, swim in the nude, and make love in the grass. After several days, they return to the city. Miss Lonelyhearts knows that Betty has failed to cure him; he cannot forget the letters. He vows to attempt to be humble. In the office, he finds a lengthy letter from Broad Shoulders, telling of her troubles with a crazy husband.

About a week later, while Shrike is pulling the same familiar jokes at Delehanty's, the bartender introduces Miss Lonelyhearts to Peter; Fay wants the columnist to have dinner at the Doyle's. After labored conversation, Peter gives him a letter about his problems: He must pull his leg up and down stairs for $22.50 a week; his wife talks money, money, money; a doctor prescribes six months' rest.

As they leave the speakeasy, very drunk, to go to the Doyle house, the cripple curses his wife and his foot. Miss Lonelyhearts is happy in his humility. When Fay tries to seduce the columnist, he fails to respond. Meanwhile, her husband calls himself a pimp and, at his wife's request, goes out to get gin. Failing to find a message to show Fay that her husband loves her, and disgusted by her obscene attempts to get him to sleep with her, Miss Lonelyhearts strikes her again and again before he runs out of the house.

Following three days of illness, Miss Lonelyhearts is awakened by five people, including Shrike and his wife, all drunk, who want to take him to a party at the editor's home. Betty is one of the group. Shrike wants to play a game in which he distributes letters from Miss Lonelyhearts's office file and makes taunting comments. When the columnist can stand it no longer, he follows Betty out, dropping unread the letter given him, which Shrike reads to the crowd. It is from Peter, accusing Miss Lonelyhearts of trying to rape his wife.

Miss Lonelyhearts tells Betty he has quit the Lonelyhearts job and is going to look for work in an advertising agency. She tells him she is going to have a baby. Although he persuades her to marry him and have the baby instead of an abortion, by the time he leaves her, he does not feel guilty. In fact, he does not feel, because his feeling, conscience, sense of reality, and self-knowledge are like a rock.

The next morning, Miss Lonelyhearts is in a fever. The Christ on his wall is shining, but everything else in the room seems dead. When the bell rings and he sees Peter coming up the stairs, he imagines the cripple has come to have Miss Lonelyhearts perform a miracle and make him whole. Mis-understanding the outspread arms, Peter puts his hand in a newspaper-wrapped package as Betty comes to the door. In the struggle, the gun Peter carries goes off and Miss Lonelyhearts falls, dragging the cripple with him.

Critical Evaluation:

Nathanael West is a tragic figure of American letters. He published four novels before his death in an automobile accident in 1940, and these novels did not meet with much acclaim during his lifetime. Subsequently, however, they were hailed as works of genius. West's vision of America is one of darkly comic absurdity. His early death robbed American letters of a great talent.

West's accidental death by modern, mechanical means has eerie echoes of his fiction. In his books, the modern world wrecks its inhabitants with a chilling indifference. Traditional orders of society have broken down, norms have vanished. West was criticized by his contemporaries; it was said that his books suffered for want of some "normal" characters to round out the absurd world West's fictions present. In West's fiction, a Murphy's law of human fate rules the roost.

West had a cartoonists' eye that exaggerated human tics, flaws, and failings. His writing is brilliantly focused and his vision intense. West appears to have been a prophet of post-World War II anomie and terror. No doubt this is why he was not appreciated until the 1950's.

West depicts a world made absurd by the disappearance of traditional orders. The paradox of reading West is that one has so much fun while dealing with insoluble miseries and repulsive sufferings. The letters that Miss Lonelyhearts receives are, amazingly, funny. They are also repulsive, depressing, and profound. West thus creates great complexity of feeling in a simple, almost cartoonlike, narrative. His characters, for example, have been termed two-dimensional by detractors. His characters are sketches of human beings, distorted by simplification, and his technique highlights exactly those qualities that his tragicomedies require. His characters show character as fate; they are trapped in being ex-

actly who they are. They remind readers of the figures of Greek drama, of myth, of biblical personages. West brings ancient concepts of fate into a modern context. Readers read about insoluble human misery, seeing it through the eyes of the compassionate Miss Lonelyhearts, yet at the same time are being made to laugh at it. This keeps readers uneasily aware of the absurdity of human life.

Additionally, *Miss Lonelyhearts* critiques capitalism. Much of the book's cruelty has to do with what the worker suffers. West's critique is also larger, less time-bound than that. It is the human condition readers are being offered, not simply the human condition under late-industrial capitalism.

An indication that the novel is more than a critique of capitalism is the theme of Miss Lonelyhearts's identification with Jesus Christ. The theme of the novel, in a nutshell, is this: Christ will always be killed by those he tries to save. He cannot help himself, any more than they. West sees that it is the very nature of Christ, to be killed for attempting to be the Savior. Miss Lonelyhearts may be suffering delusions of grandeur in identifying with Christ—but then, the book implicitly asks, what was Christ himself suffering from? Miss Lonelyhearts, like Christ, has another name. West is saying that, in his world, one's role is everything—what the workplace does not require, a person does not need. Other names in the book merit examination. Shrike, who tears savagely at Miss Lonelyhearts's idealism, bears the name of a species of fierce bird, and has no other life. Miss Lonelyhearts plays Christ or is Christ, and meets with a similar end.

The alternatives to playing Christ are likewise fatal. Who would want to be Shrike, the soulless mocker? Apart from Miss Lonelyhearts, there is no one with whom readers can identify. Identification itself, as an act, appears to be a mistake in the novel, yet it appears to be an irresistible human urge. This absurd condition stays unresolved in this novel, except through the power of the novelist's art, which holds the paradox at a certain distance so that it can be recognized for what it is. West, who wrote scripts for the Marx Brothers, sees the comedy inherent in the way things go wrong, so that a distancing—and saving—laughter is never far away, even as readers consider the dark side. The callousness with which some critics reproach West is in fact inextricable from his vision and its realization through his masterly technique.

"Critical Evaluation" by David Bromige

Further Reading

Andreach, Robert. "Nathanael West's *Miss Lonelyhearts*: Between the Dead Pan and the Unborn Christ." In *Twentieth Century Interpretations of "Miss Lonelyhearts": A*

Collection of Critical Essays, edited by Thomas H. Jackson. Englewood Cliffs, N.J.: Prentice-Hall, 1971. Analyzes the Pan-Christ antagonism as the unifying principle of West's novel and the central paradox of twentieth century life, in which paganism violates one's conscience and Christianity violates one's nature.

Barnard, Rita. "The Storyteller, the Novelist, and the Advice Columnist." In *The Great Depression and the Culture of Abundance.* New York: Cambridge University Press, 1995. Contextualizes *Miss Lonelyhearts* in the mass-media, commercial culture of the 1930's. Discusses West's critique of popular art forms.

Bloom, Harold, ed. *Nathanael West's "Miss Lonelyhearts."* Philadelphia: Chelsea House, 2005. Collection of essays analyzing West's novel, examining such subjects as the novel's modernist antihero, "debased iconography," and "rhetoric of disintegration."

Bombaci, Nancy. "Nathanael West's Aspiring Freakish Flâneurs." In *Freaks in Late Modernist American Culture: Nathanael West, Djuna Barnes, Tod Browning, and Carson McCullers.* New York: Peter Lang, 2006. Focuses on West's fascination with genetically maimed and distorted people, examining how his representation of these marginalized characters challenges modernist aesthetics and social values.

Dunne, Michael. "Nathanael West: 'Gloriously Funny.'" In *Calvinist Humor in American Literature.* Baton Rouge: Louisiana State University Press, 2007. Calvinist humor, in Dunne's definition, is the perception of humankind's imperfection. He demonstrates how this humor is used in works by West and other American writers whose fiction is populated with flawed characters.

Light, James F. *Nathanael West: An Interpretive Study.* 2d ed. Evanston, Ill.: Northwestern University Press, 1971. Claims West's compassion for people whose dreams have been betrayed fuses form and content in *Miss Lonelyhearts.* Describes the novel's imagistic style and briefly summarizes its critical reception.

Martin, Jay. *Nathanael West: The Art of His Life.* New ed. New York: Carroll & Graf, 1984. An indispensable biographical and critical source. Asserts that the dominant issue in West's life and art is the loss of value. An appendix documents West's screenwriting career.

_____. "Nathanael West: *Miss Lonelyhearts.*" In *A Companion to Modernist Literature and Culture*, edited by David Bradshaw and Kevin J. H. Dettmar. Malden, Mass.: Blackwell, 2006. Martin's analysis of West's novel is included in this student guide to modernist literature. In addition to essays examining selected works of literature, the book explores modernist art, film, music, dance, architecture, photography, and aesthetics.

_____, ed. *Nathanael West: A Collection of Critical Essays.* Englewood Cliffs, N.J.: Prentice-Hall, 1971. In addition to West's own essays and reviews by his contemporaries, this volume includes essays that study textual revisions and religious experience in *Miss Lonelyhearts.*

Veitch, Jonathan. *American Superrealism: Nathanael West and the Politics of Representation in the 1930's.* Madison: University of Wisconsin Press, 1997. Contains separate chapters on each novel, as well as an introduction discussing realism and the "crisis of representation in the 1930's."

Mister Roberts

Author: Thomas Heggen (1919-1949)
First published: 1946
Type of work: Novel
Type of plot: Satire
Time of plot: Last months of World War II
Locale: Southwest Pacific

Principal characters:
DOUGLAS ROBERTS, first lieutenant on the USS *Reluctant*
CAPTAIN MORTON, the skipper of the *Reluctant*
ENSIGN KEITH
BOOKSER, a seaman
FRANK THOMPSON, a radioman

The Story:

Douglas Roberts, first lieutenant on the *Reluctant*, a U.S. Navy supply ship in the Pacific, is the guiding spirit of the crew's undeclared war against the skipper, Captain Morton, an officious, childish, and unreasonable officer. The *Reluctant* is noncombatant, plying among islands left in the backwash of the war. None of its complement has seen action, and none wants action except Roberts, who has applied without success for transfer to a ship on the line.

In the continuously smoldering warfare between the captain and the other officers and the men of the ship, Roberts scores a direct hit on the captain's fundament with a wad of lead-foil shot from a rubber band while Captain Morton is watching motion pictures on board. Ensign Pulver, who spends most of his time devising ways of making the skipper's life unbearable, manufactures a giant firecracker to be thrown into the captain's cabin at night. The premature and violent explosion of the firecracker puts the entire *Reluctant* on a momentary battle footing. Ensign Pulver is burned badly.

Ensign Keith comes to the *Reluctant* by way of middle-class Boston, Bowdoin College, and accelerated wartime naval officer training. He is piped aboard in the blazing sunshine of Tedium Bay, hot in his blue serge uniform but self-assured because Navy regulations prescribe blues when reporting for duty. Despite the discomfort of a perspiration-soaked shirt and a wilted collar, Ensign Keith immediately shows the crew that they will have to follow naval regulations if he has his way aboard ship. One night, however, while he is on watch, he comes upon a drinking and gambling party presided over by Chief Dowdy. Keith is hoodwinked by the men into trying some of their drink. Not much later, under the influence of Chief Dowdy's "pineapple juice," Keith becomes roaring drunk, all regulations and service barriers forgotten. His initiation completed, Ensign Keith never again refers to rules and regulations.

At a forward area island base, where the *Reluctant* has docked to unload cargo, the crew quickly learns that the military hospital is staffed by real nurses. Every available binocular, telescope, and rangefinder on board is soon trained on the nurses' quarters. Interest rises to a fever pitch when it is discovered that a bathroom window shade in the quarters is never lowered. Officers and crew soon come to know the nurses by their physical characteristics, if not by formal introduction. One day, a nurse comes aboard and overhears two seamen making a wager concerning her physical characteristics. That same day, the bathroom shade is lowered, never to be raised again.

For days in advance, the ship's complement plan their shore leave in Elysium, a civilized port of call. Seaman Bookser, the spiritual type, is the butt of many jokes concerning his liberty plans. At Elysium, half the men are given shore leave. From sundown until the following dawn, they are brought back by jeep and truck. They had fought with army personnel, insulted local citizens, stolen government property, wrecked bars and saloons, and damaged the house of the French consul. Further shore leave is canceled. Bookser, the spiritual seaman, is driven up to the dock in a large car on the day of departure. Beside him is a beautiful young woman whom he kisses long and passionately before leaving her. Astonished at Bookser and proud of him at the same time, the crew makes him the hero of the stop at Elysium.

Roberts listens to V-E Day reports on the ship's radio. The apathy of his fellow officers toward events happening in Europe leads him to pitch the captain's cherished potted palm overboard late that night. At the same time, Roberts stirs up the noise-hating captain by slamming a lead stanchion against a stateroom bulkhead. Roberts is not caught, nor does he give himself up during the captain's mad search for the culprit. The crew manufactures a medal and presents it to Roberts for valor above and beyond the call of duty—a seaman had seen Roberts in action on V-E night.

Frank Thompson, a radioman and the ship's expert at the board game Monopoly, is informed by wire that his baby, whom he has never seen, has died in California. Thompson, anxious to go to the funeral and to be with his wife, applies for permission to fly to home. The captain refuses. Roberts advises him to go to a nearby island to see the chaplain and the flag secretary. Thompson goes, but he is told that no emergency leave could be permitted without his captain's approval. He then walks alone in a deserted section of the island for several hours before he returns to the *Reluctant* and takes his usual place at the head of the Monopoly table.

Not long after V-E Day, Roberts receives orders to report back to the United States for reassignment. He spends the night before he leaves the *Reluctant* with his special friends among officers and crew, drinking punch made of crew-concocted raisin brew and grain alcohol from dispensary supplies. The effect of Roberts's leaving is immediate. No longer is there a born leader aboard. All functions and activities in the ship's routine go wrong; no longer is there any one man upon whom the officers could depend to maintain their balance in the tedium of a dull tropic supply run. No longer do the enlisted men have an officer upon whom they could depend as a link between them and the ship's authorities.

Roberts is assigned to duty aboard a destroyer that is part of a task force bombarding the Japanese home islands. Not long before V-J Day, Ensign Pulver receives a letter from a friend aboard the same ship. The letter states that a Japanese kamikaze plane had broken through antiaircraft defenses and crashed into the bridge of the destroyer. Among those killed in the explosion was Roberts, who had been in the officers' mess drinking coffee with another officer. Mr. Roberts had seen action at last.

Critical Evaluation:

Mister Roberts is an ancestor of such works as Joseph Heller's *Catch-22* (1961). What *Mister Roberts* embodies—and this has also been absorbed by Heller—is the irreverent tone of the novel and its sometimes stunning mix of the wildly comic and the deeply tragic. The often sudden switch from verbal comedy or even slapstick to dramatic is something many may readily identify with *Catch-22* and the film *MASH* (1970) in which death, pain, passion, and foolishness follow one another very quickly.

Mister Roberts, published in 1946, is certainly one of the first texts to deal with the U.S. military, patriotism, and heroism, in the context of World War II, with something less than rigid respect. At least half of Thomas Heggen's novel is comic and satiric, designed to amuse the reader and make fun of military procedure, structures, and what passes for military service in some contexts.

Occasionally, the comedy in *Mister Roberts* is very broad, almost surreal. The name of the ship, the USS *Reluctant*, and the names of Pacific Ocean islands it passes or visits (Apathy, Tedium, Ennui, Elysium, and the Limbo Islands), are conceived as either humorous description or parody of the strange names of the real Pacific islands that figured in campaigns waged during the war.

Many of the comic activities in *Mister Roberts* are things associated with the lighter side of military life: discussions about sex, parties fueled by homemade alcoholic beverages, practical jokes, conspiracies against difficult officers, and gambling. In the novel's last half, Heggen changes his tone radically in several instances, and this narrative move toward tragedy culminates in the title character's death. Heggen's narrative takes a serious turn with the story of Big Gerhart's bullying of one of the young seamen, Red Stevens, who had shipped out fourteen months after his marriage. Gerhart is a man who delights in being cruel to those seemingly weaker than he; in the chapter devoted to the confrontation between him and Stevens, he is first seen mistreating a dog. Later, looking for another target, he picks on Stevens.

Gerhart begins to needle Stevens about being away from his young wife, gradually increasing the suggestiveness of his remarks, asking about Stevens's sexual activities and finally pointing out that Stevens can hardly expect such a pretty young wife to remain faithful while her husband is at sea. To Gerhart's surprise and to the surprise of onlookers, Red hits Gerhart with a wrench. Stevens is given a harmless summary court-martial, but he wins the sympathies of his shipmates and of the reader. In another moving episode, Frank Thompson receives word that his child has drowned. He asks for emergency leave to attend the funeral and see his wife, but permission is denied. The last image readers have of Thompson is of him maniacally playing Monopoly, as was his frequent custom, the image of a man driven to frantic despair by grief and frustration.

Eventually, in the spring of 1945, Roberts comes to suspect that the war has passed him by, that he has spent his years of service aboard the *Reluctant* while other men elsewhere have seen action and have perhaps distinguished themselves. What worries Roberts is that he has missed his chance at heroism—again. He had tried to join the Lincoln Brigade during the Spanish Civil War in the 1930's, but that war ended before he could participate; he had tried to join the British Royal Air Force in 1940, but had been denied because of a dental problem.

In a conversation with the *Reluctant*'s doctor, Roberts cannot really explain why he wants to fight in the war; he can only indicate that he has a compulsion to do so. While he has no illusions about heroism (he bemoans the fact that people forget too easily those who died in the war), he feels that the best men were those who, through some strange natural-selection process, were good enough to do the fighting. As for Roberts, all he has to show for his service is a medal struck by his friends in recognition of his pitching the captain's beloved palm tree overboard. Nevertheless, he does eventually succeed in being transferred to another ship—a destroyer still active in the Pacific theater.

The terrible irony is that, as *Mister Roberts* ends, Roberts becomes an example of war's tragic waste. He dies in a kamikaze attack on the ship on which he is serving—a perfect example, as he had thought, that not all casualties are heroes. What is worse is that his death is a horrible accident, a meaningless incident near the end of a war already won, and one then being waged by desperate Japanese pilots who hope only to inflict the most damage possible before defeat. In the same attack, another officer on the ship is killed while drinking coffee in the wardroom. Roberts's death has no more significance in the broad picture of the war than does the death of the other officer.

In the novel's moving denouement, Ensign Pulver creates a memorial for Roberts—by doing what Roberts would do if he were still alive and still aboard the *Reluctant*. He throws the rest of the captain's palm trees over the ship's side.

"Critical Evaluation" by Gordon Walters

Further Reading

Beidler, Philip D. "*Mr. Roberts* and American Remembering: Or, Why Major Major Major Major Looks Like Henry Fonda." *Journal of American Studies* 30, no. 1

(1996): 47-64. An analysis of Heggen's *Mister Roberts*, comparing it with Joseph Heller's *Catch-22*. Provides an overview of Heggen's career and discusses the novel's adaptation for the stage and screen.

Cohn, Victor. "Mister Heggen." *Saturday Review of Literature* 32 (June 11, 1949). A brief but interesting consideration of Heggen and his work. This article was published not long after Heggen's suicide in May of the same year.

Feeney, Mark. "*Patton/Mister Roberts*." In *Nixon at the Movies: A Book About Belief*. Chicago: University of Chicago Press, 2004. Although this chapter primarily deals with the film adaptation of *Mister Roberts*, its comments also pertain to the novel. Feeney describes how the film's (and the novel's) depiction of the dullness of military life resonates with veterans, leading to the success of the novel and its various adaptations.

Leggett, John. *Ross and Tom: Two American Tragedies*. New York: Simon & Schuster, 1974. Rev. ed. New York: Da Capo Press, 2000. Leggett's book is primarily a biographical study of Heggen and novelist Ross Lockridge, who both killed themselves, rather than a critical work on *Mister Roberts*. It is indispensable to understanding Heggen's state of mind when he wrote the novel. The revised edition has a new afterword by Leggett.

Mistero Buffo
Comic Mysteries

Author: Dario Fo (1926-   )
First produced: Mistero buffo: Giullarata popolare, 1969; first published, 1970 (English translation, 1983)
Type of work: Drama
Type of plot: Tragicomedy
Time of plot: Early first century C.E.
Locale: The Holy Land

Principal characters:
NARRATOR/HEROLD/INTRODUCER
VIRGIN MARY
MAD WOMAN
GIULLARE (JONGLEUR)
PEASANT
THE FOOL
DEATH
CHRIST

The Story:

A group of flaggelants bemoan the slaughter of the innocents, which is itself portrayed onstage. The slaughter is followed by a maddened mother addressing a wooden figurine representing the Madonna. The mother asks God how many innocents, including her child, need be slaughtered so Jesus can live. Then she spots what she says is her child, who has survived, and shows him to the wooden Madonna. It is a lamb.

Two beggars, one blind and one crippled, cooperate. The blind man carries the cripple, who spots Christ being flagellated. The cripple has heard that Jesus performs miraculous cures, so he wants to get away to avoid losing his affliction, which enables him to beg successfully. The blind man will not move, however, and both are cured as Christ passes. One rhapsodizes about his restored vision; the other bemoans his repaired legs.

A print of Christ as a Bacchus-like figure appears beside an angel recounting Christ's first miracle at the marriage at Cana. The angel is interrupted by a drunk, who says Jesus transformed water not for the benefit of others but simply to enjoy the wine himself. The drunk describes a semi-inebriated Christ jumping on the table and exhorting the wedding guests to drink up.

A peasant successfully plants fallow land. A priest rules that the land belongs to a noble, but the peasant refuses to yield the land he has planted. His barn and animals are burned; his wife is raped before his children, who go on to die. Despondent, the peasant decides to hang himself. Christ passes by and asks for water, however, and, when he is sated, he gives the peasant the wit and eloquence to convey Christ's message. He uses this power and intelligence to become a *jongleur*, or itinerant folk-actor

A peasant is born to sleep on the floor. His months of toil are prescribed in poetry: January, muck out the barn; February, sweat in the fields; and so forth. All he owns or does is taxed. A postscript informs the audience that paradise on earth is for bosses; for farmers or laborers, paradise comes after death. In the next scene, based on a picture of a pick-pocket at the opening of Lazarus's tomb, a bet is taken on whether Christ can revive Lazarus, and when he succeeds, the loser goes to pay, only to find his purse stolen. As the crowd cheers, the loser yells, "Stop, thief!"

Pope Boniface VIII, richly attired, lamely conducts a liturgical chant while carrying a crucifix. The Christ comes to life. The pope struggles to hide his finery, but Jesus kicks him in the posterior, leading Boniface to say he relishes Christ's crucifixion, which he will celebrate by drinking, dancing, and whoring, because he is Boniface.

The Fool is at an inn. The landlady announces Christ's arrival for what will be the Last Supper. Death appears as a woman, come for Jesus. The Fool waylays her in conversation and says he likes Death's smell of chrysanthemums and would happily go with her to death. She deems him either mad or a poet. Replying that every poet is a fool and every fool a poet, he sets about seducing her.

The Madonna meets friends on the street who try to block her from a crowd. Mary sees three crosses, and one friend tells her that two are to be used to crucify thieves. Mary sympathizes for the thieves' mothers, who probably do not know their sons' fate. Mary Magdalene enters and starts talking about Jesus before the friend silences her. The friend blurts that Magdalene is a prostitute and protests Jesus' pity for such undesirables. Mary replies that Christ works to give such people hope. Veronica enters, carrying a bloody cloth. She says that when she used it to wipe the face of the third condemned person, an imprint formed. Seeing it, Mary recognizes her son. The friend berates Veronica for upsetting Mary.

The Fool is working as a barker at the crucifixion. He helps the crucifiers when they say they will throw dice with him. After he wins, the Fool offers to return their money if they will free Christ. The foreman calls the Fool the fool of all fools, as they would be crucified themselves if they took Christ down from the cross. He then agrees when the Fool proposes replacing Jesus with Judas's corpse, but Christ declines to be taken down. The Fool reports that Jesus said that Death told Him that His crucifixion would redeem others. The Fool foretells that Jesus' principles will be betrayed and wars will be fought over Him. Christ replies that if but one person follows His path, His death will not be in vain, whereupon the Fool calls Christ the fool of fools. Telling the crucifiers he has changed his mind, the Fool leaves furiously.

Mary, breaking through a chorus trying to shield her from Calvary, wails, asking why her son is being crucified. She vows revenge, but Jesus asks her not to shout. Mary rails against the Archangel Gabriel, who had promised her she would be blessed. Christ says He must die, and Mary, after fainting, attacks Gabriel, telling him he cannot understand earthly suffering or her grief, especially as he has never birthed or raised a child. Gabriel acknowledges that Mary's loss will enable humankind, for the first time, to enter Heaven.

Critical Evaluation:

Since its first performance on a square in the Italian seaport town of Sestri Levante in 1969, *Mistero Buffo* has been an extremely popular play. In Italy, tens of millions of people have seen it, in union halls, on factory floors, and most often, on public squares. Almost always, it has taken the form of a one-man show starring playwright Dario Fo himself. Over the years, the play has been amplified and revived, with eleven new scenes added for the Millennium revival. To make room for new scenes, many of the introductions to existing scenes were cut or reduced as audiences grew familiar with the history involved and with Fo's project of reviving medieval Scriptural entertainments. The English translation (1983) contains at minimum the original twelve scenes of Fo's ever-evolving play.

With no conventional linear plot, *Mistero Buffo* is a series of skits, each giving voice to ordinary onlookers at Gospel events. Introductions are provided to many of the skits, explaining their links to specific medieval images that inspired them. The tragic situations portrayed are often mitigated by comedy.

Much of the play's popularity in Italy has been due to Fo's performances of it. Such performances are usually free, and, given Fo's high profile as a controversial public figure and broadly comic actor, they often draw large audiences. Fo's approach to the play builds on traditions with which Italians are familiar of open air performances and speeches given in public squares. Beyond Italy, Western audiences in general have found appeal in the play's snippy, borderline irreverent tone and its mild slaps in the face of authoritative clericalism. The suffering of the characters, mitigated by comedy, makes *Mistero Buffo* an inviting play for performance. Its unusual quantity of introductory prose also attracts readers. Its international appeal may also result from the play's unexpected presentation of, mostly, New Testament stories that skirt close to irreverent parody without crossing that line and that require nearly farcical acting. Audiences often react strongly to the play's vigorous, life-affirming characters and, in its final scene, to Fo's tragically heroic Christ.

No other playwright has borrowed as blatantly as Fo has from Bertolt Brecht, the twentieth century playwright whose work usually features characters from the bottom rungs of society. Brecht, like Fo, uses theater to intervene in sociopolitical discourse. Fo keeps the Brechtian tradition alive by including in *Mistero Buffo* several important aspects of Brechtian theater: He keeps the audience aware that it is watching a theatrical production, not a realist representation; he uses broad, grotesque acting to distance the audience emotionally from the play, so that spectators think rather than feel; he forsakes many elements of traditional theater, such as the curtain going up on a scene; he dispenses with props and costumes; and one actor plays multiple parts, even those of the opposite gender. In addition to being influenced by Brecht, Fo also borrowed, without attribution, from a predecessor play, *Mystery Bouffe* (1918/1921), by the Soviet author Vladimir Mayakovsky (1893-1930). These borrowings arguably contribute, together with the play's Christian and popular features, to *Mistero Buffo*'s stature as a drama.

Fo received the Nobel Prize in Literature in 1997. The award was denounced as scandalous by many critics, who called the author a literary lightweight better known for his acting. Indeed, many of his plays may be so tied to events of the time of their composition that they do not stand the test of time well. Fo, however, has been prolific: The 2005 Italian edition of his plays is 1,230 pages thick. Among his master plays are *Morte accidentale di un anarchico* (pr., pb. 1970; *Accidental Death of an Anarchist*, 1979), *Non si paga! Non si paga!* (pr., pb. 1974; *We Can't Pay! We Won't Pay!*, 1978), and *Papa e la strega* (pr. 1989, pb. 1994; *The Pope and the Witch*, 1992). *Mistero Buffo* enjoys popularity as a publication and fair success when produced as a play by multiactor theater groups in, and occasionally outside, the Western world—mostly because of the shared literary patrimony that emanates from the stories of Christ's life.

Robert B. Youngblood

Further Reading

Behan, Tom. *Dario Fo: Revolutionary Theatre*. Sterling, Va.: Pluto Press, 2000. Excellent discussion of *Mistero Buffo* and very useful bibliography, both on *Mistero Buffo* and on Italian politics of the 1960's.

Ghelardi, Marco. "Doing Things with Words: Directing Fo in the UK." In *Research Papers on the Theatre of Dario Fo and Franca Rame: Proceedings of the International Conference on the Theatre of Dario Fo and Franca Rame, Cambridge, 28-30 April 2000*, edited by Ed Emery. London: Red Notes, 2002. Edited by a major translator of *Mistero Buffo*. In addition to Ghelardi's essay, this collection includes cogent discussions of translating Fo; puppets; Fo's coproductions with his wife, actor Franca Rame; and the theater they founded in the 1990's.

Hirst, David. *Dario Fo and Franca Rame*. New York: Macmillan, 1989. Best book on bibliography; crucial chapters on the monologues and on politics and the theater.

Jenkins, Ron. *Dario Fo and Franca Rame: Artful Laughter*. New York: Aperture Foundation, 2001. A trove of information, including photographs of Fo in life and on stage, discussion of his artwork, and details of stagings of *Mistero Buffo* without any scenery or with "historical" flats painted by the playwright.

_____. "Dario Fo: The Roar of the Clown." In *Acting (Re)considered: Theories and Practices*, edited by Phillip B. Zarrilli. New York: Routledge, 1995. Excellent essay on Fo's views on acting and his performance technique.

Maeder, Costantino. "*Mistero Buffo*: Negating Textual Certainty, the Individual, and Time." In *Dario Fo: Stage, Text, and Tradition*, edited by Joseph Farrell and Antonio Scuderi. Carbondale: Southern Illinois University Press, 2000. Addresses many aesthetic features of the 1969 and 1977 versions of the play and their geneses. A clearly written, cogent, and important essay.

Mitchell, Tony. *Dario Fo: People's Court Jester*. London: Methuen, 1985. Indispensable chapters include "*Mistero Buffo*: Popular Culture, the *Giullari* and the Grotesque" and "Biography and Output, 1951-1967." *Giullari* is Italian for medieval and early Renaissance street actors. The subchapter "*Mistero Buffo* in London" contains a trove of information about Fo's type of theater and its reception in the United Kingdom into the 1980's.

Scuderi, Antonio. *Dario Fo and Popular Performance*. New York: Legas, 1998. Indispensable. In addition to the many *Mistero Buffo* sections, it includes important sections on adapting popular techniques, the dialectic of text and performance, subverting religious authority, and the power of humor.

The Mistress of the Inn

Author: Carlo Goldoni (1707-1793)
First produced: La locandiera, 1753; first published, 1753
   (English translation, 1912)
Type of work: Drama
Type of plot: Comedy
Time of plot: Mid-eighteenth century
Locale: Florence, Italy

Principal characters:
MIRANDOLINA, the mistress of the inn
CAVALIER DI RIPAFRATTA, a woman-hater
MARQUIS DI FORLIPOPOLI, in love with Mirandolina
COUNT D'ALBAFIORITA, in love with Mirandolina
FABRICIUS, a serving-man who is also in love with
  Mirandolina

The Story:

A Florentine innkeeper dies and leaves his young and pretty daughter, Mirandolina, mistress of his inn. The young woman runs the hostelry with much success, for she is as shrewd as she is pretty. On his deathbed, her father had made her promise to marry Fabricius, a faithful young serving-man in the inn. She promised her father to obey his wishes, but after his death she made excuses for not marrying. She tells Fabricius that she is not yet ready to settle down to married life, although she loves him very much. Actually, Mirandolina likes to have men fall in love with her, and she does her best to make fools of them in every way possible. She takes all and gives nothing.

A short time after her father's death, two noblemen staying at her inn fall in love with her. One is the Marquis di Forlipopoli, a destitute man who, despite his lack of money, is excessively proud of his empty title. The other love-smitten lodger is the Count d'Albafiorita, a wealthy man who boasts of his money. The two men are constantly at odds with each other, each feeling that Mirandolina should prefer him to his rival. In private she laughs at both of them.

The count gives Mirandolina expensive diamond brooches and earrings, and he also spends a great deal of money as a patron of the inn. The marquis, having no money to spend, tries to impress Mirandolina with his influence in high places and offers her his protection. Occasionally, he gives Mirandolina small gifts, which he openly states are much better than the count's expensive presents because little gifts are in better taste.

Pleased at the attentions of the count, the marquis, and her faithful Fabricius, Mirandolina is somewhat taken aback when a new guest arrives, the Cavalier di Ripafratta, who professes to be a woman-hater. When he receives a letter telling him of a beautiful girl with a great dowry who wishes to marry him, he becomes disgusted and angry and throws away the letter. Although his attitude toward Mirandolina is almost boorish, Mirandolina nevertheless seems much taken with a man who is immune to her charms. More than a little piqued by his attitude, she vows to make him fall in love with her.

When the cavalier demands better linens, Mirandolina goes to his room and, engaging him in conversation, strikes up a friendship of sorts. She tells him that she admires him for being truly a man and able to put aside all thoughts of love. The cavalier, struck by her pose, says that he is pleased to know such a forthright woman, and that he desires her friendship.

Mirandolina follows up her initial victory by cooking extra dishes for the cavalier and serving them to him in his room with her own hands, much to the displeasure of her other two admirers. The marquis is of much greater rank and the count is far more wealthy than the cavalier. Mirandolina's strategy has immediate success. Within twenty-four hours, the cavalier finds himself in love with the woman who serves him so well and is so agreeable to his ways of thinking.

The cavalier, however, is much disturbed by his newfound love and vows that he will leave for Leghorn immediately. He believes that out of Mirandolina's sight he will soon forget her. He orders his servant to pack for his departure, then Mirandolina learns of his plans. She herself goes to present his bill and has little trouble in beguiling him to stay a little longer. At the end of the interview, during which the cavalier professes his love, Mirandolina faints. The marquis and the count run into the room to see what has happened. The cavalier, furious at them for discovering Mirandolina in his room, throws the bottle of restorative at them. The marquis vows to have satisfaction, but when the cavalier accepts his challenge the marquis shows his cowardice by refusing to fight a duel.

The cavalier, now almost beside himself with love, sends a solid gold flask to Mirandolina, who refuses to accept it and throws it into a basket of clothes to be ironed. Fabricius, seeing the flask, gets jealous. He is also displeased by the off-handed treatment he has been receiving from the woman who had promised to marry him. Mirandolina finally appeases him by saying that women always treat worst those whom they love best.

Later in the day, while Mirandolina is busy ironing the linen, the cavalier comes to her and asks why she had rejected his suit. He refuses to believe that she had been playing a game with him, just as she had been doing with the count and the marquis. He becomes all the more angry because Fabricius continually interrupts the interview, bringing in hot flatirons for Mirandolina to use on the linen. After a lengthy argument, during which the cavalier becomes furious and refuses to let Fabricius bring in the irons, Mirandolina leaves the room.

The marquis thereupon enters and begins to taunt the cavalier for having fallen victim to the innkeeper's charms. The cavalier storms out of the room. Looking about, the marquis, very much embarrassed for money, sees the gold flask. Intending to sell it, he picks it up and puts it in his pocket. At that moment, the count enters and the two begin to congratulate themselves on Mirandolina's success in making a fool of their latest rival. They cannot help remembering, however, that she has done things for him that she has not done for them: cooked special foods, provided new bed linen, and visited with him in his room. Finally, having come to the conclusion that they are as foolish as the cavalier, they resolve to pay their bills and leave the inn.

While Mirandolina is bidding them goodbye, the cavalier pushes his way into the room and tries to force a duel upon the count. When he seizes the marquis' sword, however, and attempts to pull it from the scabbard, he finds only the handle. Mirandolina tries to calm him and to send all three away. She bluntly tells the cavalier that she has simply used her wiles to make him love her because he had boasted of being a woman-hater. Then, announcing that she had promised her father to marry Fabricius, she takes the serving-man by the hand and announces her betrothal to him. The cavalier leaves angrily, but the count and the marquis receive the news more gracefully. The count gives the newly betrothed couple a hundred pounds, and the marquis, poor as he is, gives them six pounds. Both men leave the inn wiser in the ways of women than they were when they arrived.

Critical Evaluation:

The humor of Carlo Goldoni's *The Mistress of the Inn* is based on certain assumptions of class and social structure, as well as on the positions of man and woman relative to each other in society. The heroine's contacts in the play are made possible by virtue of her being an innkeeper, for, as a rule, women of a nobler class did not encounter large numbers of men in eighteenth century Italy. Although Goldoni under-

scores Mirandolina's virtue often, her position suggested a certain moral looseness to audiences of the time. Indeed, a woman of mid-eighteenth century Italy would not have conducted herself with Mirandolina's freedom; such behavior toward men would have been judged as being immoral and unfeminine, and such a woman would have lost her social position.

Nevertheless, a woman who defied men was an ideal subject for laughter, and Mirandolina's self-assurance and cleverness were considered admirable then as in later times, though for different reasons. Goldoni's contemporaries delighted in seeing Mirandolina triumph over the foolish men in the play, not because her conquests were men, but because they were fools. In truth, Goldoni's audience would not have wanted women to be victorious over men in actuality, or even to challenge long-established male prerogatives. The humor of this battle between the genders is safe and acceptable in *The Mistress of the Inn* because it is not in any way realistic, at least for the time.

Another way in which Goldoni uses social distinctions for humorous effect is through the opposition between the old gentry and the nouveau riche. The count represents the newly moneyed class, whereas the marquis is of the old nobility, impoverished but clinging to his pride in his ancient rank. He scorns the bought title of the count, insisting that lineage cannot be purchased. Yet in the practical world, the man with money has the advantage, and the prestige of an old family is easily swept aside. The marquis babbles about the refinements that come from breeding, about "taste" and "protection" and "honor," but when the count flashes a diamond ring, Mirandolina cannot resist. Eighteenth century Italy was a country in transition, lagging behind the other European countries in economic and political developments, and the contest between these two absurd figures reflects the conditions that existed at the time. Many of the old families were being overwhelmed by the newly affluent commercial families; power was changing hands, being yielded to the ruthless and shrewd, and soon the supreme upstart of them all, Napoleon Bonaparte, would appear on the scene.

In *The Mistress of the Inn*, Goldoni combines old dramatic traditions with his own innovations. The convention of the insolent, shrewd servant, Fabricius, for example, goes back to ancient Roman and even Greek comedy, and the character of Mirandolina suggests some of the independent courtesans of the old Roman comedies. On the other hand, the sense of the momentary scene is new to Goldoni; the audience is always aware that life is going on around these characters on the stage and that the events of the comedy are not occurring in a vacuum. Part of the vitality of the play stems from this feeling of the ever-changing quality of human life.

The characters themselves are the primary reason for the play's long success. They are broadly sketched, but each possesses a good-natured vitality. Mirandolina does not marry out of her class, which would have shocked eighteenth century audiences, but the possibility that she might do so tantalizes them until the very end. Her gaiety and cleverness control the proceedings as she plays on the self-centered men as on musical instruments. They, in turn, respond to her efforts according to their personalities, ever jealous of one another, ridiculing one another, proud and arrogant, yet not one of them is a match for this earthy, witty woman.

Goldoni was a prolific dramatist, and his work completely reformed the comedy of his day. The son of a Venetian doctor, he ran away from school with a company of players. Although he eventually took a degree in law, the theater was always his first love. After making a false start with a lyric tragedy, he found his natural bent with a comedy in verse. Believing that a radical change was necessary in the Italian theater, he followed Molière's example by attempting to depict the realities of social life in as natural a manner as possible. To later audiences, his plays do not seem realistic, but they were a startling departure from what came before him. Goldoni freed his actors from the traditional practice of wearing masks on the stage, and he suppressed improvisation by writing out the parts in full. He eventually replaced the haphazard Italian farces of the day, the commedia dell'arte, with his own style of comedy of manners. His plays were both earthy and moral in tone and attempted a faithful mirror of life. Goldoni's best plays, which reflect the true life of the varied social classes in his native land, have endured and will continue to be enjoyed by audiences around the world. They possess a gaiety and shrewdness unsurpassed in later drama, and they present a tantalizing picture of a dynamic and rapidly changing moment in history.

"Critical Evaluation" by Bruce D. Reeves

Further Reading

Carlson, Marvin. *The Italian Stage from Goldoni to D'Annunzio*. Jefferson, N.C.: McFarland, 1981. Excellent background for understanding the conditions under which Goldoni produced *The Mistress of the Inn* and other comedies. Also describes the efforts of actor Eleanore Duse in popularizing the play for twentieth century audiences.

Farrell, Joseph, ed. *Carlo Goldoni and Eighteenth-Century Theatre*. Lewiston, N.Y.: Edwin Mellen Press, 1997. Collection of essays considering Goldoni's work in relation to other European playwrights of the Enlightenment era. Among other topics, the essays examine Goldoni's female characters and the forms of address in his plays.

Goldoni, Carlo. *Three Comedies*. London: Oxford University Press, 1961. The introduction by Gabriele Baldini discusses Goldoni's abilities as a comic dramatist and examines his use of stock materials in *The Mistress of the Inn*. Also provides an assessment of Mirandolina, "the most fascinating female character" to appear in Italian literature in centuries.

Günsberg, Maggie. *Playing with Gender: The Comedies of Goldoni*. Leeds, England: Northern Universities Press, 2001. Focuses on the depiction of femininity and masculinity in Goldoni's plays, placing this representation within the historical, cultural, and socioeconomic context of his times.

Riedt, Heinz. *Carlo Goldoni*. Translated by Ursule Molinaro. New York: Frederick Ungar, 1974. General survey of Goldoni's achievements as a dramatist. A chapter on *The Mistress of the Inn* explains it as "a portrayal of feminine psychology," comments on its structure, and remarks on twentieth century productions and adaptations.

Steele, Eugene. *Carlo Goldoni: Life, Work, and Times*. Ravenna, Italy: Longo Editore, 1981. Brief comments about the drama, including a general assessment of Goldoni's accomplishments as a playwright. Includes Goldoni's own comments about *The Mistress of the Inn*, and focuses critical attention on the development of Mirandolina.

Vescovo, Piermario. "Carlo Goldoni, Playwright and Reformer." In *A History of Italian Theatre*, edited by Joseph Farrell and Paolo Puppa. New York: Cambridge University Press, 2006. This chapter on Goldoni helps place his work within the broader context of Italian Enlightenment theater.

Mithridates

Author: Jean Racine (1639-1699)
First produced: Mithridate, 1673; first published, 1673
 (English translation, 1926)
Type of work: Drama
Type of plot: Tragedy
Time of plot: First century B.C.E.
Locale: Nymphée, on the Bosporus

Principal characters:
MITHRIDATES, king of Pontus
MONIME, betrothed to Mithridates and already declared
 queen
PHARNACE and XIPHARES, sons of Mithridates by different
 wives
ARBATE, Mithridates' confidant and governor of Nymphée
PHOEDIME, Monime's confidante
ARCAS, a servant

The Story:

Mithridates, the Pontine king who was fighting the Romans for forty years, is defeated and believed dead. Xiphares, the son who is, like his father, an enemy of Rome, deplores sincerely the loss of Mithridates. The other son, Pharnace, favorable to the Romans, is all the more pleased because he is in love with Monime, the old king's betrothed; now he hopes to win her for himself.

Xiphares tells Arbate that he, Xiphares, has no claims to the states Pharnace is to inherit and that his brother's feelings toward the Romans are of little interest to him. His concern for Monime is another matter. The truth is that Xiphares himself was long in love with Monime, even before his father saw her. Although he remains silent as long as she is betrothed to his father, he is now convinced that Pharnace will be compelled to kill him in order to have her.

When Monime begs Xiphares to protect her against Pharnace, whom she does not love, Xiphares finally declares his love to her. At first he is afraid that she might receive his avowal with anger. Monime, however, is secretly in love with Xiphares. They do not open their hearts to each other because Pharnace appears. Pharnace urges Monime to support his cause in Pontus. She thanks him but explains that she cannot favor a friend of the Romans who killed her father. When Pharnace hints that another interest is prompting her, Xiphares confirms his suspicions by defending Monime's freedom. The brothers then realize that they are rivals.

At that moment Phoedime, Monime's confidant, arrives to tell them that the report of Mithridates' death is false and that the king is returning. Monime and Xiphares, each sensing at last the other's feelings, are stunned. Monime deliberately bids them farewell and leaves. Now Pharnace knows that Monime and Xiphares love each other, and Xiphares knows that Pharnace loves Monime and is expecting the arrival of the Romans. Both, afraid of their father's anger, will be forced to keep each other's secret when they meet him.

After everyone goes to meet Mithridates at the harbor, Phoedime is surprised to find Monime still in the palace. Monime explains her realization that Xiphares suffered as much as she did all the time they were separated after their first meeting in Greece. Aware that she betrays her love without even speaking, she feels that she can never see Xiphares again because she also fears Mithridates' anger. She leaves hurriedly because she hears the noise of Mithridates' arrival and she does not want to face him.

The king is surprised to find his sons in Nymphée instead of in their own states. Suspiciously, he asks whether they are in love with Monime and inquires of Arbate why he allowed them to enter the city. The governor tells him that Pharnace declared his love to Monime. Arbate says nothing, however, about Xiphares' feelings. Mithridates, relieved that his favorite son remains faithful, is afraid that Monime might respond to Pharnace's love. At that moment Monime appears and he asks to be left alone with her. Mithridates tells her that he wishes to have their wedding performed as soon as possible. Seeing her sad resignation and suspecting that she is in love with Pharnace, he summons Xiphares and asks his trusted son to try to turn her affections away from his brother. Xiphares also fears that Monime might love Pharnace. Aware of his fear, Monime is unable to hide her true feelings. At the same time she declares her intention to follow her duty to Mithridates.

A short time later Mithridates calls for his two sons and explains to them his plan to attack the Romans in Italy. Pharnace will leave on a mission to the Parthians, his purpose being to marry the daughter of their king, with whom Mithridates wishes to make an alliance necessary to his plans. When Pharnace refuses, his resistance arouses his father's anger. Pharnace, thinking that his brother betrayed him, tries to get revenge by disclosing the love of Xiphares for Monime.

At first Mithridates refuses to listen to Pharnace. Then, tortured by jealousy, he resorts to a stratagem in order to learn the truth. He announces to Monime his desire to have her marry Xiphares. When she shows surprise, asking if he is trying to test her love, he pretends to believe that she wants to marry Pharnace instead. He declares that he will go with Xiphares to find death in battle, while she will stay with Pharnace. Monime, misled by the king's apparent sincerity, admits that she loves Xiphares and is loved by him. After her departure Mithridates prepares to take a terrible revenge on his son.

When Xiphares comes to bid Monime farewell, she accuses herself of having caused his ruin by her weakness. Hearing the king approaching, he leaves hurriedly. Monime then reproaches Mithridates for his stratagem. Ordered to marry him at once, she gently but firmly refuses. At that point Mithridates is in a quandary over killing Xiphares, the son who is not only his rival in love but also his best ally against the Romans. While he debates with himself, Arbate appears with the announcement that Pharnace, aided by the Romans, rises in revolt. Believing that Xiphares also betrayed him, the king orders Arcas, his faithful servant, to kill Monime.

Meanwhile, convinced that Xiphares is dead, Monime attempts to strangle herself, but Phoedime prevents her. Still wishing to die, she welcomes the poison Arcas brings her. Before she can drink it, however, Arbate comes on the run and takes the potion away from her. He brings word that Xiphares routed the Romans and that Mithridates is dying. The king, believing himself defeated, chooses to die by his own sword. Forgetting all jealousy, Mithridates blesses Monime and Xiphares, the faithful son who will succeed to the throne and avenge his father's death.

Critical Evaluation:

Presenting a theme borrowed from history, *Mithridates* is a tragedy that conforms absolutely to Jean Racine's literary ideal: a simple action with few events. In this work Racine was much more faithful to fact than he was in his earlier plays. He simply adds a love interest to the historical story in order to turn it into a drama. The two main characters are memorable in their complexity. Mithridates offers a contrast between the indomitable willpower of the warrior and the blindness and confusion of the unhappy lover. Monime seems to combine harmoniously all the gentleness and strength of Racine's heroines. The rhetorical style is versatile. Sometimes epic in Mithridates' speech, it also takes on an exquisite softness to express the subtlest shades of sentiments. *Mithridates* is the only one of Racine's tragedies in which the ending is mitigated by a promise of future happiness.

Partly because of his bellicose nature and partly because of the envy inspired by his talent, Racine was regularly involved in one imbroglio or another. In the case of *Mithridates*, however, from its first performance early in 1673, even his adversaries agreed that he created a triumph. The play was greatly admired at the royal court. Since the seventeenth century, however, *Mithridates* has not maintained a degree of popularity equal to that of others of Racine's tragedies. For example, from 1680 to 1965 *Phèdre* (1677; *Phaedra*, 1701) and *Andromaque* (1667; *Andromache*, 1674) were each produced slightly in excess of thirteen hundred times, whereas *Mithridates* was played 644 times.

For Racine, particularly adept at portraying the subtleties of the feminine heart, *Mithridates* is an unusually masculine play. The choice of a male historical figure, in this case a despotic Eastern king, as the central character in his new play was no doubt influenced by his desire to compete with the allegedly more virile theater of the aging Pierre Corneille and to silence those critics prone to blame the softness, or femininity, of plays such as *Bérénice* (1670; English translation, 1676) and *Bajazet* (1672; English translation, 1717), his two previous tragedies. The plot is more complex than that of Racine's earlier plays. Its basic element is the secret: New revelations serve to develop the plot. Xiphares reveals his love to Monime in the first act. Not until late in the second act does Monime reveal her love for him. In act 3, Mithridates discloses his plan to attack Rome. Then, threatened with imprisonment, Pharnace informs Mithridates of Xiphares' love for Monime. Finally, Monime, tricked by Mithridates, admits that she loves Xiphares. In act 4, Monime discloses the truth to Xiphares: It is she who revealed their secret to Mithridates. Throughout the play, Pharnace guards his secret: The Roman legions are on the way to Nymphée.

The old king is the central figure whose presence links closely the otherwise disparate elements of the dramatic action. The audience sees him in a double focus: As an implacable enemy of Rome, he is an adversary to his son Pharnace, who seeks conciliation with Rome; as a passionate lover, he becomes a rival of Xiphares, who also is in love with the queen, although otherwise loyal. The entanglement is further complicated by incidents that take place before the action of the play. Xiphares' mother betrayed Mithridates to the Romans; Mithridates, as the result of his "cruel suspicions," sacrificed two of his sons.

Mithridates is a complex and ambiguous character. There is a strong hint of fatality in his character, constantly evoked by the king's frequent references to his long series of past misfortunes. These misfortunes, of a sentimental and heroic nature, assure sympathy for the aging warrior. The audience feels a natural sympathy for Monime and Xiphares, young lovers struggling to find a basis on which to approach each other, and so, in this light, Mithridates is hateful in his efforts to coerce the queen into granting him her affection. There is a curious and most delicate balance between, on one hand, the grandeur of the old king, inspired for the most part by the narration of his past greatness as a warrior, and, on the other hand, the meanness of his present machinations, the duplicity of his dissimulations, and the violence of his outbursts of anger and jealousy.

Mithridates, although imperious and passionate, is really little more than a shell of his former self. His past power evaporates; the effort to marry Monime represents a last opportunity to reestablish evidence of his manhood. Except for his age—which, were there the slightest hint of anything grotesque in his character or actions, would instantly situate him with Molière's comic lovers, given to infatuations with women much younger than themselves—Mithridates is like Othello. His destruction is brought about by a blind passion that easily, or perhaps inevitably, gives rise to a fatal jealousy. Therein lies the tragic flaw of this king.

The evolution of the dramatic action depends, in a large measure, on the undercurrent of secrecy, intrigue, and deception that informs the play. Mithridates relentlessly strives to determine the hidden motives of others. For example, on his arrival in Nymphée he must know why his sons are not at their assigned posts. There is an unusual amount of misunderstanding. Mithridates, particularly, is constantly manipulating people through ruse. He has a proclivity for expressing himself in ambiguous terms, especially in talking about his sons; instead of naming them, he uses terms such as "treacherous son" and "audacious son." Other characters cannot be sure about whom he is talking. Monime is easily tricked by the duplicity of his language. The result is that Mithridates is a completely isolated figure, having no one in whom he can confide. He has three soliloquies, more than any other Racinian hero.

Unlike other tragedies of Racine, notably *Bajazet*, *Mithridates* does not end in general slaughter. At the end, the doomed king is torn between opposing sentiments: In his decision to unite Xiphares and Monime he triumphs over the base emotions of jealousy and desire for revenge that, at least until then, appear to motivate him consistently. The "happy ending" applies, of course, only to the young couple. The king's noble death assures a properly tragic denouement to the play.

"Critical Evaluation" by Robert A. Eisner

Further Reading

Abraham, Claude. *Jean Racine*. Boston: Twayne, 1977. Contains an excellent introduction to Racine's theater and an annotated bibliography of important critical studies of Racine. The chapter on *Mithridates* explores the contrasts between Mithridates and his two sons.

Barthes, Roland. *On Racine*. Translated by Richard Howard. New York: Hill & Wang, 1964. An influential structuralist study that explores representations of love and tragic space in Racine's tragedies. Barthes's chapter on *Mithridates* examines the death of the title character and the presence of evil and deception in the tragedy.

Campbell, John. *Questioning Racinian Tragedy*. Chapel Hill: University of North Carolina Press, 2005. Analyzes individual tragedies, including *Mithridates*, and questions if Racine's plays have common themes and techniques that constitute a unified concept of "Racinian tragedy."

Goldmann, Lucien. *Racine*. Translated by Alastair Hamilton. Cambridge, England: Rivers Press, 1972. Contains an insightful sociological reading of Racine's tragedies that examines them in the light of French seventeenth century politics and social change. Explains carefully the influence of Jansenism, a Catholic religious movement, on Racine's tragic view of the world.

Maskell, David. *Racine: A Theatrical Reading*. New York: Oxford University Press, 1991. Explores problems involved in staging Racine's eleven tragedies and one comedy. Discusses how different theatrical styles have influenced performances of Racine's plays. Chronicles the critical reception of his plays since the seventeenth century.

Racevskis, Roland. *Tragic Passages: Jean Racine's Art of the Threshold*. Lewisburg, Pa.: Bucknell University Press, 2008. Examines *Mithridates* and Racine's other secular tragedies, demonstrating how these works construct space, time, and identity. Argues that the characters in these plays are in various stages of limbo, suspended between the self and the other, onstage and offstage, or life and death, and the plays emphasize this predicament of being "in-between."

Weinberg, Bernard. *The Art of Jean Racine*. Chicago: University of Chicago Press, 1963. Examines in chronological order each of Racine's eleven tragedies and describes the significance of each play in the development of Racine's career as a playwright. The chapter on *Mithridates* explores the complex psychological motivation for the behavior of the title character.

Moby Dick
Or, The Whale

Author: Herman Melville (1819-1891)
First published: 1851
Type of work: Novel
Type of plot: Adventure
Time of plot: Early nineteenth century
Locale: High seas

Principal characters:
ISHMAEL, the narrator, a sailor
QUEEQUEG, a harpooner
AHAB, captain of the *Pequod*
STARBUCK, the first mate
STUBB, the second mate
FEDALLAH, Captain Ahab's Parsee servant

The Story:

Ishmael is a schoolmaster who often feels that he must leave his quiet existence and go to sea. Much of his life has been spent as a sailor, and his voyages are a means of ridding himself of the restlessness that frequently seizes him. One day, he decides that he will sign on a whaling ship, and packing his carpetbag, he leaves Manhattan and sets out, bound for Cape Horn and the Pacific.

On his arrival in New Bedford, Ishmael goes to the Spouter Inn near the waterfront to spend the night. There he finds he can have a bed only if he consents to share it with a harpooner. His strange bedfellow frightens him when he enters the room, for Ishmael is certain that he is a savage cannibal. After a few moments, however, it becomes evident that the native, whose name is Queequeg, is a friendly person, for he presents Ishmael with an embalmed head and offers to share his fortune of thirty dollars. The two men quickly become friends and decide to sign on the same ship.

Eventually they sign on the *Pequod*, a whaler out of Nantucket, Ishmael as a seaman, Queequeg as a harpooner. Although several people seem dubious about the success of a voyage on a vessel such as the *Pequod*, which is reported to be under a strange man, Captain Ahab, neither Ishmael nor Queequeg has any intention of giving up their plans. They are, however, curious to see Captain Ahab.

For several days after the vessel has sailed, there is no sign of the Captain, as he remains hidden in his cabin. The running of the ship is left to Starbuck and Stubb, two of the mates, and though Ishmael becomes friendly with them, he learns very little more about Ahab. One day, as the ship is sailing southward, the Captain strides out on deck. Ishmael is struck by his stern, relentless expression. In particular, he notices that the Captain has lost a leg and that instead of a wooden leg, he now wears one cut from the bone of the jaw of a whale. A livid white scar runs down one side of his face and is lost beneath his collar, so that it seems as though he were scarred from head to foot.

For several days, the ship continues south looking for whale schools. The sailors take turns on masthead watches to give the sign when a whale is sighted. Ahab appears on deck and summons all his men around him. He pulls out a one ounce gold piece, nails it to the mast, and declares that the first man to sight the great white whale, known to the sailors as Moby Dick, would get the gold. Everyone expresses enthusiasm for the quest except Starbuck and Stubb, Starbuck especially deploring the madness with which Ahab has directed all his energies to this one end. He tells the Captain that he is like a man possessed, for the white whale is a menace to those who would attempt to kill him. Ahab lost his leg in his last encounter with Moby Dick; he might lose his life in the next meeting, but the Captain does not listen to the mate's warning. Liquor is brought out and, at the Captain's orders, the crew drinks to the destruction of Moby Dick.

Ahab, from what he knows of the last reported whereabouts of the whale, plots a course for the ship that will bring it into the area where Moby Dick is most likely to be. Near the Cape of Good Hope, the ship comes across a school of sperm whales, and the men busy themselves harpooning, stripping, melting, and storing as many as they are able to catch. When the ship encounters another whaling vessel at sea, Captain Ahab asks for news about the white whale. The captain of the ship warns him not to attempt to chase Moby Dick, but it is clear by now that nothing can deflect Ahab from the course he has chosen.

Another vessel stops them, and the captain of the ship boards the *Pequod* to buy some oil for his vessel. Captain Ahab again demands news of the whale, but the captain knows nothing of the monster. As the captain is returning to his ship, he and his men spot a school of six whales and start after them in their rowboats. While Starbuck and Stubb rally their men into the *Pequod*'s boats, their rivals are already far ahead of them. The two mates, however, urge their crew until they outstrip their rivals in the race, and Queequeg harpoons the largest whale.

Killing the whale is only the beginning of a long and arduous job. After the carcass is dragged to the side of the boat and lashed to it by ropes, the men descend the side and slash off the blubber. Much of the body is usually demolished by sharks, who stream around, snapping at the flesh of the whale and at each other. The head of the whale is removed and suspended several feet in the air, above the deck of the ship. After the blubber is cleaned, it is melted in tremendous try-pots and then stored in vats below deck.

The men are kept busy, but their excitement increases as their ship nears the Indian Ocean and the probable sporting grounds of the white whale. Before long, they cross the path of an English whaling vessel, and Captain Ahab again demands news of Moby Dick. In answer, the captain of the English ship holds out his arm, which from the elbow down consists of sperm whalebone. Ahab demands that his boat be lowered at once, and he quickly boards the deck of the other ship. The captain tells him of his encounter and warns Captain Ahab that it is foolhardy to try to pursue Moby Dick. When he tells Ahab where he had seen the white whale last, the captain of the *Pequod* waits for no civilities but returns to his own ship to order the course changed to carry him to Moby Dick's new feeding ground. Starbuck tries to reason with the mad Captain, to persuade him to give up this insane pursuit, but Ahab seizes a rifle and in his fury orders the mate out of his cabin.

Meanwhile, Queequeg has fallen ill with a fever. When it seemed almost certain he would die, he requests that the carpenter make him a coffin in the shape of a canoe, according to the custom of his tribe. The coffin is then placed in the cabin with the sick man, but as yet there is no real need for it. Queequeg recovers from his illness and rejoins his shipmates. He uses his coffin as a sea chest and carves many strange designs upon it.

The sailors had been puzzled by the appearance early in the voyage of the Parsee servant, Fedallah. His relationship to the Captain cannot be determined, but that he is highly regarded is evident. Fedallah prophesies that the Captain will die only after he has seen two strange hearses for carrying the dead upon the sea, one not constructed by mortal hands and the other made of wood grown in America. He also says that the Captain himself will have neither hearse nor coffin for his burial.

A terrible storm arises one night. Lightning strikes the masts so that all three flame against the blackness of the night, and the men are frightened by this omen. It seems to them that the hand of God is motioning them to turn from the course to which they had set themselves and return to their homes. Only Captain Ahab is undaunted by the sight. He plants himself at the foot of the mast and challenges the god of evil, which the fire symbolizes for him. He vows once again his determination to find and kill the white whale.

A few days later, a cry rings through the ship. Moby Dick has been spotted. The voice is that of Captain Ahab. None of the sailors, alert as they had been, had been able to sight the whale before their captain. Boats are lowered and the chase begins, with Captain Ahab's boat in the lead. As he is about to dash his harpoon into the side of the mountain of white, the whale suddenly turns on the boat, dives under it, and splits it into pieces. The men are thrown into the sea, and for some time the churning of the whale prevents rescue. At length, Ahab orders the rescuers to ride into the whale and frighten him away, so he and his men could be rescued. The rest of that day is spent chasing the whale, but to no avail.

The second day, the men start out again. They catch up with the whale and bury three harpoons into his white flanks, but he so turns and churns that the lines become twisted, and the boats are pulled every way, with no control over their direction. Two of them are splintered, and the men hauled out of the sea, but Ahab's boat has not as yet been touched. Suddenly, it is lifted from the water and thrown high into the air. The Captain and the men are quickly rescued, but Fedallah is nowhere to be found.

When the third day of the chase begins, Moby Dick seems tired, and the *Pequod*'s boats soon overtake him. Bound to the whale's back by the coils of rope from the harpoon poles, they see the body of Fedallah. The first part of his prophecy had been fulfilled. Moby Dick, enraged by his pain, turns on the boats and splinters them. On the *Pequod*, Starbuck watches and turns the ship toward the whale in the hope of saving the Captain and some of the crew. The infuriated monster swims directly into the *Pequod*, shattering the ship's timbers. Ahab, seeing the ship founder, cries out that the *Pequod*—made of wood grown in America—is the second hearse of Fedallah's prophecy. The third prophecy, Ahab's death by hemp, is fulfilled when rope from Ahab's harpoon coils around his neck and snatches him from his boat. All except Ishmael perish. He is rescued by a passing ship after clinging for hours to Queequeg's canoe coffin, which had bobbed to the surface as the *Pequod* sank.

Critical Evaluation:

Although his early adventure novels—*Typee* (1846), *Omoo* (1847), *Redburn* (1849), and *White Jacket* (1850)—brought Herman Melville a notable amount of popularity and financial success during his lifetime, it was not until the

1920's and 1930's, nearly fifty years after his death, that he received universal critical recognition as one of the greatest nineteenth century American authors. Melville took part in the first great period of American literature—the period that included Edgar Allan Poe, Ralph Waldo Emerson, Nathaniel Hawthorne, Walt Whitman, and Henry David Thoreau. For complexity, originality, psychological penetration, breadth, and symbolic richness, Melville achieved his greatest artistic expression with the book he wrote when he was thirty years old, *Moby Dick*.

Between the time of his birth in New York City and his return there to research and write his masterpiece, Melville had circled the globe of experience—working as a bank messenger, salesman, farmhand, schoolteacher (like his narrator, Ishmael), engineer and surveyor, bowling alley attendant, cabin boy, and whaleman in the Pacific on the *Acushnet*. His involvement in the mutinous Pacific voyage, combined with accounts of a notorious whale called Mocha Dick that wrought havoc in the 1840's and 1850's, certainly influenced the creation of *Moby Dick*.

The tangled themes of this mighty novel express the artistic genius of a mind that, according to Hawthorne, "could neither believe nor be comfortable in unbelief." Many of those themes are characteristic of American Romanticism: the "isolated self" and the pain of self-discovery, the insufficiency of conventional practical knowledge in the face of the "power of blackness," the demoniac center to the world, the confrontation of evil and innocence, the fundamental imperfection of humans, Faustian heroism, the search for the ultimate truth, the inadequacy of human perception. *Moby Dick* is, moreover, a unique literary form, combining elements of the psychological and picaresque novel, sea story and allegory, the epic of "literal and metaphorical quest," the satire of social and religious events, the emotional intensity of the lyric genre (in diction and in metaphor), Cervantian romance, Dantesque mysticism, Rabelaisian humor, Shakespearean drama (both tragedy and comedy), journalistic travel book, and scientific treatise on cetology. Melville was inspired by Hawthorne's example to give his story the unifying quality of a moral parable, although his own particular genius refused to allow that parable an unequivocal, single rendering.

In style and theme, Melville also was influenced by Edmund Spenser, William Shakespeare, Dante, Miguel de Cervantes, Robert Burton, Sir Thomas Carlyle, Thomas Browne, and vastly miscellaneous reading in the New York Public Library (as witnessed by the two "Etymologies" and the marvelous "Extracts" that precede the text itself, items from the writer's notes and files that he could not bear to dis-

card). It was because they did not know how to respond to its complexities of form and style that the book was "broiled in hell fire" by contemporary readers and critics. Even today, the rich mixture of its verbal texture—an almost euphuistic flamboyance balanced by dry, analytical expository prose—requires a correspondingly unique sensitivity on the part of the reader. The most remarkable thing about the plot is that Moby Dick does not appear physically until after five hundred pages and is not even mentioned by name until nearly two hundred pages into the novel.

Whether it be the knowledge of reality, an embodiment of the primitive forces of nature, the deep subconscious energies of humanity, fate or destiny inevitably victorious over illusory free will, or simply the unknown in experience, it is what Moby Dick stands for that occupies the narrator's emphasis and the reader's attention through the greater part of the novel. In many ways, the great white whale may be compared to Spenser's "blatant beast" who, in *The Faerie Queene* (1590-1596), also represents the indeterminable elusive quarry and also escapes at the end to continue haunting the world.

Moby Dick is often considered to be the American epic. The novel is replete with the elements characteristic of that genre: the piling up of classical, biblical, historical allusions to provide innumerable parallels and tangents that have the effect of universalizing the scope of action; the narrator's strong sense of the fatefulness of the events he recounts and his corresponding awareness of his own singular importance as the narrator of momentous—otherwise unrecorded—events; Queequeg as Ishmael's "heroic companion," the folk flavor provided by countless proverbial statements; the leisurely pace of the narrative with its frequent digressions and parentheses; the epic confrontation of life and death on a suitably grand stage (the sea) with its consequences for the human city (the *Pequod*); the employment of microcosms to explicate the whole (for example, the painting in the Spouter Inn, the Nantucket pulpit, the crow's nest); epithetical characterization; a cyclic notion of time and events; an epic race of heroes (the Nantucket whalers with their biblical and exotic names); the mystical power of objects (Ahab's chair, the gold coin, or the *Pequod* itself); the alienated, sulking hero (Ahab); and the use of lists to enhance the impression of an all-inclusive compass. Finally, *Moby Dick* shares the usually didactic purpose of a folk epic; on one level, its purpose is to teach the reader about whales; on another level, it is to inspire the reader to become an epic hero.

All this richness of purpose and presentation is somehow made enticing by Melville's masterly invention of his narrator. Ishmael immediately establishes a comfortable rapport with the reader in the unforgettable opening lines of the novel. He is both the objective observer and a participant in the events observed and recounted, both spectator and narrator. Yet he is much more than the conventional wanderer/witness. As a schoolmaster and sometime voyager, he combines his intellectual knowledge with firsthand experience to make him an informed observer and a convincing, moving reporter. Simply by surviving, he transcends the Byronic heroism of Ahab, as the wholesome overcoming the sinister.

"Critical Evaluation" by Kenneth John Atchity

Further Reading

Bloom, Harold, ed. *Herman Melville's "Moby-Dick."* New York: Bloom's Literary Criticism, Chelsea House, 2007. Collection of reprinted and original essays about the novel, including an introduction to the novel by noted literary critic Alfred Kazin; discussions of cannibalism, slavery, and self-consumption in the tale; *Moby Dick* and antebellum popular culture; and the madness of Ahab.

Brodhead, Richard H., ed. *New Essays on "Moby Dick."* 1986. Reprint. New York: Cambridge University Press, 1994. Contains essays discussing the complexity of *Moby Dick*'s first sentence, the novel's Calvinist themes, and the multiplicity of sources used by Melville, among other subjects.

Davey, Michael J., ed. *A Routledge Literary Sourcebook on Herman Melville's "Moby-Dick."* New York: Routledge, 2004. Collection of essays providing an overview of Melville's career and placing the novel within the context of antebellum America, as well as numerous reviews and critiques of the book published from 1851 through 1998 that chart the changing reception of *Moby Dick*. Also analyzes the principal biblical allusions in the novel.

Delbanco, Andrew. *Melville: His World and Work.* New York: Knopf, 2005. Delbanco's critically acclaimed biography places Melville in his time, including discussion of the debate over slavery and details of life in 1840's New York. Also examines the significance of Melville's works at the time of first publication, and their reception in the twenty-first century.

Higgins, Brian, and Hershel Parker, eds. *Critical Essays on Herman Melville's "Moby Dick."* New York: G. K. Hall, 1992. A comprehensive selection of contemporary reviews and later essays about Melville's themes, techniques, literary influences, and affinities; Ahab and Ishmael; and Melville in the context of antebellum culture.

James, C. L. R. *Mariners, Renegades, and Castaways: The Story of Herman Melville and the World We Live In.* 1953. New ed. Hanover, N.H.: University Press of New England, 2001. A powerful reading of *Moby Dick* from the perspective of and in the context of twentieth century politics, arguing that Ahab's sway over his crew symbolizes the power of totalitarianism. This new edition includes an introduction by Donald E. Pease.

Matthiessen, F. O. *American Renaissance: Art and Expression in the Age of Emerson and Whitman.* 1941. Reprint. Whitefish, Mont.: Kessinger, 2009. This classic book gave the name American Renaissance to the period in which Melville lived and wrote, and discusses Melville's work alongside that of Walt Whitman, Ralph Waldo Emerson, Nathaniel Hawthorne, Henry David Thoreau, and others.

Miller, Edwin Haviland. *Melville.* New York: George Braziller, 1975. Psychoanalytic biography of Melville, especially attentive to his acquaintance with Nathaniel Hawthorne during the time he was composing *Moby Dick*.

Olson, Charles. *Call Me Ishmael.* San Francisco: City Lights Books, 1947. Reprint. 1997. Baltimore: Johns Hopkins University Press, 1997. A literary work of art in its own right, written by an influential postmodern American poet. Olson found Melville's library fifty years after the author's death and used it to base his theories of Melville's compositional process and his use of whaling lore and Shakespearean inspiration in *Moby Dick*.

Peretz, Eyal. *Literature, Disaster, and the Enigma of Power: A Reading of "Moby-Dick."* Stanford, Calif.: Stanford University Press, 2003. Although *Moby Dick* was published in the nineteenth century, Peretz argues that it presents a concept of disaster, violence, and catastrophe that became widely accepted in the twentieth century. Demonstrates how Melville altered traditional novel structures and vocabulary to create this depiction.

Stein, Suzanne. *The Pusher and the Sufferer: An Unsentimental Reading of "Moby Dick."* New York: Garland, 2000. Examines Melville's connections with his readers. Stein maintains that Melville and his narrator Ishmael are completely seduced by Ahab's charismatic charm; they, along with most readers and critics, fail to see that Ahab is not a tragic hero but is really a demonic character.

Stuckey, Sterling. *African Culture and Melville's Art: The Creative Process in "Benito Cereno" and "Moby-Dick."* New York: Oxford University Press, 2009. A new interpretation of the two works, in which Stuckey argues that Melville's worldview and his literary innovations were shaped by African cultural forms.

A Modern Instance

Author: William Dean Howells (1837-1920)
First published: 1882
Type of work: Novel
Type of plot: Domestic realism
Time of plot: Nineteenth century
Locale: New England

Principal characters:
MARCIA GAYLORD, a small-town young woman
SQUIRE GAYLORD, her father
BARTLEY HUBBARD, her husband
ATHERTON, a Boston lawyer
BEN HALLECK, a moral man
KINNEY, a vagabond

The Story:

In the little town of Equity, in northern New England, Bartley Hubbard is an up-and-coming young man. An orphan whose life has so far been one of great promise, he has a free and easy way about him and a ready tongue that makes him a general favorite. Squire Gaylord is pleased with his work as editor of the village paper, the *Free Press*, but not so pleased when Bartley becomes engaged to Marcia Gaylord, the squire's only daughter.

One afternoon, Bartley and Marcia go for a sleigh ride. In a swamp, they meet another cutter that has overturned in deep snow while trying to pass them on the narrow trail. The women in the overturned vehicle are Mrs. Morrison and her daughter, Hannah, who work in the office of the *Free Press*. Bartley jumps out to help them. Mrs. Morrison gets into the cutter by herself. Bartley lifts Hannah Morrison to her place, however, and Marcia is angry enough to participate in their first quarrel.

Hannah is the daughter of the town drunkard. Young Bartley encourages her greatly, thinking to improve the quality of her work, but she interprets his interest as love. Her father calls on Bartley one morning, drunk as usual, and asks Bartley's intentions toward his daughter. The young editor is so vexed and infuriated that he ejects Hannah's father bodily. His foreman, Henry Bird, in his turn accuses Bartley of stealing Hannah's affections. When he hits Bartley in the face, the latter retaliates with an openhanded slap. Henry falls, suffering a concussion when his head hits the floor.

The scandal is immense. Squire Gaylord takes a legal view of the possibility that Bird might die. Marcia interprets the fight as proof of an affair between Bartley and Hannah and breaks their engagement. Bartley resigns his job, even though Bird soon recovers. Bartley stays with Kinney, a crackerbox philosopher who cooks in a nearby logging camp. At the camp, Willett, the owner, visits with a fashionable party. Mrs. Macallister, one of the guests, flirts with Bartley, and he tries to curry favor by poking fun at the quaint Kinney.

That same night, Bartley and Kinney part in anger, and the young man walks back to town.

After selling his horse and cutter, Bartley goes to the station to catch the Boston train. Marcia catches up with him at the depot. Asking his forgiveness, she begs him to take her back. They are married the same day and leave for Boston together. In the city, Bartley goes to work. He turns his visit to the logging camp into a feature article that he sells for twenty-five dollars, marking the start of his fairly comfortable, although uncertain, income as a freelance writer. Marcia and he can afford only one room, but they are happy together. Marcia's father, Squire Gaylord, visits her once, to make certain she is married. He refuses to meet her husband again.

About the time Marcia learns that she is pregnant, Bartley is offered a job as managing editor of *Events*, whose publisher is a shrewd, unprincipled man named Witherby. With a regular salary at last, Bartley moves his wife into a private house. In college, Bartley had known Ben Halleck, a member of one of Boston's older families. Marcia knows no one at all, and she often wonders why Bartley does not resume his acquaintance with the Hallecks. Now that Bartley has a better job, he does call on the Hallecks, and they at once befriend the Hubbards. Through them, the young couple also gets acquainted with Atherton, a conservative lawyer. Halleck cares no more for Bartley than he ever had, but he is sorry for the trusting Marcia, saddled with a shallow husband. After the birth of her child, Flavia, Marcia sees less and less of Bartley, who spends many of his evenings away from home.

Witherby offers to sell some stock in the newspaper. For this deal, Bartley borrows fifteen hundred dollars from Halleck. Before long, he has assumed a prosperous air, and his drinking adds greatly to his girth. One night, after a quarrel with Marcia, he stays out late and gets quite drunk. Halleck sees him on the street and rescues him from a police officer. When Halleck takes the drunken man back to Marcia, his pity for the poor wife increases.

Kinney, visiting the Hubbards, amuses Bartley and another newspaperman with stories of his picturesque life. After he leaves, Bartley writes up the tales and sells them to another paper without Kinney's permission. Witherby is upset at seeing Bartley's work in a rival newspaper, and when he learns that his managing editor had written the article in violation of ethical considerations, he dismisses Bartley.

Bartley returns to freelancing. Halleck is absent from the city; hence Bartley cannot repay him fifteen hundred dollars. He intends to do so, but he gambles with the money and before long loses several hundred dollars. Atherton and Halleck are confirmed in their suspicions of Bartley's moral weakness. Marcia, returning from the Halleck house one evening, sees a drunken woman on the street. To her surprise, she recognizes Hannah Morrison. When she tries to talk with Hannah, the latter insists that Bartley is to blame for her present status in life. Suspecting and believing the worst of Bartley, Marcia rushes home and accuses him of having seduced Hannah. During the ensuing quarrel, they separate, and Bartley takes a train for Cleveland.

On the train, Bartley's wallet is stolen; in consequence, he is unable to send money back to Halleck. In Boston, Marcia regrets her hasty conclusions and stays on at their house awaiting her husband's return. When creditors begin to hound her, she enlists Atherton's sympathetic aid. He and Halleck continue to look after the deserted wife. In time, she thinks of Bartley as dead, and Halleck wonders when he will be free to speak to her of his love.

By chance, a western newspaper comes into Halleck's hands, a paper in which Bartley had given notice of suit for divorce. Marcia, her small daughter, Squire Gaylord, and Halleck take a train to Indiana to contest the suit. They arrive in time to have the divorce set aside, but during the trial, Marcia's father has a stroke from which he never recovers. After the trial, Bartley drifts further west and becomes the editor of a weekly paper in Whited Sepulchre, Arizona. He is shot and killed there by a citizen of the town. When Bartley's death is reported, Halleck wonders whether he is morally free to ask Marcia to marry him.

Critical Evaluation:

Born the son of a printer in Ohio in 1837, William Dean Howells pursued a career in printing, journalism, publishing, and fiction. His career began in his teens and eventually established him as the most influential force in American letters in the latter part of the nineteenth century. During the decade he acted as editor of the prestigious *Atlantic Monthly* (1871-1881), Howells shaped the direction of American literature as perhaps no single person before or since has done.

He resurrected the writings of such great talents as Herman Melville and Emily Dickinson, who had been either forgotten or overlooked. He mentored several gifted young authors, including Hamlin Garland, Bret Harte, and Stephen Crane, helping to introduce their work to the world, and he acted as confidant and valued critic for two of the literary giants of his time, Mark Twain and Henry James. Perhaps most important, Howells explicitly defined the style that dominated American literature in the years following the Civil War.

Howells believed that literature should impart a moral message. He argued that the only way it could convincingly do this was to depict life as real people actually lived it. Like Twain, Howells rejected the fanciful, sentimental, and melodramatic elements associated with Romantic fiction. Howells disliked works that appealed primarily to readers' emotions, that relied on unrealistic or overblown situations, that featured gaudy heroes and heroines, and that suggested that romantic love, or some idealized code of conduct, such as chivalry, was an appropriate basis for values and goals. Howells believed that works based on such romantic ideals had no connection to the lives of ordinary readers and, consequently, offered them no moral message. According to Howells, the best way to impart a moral was to present situations and characters to which readers could relate. He maintained that the story of highly individualized characters could easily have a general moral so long as the story rang true. Howells emphasized character over plot and the commonplace over the unusual. For Howells, such an approach created a more democratic literature, which reflected the needs (and the best interests) of the American reader.

Howells's *A Modern Instance* exemplifies the principles of realism. Its characters are ordinary people with rather modest aspirations, numerous failings, and complex personalities and motivations. Each has a unique view of the world, and all show little ability to see beyond their own narrow perspectives; consequently, they frequently act impulsively, often against their own self-interests. By the same token, the plot of the novel, rather than reflecting some highly structured scheme, seems to evolve naturally, driven by the personalities of its characters and by the sorts of coincidences common to everyday life. For example, Bartley does not really plan to leave Marcia. When he discovers that his wallet has been stolen in Chicago, he reacts to this chance occurrence by choosing a path he almost certainly would not have otherwise taken. Bartley's decision to continue westward, as well as Marcia's stubborn faith in his imminent return, depend on the unique personality traits of these two individualized characters, namely Bartley's desire to avoid conflict and follow the path of least resistance and Marcia's tendency to deny any evidence that threatens her unrealistic image of herself and her marriage.

As an early example of realism, *A Modern Instance* breaks new ground in its techniques and subject matter. Howells's novel is quite innovative in its reliance on psychology, a hallmark of realistic fiction. Howells attempts to portray the processes of perception and judgment; his effort leads to one of the most vivid descriptions of becoming drunk ever penned. Moreover, Howells repeatedly focuses on decision making, depicting it to be often a process beyond his characters' conscious control. For instance, Bartley gives little if any forethought to marrying Marcia. He capriciously decides to propose when he is feeling ill, and she fails to offer the sympathy he craves from her. Howells portrays Bartley's momentous decision as a response to an extremely insignificant and transitory discomfort—but it is exactly the discomfort that Bartley's unique psyche cannot bear.

While Howells is often accused of being overly prudish in his criticism and his fiction, in *A Modern Instance* he tackles a traditionally taboo subject, divorce. Inspired by the ancient play *Medea* and by several arguments he had witnessed between a couple while he was vacationing, Howells determined to deal with this subject, which he thought important to American life. Divorce was not given serious literary treatment again until well into the twentieth century. Moreover, given the strictures of his time, Howells deals as best he might with the more passionate side of human nature. While it is not directly stated, sexual desire clearly forms a major impetus for Bartley and Marcia's decision to marry.

Howell's principles were readily adopted by most of the great writers of his age; however, many soon began moving from Howells's brand of realism into naturalism, a trend that Howells found distasteful and argued vehemently against. Naturalism, while retaining the commonplace situations and ordinary characters of realism, depicts individuals as relatively powerless entities swept along by immense social and natural forces and driven by passions and urges beyond their control. For Howells, such a fatalistic view of life removed the moral component of literature.

Naturalism suggests that people are not responsible for their situations, actions, or even choices. Nevertheless, some of Howells's favorite writers, most notably Crane, were solidly naturalistic, and others, Twain among them, became more naturalistic as their careers progressed. Howells himself struggled to keep naturalistic themes from creeping into his own fiction. The difficulty of this struggle is evident in *A Modern Instance*, which reveals many naturalistic elements, particularly toward the end of the novel. For example, as the novel progresses, Bartley's drinking increases, causing more difficulties for him and Marcia. Bartley's drinking problem can just as easily be read as an inherited predisposition as it can be read as a flawed moral choice. Indeed, Howells risks denying his characters responsibility by taking such great care to create unique psychological underpinnings for their actions. Many of the characters' personalities—especially those of Marcia, Bartley, and Ben Halleck—seem to have been shaped greatly by the circumstances of their upbringing and events in their early lives. As a result, much of their behavior seems to stem less from conscious choice than from deeply rooted anxieties they cannot control.

"Critical Evaluation" by Thomas Hockersmith

Further Reading

Cady, Edwin H. "The Chief American Realist: 1881-1885." In *The Road to Realism: The Early Years, 1837-1885, of William Dean Howells*. Syracuse, N.Y.: Syracuse University Press, 1956. Places *A Modern Instance* in the broader context of Howells's life and work while offering a general critical overview of the novel.

Goodman, Susan, and Carl Dawson. *William Dean Howells: A Writer's Life*. Berkeley: University of California Press, 2005. Broad and compelling biography providing a comprehensive account of Howells's life and work. Among other topics, the biographers discuss Howells's friendships with and support of contemporary writers and his significance in American letters. Includes illustrations and a bibliography.

Graydon, Ben. "Product Branding in Howells's *A Modern Instance*." *ANQ* 20, no. 2 (Spring, 2007): 35-39. Graydon discusses the product branding of Bartley's beer in the novel, arguing that Howells's critique of modern culture had economic, as well as social, dimensions.

Smith, Geoffrey D. "Bartley Hubbard and Behavioral Art in William Dean Howells's *A Modern Instance*." *Studies in American Fiction* 7 (1979): 83-91. Explores Howells's literary techniques for depicting psychological processes in the novel.

Spangler, George M. "The Idea of Degeneration in American Fiction, 1880-1940." *English Studies* 70, no. 5 (October, 1989): 407-435. Discusses *A Modern Instance*'s place in American literature and identifies the novel as beginning a reversal of the traditional theme of regeneration. According to Spangler, Bartley Hubbard's degeneration paves the way for a new type of character, one that dominates much of the great fiction of succeeding years.

Stratman, Gregory J. *Speaking for Howells: Charting the*

Dean's Career Through the Language of His Characters. Lanham, Md.: University Press of America, 2001. Analyzes Howells's interest in language, focusing on the language of his characters and his use of literary dialect. Stratman argues that Howells's use of and writing about language demonstrates how his career moved in a circular path, from Romanticism to realism and back to Romanticism.

Tavernier-Courbin, Jacqueline. "Towards the City: Howells' Characterization in *A Modern Instance*." *Modern Fiction Studies* 24, no. 1 (Spring, 1978): 111-127. Examines the novel in the light of the conventions of nineteenth century popular fiction. According to Tavernier-Courbin, Howells uses setting and character in the novel to undermine typical romantic stereotypes.

Wright, Ellen F. "Given Bartley, Given Marcia: A Reconsideration of Howells' *A Modern Instance*." *Texas Studies in Language and Literature* 23, no. 2 (Summer, 1981): 214-231. By examining the many married couples in the novel, Wright argues that Howells does not intend to indict either American culture in general or the institution of marriage in particular.

Modern Love

Author: George Meredith (1828-1909)
First published: 1862
Type of work: Poetry

George Meredith's *Modern Love* is his longest poem, and when it was published (a year after his wife died), it was seen as a disturbed work. It is a sonnet sequence consisting of fifty separate sonnets rhyming *abba cddc effe ghhg*. Meredith's sixteen-line sonnets—a variation on the traditional fourteen-line sonnet—provide an apt structure for presenting interconnected but frequently contradictory feelings and reactions. Noted for their complex imagery, these sonnets present the speaker's diverse emotions, which are constantly shifting, subtly and not so subtly, in both intensity and distance from his subject. The poem is about his love for his wife.

He discovers that his wife is unfaithful, and to the husband, like a courtly lover, her faithlessness is unforgivable. Her deception is devastating. If her appearance has nothing to do with reality, he is without moorings at all. He does not know himself without her. When man is nothing more than clay and discord, death is preferable, but of death and oblivion he wants no part. Unlike May, whose annual glory defies the passage of time, the husband's foot rests precariously on a unique but unverifiable past that may neither be seen clearly nor blotted out. It remains to mock him, unless he wishes to consign himself and the past that created him to oblivion.

The brilliance and lucidity of the speaker make it too easy for the reader to forget that, although two people are engaged in the most personal of conflicts, only one side, the husband's, is available. The husband, the speaker in *Modern Love*, shifts from third to first person and back as convenience serves ("he" and "I" are mingled throughout the sonnet sequence), and the imagery becomes more densely evocative the more closely it is examined. When the poem was published, Meredith was accused of indecency. The public was not ready to accept the intimate, passionate relationship between a husband and wife as proper subject matter for a writer. The fact that Meredith's first marriage to Mary Peacock Nicolls ended in separation and her death in 1861 complicated critical opinion even more. Since the poem was read biographically, recognition of *Modern Love* as a powerful work of art complete unto itself was hard to win. After the 1862 edition, the poem was not reprinted until 1892. Worse yet, the poem was misread as somehow didactic.

The husband perceives love as the earthly state most nearly divine, the loss of which will be intolerable. Such love is a garden, suggesting both the Garden of Eden and the gardens of pagan mythology. When it becomes blighted, however, this garden is most deadly, not only to the lovers (in this case husband and wife, referred to as Madam) but also to any unsuspecting serpents. The golden-haired Lady is a serpent because she is the other woman. The other man, who in this double set of triangles comes first, will undoubtedly meet a serpent's fate and be crushed beneath a heel until he cannot feel or, if he is so unfortunate as to be callous, until he can.

These two, the other man and the other woman, have hearts into which despair can be, and finally is, struck. The wife does not hesitate but crushes the other woman's rose under her heel as if she were crushing the Lady herself out of her husband's life. Such serpents are, however, innocuous in comparison to the serpent struggle between the wife and the husband (see sonnets 1, 6, 14, 34, and 44), who apostrophizes to Raphael, the Italian painter, whose figures never show signs of inner conflict (sonnet 33). Although the speaker occasionally, briefly, quotes his wife directly (sonnets 9, 34, 35, 42, and 49) and seems to be addressing her at other times (sonnets 6, 8, 9, 11, 14, 24, 25, and 26), *Modern Love* remains the husband's soliloquy, a soliloquy where there should be a dialogue. The husband's passionate, at times violent, intensity leads him to accuse his wife of killing their love (sonnet 11). He shows her love letters she wrote but not all to him (sonnet 15). At another moment, he is aware that he should be able to give charity, when he must ask for charity in return (sonnet 20). In sonnet 43, he recognizes their joint responsibility: "I see no sin:/ The wrong is mixed. In tragic life, God wot,/ No villain need be! Passions spin the plot:/ We are betrayed by what is false within." His desperate need to survive the truth, to reconsider his marriage and the love between him and his wife (which he had accepted as the greatest treasure life had to offer), and to escape despair requires some greater absolute than their love. Long ago, he casually admitted that love dies, but at that time he never thought much about such a possibility (sonnet 16). The husband, who often tries to assume a position of objectivity, seems to attain compassionate detachment only with his wife's suicide. (That *Modern Love* should be examined as poetry, not biography, is indicated by the fact that there is no evidence that Meredith's first wife committed suicide.)

The husband's struggle with the discouraging truth of self-recognition is revealed. To deny him the ability to describe himself in the third person as well as in the first will not only rob the poem of part of its richness but undercut the variety of the speaker's reactions: noble, ignoble, cruel, compassionate, rigid, yearning, righteous, wrenching. The emotional crisis the speaker undergoes is such that there is no way to predict how he will react. The husband's approach to the realization that there is no crime—that neither of them is to blame for the other's actions (sonnet 43)—is in no way direct. His lament is that a woman's intellect cannot function independently of her physiology and that the undue subtleties resulting from this given lead to her destruction. He assumes that woman needs "more brain." Such an assertion attests the fact that his own knowledge is still incomplete, his own sense mixed up in his senses (sonnet 48). Initially, the husband sees complete ruin: himself and his wife lying like Tristran and Iseult (sonnet 1). He believes that their love, in spite of all its vicissitudes, is somehow immortal, hence the allusion to Tristan and Iseult, the couple who most exemplifies courtly love.

Husband and wife, however, no longer have a common fate or share a common history. His wife does not know what is going on in his mind, and her lack of awareness, genuine or feigned, infuriates him. When their superficial smiles meet, his inward rage churns until the world he sees is bloodstained (sonnet 2). While he rages against her, she, completely unaware of his inward soliloquy, sits laughing gently with another (sonnet 6). He is still desirous of his wife. She has meaning for him that no one else has. He nevertheless asserts that he knows it is too late to seek the spiritual in love when "the fire is dying in the grate" (sonnet 4), even though the throes of his passion remain anything but cool. Her beauty enables him to see her with the eyes of other men (sonnet 7). The fact that what is familiar to him is currently even more familiar to another man, however, so distorts his perception that he asks himself if they can actually be married. Only later, in the second part of *Modern Love* (sonnets 27-39), does he see her once again as his wife and address her as such (sonnet 33).

The sea imagery in *Modern Love*, including the wreck, is critical. Wrecked or not, wicked or innocent, the speaker will be taken as nothing less than pilot of his own life, no matter what the effect of the wind and the waves. Resolved against ever again leaving his heart in the control of another (sonnet 19), he enters with the Lady in the game of love or sentiment (sonnet 28). There is nothing here to carry him beyond the physical. Even a love seemingly superior in every way to young love has insufficient weight and force (sonnet 39). He is helplessly adrift. Dreading that his original love is still alive prevents him from attending to a new one. How, he asks, can he love one woman and simultaneously be jealous of another (sonnet 40)? Love is increasingly contemplated in the purely earthly realm where a person is nothing but clay. In struggling against his fate, the individual who becomes half serpent, like the Fiend (sonnet 33), may grow again to be half-human. From the very beginning of *Modern Love*, as in the courtly love tradition, love is associated with death. Even dead, love is terrible in its effect. Aside from the imagery linking love and death, as the sonnet sequence develops the wife is linked with images of death, losing substance, never joining her husband's present.

Toward the end of the summer, the husband and wife have no shared joys. They are present in the same place and at peace, but not together (sonnet 47). The speaker learns that passion without love allays no torments (sonnet 32), and the Lady, an asp, is no antidote for the "serpent bites" inflicted by Madam. The husband seeks to salvage his capacity to love. Beneath his agony and frustration, a belief in the reality of his past love is gradually to be perceived. Was this love lost (sonnet 50) because it did not develop in time?

He talks about his wife going among "the children of illusion" (sonnet 12); her illusion is no longer his. He marvels that men should prize the love of woman (sonnet 31), but this feeling is only sour grapes, and he admits that being approved by his Lady is not half as fine as being loved (sonnet 31). Midnight may perhaps be regarded as the hour of truth, or less melodramatically, the moment when pretense may no longer pass for reality. Husband and wife succeed in making others envy their love (sonnet 17), but in the country at Christmas, he recognizes that while they fool others, the abyss of midnight, in which they will recognize themselves as hypocrites, still awaits them (sonnet 23). Later, as the clock approaches midnight (sonnet 41), he no longer has any doubt about the death of love, and finally, he recalls that it was "the middle of the night" when he heard her call just before she died (sonnet 48).

The fact that there is a reference to spring in sonnet 11, to Christmas in sonnet 23, and to summer in sonnet 45 has led some critics to assert that *Modern Love* covers a little more than a year, but a chronology of the poem provides no insight into the husband's anguished consciousness that is at issue in this poem. Similarly, seeing the poem as divided into three parts (1-26, 27-39, 40-50) does not provide much insight.

In sonnet 43, the images of love and death and water are synthesized. The force of the wind impels the waves that, forced into hissing serpents, leave their mark far up on the sand that they momentarily devour. The same image is used at the end: "In tragic hints here see what evermore/ Moves dark as yonder midnight's ocean's force,/ Thundering like ramping hosts of warrior horse,/ To throw that faint thin line upon the shore!" There is an attempt on the speaker's part to draw some kind of moral in the last two sonnets. Only confusion results. The major achievement of this poem is its depiction of the vivid intensity of a husband's failing love for his wife. *Modern Love* remains an oddly undated poem, written one hundred years ahead of its time.

Carol Bishop

Further Reading

Fletcher, Ian, ed. *Meredith Now: Some Critical Essays*. New York: Barnes & Noble, 1971. Particularly useful in this collection of critical essays on Meredith's work is John Lucas's essay "Meredith as Poet."

Jones, Mervyn. *The Amazing Victorian: A Life of George Meredith*. London: Constable, 1999. Jones's biography aims to recover Meredith from obscurity and introduce the author to a new generation of readers. Jones links Meredith's life to his writing and includes a forty-page appendix recounting the plot summaries of all of Meredith's novels.

Priestley, J. B. *George Meredith*. New York: Macmillan, 1970. Contains useful information on Meredith's life and good insight into his work. First published in 1926.

Trevelyan, G. M. *The Poetry and Philosophy of George Meredith*. New York: Russell & Russell, 1966. This study provides helpful commentary on Meredith's poetry from a contemporary admirer. First published in 1920.

Williams, Joan, ed. *Meredith: The Critical Heritage*. New York: Barnes & Noble, 1971. Provides a lengthy, invaluable record of the early criticism, including Algernon Charles Swinburne and Robert Louis Stevenson's different statements of defense of Meredith against the charge of indecency.

Wright, Walter F. *Art and Substance in George Meredith: A Study in Narrative*. Lincoln: University of Nebraska Press, 1953. Argues for a congruity among Meredith's emotional life, intellectual life, and creative work. Index.

A Modest Proposal

Author: Jonathan Swift (1667-1745)
First published: 1729, as *A Modest Proposal for Preventing the Children of Poor People of Ireland from Being a Burden to Their Parents or the Country, and for Making Them Beneficial to the Public*
Type of work: Essay and social criticism

A Modest Proposal, by Jonathan Swift, is probably the most famous satirical essay in the English language. It was first published in Dublin as a short, anonymous pamphlet. The essay begins as a seemingly dispassionate diagnosis of the extreme poverty in eighteenth century Ireland. With nary a shift in tone, the essayist discloses his remedy: Render the children of the poor as food for the table. The children of Ireland should be sold and consumed, for sustenance of the destitute, as delicacies for the wealthy, and for the general progress of society. The essayist proceeds to furnish ironically logical reasons in support of this shocking and repulsive proposal.

Swift was born in Dublin in 1667 to English parents. He wrote poetry, essays, fiction, and political tracts, all with a biting satirical wit. His novel *Gulliver's Travels* (1726; originally titled *Travels into Several Remote Nations of the World, in Four Parts, by Lemuel Gulliver, First a Surgeon, and Then a Captain of Several Ships*) is a mix of travelogue, fantasy, adventure, and satire, making it one of the world's masterpieces of literature.

While Swift was advancing in the world of popular and polemical literature and aspiring to literary greatness, he was also rising through the ranks of the established clergy. In 1713, he was appointed dean of St. Patrick's Anglican Cathedral in Dublin. There, he saw firsthand the poverty and oppression of the Irish. He wrote tracts, letters, and essays on their behalf, including "A Letter to a Member of Parliament, in Ireland" (1708), "The Story of an Injured Lady" (1720), *A Proposal for Universal Use of Irish Manufacture* (1720), "Drapier's Letters" (1724), and "A Short View of the State of Ireland" (1728). Of these efforts, which would earn Swift a reputation as a champion of Ireland, *A Modest Proposal* is the most famous.

By the time he wrote *A Modest Proposal*, Swift's satirical methods, rooted in the classical techniques of Roman satirists such as Juvenal, had been perfected. His prose style—muscular, compact, sinewy, and expressive—can lay claim to being the most exact and forceful in the English language.

His fertile imagination was able to lay down layer upon layer of irony in almost bewildering succession. *A Modest Proposal*, like *Gulliver's Travels*, transcends the political, social, and economic crises that gave birth to it, woeful as they were. Packed with irony and satirical revelations of the human condition, this fantastical tract rises to timeless literature.

A Modest Proposal was published as a short pamphlet of fewer than two thousand words in September, 1729. It was written anonymously, although readers quickly deduced that the author was the master satirist Dean Swift. It is crucial to note that Swift, while the author of the essay, is not its speaker. Rather the authorial voice, perhaps best called the proposer, is an unnamed and unknown personage whose intellectual characteristics and prejudices can be gleaned from his proposals. What is stated in a straightforward manner by the proposer is meant satirically by Swift. The distance maintained between Swift and the proposer is necessary for the many layers of irony in the essay. The proposer, like the narrators in Swift's fiction, himself becomes a character in the intricate interplay of realism and fable, irony and satire. *A Modest Proposal* therefore combines Swift's outrage at the cruelties and stupidities of society with satirical rhetoric and his skill at creating fiction.

The proposer begins the tract by bemoaning the state of the poor in Ireland. Mothers begging for alms, with a crowd of children in their arms, are a common sight. The vast majority of the population is poor, with little useful employment. Poverty drives the youths of Ireland into crime, slavery, or the armies of the deposed Stuart kings in Spain. The proposer has an advantageous solution, to which he cannot imagine a single objection. Up to this point, the proposer has shown himself to be a reasonable if somewhat pedantic thinker, armed with a host of statistics about demography and economics in Ireland. Certainly his critique reflects no credit on the Whig government in London, which Swift, a High Church Tory in religion and politics, despised. The English colonial rule of absentee landlords, vast plantations, and enforced settlements is discredited.

Following immediately upon these trenchant observations comes the solution:

a young healthy child well-nursed is, at a year old, a most delicious nourishing and wholesome food, whether stewed, roasted, baked, or boiled; and I make no doubt that it will equally serve in a fricassee, or a ragout.

To be exact, the modest proposal is that of the 120,000 infants computed to be born every year in Ireland, 100,000 would be sold to the wealthy to be consumed at table, 20,000 children being reserved for breeding. The proposer calculates that a plump infant of 30 pounds would provide food for many dinners and, preserved with pepper or salt, will last well into winter. The price of each child is estimated to be about ten shillings (about one thousand modern U.S. dollars), providing about eight shillings of profit to the parents. In addition, the skin of the child would make fine gloves for wealthy ladies and summer boots for wealthy gentlemen. However, the proposer rejects the idea of converting adolescents to food, as their flesh is likely to be tough and lean.

The proposer supports his suggestions with a mass of coldly delivered statistics, demographic data, and calculations, as if writing one of the then-popular tracts on mercantilism or trade with the colonies. He pedantically weighs the pros and cons of his proposal, as he would any political argument. He lists six weighty and obvious advantages. First, his proposal would reduce the number of Catholics in Ireland, the traditional enemy of the Protestant settlers. Second, it would give farmers the means to pay their absentee landlords, since their agricultural products and livestock had already been seized under the English tenancy system. Third, it would increase the domestic revenue of Ireland, with no money being sent abroad.

Fourth, the parents—"breeders" as they are called in the tract—would not only receive a generous income, but would also be relieved of the expense of raising their children. Fifth, this new variety of cuisine would produce fine recipes for culinary gentlemen and their dining establishments. Finally, the possibility of selling one's children would be an inducement to enter into the vital institution of marriage, as parents would better care for their children (and husbands for their pregnant wives) given the happy profits that could be expected from well-nourished infants.

Once he has listed these benefits, the proposer answers the one possible objection that he incredulously predicts one might raise to his scheme. It is true, he says, that this proposal would greatly reduce the population of Ireland, but this very reduction of population would be beneficial, as there is no

hope of more humane measures being taken to alleviate Irish misery, such as taxing absentee landlords, replacing profligacy with industry, or cultivating a spirit of mercy from landlords toward their tenants. Finally, the proposer vouches for his own disinterest and lack of self-motivation in his proposal, as his own children are all grown and his wife past child-bearing age. (Swift himself was a lifelong bachelor.)

A Modest Proposal is a devastating critique on many levels. The most obvious object of the satire is the impoverished condition of the Irish, blamed on the oppressive plantation system by which the labor of farmers was exploited by grasping landlords. *A Modest Proposal* can be seen as an early warning about the distorted economic system that would produce the ruinous potato famine of the 1840's. The miseries of the Irish were of long standing, but Swift's critique went right to the heart of the enlightened Whiggery then reigning in London. Indeed, the character of the proposer is a caricature of the modern theorist, stuffed full of economics, statistics, and arithmetic, but blind to fundamental human values. In this manner the proposer resembles the "projectors" of the island of Lagado in *Gulliver's Travels*, whose new designs for constructing a mill leave the thitherto prosperous countryside in shambles.

Swift's critique goes beyond the miserable conditions of Ireland or the vapid theories of modernism. In a terse manner, it touches on many of the vices of the human condition. Targets of this satire include the cruelty of parents and governments that value children as commodities; voluntary abortions and infanticide, which are equated with each other and equally abhorred; eugenics or euthanasia as solutions to human want; the greed of merchants and the indolence of the poor; and even colonialism (at the time, all of Ireland was governed from London as part of the United Kingdom). Generosity, decency, and tenderness are scorned, and the metaphoric cannibalism of modern society, in which neighbor preys upon neighbor, is vividly suggested by being made literal.

In Swift's other great satirical essay, *Argument Against Abolishing Christianity* (1708; originally titled *An Argument to Prove That the Abolishing of Christianity in England May, as Things Now Stand, Be Attended with Some Inconveniences, and Perhaps Not Produce Those Many Good Effects Proposed Thereby*), Swift portrays a parliamentary act removing burdens on religious dissenters as an attack on religion, prompting a savage satire on human unbelief. The authorial voice of that essay is a modern thinker, who ironically proposes a nominal and hypocritical Christianity as the solution for England. Likewise, in *A Modest Proposal*, Swift leaps from the sorry conditions of Ireland into a savage attack on human indifference and cruelty, writing in the assumed voice of a modern theorist who ironically proposes death to improve life.

A Modest Proposal has become one of the most imitated and cited of all satirical essays to this day. Unfortunately, thousands of writers title their straightforward ideas "modest proposals," without any apparent irony, indicating a lack of knowledge of the irony inherent in Swift's title. Even more unfortunate, writers such as Garett Hardin in his influential essay on population "Tragedy of the Commons" (1968) refer to parents as "breeders," following Swift but without Swift's irony. On the other hand, some members of the gay rights movement have also appropriated the term, irony and all, to refer to heterosexuals.

The cold rationality of modern theoreticians is implied in Swift's essay. The essay is also a warning against modernity's potential for genocide that may be seen to foreshadow a host of events, from the Irish massacres of Oliver Cromwell in the seventeenth century to the horrors committed during the Holocaust in the twentieth century. It may not be too much of a leap to see the modest proposal as hinting at the eugenics movements, murderous purges, Five-year Plans, Final Solution, Great Leap Forward, and Killing Fields of modern times. As a cry to succor the Irish, this essay earned Swift the title of patriot. As a stylistically masterful satire on the propensity of modern human "cannibalism"—the murder of some humans in the name of bettering the lives of others—it ensures Swift's reputation as a perennially significant author.

Howard Bromberg

Further Reading

Akroyd, Clarissa. *Savage Satire: The Story of Jonathan Swift.* Greensboro, N.C.: Morgan Reynolds, 2006. Intended for young adults, this biography includes commentary on Swifts's greatest works, *Gulliver's Travels* and *A Modest Proposal.*

Barnett, Louise. *Jonathan Swift in the Company of Women.* New York: Oxford University Press, 2007. A study of Swift's relations to women in his life and writings; links *A Modest Proposal* to Swift's repugnance at overpopulation, untrammeled human reproduction, and coldly biological motherhood.

Bloom, Harold, ed. *Jonathan Swift: Modern Critical Views.* New York: Chelsea House, 2000. In this critical biography for young adult readers, the noted literary critic Harold Bloom describes *A Modest Proposal* as a preeminent example of Swift's satire, the most savage and merciless in the history of Western literature.

DeGategno, Paul, and R. Jay Stubblefield. *Critical Companion to Jonathan Swift: A Literary Reference to His Life and Work.* New York: Facts On File, 2006. Comprehensive survey and analysis of Swift's life and writings, topically arranged.

Fox, Christopher, ed. *The Cambridge Companion to Jonathan Swift.* New York: Cambridge University Press, 2003. In this collection of essays on Swift's life and literature, essayist Patrick Kelly finds *A Modest Proposal* rhetorically brilliant but mistaken in its economic diagnosis of Irish poverty.

Kelly, Ann. *Jonathan Swift and Popular Culture: Myth, Media, and the Man.* New York: Palgrave, 2002. Study of Swift as a maker of his own cultural myth and as a modern mythologized literary celebrity. Argues that, in modern culture, Swift as the author of *A Modest Proposal* represents the epitome of the artist as hero, presenting truths that polite society finds offensive.

Meyers, Jeffrey. "Swift and Kafka." *Papers on Language and Literature* 40, no. 3 (Summer, 2004): 329-336. Short study of Swift's influence on the writer Franz Kafka. Meyer's description of the animalistic imagery favored by Swift and Kafka is well exemplified in *A Modest Proposal*, with its farm-animal references to breeders and to humans as table fare.

Rawson, Claude, and Ian Higgins. *The Essential Writings of Jonathan Swift.* New York: W. W. Norton, 2009. A volume in the masterful Norton Critical Edition series, including the best editions of Swift's major works, with biographical and critical annotations and essays.

Wittkowsky, George. "Swift's *Modest Proposal*: The Biography of an Early Georgian Pamphlet." *Journal of the History of Ideas* 4, no. 1 (January, 1943): 74-104. Pioneering literary study of *A Modest Proposal*, demonstrating its parody of contemporary political tracts that proposed newfangled economic solutions to Great Britain's woes.

Moll Flanders

Author: Daniel Defoe (1660-1731)
First published: 1722, as *The Fortunes and Misfortunes of the Famous Moll Flanders, Who Was Born in Newgate, and During a Life of Continued Variety, for Threescore Years, Besides Her Childhood, Was Twelve Years a Whore, Five Times a Wife (Thereof Once to Her Own Brother), Twelve Years a Thief, Eight Years a Transported Felon in Virginia, at Last Grew Rich, Lived Honest, and Died a Penitent. Written from Her Own Memorandums*
Type of work: Novel
Type of plot: Picaresque
Time of plot: Seventeenth century
Locale: England and the American colonies

Principal characters:
MOLL FLANDERS, a rogue
ROBIN, her first husband
A SEA CAPTAIN, Moll's half brother and husband
JEMMY E., a rogue

The Story:

When her mother is transported to the American colonies as a felon, eighteen-month-old Moll Flanders is left without family or friends to care for her. For a time, she is befriended by a band of gypsies, who desert her in Colchester. There the child is a charge of the parish. Becoming a favorite of the wife and daughters of the mayor, Moll receives gentle treatment and much attention and flattery.

At the age of fourteen, Moll Flanders is again left without a home. When her indulgent instructor dies, she is taken in service by a kindly woman of means, and she receives instruction along with the daughters of the family. Moll is superior to these daughters in all but wealth. During her residence there, she loses her virtue to the oldest son of the family and secretly becomes his mistress. Later, Robin, the youngest son, makes her a proposal of marriage, and she accepts him. Five years later, Robin dies. Soon afterward, Moll marries a spendthrift draper who quickly depletes her savings and is imprisoned. In the meantime, Moll takes lodgings at the Mint. Passing as a widow, she calls herself Mrs. Flanders.

Her next venture in matrimony is with a sea captain, with whom she sails to the Virginia colony. There she discovers to her extreme embarrassment that she is married to her own half brother. After eight years in Virginia, she returns to England to take up residence at Bath. In due time, she becomes acquainted with a gentleman whose wife is demented. Moll helpfully nurses him through a serious illness and later becomes his mistress. During the six years in which they live together, she gives birth to three children and saves enough money to support herself after the gentleman has regretted his indiscretions and left her.

Next, the ambitious Moll meets a banker with whom she carries on a mild flirtation, but she leaves him to marry an Irishman named Jemmy E., supposedly a very wealthy gentleman of Lancashire. Moll has allowed him to believe that she has means, and she soon learns that her new husband is penniless. He has played the same trick on her that she has used on him. Moll and Jemmy E. are both rogues and therefore make a congenial couple, but eventually they decide to separate; he follows his unlawful profession of highway robbery, and she returns to the city. After Jemmy has left her, Moll finds that she is again to become a mother. She gives birth to a healthy boy who is quickly boarded out.

In the meantime, Moll has been receiving letters from her admirer, the bank clerk. They meet at an inn and are married there. On the day after the ceremony, she sees her Lancashire husband, the highwayman, in the courtyard of the inn, and she is able to save him from arrest. For five years, until his death, Moll lives with the banker in great happiness. After his death, she sells her property and takes lodgings. Forty-eight years old and with children to support, she is prompted by the devil to steal a bundle from an apothecary shop. Next, she steals a necklace from a pretty little girl on her way home from dancing school. With these acts Moll Flanders embarks on a twelve-year period as a thief. Sometimes she disguises herself in men's clothing; her favorite disguise is that of a beggar woman. After a period of apprenticeship, Moll becomes the richest thief in all England. During her years as a thief, a chance encounter with a gentleman at Bartholomew Fair results in an affair, which the two carry on for some time.

Finally, Moll is seized while trying to steal two pieces of

silk brocade and is locked up in Newgate prison. There she again sees her former husband the highwayman, who has been committed at Newgate for a robbery on Hounslow Heath. Before going up for trial and sentence, Moll repents of her sins; nevertheless, she is sentenced to death by the court. Through the kind offices of a minister, however, the truly repentant Moll is given a reprieve. The next day, she watches her fellow prisoners being carried away in carts to meet the fate that she has been spared. She is finally sentenced to transportation to America.

The highwayman, with whom she has become reconciled, is awarded a like sentence, and the pair embark for Virginia in the same ship. They have made all arrangements for a comfortable journey and have stocked themselves with the tools and materials necessary for running a plantation in the new world. Forty-two days after leaving an Irish port, they arrive in Virginia. Once ashore, Moll learns that her mother has died. Her half brother, to whom she had once been married, and her son are still living near the spot where she had disembarked years before.

Not yet wishing to meet her relatives and not desiring to be known as a transported criminal in America, she arranges for transportation to the Carolina colony. After crossing Chesapeake Bay, she and the highwayman find the ship already overloaded. They decide to stay in Maryland and set up a plantation there. With two servants and fifty acres of land under cultivation, they soon prosper. Then Moll arranges an interview with her son in Virginia, across the bay.

In due course, Moll learns that her mother has willed her a plantation on the York River, a plantation complete with stock and servants. She presents her son with one of the stolen watches she has brought from London. After five weeks, she returns to Maryland, where she and her husband become wealthy and prosperous planters of good repute throughout all the colonies. This prosperity is augmented by the arrival of a second cargo of goods from England, for which Moll had arranged before she sailed. In the meantime, the man who was both brother and husband to Moll dies, and she is now able to see her son without any embarrassment.

At the age of seventy years, Moll returns to England. Her husband soon joins her there, and they resolve to spend the rest of their lives in repentance for their numerous sins.

Critical Evaluation:

As the novel's full original title suggests, the heroine of *Moll Flanders* is perhaps the world's best-known female picaro. Ever since it was first published in 1722, *Moll Flanders* has entertained the reading public with its lusty, energetic tale of a seventeenth century adventurer and manipula-

tor. The book is so convincingly written and contains such a wealth of intimate detail that many readers have assumed the story is true biography. Daniel Defoe himself rather coyly suggested as much, perhaps because he feared such a scandalous story could not be published or would not be popular if it was known to be a work of the imagination.

In this as in his other great novels, such as *Robinson Crusoe* (1719) and *A Journal of the Plague Year* (1722), Defoe achieves his realistic effect by incorporating a wealth of authentic detail. Having been a pamphleteer and journalist much of his life, Defoe knew well how concrete facts and specific examples build plausibility. He has Moll relate her remarkable story simply, thoroughly, and with candor. She is literal-minded and bothers little with description or metaphor. (In his preface, Defoe claims to have cleaned up the language and omitted some of the more "vicious part of her life"; thus Moll's sexual adventures are related in curious, sometimes amusing circumlocutions.) Moll sticks mainly to the stark realities of her life except for passages in which she moralizes about her misdeeds.

Despite the verisimilitude, however, the novel has a problem of tone that frequently puzzles modern readers and has stirred a lively controversy among critics. The question may be stated thus: Is the story full of conscious irony, or is it told in utter sincerity? If the former is the case, most scholars agree that *Moll Flanders* is a masterwork of social commentary and of fictional art. If the latter, there are lapses in the author's moral scheme.

The problem centers more on Moll's attitude than on her actions. Given her situation—that of a woman of no status but with large ambitions—her behavior is entirely plausible. In her childhood, Moll is dependent for her survival on the whims and kindnesses of strangers. By the time she is eight years old, she is already determined to be a "gentlewoman"—an ambition very nearly impossible for a woman to fulfill in seventeenth century England when she has neither family nor, more important, money. Moll is quick to recognize the value of money in assuring not only one's physical security but also one's place in the world—and she aims for a comfortable place. Money thus becomes her goal and eventually her god. To attain it, she uses whatever means are at hand; as a beautiful woman, she finds sex the handiest means available. When, after a number of marriages and other less legitimate alliances, sex is no longer a salable commodity, she turns to thieving and rapidly becomes a master of the trade.

Readers know from other of Defoe's writings that the author sympathized with the plight of women in his society; education and most trades (except the oldest profession) were closed to them. For the most part, a woman was entirely dependent for her welfare on her husband or other men in her life. As a hardheaded pragmatist who finds herself in straitened circumstances, Moll is much akin to Becky Sharp of William Makepeace Thackeray's *Vanity Fair* (1847-1848, serial; 1848, book) and Scarlett O'Hara of Margaret Mitchell's *Gone with the Wind* (1936); all three use their ingenuity to survive in a hostile world, and although readers do not entirely condone their behavior, they can understand it.

After Moll has acted, however, she reflects; it is this reflection that poses a problem. For convenience, she marries the younger brother of the man who first seduced her. After he dies, she remarks, "He had been really a very good husband to me, and we lived very agreeably together," but then she quickly complains that because he had not had time to acquire much wealth, she was "not much mended by the match." Another five-year marriage also ends in her widowhood; she wastes not a word in grieving the husband who has given her "an uninterrupted course of ease and content" but laments the loss of his money at excessive length. Soon afterward, she steals a gold necklace from a child and admits that she was tempted to kill the child to prevent any outcry. She rationalizes that "I only thought I had given the parents a just reproof of their negligence in leaving the poor lamb to come home by itself, and it would teach them to take more care another time."

These recollections are told from the point of view of a seventy-year-old woman. Moll spends a good deal of time explaining that poverty and fear of poverty drove her to all her wickedness, yet she never admits that even when she is relatively secure, she keeps on scheming and thieving. Like many other entrepreneurs, she has come to find excitement and fulfillment in the turning of a profit, the successful clinching of a deal, the accumulation of wealth for its own sake. Although she repents her flagrant sins—deception, thieving, whoring—she apparently never recognizes the sin of her spirit in basing all human relationships on their monetary worth. Furthermore, although she closes her account by declaring that she and her husband are "resolved to spend the remainder of our years in sincere penitence for the wicked lives we have lived," they are now free from want, partly because of an inheritance but also because of the proceeds from her years as a thief. Readers see no indication that penitence goes any deeper than a rather gratified feeling that she has made peace with her Maker (a peace made, by the way, in Newgate prison while Moll was under sentence of death). There is no evidence that she intends to make restitution of stolen goods or apply herself in positive good works to offset some of her wicked deeds.

The question, then, is whether Defoe expects readers to see the irony in what one critic has called Moll's moral "muddle" or whether he is so outraged at what poverty and the lack of opportunity can do that he himself fails to see the lapses in her moral system. A few clues are presented from Defoe's life, but they are contradictory. Like Moll, Defoe was frequently haunted by poverty and spent months in the hell of Newgate. His steadfast stand as a Dissenter (which made him a lifelong outsider in English society), his humane views of the treatment of the poor and of women, his dogged and successful efforts to pay every penny of a £17,000 bankruptcy—all give evidence of a man of high and stern principles. On the other hand, he worked for the Tories and then for the Whigs, writing with passion and conviction on both sides of controversial issues, and in his numerous business ventures he was not above swindling others (even his own mother-in-law). His own dreams of status are attested by his love for trade—"the whore I doated on"—and his addition of "De" to his name (his father was James Foe) to provide a touch of gentility.

Critics have not resolved the debate over morality and irony in *Moll Flanders*. Few, however, will dispute that the novel offers a fascinating account. It has held the attention of readers for centuries. Virginia Woolf called *Moll Flanders* one of the "few English novels which we can call indisputably great."

"Critical Evaluation" by Sally Buckner

Further Reading

Backscheider, Paula R. *Daniel Defoe: His Life*. 1986. New ed. Baltimore: Johns Hopkins University Press, 1992. Provides biographical data and critical interpretations of Defoe's novels, placing emphasis on his innovative point of view.

Bell, Ian A. *Defoe's Fiction*. New York: Barnes & Noble, 1985. Examines the elements of Defoe's writing style and his characters. Discusses the problem of morality in *Moll Flanders*.

Boardman, Michael M. *Defoe and the Use of Narrative*. New Brunswick, N.J.: Rutgers University Press, 1985. Provides a discussion of Defoe's narrative technique, with a focus on how the author structures his stories.

Defoe, Daniel. *Moll Flanders: An Authoritative Text, Contexts, Criticism*. Edited by Albert J. Rivero. New York: Norton, 2004. In addition to the text of the novel accompanied by detailed annotations, this edition includes an essay outlining the novel's textual history, several modern critical analyses of the novel, and various eighteenth century materials on criminal transportation, criminals' lives, and colonial laws applying to servants, slaves, and runaways.

Lund, Roger D., ed. *Critical Essays on Daniel Defoe*. New York: G. K. Hall, 1997. Collection of essays addresses the full range of Defoe's writings, including his domestic conduct manuals, his travel books, and his novels, with two essays devoted to *Moll Flanders*. Among the topics discussed are Defoe's treatment of slavery and his treatment of the city.

Novak, Maximillian E. *Daniel Defoe: Master of Fictions— His Life and Ideas*. New York: Oxford University Press, 2001. Comprehensive biographical study by a leading Defoe scholar places Defoe's work within the context of the events of his life. Includes analysis of *Robinson Crusoe*, *Moll Flanders*, and other novels as well as discussion of Defoe's works in other genres.

_____. *Realism, Myth, and History in Defoe's Fiction*. Lincoln: University of Nebraska Press, 1983. Provides an excellent starting place for the student of Defoe's novels. Discusses his use of realistic characters, such as Moll Flanders, and examines how he overcomes the myth of female inferiority by having Moll succeed in realistic situations.

Richetti, John J. *Life of Daniel Defoe: A Critical Biography*. Malden, Mass.: Blackwell, 2005. Presents a thorough look at Defoe's writing within the context of his life and opinions, including analysis of his fiction and his political and religious journalism. Focuses on Defoe's distinctive literary style.

_____, ed. *The Cambridge Companion to Daniel Defoe*. New York: Cambridge University Press, 2008. Collection of essays includes analyses of Defoe's political and religious journalism as well as examinations of the topics of money and character in his fiction, Defoe as a narrative innovator, and gender issues in *Moll Flanders* and *Roxana*.

Molloy

Author: Samuel Beckett (1906-1989)
First published: 1951 (English translation, 1955)
Type of work: Novel
Type of plot: Absurdist
Time of plot: Mid-twentieth century
Locale: Unnamed

Principal characters:
MOLLOY, a derelict old man
A and C, two men observed by Molloy
LOUSSE, an old widow
JACQUES MORAN, a man assigned to look for Molloy
JACQUES MORAN, Moran's son
YOUDI, Moran's employer
GABER, Youdi's messenger

The Story:

Chapter 1. Molloy is in his mother's room, having been brought there after he ceased to walk. He is obliged to write out the story of how he ended there under orders from a thirsty man who collects his pages once a week on Sundays. He remembers what happened to bring him to this room. He remembers that he had been on a hilltop from which he watched two men, A and C, walking toward each other along a country road. The two meet, exchange a few words, and then go their separate ways. It is after he watches this encounter that Molloy decides to go on a quest for his mother. With his crutches fastened to his bicycle, he sets off, but when he reaches the walls of his town, he is arrested and questioned by a hostile police officer.

After his release, Molloy feels unwell, wanders to the countryside, and then returns to the town, where he runs over a dog. The dog's owner, an old widow, Lousse, decides to adopt Molloy as a replacement for her lost pet. Lousse causes Molloy to recall other love affairs, and he realizes they all remind him of his mother. Although Lousse gives him a haven in her garden, Molloy feels trapped and threatened, and he worries that Lousse is drugging his food. Having lost his bicycle, Molloy escapes Lousse's house on his crutches. He wanders around, considers suicide, and then finds himself at the seaside, where he renews the stock of sucking stones that keep him from feeling hungry. He spends some time trying to devise a mathematical order for the carrying and sucking of the stones.

Molloy moves into a forest, but his progress becomes slower and slower as he gets more decrepit. He finds a charcoal burner in the forest, whom he assaults after the charcoal burner makes unwanted advances. No longer able to hobble, Molloy crawls and then sinks to the bottom of a ditch at the very edge of the forest. It is from this ditch that he is somehow rescued, brought to his mother's room, and ordered to write his story.

Chapter 2. Jacques Moran is a fastidious man, a scrupulous Catholic, and an affluent householder. He has a subservient housekeeper named Martha and a closely monitored young son, Jacques. Moran is employed in an agency by a man named Youdi, who pays him to detect and track down certain individuals. It is Youdi who asks for the report about the events that begin one Sunday in the summer when Gaber, a thirsty agency messenger, comes to him with an urgent assignment. Moran is to leave at once with his son to look for a man named Molloy.

Disquieted and confused by these instructions, Moran rapidly becomes unwell. Not soon after starting out, he hurts his leg and sends his son to the nearest town to buy a bicycle. When a man with a stick approaches Moran, he gives him bread and breaks off a heavy stick for himself. The next day, another more respectable-looking man, who is looking for the man with the stick, approaches Moran. Moran clubs him to death. After being away for three days, his son returns with the bicycle; Moran and his son quarrel violently and the son abandons Moran. Then Gaber appears with an order for Moran to return home. By this time, Moran has deteriorated to such a degree that he is barely able to get home. He attempts to devise a mathematical order for the wearing of his shirt for his journey and grows even more decrepit, eventually finding it difficult to walk. He subsists on roots and berries and becomes such a suspicious character that a farmer accosts him and orders him off his land. When spring arrives, Moran finally returns home, but he finds the house deserted. He begins to write his report.

Critical Evaluation:

Samuel Beckett, who was awarded the Nobel Prize in Literature in 1969, is best known for his avant-garde plays, but he is also considered one of the most important experimental novelists of the twentieth century. *Molloy*, the first novel of a trilogy that is followed by *Malone meurt* (1951; *Malone Dies*, 1956) and *L'Innommable* (1953; *The Unnamable*, 1958), is considered his single greatest work of fiction. Although *Molloy* has been interpreted from many perspectives, including Jungian, Freudian, Christian, and existential, Beckett has made it impossible for any one theory entirely to explain his novel. He has deliberately created an ambiguous text, which, although it includes mythic and philosophical aspects, constantly subverts the attempt to secure clarity and

order. Beckett blends irony, despair, lyrical poetry, tragedy, and an anarchic comedy in a narrative that is both realistic and dreamlike. The work can appear to be both about everything that matters and about nothing at all.

Although there are many theories concerning the meaning of the novel, a useful starting point is to explore its structure, which appears to be one of division. The small episode involving the characters of A and C at the beginning of the novel is often seen as an outline for the novel as a whole, because it gives us an image of "twoness." The novel itself is divided into two chapters of roughly equal length. Like A and C, who come from opposite directions, the two first-person narratives, one by Molloy and one by Moran, seem to represent opposite points of view.

Each section of this novel is a psychological character study of a different man. The first chapter, narrated by Molloy, dispenses with traditional storytelling, instead using an unparagraphed, rambling, stream-of-consciousness style. Molloy is a dilapidated vagabond, with little sense of personal worth or significance. Obsessed with excrement and bodily functions, often helpless, moody, and confused, he seems to have entered a second childhood. Miserable, despairing, surrounded by a clutter of unmanageable objects, Molloy finds time to be slow, empty, and punctuated by trivial flurries of fruitless energy. He is filled with anxiety and boredom. Although he still possesses an astute analytical mind, he is utterly convinced that his experience is incomprehensible, and he ends up using his sharp intellect to sort out matters of tremendous inconsequence, such as the order of his sucking stones. Molloy does pursue one real goal, that of being reunited with his mother, with whom he has a love-hate relationship and who is psychologically present in all his relationships with women, but his quest is only ambiguously resolved by his return to his mother's room. Molloy's narrative also touches on the master-narratives of such figures as Ulysses, Aeneas, Christ, and Dante, but Beckett deploys these parallels tentatively or even ironically. Although Molloy represents a kind of life force, eternally ongoing even when only going in circles, the sense of continuation must always take into account the desolate nature of his existence.

Molloy is obsessed with his mother; Moran is a father living in a world of fathers. The sole woman in Moran's life is a servant, Martha. His employer, Youdi, suggests the Hebrew God Yahweh, with Gaber as the angel Gabriel. To further consolidate this hint of a theological order, Moran also consults with the local priest, Father Ambrose. Moran exists within a network of conformity, religious scruples, routines, and material possessions, at the center of which is the authority of the father. Within this patriarchal hierarchy, Moran is an obsessional and paranoid domestic tyrant, punctilious to the point of sadism in his role as a father to his own resentful son.

As soon as he is sent on his quest for Molloy, however, Moran begins to undergo an identity crisis. One can interpret Moran's story as that of a psychological breakdown and, more specifically, a breakdown into the side of himself that is like the hobo Molloy. As his journey unfolds, he fails to do his job and instead kills a man in the forest who closely resembles him. Although Moran's character begins with a sense of distinction between himself and Molloy (Moran is the detective, Molloy the object of his search; Moran is a respectable householder, Molloy is homeless) Moran's narrative ultimately undercuts these surface distinctions as the various meanings that have given shape and coherence to his life fail him. Increasingly, Molloy becomes a reference with which to understand what is happening to Moran. Moran's journey, which can be said to be a journey into his own unconscious, is one of disintegration and loss. It is significant that it is only when Moran has psychically dissolved into Molloy that we find a reference to a mother—the earth mother or "turdy Madonna." Moran's conventionally successful adult persona is exposed as a false self, and as his identity merges with Molloy's, the division between the two narratives is called into question.

Molloy and Moran can be viewed as one of Beckett's famous "pseudocouples," that is, as two parts of the same psyche. Their narratives features many parallel details: Both Moran and Molloy are in a house writing; both have a visitor who is always thirsty; both assault someone in the forest; both ride a bicycle and use crutches; both follow a pattern of quest, disintegration, and failure; and both circle back home. Moran's search for Molloy and Molloy's search for his mother can be viewed as the same quest pursued on different levels, and for both the creative activity of writing is the end product of their quest. Molloy, however, remains the foundation of the novel, especially since Moran disintegrates, and the style with which he tells his story evolves into that of Molloy. Although Molloy appears to be older and more sickly than Moran, a Moran yet-to-come, he also seems to be archaeologically first, existing in an earlier, repressed layer of Moran's unconscious. Considered in this light, *Molloy* is above all a psychological study.

Margaret Boe Birns

Further Reading

Abbott, H. Porter. *The Fiction of Samuel Beckett: Form and Effect.* Berkeley: University of California Press, 1973.

Examines Beckett as a cunning literary strategist who wrote with an acute awareness of the effect his fiction had on readers. Includes a useful examination of the parallels in the two stories of Moran and Molloy.

Astro, Alan. *Understanding Samuel Beckett.* Columbia: University of South Carolina Press, 1990. Offers an accessible analysis of *Molloy* and suggests that incomprehensibility is one of the novel's major themes. Includes a useful chronology and a brief bibliography of works up to 1988.

Ben-Zvi, Linda. *Samuel Beckett.* Boston: Twayne, 1986. Concludes that the fictive process is the novel's central issue and is intimately connected to the novel's quest motif. Includes a useful, simple summary of *Molloy*, a chronology, and a selected bibliography.

Cousineau, Thomas. *After the Final No: Samuel Beckett's Trilogy.* Newark: University of Delaware Press, 1999. Cousineau analyzes each of the three books in order of its respective publication, describing how in the course of the work Beckett demystifies each of the principal authority figures from whom Molloy has sought protection and guidance.

Fletcher, John. *The Novels of Samuel Beckett.* 2d ed. New York: Barnes & Noble, 1972. Important guide to Beckett's fiction, tracing the evolution of the hero in his novels, and concluding that the question of identity is at the center of Beckett's fiction. Includes a helpful analysis of *Molloy*, which Fletcher suggests is Beckett's greatest work of fiction.

McDonald, Rónán. *The Cambridge Introduction to Samuel Beckett.* New York: Cambridge University Press, 2006. Chapter 4 of this concise overview of Beckett's life and work includes a discussion of the trilogy that includes *Molloy*.

Pultar, Gönül. *Technique and Tradition in Beckett's Trilogy of Novels.* Lanham, Md.: University Press of America, 1996. Analyzes each of the three books in the order of publication, devoting a chapter to each. The chapter on *Molloy* views the protagonist as an alienated writer and a modern-day Everyman. Other chapters compare the three novels to other works of European literature and philosophy.

Rabinovitz, Rubin. *Innovation in Samuel Beckett's Fiction.* Champaign: University of Illinois Press, 1992. Suggests that what seems baffling or purposeless in Beckett results from judiciously considered formal strategies. Posits that although the novels may seem chaotic and rambling, they are ingenious works of art that use repetition as a deliberate strategy to create structure and meaning.

A Mölna Elegy

Author: Gunnar Ekelöf (1907-1968)
First published: En Mölna-elegi: Metamorfoser, 1960
    (English translation, 1984)
Type of work: Poetry

In 1946, Gunnar Ekelöf wrote that his *A Mölna Elegy* has as its theme the relativity of time and experiences in the flow of time. The poet attempts to capture one such moment, a cross-section of time, as it were, in which experiences and re-experiences combine, both remaining separate occasions and becoming a unified instant. In the *A Mölna Elegy*, Ekelöf also questions the idea of identity. The poem's first-person narrator represents a variety of personalities who focus on the lack of constancy in life and on the overwhelming transitory nature of existence. These themes, fragmented in the poem's complex structure, imbue the elegy with a tone of uncertainty and mystery. In that tone and in the disjointed structure, the work clearly echoes the style of American, English, and French surrealists and modernist poets of the early twentieth century. Particularly strong influences were T. S. Eliot's *The Waste Land* (1922) and "The Love Song of J. Alfred Prufrock," a poem Ekelöf translated into Swedish.

For English readers, the complexity of *A Mölna Elegy* is partly due to Ekelöf's use of Swedish settings and history as well as to the poem's dense content and form. The poem functions on a number of levels, for it is a web of allusions, symbols, and points-of-view of many voices inside one character's mind. It is not, however, obvious or necessarily important to know, for example, that the elegy is set at the beginning of World War II, as this information provides no insight into the poem's meaning.

It is important to know *A Mölna Elegy* takes place in a yellow autumn on a jetty on the Mölna river near Stockholm, Sweden. The setting includes descriptions of old buildings on Lidingö Island, symbolizing the nature of the past, which is alive only in memory. Through the many Roman and Greek classical allusions, the scope of the setting broadens to include the Mediterranean region, reflecting the places Ekelöf visited in his lifelong travels and his interest in classical mythology. The poem begins and ends speaking to a wanderer, the spokesman first saying "Hail" to him and finally "farewell." These lines echo phrases from Roman gravestones. Other allusions refer to William Shakespeare's *The Tempest* (pr. 1611, pb. 1623), the Bible, Swedish history, and images borrowed from Ekelöf's favorite writers.

A reader need not be aware of each of these allusions to gain an understanding of the poem; however, some attention to the elegy's difficult structure is required to understand the interconnected themes and subjects throughout the poem's sections and subsections. The poem's structure includes monologues, imagined dialogues, marginal headings, parenthetical asides and stage directions, illustrations, and a graphic layout. Meter and phrasing alternately flow and fragment in stream-of-consciousness images, creating a dense and complex interior monologue that comments on the past, present, and imagined future.

The poem opens with the poet sitting on a "bench of the past," writing of the past, merging what he sees with his memory and imagination. He sees a crazy-eyed fool playing wordless, soundless music and rending the illusion of the past in a swirling, mysterious world of nature. The poet's own life, however, stands still, the frame of reference around which all his images revolve. The repeated image of the "flying moment" is introduced when it robs the poet of his future.

The "Wave Song" section describes waves of tides and winds in an "eternal *then* which is now"; the eternal now is the past arrested in time. The sun sets beyond the river's canal as the poet describes boating scenes and memories of the past summer. Transformation begins in the cool air as past, present, and future merge, as time runs wild and years equal minutes, in the isolation of the moment.

In "Old Actor," an old man has an appointment with the past, but sleep overtakes him as the narrator remembers the actor as Prospero in Shakespeare's *Tempest*. The poet muses on the past and identity, asking "Who were you yourself?" He remembers singing in the past; in the present, clocks tick, and the poet looks through "a blind window" wondering, in the first of many window images, how Prospero can be alive. The actor awakens, and the poet seems to dream of conversations with dead ancestors who recall his childhood.

Sea imagery dominates the "1809" and "1786" sections, linking the past with the poet's Swedish history; treasured objects from various lands, music, sea travel, and stars and storms lead him to reflect on death and the dead. These memories interact and point to ancient, eternal truths evoking the idea of the interdependence of everything. The poet "remembers Time," "carries it" and "hears it" in his present where it brings together the elements of the past. Time is "complete and unknown" in the poet, ending the first half of *A Mölna Elegy*.

A Swedish "King over all that has gone before" reflects on the autumn of his lineage, himself a vestige of past traditions. He speaks of change and of the importance of action to make change, and he says that one cannot find truth in the rational and must be assimilated into the flow of time to avoid being absurd. Other voices merge hours with seasons. Images of children wanting to "hold tight" to the secure present give way to dream images of grief over the passing of history. The poet sees ancient battles and funeral pyres on the beach of the Mölna River, bringing the distant past into the present setting.

The poet's vision, now reanchored in his riverside setting, expands outward and upward, exploring the elements of nature to dramatize the vastness of time and space. Fire and land imagery, in which fire is a purifying force, is juxtaposed against the earlier water images. The "flames and waves" and land merge in a holy union. The poet sees the fire of the sun in perpetual sunset as a desolate city wind brings the poet back to the present. In a feverish state—bringing the natural elements into his own mind—the past, present, and future fuse in a dizzying, flying moment. The poem ends in a brief, calm remembrance of a near-death experience in childhood, followed by a short reflection that life, in the past or future, is still rarely fully experienced.

A result of twenty years work by Ekelöf and ten by the translators, the first English version of *A Mölna Elegy* helped expand Ekelöf's reputation. He is considered Sweden's most important twentieth century poet, highly regarded for his verse, essays, and studies of European and Middle Eastern languages and literature. As American poet Robert Bly observed, there is no English-language poet like him. Throughout his work, Ekelöf emphasized the importance of the subconscious, and critics praise his cohesiveness and his ability to synthesize varying influences, particularly Eastern and Western philosophies, and to draw on Persian, Indian, and Taoist sources. The Hindu notion that alone is the only place an individual can trust is a very important theme in *A Mölna Elegy*.

Nevertheless, Ekelöf maintains a distinctly Swedish voice, largely because of his choice of landscapes and of characters. He is considered innovative in his technique, especially in his use of musical forms in his verse. Music, particularly singing, is a central motif in *A Mölna Elegy*, for Ekelöf uses music both as sensory imagery and as a means to evoke the past.

Wesley Britton

Further Reading

Ekelöf, Gunnar. *Skrifter*. Edited and compiled by Reidar Ekner. Vol. 8. Stockholm: Bonniers, 1993. The complete Swedish edition of Ekelöf's works contains *A Mölna Elegy* with the original illustrations.

Shideler, Ross. "Gunnar Ekelöf." In *Multicultural Writers Since 1945: An A-to-Z Guide*, edited by Alba Amoia and Bettina L. Knapp. Westport, Conn.: Greenwood Press, 2004. A brief critical essay, containing a biography of Ekelöf, a discussion of the themes of his work, and a survey of criticism. Includes bibliographies of primary and secondary sources.

Sjoberg, Leif. "The Attempted Reconstruction of a Moment." In *A Mölna Elegy: Metamorphoses*, translated by Muriel Rukeyser and Leif Sjoberg. Greensboro, N.C.: Unicorn Press, 1984. The introduction to the first English translation of *A Mölna Elegy* provides a detailed interpretation of the poem and of specific allusions, sources, and possible meanings in the imagery. Includes comments by Ekelöf and a bibliography.

_____. *A Reader's Guide to Gunnar Ekelöf's "A Mölna Elegy."* New York: Twayne, 1973. A book-length overview of the poem, its sources, and the biographical and historical contexts that helped shape it. Sjoberg analyzes the poem section by section and discusses the critical reception to the 1960 edition.

Thygesen, Erik. *Gunnar Ekelöf's Open-Form Poem "A Mölna Elegy": Problems in Genesis, Structure, and Influence.* Uppsala, Sweden: Almqvist & Wiksell, 1985. Based on the author's dissertation, the study compares *A Mölna Elegy* with T. S. Eliot's *The Waste Land* and explores Eliot's influence on the Swedish poet. Describes Ekelöf's poem as a "quotation-mosaic" and refutes critics who find the poem a chaotic, structureless reflection of Ekelöf's contradictory notions of art.

Warme, Lars G., ed. *A History of Swedish Literature*. Lincoln: University of Nebraska Press, 1996. Two chapters, "Turning the Tide for Modernism" and "The Modernist Breakthrough," contain most of this book's information about Ekelöf, and other references to his work are listed in the index.

Money
A Suicide Note

Author: Martin Amis (1949-   )
First published: 1984
Type of work: Novel
Type of plot: Satire
Time of plot: Spring, 1981-Winter, 1982
Locale: New York and London

Principal characters:
JOHN SELF, a former ad executive turned film mogul
SELINA STREET, his faithless girlfriend
ALEC LLEWELLYN, his best friend
BARRY SELF, his father
FAT VINCE and FAT PAUL, bouncers and bartenders at
    Barry's pub
FIELDING GOODNEY, an American movie producer and
    cross-dressing stalker
SPUNK DAVIS, an actor who plays Self
LORNE GUYLAND, an actor who plays his father
CADUTA MASSI, an actress who plays his mother
BUTCH BEAUSOLEIL, an actress who plays the mistress
DORIS ARTHUR, a script writer
MARTIN AMIS, a writer hired to replace her
OSSIE TWAIN, an American capitalist
MARTINA TWAIN, his wife

The Story:

John Self has just traveled from London to New York City to make arrangements for his movie, alternatively titled *Money*, *Good Money*, and *Bad Money*. He takes a horrific taxi ride through Manhattan and engages in excessive drinking that leads to blackouts. He also consumes pornography, both live and simulated. Self meets with producer Fielding Goodney and fends off the stars who are courting him while trying in vain to contact his girlfriend Selina before a massive blackout convinces him that it is time to return to London.

Back in London, Self grounds himself at his father's pub, the Shakespeare, and makes a bad loan to his best friend, Alec. In a meeting with lesbian screenwriter Doris Arthur, Self describes his movie's plot—a love triangle between a father, his mistress, and his son that ends with a violent confrontation in the son's favor. When Arthur questions the mistress's motivation, Self offers her a tour of the backroom strip club and a slap on the bottom, at which point she storms out before deciding that the paycheck makes his bad behavior more palatable.

Back at his apartment, Self riffles through his mail to discover that he apparently threw Selina out before leaving for New York. She agrees to return on the condition that he open a joint checking account for them. He then visits an oral hygienist for chronic tooth pain that he likens to the hustle of the big city and checks in with his ad agency, whose executives

offer him an afternoon on the town but no details on his severance package.

Self flies back to New York to meet with several actors. Caduta Massi convinces him of her maternal tendencies before Goodney takes him on an extravagant tour of New York. Self is stalked by an anonymous telephone voice he calls Frank the Phone and an exceptionally tall, ginger-haired woman. On his thirty-fifth birthday, Self blacks out an entire dinner party with his old friends the Twains, coming to the next morning lying face down on the street. In the midst of several unsuccessful meetings, he lunches apologetically with Martina Twain, and she buys him George Orwell's *Animal Farm* (1945). The gift contrasts sharply with the mysterious pornographic package he receives at his hotel.

Once again in London, Self meets his father's new mistress Veronica, who has just done a nude magazine shoot. His car, a Fiasco, gives him some mechanical trouble while he kills time waiting for the next phase in the movie's production. After Selina accuses him of having real feelings for Martina, he invites Selina to move in with him. Her presence offers a temporary reprieve from his fears that he will end up in jail, as Alec has recently done. Finally, Self confesses that his father once sent him a detailed invoice for the expenses incurred raising him. He paid it; his father bet the money and won enough to buy the Shakespeare.

Meanwhile, Lorne Guyland has been rewriting the father

figure in the movie into an educated connoisseur. Self ignores him and tries to see Martina, but she refuses until he finishes reading *Animal Farm*, and his spirit-befuddled memory leads him into another painfully embarrassing evening adventure he cannot recall. When he finally endures his own company for long enough to read, Martina explains that it was an allegory and offers him another Orwell novel, *Nineteen Eighty-Four* (1949). His second attempt at culture is interrupted by the arrival of the script. As soon as he reads the script, Self goes to Goodney's hotel room to demand that he fire Arthur. Since Goodney is sleeping with her, neither of them are amenable to Self's suggestions, and yet another botched date with Martina sends him back to London.

There, Selina distresses him by refusing sex and, more poignantly, by refraining from any extravagant shopping sprees. Self experiences a surge of patriotism from Prince Charles's impending marriage to Lady Diana, and the writer Martin Amis agrees to rewrite the script for an exorbitant fee. Self then attempts to rape Selina before visiting Alec in prison and trying once more to obtain his severance package. While he is not successful, he does learn that Selina has been having an affair. She confirms that she is pregnant and that her relationship with Self is her alibi so she can prove Ossie Twain's paternity and sue for maintenance.

Self has sex with Butch Beausoleil; the act is videotaped, to Self's horror. Butch agrees to erase the tape only after Self beats her. Shortly thereafter, Martina takes Self to the opera *Otello* (1887) and confesses her knowledge of the affair between her husband and his girlfriend. They begin living together, but Self finds it nearly impossible to attain the nakedness of self that comes naturally to Martina. Finally, Selina seduces him and arranges for Martina to discover them, at which point his credit suddenly loses currency.

Self and Frank the Phone tangle in a dark alley. His attacker is also the ginger-haired woman, revealed to be Fielding Goodney in drag, who confesses to having duped Self into spending his own advance. Broke, Self barely escapes New York, sleeps with his father's mistress, and decides to kill himself. When he pauses to play chess with Amis, the author explains Goodney's deception, as well as his own part in the graft. The two fight, Self is knocked unconscious, and the author leaves. Self then describes his own suicide before revealing that he survived and is now living humbly with his girlfriend Georgina and the knowledge that Fat Vince is his real father.

Critical Evaluation:

Money was Martin Amis's fifth novel, and it firmly established him as a literary talent. Amis's earlier work suggested his interest in father-son relationships and hinted at his linguistic facility, but it had not prepared his audience for *Money*'s allegorical attack on the modern world or the explosive power of its narrative voice. Even the themes that seemed somewhat contrived in his earlier novels became in *Money* rich metaphors for the myriad ways in which the modern self is fragmented.

Money was published in the middle of Ronald Reagan's presidential administration (1981-1989), which advocated trickle-down economics as a rationale for massive spending, and several years into the similarly conservative Margaret Thatcher's term as prime minister of the United Kingdom (1979-1990). The novel seems prophetic in its attitude toward the dollar as the absolute democratizing force, if not in the prediction of its singularly corrupting influence. All of the characters are driven by their lust for capital—except Martina, who is already so wealthy she need not care. So long as money plays a factor in Self's life, he remains indecent. Only when he is left destitute can he establish a sense of self and interact responsibly with others.

The vehicle for the novel's narrative and themes, narrator and protagonist John Self, forms a formidable obstacle for Amis, who established his early credentials with an expansive vocabulary. A character who spends the entire novel either exceedingly drunk or exceptionally hungover can hardly be expected to turn a phrase as skillfully as the Oxford-educated Amis, yet Self's verbal acuity is staggering. Amis writes in a rhythmic slang, so Self reads like the street hustler he is, but Amis loads his complaints with tactile imagery and double or even triple entendres, which may be all the more pleasing to a reader because the narrator seems innocent of their implications. For example, describing the pain from his combined toothache and hangover, Self complains, "This morning was the worst yet. I heard computer fugues, Japanese jam sessions, didgeridoos. What is my head up to? I wish I had some idea what it's got in mind for me."

The novel's language, like its narrative, is allegorical and self-reflective. Both traits are exploited in the characters' names. Self's girlfriend, Selina Street, for example, lives on easy street, works John as proficiently as a streetwalker, and shows him that exploitation is a two-way street. The name of American producer Fielding Goodney pays homage to the eighteenth century British author Henry Fielding (1707-1754), but he is also "feelin' good" about living on Self's money. The sexually exhausted stud Lorne Guyland longs to recover his manhood ("lorn" is an archaism for "lost" or "ruined"). John Self, the allegory's Everyman, has such difficulty establishing himself that he cannot decide which young actor should play him.

Like the "Self" that is lost when John learns Barry is not his father, Martina Twain's eponym also complicates the novel's themes. Martina is herself split in two. Her name alludes both to the preeminent American author Mark Twain and to Martin Amis himself. The character likewise divides John, who keeps his relationship with her a secret from those involved in the film, but her English double Selina disrupts the peace John seeks with her by exposing Selina to his dark side. That side is also present in the dog Martina rescues. John adores Martina for helping him "to burst out of the world of money and into—into what? Into the world of thought and fascination." Like Shadow, however, John cannot find his way in Martina's posh neighborhood, so he ends up back on the street, shamefaced, but doggedly certain that is where he belongs.

To some extent, Martina becomes a civilizing influence, but she remains an influence. In this respect, she is essentially no different than Fielding Goodney or Martin Amis, despite her substantially more positive role in Self's life. In some respect, each of these characters makes John into something other than himself. Only when he is finally free of them, symbolized by the italicized narration of the final section, is he free to be "dead but still viable," just like his bum tooth.

L. Michelle Baker

Further Reading

Begley, John. "Satirizing the Carnival of Postmodern Capitalism: The Transatlantic and Dialogic Structure of Martin Amis's *Money*." *Contemporary Literature* 45, no. 1 (Spring, 2004): 79-105. A dense analysis of the novel's connections to postmodernism and consumer culture.

Diedrick, James. *Understanding Martin Amis*. 2d ed. Columbia: University of South Carolina Press, 2004. Begins with a substantial biography of the author. The chapters group novels into "periods" in Amis's development as a writer. *Money* is treated as the start of his mature career, and its numerous themes and narrative strategies are discussed at length.

Edmondson, Elie A. "Martin Amis Writes Postmodern Man." *Critique: Studies in Contemporary Fiction* 42, no. 2 (Winter, 2001): 145-154. Places *Money* and particularly its narrator, John Self, within the broader world of postmodern consumer culture.

Finney, Brian. *Martin Amis*. New York: Routledge, 2008. The introductory chapter provides a biography of Amis alongside a chronology of significant historical events and of his work, followed by a brief summary of each novel and then criticism. The criticism is organized by topic, and with each topical discussion spanning Amis's entire corpus.

Keulks, Gavin. *Father and Son: Kingsley Amis, Martin Amis, and the British Novel Since 1950*. Madison: University of Wisconsin Press, 2003. Keulks discusses the writers that most influenced both authors, as well as comparing their themes and structures, before concluding with an analysis of their influence on British literature.

_____, ed. *Martin Amis: Postmodernism and Beyond*. New York: Palgrave Macmillan, 2006. This dense, theoretical study is more suited to the advanced student than the beginner; however, it synthesizes the large body of criticism that Amis's work has begun to accrue while abstaining refreshingly from discussion of his personal life. Includes four essays that place *Money* within a broad critical and thematic context.

Tredell, Nicolas, ed. *The Fiction of Martin Amis*. Duxford, England: Icon, 2000. Provides a brief overview of Amis's career before reprinting interviews, reviews, and short critical essays chronologically by publication. Includes brief introductions and analyses intended to segue between and comment on each piece, as well as helpful glosses for obscure terms or allusions.

The Monk
A Romance

Author: Matthew Gregory Lewis (1775-1818)
First published: 1796
Type of work: Novel
Type of plot: Gothic
Time of plot: Spanish Inquisition
Locale: Madrid

Principal characters:
FATHER AMBROSIO, the monk
MATILDA (ROSARIO), his evil mistress
LORENZO DE MEDINA, a young nobleman
AGNES, his sister
ANTONIA, a virtuous maiden
ELVIRA, her mother
THE MARQUIS RAYMOND DE LAS CISTERNAS, a wealthy
    relative of Elvira
MOTHER ST. AGATHA, the prioress of St. Clare Convent
VIRGINIA DE VILLA FRANCA, a beautiful heir

The Story:

Whenever Father Ambrosio speaks in the church, all Madrid goes to hear him. He is the most learned, the most virtuous, and the most admired monk in the city. Such is his purity that he will tolerate no sin in others, and he berates the worshipers viciously. In the audience one day is a young woman named Antonia, who comes to Madrid with her mother to seek the financial aid of their relative, the Marquis Raymond de las Cisternas. At the church, Antonia meets Lorenzo de Medina, a wealthy young nobleman who, charmed by her sweetness, promises to petition Raymond in her behalf. Before he leaves the church, Lorenzo sees Raymond and learns that he is the man who supposedly spurned Lorenzo's sister Agnes and caused the heartbroken girl to enter the convent of St. Clare. Lorenzo challenges his former friend, but Raymond begs him to hear the story and then make his judgment.

The marquis does not know the fate at that moment befalling Agnes. Father Ambrosio intercepted a note written to Agnes by Raymond, acknowledging that the child she will soon bear is his and laying plans for her escape from the convent. Ambrosio summons Mother St. Agatha, the prioress, and Agnes is carried away to torture and probable death. The young girl begs Ambrosio for mercy, but he is cold to her pleas. Then she curses him, calling on him to remember her when he himself yields to temptation.

Ambrosio is to remember Agnes's words when he yields to the passions of Matilda, an evil woman who disguises herself as a novice at the monastery and who is known to the monks as Rosario. Ambrosio struggles with his conscience, but his lust overcomes him and he surrenders completely to Matilda. He cannot let the monks learn that a woman is in the monastery, however, for then he will be exiled and reviled by all who now honor him.

After hearing Raymond's story, Lorenzo forgives his friend for his supposed betrayal of Agnes. Agnes entered the convent of St. Clare in sorrow after she was persuaded by unscrupulous relatives that Raymond deserted her. Raymond found her there and by bribing the gatekeeper managed to see her each night. When she found that she was to have his child, she sent a note to him; it was his note, in reply, planning the escape and their subsequent marriage, that Ambrosio intercepted. Neither Raymond nor Lorenzo is aware of the fate that befell her, and they plan to rescue her together.

Before the proposed rescue, Lorenzo pays court to Antonia. Her mother, Elvira, fears, however, that his family will not permit his union with a girl without noble family or fortune, and she begs him not to call again until he secures his family's permission to marry Antonia. He is unable to consult his family until after his sister's rescue. When Agnes does not appear at the appointed time, Lorenzo goes to the convent and demands to see her. For several days, Mother St. Agatha tells him that Agnes is too ill to receive him. When he insists, the prioress tells him the girl died while delivering a stillborn child. Wild with anger, Lorenzo and Raymond swear vengeance on the prioress. Raymond refuses to believe that his beloved is really dead.

In the meantime, Ambrosio, satiated by his lust, learns to his horror that Matilda works magic and consorts with the devil. Although his desire for Matilda is gone, his passion for women is still great, and he turns his attention toward Antonia, who comes to beg him to go to her sick mother. The innocent girl does not suspect his intentions, but her mother does. Elvira comes upon them once when the monk is attempting to rape Antonia, but the girl is so innocent that she does not understand the monk's actions. Matilda comes to his aid and casts a spell so that he can rape Antonia as she sleeps. The plan would have succeeded if Elvira had not come into the room. When Elvira tries to call out for help, Ambrosio strangles her to death.

Raymond becomes ill after learning of Agnes's fate. Lorenzo learns from another nun that Mother St. Agatha murdered Agnes; he then lays plans to have the prioress seized. Ambrosio, meanwhile, does not give up his plan to possess Antonia. With the aid of a magic potion mixed by Matilda, he takes the girl to a dungeon in the monastery and rapes her there. Immediately afterward, he is penitent and begs her forgiveness, but she will not hear his pleas and tries to escape from him. Fearing the consequences if she does escape, he plunges a dagger into her heart. She lives only long enough to die in the arms of Lorenzo, who suddenly appears.

Lorenzo obtains from the cardinal an order to arrest Mother St. Agatha and to have her tried for the murder of Agnes. News of the arrest turns the fury of the mob against the prioress, and she and several of the other nuns are killed by the crowd. While the mob storms the convent, Lorenzo is led by screams for help into the cellar of the convent. There in the darkness he finds a pitiful figure clutching a baby. The woman's ravings are almost insensible, and she is almost dead of starvation. Lorenzo sends her to the home of Virginia de Villa Franca, a beautiful heir. Searching the rest of the crypt, he comes upon the dying Antonia.

Ambrosio and Matilda are arrested by the Inquisition. Lorenzo and Raymond learn that the pitiful woman they saved from death is Agnes, who was imprisoned and starved by the prioress. Raymond's love and the kind ministering of Virginia restore her to health, and she and Raymond are married. For a long time, Lorenzo lies ill of grief for his lost Antonia, but at last, Virginia's kindness heals his spirit, and they, too, are married.

The Inquisitors torture Matilda and Ambrosio to make them confess their crimes and their sorcery. Matilda confesses and is condemned to death by fire. Ambrosio refuses to confess and is to be tortured again the following day. That night, Matilda comes to his cell a free woman. The devil releases her, and she begs the monk to give his soul to Lucifer and thus escape death. The monk wrestles with his conscience, but his fear of the torture overcomes his fears of hell and he sells his soul to the devil.

His freedom is short-lived. Lucifer takes him through the sky to a high precipice. There he taunts him with the knowledge that he would have been released by the Inquisition had he been true to his faith. The monk also hears that, through the accident of a mixed-up family relationship, Antonia is his own sister and Elvira his mother. Lucifer, who promised the monk only release from prison in exchange for his soul—not freedom—holds the monk high in the heavens; then he dashes him to death on the rocks below.

Critical Evaluation:

To say that Matthew Gregory Lewis's *The Monk* was a *succès de scandale* when it was first published is an understatement. Edition followed edition, some with alterations, others with variations on the ending. A society for the prevention of vice encouraged England's attorney general to suppress the novel's publication. Samuel Taylor Coleridge thought the novel the "offspring of no common genius" and noted that the face of parents who saw the novel in the hands of a son or daughter would turn pale. A circulating library in Dublin kept the book, but underscored the passages that young ladies might find offensive. The novel shocked the scandalous Lord Byron and was high on the reading list of the Marquis de Sade. Despite all the initial attention, Lewis's work became less popular in the twentieth century, but its place in literature is important.

The Monk is a variation of the gothic novel. Restrained by rationalism, the gothic novel as written by Ann Radcliffe had to have a natural explanation for its supernatural aspects. As written by Lewis, the gothic novel works under no such constraints. The book unfolds with one supernatural encounter after another. Interfering ghosts tamper with human destiny, and magic works as demons and men interact. The plot is resolved in a deus ex machina conclusion that involves Satan himself. Lewis, who was first and foremost a playwright, does not present complex characters and motivations in *The Monk*. Because the supernatural is a controlling force in human affairs as of the novel's outset, complex characterization is impossible. Lewis denied his creation some of the elements that make a novel great, but he produced a good story, and the novel is not without moral purpose and lessons.

One such lesson is shown by Antonia's fate, for her innocence is no defense against evil. Another lesson is contained in the major theme of the novel, that pride is a vice that can pervert all virtues, even religious piety. This theme is exemplified in the decline and fall of Father Ambrosio. Lewis passes moral judgments on characters who transgress. Agnes loses her virginity and suffers Purgatory on earth. The model of virtue, Antonia, is raped by a monk, who then stabs her to death in an attack of panic and conscience.

The most tragic of these characters is Ambrosio, the monk who dedicates his life to celibacy—something in which he takes pride and that he feels sets him above other men. It is this misplaced pride that makes Ambrosio a prize for the devil, who appears in person to entice the monk to damnation. Satan is unwilling to tempt such a prize with that which damns mere mortals. Ambrosio is directed by lust, rape, perfidy, and murder. This leaves the reader at a loss to understand why the monk is deserving of Satan's attention as a man of high virtue. Satan reveals that Elivira and Antonia (the murdered mother and daughter) are Ambrosio's mother and sister, that Satan throws Matilda in Ambrosio's way (inciting lust), that Satan allows Ambrosio into Antonia's chamber (inciting him to kill his sister), and that Satan warns Elvira in her dreams of Ambrosio's designs on her daughter, which keeps Antonia awake (inciting him to rape his sister and thus adding the charge of incest). Satan's manipulations make plausible the monk's lapsed virtue.

The most intriguing of all the characters is Beatrice, the Bleeding Nun. Early in the novel, Agnes tells Raymond the story of the Bleeding Nun, a ghost that yearly haunts Agnes's family's castle. The family is opposed to Agnes's marriage to Raymond, and the couple arrange for Agnes to masquerade as the Bleeding Nun to escape the castle to marry Raymond. When Raymond comes to fetch Agnes, he carries away the Bleeding Nun instead. In a Freudian view, the nun is a projection of Raymond's guilt. A Jungian reading makes the spectral figure, like the Jungian anima, a being in conflict with a real woman—Agnes. Because she is unconsciously projected onto Agnes, she seems to emanate from her; Agnes paints her, even though she does not believe in her and ridicules anyone who does. The actual appearance of the ghost, thwarting the elopement, may be Lewis's way of arguing against rationalism.

Of all the characters in this cast of one-dimensional figures, perhaps Agnes stands out as the most human. She loses her virginity (which destroys her aura of purity for eighteenth century audiences) to her true love, Raymond. That she hopes to marry him redeems her somewhat. Lewis realizes he cannot kill off both Antonia and Agnes, so he inflicts a series of terrible events on Agnes in a chamber of horrors before she is allowed to be happily reunited with Raymond.

The female figures in *The Monk* reveal striking archetypal aspects that cannot be dismissed as conventions. Matilda, the Madonna figure, represents the ultimate wish fantasy, that the beloved echo the inner ideal; the Bleeding Nun represents the ultimate dread fantasy, that the beloved turn out to be the worst possible feminine image, an animated corpse. The character of Ambrosio can be read as an attack on the Catholic practice of celibacy, as the monk cannot overcome his destructive wish fantasy, to make love to the Madonna.

Lewis's *The Monk* relies on the psychological effects of horror and the supernatural, and it flouts the Radcliffean gothic conventions with rational explanations of the super-

natural. Plot is privileged over character. This accounts for the assertion that Lewis's true successors are such twenty-first century novelists as Peter Straub and Steven King.

"Critical Evaluation" by Thomas D. Petitjean, Jr.

Further Reading

Andriano, Joseph. "The Feminine in *The Monk*." In *Our Ladies of Darkness: Feminine Daemonology in Male Gothic Fiction*. University Park: Pennsylvania State University Press, 1993. Provides a Jungian reading of the novel, demonstrating a movement from the sublime (the Madonna in the form of the demoniac Matilda) to the supernatural (the Bleeding Nun).

Blakemore, Steven. "Matthew Lewis's Black Mass: Sexual Religion Inversion in *The Monk*." *Studies in the Novel* 30, no. 4 (Winter, 1998): 521-539. Focuses on sex and religion in the novel, including its depictions of lust, incest, and homoeroticism. Examines how the novel subverts the traditional roles of religion and sex.

Ellis, Markman. "Revolution and Libertinism in the Gothic Novel." In *The History of Gothic Fiction*. Reprint. Edinburgh: Edinburgh University Press, 2005. Ellis devotes an entire chapter to *The Monk*, discussing the novel's "compositional politics," Lewis and the French revolutionary wars, and criticism and censorship of the novel.

Euridge, Gareth M. "The Company We Keep: Comic Function in M. G. Lewis's *The Monk*." In *Functions of the Fantastic: Selected Essays from the Thirteenth International Conference on the Fantastic in the Arts*, edited by Joe Sanders. Westport, Conn.: Greenwood Press, 1995. Euridge takes exception to previous psychoanalytical studies of *The Monk*, arguing that Lewis's book, which may be the "apotheosis" of the gothic novel, contains many ironic and comic elements that critics have neglected.

Kendrick, Walter. *The Thrill of Fear: Two Hundred Fifty Years of Scary Entertainment*. New York: Grove Weidenfeld, 1991. Discusses the value of *The Monk* in its own time as a success and scandal. Emphasizes the novel's influence on Nathaniel Hawthorne, Mary Shelley, E. T. A. Hoffman, and other writers through the late twentieth century.

Lyndenberg, Robin. "Ghostly Rhetoric: Ambivalence in M. G. Lewis' *The Monk*." *Ariel: A Review of International English Literature* 10, no. 2 (1979): 65-79. Asserts that the use of Beatrice, the Bleeding Nun, suggests that the Bleeding Nun's ghost is a mere stock device and a composite of clichés.

Macdonald, David Lorne. *Monk Lewis: A Critical Biography.* Buffalo, N.Y.: University of Toronto Press, 2000. A biography in which Macdonald discusses all of Lewis's works and their connections to his personal life, particularly his position as a slave-owner who also was probably gay. Includes a bibliography and an index.

Watkins, Daniel P. "Social Hierarchy in Matthew Lewis's *The Monk.*" *Studies in the Novel* 18, no. 2 (Summer, 1986): 115-124. Discusses the social hierarchy that evolves in the novel, using the monastery and the Inquisition as the norm invaded by the supernatural.

Monsieur Lecoq

Author: Émile Gaboriau (1832-1873)
First published: 1869 (English translation, 1879)
Type of work: Novel
Type of plot: Detective and mystery
Time of plot: Nineteenth century
Locale: Paris

Principal characters:
MONSIEUR LECOQ, a young detective
FATHER ABSINTHE, a veteran detective
GEVROL, a veteran police inspector
MONSIEUR D'ESCORVAL, an examining judge
MAY, a suspect
PÈRE TABARET, a consulting detective

The Story:

Police agents leave the Barriere d'Italie to make their nightly rounds in a tough, sparsely settled district inhabited by thugs and cheap crooks. In this precinct the police are always careful to move in groups. Their leader is old Gevrol, an unimaginative, fearless inspector. About one hundred yards from Mother Chupin's wine shop they hear some loud cries, and the whole party rushes forward over the rough ground. The house is closed up tight; only bands of light through the shutters give evidence of life within. One eager young officer climbs on a box to peer through the shutters, and his evident horror at what he sees causes the officers to hasten their attempt to break into the house.

At Gevrol's order, two agents batter down the door. Inside on the mud floor are three bodies, two men dead and one wounded. Swaying on his feet is a stocky man with a revolver in his hand. On the stairs, a hysterical Mother Chupin hides her face in her apron. One agent seizes the man with the gun and disarms him, while another agent kneels beside the wounded victim, who is wearing a soldier's uniform. Murmuring that he had received his just deserts, the man dies.

Gevrol diagnoses the affair as a drunken brawl and is pleased that the assumed murderer was so quickly caught. The young agent who had peered through the shutters, however, expresses doubts about the case. Gevrol patronizingly asks him if he suspects some mystery. When the young agent says yes, Gevrol tells him he can stay with the bodies until morning and investigate to his heart's content.

The doctors leave the crime scene, and a police wagon takes away the accused murderer and Mother Chupin. The young agent stays at the scene with a stolid, seasoned companion, grizzled Father Absinthe. The young agent is Detective Lecoq, who had decided to join the police force after drifting from one job to another for several years. With Father Absinthe to help him, he eagerly looks around the house.

Lecoq's first find is an earring, half buried in the mud on the floor. It is a diamond earring, jewelry too expensive to be found in Mother Chupin's establishment. Encouraged, Lecoq goes outside. There is enough snow on the ground for him to reconstruct some of the happenings prior to the murders. Lecoq figured that two women, one young and one older, had visited the house, and that they had been running when they left. A man had met them outside the garden, leading them to a cab. Here the traces become lost.

Lecoq also remembers, however, what the murder suspect had said when he was captured: "Lost! It is the Prussians who are coming!" Only someone who knew Napoleonic history would have used that allusion. He evidently had been expecting someone to return and help him.

Lecoq presents his lucid report to the examining judge in the morning. Monsieur d'Escorval is greatly impressed with Lecoq's report. Despite Gevrol's insistence that the case is merely a wine shop brawl, Monsieur d'Escorval agrees with Lecoq and prepares to look fully into the affair. Disgruntled and jealous, Gevrol becomes Lecoq's enemy.

As soon as the preliminaries are over, Lecoq hurries to the police station to attend the examination of the prisoner. To his disappointment, d'Escorval brusquely orders him to wait in the corridor. Lecoq overhears enough of the examination to realize that the judge seems unwell or upset. He asks only a very few routine questions, and the prisoner's answers are almost nonsensical. In a very short time the judge hurries out and drives away.

Lecoq is curious. Looking into the prisoner's cell, he surprises the man in the act of strangling himself. Lecoq removes the band from the prisoner's throat just in time. Continuing his investigation, he learns that the night before, after the murders, a drunken man had created a disturbance outside the jail. He was locked up for the night in the cell with the murderer. In the morning the police let him go. From the description, Lecoq believes him to be the accomplice, the man who had waited outside the wine shop and helped the two women to their cab.

The next morning, Lecoq has a fresh disappointment. D'Escorval had fallen and broken his leg while descending from his carriage. A new judge is assigned to the examination, causing further delay. The new examiner, Monsieur Segmuller, listens attentively to Lecoq's analysis and agrees that there is a mystery behind the case. At last the prisoner is brought in for formal examination.

The murderer, giving his name as May, irritatingly insists he has no given name. He says he is a circus performer, and he gives convincing imitations of a barker in French, English, and German. His story is that he had been attacked by the three men and had shot them in self-defense. May is returned to his cell, and Lecoq continues his patient investigation.

The quest for the murderer's identity is a long hunt. Lecoq and Father Absinthe, working for weeks on fruitless clues, cannot trace the diamond earring. They do find the cab that had picked up two women at the scene of the crime, but the women had left the cab at an apartment house, gone into the courtyard, and disappeared through a back door.

So it went with all the clues. A visitor comes to see the prisoner and shows a pass issued to a relative of Mother Chupin. Father Absinthe tries to trail the visitor but loses him. Lecoq learns of the visit later. He is sure the man is the drunk who had been locked up with the murderer that first night, the man whose general build Lecoq had reconstructed from the footprints in the snow. Then, by spending six days hidden in the garret above May's cell, Lecoq learns that the prisoner received cipher notes from the outside rolled in bits of bread. Lecoq even suspects Gevrol of helping May, but he can prove nothing.

In despair, Lecoq pulls the old trick of letting the prisoner escape; then he follows him closely. May joins his accomplice outside a high wall. Lecoq watches while the accomplice boosts May over the wall into the garden of the duke of Sairmeuse. The accomplice is captured, but May cannot be found, even after Lecoq searched the duke's house thoroughly. Lecoq learns nothing from May's accomplice, a former convict.

As a last resort Lecoq consults old Père Tabaret, the oracle of the police force. The sage listens eagerly, and then logically explains Lecoq's errors. Tabaret says that D'Escorval had conveniently broken his leg because he knows who the prisoner is and dares not prosecute him. Lecoq cannot find May in the duke of Sairmeuse's house because May is the duke.

Lecoq has to agree with Tabaret; an obscure detective can do nothing against a duke who undoubtedly is engaged in some mysterious intrigue. If he persists in trying to arrest so great a noble, Lecoq himself will be convicted as a madman. Lecoq gives up the case, but he determines that sooner or later he will get to the bottom of the whole affair.

Critical Evaluation:

In the development of the modern detective story, Émile Gaboriau's two fictional investigators, Père Tabaret and Monsieur Lecoq, remain two of the most important transitional figures between Edgar Allan Poe's C. Auguste Dupin and Sir Arthur Conan Doyle's Sherlock Holmes (with the possible exception of Wilkie Collins's Sergeant Cuff). Furthermore, between them, Tabaret and Lecoq represent the two types of detectives that have dominated the genre.

Tabaret, the hero of Gaboriau's first crime novel, *L'Affaire Lerouge* (1863, serial; 1866, book; *The Widow Lerouge*, 1873), is the talented amateur who, like Sherlock Holmes, fights crime to escape boredom and exercises talents that go unused in the everyday world. He works outside official channels, entering the proceedings either at the request of the injured party or after the authorities have confessed their bafflement. Monsieur Lecoq, protagonist of Gaboriau's four other detective novels, is the professional police officer who works efficiently within the system but must struggle almost as much with the bureaucratic rigidities of the institution and the mediocrity and jealousy of his colleagues as he does with the criminals. This is especially evident in Gaboriau's most famous novel, *Monsieur Lecoq*.

Although *Monsieur Lecoq* was one of Gaboriau's last novels, it describes Lecoq's first case. He is, therefore, much more believable and human than the remote, mysterious figure who appears and disappears in the other works. *Monsieur Lecoq* is the only book in which Lecoq is physically described, minus any disguise, and given a personal history. As a young man from a rich background, Lecoq suddenly becomes penniless and is forced to take a variety of relatively menial jobs. To alleviate boredom, he amused himself by inventing theoretical crimes.

After describing one crime to his last employer, a famous astronomer, Lecoq was promptly fired and advised that "When one has your disposition, and is poor, one will either become a famous thief or a great detective. Choose." Thus, Lecoq has that touch of criminality that many detective writers have found an essential ingredient in the makeup of their fictional heroes. Lecoq is no armchair detective; he follows the evidence actively, sparing himself no discomfort or danger. Unlike many subsequent detective stories, the solution in Gaboriau's novels comes in bits and pieces. There are few moments of sudden revelation, only the dogged tracking down of clues. As one aspect of the case becomes clear to Lecoq, it raises new questions that must, in turn, be laboriously answered.

Lecoq is not only a superlative detective but also a most interesting personality. Observing his reactions to his own investigation is almost as interesting as the investigation itself. Not only must Lecoq deal with the criminal, he also must deal with the police bureaucracy and especially his supervisor, Gevrol. Consequently, he evolves a strategy in dealing with his colleagues that is as subtle and ingenious as that which he uses on the criminals. Lecoq knows that his own ambitions must ultimately conflict with Gevrol's authority and that, as a recent recruit, his career can be stifled by Gevrol before it begins. Thus, he gets permission to investigate the case by manipulating Gevrol's patronizing attitude and lack of imagination; he calls no attention to himself in the early stages of the investigation, turning the report in anonymously to avoid embarrassing his superior; and he selects Father Absinthe, a veteran officer known more for his drinking than his efficiency, as his partner, because the old detective will have no conflicting loyalties or ambitions. Once Lecoq has proven his ability to the department, he is able to stand up to Gevrol's spiteful machinations. Lecoq's emotional fluctuations between elation and depression according to the vicissitudes of the investigation, his barely controlled anger when something goes wrong, especially if it is the result of his own mistakes, his sense of humor and irony all combine to make him a colorful and engrossing figure.

When the detective dominates the action, *Monsieur Lecoq* is a lively, entertaining novel. Unfortunately, Lecoq is not always present. In fact, in all of Gaboriau's crime novels, the detective's investigation occupies only one-third to one-half of the narrative. For this reason, some historians of the genre

have even questioned the validity of *Monsieur Lecoq* as a detective novel. Gaboriau incorporates two structural elements into his novels that obscure the description of the investigation: the interrogation and the family chronicle.

Gaboriau was fascinated by legal procedures and especially by the process of interrogation, which is central to the French judicial system. In *Monsieur Lecoq*, Judge Segmuller's extremely lengthy questioning of the convict May is skillful, ingenious, and frequently witty. Even to a contemporary reader much of it is realistic and interesting. Because of his own interest, as well as the popularity of courtroom fiction, however, Gaboriau devotes excessive amounts of space to interrogations that reveal little or nothing and do not further the action appreciably.

From the standpoint of the modern reader, a much more serious defect in Gaboriau's work is his insistence on the family chronicle as a central element in his books. Following a premise that has endured from his novels through Doyle to Ross MacDonald, Gaboriau believed that the most interesting and compelling crimes must involve personal, usually familial, relationships, and these become even more engrossing if the family concerned is rich, famous, and aristocratic. The crime committed at the outset of the novel, it ultimately develops, is simply the final effect of a family scandal or crime committed many years previously. Investigating the current crime, therefore, leads the detective back to the original malefaction and threatens not only the present criminal but also the entire clan that he represents.

Unlike later writers using this assumption, Gaboriau fails to integrate the investigating side of the novel with the family scandal. Rather, the books divide into two separate parts, the investigation and the exposition. The first part traces the investigation to the point where the criminal's identity is revealed. Thereupon, Gaboriau shifts his narrative focus to describe all the factors leading to the crime from the participants' point of view. It is not until this domestic history reaches the point where the crime is committed that the two separate plot lines are joined and the mystery resolved.

This rather disjointed narrative method was popular in the nineteenth century because it allowed Gaboriau to incorporate into his crime novel many of the currently popular motifs and situations at great length. He could include family intrigues, scandals, tangled love affairs, victimized aristocratic women, blackmail, long-delayed vengeance, family betrayals, ostentatious displays of wealth, profligacy, and complex frauds and hoaxes, all presented with theatrical emphasis and moralistic overtones. For the modern reader, these family chronicles are much too long, ornate, melodramatic, and implausible; by the time they are finished, all the momentum and interest regarding the original investigation has been lost.

Thus, the end of the first volume of *Monsieur Lecoq* leaves the detective and the reader frustrated. The criminal May has been identified as the duke of Sairmeuse, but he seems untouchable, and many questions remain unanswered. Gaboriau added a second volume that answers these questions and leads, finally, to justice for May and vindication for Lecoq.

Further Reading

Brooks, William S. "Émile Gaboriau." In *Critical Survey of Mystery and Detective Fiction*. Vol. 2. Rev. ed. Pasadena, Calif.: Salem Press, 2008. The critical essay on Gaboriau includes a brief biography, an analysis of the Monsieur Lecoq mystery series, and suggestions for further reading.

Goulet, Andrea. *Optiques: The Science of the Eye and the Birth of Modern French Fiction*. Philadelphia: University of Pennsylvania Press, 2006. Goulet argues that French literature published from 1830 to 1910 reflects a competition between a traditional idealism and an emerging scientific empiricism. Her analysis of *Monsieur Lecoq* and other detective fiction demonstrates how these works express a duality between deduction and induction.

Mandel, Ernest. *Delightful Murder: A Social History of the Crime Story*. Minneapolis: University of Minnesota Press, 1984. *Monsieur Lecoq*, among other detective and mystery novels, is analyzed as a social commentary. The novel is explored as a statement on the social conditions present at the time the book was written.

Symons, Julian. *Bloody Murder: From the Detective Story to the Crime Novel—A History*. 4th ed. London: Pan, 1994. *Monsieur Lecoq* is analyzed as an exemplary and influential detective novel. Places *Monsieur Lecoq* within the tradition and development of the detective and mystery novel.

Thomson, H. Douglas. *Masters of Mystery: A Study of the Detective Story*. 1932. Reprint. Philadelphia: R. West, 1978. Explores *Monsieur Lecoq* as an influential work. Contains a detailed analysis of the structure and characterizations in the novel.

Wright, Willard Huntington. "The Great Detective Stories." In *The Art of the Mystery Story: A Collection of Critical Essays*, edited by Howard Haycraft. 1946. New ed. New York: Carroll & Graf, 1992. This chapter includes an analysis of the character Monsieur Lecoq as he develops in Gaboriau's novel. Compares Lecoq to other great mystery characters.

Mont-Oriol

Author: Guy de Maupassant (1850-1893)
First published: 1887 (English translation, 1891)
Type of work: Novel
Type of plot: Satire
Time of plot: Mid-nineteenth century
Locale: Auvergne, France

Principal characters:
CHRISTIANE ANDERMATT, a young married woman
PAUL BRÉTIGNY, Christiane's lover
WILLIAM ANDERMATT, Christiane's husband
GONTRAN DE RAVENEL, Christiane's brother
FATHER ORIOL, a wealthy peasant landowner
CHARLOTTE and LOUISE, Oriol's daughters

The Story:

The marquis of Ravenel, who is an enthusiastic patron of the baths at Enval, persuades his young daughter Christiane and her husband, William Andermatt, to join him there. On the advice of one of the doctors at the spring, Christiane agrees to take a series of baths, internal and external, in the hope that they will cure her childlessness. When the young couple arrive, they are joined by Christiane's spendthrift brother, Gontran, and his friend Paul Brétigny, who has come to the country to recover from a disappointing love affair. During their stay, they learn that Father Oriol, a wealthy peasant landowner of the district, is planning to blast out a huge rock that hinders the cultivation of one of his fields, and they all go to watch the event.

To everyone's surprise, a spring comes gushing from the ground after the explosion. Andermatt decides that if the water is of medicinal value he will make Oriol an offer for it, for he hopes to build an establishment that will give the existing baths heavy competition. That same evening, Andermatt, accompanied by Gontran, goes to the Oriol house and places his proposal before the peasant.

Oriol, who is quite skilled in bargaining, decides that he will have to be careful not to ask too much for the spring and the fields around it; on the other hand, he does not want to let the possibility of obtaining great wealth slip from his grasp. To inflame Andermatt's desire, he engages a beggar named Clovis to help him. Clovis, who is a poacher by night and feigns rheumatism by day to escape the attentions of the police, is to bathe in the spring for an hour each day—for a fee. At the end of a month he is to be examined, and if he is "cured" of his rheumatism, his condition will prove the medicinal value of the spring.

The unsuspecting Andermatt is enthusiastic about the projected plan, and he agrees to pay Clovis for undergoing treatment. Meanwhile, he and Oriol agree to sign a promise of sale. In order that the Oriol family might be won over to his project, Andermatt decides to hold a charity party and a lottery in which Oriol's daughters and Christiane will participate. Andermatt then returns to Paris, leaving Christiane at the baths. She and her family, accompanied by Paul Brétigny and the Oriol sisters, make numerous excursions about the countryside. Paul begins to confide in Christiane, telling her of his adventures and love affairs. As their conversations become more intimate, she realizes that he is paying court to her. To inflame his desire, she holds him at arm's length until, finally, as they are starting back from a jaunt at nightfall, he catches at her shawl while she walks in front of him and kisses it madly. She has to struggle to master her agitation before she joins the others in the carriage.

Several days later, when Christiane and the others go to view the ruins of a nearby castle by moonlight, Paul throws himself at Christiane's feet, and she submits to him. The following morning Andermatt returns. Losing no time, the financier sets about reaching an agreement with Oriol. According to the terms decided upon after much discussion, the company that Andermatt has formed is assigned the lands along the newly created stream and the crest and slope of the hill down which it runs. In return, Oriol is to receive one-fourth of the profits to be made.

Andermatt rushes back to Paris after completing his arrangements, and that night Paul goes to Christiane's room. During Andermatt's absence they have nearly a month for uninterrupted lovemaking. It is a blow to both of them when they learn that Andermatt is arriving within a few days and that he is planning to take Christiane back to Paris with him when he leaves again. The financier brings several members of his newly formed company with him. The terms of the purchase are read and signed before the village notary, and Andermatt is elected president of the company, over the dissenting votes of Oriol and his son. It is agreed that the new baths shall be known as Mont-Oriol.

That night Paul sorrowfully says good-bye to his love. He feels that, although they might meet later in Paris, part of the enchantment of their affair will be gone forever. Christiane, in contrast, is full of plans for future meetings and ways of carrying on the affair while evading the notice of her servants.

On the first of July in the following year, the day has come for the dedication of the new baths at Mont-Oriol. Christiane, soon expecting a baby, walks with her father, her brother, and Paul to watch the dedication of the three new springs, which are to be named for Christiane and for Oriol's two daughters, Charlotte and Louise. Clovis, however, is again doubled up with his assumed rheumatism, despite his apparently successful cure the previous summer. He threatens to become a serious menace to business because he declares to anyone who will listen that the waters ultimately did him more harm than good. At last Andermatt is forced to reckon with him, and Clovis finally agrees to undergo treatment every year. It is decided that his return annually for the same treatment will only prove to the public the medicinal value of the baths.

Andermatt has planned an operetta and display of fireworks for the evening of the dedication. Gontran, observing that his sister is suffering from the heat of the room in which the entertainment is beginning, sneaks out and sets off the rocket that is intended as the signal for the fireworks display to start. To Andermatt's disgust, everyone dashes outside, but he takes advantage of the unexpected interlude to have a serious conversation with Gontran. Having been informed that Oriol intends to give the lands around Mont-Oriol as his daughters' dowries, Andermatt proposes that Gontran, who is deeply in debt, should repair his finances by marrying either Charlotte or Louise. After meditating for a few moments, Gontran announces that he will open the ball to be held later that evening by dancing with Charlotte Oriol, the younger and prettier of the two sisters.

Christiane, too, makes use of the interruption. She proposes to Paul that they walk along the road on which they said good-bye the previous year. At that time, he had fallen to his knees and kissed her shadow, and she has hopes that he will repeat the act. Her hopes are dashed, however, for although the child she is carrying is his, her shadow betrays too clearly her changed form.

Gontran pays court to Charlotte Oriol at the ball, and the news of his interest in her soon becomes common gossip at the springs. The innocent young woman responds so freely that Christiane and Paul, who are fond of her, begin to fear that she will eventually find herself compromised. They are satisfied, however, when Gontran confides to them his intention to ask for her hand.

When he asks Andermatt to sound out Oriol about the match, the crafty peasant, realizing that his younger daughter will be easier to marry off than will the older, says that he plans to endow Charlotte with the lands on the other side of the mountain. Because those lands are of no use to Andermatt at the moment, Gontran realizes that he will have to change his tactics. He persuades Louise that he has courted Charlotte only to arouse the older sister's interest, and he manages to meet her frequently at the home of one of the local doctors and on walks. When the time seems ripe, he sends Andermatt once more to talk to Oriol. As the reward for his efforts he receives a signed statement that assures him a dowry and the promise of Louise's hand.

Paul, unaware of Gontran and Andermatt's scheming, has been incensed by Gontran's sudden desertion of Charlotte, and gradually his feeling of sympathy for her has grown into love. One day her father finds them together, and, partly because he is in love and partly because he does not want to compromise Charlotte, his immediate reaction is to propose. When he agrees to sign a statement as to his satisfactory income, the peasant gives his consent to the marriage.

The next morning, Christiane learns that Paul is to marry Charlotte. Her informant is the doctor who has come to examine her because she has been feeling ill. As soon as she hears that her lover is to marry, she goes into labor from the shock, and fifteen hours later a little girl is born. Christiane will have nothing to do with the baby at first, but when Andermatt brings the child to her, she finds the infant irresistible and wants to keep her close.

No one else is available to nurse the child, so the doctor's wife is chosen to keep Christiane company during her recovery. The talkative woman knows the Oriols well, and Christiane is able to learn from her most of the details of Paul's courtship of Charlotte. Upset by the realization that he has given Charlotte the same attentions she once received, she falls into a delirium, but the next day her condition begins to improve.

When the baby is a few days old, Christiane asks that Paul be sent to see her. He arrives planning to beg her pardon, but he finds there is no need to do so. Christiane, engrossed in the child, has only a few conversational words for him. Although he was hoping to see the infant who is half his, he notes that the curtains of the cradle are significantly fastened in the front with some of Christiane's pins.

Critical Evaluation:

In his chapter on *Mont-Oriol* in *Maupassant the Novelist*, Edward D. Sullivan writes, "In August 1885 Maupassant, visiting Chatel-Guyon in Auvergne, was profoundly impressed by the natural beauty of the region, and determined to use this setting as a background for his next novel." It is an indication of Guy de Maupassant's genius that he was confident of his ability to create a cast of believable characters to people an empty landscape. The imagination that was responsible for Maupassant's fame and fortune tortured him with horrible hallucinations and drove him to attempt suicide before his death in a sanatorium.

Henry James gives an incisive one-sentence evaluation of Maupassant's works in an essay on the French author: "M. de Maupassant sees human life as a terribly ugly business relieved by the comical, but even the comedy is for the most part the comedy of misery, of avidity, of ignorance, helplessness, and grossness." This sentence could serve as a capsule summation of the theme and thesis of *Mont-Oriol*. Maupassant's descriptions of the beauty of nature, including those of the pure water gushing from the mountain spring, are contrasted with his depictions of the ugliness of human behavior. He peoples his pristine landscape with fools and hypocrites. Maupassant was a cynic, but always an amusing cynic. His avaricious peasants and hypocritical doctors provide much of the comedy in *Mont-Oriol*.

It is noteworthy that Christiane Andermatt is the only character who changes, indicating that the novel is her story. She loses the girlish innocence, romanticism, and vulnerability that at first make her so irresistible to the jaded Paul Brétigny. Gontran de Ravenel remains a playboy from beginning to end. William Andermatt remains a greedy businessman. Paul remains an attitudinizing Don Juan. Christiane, however, ends up cynical, cunning, spiteful, and, above all, disillusioned. Her disappointment with human nature reflects Maupassant's own disappointment.

Biographers of Maupassant frequently remark on the influence on the author of the pessimistic and misanthropic German philosopher Arthur Schopenhauer, who was Maupassant's contemporary. "I admire Schopenhauer madly," Maupassant once wrote in a letter. Here is a characteristic passage from one of Schopenhauer's essays: "how little genuine honesty is to be found in the world and how often injustice and dishonesty sit at the helm, secretly and in the innermost recess, behind all the virtuous outworks, even where we least suspect them."

One by one, Maupassant's characters exhibit dishonesty, motivated by greed and selfishness. The marquis, an impecunious aristocrat, is willing to marry his tender young daughter to a much older, temperamentally unsuited man of an inferior social class for the sake of money. William Andermatt does not love Christiane; he has married her for her family name and for the business connections her family can provide. Paul proves to be a faithless lover who not only deceives Christiane's trusting husband but also betrays Christiane. Christiane's brother, Gontran, is so dishonest that dishonesty seems as natural to him as breathing. He coldly and deliberately jilts one of Father Oriol's daughters in favor of the other when he finds out where his financial advantage lies. Andermatt, to whom the wastrel Gontran is heavily in debt, encourages his brother-in-law in this heartless deed without regard for the feelings of the trusting young Charlotte Oriol, who is shamefully betrayed, and without regard for the fate of her sister Louise, who will spend a lifetime married to a faithless husband who never loved her.

Maupassant's male peasant characters are just as dishonest as his upper-class characters, but they do not pretend to be honorable gentlemen, nor do they expect others to be more honest than themselves. Maupassant liked to write about peasants and prostitutes because they were the only people who did not pretend to be other than what they were. The crafty, tightfisted Father Oriol and the totally unscrupulous poacher and malingerer Clovis are two of the most striking characters in the novel. They are human nature in the raw, undisguised by formal clothes and refined manners.

Even Christiane proves to be capable of the grossest dishonesty. She deceives her husband by carrying on an affair with Paul—right under Andermatt's nose. Her dishonesty is more shocking than that of any other character in the novel because of her youth, idealism, and innocence. Ultimately she presents Andermatt with a bastard daughter without showing the slightest remorse as she watches the cuckold cooing over the infant nestled in his arms.

As well as being an admirer of Schopenhauer, Maupassant was an admirer of the Russian novelist Leo Tolstoy, who acknowledged the genius of the younger writer and published an essay about him in which he deplored Maupassant's preoccupation with sexual matters. Maupassant's characterization of Paul and Gontran echoes the negative view of the upper classes that Tolstoy developed in his old age. Tolstoy thought that men and women who do not have to labor for their livelihoods are frustrated and thus exaggerate the importance of love and sex in order to fill their empty lives. Gontran and Paul are examples of leisure-class drones who create tragedy by playing at love.

Maupassant's cynicism about human nature, which he shared with Schopenhauer and Tolstoy, can be seen echoed in many works of modern fiction, perhaps most strikingly in the hard-boiled novels of the American crime writers Dashiell Hammett, Raymond Chandler, James M. Cain, and Jim Thompson. Maupassant may be said to have contributed to this genre in terms of style. He started as a short-story writer and had to learn economy with words. He became expert at selecting the telling detail that could create a scene and the line of dialogue that could bring a character to life.

"Critical Evaluation" by Bill Delaney

Further Reading

Bloom, Harold, ed. *Guy de Maupassant*. Philadelphia: Chelsea House, 2004. Collection of essays focuses primarily on Maupassant's short stories, but some discussion of his novels is presented, including critiques by Anatole France and Joseph Conrad. Among the topics addressed is the influence of Maupassant's realism.

Duffy, Larry. "Conclusion: 'Ce Parasite Supplémentaire.'" In *Le Grand Transit Moderne: Mobility, Modernity, and French Naturalist Fiction*. New York: Rodopi, 2005. Analyzes the depiction of motion in *Mont-Oriol*. Includes many quotations from the original French-language edition of the novel.

Gregorio, Laurence A. *Maupassant's Fiction and the Darwinian View of Life*. New York: Peter Lang, 2005. Describes how evolutionary theory and social Darwinism figure significantly in Maupassant's fiction, demonstrating how these writings reflect the concepts of natural selection, heredity, and materialism.

Harris, Trevor A. Le V. "Maupassant's *Mont-Oriol*: Narrative as Declining Noun." *Modern Language Review* 89, no. 3 (July, 1994): 581-594. Presents a close reading of *Mont-Oriol*, with special attention to the meanings in the names of the novel's characters. Emphasizes decline as a major theme and technical device.

James, Henry. *Partial Portraits*. Westport, Conn.: Greenwood Press, 1970. Contains the frequently quoted essay "Guy De Maupassant." Originally published in 1888, this succinct and lucid analysis of Maupassant's literary merits and shortcomings, containing some discussion of *Mont-Oriol*, has never been surpassed by a critic writing in English.

Lerner, Michael G. *Maupassant*. Winchester, Mass.: Allen & Unwin, 1975. Devotes balanced attention to the transmutations of Maupassant's life experiences into material for his short stories and novels, including *Mont-Oriol*. Includes photographs.

Sullivan, Edward D. *Maupassant the Novelist*. Westport, Conn.: Greenwood Press, 1978. Study of Maupassant's six novels devotes a chapter to *Mont-Oriol*. Examines Maupassant's letters, articles, essays, stories, and other works to trace the painful struggle of an acknowledged master of the short story to develop into an equally accomplished novelist.

Wallace, A. H. *Guy de Maupassant*. New York: Twayne, 1973. Excellent introduction to the life and works of Maupassant includes a section devoted to discussion of *Mont-Oriol*. Supplemented with a chronology and a bibliography.

Mont-Saint-Michel and Chartres
A Study of Thirteenth Century Unity

Author: Henry Adams (1838-1918)
First published: 1904, private printing; 1913, republished
Type of work: Essay

Mont-Saint-Michel and Chartres is the study of two great medieval buildings, one a Norman abbey and the other a Gothic cathedral. In the author's mind, however, the book has a far wider purpose. Henry Adams set out to evoke the mood of an era in France, the eleventh to the thirteenth century, in all aspects: art, theology, philosophy, and music. Behind this wider purpose is still another. Adams subtitled the book *A Study of Thirteenth Century Unity*, asking that it be read along with his autobiography, *The Education of Henry Adams* (1907), in which he discusses what he called twentieth century multiplicity.

Adams was a historian, and his two books suggest a theory of history and an attitude toward history. Western civilization had moved from unity to multiplicity, from a God-centered culture in which faith was the major force to an uncentered culture of competing ideologies and conflicting scientific theories. Adams's attitude is one of quiet regret, and his survey of medieval France is informed by an intellectual's poignant yearning. This emotional longing for the order of a medieval culture is more than balanced, however, by the rigorous intellection Adams exercises. Translations of old French lyrics, incisive summaries of Thomist theories, detailed analyses of architectural subtleties—these are among Adams's self-imposed duties in the book. Scholars agree that Adams fulfilled his duties with grace and considerable accuracy.

Adams's method is deceptively casual. In the preface he announces the desired relationship between himself and the reader: An uncle is speaking to a niece, as a guide for a summer's study tour of France. Readers soon see that the genial uncle has planned the course of study quite rigorously. It operates partly in the way that Adams's own mind tended to

operate, by emphasizing opposites. Adams concerns himself with contrasts: St. Michel and Chartres, the masculine temperament and the feminine, Norman culture and French culture. All this is within the major contrast of the thirteenth century and twentieth century. Adams also uses the device of paradox. He insists that his purpose is not to teach, yet the book is a joy only if the reader's intellect stands alert to follow Adams's careful exposition.

By 1904, when the book was privately printed, Adams had befriended several of the young American scholars who were awakening universities in the United States to the importance of the medieval period. Adams himself had done sporadic writing and study in this realm years before. The book can be usefully thought of as an old person's legacy to a new generation, an unpretentious structure of affectionate scholarship, carefully built with some of Adams's finest prose.

Basically, the book contains three parts. The opening chapters deal with Mont-Saint-Michel on the Normandy coast. A transition chapter enables Adams to traverse the route to the cathedral town of Chartres. Six chapters examine the great cathedral, leading the reader to see its full symbolic meaning. The six concluding chapters then attend to history, poetry, theology, and philosophy—the medieval setting in which the jewel of the cathedral shines. Adams's focus is medieval France, and his book begins at the offshore hill of St. Michel, where the great abbey was built between 1020 and 1135. Instantly, the salient characteristics accumulate, for later contrast with those of Chartres: isolation, height, energy, modest size, utter simplicity, dedication to the archangel St. Michael (representing the Church militant).

As Mont-Saint-Michel "was one of the most famous

shrines of northern Europe," so in French *The Song of Roland* (twelfth century) achieved unequaled eminence. How song and shrine complement each other is Adams's theme in the second chapter. The song and the shrine represent the militant temper of the time just before the Battle of Hastings; both exalt simplicity, directness, and intensity, and both display a certain naïveté. This was France of the eleventh century. Next it is the early thirteenth century that draws his attention, "the early and perfect period of Gothic art." On the Mount this period is seen in the ruins of the ancillary buildings (the "Merveille"): great hall, refectory, library, cloisters. The tour of the Mount completed, Adams sums up the meaning of the entire complex, using his key word, "unity": "It expressed the unity of Church and State, God and Man, Peace and War, Life and Death, Good and Bad; it solved the whole problem of the universe."

The uncle goes now to Chartres. As the fenestration of St. Michel's great hall looked ahead to the glass of Chartres, so the choir and facades of Coutances, along the way, prepare the niece for Chartres, as do Bayeux and Saint-Germain-des-Prés. For Adams, Chartres is the climactic shrine, the central symbol of its age and of his book. Readers arrive at Chartres in chapter 5, with a distant glimpse of the two spires. Adams, perhaps at his most genial, explores the facade, especially noting the contrast between the magnificent "old" tower of the twelfth century and the "new" tower completed in 1517. This is a chapter of immense detail perfectly handled. The detail gradually rises into symbolism. For Chartres is the church of the Virgin, "the greatest of all queens, but the most womanly of women." It is her palace, the utter opposite of St. Michel: feminine, elaborate, gracious, a building larger and later than the abbey. Minute examination of the portals and porches concludes chapter 5.

With a bit of the avuncular humor that accounts for the charm of the book, Adams insists on another chapter of delay—"ten minutes to accustom our eyes to the light." This is a ruse. The interior dimness symbolizes the dim past that Adams's literary art seeks to evoke. This chapter characterizes the Queen of Heaven, who demanded light, convenience, and color in her church space.

Next follow one hundred pages that function on several levels. There is narrative, a progressive tour through the church; description, an examination in detail of windows, apses, chapels; evocation, of an era and its art and faith; symbolism, the meaning of the Lady to the architects and worshipers; the meaning of the iconography; and the significance of the age itself. Adams reaches the high point of his interest and his art, besides demonstrating considerable proficiency as a master of architectural detail.

In his chapter on "The Three Queens," Adams next turns to one of his favorite doctrines. He has been posing as one of the Virgin's faithful, so that it is no surprise to see him declaring the doctrine of woman's superiority. The twelfth century held this view, insists Adams: Chartres was built for the Virgin. Secular women of the century held power also. These were Eleanor, queen of France; Mary of Champagne; and Blanche, queen of France. They created the institution of courtly ("courteous") love. The subject of courtly love leads Adams on to a lighthearted discussion of thirteenth century song, chiefly a synopsis of *Auscassin et Nicolette*, Adam de la Halle's "Li Gieus de Robin et de Marion," and the famous *Roman de la Rose*. In his discussion of poetry and architecture Adams says that in this period, "Art leads always to the woman." Specifically, art leads to the Virgin. Adams now takes up the miracles of the Virgin. They make up a special branch of literature and demonstrate that the sympathetic Virgin "was by essence illogical, unreasonable and feminine"—a pitying "power above law." Here again is the contrast between the Virgin and St. Michael.

Abruptly turning from the "feel" of the Middle Ages, achieved through study of its art, Adams now attends to its "mind." This subject is introduced by way of Abelard, theologian and dialectician at Notre Dame de Paris. Adams constructs an abstract debate between Abelard and his teacher, William of Champeaux, to bring up the issue of unity versus multiplicity, which will concern him through the rest of the book. The problems of unity and multiplicity were several: How can God be One and yet be a Trinity? How can people in their diversity become one with God? For the moment the focus is on Abelard, the man who sought God by the force of reason. He is the direct opposite of the "illogical" Virgin and of the equally illogical mystic, Francis of Assisi, whom readers meet also. Adams thus continues his method of displaying the age by means of its opposites.

Whether such opposites as scholasticism and mysticism could be reconciled is part of Adams's problem in the last chapter. The great reconciler was Thomas Aquinas, whose all-encompassing *Summa Theologica* (c. 1265-1273; English translation, 1911-1921) Adams elaborately compares to the detail and grandeur of the Gothic cathedral. Aquinas showed how to fuse God's trinity with His unity. Even more important, he showed how God, the One, permeates all being, creating the great multiplicity and diversity of humankind and the universe.

Adams sums up some of the paradoxes and polarities he has already dealt with. One unusual thing about the Church of the Middle Ages was its multiplicity: It harbored mystics and rationalists, the holy Virgin and the abject sinners she pitied. Even greater was the Church's unity. Aquinas demonstrated how God and the individual, Creator and created, formed a grand unity that the age celebrated instinctively in art, architecture, and song. Here was the medieval worldview.

Adams's final point is comparison. The Thomist explanation of God's creativity can be compared usefully to a modern dynamo and its production of energy. The dynamo is the key symbol of *The Education of Henry Adams*, the sequel to *Mont-Saint-Michel and Chartres*. The true subject of the autobiography is the century in which multiplicity won.

Further Reading

Adams, Henry. *Mont-Saint-Michel and Chartres*. New York: G. P. Putnam's Sons, 1980. Contains a helpful introduction and place of this work in the writings of Adams. Illustrations of Mont-Saint-Michel, Chartres, other works of medieval architecture, and scenes of medieval life from illuminated manuscripts aid in visualizing Adams's description of medieval monuments, culture, and society.

Byrnes, Joseph F. *The Virgin of Chartres: An Intellectual and Psychological History of the Work of Henry Adams*. London: Associated University Presses, 1981. Studies the intellectual and psychological development of Adams, particularly regarding women. His ideals culminate in the medieval symbol of the Virgin as expressed in Chartres Cathedral.

Kazin, Alfred. "Religion as Culture: Henry Adams's *Mont-Saint-Michel and Chartres*." In *Henry Adams and His World*, edited by David R. Contosta and Robert Muccigrosso. Philadelphia: American Philosophical Society, 1993. Kazin, a prominent literary critic, interprets the book as reflecting Adams's desire for unity, a quality Adams discovered in thirteenth century French architecture.

McIntyre, John P. "Henry Adams and the Unity of *Chartres*." *Twentieth Century Literature* 7 (January, 1962): 159-171. Explains the historical method that Adams used in writing *Mont-Saint-Michel and Chartres*. Demonstrates how Adams achieves a unified conception of medieval history by using Romanesque and Gothic architectural monuments as documents of social and cultural history.

Mane, Robert. *Henry Adams on the Road to Chartres*. Cambridge, Mass.: Harvard University Press, 1971. Examines *Mont-Saint-Michel and Chartres* by looking at the personal and educational background that led Adams to write on Chartres. Also analyzes the literary work itself.

Samuels, Ernest. *Henry Adams: The Major Phase*. Cambridge, Mass.: Belknap Press, 1964. The third of a three-volume biography of Adams. Contains an extensive examination of *Mont-Saint-Michel and Chartres* within the context of Adams's life.

Schroth, Raymond A. *Dante to "Dead Man Walking": One Reader's Journey Through the Christian Classics*. Chicago: Loyola Press, 2001. *Mont-Saint-Michel and Chartres* is one of the works included in this overview of Christian literature. Schroth describes Adams's book as "all of Christian history symbolized in one cathedral."

A Month in the Country

Author: Ivan Turgenev (1818-1883)
First produced: Mesyats v derevne, 1872; first published, 1855 (English translation, 1924)
Type of work: Drama
Type of plot: Psychological realism
Time of plot: 1840's
Locale: Russia

Principal characters:
ARKADY ISLAYEV, a wealthy landowner
NATALYA (NATASHA), his wife
KOLYA, their son
VERA, Natalya's ward
LIZAVETA, a companion
RAKITIN, a family friend
BELYAYEV, a young tutor
SHPIGELSKY, a doctor

The Story:

In her drawing room, Natalya, a twenty-nine-year-old wife and mother, is talking confidentially to her good friend, Rakitin. She admits that her husband, Islayev, has one fault: He goes into things too enthusiastically. He is with his workmen constantly, and he himself demonstrates how they should do their work. Her complaint ends, and she asks Rakitin to continue reading to her. She really has no interest in the book, but it is being discussed by her friends.

The book is read aloud in the big room, where a card game is in progress. Schaaf, the German tutor, has been winning until Lizaveta, companion to Islayev's mother, makes a mistake; the German grumbles at her ineptness. The doctor, Shpigelsky, breezes in and, as is his wont, tells a long, pointless story. He had really come to talk privately with Natalya about a friend of his who wishes to marry Vera. Natalya, claiming that at seventeen Vera is too young, puts off a definite answer.

Kolya, Natalya's little son, runs up, full of news about his tutor Belyayev's doings. The energetic young tutor, who had been there nearly a month, is making a kite. Vera, also coming from play, tells how Belyayev can climb trees as nimbly as a squirrel. Islayev tries to induce Natalya and Rakitin to look over his new blowing machine, but only Rakitin is interested.

As the room gradually clears, Natalya has a chance to talk with Belyayev at some length. She compliments him on his good singing voice and asks about his family. She is touched to learn that his mother is dead and that he has a sister also named Natalya. In spite of her friendly attitude, Belyayev is nervous and persists in being formal and polite with her.

In the garden, Katya, the maid, is listening to the butler's proposal. She has some trouble in fending him off, and the arrival of Schaaf makes matters a little more complicated. Schaaf archly sings a love song and tries to kiss her. She escapes by running into a raspberry patch. Vera and Belyayev call her out after Schaaf leaves. They are working on the kite and, as they work, they companionably share Katya's raspberries. Belyayev tells Vera much of his past life, of his studies in Moscow, of his poverty. Vera describes her loneliness without friends her own age. Interrupted by the arrival of Natalya and Rakitin, they slip out of the garden.

Natalya professes to Rakitin her uneasiness about Vera; the girl is very young and probably should not be so much alone with Belyayev. Rakitin begins to suspect what is happening. Natalya has always been so frank and tender with him. Now she seems preoccupied and talks distractedly. She even accuses him of having a languid mind, and she no longer cares for his descriptions of nature. Rakitin seeks out Belyayev to get better acquainted with him. He is troubled when he discovers that the young tutor hides such an engaging manner underneath his gawky exterior. Although Belyayev thinks of Natalya only as an older woman and his employer, Rakitin senses a possible rival for Natalya's affections.

Shpigelsky brings Bolshintsov, a neighbor forty years old, to the house and coaches him carefully on what he is to say. Bolshintsov is shy with women but, having decided to make an offer to Vera, he has enlisted the busybody doctor as an intermediary. If the match comes off, Shpigelsky is to get three horses as his reward.

When Natalya can no longer disguise her increasing coldness toward Rakitin, he accuses her of being attracted to Belyayev. Although she proclaims that she still loves Rakitin, she cannot deny the young tutor's charms. Rakitin delicately hints that she owes her love to her husband and suggests that both he and Belyayev should leave the house.

With Vera, Natalya assumes a sisterly air and tells her of Bolshintsov's proposal. She does not press the point too much after Vera laughs at the idea of marrying such a funny old man. Instead, with mature skill, she probes into her ward's feelings and gets her to confess her love for Belyayev. Her suspicions confirmed, she is torn between her inclinations as a woman and her duty as wife and guardian. Sending for Belyayev, she warns him that Vera is quite immature and that it is easy for her to misinterpret friendship. When the young man finally understands that Vera is in love with him, he is amazed; he has no notions of love at all. He resigns his job and offers to leave the house immediately. Natalya, unable to bear his willingness to leave the house, asks him to defer his decision for a while.

Meanwhile, Shpigelsky is impressing Lizaveta by diagnosing the ills and attitudes of members of the family. He reminds her that she will not want to remain a companion all her life; hence, he would make her an offer of marriage. Lizaveta, adopting a coquettish manner, begins a coy reply, but the doctor keeps talking. He insists on telling her all his faults and the extent of his fortune and then states that he has proved to her he is a fine fellow because he has confessed his faults. Lizaveta promises to give him an answer the next day. To her surprise, Shpigelsky sings a peculiar song about a gray goat.

Vera tries to save the situation by telling Belyayev that she knows how Natalya had warned him of the girl's love. Bitter over Natalya's efforts to get her married off to Bolshintsov, she hopes that Belyayev will confess his love for her. The young man is unresponsive. Then, Vera assures him that Natalya herself is in love with him. When Natalya finds them, Vera is openly reproachful. She accuses her guardian of treating her as a child when she is a grown woman. Henceforth, they will be equals and probably rivals. She leaves in an emotional state. When they are alone, Natalya confirms that she is in love with Belyayev. Overwhelmed by her declaration, he can think only of leaving.

Islayev begins to suspect that all is not well in his household, for he knows that Rakitin has been much in his wife's company. Being forthright, he asks Rakitin outright if he is in love with Natalya. Rakitin admits that he is, and he adds that he is leaving immediately. Islayev does not really want him to leave, but his departure does seem a good solution. Rakitin makes no mention of Natalya's infatuation for Belyayev.

Vera tells Shpigelsky that she will accept Bolshintsov's offer because she can no longer remain under the same roof with Natalya. Belyayev, not trusting himself to meet Natalya, sends a farewell note by Vera. To Islayev, it seems peculiar that so many people are leaving at once. Lizaveta also comments to Islayev's mother that she, too, will be leaving one of these days.

Critical Evaluation:

Ivan Turgenev was one of the first Russian writers to win fame outside Russia. Although best known as a novelist, Turgenev also was a poet, journalist, and dramatist. The plays—he wrote about a dozen—came relatively early in his writing career, between 1843 and 1852. Of them, *A Month in the Country*, written in 1850, is generally considered the best, even though *The Lady from the Provinces* (1851) makes a better stage production. *A Month in the Country* was a great favorite of the Moscow Art Theater and its eminent director, Konstantin Stanislavsky. The enduring popularity of the play, however, is less important than its historical position in the evolution of the Russian theater, since Turgenev's contribution anticipated the psychological realism and rather actionless plots of Anton Chekhov's later dramas.

Two of Turgenev's strong points are especially related to what has come to be known as the Chekhovian ambience. One is style; the other is characterization. Because Turgenev was a poet, his residual poetic talents later manifested themselves in the lyrical style that marks both his prose and his drama. The delicate grace of his style in treating nature and love—the incident in the raspberry patch, for instance—anticipates such typically Chekhovian settings as are found in *Dyadya Vanya* (pb. 1897, pr. 1899; *Uncle Vanya*, 1914) and *Vishnyovy sad* (pr., pb. 1904; *The Cherry Orchard*, 1908). Likewise, in characterization, Turgenev was a trailblazer. He shaped his characters not by asking "How do they look?" or "What are they doing?" but by searching for "What do the characters think and feel?" As a consequence of this method of characterization, the action of the play becomes internalized as mental and emotional events. Physical action, as it is usually understood, is reduced to a minimum. These circumstances were ideal for depicting strong female characters for which Turgenev has rightly been acclaimed. In addition, this technique of characterization was adopted and polished by Chekhov until it became the hallmark of his dramas.

A Month in the Country is a complex play, although the plot merely revolves around a simple love triangle. The theme is also easily stated but more difficult to explain; it is frustration. All of the major characters are frustrated. Their needs and desires are unmet; their attempts at gaining satisfaction are thwarted by the indifference or the insensitivity of second parties, while they, in turn, ignore similar entreaties of third parties. They do not work at cross-purposes; rather, they work along parallel lines that never meet.

The interaction, the human relationships of which the plot is made, constitutes an emotional and intellectual pattern best described as undulating, after the manner of ocean waves: High crests are separated by wide troughs. Beneath those wide troughs, life seethes with repression, suppression, and unmet needs that occasionally boil up to the crest of a breaker only to subside again, thwarted by the immutable pattern of frustration, until the next cresting of a breaker signals another emotional crisis. The pattern repeats itself with unremitting regularity. By the end of the play, the reader is emotionally bludgeoned into a resigned submission not unlike that of Natalya or Vera. For a play whose action is psychological rather than physical, *A Month in the Country* has a remarkable impact—and a lasting one, as Belyayev learns from his brief month in the country.

Further Reading

Andrew, Joe, Derek Offord, and Robert Reid, eds. *Turgenev and Russian Culture: Essays to Honour Richard Peace*. New York: Rodopi, 2008. Topics discussed include the uses of poetry in Turgenev's prose, the dark side of the writer, and Turgenev and Russian culture. Other essays focus on *A Month in the Country*, with one analyzing a production of the play and another examining "Post-War British *Month*(s) *in the Country*."

Bloom, Harold, ed. *Ivan Turgenev*. Philadelphia: Chelsea House, 2003. Collection of critical essays about Turgenev's work, comparing his work to those of Ernest Hemingway, Willa Cather, and Sherwood Anderson.

Dessaix, Robert. *Twilight of Love: Travels with Turgenev*. London: Scribner, 2005. Dessaix, a writer and a scholar of Russian literature, visited Turgenev's former homes and conducted research at the Moscow Library to locate the "soul" of the Russian writer. The resulting memoir provides insights into Turgenev's life, particularly the writer's experience of love.

Fitzlyon, April. *"A Month in the Country": An Exhibition Presented by the Theatre Museum*. London: Victoria and Albert Museum, 1983. A useful illustrated presentation of Turgenev's work for the theater, with a bibliography of translations of his plays into English and of their productions in Great Britain. Various aspects of *A Month in the Country* are treated clearly.

Freeborn, Richard. "Turgenev the Dramatist." In *Critical Essays on Ivan Turgenev*, edited by David A. Lowe. Boston: G. K. Hall, 1989. An excellent survey of Turgenev's dramas. Considers Turgenev's work for the theater a part of his apprenticeship for future works. Demonstrates how in *A Month in the Country*, Turgenev added a dimension of forceful psychological insight, reinforced by a sharp edge of social criticism.

Magarshack, David. *Turgenev: A Life.* New York: Grove Press, 1954. An illustrated biography by Turgenev's trans-

lator, concentrating on the events shaping the writer's life, his relationships with Russian and foreign writers, and the circumstances surrounding his works, including *A Month in the Country.*

Seeley, Frank Friedeberg. "Poetry, Plays, Criticism." In *Turgenev: A Reading of His Fiction.* New York: Cambridge University Press, 1991. In this survey of Turgenev's poetry and plays, Seeley finds *A Month in the Country* to be a combination of two subtle psychological portraits—a woman in crisis and a Hamlet-type hero. Argues that this play marks the full development of the Russian psychological drama a generation before Anton Chekhov.

The Moon and Sixpence

Author: W. Somerset Maugham (1874-1965)
First published: 1919
Type of work: Novel
Type of plot: Biographical
Time of plot: c. 1897-1917
Locale: England, France, and Tahiti

Principal characters:
CHARLES STRICKLAND, an artist
DIRK STROEVE, his friend
BLANCHE STROEVE, Dirk's wife
ATA, Strickland's Tahitian wife
AMY STRICKLAND, Strickland's English wife

The Story:

Charles Strickland, a dull stockbroker, lives in England with his wife and two children. Mrs. Strickland is a model mother, but her husband seems bored with her and with his children. To everyone else, it is Strickland who seems commonplace. The family spends the summer at the seashore, and Strickland returns ahead of his wife. When she writes him that she is coming home, he answers from Paris, simply stating that he is not going to live with her anymore. With singleness of intention, Mrs. Strickland dispatches a friend to Paris to bring back her husband.

Strickland is living in a shabby hotel; his room is filthy, but he appears to be living alone. Much to the discomfort of the friend, he candidly admits his beastly treatment of his wife, but there is no emotion in his statements concerning her and her future welfare. When asked about the woman with whom he had allegedly run away, he laughs, explaining to Mrs. Strickland's emissary that he had really run off to paint. He knows he can paint if he seriously tries. The situation is incredible to Mrs. Strickland's friend. Strickland says he does not care what people think of him.

Stubbornly, Strickland begins to take art lessons. Although his teacher laughs at his work, he merely shrugs his

shoulders and continues to paint in his own way. Back in England, the friend tries to explain to Mrs. Strickland the utter hopelessness of trying to reconcile her husband. She cannot realize her defeat at first. If Strickland had gone off with a woman, she could have understood him. Mrs. Strickland, however, is not able to cope with his having left her for an idea.

Dirk Stroeve, a very poor painter with a delicate feeling for art, marries an Englishwoman and settles in Paris. Impossible as it seems, Dirk, who has become acquainted with Strickland, thinks the redheaded Englishman a great painter. Strickland, however, does not want anyone's opinion. Indifferent to physical discomfort, he has not tried to sell his paintings so that he can eat. When he needs money, he finds odd jobs in and around Paris.

It is apparent that the Stroeves are very much in love. A buffoon and a fool, Dirk is constantly berating himself, but Blanche seems to hold him in high esteem. When Strickland becomes very ill, Dirk rushes home to Blanche and pleads with her to nurse the sick artist back to health. She bitterly professes her hatred of the man who had laughed at her husband's paintings, and she tearfully begs Stroeve not to bring the monster near her. Dirk is nevertheless able to persuade her to allow Strickland to come to their home.

Although she and Strickland rarely speak to each other, Blanche proves a capable nurse. There seems to be something electrifying in the air when they are together in the same room. Strickland recovers. Dirk admires Strickland's work, and so is anxious that Strickland stay and work in Dirk's studio. Strickland takes possession of the studio. When Dirk finally gathers enough courage to ask him to leave, Blanche says that she will also leave. Dirk falls before her, groveling at her feet, and pleads with her to stay, but his adoring demonstrations only bore her. When he sees that she will indeed return with Strickland to the filthy hovel that is the Englishman's studio, Dirk's generous soul cannot bear to think that his beloved Blanche should live in such poverty. He says that she need not leave; he will go. Thanking her for having given him so much happiness, he leaves her with half of what he owns.

Dirk hangs around Paris waiting for the time to come when Blanche will need him again after Strickland tires of her. Once, he follows her shopping. He walks along with her, telling her of his devotion; she will not speak to him. Suddenly, she slaps him in the face and walks away. One day, the police inform Dirk that Blanche had swallowed oxalic acid. After she dies, Dirk feels compelled to return to his studio. There he finds a nude portrait of his wife, evidently the work of Strickland. In a mad passion of jealousy, he starts to hack at the picture with a knife, but he is arrested by the wonder of the artwork. No matter what he feels, Dirk cannot mutilate the painting. He packs his belongings and returns to Holland to live with his mother.

Strickland had chosen Blanche Stroeve as a subject because he thought she had a beautiful body to paint. When he finished the picture, he was through with her. Thinking that the picture was not satisfactory, he left it in the studio. The death of Blanche and the misery of Dirk do not move him. He is an artist.

After Blanche's death, Strickland leaves Paris for Marseilles, and finally, after many wanderings, goes to Tahiti. There he paints his vivid awkward-looking pictures and leaves them with people all over the island in payment for lodging and food. No one thinks the pictures are worth anything, but years later some who had saved the pictures were pleasantly surprised to sell them for enormous sums of money to English and French collectors who came to the island looking for the painter's work.

At one of the hotels in Tahiti, Strickland is befriended by a fat old woman, Tiare Johnson, who looks after his health and his cleanliness. She even finds him a wife, a seventeen-year-

old Tahitian girl named Ata. For three years, Ata and her husband live together in a bungalow just off the main road. These are perhaps the happiest years in Strickland's life. He paints, reads, and loafs. Ata has a baby.

One day, Ata sends to the village for a doctor. When the doctor arrives at the artist's bungalow, he is struck with horror; to his experienced eye, Strickland has the thickened features of a leper. More than two years pass. No one goes near Strickland's plantation, for the locals know well the meaning of Strickland's disease. Only Ata stays faithfully with him, and everyone shuns her just as they shun Strickland. Two more years pass. One of Ata's children dies. Strickland is now so disabled by the disease that he will not even permit the doctor to see him. He is painting on the walls of his bungalow when at last he goes blind. He sits in the house hour after hour, trying to remember his paintings on the walls—his masterpieces. Strickland is not interested in the fame his art might bring and makes Ata promise to destroy his work upon his death, a wish she faithfully carries out.

Years later, a friend of Strickland, just returned from Tahiti, calls on Mrs. Strickland in London. She seems little interested in her husband's last years or his death. On the wall are several colored reproductions of Strickland's pictures. They are decorative, she thinks, and go well with her cushions.

Critical Evaluation:

The Moon and Sixpence, W. Somerset Maugham's first novel after his long, autobiographical masterpiece, *Of Human Bondage* (1915), marks an important break in style and narrative technique. Instead of being a bildungsroman such as *Of Human Bondage*, the novel portrays the adult life of a genius. The title refers to a saying about a man gazing so intently on the moon that he fails to see the sixpence lying at his feet. Influenced by the life of Paul Gauguin, the French artist, the novel tells of Charles Strickland, whose talent as a painter remains long hidden even from himself. A forty-year-old English stockbroker leading a colorless life, Strickland decides to abandon everything he has known in pursuit of art. He represents the eccentric genius who defies social and moral conventions in pursuit of creativity.

Maugham structures the plot into three major episodes, which from internal evidence can be dated approximately 1897, 1902, and 1917. The first, set in London, introduces the protagonist, his socialite wife, and his children. Strickland's middle-class family is soon broken by his abrupt and seemingly inexplicable decision to become an artist. The London setting—with its upscale apartments, dinner parties, and drawing room conversations—is the conventional one for social comedy, especially for Maugham's earlier dramas.

The second section, set in Paris, introduces the mediocre painter Dirk Stroeve and his wife, Blanche, whose friendship with Strickland leads to disastrous consequences. The narrative introduces the reader to the Bohemian life in Paris, where Strickland is learning to paint. The third section, which takes place in Tahiti, portrays the exotic setting that marked many of Maugham's later stories and novels. From an assortment of characters who knew Strickland, the narrator learns details of his last years. A return to London for a final interview with Strickland's wife forms an ironic epilogue.

Within the context of Maugham's work, the novel effects a transition between the comic settings of his earlier writing and the exotic settings of the later stories and novels. Significantly, the loosely related episodes are united by the narrative voice, a Maugham persona reminiscent of earlier novels and stories. In later works, he becomes Willie Ashenden or Mr. Maugham. A successful author, this character is primarily but not entirely autobiographical. His interests and attitudes are usually those of Maugham, and details of his life often reflect those of the author. It is noteworthy that Maugham was in each of the novel's three major settings at approximately the time of the narrative. The narrator, a first-person speaker, is detached and observant, taking little or no part in the action. Normally he is nonjudgmental, but, after Strickland abandons his wife and children, the narrator risks Strickland's wrath by calling him a cad to his face. On the few occasions when the narrator becomes involved in the action, his participation has little effect on the plot. His futile mission to Paris on behalf of Strickland's wife is a typical example. A reluctant conversationalist, he is a good listener and can induce people to bare their most closely guarded secrets. He relishes travel and art and is fascinated by genius.

The Maugham persona observes self-imposed limitations that at times lead him to appear to be merely reporting what a character is like or what he does. He adopts the tone of ironic objectivity, as if to celebrate the comic incongruity of human beings without bothering to account for them. After seeing Strickland's paintings, the narrator muses on what determined him to make such a drastic change in his life and then adds, "If I were writing a novel, rather than narrating such facts as I know of a curious personality, I should have invented much to account for this change of heart." Maugham was writing a novel, however, and his critics have suggested that it is a novelist's responsibility to show the reader the conflicts and motivation that account for the decisions and actions of the characters created.

Although the narrator claims to know less about painting than did Maugham, he describes Strickland's genius in some detail. He acknowledges that Stroeve, the ordinary artist, was the first to recognize and appreciate Strickland's genius. Despite Stroeve's enthusiasm, the narrator maintains his skepticism about Strickland's achievement until near the novel's end. What really interests him is the single-minded, ruthless pursuit of his creativity that renders the protagonist callous and cruel to almost everyone he meets. An obscure stockbroker with a comfortable middle-class life, Strickland becomes a Nietzschean Superman, living beyond good and evil. He views his wife and Blanche Stroeve as merely means toward his own advancement and discards them when they no longer interest him. Once Blanche has served as a model for a portrait, he no longer wants anything to do with her. Only Ata, the Tahitian woman who gives all and neither asks nor expects anything of him, can live amicably with him.

Remarkably, Strickland's attitude toward his own productions is one of almost total indifference; after completing a painting he loses interest in it. He sells paintings if he must to survive, but he shows an icy indifference to anyone else's response to them. Facing death, he orders Ata to burn the house whose walls are adorned with his masterpieces. The novel never resolves Maugham's unstated question—whether genius is its own justification. The epilogue's revelation that Strickland's wife decorates her London apartment with Strickland's prints suggests the answer.

The novel introduces character types that are mainstays of Maugham's fiction, some reappearing with the same name in later writings. Strickland's proper, brave, and resourceful wife reminds one of many of Maugham's female characters in fiction and drama. Tiare Johnson, the Tahitian hotel keeper, is an energetic, obese, kindhearted woman who is an unfailing friend to those in need. Captain Nichols, who knows Strickland, is an alcoholic seaman who becomes a beachcomber. These characters belong to a group that Maugham portrays with sympathy in his fiction: those whose talents, weaknesses, genius, or vices relegate them to the fringes of society or render them complete outcasts.

"Critical Evaluation" by Stanley Archer

Further Reading

Brander, Laurence. *Somerset Maugham: A Guide.* Edinburgh: Oliver & Boyd, 1965. A chapter devoted to *The Moon and Sixpence* analyzes the novel as an effort to portray genius. It concludes that Maugham achieved only a qualified success because his primary talent was in comedy.

Burt, Forrest D. *W. Somerset Maugham.* Boston: Twayne, 1985. This highly accessible book provides a comprehensive introductory critical survey and biography. Treats *The Moon and Sixpence* as one of Maugham's major novels.

Cordell, Richard A. *Somerset Maugham: A Writer for All Seasons—A Biographical and Critical Study.* 2d ed. Bloomington: Indiana University Press, 1969. Emphasizes the biographical and autobiographical elements in the novel, and places them within the context of Maugham's other fiction.

Curtis, Anthony, and John Whitehead, eds. *W. Somerset Maugham: The Critical Heritage.* London: Routledge & Kegan Paul, 1987. A collection of early Maugham criticism and reviews. Includes three significant early reviews of *The Moon and Sixpence.*

Holden, Philip. "Envisioning the Primitive: *The Moon and Sixpence.*" In *Orienting Masculinity, Orienting Nation: W. Somerset Maugham's Exotic Fiction.* Westport, Conn.: Greenwood Press, 1996. Examines the themes of homosexuality, gender identity, and race relations in some of Maugham's works, including *The Moon and Sixpence.* Holden maintains that Maugham's writing was a way to negotiate between two different masculine identities: the private homosexual and the public writer.

Loss, Archie K. *W. Somerset Maugham.* New York: Frederick Ungar, 1987. Devotes half a chapter to an analysis of *The Moon and Sixpence,* focusing attention on the novel's major characters.

Meyers, Jeffrey. *Somerset Maugham.* New York: Alfred A. Knopf, 2004. Meyers's biography emphasizes Maugham's "otherness," particularly his homosexuality. Unlike other critics who have dismissed Maugham's work, Meyers defends Maugham as a great writer who influenced George Orwell, V. S. Naipaul, and other authors.

Rogal, Samuel J. *A Companion to the Characters in the Fiction and Drama of W. Somerset Maugham.* Westport, Conn.: Greenwood Press, 1996. An alphabetical listing of the characters—animal and human, unnamed and named—in Maugham's fiction and drama. Each entry identifies the work in which a character appears and the character's role in the overall work.

_____. *A William Somerset Maugham Encyclopedia.* Westport, Conn.: Greenwood Press, 1997. Alphabetically arranged entries on Maugham's writings, family members, friends, and settings, and the historical, cultural, social, and political issues associated with his life and work. Includes a bibliography and an index.

The Moon Is Down

Author: John Steinbeck (1902-1968)
First published: 1942
Type of work: Novel
Type of plot: Parable
Time of plot: World War II
Locale: An unnamed town

Principal characters:
MAYOR ORDEN, town mayor
MADAME, his wife
JOSEPH, his servant
ANNIE, his cook
DOCTOR WINTER, town doctor and the mayor's close friend
COLONEL LANSER, a military officer in charge
LIEUTENANT TONDER, a member of the colonel's staff
GEORGE CORELL, a shopkeeper
ALEXANDER MORDEN, a local miner
MOLLY MORDEN, his wife

The Story:

A town has been invaded with minimum casualties. Six of the local defense troops are killed, three are wounded, and three escape into the nearby hills. Mayor Orden is informed that the invading commander, Colonel Lanser, wishes to meet with him. Shortly thereafter, the colonel arrives at the mayor's residence accompanied by a local shopkeeper, George Corell, who is now known to have been a spy for the invaders. The town doctor, Winter, who is a close friend of the mayor, is also present. Colonel Lanser informs the mayor that the invaders are there primarily to obtain coal and that they want the local people to mine it for them. He also informs him that the town will be allowed to keep its government as long as the people cooperate. The mayor and the doctor tell him that they are uncertain how the people will react to these demands.

Suddenly there is a disturbance in the back of the house: The mayor's cook, Annie, has thrown boiling water on a soldier who had been looking at her through the window. The colonel orders the soldiers to move away from the house even though they had been following his earlier orders. Discussion continues about the likely reaction of the people to the idea of working for the invaders.

The colonel and his staff soon establish their headquarters on the upper floor of the mayor's house. Days later, Corell arrives to speak with the colonel, suggesting that he be allowed to replace the mayor as the leader of the town. The colonel, however, recommends that he leave the area entirely. The colonel is trying to warn him of what is likely to happen to him if he stays. A report comes in that one of the invading officers has been killed. The man who committed the crime, Alexander Morden, a local miner, is quickly arrested. A trial is scheduled to take place at the mayor's house. As the drawing room is being arranged, Joseph, the mayor's servant, informs Annie the cook that two local men had escaped the night before in a boat for England. As the trial is about to begin the colonel tells the mayor that he regrets what has happened but that he needs to take steps to maintain order in the town. The mayor tells the colonel that his soldiers had killed six men when they invaded the town; if the miner is guilty of murder, he reasons, so too are the colonel's own soldiers.

The trial begins during a day with heavy snow; the people in the streets are sullen and angry. Inside, after a brief review of the incident, the colonel declares Morden guilty. The mayor stands and speaks directly to the accused. He tells him that he is indeed going to die, but that his death will serve to unify the people against the invaders. Morden is then taken out of the house and shot to death. At nearly the same moment, a shot is fired through the window, hitting one of the invading officers in his shoulder. The colonel orders that all the guns in the town be confiscated and that all who resist be arrested.

The work of mining the coal moves forward, but there also are many accidents and delays. Young men continue to escape and go to England, and the English in turn bomb the mine. Enemy soldiers are killed or disappear, and the rest come to live in a state of constant fear.

One night, Annie visits Molly Morden, the wife of the executed Alexander Morden, and informs her that two young men who are leaving for England will be coming to her place, and that the mayor will be visiting as well to talk with them. After Annie leaves, a member of the colonel's staff, Lieutenant Tonder, arrives at Molly's house. He reads her a love poem, and she sarcastically responds by offering to go to bed with him in return for two sausages. He, however, is looking for something deeper—love and human companionship. She then tells him about her husband, Alexander. Tonder is shocked and then leaves.

A few minutes later, Annie returns to Molly's house with the two men who plan to escape. The mayor and Winter also arrive, and they tell the group of their plan to kidnap Corell and throw him overboard on their way to England. The mayor and the doctor ask the men to tell the British to send them arms to fight the invaders. As they are preparing to leave, Lieutenant Tonder knocks at the front door. The others leave by the back door. Molly opens the front door for the officer, slips a pair of large sewing scissors into her dress, and kills Tonder.

One night, soldiers on patrol hear the sound of planes overhead. The planes drop hundreds of small packages into the darkness. At dawn the townspeople come out and remove the contents of the packages. The invaders also find the packages and discover that they each contains dynamite, instructions on its use, and a small piece of chocolate. The colonel discusses methods of response with his staff, but also tells them that there is no way to stop what is about to take place.

Corell visits the colonel. He had been injured the night that Molly killed Lieutenant Tonder and had narrowly missed being taken by the men who escaped to England. He tells the colonel that he must take a stronger position against the townspeople and that he should hold the mayor and the doctor responsible for attacks and acts of sabotage. The colonel responds by having the mayor placed under house arrest.

Later the doctor visits the mayor. They discuss the words of philosopher Socrates, from his *Apology*, written as he, too, faced death because of unjust accusations against him. Another officer comes in and informs the colonel that townspeople have been found with dynamite. The colonel informs the mayor that he will hold him responsible for any violence that occurs. Explosions are heard in the distance, and then an explosion hits close by. The mayor looks at the doctor and quotes Socrates' last words: "Crito, I owe a cock to Asclepius. Will you remember to pay the debt?" The doctor says that he will.

Critical Evaluation:

John Steinbeck first conceived the idea for *The Moon Is Down* in the summer of 1941 while working for the newly organized U.S. Office of the Coordinator of Information. He intended the work he did for the novel to be propaganda in support of the Allied cause. The original setting of the novel, a fictitious town in the United States, was not acceptable to those in charge of wartime propaganda, who felt that an American setting would be bad for American morale. Steinbeck changed the setting to an unnamed country, thought by most readers to be Norway; the work was then published by Viking Press in 1942. Its title comes from a scene in William Shakespeare's *Macbeth* (pr. 1606, pb. 1623), in which Banquo and his son meet Macbeth as he is going to murder Duncan. Banquo asks his son, "How goes the night, boy?" to which his son replies, "The moon is down; I have not heard the clock," suggesting the dark events that lie ahead.

To Steinbeck's surprise, the critical response to the novel in the United States was a mix of praise and disparagement. While some reviewers wrote favorably of the work, others were troubled by its sympathetic depiction of the enemy, especially Colonel Lanser, the head of the occupying force. In Europe, however, the response was considerably more positive, especially in countries under Nazi occupation. The novel was quickly translated into Norwegian, Danish, Dutch, and French, and was secretly distributed in those countries at the height of World War II. Today the work is generally seen as a powerful parable of the inner workings of resistance and the ultimate triumph of democratic government. The sympathetic depiction of the invaders is now considered to enhance the novel's stature by giving it a deeper sense of realism.

The work's central characters, Mayor Orden and Colonel Lanser, in many ways counterbalance each other. In the beginning the mayor is a kind of bumbling buffoon whose wife fusses over him to make sure he is appropriately dressed; she even ensures that the hairs in his ears are trimmed prior to his first meeting with the colonel. By the end of the novel, however, the mayor has new stature and a sense of purpose, having faced up to the invaders. In the end, he applies the ennobling words of Socrates to himself, as he, like the Greek philosopher two millennia earlier, prepares for his own death because of an injustice. The colonel, on the other hand, is world-weary and well-experienced in the effects of war. He follows the orders he has been given, even as he knows the ultimate course that events will take. In his interactions with the mayor, he gains a sense of respect and understanding for him; likewise with the mayor. Thus, the book's message is deeply felt, far more so than if the depiction of the enemy leader had been entirely negative and superficial.

Another major theme of the work is the growth of resistance among the townspeople themselves. Both the mayor and the doctor seem to sense this likelihood as early as the book's first chapter, as they speculate on the question of whether the people will be willing to work for the invaders. As the events of the novel play out, the resistance movement grows steadily—and, largely, spontaneously—from the democratic roots that are so deeply ingrained in the people themselves. The resistance grows in their responses to the execution of Alexander Morden; their reactions to the town traitor, George Correl; their successes in opening up contact with the English; and their willingness to put their lives on the line against the invaders. The distinction between "herd men" (the invaders) and "free men" (the people of the town) is given eloquent expression by the mayor in the book's concluding pages.

As with Steinbeck's novel *Of Mice and Men* (1937), *The Moon Is Down* had been conceived in a manner that makes it easily transferable to the stage. Indeed, *The Moon Is Down* opened as a Broadway play one month after it had been published. A film adaptation was released the following year. The book's impact, both in the United States and abroad, has been significant, and it continues to be read not only for its historical importance but also for its eloquent defense of democratic values and its faith in ordinary people prevailing in the face of seemingly insurmountable obstacles—values clearly apparent also in Steinbeck's Great Depression-era classic, *The Grapes of Wrath* (1939).

Scott Wright

Further Reading

Bloom, Harold, ed. *John Steinbeck*. New ed. New York: Bloom's Literary Criticism, 2008. A collection of essays discussing various aspects of Steinbeck's work and life. Part of Bloom's series of author studies.

Coers, Donald V. Introduction to *The Moon Is Down*, by John Steinbeck. New York: Penguin Books, 1995. A clear, concise summary of Steinbeck's purpose in writing the novel and the response to the novel in the United States and abroad during wartime. Based on Coers's fuller treatment of the subject in *John Steinbeck as Propagandist: "The Moon Is Down" Goes to War*. Tuscaloosa: University of Alabama Press, 1991.

Ditsky, John. "Steinbeck's 'European' Play-Novella: *The Moon Is Down*." In *The Short Novels of John Steinbeck*, edited by Jackson J. Benson. Durham, N.C.: Duke University Press, 1990. An insightful and useful discussion of the literary techniques and themes of *The Moon Is Down*. This collection also includes the essay "Dr. Winter's Dramatic Functions in *The Moon Is Down*" by Tetsumaro Hayashi.

French, Warren. *John Steinbeck's Fiction Revisited*. New

York: Twayne, 1994. One of the best overall surveys of Steinbeck's fiction. Contains a brief but balanced assessment of *The Moon Is Down.*

George, Stephen K., ed. *John Steinbeck: A Centennial Tribute.* New York: Praeger, 2002. A collection of reminiscences from Steinbeck's family and friends as well as wide-ranging critical assessments of his works. One of several books published to commemorate the centenary of Steinbeck's birth.

George, Stephen K., and Barbara A. Heavilin, eds. *John Steinbeck and His Contemporaries.* Lanham, Md.: Scarecrow Press, 2007. A collection of papers from a 2006 conference about Steinbeck and the writers who influenced or informed his work. Some of the essays discuss his European forebears, particularly Henry Fielding and Sir Thomas Malory; and his American forebears, such as Walt Whitman and Sarah Orne Jewett. Other essays compare his work to Ernest Hemingway, William Faulkner, and other twentieth century American writers.

Meredith, James H. "Occupation, Resistance, and Espionage: An Analysis of John Steinbeck's *The Moon Is Down*, Jack Higgins' *The Eagle Has Landed*, and Paul West's *The Very Rich Hours of Count von Stauffenberg* and *Rat Man of Paris*." In *Understanding the Literature of World War II: A Student Casebook to Issues, Sources, and Historical Documents.* Westport, Conn.: Greenwood Press, 1999. This casebook is designed to help students better understand literary works about World War II, including Steinbeck's *The Moon Is Down.*

Morsberger, Robert E. "Steinbeck's War." In *The Steinbeck Question: New Essays in Criticism*, edited by Donald R. Noble. Troy, N.Y.: Whitston, 1993. Places *The Moon Is Down* in the larger context of Steinbeck's wartime writing.

Parini, Jay. *John Steinbeck: A Biography.* New York: Henry Holt, 1995. A solid biography of the author. Useful for studies of Steinbeck's personal life at the time he was writing *The Moon Is Down.*

The Moonstone

Author: Wilkie Collins (1824-1889)
First published: 1868
Type of work: Novel
Type of plot: Detective and mystery
Time of plot: 1799-1849
Locale: India and England

Principal characters:
JOHN HERNCASTLE, an adventurer
LADY VERINDER, his sister
RACHEL VERINDER, his niece
FRANKLIN BLAKE, Lady Verinder's nephew
GODFREY ABLEWHITE, a charity worker
DRUSILLA CLACK, Rachel's cousin
GABRIEL BETTEREDGE, the Verinders's old family servant
DR. CANDY, a physician
EZRA JENNINGS, his assistant
SERGEANT CUFF, an inspector from Scotland Yard
ROSANNA SPEARMAN, Rachel's maid
SEPTIMUS LUKER, a pawnbroker

The Story:

In the 1799 storming of Seringapatam, India, John Herncastle, a violent and cruel man, steals the sacred Hindu diamond called the Moonstone. The jewel had been taken years before from the forehead of the Moon-God in its Brahman shrine, and Herncastle's theft was only one of a series. Since the stone had first been stolen, three faithful Hindus followed its trail, sworn to recovering the gem and returning it to the statue of the Moon-God. Herncastle took the gem to England and now keeps it in a bank vault. He saves himself from murder by letting the Hindus know that if he were killed the stone would be cut up into smaller gems, thus losing its sacred identity. At his death, Herncastle leaves the jewel to his niece, Rachel Verinder.

The stone is to be presented to Rachel on her birthday following her uncle's death. Young Franklin Blake, Lady Verinder's nephew, is asked by Herncastle's lawyer to take the gift to his cousin's home several weeks before the event, but he barely misses death at the hands of the Hindus before reaching his destination. On the advice of Gabriel Betteredge, the Verinders's old family servant, Franklin puts the gem in the vault of a bank nearby until the birthday arrives, as the Hindus had been seen in the neighborhood. Upon meeting, Franklin and Rachel fall in love. Guests begin to arrive for the birthday celebration, including Godfrey Ablewhite, a handsome and accomplished charity worker; Dr. Candy, the town physician; and Mr. Bruff, the family lawyer.

While the guests at the birthday dinner are admiring the beauty of the jewel, they hear the beating of a drum on the terrace and three Hindus appear, disguised as jugglers. One of the guests, Mr. Murthwaite, who had traveled widely in Asia, speaks sharply, whereupon the three men retreat. Watchdogs are released to protect the house that night. All seems well, but in the morning Rachel announces that the jewel has disappeared from an unlocked cabinet in her dressing room. Despite Rachel's protests, Franklin Blake insists the police be called. The Hindus are arrested and put in jail, but to everyone's astonishment, they have alibis for the entire night.

Little about the crime is discovered until Sergeant Cuff of Scotland Yard arrives. He decides that fresh paint from the door in Rachel's dressing room must have come off on someone's clothes. Inexplicably, Rachel refuses to allow a search for the stained clothing. Sergeant Cuff suspects that Rachel had staged the theft herself, and that Rosanna Spearman, a maid with a criminal record, is a party to the plot, for he learns that Rosanna had made a new nightdress shortly after the theft. Sergeant Cuff guesses that the nightdress was to replace another dress that is stained. Because the Verinders oppose his efforts, he drops the case. The only other clue he has is that Rosanna might have hidden something in the rocks by the seashore. Rosanna commits suicide soon afterward by throwing herself into a pool of quicksand. She leaves a letter for Franklin, who had, however, departed from the country by the time the letter is found.

Rachel goes to London with her mother. In time, she is engaged to Godfrey Ablewhite. When Mr. Bruff tells her, however, that Godfrey has secretly ascertained the terms of her mother's will before asking for her hand, Rachel breaks the engagement. Franklin returns to England later in the year and visits Betteredge, who tells him about Rosanna's letter. From the letter, Franklin learns that she had thought him guilty of the crime; Rosanna also left him directions for recovering a box she had buried by the sea, just as Sergeant Cuff had thought. The box proves to have the stained nightgown in it, but it is not Rosanna's nightgown but rather that of Franklin.

Unable to account for this strange fact, Franklin returns to London, where he has a long talk with Mr. Bruff about the case. Mr. Bruff informs Franklin that the Moonstone is thought to be in a bank in London, deposited there by a notorious pawnbroker named Septimus Luker. A mysterious attack on the moneylender seems confirmation. Franklin also tells Mr. Bruff of the strange discovery of the nightgown. Mr. Bruff arranges a surprise meeting between Franklin and Rachel, at which Franklin learns that Rachel had actually seen him come into the room and steal the stone. Because she loves him, she had refused to let the investigation continue. Franklin tries to convince her that he has no memory of the deed.

On Mr. Bruff's advice, Franklin returns to the Verinder's country place and tries to discover what had happened to him that night. From Dr. Candy's assistant, Ezra Jennings, he learns that the doctor had secretly given him a dose of laudanum on the night of the theft, so that Franklin, who suffers from insomnia, would get a good night's sleep. Jennings suggests administering a like dose in the same setting, to see what Franklin will do. Mr. Bruff and Rachel come down from London to watch the experiment.

The scene is set with the help of Betteredge, and Franklin is given the laudanum. Under its influence, he repeats his actions on the night of the theft. Rachel watches him come to her room and take out a substitute stone. She is now convinced that his original act had been an attempt to protect her from the Hindus by removing the stone to another room. Before Franklin can recollect what he did with the stone after he left Rachel's room, however, the drug takes full effect, and he falls sound asleep.

The experiment explains how the stone disappeared from Rachel's room but not how it ended up in a London bank through the hands of Luker. Mr. Bruff suggests that the gem might shortly be redeemed from Luker. Sergeant Cuff is called back into the case, and a watch is set on the bank. One day, Luker comes into the bank and claims the stone. On his way out, the watchers think he could have passed it to any of three people, all of whom are followed. Two prove to be innocent citizens; the third is a bearded man who looks like a sailor, whom Bruff's office boy trails to an inn where the suspect takes lodgings for the night.

When Franklin and Cuff arrive at the inn, they find the sailor dead and the box from the bank empty. Cuff examines the dead man closely and then tears away a wig and beard to expose the features of Godfrey Ablewhite. They learn from Luker that Godfrey had seen Franklin go into Rachel's room the night of the robbery and that Franklin had given Godfrey the stone with instructions to put it in the bank. Because Franklin had remembered nothing of this request the next day, Godfrey kept the jewel. The mystery is solved, and Rachel and Franklin are happily reunited.

Several years later, Mr. Murthwaite, the explorer, tells them of a great festival in honor of the Moon-God that he had witnessed in India. When the idol is unveiled, he sees gleaming in the forehead of the stone image the long-lost treasure of the god—the sacred Moonstone.

Critical Evaluation:

T. S. Eliot claimed that "*The Moonstone* is the first, longest, and best of English detective novels," and his praise has been repeated so often as almost to have become a commonplace. This praise, however, if not precisely faint, may yet be perceived as limited, since detective novels are widely regarded as light reading.

Moreover, praise of *The Moonstone* as a detective novel pays tribute to what in Wilkie Collins is both a strength and a weakness. It is commonly believed that detective fiction stands or falls on the coherence and ingenuity of its plot. From the beginning, critics recognized Collins's gifts as a constructor of plots, but they often saw in his narratives a mechanical, manipulative quality they thought limited, if indeed it did not destroy, the human interest of his work.

Critical interest in Collins grew, however, as literature began to be less stringently divided into such categories as serious and popular, which would in any case have had little meaning for Collins or his great friend Charles Dickens. A renewed appreciation of Collins's plot constructions was accompanied by growing recognition of how much there is in *The Moonstone* besides plot and by the acknowledgment of Collins's achievement in integrating various elements to produce a whole that is both unified and vital.

To begin with, it is no small accomplishment to sustain the readers' interest in the whereabouts of a missing diamond for the entire not inconsiderable length of the novel. That the mystery of the diamond is made to bear on a romantic plot involving Rachel Verinder and Franklin Blake increases the level of narrative complexity. That Collins brings both of these narrative lines of development to resolution in the same moment of discovery is an admirable feat of craft. In fact, Collins's technical mastery, although dazzling in itself, accounts for only part of the satisfaction the novel offers its readers. The focus on the diamond means that readers are eager to reach the denouement and learn what has become of the stone, but it is the author's triumph that the readers' eagerness does not become impatience.

The plot emerges from a series of narratives conveyed by a heterogeneous set of narrators. The first, Gabriel Betteredge, is astonished to discover just how difficult it is to stick to the subject; he constantly needs to bring himself back to the point. Yet his digressions are among the greatest delights of the book. In addition to sustaining and intensifying suspense by delaying answers to narrative questions, the digressions reveal the man. In short, while contributing to the effectiveness of the plot, Betteredge's digressions satisfy the readers' interest in character, that other great concern of the novel as a literary form, especially in the nineteenth century. Collins in *The Moonstone* is a master at diverting the readers while making them wait for the denouement.

Betteredge is one of a number of strongly realized characters in *The Moonstone*. Each of the other narrators, perhaps most emphatically the evangelically inclined Miss Clack, expresses an interesting personality while telling part of the tale. Collins is, however, careful to reduce the quantity of digression as he approaches the resolution. Characters other than the narrators achieve a comparable vividness. Rosanna Spearman, the plain servant who dares to love a gentleman, and Ezra Jennings, the half-caste physician's assistant who is instrumental in solving the mystery, are fascinating characters in their own right. They also provide Collins with an opportunity to engage and extend the sympathies of readers not accustomed to acknowledge the full humanity of Rosannas and Ezras.

While Collins's portrayal of the Brahmins may have about it something of the Orientalism that was a projection of nineteenth century Western fantasies and anxieties, it is a strength of the novel for suggesting thereby a reality beyond the conscious understanding of the English characters. Within the framework of the novel, the Hindus remain the "other," and the reader is not made directly aware of them as characters. Nevertheless, they are never reduced to stock villains. This is all the more impressive given the thorough demonization of Indians in the English imagination following the Indian mutiny of 1857, little more than a decade before the publication of *The Moonstone*. Collins offers an exemplary instance of a popular novelist challenging his readers rather than simply catering to prejudices.

The Moonstone is also remarkable for the range of its thematic concerns. It remains provocative, even if the terms of the argument continue to change with the passage of time, in its exploration of Christianity and its counterfeits. It is both ironic and affectionate in its examination of English values and vigorous in its confrontation of prejudices based on race and class. The novel has even been interpreted, persuasively, as a latent indictment of British imperialism.

What is impressive is not merely that these concerns are there, but that they are integrated within a narrative structure as firm as that of any nineteenth century English novel. At one level, it has been pointed out, *The Moonstone* requires nothing more of its readers than a disposition for solving mysteries and a desire to be entertained. Yet it is also a work of considerable cultural and literary impact that generously rewards the reader's committed investigation.

"Critical Evaluation" by W. P. Kenney

Further Reading

Bachman, Maria K., and Don Richard Cox, eds. *Reality's Dark Light: The Sensational Wilkie Collins*. Knoxville: University of Tennessee Press, 2003. Collection of fourteen essays analyzing Collins's novels, focusing on the themes and techniques he introduced to these works. An analysis of *The Moonstone* is provided in Timothy L. Caren's essay "Outlandish English Subjects in *The Moonstone*."

Heller, Tamar. *Dead Secrets: Wilkie Collins and the Female Gothic*. New Haven, Conn.: Yale University Press, 1992. Applies insights derived from feminist criticism to *The Moonstone* and other works by Collins, noting the influence on Collins of the gothic novel, one of the major nineteenth century genres associated with women.

Lonoff, Sue. *Wilkie Collins and His Victorian Readers: A Study in the Rhetoric of Authorship*. New York: AMS Press, 1982. In this study of the author's relation to his contemporary audience, Lonoff finds in Collins's work a covert rebellion against public opinion coupled with an overt desire to please. The book includes an extensive, lucid, and persuasive discussion of *The Moonstone*.

Nayder, Lillian. *Wilkie Collins*. New York: Twayne, 1997. An introductory overview of Collins's life and work. *The Moonstone* is discussed in chapter 5, "Reverse Colonization and Imperial Guilt: Representations of Empire in *Armadale*, *The Moonstone*, and *The New Magdale*."

Peters, Catherine. *The King of Inventors: A Life of Wilkie Collins*. Princeton, N.J.: Princeton University Press, 1991. A biography that is sensitive to the complexities of Collins's life and appreciative of his accomplishments as an artist.

Pykett, Lyn. *Wilkie Collins*. New York: Oxford University Press, 2005. Pykett traces the various debates that have arisen since 1980, when literary critics began seriously reevaluating Collins's work. The analysis of Collins's work focuses on his preoccupation with the themes of social and psychological identity, class, gender, and power.

_____, ed. *Wilkie Collins*. New York: St. Martin's Press, 1998. An excellent introduction to Collins for the beginning student. In addition to essays that discuss Collins's place within Victorian detective fiction and the "sensation novel," three essays analyze *The Moonstone*. Includes bibliographical references and an index.

Taylor, Jenny Bourne. *In the Secret Theatre of Home: Wilkie Collins, Sensation Narrative, and Nineteenth Century Psychology*. New York: Routledge, 1988. Explores the ways in which nineteenth century theories of the workings of the mind permeate Collins's fiction. Discusses *The Moonstone* as crucially shaped by the process of interplay and transformation between models of the unconscious derived from these theories.

_____, ed. *The Cambridge Companion to Wilkie Collins*. New York: Cambridge University Press, 2006. All aspects of Collins's writing are discussed in this collection. Examines his common themes of sexuality, marriage, and religion, as well as his experiences with publishers and with adapting his works for film. A superb job of chronicling Collins's writing career. Includes a thorough bibliography and an index.

Thoms, Peter. *The Windings of the Labyrinth: Quest and Structure in the Major Novels of Wilkie Collins*. Athens: Ohio University Press, 1992. Posits the quest for design as the thematic link among Collins's major novels. In *The Moonstone*, no governing order is glimpsed behind the apparent "disorderedness" of life; design can therefore only be constructed out of the needs and desires of the characters.

Le Morte d'Arthur

Author: Sir Thomas Malory (early fifteenth century-
    1471)
First published: 1485
Type of work: Novel
Type of plot: Myth and romance
Time of plot: Sixth century
Locale: England

Principal characters:
ARTHUR, the king of England
IGRAINE, the duchess of Tintagel, Arthur's mother
KING UTHER PENDRAGON, Arthur's father
MORGAUSE, Arthur's half sister and the mother of Mordred
MORDRED, Arthur's nephew and his illegitimate son
SIR GAWAIN, Arthur's nephew
SIR LANCELOT DU LAC, sometime ruler of France
GUINEVERE, Arthur's queen
NIMUE, the Lady of the Lake
QUEEN MORGAN LA FÉE, Arthur's half sister
SIR BEDIVERE, a knight
MERLIN, a wizard

The Story:

The enchanter Merlin advises King Uther Pendragon to establish the fellowship of the Round Table, which will be comprised of the 140 greatest knights in the kingdom. Merlin is to continue his role of Uther's counselor with Uther's son, Arthur, who will maintain and immortalize the tradition of the Round Table.

Arthur's life begins as the result of an illicit affair between Igraine, the duchess of Tintagel and the wife of Gorlois, and Uther Pendragon. Merlin's magic art had allowed Uther to visit Igraine in the likeness of her husband, of whose death she is as yet unaware. Arthur is conceived as a result of this deception. Ignorant of his true origin, he is brought up from infancy by one of Uther's knights.

In Arthur's youth, the Lady of the Lake, Nimue, presents him with the sign of his kingship: Excalibur, a great sword encrusted with precious stones. Still ignorant of the identity of his mother, Arthur has a brief love affair with Morgause, the queen of Orkney and one of Igraine's three daughters— and, thus, Arthur's half sister. The product of this incestuous liaison is Mordred, who is both King Arthur's nephew and his illegitimate son. Sir Gawain, a knight intensely loyal to Arthur, is the son of King Lot of Orkney and his queen, Morgause. Gawain is, therefore, Arthur's nephew.

Arthur takes Guinevere as his queen. Lancelot, a French knight and warrior of almost superhuman capabilities, joins the Round Table and becomes the courtly lover of Queen Guinevere. He is practicing a medieval convention in which a knight chastely loves and honors a lady without regard to her marital status. This chaste love eventually becomes carnal, sowing the seeds of destruction for Arthur's kingdom.

In Camelot, seat of Arthur's court, Lancelot and Guinevere have begun a love affair. Mordred and Sir Agravain—one of Gawain's several brothers, who dislikes Lancelot intensely—plot to capture Lancelot and the queen in flagrante. The king goes hunting, allowing Mordred and Agravain the opportunity to substantiate, if they can, their charges against the lovers. Lancelot indeed visits the queen's chamber. The two conspirators and an additional twelve knights of the Round Table trap Lancelot within the queen's chamber and demand that he surrender himself to them. When Lancelot finally emerges, he slays Agravain and his twelve companions. Only Mordred, wounded, escapes. Lancelot entreats Guinevere to go away with him but, grief-stricken at the disastrous results of her adultery, she tells him she will stay.

Guinevere is to be burned at the stake for her offense. Arthur bids Gawain and his brothers, Gaheris and Gareth, to lead the queen to the fire. Gawain respectfully declines, but his brothers reluctantly obey; they refuse, however, to bear arms. Lancelot rides to the queen's rescue, slaying all who oppose him. Unfortunately, in the crush of battle, he unwittingly kills the unarmed Gaheris and Gareth. He takes Guinevere to Joyous Garde, his castle in England. Gawain, formerly Lancelot's dear friend, now becomes his implacable enemy. After the pope arranges a truce between the forces of Lancelot and the king, Lancelot returns Guinevere. He and his kin leave England to become rulers of France.

Arthur, encouraged by Gawain, invades France and renews the war. Mordred takes advantage of Arthur's absence and declares himself king. He attempts to marry Guinevere, but she escapes. Upon learning of Mordred's treachery, Arthur and his army return to England. Gawain's life is taken when a battle ensues on the landing grounds. Before he dies, however, he repents for pressing Arthur to make war on Lancelot. Arthur is urged in a dream to make a one-month truce with Mordred; the usurper agrees, but both he and the king tell their men to attack if a sword is brandished. Unluckily, a knight is bitten on the foot by an adder, and when he raises his sword to kill the serpent, a general battle breaks out. One hundred thousand participants are killed and, at the conclusion of the carnage, Arthur and Mordred meet in single combat. Arthur runs his son through with his spear but simultaneously receives a mortal wound to the head. Finally, only he and Sir Bedivere remain alive.

The dying Arthur instructs Bedivere to cast Excalibur into the lake. Bedivere, seduced by the richness of the sword, twice hides it and lies to the king. The third time, however, Bedivere obeys. A hand reaches up, grasps Excalibur, and draws it beneath the surface. Bedivere puts the king on a barge containing three queens clad in mourning—his sister, Queen Morgan la Fée; the queen of North Wales; and the queen of the Waste Lands, all accompanied by Nimue, the Lady of the Lake. As he is being rowed away, Arthur tells Bedivere he is going to Avilion (a possible earthly paradise) either to die or to recover from his wound. Bedivere later discovers a chapel where a hermit tells him of a number of ladies who had visited at midnight with a corpse for him to bury.

No one is certain that King Arthur is dead. The inscription on his tomb refers to him as the once and future king—he may come again if England needs him. Guinevere becomes a nun and Lancelot a priest, ever doing penance for their sins.

Critical Evaluation:

Sir Thomas Malory's prose achieves the impression of simplicity, while comprising words beautifully arranged. His narrative has the quality of realism, even in his most fanciful scenes. He is also a master of naturalistic dialogue. For these reasons, he serves as the model for later writers of English prose, his work behind only, perhaps, the King James version of the Bible.

Malory presents himself as a translator of the French Arthurian romances. A chief source for his own writing might have been the twelfth century romances of Chrétien de Troyes, who introduced the separate legend of the Holy Grail into the Arthurian tales. The French romancers also contributed the concept of courtly love. In short, the Arthurian legend had been growing and evolving for centuries before Malory sat down to write *Le Morte d'Arthur.*

The historical Arthur, if he had existed, is said to have been a Celtic chieftain named Artorius who resisted the Anglo-Saxon invasion in the early sixth century. One contemporary historian describes a great British victory at the Battle of Mons Badonicus (Mount Badon) around 500, but he makes no mention of Artorius. In the ninth century, Nennius places the battle somewhat later (516) and states that a person named Arthur had commanded against the invaders. By the next century, Arthur's legend had grown considerably. In the twelfth century, Welshman Geoffrey of Monmouth wrote *Historia regum Britanniae* (c. 1136; *History of the Kings of Britain,* 1718), a work that makes Arthur into a great romantic figure. Geoffrey's Anglo-French translator first mentions the Round Table, and soon Arthurian tales were appearing in Old French.

In *Merlin,* an early thirteenth century verse romance, a version is introduced wherein Arthur wins his crown by drawing a magic sword from a stone. By Malory's day, Arthur and his knights are medieval heroes projected back into an ancient Britain. In 2004, the film *King Arthur* makes Arthur the leader of a warrior band in the time of the Roman occupation, and Guinevere is a fighting Celtic princess who paints her body before battle. Malory's Knights of the Round Table are so fixed in the reading public's imagination, however, that such attempts at supposed authenticity can succeed only as curiosities.

Malory was well prepared to describe the carnage of war in feudal times. He served in France in the latter part of the Hundred Years' War (1337-1453) and supported the Lancastrian side in the War of the Roses (1453-1487). He led a turbulent life and is believed to have written *Le Morte d'Arthur* while in prison. In his conclusion, Malory states that he completed his book in the ninth year of the reign of King Edward IV (r. 1461-1470, 1471-1483). Malory died in 1471, and his book did not appear until it was printed in 1485 by William Caxton, the first English printer. The extent of Caxton's editing of Malory's work was not known until 1934, when a manuscript dating from Malory's time was discovered in the Fellows' Library at Winchester College in England. It appears that Malory thought of his book as a series of eight romances. Caxton reordered, and in some cases rewrote, parts of the narrative and divided it into twenty-one books. Malory entitled, quite understandably, the last of his romances "Le Morte d'Arthur," but Caxton chose that unrepresentative title for the entire compilation. Current editions are usually a combination of the Winchester and Caxton texts.

Critics complain that *Le Morte d'Arthur* is frequently rambling and repetitious, especially when Malory abandons his central theme to follow knight after knight, each of whom is experiencing essentially the same adventure in his quest for the Holy Grail. It is also true that while Malory appears to pay homage to chivalry, it is infidelity, recklessness, and betrayal that provide the narrative its drama. Malory is also criticized for having created one-dimensional characters who exist merely to serve the demands of the plot. These are indeed not the well-rounded characters readers will come to expect in Renaissance and later fiction.

In his most critical passages, however, Malory has a sure feel for the conflict, psychological as well as physical, which satisfying fiction must always possess. Guinevere loves her husband's lofty nature and nobility, but she loves Lancelot with passion. Lancelot loves the king he has come to serve, but he loves Guinevere with passion. Arthur loves them both but is finally forced to stand against them. He feels a paternal sense of obligation toward his son, Mordred, so when he leaves for France he makes Mordred his regent—but Mordred betrays him. In the end, father and son kill each other. The Knights of the Round Table love their king but, as events spiral out of control, they must choose sides for a final, terrible battle. The result of these conflicted emotions is the poignant destruction of Malory's idealized Merrie England.

Patrick Adcock

Further Reading

Altick, Richard D. *The Scholar Adventurers*. New York: Macmillan, 1951. Chapter 3, "The Quest of the Knight-Prisoner," traces the fascinating scholarly search for which of the several historical persons named Thomas Malory was the actual author of *Le Morte d'Arthur*.

Archibald, Elizabeth, and A. S. G. Edwards, eds. *A Companion to Malory*. Woodbridge, England: Boydell and Brewer, 1996. A collection of essays by medievalists, divided into three sections: Malory in context, the art of *Le Morte d'Arthur*, and the book's reception in later years. Includes discussion of the place of women and chivalry in Malory's story and of language and style in Malory.

Hanks, Dorrel Thomas, Jr., and Jessica Gentry Brogdon, eds. *The Social and Literary Contexts of Malory's "Morte Darthur."* Woodbridge, England: Boydell and Brewer, 2001. A collection of sociohistorical analyses of Malory's work, focusing on the its place in the history of literature.

Hardyment, Christina. *Malory: The Knight Who Became King Arthur's Chronicler*. New York: HarperCollins, 2005. Hardyment pored over the only known manuscript of Malory's novel to produce this biography. She finds evidence to suggest that *Le Morte d'Arthur* may have been influenced by Malory's reading of French romances, early English histories, and popular ballads, and she describes the originality with which Malory recounted the tales of Lancelot.

Loomis, Roger Sherman. *The Development of Arthurian Romance*. New York: Harper & Row, 1963. Though dated, this book is written by an eminent medieval scholar and remains a helpful work. Traces Arthur from his first mention in Nennius's *Historia Britonum* (c. 800) to his appearance in *Le Morte d'Arthur*.

Parins, Marylyn Jackson. *Malory: The Critical Heritage*. 1988. Reprint. New York: Routledge, 1996. An important collection of early criticism and commentary on Malory's *Le Morte d'Arthur* in chronological order, beginning with Caxton's preface to the first edition and ending with remarks by influential literary critic George Saintsbury in 1912.

Svogun, Margaret duMais. *Reading Romance: Literacy, Psychology, and Malory's "Le Morte d'Arthur."* New York: Peter Lang, 2000. A new interpretation of the novel, focusing on the book's status as one of the first literary works to be mass-produced typographically. Also analyzes the book's depiction of the personal fight to accommodate the conflicting demands of the divided self.

Morte d'Urban

Author: J. F. Powers (1917-1999)
First published: 1962
Type of work: Novel
Type of plot: Social realism
Time of plot: Late 1950's
Locale: Chicago and Minnesota

Principal characters:
FATHER URBAN ROCHE, a Roman Catholic priest
FATHER WILFRID BESTUDIK, a colleague of Urban
BILLY COSGROVE, a wealthy layman and friend of Urban
FATHER JACK and BROTHER HAROLD, members of a
    community of Roman Catholic clergy
BISHOP JAMES CONOR, the head of the local archdiocese
MONSIGNOR RENTON, another of Urban's superiors
MRS. THWAITES, an eccentric small-town philanthropist
SALLY THWAITES HOPWOOD and DICKIE, her children
SYLVIA BEAN, a member of a church that Urban visits

The Story:

Father Urban Roche, born Harvey Roche in a small town in Illinois, is fifty-four years old and a longtime member of the Order of Saint Clement, a small order of Roman Catholic priests based in Chicago. Urban spends a number of years traveling and raising money for the order when, one day after a mass he says in a suburban Chicago church, he is approached by Billy Cosgrove.

Cosgrove, a wealthy man given to frequent golfing and sailing outings, later meets Urban at South Bend, Indiana, after a Notre Dame University football game. Hailing Urban from his chauffeur-driven Rolls Royce, Cosgrove becomes a mysterious and capricious force in Urban's life. Their relationship, from the beginning, is based on a strange kind of material need—on Billy's need to give Urban money and things, and on Urban's professional courting of a generous and affluent man. Urban gives Billy a load of firewood from the Saint Clement novitiate; later, over the course of time, Cosgrove endows the Clementines with items for their foundation in Minnesota, builds a golf course for the order, and invites Urban on fishing expeditions.

In the meantime, however, Urban is banished by Father Boniface to backwoods Minnesota, where a Clementine priest, Wilfrid "Bunny" Bestudik, presides over a tiny group of men clustered in a former sanatorium. Bunny has the idea of saving the facility, and even the order, from oblivion by transforming the outpost into a retreat center. Much work needs to be done on the buildings, work which, Bunny insists, can be done by the resident clerics.

Urban has a very difficult time adjusting to his new role and, in fact, does not try very hard to work as a member of the small Clementine team. He complains of the cold and often sleeps in order to escape the boredom of daily life on the Hill, as the order's facility is called. Bunny, in his quiet way, puts up with Urban's complaints and does what he thinks is best. When the pastor of a nearby church, St. Monica's, suddenly dies, Urban manages to persuade Bunny to let him temporarily take the pastor's place. This change in assignment is much to Urban's liking, and he begins to build a small empire. He courts the goodwill of Mrs. Thwaites, a reclusive old woman of some wealth. With Billy's suspect help, property adjacent to the Hill is acquired so that the order might attract retreatants with a golf course. Cosgrove hires an architect to build a fine course; later, he endows the order with an automobile for its transportation needs.

Fate or Providence intervenes in Urban's success. During a golf match with Bishop James Conor on the Hill course, Urban is hit on the head by the bishop's ball. This proves to be a serious injury, from which Urban recovers after a convalescence but which causes him recurrent headaches and some temporary short-term memory loss. The injury also sets in motion a number of threats to Urban's status and well-being. Urban's brush with death also precipitates a fundamental change in his view of his life, his faith, and his relationship with others.

Urban finds the courage to resist the cruel demands that Billy places on him. During a fishing trip, in his frustration with not being able to catch a fish, Billy tries to drown a deer in the lake; when Urban objects, Billy simply dumps Urban in the water and leaves him there. Later, Sally Thwaites Hopwood tries to seduce Urban, not only by undressing in front of him but also by appealing to otherworldly pleasures that have tempted Urban for so long in his life.

Ultimately, Urban is elected provincial of the Order of St. Clement, which is perhaps remarkable. Instead of using his new power to achieve what the old Urban might want, however, the postaccident Urban gives repeated evidence that the world and its glories mean nothing to him. Indeed, he gained a reputation for piety, partly because of his ill health, but partly because the reputation is deserved. Moreover, Urban begins to think of the Hill as his home—rather than Chicago, which was his home base in his previous existence as traveling salesman for the order.

Critical Evaluation:

Morte d'Urban is a remarkable wedding of realism, comedy, tragedy, and redemption; indeed, the reader often feels that James Powers captures much of the spirit of the daily existence of a mid-twentieth century American Roman Catholic priest. Father Urban Roche is consistently torn between piety and commitment to his faith and a desire to engage the world outside the Church. Urban is a very worldly, urbane man, gifted with social know-how associated with small-town boosters, salesmen, and members of fraternal organizations. Similarly, the other priests whom Powers presents constitute a spectrum of incompetence, foolishness, competitiveness, and sincere intent to do good and to follow the tenets of the faith. Powers shows the delineation of church politics, the petty jealousies and ambitions that motivate priests of various kinds—parish "soldiers," priests in administrative capacities, and priests who are primarily concerned with prayer and meditation. St. Clement's Hill, for example, is run by Bunny Bestudik, who is intent on carving out a small niche of notoriety for the St. Clement order by establishing a retreat house. He and his colleagues, including Urban, however, are worried about competition from the Benedictines and by pressure or indifference from the local archdiocesan bureaucracy.

The thematic focus of the novel is Urban's struggle to determine his own course. The hero's names indicate considerable irony: Urban is not only the name of several popes but also the name of a saint, and Roche is one of several French words for rock—which constitutes an oblique reference to the Latin *petrus* and the Greek *petros*, the sources of the name Peter. Saint Peter is the "rock" on which Christ, according to Scripture, built his church. Ultimately then, Urban Roche is the modern rock of the church, Peter's heir. He is also a man who is tempted by what modern culture offers.

The reader may be amused and even appalled by Urban's social sense, his love of cigars, liquor, and fast cars, and by the pleasure he takes in glib verbal salesmanship of his religion and the Church. There is a point, however, beyond which he will not go in his spirit of compromise. He argues, for example, against Monsignor Renton's angry denunciation of Mrs. Thwaites, who leaves the Church and then returns. Renton refuses to forgive Mrs. Thwaites's trespasses; Urban refuses to judge the woman's sincerity. While serving

a local parish, Urban is called in the middle of the night to anoint a sick person; he welcomes the experience because it reminds him of his fundamental duties as a priest, something the swim of his social whirl and his concern for personal and professional success tend to obscure. On the other hand, Urban, convinced that the good to be done in the world counts for a great deal, cannot conceive of the priesthood as a kind of monasticism—nothing more than a prayer and administering the Sacraments. For example, Urban dishonestly distorts facts and figures in order to persuade the bishop and his parishioners to build a new church at St. Monica's: Certain ends justify certain means. Lest the St. Monica parishioners gain too much control of their church life, Urban institutes and busily involves himself in numerous church social and group religious activities. His goal is, at least in part, to feed his own ego. Similarly, a mission Urban preaches ends with his dramatic, showmanlike flourishes.

Ultimately, however, Urban succeeds in a number of ways at St. Monica's, the most spectacular success being the 150 percent increase in mass attendance. Powers calls into question the nature of what passes for faith in modern American society; he suggests that churches that flourish are those that entertain their members and deal in the external, superficial, social appeal of church membership.

It is with the construction of the golf course at St. Clement's Hill that Urban threatens to overstep the limits of good taste and common sense. He conceives the course as a means to reach the "un-churched," and to enhance the Hill as a retreat site, but the course becomes the focus of his odd change in personality and perspective.

During a tournament at the Hill's golf course, Bishop Conor hits a ball that strikes Urban on the head. As immediately funny as his accident seems, it turns out that Urban is seriously injured. His convalescence takes time, which he spends at Mrs. Thwaites's estate; Urban experiences bad headaches and short-term memory loss; nevertheless, the bishop decides not to take over the Hill in order to use it as a seminary. Eventually, Urban is abandoned by Billy Cosgrove and by Sally Thwaites Hopwood, Mrs. Thwaites's willful daughter. These apparent setbacks increase readers' admiration of Urban, however, because Urban resists Billy's bullying and Sally's bold attempt to make him give in to his instincts.

An irony surfaces in the story as Urban is elected provincial of the Order of St. Clement, replacing his old nemesis, Father Boniface. What his colleagues see as his disappointing lack of interest in furthering the order's standing is Urban's new lack of interest in jockeying for position in the world. Later, Urban gains a reputation among Clementines for his religious zeal, which may, in part, be disaffection brought about by his poor health. As the novel ends, Powers deliberately leaves readers in doubt—not only about his hero's status as saint or casualty but also about the very nature of faith and God's role in human affairs.

Gordon Walters

Further Reading

"Fiction in Review." *Yale Review* 91, no. 4 (October, 2003): 133-160. A detailed review of Powers's fiction, including *Morte d'Urban*.

Hagopian, John V. *J. F. Powers*. New York: Twayne, 1968. Hagopian's reading of *Morte d'Urban* is thorough and intelligent, although perhaps somewhat intolerant of possible alternative interpretations.

Henault, Marie. "The Saving of Father Urban." *America* 108 (March 2, 1963): 290-292. A study of the Arthurian references in the novel.

Hinchcliffe, Arnold P. "Nightmare of Grace." *Blackfriars* 45 (February, 1964): 61-69. A consideration of what Hinchcliffe calls the "Mammon of Iniquity" theme in the novel.

Labrie, Ross. "J. F. Powers (b. 1917)." In *The Catholic Imagination in American Literature*. Columbia: University of Missouri Press, 1997. Labrie analyzes representative works by Powers and other Catholic writers and poets to describe how these works express each writer's particular interpretation of Catholic teaching.

Long, J. V. "Clerical Character(s)." *Commonweal* 125, no. 9 (May 8, 1998): 11-16. Long offers a retrospective analysis of the leading characters in *Morte d'Urban* and *Wheat That Springeth Green* and the sacred-versus-secular issues confronting them. It is an interesting look back in the light of changes in American Catholicism since the 1950's.

Merton, Thomas. "*Morte d'Urban*: Two Celebrations." *Worship* 36 (November, 1962): 645-650. Defends Powers against charges of anticlericalism and calls the novel a work of genius.

Sisk, John P. "*Morte d'Urban*, by J. F. Powers." *Renascence* 16 (1963): 101. According to Hagopian (above), Sisk's review of the novel is one of the best early assessments.

Tartt, Donna. "The Glory of J. F. Powers." *Harper's*, July, 2000. Tartt, herself a novelist, reviews *Morte d'Urban* and other fictional works by Powers.

The Mosquito Coast

Author: Paul Theroux (1941-)
First published: 1981
Type of work: Novel
Type of plot: Dystopian and psychological realism
Time of plot: Mid-twentieth century
Locale: Hatfield, Massachusetts; Mosquito coast, Honduras

Principal characters:
ALLIE "FATHER" FOX, an inventor and farm handyman
MRS. FOX, his wife
CHARLIE and JERRY, their sons
CLOVER and APRIL, their twin daughters
TINY POLSKI, an asparagus farmer, Allie's employer
MR. HADDY, a Honduran who becomes the family's helper
THE REVEREND SPELLGOOD, a missionary to Honduras
EMILY SPELLGOOD, his daughter

The Story:

Allie "Father" Fox is an angry man, living in a valley in western Massachusetts with his wife and four children and working on Tiny Polski's asparagus farm while continuing to invent machines. Earlier, the family had lived in Maine, where Father had tried organic farming and creating solar energy, both of which were failures. He had considered the move to Massachusetts a chance to start over.

Father and his oldest son, Charlie, visit Polski with one of Father's new inventions, a self-contained box that makes ice out of fire and ammonia. Polski makes fun of the invention. Father, already fed up with American culture because of its pornography, religion, materialism, drugs, and waste, plans to move—unknown to the rest of the family. He takes the family shopping, railing at the flimsiness of the merchandise and its prices. Charlie is full of foreboding, which is intensified when he later visits Polski, who warns him that Father is the most obnoxious man he has ever met.

The family sets sail from Baltimore on the ship *Unicorn*. Aboard, they meet the family of the Reverend Spellgood, whom Father baits and toys with. Charlie learns from Emily Spellgood, the reverend's daughter, that the *Unicorn* is headed for the coast of Honduras. Reverend Spellgood has a missionary church in Guampu, upriver from the Mosquito coast. The Foxes land on the coast at La Cieba, where Father buys the deed to a remote town, Jeronimo, from a drunk he meets. He hires Mr. Haddy's motor launch to ferry them upriver to Jeronimo, which turns out to be a muddy area in the forest with one rusty, tin-roofed shack.

The locals, the Zambus, help Mr. Haddy unload his launch while the Foxes are greeted with gifts of food by the Maywit family, also consisting of two parents and four children, who inhabit the shack. Father immediately visualizes the town he will create here and hires all the men present, including Mr. Maywit, to help him build it. Soon, with Mother working alongside the men, the land is cleared.

Mr. Haddy returns from the coast with a missionary whom Father soon forces to leave. Over the next few weeks, they build a house, plant crops, pave paths, and build a pump wheel on the river that supplies water. Father then has the men build a huge plant of sorts filled with strange plumbing—a tall replica of the ice-making machine that Polski had spurned. Charlie names the machine Fat Boy.

When Fat Boy is finally operational, Father decides to bring ice up the river to the most primitive town he can find, to "enlighten" the indigenous people of the village. He wraps a block of ice in banana leaves and sets off with Charlie, Mr. Haddy, and a few Zambus to Seville, the last town up the river. After getting lost and then slogging through swampland, they come upon the empty village. The villagers creep out of the woods, and Father finally shows the leader the ice. Father soon discovers that the leader knows the word "hice" and becomes infuriated. He also finds out that the villagers are Christians as well. He stomps away from the group leaving only his angry smell behind.

After Jeronimo becomes a successful settlement with comfortable living quarters and successful crops, Father builds a huge block of ice and straps it to a sled. He brings Charlie and his younger brother, Jerry, along with the sled pulled by Zambus, and sets out to cross the mountains to a village more primitive than Seville. By the time they arrive at the remote Indian village, the block of ice has melted to a sliver. The Indians are more impressed with Father's missing finger than with the ice, but Father refuses to leave the village

until his party is fed. They are finally fed by three ragged white men, assumed to be slaves. Father brags to them of his settlement in Jeronimo.

The party returns to Jeronimo and finds that the Maywits have deserted and gone upriver with a missionary. Days later, the three white men, whom Father had assumed to be slaves of the Indians, show up in Jeronimo, carrying pistols and a rifle. When it becomes apparent the men will not leave, Father offers the three men Fat Boy to sleep in. While the men are asleep, Charlie is told by his father to seal the plant. Father then fires up the boiler. A horrible scene ensues, in which the men struggle and cry as they die in the plant. Fat Boy then explodes and destroys all of Jeronimo, and Mr. Haddy's boat as well.

Father breaks down and cries, but he soon recovers and leads the family on foot over a mountain ridge, where they discover a creek. They meet a Miskito Indian with a launch who lets Father take the launch downstream, laden with the family and Mr. Haddy. While they are poling on the Rio Sico, Father announces that the United States has been blown up and no longer exists. The party reaches Laguna Miskita, where the family builds another settlement. The rains soon come, however, and they are flooded out. Their hut is washed away, but they remain in it and head upstream.

The group travels for days until they reach Guampu, near the missionary settlement of the Reverend Spellgood. Charlie and Jerry swim ashore and convince Emily Spellgood, the reverend's daughter, to give them the key to her father's jeep. They swim back to the boat and find Father gone. They try to convince their mother to leave with them. Suddenly the mission and all its buildings explode. As they watch the flames, Father returns to the boat and tries to escape upriver. Charlie pulls Father's feet tight in the anchor chain, while mother and the children climb into the dugout. The people onshore are shooting at the boat. Mother and the children topple Father over into the dugout and reach the opposite shore. They dump Father into the jeep and climb in after him, as Mother drives toward the coast, where they make camp on the beach.

Days later, Mother goes shopping for bandages in the village, while Father lies at the beach, his legs still paralyzed. He sends Charlie on an errand, then drags himself up the beach on the sand and dies there. Mr. Haddy, hearing of the disaster, returns to help the family back to La Cieba. They head home, still in shock but thrilled to be returning home.

Critical Evaluation:

With *The Mosquito Coast*, Paul Theroux continues an American tradition of starting a new, idealistic society in the wake of disillusion with the United States and its values. This theme is a direct descendent of the works of Henry David Thoreau, James Fenimore Cooper, Herman Melville, and Mark Twain. *The Mosquito Coast* is told in the first person by fourteen-year-old Charlie Fox, who is perceptive but sees his father, Allie, or Father, through the mixed emotions of love, apprehension, fear, admiration, and terror. The major irony between Father's goal and his failure to bring self-reliance and self-improvement to the indigenous Hondurans is matched by the irony between the story Charlie tells and the story the reader interprets from the telling. Because the narrator is a teenager and sees events through emotional eyes, he is unreliable, so the reader must interpret the more disturbing aspects of Father's behavior. There is a difference between Father's actions, Charlie's interpretations of them, and the reader's interpretations, another subtle irony that serves to increase the horror of what actually takes place.

While the book adheres to the traditional novelistic structure in which the plot proceeds in a linear fashion, the development of the personalities of father and son take place within this structure. The son changes during the events and grows more mature, more equipped to judge his father's mistakes, and more responsible. Charlie is the one who takes matters into his own hands once he realizes that continuing up the river is futile; he is the one who acquires the key to the Reverend Spellgood's vehicle; and he is the one who fells his father in the anchor chain when people are shooting at the family from the mission.

Father develops in an opposite direction, becoming more cruel, obsessive, and maniacal. Although he prides himself on never striking any of his children, he devises cruel and dangerous tests and punishments for his rebellious sons, and he has no interest in nature except for how it might be manipulated by him. Although he professes to admire the simple society of the indigenous peoples, he loathes it once he sees the way they live in the jungle. Father is, in fact, a bigot. Unable to accept anything the way it is, his egomania is such that he criticizes the world as it is and does not believe in God because he cannot believe that God would design the world so poorly. He tells Charlie that whoever created the world made a mess of it. He manipulates everyone in the family, ruling unilaterally. His tirade near the end of the story criticizes how women are "made": full of excess flesh and prone to "leaks."

Theroux sets Father up as a genius, and in his individual way he is. The reader is impressed with his inventive skills and with his ability to create a village, farm, and houses from scrap and bits of remnants cast off by an organized society. Because Charlie is such a sympathetic character, the reader is willing to go along with his father, although some of the stories Charlie tells about his father are frightening. However,

when Father resorts to the evil act of killing the three strangers by blowing up his own ice factory, Father loses the reader's support. At the book's climax, when Father sets fire to the Reverend Spellgood's mission and then is immobilized by Charlie, it is apparent that there is no hope of redemption for him. His subsequent paralysis and death is a fitting end. Charlie heads home with his mother and siblings to find what Father had always wanted, to lead a "normal" life.

One of the world's most prolific travel writers, Theroux also has produced a solid oeuvre of fiction that includes more than two dozen novels, collections of short stories, and several children's books. Originally from Medford, Massachusetts, Theroux was educated at the Universities of Maine and Massachusetts and trained for the Peace Corps at Syracuse. An inveterate traveler, his first major success as a travel writer was *The Great Railway Bazaar*, published in 1975. He became known for his fiction with the 1978 novel *Picture Palace*, which was awarded the Whitbread Award in England, followed by *The Mosquito Coast* in 1982, which won the James Tait Black Memorial Prize. *The Mosquito Coast* was made into a film directed by Peter Weir and starring Harrison Ford, Helen Mirren, and River Phoenix. It was released in 1986.

Sheila Golburgh Johnson

Further Reading

Coate, Samuel. *Paul Theroux*. Boston: Twayne, 1987. An excellent criticism and interpretation of Theroux's life and fiction that analyzes themes and characters of his work. Includes an index. A volume in Twayne's U.S. Authors series.

Edwards, Thomas R. "Paul Theroux's Yankee Crusoe." *The New York Times Magazine*, February 14, 1982. A detailed and wide-ranging review of *The Mosquito Coast* at the time of its first publication.

Fujii, Hikaru. "Journey to the End of the Father: Battlefield of Masculinity in *The Mosquito Coast*." *Critique* 48, no. 2 (Winter, 2007): 168-183. Presents a detailed analysis of one of Theroux's most important novels. Applies theories of masculinity and of power relationships to explain the motivations of both the protagonist and the narrator.

Lyons, Paul. "From Man-Eaters to Spam Eaters: Literary Tourism and the Discourse of Cannibalism from Herman Melville to Paul Theroux." In *Multiculturalism and Representation: Selected Essays*, edited by John Rieder and Larry E. Smith. Honolulu: East-West Center, University of Hawaii, 1996. An exploration of the ways indigenous populations have been characterized in literature. Part of a larger study on the literary representation of diverse cultures.

Mowat, John. *Strangers Ourselves: The Adventures of Paul Theroux*. Madison, Wis.: Frog Books, 2006. Presents critical analysis of some of Theroux's novels in addition to information about his life that sheds light on his literary influences.

Pineda, Baron L. *Shipwrecked Identities: Navigating Race on Nicaragua's Mosquito Coast*. New Brunswick, N.J.: Rutgers University Press, 2006. Although focused on Nicaragua, this book describes the social conditions and race relations of the area that includes the southern tip of Honduras. Helpful for understanding the setting of *The Mosquito Coast*.

The Mother

Author: Grazia Deledda (1871-1936)
First published: La madre, 1920 (English translation, 1922)
Type of work: Novel
Type of plot: Psychological realism
Time of plot: Early twentieth century
Locale: Sardinia

Principal characters:
PAUL, a priest
MARIA MADDALENA, his mother
AGNES, his sweetheart

The Story:

Maria Maddalena is an orphan, brought up in drudgery by aunts. Part of her work is to bring flour from the mill. If there are no other customers, the old man who waits on her follows her out and kisses her by force behind the bushes. His whiskers prick her. When her aunts learn what is happening, they forbid the girl to go near the mill again. To their surprise, the old man comes to the house one day and asks for Maria in marriage.

Maria continues to live in her aunts' house, and her husband stays at the mill. Each day, when she visits him, he steals flour and gives it to her. Widowed shortly after she becomes pregnant, she supports her son by working as a servant. She refuses to become involved with the servants or masters of the places in which she works, for she wishes to make her son a priest and she feels that purity is required of her as well. When her son Paul goes to the seminary, Maria works there to be near him. The bishop often commands Paul to seek out his sacrificing mother and kiss her hand. During vacations, they sometimes go back to their native village. One summer, Paul visits the town prostitute several times. He is fascinated by her white skin; he thinks it is so pale because her house is in constant shade. After that summer, Paul throws off desires of the flesh and feels himself sanctified.

After completing his studies, Paul is assigned to the remote village of Aar, a mountainous town where strong winds blow all the time. Maria is proud that her dreams are coming true as the population gathers in the square to meet the new priest. She settles down placidly in the presbytery to keep house for her son.

Aar has had no priest for some time. The former priest was a drunkard, a gambler, and, some people say, a sorcerer. They half liked him, however, and never complained to the bishop because they were afraid of his magic. Prudently, Maria put bars in the form of a cross on the front door to ward off the evil eye, for it was common knowledge that the old priest swore to drive away any successor.

One night, Maria is desperately afraid. For some time, Paul had a mirror in his room; he cleans his nails and washes with scented soap. He even lets his hair grow long and tries to comb it over his tonsure. She knows what is happening. Agnes is the only remaining member of the family in the big house of the village, and Paul begins to visit her on his parish rounds. From the sounds in his bedroom, Paul is again getting ready to go out that night, and he leaves hurriedly. Ashamed but desperate, his mother follows him. She sees him go to the side gate of the big house and disappear inside. Finding the gate locked, she circles the grounds, but all the entrances are shut. She returns home to wait for Paul.

Dozing as she waits, she thinks the wicked old priest is sitting beside her, leering at her from his whiskered face. He draws off his socks and orders her to mend them. Calmly enough, she asks him how she can mend socks for a dead man. The priest declares he is not dead; furthermore, he will drive them out of the village. When she calls him wicked, he argues with her that God put people on earth to enjoy themselves.

With a start, she awakens and looks about her for the socks. She thinks she hears ghostly footfalls leaving the presbytery. Earlier, she considered denouncing Paul to the bishop. Not sure of his guilt, however, she resolves to face the problem at once.

When Paul comes in, he curtly tells his mother that he was calling on a sick person. Maria is determined, however, to leave the village, never to see him again unless he breaks with Agnes. She wonders if her own son can be so selfish that he cannot see he is endangering Agnes's soul as well as his own. In his chamber, Paul falls into a troubled sleep after calling on God for help.

In the morning, his mother awakens him early, and before he leaves his room he writes written a letter renouncing Agnes. With a pale face, he gives it to his mother and tells her to deliver it to the girl in person. After hearing confessions, he says mass. His sermon is cutting. The congregation grows smaller each day; only on Sunday are the pews filled. After the service, he learns that Agnes received his letter.

During the morning, word comes that King Nicodemus is dying. Nicodemus is a wild hunter who lives far up the mountain, where he removes himself so he can do no harm to other human beings. His relatives bring him into the village when he is far gone in sickness. Paul, with his server Antiochus, goes to the hut to give the hunter extreme unction. To their surprise, Nicodemus disappears. With his last strength, he leaves the hated village, to die in his own mountain cabin.

Later, a woman brings a little daughter who is having a tantrum. The mother thinks the girl is possessed by a demon, for it takes force to get her into the presbytery. Humoring the superstitious mother, Paul reads the parable of the Gadarene swine. As he reads, the girl becomes quiet and receptive. Maria and the others are sure Paul exorcised an evil spirit. The people of the village, believing him a miracle worker who can cast out demons, hold a celebration for Paul. He is thankful when some of the merrymakers go home with him. He needs help that night to keep from going to Agnes.

Antiochus lingers after the rest of the company to remind Paul of a promise to visit the boy's mother. Antiochus wants to be a priest, and Paul promises to speak about the plan. He wearily sets out. While he is impressing on his server's mother the sacrifices demanded of the priesthood, one of Agnes's servants comes with the news that Agnes fell and is bleeding from her nose. Accepting his fate, Paul goes to see her again.

Agnes is pale and looks older but not ill. She reproaches him for the letter and inquires about his promise to marry her and to take her away. Paul declares that he has only a brother's love for her. Angry, Agnes says that he comes at night and seduces young girls. She will so denounce him in church if he does not leave the village before morning.

Paul tells his mother of the threat. Both are apprehensive of going to church; they are thankful to see Agnes's pew empty, but toward the end of the service she appears, looking straight at Paul. As the services are ending, he hears a cry. His mother dropped dead. Paul goes to her side. He sees Agnes staring at him.

Critical Evaluation:

When Grazia Deledda won the Nobel Prize in Literature in 1926, there was controversy because her reputation was not yet international and her prize provided a propaganda victory for Benito Mussolini's government, which she detested. Luigi Pirandello, the Sicilian widely regarded as the leading Italian writer of the twentieth century, was so angry that he dashed off a satirical novella, with a caricatured Deledda as its heroine. Others alleged that Deledda was chosen by the Scandinavian award committee because her bleak landscapes reminded them of the gloom of their own national authors.

Deledda's writing holds up well, and she appears to be one of the more durable Nobel laureates of the 1920's. A nostalgia for a lost time and place operates in her favor. She evokes her native Sardinia as an island of peasants, small landowners, priests, and bandits. From a safe distance, city dwellers are charmed by this pastoral scene.

Simple statements and clean metaphors not easily lost in translation characterize Deledda's style. She knows how to choose the precise detail to render the flavor of a moment, the personality of a character, or the atmosphere of a place. Italian was not Deledda's native tongue. As a child, she spoke Logudoro, a dialect not even understood throughout her entire island. From Giovanni Verga, the Sicilian novelist, Deledda learned to provide the color of the actual speech of rustic people while writing in the standard literary language of Italy. Like Verga, she became skilled at convincingly converting the rhythms and images of provincial speech into recognizable, dignified, and poetic Italian.

Deledda had little formal education. Although her family was reasonably affluent by the standards of Nuoro, where they lived, education for women was not a priority among a people who equated books with laziness and wondered how a "scribbling woman" could ever find a husband. Through a program of self-directed reading, Deledda absorbed the bardic style of Homer and the Bible. Other influences were Giovanni Verga, the realist, and Gabriel d'Annunzio, the decadent romantic. Among the French, English, and Russians, she discovered Victor Hugo, Thomas Hardy, and Fyodor Dostoevski. Her affinities with these sources are evident in her writing.

The Mother is by far Deledda's best-known work, although its position as her masterpiece is less clear. The narrative approaches the classicism outlined by Aristotle, and the book is marked by consistency of mood and totality of effect. The action unfolds during a two-day span. The three principals—the priest's mother, Maria Maddalena; Paul, the priest; and Agnes, the woman he covets—are quintessential Deledda characters, whose raw emotions seem appropriate to folk inhabiting Mediterranean islands visited and ravished by Vikings, Arab conquerors, and Vandals. However, the social and spiritual crises faced by Paul are timeless.

Celibate priesthood originated before the cross was first raised on Sardinia. Paul's tragedy works itself out in a milieu that happens to be Catholic, yet his dilemma is that of the Protestant clergyman in Nathaniel Hawthorne's *The Scarlet Letter* (1850) or of the Druid priest in Vincenzo Bellini's opera *Norma* (1831). Deledda and her characters are not theologians. They do not concern themselves with the rationale behind the Roman Catholic Church demands. They do understand, however, the mystery that surrounds sacred consecration. The dimly understood teachings of Christianity mingle with the older superstitions of the island and the unspoken belief that a grim Providence presides over all.

Paul's pain is intensified by the solitude of his environment. If he possessed deep spirituality, intellectual interests, companions, or even the opportunities to fraternize with other priests and safe parishioners, his deprivations would seem less keen. If the obsessive family ties could be loosened or his life led under less scrutiny, his burden might lift.

Paul's inner resources are further depleted by his never having developed a conscience of his own. His mother remains his conscience, and God speaks in her voice. At one point, he has a vision of her lying on an altar, like a mysterious idol whose hand he is being forced to kiss. He is the victim of this woman, who is equally lonely and lives only through him. His priestly role raises her from servant to Madonna status. Having given him to the Church before his own age of consent, she never really gives him to God.

A great contrast to Paul is his altar boy, Antiochus. The young man ardently desires to be a priest, even though he must assert his choice against the wishes of his own mother, a usurer who also practices "certain other trades."

Maddalena, a mother who follows her son to assignations

and monitors his every act, is as controlling and destructive as Sophia Portnoy in Philip Roth's *Portnoy's Complaint* (1969), which, incidentally, had enormous success in Italy. However, Deledda does not pass glib judgment on this woman whom the island people view as noble, even heroic, whose struggle is the central focus of the novel.

Operatic adaptations of Deledda's writing were unsuccessful, but she has an eye and ear for the grand scene. *The Mother* builds to a climax during Sunday mass, in a village church rendered in full sensuous detail. Agnes appears, threatening publicly to expose her relationship with Paul. Although she fails in the end to denounce him, she casts a witchlike spell over his mother, who dies in anticipation of shame and scandal. Agnes is the succubus who gives Maddelena the evil eye, that fearsome glance against which Sardinians wear their horned amulets.

At one time, critics labeled Deledda as a local colorist, because she commemorated Sardinians of her generation much as Berga did Sicilians and Prosper Mérimée did Corsicans. However, her simple folk are neither the morally depraved country people of an Erskine Caldwell novel nor the noble primitives of a Victor Hugo tale. They are real people, confronting the human situation in a defined time and place, however claustrophobic.

"Critical Evaluation" by Allene Phy-Olsen

Further Reading

Deledda, Grazia. *The Mother.* Translated by Mary G. Steegmann. New York: Macmillan, 1923. Reprint. Cherokee, 1982. The introduction provides an excellent, nontechnical discussion in English of Deledda's novel.

Heyer-Caput, Margherita. *Grazia Deledda's Dance of Modernity.* Toronto, Ont.: University of Toronto Press, 2008. Examines Deledda's work within the context of literary modernism and of philosophy, including the ideas of positivism, Friedrich Nietzsche, and Arthur Schopenhauer. Heyer-Caput focuses on Deledda's novels, addressing elements of regionalism, decadence, and *verismo* and the influence of other literary movements with which Deledda has been associated

King, Martha. *Grazia Deledda: A Legendary Life.* Leicester, England: Troubador, 2005. King's biography chronicles Deledda's unlikely evolution from a young girl in nineteenth century Sardinia to a Nobel Prize-winning novelist. A good starting point to learn about Deledda. Includes bibliography.

Kozma, Janice M. *Grazia Deledda's Eternal Adolescents: The Pathology of Arrested Maturation.* Cranbury, N.J.:

Associated University Presses, 2002. A study of De-ledda's depictions of men in her novels and short stories. According to Kozma, Deledda believed that many men failed to mature and become full adults, and she superimposed her understanding of this "psychopathology" upon her male characters.

Pacifici, Sergio. *The Modern Italian Novel: From Capuana to Tozzi.* Carbondale: Southern Illinois University Press, 1973. Highly readable account of Italian achievements in modern fiction. One chapter is devoted principally to Deledda's work.

Pribic, Rado, ed. *Nobel Laureates in Literature: A Biographical Dictionary.* New York: Garland, 1990. Reviews Deledda's literary achievement, with a concise, pertinent commentary on *The Mother.* Identifies themes the novel shares with Deledda's other books and with representative international works of literary naturalism and existentialism.

Mother

Author: Maxim Gorky (1868-1936)
First published: Mat, 1906, serial; 1907, book (English translation, 1906)
Type of work: Novel
Type of plot: Naturalism
Time of plot: First decade of the twentieth century
Locale: Russia

Principal characters:
PELAGUEYA VLASOVA, a revolutionary heroine
PAVEL VLASOV, her son
ANDREY,
VYESOVSHCHIKOV,
RYBIN,
NIKOLAY IVANOVICH,
SOFYA,
SASHENKA, and
NATASHA, the Vlasovs' revolutionary friends

The Story:

The factory workers in the small Russian community of Nizhni-Novgorod are an impoverished, soulless, brutal lot. Their work in the factory dehumanizes them and robs them of their energy; as a result, they live like beasts.

When the worker Michael Vlasov dies, his wife, Pelagueya, fears that her son Pavel will lead the same anguished, brutal life. Gradually, however, she notices with joy and apprehension that Pavel is turning out differently and that he is given to reading. One day, Pavel informs his mother that he is reading subversive literature and that a group of his socialist friends are coming to visit him. Pelagueya is naturally frightened, but when his friends arrive she notices that they are much warmer, much more gentle than the people with whom she lived all of her life. Though they engage in heated arguments, no one seems to get angry at the others. Pavel's friends seem full of hope and vitality, and Pelagueya quickly warms up to them. In particular, she likes Andrey, who is bighearted and full of laughter, and Natasha, a frail, gentle girl who reads aloud during the meetings. Others in the group are Sashenka, a commanding girl who loves Pavel, and Vyesovshchikov,

the village misanthropist. They are idealistic young people, hopeful about the future of working people and prepared to put their ideas into action. Pelagueya agrees to take Andrey in as a roomer out of her motherly love for him.

Gradually Pavel's home became the center of their activities, but at the same time the group becomes the focus of village suspicion. Pavel and his comrades print leaflets and distribute them among the workers, spelling out their miserable condition. Soon afterward, the police drop in unexpectedly and arrest Andrey and Vyesovshchikov. Several others are arrested as well.

While the workers are generally hostile to Pavel because of his strangeness, he also inspires a certain confidence in them by virtue of his stern intelligence. Pelagueya is flattered that the sharp peasant, Rybin, an old bear of a man, should go to her son for advice. One day, the workers are notified that their pay will be cut. The workers are behind Pavel when he makes a speech to them and to the manager in protest against the cut; however, because of the speech, Pavel is arrested and sent to jail.

Distressed by her son's arrest, Pelagueya learns that about sixty others were arrested as well and that Andrey sent her his regards from prison. She thereupon decides to become involved in her son's activities and takes a job as a caterer to the factory laborers. Under cover of her work she distributes revolutionary literature. Meanwhile, she continues to see Pavel's socialist friends.

Soon afterward, Andrey is released from prison, and he returns to Pelagueya, who welcomes him with open arms. Rybin, claiming that the peasants are no better off than the workers, goes to the country to stir up the peasants against their oppressive masters.

With Andrey living in her house, Pelagueya feels happier. Under his friendly goading, she learns to read and write. She visits Pavel in prison and slyly tells him of her activities in distributing leaflets. Pelagueya's world expands greatly now that she is involved in the socialist cause; she has something to hope for beyond her selfish interests.

In the spring, Pavel is released from prison. The Vlasov household continues to be the hub of local socialist activities, and Pavel announces his intention of marching with the banner in the coming May Day parade, even though to do so will mean another jail sentence. One day, one of Pavel's friends rushes in to report that a spy was murdered in the street. At first Pelagueya fears that Vyesovshchikov committed the crime; later Andrey reveals that he accidentally killed the spy and feels guilty about his deed. After two weeks of inquiring into the matter, the police give up the investigation.

May Day arrives, and Pavel and Andrey are up early. The crowds gather in the streets, and the two men walk through them with Pelagueya close behind. After they make an abortive attempt to rouse the workers with speeches and songs, soldiers appear, force back the crowd, and arrest Pavel, Andrey, and their companions. Pelagueya feels depressed after their arrest. In answer to her loneliness, Nikolay Ivanovich comes to her and invites her to live with him in the city. She accepts his invitation and moves to his apartment. Nikolay and his sister Sofya are well-bred socialists. They treated Pelagueya with affection and respect, and she comes to love them as though they were members of her own family.

Pelagueya and Sofya dress as pilgrims and in that disguise distribute propaganda throughout the city and surrounding countryside. While delivering books to Rybin, Pelagueya sees the hardships of peasant life and the cruelty of the masters. She proves useful in aiding Vyesovshchikov to hide from the police after he escapes from prison. She nurses a dying comrade, and during a riot at his funeral she helps a wounded boy at some danger to herself. She also visits Pavel in prison.

Learning that many of her comrades were arrested, she decides to go alone to deliver her pamphlets in the country village. On arriving there she sees that Rybin was arrested and cruelly beaten. That night, she stays with sympathetic peasants and gives them copies of her leaflets. Returning to the city, she aids a fugitive peasant and tells Nikolay about her trip. Shortly thereafter, she helps a comrade to escape from prison. Her efforts for the workers make her realize how family allegiances interfere with loyalty to the cause; she understands now why Pavel refuses to get married.

After about six months in jail, Pavel and his comrades are finally brought to trial. The judges are cold, impersonal, and aloof. Several of Pavel's friends decline to testify in his defense. As the trial proceeds, Pavel makes a rousing speech in which he denounces the decadence of the masters and praises the youth and vision of the socialists. After Andrey further taunts the judges, Pavel and his companions are sentenced to exile in Siberia.

During this time, the police hunt down the socialists. Nikolay is arrested shortly after the trial. Pavel's speech is printed, and Pelagueya promises to deliver copies to a remote town. On the train, she recognizes a police spy and knows she is trapped. When the police try to arrest her, she shouts to the other occupants of the train about her mission and their servitude. She opens her bag and hands out the leaflets even while the police are beating her.

Critical Evaluation:

At the turn to the twentieth century, the writings of Maxim Gorky of Russia aroused interest throughout the world for their dramatic presentation of the struggles taking place in that largely unknown country. His representations of the bitter lives of Russia's people caused a sensation whenever they were published or produced on the stage. *Mother* is one of the most famous of these early works, and it is his only long work devoted entirely to the Russian revolutionary movement. Most of Gorky's early novels fail to sustain a continuous, powerful narrative, succumbing instead to frequent and irrelevant philosophical digressions, but *Mother* stands as a vivid and moving portrayal of a bitter struggle. If *Mother* is propaganda, it is propaganda raised to the level of art.

Although Gorky wrote primarily about the proletariat and in a naturalistic vein, he was not fundamentally concerned with politics, and his works exhibit a marked lyric talent that imbues his writing with a haunting poetic quality. Gorky's concern was with strong, vital, memorable characters rather than with dogma or morality. He envisioned a future in which vigorous people would free themselves from their economic degradation and live as free, independent spirits. He was a visionary rather than a dogmatist. This fact is particularly evident in *Mother*, in which Pelagueya Vlasova, through the love of her son, becomes converted to the revolutionary cause and gradually comes to love the people as her children. Gorky was strongly attracted to self-made individuals, to men and women with the courage to carry out their plans, and he makes the reader admire them as well. The lyric sweep of Gorky's vision in this novel is compelling.

Pelagueya's expanding consciousness forms the framework of the novel and serves as the catalyst that unites the parts of the story into a coherent, dynamic vision and raises the book to the level of a masterpiece. In the course of the narrative, the reader experiences the gradual growth of a movement in the radicalization first of the young man Pavel and then of his mother. The mother is only forty years old when the story opens, but already she is an old woman, brutalized by years of poverty and beatings. Spiritually, however, she is not dead, and as she painfully learns the truth about herself and her world, she begins to want to help spread this truth. The numbing fatalism that bound her when her husband was alive, her belief that the lot of women must always be despair, is gradually replaced by hope for the future.

The two aspects of love, its pain and its strength, are movingly depicted. The mother wants to protect her son, but she knows that she must let him be free. At the same time, her growing love for the members of the movement gives her the strength to remake her life and to brave hardships in contributing to the struggle. Her love in turn helps the others in the movement, and their united love for the poor, for the masses of humanity as yet unawakened, helps to keep all of them going. The party is called the "spiritual mother" of the working people, and many times it is referred to as helping the masses to be "reborn." The primary task of the mother and her compatriots is to educate the people and to distribute literature that will help them to be "reborn." Awareness must be the first step to revolution. The people are equated with Jesus Christ in several passages, most particularly when the mother washes the feet of the peasant leader Ignaty. The symbolism is unobtrusive yet effective.

The long novel is filled with powerful scenes, from the opening in which the terrified woman is beaten by her husband to the ending when she is killed while carrying on the work of her son. The trial of Pavel, her son, and his close friend Andrey, is effectively handled, as are the several riots and crowd scenes. Gorky's ability to handle large groups of people is remarkable. Each individual stands out distinctly, depicted as having human, believable eccentricities and irrationalities, yet Gorky manages to create a sense of the all-embracing tide of humanity. Human beings are not always consistent to character, and Gorky knew this; his people are realistic, and his characterizations are the principal strength of his mosaic of the early days of the Russian Revolution.

Further Reading

Borras, F. M. *Maxim Gorky the Writer: An Interpretation.* Oxford, England: Clarendon Press, 1967. One of the more astute interpretations of Gorky's works, especially of his novels and plays. Borras emphasizes Gorky's artistic achievements in such works as *Mother.*

Clark, Katerina. *The Soviet Novel: History as Ritual.* 3d ed. Bloomington: Indiana University Press, 2000. Clark's chronicle of the development of the Socialist Realist novel includes information about Gorky, his pronouncements on fiction, and *Mother.*

Cornwell, Neil, ed. *The Routledge Companion to Russian Literature.* New York: Routledge, 2001. Chapters 15 and 16 provide information about Gorky's contributions to the Russian novel.

Gifford, Henry. "Gorky and Proletarian Writing." In *The Novel in Russia: From Pushkin to Pasternak.* New York: Harper & Row, 1965. A discussion of Gorky's influence on proletarian writers, with remarks on the role of *Mother* in this respect.

Hare, Richard. *Maxim Gorky: Romantic Realist and Conservative Revolutionary.* London: Oxford University Press, 1962. Hare combines the political aspects of Gorky's biography with critical analysis of his works, including *Mother.*

Levin, Dan. *Stormy Petrel: The Life and Work of Maxim Gorky.* New York: Appleton-Century-Crofts, 1965. A general biography covering Gorky's entire life. Includes a discussion of *Mother.*

Morris, Paul D. "Representing Soviet-Russian Reality: Maxim Gorky's *Mother.*" In *Representation and the Twentieth-Century Novel: Studies in Gorky, Joyce, and Pynchon.* Würzburg, Germany: Königshausen & Neumann, 2005. A critical interpretation of Gorky's *Mother*, as well as James Joyce's *Ulysses* and Thomas Pynchon's *Gravity's Rainbow*, discussing how each novel represents a different literary tradition; Morris views Gorky's book as a paradigm of the Socialist Realist novel.

Valentino, Russell Scott. *Vicissitudes of Genre in the Russian Novel: Turgenev's "Fathers and Sons," Chernyshevsky's "What Is to Be Done?," Dostoevsky's "Demons," Gorky's "Mother."* New York: Peter Lang, 2001. Valentino analyzes Russian fictional works from the 1860's that are examples of the "tendentious novel" of this period. He describes how these novels influenced twentieth century literature, including Gorky's *Mother.*

Weil, Irwin. *Gorky: His Literary Development and Influence on Soviet Intellectual Life.* New York: Random House, 1966. The most scholarly book on Gorky in English, skillfully combining biography with critical analysis, including that of *Mother.* Valuable especially for the discus-

sion of Soviet literary life and Gorky's connection with, and influence on, younger Soviet writers.

Yedlin, Tova. *Maxim Gorky: A Political Biography.* Westport, Conn.: Praeger, 1999. Yedlin's biography focuses on Gorky's political and social views and his participation in the political and cultural life of his country. Includes bibliography and index.

Mother and Son

Author: Ivy Compton-Burnett (1884-1969)
First published: 1955
Type of work: Novel
Type of plot: Satire
Time of plot: End of the nineteenth century
Locale: An English country house

Principal characters:
MIRANDA HUME, matriarch of the Hume family
JULIUS HUME, her husband
ROSEBERY HUME, their eldest son
FRANCIS,
ALICE, and
ADRIEN, Julius's children
EMMA GREATHEART, a neighbor of the Humes
HESTER WOLSEY, her companion
MISS BURKE, her housekeeper
PLAUTUS, her cat

The Story:

Miss Burke, who has applied for the post of paid companion to Miranda Hume, finds her so rude and overbearing that she feels obliged to refuse to continue the interview with the rigid and autocratic potential employer. Instead, Miss Burke blunders into the neighboring house and accepts a position as a housekeeper to Emma Greatheart, who lives with her cat, Plautus, and her old schoolfriend, Hester Wolsey. However, Hester feels forced by economic necessity to get a job, despite her friend's willingness to provide support, and applies for the still-available position as companion to the austere and forbidding Miranda. Hester is given the position without an interview.

Although Miranda continues to fail in health, she still finds the strength to bully and intimidate her family. Her general hostility excludes, however, her son, Rosebery, on whom she dotes and who remains loyal instead of striking out on his own. However, her husband, Julius, prefers the three children of his late brother—Francis, Alice, and Adrien—who have become his wards. Their alienation from Miranda's regime, reflected in their bitter jokes, is a marked contrast to the behavior of Rosebery, who basks in his role as his mother's favorite. As Miranda's health declines further, Hester is drawn deeper into the family circle.

At a moment when Miranda is particularly unwell, her husband decides to confess that he is in reality not the guardian but the father of the three younger children. Miranda, who has based her life on a belief in her own godlike omniscience, dies as a consequence of the shock and fury she feels at the thought of her husband's secret past. The confession of Julius, which can be said to have been a murder weapon, and Miranda's consequent death are witnessed by both the appalled Rosebery and the keenly interested Hester.

Hester is also present when Rosebery learns a second secret. In a letter that Miranda had kept hidden, Rosebery discovers that Julius is not his birth father and that he is the product of an earlier liaison on Miranda's part. In short order, Rosebery sees both of his respectable Victorian parents exposed as adulterers. On an unconscious level, however, the parents seem to have known all along. The loyalty of Miranda and Julius has always been to their own gene pools, which they have privileged over other bonds, exposing their animal cunning and their human narcissism. However, Rosebery achieves a moment of nobility in surrendering his rights to Julius's estate, in favor of Julius's birth family.

Miranda's death becomes the occasion for rejoicing among the younger children and the occasion for sorrow on the part of Rosebery. Hester finds herself under pressure to assume Miranda's position within the household. Recovering from his grief with suspicious haste, however, Rosebery immediately proposes to Hester, who declines, hoping instead to marry Julius. Hester becomes infuriated when Julius proposes to Emma and when Rosebery proposes to Miss Burke. Overcome by feelings of jealousy and envy, it suits Hester's purpose at this time to reveal the Hume family secrets concerning the paternity of Rosebery and the other children. These revelations bring Miss Burke and Emma to their senses.

Emma and Hester return to their original domestic arrangement, with the addition of the helpful Miss Burke. They remain free from marriages that promised more convenience than love, but they have learned much that was distressing about human nature. The antics of their cat, Plautus, who brings, as a gift, a mouse he has captured, indicate to them the predatory, selfish animal instincts that simmer beneath the respectable appearances of the two households.

At the Hume household, Julius and Rosebery are left without mature female companionship. Instead of having a wife and family of his own, Rosebery continues to live in his mother's house. He spends his time teaching the children the games his mother had taught him. The younger children, whose teasing, especially of their servants, can be sadistic, receive from Rosebery some of the affection that had been lacking in their relationship with Miranda. Although Rosebery briefly considers doing so, he does not leave the domestic sphere for a new life in the outside world. Instead, he takes Miranda's place at home, although he also expresses a wish to find and meet his real father.

"The Story" by Margaret Boe Birns

Critical Evaluation:

Ivy Compton-Burnett's great subject is the family. Herself the product of a large and exceedingly dysfunctional Victorian family, she drew on her own experiences to explore the nature of the family as a social unity, addressing the ways in which parents tyrannize their children and how the children respond to such treatment. She also looks at the ways in which even dysfunctional families negotiate their relationships with the outside world and the fictions they construct to conceal and deceive the observer.

Mother and Son is dominated by the relationship between the autocratic Miranda Hume and her son, Rosebery. Initially, it is not clear to the reader whether Rosebery is in fact her son or her husband, such is the closeness between them. The introduction of Julius as her husband settles the legal re-

lationship, but the emotional relationship remains unclear. Such is Miranda's regard for Rosebery, her desire to have him close to her, that one begins to think in terms of some kind of emotional incest. For his own part, Rosebery seems to be content to remain close to his mother, but his motives are not entirely clear.

While both mother and son firmly emphasize that Rosebery is a confirmed bachelor, which is often social shorthand for a closeted gay man or a man in denial about his homosexuality, it is noticeable that as soon as his mother's back is turned, Rosebery becomes deeply attentive to any woman in his vicinity. It remains unclear whether he is simply habituated to behaving in such a way because of his mother's influence or whether he wants to establish a relationship with a woman his own age. Nonetheless, Rosebery insists on escorting Miss Burke back to the village after her unsuccessful interview. Later, he takes tea with Hester Wolsey when she first arrives at the house, before the rest of the family returns home. This seemingly insignificant event—having tea—is given extra resonance by the way in which Rosebery takes an almost illicit pleasure in rearranging things to his own taste. It also resonates by revealing that although his mother always serves him sugared tea, he prefers it without.

Miranda's subsequent discovery of this last fact takes on the nature of a crisis because it confirms that even her own son, kept close, can dissemble and keep secrets from her, something she finds intolerable. Secrets are always intolerable to Miranda, and it is the discovery of the greatest secret of all that kills her because, literally, she cannot contain the knowledge of it, although she has contained the actuality of the three children in her house unwittingly.

It is uncertain whether Rosebery's emotional needs are shaped by a need for companionship based on mutuality or because he is seeking a mother-substitute; that he proposes to both Miss Burke and Hester, each of whom occupies a "nurturing" role at various points within the novel, suggests the latter, yet there is something in Rosebery's manner that indicates he would prefer a more "normal" relationship with a woman; it also indicates, possibly, that he has no idea how to have such a relationship. It is equally noteworthy that Rosebery is himself finally positioned in a nurturing role, helping to care for the younger children who have already, through his own actions, effectively usurped his position within the family. Thus, he becomes an emasculated cuckoo within his own nest. Julius, by contrast, having been kept at a distance by Miranda, has had the opportunity to create his own life and his own family, but even he has been obliged to secrete his family in plain view, disguising them as his niece and nephews and maintaining an appropriate familial distance.

Francis, Adrian and Alice, the next generation of Humes, already have a cynical attitude to family life as a result of observing Miranda's behavior. The reader is left to wonder whether they will be able in turn to break away from the family house and establish their own lives, or whether they will feel obliged to remain close to Julius and Rosebery.

Emma Greatheart's establishment seems to offer a different model for living, but while Emma may live up to her own name in being able to offer the impoverished Hester a home and in espousing idealistic notions of companionship, there remains a sense, nonetheless, that even such a carefree life has hidden costs. Hester, although socially and intellectually Emma's equal, cannot match her in terms of financial security, hence her desire to make her way in the world. Her ability to take on the running of the Hume household suggests that she has taken a similar role at the Greatheart cottage, a role further emphasized by Emma's greater need for the presence of Miss Burke once Hester has departed. This in turn suggests that Emma has the capacity to take on an autocratic role similar to that of Miranda, but she avoids doing so thanks to greater self-awareness. Whereas Miss Burke and Miranda instantly took a dislike to one another, Emma and Miss Burke are able to spar, despite the difference in status. Emma's conversation, much of it conducted via Plautus the cat, suggests caution, an awareness of her somewhat tenuous position within the household.

Dialogue is key in Compton-Burnett's work. She avoids all but the minimum in terms of scene-setting and description, focusing instead on extraordinary conversational exchanges between characters. These are not plausible discussions between characters, but a complex use of stream-of-consciousness techniques, indicating thoughts that are usually left unspoken. At times it is impossible to discern whether characters have spoken aloud or are articulating unspoken thoughts. Although this approach initially might seem straightforward if not downright simplistic, closer study of Compton-Burnett's work reveals how devastating this technique is in terms of examining those things the characters attempt to conceal from one another.

"Critical Evaluation" by Maureen Kincaid Speller

Further Reading

Baldanza, Frank. *Ivy Compton-Burnett*. New York: Twayne, 1964. This work features an analysis of each of Compton-Burnett's novels as well as a treatment of her writing techniques. Includes a chronology and a bibliography.

Burkhart, Charles, ed. *The Art of I. Compton-Burnett*. London: Victor Gollancz, 1972. A compilation of critical essays and interviews by leading critics of Compton-Burnett's work. Examines the theme of domestic tyranny, and includes the important essay on Compton-Burnett's dialogue by French novelist Nathalie Sarraute.

Cavaliero, Glen. "Family Fortunes: Ivy Compton-Burnett." In *The Alchemy of Laughter: Comedy in English Fiction*. New York: St. Martin's Press, 2000. Cavaliero includes works by Compton-Burnett in his examination of comedy in English novels, in which he discusses the elements of parody, irony, satire, and other types of humor in these books.

Gentile, Kathy Justice. *Ivy Compton-Burnett*. New York: St. Martin's Press, 1991. Establishes Compton-Burnett as a feminist and adds new and important perspectives to her work, including feminist analyses of all of the novels. Includes an excellent bibliography.

Greig, Cicely. *Ivy Compton-Burnett: A Memoir*. London: Garnstone Press, 1972. An affectionate but perceptive memoir by Compton-Burnett's typist and friend. Includes some useful insights into *Mother and Son*.

Ingman, Heather. "Ivy Compton-Burnett: Tyrants, Victims, and Camp." In *Women's Fiction Between the Wars: Mothers, Daughters, and Writing*. New York: St. Martin's Press, 1998. Explores how Compton-Burnett and five other authors depict the mother-daughter relationship in their work. Argues that Compton-Burnett's novels "provide a devastating insight into the psychopathology of Victorian family life and a critique of the patriarchal power structures underpinning it."

Liddell, Robert. *The Novels of I. Compton-Burnett*. 1955. Reprint. Philadelphia: R. West, 1977. The first important interpretation of Compton-Burnett. Remains the standard critical book. Includes a detailed and appreciative analysis of each work, with particular reference to the theme of domestic tyranny.

Nevius, Blake. *Ivy Compton-Burnett*. New York: Columbia University Press, 1970. A short, appreciative, general book for students and general readers unfamiliar with Compton-Burnett's work. Also serves as a lively introduction for readers who find her novels difficult and inaccessible.

Spurling, Hilary. *Ivy: The Life of I. Compton-Burnett*. 1984. Reprint. London: Richard Cohen Books, 1995. The indispensable biography of Compton-Burnett, with much useful information about her childhood, the source material for all of her novels. Describes her happy and creative years with her companion, Margaret Jourdain.

Mother Courage and Her Children

Author: Bertolt Brecht (1898-1956)
First produced: Mutter Courage und ihre Kinder, 1941;
    first published, 1949 (English translation, 1941)
Type of work: Drama
Type of plot: Play of ideas
Time of plot: 1624-1648
Locale: Europe

Principal characters:
MOTHER COURAGE, or ANNA FIERLING, owner of a
    canteen wagon
KATTRIN, her daughter
EILIF, her older son
SWISS CHEESE, her younger son
COOK
CHAPLAIN
YVETTE POTTIER, a camp follower

The Story:

In 1624, six years into the Thirty Years' War, a recruiting officer and a sergeant discuss the difficulty of recruiting in Poland, which had been at peace and was not organized for war. Mother Courage's canteen wagon rolls on, drawn by her two sons, Eilif and Swiss Cheese. Mother Courage and her daughter, Kattrin, who cannot speak, sit on the wagon. Mother Courage sings a song that both criticizes war and entices officers to buy her wares for their soldiers because "cannon is rough on empty bellies." She tells the officers she had been given the name Mother Courage because she had driven wildly through the bombardment of Riga to sell fifty loaves of bread that were getting moldy.

When the officers try to recruit Eilif, Mother Courage angrily confronts them. In response to the sergeant's downplaying of the dangers of war, she offers to look into his future by drawing lots. He draws the black cross of death. The recruiting officer persists, so Mother Courage has Eilif and Swiss Cheese draw lots, and both draw black crosses. Mother Courage draws for Kattrin, who also gets a cross. The sergeant distracts Mother Courage by negotiating to buy a belt, while the recruiting officer convinces Eilif to leave with him.

Two years later, Mother Courage negotiates the sale of a capon to the commander's cook and helps him prepare it for the commander and his guest of honor, Eilif. Angered as she listens to Eilif recounting his daring in capturing twenty bullocks and the commander's praising him, she tells the cook that a leader who needs bravery is a bad leader. Eilif and his mother are reunited when she joins his "Song of the Wise Woman and the Soldier," in which the soldier ignores the wise woman's advice and dies.

Three years later, Swiss Cheese is paymaster of the retreating Second Protestant Regiment. Yvette, a camp follower, sings "The Fraternization Song," lamenting her first soldier lover, whom she has not seen in five years. The cook

and the chaplain brings Eilif's request for money before he leaves with his regiment. Concerned about the cash box entrusted to Swiss Cheese, Mother Courage pays, complaining that Eilif speculates in mother love.

The cook, the chaplain, and Mother Courage discuss the religious war. Mother Courage notes the Protestant king is unbeatable because, although he wages war from fear of God, he also wants a good profit, so little fellows back the war.

The Catholics defeat the Protestant soldiers, who retreat hastily, leaving Mother Courage and the others as prisoners. The group quickly gets rid of evidence that ties them to the Protestants, and Catholics ignore the obvious because they need a canteen. Mother Courage notes, "The defeats and victories of the fellows at the top aren't always defeats and victories for the fellows at the bottom."

Business is good for the canteen and for Yvette, but Swiss Cheese's cash box remains a concern. He is discovered by Catholic soldiers, confesses under torture, and is put on trial.

Hoping to save Swiss Cheese, Mother Courage negotiates with Yvette, who has formed a liaison with a Catholic colonel willing to buy her a canteen. Mother Courage is unwilling to part with the wagon, arguing for a lease, to which Yvette agrees. When Mother Courage learns Swiss Cheese had thrown the cash box, from which she had hoped to repay Yvette's loan, into the river, she tries to haggle with her son's captors over the bribe for his release. She fails, and he is condemned and shot. When soldiers bring his body for Mother Courage to identify, she denies knowing him, so his body is thrown into a carrion pit.

Mother Courage goes to the officer's tent to complain that soldiers had vandalized her wagon after Swiss Cheese's death. She talks an angry young soldier out of complaining, singing the "Song of the Great Capitulation," then she herself leaves without lodging a complaint.

Two years later the war has widened. Over Mother Courage's objections, the chaplain and Kattrin tear up officers' shirts to bind up the peasants' wounds, and Kattrin rescues a baby from its burning home. During the funeral of a fallen commander, Mother Courage, the chaplain, and the clerk argue about the possibility of peace. The chaplain asserts that war will not end, because it satisfies all needs, including the need for peace. Convinced, Mother Courage sends Kattrin and the clerk to stockpile supplies. In their absence, the chaplain unsuccessfully proposes a closer relationship to Mother Courage. Kattrin returns alone with the supplies and a disfiguring wound. They move on, all three pulling the wagon.

News of peace arrives, and the cook returns. He and Mother Courage berate the chaplain for his reasoning about peace. The argument is interrupted by Yvette's return. She had married the colonel and is now widowed and well off. Recognizing the cook as her first lover, she warns Mother Courage about him. They leave, and the cook and the chaplain receive Eilif's last visit. During this brief peace, he acts as if it were still wartime; he steals cattle and is sentenced to death. He is taken away before Mother Courage returns with news that the war has resumed. She is told only that Eilif had gone away. The cook and Kattrin pull the wagon back to the war.

As the war worsens, the cook inherits an inn and invites Mother Courage to run it with him. When he refuses to include Kattrin, she starts to leave her mother. Mother Courage, who sends the cook away, assures Kattrin they must stay together.

Mother Courage leaves Kattrin in the care of a peasant family while she goes into the Protestant town of Halle to buy supplies. Catholic soldiers, intent on ambushing Halle while the town sleeps, force these peasants to assist them. After the soldiers take the peasant son as their guide, his mother prays to God to protect her grandchildren, who are sure to be massacred in the ambush. When Kattrin hears the children mentioned, she grabs a drum and, from the roof, drums loudly to awaken the town. The soldiers shoot her, but the sound of a cannon from the town signals her success.

Mother Courage returns, mourns Kattrin briefly, then, paying the peasants to bury the body, joins the last regiment leaving Halle to resume her business. At the end, she pulls the wagon alone.

Critical Evaluation:

A major force in modern theater, German playwright Bertolt Brecht is perhaps best known for his concepts of epic theater and *Verfremdungseffekt* (alienation effect). A Marxist, Brecht reacted against what he called culinary theater,

which provides its audience with the illusion of reality. Brecht wanted theatrical productions to destroy comforting illusions, so the audience would think rather than feel.

Brecht defined the learning process of alienation as a dialectical progression, moving the audience from its familiar—and false—understanding to an estranging nonunderstanding, achieved by a defamiliarizing theatrical presentation, to the final stage of understanding in a new way. This was to be achieved through productions that used the techniques of epic theater. The ideal was a dispassionate presentation. One means was the use of a narrative voice, through projected slogans on stage, to intervene between the audience and events of the play and eliminate audience identification with the character, thus forcing the audience to maintain objectivity.

The plots of epic plays consist of loosely knit episodes, complete within themselves. The nonliterary elements—stage design, music, choreography—are designed to be autonomous, interrupting the flow of the production. Together, these elements are to create distance, resulting in an audience's viewing the play with a critical eye.

Mother Courage and Her Children, loosely based on Hans Jakob Christoffel von Grimmelshausen's *Lebensbeschreibung der Ertzbetrügerin und Landstörtzerin Courasche* (1670; *Courage: The Adventuress*, 1964), is Brecht's most successful play. It uses many epic theater techniques. The play is composed of twelve scenes of varying lengths, each introduced by a slogan designed to place it in historical context, eliminate suspense, and clarify the effect of the war on the characters. For example, the slogan for scene three is "Three years pass and Mother Courage, with parts of a Finnish regiment, is taken prisoner. Her daughter is saved, her wagon likewise, but her honest son dies."

Music is also used throughout the play to stop action and comment on it. Mother Courage's first song has a thematically important refrain: "Let all of you who still survive/ Get out of bed and look alive!" This is repeated in several scenes, and sung at the play's conclusion by the soldiers Mother Courage is rushing to join.

Two other songs are thematically important. "The Song of the Great Capitulation," sung by Mother Courage, details her progress in learning to "march in lockstep with the rest." The cook's "Song of the Great Souls of this Earth" notes problems caused by virtues such as Solomon's wisdom, concluding that only vices bring reward. Although Brecht was a Marxist, his pessimism, illustrated in these songs, was difficult for Marxist critics to accept.

Brecht considered *Mother Courage* to be a cautionary tale that shows that those who live on war have to pay. War is a metaphor for capitalistic business; the state of war is analogous to the human condition, poisoned by greed and exploitation. Brecht believed that both war and capitalism made human virtues "fatal even to those who exercise them." He considered Mother Courage to be guilty, a deformed merchant-mother, the hyena of war.

To Brecht's irritation, response to the play generally focused on its emotional impact. Mother Courage has been seen as a complex and tragic character, compared to Niobe. Spectators sympathized with her hard choices. Kattrin, whose love of children, eagerness for motherhood, and compassion make her a life force, is also a profoundly sympathetic character. Ravaged by the war (her muteness resulting from a soldier who "stuck something in her mouth when she was little"), she is normal in an abnormal world that has done its best to deform her. Her act of defiance, drumming to save the children of Halle, has been called the most emotionally moving scene in modern drama.

The emotional depth of this play derives from its ambiguity. Brecht made changes in the play before its second production in post-World War II Berlin, hoping to mitigate the emotional response. The Berlin audience, many of whom had lost relatives in the war, sat weeping at the play's conclusion, and the critics again responded to Mother Courage's Niobe-like qualities. Later critics also noted its emotional power.

Elsie Galbreath Haley

Further Reading

Demetz, Peter, ed. *Brecht*. Englewood Cliffs, N.J.: Prentice-Hall, 1962. The essay on *Mother Courage and Her Children* focuses on the "Song of the Great Capitulation," Brecht's Marxism and pessimism, and epic theater.

Esslin, Martin. *Brecht: The Man and His Work*. Garden City, N.Y.: Doubleday, 1960. Critical study of Brecht, including his biography, poetry, the theory and practice of Brechtian theater, and Brecht's relationship to communism.

Fuegi, John. *Bertolt Brecht: Chaos, According to Plan*. New York: Cambridge University Press, 1987. Discusses the theater of Brecht's time and how he changed it. Section on *Mother Courage and Her Children* focuses on the 1949 Berlin production and how Brecht's staging reinforced the play's meaning.

Horwich, Cara M. *Survival in "Simplicissimus" and "Mutter Courage."* New York: Peter Lang, 1997. A comparison of *Mother Courage and Her Children* and the work upon which it is based—the *Simplicissimus* novels, which were written by Hans Jakob Christoffel von Grimmelshausen in the seventeenth century. Horwich maintains that both works share a common concern with human survival in a dangerous world, and she demonstrates how both present lower clergymen as models of survival.

Speirs, Ronald. *Bertolt Brecht*. New York: St. Martin's Press, 1987. An introduction to Brecht's works, focusing on the balance between the intellect and the emotional response produced by the plays. Contains an analysis of *Mother Courage and Her Children* and four of Brecht's other plays.

Thomson, Peter. *Brecht: "Mother Courage and Her Children."* New York: Cambridge University Press, 1997. A history of the plays' production, beginning with Brecht's own staging in Berlin in 1949, covering British productions in 1956 and 1995, and describing some of the significant Continental presentations. Thomson also describes how the play's characters have been interpreted by Dame Judi Dench, Glenda Jackson, and other actors.

Thomson, Peter, and Glendyr Sacks, eds. *The Cambridge Companion to Brecht*. 2d ed. New York: Cambridge University Press, 2006. Essays offering numerous interpretations of Brecht's work, including examinations of Brecht and cabaret, music, and stage design; his work with the Berliner Ensemble; and key words in his theory and practice of theater. Chapter 9 discusses *Mother Courage and Her Children*.

Unwin, Stephen. *A Guide to the Plays of Bertolt Brecht*. London: Methuen, 2005. Contains analyses of many of Brecht's plays and discusses his theories of drama, his impact, and his legacy. Designed as an accessible introduction to Brecht for students, teachers, and other readers.

Mother Hubberds Tale

Author: Edmund Spenser (c. 1552-1599)
First published: 1591, as *Prosopopoia: Or, Mother Hubberds Tale*
Type of work: Poetry
Type of plot: Fable
Time of plot: Antiquity

Principal characters:
REYNOLD, the wily fox of French folk legends
THE APE, his accomplice

The Poem:

August days bring sickness to the poet. His friends visit him and tell tales of knights, fairies, and giants to while away his days of illness. What pleases him most, however, is the beast fable recounted by old Mother Hubberd. In the fable, the fox approaches his neighbor, the ape, and proposes that they set out together to seek their fortunes. The ape willingly acquiesces, wanting only to know how his friend plans to improve their sorry lot. The fox suggests a disguise and points out that if they pretend to be beggars, they will be free of all obligations and responsibilities. The two dress themselves in the tattered remains of military uniforms to win confidence and sympathy.

The comrades' first victim is an honest, unintelligent farmer who listens sympathetically to the ape's description of his misfortunes and his wounds. The ape requests employment—something that will not tax his poor, battered body—and soon he is tending the gullible husbandman's sheep with the fox as his trusty dog. The partners in crime feast lavishly on their charges for several months, then escape into the night just before they are to produce an accounting of the flock.

Weary of profitless begging, they provide themselves with a gown and a cassock to impersonate learned clergymen. They first encounter an illiterate priest who advises them on their parish duties. All that is necessary is to say the service weekly, to "lay the meat before" the faithful; they have no responsibility for helping their parishioners accept the gospel. The old days when priests prayed daily and sincerely are, fortunately, past.

Now once a week, upon the Sabbath day, "It is enough to do our small devotion,/ And then to follow any merry motion." The priest then suggests that the fox and ape go to some nobleman, feigning a grave and saintly demeanor, to request a benefice. He cannot recommend that they seek preferment at court, for "nothing there is done without a fee." Heeding this good counsel, the fox assumes the role of priest, and the ape becomes his parish clerk. They revel gaily for a time, but the complaints of their abused and exploited parishioners finally bring about their expulsion from their offices. Once

more on the road, they almost starve before they meet a richly dressed mule who tells them that he has just come from the court. He, too, has advice for achieving success. They should appear at court themselves, and do so

> with a good bold face,
> And with big words, and with a stately pace,
> That men may thinke of you, in generall,
> That to be in you, which is not at all:
> For not by that which is, the world now deemeth,
> (As it was wont) but by that same that seemeth.

The fox and ape easily win the royal favor, being suited by nature and inclination to win acceptance. The ape dresses in outlandish clothes and demonstrates his accomplishments: "For he could play, and daunce, and vault, and spring,/ And all that else pertains to reveling." He is also skilled at fortune-telling, juggling, and sleight of hand. The latter talent is especially profitable, for "what he touched came not to light again."

The ape passes his time gambling, carrying on intrigues, and composing exceedingly bad verses to corrupt the chaste ladies around him. To support his success, the fox, disguised as his confidential servant, practices all kinds of deceits and, for a large fee, promises favors from his master to poor suitors who come to court looking for preferment.

At length the fox's deceptions are discovered, and he is banished. The ape, left without resources, soon finds himself shabby and scorned, and he flees to rejoin his friend. Lamenting their lack of success, they wander into a wood where they find a lion lying asleep, his crown and scepter beside him. The ape timorously steals the lion's skin and his regalia, then claims the throne for himself as a reward for his valor. The fox reluctantly agrees, stipulating that he be allowed to make all the decisions of government. They initiate a reign of terror, extorting treasure from all the beasts of the forest.

The fox sells justice, raises the fortunes of his family by his ill-gotten gains, and defends his actions on the grounds of his long experience and his desire to build up the royal treasury. He brings about the downfall of the noblest beasts, scorns scholars and poets, and disdains the common people.

Only divine intervention can put an end to this disastrous reign; Jupiter notices the turmoil among the wild animals and sends Mercury to humble the usurper ape. Mercury awakens the lion from his unnatural sleep, and the latter goes to the door of his palace, roaring with such force that most of its inhabitants perish from fear. The ape runs to find a hiding place, and the fox skulks out to the lion, laying all the blame upon his partner. The lion punishes both, stripping the fox and casting him out, then clipping the ape's tail and ears; the story ends as a kind of myth of "why the ape has no tail."

Critical Evaluation:

The first three books of Edmund Spenser's masterpiece, *The Faerie Queene*, were published in 1590 and attracted immediate and widespread attention and praise. The next year, publisher William Ponsonby brought out a collection of shorter poems by Spenser, *Complaints Containing Sundrie Small Poemes of the Worlds Vanitie*, containing, among other works, *Prosopopoia: Or, Mother Hubberds Tale*. The *Complaints* was intended to take advantage of the poet's newly found popularity. Unfortunately, the sharp satire of some of the poems, especially *Mother Hubberds Tale*, offended the Elizabethan authorities, and the book was apparently "called in," or censored, shortly after its publication.

The satire in *Mother Hubberds Tale* that caused it to be censored was political in nature, and referred specifically to events surrounding the proposed marriage of Queen Elizabeth I to a French duke. Although the events had taken place long before the actual publication of the poem, which was probably written in 1579-1580, its offense to high officials in Elizabeth's court, including Lord Burleigh and even the queen herself, was sufficient to have the volume suppressed and Spenser, for all practical purposes, banished to Ireland.

The entire poem is framed as if spoken by Mother Hubberd herself. "Prosopopoeia" refers to the rhetorical device in which an imaginary or absent person speaks or acts out a story. The purpose of the device is to set the satire within an imaginary context, allowing the animal fable that follows to be both believable and understandable. The central character of *Mother Hubberds Tale*, the wily fox who attempts to defraud the public, comes from the popular French stories of Reynard the Fox, translated and published by England's first printer, William Caxton, in the late fifteenth century.

The format of the poem is that of the travel tale, specifically that of the picaresque story, which follows the adventures of a clever rogue. (The Spanish word for rogue, *pícaro*, gives the genre its name.) In *Mother Hubberds Tale*, there are two rogues, the fox and the ape. Their travels take them from rustic isolation to palatial splendor, since each deception they perform advances them another step up the social ladder: They begin as beggars and continue their successful trickeries until the ape becomes a king and the fox becomes his powerful first minister. At that point, Jupiter, a symbol of divine authority, bestirs the rightful monarch, the lion, into reclaiming his throne, and the fox and the ape receive their rightful punishments.

The poem falls into two sections. The largest section of the poem, up to line 950, is a general satire on human society and its ills. The fox and ape meet a succession of stock characters who symbolically represent the various levels of society. First, they encounter and dupe the honest farmer; his failing is that he is credulous to the point of stupidity, mistaking the ape for a shepherd and the fox for his faithful sheepdog. At the same time, Spenser uses this episode to point out an evil of his age, the plight of discharged veterans who were left to wander with no means of livelihood. The two rogues next encounter an illiterate priest, who suggests the benefits of a clerical occupation if religion is not taken too seriously. Spenser's account of their progress in this guise is a scathing condemnation of clerical abuses of his age. Finally, they arrive at court and, after vain efforts to win preference, they chance upon the sleeping lion, steal his skin and crown, and usurp the throne.

The description of the pair's exploits at court is the longest single section of the poem, and it was closest to Spenser's heart, for he had spent many months at court trying without success to win royal favor and patronage. Spenser also contrasts the ape's behavior with that of the true nobleman, whose primary allegiance is to his honor and personal integrity; who spends his days in riding, running, wrestling, preparing for military service, playing musical instruments, and writing poetry; who tries to learn enough about the affairs of state to be a wise counselor to his prince; and who endeavors in every way to achieve excellence.

The latter part of the poem is set entirely in the world of animals, as the two adventurers take over the throne of the lion, the traditional king of beasts. Here, the satire becomes pointedly specific. The ape, an animal not native to the land, calls in alien creatures such as griffins, minotaurs, crocodiles, dragons, beavers, and centaurs to support his rule. As the poem notes, "For tyrannie is with strange ayde supported." Spenser is clearly alluding to the proposed marriage of Elizabeth to the Duc d'Alençon. Marriage to a foreigner, Spenser warns, would bring a similar body of unnatural, decidedly un-English figures into the court. Queen Elizabeth, seldom a monarch to seek, and never one to accept, unwanted advice, would have been furious at the poet's presumption, one reason the volume was called back.

There were other reasons for its censorship. With the ape as king, the fox becomes his powerful chief minister, wielding the real power behind the throne and using the opportunity to advance his own family into positions of influence and riches and ousting the older, more legitimate aristocracy. Just such behavior had been widely alleged against Lord Burleigh, Elizabeth's lord treasurer, and the repetition of such attacks, even in disguised form, would have provided another argument for the authorities to suppress the book.

Beyond the social and political satire of *Mother Hubberds Tale*, however, is the literary and artistic level of the work. *Mother Hubberds Tale* is the most medieval of Spenser's works. As he often did, Spenser turned to the verse of the fourteenth century poet Geoffrey Chaucer for inspiration and pattern. Spenser's debt to the earlier writer includes the use of the beast fable to criticize the politics of the day and stylistic devices. His apology for his plain language, on the grounds that he is simply reproducing the words of an old woman, is reminiscent of Chaucer's excuse for the bawdy vocabulary of some of his characters. Spenser has deliberately tried to reproduce the sententious quality of an old woman's storytelling; however, he occasionally slips out of his persona, especially when he is discussing the evils of the court.

Spenser followed Chaucer's example in another important point: that of writing verse with the clarity and simplicity of prose. The action in *Mother Hubberds Tale* is clearly presented and easily grasped. The characters, although sometimes stock figures drawn from conventional morality, are realistic enough to be believable and, the fox and the ape especially, are individuals. The major flaw in the progression of the narrative is probably the personal feeling that overshadows the story in the episode at court, but this adds to the poem's interest for the modern reader.

Taken all in all, *Mother Hubberds Tale* is a minor masterpiece of narrative verse. Spenser has assimilated medieval techniques and the folk tradition brilliantly to produce a work that remains an interesting, amusing narrative, and a powerful religious and political satire. He so successfully blends the worlds of humans, beasts, and Olympian gods that there is no apparent incongruity.

"Critical Evaluation" by Michael Witkoski

Further Reading

Brown, Richard Danson. "Cracking the Nut? *Mother Hubberds Tale*'s Attack on Traditional Notions of Poetic Value." In *The New Poet: Novelty and Tradition in Spenser's "Complaints."* Liverpool, England: Liverpool University Press, 1999. Analyzes the poem and others in Spenser's *Complaints* (1591) collection of poetry. Argues that the collection demonstrates how Spenser gradually moved from a traditional poetics to a new form of poetry that emerged from his transformation of the "complaint" genre.

Cummings, Robert M., ed. *Spenser: The Critical Heritage*. 1971. Reprint. New York: Routledge, 1995. Spenser's reputation as a poet's poet has always been high. This collection of critical opinions on his work traces the course of that reputation from Elizabethan times to the twentieth century.

Fowler, Alastair. "Edmund Spenser." In *British Writers*, edited by Ian Scott-Kilvert. New York: Charles Scribner's Sons, 1979. Excellent introductory piece on Spenser and his works, highlighting his achievements in all poetic genres. Helpful for understanding the place of *Mother Hubberds Tale* in Spenser's career.

Hadfield, Andrew, ed. *The Cambridge Companion to Spenser*. New York: Cambridge University Press, 2001. Collection of essays providing an overview of Spenser's life and work. Some of the essays discuss the relevance of Spenser, the historical contexts of his work, his use of language, and his literary influence.

Jones, H. S. V. *A Spenser Handbook*. 1930. Reprint. New York: Appleton-Century-Crofts, 1958. Remains one of the most useful works dealing with *Mother Hubberds Tale*. This dated but important handbook provides a brief but excellent overview of the poem and how it fit into its time.

Lethbridge, J. B., ed. *Edmund Spenser: New and Renewed Directions*. Madison, N.J.: Fairleigh Dickinson University Press, 2006. Reprints a collection of papers originally delivered at a conference about Spenser. Includes discussions of the Spenserian stanza, Spenser's relationship to Ireland, and the trend toward a new historical criticism of his work.

McCabe, Richard A. *Spenser's Monstrous Regiment: Elizabethan Ireland and the Poetics of Difference*. New York: Oxford University Press, 2002. Analyzes how Spenser's experiences of living and writing in Ireland challenged his ideas about English nationhood. Assesses the influence of colonialism on the themes, imagery, language, and structure of his poetry.

Sanders, Andrew. *The Short Oxford History of English Literature*. New York: Oxford University Press, 1994. Good, if brief, introductory articles on Spenser and his contemporary scene that illuminate the particular conditions of Elizabethan England.

The Moths, and Other Stories

Author: Helena María Viramontes (1954-   )
First published: 1985
Type of work: Short fiction
Type of plot: Domestic realism and social realism
Time of plot: Late twentieth century
Locale: Southern California and Mexico

The Stories:

In "The Moths," a young girl experiences a rite of passage to adulthood as she cares for her dying grandmother, her Abuelita. Estranged from her family's strict demands, and especially from her domineering father, the girl finds comfort nursing her grandmother. Her grandmother dies, and the girl carries her into the bathroom, submerging herself and her grandmother in a tub of water. Gray moths begin to fill the bathroom, emerging from the grandmother's soul through her mouth.

In "Growing," a confused teenage protagonist is pulled between childhood pleasures and adult desires and is saddled with the responsibility of taking care of a younger sister. In "Birthday," Alice Johnson comes to realize that she cannot depend on a man, and that the decision to have an abortion is hers alone. In "The Broken Web," an older women tries to break free from the gender roles imposed by the Church and by society. She kills her husband in an argument but finds that she is still owned by him and their children, regardless of whether she is in Tijuana, Mexico, or in Fresno, California.

In "The Cariboo Café," two immigrant children become lost in the Los Angeles garment district. They are found by an old woman, herself an undocumented immigrant from Central America. She takes the children to her hotel room and then to the Cariboo Café, where the owner feeds the three and then later calls the police. Both the white café owner and the immigrant woman have sons who have died, the café owner's son in the Vietnam War and the woman's son in a repressive Central American regime. The two parents find substitutes in the two lost children, but the truth remains that their dreams of family had already been shattered by government repression in the United States and in Central America and Vietnam.

In "The Long Reconciliation," social and cultural roles control the triangle of a husband and wife in Mexico and the man with whom the wife betrays her husband. The three act out their fated gender roles as if living in a Greek tragedy.

In "Snapshots," Olga Ruiz, a woman divorced after thirty years of marriage, lives in memories triggered by her photo albums. A daughter's visit only reminds her of the constricted roles she had failed to fulfill in her marriage. In "Neighbors," an isolated old woman, Aura Rodriguez, is harassed by gang members in her changing Los Angeles neighborhood. She fires a pistol at someone she thinks is threatening her, but she ends up killing the homeless woman who has been staying with Fierro, the old man who lives in the house behind the home of Aura.

Critical Evaluation:

The Moths, and Other Stories, Helena María Viramontes's first short-story collection, contains eight tales and an introduction by Yvonne Yarbo-Bejarano. Two of the stories, "The Moths" and "The Cariboo Café," have been reprinted in a number of anthologies of twentieth century American literature. In the introduction the collection, Yarbo-Bejarano notes that, although Viramontes addresses the problems of racial prejudice and economic struggles, the emphasis is on the cultural and social values that shape these women. She also suggests that most of stories involve the conflict between the female character and the man who represents an oppressive authority figure.

Viramontes's writing is often characterized by shifting points of view and by fractured narratives that abruptly break off and sometimes leave readers confused. Her imagery, however, including a great deal of religious metaphor, is often poetic and occasionally merges into Magical Realism.

The short stories in *The Moths, and Other Stories* are noteworthy for raising crucial issues, especially in the growing and changing Latino and Latina communities. The girls and women in Viramontes's stories try to find their own identities in spite of oppressive institutions, especially the family and the Catholic Church, which proscribe their actions and dreams. Young women make the difficult transition from childhood to adulthood among family members who do not understand them and who therefore restrict their personal growth. Older women, both those trapped in marriage and those free but isolated and lonely, struggle to carve out meaning in their lives. Also, the stories often end violently. While Viramontes focuses on gender, she also understands how social and cultural values other than those concerning gender roles also mold women's lives. Viramontes's approach is feminist, one that explicitly addresses class and ethnic consciousness as well.

Furthermore, the stories are "border" stories in several ways. First, her characters inhabit the space between regions, that is, between the United States and Latin America. Second, her characters are young women moving between stages in human life, middle-aged women living in limbo between marriage and selfhood, and elderly women caught in the realm of isolation between society and death.

"The Moths," one of Viramontes's most celebrated stories, focuses on an adolescent girl's search for identity. The girl is estranged from the strict codes of her patriarchal family. She finds herself by rejecting her family's harsh values and by assuming responsibility for her grandmother and easing her death. The religious demands of the family are replaced by the folk-religious imagery of the grandmother's death scene, where Mexican legend is blended into traditional religious rituals: In the last scene of the story, small gray moths emerge from the grandmother's soul through her mouth (an image from Mexican folklore) as her granddaughter holds her in the bathtub.

As is so often the case in Viramontes's fiction, powerful and complex imagery underscores the theme of this story. Beneath the image of the girl and her grandmother in the tub, for example, lies the outline of Michelangelo's "Pieta," the famous statue of the Virgin Mary holding the body of Christ after the Crucifixion—an image of grief, death, and transfiguration. The bath in "The Moths" has become both a place of last rites and a place for a kind of baptism. The scene evokes both the sense of someone dying and the sense of someone being born—the girl appears to be giving birth to herself. By the end of the story, the girl has given birth to her new identity.

A similar family configuration is created in "The Cariboo Café," where an immigrant woman and then a café owner try to find their respective dead sons in the two lost children. Here, however, Viramontes evokes the workings of oppression and repression not through the family and Church but through governments in multiple countries. In the end, it is governmental policy that destroys any family. The folk imagery is present here in the La Llorona figure of Mexican legend, the weeping woman wandering in search of her lost children. "Neighbors" also finds its final resolution in violence, including the violent taking of another son. In this story as well, both the female and male characters live in isolation from society. The tragic violence of "The Long Reconciliation," too, is tempered by religious images and the music of a carousel.

Viramontes became a key figure in the emergence of Latina literature in the last quarter of the twentieth century. *The Moths, and Other Stories*, her first collection of short fiction, has firmly established in the literature her themes and her often poetic and powerful expression of them.

David Peck

Further Reading

Castillo, Debra A., and María Socorro Tabuenca Córdoba. *Border Women: Writing from La Frontera*. Minneapolis: University of Minnesota Press, 2002. An analysis of writing by women living on both sides of the U.S.-Mexican border, examining how these writers question accepted ideas about border identities.

Garza-Falcon, Leticia. *Gente Decente: A Borderlands Response to the Rhetoric of Dominance*. Austin: University of Texas Press, 1998. Chapter 6, "Media Reportage as History-in-the-Making," consists of detailed analyses of "The Cariboo Café" and "Neighbors." Part of a study of "border" literature and of cultural borderlands as places for refiguring cultural and social dominance and oppression through literature.

Green, Carol Hurd, and Mary Grimley Mason, eds. *American Women Writers*. New York: Continuum, 1994. The editors provide a brief biographical sketch of Viramontes as well as an analysis of the stories in *The Moths*. Emphasizes the portrayal of Chicana women with their strengths and weaknesses as they struggle with cultural and social restrictions. Notes, too, that many of the characters pay a price for rebelling against traditional values.

Mujcinovic, Fatima. *Postmodern Cross-culturalism and Politicization in U.S. Latina Literature: From Ana Castillo to Julia Alvarez*. Modern American Literature 42. New York: Peter Lang, 2004. Viramontes's work is examined in this literary and cultural analysis of the work of Mexican American, Puerto Rican, Cuban American, and Dominican American women writers. Mujcinovic views these writers' work from a contemporary feminist, political, postcolonial, and psychoanalytical perspective.

Saldivar-Hull, Sonia. *Feminism on the Border: Chicana Gender Politics and Literature*. Berkeley: University of

California Press, 2000. The last chapter in this study of Chicana feminist writers, "'I Hear the Women's Wails and I Know Them to Be My Own': From Mujer to Collective Identities in Helena María Viramontes's U.S. Third World," looks at several stories from Viramontes's collection in political and gender terms.

Sandoval, Anna Marie. *Toward a Latina Feminism of the Americas: Repression and Resistance in Chicana and Mexicana Literature.* Austin: University of Texas Press, 2008. Chapter 4, "Acts of Daily Resistance in Urban and Rural Settings: The Fiction of Helena María Viramontes,"

includes a long and probing analysis of "Cariboo Café" that identifies the political and social issues in the story.

Yarbo-Bejarano, Yvonne. *Introduction to "The Moths, and Other Stories."* Houston, Tex.: Arte Público Press, 1995. Yarbo-Bejarano discusses Viramontes's portrayal of women characters who struggle against the restrictions placed on them by Chicano culture, the Catholic Church, and the men in these women's lives. Provides a brief analysis of each story in the collection, showing that the stories deal with problems that Chicana women face at various stages of their lives.

Mourning Becomes Electra

Author: Eugene O'Neill (1888-1953)
First produced: 1931; first published, 1931
Type of work: Drama
Type of plot: Tragedy
Time of plot: Late 1860's
Locale: New England

Principal characters:
EZRA MANNON, a Civil War general
CHRISTINE, his wife
ORIN, his son
LAVINIA, his daughter
CAPTAIN ADAM BRANT, Christine's lover
HAZEL NILES and PETER NILES, cousins of the Mannons
SETH, the Mannons' caretaker

The Story:

The American Civil War is over, and in their New England home Christine and Lavinia Mannon await the homecoming of Ezra Mannon and his son, Orin. Lavinia, who adores her father, detests Christine because of Ezra's love for his wife. For her part, Christine is jealous of Orin's love and hates her husband and daughter. In this house of hidden hatred, Seth, the watchful gardener of the old mansion, sees that Lavinia also despises Captain Brant, a regular caller at the Mannon home.

The Mannons, descended from old New England stock, have their family skeleton. Dave Mannon, Ezra's brother, had run off with an American Indian woman named Marie Brantome. Seth, seeing the antagonism between Lavinia and her mother, discloses to Lavinia that Captain Brant is the son of Marie and Dave Mannon.

Embittered by her mother's illicit romance with Brant and jealous of her hold on Ezra, Lavinia forces Christine to send her lover away. Christine is too strong a woman to give in entirely to her daughter's dominance. She urges Brant to send her some poison. It is common knowledge that Ezra has heart trouble, and Christine plans to rid herself of the husband so that she will be free to marry Brant. Lavinia cruelly reminds

her mother that Orin, her favorite child, had been born while Ezra was away during the Mexican War.

When Ezra, a kind and just man, comes home, he realizes that Christine shrinks from him while pretending concern for his health. That night in their bedroom, Ezra and Christine quarrel over their failing marriage. Ezra has a heart attack, and when he gasps for his medicine Christine gives him the poison instead. As he lay dying in Lavinia's arms, the helpless man feebly but incoherently accuses Christine of his murder. Lavinia has no proof, but she does suspect that her mother had a part in her father's death.

After Ezra's death, Peter and Hazel Niles, cousins of the Mannons, visit the mansion. Peter is a rejected suitor of Lavinia, and Hazel is in love with Orin. Lavinia spies on her mother constantly. When Orin comes home, the two women vie for his trust, Lavinia trying to raise suspicion against her mother and Christine attempting to regain her son's close affection. Uncomfortable under her daughter's looks of silent, sneering accusation, Christine finally realizes that Lavinia found the box of poison. While Hazel, Peter, and Christine try to make a warm welcome for Orin, Lavinia hovers over the group like a specter of gloom. Able to get Orin alone before Lavinia can speak to him, Christine tells her son about Lavinia's suspicions concerning Captain Brant and Ezra's death, and she tries to convince him that Lavinia's distraction over Ezra's death has warped her mind.

Orin, whose affection for his mother makes him dislike Ezra, believes Christine, but the returned soldier swears that if he ever discovers that the story about Captain Brant were true, he would kill Brant. Desperate, Christine tells Lavinia that Orin's trust has been won and that Lavinia need not try to take advantage of his credulity. Lavinia merely stares at her mother in silent defiance, and under her daughter's cold stare, Christine's triumphant manner collapses into a pathetic plea that Lavinia not endanger Brant's life, for Orin has threatened to kill him.

When Lavinia slyly hints the truth to Orin, his childhood trust in her leads him, however unwillingly, to believe her story in part. Lavinia hints that Christine might run to Brant at the first opportunity. Orin agrees to wait for proof, but he repeats that if sufficient proof were offered he would kill Brant. Lavinia instructs Orin to maintain a pretense that he believes her to be mad.

Shortly after Ezra's funeral, Christine goes to Brant. Orin and Lavinia pretend to be paying a call on a nearby estate, but instead they follow their mother to Brant's ship, where they overhear the lovers planning to leave together. Although Orin is consumed with jealous hatred of Brant, Lavinia restrains him from impulsive action. When Christine leaves, Orin goes into the cabin and shoots Brant. Then the brother and sister rifle the ship's cabin and Brant's pockets to make the death appear to have been a robbery and murder.

Orin and Lavinia return to the Mannon mansion and tell Christine what they had done. Orin sees his mother's grief and falls to his knees, pleading with her to forgive him and to give her her love. Fearing he has lost his mother's affection, the bewildered boy rushes from the room, but Lavinia faces her mother victoriously. Christine goes into the house and shoots herself. Orin, in a frenzy of grief, accuses himself of his mother's murder.

Lavinia takes her brother on a long sea trip to help him overcome his guilt. When they return, Orin is completely under Lavinia's control, reciting in toneless speech that Christine had been an adulterer and a murderer, and that Orin had saved his mother from public hanging. He is changed in appearance and spirit; it is plain that strange thoughts of grief and guilt prey on his mind. During the trip Lavinia had grown to look and behave like Christine.

Lavinia now accepts Peter's love. When Orin sees his sister in Peter's embrace, he becomes angry for a brief moment before he congratulates them. When Orin becomes engaged

to Hazel, Lavinia is afraid to leave Orin alone with the girl for fear he will say too much about the past.

Orin begins to write a family history, urged by a remorseful desire to leave a record of the family crimes. Jealous of Lavinia's engagement to Peter, he threatens to expose her if she marries him. Orin keeps hinting to Lavinia that, like Christine, she is planning to poison him as Christine had poisoned the man who held her in bondage. Finally, driven to distraction by Orin's morbid possessive attitude toward her and by his incessantly recurring to their guilt, Lavinia suggests to the crazed Orin that he kill himself. As Peter holds Lavinia in his arms, Orin goes to the library to clean his pistol. His death is assumed to have been an accident.

Hazel suspects something vile and sinister behind Orin's accidental death. She goes to Lavinia and pleads with her not to ruin Peter by marrying him, but Lavinia denies that there is any reason to put off the marriage. While she speaks, however, Lavinia realizes that the dead Mannons will always rule her life. The others had been cowards, and had died. She will live. She sends Peter away. Then she orders Seth the gardener to board up the windows of the mansion. Alone, the last surviving Mannon, Lavinia enters the old house to spend the rest of her life with the dead.

Critical Evaluation:

Mourning Becomes Electra, a trilogy consisting of *Homecoming*, *The Hunted*, and *The Haunted*, is, though set at the end of the American Civil War, an adaptation of the greatest of Aeschylus's trilogies, *Oresteia* (458 B.C.E.; English translation, 1777). Eugene O'Neill's play illustrates the struggle between the life force and death, in which human attempts to express natural sensual desires and love of others or even of life itself are overcome by the many forms of death: repression derived from the Puritan religion, death-in-life engendered by society's values, isolation, war, and physical death. This struggle is present not only in the plot structure (each play culminates in a death) but also the setting, in the actors' faces, stances, and costumes, and in repetitive refrains.

Darkness, associated with death, pervades the plays: *Homecoming*, for instance, begins with the sunset, moves into twilight, and ends in the dark of night; *The Hunted* takes place at night; *The Haunted* spans two evenings and a late afternoon and indicates the inevitable coming of night, darkness, and death as Lavinia retreats to rejoin the host of dead Mannons.

The Mannon house itself, seen by the audience at the beginning of each play, stands amid the beauty and abundance of nature. It has a white Greek temple portico that O'Neill directs should resemble "an incongruous white mask fixed on the house to hide its somber grey ugliness." That the house is an ironic inversion of the affirmation and love of life associated with the Greeks is soon obvious. Christine thinks of the house as a tomb of cold, gray stone, and even Ezra compares it to a "white meeting house" of the Puritan Church, a temple dedicated to duty, to the denial of life and love, and to death. The house itself is not only alienated from nature but also isolated from the community, built on the foundations of pride and hatred and Puritan beliefs. Its cold facade and isolation symbolize the family that lives within it, whose name indicates their spiritual relationship to Satan's chief helper, Mammon. The curse of this house stems from the effects of materialism, Puritanism, alienation, and repression of what is natural—a death-in-life state.

The stiff, unnatural military bearing of the Mannons and the masklike look of their faces—on portraits of Orin and Ezra, on Christine's face when she is about to commit suicide, on Lavinia's face after Orin's death—are further evidence that the family is dead in the middle of life. Even the townspeople comment on the Mannons's "secret look." The look indicates the Mannons's denial of life, their repression of their sensual natures, and their refusal or inability to communicate with others. The dark costumes of the family also indicate the hold that death has on them and accentuates the green satin worn first by Christine and later by Lavinia as they struggle to break out of their tomb and reach life.

The instinct of love and life survives most strongly in the women, but even they are defeated. The search for pure love through a mother-son relationship is futile, for the Oedipal complex, as Orin finally realizes, leads beyond the bounds of a pure relationship. Family love, too, fails, as is evident in the relationships between Christine and Lavinia and Ezra and Orin. Even love between men and women is not sufficient to triumph over the alienation and loneliness of the Mannon world.

The leitmotif of the South Sea islands, symbols of escape from the death cycle of heredity and environment of New England society, is present throughout the three plays. The islands represent a return to Mother Earth, a hope of belonging in an environment far removed from Puritan guilt and materialism. Brant has been to these islands; Ezra wants to have one; Orin and Christine dream of being on one together, and they do finally travel to the islands but come to realize that they cannot become a permanent part of the island culture, but must return to the society to which they belong by birth and upbringing. The islands, symbols of escape, also finally fail the Mannons.

The Mannons try other avenues of escape from their deathly isolation. David Mannon attempts to escape with Marie Brantome but finally turns to drinking and suicide. Ezra escapes by concentrating on his business and then on the business of death—war—before he realizes the trap of death. Christine focuses her attempts to escape first on her son and then on Brant. Orin tries to escape through his mother's love, then through Hazel's, and finally, in desperation, in an incestuous relationship with Lavinia. Lavinia does not see the dimensions of the death trap and does not desire escape until her trip to the islands, where she experiences the abundance of guilt-free life. After her return, she is willing to let Orin die, just as Christine let Ezra die, to be free to love and live. Too late, however, she too feels the curse of the guilt associated with the Puritan beliefs and realizes that she cannot escape. Lavinia learns Orin was right: Those who kill also kill part of themselves each time they kill until finally nothing alive is left in them. She underscores this in her last conversation with Peter, remarking, "Always the dead between [us]. . . . The dead are too strong." Death itself is the only real escape for the alienated, guilt-ridden Mannons.

Compared to its source, Aeschylus's *Oresteia*, O'Neill's themes and characterization seem shallow. Christine, who goads Ezra into a heart attack because of her hatred of his attitude toward their sexual relationship and her love of Brant, is no match for Clytemnestra, who revenges the death of her daughter, her insulted pride, and hatred of Agamemnon with a bloody knife. The neurotic weak Orin is likewise a lesser character than Orestes, whose strong speech of triumphant justice over his mother's slain body breaks only with his horrified vision of the Furies. Ezra, however, is more human than Agamemnon, and Lavinia's complexities far outstrip those of Electra: Lavinia's recognition and acceptance of her fate is in the noble tradition of the tragic hero.

The radical difference in the intentions of the two playwrights accounts for some of these differences. Aeschylus, whose major themes are concerned with the victory of human and divine laws, concludes his trilogy with the establishment of justice on Earth and Orestes' reconciliation with society and the gods; he affirms that good has come out of evil, order from chaos, and wisdom from suffering. In *Mourning Becomes Electra*, the curse is not lifted but confirmed at the end, as Lavinia gives up her futile struggle and succumbs to the psychological "furies" that drive human beings. Although O'Neill's analysis may occasionally be oversimplified, *Mourning Becomes Electra* is one of the few twentieth century American plays that can truly be said to evoke the tragic emotions of pity, fear, and even awe.

"Critical Evaluation" by Ann E. Reynolds

Further Reading

Berlin, Normand, ed. *Eugene O'Neill, Three Plays: "Mourning Becomes Electra," "The Iceman Cometh," "Long Day's Journey into Night": A Casebook.* Basingstoke, England: Macmillan, 1989. A good introduction. Includes excerpts from O'Neill's working diary, tracing the play's development from inception to second galleys. Contains four reviews of the original production and seven critical studies dealing with character, theme, and style.

Bloom, Harold, ed. *Eugene O'Neill.* Updated ed. New York: Bloom's Literary Criticism, 2007. Collection of critical essays, including Doris Alexander's analysis of *Mourning Becomes Electra.*

Bogard, Travis. *Contour in Time.* New York: Oxford University Press, 1988. Provides a detailed comparison of *Mourning Becomes Electra* and plays by Euripides and Aeschylus, noting the shift in emphasis from the theological to the psychological. Discusses the play's importance as historical drama, focusing on Calvinist tradition and Puritan repression in New England.

Floyd, Virginia. *The Plays of Eugene O'Neill.* New York: Frederick Ungar, 1985. An excellent introduction. Includes a brief biography and interpretive analysis of each play, identifying themes, key words, and ideas. Relates *Mourning Becomes Electra* to its Greek source and to O'Neill's life.

Gelb, Arthur, and Barbara Gelb. *O'Neill.* New York: Harper & Row, 1962. Comprehensive study of O'Neill's life and work based on his writings and more than four hundred interviews with family members, friends, and critics. Traces his personal growth and his growth as an artist. Follows the development of *Mourning Becomes Electra* from idea to production.

Moorton, Richard F., ed. *Eugene O'Neill's Century: Centennial Views on America's Foremost Tragic Dramatist.* New York: Greenwood Press, 1991. Presents essays from a variety of perspectives, including theatrical arts, psychology, philosophy, and classics, which analyze and psychoanalyze character and theme in O'Neill's work.

Shaughnessy, Edward L. *Down the Nights and Down the Days: Eugene O'Neill's Catholic Sensibility.* Notre Dame, Ind.: University of Notre Dame Press, 1996. Although O'Neill renounced Catholicism when he was a teenager, Shaughnessy finds evidence that he retained some of his Catholic upbringing and brought this moral sensibility to his plays, including *Mourning Becomes Electra.*

Törnqvist, Egil. *Eugene O'Neill: A Playwright's Theatre.* Jefferson, N.C.: McFarland, 2004. Demonstrates how O'Neill was a controlling personality in the texts and performances of his plays. Describes his working conditions and the multiple audiences for his works. Examines the titles, settings in time and place, names and addresses, language, and allusions to other works in his dramas.

Voglino, Barbara. "Success at Last: Closure in *Mourning Becomes Electra.*" In *"Perverse Mind": Eugene O'Neill's Struggle with Closure.* Madison, N.J.: Fairleigh Dickinson University Press, 1999. Focuses on nine plays written at different periods of O'Neill's career to demonstrate how the failed endings of the early works developed into the successful closures of his later plays.

The Mousetrap

Author: Agatha Christie (1890-1976)
First produced: 1952; first published, 1954
Type of work: Drama
Type of plot: Detective and mystery
Time of plot: Mid-twentieth century
Locale: Berkshire, England

Principal characters:
MOLLIE RALSTON, the owner of Monkswell Manor, a guest house
GILES RALSTON, her husband
CHRISTOPHER WREN,
MRS. BOYLE,
MAJOR METCALF,
MISS CASEWELL, and
MR. PARAVICINI, the guests at Monkswell Manor
DETECTIVE SERGEANT TROTTER, a police officer

The Story:

Early one winter afternoon, a brutal murder occurs on Culver Street in Paddington. Witnesses heard someone whistling the nursery rhyme "Three Blind Mice" just before the victim had screamed. Later that afternoon, in the Great Hall of Monkswell Manor, Mollie and Giles Ralston prepare for the opening of their guest house, worrying about the effects of the severe snowstorm outside and their own inexperience in their new venture. Giles leaves, joking that since they know so little about their guests some might even be criminals. Alone, Mollie turns on the radio, where a description of the Culver Street murderer is being broadcast. The announcer mentions the suspect's dark overcoat, light scarf, and felt hat just as Mollie picks up Giles's dark coat, scarf, and hat.

Shortly afterward, the first guest, Christopher Wren, arrives, followed by Mrs. Boyle and Major Metcalf, who had been forced by the weather to share a taxi from the train station. Mrs. Boyle immediately begins to criticize the manor and the Ralstons's inexperience, but she refuses Giles's offer to take her back to the station. Moments later, the last expected guest, Miss Casewell, rings the bell. After settling the guests in their rooms, Mollie and Giles lament that they all seem either peculiar or unpleasant. To their surprise, the doorbell rings once again and an elderly foreign gentleman, Mr. Paravicini, staggers in. He tells them that his car is trapped in a snowdrift and that Monkswell Manor would soon be cut off by the snow.

The next morning, Mollie receives a call from the Berkshire police, who tell her that they have discovered a connection between the Culver Street murder and the manor; because the manor is now snowbound, a Sergeant Trotter will ski there to provide them with protection. When Trotter arrives, they learn that the victim in the Culver Street murder, together with her husband, had several years earlier been convicted of criminal neglect after the death of the youngest of three children placed in their protection. A notebook found near the crime scene held two addresses, one on Culver Street and the other of Monkswell Manor. Underneath were written the words "This is the first" and the notes of "Three Blind Mice." The police assume that one of the older children had chosen to avenge the brother. The girl in the case had disappeared long ago, and the eldest boy had deserted from the army after being diagnosed as schizophrenic. Trotter advises that anyone with a connection to the case should reveal it, since they could be in danger, but no one responds. After Trotter leaves to search the house, Major Metcalf accuses Mrs. Boyle of being the magistrate who had sent the children to the home. She admits this but denies having done anything wrong.

Trotter, returning to telephone his supervisor, finds that the phone line is dead and investigates. Mrs. Boyle enters the empty hall and shuts the door. When the door opens again, she turns nervously, but relaxes when she recognizes the person. Someone whistles the tune "Three Blind Mice" and the lights go out. A quick scuffle ensues, followed by the sound of a fall. Moments later, Mollie finds Mrs. Boyle's body.

Trotter questions the remaining guests, but no one can produce an alibi for the murder. He dismisses all but Mollie, with whom he discusses his suspicions. Wren is the right age to be the eldest child; Casewell might be the sister; Paravicini is a possibility, too, for he walks like a much younger man and is wearing makeup; Metcalf could be the children's father. When Trotter asks about Giles, Mollie reveals they had only known each other for three weeks before they were married. Mollie insists that Giles had been in the country at the time of the first murder, but Trotter shows her Giles's coat, from the pocket of which he pulls a London paper.

When he discovers that his skis are missing, Trotter reassembles everyone. After examining alibis again, he suddenly announces that he has a clue but needs to reenact Mrs. Boyle's murder. Each person is to duplicate someone else's movements, while Trotter plays the victim in the empty hall. Mollie is assigned to the drawing room. Trotter calls her in and tells her that he is the oldest child. He plans to kill her because she had not responded when his young brother had written to her, his kind young teacher, for help. Mollie pleads that she received the letter too late, but Trotter does not listen to her. He is about to strangle her when Major Metcalf and Miss Casewell enter. Casewell tells Trotter that Mollie is his sister. Metcalf reveals that he is the real detective. When Mollie and Giles discuss their both having been in London, they discover that each had gone there to buy an anniversary present for the other.

Critical Evaluation:

Agatha Christie's name is synonymous with the mystery novel, and her books have been translated into more than one hundred languages. Almost all of her novels remain in print. Although some critics consider her work to be no more than popular fiction, the mystery novel has become an increasingly respectable literary genre. Critical studies have been devoted to many aspects of the field, in particular to Christie, one of the finest writers of the classic detective tale.

The traditional mystery story has a particular set of rules, in which the writer sets a puzzle, provides clues for the reader to follow, and then delivers a solution to the puzzle that is both a surprise to the reader and consistent with the accumulated evidence of the story. *The Mousetrap* provides a perfect illustration of how Christie did precisely that and at the same time found new ways to combine those elements.

The Mousetrap, originally the short story "Three Blind Mice," which was adapted first into a radio drama and then into a full-length play, contains many Christie trademarks. One of these is the setting, which, as in most of her works, is the English countryside. Yet this frequently serves as little more than a backdrop. Christie likes to cut the setting—and thus the characters—off from the rest of the world so as to create a closed circle of suspects. In *Ten Little Indians* (1943), the characters are stranded on an island; in *Murder on the Orient Express* (1934), they are traveling on a train; and in many of the stories, including Christie's first novel, *The Mysterious Affair at Styles: A Detective Story* (1920), they are gathered together in a country house. *The Mousetrap* recreates this setting with the Great Hall at Monkswell Manor. Christie assembles her characters and then isolates them with a snowstorm; from that point on, the outside world no longer intrudes. There is no mention of politics or names and events in the news. Political realities do not exist, except in the most general of terms; Mrs. Boyle accuses Miss Casewell of being a Socialist, and she laments the lack of responsibility of the lower classes. The play's reality, its true setting, is a tightly closed circle of individuals.

In this world, plot development is paramount. Every narrative detail and character description serves to move the drama forward. In fact, Christie deleted the first nine pages of an early draft of the play, where the murder had been described at greater length, to focus more quickly on the narrow circle and the puzzle. The curtain opens on a dark stage and the audience hears shrill whistling, a scream, and police whistles. The lights go up to a radio broadcast account of the murder in an empty room; the announcer adds that a heavy snowstorm is descending on the English countryside. Before a single actor has even been seen, the audience is caught up in the middle of the puzzle.

The stage directions for the play are detailed, since much of the action depends on staging. Red herrings are thrown to the audience with both sight and sound clues. Mollie's glove contains a London bus ticket; Christopher Wren wanders about mysteriously, whistling a succession of nursery rhymes. Gestures, looks, silences, all are designed to focus suspicion on one character after another. These bits of misdirection are carefully designed to hide the clues that reveal the true murderer.

Critics have pointed out the lack of character development in Christie's books, but this is a deliberate device designed to keep attention on the puzzle. Character development would interfere with the play's momentum. Christie's characters are primarily suspects. Every character in *The Mousetrap* is made to seem guilty by at least one gesture or word. Wren is the most obvious suspect: He has many characteristics that match what has been revealed about the murderer, for he deserted from the army and suffered from the death of his mother. If Christie had provided further details about his unhappy childhood, she would have not only changed the pace and focus of the play but also eliminated one of her more promising suspects.

In her fiction, Christie relies on a set of stock characters that, like her settings, she uses over and over. These stereotypes tend to be defined more by role than by individual personality. Moreover, use of such stereotypes allows Christie to provide frequently humorous insight into the middle- and upper-middle-class social world that predominates in her writing. When personality traits emerge, they often do so as a single or defining characteristic. This is particularly true in *The Mousetrap*, where, for example, Mrs. Boyle establishes herself as an overbearing, fault-finding bully with her first few speeches, and stage directions describe Casewell as a "manly" young woman.

Although Christie's characters may be stereotypical, they are rare in the world of the classic thriller. Traditionally, the narrator, the detective, and the young lovers are automatically removed from the suspect list. There are no such guarantees with Christie. Her murderer, as in *The Mousetrap*, is often not just the last person to be suspected but the one person who is never considered at all. This clever combination of suspense and humor, which keeps the audience puzzled and entertained until the last page, is the hallmark of a Christie mystery and one of the reasons for her enduring popularity.

Mary Mahony

Further Reading

Bargainnier, Earl F. *The Gentle Art of Murder: The Detective Fiction of Agatha Christie*. Bowling Green, Ohio: Bowling Green State University Popular Press, 1980. This book takes an affectionate but clear-eyed look at Christie's faults and fortes. Especially interesting are Bargainnier's discussions of passages that parody the detective fiction of Christie and others and of Christie's indirect comments on the contemporary sociological situation.

Bunson, Matthew. *The Complete Christie: An Agatha Christie Encyclopedia*. New York: Pocket Books, 2001. Reference work containing alphabetical entries on all characters, cross-referenced to the novel or story in which they appear; plot synopses; listings of all film, television, and radio adaptations of Christie's work and of documentaries about Christie; a biography; and a bibliography.

Christie, Agatha. *Agatha Christie: An Autobiography.* New York: Dodd, Mead, 1977. Charmingly written memoir in which the author discusses her life and her attitudes about writing. Includes descriptions of incidents that inspired *The Mousetrap* and brief evaluations of characters, as well as insight into methods of plot development.

Keating, H. R. F., ed. *Agatha Christie: First Lady of Crime.* London: Weidenfeld & Nicolson, 1977. A diverse collection of essays, including a discussion of *The Mousetrap* by drama critic J. C. Trewin.

Makinen, Merja. *Agatha Christie: Investigating Femininity.* New York: Palgrave Macmillan, 2006. Makinen sets out to disprove what many critics before her have asserted: that Christie created her female characters to be weak and inferior to their male counterparts. She emphasizes the ways in which the female characters play vital roles outside the domestic sphere and therefore challenge traditional notions of femininity. Makinen proves that Christie's female characters are as successful and strong as her male characters.

Murdoch, Derrick. *The Agatha Christie Mystery.* Toronto, Ont.: Pagurian Press, 1976. Discusses the royal impetus that led to the radio play *Three Blind Mice* and the Shakespearean source of the new title *The Mousetrap.* Offers a final summing up of critical judgments by the author and others.

Osborne, Charles. *The Life and Crimes of Agatha Christie: A Biographical Companion to the Works of Agatha Christie.* New York: St. Martin's Press, 2001. Provides literary evaluations of Christie's fiction. Includes a discussion of the development and production of *The Mousetrap*, as well as interesting statistics. Helpful bibliography of Christie's fiction identifies her writing by type and by detective.

Robyns, Gwen. *The Mystery of Agatha Christie.* Garden City, N.Y.: Doubleday, 1978. Informative biography that provides literary and theatrical evaluations. Includes details about the staging of *The Mousetrap* and interviews with individuals involved in the production.

Thompson, Laura. *Agatha Christie: An English Mystery.* London: Headline Review, 2007. Comprehensive biography, written with the cooperation of Christie's family and with full access to unpublished, letters, and notebooks. Examines Christie's eleven-day disappearance in 1926, and the novels she wrote under the pseudonym Mary Westmacott.

Wagoner, Mary. *Agatha Christie.* Boston: Twayne, 1986. An extremely helpful beginner's source and a comprehensive literary analysis of Christie's fiction. Also provides insight into the rules and traditions of the classic detective story. Classifies Christie's main writing styles and humorous analyses of manners. Includes an annotated bibliography.

York, R. A. *Agatha Christie: Power and Illusion.* New York: Palgrave Macmillan, 2007. Reevaluates Christie's novels, which traditionally have been described as "cozy" mysteries. Asserts that although these works may appear to depict a stable world of political conservatism, conventional sex and class roles, and clear moral choices, this world is not as safe as it appears to be. Notes how Christie's mysteries also depict war, social mobility, ambiguous morality, and violence.

A Moveable Feast

Author: Ernest Hemingway (1899-1961)
First published: 1964
Type of work: Autobiography

Principal personages:
ERNEST HEMINGWAY
HADLEY HEMINGWAY, his first wife
F. SCOTT FITZGERALD
ZELDA FITZGERALD
JAMES JOYCE
SYLVIA BEACH, bookshop proprietor
EZRA POUND
GERTRUDE STEIN
ERNEST WALSH, a poet
EVAN SHIPMAN, a poet
JULES PASCIN, a French painter
WYNDHAM LEWIS
RALPH CHEEVER DUNNING, an opium-smoking poet
FORD MADOX FORD

Perhaps more than any other writer of the twentieth century, Ernest Hemingway laid bare the violent realities lurking beneath all human experience. His aim from the very beginning was to represent those realities as precisely as he could, never minimizing their destructive potential. Life, he wrote early in his career, was uncompromising. It punished the fine and the foul impartially, taking its own grim time, choosing its own grim methods. The bleak and simple wisdom is given form in the retreat from Caporetto, the wound of Jake Barnes, the wreckage of the old man's great fish.

In his attempts to render, and thus confront, the desolating facts of life, Hemingway was himself uncompromising. He developed a subdued and stoic prose that betokened what he thought the only meaningful response to the inevitable ruin that time visits on everyone. Through the exercise of control, individuals could confer grace and dignity on defeat, and though time would destroy it need not humiliate. Even Hemingway's symbols reflected this tight dialectic, compressing it into local realities that were images of the eternal shape of the contest, as in his picture of the bullfight. In the rituals of the arena, the bull would always die, and ultimately the bullfighter would too. The animal, however, would go down charging, whereas the fighter at his best performed a ceremony of courage, delicacy, and precision. Though neither would survive, neither would retreat from the confrontation with death.

In *A Moveable Feast*, written in the last years of Hemingway's life and published after his death, there is in one respect a disquieting relaxation of that old standard. Though much of the prose is as fine as ever, Hemingway, in remembering his early years in Paris, engages in nervous battle for first place among his writing contemporaries, those individuals whom with the passage of time had gained almost mythic stature. Ezra Pound, James Joyce, Ford Madox Ford, and F. Scott and Zelda Fitzgerald had begun to be seen as figures in a novel, endlessly alive on the streets along the Seine, in Gertrude Stein's apartment, at the sidewalk cafés, and in the warm and cluttered interior of Sylvia Beach's bookshop, Shakespeare and Company. In *A Moveable Feast*, however, Hemingway reduces these figures not by distortion of facts but by skillful placing of reductive emphases. It is as though Hemingway, before entering the ring, had drugged his bull.

Nevertheless, the writing is so compelling that the reader must make a special effort to remember that this is not an objective account of that literary generation that provoked as much interest in itself as in its works. As historical document, the book adds to an understanding of the past, sometimes striking a comic note, as in clarifying that Stein's famous remark, "You are all a generation perdue," or a lost generation, originated with an angry garage manager giving a tongue-lashing to an attendant repairing Stein's automobile.

More often there is something graceless about Hemingway's selection of detail. A delicate confidence once entrusted to him by F. Scott Fitzgerald is exposed so casually that one can only conclude Hemingway's intention was to enlarge his own stature by reducing that of his friend. Shaken by Zelda's assertion that he was built too small to satisfy a woman, Fitzgerald had brought himself, with great difficulty, to ask Hemingway's opinion. After a quick inspection in the men's room of a restaurant, Hemingway assured him that he was all right and went on to provide some typical locker-room information on technique. Fitzgerald, of course, remained doubtful. Though this may be precisely the way it all happened, the incident is tilted favorably toward Hemingway, who is clearly meant to represent hero, father, authority, potency figure. There is even a hint that Zelda may not have been entirely wrong and that Hemingway was simply being a good, sympathetic, and protective friend. The passage undercuts itself and gives itself away as not being what it proclaims to be.

An equally private detail from Stein's life is handled in the same callous manner, and Hemingway is similarly self-congratulatory in his treatment of other famous friends. Many of the sketches seem designed exclusively to deflate the competition. Hemingway seldom values someone else valued for something achieved; rather, his most complex friends are treated as though they were equal merely to the worst of their traits. Ford is presented as someone to avoid looking at, in whose presence others must hold their breath and whose arrival at an outdoor café could foul the others' drinks. Wyndham Lewis is presented as unbearably supercilious and gratuitously unkind, the nastiest looking man Hemingway had ever seen, having the eyes of a failed rapist. Sometimes the competition is shown to be downright unsavory, sometimes obtuse, sometimes merely ineffectual (perhaps the unkindest cut of all). There is cynicism in much of this, a failure of sensitivity, and frequently a smell of contrivance.

By contrast, Joyce is treated with kindness, though he is not often mentioned. Pound is depicted as a sort of saint who helped other writers by raising money, dispensing advice, and even admiring their works simply because they were friends. There is warmth, too, in the overall treatment of Fitzgerald, though he comes off as somewhat absurd. In the account of Hemingway's friendship with Stein, where he writes of helping her proofread her works, she is described serving him fine liqueurs while entertaining, encouraging, and criticizing him. There is a sense throughout, however, that the potency of his friends is limited while his is not.

Beneath these obvious qualities in the sketches runs another current, which is dreamlike and compelling: Hemingway's idyllic remembrance of the time with his first wife in their small apartment over a sawmill on the rue Notre-Dame-des-Champs. This undercurrent is a literature of nostalgia, a beautiful story of crisp winter walks, fire-heated rooms, tender conversation. This quiet world, surely more perfect in recorded memory than in lived reality, is kept apart from the other, that land of tension, celebrity, desecration. Like Huck

Finn's river, the apartment over the sawmill is a place of renewal, a sanctified region beyond the touch of ugliness. Hadley Hemingway is always both lover and mother, the couple's Paris a garden and playground. This is myth, not history. Though built on fact, the tale is transformed by selection and emphasis into a dream of perpetual childhood. In this world, hunger is not pain but a sharpening of the perceptions, an internal signal of one's youth. Poverty is in itself a condition of grace.

Despite descriptions of embarrassingly adolescent talk between Hadley and Hemingway, despite a strange shifting of guilt when the dream is finally betrayed by Hemingway (it is the rich who are responsible), the quiet, lyric power of the romance is irresistible. Even the scraps of wisdom, stripped down, fragmentary, and always too simple, seem impressive and right in their context—on the sense of loss, for instance, which all things, good or bad, evoked after the loss. The loss of the good made demands, required the reconstruction of one's life. It is not the idea here that moves readers but the world implied by it, a simplified, manageable world in which good and bad are distinguishable and capable of manifesting their qualities even in their absence. In Hemingway's prose, this is the world of the clean, well-lighted legend from which to look out upon reality, knowing that it will finally destroy what exists but knowing, too, that it is there.

Further Reading

Bloom, Harold, ed. *Ernest Hemingway*. Philadelphia: Chelsea House, 2005. Contains articles analyzing Hemingway's work by a variety of writers, including such eminent literary critics as Edmund Wilson, Robert Penn Warren, and Carlos Baker.

Brenner, Gerry. *A Comprehensive Companion to Hemingway's "A Moveable Feast": Annotation to Interpretation.* 2 vols. Lewiston, N.Y.: Edwin Mellen Press, 2001. Provides a line-by-line reading and analysis of the text, biographies of all of the people mentioned in the book, photographs of the main characters, maps, a chronology of events, and a bibliography.

Burwell, Rose Marie. *Hemingway: The Postwar Years and the Posthumous Novels*. New York: Cambridge University Press, 1996. Burwell's biographical analysis of Hemingway's last years devotes a chapter to *A Moveable Feast*.

Kert, Bernice. *The Hemingway Women*. New York: W. W. Norton, 1983. Provides biographical details of Hemingway and the women in his life, including for the years 1920 to 1926, which focus on Hadley Hemingway and Pauline Pfeiffer.

Lynn, Kenneth S. *Hemingway.* New York: Simon & Schuster, 1987. A standard biography of Hemingway, which places the writing of *A Moveable Feast* in the context of the author's approaching suicide.

Messent, Peter. "Coda: *A Moveable Feast.*" In *Ernest Hemingway.* New York: St. Martin's Press, 1992. Places the work in the context of Hemingway's larger, utopian project of a pure art that would re-create out of the historical world a linguistic one entered at will and one that is equally valid and eternally valuable. Shows how, by merging his voice at the end of his career with his voice as a young writer and the voice of his fictional young writer, Nick Adams, Hemingway achieved some of his best literary effects.

Renza, Louis A. "The Importance of Being Ernest." *South Atlantic Quarterly* 88, no. 3 (Summer, 1989): 661-689. Argues that Hemingway felt such a hunger to write true sentences that the very act of writing them created a world as real as the one to which they referred. At the same time, his need to make money threatened his dedication to high artistic standards.

Tavernier-Courbin, Jacqueline. *Ernest Hemingway's "A Moveable Feast": The Making of Myth.* Boston: Northeastern University Press, 1991. Gathering and carefully weighing extensive evidence about the play of imagination and memory in Hemingway's conceptualization and composition, Tavernier-Courbin provides an objective examination of fact and fiction and a balanced analysis of what the work reveals about its author. Includes chronologies, maps, and manuscript revisions.

Trogdon, Robert W., ed. *Ernest Hemingway: A Literary Reference.* New York: Carroll & Graf, 2002. A compendium of information about Hemingway, with photographs, letters, interviews, essays, speeches, book reviews, copies of some of his unfinished manuscripts, and his comments about his and other writers' works.

Wagner-Martin, Linda. *Ernest Hemingway: A Literary Life.* New York: Palgrave Macmillan, 2007. Examines Hemingway's life, especially his troubled relationship with his parents. Wagner-Martin makes insightful connections between the writer's personal life, his emotions, and his writing.

The Moviegoer

Author: Walker Percy (1916-1990)
First published: 1961
Type of work: Novel
Type of plot: Social realism
Time of plot: Early 1960's
Locale: New Orleans, Louisiana

Principal characters:
JOHN BICKERSON "BINX" BOLLING, an unmarried southern stockbroker
KATE CUTRER, Binx's beautiful distant cousin
EMILY CUTRER, Binx's great-aunt and Kate's stepmother
JULES CUTRER, Emily's husband and Kate's father
WALTER WADE, Kate's fiancé

The Story:

Binx Bolling is on a search—a quest for the meaning of life in modern America. He often visits his great-aunt Emily's home for lunch, where he talks to her about the cosmic importance of the lives of people they know. She wants him to go to medical school, but he frequents movies and watches television as a way of distracting himself from domestic realities and from personal involvement with those around him. He is a stockbroker who has affairs with his various secretaries.

At one of Binx's luncheons with his great-aunt, she elicits his help in warding off a "nervous break-down" that is evidently forthcoming for his distant cousin, Kate Cutrer. Aunt Emily has found Kate's hidden bottles of whiskey and sodium pentobarbital. Binx agrees to help; that is, he agrees to give Kate attention and keep her distracted. At a subsequent lunch, Walter Wade shows up to talk football and make preparations for Mardi Gras with Uncle Jules. Walter, an old fraternity brother of Binx, and Kate are engaged to marry.

Binx and Kate decide to watch the Mardi Gras parade together, in which they see Walter and after which they attend a movie. Slowly, over time, they fall in love with each other, and Kate cancels her engagement to Walter. Binx is attracted to his new secretary, Sharon Kincaid, and spends time with her. He eventually realizes, however, that it is Kate whom he really wants. It is revealed, in turn, that Sharon is in love with another man.

When Binx proposes marriage to Kate, she delays an answer. At the office the next morning, a Saturday, he invites Sharon to go swimming with him and to have a "date" for the day. She accepts, and they have a minor car accident. They exchange platitudes of love at the picnic on the beach. Binx takes Sharon to meet his mother and other family members; then, predictably, they go to yet another movie.

After going to church with his mother, Binx returns to the home of his aunt Emily, where he learns that Kate, that very morning, has attempted suicide. Emily discovered Kate before she died and had telephoned for a doctor, who came to the house and pumped the whiskey and pentobarbital from her stomach. Emily and Binx discuss what is to be done about Kate, with nothing being resolved. Binx then converses with Kate herself, but toward no immediate end. Even though both have a great understanding of each other, this understanding is self-defeating. Binx cannot lie and tells her that life has meaning, for he had found none for himself.

Binx is scheduled to make a business trip to Chicago. At the last moment he decides to take Kate with him, but he does not inform Emily. They travel by train, and both seem to be doing fine with each other and with themselves. The trip is somewhat spoiled for Kate because they discover another couple on the train whom they knew. Binx and Kate discuss the meaning of life and death and their own roles in the universe. Binx returns persistently to thoughts about his search for meaning in life. They make numerous references to movies. They conclude little of importance. Kate mutters, "Losing hope is not so bad. There's something worse: losing hope and hiding it from yourself." Kate and Binx attempt to have sex in the sleeper of the train but fail. In Chicago, Binx perfunctorily takes care of his business appointments, leaving Kate at the hotel. The two of them then go to yet another movie. Back at the hotel, Emily telephones. She is furious because Binx had taken Kate to Chicago without telling anyone. They leave Chicago by bus to return home.

Back in New Orleans, Kate and Binx avoid most of the Mardi Gras parade and activities. They return to Emily's house, where she castigates Binx, excessively, for taking Kate with him without telling anyone. The conversation becomes rather a social diatribe, with Emily making observations about manners, the class system, history, heritage, literature, art, and responsibility. Binx is dutifully apologetic but obviously cannot undo what had been done. Emily claims that "Ours is the only civilization in history which has en-

shrined mediocrity as its national ideal." Binx agrees with her. Ironically, it is Binx who understands the source of this "enshrined mediocrity."

Binx escapes his aunt's wrathful gentility. Kate is waiting for him, having overheard every word of the conversation. It is, on that day, Binx's thirtieth birthday. He concludes from his "dark pilgrimage" of thirty years that "Nothing remains but desire"—desire for sex, desire for life, desire to search. The awareness of the futility of such efforts is for him, inevitable.

In the end, Kate and Binx marry, as does his secretary, Sharon Kincaid, and her boyfriend. Two of Binx's family members (his uncle Jules and his brother Scott) die. The two newlyweds are left alone. The search for life has not concluded, but it has somehow ceased to matter.

Critical Evaluation:

Walker Percy's novel *The Moviegoer* is in many ways the first important novel of the New South. The setting is not agricultural; the characters are not grotesques, larger-than-life figureheads, "rednecks," or symbols. The plot does not hinge upon treasure buried in the backyard. Rather, it is a world in which air conditioners, fast living, color televisions, and movies have replaced mint juleps and moss trees.

In this New South, existentialism has arrived. The main character, Binx Bolling, views himself as a character in a film. He is alienated from nature, society, family, culture, and God. Only films, those impersonal images on the screen, seem to offer him any vision into the purpose and meaning of his own life. He possesses attention only for his own self as a character. Watching movies becomes, for Binx Bolling, watching life, and watching life becomes living life; or, at least, watching life is a substitute for living it. It is as close as he can get. Binx cannot live life: He cannot go to medical school as his aunt would have it. He cannot fall in love with one of his secretaries, although like characters in a movie, he can have sex with them. He cannot go to church; he cannot even go to Chicago for the week in any meaningful way. He is trapped like a character in a film—unable to control the script, the action, or the projector.

In the opening chapter of the novel, Binx realizes that all the people around him are "dead." They are far more lifeless and immobile than characters on the screen. He is attracted to and repulsed by the Elysian Fields, the nearby suburb of New Orleans. It is a place with a significant name but no substance. It is the new landscape of the South and America.

Much of Binx's efforts center on some sort of self-announced search that he is on. The author toys with this as a literary scheme and device. On one hand, Binx's search is for the meaning of life, the Holy Grail, the Helen of Troy, the Elysian Fields, the wine of communion—for union with self and God. On the other, it is only a pale imitation of these things in the shadowy no-man's-land of modern life. There is, Percy perhaps implies, not without irony, no Holy Grail in contemporary life unless it is sex. Binx is left to conclude that "Nothing remains but desire."

Binx is on a search for the meaning of life, so the novel proceeds in a formulaic fashion. Binx ponders and thinks; he has sophomoric discussions; he tries to find answers in others and in relationships; he goes to church and studies the arts and literature; he would enter a profession to find meaning in work; he has affairs with women that come to nothing, not even pain. His business trip to Chicago is something of a parody of an odyssey in which a young person leaves home a boy and returns a man. Binx, however, leaves home a boy and returns as one. Kate is something of an anti-Helen. She, too, is emotionally defunct and incapable of love. Her drugs, whiskey, and suicide attempts are also indicative of an alienation that is so complete it amounts to selfishness. It is also a renunciation of the role of women in Percy's New South.

Binx returns home (to Gentilly, Louisiana) to marry Kate, bury the dead in the family, soothe his aunt Emily, and proceed with business, which turns out to be life as usual. He learns that he can do no better than go to movies, for movies are momentary events in which life becomes interesting. The fantasy produced by the screen is more rewarding and fulfilling than the monotony of life at home and work and marriage. Watching movies affords not so much distraction as pretentious involvement with life. Binx cannot be a movie star, which is to say that he cannot have a glamorous, exciting, and rewarding life. What he can do, though, is see himself as a character in a movie and become detached from self, and all the problems that go along with having a role. This detachment is not permanent, but it is one way of dealing with life.

Binx is the prototype of all the main characters in Percy's later novels. A white, middle-class male suffering from adolescent angst, incipient middle age, distraction, alienation, and paranoia, Binx embodies and foreshadows such characters as Will Barrett in *The Last Gentleman*, Lance Lamar in *Lancelot*, and Tom More in *Love in the Ruins* and *The Thanatos Syndrome*. Binx, a self-defined and self-explained

castaway, is representative of persons living in a universe where love and meaning cannot be found.

Carl Singleton

Further Reading

Desmond, John F. *Walker Percy's Search for Community*. Athens: University of Georgia Press, 2004. Desmond examines Percy's novels to analyze his continuing concerns about community, describing how he formed his ideas about community from various philosophers and his Catholic beliefs

Hardy, John Edward. "Man, Beast, and Others in Walker Percy." In *Walker Percy: Novelist and Philosopher*, edited by Jan Nordby Gretlund and Karl-Heinz Westarp. Jackson: University Press of Mississippi, 1991. Discusses Binx Bolling by comparing him to other main characters in Percy's works.

Kobre, Michael. *Walker Percy's Voices*. Athens: University of Georgia Press, 2000. Analyzes Percy's novels from the perspective of Russian literary theorist Mikhail Bakhtin. Kobre is especially interested in Percy's characters, who must sort out the conflicting inner voices of friends, therapists, family, and others until they eventually determine their own identity.

Lawson, Lewis A. "Moviegoing in *The Moviegoer*." *Southern Quarterly* 18, no. 3 (1980): 26-42. One of the best discussions of the overall metaphor of *The Moviegoer*, seeing films. Lawson shows how, for Percy, watching films becomes an alternative to living life.

Samway, Patrick H. *Walker Percy: A Life*. New York: Farrar, Straus and Giroux, 1997. An authorized biography, written with Percy's approval and assistance. Samway portrays Percy, whom he met in a writing program, as a writer of great intellect and passion.

Tharpe, Jac. *Walker Percy*. Boston: Twayne, 1983. Provides critical discussion of Percy's philosophy and essays, as well as biographical and other background information. One chapter is devoted to *The Moviegoer*.

Wyatt-Brown, Bertram. *The House of Percy*. New York: Oxford University Press, 1994. Primarily a biography of Percy's family, this work reveals connections between Percy's family life and the characters in his novels, particularly Binx Bolling in *The Moviegoer*.

Mr. Cogito

Author: Zbigniew Herbert (1924-1998)
First published: Pan Cogito, 1974 (English translation, 1993)
Type of work: Poetry

Cogito, ergo sum, wrote René Descartes, "I think, therefore I am." Mr. Cogito, a twentieth century human being, the citizen of a small European nation, and at least occasionally the alter ego of poet Zbigniew Herbert, does a lot of thinking in this collection of Herbert's poetry from the late 1960's and early 1970's. Mr. Cogito, not surprisingly, confronts the philosophical problem as to precisely what constitutes the self; what makes up human identity in a world full of others, past and present; where Mr. Cogito ends and where others— animal, vegetable, or mineral—begin; and how one individual lives among others.

Herbert's earlier work, including *Struna światła* (1956), *Hermes, pies i gwiazda* (1957), *Studium przedmiotu* (1961), and *Napis* (1969), deal in historical and political ironies, chief among them the question of art (or form) confronted with unspeakable experience. Herbert, like many of his contemporaries throughout Central and Eastern Europe, had a thorough education. During the Nazi occupation, he began writing underground, just as he studied and fought underground; when the war ended and the Stalinization of Polish life began, that did not essentially change.

Avant-garde in its avoidance of rhyme and punctuation, its use of idiom and casual diction, and classical in its spareness and clarity, Herbert's poetry rarely makes direct mention of contemporary events, yet it expresses the collective experience of Poland with unsparing intelligence. The poet often speaks in the first person plural, reserving the "I" for a figure from history or myth, distant in time or space. However, the speech and sensibility of these figures are as close to the readers of Herbert's time as those of the morning newspaper.

In "Elegy of Fortinbras," one of his best-known pieces, Fortinbras addresses the dead Hamlet with the pragmatic coolness of a twentieth century enlightened tyrant, contemptuous of fancy and as skilled in inventories as he is in invasion: "Adieu prince I have tasks a sewer project/ and a decree on prostitutes and beggars/ I must also elaborate a better system of prisons/ since as you justly said Denmark is a prison."

The irony inherent in conversations between the powerful and powerless underlies much of Herbert's work, and his rejection of both the style and the substance of Poland under communism made publication difficult for him even after the thaw of 1956. *Report from the Besieged City* (1983), written while Poland was under martial law, was his first work to be published abroad, and even before it appeared in his homeland.

Ironic detachment (not to be confused with moral indifference) has been a hallmark of Herbert's poetry from the beginning, and *Mr. Cogito* is no exception. Mr. Cogito is not a fixed character with a stable point of view, and Herbert himself called him neither a mask nor a persona but a method for distancing, "objectifying." His points of reference are Herbert's beloved humanist tradition—Greek mythology, ancient history, philosophy—yet the book is clearly more personal than Herbert's earlier ones. This is particularly true of the opening poems, where Mr. Cogito looks at his own reflection, remembers father, mother, and sister, and contemplates returning to his birthplace. In "Mr. Cogito Looks at His Face in the Mirror," he sees features he would rather not belong to him: close-set eyes, the better to spy out invading tribes; big ears, the better to hear rumbling mammoths. Those same eyes and ears, he protests, have absorbed Veronese and Mozart, but "the inherited face" shows the descent of the species with all its animal fears and ancient passions, and Mr. Cogito regretfully concludes that it, not he, wins.

"About Mr. Cogito's Two Legs" is an anatomical version of two different attitudes toward life: one leg is boyish, well-shaped, and energetic, ready to dance or run away at any moment, to survive for the love of life; the other is thin, scarred, and rigid. One is not better than the other; rather, they might be compared to Sancho Panza and Don Quixote, and the combination is not crippling. Mr. Cogito simply staggers slightly as he makes his way through the world.

Distressed by the presence of others within himself, he is also surprised and touched by their separateness. Mr. Cogito often feels amazement, as the young boy discovers in "Sister," that he has "remained within the limits of his own skin," or as the grown man wonders at the sudden impenetrability of a dead friend's body. "Others" include things as well as people: In "Sense of Identity" Mr. Cogito looks to a sandstone that, far from being dead and inert, varies according to light and weather, struggles with the elements, and endures changes in its own nature. He is not personifying the stone in any conventional sense; it leads its own opaque, self-enclosed sandstone life, which happens to share much with human existence. Both are always subject to external pressures, to a reality outside themselves—and here is where the self in Herbert's poetry differs from the self-absorbed "I" of many other twentieth century Western poets.

Loss and dislocation lie at the core of Herbert's reality. In "Mr. Cogito Thinks of Returning to the City Where He Was Born," he expects that he will find nothing of his childhood except, and here the speculation turns to nightmarish certainty, a flagstone on which the boy draws a chalk circle. He raises one foot to hop but finds himself frozen in that pose, unable to grow up, as years pass and wars rage and the circle fills with ash, all the way up to his shoulders and mouth. On one level, the loss is universal—past lost to present, childhood irretrievably lost to the bitter taste of adult experience, lost homes to which one cannot return—but there are more levels as well, on which history and geography cease to be symbolic. After World War II, Herbert's own birthplace of łwów was suddenly no longer Poland but the Soviet Union, as far removed as if it, like hundreds of other Polish towns and villages, was razed to the ground. Warfare or camps killed roughly one-sixth of Poland's entire population, and much of Polish Jewry was indeed reduced to ash. Long used in poetry as a symbol of death and desolation, ash in postwar Poland had a quite specific and horrible meaning.

What is inhuman for Herbert the humanist is not the inanimate object but the perfect system, whether earthly or heavenly. Mr. Cogito is, in his own modest, bemused way, a continuation of what some Herbert commentators have called "the attack on transcendence," and what others have called "the rejection of 'purity.'" Purity was often represented in his earlier works by imperturbable gods or angels bent on creating an unlivable paradise. In "At the Gate of the Valley," for example,

> after a loud whisper of explosion
> after a loud whisper of silence
> this voice resounds like a spring of living water
> it is we are told
> a cry of mothers from whom children are taken
> since as it turns out
> we shall be saved each one alone
> the guardian angels are unmoved
> and let us grant they have a hard job

A philosopher's yearning for absolute perfection prompts "Mr. Cogito Tells About the Temptation of Spinoza," in which God counters Baruch Spinoza's questions about first and final causes with kindly practical advice: take care of yourself, eat better, dress better, buy a new house, forgive flawed mirrors and drunken singers.

> —calm
> the rational fury
> thrones will fall because of it
> and stars turn black
> —think
> about the woman
> who will give you a child
> —you see Baruch
> we are speaking about Great Things

Mr. Cogito may think about great things and great people, but he does not want to be one. In "Mr. Cogito's Game," which is a replay of the escape of Russian anarchist Peter Kropotkin from a czarist prison, he delights in the daring flight but prefers the inferior role, being a helper rather than a hero. This is not cowardice but temperament, as well as a refusal to strike dramatic poses and make grand gestures in the service of a grand abstraction. He clings to his earthly senses of sight, touch, and sound. There is some wistfulness in "Mr. Cogito Laments the Pettiness of Dreams," wherein he envies his grandparents their vividly colored dreams. (His are of the bill collector knocking on his door.) The tone of "Mr. Cogito's Abyss" is low-key and apologetic as he explains that his abyss—his despair, his sense of disinheritance, his isolation—is persistent and annoying, like a small pet or a skin disease, but hardly the black hole of a Blaise Pascal or a Fyodor Dostoevski.

Even at his most cartoonlike, Mr. Cogito is a small, individual bastion of human values, of the good and the beautiful, fidelity and truth. Mr. Cogito may accept imperfection and defeat; he has his limitations, being an ordinary man. Ordinary men and women are, however, faced with moral choices, and those moral choices are very much present, though Herbert presents them less starkly, more compassionately, than he did in his earlier work. In "Mr. Cogito on Upright Attitudes," the inhabitants of a threatened city surrender long before the enemy is at the gates; they are sewing white flags, teaching their children to lie, and practicing their kneeling. Herbert uses an undramatic, ordinary figure of speech for Mr. Cogito's choice, which is "to stand up to the situation," knowing full well that it is simply the choice of position in which to die. Standing up, in fact, simply makes him a better target. Upright attitudes guarantee nothing, most especially not survival. As the biblical language of "The Envoy of Mr. Cogito" argues, however, that is not the point. The point is to bear truthful witness in things great and small, and this is no less heroic than the exploits of a Gilgamesh, a Hector, or a Roland.

Perhaps no other Polish poet except the Nobel laureate Czesław Miłosz has so wide an appeal to the foreign reader as has Herbert, whose work translates into English with relative ease. The "relative" is important, because he is particularly skilled at using common idioms and clichés, which generally do not translate well, in unexpected contexts. There are allusions to Polish as well as to Roman history, and associations that non-Polish readers might not make without a footnote. However, this grounding in the local, the specific, and the individual keeps the poetry from ever seeming abstract and generalized. This and his balance between austerity and compassion, lucidity and complexity, the ideal and the real give him a voice that resonates far beyond the borders of his country.

Jane Ann Miller

Further Reading

Alvarez, A. Introduction to *Selected Poems: Zbigniew Herbert*, translated by Czesław Miłosz and Peter Dale Scott. New York: Ecco, 1968. A brief but eloquent and useful introduction to the first volume of Herbert's poetry to be published in English.

Baranczak, Stanisław. *A Fugitive from Utopia: The Poetry of Zbigniew Herbert*. Cambridge, Mass.: Harvard University Press, 1987. A thorough study of Herbert's poetry, organized around his use of antinomy, or paradox. Baranczak argues that the contradiction between Herbert's attachment to the cultural heritage of the West and his sense of Eastern European disinheritance lies at the core of his work.

Bayley, John. "The Art of Austerity: Zbigniew Herbert." In *The Power of Delight: A Lifetime in Literature, Essays, 1962-2002*. Selected by Leo Carey. New York: W. W. Norton, 2005. An examination of Herbert's work is included in this compilation of the work of literary critic Bayley.

Carpenter, Bogdana, and John Carpenter. "The Recent Poetry of Zbigniew Herbert." *World Literature Today* 51, no. 2 (Spring, 1977): 210-214. Refers specifically to *Mr. Cogito*, which the authors later translated. Discusses Herbert's relationship to his persona and the differences between this and his earlier work.

Czerniawski, Adam, ed. *The Mature Laurel: Essays on Modern Polish Poetry*. Chester Springs, Pa.: Dufour, 1991. Contains several good essays on Herbert, some devoted to analysis of individual poems. Others discuss his work in relationship to that of such leading contemporaries as Wisława Szymborska and Tadeusz Różewicz.

Heaney, Seamus. "Atlas of Civilization." In *The Government of the Tongue*. New York: Noonday Press, 1990. Heaney sees a direct connection between Herbert and Socrates, Plato, and the notion of the examined life.

Hirsch, Edward. "Zbigniew Herbert." In *Responsive Reading*. Ann Arbor: University of Michigan Press, 1999. Hirsch, himself a poet, analyzes the work of Herbert.

Levis, Larry. "Strange Days: Zbigniew Herbert in Los Angeles." In *The Gazer Within*, edited by James Marshall, Andrew Miller, and John Venable. Ann Arbor: University of Michigan Press, 2001. Levis, an American poet, reviews Herbert's work.

Popovic, Dunjal. "'The Trace of a Hand Searching for Form': Zbigniew Herbert, Classical Heritage, and Poetry After Auschwitz." *Slavic and East European Journal* 51, no. 1 (Spring, 2007): 74-86. Examines Herbert's poetry written before and after World War II to determine how he responded to Nazism and other events of the conflict.

Zagajewski, Adam, ed. *Polish Writers on Writing*. San Antonio, Tex.: Trinity University Press, 2007. Some of Herbert's correspondence and an interview with the poet are included in this anthology of works in which Polish authors describe what it means to be a writer.

Mr. Sammler's Planet

Author: Saul Bellow (1915-2005)
First published: 1970
Type of work: Novel
Type of plot: Social realism
Time of plot: Late twentieth century, specifically during the first Moon landing
Locale: New York City and suburbs, Poland, and Israel

Principal characters:
ARTUR SAMMLER, a Holocaust survivor
SHULA (SLAWA) SAMMLER, his eccentric daughter
ELYA GRUNER, Sammler's nephew
ANGELA GRUNER, Elya's daughter
WALLACE GRUNER, Elya's son
DR. GOVINDA LAL, a scientist from whom Shula steals an essay
AFRICAN AMERICAN PICKPOCKET, a nameless, majestic person
EISEN, Shula's abusive former husband
MARGOTTE ARKIN, the niece of Sammler's late wife
LIONEL FEFFER, an associate of Sammler

The Story:

Artur Sammler is a highly introspective, brilliant, and aging Holocaust survivor living in New York City. Loved by those who know him, he functions as their gentle, infinitely likable father-confessor. However, since his experience of crawling out of a mass grave in Poland he is "dry" inside. His "death" and "rebirth" in a Holocaust killing field leaves him with an eye that can distinguish only light and shade and a spirit that is often myopic and incapacitated. He is slightly confused, bitter, morally indignant, and constantly ready to sit in judgment upon others. He rarely ever expresses these feelings because he nevertheless loves and needs his circle of friends.

In spite of attempts to insulate himself from the modern world that he reluctantly was born into during the Holocaust, Sammler's life on his planet is presenting him with many problems. His customary existence is upset because of the imminent death of Elya Gruner, the man who saved Sammler and his daughter from Holocaust Poland and who supported them in America. Furthermore, he is also involved with the intrigue of spying on an African American pickpocket, and the problem of his daughter, who steals the only copy of an important manuscript.

Sammler was spying for days on an African American male who pickpockets the riders of the bus he rides. He is fascinated by this man's grace, his stylish dress, and most of all his audacity in always picking the same bus route for his exploits. Sammler next visits with his daughter Shula, who changes her name to "Slawa" that month because it is Easter, and Shula, who was brought up under that name for four years by Catholic nuns during the Holocaust, wants to participate in Ash Wednesday. Sammler is both amused and re-

pulsed at Shula-Slawa's Jewish-Christian identity and contemplates the divisions of the modern self.

Sammler then goes to Columbia University to give a lecture on H. G. Wells and the Bloomsbury Group on the insistence of a rather irresponsible student named Lionel Feffer. During the lecture, a bearded Marxist student stands up and violently attacks Sammler's speech as "effete" nonsense. The student then calls him an "old man" and even goes so far as to question Sammler's sexual prowess. Sammler abruptly leaves and, on the trip home, once again sees the pickpocket. When the pickpocket catches Sammler watching him, he follows and corners Sammler alone in his apartment lobby. Here, rather than mugging Sammler or silencing him with physical violence, the pickpocket calmly displays his genitalia as a "lesson" to the stupefied Sammler, who almost wants to watch. After this, he goes up to his apartment where Shula left him a note and a manuscript by Dr. V. Govinda Lal. Its title is "The Future of the Moon."

Next, Sammler visits Angela and Wallace Gruner. Elya describes Wallace as a "high I.Q. moron" and Angela as "insidious," "an apprentice whore," and a woman who "sent the message of gender everywhere." After talking with these two, Sammler visits Elya in the hospital, where Sammler learns that Elya is going to die soon, no matter what the doctors do. He spends more time with the Gruner family and notices their self-centered, casual attitude about their dying father. On the way home from the hospital, Sammler peruses Lal's manuscript. He then meets Feffer, who tries to apologize for the incident at the university, and then informs him that Shula stole Lal's manuscript, and it is the only copy. Sammler immediately jots off an explanatory letter to Lal, leaves the manuscript at his home so he can retrieve it, and returns to visit Elya. His anxiety about both the pickpocket and Lal's purloined manuscript causes a flashback to his Holocaust experiences.

Sammler returns to visit Elya at the hospital, then visits with Angela, Wallace, and Eisen, the last returning from Israel as a would-be artist. Sammler has a flashback about his experience visiting Israel during the Six-Day War. Margotte phones Sammler and informs him that Shula-Slawa took the manuscript again, and that Lal is at Sammler's house with a detective. Sammler talks to Lal, compliments his work, and Lal expresses his hopes to publish it before the first lunar landing. After he goes to Elya's New Rochelle home with Wallace, Sammler contemplates the thefts and confronts Shula-Slawa. She informs him that the manuscript and a copy she made are then in lockers at Grand Central Station. Sammler and Lal finally meet, Sammler gives him the keys to the lockers, and both men engage in a long, far-reaching dialogue.

They notice that the floor is wet. In his search for his father's hidden money, Wallace undoes the pipes in the attic. Lal saves the day by turning off the water, and they all retire to bed. Reflecting on the day's madness, Sammler again thinks back to the Six-Day War. The next day, Sammler is left stranded in New Rochelle by Wallace and Lal but gets a ride into New York with Elya's chauffeur, Emil. Sammler thinks deeply about Elya, but as they enter town, Emil points a fight out to Sammler, which turns out to involve none other than Feffer and the pickpocket. Feffer was spying on the man, this time with a hidden camera, and was caught. Reaching the scene, Sammler spots Eisen, who, after much confusion and struggle, ends the fight by repeatedly bludgeoning the African American with his art—crude metal figurines. The sheer murderousness of Eisen's blows on the man horrifies Sammler, who tries to stop the violence but is too late. The man falls to the ground bleeding, his face torn open. At Feffer's insistence, Sammler, weak from experiencing such violence again, leaves the scene and goes to visit Elya.

Entering the hospital, Sammler is once again delayed, this time by Angela. He offends her by asking for her to reconcile with Elya and intuits that, once Elya dies, he will probably lose all of his financial support. Sammler then gets a phone call from Shula-Slawa, who is ecstatic because she found money stuffed in a couch at Elya's. He forbids her to take it. Sammler finally reaches Elya's doctor but is told that Elya died. Sammler, distracted too long, missed Elya's passing.

He finds Elya's body and utters a prayer—almost a Kaddish—over his benefactor, friend, and nephew. Sammler then commends Elya's life to God and says that Elya met, in spite of "all the confusion and degraded clowning of life . . .

the terms of his contract," and that this is what makes any life truly authentic.

Critical Evaluation:

The backdrop for this novel is not only New York's diversity and decay; it is also the excitement then in the air about the Apollo Moon landing and the potential of a new frontier for humanity. Sammler, a character many have seen to be a thinly disguised Saul Bellow, is not so sure about humanity's potential at all. He is greatly disturbed with the many forms of madness that are destroying the planet. Leaving the planet to inhabit a more pure one is no solution; the notion of purity will do nothing but bring about more violence such as the Holocaust.

Generally in his novels, Bellow allows for a solution, hard-won to be sure, to humanity's problems, and *Mr. Sammler's Planet* is no exception. During his travails in dealing with late twentieth century America, Sammler is still able to come to a moment of peace and of rebirth as he stands over Elya's body. His prayer shows that Elya's death brings about another rebirth in Sammler—this time into a life that can overcome the narrowness of his own modern thinking. Elya's contradictory life of perfect giving to Sammler during the Holocaust and in America and his imperfection in the taking of Mafia abortion money make Sammler aware of the great contradictions in life. He sees in Elya a great life spent living out the knowledge that one must live one's life for others, not only for one's self. Although Elya showed weakness, his ability to give remained exemplary.

Upon its publication, *Mr. Sammler's Planet* was considered one of Bellow's weaker novels. It is somewhat of a departure for him. However, Bellow's insights and critiques of the major elements of modern life made *Mr. Sammler's Planet* one of his more powerful and enduring texts. Its many digressions extend and brilliantly negotiate the more important philosophical and ethical questions about life in the late twentieth century. This partially explains why Bellow received the Nobel Prize in Literature in 1976.

The scenes with the African American pickpocket, Govinda Lal, and Sammler's recollections of the Six-Day War predate many of the current debates about Jewish-African American relations, various postcolonial theories, issues surrounding the Holocaust, and Israel's treatment of Palestinians. Bellow clearly teaches that acts of violence are an affront to all and are never justified simply by one's history or political stance. For example, when Sammler sees the gashes on the pickpocket's face after he is viciously beaten by Eisen, his own damaged eye begins to throb in complete sympathy for this new victim of violence.

Angela's characterization and the lesson taught to Sammler in his apartment lobby provide valuable insights about regarding the female as other, power, and desire. *Mr. Sammler's Planet* also contains a prolonged investigation about self-construction in late twentieth century America, particularly after such events as the Holocaust and rapid technological advance. Mr. Sammler's planet is the reader's planet, Bellow seems to suggest, and it is a sphere with a movement toward a greater human goal and toward a darker future ripe with brutality, selfishness, and violence. With Sammler, Bellow shows that personal rebirth is still possible on this planet but always at a cost of great sacrifice and suffering.

James Aaron Stanger

Further Reading

Atlas, James. *Bellow: A Biography.* New York: Random House, 2000. Atlas spent ten years working on this book, which some critics consider the definitive biography of Bellow. Atlas is particularly good at finding parallels between the tone of Bellow's novels and his mood at the time he wrote them.

Bach, Gerhard, ed. *The Critical Response to Saul Bellow.* Westport, Conn.: Greenwood Press, 1995. Collection of reviews and essays about Bellow's work that were published from the 1940's through the 1990's, including pieces by Delmore Schwartz, Robert Penn Warren, Alfred Kazin, and Granville Hicks. Contains articles about all of the major novels.

Cronin, Gloria L., and L. H. Goldman, eds. *Saul Bellow in the 1980's: A Collection of Critical Essays.* East Lansing: Michigan State University Press, 1989. Essential reading for *Mr. Sammler's Planet.* See especially Allan Chavkin's article, "Bellow and English Romanticism," Susan Glickman's "The World as Will and Idea: A Comparative Study of *An American Dream* and *Mr. Sammler's Planet*," and Ellen Pifer's "Two Different Speeches: Mystery and Knowledge in *Mr. Sammler's Planet*."

Dremer, S. Lillian. *Witness Through the Imagination: Jewish-American Holocaust Literature.* Detroit, Mich.: Wayne State University Press, 1989. An essential discussion of *Mr. Sammler's Planet* as a Holocaust novel.

Fuchs, Daniel. *Saul Bellow: Vision and Revision.* Durham, N.C.: Duke University Press, 1984. Making use of Bellow's collection of unpublished manuscripts, Fuchs traces the evolution of a Bellow novel from idea through revision. He also examines the literary and intellectual milieus in which Bellow wrote.

Halldorson, Stephanie S. *The Hero in Contemporary American Fiction: The Works of Saul Bellow and Don DeLillo.* New York: Palgrave Macmillan, 2007. Halldorson describes how the two American authors redefine the concept of heroism. Her study focuses on Bellow's novels *Mr. Sammler's Planet* and *Henderson the Rain King.*

Kiernan, Robert. *Saul Bellow.* New York: Continuum, 1988. Contains analysis of Bellow's individual works as well as an introduction to his life and career. Includes chronology, bibliography of works by and about Bellow, index, and notes.

Quayum, M. A. *Saul Bellow and American Transcendentalism.* New York: Peter Lang, 2004. Quayum examines *Mr. Sammler's Planet* and four of Bellow's other novels to demonstrate the influence of American transcendentalism, particularly the writings of Ralph Waldo Emerson, Henry David Thoreau, and Walt Whitman

Stock, Irvin. *Fiction as Wisdom: From Goethe to Bellow.* University Park: Pennsylvania State University Press, 1974. Includes a chapter on Bellow that provides an excellent overview of *Mr. Sammler's Planet*'s debt to British Romantic literature.

Mrs. Dalloway

Author: Virginia Woolf (1882-1941)
First published: 1925
Type of work: Novel
Type of plot: Psychological realism
Time of plot: 1920's
Locale: London

Principal characters:
CLARISSA DALLOWAY
RICHARD DALLOWAY, her husband
PETER WALSH, a former suitor of Clarissa
ELIZABETH, Mrs. Dalloway's daughter
MISS KILMAN, Elizabeth's friend
SALLY SETON, an old friend of Clarissa and Peter
SEPTIMUS SMITH, a war veteran

The Story:

Clarissa Dalloway makes last-minute preparations for an evening party. During her day in the city, she enjoys the summer air, the many sights and people, and the general bustle of London. She meets Hugh Whitbread, now a court official and a handsome and sophisticated man. She has known Hugh since her youth, and she also knows his wife, Evelyn, for whom she does not particularly care. Other people come to London to see paintings, to hear music, or to shop, but the Whitbreads come to consult doctors, for Evelyn is always ailing.

Mrs. Dalloway shops. While she is in a flower shop, a luxurious limousine pulls up outside. Everyone speculates on the occupant behind the drawn curtains of the car, and everywhere the limousine goes, it is followed by curious eyes. Mrs. Dalloway, who suspects that the queen is inside, feels that she is right when the car drives into the Buckingham Palace grounds.

The sights and sounds of London remind Mrs. Dalloway of many things. She thinks back to her youth, to the days before her marriage, to her husband, and to her daughter, Elizabeth. Her daughter is a problem, mainly because of her horrid friend Miss Kilman, a religious fanatic who scoffs at the luxurious way the Dalloways live. Mrs. Dalloway hates her. Miss Kilman is not at all like the friend of her own girlhood, Sally Seton, whom Mrs. Dalloway truly loves.

Mrs. Dalloway wonders what love really is. She has loved Sally, but she has loved Richard Dalloway and Peter Walsh, too. She married Richard, and then Peter had left for India. Later, she learns that he had married someone he met on board ship. She has heard little about him since his marriage. The day, however, is wonderful and life is wonderful. The war is over, and Mrs. Dalloway is giving a party.

While Mrs. Dalloway is shopping, Septimus Smith and his wife are sitting in the park. Septimus had married Lucrezia while he was serving in Italy, and she had given up her family and her country for him. Now he frightens her because he acts so strangely and talks of committing suicide. The doctor said that there is nothing physically wrong with him. Septimus, one of the first to have volunteered for war duty, had gone to war to save his country, the England of William Shakespeare. When he got back, he was a war hero and was given a good job at the office. The couple has nice lodgings, and Lucrezia is happy. Septimus begins reading Shakespeare again, but he is unhappy and broods. He and Lucrezia have no children. To Septimus, the world is in such horrible condition that it is unjust to bring children into such a world.

Septimus begins to have visits from Evans, a comrade who had been killed in the war, and Lucrezia becomes even more frightened; she calls in Dr. Holmes. Septimus feels almost completely abandoned by that time. Lucrezia cannot understand why her husband does not like Dr. Holmes, for he is so kind and so much interested in Septimus. Finally, she takes her husband to Sir William Bradshaw, a wealthy and noted psychiatrist.

Septimus has a brilliant career ahead of him, and his employer speaks highly of his work. No one knows why he wants to kill himself. Septimus says that he had committed a crime, but his wife says that he is guilty of absolutely nothing. Sir William suggests a place in the country where Septimus could be by himself, without his wife. It is not, Sir William says, a question of preference. Since he has threatened suicide, it is a question of law.

Mrs. Dalloway returns home from shopping. Lady Bruton has invited Richard Dalloway to lunch. Mrs. Dalloway never liked Millicent Bruton because she is far too clever. When Peter Walsh calls, Mrs. Dalloway is surprised and happy to see him again. She introduces him to Elizabeth, her daughter. He asks Mrs. Dalloway if she is happy; she wonders why. When he leaves, she calls out to him not to forget her party. Peter thinks about Clarissa Dalloway and her parties: That is all life means to her.

Peter is divorced from his wife and had come to England. Life is far more complicated for him. He has fallen in love with another woman, one who has two children, and he has come to London to arrange for her divorce and to find a job. He hopes Hugh Whitbread will help him find one in government.

That night, Clarissa Dalloway's party is a great success. She initially was afraid that the party might not be, but when the prime minister arrives, her evening is complete. Peter meets Lady Rossetter, who turns out to be Sally Seton. She was not invited but just dropped in. She has five sons, she tells Peter. They chat. When Elizabeth comes in, Peter notices her beauty.

Later, Sir William Bradshaw and his wife enter. They are late, they explain, because one of Sir William's patients had committed suicide. Feeling altogether abandoned, Septimus Smith had jumped out of a window before they could take him to the country. Clarissa is upset. Although the person who had committed suicide is completely unknown to her, she feels the death is her own disaster, her own disgrace. The poor young man had thrown away his life when it had become useless. Clarissa has never thrown away anything more valuable than a shilling. Once she had stood beside a fountain while Peter Walsh, angry and humiliated, had asked her whether she intended to marry Richard. Richard had never become prime minister. Instead, the prime minister came to her parties. Now she is growing old. Clarissa Dalloway knows herself at last for the beautiful, charming, inconsequential person she is.

Sally and Peter talk on. They think idly of Clarissa and Richard and wonder whether they are happy together. Sally agrees that Richard has improved. She leaves Peter and talks with Richard. Peter is feeling strange. A sort of terror and ecstasy take hold of him, and he cannot be certain what it is that excites him so suddenly. It is Clarissa, he thinks. Even after all these years, it is Clarissa.

Critical Evaluation:

Mrs. Dalloway comes midway in Virginia Woolf's fiction-writing career and near the beginning of her experiments with form and technique, just after *Jacob's Room* (1922), her first experimental novel. The book is really two stories—that of Clarissa Dalloway and that of Septimus Smith—and the techniques by which Woolf united the two narrative strands are unusual and skillful. While writing the novel, Woolf commented in her diary on her new method of delineating character. Instead of explaining the characters' pasts chronologically, she uses a "tunnelling process": "I dig out beautiful caves behind my characters." The various characters appear in the present without explanation; various sense impressions—a squeaky hinge, a repeated phrase, a particular tree—call to mind a memory, and past becomes present. Such an evocation of the past is reminiscent of Marcel Proust, but Woolf's method does not involve the ego of the narrator.

Woolf's "caves" reveal both the past and the characters' reactions to present events. Woolf structurally connects the "caves" and her themes by spatial and temporal techniques; her handling of the stream-of-consciousness technique—unlike that of James Joyce—is always filtered and indirect; the narrator is in command, telling the reader "Clarissa thought" or "For so it had always seemed to her." This ever-present narrative voice clarifies the characters' inner thoughts and mediates the commentary of the novel; at times, however, it blurs the identity of the speaker. Woolf's use of the "voice" became more prominent in *To the Lighthouse* (1927), then disappeared in *The Waves* (1931).

With its disparate characters and various scenes of street life, the structure of the book seems at first to lack unity. Woolf, however, uses many devices, both technical and thematic, to unite elements. The day, sometime in mid-June, 1923, is a single whole, moving chronologically from early morning to late evening. The book is not divided into chapters or sections headed by titles or numbers, but Woolf notes some of the shifts in time or scene by a short blank space in the manuscript. More often, however, the transition from one group of characters to another is accomplished by the remarking of something public, something common to the experience of both, something seen or heard.

The world of Clarissa and her friends alternates with the world of Septimus. The sight of a motorcar, the sight and sound of a skywriting plane, a running child, a woman singing, an omnibus, an ambulance, and the clock striking are the transitions connecting those two worlds. Moreover, the striking of the clocks ("first a warning, musical; then the hour, irrevocable") is noted at various other times to mark a shift from one character's consciousness to another. The exact time, which is given periodically, signals the day's progress (noon comes at almost the exact center of the book) and stresses the irrevocable movement toward death, one of the book's themes. Usually at least two clocks are described as striking—first Big Ben, a masculine symbol, then, a few seconds later, the feminine symbol St. Margaret's; this suggests again the two genders of all existence united in the echoes of the bells, "the leaden circles."

The main thematic devices used to unify the book are the similarity between Clarissa and Septimus and the repetition of key words and phrases in the minds of various characters. The likeness between Clarissa and Septimus is most important, as each helps to explain the other, although they never meet. Both are lonely and contemplate suicide. Both feel guilty for their past lives, Septimus because he "cannot feel" the death of Evans, Clarissa because she rejected Peter and has a tendency to dominate others. Both have homosexual feelings, Septimus for Evans, Clarissa for Sally Seton. More important, both want desperately to bring order into life's chaos. Septimus achieves this momentarily with the making of Mrs. Peters's hat, Clarissa with her successful party. Septimus understands that the chaos will return and so takes his own life to unite himself with death, the final order. Septimus's suicide forces Clarissa to see herself in a new and more honest way and to understand for the first time her schemings for success. Clarissa "felt somehow very like him"; she does not pity him but identifies with his defiant "embracing" of death.

Certain phrases become thematic because they are so often repeated and thus gain richer overtones of meaning at each use, as different characters interpret differently such phrases as "Fear no more" and "if it were now to die" and such concepts as the sun and the waves. The phrases appear repeatedly, especially in the thoughts of Septimus and Clarissa.

The disparate strands of the story are joined at Clarissa's

party, over which she presides like an artist over her creation. Not inferior to the painter Lily Briscoe as a creator, Clarissa's great talent is "knowing people almost by instinct," and she is able triumphantly to combine the right group of people at her party. Clarissa, Richard, and Peter all come to new realizations about themselves at the party. Richard, who has been unable to verbalize his love for Clarissa, is finally able to tell his daughter, Elizabeth, that he is proud of her. At the end, Peter realizes that the terror and excitement he feels in Clarissa's presence indicate his true feelings for her.

The two figures who are given unfavorable treatment—Sir William, the psychiatrist, and Miss Kilman, the religious fanatic—insist on modes of existence inimical to the passionate desire of Clarissa and Septimus for wholeness. Claiming that Septimus "lacks proportion," Sir William nevertheless uses his profession to gain power over others and, as Clarissa understands, makes life "intolerable" for Septimus. Miss Kilman's life is built on evangelical religion; she considers herself to be better than Clarissa, whom she wants to humiliate. She proudly asserts that she will have a "religious victory," which will be "God's will."

The real action of the story is all within the minds of the characters, but Woolf gives these inner lives a reality and harmony that reveal the excitement and oneness of human existence. Clarissa and Septimus are really two aspects of the same being—the feminine and the masculine—united in Clarissa's ultimate awareness. *Mrs. Dalloway* remains the best introduction to Woolf's characteristic style and themes.

"Critical Evaluation" by Margaret McFadden-Gerber

Further Reading

Abel, Elizabeth. "Narrative Structure(s) and Female Development: The Case of *Mrs. Dalloway*." In *Virginia Woolf: A Collection of Critical Essays*, edited by Margaret Homans. Englewood Cliffs, N.J.: Prentice Hall, 1993. Analysis of *Mrs. Dalloway* as a "typically female text" that hides its "subversive impulses," which resist the typical narrative structure. Points out that Clarissa's real passion was not for Peter but for Sally, whose kiss gave Clarissa "a moment of unparalleled radiance and intensity." Many of the other essays in this collection connect *Mrs. Dalloway* to Woolf's other works, including a piece examining the images of space, darkness, and affirmation in *Mrs. Dalloway* and *To the Lighthouse* (1927).

Barrett, Eileen, and Patricia Cramer, eds. *Virginia Woolf: Lesbian Readings*. New York: New York University Press, 1997. Part 2 of this collection of conference papers focuses on Woolf's novels, with interpretations of the les-bian eroticism in *Mrs. Dalloway* and six of Woolf's other books.

Blair, Emily. *Virginia Woolf and the Nineteenth-Century Domestic Novel*. Albany: State University of New York Press, 2007. Describes the influence of nineteenth and early twentieth century literature, particularly its descriptions of femininity, upon Woolf's work, Compares her novels to those of Elizabeth Gaskell and Margaret Oliphant, two popular Victorian novelists.

Briggs, Julia. *Virginia Woolf: An Inner Life*. Orlando, Fla: Harcourt, 2005. Biography focusing on Woolf's work and her fascination with the workings of the mind. Briggs traces the creation of each of Woolf's books, from *The Voyage Out* (1915) through *Between the Acts* (1941), combining literary analysis with details of Woolf's life.

Daiches, David. *The Novel and the Modern World*. Rev. ed. Chicago: University of Chicago Press, 1984. Includes a chapter examining the rhythms of Woolf's style, her works' repetitions and qualifications of impressionistic "patterns of meaning" that are almost "hypnotic." Focuses on time, death, and personality as key themes and compares Woolf favorably to James Joyce in her stream-of-consciousness technique, which limits space and time to reveal individual consciousness and memory.

De Gay, Jane. "Literature and Survival: *Jacob's Room* and *Mrs. Dalloway*." In *Virginia Woolf's Novels and the Literary Past*. Edinburgh: Edinburgh University Press, 2006. Examines Woolf's preoccupation with the fiction of her predecessors. Analyzes eight novels and other works to explore her allusions to and revisions of the plots and motifs of earlier fiction.

Harper, Howard M. *Between Language and Silence: The Novels of Virginia Woolf*. Baton Rouge: Louisiana State University Press, 1982. In *"Mrs. Dalloway*," reveals the genesis of the novel and its characters, who are based on Woolf's friends and family members. Discusses the absence of a mother, Clarissa's own ambivalence about her life, the imagery of sea and wind, and the work's parallels in *Night and Day* (1919), *The Voyage Out* (1915), and *To the Lighthouse*.

Henke, Suzette A. "*Mrs. Dalloway*: The Communion of Saints." In *New Feminist Essays on Virginia Woolf*, edited by Jane Marcus. 1981. Reprint. London: Macmillan, 1985. Discusses *Mrs. Dalloway* as a "scathing indictment of the British class system" and of patriarchy, focusing on Woolf's use of Greek tragedy and Christian doctrine to create a symbolic story of good versus evil, art versus war, privacy versus passion, homosexuality versus heterosexuality, and sacrifice versus revelation.

Minow-Pinkney, Makiko. *Virginia Woolf and the Problem of the Subject.* New Brunswick, N.J.: Rutgers University Press, 1987. An examination of five of Woolf's novels in terms of her "feminist subversion of conventions." The chapter on *Mrs. Dalloway* explains how Woolf deliberately confuses past and present thoughts and actions to diminish the "linear progress" of the narrative to blur the identity of the subject, thus producing a feeling of fluidity, spontaneity, and sensibility.

Roe, Sue, and Susan Sellers, eds. *The Cambridge Companion to Virginia Woolf.* New York: Cambridge University Press, 2009. A collection of essays by leading scholars that addresses Woolf's life and work from a range of intellectual perspectives. Includes analyses of her novels and discussions of Woolf and modernism, feminism, and psychoanalysis. Indexed references to *Mrs. Dalloway.*

Warner, Eric, ed. *Virginia Woolf: A Centenary Perspective.* New York: St. Martin's Press, 1984. Includes some of the best available articles on Woolf's symbolism and purpose. The images of reflections in glass, sight, and mirroring are key to her sense of being and to the creation of continuity between people. One article examines the paradoxes of love and silence, duality and time; another discusses Woolf's concern with the self and with consciousness.

Woolf, Virginia, et al. *The "Mrs. Dalloway" Reader.* Edited by Francine Prose. Orlando, Fla.: Harcourt, 2003. In addition to the text of the novel, this edition contains an incisive introduction by Prose, herself a novelist, describing what Woolf achieves in *Mrs. Dalloway.* The book also includes Woolf's story *Mrs. Dalloway's Party,* selected short stories, diary entries, and critical essays by Michael Cunningham, Mary Gordon, E. M. Forster, and others.

Mrs. Dane's Defence

Author: Henry Arthur Jones (1851-1929)
First produced: 1900; first published, 1905
Type of work: Drama
Type of plot: Social realism
Time of plot: Early twentieth century
Locale: Near London

Principal characters:
MRS. DANE, a woman of questionable reputation
SIR DANIEL CARTERET, a distinguished jurist
LIONEL CARTERET, his adopted son, in love with Mrs. Dane
MRS. BULSOM-PORTER, a gossip
MR. JAMES RISBY, her nephew
LADY EASTNEY, Mrs. Dane's friend
JANET COLQUHOUN, her niece

The Story:

Young Lionel Carteret is madly in love with Mrs. Dane, a woman three years older than he. The difference in their ages is not too important to those who love the young man, but Mrs. Dane's reputation makes them try to dissuade Lionel from his attachment. Mrs. Bulsom-Porter, a local gossip, has been told by her nephew, James Risby, that Mrs. Dane is actually Felicia Hindemarsh.

Miss Hindemarsh had, five years previously, been involved in a horrible scandal in Vienna, in which she had had an affair with a married man for whom she worked as a governess. The wife, learning of the affair, had committed suicide, and the man himself is still in an insane asylum. Risby, however, had since told Mrs. Bulsom-Porter that he had been mistaken. Although he thought that Mrs. Dane is Felicia

Hindemarsh, he is now completely convinced that he had been wrong. In fact, he now declares that Mrs. Dane hardly resembles the sinful Miss Hindemarsh. His retraction means little to Mrs. Bulsom-Porter, who knows absolutely nothing of Mrs. Dane except that she is attractive and charming. Those qualities are enough to make Mrs. Bulsom-Porter hate her, and she continues to spread the story about Mrs. Dane's past, without admitting that there might be some doubt about her story.

Lionel had been deeply in love with Janet Colquhoun the year before, but is persuaded by Sir Daniel Carteret, his foster father, to wait before he asks her to marry him. Sir Daniel tries to make Lionel see that his latest infatuation might also pass away, but Lionel will not listen to that well-meaning advice. He accuses Sir Daniel of never having known love. The young man does not know that many years before, Sir Daniel had been in love with a married woman. They had decided to defy the conventions and go away together, but on the night of their departure, her son had become dangerously ill. She stayed with her child, and she and Sir Daniel renounced their affections. The woman had been Lionel's mother. After her death, and the subsequent death of her husband, Sir Daniel adopted Lionel, giving him his name and his love. The young man is so dear to Sir Daniel that he cannot stand to see the boy ruin his life by marrying Mrs. Dane, at least while her reputation is clouded.

Sir Daniel and Lady Eastney, Mrs. Dane's friend, set about to try to solve the mystery once and for all. Although Risby has retracted his story, Mrs. Bulsom-Porter will not stop spreading the scandal until she is proved wrong beyond a doubt. Mrs. Dane herself will do nothing to stop the gossip, but at last Sir Daniel persuades her to tell him enough about her background to allow an investigation. While he is trying to piece together the facts, Mrs. Bulsom-Porter employs a detective to go to Vienna and find evidence to prove Mrs. Dane is Miss Hindemarsh.

When the detective returns from Vienna, Mrs. Dane meets him first and begs him to declare her innocence. She offers him any sum not to reveal what he has learned. Consequently, when he is asked by Mrs. Bulsom-Porter and Sir Daniel to reveal his findings, he says that those in Vienna who had known Felicia Hindemarsh swore that there is absolutely no resemblance between her and the photograph of Mrs. Dane that he had shown them. His account satisfies everyone but Mrs. Bulsom-Porter. Sir Daniel, Lady Eastney, and even Mr. Bulsom-Porter insist that she sign a retraction and a public apology, but she refuses. She still hopes to catch Mrs. Dane in a lie.

It might be necessary for Mrs. Dane to sue Mrs. Bulsom-Porter for slander, so Sir Daniel continues his own investigation. He talks again with Mrs. Dane, in an attempt to find out everything about her history. She tells him that she had lived in Canada for several years, which made it difficult to trace her past. Then she betrays herself by mentioning her uncle's name. When Sir Daniel looks up that name and her relative's place of residence, he finds a reference to a Reverend Hindemarsh.

At first, Mrs. Dane claims that Felicia Hindemarsh is her cousin, and that she had tried to conceal the fact because of the disgrace, but at last she is forced to confess that she is Felicia. Risby and the detective had known the truth but had shielded her because they thought she had suffered enough for her sin.

Mrs. Bulsom-Porter is a troublemaker who needs to be cured of her vicious ways, and no one else wishes to make Mrs. Dane suffer more, so Sir Daniel and Lady Eastney force Mrs. Bulsom-Porter to make a public apology for the scandal she had caused. No one will ever know that she had been right. Lionel wants to marry Mrs. Dane anyway, but Sir Daniel persuades her to forsake him, even though she loves him sincerely. Mrs. Dane had had a child as a result of her unfortunate earlier affair, and Sir Daniel knows that, although Lionel loves her, he will forever remember that she had lied once and might lie again. Also, the man in the case is still living, although insane, and the wise Sir Daniel knows that these facts are no foundation for a successful marriage. Since Lionel will never forsake her, Mrs. Dane must use her love for him wisely and disappear from his life forever. She agrees, never doubting the wisdom of Sir Daniel's decision, and leaves the region without telling Lionel good-bye.

Because Sir Daniel has been so kind and wise in dealing with Mrs. Dane and Lionel, Lady Eastney accepts the proposal that Sir Daniel had made to her some time before. She knows that she will always feel secure with him. Although Lionel thinks that he could never be happy or fall in love again, he promises to try to carry out his foster father's wishes. Janet, who tries hard to pretend that their last year's love is over, kisses Lionel understandingly, promising him better times to come.

Critical Evaluation:

Henry Arthur Jones was one of the early modern dramatists, the school begun by Henrik Ibsen at the end of the nineteenth century. *Mrs. Dane's Defence* belongs to the period of dramatic literature that saw the introduction of naturalism into the English theater. The attempt to portray people as they really are was coupled with another new tendency in drama—humanitarianism. Although Mrs. Dane's sin was not condoned, her weakness was forgiven by those who were really her friends.

The realistic British "well-made play" provided the transition between the artificial, elaborate, pseudopoetic dramatic spectacles of the early nineteenth century and the realistic, iconoclastic theater of George Bernard Shaw and his successors. On the one hand, the genre brought realism to the English stage—recognizable domestic scenes with actual furniture, doors and windows that opened and closed, functional props, colloquial dialogue, and natural acting. On the other hand, for all its surface realism and apparent concern with serious social issues, the British well-made play typically reflected assumptions and attitudes that reinforced, rather than challenged, the middle-class Victorian society that supported it. If the best of these plays did not actually attack the prevalent social and moral values, they did posit interesting questions and, occasionally, suggested ambiguous difficulties beneath the smug, placid surface of Victorian society. There is perhaps no better example of the powers and limits of the British well-made play than Henry Arthur Jones's *Mrs. Dane's Defence*.

For the first three acts, *Mrs. Dane's Defence* is a typical well-made play, although the action seems less contrived and the characters more natural than usual. As in most examples of the genre, the action turns on concealed information that is gradually revealed in the course of the play, in this case the true identity and "notorious" past of the heroine, Mrs. Dane. Although her efforts to clear her name seem to be going well, the audience receives several hints that the gossip regarding her is really true. With mechanical precision the play builds to the powerful *scène à faire* (obligatory scene) in which Judge Daniel Carteret cross-examines Mrs. Dane and painfully extracts the truth from her. Having had her true identity revealed and her shady past exposed, Mrs. Dane would normally fall victim to Victorian convention, which demanded punishment (if not death, at least social ostracism) for a woman of Mrs. Dane's sort. In the ambiguous denouement of act 4, *Mrs. Dane's Defence* veers somewhat from the well-made play pattern and introduces complexities that give the play a modernity that most plays of the genre—including all of Jones's others—conspicuously lack.

Beneath the surface problems of false identity and thwarted romance is a very subtle and interesting battle of the genders. Sir Daniel Carteret represents the conventional masculine view; he demands truth at all costs and insists that the person exposed pay the price of the misdeeds without regard to extenuating circumstances. This attitude clashes with the feminine approach advocated by his intended, Lady Eastney, who considers only the "human" aspects of the problem and weighs motive and essential character more heavily than technical fact. Even after she learns Mrs. Dane's actual identity, Lady Eastney says, "Mrs. Dane shall leave this place, if she does leave it, without a stain on her character. And I intend that Mrs. Bulsom-Porter shall stay in it, if she does stay in it, as a self-confessed scandal-monger."

Lady Eastney wins the public battle, in that Mrs. Dane's name is cleared and Mrs. Bulsom-Porter is openly embarrassed. In a sense, she also wins in her conflict with Sir Daniel, since she coerces him into accepting her strategy, even though he knows it is based on false information. On the more important question of Mrs. Dane's engagement to Lionel Carteret, it is the judge's view that prevails.

The central irony is that to impress his view of things on Lionel and Mrs. Dane, Sir Daniel, the apostle of truth at all costs, tells lies. He tells his son that he once made a similar sacrifice, when the opposite was true, and he threatens Mrs. Dane with ultimate exposure, when he knows that the secret is safe. Mrs. Dane analyzes the problem correctly when she says, "Only we mustn't get found out. I'm afraid I've broken that part of the law." Thus, the essential hypocrisy and moral self-righteousness of upper middle-class Victorian society is exposed, in the character of its most respectable advocate, to a degree that Jones himself may not fully have intended or realized.

Further Reading

Cordell, Richard A. *Henry Arthur Jones and the Modern Drama*. Port Washington, N.Y.: Kennikat Press, 1968. Critical study of the playwright's major works. Describes the genesis of *Mrs. Dane's Defence* and comments on its characteristics as a well-made play. Claims Jones succumbed to contemporary pressures that upheld a double standard of morality for men and women.

Dietrich, Richard F. *British Drama, 1890 to 1950: A Critical History*. Boston: Twayne, 1989. Places Jones in the context of late nineteenth century British drama, highlighting his essential conservatism. Describes *Mrs. Dane's Defence* as a problem play in which the author expertly counterpoints character.

Emeljanow, Victor. *Victorian Popular Dramatists*. Boston: Twayne, 1987. Chapter on Jones explains his popularity with nineteenth century audiences. Comments on the first production of *Mrs. Dane's Defence*, asserting that Jones's characters serve as mouthpieces for conventional British values.

Foulkes, Richard. "Henry Arthur Jones and Wilson Barrett." In *Church and Stage in Victorian England*. New York: Cambridge University Press, 1997. Examines the relationship of Victorian theater to the era's religious movements, describing how playwrights, including Jones, and religious figures sought to create a common nineteenth century British culture.

Jenkins, Anthony. "Terrible Leanings Toward Responsibility." In *The Making of Victorian Drama*. New York: Cambridge University Press, 1991. Discusses Jones as one of seven influential nineteenth century British dramatists. Accuses him of succumbing to conventional morality in *Mrs. Dane's Defence*. Claims his defense of the facade of respectability places him on the side of those who believed in preserving traditional British values at all costs.

Powell, Kerry, ed. *The Cambridge Companion to Victorian*

and Edwardian Theatre. New York: Cambridge University Press, 2004. Although no essay in this book focuses on Jones, the index lists numerous references to Jones and his work. These references help place his work in the context of Victorian-era theater.

Taylor, John Russell. *The Rise and Fall of the Well-Made*

Play. London: Methuen, 1967. One chapter discusses Jones's career and the popularity his plays enjoyed at the beginning of the twentieth century. Considers *Mrs. Dane's Defence* "one of the classics of English well-made drama." Analyzes the play's structure and explains why Jones fails to be convincing in his ending.

Mrs. Ted Bliss

Author: Stanley Elkin (1930-1995)
First published: 1995
Type of work: Novel
Type of plot: Comedy and bildungsroman
Time of plot: 1980's
Locale: Miami

Principal characters:
DOROTHY "MRS. TED" BLISS, an elderly Jewish woman
MANNY TRESSLER, a retired real-estate lawyer
ALCIBIADES CHITRAL, a Venezuelan and a reputed drug dealer
TOMMY "OVEREASY" AUVERISTAS, a South American importer
HECTOR CAMERANDO and JAIME GUTTIEREZ, South American gentlemen of means
HOLMER TOIBB, a counselor
MILTON "JUNIOR" YELLIN, a small-time hustler
MAXINE, Dorothy's daughter
FRANK, Dorothy's son
ELLEN BLISS, Dorothy's daughter-in-law
LOUISE MUNEZ, a guard at Dorothy's condominium

The Story:

Dorothy "Mrs. Ted" Bliss has lived in her Towers condominium ever since she and her late husband, Ted, first retired to Florida. Now in her early seventies and alone, she appears to her neighbors a pleasant but insubstantial woman, a sort of mascot to the Towers' self-contained society.

Things are about to change in Dorothy's life. As the older condo dwellers begin to die, émigrés from South America buy up their units. The original Jewish residents are older and comfortably fixed, but stuffy and set in their ways. The Latinos are younger, stylish, and proud, and are given to the grand gesture and the application of discreet gratuities. The men, especially, project a reined-in animal magnetism that stirs Dorothy's imagination.

The Towers' social committee, aware of the growing culture gap between these two groups, tries to counter it with what they call Good Neighbor Nights and international-theme parties. These efforts strike the South Americans as naïve and cheesy, but occasionally some of them attend. In the middle of a card game at one of these parties, Dorothy has her first encounter with two Latin gentlemen, Hector

Camerando and Jaime Guttierez. Her life begins to take unexpected turns.

Some weeks after her husband's death, Dorothy receives a bill from the city for almost two hundred dollars in taxes on Ted's car. Dorothy does not drive and had always left business matters to her husband. She cannot understand owing money on a car that is already paid for. The two hundred dollars seem an enormous amount for what she thinks is nothing.

Alcibiades Chitral, a gallant Venezuelan, shows up at her front door asking if he can buy Ted's 1978 Buick LeSabre, making her feel both rescued and flustered. The test drive has some of the undertones of a date to Dorothy, and when Alcibiades offers her five thousand dollars more than the market value for the car, she makes the deal.

Some weeks later, Alcibiades is brought to federal court on drug-dealing and money-laundering charges. Dorothy receives a subpoena to testify as a witness. Her Buick is somehow involved in Alcibiades's activities. Dorothy's children, Maxine and Frank, hire her a high-priced local attorney. Dorothy, aghast at the lawyer's charges, fires her and prevails on retired real-estate lawyer Manny Tressler to represent her pro bono. He gets her through the court appearance but cannot help when drug enforcement officers lay claim to her basement parking space as well as the car. Still, in asking Manny to help, she had made a friend of him. He shows her how to use a checkbook and becomes a sort of counselor-on-life to her, countering her loneliness and ineptness at dealing with the outside world.

Attending a party in importer Tommy Auveristas's penthouse apartment, Dorothy fidgets uncomfortably at the exotic food and conversation, but she perks up when Tommy treats her as the guest of honor. He offers to get the LeSabre and to have the police blocks removed from Dorothy's basement parking space. Her children suspect the Latino men's sudden attentions. They decide their mother needs to be under a local professional's care. Persuading her to see a doctor is a lost cause. Finally, Manny suggests she might be willing to see a recreational therapeusist, whose specialty is treating bored old people who lack inner resources.

Holmer Toibb, the therapeusist, talks in medical analogies, which confuses Dorothy, and asks her to bring a list of her interests to her next appointment. Dorothy can only list playing cards, watching television, and seeing other people's apartments. Holmer, however, is fascinated by her supposed connection with the notorious Tommy, also known as Overeasy.

Waiting at the bus stop after one of her appointments, Dorothy is surprised by Hector, who offers her a ride home. On the drive, Hector's conversation half-insults, half-fascinates her. Appalled at his own words, Hector explains that he is a big player in jai alai and in greyhound racing, and that he can make her much money with his betting tips.

Hector is as good as his word. Dorothy bets cautiously and infrequently—mostly to avoid hurting Hector's feelings—but she always wins. Her regard for South American gentlemen revived, she offers to visit Alcibiades in prison. She had always felt guilty about her part in his conviction. In due time a driver and limousine arrive to take her to the minimum-security prison on the edge of the Everglades. To Dorothy the prison resembles an upscale retreat center more than a penitentiary, but Alcibiades's ninety-nine-year sentence still preys on her mind. They have a good visit, only slightly marred by Alcibiades's rant against the "passivity" and naïveté of Jews when she asks why he had picked her as the stooge for his gambit.

The years go by. Dorothy's children bring her to son Frank's new home in Rhode Island for the Passover holidays. Frank's new religiosity surprises her, and she is upset to learn that he had lost his previous job in Pittsburgh because of campus politics. Mostly, however, the visit reminds her of how far apart she is from her children's daily lives, and vice versa.

Dorothy is now in her eighties. Manny has died. Before her trip to Rhode Island, she had returned to the therapeusis center. Holmer was gone, but to her shock, her new therapist is Milton "Junior" Yellin, her husband's onetime business partner, who had changed vocations. Junior has conveniently forgotten that he once made a pass at her, but to Dorothy, it now merely adds to their shared history. They chat, and she finds that apparently, Junior is lonely, too. The two begin to spend time together, not as a couple but as friends. Dorothy had never had a friend before; family duties had always absorbed her. They go to jai alai matches together. Junior becomes intrigued with metal detectors, and they visit the beach, trolling for buried treasure.

Dorothy receives a letter from her daughter-in-law Ellen, who was married to Dorothy's son Marvin. Ellen invites herself to a free Florida vacation in Dorothy's apartment, but Dorothy is not keen on this idea; but she cannot say no to her daughter-in-law. They spend a week being elaborately polite to each other. One night, Dorothy invites Junior to dinner. He arrives drunk, sets off an incipient quarrel between the two women, and makes a mess in Dorothy's bathroom, which upsets Dorothy the most. While Junior figures the mess is a minor faux pas, mended with an apology, house-proud Dorothy views it as a sort of ritual defilement. She throws away the guest towels that Junior used in a clean-up effort, convinced she has lost the last person to whom she was close.

A few days later, Dorothy receives a ship-to-shore telegram announcing Ellen and Junior's marriage. The note had been sent from a Caribbean cruise ship; the couple is at sea on their honeymoon. Unfortunately, Hurricane Andrew is forming in the Atlantic near their ship. Dorothy sits watching the weather coverage, at first reluctant to believe a storm is directly on course to hit Miami. As it approaches, she refuses evacuation and then refuses boards to protect her condo's windows. She wants to watch, she says, not sure at this point even why she is staying. When the hurricane hits, the electricity goes off and she thinks the building is deserted. As the winds lash the palm trees, she sees a light playing over her darkened living room. She opens the door and sees Louise, the guard, making her rounds. Louise offers to wait out the storm with her, and the two clasp hands and comfort each other.

Critical Evaluation:

To read *Mrs. Ted Bliss* for plot is to miss half the point of this last novel by award-winning writer Stanley Elkin. The novel does have a storyline, a somewhat quirky one, but one that lacks the coherence of a conventional cause-and-effect plot. The story is a bildungsroman of a seventy-plus-year-old woman, if such a novel can exist for an older person. As such, it is basically a quest story, with the poignant feature that Dorothy "Mrs. Ted" Bliss has absolutely no idea of what she is questing. In the end, with a hurricane battering at her picture windows, the answer becomes clear: She is seeking connection.

The connections that defined most of her adult life—those primary bonds to husband and family—are now broken by death or are weakened by distance and the generation gap. The book's very title, implying Dorothy's persistence in thinking of herself as Mrs. Ted Bliss instead of Dorothy Bliss, highlights the significance to her of her role as wife and mother. Her Passover visit to Rhode Island shows how peripheral she has become in the lives of her surviving children and grandchildren. There is both sadness and irony in the way she has always identified herself as "just a baleboosteh"—a Yiddish term meaning, approximately, "praiseworthy homemaker." Her ingrained, praiseworthy-homemaker routine continues even without a family to care for.

Still, other connections begin to fall into Dorothy's life, almost as if summoned by her need for them. Some connections, like the South American gentlemen, are suspect connections by the standards of her former life, yet they provide delicious frissons of the exotic and romantic, to which she was oblivious in that earlier life. Others, like Manny Tressler and Junior Yellin, she trusts more; they offer a mix of a familiar Jewish background and a brisk openness to new ventures.

These acquaintances drag Dorothy into encounters with the wider world that are unexpected in women of her age—at least in fiction. What she finds baffles her, often leading to comedic misunderstandings. Dorothy's basic personality changes very little; nevertheless, she is a different person at the novel's end. Indeed, the theme of the novel could be that one is never too old for adventure.

Reviewers of Elkin's fiction make note of his intoxication with language. *Mrs. Ted Bliss* shows off this trademark style in full form; the text is so packed with riffs and digressions that readers may have trouble teasing out what is actually happening. Elkins was proud of this approach, which stands in opposition to both the minimalism of much contemporary literary fiction and the straightforward storytelling of popu-

lar novels. His books have been much more admired by literary figures than by the general reading public. *Mrs. Ted Bliss* won the National Book Critics Circle Award for 1995.

An elderly Jewish widow is an unusual protagonist in any fiction today, and even less so in a comedic novel of character. That Elkin succeeds with the idea, even with the eccentricities of voice and event that dot the story, is testament to his talent. That he chose to write the novel near the end of his life as a longtime survivor of multiple sclerosis is testament to his humanity.

Emily Alward

Further Reading

Dougherty, David. "A Conversation with Stanley Elkin." In *The Muse upon My Shoulder: Discussions of the Creative Process*, edited by Sylvia Skaggs McTague. Madison, N.J.: Fairleigh Dickinson University Press, 2004. Elkin is one of thirteen authors who discuss the process of writing, their inspiration to write, and their relationship to their readers in this collection of interviews.

Gass, William H. *A Temple of Texts: Essays.* New York: Knopf, 2006. Another writer obsessed with the workings of language offers an appreciation of Elkin's writing in the essay "Open on the Sabbath."

Goodman, Walter. "Twilight of a Baleboosteh." *The New York Times Book Review,* September 17, 1995. A long, appreciative review of *Mrs. Ted Bliss*, with quotations and images that illustrate Elkin's unique writing style.

Review of Contemporary Fiction 15, no. 2 (Summer, 1995). A special issue on Elkin that features contributions by Jerome Klinkowitz, Jerome Charyn, William H. Gass, and others. Includes an interview with Elkin in which he discusses the mystery in his fiction, the nature of plot, the essence of story, and his prose style.

Saltzman, Arthur M. "*Mrs. Ted Bliss.*" *Review of Contemporary Fiction* 16, no. 1 (Spring, 1996): 145. A short but incisive review focusing on the tensions between physical decline and the ego's continuing vitality in *Mrs. Ted Bliss*.

Tristman, Richard. "Tragic Soliloquy, Stand-up Spiel." *New England Review* 27, no. 4 (Fall, 2006): 36-40. Presents an analysis of the comic themes in Elkin's writing, including a discussion of the characters, whom Tristman describes as being "drawn from the ordinary and even tawdry precincts of life."

Much Ado About Nothing

Author: William Shakespeare (1564-1616)
First produced: c. 1598-1599; first published, 1600
Type of work: Drama
Type of plot: Comedy
Time of plot: Thirteenth century
Locale: Italy

Principal characters:
DON PEDRO, prince of Arragon
DON JOHN, his bastard brother
CLAUDIO, a young lord of Florence
BENEDICK, a young lord of Padua
LEONATO, the governor of Messina
HERO, Leonato's daughter
BEATRICE, Leonato's niece
DOGBERRY, a constable

The Story:

Don Pedro, prince of Arragon, arrives in Messina accompanied by his bastard brother, Don John, and his two friends, the young Italian noblemen Claudio and Benedick. Don Pedro had vanquished his brother in battle. Now, reconciled, the brothers plan to visit Leonato before returning to their homeland. On their arrival in Messina, young Claudio is immediately smitten by the lovely Hero, daughter of Leonato, the governor of Messina. To help his faithful young friend in his suit, Don Pedro assumes the guise of Claudio at a masked ball and woos Hero in Claudio's name. Then he gains Leonato's consent for Claudio and Hero to marry. Don John tries to cause trouble by persuading Claudio that Don Pedro means to betray him and keep Hero for himself, but the villain is foiled in his plot and Claudio remains faithful to Don Pedro.

Benedick, the other young follower of Don Pedro, is a confirmed and bitter bachelor who scorns all men willing to enter the married state. No less opposed to men and matrimony is Leonato's niece, Beatrice. These two constantly spar with one another, each trying to show intellectual supremacy over the other. Don Pedro, with the help of Hero, Claudio, and Leonato, undertakes the seemingly impossible task of bringing Benedick and Beatrice together in matrimony in the seven days before the marriage of Hero and Claudio.

Don John, thwarted in his first attempt to cause disharmony, forms another plot. With the help of a servant, he arranges to make it appear as if Hero is being unfaithful to Claudio. The servant is to gain entrance to Hero's chambers when she is away. In her place will be her attendant, assuming Hero's clothes. Don John, posing as Claudio's true friend, will inform him of her unfaithfulness and lead him to Hero's window to witness her wanton disloyalty.

Don Pedro pursues his plan to persuade Benedick and Beatrice to stop quarreling and fall in love with each other. When Benedick is close by, thinking himself unseen, Don Pedro, Claudio, and Leonato talk of their great sympathy for Beatrice, who loves Benedick but is unloved in return. The three tell one another of the love letters Beatrice had written to Benedick and had then torn up, and that Beatrice beats her breast and sobs over her unrequited love for Benedick. At the same time, on occasions when Beatrice is nearby but apparently unseen, Hero and her maid tell each other that poor Benedick pines and sighs for the heartless Beatrice. The two unsuspecting young people decide not to let the other suffer. Each will sacrifice principles and accept the other's love.

Just as Benedick and Beatrice prepare to admit their love for each other, Don John is successful in his base plot to ruin Hero. He tells Claudio that he has learned of Hero's duplicity, and he arranges to take him and Don Pedro to her window that very night to witness her unfaithfulness. Dogberry, a constable, and the watch apprehend Don John's followers and overhear the truth of the plot, but in their stupidity the petty officials cannot get their story told in time to prevent Hero's disgrace. Don Pedro and Claudio witness the apparent betrayal, and Claudio determines to allow Hero to arrive in church the next day still thinking herself beloved. Then, instead of marrying her, he will shame her before all the wedding guests.

All happens as Don John had hoped. Before the priest and all the guests, Claudio calls Hero a wanton and forswears her love for all time. The poor girl protests her innocence, but to no avail. Claudio says that he had seen her foul act with his own eyes. Hero swoons and lays as if dead, but Claudio and Don Pedro leave her with her father, who believes the story and wishes his daughter really dead in her shame. The priest believes the girl guiltless, however, and he persuades Leonato to believe in her, too. The priest tells Leonato to let the world believe Hero dead while they work to prove her innocent. Benedick, also believing in her innocence, promises to help unravel the mystery. Then, Beatrice tells Benedick of her love for him and asks him to kill Claudio and so prove his love for her. Benedick challenges Claudio to a duel. Don John had fled the country after the successful outcome of his plot, but Benedick swears that he will find Don John and kill him as well as Claudio.

At last, Dogberry and the watch get to Leonato and tell their story. When Claudio and Don Pedro hear the story, Claudio wants to die and to be with his wronged Hero. Leonato allows the two sorrowful men to continue to think Hero dead. In fact, they all attend her funeral. Leonato says that he will be avenged if Claudio will marry his niece, a girl who much resembles Hero. Although Claudio still loves the dead Hero, he agrees to marry the other girl so that Leonato should have his wish.

When Don Pedro and Claudio arrive at Leonato's house for the ceremony, all the women are masked. Leonato brings one young woman forward. After Claudio promises to be her husband, she unmasks. She is, of course, Hero. At first, Claudio cannot believe his senses, but after he is convinced of the truth he takes her to the church immediately. Then, Benedick and Beatrice declare their true love for each other, and they, too, leave for the church after a dance in celebration of the double nuptials to be performed. Best of all, word comes that Don John had been captured and is being brought back to Messina to face his brother, Don Pedro, the next day. On this day, however, all is joy and happiness.

Critical Evaluation:

William Shakespeare's *Much Ado About Nothing* has in fact very much to do with "noting" (an intended pun on "nothing") or half-seeing, with perceiving dimly or not at all. Out of a host of misperceptions arises the comedy of Shakespeare's drama. Indeed, if it can be said that one theme preoccupies Shakespeare more than any other, it is that of perception, which informs not only his great histories and tragedies but also his comedies. An early history such as *Richard II* (pr. c. 1595-1596, pb. 1600), for example, which also involves tragic elements, proceeds not only from the title character's inability to function as a king but also from his failure to apprehend the nature of the new politics. Both *Othello* and *King Lear* are perfect representatives of the tragic consequences of the inability to see. Hindered by their egos, they live in their own restricted worlds oblivious to reality. When they fail to take the real into account, whether it is the nature of evil or their own limitation, they must pay the cost.

Although the blindness of Leonato, Don Pedro, Claudio, and Benedick in *Much Ado About Nothing* very nearly results in tragedy, it is the comic implications of noting rather than seeing that Shakespeare is concerned with here. Yet if his mode is comic, his intention is serious. Besides the characters' inability to perceive Don John's villainy, their superficial grasp of love and their failure to understand the nature of courtship and marriage reveal their moral obtuseness. In fact, the whole society is shot through with a kind of civilized shallowness. The play begins as an unspecified war ends, and the audience is immediately struck by Leonato's and the messenger's lack of response to the casualty report. To the governor of Messina's question, "How many gentlemen have you lost in this action?" the messenger replies, "But few of any sort, and none of name." Leonato comments, "A victory is twice itself, when the achiever brings home full numbers." The heroes of the war—Don Pedro, Claudio, and Benedick—return in a high good humor, seemingly untouched by their experiences and now in search of comfort, games, and diversion.

Only Beatrice is unimpressed with the soldiers' grand entrance, for she knows what they are. Between their "noble" actions, they are are no more than seducers, "valiant trenchermen," gluttons and leeches, or, like Claudio, vain young boys ready to fall in love on a whim. Even the stately Don Pedro is a fool who proposes to Beatrice on impulse after he has wooed the childish Hero for the inarticulate Claudio. In contrast to their behavior, Beatrice's initial cynicism—"I had rather hear my dog bark at a crow, than a man swear he loves me"—is salutary and seems like wisdom.

Beatrice, however, is as susceptible to flattery as is Benedick. Like her eventual lover and husband, she is seduced by Don Pedro's deception, the masque he arranges to lead both Beatrice and Benedick to the altar. Both of them, after hearing that they are adored by the other, pledge their love and devotion. To be sure, the scenes in which they are duped are full of innocent humor, but the comedy does not obscure Shakespeare's rather bitter observations on the foppery of human love and courtship.

Nor is their foppery and foolishness the end of the matter. Don John realizes that a vain lover betrayed is a cruel and indeed inhuman tyrant. With little effort he convinces Claudio and Don Pedro that the innocent Hero is no more than a strumpet. Yet rather than break off the engagement in private, they wait until all meet at the altar to accuse the girl of "savage sensuality." Without compunction they leave her in a swoon, believing her dead. Even the father, Leonato, would have her dead rather than shamed. It is this moment that reveals the witty and sophisticated aristocrats of Messina to be grossly hypocritical, for beneath their glittering and refined manners lies a vicious ethic.

In vivid contrast to the decorous soldiers and politicians are Dogberry and his watchmen, although they certainly function as no more than a slapstick diversion. Hilarious clowns when they attempt to ape their social betters in manners and speech, they are yet possessed by a common sense or—as one critic has observed—by an instinctual morality, which enables them to uncover the villainy of Don John's henchmen, Conrade and Borachio. As the latter says to the nobleman, Don Pedro, "I have deceived even your very eyes: what your wisdoms could not discover, these shallow fools have brought to light." Like the outspoken and bawdy Margaret, who knows that underlying the aristocrats' courtly manners in the game of love is unacknowledged lust, Dogberry and his bumbling followers immediately understand the issue and recognize villainy, though they may use the wrong words to describe it.

Shakespeare does not force the point home in the end. He is not dealing here with characters of great stature, and they could not bear revelations of substantial moral consequence. They may show compunction for their errors, but they exhibit no significant remorse and are ready to get on with the rituals of their class. It does not seem to matter to Claudio whether he marries Hero or someone who looks like her. Even Beatrice has apparently lost her maverick edge as she joins the strutting Benedick in the marriage dance. All ends well for those involved (with the exception of Don John), but through no great fault of their own.

"Critical Evaluation" by David L. Kubal

Further Reading

Bloom, Harold, ed. *William Shakespeare's "Much Ado About Nothing."* New York: Chelsea House, 1988. Contains eight significant articles on the play. Especially good is the essay by Richard A. Levin, who looks beneath the comedic surface to find unexpected, troubling currents, and the essay by Carol Thomas Neely, who contributes an influential feminist interpretation.

Evans, Bertrand. *Shakespeare's Comedies.* Oxford, England: Clarendon Press, 1960. Important critical study. Concludes that Shakespeare's comic dramaturgy is based on different levels of awareness among characters and between them and the audience. Argues that the comedy in *Much Ado About Nothing* reflects an intricate game of multiple deceptions and misunderstandings that the audience enjoys from a privileged position.

Greenblatt, Stephen. *Will in the World: How Shakespeare Became Shakespeare.* New York: Norton, 2004. Critically acclaimed biography, in which Greenblatt finds new connections between Shakespeare's works and the bard's life and engagement with Elizabethan society.

Hunter, Robert Grams. *Shakespeare and the Comedy of Forgiveness.* New York: Columbia University Press, 1965. Argues persuasively that the thematic core of several Shakespearean comedies derives from the tradition of English morality plays. In *Much Ado About Nothing*, Claudio sins against the moral order by mistrusting Hero and is saved by repentance and forgiveness.

Macdonald, Ronald R. *William Shakespeare: The Comedies.* New York: Twayne, 1992. Compact introduction to Shakespeare's comedy that is both critically sophisticated and accessible to the general reader. The essay on *Much Ado About Nothing* reveals various subtextual relationships of class and gender by probing the characters' semantically complex and ironic verbal behavior.

Ornstein, Robert. *Shakespeare's Comedies: From Roman Farce to Romantic Mystery.* London: Associated University Presses, 1986. Award-winning book by a major Shakespeare scholar. The chapter on *Much Ado About Nothing* offers a sensitive, graceful analysis of the play that focuses primarily on characterization, plot, and moral themes.

Shakespeare, William. *Much Ado About Nothing.* Edited by Michael Clamp. New York: Cambridge University Press, 2002. In addition to the text of the play, this edition contains more than ninety pages of introductory material, including discussions of the play within the context of romantic comedy, and the play's date, sources, title, place and setting, characters, plot construction, and performance history.

Simpson, Matt. *Shakespeare's "Much Ado About Nothing."* London: Greenwich Exchange, 2007. Discusses the importance of honor and ritual in the lives of the characters, describing how their need to behave in a virtuous manner sometimes causes them to do the wrong things for the right reasons. Argues that the play is about redemption and renewal.

Wynne-Davies, Marion, ed. *"Much Ado About Nothing" and "The Taming of the Shrew."* New York: Palgrave, 2001. Collection of essays about the two plays, including discussions about *Much Ado About Nothing* as an "unsociable comedy," and the sexual and family politics and "workings of ideology" in this play.

Mumbo Jumbo

Author: Ishmael Reed (1938-   )
First published: 1972
Type of work: Novel
Type of plot: Satire
Time of plot: 1920's
Locale: Harlem, New York City

Principal characters:
PAPA LABAS, a conjure man of Jes Grew Kathedral
BERBELANG, LaBas's former assistant and a Mu'tahfikah leader
BLACK HERMAN, a famous African American occultist
HINCKLE VON VAMPTON, the Atonist publisher of *The Benign Monster*
HUBERT "SAFECRACKER" GOULD, Von Vampton's assistant
WOODROW WILSON JEFFERSON, Von Vampton's African American tool
BIFF MUSCLEWHITE, curator for the Center of Art Detention

The Story:

One night in 1920, the mayor of New Orleans is drinking bootlegged gin with his mistress when a messenger announces the outbreak of Jes Grew, a "psychic epidemic" causing African Americans to thrash in ecstasy and to lust for meaning in life. By the next morning, ten thousand people had contracted the disease, which is spreading rapidly across America.

PaPa LaBas, a conjure man who carries "Jes Grew in him like most other folk carry genes," runs Jes Grew Kathedral and represents the old ways of Jes Grew, specializing in "Black astrology charts, herbs, potions, candles, talismans." His former assistant, Berbelang, moved away from old ways and worked to expand Jes Grew to other non-Western peoples such as Native Americans, Asians, and Muslims, as well as to more people of African descent. Berbelang leads the Mu'tahfikah, a radical group of Jes Grew Carriers who loot Centers of Art Detention (museums) to return treasures to their native lands in Africa, South America, and Asia.

Attempting to halt Jes Grew, the Wallflower Order of the Atonist Path (Western culture) forms a two-step plan. Its first step is to install Warren Harding as anti-Jes Grew president of the United States; their next step is to implant a Talking Android within Jes Grew to sabotage the movement. Atonist Biff Musclewhite gives up his job as police commissioner and becomes a consultant to the Metropolitan Police to qualify for a higher paying job as Curator for Art Detention.

One day, LaBas is in court facing charges that he allowed his "Newfoundland HooDoo dog 3 Cents" to defecate on the altar at St. Patrick's Cathedral. The Manhattan Atonists use charges like this, fire inspections, tax audits, censorship of writings, and other means to deter LaBas and Jes Grew.

Atonist Hinckle Von Vampton works in the copy room of the *New York Sun*, a Wallflower Order newspaper. One night, his landlady sees him performing secret rituals. At work, when he forgets to keep a headline in present tense, his boss thinks he is "losing his grip." Later, Von Vampton is fired for printing the headline "Voo Doo Generals Surround Marines at Port-au-Prince," violating the paper's policy against mentioning U.S. military action in Haiti. Their reason is that "Americans will not tolerate wars that can't be explained in simple terms of economics or the White man's destiny." Von Vampton is later seized at gunpoint and taken to Wallflower Order headquarters, which is buzzing with activity monitoring the Jes Grew epidemic.

The person in charge of the headquarters, Hierophant 1, explains to Von Vampton that the Wallflower Order needs The Text, the sacred Jes Grew writings. Von Vampton had divided The Text into fourteen parts and sent it to fourteen individual Jes Grew Carriers in Harlem. Only Von Vampton had the power to reassemble The Text, so the Wallflower Order agrees to let him control the project. First, he must burn The Text. Second, he must create the Talking Android that would infiltrate and undercut the Jes Grew movement. Von Vampton recruits Hubert "Safecracker" Gould to help run *The Benign Monster*, the magazine he will use to carry out the project.

Woodrow Wilson Jefferson, a young man who left rural Mississippi to begin a journalism career in New York City, is laughed out of the *New York Tribune* because of his ragged, rural appearance and because he wants to meet Karl Marx and Friedrich Engels. Later, Jefferson sees a sign outside the offices of *The Benign Monster*, stating, "Negro viewpoint wanted." Von Vampton hires Jefferson and gives him an office in his estate, Spiraling Agony. Jefferson is like putty waiting to be formed and would have made a perfect Talking Android, except Von Vampton thinks his skin is too dark. The Talking Android has to be black, but Von Vampton believes people will not accept anyone too dark.

Von Vampton learns that Abdul Hamid has acquired and is trying to publish The Text. Von Vampton, Gould, and Jefferson go to Abdul's office and offer to buy it, but Abdul refuses to sell. When Gould pulls out a gun and demands to see the safe, Abdul resists, so Von Vampton stabs him in the back. Gould opens the safe but finds it empty. The *Sun* headline distorts the incident by suggesting that Mu'tahfikah is responsible for Abdul's death.

Charlotte, a young French translator at the Kathedral, quits her job to perform Neo HooDoo dances at the Plantation House cabaret, despite LaBas's warning against using The Work for profit. She also entertains customers outside the club.

The Mu'tahfikah—Berbelang, Yellow Jack, Thor Wintergreen, and José Fuentes (whom La Bas had met during an art history class in college)—plan to recover some cultural artifacts. Biff Musclewhite is in Charlotte's apartment when the Mu'tahfikah kidnaps him to gain access to the Center for Art Detention. As ransom, they demand the return of the Olmec Head, a Central American sculpture.

Left to guard the hostage, Thor Wintergreen is tricked into helping Musclewhite and the police ambush Berbelang, who is shot and killed. Musclewhite convinces Wintergreen that the Mu'tahfikah members not only are taking back their culture but also getting ready to take over the country. Once free, Musclewhite makes an appointment to see Charlotte, but before he arrives, she sees the headline announcing Berbelang's death. When she accuses Musclewhite of having something to do with the incident, he strangles her.

Making his last run of the night, a trolley operator is seduced by LaBas's assistant Earline, who had picked up a *loa*, the sensuous spirit of the Voodoo goddess Erzulie. When PaPa LaBas leaves to tell Earline of Berbelang's death, she faints and LaBas calls Black Herman to exorcise the *loa*.

The next morning, Black Herman takes LaBas to see Haitian Benoit Battraville aboard the freighter *The Black Plume* in the harbor. Battraville explains the Atonist role in Haiti and reveals the Wallflower Order plot to install a Talking Android. LaBas and Black Herman volunteer to track the Talking Android.

Meanwhile, Von Vampton is still looking for someone to become the Talking Android when he sees an advertisement for skin bleaching cream. He is applying the cream to Jefferson's face when the young man's father rushes in and then takes his son back home to Mississippi. The skin-lightening

plot failed. Instead, Von Vampton settles on an opposite plan when Gould accidentally falls facedown into black mud. Gould becomes the Talking Android.

Concerned about President Harding's political blunderings and alleged black ancestry, the Wallflower Order decides to do away with him by sending him on a train trip to California and slowly poisoning him along the way. Harding dies in San Francisco. The order also takes defensive moves to combat the spread of Jes Grew. The federal government seizes control of the arts and decentralizes art objects away from the Centers for Art Detention to protect them from the Mu'tahfikah.

At a gathering north of New York City, the Talking Android is reading his epic poem "Harlem Tom Toms" when LaBas and Black Herman break in and expose Gould as a fake. Asked to defend their charges, LaBas gives an extended history of the mythology behind Jes Grew, dating back thousands of years to ancient Egypt. Having brought Jes Grew history up to the present, LaBas explains how he solved the mystery and located the box that should have held Abdul's copy of The Text underneath the floor of the Cotton Club where Abdul had hidden it. A seal on the box reminds LaBas of Von Vampton's pendant, connecting the Atonist to the mystery. Then Buddy Jackson, operator of several Harlem speakeasies, steps forward and announces that he had given The Text to Abdul. PaPa LaBas and Black Herman seize Von Vampton and Gould and turn them over to Benoit Battraville.

Jes Grew dies down, but PaPa LaBas continues telling its history, giving yearly university lectures. The novel ends with a philosophical discussion of the psychic power of blackness in the American imagination.

Critical Evaluation:

First-time readers of Ishmael Reed's *Mumbo Jumbo* are overwhelmed by the amount of information contained in the novel, including history, mythology, politics, literary history, music, and photography. Critic Henry Louis Gates, Jr., offers the best way to deal with this confusion: Think of it as "gumbo," a complex stew of irregularly shaped chunks and spicy seasonings. Like gumbo, the novel has a cumulative effect, which builds and changes as one reads and lingers long after one has finished the novel.

Mumbo Jumbo is a satire, but the objects of Reed's critiques are not always clear because there are so many. He satirizes politics by having Cab Calloway run against Warren Harding for president of the United States and by naming Hinkle Von Vampton's estate Spiraling Agony after Spiro Agnew. He critiques music history by having Moses steal rock lyrics from The Work and by including a photograph of the rock group Black Sabbath. Satires of literary history also flood the book, including a stab at James Baldwin—"King Baldwin 1 grants the Templars his palace as their headquarters"—and a condemnation of *Confessions of the Black Bull God Osiris* by Bilious Styronicus (a stab at William Styron's *The Confessions of Nat Turner,* 1967). Reed even critiques formal education by having PaPa LaBas give university lectures on Jes Grew in the 1960's.

In addition, *Mumbo Jumbo* is a parody of literary form. Reed uses the structure of thriller detective fiction (mystery, clues, whodunits, rational order) but undermines detective fiction's reliance on reason. The discoveries, deductions, and conclusions in *Mumbo Jumbo* are not rational; they defy "order" as defined by Western culture.

Mumbo Jumbo is Reed's most comprehensive study of his "Neo-Hoodoo" aesthetic based on pantheistic voodoo culture rather than on monotheistic Western culture. Reed urges people of color to reclaim their art and culture, a message that echoes the Harlem Renaissance of the 1920's and the Black Arts movement of the 1960's. *Mumbo Jumbo* creates a history of the Jes Grew movement, a history of African American experience, which stands as an alternative version to the linear grand narrative of Western history. In presenting data, Reed employs devices common to history textbooks: footnotes, definitions, charts, illustrations, and a bibliography. The novel is encyclopedic of African American culture, tracing its origins and roots by examining instances of rapid expansion in the fictional Jes Grew movement.

Reed's resistance of an orderly linear narrative and his technique of bombarding the reader with information place *Mumbo Jumbo* in the realm of postmodern fiction, such as Thomas Pynchon's *Gravity's Rainbow* (1973), Robert Coover's *The Public Burning* (1976), and Salman Rushdie's *Midnight's Children* (1980). All of these works critique history by offering alternatives to a master narrative, and each is a sociopolitical satire.

Geralyn Strecker

Further Reading

Byerman, Keith E. "Voodoo Aesthetics: History and Parody in the Novels of Ishmael Reed." In *Fingering the Jagged Grain: Tradition and Form in Recent Black Fiction.* Athens: University of Georgia Press, 1985. Focuses on Reed's use of parody and reworking of history. Analyzes six novels and traces the development of a new aesthetic of African American sensibility that Reed calls Neo-Hoo-Doo art.

Carter, Steven R. "Ishmael Reed's Neo-Hoodoo Detection." In *Dimensions of Detective Fiction,* edited by Larry N. Landrum, Pat Browne, and Ray B. Browne. Bowling Green, Ohio: Bowling Green State University Popular Press, 1976. Argues that Reed's parody of detective fiction leads readers from the mysteries within the text to the mysteries in life, to consider the culprits in history, to question the alleged truths of Western culture, and to discover distortions of reality in written history.

Cooke, Michael G. "Tragic and Ironic Denials of Intimacy: Jean Toomer, James Baldwin, and Ishmael Reed." In *Afro-American Literature in the Twentieth Century: The Achievement of Intimacy.* New Haven, Conn.: Yale University Press, 1984. Recognizes *Mumbo Jumbo* as a high-spirited satire but criticizes Reed for not developing the concept of the Jes Grew Text into something more positive for African Americans.

Dick, Bruce, and Amritjit Singh, eds. *Conversations with Ishmael Reed.* Jackson: University Press of Mississippi, 1995. A compilation of twenty-six interviews with Reed that were conducted from 1968 through 1995. Includes one "self-interview" and a chronology of significant events in Reed's life.

Dick, Bruce Allen, and Pavel Zemliansky, eds. *The Critical Response to Ishmael Reed.* Westport, Conn.: Greenwood Press, 1999. Chronological account of the critical response to Reed's novels. Contains book reviews, essays, an interview with Reed, a chronology of his life, and bibliographical information.

Gates, Henry Louis, Jr. "On 'The Blackness of Blackness': Ishmael Reed and a Critique of the Sign." In *The Signifying Monkey: A Theory of Afro-American Literary Criticism.* New York: Oxford University Press, 1988. Recognizes Reed's importance in the tradition of African American literature. Finds *Mumbo Jumbo* to be an elaboration on the detective novel and a postmodern text because of its use of intertextuality.

Martin, Reginald. *Ishmael Reed and the New Black Aesthetic Critics.* New York: St. Martin's Press, 1988. Closely analyzes Reed's evolving notion of Neo-HooDoo aesthetics and how it relates to black aesthetic critics such as Clarence Major, Houston Baker, Jr., Addison Gayle, Jr., and Amiri Baraka. Concludes that Reed refuses to acknowledge any mode of criticism. Discusses *Mumbo Jumbo* as a satiric allegory that is in itself the Text that is searched for in the novel.

Mvuyekure, Pierre-Damien. *The "Dark Heathenism" of the American Novelist Ishmael Reed: African Voodoo as American Literary Hoodoo.* Lewiston, N.Y.: Edwin Mellen Press, 2007. Defines Reed's novels as postcolonial writings characterized by Neo-HooDooism, an aesthetic derived from African voodoo. Demonstrates how Reed transforms the English language and debates about colonialism into discourses about self-empowerment and self-representation, reconnecting African Americans with Africa.

Weisenburger, Steven. *Fables of Subversion: Satire and the American Novel, 1930-1980*. Athens: University of Georgia Press, 1995. A discussion of Reed's use of Menippean satire in *Mumbo Jumbo* is included in this study of satire in thirty postmodern American novels.

Whitlow, Roger. "Ishmael Reed." In *Black American Literature: A Critical History*. Rev. ed. Chicago: Nelson Hall, 1976. Covers Reed's early work, including his poetry, and makes a strong argument for his inclusion in the absurdist literary tradition. Sees many connections to the style and satiric content of such American writers as Joseph Heller, Norman Mailer, and J. D. Salinger.

Murder in the Cathedral

Author: T. S. Eliot (1888-1965)
First produced: 1935; first published, 1935
Type of work: Drama
Type of plot: Historical
Time of plot: 1170
Locale: Canterbury, England

Principal characters:
ARCHBISHOP THOMAS BECKET
PRIESTS
TEMPTERS
KNIGHTS
CHORUS OF WOMEN OF CANTERBURY

The Story:

The women of Canterbury are drawn to the cathedral, knowing instinctively that they are drawn there by danger. There is no safety anywhere, but they have to bear witness. Archbishop Thomas Becket has been gone seven years. He had always been kind to his people, but he should not return. During the periods when the king and the barons ruled alternately, the poor had suffered all kinds of oppression. Like common people everywhere, the women had tried to keep their households in order and to escape the notice of the various rulers. Now they could only wait and witness.

The priests of the cathedral are well aware of the coming struggle for power. The archbishop has been intriguing in France, where he has enlisted the aid of the pope. Henry of Anjou is a stubborn king, however. The priests know that the strong rule by force, the weak by caprice. The only law is that of seizing power and holding it.

A herald announces that the archbishop is nearing the city and that they are to prepare at once for his coming. Anxiously, they ask whether there will be peace or war, whether the archbishop and the king have been reconciled or not. The herald is of the opinion that there had been only a hasty compromise. He does not know that when the archbishop had parted from the king, the prelate had said that King Henry would not see him again in this life.

After the herald leaves, one priest expresses the pessimism felt by all. When Thomas Becket was chancellor and in temporal power, courtiers flattered and fawned over him, but even then he had felt insecure. Either the king should have been stronger or Thomas weaker. For a time, the priests are hopeful that when Thomas returns he will lead them. The women think the archbishop should return to France. He would remain their spiritual leader, but in France he would be safe. As the priests start to drive out the women, the archbishop arrives and asks them to remain. Thomas Becket tells his priests of the difficulties he has encountered, and that rebellious bishops and the barons had sworn to have his head. They sent spies to him and intercepted his letters. At Sandwich, he had barely escaped with his life.

The first tempter arrives to talk with Thomas. When he was chancellor, Thomas had known worldly pleasure and worldly success. Many had been his friends, and at that time he knew how to let friendship dictate over principles. To escape his present hard fate, he needs only to relax his severity and dignity, to be friendly, and to overlook disagreeable principles. Thomas has the strength to give the tempter a strong refusal.

The second tempter reminds Thomas of his temporal power as chancellor. He could be chancellor again and have lasting power. It is well known that the king only commands, whereas the chancellor rules. Power is an attribute of the present; holiness is more useful after death. Real power has to be purchased by wise submission, and his present spiritual authority leads only to death. Thomas asks about rebellious bishops whom he had excommunicated and barons whose privileges he had curtailed. The tempter is confident that these dissidents will come to heel if Thomas were chancellor with the king's power behind him. Again, Thomas has the strength to say no.

The third tempter is even easier to deal with. He represents a clique intent on overthrowing the throne. If Thomas will lead them, they can make the power of the Church supreme. No more will the barons as well as the bishops be ruled by a king. Thomas declines the offer to lead the malcontents.

The fourth tempter is unexpected. He shows Thomas how he can have eternal glory. As plain archbishop, the time will come when men will neither respect nor hate him; he will become a fact of history. So it is with temporal power, too: King succeeds king as the wheel of time turns. Shrines are pillaged and thrones totter. If, however, Thomas continues in his present course, he will become a martyr and a saint, to dwell forevermore in the presence of God. The archbishop faces a dilemma. No matter whether he acts or suffers, he will sin against his religion.

Early on Christmas morning, Thomas preaches a sermon on peace, saying that Christ left people his peace but not peace as the world thinks of it. Spiritual peace does not necessarily mean political peace between England and other countries or between the barons and the king.

After Christmas, four knights come to Canterbury on urgent business. Refusing all hospitality, they begin to cite charges against Thomas, saying that he owes all his influence to the king, that he has been ignobly born, and that his eminence is due solely to King Henry's favor. The knights try to attack Thomas, but the priests and attendants interpose themselves.

The charges are publicly amplified. Thomas had gone to France to stir up trouble in the dominion and to intrigue with the king of France and the pope. In his charity, King Henry had permitted Thomas to return to his see, but Thomas had repaid that charity by excommunicating the bishops who had crowned the young prince; hence the legality of the coronation is in doubt. The knights then pronounce his sentence: He and his retinue must leave English soil.

Thomas answers firmly. In France he had been a beggar of foreign charity; he would never leave England again. He had no dislike for the prince; rather, he had only carried out the pope's orders in excommunicating the bishops. These words availed little. In the cathedral proper, the knights fall on Thomas Becket and slay him.

The knights justify the slaying. It may have looked like four against one, an offense against the English belief in fair play, but before deciding, the people should know the whole story. First, the four knights would not benefit from the murder, for the king, for reasons of state, would deplore the incident, and the knights would be banished.

Second, the king had hoped, in elevating Thomas to the archbishopric, to unite temporal and spiritual rule and to bring order to a troubled kingdom; but as soon as Thomas was elevated, he had become more priestly than the priests and refused to follow the king's orders. Third, he had become an egotistical madman. There is evidence that before leaving France he had clearly prophesied his death in England and he had been determined to suffer a martyr's fate. In the face of this provocation, the people must conclude that Thomas had committed suicide while of unsound mind. After the knights leave, the priests and populace mourn. Their only solace is that so long as people will die for faith, the Church will be supreme.

Critical Evaluation:

Unlike those artists who maintain an unchanged view of the world and of the development of their art, T. S. Eliot's life was one of growth. In his youth, he was primarily a satirist, mocking the conventions of society in poems such as "The Love Song of J. Alfred Prufrock" or "Portrait of a Lady." Later, he became a mosaic artist of exquisite sensibility when, fragment by fragment, he pieced together his damning portrait of post-World War I civilization in *The Waste Land* (1922). Still later, finding his ethical pessimism essentially sterile, he climaxed his long interest in philosophy, theology, literary history, and government by becoming a royalist in politics, a classicist in literature, and an Anglo-Catholic in religion.

Born in the United States and educated at Harvard, Eliot early settled in England. Throughout his early career he had developed more than a casual interest in the drama, not merely as an art form in and of itself, but in the theater as a means of instruction. Such early fragments as *Sweeney Agonistes* (1932) tantalize by their incompleteness, but *Murder in the Cathedral* demonstrates Eliot's mastery of the classic tragic form.

In this remarkably effective play, Eliot links devices derived from the Greeks—the chorus, static action, and Aristotelian purgation—with his profound commitment to the Anglo-Catholic liturgy. *Murder in the Cathedral* in many ways resembles a medieval morality play whose purpose is to enlighten as well as entertain. Yet the work is never merely morally instructive. It rises above didacticism because Archbishop Thomas Becket's internal anguish is made so personal and timeless. Becket's assassination becomes more real by the subsequent political and temporal events it evokes.

Eliot firmly believed that twentieth century drama, to be most effective, had to be written in poetry, a belief he shared with William Butler Yeats, his Irish contemporary. Eliot's poetry is moving without being ostentatiously poetic because it reaches the audience on a level that Eliot himself termed the auditory imagination. Responding from the unconscious, the spectators are drawn deeply into the drama and begin to share Becket's internal agonies by participating in the almost primitive rhythmic manipulations of Eliot's deceptively simple verse.

What makes Eliot's play so timely is that the four allurements offered to Thomas by the tempters are precisely those faced, whether consciously or unconsciously, by the twentieth century audience: those of worldly pleasure, temporal power, spiritual power, and, finally and most subtly, eternal glory. Thomas refutes all of them, quite directly, but is entranced for a time by the fourth tempter, who indicates that if Thomas were to proceed on his course, he would be deliberately courting martyrdom to achieve eternal happiness with God. Eventually, Thomas counters the argument with one of the most effective lines in the play: "The last temptation and the greatest treason/ Is to do the right deed for the wrong reason." Thomas's certainty of the spiritual correctness of his own actions mirrors that of members of the audience, who slowly become aware of their own culpability in acting correctly for insufficient reason in any matter, or even of acting selfishly for a good end. The involvement of the audience so profoundly is another tribute to Eliot's genius.

Eliot also works on still another level, that of the conflict of powers. Each power may perhaps be justified in its own way, and Thomas recognizes that the king and the temporal power he represents have some justification. The king, moreover, had once been Thomas's closest friend and had, in fact, made him archbishop. Thomas ponders on the debts to the temporal realm, to friendship, and to gratitude, but he continues to maintain the primacy of the spiritual order over the temporal. If some things are Caesar's, they are Caesar's only because God permitted that to be so.

Murder in the Cathedral was first staged in Canterbury Cathedral, a magnificent Gothic antiquity providing a most striking setting. Still often produced in a church edifice, the play gains immediacy through the verisimilitude achieved by the combination of setting, liturgy, verse, and chorus. Despite Thomas's brilliant Christmas sermon, which opens the second act, Eliot does not preach. He does not reduce the situation to a simple case of good versus evil. Rather, he creates a conflict of mystiques, each with a well-developed rationale. The choice is between alternatives, not opposites. Thomas, who fears that he may be a victim of the sin of pride, must nevertheless choose either damnation or salvation.

Eliot, always conscious of history, knew that the Shrine of Saint Thomas Becket at Canterbury was among the most famous of medieval objects of devotion and pilgrimage. Thus, even the justifications of the knights who killed Thomas deserve serious attention. More than one twentieth century historical critic has wondered if Thomas were not "hell-bent" on heaven, a question that Thomas himself ponders. If the knights' justification is to be rejected, the question remains as to how much of their own rationalizations does not continue to be part of what motivates individual action.

Murder in the Cathedral is a compelling drama for celebrating the themes of faith, justification, power, and conflict, which continue to recur through the ages. Eliot created a timeless work that anticipates his profoundly religious and mystical collection of poems *Four Quartets* (1943) and his later treatments of very similar themes in plays such as *The Cocktail Party* (1949) and *The Confidential Clerk* (1953). All of Eliot's later poetry and plays, however, must be read with *Murder in the Cathedral* in mind, for it represents a pivotal achievement in his distinguished career.

"Critical Evaluation" by Willis E. McNelly

Further Reading

Ackroyd, Peter. *T. S. Eliot: A Life*. New York: Simon & Schuster, 1984. A readable biography providing useful and interesting details about the making of *Murder in the Cathedral*, its critical reception, and its importance to Eliot's rising career as a playwright. Ackroyd finds the play a success and discusses it in connection with other Eliot works.

Badenhausen, Richard. "T. S. Eliot Speaks the Body: The Privileging of Female Discourse in *Murder in the Cathedral* and *The Cocktail Party*." In *Gender, Desire, and Sexuality in T. S. Eliot*, edited by Cassandra Laity and Nancy K. Gish. New York: Cambridge University Press, 2004. This discussion of gender issues in the two plays is included in a collection of essays that examine the treatment of desire, homoeroticism, and feminism in Eliot's poetry, plays, and prose.

Bloom, Harold, ed. *T. S. Eliot's "Murder in the Cathedral."*

New York: Chelsea House, 1988. A collection of eleven important essays by prominent literary critics, such as Helen Gardner, David Ward, and Stephen Spender. Wide range and balance of approaches, along with a useful chronology and bibliography.

Clark, David R., ed. *Twentieth Century Interpretations of "Murder in the Cathedral": A Collection of Critical Essays.* Englewood Cliffs, N.J.: Prentice-Hall, 1971. A collection of fourteen essays by prominent critics, such as E. Martin Browne, Louis L. Martz, Grover Smith, William V. Spanos, and David E. Jones. Includes a substantial chronology of the author's life and a concise bibliography.

Gordon, Lyndall. *T. S. Eliot: An Imperfect Life.* New York: W. W. Norton, 1999. An authoritative, thoroughly researched biography that concedes Eliot's many personal flaws as well as describing his poetic genius.

Moody, A. David, ed. *The Cambridge Companion to T. S.*

Eliot. New ed. New York: Cambridge University Press, 2006. Collection of essays, including discussions of Eliot's life; Eliot as a philosopher, a social critic, and a product of America; and religion, literature, and society in Eliot's work. Also features the essay "Pereira and After: The Cures of Eliot's Theater" by Robin Grove.

Raine, Craig. *T. S. Eliot.* New York: Oxford University Press, 2006. In this examination of Eliot's work, Raine maintains that "the buried life," or the failure of feeling, is a consistent theme in the poetry and plays. Chapter 5 focuses on Eliot's plays. Part of the Lives and Legacies series.

Smith, Carol H. *T. S. Eliot's Dramatic Theory and Practice: From "Sweeney Agonistes" to "The Elder Statesman."* Princeton, N.J.: Princeton University Press, 1963. Chapter 3 provides a useful summary of the play's main features and concludes that the play succeeds on the level of poetic rhythm and imagery. A good introduction.

Murder on the Orient Express

Author: Agatha Christie (1890-1976)
First published: 1934
Type of work: Novel
Type of plot: Detective and mystery
Time of plot: 1930's
Locale: Central Europe

Principal characters:
HERCULE POIROT, a Belgian private detective
M. BOUC, the train company's director
PIERRE MICHEL, a conductor on the train
DR. CONSTANTINE, a Greek physician
COLONEL ARBUTHNOT, an English gentleman
MR. RATCHETT, a rich American
HECTOR MACQUEEN, his personal secretary
PRINCESS DRAGOMIROFF, an elderly Russian aristocrat
GRETA OHLSSON, a Swedish nurse
MRS. HUBBARD, a loud American woman
COUNTESS ANDRENYI, an American-born noble

The Story:

Hercule Poirot finds himself the uninvited guest at the scene of an elaborately planned murder on wheels. The Belgian detective is making his way from Istanbul, Turkey, to London, and he is looking forward to a leisurely trip and a chance to clear his head, a chance to rest his "little grey cells," as Poirot refers to his brain.

A good friend of Poirot, M. Bouc, is an administrator with Wagon Lit, the train company that operates the Orient Express. Poirot prefers to travel first class. Because it is winter, off season for tourists, the detective is assured by Bouc that

finding a first-class cabin on the train will be easy. To their surprise, the car leaving Istanbul, the Calais Coach, is nearly full. There is, however, one no-show, and Poirot finds himself sharing a compartment with Hector MacQueen, the private secretary to a wealthy American, Mr. Ratchett.

Poirot is introduced by Bouc to Dr. Constantine, a Greek physician, traveling in the next car. On the first night of the journey, as they sit in the dining car, Bouc points out to Poirot the variety of travelers in the dining car: the rich and the poor. Some are English, some American, some French, some Italian, some Russian, some Hungarian—an array of passengers from differing socioeconomic backgrounds and different cultures. Where else in the world, Bouc wonders aloud, could one find such an assortment of people beneath one roof? Yes, Poirot thinks to himself, perhaps only in America.

The first night passes peacefully, and Bouc moves Poirot from his shared cabin with MacQueen to a private one next door to Ratchett. During the second night of the trip, Poirot has trouble sleeping, awakened by voices, service bells summoning conductor Pierre Michel, and thumping on his cabin door. At about 1:15 A.M., Poirot sticks his head out of his cabin and sees a woman wearing a kimono with a dragon print walking down the corridor. He hears his neighbor, Ratchett, tell the conductor in perfect French that nothing is wrong and that he had not meant to ring his service bell. The train is stopped, too, as an avalanche of snow covers the tracks.

Ratchett, Poirot has determined, is an evil man. The evil shows on his face, and Poirot has taken an instant dislike in him. Earlier in the evening, Poirot had been approached by Ratchett and was offered a job—to keep Ratchett alive. Ratchett has been receiving hate mail and otherwise threatening letters. Poirot turns down the offer of employment.

The next day, Ratchett is discovered dead in his cabin, and there are many clues. A pipe cleaner belonging to the Englishman, Colonel Arbuthnot, is found on the floor of the murdered man's compartment. An expensive lady's handkerchief, belonging to Princess Dragomiroff, also is found on the floor. The dead man's watch is in the pocket of his pajamas, broken and stopped at 1:15 A.M. The window of the cabin is open. A button from a conductor's uniform is found near the bed of Mrs. Hubbard, Ratchett's American neighbor in the connecting cabin, who had complained of a man lurking in her room during the night.

For Poirot, there are too many clues. Too many clues at a crime scene means tampering, Poirot thinks. How does one separate the real clues from the planted ones? One of the best clues, one that Poirot thinks is real, is a piece of burned paper in an ashtray. The tray has two different types of matches in it. One type of match had also been found in the cabin of the dead man; the other type of match had not. Using wire mesh from a woman's hatbox, Poirot carefully places the burned paper between two layers of wire mesh and lights a match beneath it to reveal the words once written on the paper. These few words on the burned piece of paper become the best clue, leading Poirot to the dead man's true identity. Ratchett is, in reality, a killer and kidnapper of children. His real name is Cassetti.

Cassetti had been arrested and acquitted in the infamous Daisy Armstrong kidnapping and murder case in the United States. The kidnapping and murder of Daisy Armstrong destroyed her entire family; her father and mother, an unborn child, and her nursery maid all died as a consequence of this hideous action.

As Poirot inspects the body of the dead man, he thinks Cassetti has finally received justice, if not strictly via the letter of the law. The corpse has twelve dagger wounds, the range in severity of puncture wounds suggesting some made by a right-handed killer, others made by a left-handed killer. Some wounds are deep, while others only break the skin's surface. After interviewing each passenger in the Calais Coach and after examining everyone's luggage, Poirot learns several facts that seem unimportant and unrelated. For example, there is a spot of grease on Countess Andrenyi's passport, partially obscuring her first name. A conductor's uniform with a missing button is found in the luggage of Greta Ohlsson, a Swedish nurse. Even more interesting, the kimono with the dragon print is found in Poirot's own luggage.

In the dining car of the Calais Coach aboard the Orient Express, Detective Poirot identifies the killer, but only after he details the evidence and slowly puts the proverbial noose around the neck of the guilty. The kicker, the surprise, is that everyone is guilty: They all did it.

Poirot has been an audience of one surrounded by a cast of twelve killers, each suspect playing a role, acting out his or her part, trying to mislead the detective. From Poirot's vantage point, he is challenged to match his wits against the collected intelligence of a dozen minds bent on revenge.

Poirot, in the end, reveals two truths: what really happened and the agreed-upon truth that Poirot offers to the killers. Poirot, during his big reveal, presents both possibilities to his cast of suspects; the second possibility is deemed fairer and more just and so becomes the official truth. Cassetti, the murdered killer, had received an alternative form of justice at the hands of those he had victimized by his actions. Although he had been intent on solving the crime aboard the Orient Express, Poirot, now, is not as intent on seeing the guilty punished.

Critical Evaluation:

Agatha Christie wrote sixty-six detective novels, sixteen volumes of short stories, and nineteen plays under her own name; she also wrote five romantic novels as Mary Westmacott. Surpassed by only William Shakespeare, Christie's work has been more widely published, in more languages, than any other author in the English language. Not surprisingly, this amount of literary output, written with the sole purpose of entertaining mystery fans but nonetheless still going strong decades after the author's death, would eventually invite a closer inspection by critics.

Many of Christie's themes are found in *Murder on the Orient Express*: physical isolation, loose associations among suspects, the truism that "everyone has something to hide," and an alternative brand of justice. The dead man's killers did not plan on Detective Hercule Poirot's presence on the train, and they did not count on the weather being so bad that the train would be stuck in the middle of what was then Yugoslavia. Without these two unexpected developments, the well-planned murder might have succeeded without a hitch, but the twelve murderers on the train had to improvise, had to alter their plans for revenge to account for the weather and for Poirot. The little improvisations, the little changes made by the suspects for the detective's benefit, eventually led Poirot and his "little grey cells" to the truth.

Literary critics who have found their way to the detective and mystery genre have rightly applauded Christie for her ingenious plots, her clever twists and turns. Even so, there are few Christie novels that have drawn more attention, with equal amounts of admiration, imitation, and parody than *Murder on the Orient Express*.

Christie had already broken one of the commandments of the mystery genre, when *The Murder of Roger Ackroyd* was published in 1926. In this novel, the book that made Christie famous around the world, she dared to make the narrator the murderer, demonstrating the quintessential example of the unreliable narrator. By 1934, when *Murder on the Orient Express* was first released—but as *The Calais Coach Murder*—Christie's fans had come to expect the unexpected.

A common theme in Christie's works is that everyone, if not actually guilty of some crime, has, at minimum, something to hide. Past indiscretions, embarrassing financial woes, a misspent youth, and love affairs gone bad are all better left hidden. During the course of an investigation, however, the detective may find it necessary to shine a bright light into the dark corners of a character's life to bring out all the evidence required to solve the case.

In this respect, the Orient Express mystery can be compared with another Christie work, *And Then There Were None*, published in 1939. This later Christie novel is similar because all the characters are guilty of actual crimes, though they have gone unpunished. The characters are invited to a secluded mansion and are then murdered one by one by an impostor among them. In both novels, Christie takes personal guilt to the next level, making all the characters not only suspects but also actual killers.

Poirot, the hero in thirty-three of Christie's novels, is the outsider on the Calais Coach, the only person not associated with the Daisy Armstrong kidnapping and murder case, which ties all the characters together. Poirot is always the outsider in Christie's novels, the Belgian among Englishmen, the retired, older, meticulous gentlemen among the younger, less-self-conscious crowd. Poirot's detachment is by design, separate from the scene. He is the all-knowing, all-seeing hand of righteousness, setting the world right.

Christie's novels are studies in order and chaos theory. The reader is introduced to a miniature well-ordered world where things make sense. Beneath the surface, troubles boil and eventually erupt, usually taking the form of murder. Poirot explores the scene and the characters, gathers information, stores facts and impressions, and then slowly rebuilds the miniature world, removing the chaos and restoring order. To accomplish this, he must be misunderstood and underestimated. His strangeness, foreignness, and personal idiosyncrasies disarm his cast of suspects. After meeting him, these suspects often believe his reputation for intelligence, for crime-solving, is exaggerated. He is more amusing than intimidating. Poirot's fellow passengers on the Orient Express work as a team to lead the detective away from the truth, but their deceptive tricks backfire when they insult Poirot's intelligence.

Randy L. Abbott

Further Reading

Arnold, Jane. "Detecting Social History: Jews in the Works of Agatha Christie." *Jewish Social Studies* 49, nos. 3/4 (Summer/Autumn, 1987): 275-282. Christie's novels are not character driven, and they are often criticized for their lack of character development and for often reverting to stereotypes. Christie wrote works of entertainment and discouraged scholarly study of her work, yet her writing is nonetheless open to study. Twenty-three Jewish characters appear in her stories, including *Murder on the Orient Express*.

Bunson, Matthew. *The Complete Christie: An Agatha Christie Encyclopedia.* New York: Pocket Books, 2001. A comprehensive reference volume that contains alphabetical entries on all characters in Christie's works, cross-referenced to the works in which they appear; plot synopses; listings of all film, television, and radio adaptations of Christie's works and of documentaries about Christie; a biography; and a bibliography.

Makinen, Merja. *Agatha Christie: Investigating Femininity.* New York: Palgrave Macmillan, 2006. Sets out to disprove what many critics have asserted: that Christie created her female characters to be weak and inferior to their male counterparts. Emphasizes the ways in which the female characters play vital roles outside the domestic sphere and therefore challenge traditional notions of femininity.

Osborne, Charles. *The Life and Crimes of Agatha Christie: A Biographical Companion to the Works of Agatha Christie*. New York: St. Martin's Press, 2001. Presents a chronological listing of Christie's works accompanied by biographical notes that place the writings within the context of the events of the author's life. Includes bibliographical references and an index.

Singer, Eliot A. "The Whodunit as Riddle: Block Elements in Agatha Christie." *Western Folklore* 43, no. 3 (July, 1984): 157-171. An analysis of the detective novel as a puzzle or riddle, exploring how a puzzle is solved and offering examples from Christie's novels, including *Murder on the Orient Express*.

Thompson, Laura. *Agatha Christie: An English Mystery*. London: Headline Review, 2007. A comprehensive biography, written with the cooperation of Christie's family

and with full access to the author's unpublished letters and notebooks. Includes information about Christie's eleven-day disappearance in 1926 and about the novels she wrote as Mary Westmacott.

Vagstad, Kristi. "Yankees on the Orient Express." *Armchair Detective* 28, no. 1 (Winter, 1995): 82-90. Golden age detective fiction is known for its xenophobic tendencies, for stereotyping foreigners as outsiders with undesirable traits. This article explores Christie's treatment of Americans in *Murder on the Orient Express*. Christie's father was an American.

York, R. A. *Agatha Christie: Power and Illusion*. New York: Palgrave Macmillan, 2007. Reevaluates Christie's novels, which traditionally have been described as "cozy" mysteries. Asserts that although these works may appear to depict a stable world of political conservatism, conventional sex and class roles, and clear moral choices, this world is not as safe as it appears to be. Notes how Christie's mysteries also depict war, social mobility, ambiguous morality, violence, and, of course, murder.

The Murder Room

Author: P. D. James (1920-   )
First published: 2003
Type of work: Novel
Type of plot: Detective and mystery
Time of plot: October and November, 2003
Locale: Hampstead Heath, near London

Principal characters:
ADAM DALGLIESH, a commander, New Scotland Yard
KATE MISKIN, detective inspector
PIERS TARRANT, detective inspector
MARCUS DUPAYNE, staff member and trustee of the Dupayne Museum
CAROLINE DUPAYNE, girls' school principal and museum trustee
NEVILLE DUPAYNE, psychologist and museum trustee
JAMES CALDER-HALE, museum curator
MURIEL GODBY, museum receptionist
TALLY CLUTTON, museum custodian
RYAN ARCHER, a part-time museum general laborer
MRS. FARADAY, part-time museum gardener
CELIA MELLOCK, a murder victim

The Story:

Scotland Yard commander Adam Dalgliesh meets an old friend, and the two visit the Dupayne Museum. The Dupayne is a private museum that focuses on Great Britain in the years between World War I and II, and its most famous collection is the Murder Room, which contains memorabilia related to

some of the most famous murder cases of the period. As he leaves, Dalgliesh notes that he is glad to have visited, but that he has no interest in returning.

The three adult children of museum founder Max Dupayne serve as trustees and hold the future of the museum in their hands. Neville Dupayne, the eldest, is a psychologist, Caroline Dupayne works as the assistant principal at a girls' school, and Marcus Dupayne is a freshly retired civil servant. Because of low revenues and a soon-to-expire lease, the museum is at a crisis point. Caroline, who lives in a luxurious apartment located in the mansion that houses the museum, and Marcus, who wants to be more involved with the administration of the museum during his retirement, want things to continue as they have. Neville, who, of the three siblings is the least directly involved with the museum, and whose daughter needs money, makes clear his intention to vote for closure. The three meet, and although Caroline and Marcus attempt to influence Neville, the older brother stands firm.

Museum staff members include curator James Calder-Hale, who is dying of cancer. He sees the museum and the work he has done to create and sustain it as his legacy. Custodian Tally Clutton, after years of surviving in unhappy circumstances, is content for the first time in her life with her work and her cottage on the museum grounds. Muriel Godby, an officious receptionist who previously worked for Caroline at the school, comes from a dysfunctional family, has suffered a difficult life, and is loyal to Caroline. All of these museum employees have a vested interest in the continued existence of the facility.

Tally, returning to the museum grounds on a Friday evening, is struck by a car. The motorist stops to check on her, but leaves quickly after making a familiar comment, later recognized by all as the same comment Alfred Arthur Rouse, one of the murderers highlighted in the museum, said to a witness as he fled the scene of his crime. Tally is able to recover enough from the accident to continue down the road, until she finds Neville's car ablaze, in the museum garage. Neville had burned to death inside his car.

Dalgliesh, now heading the special investigation squad, is asked to take the case, owing to its "sensitive nature." It turns out that the curator, Calder-Hale, is a sometimes agent of MI5, the British intelligence service. A suitably vague explanation of the case is concocted to appease the local police. Dalgliesh then contacts his two top detectives, Kate Miskin and Piers Tarrant. Miskin and Tarrant happen to be dining together, discussing their possible futures with the Metropolitan Police. The trio arrives at the scene and begins the investigation. They speak to Marcus and Caroline that evening, along with Tally and Muriel, and Dalgliesh quickly recognizes the complicated situation he faces. Among their initial discoveries are that Neville had been having an affair with Angela Faraday, his secretary, who also happens to be the daughter-in-law of the gardener at the museum. Ryan Archer, the unreliable general laborer who works a the museum

part-time, has disappeared, and a disgruntled patron, whose grandfather's treasured painting had been lost to Max Dupayne, is tentatively identified as the driver who hit Tally. Dalgliesh and his team begin piecing together the facts and weaving together the strands of Marcus's, Caroline's, and Neville's recent encounters.

During the investigative tour of the Murder Room, a cell phone begins ringing. The sound seems to be coming from a trunk, which is part of a display. In the trunk where murder victim Violette Kaye had been found decades earlier, another body is discovered. The victim is soon identified as Celia Mellock, who had attended Caroline's school for a short time. Later, Celia's belongings are uncovered in the donations bin at a thrift shop. Interviews with her mother and stepfather, who had flown to London from Bermuda to meet with the police, are less than satisfactory.

On a whim, Tally takes a trip into London, feeling the need to get away for the day. She wanders into the public gallery at the House of Lords and recognizes Lord Martlesham as the man at the museum on the night of Neville's murder. She reports this to Dalgliesh, who now has another angle to investigate.

Lord Martlesham agrees to discuss matters with police, and it is revealed that he had known Celia and had arranged to meet her at the museum the night she was murdered. He says that she did not appear and that he could not reach her by phone. He admits they were involved in a sexual relationship, but adds that he had tried to break things off with her. Dalgliesh presses further, and Martlesham admits that they were to meet in Caroline's flat, not the parking lot of the museum. Dalgliesh's hunch about Caroline having something to hide is confirmed: She runs a private, exclusive sex club through her apartment. A subsequent interview with Caroline reveals details about the club, but not a strong connection to the murders.

That night, Tally is attacked and left for dead. The scene had been made to look like yet another true crime case highlighted in the museum. Luckily for Tally, Dalgliesh and Miskin had been on their way to interview her when she was attacked; her wounds were not fatal. Also, a motorcyclist had been hit by the car driven by the fleeing murderer.

Dalgliesh soon finds out that Caroline had earlier told her receptionist, Muriel, to look for other work. Muriel, extremely loyal to Caroline and in stable circumstances for the first time in her life, wanted to kill Neville—the lone sibling in favor of closing the museum. With Neville dead, she reasoned, the museum could continue on. She then killed Celia because she had witnessed the murder. Muriel then became convinced that Tally had realized the truth as well, and had attempted to kill her, too, to protect the museum and, thus, her job.

Critical Evaluation:

P. D. James, dubbed the "queen of crime" by critic Julian Symons, has contributed extensively to the mystery genre since the introduction of Inspector Adam Dalgliesh in *Cover Her Face* (1962). James has won numerous awards for her works, including the 1987 Diamond Dagger, the highest honor bestowed by the British Crime Writers' Association.

The Murder Room is a fine example of James's talents with plot development and narrative techniques. The opening section of the novel outlines a situation with an obvious victim and a whole host of potential suspects with a variety of motives. Neville Dupayne as the first victim seems a foregone conclusion, but the reader may be surprised when James signals the existence of a second victim. It is certainly a surprise to see that the second victim is a character James had yet to introduce. When the reader encounters a third victim, yet another twist is in store.

James has particular skill in painting her novels' settings, especially the architecture, and she skillfully describes the mundane, such as the sights and the smells of the city. Several critics and scholars, thus, have written about the importance of place in James's works.

James also drops clues that even a careful reader might miss, such as the description of Muriel Godby's extreme devotion to Caroline that jumps off the page upon rereading, and the note during James Calder-Hale's introduction that mentions him paying for discreet sex.

Some reviews of *The Murder Room* found it to be just an average entry in a series, chiding James for not doing anything new. Whether one believes the plot to be distinctive or mundane, no one can fault James's skilled prose and mastery of ironic commentary.

Elizabeth Blakesley Lindsay

Further Reading

Breen, Jon L. "Murder Most British: P. D. James Strikes Again." *Weekly Standard*, November 29, 2003. Discusses *The Murder Room*, noting that a museum devoted to Great Britain between the world wars is an appropriate setting for one of James's novels, as James is the strongest contemporary link to England's detective fiction of that era.

Kotker, Joan G. "P. D. James's Adam Dalgliesh Series." In *In the Beginning: First Novels in Mystery Series*, edited by Mary Jean DeMarr. Bowling Green, Ohio: Bowling Green State University Popular Press, 1995. Although this chapter predates *The Murder Room*, Kotker's analysis of the first Dalgliesh series novel, *Cover Her Face*, remains important. Describes the evolution of the series from 1962 to the 1990's.

Kresge-Cingal, Daphne. "Intertextuality in the Detective Fiction of P. D. James: Literary Game or Strategic Choice?" *Clues* 22, no. 2 (2001): 141-152. This article explores connections between James and Agatha Christie, although it does not include specific information on *The Murder Room*. Also discusses intertextuality in general in the mystery genre.

O'Conner, Patricia T. "Grisly Pictures from an Institution." *The New York Times Book Review*, December 7, 2003. This well-written review of *The Murder Room* also provides a succinct outline of many aspects of James's work and the characteristics of her writing style.

Rowland, Susan. "The Horror of Modernity and the Utopian Sublime: Gothic Villainy in P. D. James and Ruth Rendell." In *The Devil Himself: Villainy in Detective Fiction and Film*, edited by Stacy Gillis and Phillippa Gates. Westport, Conn.: Greenwood Press, 2002. Rowland focuses on several novels in the Dalgliesh series through the lens of the gothic. Good background on James, but without discussion of *The Murder Room*.

Sizemore, Christine Wick. *A Female Vision of the City: London in the Novels of Five British Women*. Knoxville: University of Tennessee Press, 1989. Many critics and scholars note the importance of setting in James's work, and one of the chapters in this monograph provides analysis of James's depictions of London. Sizemore also offers a good overview of James's works and themes.

Upson, Nicola. "Behind the Scenes at the Museum." *New Statesman* 28 (July, 2003): 38-39. This insightful review focuses on James's concern with social issues of the past and present, praising *The Murder Room* as a "thoughtful exploration of human motivation, not just for murder but for simple acts of love and hate and faith."

Vanacker, Sabine. "The Family Plot in Recent Novels by P. D. James and Reginald Hill." *Critical Survey* 20, no. 1 (2008): 17-28. A critical essay that analyzes James and Reginald Hill as exemplars of increased complexity and scope in the genre, using Tzvetan Todorov's 1977 work on mystery plot structure as a theoretical base. Explores the narrative structure of the novel while arguing that the work is driven by James's use of the plot device that Vanacker calls the family melodrama.

Mutiny on the Bounty

Authors: Charles Nordhoff (1887-1947) and James
    Norman Hall (1887-1951)
First published: 1932
Type of work: Novel
Type of plot: Adventure
Time of plot: Late eighteenth century
Locale: England, the South Pacific, Tahiti, and the
    Dutch East Indies

Principal characters:
WILLIAM BLIGH, captain of the HMS *Bounty*
ROGER BYAM, a midshipman
FLETCHER CHRISTIAN, master's mate and leader of the
    mutiny
GEORGE STEWART, a midshipman and a friend of Byam
TEHANI, a Tahitian woman

The Story:

In late 1787, young Roger Byam accepts Lieutenant William Bligh's offer of a berth as midshipman on the HMS *Bounty*, an armed British transport commissioned to ship breadfruit trees from Tahiti to the West Indies to provide a cheap source of food for the black slaves of English planters. Byam's special duty, under the aegis of Sir Joseph Banks, a family friend and president of the Royal Society, will be to complete a Tahitian dictionary and grammar for the benefit of English seamen.

While still in port, Byam witnesses a brutal example of British naval law: A sailor is subjected to dozens of lashes with a cat-o'-nine-tails for striking an officer, and the punishment is carried out to its conclusion, even though the man dies midway through the flogging. Once the full complement of officers and crew—a total of forty-five men—is aboard and favorable winds prevail, the *Bounty* sets sail.

Byam, a novice sailor from a sheltered, well-to-do background, begins to learn the ways of a ship at sea and comes to realize that Captain Bligh, though a competent navigator, represents the worst traits of British naval commanders. Bligh's unbending adherence to discipline, demonstrated through excessive floggings for minor infractions and his insensitivity toward the crew as human beings, is exacerbated by his exploitation of the men: Their food rations, barely edible, are reduced so the captain can profit.

After sailing ten months and 27,000 miles, the *Bounty* arrives in Tahiti. In contrast to the tyrannical atmosphere aboard ship, the islands offer almost unbounded freedom. Crewmembers submit to tattooing, exchange their clothing for local garb, and acquire deep suntans. Eagerly adopting a traditional Tahitian custom, the men each choose a *taio*, or special friend, from among the indigenous people of the islands. During a sailor's stay in Tahiti, the *taio* will supply him with all the delicacies the islands have to offer. Byam's *taio* is Hitihiti, a respected chieftain who knows Captain Bligh from his previous visit to Tahiti accompanying the famous explorer Captain Cook.

During the stay at Tahiti, Byam, living ashore, collects information for his language study. Most of the sailors find women with whom they live on the island and to whom some of them marry. Fletcher Christian chooses as his female companion a woman named Maimiti, the niece of Byam's *taio*. George Stewart chooses a Tahitian he calls Peggy. Byam is too devoted at the time to absorbing the culture, learning the language, and preparing his lexicon to become involved with a woman.

Unlike the rest of the crew, Captain Bligh seldom ventures from the *Bounty* and maintains the strictest decorum. He continues to exercise the cruelties that most of his underlings consider excessive, unfair, and illegal. One practice in particular that galls the crew is the captain's insistence upon confiscating the sailors' property, gifts from the island, when the *Bounty* sails again. These gifts include *tapa* cloth garments, fresh fruits, wildlife, handmade crafts, and pearls, which the friendly islanders regularly bestow upon the Englishmen and which the sailors feel rightfully belongs to them. Bligh orders such gifts to be put into the ship's stores. He further places the men on unpalatable salt pork rations, in the middle of the abundance of the islands. Just before leaving Tahiti, Bligh alienates Christian by doing the unthinkable: He publicly and falsely accuses the proud master's mate of stealing coconuts.

After nearly six months, the collection of the breadfruit trees is finally completed, and the *Bounty* sets sail for the West Indies, but not before four crewmen attempt desertion. Caught and returned, they are flogged before the crew. This adds to the already sullen attitude of the sailors. Feelings continue to run high against Bligh during the early part of the voyage, until one fateful morning when impulse leads Christian to mutiny. With like-minded companions, he gains control of the ship and subsequently sets Bligh adrift in the *Bounty*'s launch, with eighteen loyal crewmen, as many as the launch will safely contain; seven loyal hands, among them Byam and Stewart, his close friend, must stay behind on the ship because there is no room in the small boat.

With Christian in command, the *Bounty*, now with a crew of twenty-three, jettisons the breadfruit trees and sails the South Seas in search of a suitable, uncharted island on which to establish a permanent settlement. After several attempts to land are thwarted by islanders, the *Bounty* returns to Tahiti. Here, the crew again splits: Most of the mutineers continue to sail with Christian in their search for refuge, while others, including Byam and Stewart, remain in Tahiti. They expect eventually to be found and returned home to resume their naval careers.

Christian and the mutineers sail off in the *Bounty* to an unknown destination. Byam, Stewart, and the other crewmen left behind renew their idyllic existence in Tahiti. Byam falls in love with a noble local woman, Tehani, and they marry. He continues to work on his language manuscripts. They have a child, and they name her Helen. For eighteen months, time passes pleasantly. Then the HMS *Pandora* arrives at the islands. Unbeknownst to Byam and the other sailors happily marooned on Tahiti, Bligh has survived his long voyage in the overloaded launch to reach England. In making his report to the British Admiralty, the former captain of the *Bounty* has not distinguished between mutineer and loyal sailor among the men who remained behind. When Byam, Stewart, and their companions from the *Bounty*, eager for word of home, greet the newly arrived ship, they are promptly clapped in irons and imprisoned. They are placed on the ship for return to England and for trial for mutiny, a hanging offense. The prisoners suffer great privation during their voyage until the *Pandora* founders on a reef and sinks; Stewart drowns during the wreck. The survivors, duplicating Bligh's feat, sail in open boats and endure incredible hardships until arriving safely at Timor in the Dutch East Indies, from which they are shipped to England.

Back home, the prisoners await months to be court-martialed for mutiny. Byam, supported by the sympathetic Sir Joseph Banks, learns his beloved mother has died, perhaps hastened to her grave by a cruel letter from Captain Bligh. Two loyal men falsely accused of the crime, Morrison and Muspratt, are pardoned. The innocent Byam and three mutineers who stayed in Tahiti—Ellison, Burkitt, and Millward—are convicted and condemned to be hanged. Several *Bounty* crewmen (Nelson, Norton, and Tinkler), who could have given evidence clearing Byam, have apparently perished. At the last moment, Tinkler, presumed lost at sea, is found alive, and he gives testimony that produces an acquittal for Byam. Nothing, however, can save Ellison, Burkitt, and Millward, who must swing from the yardarms for their part in the mutiny.

Following the trial, Byam continues his naval career and eventually becomes captain of his own ship. He participates in a series of wars—against the Dutch, the Danes, the Spanish, and the French—and though he thinks often of the family he left in Tahiti, he is unable to return to the islands until 1810. When he arrives there, eighteen years after leaving, he discovers that the friendly, happy place he once knew had been ravaged by war and disease, mercilessly exploited for its natural resources. He learns that Tehani, his wife, has long been dead. He finds his daughter, Helen, who closely resembles her mother, alive and now a mother herself. An older, wiser Byam sees no purpose in identifying himself to his daughter, and he sadly leaves Tahiti for the final time, realizing that the formerly beautiful green islands are now filled with ghosts, the young midshipman he once was among them.

"The Story" revised by Jack Ewing

Critical Evaluation:

One of the primary issues examined in Charles Nordhoff and James Norman Hall's *Mutiny on the Bounty* is the passage of time. More than five decades elapse over the course of the novel, which is narrated in the first-person by Roger Byam, a midshipman on the *Bounty*. Seventy-three years old when the story is told, Byam refreshes his memory, which time has dimmed, via a daily journal he had kept when he was a callow youth in his impressionable teens. Another one hundred years elapsed between the period of Byam's reminiscence and the date of the novel's original publication. The images related in the novel remain as vivid, and the story remains as relevant, as if events of the novel occurred just yesterday.

Although the 1789 incidents upon which the story is based are real, and are supported with the facts of exhaustive research (some of which was ignored by Nordhoff and Hall for dramatic reasons), the character of Byam is a fabrication. The authors had several purposes in using a fictionalized participant to relate an essentially true story. First, in the time-honored literary tradition of tall sea stories, represented by such works as Samuel Taylor Coleridge's long poem *The Rime of the Ancient Mariner* (1798) and Herman Melville's 1851 classic, *Moby Dick: Or, The Whale* (also based on actual occurrences), Byam has survived an ordeal to which persons weaker in mind, body, or spirit would have succumbed and has lived to tell a cautionary tale.

Like all such stories, which have unfolded from the age of Homer, the ocean is an implacable presence, constantly testing the mettle of those who venture the sea. The deep, dark waters that cover three-quarters of the earth's surface display incredible beauty and abundance; they also display unimaginable violence and terror. The unpredictable nature of large bodies of water is a force that can shape, reveal, or destroy the character of individuals: It also is a force that challenges the concept of the survival of the fittest at its most basic and elemental.

Second, Byam puts a human face on the long-ago events that led to mutiny. Such a character allows the authors, as in all historical novels, to invent dialogue that might have been spoken, to extrapolate from bald facts, to make educated suppositions, and to draw conclusions, about which the evidence is silent. A single, unified perspective makes the novel's complex themes—law versus justice, the order of discipline as opposed to the chaos of freedom, the comfort of the familiar in contrast to the appeal of the exotic—more immediate and understandable to modern readers. This perspective also helps modern readers understand the novel's sequels. Byam is a sympathetic eyewitness to history: He is idealistic, well spoken, ambitious, and likeable, and as someone easy to identify with, he serves to involve the reader emotionally with the story.

Third, Byam provides the authors an opportunity to present their own answers to the overriding questions posed by the events themselves. Was Captain Bligh as brutal as portrayed, and was Fletcher Christian truly justified in leading a mutiny? The simple answer to both questions is, probably not. Records reveal that flogging was practiced less often on the *Bounty* than on other British ships of the day. Likewise, there is no concrete evidence that Bligh used his position to benefit himself financially, and it is unlikely that the real Bligh—an educated, highly experienced, and certainly a blunt, sharp-tongued individual—whose distinguished naval career spanned more than fifty years, would have risen to the position of vice admiral if his leadership qualities did not outweigh his flaws. By contrast, though Christian seems noble, subsequent events show him to be inconsistent in his actions, a characteristic that detracts from his abilities as a leader.

Because Byam has transparent attitudes toward his shipmates and because he is drawn with preconceived notions of guilt and innocence, he is not necessarily a reliable narrator. He reflects the authors' prevailing attitudes about the living, breathing persons who actually existed. Paradoxically, though a fictional creation, Byam is the most fully rounded and believable of all the characters in the novel. Captain Bligh is a one-dimensional, though memorable creation. Christian, presented as a courageous man of principle, is shown to have apparently initiated the mutiny for reasons of wounded pride rather than for compassion for his beleaguered shipmates. When Christian assumes command of the ship he becomes as autocratic as Bligh, illustrating a sad truth that revolutions often only replace one form of tyranny with another. The impetus for the voyage—to procure a cheap source of food for slaves—is never questioned by any of the characters. Slavery, of various forms, is a recurring theme in the novel: in the onboard relationships between officers and crew, in the hierarchy of Tahitian society, and, more subtly, in the class structure of British culture itself.

Whatever its weaknesses as an accurate depiction of history, *Mutiny on the Bounty* is excellent fiction, one of the most popular sea stories ever written. It is a contest of wills between the domineering protagonist, Captain Bligh, and his antagonist, the proud, headstrong aristocrat Christian. The novel can ultimately be reduced to a collision between the principles and temperaments of two unyielding men against the backdrop of the primeval forces of nature and to the consequences of their actions. The story of the mutiny is so dramatic and so colorful that it has served as the basis for several motion pictures, beginning in 1916, with others, the first in 1935, drawing upon the novel.

Nordhoff and Hall capitalized on the popularity of *Mutiny on the Bounty* by producing two subsequent novels, completing the Bounty trilogy. The first sequel, *Men Against the Sea* (1934), follows a similar structure as *Mutiny on the Bounty* by presenting information through a first-person narrator. The story tracks Bligh and his companions as they courageously battle the elements in voyaging thousands of miles toward salvation in a small boat. The second sequel, *Pitcairn's Island* (1934), which is written in the third-person, traces the violent struggles of Christian and his English and Polynesian cohorts to establish a safe haven on a remote Pacific outpost, Pitcairn Island. Descendants of the real mutineers still eke out an existence on this island.

"Critical Evaluation" by Bill Delaney;
revised by Jack Ewing

Further Reading

Alexander, Caroline. *The Bounty: The True Story of the Mutiny on the Bounty.* New York: Viking, 2003. Recounts the actual events aboard the ship and subsequent efforts to round up and court-martial the mutineers. Enlivened by excerpts from crewmembers' letters and court documents. Portrays Bligh as a brilliant navigator and not as the brutal taskmaster depicted in fictional accounts.

Bligh, William. *The Bounty Mutiny: Captain William Bligh's Firsthand Account of the Last Voyage of the HMS Bounty.* St. Petersburg, Fla.: Red and Black, 2008. An authoritative account from the oft-vilified subject of the mutiny, detailing the original purpose of the *Bounty*'s voyage, a detailed account of the ship's takeover, and the captain's forty-one-day journey in the ship launch to Indonesia.

Hall, James Norman. *My Island Home: An Autobiography.* 1970. Reprint. Westport, Conn.: Greenwood Press, 1970. Includes Hall's recollections of how he and Charles Nordhoff came to write *Mutiny on the Bounty*. Discusses their research and their fictionalizing of the historical material. Also examines how they envisioned the material as leading to a trilogy of novels.

Hough, Richard Alexander, and Richard Hough. *Captain Bligh and Mister Christian: The Men and the Mutiny.* Annapolis, Md.: U.S. Naval Institute Press, 2000. This overview covers three major aspects of the *Bounty* incident: the mutiny, Bligh's voyage, and the mutineer's settlement on Pitcairn Island. Emphasizes the roles and the characters of the main participants.

Kirk, Robert W. *Pitcairn Island, the Bounty Mutineers and Their Descendants: A History.* Jefferson, N.C.: McFarland, 2008. This detailed study, complete with maps and photographs, traces the history of the island from its settlement by the *Bounty* mutineers in the late eighteenth century through the current status of its inhabitants.

Roulston, Robert. *James Norman Hall.* Boston: Twayne, 1978. In the first book-length critical study of Hall's work, Roulston examines in some detail the Bounty trilogy. He declares the novel a melodrama, perhaps something short of true literature, but finds it to be among the best of the genre.

My Ántonia

Author: Willa Cather (1873-1947)
First published: 1918
Type of work: Novel
Type of plot: Regional
Time of plot: Late nineteenth and early twentieth centuries
Locale: Nebraska

Principal characters:
JIM BURDEN, the narrator and Ántonia's friend
ÁNTONIA SHIMERDA, a Bohemian peasant girl

The Story:

Jim Burden's father and mother die when he is ten years old, and the boy makes the long trip from Virginia to his grandparents' farm in Nebraska in the company of Jake Marpole, a hired hand who is to work for Jim's grandfather. Arriving by train in the prairie town of Black Hawk late at night, the boy notices an immigrant family huddled on the station platform. Jim and Jake are met by a lanky, scar-faced cowboy named Otto Fuchs, who drives them in a jolting wagon across the empty prairie to the Burden farm.

Jim grows to love the vast expanse of land and sky. One day, Jim's grandmother suggests that the family pay a visit to the Shimerdas, an immigrant family just arrived in the territory. At first, the newcomers impress Jim unfavorably. The Shimerdas are poor and live in a dugout cut into the earth. The place is dirty, and the children are ragged. Although he cannot understand her speech, Jim makes friends with the oldest girl, Ántonia.

Jim often finds his way to the Shimerda home. He does not like Ántonia's surly brother, Ambrosch, or her grasping mother, but Ántonia wins an immediate place in Jim's heart with her eager smile and great, warm eyes. One day, her father, with his English dictionary tucked under his arm, corners Jim and asks him to teach the girl English. She learns rapidly. Jim respects Ántonia's father, a tall, thin, sensitive man who had been a musician in the old country. Now he is worn down by poverty and overwork. He seldom laughs any more.

Jim and Ántonia pass many happy hours on the prairie. Then, during a severe winter, tragedy strikes the Shimerdas when Ántonia's father, broken and beaten by the prairie, shoots himself. Ántonia had loved her father more than anyone else in her family. After his death, she shoulders his share of the farmwork. When spring comes, she goes with Ambrosch into the fields and plows like a man. The harvest brings money, and the Shimerdas soon have a house. With the money left over, they buy plowshares and cattle.

Because Jim's grandparents are growing too old to keep up their farm, they dismiss Jake and Otto and move to the town of Black Hawk. There, Jim longs for the open prairie land, the gruff, friendly companionship of Jake and Otto, and the warmth of Ántonia's friendship. He suffers at school and spends his idle hours roaming the barren gray streets of Black Hawk. At Jim's suggestion, his grandmother arranges with a neighbor, Mrs. Harling, to bring Ántonia into town as her hired girl. Ántonia enters into her tasks with enthusiasm. Jim notices that she is more feminine and laughs more often; though she never shirks her duties at the Harling house, she is eager for recreation and gaiety.

Almost every night, Ántonia goes to a dance pavilion with a group of hired girls. There, in new, handmade dresses, the girls gather to dance with the village boys. Jim goes, too, and the more he sees of the hired girls, the better he likes them. Once or twice, he worries about Ántonia, who is popular and trusting. When she earns a reputation for being a little too loose, she loses her position with the Harlings and goes to work for a cruel moneylender, Wick Cutter, who has a licentious eye on her.

One night, Ántonia appears at the Burdens and begs Jim to stay in her bed for the night and let her remain at the Burdens. Wick Cutter is supposed to be out of town, but Ántonia suspects that, with Mrs. Cutter also gone, he might return and try to harm her. Her fears prove correct, for Wick returns and goes to Ántonia's bedroom, and finds Jim.

Ántonia returns to work for the Harlings. Jim studies hard during the summer, passes his entrance examinations, and in the fall leaves for the state university. Although he finds a whole new world of literature and art, he cannot forget his early years under the blazing prairie sun and his friendship with Ántonia. He hears little from Ántonia during those years. One of her friends, Lena Lingard, who had also worked as a hired girl in Black Hawk, visits him one day. He learns from her that Ántonia is engaged to be married to a man named Larry Donovan.

Jim goes to Harvard to study law and for years hears nothing of his Nebraska friends. He assumes that Ántonia is married. When he makes a trip back to Black Hawk to see his grandparents, he learns that Ántonia, deceived by Larry, had left Black Hawk in shame and returned to her family. There she works again in the fields. When Jim visits her, he finds

her the same lovely girl, though her eyes are somber, and she has lost her old gaiety. She welcomes him and proudly shows him her baby.

Jim believes that his visit will be the last time he will see Ántonia. He tells her how much a part of him she has become and how sorry he is to leave her again. Ántonia knows that Jim will always be with her, no matter where he goes. He reminds her of her beloved father who, though he had been dead many years, still lives on in her heart. She tells Jim good-bye and watches him walk back toward town along the familiar road.

Jim does not see Ántonia again for twenty years. On a Western trip, he finds himself not far from Black Hawk and, on impulse, drives in an open buggy to the farm where she lives. He finds the place swarming with children of all ages. Small boys rush forward to greet him, then fall back shyly. Ántonia has married well, at last. The grain is high, and the neat farmhouse seems to be charged with an atmosphere of activity and happiness. Ántonia seems as unchanged as she was when she and Jim used to whirl over the dance floor together in Black Hawk. Cuzak, her husband, seems to know Jim before they are introduced, for Ántonia had told her family about Jim. After a long visit with the Cuzaks, Jim leaves, promising that he will return the next summer and take two of the Cuzak boys hunting with him.

Waiting in Black Hawk for the train that will take him East, Jim finds it hard to realize the long time that has passed since the dark night, years before, when he saw an immigrant family standing wrapped in their shawls on the same platform. All his memories of the prairie come back to him. Whatever happens now, whatever they had missed, he and Ántonia had shared precious years between them, years that will never be forgotten.

Critical Evaluation:

Perhaps the most beautiful aspect of this book is its disarming simplicity. There are no witty phrases, no complicated characters, indeed, there is scarcely any plot. Yet there is a quiet, probing depth in Willa Cather's writing. The figure of the pioneer woman Ántonia Shimerda concentrates in itself a complex of values, an axis about which *My Ántonia* revolves. The novel illustrates two classical themes of American literature, reaching back into the nineteenth century for its plot and beyond its time for its artistic and moral direction.

Cather, the product of a genteel Virginia upbringing, was early in life transplanted to the frontier and forced to confront those vast blank spaces over which humans had not yet succeeded in establishing the dominion of custom and convention. She saw a few brave settlers in the wilderness, meeting the physical and moral challenges of having to act straight out of their instincts without benefit of civilized constraints; for her these people, particularly the women, are a race apart. Ántonia, with her noble simplicity, is among other things a monument to that vigorous race.

Ántonia is also an embodiment of a long tradition of fictional heroes of British and American romantic tales. At the time the novel was written, literature and criticism in the United States were undergoing a change. The direction of literature in the new century owed much to the developing sciences; Sinclair Lewis and Theodore Dreiser appeared with their sociological novels that signaled the rise of naturalism. Fictional characters began to be viewed as interpreting in their acts the flaws and beauties of laws, institutions, and social structures. *My Ántonia* fits an older mold, in which the effects of colonial Puritanism can be detected. That mode demanded that the hero overcome or fail to overcome the strictures and hazards of his or her situation by wit, strength, or courage. This convention draws from the very wellspring of American life, the democratic belief in the wholeness and self-sufficiency of the individual, in personal culpability, and in the absolute value of the personal conscience.

Cather makes no indictment of the society that scorns and undervalues Ántonia and the other hired girls; the social conventions are, with the land, simply the medium through which she relates the tale. It is the peculiarly American sense of starting afresh in a new land, that sense of moral isolation, that adds poignancy to the struggles of individuals. This theme of American newness and innocence, which R. B. Lewis calls "The Theme of the American Adam," has as a natural concomitant elements of temptation and fortunate fall. The serpent in Ántonia's story is the town of Black Hawk, where she quarrels with her benefactors and runs afoul of Larry Donovan. Seduced and abandoned, she returns to the land but, as she tells Jim Burden, her experience made it possible for her to prepare her own children how to face the world.

If the town in one sense represents Ántonia's downfall, it is also the grey backdrop against which she shines; in the same way, the prairie is both her antagonist and the natural force of which she is the flower. Significantly, Jim first finds her actually living in the earth. Early in the novel, she begins to take on characteristics of the land: "Her neck came up strongly out of her shoulders, like the bole of a tree out of the turf." "But," the novel continues, "she has such splendid color in her cheeks—like those big dark red plums." She works the land, makes gardens, and nourishes the Harling children with food and stories. Cather insists on her connection with the fertile earth, the virgin land, which is in this novel the source of physical vigor and the best resource of the soul. Jim describes his first experience of the land as a feeling of cosmic unity:

> Perhaps we feel like that when we die and become part of something entire, whether it is sun and air, or goodness and knowledge. At any rate, that is happiness; to be dissolved into something complete and great.

The people who live on the prairie seem to him open and giving like the land; he says of Ántonia that "everything she said seemed to come right out of her heart." By contrast, the life of the town is pinched and ungenerous: "People's speech, their voices, their very glances, became furtive and repressed. Every individual taste, every natural appetite, was bridled by caution."

Ántonia, in all her acts, shows the naturalness and boundless generosity of the plains; she gives unstintingly of her strength and loyalty to her surly brother, to Jim, and the Harling children, to Larry Donovan, and to her husband, Cuzak; and she pours out a flood of love and nurture upon her children. She alludes several times to her dislike of towns and cities and to her feeling of familiar friendship with the countryside. Toward the end of the book, the figure of Ántonia and the infinite fertility of the land come together symbolically in an extremely vivid and moving image. Ántonia and her children have been showing Jim the contents of their fruit cellar, and as they step outside, the children "all came running up the steps together, big and little, tow heads and gold heads and brown, and flashing little naked legs; a veritable explosion of life out of the dark cave into the sunlight." The cave might be the apotheosis of Ántonia's first home on the prairie, the latter redeeming the former by its fruitfulness.

Above all, the novel celebrates the early life on the plains of which Jim and Ántonia were a part. The long digressions about Peter and Pavel, Blind D'Arnault, the Cutters, and others; the profoundly elegiac descriptions of Jake Marpole and Otto Fuchs; and the sharply caught details of farm life, town life, and landscape are all elements employed in the re-creation of a simpler and better time, a hard life now beyond recall but lovingly remembered.

"Critical Evaluation" by Jan Kennedy Foster

Further Reading

Bloom, Harold, ed. *Willa Cather's "My Ántonia."* New York: Chelsea House, 1987. Collection of eleven reprinted articles, selected by a leading literary critic. Includes a Cather chronology and a bibliography.

_____. *Willa Cather's "My Ántonia."* New ed. New York: Bloom's Literary Criticism, 2008. The updated edition contains additional essays about *My Ántonia*, including discussions of sexuality, autonomy, and the representation of immigration, sacrifice, and empire in the novel.

Brown, Edward Killoran. *Willa Cather: A Critical Biography.* New York: Alfred A. Knopf, 1953. Brown, Cather's first biographer, presents a gracefully written book with insights into Cather's writings. Penetrating in its discussion of Cather's use of feelings and nostalgic memories in *My Ántonia*. Brown died before he finishing this biography, and Leon Edel completed the work.

De Roche, Linda. *Student Companion to Willa Cather.* Westport, Conn.: Greenwood Press, 2006. An introductory overview of Cather's life and work aimed at high school and college students and general readers, with discussion of the character development, themes, and plots of six novels. Chapter 6 focuses on of *My Ántonia*.

Jessup, Josephine Lurie. *The Faith of Our Feminists.* New York: Richard R. Smith, 1950. An early feminist scholar, Jessup compares Cather favorably with Edith Wharton and Ellen Glasgow, particularly Cather's development of strong female characters. This is a short but important book.

Lee, Hermione. *Willa Cather: Double Lives.* New York: Pantheon Books, 1989. Lee presents a sweeping, multilayered examination of Cather's life and art. Studies all the writings, often producing original and controversial interpretations. Discussion of the pastoral is a significant contribution to understanding Cather's use of the land motif. Includes a valuable short bibliography.

Lindermann, Marilee. *The Cambridge Companion to Willa Cather.* New York: Cambridge University Press, 2005. Thirteen essays include examinations of Cather's politics and sexuality and a study of her works in the context of modernism. One essay focuses on *My Ántonia*.

Meyering, Sheryl L. *Understanding "O Pioneers!" and "My Ántonia": A Student Casebook to Issues, Sources, and Historical Documents.* Westport, Conn.: Greenwood Press, 2002. Contains analysis of the two novels, as well as excerpts from journals, letters, government reports, and other primary documents that provide historical context about life on the plains, farming, the railroad, women on the frontier, and foreign-born pioneers.

Murphy, John J. *"My Ántonia": The Road Home.* Boston: Twayne, 1989. Places the novel in historical and literary context and provides a reading of the text. Includes a chronology and bibliography.

Woodress, James. *Willa Cather: Her Life and Art.* Lincoln: University of Nebraska Press, 1982. Woodress, a Cather expert, provides a clear, enthusiastic treatment of Cather's accomplishments as an author. He argues that *My Ántonia* is her finest novel and one of the best written by an American.

My Brilliant Career

Author: Miles Franklin (1879-1954)
First published: 1901
Type of work: Novel
Type of plot: Psychological realism
Time of plot: 1890's
Locale: Australian Bush

Principal characters:
SYBYLLA MELVYN, the teenage narrator
RICHARD MELVYN, Sybylla's father
LUCY MELVYN, Sybylla's mother
GERTIE, Sybylla's sister
AUNT HELEN and GRANNIE, with whom Sybylla goes to live
UNCLE JULIUS, Aunt Helen's brother
HAROLD BEECHAM, a wealthy bushman, in love with Sybylla
EVERARD GREY, a young English aristocrat who befriends Sybylla
FRANK HAWDEN, suitor to Sybylla
THE M'SWAT FAMILY, who employ Sybylla as governess

The Story:

Sybylla is the daughter of wealthy cattle station owner Richard Melvyn. When the family falls on hard times, Richard sells his three stations and buys Possum Gully, a small farm. Richard's drinking habit undermines his livestock deals. He mortgages Possum Gully and uses the money to set up a dairy farm. The entire family slaves long hours for little return; the family drops from swelldom to peasantry. Sybylla's previously gentle and refined mother becomes angry, thin, and careworn, while her father becomes slovenly and withdrawn; he loses all love for, and interest in, his family. Sybylla, fond of music and literature, longs for something better than the daily grind of work and sleep.

When Sybylla is fifteen years old, a drought brings the dairy farm to ruin. A dishonest moneylender's agent absconds with Richard's repayments, and the bailiffs are sent in; everything the family owns is sold. Their friends and neighbors, however, come to the rescue; they bid low for the family's possessions and return them.

Because Lucy Melvyn finds her daughter's presence a burden to her, Sybylla's grandmother offers to have Sybylla stay with her. Sybylla leaves the farm to live at Caddagat, the home of Aunt Helen and Grannie. They welcome Sybylla warmly, in contrast to the cold farewell she received from her parents. Sybylla thrives in this loving and refined environment; she reads and plays the piano for hours.

Sybylla feels sad, however, convinced that she is so ugly and hence unlovable. Aunt Helen takes pity on Sybylla and takes her in hand to bring out her beauty. Sybylla's "coming out" is to meet Uncle Julius (Uncle Jay-Jay) and a young English aristocrat, Everard Grey. Grey, impressed with Sybylla's striking looks and talent for acting and singing, expresses a desire to introduce her to the stage, where, he believes, she will have a brilliant career. The notion of such a career, however, is dismissed by Grannie and Aunt Helen as unsuitable.

Aunt Helen and Grannie are friends of a neighboring wealthy squatter family, the Beechams. Sybylla meets Harry Beecham—described as her only real sweetheart—when she is dressed in one of the servant's dresses and a pair of men's boots. Mistaking her for a servant, he tries to kiss her and then tests her mettle by having her stand still while he cracks his stockman's whip around her. When he finds out who she is, he is embarrassed, and Sybylla is delighted at having the power to make him so.

Harry and Sybylla continue to spend time together. Perplexed, yet intrigued by her wild nature, Harry proposes to Sybylla. She expresses surprise, because he had never uttered a word of love to her. She accepts the engagement, but she tells herself that it will be only for a little while. As he

stoops to kiss her, she picks up a riding whip and strikes him in the face. He makes light of the incident.

When Harry presents her with an engagement ring, she takes it, but she refuses to put it on; she tells him that they will have a three-month probation period to see how they get along, during which time she will sometimes wear the ring.

Harry suddenly loses his money and station property. Sybylla offers to accept his engagement, now that he needs her. She will marry him when she reaches age twenty-one, whether he is rich or poor. Delighted by her response, Harry leaves to remake his fortune. Sybylla receives a letter from her mother, telling Sybylla that Sybylla must help the family by working as a governess for the M'Swat family. Sybylla's father owes money to Peter M'Swat, who is willing to take twenty pounds per year off the debt if Sybylla teaches his children.

Sybylla unwillingly leaves her happy home to do her duty by her family. Life with the M'Swats is a kind of hell. The family lives in filth and does not possess a trace of refinement. Sybylla falls ill under the strain and is sent home. Her life has reached a dead end. Her mother is displeased, and Grannie has replaced her with her younger, prettier sister, Gertie. The presents Uncle Jay-Jay brings back from his travels are given to Gertie, instead of Sybylla.

Harry Beecham has remade his fortune; he returns to ask for Sybylla's hand, but she cannot bring herself to marry him. In his disappointment, Harry sets off to travel the world.

Critical Evaluation:

Miles Franklin was the pseudonym for Stella Maria Sarah Miles Franklin, one of Australia's most distinguished novelists. She was born into the "squattocracy," and she was the fifth generation of a pioneering family. Franklin's novels draw on her upbringing in the Australian Bush, and the novels reflect her love for her homeland. They also reveal her iconoclastic nature: her devotion to women's rights and her scorn of marriage as the only viable option for women, her contempt for filial duty, and her irrepressible spirit, which often led to behavior seen as unladylike.

Franklin wrote *My Brilliant Career* at the age of sixteen, though it was not published until she was twenty-two years old. The novel was greeted by the critic A. G. Stephens as "the very first Australian novel," in the sense that it was the first to embody an Australian outlook in vigorous Australian idiom. Modern critics are still divided over its merit. Some consider it Franklin's best, most original work. Certainly, her characters and her authorial stance were developed in this novel, and they did not progress greatly in future works.

The novel is the first part of the life story of Sybylla Melvyn, the daughter of a once-wealthy squatter family that has fallen on hard times. Franklin continues Melvyn's life story in her later novel, *My Career Goes Bung* (1946). Although *My Brilliant Career* was not intended to be autobiographical, Sybylla's life has some aspects in common with the early life of the author. The similarities did not escape Franklin's relatives and neighbors. Many took offense at her sardonic portrayal of what they mistakenly believed to be their own lives and characters. Their response caused Franklin great distress, and she forbade the novel's republication until ten years after her death.

The title *My Brilliant Career* is ironic; Franklin initially placed a question mark in parentheses after the word "Brilliant." The high-spirited tomboy narrator, Sybylla, has a more than usual share of intelligence, talent, and maturity. Her ambitions reach far beyond her small-town life in the Australian Outback—but she finds no outlet for her gifts, and she is doomed to a frustrated and limited existence of mundane chores and unstimulating company.

This existence could easily be a recipe for a whiny character and a depressing story, but Sybylla is a tremendously vital and exhilarating creation. She tells her story with unerring humor and razor-sharp insight. While the storyline of *My Brilliant Career* is slight, and its structure is rambling and inconsequential, the character of Sybylla etches itself indelibly into the memory.

As a feminist, Sybylla is remarkably ahead of her time. Marriage, in her opinion, is "the most horribly tied-down and unfair-to-women existence going." She despises marriage as a "degradation" that she refuses to "perpetuate." She laments that it is only men who can be masters of their fate, whereas women are forced to sit with tied hands and patiently suffer as the waves of fate toss them this way and that.

With her passion for music and literature, with her revolutionary notions of readjusting the wheels of society, and with her determination never to marry, Sybylla is without a sphere. Uncle Jay-Jay gives her a birthday present of a doll, but for a young woman who numbers among her priorities the devising of social and economic solutions to the problems of tramps, this present is inappropriate. On another occasion, she tells Uncle Jay-Jay that instead of wasting money on presents, she wishes that he will set her up in an independent profession.

Readers cannot help but cheer Sybylla as her sharp tongue and impetuous nature cut through the conventions and hypocrisies of her world. She is the antithesis of the romantic heroines of the literature of the 1890's; she is plain, difficult, egotistical, and hard to please. Told by her mother that the famous writers whom she idolizes should teach her to be grate-

ful for her lot, Sybylla blasts such homespun philosophy: "It was all very well for great people to point out the greatness of the little, empty, humdrum life. Why didn't they adopt it themselves?" She repeatedly gets into trouble for her "unwomanly" actions, such as her behavior toward Frank Hawden, a despised suitor. When she says that she will drive the buggy to collect the mail, Grannie insists that Frank accompany her. Sybylla acquiesces, but when he gets out of the buggy to open a gate, she seizes her chance and whips up the horses, leaving an enraged Frank to walk home in the dust.

Without doubt, Sybylla has acted like a spoiled brat, but Frank's boorish behavior places readers' sympathies firmly on her side. He is an extreme example of the apparent weakness displayed by most of Franklin's male characters. Time and again, it is left to women to provide the strength, the responsibility, and the glue that holds the family units together. Richard Melvyn begins well, but he ends as an irresponsible drunk who shows no love to his family; Everard Grey is revealed as a person without depth of feeling; and even Harry Beecham fails to prove himself exceptional enough to win Sybylla. Sybylla effortlessly dominates and emasculates them all. She picks up her father from his drinking sprees and drives him home like a delinquent child, she scorns Grey, and when Harry proposes to her, she strikes him with a whip. She even sees Harry's restrained response as a weakness, and she seems secretly to long for him to wield power over her.

In spite of her prickly, touch-me-not nature, Sybylla is aware of the value of marriage; she knows that "our greatest heart-treasure" is the knowledge that there is in creation an individual to whom a person's existence is necessary. She asks who can this be but a husband or a wife? This moving passage does a great deal to transform the outcome of the Harry-Sybylla plot. The passage lifts Sybylla's final rejection of Harry out of the region of the wild adolescent perversities that have previously governed her behavior toward him and raises the rejection to the loftier status of a mature affirmation of independence. Despite the inevitable trace of sadness that Sybylla does not ride off into the sunset with her beau, many readers will applaud her courageous decision to journey alone.

Claire J. Robinson

Further Reading

Barnard, Marjorie. *Miles Franklin*. New York: Twayne, 1967. A lucid and comprehensive guide to Franklin's life and works. An excellent starting point.

Callil, Carmen. Introduction to *My Brilliant Career*, by Miles Franklin. New York: St. Martin's Press, 1980. This introductory essay establishes the initial modern perspective on the novel, a perspective debated since this reprinting.

Coleman, Verna. *Miles Franklin in America: Her Unknown (Brilliant) Career.* London: Sirius, 1981. Discusses Franklin's novels in relation to the author's life and her reception among readers and critics in the United States.

Ewers, John K. *Creative Writing in Australia: A Selective Survey.* Rev. ed. Melbourne, Vic.: Georgian House, 1966. Ewers finds Franklin's *My Brilliant Career* true to Australia, with a clear vision of reality and a scorn of pretense, and advises reading it together with its sequel, *My Career Goes Bung* (1946), for a clear picture of an "extraordinary mind."

Garton, Stephen. "Contesting Enslavement: Marriage, Manhood, and *My Brilliant Career.*" *Australian Literary Studies* 20, no. 4 (October, 2002): 336-349. Focuses on issues of enslavement in the novel. Discusses the novel's depiction of marriage, the character of Harold Beecham, masculinity, and femininity. Garton's piece is one of several articles in this issue that examine various aspects of *My Brilliant Career.*

Hadgraft, Cecil. "The New Century: First Harvest of Fiction." In *Australian Literature: A Critical Account to 1955.* London: Heinemann, 1960. Although Hadgraft finds *My Brilliant Career*'s literary value to be unequal to its human interest and the dominating personality to be odd, he praises its setting, vocabulary, and circumstances as convincingly Australian, a "remarkable" achievement.

Mathew, Ray. *Miles Franklin.* Melbourne, Vic.: Lansdowne Press, 1963. Psychological study of Franklin's novels. Contains valuable observations on Sybylla's almost pathological mistrust of emotion.

Roe, Jill. *Her Brilliant Career: The Life of Stella Miles Franklin.* Cambridge, Mass.: Belknap Press, 2009. A comprehensive biography of Franklin, a work developed from "decades of research in thousands of papers" left by Franklin upon her death. The "definitive life of this remarkable writer and feminist."

Sheridan, Susan. "Louisa Lawson, Miles Franklin, and Feminist Writing." In *Along the Faultlines: Sex, Race, and Nation in Australian Women's Writing, 1880's-1930's.* St. Leonards, N.S.W.: Allen & Unwin, 1995. Examines the relation between Australian women's fiction and feminist theories of cultural change, focusing on how women writers in the Australian colonies treated questions of nation, gender, and racial difference within the context of a settler society. This chapter compares the work of Franklin and Lawson, two Australian feminist writers.

My Kinsman, Major Molineux

Author: Nathaniel Hawthorne (1804-1864)
First published: 1832
Type of work: Short fiction
Type of plot: Romance
Time of plot: Shortly before the Revolutionary War
Locale: Colonial Massachusetts

Principal characters:
ROBIN MOLINEUX, a teenager setting out to find a future for himself
MAJOR MOLINEUX, the boy's relative and would-be patron, who is humiliated by a mob

The Story:

On a moonlit evening just before the American Revolution in a time of political rebellion against British rule, Robin Molineux arrives at the ferry landing of a sizeable Massachusetts town. A country boy of about eighteen, Robin wears secondhand and homemade clothing, and he carries a cudgel consisting of an oak sapling with part of its root attached. He assumes that any passerby will be eager to tell him the way to the home of his kinsman, Major Molineux. However, he soon finds that directions will not be so easy to obtain.

The first person Robin meets is a well-dressed old man who coughs repeatedly. Robin takes hold of the old man's skirt and asks if he knows the way to Major Molineux's home. The gentleman responds angrily that he does not know the man, demands that Robin remove his hand, and threatens to have him put in the stocks for lack of respect. A nearby barbershop door is open, and those inside are delighted to witness Robin's humiliation. Surprised, "shrewd" Robin, as he is repeatedly designated by the narrator, attributes the behavior to the old man's being from the country and lacking the breeding to be civil to strangers. He even considers hitting the man on the nose.

Robin proceeds to an inn, where the cordial innkeeper assumes he is a possible patron. Robin infers that the innkeeper treats him well because he sees a family resemblance to Major Molineux, so with a great deal of confidence he admits that he is nearly penniless and is only there to inquire the way to Major Molineux's home. Immediately, everyone in the tavern becomes hostile. The innkeeper pretends to see a resemblance between Robin and a runaway apprentice depicted on a wanted poster, and he rudely urges the boy to move on. Robin, again "shrewdly," assumes the change in behavior is due to his confession of an empty pocket, but he thinks it strange that his poverty should outweigh his connection to his important kinsman. Once again, he contemplates physical retaliation, thinking that, if he could only meet the hostile men back in the woods where he and his oak sapling grew up, he would teach them some manners.

Robin's next encounter is with a young woman wearing a scarlet petticoat who behaves with a sly freedom. When he asks about his kinsman, she replies that he dwells with her and invites Robin in, but he doubts that she is telling the truth. Before Robin succumbs to the woman's temptations, the night watchman appears, and she disappears back into her house. The watchman is rude to Robin, threatening to put him in the stocks and laughing to himself when Robin asks about Major Molineux. Robin begins to believe he is under a spell.

After meeting groups of men who talk to him in a strange language and curse him when he cannot reply, the frustrated Robin determines to find answers. Using his cudgel as a barrier, he stops the next passerby and demands to know where his kinsman lives. Robin is astonished to see that the man's face is painted half black and half red so that he looks fiendish. The stranger advises Robin that if he waits at that spot for an hour, he will see Major Molineux pass by. The ever-shrewd Robin categorizes the encounter as one of the many strange sights a traveler is likely to see on a journey.

Robin sits before a church contemplating his experiences and, in a dreamlike state, visualizing his family back home. This pleasant reverie ends, however, as he imagines his family entering the house, and the door closes, latches, and excludes him. Struggling to stay awake, Robin has one more encounter, this time with a gentleman who speaks to him with real kindness. Robin explains to him that his father and Major Molineux are brothers' sons and the major has offered to help Robin become established in life. Now that Robin is grown and ready to begin life on his own, he is seeking his kinsman. The gentleman confirms that the fiendish-looking man's advice was accurate, and he and Robin wait together for the major to pass.

Soon, a raucous parade appears led on horseback by the bicomplexioned man, who looks at Robin as if he has a part to play in the entertainment. Prominently displayed in the parade on a cart and covered in tar and feathers sits Major Molineux. To complete his disgrace, Molineux recognizes his kinsman Robin immediately upon seeing him. First filled with pity and terror, Robin is soon affected by both the excitement and the expectations of the crowd, which includes most of the people he has earlier encountered. Suddenly, he laughs more loudly than anyone.

After the parade goes on, a downcast Robin turns to the kindly gentleman sitting with him and asks that he show him the way to the ferry so he can return home. His companion overrules him, saying that he will be glad to do so in a few days if Robin should still wish to go. In the meantime, he urges the young man to stay in town for awhile and, seeing that he is a shrewd youth, discover whether he can be successful in the world without the help of his kinsman.

Critical Evaluation:

Nathaniel Hawthorne wrote "My Kinsman, Major Molineux" when he was about twenty-five years old. Most modern literary critics consider the work one of his finest stories. However, the author himself may not have felt so. He did not include it in his first two collections of stories, and literary critics before the 1950's gave it little attention. Like many of Hawthorne's early stories, it was first published anonymously in *The Token*, an annual collection marketed as a gift book for parlors. Hawthorne finally published the story under his own name in his third collection of short stories, *The Snow-Image, and Other Twice-Told Tales* (1851).

Many critics see in "My Kinsman, Major Molineux" an archetypal coming-of-age tale. Robin's journey essentially marks his transition from childhood to adulthood. He is leaving home to make his way in the world, and Major Molineux has offered him his help. He is naïvely proud of his connection to the major, apparently never considering that others might not regard his cousin so highly. He is slow to understand why he encounters so much hostility and deception in the town, and he considers resorting to a childish violence to solve the problems he encounters. That he carries a young tree with him, roots and all, marks him as a country bumpkin, innocent of the ways of the world, particularly the urban world. However, at the end of the story Robin's false shrewdness may have become real shrewdness, as he finally realizes that his relative is hated in the community and that he has participated in his usurpation. He is a sadder and wiser man than he was, a fact that his companion notes when he suggests that he try standing on his own two feet rather than depending on the patronage of a relative.

Some critics see the story as a historical allegory. Q. D. Leavis, for example, feels that the subtitle of the tale might be "America Comes of Age." The opening paragraph, which details a history of abuses the colonists inflicted on their royal governors, provides readers with a preview of the story's outcome. Major Molineux is one of the representatives of the British government who has annoyed the American colonists to the point that they stage a political demonstration to supplant him and assert their freedom. Many Americans, like Robin, had British relatives and faced a choice of standing with them or with their new American neighbors. Although he is not particularly proud of laughing at his cousin, Robin's laughter allies him with the rebellious colonists. Young Robin, like young America, asserts his independence from past associations.

Some psychoanalytic critics see the essence of the tale not in the outward events it portrays but in the anxieties those events cause in the psyche of young Robin. He wants approval and success, and he fears punishment and failure. As he tries to fit into the adult world of the town, Robin searches for an idealized father figure on whom he may depend, but instead he is forced to handle alone the contempt of various male conspirators, the temptation of a woman of the evening, and the sight of his father figure being humiliated. Hyatt Waggoner and Roy R. Male emphasize Robin's guilt over being a coconspirator in the destruction of his father figure, while Frederick Crews argues that Robin is free at the end, no longer dependent on or resentful of authority. An emerging man, he has a healthy dependence on himself.

Other critics have tried to reconcile psychological and historical interpretations of the story. Terence Martin sees the story as a fusion of the two frames, a tale of both individual and national maturity. Daniel G. Hoffman agrees, arguing that the central theme of the narrative, self-determination and its consequences, applies to both the personal story of Robin and the political history of the American colonists on the verge of autonomy. Hoffman believes that Robin and the young country must learn a harsh lesson: that the impulse to be self-determining comes from demonic depths and leaves a burden of freedom. Neal Frank Doubleday argues that the tale is a personal one set in a historical context. At the end, Robin is bitterly aware that he has betrayed himself and abandoned his loyalties in order to conform to society and avoid further rejection.

Using a new historicist approach, Michael J. Colacurcio argues that Hawthorne sought to deflate some of the bloated rhetoric that surrounded the 1826 fiftieth-anniversary celebrations of the American Revolution. Hawthorne's version of the revolution rather grimly demonstrates that plotting and petty cruelty characterized revolutionary activities more than God's providence did.

A story rich in interpretative possibilities, "My Kinsman, Major Molineux" is replete with the ambiguity for which Hawthorne is known. Written when many Americans were calling for a uniquely American literature, it is part of Hawthorne's distinctive contribution to what many believe is the period of that produced America's most significant literature, the American Renaissance.

William L. Howard

Further Reading

Becker, John E. *Hawthorne's Historical Allegory: An Examination of the American Conscience*. Port Washington, N.Y.: Kennikat Press, 1971. Argues that Hawthorne used historical allegory to interpret America to itself. Particularly useful for stories set in clearly defined eras of America's past, such as "My Kinsman, Major Molyneux."

Bunge, Nancy. *Nathaniel Hawthorne: A Study of the Short Fiction*. New York: Twayne, 1993. An easy-to-read guide to the short stories.

Colacurcio, Michael J. "The Matter of America: 'My Kinsman, Major Molineux.'" In *Modern Critical Views: Nathaniel Hawthorne*, edited by Harold Bloom. New York: Chelsea House, 1986. A complex reading of the story using a new historicist approach.

Crews, Frederick C. *The Sins of the Fathers: Hawthorne's Psychological Themes*. New York: Oxford University Press, 1966. Uses a psychoanalytic approach, showing how Freudian themes recur in Hawthorne's works, including "My Kinsman, Major Molyneux."

Doubleday, Neal Frank. *Hawthorne's Early Tales: A Critical Study*. Durham, N.C.: Duke University Press, 1972. Contains a wealth of information on the conventions of American publishing, magazines as a venue for short stories, and the influence of Sir Walter Scott on American writers. Excellent source of background on "My Kinsman, Major Molyneux" in particular.

Hoffman, Daniel G. *Form and Fable in American Fiction*. New York: Oxford University Press, 1961. Useful for identifying the influences of folklore and myth in Hawthorne's work.

Reynolds, Larry J., ed. *A Historical Guide to Nathaniel Hawthorne*. New York: Oxford University Press, 2001. A basic guide to Hawthorne's times. Includes a brief biography, as well as essays by various contributors on mesmerism, children, the visual arts, and slavery. Also includes a valuable bibliographical essay surveying the many critical approaches to Hawthorne.

My Life and Hard Times

Author: James Thurber (1894-1961)
First published: 1933
Type of work: Autobiography

Principal personages:
JAMES THURBER
CHARLES, his father
MARY, his mother
HERMAN and ROY, his brothers
GRANDFATHER

To say that there are two worlds—the world of ordinary men and the world of James Thurber—is a cliché that would never have been tolerated by Thurber himself, for one of the charms of his style is a scrupulous avoidance of anything resembling the trite. Among his many phobias there must have existed the dread of turning a corner in a sentence and being waylaid with a cliché. His precision of language and careful attention to detail are the qualities that infuse his writing with interest and charm, as is his ability to impose a world of fantasy on a world of reality and to achieve an interrelationship of the external and the internal, the factual and the imaginative.

In his preface to *My Life and Hard Times*, Thurber apologizes for writing an autobiography before he had reached the age of forty and for not conforming to Ford Madox Ford's dictum that one's memoirs should paint a picture of one's time. Thurber more or less admits that there is no time and that all he intends to tell is what happened to this one writer. Since what follows could have happened to no one but Thurber, he thus implicitly admits the existence of the Thurber world.

This world reaches beyond the boundaries of the real or the commonplace and extends into a region of fable, peopled by such figures as the cook Emma Inch and her asthmatic dog, Feely; Della, who made cretonnes for the soup and whose brother worked in an incinerator where they burn refuse; Barney Haller, the hired man, whom thunder followed like a dog; and Walter Mitty, that frustrated, comic Prufrock with his dreams of heroism and glory. Strange things happen in this world because Thurber sees it that way: An old woman with a parasol is seen to walk through a truck, a cat rolls across the street atop a striped barrel, and an admiral in full uniform rides a bicycle across the highway in the path of an oncoming car. That these things are never what they seem but fragments of the ordinary world suddenly revealed in a new light or a different perspective is the secret of Thurber's humor. It is a form of humor little concerned with the conventional or the obvious. It arises quite naturally from a rec-ognition of the inner, emotional chaos of a sensitive, individualistic man trapped in the affairs of the practical, demanding world, with no weapon of defense but his own resistances and inferiorities.

Hence that air of the fabulous that also invests Thurber's drawings: the meek, rotund men with poses of resignation, whose faces reveal long-thwarted efforts to think and act in a positive manner; the aggressive, rather frightening women who never seem disturbed by doubts as to their superiority; the huge, sadly patient dogs. They belong in a world in which life has grown complicated for men and animals, from which one way of escape leads into a Cloud-Cuckoo Land where the illogical becomes the logical and the fantastic reveals the dilemma of people facing the psychological confusion and insecurity of their place in a world almost devoid of sense and meaning.

Nowhere does Thurber display to better advantage his genius for uncovering the incongruous in everyday human affairs, in the daydream escapes from personal confusion or catastrophe, than in the nine episodes that center on Thurber's youth in Columbus, Ohio, as told in *My Life and Hard Times*.

"The Night the Bed Fell" is about the night the bed did not fall on Thurber's father while he slept in the attic where Grandfather was supposed to sleep. Grandfather, who refused to believe that the army of the Potomac was not still trying to take Richmond, had wandered off some days before; eventually he would turn up with profane criticism of the campaign, its military leaders, and the administration in Washington. Actually, James Thurber rolled out of his cot; his mother was convinced that the bed had fallen on Father and he must be pulled from the wreckage; a visiting cousin poured a glass of camphor over himself, and Father was sure that the house was on fire. Mother, who always called it the night on which the bed fell on Father, was looking on the bright side of things when she said she was glad Grandfather had not been there.

"The Car We Had to Push" is about all sorts of things, but mostly about Grandfather's brother, Zenas, who contracted the chestnut tree blight and died of that strange malady in 1866. "The Day the Dam Broke" is about the day the dam did not break. Expected catastrophes have a way of not happening in the Thurber world, but the effects are very much the same. The citizens of Columbus, thinking it had broken, fled in panic. The police were summoned to the Thurber household on "The Night the Ghost Got In," and Grandfather shot one police officer in the shoulder under the hallucinated impression that the men in blue uniforms were deserters from General Meade's army.

"More Alarms at Night" deals with brother Roy's feigned delirium; even at the best of times Roy was likely to sing "Onward, Christian Soldiers" or "Marching Through Georgia" in his sleep. He awakened Father in the small hours, called him Buck, and announced that his time had come. Father, a mildly nervous man, aroused his family. Everyone assured him that he had had a bad dream. The sketch also deals with another night when James awoke poor Father to get help in remembering the name of a New Jersey city, Perth Amboy. Sure that his son had gone mad, Father ran from the room.

"A Sequence of Servants" tells of 162 servants, including Vashti, who told her lover that he must never tangle with her jealous stepfather, who had married her mother just to be near Vashti; it turns out that Vashti had invented her stepfather to pique the lover.

A memorable Airedale named Muggs is "The Dog That Bit People." When he died, after biting almost everybody in Ohio—including Lieutenant-Governor Malloy—Mother wanted to bury him in the family plot under "Flights of angels sing thee to thy rest" or some equally misappropriate inscription. The family dissuaded her, however, and Muggs was interred along a lonely road beneath an epitaph of Thurber's choice: "Cave canem." Mother was always quite pleased with the classic dignity of that simple Latin phrase.

"University Days" presents Bolenciecwcz, star tackle on the Ohio State football team, whom an economics professor tried to make eligible for the Illinois game by asking him to name one means of transportation; after hints, prods, and auditory and visual demonstrations by the professor and the whole class, Bolenciecwcz mentioned a train and the day was saved. There is also an agricultural student named Haskins, who wanted to be a journalist and whose beat for campus news covered the cow barns, the horse pavilion, the sheep house, and the animal husbandry department in general.

The final sketch, "Draft Board Nights," describes Thurber being repeatedly called before the draft board, which always turned him down because of poor eyesight, and then,

through some repetitive mistake, called him back. He eventually drifted into service, not in the U.S. Army, but as an unauthorized and undetected examiner of draftees—a pulmonary man, to be exact. What put a merciful end to that was the Armistice.

It is useless for critics to debate the place of Thurber in the literature of his time. His humor, which creates its effects according to the laws of its own logic and yet always with a savoring of common sense, is superbly his own, as his would-be imitators have discovered. His manner is nimble without being racy; it has poignancy without sentimentality. His touch with words is delicate yet precise. Best of all, he illustrates his own books with inimitable drawings that, like his prose pieces, distort the familiar into the fantastic without losing touch with reality.

Further Reading

Bernstein, Burton. *Thurber: A Biography.* 1975. New ed. New York: Arbor House, 1985. A thorough treatment, beginning with Thurber's ancestry. Examines his works in relation to his life. The discussion of *My Life and Hard Times* includes critical reactions of Ernest Hemingway and other contemporaries, and the work is also compared to Thurber's other writings.

Gopnik, Adam. "The Great Deflater." *The New Yorker,* June 27-July 4, 1994. A profile of Thurber, chronicling his life and literary career. Discusses the success of *My Life and Hard Times,* Thurber's ability to express inner experience, and the declining popularity of his work in the 1990's.

Grauer, Neil A. *Remember Laughter: A Life of James Thurber.* Lincoln: University of Nebraska Press, 1994. A concise yet thorough biography, relating Thurber's work to his life and analyzing his humor. Illustrated with twelve of Thurber's cartoons.

Holmes, Charles S. *The Clocks of Columbus: The Literary Career of James Thurber.* New York: Atheneum, 1972. A thorough and insightful overview of Thurber's works. Chapter 9, "Columbus Remembered: *My Life and Hard Times,*" discusses Thurber's autobiography in relation to reality, drawing on news stories and reminiscences of friends and relatives. Provides a scholarly critique of the protagonist, dominant themes, and style.

Kinney, Harrison. *James Thurber: His Life and Times.* New York: H. Holt, 1995. Comprehensive and revealing biography containing many excerpts from Thurber's letters, essays, conversations, and poems and illustrated with his cartoons. Describes how Thurber drew his self-deprecating humor from his personal experiences.

Tanner, Stephen L. "James Thurber and the Midwest." *American Studies* 33, no. 2 (Fall, 1992): 61-72. Compares *My Life and Hard Times* with *The Thurber Album*, which reveals his changing view of Columbus over time. Focuses on the Ohio roots of much of his writing.

Thurber, James. *The Thurber Letters: The Wit, Wisdom, and Surprising Life of James Thurber.* Edited by Harrison Kinney. New York: Simon & Schuster, 2003. This biographical account, based on letters and other correspondence provided by Thurber's daughter, Rosemary A. Thurber, gives "unprecedented insight into the life and career of one of America's greatest and most enduring humorists."

Tobias, Richard C. *The Art of James Thurber.* 1970. New ed. Athens: Ohio University Press, 1975. An excellent appraisal with valuable insights, which compares Thurber's comic writing with that of such writers as Sir Thomas Malory, William Wordsworth, and William Shakespeare. Devotes one chapter to *My Life and Hard Times*, viewing it as a "comic mask."

My Name Is Asher Lev

Author: Chaim Potok (1929-2002)
First published: 1972
Type of work: Novel
Type of plot: Domestic realism
Time of plot: Mid-twentieth century
Locale: Crown Heights, Brooklyn, New York

Principal characters:
ASHER LEV, a young Hasidic artist
RIVKEH LEV, Asher's mother
ARYEH LEV, Asher's father
YITZCHOK LEV, Asher's uncle, a successful jeweler and watch repairer
YUDEL KRINSKY, Asher's friend and confidant, a Russian Jew employed in a stationery store
JACOB KAHN, an artist, Asher's mentor
ANNA SCHAEFFER, an art gallery owner who shows Jacob Kahn's and Asher Lev's work

The Story:

Asher Lev is the only child of a devout, Orthodox Jewish couple, Rivkeh and Aryeh Lev. By the age of four, Asher shows an unusual talent for drawing. His mother urges him repeatedly to make pretty drawings, while his father views Asher's preoccupation with suspicion, labeling it "foolishness."

When Asher is six years old, his family receives the news of the death of his Uncle Yaakov, Rivkeh's only brother. Yaakov, who was studying history and Russian affairs, died in a car accident while traveling for the Rebbe, a religious leader. The death plunges Rivkeh into a prolonged depression. Asher's father works and travels for the Rebbe, and Asher is often left alone with a housekeeper.

While visiting Asher's family, Asher's uncle, Yitzchok (Aryeh's brother), notices his nephew's drawings and proclaims the boy "a little Chagall." He tells Asher that Chagall is the greatest living Jewish artist, and he adds that Picasso is the greatest artist of all. Uncle Yitzchok buys one of Asher's drawings so that he can own an "early Lev," but Asher's father opposes this gesture and insists that Yitzchok return the drawing.

During Rivkeh's depression, Asher begins to be haunted by nightmares of his father's great-great-grandfather. Asher comes to regard this figure as his mythic ancestor. The figure appears to him repeatedly at night and comes to symbolize Asher's religious and cultural heritage and the accompanying burdens and expectations.

Rivkeh eventually recovers and becomes convinced that she must continue her brother's work. She receives special permission from the Rebbe to attend college and to study Russian history, eventually earning a doctorate. With both his parents so involved with the post-World War II affairs of Jews around the world, and particularly in Russia, young Asher is often alone. He stops drawing for a time and later comes to view this period as the time when his gift is taken away. He vows never to let that happen again.

Asher befriends Yudel Krinsky and often visits the stationery store where Yudel works. Asher encounters artists' supplies for the first time. Krinsky also answers Asher's many questions about life in Russia.

With the death of Stalin, Asher's father is able to travel more freely in Europe. The Rebbe asks Aryeh to move to Vienna, but Asher refuses to move with his family. Asher's attachment to his home and neighborhood is fierce, and he fears that he will lose his artistic gift if he leaves. Asher begins to draw again and senses that "something was happening to my eyes. . . . I could feel with my eyes."

Asher is doing poorly in school. One day he unconsciously draws a sinister-looking picture of the Rebbe in a religious text. The drawing is discovered, and Asher's instructor and his classmates view it as a defilement of a holy book. The rift among Asher, his classmates, and his instructors grows. Asher feels increasingly isolated.

Aryeh's opposition to Asher's preoccupation with art intensifies, and Rivkeh frequently finds herself caught between her husband and her son. Asher still refuses to accompany his parents to Vienna. Eventually Asher's father makes the trip alone, leaving Asher and his mother at home together.

Rivkeh takes Asher to the museum, where Asher begins to study the great masterpieces. In his exposure to the history of art, Asher encounters Christian images and themes. Rivkeh buys Asher a set of oil paints from Yudel Krinsky. When Aryeh returns from his travels, he remains unreconciled to his son's gift, and the gulf between father and son widens.

Asher is sent to talk with the Rebbe. The Rebbe tells him, "A life is measured by how it is lived for the sake of heaven," and arranges for Asher to meet Jacob Kahn, a successful artist who is a nonpracticing Jew. Jacob is in his seventies. Asher is thirteen. Asher begins studying with this great master who worked with Picasso in Paris and who knows many of the century's great artists. Jacob introduces Asher to gallery owner Anna Schaeffer. Her gallery handles Jacob's art, and Asher learns that Anna will eventually introduce his art to the world.

Asher spends a lot of time with Jacob and his wife, including summer vacations in Provincetown, Massachusetts. Rivkeh joins Aryeh in Europe, leaving Asher in the care of his uncle Yitzchok, who converts an attic into Asher's first studio. Asher later joins his family in Vienna for a short time, but the stress and the separation from his world and his art prove too great for him. He returns home.

Anna arranges for Asher to have a show, noting that he is "the youngest artist ever to have a one-man show in a Madison Avenue gallery." She bills him as "Asher Lev, Brooklyn Prodigy." Asher's work is well received, leading to subsequent shows and sales. Asher's parents return after living abroad for several years, and Asher moves back home. Asher

continues to paint with Jacob and in his own studio in his uncle's home.

After one of his shows, Asher decides that he must go to Europe to study and paint. Following his graduation from college, he travels alone to Italy and France. He settles in Paris and works there. Anna visits him in order to arrange for another New York show. She is particularly moved by two paintings Asher did—crucifixion scenes that depict his mother's suffering as she is torn between her husband and her son. Anna names these paintings "Brooklyn Crucifixion I" and "Brooklyn Crucifixion II." Asher knows these paintings will cause his parents and his religious community great pain. He knows that few in his community will be able to understand his choice of the Crucifixion as a way to depict suffering. He knows, though, that to be true to his artistic calling, he has to paint what he sees and what he feels.

Asher is unable to bring himself to tell his parents about these paintings. His parents see them for the first time at his show. The impact on them is as Asher guesses it would be. The show is a critical success. A museum buys the two crucifixion paintings, but the rift now among Asher and his family and his religious community is irreparable. The Rebbe tells Asher that he must leave. Asher understands and accepts what is essentially an exile. He leaves for Europe, taking with him the memory of his parents watching him from their window.

Critical Evaluation:

In writing about Orthodox Jewish life, Chaim Potok speaks with considerable authority: He was a rabbi and a respected academic, and he served as the editor-in-chief of the Jewish Publication Society of America. In *My Name Is Asher Lev*, Potok focuses on the role of the artist in a particular community—a community he locates in Crown Heights, Brooklyn, and calls Ladover Hasidism. Potok models his Ladover Hasidism on Lubavitch Hasidism.

My Name Is Asher Lev, like Potok's other novels including *The Chosen* (1967), *The Promise* (1969), *In the Beginning* (1975), and *Davita's Harp* (1985), probes the specific struggles of one member of a community who comes into conflict with the norms and expectations of that community. Asher Lev's community expects him to follow in his parents' footsteps and to work in some way for the preservation and the betterment of Judaism worldwide. Asher, however, is seen as responding to a radically different calling: art. A very familiar pattern of conflict in the world of the novel—the individual versus society—becomes apparent early in the book. On the first page, Asher lists some of the charges he has to face. These include "traitor, an apostate, a self-hater, an inflicter of shame upon my family, my friends, my people." Asher's own struggle to come to terms with these labels is also sensed when he adds: "In all honesty, I confess that my accusers are not altogether wrong: I am indeed in some way, all of those things." *My Name Is Asher Lev*, then, becomes a defense, a defense of the individual and a defense of art.

The particular society to which Asher belongs is bound together by religious beliefs, and the decisions of the individuals and of the corporate body are seen as having eternal consequences. Asher is taught to view all of his decisions, including those of vocation, not simply in terms of how best to fill his days but also in terms of how best to contribute to eternity. To some, including Asher's father, the world of art is viewed with extreme fear and suspicion; if Asher does not use his art to serve the Master of the Universe, then clearly he aligns himself with the Other Side. Asher's decision to become an artist ultimately results in banishment from his home and his community. The spiritual parallels of this exile are inescapable.

It is no accident that Asher's father's name means "lion." Aryeh is presented to the reader as a mighty defender of his beliefs and as a protector and a rescuer of those with whom he shares beliefs. His opposition to Asher's art becomes as fierce as his devotion to his own causes—causes he sees as incompatible with Asher's worldly pursuits. While both of Asher's parents devote their energies to the liberation and the resettling of Russian Jews, Asher seeks to master the traditions of Western art, including Christian symbols and images. Asher ultimately establishes a name and a place for himself within that tradition, a tradition that Aryeh views as particularly threatening. In borrowing forms from that tradition, particularly the cross, Asher acknowledges the affront this presents to his father: "The Crucifixion had been in a way responsible for his own father's murder on a night before Easter decades ago."

While the role of the artist in society and the relationship of the individual to society are familiar themes in literature, this novel also explores other related themes, including isolation and the search for and the creation of identity. The nature of art and of suffering and the artist as exile are explored through the character of Asher as well. The sacrifices inherent in following one's calling are traced not only in the character of the young artist but also through Asher's parents; the parents make great personal sacrifices in order to live out their most cherished beliefs.

Potok begins his novel with an epigraph from Picasso: "Art is a lie which makes us realize the truth." This epigraph immediately draws the reader's attention to such philosophical considerations as the nature of truth. The novel is rich in its exploration of paradox and inherent contradictions; on one hand, Asher pays his parents the highest possible honor by immortalizing them and their struggles in his art; on the other hand, this depiction is viewed as the act of a traitor and blasphemer. Asher's greatest triumph becomes the source of his greatest pain. Potok continues the story of Asher in *The Gift of Asher Lev*, published in 1990.

Beverly J. Matiko

Further Reading

Abramson, Edward A. *Chaim Potok*. Boston: Twayne, 1986. Chapter four is devoted entirely to *My Name Is Asher Lev* and includes sections on "Judaism and the Visual Arts," "The Individual and the Community," "Ancestors and Fathers," and "Artistic and Stylistic Development." Also of interest are the book's first and last chapters, entitled "From Rabbi to Writer" and "The Writer Arrived." Abramson includes a six-page selected bibliography.

Daum, Robert A. "Crossing Cruci-Fictional Boundaries: Transgressive Tropes in Chaim Potok's *My Name Is Asher Lev*." In *Jesus in Twentieth-Century Literature, Art, and Movies*, edited by Paul C. Burns. New York: Continuum, 2007. This analysis of Potok's novel focuses on its treatment of a crucified Jesus; it is included in a collection of essays that analyze the representation of Jesus in the work of twentieth century novelists, artists, and filmmakers.

Jewish Studies Program, University of Pennsylvania. *Chaim Potok and Jewish-American Culture: Three Essays*. Philadelphia: Author, 2002. These essays, delivered at a memorial symposium for Potok, reappraise *The Chosen*, discuss "Potok and the Question of Jewish Writing," and examine how the author was a *Zwischenmensch*, or a person who negotiated between two cultures

Kremer, S. Lillian. "Dedalus in Brooklyn: Influences of *A Portrait of the Artist as a Young Man* on *My Name Is Asher Lev*." *Studies in Jewish American Literature* 4 (1985): 26-38. Finds "the mark of James Joyce indelibly stamped on the third and fourth novels of Chaim Potok," particularly in the use of "monologue, stream of consciousness techniques, and epiphany."

Pinsker, Sanford. "The Crucifixion of Chaim Potok/The Excommunication of Asher Lev: Art and the Hasidic World." *Studies in Jewish American Literature* 4 (1985): 39-51. Calls the novel a *Kunstlerroman*, or a novel of an artist's education, and views Asher Lev's departure at the novel's end as "a kind of exile, a kind of excommunication."

Sternlicht, Sanford. *Chaim Potok: A Critical Companion.* Westport, Conn.: Greenwood Press, 2000. A straightforward and useful guide to the novelist's works. Summarizes Potok's life, assesses his literary heritage and achievements, and devotes a chapter to an analysis of *My Name Is Asher Lev.*

Studies in American Jewish Literature 4 (1985). This issue, entitled "The World of Chaim Potok," contains various articles, including one by Potok, and an interview with him.

Walden, Daniel, ed. *Conversations with Chaim Potok.* Jackson: University Press of Mississippi, 2001. Reprints numerous interviews with Potok in which he discusses a range of topics, including his views on writing and other writers, his religious faith, and his novels.

My Name Is Red

Author: Orhan Pamuk (1952-   )
First published: Benim Adım Kırmızı, 1998 (English translation, 2001)
Type of work: Novel
Type of plot: Historical and murder mystery
Time of plot: 1591
Locale: Istanbul

Principal characters:
ELEGANT EFFENDI, a court miniaturist
ENISHTE EFFENDI, a master court miniaturist and confidant of Sultan Murat III
BLACK, a miniaturist, bookmaker, and diplomat
MASTER OSMAN III, the master miniaturist of Murat's court
BUTTERFLY,
OLIVE, and
STORK, court miniaturists and murder suspects
SHEKURE, the beautiful widowed daughter of Enishte Effendi, and Black's love interest

The Story:

A dead man calls out from the bottom of a well, into which his battered body had been dumped. The souls of the dead can still interact with the living in the world of late sixteenth century Istanbul, the center of the Ottoman Empire.

A former miniaturist apprentice named Black returns to Istanbul after a twelve-year absence to visit his uncle Enishte Effendi, also his former teacher. Black learns that miniaturist Elegant Effendi has been missing and may have been harmed. He also learns that Enishte Effendi has been secretly commissioned by the sultan to illustrate a book in the European manner to extol the glories of the sultan and his reign. The plan is for this illustrated volume to be presented to Western diplomats to circulate through Europe as evidence of Sultan Murat III's power, wealth, and intellect.

While Black and Enishte Effendi are discussing art in general as well as the sultan's secret commission (an open secret at the sultan's court), a messenger arrives with news that Elegant Effendi has in fact been murdered and that his corpse has been found at the bottom of a well. Murat is angry that one of his illustrators has been murdered. As a knowledgeable outsider, Black is charged with finding the murderer within three days, or he will suffer the consequences. Disturbing his mental equilibrium even further, Black catches a glimpse of Shekure, Enishte Effendi's widowed daughter. Black has long been infatuated with Shekure and devises strategies to be alone with her so that he might declare his love, a passion about which Shekure is ambivalent.

Black interviews all the illustrators attached to the sultan's court, men he had known as boys when they all apprenticed together. Black attempts to ascertain which camp each illustrator falls into—traditionalist or innovator. He needs to know the vehemence with which each illustrator holds opinions of individual artistic style as well as their opinions about Elegant Effendi's talent. Master Osman III, Butterfly, Stork, and Olive are asked the same three questions on artistic style. Their responses do not provide conclusive evidence about the murderer's identity. A partially completed illustration had been found on Elegant Effendi's corpse. The murderer is likely the man who drew this illustration and then had given it to Elegant Effendi to draw a frame around it.

Each illustrator is commanded to quickly draw a picture of a horse, without putting conscious thought into the work. In this way, Black hopes to trick the murderer into revealing himself. Subtle differences among the pictures leads Black and the presumed-innocent Master Osman to the sultan's palace, where they are granted extraordinary access to the treasury, including the sultan's private collection of staggeringly precious and exotic illuminated books. Locked into the private vaults with the librarian, the two sleuths journey through the history of Islamic art and literature. Black's thoughts turn increasingly toward Shekure, however, while Master Osman slips further and further into the mystical realm of communion with his artistic predecessors and their desire to see into the impenetrable darkness of Allah's own creativity. Given the opportunity, Master Osman chooses to blind himself to see more clearly, as Allah sees, without the distraction of actual physical objects.

While Black and the now-blind Master Osman continue their search for clues, the murderer strikes again. Enishte Effendi is killed this time, and his studio is ransacked, in a desperate attempt to find the incriminating illustration. The murderer escapes undetected.

Shekure, meantime, has slipped away to meet with Black, whom she finally agrees to marry—more out of fear than love, however. The wedding is a hurried ceremony to protect Shekure from the machinations of her dead husband's relatives. Shekure refuses to consummate her marriage to Black until the killer is found and arrested.

All who align themselves with those advocating the development of individual artistic styles remain in danger both from a murderer who has already killed twice and from the followers of a popular religious leader dead set against the rise of foreign influences in Ottoman society. Finally, the murderer is tricked into revealing himself when presented with the evidence against him. Naturally, he justifies his actions by arguing that art must capture the intensity of divine creativity. To allow artists such as Elegant Effendi to develop individual styles, he says, and to present illustrations of the physical world from any perspective other than that of the divine, is to desecrate both art and faith.

Critical Evaluation:

Orhan Pamuk's novel *My Name Is Red* is a historical murder mystery, and much of the plot is focused on figuring out why court miniaturist Elegant Effendi was murdered, and by whom. The novel also is an exploration of the proper relationship between human and divine creativity and the quite possibly unbridgeable difference between post-Enlightenment European society and the traditional Muslim society of Ottoman Istanbul.

The sultan's secretly commissioned illuminated book, and responses to its rumored existence, divide the main characters into two mutually exclusive camps. On the one side are the traditionalists, those who believe that any illustration an artist constructs will be, by definition, flawed. Human art is merely an attempt to mimic the perfect creation of Allah. Such attempts not only are doomed to failure but also are insults to the magnificent creativity of Allah; they border on apostasy against Islam. The best that an artist or illustrator can hope to achieve is blindness brought on by years of painstaking reproduction of forms and illustrations produced by master miniaturists in previous centuries. As long as an artist has his own ego, his own sight and insight, and his own creativity, he will always be distanced from seeing and illustrating the world as Allah sees it. Only in the darkness of blindness can the artist's mental image, untainted by the physical representation of objects, approach the vision of Allah. The most traditional illustrators would deliberately blind themselves in order not to be distracted by the impurity of physical sight.

In contrast to the traditional school are those who see value in an artist's individual style as a mark of the importance of human creativity. These innovators wish to illustrate in the Western (Frankish) style in which artists include clues about not only their own identities but also the psychological characteristics of their subjects. Some innovators even sign their own name—visibly—to their work. Artistic innovators no longer wish to depict persons and stories in a highly stylized manner. They wish to draw their subjects as individuals so that one might recognize a person from their portrait. Such is the Western style with which the sultan has become intrigued, even to the point of having his own portrait painted in the innovative fashion. Traditionalists, both artistic and religious, fear what they see as growing foreign (infidel) influence on the sultan and in his court. Opinions about art and human creativity thus serve as metaphors for religious conservatism versus European secularism, for ahistorical concepts versus changes in traditions.

My Name Is Red comprises fifty-nine short chapters, each narrated by a different character, including the murder victim, the murderer, a dog, and even a gold coin. Each character conveys information about the murdered Elegant Effendi as well as opinions about art, love, and daily life on the fringes of the sultan's court. Framed as a murder mystery, Pamuk's novel weaves together multiple plot lines. Against the backdrop of the murder investigation, the reader follows the clandestine but increasingly dangerous romance between Black and Shekure, the growing power of religious fundamentalism and its threat of physical violence against opponents, and rising tensions from an increase of foreign influences in Ottoman society.

Many reviewers note that Pamuk plays with literary conventions in *My Name is Red*. The story is told from multiple first-person points of view and even incorporates nonhuman narrators, such as the talking dog and the gold coin. Readers with knowledge of medieval Islamic art and philosophy texts, which form the substrate of the novel, will interpret the narrative on a much deeper level. Readers unacquainted with Islamic history, art, philosophy, and theology will learn much about Ottoman legal practices and social customs, among other topics.

Pamuk's use of clashing symbols for East-West relations surfaces in many of his novels and was one of the reasons Pamuk was awarded the Nobel Prize in Literature in 2006. His books have been translated into more than forty languages. Recognized worldwide for his literary accomplishments, Pamuk remains controversial in Turkey for his public statements regarding the Turkish genocide against Armenian civilians in the early twentieth century. He had been charged with crimes against the Turkish government, but the case was dismissed on a technicality. Pamuk maintains that he speaks out on atrocities against Kurds and Armenians precisely because Turkey needs stronger laws to ensure freedom of the press. He insists that the country must acknowledge its own culpability for actions against minority populations if Tur-

key is to join the European Union and progress both socially and economically.

Victoria Erhart

Further Reading

Anadolu-Okur, Nilgun, ed. *Essays Interpreting the Writings of Novelist Orhan Pamuk*. New York: Edwin Mellen Press, 2009. A scholarly critique of Pamuk's work. Essays discuss his overarching themes that, despite being specific to Turkish history, remain deeply relevant to modern-day East-West relations.

Brahm, Gabriel Noah, Jr. "Reading *City of Quartz* in Ankara: Two Years of Thinking in Orhan Pamuk's Middle East." *Rethinking History* 11, no. 1 (March, 2007): 79-102. A discussion of so-called Occidentalist prejudices and the construction of a false Orientalist perspective that only reinforces Western prejudices against traditional Middle East culture and history.

De Bellaigue, Christopher. "There Is No East." *Harper's Magazine* 315 (September, 2007): 73-79. Reviews Pamuk's themes and stylistic models in his later novels. Discusses how the theme of religious alienation has affected East-West relations.

Goknar, Erdag. "Orhan Pamuk and the 'Ottoman' Theme." *World Literature Today*, November/December, 2006, 34-38. Studies how Pamuk uses Ottoman identity in all of his novels and how this identity is perceived in a European context.

Myra Breckinridge

Author: Gore Vidal (1925-   )
First published: 1968
Type of work: Novel
Type of plot: Social realism
Time of plot: 1968
Locale: Hollywood, California

Principal characters:
MYRA BRECKINRIDGE, co-owner of a Hollywood acting academy
BUCK LONER, co-owner of the acting academy
RUSTY GODOWSKY, a handsome student at the academy
MARY-ANN PRINGLE, a beautiful student at the academy
RANDOLPH SPENSER MONTAG, Myra's analyst
LETITIA VAN ALLEN, an agent

The Story:

Myra Breckinridge is twenty-seven years old when she inherits her dead husband's portion of an acting academy, which is co-owned by a former "singin', shootin', cowboy" star of radio and movie fame. Myra, who begins her narrative

by describing herself as a woman "whom no man will ever possess," in appearance imitates such former film stars as Fay Wray, Jean Harlow, and Lana Turner. Myra declares that the novel form is dead and that there is no point "to writing made-up stories." As far as Myra is concerned, the films of the 1940's were the high point of Western artistic creation, although she believes it is in her time being surpassed by a higher art form, the television commercial. According to Myra, her real mission in Hollywood is to fulfill her destiny of reconstructing the genders.

Myra characterizes herself as the "New Woman" whose "astonishing history" she is recording as part of therapy for her "analyst, friend, and dentist," Dr. Randolph Spenser Montag. Myra characterizes her co-owner in the acting academy, Buck Loner, as "not the man he had been when he made eighteen low-budget Westerns; now he is huge, disgusting, and old." He is also trying to seduce Myra, despite her being the widow of his only nephew, Myron Breckinridge, who had drowned the previous year while riding on the Staten Island ferry. Myra implies that Myron had not taken his own life.

In his part of the narrative, Buck details his deceased nephew's homosexuality and career as a movie reviewer. Loner has hired a private investigation agency, Flagler and Flagler, to examine the deed to the academy and make a careful investigation of his nephew's widow, Myra; he is hoping to find a loophole that will prevent her from inheriting a property he feels is his alone, despite the academy having been built with money from Myron's mother, Gertrude.

Myra considers it her mission in life to teach such aspiring young stars as Rusty Godowsky and such old cowboy stars as Loner what it means to be a man in the age of "Woman Triumphant." As Myra declares, "To be a man in a society of machines is to be an expendable, soft auxiliary to what is useful and hard." Myra believes there is nothing left for the old-fashioned male to do, no physical struggle to survive and mate. She defines men as travesties who can only act out the classic hero who is a law unto himself, moving at ease through a landscape filled with admiring women. Thrilled that that period of masculine domination has ended, Myra suggests that women are living at the dawn of the age of "Women Triumphant, of Myra Breckinridge!"

Myra reveals that her dead gay husband, Myron, had been abused and humiliated by many men. Myra plans to avenge Myron with a three-point plan that calls for reviving the "Female Principle"; forcing Buck to submit to her demand that she take over his acting studio; and demeaning the macho, all-American Rusty Godowsky by first breaking up his relationship with his girlfriend, Mary-Ann Pringle, and then raping him with a dildo.

Loner is informed by Flagler and Flagler that the will is valid and that Myra can indeed inherit her dead husband's portion of the acting academy. Myra thereupon assumes her place in the academy. She befriends Mary-Ann, who is, as

Myra puts it, "as stupid as she seemed." Mary-Ann, believing everything that Myra says, forces her macho boyfriend to enroll in posture-training classes with Myra. Myra thus has her pawns in place. Buck is lusting after her, Mary-Ann believes her, and Rusty is continually being humiliated in posture-training class.

When Loner hires the Golden State Detective Agency to tape phone calls between Myra and Dr. Montag in New York, he draws mistaken conclusions from a reference to Montag's having witnessed a "marriage" in Monterey. He is flabbergasted when the agent, his former lover, Letitia Van Allen, takes a shine to Myra.

Myra and Letitia have lunch and become fast friends. Letitia questions Myra's involvement with Mary-Ann, asking if their relationship is lesbian in nature. Myra denies it and implies, on the contrary, that she is interested in Mary-Ann because of Rusty. Letitia confides about her past, when she had bedded every "stud in town who wants to be an actor," but when she asks Myra if she is shocked, Myra tells her that she considers herself the new American woman who "uses men the way they once used women." Myra confides to the reader, however, that she is not so sure of herself. She wonders who she is and how she feels. Eventually, she questions her own existence: "Do I exist at all? That is the unanswerable question."

Myra's plan is put into full effect when she has a nighttime posture lesson with Rusty. She has him strip, ostensibly for a preliminary health examination before referring him to a doctor who specializes in correcting spinal problems. Myra conducts the examination as a professional might. She probes his rectum with a thermometer and questions him about his sexual history. Finally, she manipulates his genitalia before subjecting him to what she calls "the final rite." Myra feels triumphant, believing that she has completed the young man's humiliation. She does not guess that Rusty enjoyed the experience.

Myra Triumphant is, however, brought down by an automobile accident. Her hormonal balance is upset, her breasts vanish, and she sprouts a beard. Buck discovers that she is, in fact, Myron, who had changed his gender. Rusty becomes actively gay, and Myron/Myra marries Rusty's former girlfriend, Mary-Ann, and lives happily ever after.

Critical Evaluation:

Gore Vidal, whose literary oeuvre includes plays and poetry, is best known for his novels. His first novel, *Williwaw* (1946), was written when Vidal was nineteen years old, and his second, *In a Yellow Wood*, came the next year, 1947. With the publication of his third novel, however, *The City and the*

Pillar (1948, revised and expanded in 1965 with an essay, "Sex and the Law," and an afterword), Vidal first touched on a subject very important to him, homosexuality.

In this work, which he saw as a study of obsession, Vidal probed the boundaries of society's sexual tolerance. The novel affected the rest of his career. Some of his readers saw the work as a glorification of homosexuality, for in American fiction until that time gay and lesbian characters had been presented as doomed or bizarre figures. By contrast, the protagonist of *The City and the Pillar* is an average American male confused by his feelings about gay sex and obsessed with the memory of a weekend encounter with another young man. If the protagonist is doomed, it is only because he is obsessed with this past event, not because he prefers men to women. The protagonist tries to revive the affair later, and when he is rejected, he kills his former lover. Vidal later issued a revised edition in which the protagonist comes to realize the sterility of his obsession.

Vidal considers himself a sexual libertarian. He believes that sex between consenting adults is something to be enjoyed, a gift, and that a "heterosexual dictatorship" has distorted human sexuality. He declared that

There is no such thing as a homosexual or heterosexual person. There are only homo- and heterosexual acts. Most people are a mixture of impulses if not practices, and what anyone does with a willing partner is of no social or cosmic significance.

However, the reading public in 1948 was not ready for Vidal's message.

Myra Breckinridge in 1968 found a somewhat more receptive audience. The book went through more than twenty printings, although it came out in a censored form in England (with Vidal's cooperation), and it was made into a 1970 feature film. The novel appeared during a burgeoning sexual revolution and the mid-twentieth century women's movement. Beneath the gaiety of Myra's campy narrative is a novel of serious purpose with much to say about popular culture, mass media, and human sexuality.

Myra's questions about her own—"But who am I? What do I feel? Do I exist at all?"—are not questions limited to gays and lesbians but are germane to the human condition. It is Myra's purpose, as it was the early purpose of the women's movement and of the nascent gay and lesbian rights movement, subjectively to destroy the masculine principle. Myra achieves her purpose objectively by raping Rusty Godowsky.

In *Myron*, a 1974 sequel to *Myra Breckinridge*, Vidal returns to the same theme he approached in the first novel: the struggle for domination of a single body between the personas of Myra and Myron. This struggle can be interpreted both as the struggle for domination between men and women and as the struggle for domination between heterosexuals and homosexuals.

Vidal's novels—especially *The City and the Pillar, Myra Breckinridge*, and *Myron*—continue to intrigue, stimulate, and anger. Since publishing *The City and the Pillar*, Vidal lived his life and conducted his artistic career on his own terms. To his many admirers, he became a symbol of freedom, just as his character Myra succeeded in liberating women—and by extension, gay men—in *Myra Breckinridge*. Many readers who were once shocked by Vidal's comments on contemporary society eventually realized that Vidal's vision corresponded closely to twentieth century realities.

Thomas D. Petitjean, Jr.

Further Reading

Altman, Dennis. *Gore Vidal's America*. Malden, Mass.: Polity Press, 2005. Examines all of Vidal's writings, including *Myra Breckinridge*, discussing how his works chronicle the evolution of post-World War II American society, history, and politics.

Baker, Susan, and Curtis S. Gibson. *Gore Vidal: A Critical Companion*. Westport, Conn.: Greenwood Press, 1997. Provides a brief biography and examines Vidal's writing, pointing out its common theme of the decline of the West in general and of the United States in particular. Chapter 13 focuses on *Myra Breckinridge* and its sequel, *Myron* (1974), discussing the novels' point of view, character development, and thematic issues, and offering a feminist reading of the works.

Dick, Bernard F. *The Apostate Angel: A Critical Study of Gore Vidal*. New York: Random House, 1974. A balanced critical assessment of Vidal's major works, including *Myra Breckinridge*.

Eisner, Douglas. "*Myra Breckinridge* and the Pathology of Heterosexuality." In *The Queer Sixties*, edited by Patricia Juliana Smith. New York: Routledge, 1999. An analysis of the novel from the perspectives of feminism and 1960's New Left politics.

Kiernan, Robert F. *Gore Vidal*. New York: Frederick Ungar, 1982. Takes a biographical approach to Vidal's works, including *Myra Breckinridge*.

Parini, Jay, ed. *Gore Vidal: Writer Against the Grain*. New York: Columbia University Press, 1992. Collection analyzing Vidal's works, including the essay "My O My O Myra" by Catharine R. Stimpson and pieces by Harold

Bloom, Italo Calvino, and Stephen Spender. Includes an interview in which Vidal discusses his career and his rocky relationship with literary critics.

Summers, Claude J. *Gay Fictions: Wilde to Stonewall.* New York: Continuum, 1990. Includes a chapter on Vidal, which primarily discusses *The City and the Pillar* but also refers to the themes in *Myra Breckinridge* with deft understanding.

White, Ray L. *Gore Vidal.* New York: Twayne, 1968. A basic introduction to the life and work of Vidal. Includes a discussion of *Myra Breckinridge.*

Woodhouse, Reed. "Gore Vidal's *Myra Breckinridge.*" In *Unlimited Embrace: A Canon of Gay Fiction, 1945-1995.* Amherst: University of Massachusetts Press, 1998. Erudite analysis of Vidal's novel and other works of post-World War II gay male fiction.

The Mysteries of Paris

Author: Eugène Sue (1804-1857)
First published: Les Mystères de Paris, 1842-1843
  (English translation, 1843)
Type of work: Novel
Type of plot: Melodrama
Time of plot: Mid-nineteenth century
Locale: France and Germany

Principal characters:
RODOLPH, the grand duke of Gerolstein
LADY SARAH MACGREGOR, his wife
FLEUR-DE-MARIE, their daughter
CLÉMENCE D'HARVILLE, the wife of one of Rodolph's friends
LA CHOUETTE and SCHOOLMASTER, two Paris criminals
JACQUES FERRAND, a hypocritical and cruel lawyer
MADAME GEORGES, a woman befriended by Rodolph
RIGOLETTE, Fleur-de-Marie's friend

The Story:

Rodolph, the grand duke of Gerolstein, a small German state, is a handsome young man in his thirties in 1838. Behind him lay a strange past. As a youth, he had been brought up in his father's court by an evil tutor named Polidori, who had done his best to warp and confuse the young prince's mind. Polidori had been urged on by the beautiful but sinister Lady Sarah Macgregor, who was told in her youth that she was destined someday to be a queen.

Sarah has decided that Rodolph, heir to a duchy, will be the perfect husband for her. With the aid of Polidori, she forces Rodolph into a secret morganatic marriage. In England, where she has fled, she gives birth to a daughter. Rodolph's father is furious, and he has the marriage annulled. One day, after he threatens to kill his father, Rodolph is sent into exile. Before long, Sarah loses all interest in her child and pays her Paris lawyer, Jacques Ferrand, to find a home for the girl. Ferrand gives the child into the care of some unscrupulous child takers and, after a few years, writes to Sarah and says, falsely, that the child has died. Sarah forwards the letter to Rodolph.

Rodolph moves to Paris, where he amuses himself by roaming through the slums in disguise. Although he is strong, agile, and a fine fighter, the young duke is always followed by his faithful servant, Sir Walter Murphy. Together they ferret out the secrets and mysteries of Paris streets. One night, Rodolph chances to save a young girl who is being attacked. When he has heard her story, he is so touched by it that he decides to help her. Fleur-de-Marie, as she is called, is an orphan who had been brought up by criminals and had been in prison. After being freed, she was recognized by her old tormentors and captured by them, drugged, made a prisoner, and compelled to suffer great indignities. Feeling that she is really innocent of the crimes into which she has been forced, Rodolph takes her to the farm of Madame Georges. The girl's beauty, her sad plight, and her being the age his dead daughter would have been arouse his interest and pity.

Madame Georges is likewise a woman whom the duke has befriended. Her criminal husband had deserted her, and he took their son with him. Rodolph searched the streets of Paris for a clue to the whereabouts of Madame Georges' son. At the farm, Fleur-de-Marie soon develops into a devout and delightful young woman.

Rodolph continues to live his double life. He attends diplomatic balls and the parties of thieves, and on both planes he finds much to do to help people to live better lives. At last, to learn better the secrets of Paris, he takes lodgings in a boardinghouse in one of the poorer sections of town. There he meets many needy families, and in countless ways he helps them all. One of the occupants of the house is a girl named Rigolette, who had been Fleur-de-Marie's friend in prison. Rigolette is hardworking and kind, and Rodolph learns a great deal from her about the people of the house.

One day, Rodolph learns that Clémence d'Harville, the wife of one of his good friends, is involved in an affair with a lodger in the house. It does not take him long to discover that the person behind this affair, plotting the destruction of d'Harville and his wife, is Lady Sarah Macgregor. As soon as he can, Rodolph warns Clémence and saves her from her folly. Clémence is unfortunate in that she has been forced into marriage with d'Harville by her mother-in-law, for she does not love her husband. Because he and their daughter are subject to epileptic seizures, her life is an unhappy one. By chance, d'Harville learns of his wife's unhappiness and contrives to commit suicide in such a way that everyone thinks his death accidental. By this act, he saves Clémence from greater unhappiness and atones for the evil he had committed in marrying her.

While staying at the lodging house, Rodolph learns of the numerous evil deeds of the hypocritical lawyer, Jacques Ferrand. When Rodolph learns that Ferrand is planning the murder of Clémence's father, he and Sir Walter Murphy succeed in thwarting the lawyer's evil scheme. Ferrand is also responsible for the imprisonment of Rigolette's lover. To get to the bottom of Ferrand's plans, Rodolph remembers Cecily, a beautiful woman who had once been married to his private doctor, but who later became a depraved creature. Rodolph secures her release from prison and has her introduced into Ferrand's household, where she can spy on his activities and learn his secrets.

Meanwhile, Sarah asks Ferrand to find a young girl whom she could claim is really her child by Rodolph, for she hopes that if she can produce the dead girl she could effect a reconciliation, now that Rodolph is the reigning duke of Gerolstein. Ferrand, learning the whereabouts of Fleur-de-Marie, hires La Chouette, an ugly one-eyed woman, and a criminal called the Schoolmaster to kidnap the girl from the farm of Madame Georges. When the Schoolmaster arrives at the farm, he discovers that Madame Georges is his wife, the woman he had deserted. He does not succeed in getting Fleur-de-Marie. Instead, she is put in jail for failing to give testimony concerning a crime she had witnessed before

Rodolph had saved her from the slums. By chance, Clémence finds the girl while on a charitable errand. Not knowing that Fleur-de-Marie knows Rodolph, she tries to make the girl's life more pleasant in prison.

When Sarah learns that Fleur-de-Marie has been under the care of Rodolph's friends, she gets jealous and makes arrangements to have Fleur-de-Marie killed as soon as she is released from the prison. Ferrand, entrusted with plans for her death, has her released from prison by an accomplice who pretended to be an agent of Clémence d'Harville. On leaving the prison, Fleur-de-Marie meets Rigolette and tells her old friend of her fortune. Rigolette, who knows Clémence through Rodolph, is pleased. After they part, Fleur-de-Marie is seized by Ferrand's hirelings and taken into the country, where she is thrown into the river. Some passersby, however, see her in the water and pull her ashore in time to save her life.

Meanwhile, La Chouette, learning that Fleur-de-Marie is really the daughter of Rodolph and Sarah, hurries to Sarah with her information. Sarah is shocked at the discovery. La Chouette, seeing a chance to make more money by killing Sarah and stealing her jewels, stabs her protector. The attacker escapes with the jewels and returns to the Schoolmaster to taunt him with her success. The two get into a fight, and the Schoolmaster kills La Chouette. He is captured and put into prison.

Through Cecily, Rodolph also learns that his daughter is not really dead. Cecily had had little difficulty in uncovering Ferrand's past. As soon as he finds out what Sarah has done, Rodolph sees her; despite her terrible wound, he accuses her violently of the shameful and criminal neglect of her daughter.

Returning home, Rodolph is surprised to hear that Clémence had visited him. Clémence had had the fortune to find Fleur-de-Marie in the home where she had been cared for after her escape from drowning, and she had brought the girl to Rodolph. Clémence does not know that events had proved that Fleur-de-Marie is Rodolph's daughter, so the reunion of father and child is not without pain as well as pleasure, for Clémence and Rodolph had long secretly known that they love each other. Rodolph begs Clémence to marry him and to be a mother to his child. He feels sure that Sarah will die and the way will thus be clear for their happy life together.

Rodolph remarries Sarah on her deathbed so that their daughter can be called truly legitimate. Information that Rodolph receives from Cecily also makes it possible for him to free Rigolette's lover from prison, and it turns out that he is the long-lost son of Madame Georges. With these problems solved, Rodolph plans to return to Germany. First, however, he uses his knowledge of Ferrand's activities to force the lawyer to establish many worthy charities. His money gone, Ferrand goes into a decline and dies soon afterward. Rigolette's lover becomes administrator for one of the charities and, after their marriage, he and Rigolette live happily with Madame Georges.

Rodolph returns to Germany with Fleur-de-Marie as his legitimate daughter and Clémence as his wife. For a time the three live together with great happiness. Then Rodolph notices that Fleur-de-Marie seems to have moods of depression. One day, weeping, she explains that his goodness to her is without compare but that the evil life that she had led before he had rescued her from the slums preyed constantly on her mind. She begs to be allowed to enter a convent. Rodolph, realizing that nothing he could say will change her mind, gives his permission.

While serving as a novice at the convent. Fleur-de-Marie's conduct is so perfect that when she is admitted to the order, she immediately becomes the abbess. This honor is too much for her gentle soul to bear, or for her weak, sick body to withstand, and that very night she dies. Rodolph, noting that the day of her death is the anniversary of the day on which he had tried to kill his father, feels that the ways of fate are strange.

Critical Evaluation:

One of the legacies of the French Revolution of 1789 was that the movement toward universal literacy proceeded more rapidly in France than anywhere else in Europe. A circulation war developed among French daily newspapers, and one of the weapons with which the war was fought was serial fiction of a melodramatic kind, whose relentless narrative thrust made readers anxious to acquire every episode. *The Mysteries of Paris* was the breakthrough work that demonstrated the potential of this curious new medium, revealing the remarkable truth responsible for the seemingly paradoxical face of modern journalism: that most newspaper readers are not much interested in news of political and economic significance; instead, they prefer human interest stories, the more sensational and scandalous the better, preferably spiced with a little local interest and some connection to royalty. Eugène Sue imported this idea into his fiction with great enthusiasm.

The plot of *The Mysteries of Paris* is firmly located in the well-known streets, prisons, hospitals, and asylums of contemporary Paris. It features a host of nasty villains who add to the cruel blows inflicted by ill-fortune and bad laws upon honest working folk. The desperate attempts made by hum-

bly virtuous individuals to get by in life are here aided by the charitable efforts of a princely paragon of nobility who goes among them in disguise (as some princes have been reputed by legend to do). The multistranded story moves from drinking dens and dungeons to grand houses and palaces but is careful to bind its disparate elements together with a series of careful contrivances. As the plot unwinds, everyone eventually turns out to be related to everyone else, either by blood or by virtue of being unluckily enmeshed in the same evil conspiracies. No previous work had ever offered the poor such a sense of being a part of the affairs of the world or such wild fantasies of salvation from their most desperate plights. Nor had any previous work of popular fiction addressed the rich with such frankness on the subject of the desperate plight of the poor and the practical possibilities of its alleviation.

Such scenes as the deliberate blinding of the Schoolmaster and the death of La Chouette led Sue's detractors to accuse him of sadism, but the charge is mistaken. What such scenes actually attempt to give is an appropriate expression of an outrage so profound that nothing but extremes of horror can possibly contain it. There is a key scene set in La Force (the main prison of Paris at the time) in which a petty thief must unwittingly play Scheherazade, spinning out a story to frustrate the planned murder of the unjustly imprisoned Germain. The thief points out—presumably echoing the author's fascination with an equivalent discovery—that, although the criminals who constitute his audience have no liking for tales in which men like themselves go to the guillotine, they retain a more profound sense of morality that gladly and greatly rejoices in the unusual punishment of the unusually wicked.

Pursuing this aim, Sue distinguishes between those criminals who retain a certain essential "heart" and "honour" and those who give themselves over entirely to predatory cruelty. For the latter, fates as hideous as he can contrive are carefully and fervently designed. The worst of crimes inflamed such indignation in Sue that nothing within the law would serve as recompense, and for him the worst crimes of all were crimes of greed and ambition masked by respectable appearances: the crimes of crooked lawyers, corrupt bailiffs, and poison-supplying doctors. There were many readers ready to agree with him.

In the end, though, Sue could not contrive a wholehearted escape from the prison of contemporary morality, and his failure to carry through the bold thrust of his own ideals is evident in the concluding passage, in which the happy ending he has so cunningly contrived is eaten away as if by a cancer. Sue does not allow Fleur-de-Marie to forget that, no matter how little choice she had in the matter, she had briefly been a whore. That her true place in the world is that of a princess there is not a shadow of doubt, and her saintliness continues to increase when she belatedly comes into that inheritance, but her sense of guilt and shame poisons her peace of mind.

"Critical Evaluation" by Brian Stableford

Further Reading

James, Louis. *Fiction for the Working Man, 1830-1850: A Study of the Literature Produced for the Working Classes in Early Victorian Urban England.* New York: Oxford University Press, 1963. *The Mysteries of Paris* and other works by Sue are discussed in chapter 8, "Fiction from America and France."

Palmer Chevasco, Berry. *Mysterymania: The Reception of Eugène Sue in Britain, 1838-1860.* New York: Peter Lang, 2003. Charts the reaction of Victorian England to *The Mysteries of Paris* and, by extension, the effects of Sue's writing on the development of Victorian crime fiction.

Prendergast, Christopher. *For the People by the People? Eugène Sue's "Les Mystères de Paris"—A Hypothesis in the Sociology of Literature.* Oxford, England: European Humanities Research Centre, 2003. Offers a sociological and historical interpretation of *The Mysteries of Paris.* Examines social historian Louis Chevalier's claim that the novel is a collective production of Sue and his reader-correspondents, who initially read the novel in serial form.

Rye, Marilyn. "Eugène Sue." In Vol. 4 of *Critical Survey of Mystery and Detective Fiction*, edited by Carl Rollyson. Rev. ed. Pasadena, Calif.: Salem Press, 2008. Provides a brief overview of Sue's life and work, focusing on *The Mysteries of Paris.* Describes this work as the first novel to present a realistic portrait of the criminal underworld of Paris.

The Mysteries of Pittsburgh

Author: Michael Chabon (1963-   )
First published: 1988
Type of work: Novel
Type of plot: Bildungsroman
Time of plot: Early to mid-1980's
Locale: Pittsburgh, Pennsylvania

Principal characters:
ART BECHSTEIN, the narrator, a man in his early twenties
JOE "THE EGG" BECHSTEIN, Art's father, a gangster
ARTHUR LECOMTE, Art's lover
PHLOX LOMBARDI, Art's lover
LENNY STERN ("UNCLE LENNY"), Joe's business associate
CLEVELAND ARNING, Arthur's best friend
JANE BELLWETHER, Cleveland's girlfriend

The Story:

Art Bechstein is a drifting young Jewish man in conflict with both his sexuality and his father, Joe Bechstein, a widowed gangster. They meet for lunch while Joe is visiting Pittsburgh on business. Art is uncomfortable with his father's work and keeps it a secret from everyone in his life; in turn, Joe is puzzled and dismayed by his son's choices. The two men struggle to relate to one another.

Art has just finished college. On a final trip to the library, he meets Arthur Lecomte, a handsome, sophisticated young man. Art immediately identifies Arthur as gay and strains to appear comfortable with that fact. Their impromptu conversation turns into a long drunken evening that ends at a house party. There, Art is introduced to Jane Bellwether, who is dating Arthur's best friend Cleveland. She and Arthur swap sto-

ries about Cleveland, who is an adventurous and unpredictable alcoholic. Arthur is clearly attracted to Art, who deflects the attention by asking about Phlox, a beautiful girl who works with Arthur.

A few days later, Art's shift at Boardwalk Books is interrupted by the appearance of a large, leather-clad biker who forces Art away from work by mentioning his gangster father. After the two speed off on his motorcycle, the man reveals himself to be Cleveland and tells Art that he works as a debt collector for Uncle Lenny, one of Joe's underlings. They find Arthur and spend the night drinking, after which Arthur tries to kiss Art but is rebuffed.

Over the next few weeks, Art becomes close friends with Arthur. The two alternately spend their time drinking and hanging out on a hill overlooking an area of the city they call the Lost Neighborhood. The area includes the Cloud Factory, whose only product seems to be the perfect white puffs of smoke drifting from its stacks.

At the same time, Art develops a romantic and sexual relationship with Phlox, though they argue about Arthur and homosexuality, which she considers disgusting. Cleveland asks Art to introduce him to his father, but he refuses, uncomfortable that Cleveland has access to a part of his life that he tries so hard to keep secret. Jealous tension builds between Arthur and Phlox. One day, while lounging at a swimming pool, Art is flustered to be caught admiring Arthur's body and finally admits to himself that he is in love with another man.

One day, Cleveland convinces Art to go on his loan collection rounds with him. An altercation with a couple of small-time gangsters turns out to be a setup orchestrated by Cleveland in order to meet Art's father. The two interrupt Joe Bechstein in the middle of a meeting, and though the situation is tense, Cleveland lands a job with one of Joe's associates.

Upset by the scene with his father, Art goes to Arthur and they have sex. He confesses to Phlox that he cheated on her, inventing a female partner. When she runs into Art and Arthur together, however, she realizes the truth. After the confrontation, Art goes home alone.

Cleveland tells Art that he must choose between his two lovers. When Art learns that Cleveland is training to be a jewel thief, they argue; Art is both worried for his friend and uncomfortable about the blurred boundary between his family life and his friends. Leaving abruptly, Cleveland accidentally takes a letter from Phlox to Art that mentions his affair with Arthur.

Meanwhile, Phlox fades into the background of Art's life as he pursues his relationship with Arthur at the luxurious home where Arthur is house-sitting. One day, Arthur's mother visits, and Art realizes that Arthur has a working-class background and that his air of sophistication and worldliness is manufactured. Their brief domesticity ends when the owners of the home return.

Phlox arranges a meeting with Art at the library under false pretenses. They reconcile and have sex, but his heart is not in it. He sneaks out while she is sleeping to confess to Arthur. He asks Arthur not to make him choose between the two of them, and Arthur agrees, begging him not to end their relationship.

When Cleveland attempts his first heist, things go horribly awry. He is drunk and breaks into a house while the family is downstairs eating dinner. Angered that his son is hang-

ing out with low-level criminals, Joe Bechstein tries to teach Cleveland a lesson by informing the police of Cleveland's crime. After leading a high-speed chase on his motorcycle, Cleveland evades capture. Art tries to call his father to convince him to leave Cleveland alone, but Joe will not accept his collect call. Meanwhile, the police find Cleveland. While Art watches, his friend attempts to escape by climbing to the top of the Cloud Factory and falls to his death.

In the aftermath, Art refuses to see his father. Joe learns of his son's relationship with Arthur when Phlox's letter is found on Cleveland's body. Joe's thugs threaten Arthur and tell him to leave town. Art and Arthur run away to New York and then to Europe, where eventually their relationship dissolves. Art never sees Phlox or his father again.

Critical Evaluation:

Michael Chabon was twenty-four years old when his master of fine arts thesis was published. That thesis, *The Mysteries of Pittsburgh*, had been sent by his adviser to an editor to consider for publication. The work immediately sold for $155,000—a record figure for a first book. Reviewers hailed Chabon as a bold, original new voice. His early supporters were not wrong; in the years since then, Chabon has become one of the most important figures in the contemporary American literary landscape, writing such novels as *Wonder Boys* (1995), *The Yiddish Policemen's Union* (2007), and *The Amazing Adventures of Kavalier and Clay* (2000), which won the 2001 Pulitzer Prize in fiction.

The characters in *The Mysteries of Pittsburgh* are young, beautiful, and directionless. What makes this coming-of-age tale more than just another glib story about hard-drinking, privileged youth is Chabon's lyrical and evocative prose. He manipulates language, images, and metaphor with playful mastery. The connection between the characters and their environment is continually reinforced, as when one of Art and Arthur's confrontations occurs under a sky that

> glowed and flashed orange . . . as if volcano gods were fighting there or, it seemed to me, as if the end of the world had begun—it was an orange so tortured and final.

The images in this book function on multiple levels. The Cloud Factory, for example, is a physical place that serves as a plot device, but it is also a symbol of the beauty and mystery that even an industrial city such as Pittsburgh is capable of producing. It evokes as well the fragile and ephemeral nature of the characters' youth. When Cleveland falls from the heights of the Cloud Factory, then, his death is both literal and heavily symbolic.

The Mysteries of Pittsburgh takes place over the course of a summer—a structure whose idea, according to Chabon, came from reading Philip Roth's *Goodbye, Columbus* (1959). The passing of June, July, and August provides a framework for the plot and maps the action sequence onto the shifting dynamics of the characters' relationships.

Chabon is insightful and compassionate about young love and loss—the primary preoccupations of his characters. These men and women are deeply ambivalent, contradicting themselves from one moment to the next. They drift, they flail, and they fail, but their humanity is always recognizable, as when Art says,

> I felt happy—or some weak, pretty feeling centered in my stomach, brought on by beer . . . but it was a happiness so like sadness that the next moment I hung my head.

With her complicated outfits and vehement rejection of homosexuality, Phlox is an effective foil to Arthur's crisp appearance and uncomplicated sexuality. That these rivals for Art's affection are polar opposites in multiple ways inflates the conflict into something greater than male versus female.

In many ways, *The Mysteries of Pittsburgh* is a typical bildungsroman, in which Art struggles to understand himself in relation to the world around him: He must reconcile himself to his own lack of direction, his dead mother, his father's unsavory business, and Joe's implied but never articulated role in his wife's death. The fact that Art is also coming to terms with his sexuality (which led many to falsely assume that Chabon was gay) adds a twist to the established genre.

Art chooses Arthur over Phlox repeatedly, both before and after the two men become sexually involved, but those choices often seem born out of circumstance more than anything else. The novel ends before Art is willing to make any definite conclusions about his sexuality, so readers are left to imagine how he will ultimately live his life. This ambiguity points to a complicated sexuality that cannot be answered with a simple yes or no. At one point, Arthur compares love to falconry, and Cleveland responds: "Never say love is like anything. . . . It isn't." The lesson is that love and sex are complex and highly individual. Ultimately, as Arthur claims, all that can happen is "you turn into whoever you're supposed to turn into."

At times, the novel's plot feels inorganic and overly manipulated, especially regarding Cleveland's dalliances with the criminal underworld and his ultimate death. A later novel by Chabon, *Wonder Boys*, is also set in Pittsburgh. In that work, the zany over-the-top details—a dead dog in a car trunk, the theft of Marilyn Monroe's sweater, an omnipresent tuba—and the antic, off-kilter velocity of the characters' lives feel true to the story (and undermine readers' expectations of this gritty and pedestrian city). In *The Mysteries of Pittsburgh*, however, Chabon has yet to come into his full powers as a writer, and the intricate subplot feels forced upon the characters.

If Chabon had stopped writing after *The Mysteries of Pittsburgh*, this book would have been thoroughly enjoyable but ultimately not a text of great import. For all the attention the book received when it was first published, relatively little has been written about it since the original reviews. It derives its primary significance in the world of serious literature from what followed: It is the first book of a great writer. In it, one can see the nascent strengths of Chabon's writing that would come to fruition in his subsequent work. Many of its themes and concerns reappear in his later, more mature writing, including male Jewish protagonists, the struggle for identity, a queering of traditional narratives, and a tendency to combine genre fiction with sophisticated literary writing in unexpected ways.

Chris Hartman

Further Reading

Caveney, Graham. "French Kissing in the USA." In *Shopping in Space: Essays on America's Blank Generation Fiction*, edited by Elizabeth Young and Graham Caveney. New York: Atlantic Monthly Press, 1992. An analysis of language, sexuality, and description in *The Mysteries of Pittsburgh*, seen through the lens of a tension between American and European cultures.

Chabon, Michael. "On *The Mysteries of Pittsburgh*." *The New York Review of Books* 52, no. 10 (June 6, 2005): 38-39. Chabon describes the circumstances under which he wrote his first novel, citing F. Scott Fitzgerald's *The Great Gatsby* (1925) and Philip Roth's *Goodbye, Columbus* as inspirations.

_____. "Writer, Be Afraid." In *The Writing Life: Writers on How They Think and Work*, edited by Marie Arana. New York: PublicAffairs, 2003. In his chapter of this collection, Chabon discusses his fear of creating nonheterosexual characters, including Art and Arthur in *The Mysteries of Pittsburgh*.

Fowler, Douglas. "The Short Fiction of Michael Chabon: Nostalgia in the Very Young." *Studies in Short Fiction* 31, no. 1 (Winter, 2005): 75-82. The main focus of this article is Chabon's book of short stories *A Model World, and Other Stores* (1991). In the introduction, however, Fowler discusses *The Mysteries of Pittsburgh* and argues that the failings of the earlier novel are corrected in the short stories.

Lott, Brett. "Lover in a World Too Full for Love." *Los Angeles Times Book Review*, April 17, 1988, pp. 1, 11. A review of *The Mysteries of Pittsburgh* that highlights the strengths and weaknesses of the novel.

McDermott, Alice. "Gangsters and Pranksters." *The New York Times Book Review*, April 3, 1998, p. 7. Argues that *The Mysteries of Pittsburgh* contains "all of the delights, and not a few of the disappointments" typical of first novels.

The Mysteries of Udolpho

Author: Ann Radcliffe (1764-1823)
First published: 1794
Type of work: Novel
Type of plot: Gothic
Time of plot: 1584
Locale: France and Italy

Principal characters:
EMILY ST. AUBERT, a young French aristocrat
SIGNOR MONTONI, a villainous Italian who is married to Emily's aunt
VALANCOURT, Emily's sweetheart
COUNT MORANO, a Venetian nobleman who is in love with Emily
MADAME MONTONI, Emily's aunt

The Story:

After the death of his wife, Monsieur St. Aubert, a French aristocrat, takes his daughter on a trip in the Pyrenees. High on a mountain road, the St. Auberts meet a young nobleman dressed in hunting clothes. He is Valancourt, the younger son of a family with which Monsieur St. Aubert is acquainted. Joining the St. Auberts on their journey, the young man soon falls in love with eighteen-year-old Emily St. Aubert, and the girl feels that she, too, might lose her heart to him.

St. Aubert becomes gravely ill and dies in a cottage near the Chateau-le-Blanc, ancestral seat of the noble Villeroi family. After her father's burial at the nearby convent of St. Clair, Emily returns to her home at La Vallée and, as her father had requested, promptly burns some mysterious letters. She finds a miniature portrait of a beautiful unknown woman among the letters. Since she was not told to destroy the portrait, she takes it with her when she leaves La Vallée to stay with her aunt in Toulouse.

Valancourt follows Emily to Toulouse to press his suit. After some remonstrance, the aunt gives her permission for the young couple to marry. A few days before the ceremony, the aunt herself marries Signor Montoni, a sinister Italian, who immediately forbids Emily's nuptials. To make his refusal doubly positive, he takes Emily and her aunt to his mansion in Venice.

There, Emily and Madame Montoni are in unhappy circumstances, for it soon becomes apparent that Montoni has married to secure the estates of his new wife and her niece for himself. When he tries to force Emily to marry a Venetian nobleman, Count Morano, Emily is in despair. On the night before the wedding, Montoni suddenly orders his household to pack and leave for his castle at Udolpho, high in the Apennines.

When the party arrives at Udolpho, Montoni immediately begins repairing the fortifications of the castle. Emily does not like the dark, cold castle from which the previous owner, Lady Laurentini, had disappeared under mysterious circumstances. Superstitious servants claim that apparitions flitted about the halls and galleries of the ancient fortress.

Shortly after Montoni and his household have settled there, Count Morano attempts to kidnap Emily. Foiled by Montoni, who wounded him severely in a sword fight, Morano threatens revenge. A few days later, Montoni tries to force his wife to sign over her estates to him. When she refuses, he locks her up in a tower of the castle. Emily tries to visit her aunt that night. Terrified to find fresh blood on the tower stairs, she concludes that her aunt has been murdered.

Ghostly sounds and shadows about Udolpho begin to make everyone uneasy. Even Montoni, who had organized a band of marauders to terrorize and pillage the neighborhood, begins to believe the castle is haunted. Emily hears that several hostages have been taken. She is sure that Valancourt is a prisoner, for she has heard someone singing a song he had taught her, and one night a mysterious shadow calls her by name. Her life is tormented by Montoni's threats that unless she sign away her estates to him she will suffer the same fate as her aunt. As Emily discovers from her maid, her aunt had not been murdered except indirectly, for she had died after becoming very ill from the harsh treatment. She had been buried in the chapel of the castle.

Morano makes another attempt to steal Emily away from the castle, this time with her assistance, as she is now afraid for her life. Montoni and his men, however, discover the attempt in time to seize the abductors outside the castle walls. Shortly afterward, Montoni sends Emily away after forcing her to sign the papers that give him control of her estates in France. At first, she thinks she is being sent to her death, but Montoni sends her to a cottage in Tuscany because he had heard that Venetian authorities are sending a small army to attack Udolpho and seize him and his bandits after the villas of several rich Venetians had been robbed.

When Emily returns to the castle, she sees evidence of a terrible battle. Emily's maid and Ludovico, another servant, disclose to Emily that a prisoner who knows her is in the dungeons below. Emily immediately guesses that it is Valancourt, and she makes arrangements to escape with him. The prisoner, however, is Monsieur Du Pont, an old friend of her father. Emily, Monsieur Du Pont, the girl's maid, and Ludovico make their escape and reach Leghorn safely. There they take a ship for France. Then a great storm drives the ship ashore, close to the Chateau-le-Blanc, near which Emily's father had been buried.

Emily and her friends are rescued by Monsieur Villefort and his family. The Villeforts had inherited the chateau and are now attempting to live in it, although it is in disrepair and said to be haunted. While at the chateau, Emily decides to spend several days at the convent where her father is buried. There she finds a nun who closely resembles the mysteriously missing Lady Laurentini, whose portrait Emily had seen at the castle of Udolpho.

When Emily returns to the chateau, she finds it in a state of turmoil; weird noises seem to come from the apartments of the former mistress of the chateau. Ludovico volunteers to spend a night in the apartment. Although all the windows and doors are locked, he is not in the rooms the next morning. When the old caretaker tells Emily this news, she notices the miniature portrait that Emily had found at La Vallée. The miniature, says the servant, is a portrait of her former mistress, the Marquise de Villeroi. She also points out that Emily closely resembles the portrait.

Valancourt reappears and once again makes plans to marry Emily, but Monsieur Villefort tells her of gambling debts the young man had incurred and of the wild life he had led in Paris while she was a prisoner in Italy. Emily thereupon refuses to marry him and returns in distress to her home at La Vallée, where she learns that Montoni has been captured by the Venetian authorities. Because he had secured the deeds to her lands by criminal means, the court restored them to her. She is once again a young woman of wealth and position.

While Emily is at La Vallée, the Villefort family makes a trip high into the Pyrenees to hunt. They are almost captured by bandits, but Ludovico, who had inexplicably disappeared from the chateau, rescues them. He had been kidnapped by smugglers who used the vaults of the chateau to store their treasure. He disclosed that the noises in the chateau were caused by the outlaws in an effort to frighten away the rightful owners.

When she hears this, Emily returns to the chateau to see her friends. While there, she again visits the convent of St. Clair. The nun whom she had seen before, and who resembles the former mistress of Udolpho, is taken mortally ill while Emily is at the convent. On her deathbed, the nun confesses that she is Lady Laurentini, who had left Udolpho to go to her former lover, the Marquis de Villeroi. Finding him married to Monsieur St. Aubert's sister, she ensnared him once more and made him an accomplice in her plot to poison his wife. When the marquis, overcome by remorse, fled to a distant country and died there, she had retired to the convent to expiate her sins.

Emily's happiness is complete when Monsieur Du Pont, who had escaped with her from Udolpho, proves that Valancourt had gambled only to secure money to aid some friends who were on the brink of misfortune. Reunited, they are married and leave for La Vallée, where they live a happy, tranquil life in contrast to the many strange adventures that had separated them for so long.

Critical Evaluation:

Christmas Eve of 1764 saw the publication of Horace Walpole's *The Castle of Otranto*, a story of supernatural terror set in a vaguely medieval past and complete with a gloomy castle, knights both chivalrous and wicked, and virtuous fair maidens in distress—the first English gothic novel. During the preceding summer, while Walpole was transforming a nightmarish dream into a gothic novel at Strawberry Hill, Ann Ward was born in London. By the time she married the law student William Radcliffe twenty-three years later, the era of the gothic novel was under way, having begun to flourish with Clara Reeve's professed imitation of *The Castle of Otranto* in *The Old English Baron* (1777). Ann

Radcliffe, born in the same year as the genre itself, was to be supreme among the gothic novelists, whose works were so popular in the last decades of the eighteenth century.

Apart from one posthumously published novel, Radcliffe's total output as a novelist consists of five immensely successful gothic novels. *The Mysteries of Udolpho* was her fourth and most popular. Anna Laetitia Barbauld in her preface to this novel for *British Novelists* (1810) notes that a "greater distinction is due to those which stand at the head of a class," and she asserts that "such are undoubtedly the novels of Mrs. Radcliffe." This estimate continues to be valid.

Radcliffe, however, might have been relegated entirely to the pages of literary history had it not been for Jane Austen's delightful burlesque of gothic novels, *Northanger Abbey* (1818), in which a sentimental heroine under the inspiration of *The Mysteries of Udolpho* fancies herself involved in gothic adventures. Through the exaggerated sentiment of her heroine, Austen ridicules a major element in gothic novels in general—sensibility. A reliance on feeling, in contradiction to the dominant rationalism of the eighteenth century, the cult of sensibility was nonetheless a vital part of the age. Individuals of sensibility were peculiarly receptive to the simple joys of country life, to the sublime and beautiful aspects of nature, and above all, to benevolence; their own depth of feeling compelled sympathy, and it was considered proper to manifest sensibility through such traits as a readiness to weep or faint and a touch of melancholia.

In *The Mysteries of Udolpho*, the good characters are endowed with sensibility, the bad are not. Emily St. Aubert, her father, and her lover, Valancourt, are exemplars of a highly refined capacity for feeling. St. Aubert scorns worldly ambition and is retired from the world, represented by the city of Paris, to his rural estate, La Vallée, where his days are spent in literary, musical, and botanical pursuits; these pleasures are heightened by a pensive melancholy. The villainous Montoni, by contrast, loves power, and he responds to the idea of any daring exploit with eyes that appear to gleam instantaneously with fire. At home in cities, with their atmosphere of fashionable dissipation and political intrigue, he thrives in the solitary Castle of Udolpho only when he has made it a bustling military fortress. Cold, haughty, and brooding, he is—unlike the ingenuous St. Aubert—adept at dissimulation.

Much of Emily's anguish is caused by the lack of sensibility in Montoni's world; her own ingenuousness and benevolence is misinterpreted as mere policy, spurring her enemies to further mischief. Emily's sensibility, however, sometimes functions as an effective defense, for her profuse tears and spells of fainting postpone immediate confrontations. Sometimes, too, sensibility assists discovery, as when Emily, shutting herself away to read, play her lute, sketch, or simply meditate and gaze rapturously upon the landscape at hand, could become vulnerable to mystery.

In this novel, the conventionally spurious medieval setting serves well the solitude of sensibility and gives scope for a range of feelings as the heroine is forced to travel about France and Italy; inhabit gloomy, ruined castles; and encounter chevaliers, noble ladies, courtesans, mercenary soldiers, bandits, peasants, monks, nuns, war, and murder. She encounters deaths by poisoning, stiletto, sword, torture, pistol, and cannon fire. Emily's wide-ranging adventures in a remote, dark age are the fit trials of her sensibility, foreshadowed in her dying father's lecture on the danger of uncontrolled sensibility; and if later readers are overwhelmed by evidence of her frequent trembling, weeping, and fainting, Emily herself is more conscious of her constant endeavor to be resolute, her ultimate survival with honor unscathed being sufficient proof of her strength of sensibility.

Although Austen ridicules excessive sensibility, she also allows Henry Tilney, her spokesperson for reason in *Northanger Abbey*, to praise Radcliffe's novel, however facetiously, by claiming that he could hardly put down *The Mysteries of Udolpho* once he had begun reading it, and had finished the novel, hair standing on end, in two days. Henry's count of two entire days accurately indicates average reading time; even more important, his appreciation of the suspense that is maintained throughout the book pays tribute to Radcliffe's narrative powers.

The essential quality that sustains gothic suspense is a pervasive sense of the irrational elements in life. Emily herself provides the appropriate image when she describes her life as appearing to be like the dream of a distempered imagination. Although basically a straightforward, chronological narrative, *The Mysteries of Udolpho* seems timeless and dreamlike, the sweeping length of the story suggesting the cinematic technique of slow-motion photography. The novel accomplishes shifts in scenery with the rapidity peculiar to dreams: Now Emily is in Leghorn; now she is in a ship tossed amid white foam in a dark and stormy sea, incredibly, upon the very shores where lies the mysterious Chateau-le-Blanc. Written in the generalizing poetic diction of the eighteenth century, the vast amount of scenic description contributes to the unreal atmosphere and is suggestive of a dream world where forms are vague and time and space ignore ordinary delimitations. Therefore, the Castle of Udolpho seems limitless in size; its actual shape and substance, typically viewed in the solemn evening dusk, seems indefinite, gloomy, and sublime with clustered towers. Other scenes call up boundless space, as in the recurrent images of blue-tinged views of distant mountaintops.

The repetitive pattern of Emily's adventures is also dreamlike: She is repeatedly trapped in a room with no light, and again and again she flees down dark, labyrinthine passages or seemingly endless staircases. People who are rationally assumed to be far away suddenly materialize, often in shadowy forms; their features are obscure and are known to Emily only intuitively. Disembodied voices and music from unseen instruments are commonplace. Continually beset with a dread of undefined evil, she recurrently experiences a paralysis of body and will before an imminent yet concealed danger.

In post-Freudian times, readers detect the realm of the subconscious emerging in Emily's nightmare world, not only in the repetitive, dreamlike patterns but also in the very nature of her predicament—that of the pure, innocent "orphan child" whose physical attractions precipitate sword fights, subject her to would-be rapists who pursue her down the dark corridors, and render her helpless before the cold, cruel Montoni, whose preposterous depravity holds for her the fascination of the abomination.

Radcliffe, however, is too much a part of the Age of Reason to permit irrationality to rule. Emily is preserved by her innate strength of sensibility from assaults on her person and her mind. In all of her melancholy meditations, once her ordeal has ended, she is never required to wonder why Montoni appealed to her as he did when he was triumphant, bold, spirited, and commanding. Instead, her mind dismisses him as one who was insignificant, and she settles down to a secure life with Valancourt, a candid and openhanded man. In her retirement to La Vallée, Emily may never be able to avoid counterparts of Madame Montoni, whose fashionable repartee recalls the comedy of manners in which Austen was to excel, but she will be safe from such men as Montoni.

In the spirit of reason, the author also banishes the mystery of the supernatural happenings that provide so much suspense. Every inexplicable occurrence finally has its rational explanation. Some critics have complained, with some justice, about the protracted suspense and the high expectations that defuse Radcliffe's increment of horrors and nebulous challenges to the imagination. Nevertheless, when a reader, like Henry Tilney, has kept pace with this lengthy novel, the impression of Emily St. Aubert's nightmare world is more vivid than the skepticism of reason that explains away all the dark secrets. Ultimately, the vague shapings of the imagination triumph.

"Critical Evaluation" by Catherine E. Moore

Further Reading

Castle, Terry. "The Spectralization of the Other in *The Mysteries of Udolpho*." In *The New Eighteenth Century: Theory, Politics, English Literature*, edited by Felicity Nussbaum and Laura Brown. New York: Methuen, 1987. Examines the neglected segments of *The Mysteries of Udolpho* and asserts that the supernatural is "rerouted" rather than explained.

Ellis, Markman. "Female Gothic and the Secret Terrors of Sensibility." In *The History of Gothic Fiction*. Reprint. Edinburgh: Edinburgh University Press, 2005. This extensive chapter on Radcliffe and other women writers of gothic literature examines Radcliffe and the politics of female and male sensibility, gothic masculinity, and other topics. Book's preface includes discussion of "the pleasure derived from objects of terror."

Gordon, Scott Paul. "Ann Radcliffe's *The Mysteries of Udolpho* and the Practice of Quixotism." In *The Practice of Quixotism: Postmodern Theory and Eighteenth-Century Women's Writing*. New York: Palgrave Macmillan, 2006. Radcliffe's novel is included in this study of how eighteenth century British women writers used quixotic motifs in unexpected ways. Includes bibliographical references and an index.

Graham, Kenneth W. "Emily's Demon-Lover: The Gothic Revolution and *The Mysteries of Udolpho*." In *Gothic Fictions: Prohibition/Transgression*, edited by Kenneth W. Graham. New York: AMS Press, 1989. Places Radcliffe's *The Mysteries of Udolpho* in the historical moment of the revolution in gothic literature.

Howells, Coral Ann. *Love, Mystery, and Misery: Feeling in Gothic Fiction*. London: Athlone Press, 1978. Analyzes Emily St. Aubert as a character through whom Radcliffe experimented with subjectivity and points of view.

Kickel, Katherine E. "Seeing Imagining: The Resurgence of a New Theory of Vision in Ann Radcliffe's *The Mysteries of Udolpho*." In *Novel Notions: Medical Discourse and the Mapping of the Imagination in Eighteenth-Century English Fiction*. New York: Routledge, 2007. Describes how fiction by Radcliffe reflects new medical discoveries about the area of the brain that spurs the imagination. Argues that Radcliffe and other contemporary writers similarly sought to map the area of the brain responsible for imagination by creating narrators who reflect on the process of writing.

Kiely, Robert. *The Romantic Novel in England*. Cambridge, Mass.: Harvard University Press, 1972. Kiely observes innovative aspects in the character of Emily St. Aubert, including that she is aware of her own thinking and that she is astute rather than helpless in finding her way in her gothic situation.

Miles, Robert. *Ann Radcliffe: The Great Enchantress.* New York: Manchester University Press, 1995. Explores the historical and aesthetic context of Radcliffe's fiction, with separate chapters on her early works and mature novels. *The Mysteries of Udolpho* is discussed in chapter 7. Considers Radcliffe's role as a woman writer. Includes notes and a bibliography.

Moers, Ellen. *Literary Women: The Great Writers.* Garden City, N.Y.: Doubleday, 1976. A groundbreaking work that begins to delineate a female literary tradition. Moers discusses how Radcliffe used the gothic novel to explore the nature of the heroine. Compares Radcliffe to novelist Fanny Burney.

Roberts, Bette B. "The Horrid Novels: *The Mysteries of Udolpho* and *Northanger Abbey.*" In *Gothic Fictions: Prohibition/Transgression*, edited by Kenneth W. Graham. New York: AMS Press, 1989. Challenges conventional notions of Jane Austen's evaluation of Radcliffe's art by examining Austen's treatment in *Northanger Abbey* of both Radcliffe's *Mysteries of Udolpho* and other contemporary "horrid" novels.

Todd, Janet. *The Sign of Angellica: Women, Writing, and Fiction, 1600-1800.* New York: Columbia University Press, 1989. Discusses female authorship by the signs it creates to identify itself. Suggests that Radcliffe maintains the image of female gentility—the lady—in her life and works.

The Mysterious Island

Author: Jules Verne (1828-1905)
First published: L'Île mystérieuse, 1874-1875 (English translation, 1875)
Type of work: Novel
Type of plot: Adventure
Time of plot: 1865-1869
Locale: An island in the South Pacific

Principal characters:
CAPTAIN CYRUS HARDING, an army engineer
NEBUCHADNEZZAR, his black servant
GIDEON SPILETT, a reporter
JACK PENCROFT, a sailor
HERBERT BROWN, an orphan
AYRTON, a mutineer
CAPTAIN NEMO, the captain of the *Nautilus*

The Story:

On March 24, 1865, a balloon carrying five persons escaping from Richmond, capital of the Confederacy during the American Civil War, falls into the sea. Caught in a storm, the balloon had flown some seven thousand miles in five days. The five passengers are Captain Cyrus Harding, an engineer in General Grant's army; his black servant, Nebuchadnezzar, known as Neb; Gideon Spilett, a reporter; Jack Pencroft, a sailor; and Herbert Brown, the fifteen-year-old orphan son of one of Pencroft's former sea captains.

The balloon falls near an uncharted island, and Harding, together with his dog, Top, is washed overboard. Once its load is lightened, the balloon then deposits the other travelers on the shore of the island. The next morning, Neb looks for his "master" while the others explore the island. The next day, Herbert, Pencroft, and Spilett take stock of their resources, which consist of the clothes they wear, a notebook, and a watch. They suddenly hear Top barking. The dog leads them to Captain Harding, who, having been unconscious, is at a loss to explain how he arrived at a place more than a mile away from the shore.

When Harding gets stronger, the group decides to consider themselves colonists rather than castaways, and they call their new home Lincoln Island. Harding finds on the island samples of iron, pyrite, clay, lime, coal, and other useful minerals. The colonists make bricks, which they use to construct an oven in which to make pottery. From Top's collar, they are able to make two knives, which enable them to cut bows and arrows. Eventually, they make iron and steel tools.

Under the brilliant direction of Harding, who seems to know a great deal about everything, the colonists work constantly to improve their lot. After discovering a cave within a cliff wall, they plan to make this their permanent residence; they call it Granite House. They make a rope ladder up the side of the cliff to the door of the cavern, which they equip with brick walls, furniture, and candles made from seal fat.

One day, Pencroft finds washed up on the beach a large chest containing many useful items, including books, clothes, instruments, and weapons. On another occasion, the colonists return to Granite House to find that their home has been invaded by orangutans, who suddenly become terrified by something and begin to flee. The colonists kill all but one, which they domesticate and call Jup.

The colony prospers. They domesticate various animals, use a stream to power an elevator to Granite House, and make glass windows. They build a boat designed by Harding and name it the *Bonadventure*. As they are sailing it, they find a bottle with a message, saying that there is a castaway on nearby Tabor Island. Pencroft, Spilett, and Herbert sail to Tabor Island, where Herbert is attacked by a strange wild man. Pencroft and Spilett succeed in capturing him and take him back to Lincoln Island, where he begins to become civilized again. One day he confesses with shame that his name is Ayrton, that he had attempted mutiny on one ship, had tried to seize another, and had finally been put ashore on Tabor Island by Captain Grant, of the *Duncan*. Ayrton, who repents his past life, is accepted by the colonists as one of them. He lives at a corral that the colonists had built some distance from Granite House.

One day the colonists sight a pirate ship. A battle between the pirates and the colonists develops, and just when things are going badly for the colonists, the pirate ship seems to explode. Later, the colonists find the remains of a strange torpedo that had destroyed the ship. A short time later, the colonists discover that the telegraph system that Harding had built to the corral was broken down. When they go to the corral to investigate, they are attacked by some of the pirates from the destroyed ship, and Herbert is seriously wounded. Ayrton, moreover, is gone. While the colonists are trying desperately to keep Herbert alive, the pirates set fire to the mill and sheds close by Granite House and destroy the plantation. By the time the colonists make their way back to Granite House, Herbert has weakened seriously. The one thing needed for his recovery, sulphate of quinine, is lacking on the island, but on the crucial night that might have been Herbert's last, the colonists find a box of quinine beside Herbert's bed, and the medicine enables him to recover.

The colonists set out to find their mysterious benefactor and to exterminate the pirates. When the expedition arrives at the corral, they find Ayrton, who had been tortured by the pirates but who is still alive. Top then discovers the corpses of all the remaining pirates, who had been killed in a mysterious way. The colonists make plans to build a ship large enough to carry them back to civilization. When they discover smoke rising from the crater of the volcano, they redouble their efforts to complete the boat.

One day the colonists receive a call on the telegraph telling them to go to the corral immediately. There they find a note telling them to follow the wire that was attached to the telegraph line. They follow the wire into a hidden cove, where they find the fantastic submarine *Nautilus* and its captain, Nemo, who, it turns out, is also their benefactor. He tells them how he had been a rich nobleman in India, how he had been defeated in his fight for the independence of his country, and how he and his followers, disgusted with the ways of humanity, had built a gigantic undersea craft. His followers had died, and Nemo, old and alone, had taken the *Nautilus* to Lincoln Island, where he has lived for the past six years, giving aid to the colonists because he believes them to be good people. After presenting Harding with a box of jewels and pearls and making a last request that he be buried in his ship, he dies. The colonists seal the *Nautilus* with Captain Nemo's body inside and then open the flood valves to sink the ship.

Following advice Captain Nemo had given him, Harding investigates the caverns beneath the island and sees that, as soon as the seawater penetrates to the shaft of the volcano, the entire island will explode.

The colonists work with all haste to complete work on the boat. By March of their fourth year on the island, the hull is built, but on the night before the launching, the entire island is shattered with a tremendous roar. All that is left of Lincoln Island is a small rock formation. The colonists all reach safety there, but their ship has vanished. The colonists stay on the rock formation for nine days.

On March 24, they sight a ship. It is the *Duncan*, which has come to rescue Ayrton after his twelve-year exile on Tabor Island. The colonists go to the United States. With the treasure Captain Nemo had given them, they buy land in Iowa. They prosper in their new home.

Critical Evaluation:

The Mysterious Island is, in a sense, a sequel to Jules Verne's famous *Twenty Thousand Leagues Under the Sea* (1870), for in this work, Verne describes the death of Captain Nemo. Primarily, however, it is a story of survival and a celebration of the adaptability and ingenuity of intelligent, hard-working people. Verne shows the great satisfaction that can be derived from personal accomplishment. The wealth of detail and description and the valid explanations of mysterious happenings create a sense of realism. At the urging of his publisher, Pierre-Jules Hetzel, Verne turned an early, rather unpromising manuscript into *The Mysterious Island* by adding scientific data, mystery, dramatic complications, and a startling, original conclusion.

Apart from its interest as a story, *The Mysterious Island* is significant for its technological detail. Unlike many tales of the shipwreck variety, unlike even many science-fiction stories of the twentieth century, the novel includes not merely the trappings of science; it also includes scientific substance. Verne goes into detailed accounts of the ways in which tools, chemicals, and communications equipment can be manufactured from elementary materials. All of this description, which may appear to be unrelated to the plot, is significant because it reflects the optimism of nineteenth century European society and especially the widespread confidence placed in technology. Although in some stories, Verne suggests the danger of this new power, for the most part, he embraces industrialism and especially the revolutionary technology that gives birth to it. Industrialization and technology, however, were also massively abused during this period, largely for reasons of profit; so Verne's celebration was generally placed either in the future or in some imaginary place, as in *The Mysterious Island*. The novel's technological descriptions show, in effect, technical history from the most primitive beginnings to a reasonably advanced state; these descriptions may be said to recapitulate, in capsule form, the progress of humanity. Thus it is significant that the heroes are from the United States, because it was seen, at the time, as a rising, dynamic industrial power, leading the world into a new age.

Although Verne's ideas, and his enthusiasm for his ideas, are a pleasure in the novel, there are serious literary flaws in the work. The most damaging of these is probably Verne's shallow characterizations; although his characters are generally adequate, they are never wholly successful or convincing. Nebuchadnezzar, for example, is little more than a stereotype. Verne is not interested in exploring the depths of people's characters, although he is vitally interested in their achievements.

Further Reading

Angenot, Marc. "Jules Verne: The Last Happy Utopianist." In *Science Fiction: A Critical Guide*, edited by Patrick Parrinder. New York: Longmans, 1979. Focuses on a concept of circulation, seen as underlying the mainstays of Verne's narratives: characters, forces of nature, and scientific innovation. Describes Verne as happy in that mobility; views the knowledge that accompanies it as continual and positive.

Butcher, William. *Jules Verne: The Definitive Biography*. New York: Thunder's Mouth Press, 2006. An exhaustive examination of Verne, revealing rich—and sometimes controversial—details of his life. Contradicts some previous biographies, which depict Verne as stodgy and boring.

Costello, Peter. *Jules Verne: Inventor of Science Fiction*. New York: Charles Scribner's Sons, 1978. A detailed and lucid study of Verne's life and works. Includes a thoughtful review of and commentary on *The Mysterious Island*'s events and character significance.

Evans, Arthur B. *Jules Verne Rediscovered: Didacticism and the Scientific Novel*. Westport, Conn.: Greenwood Press, 1988. Scholarly, forthright discussion explores and clarifies myths and misunderstandings about Verne's literary reputation and achievements. Perceives Verne as the inventor not of science fiction but of scientific fiction.

Jules-Verne, Jean. *Jules Verne: A Biography*. Translated by Roger Greaves. New York: Taplinger, 1976. Readable volume by Verne's grandson, with illustrations and quotations adding an intimate flavor. Recounts highlights of *The Mysterious Island* and circumstances related to its development.

Lynch, Lawrence. *Jules Verne*. New York: Twayne, 1992. A critical assessment of Verne's complete works. Includes a generous synopsis of *The Mysterious Island* and analysis of major themes, such as the island itself, and its interconnection with themes from other Verne epics. Excellent introductory resource.

Saint Bris, Gonzague. *The World of Jules Verne*. Translated by Helen Marx. New York: Tuttle Point Press, 2006. Collection of anecdotes, extracts from the novels, and illustrations that attempts to re-create the settings and characters of Verne's visionary fiction. Illustrated by Stéphane Heuet, with a foreword by Arthur C. Clarke.

Smyth, Edmund J., ed. *Jules Verne: Narratives of Modernity*. Liverpool, England: Liverpool University Press, 2000. Collection of essays by Verne scholars that examine, among other topics, Verne, science fiction, and modernity; Verne and the French literary canon; and "the fiction of science, and the science of fiction."

Unwin, Timothy. *Jules Verne: Journeys in Writing*. Liverpool, England: Liverpool University Press, 2005. A reexamination of Verne's fiction. Argues that he was a skillful creator of self-conscious, experimental novels. Compares Verne's work to that of Gustave Flaubert and other nineteenth century French writers.

The Mystery of Edwin Drood

Author: Charles Dickens (1812-1870)
First published: 1870
Type of work: Novel
Type of plot: Detective and mystery
Time of plot: Mid-nineteenth century
Locale: England

Principal characters:
EDWIN DROOD, a young engineer
JACK JASPER, Edwin's young uncle and guardian
ROSA BUD, Edwin's fiancé
NEVILLE LANDLESS, an orphaned young man
HELENA LANDLESS, his sister and Rosa Bud's schoolmate
DURDLES, a stonemason and acquaintance of Jack Jasper
MR. CRISPARKLE, Neville Landless's tutor and friend

The Story:

Jack Jasper is the choirmaster of the cathedral at Cloisterham. Young as he is, he is also the guardian of his orphan nephew, Edwin Drood, who is only a few years Jasper's junior. Edwin Drood is an apprentice engineer who expects one day to become a partner in the firm that employs him, for his father had been one of the owners. Drood's profession takes him all over the world, but he comes back at every opportunity to Cloisterham to see his uncle and his fiancé.

Drood's fiancé, Rosa Bud, is attending a finishing school in Cloisterham. She has been there for several years, for both her parents are dead. The fathers of the two young people had been extremely close friends, and both had requested in their will that their two children become engaged and, at the proper time, married. As the years passed, Edwin and Rosa realized that they were not in love and had no desire to marry. During Rosa's last year at the finishing school, they agree to remain friends but to put aside all ideas of marriage. No one except Rosa realizes that Jasper is in love with her. Rosa is very much afraid of Jasper, so much so that she dares not tell anyone of Jasper's infatuation, but she almost gives her secret away when she ceases taking music lessons from him.

During one of Drood's visits to Cloisterham, a young English couple arrives there from Ceylon, where they had been orphaned. The young woman, Helena Landless, who is Rosa Bud's age, enters the finishing school, and the young man, who is the age of Edwin Drood, begins studies under one of the minor officials at the cathedral, Mr. Crisparkle. Crisparkle, a friend of Jasper and Drood, introduces his charge, Neville Landless, to Jasper and Edwin, in the hope that they will all become fast friends.

As it turns out, however, young Landless was immediately smitten with Rosa and becomes irritated by Drood's casual attitude toward her. The very first evening the three men spend together in Jasper's lodgings, the two quarrel; Jasper claims that if he had not interceded, Landless would have killed Drood.

Rosa and Helena become close friends, and Rosa confesses to Helena that she is in love with Helena's brother. Jasper soon deduces this fact for himself and becomes exceedingly jealous. Jasper, who is addicted to opium, is extremely peculiar and mysterious at times. He becomes acquainted with Durdles, a stonemason, who takes him about the cathedral and points out the various old tombs under the ancient edifice. On one of the visits, which took place in the dead of night, Durdles became very drunk. While he was asleep, Jasper took the key to an underground tomb from Durdles's pocket. What he did with it later on remains a mystery.

During the following Christmas season, Mr. Crisparkle tries to patch up the quarrel between Landless and Drood. He proposes that they meet together at Jasper's lodgings and, after mutual apologies, have a congenial evening together. The two young men agree. On Christmas morning, however, Drood is reported missing by his uncle, with whom the nephew is staying. Jasper says that late the night before the two young men had walked out of his lodgings and turned toward the river. No one has seen them after that. When Mr. Crisparkle appears, he reports that young Landless had left earlier that morning on a solitary walking trip. A search party sets out after him and brings him back to Cloisterham. Young Landless is unable to convince anyone of his innocence, although there is not enough evidence to convict him of any crime. Indeed, the body of Drood is not found, although Mr. Crisparkle discovers his watch and tiepin in the river.

At first, only Rosa and Helena are convinced of Landless's innocence. They soon win Mr. Crisparkle over to their side, and he helps Landless to leave Cloisterham for a refuge in London. Jasper vows that he will find evidence to incriminate the murderer. He also intimates that he has some evidence that Landless is the guilty person. Publicly, however, there is no evidence that Drood has actually been killed.

After a few months, Jasper appears at the school and requests an interview with Rosa. As they walk in the school gardens, Jasper tells her of his love for her and warns her that he has sufficient evidence to send Landless to the gallows. He also implies that he will use his knowledge unless Rosa returns his love. After he leaves, Rosa leaves, too, for London, where she seeks the protection of her guardian, Mr. Grewgious, an odd man who loves her because he had been in love with her mother years before. Mr. Grewgious arranges for Rosa to remain in safe lodgings in London. Mr. Crisparkle arrives the next day and begins to lay plans to extricate Landless and Rosa from their troubles.

One day, a white-haired stranger arrives in Cloisterham. His name is Datchery, and he says he is looking for quiet lodgings where he can end his days in comfort and peace. Looking for a place of residence that will reflect the quaintness of the past, he takes a room across from Jasper's home in the old postern gate. Passersby see him sitting by the hour behind his open door. Every time he hears a remark about Jasper, he makes a chalk mark, some long, some short, inside his closet door.

A short time later, Jasper begins to be followed, almost haunted, by a haggard old woman from whom he has in the past bought opium. She apparently learned something about the choirmaster and suspects a great deal more. Datchery notes her interest in Jasper and follows her to a cheap hotel. The next morning, he and the strange woman attend a service in the cathedral. When the woman tells him that she knows Jasper, old Datchery returns home and adds another chalk mark to those behind his closet door.

Critical Evaluation:

Charles Dickens died before this novel was completed, and he left no notes among his papers to show how he intended to end the story. Undoubtedly, *The Mystery of Edwin Drood* owes some of its popular appeal to its being unfinished. Dickens had only completed half of the work at the time of his death, and this missing ending has spawned dozens of conclusions, the first four only months after his death, as well as a play in which the audience can choose Drood's murderer. Nevertheless, the existent fragment stands on its own as a good example of Dickens's style and literary technique. An indication of the narrative's power is its invariable inclusion in lists of the best works of mystery and suspense.

Although the titular protagonist is Edwin Drood, the action and psychological drama center on his uncle, John Jasper. There are, in reality, two Jaspers, the seemingly devoted friend and quiet and dedicated choirmaster, and the resentful opium addict who is madly in love with Rosa. This duality does not, however, represent a split personality. Although some critics have seen in Dickens's portrayal of Jasper a pre-

cursor to Robert Louis Stevenson's *The Strange Case of Dr. Jekyll and Mr. Hyde* (1886), Jasper the benevolent choirmaster is a conscious facade that enables him to indulge his drug habit in secret. John Jasper's envy of Drood, his lust for Rosa, and his scorn for his job and environs are never hidden in the narrative. The clues to the choirmaster's true personality, which is uniformly negative, gradually mount. Indeed, there is not much mystery about what happened to Drood; it is quite clear that he is murdered by Jasper. From Dickens's notes and conversations with friends, family, and artistic collaborators, it is clear that for Dickens the important element of the novel is not the question of guilt but the manner of its disclosure. There is also substantial evidence to indicate that some of the final chapters would have contained Jasper's confession in his prison cell as he awaited execution. In any case, even a superficial reading of the text points rather unmistakably to Jasper.

Although Jasper's true nature is not an enigma to the reader, there are a number of other mysteries, plot intricacies, and personality quirks that fascinate and provide material for speculation. Indeed, the cast of characters of *The Mystery of Edwin Drood* is one of Dickens's finest. Jasper, as villain, stands alone, his portrait being that of a withdrawn, moody man who first releases his inhibitions in his opium dreams and then tries to convert fantasy to fact. The other principal figures can be roughly organized into two groups, the victims and their defenders and protectors, but, as in all of Dickens's best work, there is an infinite variety and psychological detail in their very distinct personalities. The victims—Edwin Drood, Rosa Bud, and the falsely accused Neville Landless—are all orphans. Their protectors are Mr. Grewgious, Rosa's guardian, and the Canon Crisparkle, Neville's temporary guardian. The betrayal of Jack Jasper, who is Drood's guardian and responsible for his happiness and well-being, is seen as doubly odious for being juxtaposed with the conduct of the other two guardians.

The betrayal and persecution of the innocent is, of course, a common Dickensian theme. In *The Mystery of Edwin Drood*, that theme is emphasized by the sense of fatality that hangs over the first part of the novel. Allusions to William Shakespeare's *Macbeth* (pr. 1606, pb. 1623) are frequent (the chapter preceding Drood's disappearance is explicitly entitled "When Shall These Three Meet Again"), and the cold, gray, dismal landscape positively drips pessimism. Drood's disappearance takes place on Christmas Eve; instead of this being a time of joyous celebration and reunion, Rosa and Drood break off their engagement and the opium dealer silently stalks Jack Jasper; instead of being a quiet, beautiful night of carols, a fierce shrieking wind scatters everything before it, forcing people inside and leaving the streets empty and echoing.

Much has been made of Dickens's jealousy of Wilkie Collins's success with *The Moonstone* (1868) and that he may have tried to outdo his former close friend on his own terrain, the novel of mystery and suspense (even going so far as to use the effects of opium as a central plot device). Dickens used suspense and mystery, but not in connection with the central action, the disappearance of Drood; any doubt concerning the identity of murderer and victim seems to be wishful thinking on the part of would-be literary detectives. The question of identity is, however, an important theme in the novel. Indeed, the real mystery of *The Mystery of Edwin Drood* concerns the identities of several of the other major characters.

Who are Neville and Helen Landless, and what is their past? Who was the Princess Puffer? Why does Jasper seem to be more than just a present client to her? Above all, who is Datchery, the mysterious, obviously disguised stranger, who takes up residence opposite Jasper's lodgings and closely observes the choirmaster? Most close readers of the text believe that Datchery is one of the other characters, Mr. Grewgious, Bazzard, his clerk, Helen Landless, Tartar, or even Drood himself. In one ingenious suggestion, Datchery is none other than Dickens himself, who enters his own novel not just as omniscient narrator but as main character. In *The Moonstone*, Collins had introduced the figure of the great detective with Sergeant Cuff. Perhaps Dickens was again trying to best the younger man by explicitly introducing himself as the great "unraveler" of mystery, the better detective, just as implicitly he was trying to prove himself the better novelist. In any case, the appearance of Datchery, who has obviously come to find out the truth, marks a turning point in the novel. The exposition has ended and the denouement begins, but here the fragment ends.

"Critical Evaluation" by Charlene E. Suscavage

Further Reading

Baker, Richard M. *The Drood Murder Case: Five Studies in Dickens's Edwin Drood.* Berkeley: University of California Press, 1951. Particularly good for its discussion of possible influences on the novel and antecedents in Dickens's own work.

Collins, Philip. *Dickens and Crime.* 3d ed. New York: St. Martin's Press, 1994. Interesting attempt to relate Dickens's writings about crime to events in his own life and time. A prime source for the many theories about the personality of the novel's character Jack Jasper and his role as murderer.

Frank, Lawrence. "News from the Dead: Archaeology, Detection, and *The Mystery of Edwin Drood.*" In *Victorian Detective Fiction and the Nature of Evidence: The Scientific Investigations of Poe, Dickens, and Doyle.* New York: Palgrave Macmillan, 2003. Examines how nineteenth century detective fiction was influenced by and responded to contemporary writings about archaeology, evolutionary biology, and other fields. Frank argues that in this era, detective fiction became more secular and worldly, with writers questioning scientific inquiry.

Fruttero, Carlo, and Franco Lucentino. *The D Case: Or, The Truth About "The Mystery of Edwin Drood."* Translated by Gregory Dowling. New York: Harcourt, Brace, Jovanovich, 1993. A tour de force, in which the world's most famous fictional detectives try to finish Dickens's novel. The first half contains a good edition of the work, while the second demonstrates an extremely close reading of the text with excellent and witty discussions of current and past theories.

Hardy, Barbara. *Dickens and Creativity.* London: Continuum, 2008. Focuses on the workings of Dickens's creativity and imagination, which Hardy argues is at the heart of his self-awareness, subject matter, and narrative. *The Mystery of Edwin Drood* is discussed in chapter 6, "Imaginative Extremes, Negations, and Norms."

Jordan, John O., ed. *The Cambridge Companion to Charles Dickens.* New York: Cambridge University Press, 2001. Collection of essays that examine Dickens's life and times, analyze his novels, and discuss topics such as Dickens and language, gender, family, domestic ideology, the form of the novel, illustration, theater, and film.

Paroissien, David, ed. *A Companion to Charles Dickens.* Malden, Mass.: Blackwell, 2008. Collection of essays discussing Dickens as a reformer, Christian, and journalist. Also examines Dickens and the topics of gender, technology, the United States, and the uses of history.

Rowland, Peter. *The Disappearance of Edwin Drood.* New York: St. Martin's Press, 1992. A good addition to the unending scholarly pursuit of finishing *The Mystery of Edwin Drood.*

The Myth of Sisyphus

Author: Albert Camus (1913-1960)
First published: Le Mythe de Sisyphe, 1942 (English
    translation, 1955)
Type of work: Essay

Regarded as one of the foremost thinkers and writers of modern France, Albert Camus reached maturity at a time when Adolf Hitler came to power. Camus's writings express the horror of living during Hitler's rise and during World War II, and the desire to establish a meaningful life in a meaningless world of war and futile conquest. Not content with the nihilism of his age, and unable to ignore the catastrophe of modern life, Camus developed two related concepts, the absurd and revolt, into a significant philosophy of personal life. He examined the concept of revolt at length in *The Rebel* (1951), but in *The Myth of Sisyphus* he presents the concept of the absurd and thus outlines the belief that the individual has worth but lives in a world that denies such worth. The absurd is the clash between the order for which the human mind strives and the lack of order that one finds in the world.

Camus begins *The Myth of Sisyphus* by categorically stating that the one truly serious problem of philosophy is suicide, because suicide is the confession that life is not worth living. Why, he asks, do people not commit suicide? From this springboard he goes on to describe the absurdity of existence. People are not logical in the act of killing themselves, but they do believe in the absurdity of their lives. The absurd, Camus explains, forces itself upon a person when that person desires to find absolutes by which to guide his or her life; a person searches for absolutes but finds that the world is not reasonable. Once one realizes that existence is absurd, two solutions emerge: suicide or recovery. In short, one's experiences bring the necessity of choosing between suicide and life in absurdity. If one chooses life, then one must accept the absurd. This absurdity is neither in the person (who has an internally consistent understanding) nor in the world (which also is consistent), but is the bond uniting them; therefore, physical suicide does not answer the question of absurdity—such an act merely destroys one of the terms.

Having stated this thesis, Camus then considers the alternatives to physical suicide. Philosophical suicide, the existential "leap of faith," is an antirational acceptance of the limits of reason. Reason's limitations are an excuse to transcend to God. Camus calls this attitude an escape; the absurd does not lead to God but only to itself. Hence, to speak of a "leap of faith" is like advocating physical suicide since both are escapes and, therefore, seek to contradict or negate the absurdity of existence. Physical suicide attempts to have value or meaning in a meaningless existence; the existential "leap" tries to evade the condition of life. Rejecting physical and philosophical suicide, Camus reaches the final alternative: A person must fully confront the truth of his or her existence and accept it. Continually tempted to either kill oneself or make a "leap," a person must live only with the certainty that nothing is certain except the absurd. A person must find whether it is possible to live without appeal. Such a person is indifferent to the future but wants to live the now to its fullest; such a person is interested not in the best life but in the most living, realizing that the condition of life is contradictory.

In the second part of this slender volume, Camus treats the ethical implications of life in the absurd. Having chosen absurdity, how does one act positively while consciously aware of the negative character of the choice? Although all systems of morality are based on the idea that every action has consequences, one who recognizes the unpredictable and unreasonable condition of life cannot judge an act by its consequences. Instead, such a person sees action as an end in itself—the value of life being measured by its sterility, indifference, and hopelessness. Don Juan, for example, goes from one affair to another, not because he searches for total love but merely because he needs the repetition. Yet Don Juan is not melancholy; he knows his condition of life—seducing— and does not hope (the desire to have life other than it is). He can live in neither the past nor the future; he lives entirely in the now. He fully realizes that there is no such thing as eternal love, so he has chosen to be nothing. If he was punished as Christians say, it was because he achieved knowledge without illusion. Like Don Juan, the actor is also absurd, because he (or she) applies himself wholeheartedly to being nothing—a mask that lives only three or so hours. He seeks the sterile life that accepts the absurd as its basic condition.

Finally, Camus describes the conqueror, the third example of the absurd man. Conquerors live completely within time; they are the rebels who shall never succeed, for revolution is always against God and no person can be victorious.

Still the conqueror fights on, knowing that conquest is futile. These examples—the seducer, the actor, and the conqueror—represent the extremes of absurd action. The ordinary person, who knows but hides from nothing and who squarely faces life without hope, represents the typical absurd person, but it is the creator who is the most absurd character of all.

Each type of absurd person puts his or her entire effort into a struggle that is doomed from the beginning, but the creator is one who attempts to examine and to enrich the world that is ephemeral and meaningless. Art is the death and propagation of experience, the absurdly passionate repetition of monotonous themes; it is not escape from existence but the portrayal of the blind path of all people. The artist and the art "interlock"; the work of art illustrates the mind's repudiation of itself, the desire of the mind to cover nothing with the appearance of something. Thinking is creating a world of images; the novelist who is philosophical creates the full complexity and paradox of life. Fyodor Dostoevski, for example, was not interested in arguing philosophical problems but rather in illustrating the implications of such speculation. Dostoevski's novels are filled with absurd judgments, the greatest of which is that existence is illusory and eternal. The absurd novelist, then, negates and magnifies at the same time; such a novelist does not preach a thesis but describes the contradictions of life. The absurd novel has no depth beyond human suffering. Thus the creator passionately describes the fleeting, trying to capture the ephemeral that cannot be captured; a human creator, too, is doomed to failure from the beginning.

The closing section of the volume gives the book its title. In the classical myth of Sisyphus's punishment, Camus finds the absurd hero. Sisyphus is condemned to an eternity of futile and hopeless work. He rolls a huge stone up a mountain, a struggle that takes superhuman strength. The moment that the stone reaches the pinnacle, he cannot keep it balanced; it rolls back to the valley. He knows that his strength and effort are hopeless, yet he silences the gods by his determination to do the hopeless. Actually Sisyphus's consciousness of his torment and its hopelessness makes him superior to it—his very act is a revolt because his consciousness makes him happy and happiness negates punishment.

Not until *The Rebel* did Camus analyze the nature and implications of this revolt from the absurd; however, in his lucid, often lyrical *The Myth of Sisyphus*, he clearly describes the condition of life that he found in Hitler's Europe. The result of this description, the concept of the absurd, formed the basis for his works and became one of the fundamental essays in modern French philosophy and letters.

Further Reading

Carroll, David. *Albert Camus, the Algerian: Colonialism, Terrorism, Justice.* New York: Columbia University Press, 2007. Analyzes Camus's novels, short stories, and political essays within the context of the author's complicated relationship with his Algerian background. Carroll concludes that Camus's work reflects his understanding of both the injustice of colonialism and the tragic nature of Algeria's struggle for independence. Includes a bibliography and an index.

Hughes, Edward J., ed. *The Cambridge Companion to Camus.* New York: Cambridge University Press, 2007. Collection of essays, including "Rethinking the Absurd: *Le Mythe de Sisyphe*" by David Carroll. Other essays discuss Camus's life and times, his formative influences, his relationship with Jean-Paul Sartre, Camus and the theater, and social justice, violence, and ethics in his work.

Lazere, Donald. *The Unique Creation of Albert Camus.* New Haven, Conn.: Yale University Press, 1973. This fascinating psychoanalytical study helps readers recognize many new levels of meaning in Camus's works. Explores the metaphysical dimension and the search for moral values in *The Myth of Sisyphus*.

Lottman, Herbert R. *Albert Camus: A Biography.* Garden City, N.Y.: Doubleday, 1979. This well-documented biography of Camus examines the historical context in which Camus wrote his major works. Explains why *The Myth of Sisyphus* can be read as a philosophical justification of the need to resist the evil of the Nazi occupation of France.

McBride, Joseph. *Albert Camus: Philosopher and Littérateur.* New York: St. Martin's Press, 1992. Contains a thoughtful analysis of the profound influence of Saint Augustine and Friedrich Nietzsche on Camus. Explores the philosophical and theological aspects of *The Myth of Sisyphus*.

Parker, Emmett. *Albert Camus: The Artist in the Arena.* Madison: University of Wisconsin Press, 1965. Discusses the political dimensions of Camus's works written both during the Nazi occupation of France from 1940 to 1944 and after that country's liberation. Describes Camus's role in the French Resistance.

Rhein, Phillip H. *Albert Camus.* Rev. ed. Boston: Twayne, 1989. Describes the meaning of the absurd as well as the political aspects of *The Myth of Sisyphus*. Contains an excellent annotated bibliography of critical studies in English on Camus.

Solomon, Robert C. "Camus' Myth of Sisyphus and the Meaning of Life." In *Dark Feelings, Grim Thoughts: Ex-*

perience and Reflection in Camus and Sartre. New York: Oxford University Press, 2006. Solomon argues that "despite their very different responses to the political questions of their day" both Camus and Jean-Paul Sartre were "fundamentally moralists," and that "their philosophies cannot be understood apart from their deep ethical commitments."

Todd, Olivier. *Albert Camus: A Life*. Translated by Benjamin Ivry. New York: Alfred A. Knopf, 1997. Making use of material such as unpublished letters made available after the death of Camus's widow, this detailed biography reveals much about Camus's love affairs and his many important friendships.

N

The Naked and the Dead

Author: Norman Mailer (1923-2007)
First published: 1948
Type of work: Novel
Type of plot: Social realism
Time of plot: World War II
Locale: Anopopei, an island in the South Pacific

Principal characters:
GENERAL CUMMINGS, commander of the Anopopei campaign
MAJOR DALLESON, a U.S. Army bureaucrat
LIEUTENANT ROBERT HEARN, Cummings's aide
SERGEANT SAMUEL CROFT, a platoon leader
SERGEANT BROWN,
ROTH,
GOLDSTEIN,
RED VALSEN,
JULIO MARTINEZ,
ROY GALLAGHER,
WOODROW WILSON,
OSSIE RIDGES,
STANLEY,
MINETTA,
TOGLIO,
WYMAN, and
HENNESSEY, the men in Croft's platoon

The Story:

In the campaign against the Japanese during World War II, U.S. Army troops commanded by General Cummings land on the beach of Anopopei, an 150-mile-long South Pacific island held by the Japanese army. The platoon of Sergeant Samuel Croft is assigned to conduct reconnaissance on the beach. Croft's men consider themselves lucky because this duty would keep them busy for a week or so while other troops go on the more dangerous patrols into the interior of the island. Red Valsen, however, resents any duties because of his disdain for authority. Croft is able to control all the men but Red. Sergeant Brown considers Croft the best and meanest platoon sergeant in the Army because he seems to love combat. Despite Croft's courage and leadership, some of his men are fearful, especially after young Hennessey is killed by a mortar shell. After Croft begs for a replacement for Hennessey, he is given Roth, a pessimistic clerk who resents never getting anywhere in the civilian world despite his education. Of all his men, Croft likes only Julio Martinez, a reliable scout.

Lieutenant Robert Hearn, General Cummings's aide, admires the general's ability to put his thoughts into action but resents his own position, longing for a combat role. A snob who claims to know everything worth knowing, Cummings picks Hearn as his aide because he considers the lieutenant to be the only officer on his staff with the intellect to understand him. Cummings likes to remind Hearn that Hearn would be nothing without the general.

Croft's platoon grows restless for combat. Most of them instantly dislike Roth, whom Brown considers lazy and shiftless. Moving antitank guns into the jungle after a storm, they drop one into a muddy creek bed, and Wyman blames Goldstein. Confronted by a Japanese platoon, Roy Gallagher wants to surrender, but the enemy troops are repelled, with Toglio slightly wounded. For the first time in combat, Croft is afraid. He orders Red to shoot four already dead Japanese and then execute a prisoner after being friendly to him, upsetting Red even more. Martinez steals gold teeth from the mouths of Japanese corpses.

Gallagher is told that his wife, Mary, died in childbirth, but he refuses to accept her death. The other men are made uneasy by Gallagher's loss, made even more painful by his continuing, because of the delay of mail from home, to receive letters from Mary for weeks after her death. After the failure of the Japanese attack, Cummings's campaign stalls for no apparent reason, and he feels powerless to change matters. The general begins harassing Hearn, who responds by grinding out a cigarette in the middle of Cummings's spotless floor. Cummings forces Hearn to choose between being imprisoned for insubordination and picking up a cigarette the general throws down. Hearn gives in, picks up the cigarette, but asks for a transfer. Cummings refuses and sends him to work under Major Dalleson.

The slightly wounded Minetta fakes insanity to keep from returning to combat but changes his mind after another patient dies of his wounds. Woodrow Wilson agonizes over the discomfort of his sexually transmitted disease. Cummings decides that sending in a battalion to drive out the enemy without naval support would result in a massacre of his troops. The general devises a plan of attack but decides to send in a reconnaissance patrol first. Based on Dalleson's recommendation, Cummings decides to send Croft's platoon, and he assigns Hearn to lead it just before the mission begins. Hearn distrusts the general's motives, and Croft resents giving up his platoon to the untested lieutenant. Croft had always thought that a man either was destined to be killed or not, and saw himself as exempt from death; suddenly, though, he was not so certain. He also dislikes Hearn's efforts to make the men like him. Hearn realizes how easy it would be to let Croft make all the decisions. Croft thinks the best way to accomplish the mission is to climb Mount Anaka in the center of the island.

When the platoon is ambushed, Wilson is seriously wounded in the stomach. Brown, Stanley, Ridges, and Goldstein are chosen to carry Wilson back to the beach. The remaining men experience a respite from the shock of battle when Roth discovers an injured bird, but Croft kills it. After Red challenges Croft, Hearn stops the dispute before blows are struck. Later, the remaining men in the patrol want to go back, but Hearn, at first, does not want to seem a failure to the general. When he changes his mind, Croft argues that a successful mission could end the entire campaign. Hearn gives in but decides to resign his commission after the campaign. Sent ahead as a scout, Martinez finds Japanese in their path and kills one of them. Croft lies to Hearn about what Martinez had seen, and when the patrol proceeds, the lieutenant is killed. Croft then orders them to climb the mountain. Meantime, after Brown and Stanley collapse under the burden of carrying Wilson, Goldstein and Ridges continue with the stretcher on their own.

When Dalleson is left in command after Cummings seeks

the support of a destroyer, the situation of the campaign changes suddenly. Not knowing what to do, the major accidentally launches a complete attack. In a few hours, the Japanese are completely routed and Croft's platoon forgotten.

Their sacrifices made pointless by Dalleson's bumbling, the patrol directs their frustration at the weak Roth. Attempting to show them he is as good as they are, Roth jumps awkwardly from a ledge and falls to his death. Wilson also dies, but Goldstein and Ridges continue carrying his body until they lose it in a river. Martinez tells Croft he will not continue up the mountain, and a rebellion stirs. Croft threatens to shoot Red, and the men give in again. Shortly afterward, they are attacked by hornets and run down the mountain. Croft finally gives up on their mission, and all the survivors return to the beach. Back on their landing craft, they quickly forget all their hostility toward one another. Cummings is upset that Dalleson had blundered his way to victory and was nevertheless congratulated. As Dalleson plans trivial projects, anonymous soldiers on a mopping-up mission execute some Japanese prisoners.

Critical Evaluation:

Norman Mailer's career as one of the most highly regarded novelists in the United States got off to a resounding start with *The Naked and the Dead*, the first major treatment of World War II in American fiction. The novel is considered, along with James Jones's *From Here to Eternity* (1951) and Joseph Heller's *Catch-22* (1961), to be one of the few American masterpieces about the war. It is one of the best realistic treatments of combat since Erich Maria Remarque's *Im Westen nichts Neues* (1929; *All Quiet on the Western Front*, 1929). Mailer based the novel on the eighteen months he spent overseas in Leyte, Luzon, and Japan (with the occupation forces) from 1944 to 1946.

As is usually the case in a first novel, the influences on the book are fairly clear. Critics cite stylistic echoes of Ernest Hemingway, social concerns like those of John Steinbeck, naïve young men in search of maturity as with the characters of F. Scott Fitzgerald and Thomas Wolfe, and a flashback structure similar to John Dos Passos's *U.S.A.* trilogy (1930-1936). The style of *The Naked and the Dead* is simpler, partly because of the Hemingway influence, than Mailer's later self-conscious, often ornate writing, but the thematic concerns—among them, the conflict of the individual with a hostile, indifferent society—are the same as in his more mature fiction. Mailer intends the Anopopei campaign to be a microcosm not only of the war in the Pacific but of any war at any time or place. In showing the disconnect between the worlds of command and combat, Mailer emphasizes how war creates alienation in all its participants. As represented in figures like Cummings and Croft, the Army seems the worst possible version of American society. Not only are the most sensitive, humane, and liberal characters, such as Hearn and Roth, defeated by their experiences; so are their cynical, amoral opposites.

Croft loses control of the patrol and fails to climb the mountain that represents his irrational need for order. Cummings cannot claim credit for the campaign's success and has difficulty in communicating his needs to those above and below him. That only the bureaucratic Dalleson comes out ahead points out how America is a society controlled not by people of action, such as Croft, or thinkers, such as Cummings, but by mere paper pushers, such as Dalleson.

Mailer is concerned with much more than men at war and uses his characters to explore what he considers to be sicknesses within society. The novel's characters are petty, scheming, sensitive to slights, and insensitive to others. They are unable to communicate effectively in any situation. There are huge communication gaps between Cummings and Dalleson, between Hearn and Croft, and between the corporals and privates in Croft's platoon. In Mailer's view of the world, men at war are at least as dehumanized by their own weaknesses as they are by the war itself.

Neither courage nor education nor religious values seem to count for much. The failure of the latter can be seen in the quest of Ridges, with his traditional, southern Christianity, and Goldstein, with his struggle to be a good man in an anti-Semitic world, to give Wilson a decent burial. That they fail because of a river points out nature's indifference to human needs, as do the hornets who end Croft's attempt to conquer the mountain. At least in making the effort to save and then to bury Wilson, Goldstein and Ridges are admirable. In their attempt to find meaning and, possibly, redemption, they try to define themselves while the weaker Brown and Stanley allow the Army to determine who they are.

As the flashbacks to their lives before the war indicate, Mailer's protagonists were little different in their peacetime lives. Mailer's civilian America is as chaotic as the war. Throughout *The Naked and the Dead*, Mailer illustrates how humanity's destiny is at the whim of illogical forces over which it is impossible to exert control.

Michael Adams

Further Reading

Aichinger, Peter. *The American Soldier in Fiction, 1880-1963: A History of Attitudes Toward Warfare and the Military Establishment*. Ames: Iowa State University Press, 1975. Places the novel in the context of other treatments of World War II in American fiction. Complains that Mailer is unable to comprehend the character of the professional officer and that the novel is undermined by turgid ideological discourse.

Glenday, Michael K. "The Hot Breath of the Future: *The Naked and the Dead*." In *Norman Mailer*. New York: St. Martin's Press, 1995. Offers a reassessment of Mailer's novels, including *The Naked and the Dead*, and their importance to American literature.

Gordon, Andrew. *An American Dreamer: A Psychoanalytic Study of the Fiction of Norman Mailer*. Madison, N.J.: Fairleigh Dickinson University Press, 1980. Considers the novel in the context of other Mailer fiction that contrasts weak, liberal, masochistic characters with strong, reactionary, sadistic ones. Argues that the novel's central psychological conflict is the doomed struggle for control over the self and outside forces.

Kaufman, Donald L. *Norman Mailer: The Countdown—The First Twenty Years*. Carbondale: Southern Illinois University Press, 1969. Analyzes the contrast between bestial and humane values in the novel and Mailer's depiction of obstacles to the creative urge. Argues that the novel is a commentary on isolation from space, time, and humanity.

Kinder, John M. "The Good War's 'Raw Chunks': Norman Mailer's *The Naked and the Dead* and James Gould Cozzens's *Guard of Honor*." *Midwest Quarterly* 46, no. 2 (Winter, 2005): 187-202. Kinder compares the two World War II novels, arguing that the books do not share the "sense of moral rectitude" about the war that is common to most other novels about the conflict. Maintains these novels do not romanticize the war or its fighters, and they take exception to the conventional wisdom that Americans during wartime were united around a common goal.

Leeds, Barry H. *The Structured Vision of Norman Mailer*. New York: New York University Press, 1969. Interprets the novel as a pessimistic examination of the sickness of society and of the flawed nature of the individual. Shows how Mailer is an acerbic social critic.

Manso, Peter. *Mailer: His Life and Times*. New York: Washington Square Press, 2008. An exhaustive biography based on more than two hundred interviews, some of which provide multiple versions of the events in Mailer's life.

Solotaroff, Robert. *Down Mailer's Way*. Champaign: University of Illinois Press, 1974. Argues that the novel is an allegory for what Mailer saw as the coming of fascism to America. Maintains that Mailer loses control of the novel because the values he seemingly endorses go against his deepest beliefs.

Naked Lunch

Author: William S. Burroughs (1914-1997)
First published: 1959
Type of work: Novel
Type of plot: Fantasy
Time of plot: Mid-twentieth century
Locale: New York; Texas; New Orleans, Louisiana; the
  "Interzone"

Principal characters:
WILLIAM LEE, a drug addict
JANE, his companion
DR. BENWAY, a charlatan doctor
A. J., a carnival con man
DOC PARKER, a druggist

The Story:

William Lee, a drug addict and hustler, and Jane, his companion, travel by automobile across the United States to Texas in search of drugs. After picking up a quart of paregoric and a quantity of Nembutal, they drive on to New Orleans. There they buy some heroin and continue on to Mexico. During this trip, Lee, the narrator, delivers a rambling monologue about drug addicts, addiction, pushers, American cities, the police, narcotics agents, and the drag of life in suburban America where the neighborhoods are all the same and the people all dull and boring. In his monologue Lee concentrates on the terrible agony of need that the drug addict suffers. In Mexico, Lee needs to locate a drug supplier, and he finds one in Old Ike, a local junkie who receives a monthly drug allowance from the government. Jane meets a pimp who is a ritual marijuana user and who attempts to put her under his spell.

Lee then goes to Interzone, an imaginary city, which is a combination of the southern United States, South America, Tangier, New York, and Panama. There he meets Dr. Benway, a master at controlling human behavior who works for Islam, Inc. Benway gives Lee a tour of the Reconditioning Center in Freeland, a place where pseudoscience is practiced in bizarre experiments to brainwash human beings. Lee sees the monstrous results of Benway's "science" in creatures called INDs, or humans who had had their minds stripped. INDs are human vegetables who behave like zombies.

Dr. Benway tells Lee about his twisted theories of addiction and describes in explicit detail the effects of various drugs, including morphine, LSD, and heroin. Benway shows Lee the criminal ward and gives him his opinions concerning homosexuality, specifically that it is a political crime. When a computer malfunctions, Benway and Lee have to leave the Reconditioning Center. As they depart, Lee describes the horrible mutants, English colonials, bores, explorers, Arab rioters, hypochondriacs, and rock-and-roll hoodlums in the streets and at the cafés they pass.

Interzone, the city, is described as a criss-crossing network of streets that run through and beneath dwelling cubicles, cafés, and odd-shaped rooms. Merchants sell Black Meat, the addictive flesh of a giant centipede. Mugwumps, subhuman, reptilelike creatures, sit on café stools and dispense mugwump fluid to addicts. In the hospital, Lee experiences withdrawal from narcotics and tells how horribly sick it makes him. Dr. Benway explains to the nurses and patients how he practices surgery. In an insane speech, Benway insults every standard of medicine and sanitary medical procedure. Lee continues to describe the effects of various addictive drugs, as he tries to take the cure.

In a plushly decorated Interzone bar, a mugwump has perverted sex with a young boy. The boy is tied up and hung from a wooden gallows. He is sodomized by the mugwump. At the point of orgasm the boy's neck snaps. Satyrs, Arab women, Javanese dancers, Aztec priests, and various bizarre inhabitants of Interzone have outrageous sex with boys and with one another. At the campus of Interzone University, a professor lectures on perversions and "The Rime of the Ancient Mariner," by Samuel Taylor Coleridge. A. J. operates as an undercover agent disguised as a playboy and practical joker. At A. J.'s Annual Party, pornographic movies are shown to an audience of depraved sexual perverts who engage in bizarre acts of sadomasochism.

Lee describes Interzone as a Composite city, where all the houses are joined. In the Interzone Market at the Meet Café, wanderers, bums, junkies, drug pushers, dwarfs, and black marketeers meet to discuss drugs, philosophy, and Dr. Benway's projects. Male prostitutes debate politics with members of the Nationalist Party. Lee recounts a number of short, perversely comic tales. Benway continues his pseudoscientific experiments with the assistance of Dr. Berger and a technician. They try to "cure" homosexuals by brainwashing them.

Islam, Inc., and several of the political parties of Interzone hold meetings at which the delegates and speakers are tortured and put to death. A. J. engages in disgusting behavior at the restaurant Chez Robert, calling a hundred starving hogs into the restaurant. After he leaves the restaurant, A. J. takes a baboon to the opera.

Lee tells the stories of a number of Interzone characters, including Clem and Jody, two vaudeville hoofers, and Salvador, an Italian pimp and drug dealer. Various parties—the Divisionists, Liquefactionists, and Senders—compete for control of the people in Interzone. Lee is forced to file an affidavit to avoid being evicted from his apartment. The County Clerk tells Lee about Doc Parker's drugstore, where one can buy drugs. The Clerk also tells a story about the vicious murder of a black service station attendant in Texas. Lee tells of the lost and unlucky inhabitants of Interzone, who fail miserably at every enterprise they attempt. Carl Peterson, who lives in Freeland, a welfare state, is summoned by Dr. Benway to undergo tests at the Ministry of Mental Hygiene. Benway tells Carl that homosexuality is a sickness and that Carl might need treatment. Carl undergoes several tests to determine his sexual orientation. Finally, in disgust, Carl walks out of Benway's clinic.

A sailor, who is in the throes of addiction, describes the Exterminator. The Exterminator is actually Lee, and his main job is to poison roaches with pyrethrum powder. Hauser and O'Brien, two narcotics officers, are ordered to arrest Lee at his apartment. After they arrive, Lee tries to take more drugs. Lee ends up murdering the two officers. The road through withdrawal and toward recovery is described by Lee as a horrible nightmare in which the junkie faces thoughts of suicide to cleanse his "rotting, phosphorescent bones," and silence the "mangled insect screams." Finally, Lee utters a few desperate words about drug sickness and the pathos of drug commerce and the smells of gasoline and slow, cold fires, burning endlessly.

Critical Evaluation:

Since its first publication in Paris in 1959, *Naked Lunch* has received both praise and censure. While noted authors and critics such as John Ciardi, Norman Mailer, and Mary McCarthy have applauded *Naked Lunch* as a novel of genius and terrible beauty, its publication in the United States in 1962 was met with seizure by the U.S. Postal Service and U.S. Customs on the grounds it was pornographic. *Naked Lunch* was found to be obscene by a Massachusetts Superior Court in 1965, a decision that was later overturned by the Massachusetts Supreme Court.

Naked Lunch is a disjointed account of the horrors of a junkie's addiction, withdrawal, and cure. William Burroughs, one of the original Beat writers, arrived in Tangier,

Morocco, in 1953, after spending months in the jungles of South America in search of the hallucinogenic plant Yage. At that time Burroughs was heavily addicted to narcotics such as morphine and codeine. He was perhaps drawn to Tangier because of its reputation as a zone of permissiveness where drugs were plentiful and expenses were low. Tangier was an International Zone, where there was unregulated free enterprise. It was also known to expatriate writers and artists as a sanctuary where they could live without being scrutinized by the authorities. Once settled in Tangier, Burroughs tried to write, but his drug addiction made that process both painful and difficult. As he attempted various cures, his writing slowly progressed. The novel that began to develop would be a narrative based on his addiction and withdrawal and his impressions of Tangier.

Burroughs first compiled a large volume of notes, which contained his travel and drug experiences, hallucinations, dreams, and satirical fantasies about American society. To complete the manuscript, Burroughs had to face his addiction and undergo drug treatment. While he made various attempts to withdraw in Tangier, he was finally cured after seeking the help of Dr. John Yerbury Dent of London. His friends Allen Ginsberg, Jack Kerouac, and Alan Ansen visited him in Tangier in 1957, where they helped type, select, and edit the final manuscript and prepare it for publication.

In *Naked Lunch*, Burroughs tells his story metaphorically through a series of episodes, visions, and myths. These fantasies work to describe a state of mind rather than create a traditional narrative. The technique used in *Naked Lunch* is similar to collage or montage. Scenes, episodes, and routines are juxtaposed in a way that makes it possible to read them in almost any order. The episodes are indicated by titles that refer to the subject or theme. The episodes vary from two or three pages in length to more than twenty pages. Within the episode there is usually an introduction in which characters, setting, or a situation is defined, followed by improvisations that may end in a violent or dramatic climax.

The main setting of *Naked Lunch* is Interzone, a city based on a composite of the places where Burroughs had gone in search of drugs: New York, Louisiana, South America, and Tangier. Interzone is inhabited by hustlers, addicts, con men, losers, and petty officials. These inhabitants spend their time taking drugs, having pornographic sex, and engaging in sleazy commerce. There are political and economic conspiracies everywhere, usually made up of groups involved in a struggle for power and control over the "consumers." The control the conspirators exercise is based on the consumer's need for drugs, sex, or power. Through the many satirical, hallucinatory scenes, Burroughs exposes the hypocrisy and destructiveness of American society. Doctors, bureaucrats, and politicians are the chief examples of the power elite who manipulate the masses. For example, Dr. Benway and Dr. Berger create "healthy" men by torturing and brainwashing them. The three main political parties are like parasites, seeking to gain control over Interzone through demoniac possession.

In *Naked Lunch*, Burroughs uses a variety of literary forms derived from popular culture, including newspapers, advertising, magazines, comics, paperbacks, movies, radio, and television. His characters are all pop-culture types: the crazed doctor, secret agent, private eye, gangster, drug pusher, mad scientist, vampire, and zombie. Bill Lee and A. J. represent Burroughs's alter egos. The episodes are arranged in random order, to create an improvised text that can be entered at any point. While the untraditional, shocking nature of the subject matter and the experimental form of the novel resulted in many negative reviews when *Naked Lunch* was published, there was much praise for its boldness and unrelenting power. *Naked Lunch* has been vindicated as a work of literary merit that is still capable of artistic and moral revelation.

Francis Poole

Further Reading

Dittman, Michael J. "*Naked Lunch*, William S. Burroughs." In *Masterpieces of Beat Literature*. Westport, Conn.: Greenwood Press, 2007. This book, designed to introduce students to works of Beat literature, includes a biography of Burroughs, a synopsis of the plot of *Naked Lunch*, a discussion of the novel's themes and style, study and discussion questions, and suggestions for further reading.

Goodman, Michael Barry. *Contemporary Literary Censorship: The Case History of Burroughs' "Naked Lunch."* Metuchen, N.J.: Scarecrow Press, 1981. A narrative history of the writing, publication, critical reception, and censorship of *Naked Lunch* in the United States. Well documented, it includes much previously unpublished material.

Harris, Oliver. *William Burroughs and the Secret of Fascination*. Carbondale: Southern Illinois University Press, 2003. A critical analysis of *Naked Lunch* and the other novels published in the 1950's, placing these works within the context of their critical history and in relation to Burroughs's method of writing. Focuses on how Burroughs's fiction was shaped by his letter writing.

Miles, Barry. *William Burroughs: El Hombre Invisible*. London: Virgin Books, 1992. An entertaining overview of Burroughs's literary and artistic output. Includes chapters devoted specifically to Tangier and to *Naked Lunch*. Offers a personal portrait of Burroughs the man and artist.

Morgan, Ted. *Literary Outlaw: The Life and Times of William S. Burroughs*. New York: Henry Holt, 1988. A detailed biography of Burroughs which discusses *Naked Lunch*, its style, themes, and organization. Includes interesting photographs of Burroughs taken throughout his life.

Mottram, Eric. *William Burroughs: The Algebra of Need*. London: Marion Boyars, 1977. A study of Burroughs's work as a radical critique of Western power structures and the myths that support them. Mottram analyzes *Naked Lunch* and other works of Burroughs's fiction in comparison with other radical thinkers.

Russell, Jamie. *Queer Burroughs*. New York: Palgrave, 2001. Focuses on the relationship of Burroughs's writing to his homosexuality. Russell seeks to chart the progression of gay themes in Burroughs's novels, including *Naked Lunch*; he explores how the novels imagine a radical gay identity and respond to the gay rights movement.

Schneiderman, Davis, and Philip Walsh, eds. *Retaking the Universe: William S. Burroughs in the Age of Globalization*. London: Pluto Press, 2004. Collection of essays examining Burroughs's life and work, including discussions of Burroughs and contemporary theory; Burroughs, Dada, and Surrealism; and the social and political relevance of his work in the emerging global age.

Skerl, Jennie. *William S. Burroughs*. Boston: Twayne, 1985. A very good introduction to Burroughs's life and work until 1981 and the publication of *The Cities of the Red Night*. Provides insight into the creation, themes, and techniques of *Naked Lunch*.

The Naked Year

Author: Boris Pilnyak (Boris Andreyevich Vogau, 1894-1938)
First published: Goly god, 1922 (English translation, 1928)
Type of work: Novel
Type of plot: Regional
Time of plot: Early twentieth century
Locale: Russia

Principal characters:
DONAT RATCHIN, a merchant's son and a young revolutionist
NASTIA, a chambermaid
ARKHIP, a peasant member of the party
ARKHIPOV, his father
NATALIA ORDYNIN, a young doctor
BORIS,
GLEB, and
EGOR, her brothers
CATHERINE and LYDIA, her sisters
ANDREY, a fugitive

The Story:

Ordynin Town is a citadel that existed for years in a normal fashion, where poets, artisans, and merchants dwell, busy with their tasks. The Ratchin family members were merchants for two hundred years, and for much of that time they leased the salt trade. Donat, a curly-headed youth, is the youngest son. Already he counts on taking his place in the market, on buying and selling and ruling his clerks.

The monastery holds an important place in the lives of the people, for its bells regulate their lives. At nine o'clock the town goes to bed; anyone up and about after that hour has to identify himself to the watch. Pranks of boys and dwarfs provide the only excitement, and the stationer's store is the intellectual center of the town.

At the age of fifteen, Donat falls in love with a chambermaid named Nastia. Every evening he goes to her kitchen and reads church history aloud to her. When Ivan, his father, hears of the attachment, he has both Donat and Nastia whipped; that same night, Ivan sends his housekeeper to Donat's bed. Afterward Donat learns how to get out of the house at night. For a while he clambers out of a window and goes to see the persecuted widow of a rich moneylender.

In 1914 war comes, and in 1917 revolution. From ancient Ordynin the inhabitants are called up to learn the craft of murder, to kill and to die. Donat is sent to the Carpathians. The first casualty of Ordynin is Classic-Spark, a loafer who commits suicide when the vodka runs out. Because the merchants of Ordynin refuse to pay a sufficient bribe to the engineers who are laying the railroad tracks, the railway station is put some distance away. Ordynin is doomed to remain in the backwash of progress and change.

The Ratchin house is requisitioned by the Red Guard, and the salt market is broken up. Donat returns from the war full of hatred for the old order. He orders that the salt building be destroyed and a house for the people erected in its place.

In the monastery, Olly Kuntz prints blank orders for arrest and imprisonment. Arkhip, a peasant unused to writing, is in command, and he frequently laboriously pens orders of execution. Comrade Laitis takes Olly to the cinema and sees her home. Later he comes back with his soldiers to arrest Andrey, a lodger, but Andrey cleverly gives them the slip and gets away. The soldiers break into Olly's room when they search the building, and Olly weeps out of sympathy for Andrey. Semyon, a bookish man interested in masonry, is much impressed by Andrey's cleverness.

Old Arkhipov, Arkhip's father, goes to see the doctor. His fears are confirmed when his doctor, Natalia Ordynin, tells him that he has cancer of the stomach. At the moment that Arkhipov decides that he must die, Arkhip is signing an execution warrant. That evening the father asks Arkhip's advice, and upon his son's suggestion, he shoots himself in the mouth.

After two years, Gleb returns to the manor. No one can remember whether the town is named for the Ordynin family or whether the family takes its name from the town. At any rate the Ordynins were lords for a long time; now the seal of Cain is on them. In the run-down house no one greets Gleb, but soon Egor, his brother, half naked and dirty, comes stumbling in with the servant Martha. Martha finds her master in a brothel and brings him home. Egor pays for the spree by selling his sister Natalia's coat.

Gleb learns that Boris, his older brother, locked Egor in his room and then raped Martha. Since Egor is half in love with her, the crime seems particularly serious. When Boris comes into Gleb's room, Boris announces gloomily that he is suffering from syphilis, a family disease. Then Gleb thinks of his lunatic father, a religious fanatic in his old age, and of the brothers and sisters who died in infancy.

Arina, the mother, sells clothes and furniture to make ends meet. Natalia, already suspected of being too fond of Arkhip, alienates herself further from the family by going to live at the hospital where she works. Catherine, the youngest daughter, is pregnant, and the other sister, Lydia, advises her to have an abortion. To her dismay, Catherine learns that she also has syphilis, but when she runs to Lydia for comfort, her sister, under the influence of morphine, pays little attention to her.

Andrey joins a brotherhood near the Black Streams. The peasant girls call him out to their dances at night, and he is happy for a time. Aganka, the merriest and hardest-working of the girls, attracts him greatly, but she dies during the hot summer. Smallpox and typhus break out, and all Russia suffers from pestilence and famine and war. Andrey becomes Irina's betrothed, although the comrades frown on marriage as sentimental nonsense. Donat is the unbending leader of their anarchistic commune.

The commune ceases to be a haven when the band of armed strangers arrives. At the instigation of Harry, their English leader, they kill most of the men and then ride on to join an uprising in the Ukraine. Andrey is lucky to get away.

At first, Boris is furious when Ivan, president of the poverty committee, requisitions the Ordynin manor. He knew Ivan for years and despises him as an unlettered peasant. In a spirit of bravado, Boris leaves home on foot. A friendly peasant gives him shelter the first night, but the apprehensive peasant makes him leave early the next morning. Later that day, Boris finds space in a refugee wagon.

The famine becomes worse. The old men barter with traveling merchants because there is no money with which to buy anything. There are no young men left to work; they all went off with the Reds or the Whites. People do anything they can for bread. At Mar Junction, the railway station, the Red Guards often requisition young women who come in on the refugee train.

The Whites occupy Ordynin, and when they leave, the Reds swarm back. Committees and commissions spring up all over the town. The Moscow functionaries even reopen a mine outside the town. Although the mine, with its antique equipment, is a deathtrap, men are forced to work in it.

Busy with his many duties, Arkhip feels keenly his lack of education. Natalia, the only normal Ordynin, is a doctor under the new government. Arkhip knew Natalia for a long time, and at last, needing an educated partner and wanting

children, he asks her to marry him. Natalia thinks of her university days, when she was in love. It is a painful memory. She would welcome this new kind of mating, with neither love nor pain. Despite her resolutions, however, she feels close to Arkhip and talks of the coziness of their union. Arkhip goes home and thumbs in vain through his dictionary. He does not know the meaning of the word coziness, nor can he find it in the dictionary.

Critical Evaluation:

The "naked year" is 1917, the year of the Bolshevik Revolution, and Boris Pilnyak's attempt to capture its essence in his narrative established him as Russia's first important postrevolutionary novelist. It can be strongly argued that *The Naked Year* is neither in form a novel nor in substance a communistic document. The fragmentary, lyrical, relatively plotless and characterless series of vignettes that make up the book are more like a sequence of random impressions and rhetorical digressions, thinly tied together in time and place, than a controlled, directed narrative. The origins and essence of the revolution, as Pilnyak presents them, do not conform to the tenets of Soviet political dogma.

Despite its narrative difficulties and ideological impurity, *The Naked Year* was generally hailed as a masterpiece upon its publication in 1922. The main character of the book is the Russian people, and the substance of it is their diverse reactions to the civil turmoil that swept across Russia from 1914 to the early 1920's. Although Pilnyak uses a mixture of prose styles and jumps from character to character and event to event with few formal transitions, he does focus most of the action in the town of Ordynin and on characters who represent all levels of Russian society—the Ratchin family belongs to the middle class, the Ordynins are aristocratic, Arkhip represents the rising peasantry—in a fairly complete, if unsystematic fashion. Thus the reader comes away from *The Naked Year* with a coherent impression of life in revolutionary Russia.

The historical vision Pilnyak presents in the novel is that of a spontaneous peasant revolt overthrowing the old order. He sees the conflict not so much in terms of the bourgeoisie versus the proletariat as the "natural" Eastern side of Russian culture, represented by the peasantry, in conflict with the "artificial" European urbanized Russia. The revolution was, in his opinion, the necessary cleansing force, and the Bolsheviks were merely the agents of historical change, not the inevitable culmination of it.

Such unorthodox views displeased the revolutionary hierarchy, but the power and the popularity of the novel, coupled with the relative instability of Soviet politics at the time, kept Pilnyak in the ranks of accepted writers. In such later works, however, as "The Tale of the Unextinguished Moon" (1927)—a direct attack on Stalin—and *Krasnoye derevo* (1929; *Mahogany*, 1968), he provoked the dictator's wrath. Despite abject disavowals of his works, pitiable recantations, and several orthodox writings, Pilnyak was imprisoned during the Stalinist purges of the mid-1930's and presumably perished in neglect and disgrace.

Further Reading

Brown, Edward J. "Boris Pilnyak: Biology and History." In *Russian Literature Since the Revolution*. Rev. ed. Cambridge, Mass.: Harvard University Press, 1982. Considers *The Naked Year* a virtuoso performance both in its symphonic structure of themes and ideas and its presentation of the primitive and elemental forces of the Russian Revolution. A good survey of Pilnyak's works.

Erlich, Victor. "Two Pioneers of the Soviet Novel: Konstantin Fedin and Boris Pilnyak." In *Modernism and Revolution: Russian Literature in Transition*. Cambridge, Mass.: Harvard University Press, 1994. Examines works by Pilnyak and other writers to explore the complex and ambiguous relationship of literary modernism and the Soviet government in the years immediately following the Russian Revolution. Describes how Russian literature, which prior to the revolution was characterized by experimentation, eventually became more regimented and conformist as the avant-garde's relationship to the Soviet state became increasingly precarious.

Maguire, Robert. "The Pioneers: Pil'nyak and Ivanov." In *Red Virgin Soil: Soviet Literature in the 1920's*. New ed. Evanston, Ill.: Northwestern University Press, 2000. A useful discussion of Pilnyak's role in Russian literature of the 1920's, especially of his iconoclastic approach to literature. Asserts that Pilnyak lacks greatness but was influential in shaping the Russian literature of his time.

Reck, Vera T. *Boris Pil'niak: A Soviet Writer in Conflict with the State*. Montreal: McGill-Queen's University Press, 1975. Extensive account of Pilnyak's celebrated troubles with the authorities, to whom Joseph Stalin gave the tone by declaring that Pilnyak expressed his anarchism already in *The Naked Year*.

Shentalinsky, Vitaly. "A Bullet in Place of a Full Stop: The File on Boris Pilnyak." In *Arrested Voices: Resurrecting the Disappeared Writers of the Soviet Regime*. Translated by John Crowfoot. New York: Martin Kessler Books, Free Press, 1996. In the late 1980's, Shentalinsky was able to obtain government documents regarding the arrest of many writers during the regime of Joseph Stalin. His book describes the contents of the documents he retrieved about Pilnyak and other authors.

Slonim, Marc. "Boris Pilnyak: The Untimely Symbolist." In *Soviet Russian Literature: Writers and Problems, 1917-1977*. 2d rev. ed. New York: Oxford University Press, 1977. Substantive historical survey of Pilnyak's works and his place in the early Russian literature of the Soviet period.

Struve, Gleb. *Russian Literature Under Lenin and Stalin, 1917-1953*. Norman: University of Oklahoma Press, 1971. Contains a brief but excellent account of Pilnyak's writings, including *The Naked Year*, and of his conflicts with the state that eventually led to his death.

The Name of the Rose

Author: Umberto Eco (1932-   )
First published: Il nome della rosa, 1980 (English translation, 1983)
Type of work: Novel
Type of plot: Detective and mystery
Time of plot: 1327
Locale: Northern Italy

Principal characters:
WILLIAM OF BASKERVILLE, a Franciscan monk and former inquisitor, now a detective
ADSO OF MELK, the narrator, a Benedictine novice assigned as William's scribe
ABO, the abbot of the Benedictine monastery
JORGE DE BURGOS, an aged, blind monk
MICHAEL OF CESENA, the leader of the Franciscan order
BERNARD GUI, a Dominican inquisitor
THE UNNAMED EDITOR AND TRANSLATOR

The Story:

It is in late November, 1327, that the learned Franciscan William of Baskerville, student of Roger Bacon and friend of William of Occam, arrives at a Benedictine abbey in northern Italy, accompanied by his young Benedictine scribe, Adso of Melk. William had been assigned the difficult task of arranging a meeting between representatives of Pope John XXII and the leader of the Franciscans, Michael of Cesena, at a time of great religious, political, social, and economic upheaval. The pope held the entire Franciscan order responsible for the extremist position on poverty held by its most radical members. The emperor supported the Franciscans, an odd alliance until one realized his motive: to weaken the pope's power. The Benedictines also supported the Franciscans, but for a very different reason: They feared that a strong centralized Church, especially one located in Avignon, would undermine the spiritual and economic control that individual monasteries had long exerted over surrounding areas.

When William arrives, he is informed by the abbot of a recent event that, although not directly related to William's mission, could threaten both its success and the abbot's sovereignty. The body of a young and handsome monk, a master illustrator named Adelmo, had been found earlier that day. The abbot charged William with clearing up the mystery surrounding Adelmo's death—whether it was murder or suicide—before the arrival of the papal legation. Although allowed considerable latitude in conducting the investigation, William is barred from entering the monastery's great library located on the Aedificium's top floor. The prohibition only piques William's interest, especially when the body of another monk connected with the library, the Greek scholar Venantius, is found head down in a great jar filled with pigs' blood the very next day. The old monk Alinardo sees in the two deaths signs of the apocalypse announced in the book of Revelations. William does not believe that the end is near, but he does believe that the book of Revelations has something to do with the deaths. As a result, he becomes even more determined to penetrate the mysteries of the forbidden, labyrinthine library.

Adso finds his naïve faith just as challenged as William's wits, first by his master's revelations, then by his own curiosity. The abbey, he learns, is not a world apart from, but a microcosm of, the secular world outside its walls. Divine order and absolute truth give way to human-made, relativistic pronouncements and interpretations. Adso proves only slightly better at resisting these seeming snares than he does the sexual advances of the young woman he comes upon in the kitchen one night after becoming separated from William during one of their forays into the library. After first trans-

mogrifying her into the whore of Babylon, Adso's fevered, book-bound imagination transforms her into the beauty extolled in the Song of Songs.

Adso's postcoital reverie is cut short by the discovery of a third corpse—the second with mysteriously blackened fingers—and the arrival of the papal legation led by the infamous inquisitor Bernard Gui. In the world according to Gui, a man more inquisitorial than inquisitive, all is clear, despite the fog that has descended on the abbey. The girl is not an impoverished peasant but a witch; Remigio is not a lustful cellarer who has his assistant, the grotesque and babbling Salvatore, procure village girls willing to exchange their virtue for bits of meat, but a heretic and the murderer of all four monks, the herbalist Arvenius being his most recent victim. The death of a fifth monk, the illiterate librarian Malachi, provides the most visible proof of the inadequacy of the inquisitor's theory. Much to Adso's dismay, it does not prove the girl's innocence; she is, William claims, "dead meat" whom Adso would do well to forget.

Adso does not save the girl, but he does save the day with the chance remark that provides William with the clue he needs to solve yet another of the library's mysteries. Once again, however, solving a mystery does not save a life, that of the abbot sealed in a secret stairway leading to the library. This William learns when he finally reaches the library's Finis Africae and confronts his nemesis, the blind monk Jorge de Burgos, mastermind of the murders, although not technically a murderer. Just as William suspects, all the victims died for lust: in some cases sexual, in others intellectual. Most died by their own hand, three of them literally so, wetting their fingers before turning the fatal book's poisoned pages. This was the book that Jorge was determined no one else should ever read, the one hidden away in the library's labyrinthine recesses. It was bound with a number of other very different manuscripts, each in a different language: the manuscript

> in Greek, made perhaps by an Arab or by a Spaniard, that you found when, as assistant to Paul of Rimini, you arranged to be sent back to your country to collect the finest manuscripts of the apocalypse in Leon and Castile.

It was not a manuscript that deals with the Apocalypse, but one that Jorge fears would bring about a more catastrophic end than the one foretold in the book of Revelations.

Although his lust for books prevents him from destroying it, Jorge greatly feared the consequences should this "second book of the *Poetics* of Aristotle, the book everyone has believed lost or never written, and of which you hold perhaps the only copy," become known. Jorge believes that Aristotle had, through Thomas Aquinas's writings, already undermined the Church's teachings and authority. What he fears even more is the manuscript's elevating comedy to the level of art, thus giving it a power far greater than the heresies and carnival inversions whose subversive potential the Church could control. In a final act of defiance—at once horrific, childish, and comic—Jorge destroys the manuscript and himself by eating its poisoned pages and then accidentally starting the fire that destroys first the library and then the entire abbey: endgame becomes Armageddon in the tale's fiery conclusion.

Critical Evaluation:

The Name of the Rose is that rarest of books: a work that manages to be enjoyable without being escapist, an international best seller that crosses literary borders as readily as it does national ones, offering something for all its readers and most for those willing to appreciate the playful plural of this inviting yet intricate novelistic labyrinth. Part of its appeal stems from the fullness with which Umberto Eco depicts his medieval world, a world already made appealing by Barbara Tuchman's *A Distant Mirror* (1978) and films such as *Excalibur* (1981).

The Name of the Rose is not merely a historical novel with gothic shadings. It is also, and more obviously, a detective story (according to Eco, "the most metaphysical and philosophical" kind of plot), although in a parodic, metafictional, postmodern key. As indebted to the great Argentinean writer and national librarian Jorge Luis Borges as to Sherlock Holmes's creator Arthur Conan Doyle, the novel presents "a mystery in which very little is discovered and the detective is defeated."

The novel's impure form constitutes a virtual library of literary echoes, ranging from whole genres to specific authors and works, a towering babel of intertextualized voices in the form of a seamless story, a celebration of narrative on one hand, a work not without political and pedagogical import on the other. Among its many pleasures is the way the novel, like the essays in Eco's *Travels in Hyper Reality* (1986), makes the subject of Eco's scholarly writings, semiotics, accessible to a nonacademic audience. *The Name of the Rose* is not, however, merely a medieval exemplum or detective story dressed up as a *roman à these*. Eco's novel is "a machine for generating meanings," a narrative version of the monastery's labyrinthine library in which one finds the "maximum of confusion achieved with the maximum of order," but a confusion intended to seduce, not repel. In this

sense, the novel resembles the rose that figures so prominently in the novel's first words, the title, and its last, where its meaning is both declared and disguised in the unattributed line from Bernard de Cluny's *De contemptu mundi* (c. 1140; on contempt for the world): "Stat rosa pristina nomine, nomina nuda tenemus" ("Yesterday's rose endures in its name, we hold empty names"). As Eco explains in his postscript, as a symbol, the rose is so full of meanings as to be virtually empty of meaning—a floating signifier.

Such a novel might have proved—like the numerous passages in Latin—too daunting for most readers were it not for Eco's decision "to make everything understood through the words of one who understood nothing." In this way, the reader experiences the shock of the new in much the same way the befuddled Adso does. Because Adso is everything the erudite and ironic William of Baskerville is not—young, naïve, literal-minded, faithful, obedient, credulous—the reader is also allowed, or encouraged, to feel superior to William's scribe and disciple. In this way, the reader comes to experience some of the same doubleness of vision as Adso the eighty-year-old narrator does in trying to reconstruct himself and his world as they existed in 1327 when he was a differently befuddled eighteen-year-old novice.

A similar dualism is at work, and at play, in the novel's overall structure. Adso's manuscript is divided into seven days, or chapters, each chronicling that day's events and subdivided according to the eight canonical hours (matins, lauds, and so on). The structure is apt and easy to follow, but it is also arbitrary. It organizes time and narrative space and orients the reader, but it also serves as a sign of Adso's acceptance of the Benedictine rule and of a divinely ordered universe. The novel is further complicated—denaturalized, made enigmatic and therefore suspect—by the unnamed and, therefore, mysterious editor's untitled preface, dated January 5, 1980. Even as he or she explains how the manuscript came briefly into his possession, the editor's remarks cast doubt on both the authenticity of Adso's manuscript and the accuracy of the editor's translation. Thus, just as there are two worlds at the abbey—one daytime, one nighttime, with the latter being by far the more intriguing—so, too, does *The Name of the Rose* comprise a whole succession of stories, one inside another, each requiring a certain kind of sleuthing: there is the one Adso tells and then there are the stories of his telling and the editor's, to which Adso's narrative serves as a five-hundred-page postscript.

The "game of strange alliances" played out in 1327 infects the novel at every level. Absolute truths and univocal utterances give way to ambiguous relations, the meaning of which involves interpretive codes and contexts. "Books,"

William explains, "are not meant to be believed, but to be subjected to inquiry." Inquiry does not necessarily save or solve, however, as William admits when he finds Jorge at the center of the interpretive web: "There was no plot, and I discovered it by mistake," reaching the right destination by following a series of wrong guesses (abductions). Even in failure, though, there is a certain success of a decidedly humbling kind. As William says and as Eco's apocalyptic yet comic novel reveals, "Perhaps the mission of those who love mankind is to make people laugh at the truth, to make truth laugh, because the only truth lies in learning to free ourselves from insane passion for the truth."

Robert A. Morace

Further Reading

Bouchard, Norma, and Veronica Pravadelli, eds. *Umberto Eco's Alternative: The Politics of Culture and the Ambiguities of Interpretation.* New York: Peter Lang, 1998. Collection of essays analyzing Eco's fiction and scholarly works. "Desperately Seeking Satan: Witchcraft and Censorship in *The Name of the Rose*" discusses this novel.

Capozzi, Rocco, ed. *Reading Eco: An Anthology.* Bloomington: Indiana University Press, 1997. Essays by some of the top Eco scholars exploring his ideas about literary semiotics and analyzing how these concepts are expressed in both his fiction and scholarly writing. Includes three essays on *The Name of the Rose* by Teresa De Lauretis, David H. Richter, and Thomas Sebeok.

Coletti, Theresa. *Naming the Rose: Eco, Medieval Signs, and Modern Theory.* Ithaca, N.Y.: Cornell University Press, 1988. Discusses Eco's mingling of medieval and modern and what this means in the light of the novel's reception.

Eco, Umberto. *Postscript to "The Name of the Rose."* San Diego, Calif.: Harcourt Brace Jovanovich, 1984. In the spirit of Poe's "Philosophy of Composition," Eco discusses how the novel came to be written, not how it should be read.

Farronato, Cristina. *Eco's Chaosmos: From the Middle Ages to Postmodernity.* Buffalo, N.Y.: University of Toronto Press, 2003. Farranato examines the tension between cosmos and chaos, or "chaosmos," and the struggle for a composition of opposites in Eco's work, including *The Name of the Rose.*

Ford, Judy Ann. "Umberto Eco: *The Name of the Rose.*" In *The Detective as Historian: History and Art in Historical Crime Fiction,* edited by Ray B. Browne and Lawrence A. Kreiser, Jr. Bowling Green, Ohio: Bowling Green State University Popular Press, 2000. Eco's novel is included in this study of detective stories set in various eras of history.

Haft, Adele J., Jane G. White, and Robert J. White. *The Key to "The Name of the Rose."* Harrington Park, N.J.: Ampersand, 1987. A useful source that identifies the novel's literary references and provides translations of all non-English passages.

Inge, M. Thomas. *Naming the Rose: Essays on Eco's "The Name of the Rose."* Jackson: University Press of Mississippi, 1988. Ten essays with a foreword by Eco, a reader-response postscript, and a useful annotated checklist of English-language criticism.

Richter, David H. "Eco's Echoes: Semiotic Theory and Detective Practice in *The Name of the Rose.*" *Studies in Twentieth Century Literature* 10, no. 2 (Spring, 1986): 213-236. Densely detailed and finely argued discussion of the relation between Eco's parodic novel and semiotic theory.

Nana

Author: Émile Zola (1840-1902)
First published: 1880 (English translation, 1880)
Type of work: Novel
Type of plot: Naturalism
Time of plot: 1860's
Locale: Paris and rural France

Principal characters:
NANA, a beautiful courtesan
FAUCHERY, a dramatic critic
STEINER, a wealthy banker
GEORGE HUGON, a student
PHILIPPE HUGON, his brother and an officer
FONTAN, an actor
COUNT MUFFAT DE BEUVILLE
SABINE, his wife
MARQUIS DE CHOUARD and COUNT XAVIER DE
VANDEUVRES, well-known figures of the Parisian world
of art and fashion

The Story:

Monsieur Fauchery, theatrical reviewer for a Paris paper, is attending the premiere of *The Blonde Venus* at the Variety Theatre because he had heard rumors of Nana, the Venus of the new play. Paris's smart set is well represented at the theater that night, and Fauchery and his cousin Hector de la Faloise note a few of the more interesting people. In the audience are Steiner, a crooked but very rich banker who is the current lover of Rose Mignon, an actor in *The Blonde Venus*; Mignon, who serves as procurer for his own wife; Daguenet, a reckless spender reputed to be Nana's lover for the moment; Count Xavier de Vandeuvres; Count Muffat de Beuville and his wife; and several of the city's well-known courtesans.

The play, a vulgar travesty on the life of the Olympian gods, is becoming boring until Nana finally appears; with beautiful golden hair floating over her shoulders, she walks confidently toward the footlights for her feature song. When she begins to sing, she seems such a crude amateur that murmurs and hisses begin to sound. Suddenly a young student exclaims loudly that Nana is stunning. Everyone laughs, including Nana. It was as though she frankly admitted that she had nothing except her voluptuous self to offer. Nana, however, knew this was sufficient for her audience. As she ends her song, she retires to the back of the stage amid a roar of applause. In the last act, Nana's body is veiled only by her golden locks and a transparent gauze. The house grows quiet and tense. Nana smiles confidently, knowing that she had conquered them with her flesh.

Thus Nana, product of the streets of Paris, starts her career as mistress of the city. To get money for her scrofulous little son, Louis, and for her own extravagant wants, she sells herself at varying prices to many men. She captivates Steiner,

the banker, at an all-night party after her initial success as Venus. He buys her a country place, La Mignotte, a league from Les Fondettes, home of Madame Hugon, whose seventeen-year-old son, George, was the one who called Nana stunning the opening night of *The Blonde Venus* and who had been enraptured with her at Nana's party. Nana, making no pretense of belonging exclusively to Steiner, invites a number of friends to visit her at La Mignotte.

Madame Hugon entertains Count Muffat, his wife, Sabine, and their daughter, Estelle, at her home in September. George, who had been expected several times during the summer, suddenly comes home. He had invited Fauchery and Daguenet for a visit. Mme Vandeuvres, who had promised for five years to come to Les Fondettes, was likewise expected. Mme Hugon is unaware of any connection between the coming of Nana to La Mignotte and the simultaneous visits of all of these men to Les Fondettes.

George escapes from his doting mother and leaves in the rain to Nana, who finds him soaking wet as she is gathering strawberries in her garden. While his clothes are drying, he dresses in some of Nana's clothes. Despite Nana's feeling that it is wrong to submit to such an innocent boy, she finally gives in to George's entreaties, and she is faithful to him for almost a week. Muffat, who had lived a circumspect life for forty years, becomes increasingly inflamed by passion as he pays nightly visits to Nana's place, only to be rebuffed each time. He talks with Steiner, who likewise was being put off by Nana with the excuse that she was not feeling well. Meanwhile Muffat's wife attracts the attention of Fauchery, the journalist.

Eleven of Nana's Parisian friends arrive in a group at La Mignotte. George is seen with Nana and her friends by his mother, who later makes him promise not to visit the actor, a promise he has no intention of keeping. His brother, Philippe, an army officer, threatens to bring him back by his ears if he has anything more to do with Nana.

Being true to George is romantically pleasing, but financially it is unwise, and Nana at last gives herself to the persistent Muffat the night before she returns to Paris to see if she can recapture the public that had acclaimed her in *The Blonde Venus*.

Three months later, Muffat, who has taken the place of castoff George, is having financial troubles. During a quarrel with Nana he learns from Nana that his wife, Sabine, and Fauchery are making a cuckold of him. Nana, by turns irritated or bored by Muffat and then sorry for him, chooses this means of avenging herself on Fauchery, who had written a scurrilous article about Nana.

Having now broken with Muffat and Steiner, Nana gives up her place in the Boulevard Haussmann and lives with the actor Fontan. Fontan, however, becomes increasingly difficult and even vicious, beating her night after night and taking all of her money. Nana returns to her old profession of streetwalking to pick up a few francs. After a close brush with the police, Nana grows more discreet. She leaves the brutal Fontan and seeks a part as a grand lady in a new play at the Variety Theatre. Given the part, she fails miserably in it; but she begins to play the lady in real life in a richly decorated house that Muffat purchases for her. Despite Nana's callous treatment of him, Muffat can not stay away from her.

In her mansion in the Avenue de Villiers, Nana squanders money in great sums. Finding Muffat's gifts insufficient, she adds Count Xavier de Vandeuvres as a lover. She plans to get eight or ten thousand francs a month from him for pocket money. George Hugon reappears, but he is less interesting than he had once been. When Philippe Hugon tries to extricate his young brother from Nana's net, he also gets caught. Nana grows bored. From the streets one day she picks up the prostitute Satin, who becomes her vice.

In a race for the Grand Prize of Paris at Longchamps, Nana wins two thousand louis on a horse named for her, but de Vandeuvres, who owns the filly Nana as well as the favorite Lusignan, loses everything through some crooked betting. He sets fire to his stable and dies with his horses.

Muffat finds Nana in George's arms one evening in September; from that time on, he ceases to believe in her sworn fidelity. He becomes more and more her abject slave, submitting meekly when Nana forces him to play woolly bear, horse, and dog with her and then mocks his ridiculous nudity. Muffat is further degraded when he discovers Nana in bed with his father-in-law, the ancient Marquis de Chouard.

George, jealous of his brother Philippe, stabs himself in Nana's bedroom when she refuses to marry him. He dies of his self-inflicted wound, and Nana is briefly sorry for him. Nana also breaks Philippe. He is imprisoned for stealing army funds to spend on her.

Nana thrives on those she destroys. Fate catches up with her at last. Visiting her dying son after his long absence and many conquests in foreign lands, she gets smallpox from him and dies a horrible death in a Paris hospital. The once-beautiful body that had destroyed so many men lay a rotting ruin in a deserted room; outside were the sounds of the French battle cry. The Franco-Prussian War of 1870 had begun.

Critical Evaluation:

Émile Zola's Rougon-Macquart series (1871-1893), including *Nana*, ran to an aggregate of twenty novels, exploring the naturalistic philosophy of literature. This philosophy was strongly influenced by the scientific method outlined in Claude Bernard's *Introduction a l'étude de la médecine expérimentale* (1865; *An Introduction to the Study of Experimental Medicine*, 1927). Zola himself explained the relationship between science and literature in his theoretical works: *Le Roman expérimental* (1880; *The Experimental Novel*, 1893; a direct application of Bernard's principle to literature), *Les Romanciers naturalistes* (1881; *The Naturalist Novel*, 1964), and *Le Naturalisme au théâtre* (1881; *Naturalism on the Stage*, 1893). According to Zola, naturalism combines scientific determinism, pessimistic and mechanistic views of human behavior, pathological assumptions about human motivation, and a predilection for examining the life of the lower socioeconomic classes. Thus, Zola's Rougon-Macquart series, designed after the model of Honoré de Balzac's seventeen-volume *La Comédie humaine* (1829-1848; *The Human Comedy*, 1895-1896, 1911), seeks to portray the society of the Second Empire by "scientifically" describing conditions of life.

Zola, however, did not recognize that hereditary (biological) determinants cannot rationalize behavior. His attempt to trace through twenty novels a family epic of neuroses and alcoholism was therefore less than successful. Nevertheless, it did produce some memorable character studies—among them, *Nana*—in the multifaceted collection of one-thousand-odd characters who appear in the series, depicting various social classes, circumstances, and places that Zola knew well.

Indeed, so attentive is Zola to naturalism's scientific principles that he paints in words as vivid a portrait of Nana as could be painted by the most adept realists. Of course, attention to detail as well as to psychological motivation is paramount in the naturalistic canon. Just as scientific experiments require exacting attention to statistical data, so also do naturalistic novels demand factual accounting. Thus, *Nana* satisfies its philosophical imperatives by providing such meticulous details as would be necessary for a laboratory report. These details evolve not only from the physical description of Nana herself but also from the development of the plot. Each twist and turn in Nana's life and fortune, for example, is as carefully documented as a research paper. No phenomenon is left unexplained. Zola's approach to *Nana*—novel and character—is that of a scientist who leaves no possibility unexplored. Hence, in *Nana*, the protagonist is fully explored, fully psychologized.

While Nana is being thoroughly explored, Zola also develops the theme of the novel. He presents in the novel an unrelenting account of a fashionable but decadent society. In much the same manner as a twentieth century commentator on the jet-set phenomenon, Zola chronicles the debaucheries of mid-nineteenth century Paris. Money, power, and sex dominate French society, according to Zola: Money buys power, and power gets sex. Thus the central characters, obsessed with the power of money, buy and sell themselves and one another with kaleidoscopic turnover. Monsieur Mignon pimps for his wife; Madame Hugon, wittingly or unwittingly, sets up her son, George, for seduction by Nana; Nana herself accumulates an incredible number of lovers from Daguenet to Steiner to George Hugon to Count Muffat to Fontan to Count Xavier de Vandeuvres to Philippe Hugon to Satin to the Marquis de Chouard. The moral rot endemic in all of these people reaches its culmination in Nana's literal and symbolic contracting of smallpox from her neglected son.

Zola lays bare the political, social, and ethical bankruptcy of the Second Empire. He does it through plot development and characterization. Nana's sequential—and sometimes simultaneous—liaisons constitute the thread of plot development. Her fortunes depend not upon her theatrical talents but upon her contacts with monied men who can keep her in style. Her only errors are those that involve sentiment rather than cold analysis and rational evaluation of her prospects for survival. Plot development reveals the theme of the novel as a study in how the economically disadvantaged cope with an inherently inequitable system. Zola's implication is that they do it tenuously and insecurely. For in his characterization of Nana, Zola depicts a woman who is utterly insecure. Nana has no solid resources of her own other than her gorgeous body. She is vulgar; she is cheap; she is sordid. She is all of these degraded things because she has no confidence in her own worth as a human being. Hence, in her view, and in society's view, once she has lost her attractiveness to the debilities of disease, she is worthless.

Still, for all of Zola's professed adherence to naturalistic principles, his work has been judged at its artistic best precisely where he lapses from his systematic method into the natural rhythms of a novelist. The kernel of truth in this judgment certainly applies to *Nana*. Although the protagonist is most often described in great detail, she appears in the mind's eye of the reader at her seductive best when she is limned in only a few bold strokes. Likewise, the inexorable logic of the sordid and predominantly deterministic plot is occasionally softened, and not a little enhanced, by such tender scenes as Nana's meeting with George in the rain-drenched strawberry patch.

Similarly, Zola's dispassionately analytical language is brightened from time to time with passages of near-poetic prose. Above all, the naturalistic dictum that all characters, including the protagonist, must represent types and not be extraordinary is belied by Nana herself, for Nana is nothing if not extraordinary—in her beauty, in her greed, in her vulgarity. Indeed, these contradictions, the unlikely combination of qualities, render her character atypical. Zola was quite distressed over his romantic tendencies, seeing them as flaws in the naturalistic scheme of things; however, he seemed blind to the flaws of naturalism systematically applied, especially its morbidity, its monotony, and its fundamental mediocrity. In the final analysis, however, Zola's genius as an artist stems from his inability to follow any one theory undeviatingly, and the best of *Nana* can be attributed to that characteristic.

"Critical Evaluation" by Joanna G. Kashdan

Further Reading

Baguley, David, ed. *Critical Essays on Émile Zola*. Boston: G. K. Hall, 1986. In "The Man-Eater," Roland Barthes discusses the symbolic movement of *Nana* and the novel's epic scope. He also lauds Zola's comprehensive treatment of the Second Empire. Includes bibliography.

Berg, William J., and Laurey K. Martin. *Émile Zola Revisited*. New York: Twayne, 1992. Focuses on the Rougon-Macquart series, using textual analysis and Zola's literary-scientific principles to analyze each of the twenty novels.

Brooks, Peter. "Zola's Combustion Chamber." In *Realist Vision*. New Haven, Conn.: Yale University Press, 2005. Zola's novels are among the works of literature and art that are examined in this study of the realist tradition in France and England during the nineteenth and twentieth centuries.

Brown, Frederick. *Zola: A Life*. New York: Farrar, Straus and Giroux, 1995. A detailed and extensive biography of Zola that discusses his fiction and the intellectual life of France, of which he was an important part. Shows how Zola's naturalism was developed out of the intellectual and political ferment of his time; argues that this naturalism was a highly studied and artificial approach to reality.

Gallois, William. *Zola: The History of Capitalism*. New York: Peter Lang, 2000. Interprets the Rougon-Macquart novels as a history of capitalism, drawing connections between Zola's novels and the work of economists and sociologists Karl Marx, Max Weber, and Émile Durkheim. Includes a bibliography and an index.

Grant, Elliott M. *Émile Zola*. New York: Twayne, 1966. Chapter 6 discusses one of Zola's prevalent themes, the destructiveness of love. Explores Zola's knowledge of the world of prostitutes and Nana's symbolic significance. Includes chronology, notes, and bibliography.

Knapp, Bettina L. *Émile Zola*. New York: Frederick Ungar, 1980. Chapter 4 discusses the role of prostitutes and coquettes in the Second Empire and Zola's handling of them as symbolic characters. Includes chronology, notes, and bibliography.

Nelson, Brian, ed. *The Cambridge Companion to Émile Zola*. New York: Cambridge University Press, 2007. Collection of essays, including discussions of Zola and the nineteenth century; his depiction of society, sex, and gender; and "*Nana*: The World, the Flesh, and the Devil" by Valerie Minogue. Includes a summary of Zola's novels, a family tree of the Rougon-Macquarts, a bibliography, and an index.

Richardson, Joanna. *Zola*. New York: St. Martin's Press, 1978. Chapter 16 discusses the conditions under which Zola wrote *Nana* and the reception of the novel. Analyzes Nana's character and Zola's rich evocation of society. Includes notes and bibliography.

Walker, Philip. *Zola*. London: Routledge & Kegan Paul, 1985. Chapter 4, "First Great Triumphs," explores *Nana*'s impact on the public, its analysis of society's susceptibility to corruption, Zola's painstaking efforts to make his scenes real and accurate, and Nana's symbolic presence.

The Napoleon of Notting Hill

Author: G. K. Chesterton (1874-1936)
First published: 1904
Type of work: Novel
Type of plot: Fantasy
Time of plot: 1984-2014
Locale: London

Principal characters:
ADAM WAYNE, provost of Notting Hill
AUBERON QUIN, king of England
JAMES BARKER, provost of South Kensington
RED BUCK, provost of North Kensington

The Story:

Walking to work on a wintry day in 1984, powerful bureaucrat James Barker, idler Wilfred Lambert, and prankster Auberon Quin meet the exiled president of Nicaragua, a country that has been swallowed up by more powerful nations. Despite the Nicaraguan's argument that imperialists annihilate the customs of the conquered, Barker defends imperialism, insisting on the superiority of English civilization, which has evolved from democracy to despotism. He explains that the country needs neither a parliament nor a king; the latter, whose duty is simply to sign papers, is now chosen through a rotation system. The Nicaraguan, appalled by Barker's words, dies three days later. Quin, meanwhile, is stirred by the Nicaraguan's patriotism.

Quin, to Barker's horror, is named king. Unlike Barker, he realizes that London's people are sunk in a deadening, joyless routine. He mingles among common people to determine their needs. A child named Adam Wayne attacks him with a toy sword, and Quin, amused by this childish imitation of knighthood, decides, as a joke, to revive medievalism. He issues a Great Proclamation of the Charter of Free Cities. Suburbs become cities, each with a city wall, a guard, banners, official colors, and coats of arms. Their provosts are selected by a rotation system. Quin happily assigns the cities their official colors, garb, guards, heralds, and trumpeters.

The selected provosts, who include Barker and Red Buck, conspire to create, through bribery, purchase, and bullying, a road that will destroy five old stores on Pump Street in Notting Hill. Ten years later, negotiations for the road encounter an obstacle in Adam Wayne, who has become the provost of Notting Hill. Objecting to the destruction of the shops, he vows to preserve his city. The other provosts appeal to the king. Barker regards Wayne as a madman, since any sane man would accept the provosts' financial offers. Having tried unsuccessfully to convince the king to force sale of the Notting Hill property or to have Wayne certified as insane, the provosts prepare for war. Quin notes that the provosts, obsessed with money, power, and respectability, are as mad as Wayne, but Quin is stunned that his joke has inspired Wayne's passion and patriotism. He sadly expects Wayne to lose the war.

Wayne finds it difficult to inspire others to his cause. Notting Hill's merchants conduct their transactions without interest or joy; Wayne cannot break through their torpor, until he reaches Mr. Turnbull. Turnbull is the proprietor of a toy or curiosity shop, a collector of toy soldiers, and a student of military history. While Buck is assuring the others on his side that their victory is certain—because battle, like everything else, is a matter of numbers—Turnbull becomes Wayne's military strategist. From their Pump Street headquarters, Turnbull sends forty London boys for hansom cab rides. The boys bring the cabs to Turnbull; the horses, once properly fed, become cavalry horses, the cabs become barricades, and their drivers, soldiers.

Thanks to Turnbull's genius, Wayne's army defeats a far larger force. Still convinced that greater numbers inevitably win, Buck insists that the battle resume at night under the illumination of gaslights. Wayne's forces cut off the gas, leaving their enemies to fight one another in the dark. Wayne's opponents regroup. With an enormous army, they are certain of victory, until Wayne announces his capture of a water tower. Unless his enemies surrender, he will release the water and they will drown. His victory is complete.

Twenty years later, Notting Hill's council has become imperialistic, and Wayne anticipates their inevitable defeat because their cause is unjust. Quin and Wayne survive. Quin admits he began the whole thing as a joke. Wayne explains that they need each other: Quin needs Wayne's seriousness, and Wayne needs Quin's humor. They are, Wayne says, two halves of the same brain. They go off together.

Critical Evaluation:

G. K. Chesterton was a well-known journalist and essayist when his first novel, *The Napoleon of Notting Hill*, appeared. He had formed firm opinions on important issues of the day, and he used the novel to attack the popular nine-

teenth and twentieth century notion that evolution is synonymous with material and technological progress. He sought to oppose imperialism and social theorists and, more subtly, to define creativity and the vital social role of the artist. In doing this, as Stephen R. L. Clark has shown, Chesterton established many of the ideas on which later science-fiction, utopian, and dystopian writers would base their work.

Unlike most of his contemporaries, Chesterton denied that the future was knowable. In an introduction to the novel, he directly attacked such social theorists as playwright and pamphleteer George Bernard Shaw, whose Fabian socialism anticipated a world run by bureaucrats, and novelist H. G. Wells, who envisioned a world run by scientists. Chesterton posited that change happens through evolution, not revolution; thus, at any given time, the present contains elements of the past that have not yet, and may never be, evolved away, as well as elements of the future that are struggling to be born. The future, to Chesterton, is a fertile field for fantasy; what happens rests on the wills of men, not on the ideas of theorists. In creating a novel as a vehicle for his ideas, he implicitly opposed the Utopian socialist novelists of his age, Edward Bellamy (*Looking Backward, 2000-1887*, 1883) and William Morris (*News from Nowhere*, 1890). Chesterton believed that humans prefer a world of risk and challenge to the socialists' world of stasis and security.

In Chesterton's 1984, the bureaucrat-controlled suburbs have evolved into a world of stultifying monotony for the common man. (No women appear in the novel.) Twice, Chesterton states that England in 1984 has not changed significantly since 1904. His contemporaries would have smiled at the changes he regarded as insignificant, but later readers, taking Chesterton's words seriously, may conceive a skewed view of life in 1904. Supposedly unnecessary institutions that have disappeared include Parliament and the hereditary monarchy. Few police are needed, suggesting that London's headline-making social problems have not spread to the suburbs, have evolved away, or have disappeared as a result of the passivity of the city's inhabitants. Much technology has vanished. Chesterton's characters generally walk or ride in horse-drawn cabs, although by 1904 automobiles had appeared on London's streets. Warfare is waged with hand-to-hand weapons such as battle-axes and swords, not guns. London is illumined by gaslight, although in 1904 electrification was spreading. Chesterton again indicates that no one can predict the future and that, for him, people and ideas, not mere inventions, are important.

Greed, however, is not dead in Chesterton's future, and the author associates greed with imperialism. Theorists, including Wells and Shaw, supported British imperialism. Always insistent on the rights of common people, Chesterton opposed the expansion of the British or any other empire: It was his opposition to the recently ended Boer War (1899-1902) that inspired him to write the novel. The road that provosts propose to drive through Notting Hill resembles the railroad that earlier imperialist Cecil Rhodes proposed to drive through African territory populated by Boers (Dutch settlers and their descendants) as an excuse to acquire Boer land. Imperialism, Chesterton argues in this novel, is a false and immoral cause. When Notting Hill is victim, it outwits its oppressors. When it becomes imperialistic, it fails, as it should. Again, in this novel, people and their traditions remain of primary importance, as does the need for joy and beauty.

The novel's two principal characters are Auberon Quin and Adam Wayne. Not all of Chesterton's characters have significant names, but the name "Auberon" is evocative of the magical fairy king Oberon from William Shakespeare's comedy *A Midsummer Night's Dream* (pr. c. 1595-1596, pb. 1600), and, in fact, Auberon is described as the godson of a fairy king. Quin's last name suggests Harlequin, a mischievous British pantomime character derived from the Italian *commedia dell'arte* character Arlecchino. Adam is the biblical figure in the Garden of Eden; Wayne may derive from "wain" (vehicle) or "way."

Both men are artists and published poets. Wayne's *Hymns on the Hill* celebrates the beauty of London and is unsuccessful; it has substance, but not style. Quin's own elaborately styled verses about London are published under the pen name Daisy Daydream; Quin has style, but not substance. As he reinvents medievalism, Quin finds pleasure in designing uniforms, coats-of-arms, and official colors, but Wayne alone is comfortable in these. Under Wayne's government, merchants' shops and attire take on great beauty. Chesterton's contemporaries immediately identified Quin's physical appearance with that of essayist and caricaturist Max Beerbohm, but Quin actually is associated with the entire turn-of-the-century aesthetic, or decadent art movement, which, to Chesterton, entailed a self-centered, often hedonistic, boredom and pessimism. Quin himself is bored and must learn that, contrary to aesthetic creeds, art is neither superior to life nor detached from it.

In stirring Londoners, Quin stirs himself. Excited by battle, he becomes a newspaperman criticizing the king (himself) and a colonel in a regiment he has created, the First Decadents Green. As Wayne's passion makes Quin's pseudo-medievalism real, Quin's revival of medievalism points to another kind of decadence. Chesterton, much influenced by the chivalric romances of Sir Walter Scott, considered the concepts of chivalry and honor to be highly important, but, by his day, chivalry had decayed into an excuse for lavish aristocratic entertainments, a sentimental subject for poets and painters, or a romantic justification of imperialism. Chivalry reassumes its original power when Wayne fanatically defends Notting Hill. Wayne's passion, in turn, has the power to inspire others, turning Turnbull into a brilliant military strategist and Pump Street store windows into works of beauty. Even the idler Lambert dies as a military hero.

Wayne is opposed primarily by Barker and Buck, both of whom are limited by their rigidly constructed theories. They repeatedly illustrate Chesterton's point that men do what they want, not what theorists plan. Barker assumes that routinely appointed monarchs will simply sign papers given to them by bureaucrats; he is frustrated and angry, but helpless, when Quin chooses how to use the absolute power that has been given to him. Ten years later, Barker and Buck are again frustrated when Quin refuses either to confiscate Notting Hill property or to institutionalize Wayne. Wayne and Turnbull, imaginative men, repeatedly outwit Barker and Buck in battle, despite Barker and Buck's absolute conviction that victory invariably lies in numbers. Buck insists on fighting at night under the gaslights, not anticipating that someone might turn off the gas. Stubbornly, Buck and Barker respond to their opponents' superior tactics simply by amassing a greater force, which is again outwitted by Wayne's capture of the water tower.

Twenty years later, however, Notting Hill takes up a morally wrong, imperialistic, cause, intent on conquest, and it is defeated. As the now-mature Wayne tells Quin, however, he and Quin are unconquered but must accept the need for each other's strength. When Wayne describes them as two parts of the same brain, he is saying that his own linear, dedicated thought must be balanced by Quin's humor and joyousness. Both halves are necessary to an artist. Artists, in turn, are necessary for the world. Common people know the need for love and laughter, although arid intellectuals and theorists may not understand this need. In so saying, Chesterton is defining his own role as creator, and, as he suggests in such later works as *The Victorian Age in Literature* (1913), he is defining the qualities vital to true creativity. Thus, Wayne and Quin must go off into the world together.

Betty Richardson

Further Reading

Barker, Dudley. *G. K. Chesterton.* New York: Stein & Day, 1973. Brief biography that is primarily concerned with Chesterton's early years and fiction.

Clark, Stephen R. L. *G. K. Chesterton: Thinking Backward, Looking Forward.* Philadelphia: Templeton Foundation Press, 2006. Places *The Napoleon of Notting Hill* within the context of futuristic science fiction, studying Chesterton's individual novels and the themes he introduced for later writers.

Coren, Michael. *Gilbert: The Man Who Was Chesterton.* New York: Paragon House, 1990. Examines Chesterton's early years and influences, as well as *The Napoleon of Notting Hill.*

Dale, Alzina Stone. *The Outline of Sanity: A Biography of G. K. Chesterton.* 1982. Reprint: Lincoln, Nebr.: Authors Guild Backinprint.com, 2005. Provides a detailed examination of Chesterton's objections to the Boer War and imperialism.

Gardner, Martin. *The Fantastic Fiction of Gilbert Chesterton.* Shelburne, Ont.: George A. Vanderburgh, 2008. Includes Gardner's valuable introduction to the 1991 Dover Press edition of *The Napoleon of Notting Hill*, as well

as an essay originally published in the May 10, 1991, issue of *Midwest Chesterton News.*

McCleary, Joseph R. *The Historical Imagination of G. K. Chesterton: Locality, Patriotism, and Nationalism.* New York: Routledge, 2009. Chapter 4 focuses on *The Napoleon of Notting Hill, The Man Who Was Thursday: A Nightmare* (1908), and *The Ball and the Cross* (1909) as expressing Chesterton's political and historical views.

Payne, Randall. Introduction to *The Autobiography of G. K. Chesterton.* San Francisco: Ignatius Press, 2006. The novel's setting is strongly influenced by the setting of Chesterton's childhood. Payne's annotations to Chesterton's autobiography make this work accessible to modern readers.

Pearce, Joseph. *Wisdom and Innocence: A Life of G. K. Chesterton.* San Francisco: Ignatius Press, 2004. Relates *The Napoleon of Notting Hill* to other Chesterton writings and includes comments by other writers and critics.

The Narrative of Arthur Gordon Pym

Author: Edgar Allan Poe (1809-1849)
First published: 1838
Type of work: Novel
Type of plot: Adventure
Time of plot: Early nineteenth century
Locale: High seas

Principal characters:
ARTHUR GORDON PYM, an adventurer
AUGUSTUS BARNARD, his friend
DIRK PETERS, a sailor

The Story:

Arthur Gordon Pym was born the son of a respectable trader in Nantucket. While still young, he attends an academy and there meets Augustus Barnard, the son of a sea captain, and the two become close friends. One night after a party, Augustus wakes Pym from his sleep, and together they set off for the harbor. There, Augustus takes charge of a small boat, and they head out to sea.

Before long, Pym, seeing that his companion is unconscious, realizes the sad truth of the escapade. Augustus is drunk and, now in the cold weather, is lapsing into insensibility. As a result, their boat is run down by a whaler, and the two narrowly escape with their lives. They are taken aboard the ship that had run them down and returned to port at Nantucket.

The two friends become even more intimate after this

escapade. Captain Barnard had been preparing to fit out the *Grampus*, an old sailing hulk, for a voyage on which Augustus was to accompany him. Against his father's wishes, Pym plans to sail with his friend. Since Captain Barnard would not willingly allow Pym to sail without his father's permission, the two boys decide to smuggle Pym aboard and hide him in the hold until the ship should be so far at sea that the Captain would not turn back.

At first, everything goes according to schedule. Pym is hidden below in a large box with a store of water and food to last him approximately four days. At the end of the fourth day, Pym finds that his way to the main deck is barred. His friend Augustus does not rescue him. He remains in that terrible state for several days, coming each day closer to starvation or death from thirst.

At last, Pym's dog, who had followed him aboard the ship, finds Pym. Tied to the dog's body is a paper containing a strange message concerning blood and a warning to Pym to keep silent if he values his life. Pym is sick from hunger and fever when Augustus at last appears. The story he tells is a terrible one. Shortly after the ship had put to sea, the crew mutinied, and Captain Barnard had been set adrift in a small boat. Some of the crew had been killed, and Augustus himself was a prisoner of the mutineers. Pym and Augustus locate a place of comparative safety where it is agreed that Pym should hide.

Pym now gives his attention to the cargo, which seems not to have been stowed in accordance with the rules for safety. Dirk Peters, a drunken mutineer, helps both Pym and Augustus and provides them with food.

When the ship runs into a storm, some of the mutineers are washed overboard. Augustus is once more given free run of the ship. Augustus, Pym, and Peters plan to overcome the other mutineers and take possession of the ship. To frighten the mutineers during a drunken brawl, Pym disguises himself to resemble a sailor recently killed. The three kill all the mutineers except a sailor named Parker. Meanwhile, a gale comes up, and in a few hours, the vessel is reduced to a hulk by the heavy seas. Because the ship's cargo is made up of empty oil casks, there is no possibility of its sinking from the violence of the heavy seas. When the storm abates, the four survivors find themselves weak and without food or the hope of securing stores from the flooded hold. One day, they sight a vessel, but as it draws near, those aboard the *Grampus* see that it is adrift and all of its passengers are dead.

Pym tries to go below by diving, but he brings up nothing of worth. His companions are beginning to go mad from strain and hunger. Pym revives them by immersing each of them in the water for awhile. As their agony increases, a ship comes near, but it veers away without coming to their rescue. In desperation, the men consider the possibility of eating one of their number. When they draw lots, Parker is chosen to be eaten. For four days, the other three live upon his flesh.

At last, they make their way into the stores and secure food. Rain falls, and the supply of fresh water, together with the food, restores their hope. Augustus, who had suffered an arm injury, dies. He is devoured by sharks as soon as his body is cast overboard.

A violent lurch of the ship throws Pym overboard, but he regains the ship with Peters's help just in time to be saved from sharks. The floating hulk having overturned at last, the two survivors feed upon barnacles. Finally, when they are nearly dead of thirst, a British ship comes to their rescue. It is the *Jane Guy* of Liverpool, bound on a sealing and trading voyage to the South Seas and Pacific. Peters and Pym begin to recover. Within two weeks, they are able to look back upon their horrible experiences with almost the same feeling with which one recollects terrible dreams.

The vessel stops at Christmas Harbor, where some seals and sea elephants are killed for their hides. The captain is anxious to sail his vessel into Antarctica on a voyage of exploration. The weather turns cold. There is an adventure with a huge bear, which Peters kills in time to save his companions. Scurvy afflicts the crew. Once the captain decides to turn northward, but later he foolishly takes the advice of Pym to continue on. They sail until they sight land and encounter some "savages" whom they take aboard.

The animals on the island are strange, and the water is of some peculiar composition that Pym cannot readily understand. The natives on that strange coast live in a state of complete savagery. Bartering begins. Before the landing party can depart, however, the sailors are trapped in what seems to be an earthquake, which shuts off their passage back to the shore. Only Pym and Peters escape, to learn that the natives had caused the tremendous landslide by pulling great boulders from the top of a towering cliff. The only white men left on the island, they face the problem of evading the natives, who are now preparing to attack the ship. Unable to warn their comrades, Pym and Peters can only watch helplessly while the natives board the *Jane Guy* and overcome the six white men who had remained aboard. The ship is almost demolished. The natives bring about their own destruction, however, for in exploring the ship they set off the ammunition, and the resulting explosion kills about one thousand of them.

In making their escape from the island, Pym and Peters discover ruins similar in form to those marking the site of Babylon. When they come upon two unguarded canoes, they take possession of one and push out to sea. Natives chase them but eventually give up the pursuit. They begin to grow listless and sleepy when their canoe enters a warm sea. Ashy material falls continually upon them. At last, the boat rushes rapidly into a cataract, and a human figure, much larger than any person and as white as snow, arises in the pathway of the doomed boat. So ends the journal of Arthur Gordon Pym.

Critical Evaluation:

The reception of Edgar Allan Poe's *The Narrative of Arthur Gordon Pym* after its publication was in no way an unqualified approval. On the contrary, its misreading was the general result. Literal-minded reviewers jumped immediately to the conclusion that the narrative amounted to a fraudulent attempt to bamboozle the unwary. That its author intended to parody the popular voyage literature of the time was not considered. Not all the reviews were hostile. In Great Britain, *The Narrative of Arthur Gordon Pym* went through two editions. It was generally treated as the report of an actual voyage. Therefore, it remained for the French to be the first to recognize *The Narrative of Arthur Gordon Pym* as an extraordinary romance of adventure and as an important work of art. In 1858, French poet Charles Baudelaire admired *The Narrative of Arthur Gordon Pym* enough to translate it.

Meanwhile, in the United States the work was neglected and practically forgotten, except for Henry James's praise, recorded in his great novel *The Golden Bowl* (1904), of *The Narrative of Arthur Gordon Pym* as "a wonderful tale" fondly remembered by Prince Amerigo. Not until 1950 was *The Narrative of Arthur Gordon Pym* to be taken seriously, when poet and critic W. H. Auden included the romance in his anthology *Edgar Allan Poe: Selected Prose, Poetry, and Eureka*. In his introduction, Auden declares *The Narrative of Arthur Gordon Pym* and *Eureka: A Prose Poem* (1848) to be among Poe's most important works.

Soon even academia woke from its sleep. Patrick F. Quinn, in 1952, emphasized that the narrative is structured by the pattern of deception and revolt. He also discussed the 1933 psychoanalytical interpretation of *The Narrative of Arthur Gordon Pym* by Marie Bonaparte, who saw its central meaning as "the passionate and frenzied search for the Mother." The philosopher Gaston Bachelard held that *The Narrative of Arthur Gordon Pym* derived "from the deepest psychological center of Edgar Poe." Bachelard termed *The Narrative of Arthur Gordon Pym* "one of the great books of the human heart." Edward Davidson viewed *The Narrative of Arthur Gordon Pym* as a philosophical narrative that shows nature to be deceptive, untrustworthy, and destructive. The plot is based on a quest to find the axis of reality on which the world turns. Everything is uncertain and an illusion; to find oneself is to lose one's self and to slip away into nothingness. According to Davis, "terror is the way to a knowledge of the world's primal unity." Quinn's and Davidson's essays proved the launching pads for the many future studies of *The Narrative of Arthur Gordon Pym* and its increasing importance in the Poe canon.

The Narrative of Arthur Gordon Pym reveals Poe's philosophy of the relation of the self to nature, to the world, and to the universe. It also depicts a psychic quest to discover the core of the self. The narrative structure has been explored, as have the narrative voices and their tones. The problematics of narrative unity, the use of enclosure, the truncated conclusion, and the use of satire, irony, and ways of deception have

also been studied. The ideas of the Freudian quest for the mother and of Jungian archetypes, of the roles of dream and wakefulness, of the conscious and the unconscious, of illusion and reality, and of empirical versus intuitive knowledge have been considered as well, in addition to the role of allegory and symbolism.

Some critics have been amazed to discover the way Poe calls attention to his textual and narrative space by questioning whether language can ever be clearly understood, whether human life is governed by uncertainty and chance, and whether nature and the universe are completely indifferent to human happiness and welfare. There has been much speculation about the meaning of the great white human figure that appears at the end of the tale, the role of the racial colors of white, black, and red, and whether writing is favored over speech.

"Critical Evaluation" by Richard P. Benton

Further Reading

Ackroyd, Peter. *Poe: A Life Cut Short*. London: Chatto & Windus, 2008. Ackroyd, a novelist, provides a concise chronicle of Poe's brief, unhappy life.

Eakin, Paul J. "Poe's Sense of an Ending." *American Literature* 45 (1973): 1-22. Examines the abortive ending relative to the whole and concludes that the narrative is complete.

Fisher, Benjamin F. *The Cambridge Introduction to Edgar Allan Poe*. New York: Cambridge University Press, 2008. Overview of Poe's literary career and writings. Describes how Poe's fiction advanced from gothic fantasy to more sophisticated explorations of human psychology. The references to *The Narrative of Arthur Gordon Pym* are listed in the index.

Harvey, Ronald C. *The Critical History of Edgar Allan Poe's "The Narrative of Arthur Gordon Pym": "A Dialogue with Unreason."* New York: Garland, 1998. Charts the complex critical response to the novel since its publication, demonstrating how the novel's theme and narrative have eluded most critics' understanding. Demonstrates how critics have disagreed over the novel's genre, author's intent, and whether the book is a work of a genius, a hack, or something in between. Includes an extensive bibliography of criticism of the novel published from 1838 through 1993.

Hayes, Kevin J., ed. *The Cambridge Companion to Edgar Allan Poe*. New York: Cambridge University Press, 2002. Collection of essays, including discussions of Poe's aesthetic theory, humor, feminine ideal, Poe and the gothic tradition, and Poe, sensationalism, and slavery. Geoffrey Sanborn's essay, "A Confused Beginning: *The Narrative of Arthur Gordon Pym, of Nantucket*," analyzes this work.

Irwin, John T. *American Hieroglyphics: The Symbol of the Egyptian Hieroglyphics in the American Renaissance*. Baltimore: Johns Hopkins University Press, 1980. Examines the relationships of writing, doubling, and the use of hieroglyphics, including a considerable examination of *The Narrative of Arthur Gordon Pym*. An outstanding study of its subject.

Kennedy, J. Gerald. *The Narrative of Arthur Gordon Pym: And the Abyss of Interpretation*. New York: Twayne, 1995. A reconsideration of the novel, analyzing it in the light of the political and racial unrest at the time of its publication. Examines critics' divided views of the novel.

_____. "Unreadable Books, Unspeakable Truths." In *Poe, Death, and the Life of Writing*. New Haven, Conn.: Yale University Press, 1987. Calls attention to the "self-consciousness" of the text regarding its indefiniteness and insufficiency of language.

Peirce, Carol, and Alexander G. Rose III. "The White Vision of Arthur Gordon Pym." In *Poe's Pym: Critical Explorations*, edited by Richard Kopley. Durham, N.C.: Duke University Press, 1992. Seeks to explain Poe's knowledge of Arthurian legend and the myth of the White Goddess.

Narrative of the Life of Frederick Douglass

Author: Frederick Douglass (1817?-1895)
First published: 1845
Type of work: Autobiography

There are about six thousand records in existence of slaves who either wrote their own stories or told them to others. Of these works, commonly known as slave narratives, Frederick Douglass's *Narrative of the Life of Frederick Douglass, an American Slave* is nearly universally considered to be the most compelling and well written. Douglass went on to write two more autobiographies, *My Bondage and My Freedom* (1855) and *Life and Times of Frederick Douglass, Written by Himself* (1881), to found several abolitionist magazines—most notably *North Star*—and to become the greatest African American orator and statesman of his age. However, he is primarily known for his first book, which he wrote before the age of thirty and despite the fact that he had never gone to school. Douglass's autobiography came to be one of the most frequently taught books at American colleges and universities, where together with *Moby Dick* (1851), *The Scarlet Letter* (1850), and *Uncle Tom's Cabin* (1851-1852) it was regarded as a seminal source for understanding the United States in the antebellum period of the nineteenth century.

Douglass's story began humbly. Douglass describes how, as a young boy growing up as a slave in Talbot County, Maryland, he never knew his age or the identity of his father. Slave owners did not consider it necessary to tell slaves such facts or to try to keep families together. His mother, Harriet Bailey, was separated from him when he was an infant. Douglass saw her only four or five times during his life, and then only at night when she paid surreptitious visits from the plantation twelve miles away where she was sold; she always had to leave before her young son woke up, and she died when Douglass was seven.

It is possible that the man who owned Douglass, Captain Anthony, was his father. Owners often took sexual advantage of their slave women, and as a boy, Douglass saw his master beat his Aunt Hester out of jealousy because a slave from a neighboring plantation paid attention to her. The pain slaves experienced from mistreatment and beatings often led them to sing songs with "words which to many would seem unmeaning jargon" but which conveyed the depths of their hardship. Such songs were their only outlet for expression.

Throughout his childhood on the plantation, Douglass (who did not then have a last name and was simply known as Frederick) witnessed many acts of cruelty, ranging from unjust beatings to unwarranted and unpunished murder of slaves by white owners or their overseers. As a child, he owned only one shirt, had to sleep on the ground, and ate his meals of corn mush from a common trough. It was his good fortune to be sent to Baltimore to the home of Hugh Auld, a relation of Captain Anthony. There, he not only enjoyed better living conditions but also was closer to the North. Had he not been sent to Baltimore, Douglass might never have escaped slavery.

In Baltimore, Mrs. Auld began to teach Douglass his *abc*'s. When Mr. Auld discovered this, he was furious, telling her that teaching a slave how to read was the quickest way to "spoil" him. Deciding that anything his master deemed bad must be good for him, Douglass became determined to teach himself to read. He devised a way to trick other little boys into inadvertently giving him lessons by pretending to know more than they did and making them prove otherwise.

By the age of twelve, Douglass could read essays from a book of famous speeches he acquired. Reading, however, showed him for the first time the true injustice of his own position. For the first time, he realized that there were people opposed to slavery and that there were compelling arguments against the practice. He resolved to run away as soon as he was old enough and the right opportunity presented itself.

Along with understanding the potential power inherent in the ability to read—nothing less than "the power of the white man to enslave the black man"—Douglass also began to understand his own condition by reading essays on liberty. The passages in which he describes his awakened understanding are among the most stirring in all of American literature. A succession of metaphors follows the description of his first reading experiences: Slavery is a "horrible pit" with "no ladder upon which to get out"; preferable to his own condition is that of "the meanest reptile." Perhaps no other work, fiction or nonfiction, so clearly demonstrates the effect of literacy in developing the associative powers of the thinking mind. Mr. Auld was, in a sense, correct when he says that learning to read and write would "spoil" a slave. Once Douglass developed a figurative capacity of language, he was forever unfit to serve slaveholders obediently. Everything in the world reminded him of the injustice of his own enslavement: "It looked from every star, it smiled in every calm, breathed in every wind, and moved in every storm."

Until he became old enough to escape, Douglass did his best to tolerate his condition. As a consequence of his small acts of rebellion, however, he was sent to a slave breaker, Mr. Covey, whose job it was to destroy the will of a slave and create an obedient worker and servant. During his first six months with Mr. Covey, Douglass was subjected to strict discipline and endless work. The slave breaker destroyed wills not just by working the slaves hard but by disorienting them and surrounding them with constant observation and deception. There were various ways in which Mr. Covey created an oppressive atmosphere, as when he told the slaves that he was leaving for town, only to return and spy on them. One day, Douglass fought back when Covey hit him; they fought for two hours, until both men were exhausted, but Douglass held his own. He resolved then that "however long I might remain a slave in form, the day had passed forever when I could be a slave in fact."

The first time he tried to escape, Douglass drew on his ability to write to forge protection papers for himself and several friends. They were caught and jailed, and Douglass was threatened with being sent to Alabama, from where escape was almost impossible. Instead, he was fortunately sent back to Baltimore, and it was determined that he should learn a trade. Douglass worked in a shipyard for one year and became a skilled caulker. When he contracted jobs on his own, earning six or seven dollars a week, he had to give the money to his master.

Douglass eventually escaped to the North. He did not provide details of his flight in the *Narrative of the Life of Frederick Douglass* because he did not wish to create additional obstacles for others who were trying to escape from slavery. He fled first to New York, from where he sent for the woman he planned to marry, a free black woman named Anna. Together, the couple moved to New Bedford, where they sought out the abolitionist Nathan Johnson, who advanced them money and helped them in other ways. Douglass changed his name to Johnson upon reaching New York, but because there were so many Johnsons in New Bedford, he accepted Nathan's suggestion that he call himself Frederick Douglass. In New Bedford, Douglass found white abolitionists as well as blacks who abhorred slavery and tried to protect one another from being sent back south.

Moved by the abolitionist cause, Douglass stood up to speak at an antislavery convention in Nantucket. At first, still feeling like a slave, he was abashed at the thought of speaking to white people, but the words soon came more easily. Douglass became an influential abolitionist himself, which eventually led to his writing the story of his life under slavery.

Those who read the book are astonished that such a document could be produced by a man with no formal education less than seven years after escaping from slavery. In Douglass's own time, this remarkable feat led to incredulity among his readership. All slave narratives were subject to charges of fraud from apologists for slavery, for which reason Douglass's book and others open with testament letters from respected white abolitionists. Many of those who heard Douglass speak and found him to be as forceful an orator as he was a writer found it difficult to credit that he was so lately a slave. In an era marked by P. T. Barnum's famous hoaxes, an era when even the best-intentioned Northern whites believed that African Americans were intellectually inferior to whites, Douglass faced skepticism on all sides. A strong motivation for publishing his story was to provide details of his life that could not be faked. When one early Southern detractor of the book claimed to have been acquainted with Douglass as a slave and to know that he was too uneducated to have written a book, Douglass replied by thanking him for substantiating the book's main claim, that he was indeed an American slave.

Douglass's accomplishments after escaping slavery fit well into the tradition of American self-sufficiency and success. By rising above the subjugating conditions of his early years, Douglass provided hope for others that through strength and self-reliance they, too, could achieve great things. His later autobiographies and writings testify to the persistence of prejudice as a limiting force on African Americans even after the end of institutionalized slavery, in the North as well as in the South. However, in the argument for the possibility of human achievement and for the liberty for all humans to pursue their potential, there is perhaps no more heroic example in American letters than Douglass provides in his *Narrative of the Life of Frederick Douglass*.

Ted Pelton

Further Reading

Andrews, William. *To Tell a Free Story: The First Century of Afro-American Autobiography, 1760-1865*. Normal: University of Illinois Press, 1986. A comprehensive account of slave narratives, which includes an extensive interpretation of Douglass's writings.

Gates, Henry Louis, Jr., ed. *The Classic Slave Narratives*. New York: Penguin Books, 1987. Contains narratives by Olaudah Equiano, Mary Prince, and Harriet Jacobs, in addition to that of Douglass, as well as an excellent short introduction to the form.

Hall, James C., ed. *Approaches to Teaching "Narrative of the Life of Frederick Douglass."* New York: Modern Language Association of America, 1999. In addition to suggesting approaches for teaching the *Narrative*, the book's essays provide historical and literary background to further understanding of the work as well as critical analyses of its rhetoric, the relationship of the *Narrative* to Douglass's oratory, the *Narrative* and nineteenth century American protest writing, and other aspects of the work.

Huggins, Nathan Irvin. *Slave and Citizen: The Life of Frederick Douglass*. Boston: Little, Brown, 1980. Offers a succinct and lucid biography for the general reader; Huggins is a good storyteller.

McFeely, William S. *Frederick Douglass*. New York: W. W. Norton, 1991. A comprehensive biography with an excellent bibliography. McFeely is particularly good in describing Douglass's relationship with family and friends.

O'Meally, Robert G. "Frederick Douglass' 1845 Narrative: The Text Was Meant to Be Preached." In *Afro-American Literature: The Reconstruction of Instruction*, edited by D. Fisher and R. Stepto. New York: Modern Language Association of America, 1979. Argues that the *Narrative* has recognizable affinities with the sermons of black preachers. The audience, according to O'Meally, is white, and "preacher" Douglass is exhorting them to end the abysmal institution of slavery.

Quarles, Benjamin. *Frederick Douglass*. New York: Atheneum, 1970. Presents an excellent first chapter that demonstrates how Douglass's years in slavery influenced his later life. The epigraphs that introduce each chapter, most of which are by Douglass, give a sense of the man and his age.

Starling, Marion Wilson. *The Slave Narrative: Its Place in History*. 1947. Reprint. Washington, D.C.: Howard University Press, 1988. The first book about the slave narrative as a form and a good introduction to its historical importance.

Sundquist, Eric L. *Frederick Douglass: New Literary and Historical Essays*. New York: Cambridge University Press, 1990. Scholarly interpretations of Douglass's life and writings, including analyses of the *Narrative*.

Waters, Carver Wendell. *Voice in the Slave Narratives of Olaudah Equiano, Frederick Douglass, and Solomon Northrup*. Lewiston, N.Y.: Edwin Mellen Press, 2002. A close reading of three slave narratives, examining the authors' use of language, symbolism, and personal experience to describe and attack slavery.

The Narrow Road to the Deep North

Author: Matsuo Bashō (1644-1694)
First published: Oku no hosomichi, 1694 (English
    translation, 1933)
Type of work: Diary and poetry

Matsuo Bashō, known as Bashō, combines his talents as a poet and essayist in the writing of the poetic diary, a form of literature that was prized highly during Bashō's time. Bashō, whose name is a nickname meaning "banana tree," had been called Kinsaku as a child and Matsuo Munefusa as an adult. When he first began writing poetry, he called himself Sobo, and later, for about eight years, he used the name Tosei.

Planted in the garden near one of Bashō's residences was a banana plant that had wide leaves, especially enjoyed by Bashō. When people sought directions to his house, they were told to go to the house with the banana tree; gradually Bashō came to be referred to as the "banana tree person." Around 1681, he took Bashō as his pen name. Changing names and taking pen names was not unusual in Japan at the time, especially for a person such as Bashō, who was of samurai, or feudal warrior, stock.

After Bashō moved to Edo, now Tokyo, he became a teacher of *haikai*, a special kind of poem that was at first something of a light-hearted diversion from the more serious *renga*, or linked verse. This type of poetry has an opening stanza composed by one person and is completed by another person, hence the name "linked verse." Largely because of Bashō's artistry, the *haikai* developed into a serious kind of poem. The word *haiku* developed from the *hokku*, or "starting verse" of a linked verse. A *haiku*, then, is an independent poem derived from the *haikai*; thus, the *haiku* is literally the *hokku* of a *haikai*. This miniature poem has seventeen syllables, which usually follow a pattern of three lines of five, seven, and five syllables, respectively, as in "a ya me ku sa (blue flag herbage, or iris)/ a shi ni mu su ba n (feet on bind)/ wa ra ji no o (straw sandals of cord)," which can be translated, without following the syllabic pattern, as "I will bind irises/ Around my feet/ Thongs for my sandals."

Bashō wanted to go beyond traditional *haikai* forms and find fresh ways of writing poetry. He thought that traveling would provide a means of broadening the scope of his life and his poetry, so he made four journeys between 1684 and 1689. These journeys can be considered spiritual pilgrimages as well as physical journeys to seek the ultimate of beauty.

The first journey, westward, began in the fall of 1684 and was completed in the summer of 1685. On returning, Bashō wrote the first of several travel diaries, *Norarashi kikō* (1687; *The Record of a Weather-Exposed Skeleton*, 1966). A second journey westward in 1687 resulted in two more diaries, *Oi no kobumi* (1709; *The Records of a Travel-Worn Satchel*, 1966) and *Sarashina kikō* (1704; *A Visit to Sarashina Village*, 1966). It was Bashō's third journey, his longest, that provided the material for *The Narrow Road to the Deep North*. This time, Bashō went northward into the least developed areas of Japan, the northern part of Japan's largest island, Honshu. The diary in its published form took about four years to complete, although it is only about thirty pages long in English translation.

The book's original title, *Oku no hosomichi*, has been translated several ways; it is difficult to express in English all that the word *oku* includes. On one hand, the name is that of an actual road that Bashō traveled; *oku* is also a short form for *Michi-no-Oku* (or *Michinoku*), generally translated as "the road's far recesses." *Michi-no-Oku* was a popular name for a region called Ōshu, or the "far provinces." Over and above the literal explanations of the word, it carries a sense of an "inner recess" or something "within oneself." Bashō was known for choosing titles that could be interpreted on more than one level, in this case, an actual journey as well as an inward search.

The Narrow Road to the Deep North traces Bashō's fifteen-hundred-mile route from Edo to Ogaki, describing activities and places he visits or stays during the 156-day trip. The diary is by no means just an ordinary travel journal with a few poems. Bashō sometimes changes actual facts about the trip—dates, itinerary, and the like—to improve the effect of the work as literature. The *haiku* interspersed with prose passages are some of his finest poems. The diary opens with a prologue that announces Bashō's yearning to travel and reminds the reader that life is a journey. The introduction ends, as many sections do, with a *haiku* that expresses his feeling about his departure.

As Bashō and his companion, Kawai Sora, make their way northward to the well-known temple and mountain at Nikko, and on to Kurobane, Bashō records in his prose commentary the noteworthy sights they visit. Much of the richness of both the prose and the poetry is realized because so many of the places the travelers visit are historical sites of which most Japanese have heard. It is characteristic of Japanese literature, especially of earlier works, to allude to places, sites, and people from ancient classical writing that Japanese people will recognize. The association with the earlier works makes the passage all the more meaningful and evocative of the glory of days long past.

Sometimes Bashō stops only briefly in a village after seeing some famous landmark; at other times he stays several days and visits friends or acquaintances in the area. His *haiku* are evoked by his reaction to or reflection on something associated with what he experiences. At Ashino, for example, going to see a famous willow tree provides his topic; a famous stone at Shinobu inspires another, as does the Tsubo Stone, so called because the dimensions of the stone are approximately three by six feet, or one *tsubo* in Japanese measurement of the day. It was near Ichikawa, where the Tsubo Stone was located, that Bashō found the road called Oku-no-hosomichi, which provided the diary's title.

As Bashō advances from one village to another, visiting castles, mountains, and other famous sites or simply noting the natural beauty of a place, he is often overcome with something of awe-inspiring beauty and writes a *haiku* on the spot. Some things had been more meaningful than others. At Hiraizumi, on approaching the ruins of the Castle-on-the-Heights, he finds the site now reduced to nothing more than an untended field of grass. Bashō thought of the days long past when the renowned Yoshitsune had fortified himself at this place, glory now reduced to wilderness of grass. He is reminded of a line in a classical Chinese poem by Tu Fu, an eighth century poet, which says, "Countries may fall, but their rivers and mountains remain." These reflections cause Bashō to sit at the site weeping, oblivious to the passing of time. These strong feelings brought forth one of his often-quoted *haiku*: "Natsugusa ya/ Tsuwamono domo ga/ Yume no ato" (The summer grasses/ Of brave soldiers' dreams/ The aftermath). Because the proper English punctuation is not clearly indicated in the Japanese version, some translations render the last two lines as a question: Are warrior's heroic deeds/ Only dreams that pass?

Moving on, Bashō continues to record his impressions, sometimes comparing or contrasting one with another. When he visits Matsushima, a group of many small islands, he is overcome with its beauty and declares that Matsushima is "the most beautiful place in all Japan!" Later, when he comes to the northernmost point of his journey, Kisakata, he records his visit to a famous lagoon, which he describes as having a "sense of desolate loneliness and sorrow of a tormented soul" that is, nevertheless, beautiful, like Matsushima.

Beginning the southwesterly descent from the northern country, Bashō passes through the Etchigo Province. At one point, near present-day Niigata, Sado Island is visible from the mainland, and Bashō writes several *haiku* that are among his best largely because they manifest *sabi*, a kind of loneliness in which the immensity and strength, or even indifference, of the universe is set in contrast to human finiteness and insignificance. A reader may experience the feeling of being overpowered or dissolved in the face of the infinite. One poem, in which there is no trace of humanity, but only an expression of the primitive universe, illustrates this concept: "Araumi ya/ Sado ni yokotau/ Amanogawa" (The rough sea/ Extending toward Sado Isle,/ The Milky Way). Sometimes *amanogawa* is translated more literally as "Heaven's River"; the effect, however, is that of the configuration of the stars in such an arrangement that they look something like a river flowing across the sky, forming what is called the Milky Way in English.

Sometimes Bashō makes associations with older poems in the Japanese tradition. On August 30, 1689, he reaches the castle town of Kanazawa and then makes his way to Daishoji and on to Maruoka. By this time, fall has arrived. His companion Sora becomes ill and returns to relatives in the Ise Province, but Bashō travels on after a student of *haiku* comes to accompany him the rest of the way, arriving in Ogaki around October 18. Bashō comments that, though he has not recovered from the fatigue of the journey, he does not want to miss going to the renowned Ise Shrine to see the ceremony of the Shinto deity being transferred to a newly built shrine, a special occasion that takes place only once every twenty-one years.

Soryū, a scholar-priest who helped prepare the final draft of Bashō's journal, writes a brief epilogue in which he tells readers, "At times you will find yourself rising up to applaud. At other times you will quietly hang your head with emotion." Bashō is said to have had more than two thousand students at the time of his death. There is no doubt about his reputation among his contemporaries and later Japanese poets. His work elevated the *haiku* into a mature art form. Because of the variety of his poems, he appealed to readers of various tastes. Some readers like his early witty verse; rural poets have preferred the later poems in a plainer style. The poet Issa is said to have emulated him as a diarist. In the twentieth century, Bashō was compared by some to England's William Wordsworth because of his seeking a mystic union with nature. Largely because of Bashō, there is an interest around the world in the *haiku* as a literary form.

Victoria Price

Further Reading

Bashō, Matsuo. *A Haiku Journey: Bashō's "Narrow Road to a Far Province."* Translated by Dorothy Britton. New York: Kodansha International, 2002. Especially valuable for the translator's introduction, which provides valuable insights into the *haiku* and into Bashō's poetic artistry.

Katō, Shūichi. *A History of Japanese Literature: From the Man'yoshu to Modern Times.* Translated and edited by Don Sanderson. New ed. 1979. Richmond, England: Curzon Press, 1997. In addition to placing Bashō in the context of Japanese literature, this treatment discusses Bashō's association with both the *haiku* and the poetic diary as a literary genre.

Kerkham, Eleanor, ed. *Matsuo Bashō's Poetic Spaces: Exploring Haikai Intersections.* New York: Palgrave Macmillan, 2006. Collection of essays examining Bashō's contributions to literature and philosophy. Some of the essays analyze his geographical imagination, his views of art and nature, and his influence on Japanese poets.

Qiu, Peipei. *Bashō and the Dao: The Zhuangzi and the Transformation of Haikai.* Honolulu: University of Hawaii Press, 2005. Describes how Bashō and other *haikai* poets in the seventeenth century adapted the *Zhuangzi* and other works of Daoist literature, eventually transforming *haikai* from comic verse to a form of high poetry.

Ueda, Makoto. *Literary and Art Theories in Japan.* 1967. New ed. Ann Arbor: Center for Japanese Studies, University of Michigan, 1991. Examines the literary theories of a number of writers. Bashō receives thorough discussion in the light of his contribution to the principles that govern the writing of *haiku.* Part of the Michigan Classics in Japanese Studies series.

_____. *Matsuo Bashō.* New ed. New York: Kodansha International, 1989. One of the most valuable books on Bashō, this work provides substantive discussion of his life and his literary development, as well as critical commentary and an evaluation of his place in literature.

Nathan the Wise

Author: Gotthold Ephraim Lessing (1729-1781)
First produced: Nathan der Weise, 1783; first published, 1779 (English translation, 1781)
Type of work: Drama
Type of plot: Philosophical
Time of plot: Twelfth century
Locale: Jerusalem

Principal characters:
NATHAN, a Jewish merchant
RECHA, his adopted daughter
SULTAN SALADIN, the son of the ruler of all the Saracens
SITTAH, his sister
CONRAD VON STAUFFEN, a Templar who was spared by the sultan
DAJA, a Christian woman and Recha's companion

The Story:

Nathan, a wealthy Jewish merchant, has just returned to Jerusalem from Babylon when Daja, the deeply prejudiced Christian companion to Nathan's adopted daughter, a woman orphaned during the Third Crusade, tells him of the dramatic rescue of his beloved Recha from their burning house. Nathan, in spite of having suffered severely at the hands of Christians and Saracens alike, wishes to reward the young man who had so courageously saved Recha's life. The hero proves to be a young Templar who recently had been pardoned by the sultan.

Each day, at Recha's urging, Daja attempts to thank and reward the young man as he makes a daily visit to Christ's tomb, but each time he rudely repulses her. Recha, as the result of shock over her narrow escape as much as from gratitude to her benefactor, suffers hallucinations in which she believes that the young Templar is her guardian angel. Nathan thinks it miraculous that Sultan Saladin should spare a Christian knight's life or that the Templar would desire to be so spared. The truth is that the Saracen's leniency is based on the young man's resemblance to his own dead brother, Assad.

Daja, told by Nathan to seek out the young man and invite him to their home, finds him in a bad mood after he rejects a friar's request from King Philip that he spy on and murder Saladin. The young man vehemently refuses to consider performing such a deed. The knight again tells Daja that he had performed his rescue of Recha through happenstance and therefore would accept no reward. Nathan then meets with and begs the youth, a penniless stranger in a strange land, to accept aid and friendship. Boorish though the young knight is, he offers to let Nathan buy him a mantle to replace his own, which had burned in the fire. At this suggestion the Jew sheds a tear and dissolves the intolerant Templar's disdain and suspicion. They shake hands, friends. Nathan learns that the young man is Conrad von Stauffen, a name somehow associated in the Jew's mind with the name Filneck, but before he could inquire further the Jew receives a message demanding his presence at the sultan's palace.

The young knight, in the meantime, calls on Recha. Something immediately draws them together, some mutual feeling not unlike romantic love. He hastens off, however, to avert any disaster that might befall Nathan at the hand of Saladin, who had summoned the Jew to obtain from him money to replenish the treasury so that the war against the crusaders might continue. To put the Jew somewhat at a disadvantage, Saladin asks enlightenment from Nathan, who is called the Wise (which Nathan denies he was), on the paradox of the several "true" religions.

Nathan then tells the story of a father who possesses a ring traditionally passed on to the favorite son, who would then be lord of the house. Since he loves his three sons equally well (as the Father in heaven loves all people, said Nathan), the father makes exact copies of the ring and gives one to each son. None knows which ring is the true ring, and after the father's death a controversy arises. The problem of the "true" ring can be resolved no more than the argument over the "true" faith—Jewish, Christian, or Muslim. A judge suggests that each son act as if his were the true ring and live and rule as well as he can. Finally, generations hence, it is decided in a higher, greater court, with religions as with the ring, which ring is the true one.

When Nathan returns from the palace, young Conrad von Stauffen asks for Recha's hand in marriage. Astounded, Nathan says that he cannot consent without due reflection. Daja, on an amorous mission, tells the Templar that Recha had been born Christian but was reared as a Jew, a crime punishable by death. The Templar assumes that Recha was stolen from her proper parents. Dismayed by Daja's story, the knight guardedly asks counsel of the Patriarch of Jerusalem, who says that in such a case the Jew must die at the stake for holding back salvation from an innocent child. Perplexed and unhappy, the young man confers with the sultan.

Saladin, amazed at such accusations, refuses to believe ill of Nathan and asks the Christian to exercise prudence and charity. As the young Templar leaves to save Nathan from the patriarch's wrath, the sultan and his sister remark the resemblance the young man bore to their long-lost brother, believed dead.

In the meantime, a friar sent to spy on Nathan reveals that eighteen years ago he, the friar, then a squire, delivered Recha to the Jew for his master, Lord Wolf von Filneck, who was later killed in battle; the child's mother, a von Stauffen, was already dead. Nathan confides that his own wife and seven sons had been killed by Christians only shortly before he adopted Recha as his own, an act that saved his sanity and restored his faith in God.

Saladin, who favors the marriage of the two young people, then learns from Nathan that Wolf von Filneck's breviary, turned over to Nathan by the friar, contains a strange story. Crusader Filneck's rightful name is Assad. The sultan's brother, having married a Christian and accepted her faith, had left his son to his deceased wife's brother, Conrad von Stauffen, after whom he was named. The boy's sister he left indirectly to Nathan. The Jewish child and the Christian child both were Muslim; their uncle is a sultan, and their godfather is a wise man and a Jew.

Critical Evaluation:

As Gotthold Ephraim Lessing's final dramatic work, completed only two years before his death, *Nathan the Wise* has invited speculation that it is a summing up of its author's life and thought. Such scrutiny is intensified by Lessing's reputation as possibly the German Enlightenment's most outstanding figure. Confronting fundamental issues in philosophy, literature, and drama at a critical period in Western culture, Lessing's writings have invariably provoked debate.

A theological controversy that embroiled Lessing in 1778 is considered the inspiration for *Nathan the Wise*. After failing in his dream of creating a national theater, Lessing accepted an invitation to head the highly regarded and amply stocked library in Wolfenbuttel. In this position, he undertook a series of publishing projects, which he was assured would escape the censor's desk. Lessing's subsequent publication of a posthumous apologia for the Deist position by Hermann Samuel Reimarus unleashed a series of attacks against him by the religious orthodoxy. Lessing was accused of championing Deism, which challenged religious dogma from the perspective of rationalism. Consequently, the exemption from censorship that his projects had been granted was revoked. Under these conditions, Lessing began reworking an old sketch whose situation, he wrote in a letter to his brother Karl, presented an analogy to his own, that of a man embattled by the forces of prejudice and fanaticism.

As Lessing predicted in another letter to Karl, theaters were reluctant to perform the resulting drama. Censorship was an impediment, but not the only one. The play's length and the demands it made on audiences and on actors posed practical problems. Subtitling his work "a dramatic poem," Lessing invented a form suited to his metaphysical purposes, which diminished the play's theatricality. This form consisted of a succession of scenes that prompted the characters to reveal themselves through a dialectical exchange of ideas, rather than through actions.

Consistent with its elevated aim, the play is written in verse, specifically iambic pentameter, or blank verse. This metered, poetic style, along with the poem's philosophic ambitions, marks *Nathan the Wise* as an innovation. Such qualities also distinguish it as a forerunner of classical idea dramas such as Johann Wolfgang von Goethe's *Iphigenie auf Tauris* (pr. 1779; *Iphigenia in Tauris*, 1793).

During Lessing's lifetime, the play, which caused a sensation in the literary world, was known primarily in its published form. *Nathan the Wise* finally premiered in Berlin on April 14, 1783, two years after Lessing's death. There were only three performances. The general public became familiar with the work largely through a number of popular parodies. The majority of these satirized Lessing's positive presentation of a Jewish character. *Nathan the Wise*, which was banned from school curricula under Nationalist Socialist rule, became the first play produced in postwar Germany. Presumably, it was revived to demonstrate that a tradition of tolerance existed in German culture.

While the play's advocacy of religious tolerance is universally acknowledged, judgment varies regarding its legacy. Most Jewish critics commend it for allying itself with the cause of emancipation. Others, particularly in the Zionist camp, have assailed the play, contending that it promotes assimilation, which in the long run is destructive to Jewish culture.

Critics also disagree on the nature of Lessing's religious convictions as articulated in the play. The focus of debate is the parable of the rings, which lies at the center of the drama, structurally as well as thematically. The first recorded version of the parable of the rings is found in Spanish Hebrew literature about the time of the Crusades, which Lessing chose for the setting of his play. Lessing's primary source, however, is probably Giovanni Boccaccio's version in his *Decameron* (1348-1353). While Lessing clearly expands the tale, conflict arises over the meaning and import of this development.

Some critics discern in Lessing's account of the parable a utopian religious message. They highlight its mythic qualities and point to Lessing's closing image: a loving circle comprising Jew, Christian, and Muslim. According to this conception, the magic of the ring in the parable parallels the magic that appears to generate Nathan's inexhaustible riches. It is the triumphant power of active, divine love operating through human beings, no matter what faith.

Other critics find in the parable intimations of a modern ambivalence toward faith. They emphasize its implied skepticism toward absolute truth. In this view, the message of the parable is that the power of the ring, apart from any inherent quality of the ring itself, is the power of human beings to believe. Of note is that the father in the tale, who ordered the ring's duplication, is himself unable to discern the original ring—suggesting that it no longer exists. Moreover, these critics point out, judgment in the parable is left open.

Such contradictory inferences are likely the result of the play's absorption in doubts regarding the limits of knowledge, which was endemic to the eighteenth century. *Nathan the Wise* may thereby be anticipating Immanuel Kant's *Kritik der reinen Vernunft* (1781; *Critique of Pure Reason*, 1838). Belief cannot be knowledge, Lessing apparently argues, so tolerance regarding matters of faith becomes a necessity. Religious faith, his parable demonstrates, is best understood in terms of tradition, which shapes and is shaped by history. Positively understood, the interpretation and application of tradition, which transmits culture and values, is the property of any and all religions. Lessing would appear to illuminate a paradoxical vision that sees unity in diversity.

Lessing's designation of the parable as the kernel from which his play developed suggests the transforming power he intended for *Nathan the Wise*. A parable, while conveying an accessible message, does so indirectly. The listener or reader is thereby challenged to interpret and act on its meaning. Even as the parable in *Nathan the Wise* denies authoritative proof for the primacy of any particular faith, audiences are called upon to authenticate, in acts of beauty and substance, their own traditions.

"Critical Evaluation" by Amy Spitalnick

Further Reading

Brown, Francis. *Gotthold Ephraim Lessing*. New York: Twayne, 1971. Surveys Lessing's accomplishments as dramatist, critic, and theologian. Sees in *Nathan the Wise* his signature emphasis on the virtue of acting with conscious intent. Concludes that Lessing was a product and a prophet of his era.

Eckardt, Jo-Jacqueline. *Lessing's "Nathan the Wise" and the Critics, 1779-1991*. Columbia, S.C.: Camden House, 1993. Collection of chronologically arranged criticism about the play, revealing the recurrence of motifs and themes, as well as the historical development of certain interpretations. Very helpful in shedding light on the ideological orientation of various critics.

Fischer, Barbara, and Thomas C. Fox, eds. *A Companion to the Works of Gotthold Ephraim Lessing*. Rochester, N.Y.: Camden House, 2005. Collection of essays, including discussions of Lessing's life and times, his place within the European Enlightenment, his theory of drama, and Lessing and philosophy, theology, and the Jews.

Garland, Henry B. *Lessing: The Founder of Modern German Literature*. 1937. Reprint. Folcroft, Pa.: Folcroft Library Editions, 1973. Determines Lessing's primary role as a dramatist to be that of an innovator. Argues that what matters most in *Nathan the Wise* is its underlying ethical content.

Graham, Ilse. *Goethe and Lessing: The Wellsprings of Creation*. New York: Barnes & Noble, 1973. Analyzes the play's structure in terms of central, unifying symbols. Focuses on poetic elements, such as image patterns and language.

Lessing, Gotthold Ephraim. *Nathan the Wise: With Related Documents*. Edited, translated, and with an introduction by Ronald Schechter. Boston: Bedford/St. Martin's, 2004. In addition to the text of the play, this edition contains Schechter's introduction, in which he discusses the drama, Lessing's place within the Enlightenment, and the situation of the European Jews in the eighteenth century. Also contains five historical documents to place the play within its context.

Leventhal, Robert S. "The Parable as Performance: Interpretation, Cultural Transmission, and Political Strategy in Lessing's *Nathan der Weise*." *German Quarterly* 61, no. 4 (Fall, 1988): 502-527. Argues compellingly that Lessing questioned basic premises of eighteenth century interpretive theory. Stresses Lessing's skepticism of absolute principles.

Ottewell, Karen. *Lessing and the Sturm und Drang: A Reappraisal Revisited*. New York: Peter Lang, 2002. Analyzes Lessing's dramas within the context of the Sturm und Drang movement. Ottewell views Lessing as an important precursor of the movement, and she analyzes his attitudes toward and his impact upon writers associated with the movement, including Johann Gottfried Herder and Friedrich Schiller.

Native Son

Author: Richard Wright (1908-1960)
First published: 1940
Type of work: Novel
Type of plot: Social realism
Time of plot: 1930's
Locale: An American city

Principal characters:
BIGGER THOMAS, a young African American
MR. DALTON, Bigger's employer
MRS. DALTON, his wife
MARY DALTON, their daughter
JAN ERLONE, Mary's sweetheart
BRITTEN, Dalton's private detective
BESSIE MEARS, Bigger's mistress
BUCKLEY, a state prosecutor
BORIS A. MAX, Bigger's lawyer

The Story:

Bigger Thomas lives in a one-room apartment with his brother, sister, and mother. Always penniless, haunted by a pathological hatred of white people, driven by an indescribable urge to make others cringe before him, Bigger has retreated into an imaginary world of fantasy.

Through the aid of a relief agency, he obtains employment as a chauffeur for a wealthy family. His first assignment is to drive Mary Dalton, his employer's daughter, to the university. Mary, however, is on her way to meet Jan Erlone, her sweetheart. The three of them, Mary and Jan—white people who are crusading with the Communist Party to help African Americans—and Bigger—a reluctant ally—spend the evening driving and drinking. Bigger brings Mary home, but Mary is too drunk to take herself to bed. With a confused medley of hatred, fear, disgust, and revenge playing within his mind, Bigger helps her to her bedroom. When Mary's blind mother enters the room, Bigger covers the girl's face with a pillow to keep her from making any sound that might arouse Mrs. Dalton's suspicions. The reek of whiskey convinces Mrs. Dalton that Mary is drunk, and she leaves the room. Then Bigger discovers that he had smothered Mary to death. To delay discovery of his crime, he takes the body to the basement and stuffs it into the furnace.

Bigger then begins a weird kind of rationalization. The next morning, in his mother's home, he begins thinking that he is separated from his family because he had killed a white girl. His plan is to involve Jan in connection with Mary's death.

When Bigger returns to the Dalton home, the family is worrying over Mary's absence. Bigger feels secure from incrimination because he had covered his activities by lying. He decides to send ransom notes to her parents, allowing them to think Mary had been kidnapped. There are too many facts to remember, however, and too many lies to tell. Britten, the detective whom Mr. Dalton had hired, tries to intimidate Bigger, but his methods only make Bigger more determined to frame Jan, who, in his desire to protect Mary, lies just enough to help Bigger's cause. When Britten brings Bigger face to face with Jan for questioning, Bigger's fear mounts. He goes to Bessie, his mistress, who gets from him a confession of murder. Bigger forces her to go with him to hide in an empty building in the slum section of the city. There he instructs her to pick up the ransom money he hopes to receive from Mr. Dalton.

Bigger is eating in the Dalton kitchen when the ransom note arrives. Jan had already been arrested. Bigger clings tenaciously to his lies. It is a cold day. Attempting to build up the fire, Bigger accidentally draws attention to the furnace. When reporters discover Mary's bones, Bigger flees. Hiding with Bessie in the deserted building, he realizes that he cannot take her with him. Afraid to leave her behind to be found and questioned by the police, he kills her and throws her body down an air shaft.

When Bigger ventures from his hideout to steal a newspaper, he learns that the city is being combed to find him. He flees from one empty building to another, constantly buying or stealing newspapers to judge his chances for escape. Finally, he is trapped on the roof of a penthouse by a searching police officer. Bigger knocks him out. The police finally capture Bigger after a chase across the rooftops.

In jail, Bigger refuses to eat or speak. His mind turns inward, hating the world, but he is satisfied with himself for what he had done. Three days later, Jan Erlone comes to see Bigger and promises to help him. Jan introduces Boris A. Max, a lawyer for the Communist front organization for which Jan works. Buckley, the prosecuting attorney, tries to persuade Bigger not to become involved with the Communists. Bigger says nothing even after the lawyer tells him that Bessie's body had been found. When Buckley begins listing the crimes of rape, murder, and burglary charged against him, Bigger protests, vigorously denying rape and Jan's part in Mary's death. Under a steady fire of questions from Buckley, Bigger breaks down and signs a confession.

The opening session of the grand jury begins. First, Mrs. Dalton appears as a witness to identify one of her daughter's earrings, which had been found in the furnace. Next, Jan testifies, and, under the slanderous anti-Communist questioning, Max rises in protest against the racial bigotry of the coroner. Max questions Mr. Dalton about his ownership of the high-rent, rat-infested tenements where Bigger's family lives. Generally, the grand jury session becomes a trial of the race relations that had led to Bigger's crime rather than a trial of the crime itself. As a climax to the session, the coroner brings Bessie's body into the courtroom to produce evidence that Bigger had raped and murdered his sweetheart. Bigger is returned to jail after Max promises to visit him. Under the quiet questioning of Max, Bigger at last talks about his crime, his feelings, his reasons. He had been thwarted by white people all of his life, he says, until he killed Mary Dalton; that act had released him.

At the opening session of the trial, Buckley presents witnesses who attest Bigger's sanity and his ruthless character. The murder is dramatized even to the courtroom reconstruction of the furnace in which Mary's body had been burned. Max refuses to call any of his own witnesses or to cross-examine, promising to act in Bigger's behalf as sole witness for the defense. The next day, in a long speech, Max outlines an entire social structure, its effect on an individual such as Bigger, and Bigger's inner compulsions when he killed Mary Dalton. Pleading for mitigation on the grounds that Bigger is not totally responsible for his crime, he argues that society, too, is to blame.

After another race-prejudiced attack by Buckley, the court adjourns for one hour. It reopens to sentence Bigger to death. Max's attempts to delay death by appealing to the governor are unsuccessful.

In the last hours before death, Bigger realizes his one hope is to communicate his feelings to Max, to try to have Max explain to him the meaning of his life and his death. Max helps him see that the people who persecute African Americans, poor people or others, are themselves filled with fear. Bigger forgives them because they are suffering the same urge that he suffers. He forgives his enemies because they do not know the guilt of their own social crimes.

Critical Evaluation:

When it appeared in 1940, *Native Son* was without precedent in American literature. Previous African American writing, including Richard Wright's *Uncle Tom's Children* (1938), had treated blacks as passive and innocent victims of racism suffering their lot in dignified silence. As Wright said of his own earlier work, the reading audience could escape into the self-indulgence of pity on reading such work rather than truly face the hard facts of racism. In Bigger Thomas, Wright created a character who was neither a passive sufferer nor an innocent victim. Instead, Wright reminded Americans of the full cost of bigotry in social and human terms by dramatizing the deep anger, hate, and fear that many blacks felt.

Years after *Native Son*'s appearance, James Baldwin would assert that every black person carries some degree of Bigger Thomas within him- or herself. Perhaps so, and it is to Wright's credit that he was the first American writer to bring those feelings into the open. Readers are reminded that Bigger is a "native son," and his experience is quintessentially a part of the American experience. On the psychological, the sociological, and the philosophical levels, Wright explores the most disturbing implications of what it means to be African American.

The basic tone of Wright's psychological treatment of Bigger is set in the opening scene in which Bigger and Buddy battle the rat. Here is a symbolic paradigm for the entire novel in which Bigger, like the rat, will be hunted and destroyed. The rat, it must be understood, operates entirely at the instinctual level, and its viciousness is in response to fear. Recalling that "Fear" is the title of the first section of the novel, as "Flight" is of the second, suggests that Bigger, too, is a creature motivated by fear and acting instinctively. This is demonstrably true of his killing Mary Dalton while avoiding detection, and it shows up even earlier in the fight with Gus. Fearful of outside forces, particularly white people, Bigger is equally fearful of the repressed anger within himself, as his several comments referring to his concern that he is destined to commit some terrible act indicate. Thus, in at least the first two sections of the novel, Bigger, before and after the murder, is operating at an instinctual level, and it is against this background that his development takes place.

Bigger's psychological state is an obvious result of the sociological conditions prevailing in the novel. As Bigger dramatizes the anger and pain of his race, the Daltons effectively represent the ruling white power structure. It is to Wright's credit that he does not give way to the temptation to create villains, but makes these whites generous, liberal, and humanitarian. It is ironic that even while giving a "chance" to

Bigger and helping in ghetto programs, the Daltons are reaping the proceeds of ghetto housing. Appropriately, Wright uses the metaphor of blindness to characterize the attitude of the Daltons here, as he will later, to account for Max's failure to comprehend Bigger. Bigger, too, is described as blind, because, in this world of *Native Son*, there is no real possibility of people seeing one another in clear human perspective. All the characters respond to one another as symbols rather than as people.

Wright's use of the polarities of black and white symbolism is not limited to the literal and racial levels of the novel. The entire world of *Native Son*, as the story unfolds, is increasingly polarized into a symbolic black-white dichotomy. Especially during part 2, the snow that buries the city under a cold and hostile blanket of white becomes a more complicated manifestation of the white symbolism than that limited to the sociological level. At the same time, not only does Bigger escape into the black ghetto in search of safety and security, he also seeks out the black interiors of abandoned buildings to hide from both the freezing snow and the death-dealing white mob. Finally, Bigger's flight ends when he is spread out against the white snow as though he were being crucified.

It is not probable that Wright had heard of European existentialism when he wrote *Native Son*, so it is all the more remarkable that this novel should so clearly demonstrate concepts that anticipate Wright's embracing of existentialist philosophy when he went to Europe in the late 1940's. Though Bigger very obviously commits the first murder without premeditation, he quickly comes to the realization that somehow the act is the sum of his entire life. Rather than repudiating responsibility for his crime, or seeing himself as a victim of circumstances, either of which would be understandable, Bigger consciously and deliberately affirms the killing as the most creative act of his life. Whereas before he was in the position of constantly reacting—like the rat—he now sees himself as having responsibility for his own fate. Further, the world that before had seemed frighteningly ambiguous is now clearly revealed to him. For the first time in his life, Bigger has a positive sense of his own identity and a concrete knowledge of how he relates to the world around him. Ironically, Max's case that Bigger is a victim of society threatens to deprive Bigger of the identity he has purchased at such terrible cost to himself, but, facing death at the end of the novel, he reaffirms his belief that he killed for something, and he faces death with the courage born of his one creative moment.

Wright's novel is not without faults, particularly the tedious final section in which Max argues a doctrinaire Marxist interpretation of Bigger's crime. Apparently, however, Wright himself could not fully accept this view, since Bigger's reaffirmation of responsibility contradicts Max's deterministic justification. In the final analysis, Bigger's insistence upon responsibility for his act demonstrates the human potential for freedom of act and will and asserts human possibility in contrast to the Marxist vision of people as animals trapped in a world they cannot control.

"Critical Evaluation" by William E. Grant

Further Reading

Bloom, Harold, ed. *Richard Wright's "Native Son."* New ed. New York: Bloom's Literary Criticism, 2009. Compilation of critical essays about the novel, including discussions of the book's contemporary critical context, Bigger as an oppressor, spectacle and event in the novel, and a comparison of the novel with Fyodor Dostoevski's *Crime and Punishment* (1866).

Felgar, Robert. *Student Companion to Richard Wright.* Westport, Conn.: Greenwood Press, 2000. Provides an overview of Wright's life and literary career and analyses of the plots, character development, themes, and other elements of his works. Chapter 4 is devoted to *Native Son.*

Fraile, Ana María, ed. *Richard Wright's "Native Son."* New York: Rodopi, 2007. Collection of essays interpreting the novel, including discussions of its reception, Wright and his white audience, the depiction of black women, biblical imagery in the book, and Bigger Thomas figures in hip-hop culture.

Kinnamon, Keneth, ed. *Critical Essays on Richard Wright's "Native Son."* New York: Twayne, 1997. A collection of contemporary essays and book reviews, reprinted criticism, and original essays on the novel. Contributors include Malcolm Cowley, Ralph Ellison, and Sterling A. Brown.

_____. *New Essays on "Native Son."* New York: Cambridge University Press, 1990. Presents a thorough examination of the genesis and background of *Native Son.* Kinnamon analyzes Wright's own essay "How 'Bigger' Was Born" along with letters, notes, manuscripts, and galley and page proofs to show how external forces influenced the writing of the novel.

Mitchell, Hayley R., ed. *Readings on "Native Son."* San Diego, Calif.: Greenhaven Press, 2000. A collection of essays in which contributors advance various arguments to interpret the novel, including assertions that Wright's craft is as important as the content of *Native Son,* the book's conclusion is often misunderstood, Wright's male heroes and female characters are archetypes, Bigger Thomas is a product of mass culture, and Bigger represents the "social plight of the lower classes."

Warnes, Andrew. *Richard Wright's "Native Son."* New York: Routledge, 2007. A guide to the novel, with information about Wright's life; *Native Son*'s texts, contexts, and critical history; and several essays interpreting the book.

Williams, John A. *The Most Native of Sons: A Biography of Richard Wright.* Garden City, N.Y.: Doubleday, 1970. Provides a solid biography. Places Wright in his historical context both at home and abroad, giving a sense of the man and his times.

Wright, Richard. *Early Novels: "Lawd Today!" "Uncle Tom's Children," "Native Son."* Vol. 1 in *Works,* edited by Arnold Rampersad. New York: Library of America, 1991. Reinstates significant cuts that were made in *Lawd Today!* and *Native Son.* The volume also deserves attention for its detailed chronology, which reads like an excellent biography.

_____. "How 'Bigger' Was Born." In *Native Son.* Reprint. New York: Perennial Library, 1987. Wright details the genesis of *Native Son,* describing five Bigger Thomases, dating back to his childhood. Wright is his own best critic.

The Natural

Author: Bernard Malamud (1914-1986)
First published: 1952
Type of work: Novel
Type of plot: Fable
Time of plot: 1930's-1940's
Locale: Chicago and New York

Principal characters:
ROY HOBBS, nineteen-year-old ballplayer
POP FISHER, manager of the New York Knights baseball team
MEMO PARIS, niece of Pop Fisher
IRIS LEMON, thirty-three-year-old grandmother

The Story:

In section one, "Pre-Game," nineteen-year-old pitcher Roy Hobbs journeys by train to Chicago for a tryout with the Cubs. He is accompanied by Sam Simpson, an alcoholic former major-league catcher and scout who hopes to use his discovery of Roy to resurrect his scouting career. Roy is naïve, self-centered, and unsophisticated. With his homemade bat, Wonderboy, fashioned from a tree that had been split by lightning and seems to possess an energy all its own, Roy is, however, a superbly gifted ballplayer.

Also on the train is Walter "the Whammer" Wambold, aging American League batting champion and three-time winner of the Most Valuable Player Award. When the train is mysteriously delayed, Roy and the others wander over to a nearby carnival, where the Whammer displays his prowess in a batting cage and Roy attracts a crowd by throwing baseballs at milk bottles. As the rivalry builds to its confrontation, Sam bets that Roy can strike out the Whammer with three pitches. After the third pitch, the Whammer drops the bat and returns to the train, "an old man."

Roy's triumph brings him to the attention of Harriet Bird, who guards a shiny black box as jealously as Roy guards Wonderboy. Excited by Roy's victory in "the tourney," she tells him he is like "David jawboning the Goliath-Whammer, or was it Sir Percy lancing Sir Maldemer, or the first son (with a rock in his paw) ranged against the primitive papa?" Roy responds, "I'll be the best there ever was in the game." "Is that all?" Harriet asks. Harriet turns out to be the mysterious woman Roy had heard about who shot promising young athletes with silver bullets. Soon after, in a Chicago hotel room, Roy reaffirms his determination to become the best player who ever lived. Harriet reaches into her mysterious hatbox, draws out a gun, and shoots Roy in the stomach with a silver bullet.

Section two, "Batter Up," takes place fifteen years later. Ashamed of his nearly fatal "accident" in Chicago, Roy is determined to begin a new life after years of wandering and working at odd jobs. As an outfielder, Roy tries out with the New York Knights, a team that had amassed a record number of losses. To win a starting spot in the lineup, Roy has to displace the Knight's current left fielder, batting champ Bump Bailey, who looks out solely for himself and whose batting prowess does little to inspire his teammates. The rivalry ends when Bump, trying valiantly to match Roy's flawless fielding, crashes into the left field wall and dies of his injuries. With the aid of Roy's superhuman skills, the team begins a miraculous drive for the pennant.

Pop Fisher, the aging manager of the Knights and a former major-league player himself, hopes to lead the Knights to the world championship. He becomes Roy's spiritual father. Pop's ambition, however, is being thwarted by the forces of evil in the form of Judge Banner, a profit seeker who owns sixty percent of the Knights' stock. Pop had sold stock to the judge with the stipulation that the manager would retain control over player deals "as long as he lives." Yet he is slowly losing control. The judge harasses the manager in an effort to force Pop to resign so that the judge can seek profits rather than victory. The power behind the judge is Gus, the supreme bookie, who uses the magic of statistics and knows that playing the percentages pays off in the long run.

As the team makes its final drive for the pennant, Roy is distracted by his fatal attraction to Memo Paris, the niece of Pop Fisher and former girlfriend of Bump Bailey. Pop warns Roy that she will "weaken your strength," but even after Roy discovers that she is in league with Gus and the judge, his passion for her continues unabated. Roy also has an affair with Iris Lemon, a woman in Chicago who brings Roy out of his batting slump by rising up in the stands as an expression of support.

One night Roy eats so much that he becomes sick and ends up in a maternity hospital. He is told by the doctor that he will recover in time to play in the final game of the season, on whose outcome the elusive pennant rests—but that the game will be his last. Memo tells him that she demands a husband who can provide her with expensive things. To have Memo, Roy accepts a payoff from the judge to throw the crucial playoff game. Near the end of the game, however, Iris's presence in the stands causes Roy to decide he cannot go through with the fix. Wonderboy splits in half when Roy swings at the ball with fierce determination. Without Wonderboy, Roy strikes out "with a roar" on three pitches and walks away, like the Whammer before him, an old man.

In the final scene, Roy repudiates the betrayal by throwing the bribe money at the judge. On the street outside, Roy, like Shoeless Joe Jackson in 1919, painfully listens as a newsboy, carrying a stack of papers spreading word of the suspected fix to the world, implores mournfully, "Say it ain't true, Roy."

Critical Evaluation:

The Natural is a fable in which the fortunes of its hero parallel those of Parzival, the medieval knight. Bernard Malamud uses myth and American culture's heroic ritual to explore the psychology of American life. The novel is enriched by drawing on events out of baseball lore and legend, such as the 1949 hotel-room shooting of Philadelphia Phillies infielder Eddie Waitkus by a crazed woman sports fan, the infamous game-fixing scandal of 1919, the many achievements of Babe Ruth, and the fate of Casey at the bat.

Roy Hobbs is a knight and a fool. An aging rookie who comes to play for the hapless New York Knights, he is also a natural baseball player with outstanding talent. After he became a knight, Parzival was given the quest of finding and healing the Fisher King of the Wasteland. He failed because he did not ask, rather than answer, the right question. Like Parzival, Roy fails because of his inability to answer Harriet Bird's question about what he hopes to accomplish in his career. His reply is limited and selfish: to be the best there ever was in the game. After Harriet gives him a second chance and he fails again, she discharges a silver bullet into him. It is not enough for the hero to have talent; he must have a purpose in life. Parzival and Roy are heroes who are too wrapped up in their self-image to recognize the responsibility that comes with their great talent.

After fifteen years, Roy returns to baseball, this time, like Babe Ruth, as a home-run hitter rather than a pitcher. He joins the Knights, a team so bad that even its field, like the Wasteland, suffers from drought. The team's manager, Pop Fisher, the Fisher King, has spent a career without winning a pennant. In the medieval myth the Wasteland cannot become fertile until the Fisher King is replaced by the young, innocent hero. In *The Natural*, Roy is the mythic hero who can undo the bad luck of his spiritual father, Pop Fisher, and bring relief to the drought. When Roy starts hitting, the team begins winning, torrential rains come down, and the field turns green.

As fertility god, Roy has to choose the proper woman to be his companion. Like other Malamud heroes, he has a choice between a woman who represents life-giving fertility and one whose power lies in her seductive vanity. Iris Lemon, named for a fruit and a flower, is the woman Roy should choose. Roy, however, is attracted to Memo Paris, whose name suggests someone who uses memory rather than imagination and who uses her powers to destroy, as Paris did Achilles, the men in her life. Her condition is symbolized by her sick breast, a sign that she is incapable of either nurturing the hero or having her own children.

Iris, on the other hand, is connected with Roy's first selfless act. Roy promises to hit a home run for an injured boy, a boy who has given up struggling for his life (the incident is taken from the career of Ruth). Roy understands for the first time that as a hero he has responsibility for other human beings. When Iris stands up in the crowd for him, he responds by hitting a home run. Iris urges upon Roy the responsibility inherent in being a hero. A hero must become a moral example for ordinary people, especially for children.

Later, Iris tries to explain to Roy the sacrifice of ego that is required of a hero. The hero is not for himself, but for others. Iris explains to Roy the theory that every person has two lives: One life teaches through experience how to live, and the other life is the life lived out of that knowledge. The life that teaches is always built out of suffering and sacrifice so that the life that is lived can move toward happiness by choosing the right things.

Iris can bring Roy to that life only by freeing him from his fear of mortality. She must make him see that playing baseball with the aim of making himself immortal by setting records is immoral, self-centered, and counterproductive. Roy is not mature enough, however, to accept her wisdom. Malamud believes that redemption lies in the hero's understanding of his own past and his ability to transcend it. Roy's inability to do this is the basis of his failure. A woman laments at the end of the novel, "He coulda been a king." Roy is left only with his self-hatred. As the ballplayer tells himself in the final page, "I never did learn anything out of my past life, now I have to suffer again."

Roy's dismal failure makes *The Natural* a clear introduction to the morality that informs Malamud's later work. Malamud's moral understanding is based upon his insistence that submission to suffering is the only avenue of redemption. Readers see in Roy their own limitations and the possibility that exists to overcome those limitations. Malamud's qualified affirmation comes out of a belief in the resources of the human spirit, with an understanding of the social and economic pressures that can suffocate it. In its use of myth, moral, and symbol, *The Natural* is a necessary text for reading Malamud's subsequent fiction.

Milton S. Katz

Further Reading

Alter, Isaka. "The Good Man's Dilemma: *The Natural*, *The Assistant*, and American Materialism." In *Critical Essays on Bernard Malamud*, edited by Joel Salzberg. Boston: G. K. Hall, 1987. Focuses on the social criticism in Malamud's fiction and how in *The Natural*, Roy chooses materialism over love and morality.

Avery, Evelyn, ed. *The Magic Worlds of Bernard Malamud*. Albany: State University of New York Press, 2001. A wide-ranging collection of essays on Malamud and his writings, including personal memoirs by members of his family and friends and analyses of some of his works.

Bloom, Harold, ed. *Bernard Malamud*. New York: Chelsea House, 2000. A collection of essays assessing the entire spectrum of Malamud's works, as well as a chronology of his life and a bibliography. "*The Natural*: Malamud's World Ceres" by Earl R. Wasserman provides a comprehensive analysis of how Malamud weaves historical episodes into an epic.

Davis, Philip. *Bernard Malamud: A Writer's Life*. New York: Oxford University Press, 2007. The first full-length biography. Davis chronicles the events of Malamud's life, describes his writing methods, and connects the events of his life to his work. He also provides literary analysis of Malamud's novels and other fiction. References to *The Natural* are listed in the index.

Helterman, Jeffrey. *Understanding Bernard Malamud*. Columbia: University of South Carolina Press, 1985. A highly readable guide for students and nonacademic readers about what Malamud expresses and the means by which it is conveyed. Chapter 2 discusses mythic dimensions, themes, and symbolism in *The Natural*.

Hershinow, Sheldon. *Bernard Malamud*. New York: Frederick Ungar, 1980. Chapter 2 offers an analysis of *The Natural* as depicting the plight of the mythic hero in the modern world.

Richman, Sidney. *Bernard Malamud*. Boston: Twayne, 1966. Chapter 3 provides an excellent, detailed analysis of *The Natural* as a novel of ideas laced with moral ambiguity and pessimism.

Nausea

Author: Jean-Paul Sartre (1905-1980)
First published: La Nausée, 1938 (English translation, 1949)
Type of work: Novel
Type of plot: Philosophical realism
Time of plot: 1930's
Locale: France

Principal characters:
ANTOINE ROQUENTIN, a French historian
ANNY, Roquentin's former sweetheart
OGIER P., The Self-Taught Man and an acquaintance of Roquentin
FRANÇOISE, the congenial owner of a café, and Roquentin's friend

The Story:

After traveling through Central Europe, North Africa, and Asia, a thirty-year-old Frenchman named Antoine Roquentin settles down in the seaport town of Bouville to finish his historical research on the Marquis de Rollebon, an eighteenth century figure in European politics whose home had been at Bouville. For three years, Roquentin searches the archives of the Bouville library reconstructing the nobleman's life. All Roquentin's energies are concentrated on his task; he knows few people in Bouville except by sight, and he lives more in the imaginary world he is re-creating than in the actual world.

In the third year of his residence in Bouville, during the winter of 1932, Roquentin begins to have a series of disturbing psychological experiences that he terms "the nausea." He feels there is something new about commonplace articles, and even his hands seem to take on new aspects, to have an existence all their own. It is then that Roquentin's loneliness becomes a terrible thing to him, for there is no one to whom he can speak of his experiences. His only acquaintances are Ogier P., whom Roquentin has nicknamed The Self-Taught Man because he was instructing himself by reading all the books in the library, and a woman named Françoise, who operates a café called the Rendezvous des Cheminots. Françoise, who had become fond of Roquentin, is the outlet for his physical sexuality, but their acquaintance had not gone beyond that. In his loneliness, Roquentin begins to think of Anny, an English girl who had traveled with him some years before and whom he had loved; he had not heard from her in more than three years. The nausea comes increasingly often to plague Roquentin; it passes from objects into his body through his hands, and the only way he can describe it is that it seems like a sweetish sickness.

One evening, shortly after the nausea first appears, Roquentin goes to the café, only to find that Françoise is gone for a time. He sits down to listen to music on a battered old phonograph and, for the first time, the nausea creeps upon him in a place with bright lights and many people; even more horrible, it seems as if the sickness is outside himself, in other objects.

Strangely enough, as the days pass, The Self-Taught Man makes an effort to be friendly with Roquentin. Learning that Roquentin had traveled extensively, The Self-Taught Man asks to see some of the photographs he had collected and to hear some of his adventures. He even goes to Roquentin's rooms one evening for that specific purpose. These friendly overtures are not entirely welcome to Roquentin, since he is immersed in his psychological problems, but he acquiesces and sets a date to have dinner with The Self-Taught Man a few days later.

In the interval before the dinner engagement, the book about the Marquis de Rollebon comes to a halt. One day, Roquentin suddenly stops writing in the middle of a paragraph and knows that he will write no more, although he has spent more than three years of his life on the work. Roquentin suddenly feels cheated, as if his very existence was stolen by the Marquis de Rollebon during those years, as if the marquis had been living in place of himself. Roquentin realizes that he will never be able to be certain of the truth about the marquis, who all of his life had used men for his own ends.

Once he realizes that he will no longer write, Roquentin finds little purpose in his life. Indeed, there seems to be no reason for his existence. For three years, Roquentin has not reacted to his own existence because he has been working; now his existence is being thrust on him with disquieting abruptness.

One Wednesday, Roquentin and The Self-Taught Man meet for the prearranged dinner, a rather stiff affair, during which The Self-Taught Man tries to convince Roquentin that he, like himself, ought to be a humanist, that in the humanity of the world is to be found the true reason for the universe. Roquentin becomes so disquieted that the nausea comes over him during the discussion, and he abruptly leaves the restaurant.

A day or two later, Roquentin receives an unexpected letter from Anny, which had been forwarded from his old address in Paris. She writes that she will be in Paris for a few days and wishes to see him. Roquentin looks forward to seeing her and plans to leave Bouville for the first time in three years to visit with her in Paris. When the day arrives, he presents himself at her address.

Anny is not the same; she became fat, but the changes that bother him the most are those he feels rather than sees. The interview is a dismal failure; Anny accuses him of being worthless to her and finally throws him from the room. Later, he sees Anny getting on a train with the man who kept her, and he goes back to Bouville with a sense of numbness. He believes that both he and Anny had outlived themselves. All that is left to do, he feels, is eating and sleeping, an existence not unlike that of an inanimate object.

Roquentin remains in Bouville only a few days more. Unhappy and lonesome, he seeks out The Self-Taught Man and finds him in the library. Because The Self-Taught Man is reading to two young boys, Roquentin sits down to read until The Self-Taught Man has finished. He never gets a chance to resume his conversation with his acquaintance, for The Self-Taught Man reveals that he is gay and is brutally ejected from the library by the librarians. The only other person to whom Roquentin wishes to say good-bye is the congenial woman who owns the Rendezvous des Cheminots. She spares him only a moment, though, because another patron claims her time.

Roquentin goes to the railway station for the train to Paris. His only hope is that he might write a book, perhaps a novel, that would make people think of his life as something precious and legendary. He knows, however, that his work on such a book, unlike his attempts at the history of the Marquis de Rollebon, will not keep from him the troublesome problem of existence.

Critical Evaluation:

Throughout Jean-Paul Sartre's *Nausea*, Antoine Roquentin attempts to define the relationship between himself and the world so that he can understand the powerful sense of nausea that overwhelms him. He hopes that in so doing he can define the meaning of his existence. Roquentin, an existential man, is destined to fail in his search. As Sartre's personification of existentialism, Roquentin cannot but find his own existence abhorrent and ultimately meaningless; his nausea reflects not only the vertigo of existence but also his realization that existence, which is a dispensable element of reality itself, comprises only suffering and despair.

When the novel commences, Roquentin is focused on his historical research in the town library, his frequent visits to cafés, his memory of the past, and occasional sexual trysts with Françoise, the woman who runs one of the cafés he frequents. Other than with Françoise, Roquentin has no contact with anyone except The Self-Taught Man, who "doesn't count." By his own account, Roquentin neither gives nor receives anything from anyone; thus, his existence is isolated.

Through the nausea, Roquentin discovers that all of his pleasures and activities are meaningless. Initially, for example, his trips to cafés provide him with some pleasure, and he is safe from the nausea when he sits in the well-lighted, crowded cafés of Bouville. Eventually, however, the nausea invades the café as well, and he is horrified by the people and objects around him. His sexual encounters with Françoise have little meaning to begin with; they merely serve a need that, according to Roquentin, is "mutual." Whatever pleasure Roquentin may have found in these encounters is lost, however: He is suddenly disgusted by her appearance, her smell, her very existence. The meaninglessness of their relationship is intensified by his final conversation with her before he leaves to board the train for Paris. Françoise barely speaks to him, and she spends Roquentin's final moments in the café doting on another customer.

Another element of Roquentin's life is his walks about town, yet these walks eventually serve only to reinforce his perception of the futility of existence. He watches people interact with each other and condemns the regularity and predictability of their lives. They are "idiots" with "thick, self-satisfied faces" and empty lives. Occasionally, he focuses on the self-confidence and purpose that he sees in wealthy men, but their world is completely alien to him. In any case, he knows that they, too, must die, that their lives, too, are ultimately an illusion. Even the beauty of nature becomes abhorrent to Roquentin when he realizes that trees "*did not want* to exist, only they could not help themselves." Finally, Roquentin concludes that all that exists, exists "without reason, prolongs itself out of weakness and dies by chance."

As Roquentin realizes the pointlessness of the simple pleasures he had previously enjoyed, he focuses on the remaining significance of his life: his research on the history of the Marquis de Rollebon and the memory of his own personal history, the highlights of which are adventure and love. The primary difficulty that Roquentin has with searching for meaning in the past is that recollection of the past is subjective. As he explores his personal past, for example, he encounters only "scraps of images"; significantly, he is unsure whether they are "memories or just fiction." In this context, his adventures, which previously held great import, lose their significance. His sense as to whether or not he has even experienced adventures, in the light of his perception of the complexity of truth and memory, begins to waver. Ultimately, he concludes that "things have happened" to him, but that he has had no adventures and that he has deceived himself for years. He then turns his attention to the Marquis de Rollebon, to whom he had lent his own life.

Through his recent discovery of the questionable nature of his own recollection of the past, Roquentin cannot but ask, "How can I, who have not the strength to hold to my own past, hope to save the past of someone else?" Consequently, Roquentin discovers that the past cannot exist in the true concept of that term. Only the present can exist, as the subjectivity of memory destroys the possibility of historical truth. Without truth, there can be no existence, just as existence, in its indifference, is truth.

Seeking yet another reason for existence, Roquentin turns not to the memory of his love for Anny but to his hope for the future in the form of his impending meeting with her, which serves as his "sole reason for living." Within *Nausea*, however, as within all of Sartre's works, there is to be no salvation through others. The individual, in his or her own search for meaning, is always let down by the other, much as The Self-Taught Man is ultimately let down by his own belief system, rational humanism, when he is rejected by the librarian and the library's patrons. Anny, reinforcing Roquentin's sense of the inauthenticity of the past, is not as he remembers her. She has grown fat, she talks only about herself, and though her experiences of life seem to parallel Roquentin's, she refuses to acknowledge any correlation between these experiences. Like Françoise and so many of Sartre's women characters, she is self-centered and two-dimensional, incapable of complex thought or tenderness. Again, Roquentin is left with only his existence in all of its futility. In the end, he looks forward to the possibility of writing a novel and to living in Paris, even though he knows that his existence is meaningless. It is this awareness that gives him a sense of freedom.

Roquentin serves as the embodiment of Sartre's existential man. Rational humanism, as personified by The Self-Taught Man, serves as a parallel, yet inferior, belief system. Ironically, Roquentin, who never attempts to help anyone, even though he encounters others in need, reaches out to The Self-Taught Man, as if to reinforce the validity of rational humanism itself. The Self-Taught Man, however, refuses Roquentin's help, choosing instead to face his grief alone. According to Sartre's existentialism, there is no other valid choice.

"Critical Evaluation" by Dana Reece Baylard

Further Reading

Barnes, Hazel E. *The Literature of Possibility: A Study in Humanistic Existentialism*. Lincoln: University of Nebraska Press, 1959. A philosophical and psychological examination of Sartre's literary output, written by one of his leading translators. Refutes the charge of antihumanism that has been made against Sartre's work.

Danto, Arthur C. *Jean-Paul Sartre*. New York: Viking Press, 1975. The first chapter, "Absurdity: Or, Language and Existence," examines *Nausea* at length and discusses Sartre's views on language, the analytic "philosophy of mind," and the structural representation of reality.

Magny, Claude-Edmonde. "The Duplicity of Being." In *Sartre: A Collection of Critical Essays*, edited by Edith Kern. Englewood Cliffs, N.J.: Prentice-Hall, 1962. Discusses the experience of nausea as "the sudden revelation" of the mutability and impermanence of existence and existing things. Interprets the characters of *Nausea* as "cheaters" who attempt a sequential, and hence "fictitious," narration of their lives. Recommended for more advanced readers.

Murdoch, Iris. *Sartre: Romantic Rationalist.* 1953. New ed. New York: Viking Press, 1987. Includes a new, well-written introduction to Sartre's thought. Discusses *Nausea* in chapter 1, "The Discovery of Things," and refers to the work throughout. An excellent guide to Sartrean themes.

Peyre, Henri. *French Novelists of Today.* New York: Oxford University Press, 1967. An amplified version of Peyre's earlier *The Contemporary French Novel* (1955). Chapter 9 covers *Nausea* and other novels by Sartre. Includes a short but helpful bibliography.

Rolls, Alistair, and Elizabeth Rechniewski, eds. *Sartre's "Nausea": Text, Context, Intertext.* New York: Rodopi, 2005. A reappraisal of the novel, in which contributing essayists assess its relevance in the twenty-first century.

Includes discussions of Sartre's autodidacticism, art and illumination in the novel, and travel, displacement, and intertextuality in the book.

Rowley, Hazel. *Tête-à-Tête: Simone de Beauvoir and Jean-Paul Sartre.* New York: HarperCollins, 2005. Rowley chronicles the relationship between the two French writers, discussing their writing, their politics, their philosophical legacy, and their commitment to each other. Includes bibliography and index.

Solomon, Robert C. "Meditations on *Nausea*: Sartre's Phenomenological Ontology." In *Dark Feelings, Grim Thoughts: Experience and Reflection in Camus and Sartre.* New York: Oxford University Press, 2006. Examines Sartre's pre-1950 works, including *Nausea*, to highlight what is especially interesting and valuable in his philosophy and to compare it with the philosophy of Albert Camus. Concludes that both men were fundamentally moralists, and one must understand their political commitments to understand their philosophies.

The Necklace

Author: Guy de Maupassant (1850-1893)
First published: "La Parure," 1884 (English translation, 1903)
Type of work: Short fiction
Type of plot: Naturalism
Time of plot: 1880's
Locale: Paris

Principal characters:
MADAME MATHILDE LOISEL, a middle-class housewife
MADAME FORESTIER, a wealthy former classmate of Mathilde
MONSIEUR LOISEL, Mathilde's husband, a clerk at the Ministry of Public Instructions

The Story:

Mathilde Loisel is miserable as the wife of a middle-class Parisian clerk. She suffers constantly from what she views as a life of poverty. Although her husband's income from his position as a clerk at the Ministry of Public Instructions sufficiently meets the couple's needs, Mathilde dreams of attending the local salons, which host intimate gatherings of the upper class. She assumes airs at the dinner table, fantasizing that she is eating a higher quality of food and imagining herself dining with the wealthy. Mathilde focuses on her lack of jewels and fine clothing rather than on enjoying her life. She is jealous of one acquaintance in particular with whom she attended convent school, Madame Forestier, who has made a good marriage to a wealthy man.

Thinking Mathilde will be pleased, Monsieur Loisel brings her an invitation to a ball at the Palace of the Ministry.

Mathilde surprises him by throwing down the invitation. Because Mathilde lacks a beautiful gown and jewels, she does not feel she can attend the ball. Monsieur Loisel reluctantly agrees to finance the purchase of a four-hundred-franc gown, understanding that he must sacrifice a planned hunting vacation with friends to do so. Mathilde buys the dress but complains that she has no jewels. Monsieur Loisel suggests that she visit her friend Madame Forestier and ask to borrow some jewelry. For once, Mathilde is pleased by a suggestion made by her husband.

Madame Forestier offers Mathilde the choice of her jewels. Mathilde selects a superb diamond necklace from a black satin box. She feels euphoric when she tries it on. When Madame Forestier immediately agrees to let her borrow the necklace, Mathilde kisses her in gratitude.

At the ball, Mathilde's beauty attracts much attention. She is ecstatic when many men ask her name. She dances with all of the attachés from the cabinet and is even noticed by the minister. Intoxicated with pleasure and passion, Mathilde exists for a time in a fantasy haze. She believes she has at last succeeded in her quest to excel in high society.

Monsieur Loisel finds a room in which to sleep while Mathilde enjoys dancing and socializing. At 4:00 A.M., she is ready to leave. As Monsieur Loisel places her everyday wrap over his wife's shoulders, it contrasts so much with her beautiful gown that she hurries to depart before the other women notice. Although Monsieur Loisel asks her to wait inside and avoid the cold as he calls a cab, she races down the stairs. They fail to hail a cab and walk miserably in the cold until they find an enclosed carriage, the transportation mode of the middle class, in which to ride.

The Loisels arrive home at the Rue des Martyrs, and Mathilde pauses to enjoy her reflection in the mirror. She screams when she sees that the necklace is missing. She and Monsieur Loisel search frantically, but they cannot find the necklace. Monsieur Loisel volunteers to walk back to the ball's location, searching as he goes. He returns home exhausted and without the necklace. At his instruction, Mathilde writes a letter to Madame Forestier, explaining she will delay in returning the necklace. She lies, claiming that its clasp broke so she is having it repaired. This ruse allows them time to continue the search.

When the Loisels are unable to find the necklace, they use its jewel box to search for a jeweler from whom it might have been purchased. They discover the value of the necklace to be forty thousand francs; a jeweler offers to sell them a duplicate for thirty-six thousand francs. They buy the necklace using Monsieur Loisel's inheritance of eighteen thousand francs and borrowing the balance, imperiling their future security. Still hopeful of finding the necklace, they secure a promise from the jeweler to buy back the duplicate for thirty-four thousand francs if they return it within three months. However, they do not find the necklace, and they assume crippling debt that forever changes their lives. Monsieur Loisel anticipates a "black misery" that will befall them as a result not only of future physical sacrifice but also of "moral tortures."

When Mathilde takes the newly purchased necklace to Madame Forestier, she fears her acquaintance will discover that the necklace is a replacement. Her greatest concern is that her friend would consider her a thief. Although Madame Forestier scolds Mathilde for delaying the necklace's return, she never opens the case to inspect it.

The next years are torturous for Mathilde, who works like a servant, her own servant having been dismissed. The Loisels move to poor housing. Mathilde dresses in work clothing suiting her position and assumes all the family's "odious" housekeeping duties. Monsieur Loisel works a second job at night. They work for ten years to repay their debts. The strain of deprivation exacts a toll, and Mathilde ages rapidly. Occasionally, she fantasizes, remembering the wonders of the ball. Finally, their debt is paid in full.

One day on the street, Mathilde meets Madame Forestier, still youthful and lovely. At first not recognizing Mathilde, Madam Forestier is shocked by her friend's haggard appearance. She cries out with sympathy over Mathilde's transformation. Mathilde explains that her life has been hard because of Madame Forestier. Mathilde shares the truth regarding her loss and replacement of the necklace that she had borrowed. She explains it was purchased with ten years of hard labor. She proudly describes how she met her obligation both to Madame Forestier and to society.

Madame Forestier takes Mathilde's hands in her own and tells her the truth. The necklace that she had loaned Mathilde was mere costume jewelry worth only five hundred francs.

Critical Evaluation:

Following his service in the Franco-Prussian War of 1870-1871, Guy de Maupassant studied with the seminal French writer Gustave Flaubert. From Flaubert, de Maupassant learned that his job as a writer was to observe and then report common occurrences in an original way. His stories would show less sympathy for their characters than did those of Anton Chekhov, another writer of his era with whom de Maupassant is often associated. De Maupassant began his career by publishing the story "Boule de Suif" (1880; ball of fat), which sparked a strong reaction to its topic of prostitution and bourgeois hypocrisy in France. He published almost three hundred stories written in the naturalist style before suffering a lingering illness and death from syphilis. His own experience serving as a clerk for the Ministry of Public Instructions informed his writing of "The Necklace."

Much of de Maupassant's discourse resembles conversation, echoing the conventions of oral storytelling. His narrator acts as a nonjudgmental observer. Readers are left to draw their own conclusions regarding his characters' actions, morality, or lack of morality. One of the most prolific writers of his era, de Maupassant influenced many writers, including the American Kate Chopin, whose widely anthologized short story "The Story of an Hour" (1894) owes much to de Maupassant's enigmatic style.

Formalist critics have noted de Maupassant's employment of repetition for emphasis. For example, of the first seven paragraphs in "The Necklace," six begin with the word "She," clarifying that the focus of the story will remain on Mathilde. De Maupassant sets a cynical tone early in the tale though his vocabulary choice: Words such as "suffered," "poverty," "wretched," "ugliness," "tortured," and "angry" all appear in the third paragraph. He then lightens his tone through playful alliteration used to frame Mathilde's fantasies. Examples include the phrases "dainty dinner," "shining silverware," "fairy forest," "delicious dishes," and "sphinx-like smile" (all of which are also alliterative in French). De Maupassant's use of detail helps emphasize the value placed upon objects, the fantasized Oriental tapestry in the story's opening serving as a fine example. His short cryptic sentences aid in building narrative momentum, and he bolsters imagery through quick staccato descriptions that resemble stage directions, such as "She turned madly toward him," or "He stood up, distracted."

"The Necklace" is framed by heavy irony, especially in its conclusion, which helps impart its observations regarding the costs of pride. The Loisels pay an incalculable personal price, both literally and figuratively, for Mathilde's vanity. De Maupassant provides no evidence of an epiphany that might demonstrate that Mathilde has learned or benefited in any way from her foolish actions. However, readers may realize that her failure to take responsibility for her actions is the flaw that leads to her fall. Although the conclusion of "The Necklace" is meant to surprise, de Maupassant inserts foreshadowing that might be noted by an astute reader, such as the facts that Madame Forestier freely loans the necklace and then does not care even to examine the piece that Mathilde returns to her, suggesting its low value.

With its emphasis on Parisian class structure, "The Necklace" is a prime candidate for application of Marxist criticism. Mathilde is born into a family of clerks, lacks a dowry, is unable to perform any service, and, most important, lacks any expectations: She is thus destined to remain in her low station. However, she possesses a strong sense of imagination that prevents her from accepting her "place." She fantasizes details about the upper class based on stories she has heard, her daydreams containing a strong emphasis on material things. She pretends through role-playing to be a member of the upper class, and her longings promote dissatisfaction with her middle-class life. A member of the "petite bourgeoisie," Monsieur Loisel works for wages at the pleasure of the upper class. By the story's end, Mathilde bears the burdens of the servant class.

Some Marxist critics focus on power structures and control of one group by another based on material possessions.

Not only does class structure limit Monsieur Loisel's income, but it also limits Mathilde's happiness. In contrast, Monsieur Loisel is accepting of his social place. Any regrets he holds are on behalf of his wife, whose misery greatly affects his existence. Madame Forestier's reserved attitude toward Mathilde makes clear that, although they began life on the same level, she believes herself superior to Mathilde because she has become a member of the upper class, the haute bourgeoisie, through marriage.

Marxist ideology promotes revolution by the working class, which see all surplus value extracted from the products of its labor for the benefit of the upper classes. Rather than physically revolting against her circumstances, however, Mathilde escapes her circumstances through fantasy, desiring the things that the upper classes possess and thereby accepting bourgeois values as her own. Her situation is untenable, as she can never become a part of the class she longs to join, but neither can she accept her own position.

When Mathilde attempts a temporary shift to the upper class, it is not through revolution but through capitulation, an act that supports the story's irony. By accepting an invitation to interact on a temporary basis with the members of the upper class, Mathilde complies with their requirements. Not only do these requirements effectively force the Loisels to retain their lower social status, but they also cause a further loss of income by requiring Monsieur Loisel to spend money he cannot afford to dress Mathilde as she desires. Ironically, the Loisels do descend to the working class as a result of Mathilde's pride.

Other critical schools that may provide useful readings of "The Necklace" include feminism, which would tend to focus on Mathilde's restrictions as a member of a nineteenth century patriarchal society. Because women cannot work for success, they must depend upon the confines of marriage to advance their social standing, as Madame Forestier does. Women succeed in this society only as fashion objects. A crucial symbol for feminist critics is the mirror in which Mathilde admires herself, which represents objectification. Deconstructionist critics might focus on the binary opposition between wealth and poverty, discussing how in this instance poverty is the preferred condition, because through poverty Mathilde sees that she was not poor in her previous circumstance.

Virginia Brackett

Further Reading

Bloom, Harold, ed. *Guy de Maupassant*. Philadelphia: Chelsea House, 2004. Collection of essays on de Maupassant's short fiction, divided into sections. The section on "The Necklace" includes a plot summary, a list of characters, a summary of critical views on the work, and four full essays relevant to the story.

Bryant, David. *The Rhetoric of Pessimism and Strategies of Containment in the Short Stories of Guy de Maupassant.* Lewiston, N.Y.: Edwin Mellen Press, 1993. Using several stories as examples, Bryant discusses de Maupaussant's depiction of a world hostile to humanity. He describes three constants in the stories that contribute to de Maupassant's overall unity of vision: the world as a metaphysical farce in which the narrator's detachment transforms suffering, the power of chance, and writing as a response to fate.

MacNamara, Matthew. "A Critical Stage in the Evolution of Maupassant's Story-Telling." *Modern Language Review* 71, no. 2 (April, 1976): 294-303. Emphasizes the extent to which de Maupassant was influenced by oral tradition and spoken conversation.

Powys, John Cowper. "Guy de Maupassant." In *Essays on de Maupassant, Anatole France, and William Blake.* Whitefish, Mont.: Kessinger, 2006. Highlights de Maupassant's realist approach and his focus on physical reality.

Worth, George J. "The English 'Maupassant School' of the 1890's: Some Reservations." *Modern Language Notes* 72, no. 5 (May, 1957): 337-340. Chronicles de Maupassant's career and the metamorphosis of his anecdotal conversational style.

A Nest of Simple Folk

Author: Seán O'Faoláin (1900-1991)
First published: 1933
Type of work: Novel
Type of plot: Regional
Time of plot: 1854-1916
Locale: Ireland

Principal characters:
LEO FOXE-DONNELL, an Irish patriot
JUDITH, his mother
JULIE, his wife
JOHNO O'DONNELL, the son of Julie and Leo
JOHNNY HUSSEY, a police officer
BID, his wife
DENIS, the son of Bid and Johnny

The Story:

Foxehall is a bleak, remote manor house, and the family that owns it keeps to themselves. Rachel and Anna Foxe are content to live prim maiden lives, poverty-stricken remnants of a landed family. Judith Foxe, however, marries Long John O'Donnell, a secretive farmer. Judith is cut off with a dowry of five fields as a punishment for marrying beneath her station; for seventeen years, she does not see her sisters. The marriage is a good one for Long John. Poor as he is, he feels that Judith's five fields were good pay for taking an unattractive wife. When their tenth child, Leo, is born, Rachel condescends to sponsor him. Afterward, it seems to Judith that Leo is her only true son. When her husband is near death, she is determined that Leo should be the heir.

James, the oldest son, works like a servant for his harsh father. As the oldest, he will inherit the home farm. Phil is next in line; by rights, he should have had the five fields. Long John obstinately refuses to make a will; as he grows weaker, however, Judith harries him into telling a lawyer how the

property should be distributed. She also dresses Leo in Phil's clothes and tricks her weak, dying husband into pointing to Leo as the heir to the five fields. By this act, James inherits only the heavily mortgaged home farm and the obligation to find husbands for his numerous sisters. Leo is given the five free fields, with Phil receiving only what James will share with him.

After the funeral, James drives the family home. Young Leo senses James's state of mind and offers to give him all the land, an offer which infuriates the older brother. James whips Leo savagely and drives him off the farm. Leo goes to live with his maiden aunts. Rachel and Anna do their best to make a genteel aristocrat of their rough and surly nephew. Nicholas, a ne'er-do-well, is his tutor, and Nicholas himself is rough. A long debate ensues over Leo's future as a doctor or a gentleman farmer. Leo has little preference, but when he is sent to Limerick to study with Dicky, his doctor cousin, he goes willingly enough.

Nicholas is influential in molding the boy's sympathies and accompanies him on the journey. Because the tutor had told him of the past insults and atrocities by the aristocracy, Leo becomes angry at the injustices suffered by the poor farmers. In Limerick, the two call on Frankie O'Donnell, Leo's uncle, a tavernkeeper who is a revolutionary at heart. The rough welcome there is in sharp contrast with his treatment at Doctor Dicky's house. The old doctor is a gruff Protestant and a teetotaler. Leo is out of place in his country clothes. After a trial term, Leo is sent home in disgrace; he has no aptitude for medicine.

For years, Leo lives an idle and dissolute life. After his aunts die, he becomes the owner of Foxehall. Taking no care of the property, he hunts, carouses, and chases girls. One of them, Philly Cashen, is turned out of old Mag Keene's house because of her pregnancy. Distraught, Philly goes to Foxehall. Although she knows that Leo is guilty, Judith refuses to help the girl. At last, Judith leaves her youngest son and his fine house and returns to live with James. Philly is not the only girl Leo ruins; another is Julie Keene, who is too young to have been able to resist him successfully.

The Fenian spirit pervades the countryside. Although a landowner, Mad Leo joins the plotters and leads a raid on the police post. By chance, Julie sees them and runs to warn another sweetheart of hers, a detective. The plotters are seized, and Leo is sentenced to fifteen years in jail. While he is in prison, his mother dies, but Leo does not know of her death; his family never informs him. A change of government brings an amnesty, and after ten years, Leo is released.

Julie is still unmarried. Holding no grudge against her, Leo courts her again, and when she becomes pregnant, he mortgages his land to raise money to send her to Dublin. Julie gives birth to a boy, gives him away, and returns as happy as ever. Leo continues his shiftless ways and eventually loses his land to his grasping brother, James. Finally, with the help of a neighborhood priest, Leo is bullied into marrying Julie, and the strange couple set themselves up in a small paper shop in Rathkeale.

Bid, Julie's pretty youngest sister, comes to live with them after a time. Before long, she is walking out with Johnny Hussey, a police officer. After innocent Bid visits the police barracks with Johnny, Leo questions her closely about the visit, for at the age of sixty, he is still an ardent Fenian. Bid assures Leo that the police officer has said nothing about him, but she half guiltily remembers some joking remarks she had heard. Leo is perturbed. Julie is almost hysterical and demands that Leo bring back their lost son. To quiet her, he finds Johno O'Donnell, now a twenty-year-old sailor, and brings him as a nephew to Rathkeale.

After Johnny searches Leo's room and finds suspicious letters, the police begin to watch Leo carefully. Still a fiery patriot, Leo plans with his son, Johno, to bring into a river port a shipment of rifles that Johno smuggled aboard his ship. Leo and a few Fenians are waiting with a skiff to take them off when the police surprise them. Leo fires a warning shot. When an officer is wounded, the conspirators quickly row out into the foggy harbor and escape. Leo lands on the other shore. Returning to Rathkeale, he is arrested and sentenced to five years in prison.

Meanwhile, Johnny marries Bid. When he is transferred to Cork, they take Julie, now old and broken, with them. After Leo's release from prison, the old couple see nothing to do but to live with Johnny, who had been promoted to the post of acting sergeant. Johno and his wife complete the family circle. Denis, Bid's oldest boy, was always prim. Because Leo and Johno are gusty and loud, Johnny encourages his son to be different. Bid regards Denis as a potential scholar and plans for his education. Old Leo has a small shop where he sometimes takes bets. As always, he knows what is going on among the revolutionaries.

Bid takes in lodgers to get money for the boy's schooling. Although she is always tired, her efforts seem worthwhile. Nevertheless, Denis is a disappointment to her. He has no head for studies and gives up his ambitions after he fails the civil service examination three times. Worse than that, he quarrels with his father.

Rifles are cracking all over Ireland. When an uprising breaks out in Dublin, Denis, after helping Leo and Johno to escape arrest, calls his father a police spy and takes shelter with the O'Donnells. Like Ireland, his is a house divided.

Critical Evaluation:

Seán O'Faoláin was the leading Irish man of letters of his generation whose literary reputation rests largely on his short stories. *A Nest of Simple Folk* is the first of his three novels, and the one that draws most directly on his personal and historical experiences. For various reasons, however, the work is not to be considered as simply an autobiographical first novel. Like many Irish writers of his generation, O'Faoláin was careful to resist the influence of James Joyce, whose *A Portrait of the Artist as a Young Man* (1916) set the standard for Irish first novels in theme, structure, and artistry. O'Faoláin sought his creative model elsewhere, as the title of *A Nest of Simple Folk*—deliberately echoing that of a novel by Ivan Turgenev, *Dvoryanskoye gnezdo* (1859; *A House of Gentlefolk*, 1894)—is intended to suggest.

The invocation of Turgenev does not end with titles. The atmosphere, depiction of the landscape, economic reality, and pace of narrative development all resemble the Russian author's works. O'Faoláin, however, is not merely being a mimic. The clouds and river mists that recur throughout the novel are not just picturesque details. They function as a means of conveying the sense of the recurrent and inescapable conditions of existence. These meteorological and atmospheric features are so prevalent, they constitute the equivalent of a destiny. The view of the landscape, of rural family life, of commercial life in the town of Rathkeale and the city of Limerick, is of such a repetitive and claustrophobic nature as to suggest the title of another nineteenth century Russian novel, Nikolay Chernyshevsky's *Chto delat'* (1863; *What Is to Be Done?*, c. 1863). The challenge for the characters is how to resist the destiny inscribed for them by the undramatic but insidious powers of nature, and the powerfully inert forces of custom and social class that are their counterparts.

This challenge is presented in terms of the characters, in their various ways, attempting to act as though they had a nature of their own, a life distinct from the one arising from the conditions into which they were born. Inasmuch as such preoccupations constitute the overall narrative interest of *A Nest of Simple Folk*, the novel may be considered a meditation on the origins of the modern, and by virtue of that is a work of more than local Irish interest. It is not coincidental that the work concludes in a setting that, for all its ostensible lack of urban features, is in fact the city of Cork. Unlike his forebears, the landscape that Denis Hussey—heir to his family's two-faced history and to the conflicting tendencies in national history which that family history exemplifies—contemplates in his formative years is one composed entirely of human-made structures.

Although the city and county of Cork were to play a leading role in the violent political events set in motion by the rebellion of Easter, 1916, the novel quite accurately and tellingly presents the rebellion itself as both a shock, a mere skirmish, and the unlikely culmination of the years of suffering and commitment of the novel's protagonist, Leo Foxe-Donnell. The Easter Rising, as it is known in Irish history, accelerated the movement toward political self-determination for the Irish people, whose progress until that juncture had been at best tragically disappointing and at worst stagnantly counterproductive. *A Nest of Simple Folk*, however, is careful not to become the historical novel it easily might have been. The career of Leo is not of great political or historical moment. It represents a reaction against conditions more than an action in favor of alternative conditions. Policy, ideology, strategy, and recruitment play little or no part in Leo's exploits.

On the contrary, he attains his reputation through action—or rather, through abortive action—or through the periods of imprisonment that not only sanctify his efforts in the eyes of the authorities and his fellow nationalists but also confirm the intrinsic historical and political insignificance of those actions. A similar perspective may be applied to those who betray Leo, as his intimate acquaintance and family connection with them suggest. Julie, his wife-to-be, has little thought of the political dimension of her betrayal, nor does her sister, Bid. Neither woman's involvement with a police officer alerts her to the political context of her life. They have no particular sense of themselves as members of an Irish nation in the making. They would hardly know what to make of the term "folk" if it were directly applied to them. Such a lack of self-awareness and critical distance is part of what O'Faoláin intends to convey by the term "simple."

It should also be noted, however, that O'Faoláin is also carrying out a complex and sophisticated maneuver in the realm of contemporary cultural ideology. One of the important ideological preconditions of the Easter Rising was the projection of a certain image of essential Irishness, based on a conception of the countryside and its inhabitants. Such an image was intended to make a claim for a pure, long-suffering populace, in whose name the struggle for Irish freedom could justifiably be waged. The hybrid, prefabricated character of Leo, his siblings' excruciating and embittering demands for land, the complicated morality—or lack of it—that underlies Leo's behavior, and the debatable quality of all the characters' consciousness may be regarded as O'Faoláin's critique of the preceding generation's ideology, and also perhaps of the literature that was that ideology's most important vehicle.

Pertinent as O'Faoláin's awareness of cultural and political history is to an appreciation of *A Nest of Simple Folk*, that awareness, however, does not overwhelm the novel. The author's detached but sympathetic manner ensures that the focus remains on his characters' frailty. The significance of their frailty for the themes of attempted change and putative self-realization gives the narrative its dramatic interest. Those themes, in turn, attain a wider, emblematic, significance when seen in the context of Irish political and cultural history.

"Critical Evaluation" by George O'Brien

Further Reading

Arndt, Marie. *A Critical Study of Sean O'Faolain's Life and Work*. Lewiston, N.Y.: Edwin Mellen Press, 2001. Critical biography that places O'Faoláin's achievements in their historical and political context. Argues that despite

O'Faoláin's attempts to portray himself as an internationalist, he remained attached to his Irish roots.

Bonaccorso, Richard. *Seán O'Faoláin's Irish Vision*. Albany: State University of New York Press, 1987. A survey of the main phases of O'Faoláin's career, evaluating *A Nest of Simple Folk* within that career. The analysis of the novel concentrates on its treatment of individuality. Includes a comprehensive bibliography.

Doyle, Paul A. *Seán O'Faoláin*. New York: Twayne, 1968. A general introductory survey of all O'Faoláin's writings. The discussion of *A Nest of Simple Folk* deals with its sense of historical context and its narrative development. Contains a chronology and a bibliography.

Harmon, Maurice. *Seán O'Faoláin: A Critical Introduction*. 2d ed. Dublin: Wolfhound Press, 1984. An insightful overview of O'Faoláin's career. Discusses his contributions to Irish intellectual life and his major works. The evaluation of *A Nest of Simple Folk* is guided by a sense of the conflict between the individual and society in O'Faoláin's novels. Includes an extensive bibliography.

Kiely, Benedict. "Sean O'Faolain: A Tiller of Ancient Soil." In *A Raid into Dark Corners, and Other Essays*. Cork, Ireland: Cork University Press, 1999. Kiely, an Irish writer and literary critic, assesses O'Faoláin's novels and short stories.

O'Brien, Conor Cruise. "The Parnellism of Seán O'Faoláin." In *Maria Cross: Imaginative Patterns in a Group of Catholic Writers*, edited by Donat O'Donnell. 2d ed. London: Burns and Oates, 1963. Intellectually sophisticated, culturally wide-ranging, critically incisive analysis of certain key features in O'Faoláin's major works, among them history, tradition, and memory. Assesses how these features shape the narrative of, and constitute authorial identity in, *A Nest of Simple Folk*.

O'Faoláin, Seán. *Vive Moi!: An Autobiography*. Boston: Little, 1964. Author's autobiography presents prototypes of the landscape, characters, and rural sensibility featured in *A Nest of Simple Folk*. The contrast between fictional and autobiographical perspectives is critically revealing.

The Neuromancer Trilogy

Author: William Gibson (1948-   )
First published: 1984-1988; includes *Neuromancer*, 1984; *Count Zero*, 1986; *Mona Lisa Overdrive*, 1988
Type of work: Novels
Type of plot: Science fiction
Time of plot: Twenty-third century
Locale: Freeside, in Earth orbit; Chiba City, Japan; Istanbul, Turkey; London; Nevada; Barrytown, New York; rural Georgia; the Sprawl

Principal characters:
HENRY DORSETT CASE, a cyberspace cowboy (computer hacker)
MOLLY (SALLY SHEARS), a street samurai (killer for hire)
THE FINN, a fence and computer hardware expert
ARMITAGE (COLONEL CORTO), an unstable manufactured personality built from the shell of the catatonic Corto
DIXIE FLATLINE, the computer-encoded mind (ROM construct) of a dead master cyberspace cowboy
PETER RIVIERA, a drug-addicted sadist capable of projecting his fantasies holographically
LADY 3JANE TESSIER-ASHPOOL, a slightly mad and perverted heir to a vast empire
WINTERMUTE, an artificial intelligence (AI) programmed to arrange its integration with a second AI
NEUROMANCER, the second AI, the romantic and imaginative counterpart to Wintermute's hard reasoning and logic
TURNER, a street samurai who specializes in security and assisting corporate defectors
RUDY TURNER, Turner's brother, who lives in rural Georgia

Principal characters (continued):

CONROY, his employer

ANGELA "ANGIE" MITCHELL, the seventeen-year-old daughter of Christopher Mitchell, who created the first biosofts; later a simstim star

JAYLENE SLIDE, a female cyberspace cowboy working for Conroy

JOSEF VIREK, a vastly wealthy man kept alive in tanks

MARLY KRUSHKHOVA, an art expert whom Virek hires

BOBBY NEWMARK (COUNT ZERO), a beginner computer hacker from the New Jersey Projects

TWO-A-DAY, a computer contraband dealer who gives an icebreaker to Bobby and who engineers his rescue after he is attacked

BEAUVOIR and LUCAS, black professionals who do the bidding of voodoo deities found in cyberspace

WIGAN LUDGATE (THE WIG), an insane former cyberspace cowboy living in orbit in abandoned Tessier-Ashpool data cores

JAMMER, a former cyberspace cowboy who owns a nightclub in the New York area of the Sprawl

KUMIKO YANAKA, the thirteen-year-old daughter of a Yakuza overlord

COLIN THE GHOST, a biosoft ROM construct with the persona of a young Englishman

ROGER SWAIN, Yanaka's subordinate in London

PETAL, Swain's subordinate

TICK (TERRANCE), a cyberspace cowboy who helps Molly and Kumiko

KID AFRIKA, the agent who brings the comatose Bobby Newmark to the Factory

THOMAS TRAIL GENTRY, a part criminal, part mystic who runs the Factory

SLICK HENRY, a former convict with Induced Korsakov's syndrome who creates large, mechanical, remote-controlled creatures from scrap parts at the Factory

CHERRY-LEE CHESTERFIELD, a nurse who accompanies the comatose Bobby Newmark

HILTON SWIFT, controller of Angie Marshall

MONA LISA, a sixteen-year-old street addict

PROPHYRE, Angie Marshall's hairdresser and protector

PRIOR, a criminal who transforms Mona Lisa into Angie's double

ROBIN LANIER, Angie's simstim costar

CONTINUITY, a computer entity assisting and managing Angie

The Story:

In *Neuromancer*, Henry Dorsett Case is a cyberspace cowboy, or computer hacker. He is running toward suicide because the criminals he was working for have chemically altered his brain so he can no longer enter cyberspace, the visualization of the computer universe accessed through a keyboard. He is captured by Molly, who is working for Armitage. Armitage restores Case's ability and sends him on a "run" into cyberspace, but he also has toxin sacs sewn into his arteries that will maim him again if he fails to complete his assignment. Case and Molly employ the services of the Finn, a fence and computer expert, to find out who is employing Armitage. They all travel to the Sprawl—a vast megalopolis that covers all of the territory between Boston and Atlanta—where Armitage instructs them to steal the Dixie Flatline, the ROM construct (computer-encoded mind) of a dead cyberspace cowboy. Shortly afterward, they discover that an artificial intelligence (AI) called Wintermute is the moving force behind Armitage.

The group travels to Istanbul, where Peter Riviera joins them, and they then take the JAL Shuttle, transferring to Zion Cluster, an orbiting miniworld run by Rastafarians, several of whom Wintermute has coopted. They move on to Freeside, a vast entertainment and commercial vacation paradise in high orbit, where they prepare to enter Straylight Villa, a private enclave at its tip. Straylight Villa is the family home of Lady 3Jane Tessier-Ashpool, and the group has been instructed to force Lady 3Jane to assist them by providing them with a password in the physical side of their run.

The run turns out to be the illegal amalgamation of two AIs, Wintermute and Neuromancer. On the way to its completion, Armitage commits suicide, Riviera dies of poisoned drugs, and Case experiences "flatlining," a temporary death of the body, while first Wintermute and then Neuromancer place him in virtual worlds. With the assistance of the Dixie Flatline construct and his own immense anger at the manipulations of which he has been a victim, Case finally breaks through and allows the AIs to merge. As the story ends, Molly and Case have been made rich, the toxin sacs have been removed, and the couple go their separate ways. The entity created from the combined AIs announces that it now is the cyberspace matrix and has discovered another intelligence in Alpha Centauri.

In *Count Zero*, Turner is hired by Conroy to assist in the defection of Christopher Mitchell. The project goes very wrong, as the transfer site is destroyed and only Turner and Mitchell's daughter Angie escape alive. Unsure of who has betrayed the operation, Turner retreats to his brother Rudy's rural hideaway and then takes a hovercraft to the New York portion of the Sprawl, constantly on the run from attackers. Angie's brain has been augmented with biosofts by her father, and she is therefore a target. She has seizures when she is possessed and guided by voodoo gods who dwell in the network matrix of cyberspace.

Meanwhile, Bobby Newark—a would-be cyberspace cowboy living in the slums of Barrytown—nearly loses his life when he tries to run an "icebreaker," or hacking program. He escapes brain death only when Angie (unbeknown to him) intervenes in cyberspace. Bobby is pursued by those alerted by his attempt, until he is rescued by Two-a-Day's helpers after he has been badly cut up and robbed. He meets the black lawyer Beauvoir and his friend Lucas, who are interested in him because they think their voodoo god was the source of the voice that saved him in cyberspace. Beauvoir and Lucas shepherd Bobby to the Sprawl, where he ends up in Jammer's eighth-floor nightclub, under siege from Conroy and Josef Virek. Turner eventually brings Angie to the same club.

Marly's art gallery has collapsed because her lover Alain perpetuated a fraud. She is hired by Virek to track down the creator of seven small artworks in the form of boxes with arrangements of objects inside them. Virek is suffering from expanding cancers and is stored in life-sustaining tanks. He appears to Marly in a virtual representation.

Marly's pursuit of the objects leads her to Alain, who tries to sell her information but is murdered. Marly finds the information, but she decides that Virek's overpowering wealth and his security apparatus, led by a Spaniard named Paco, are corrupt. She escapes into high orbit, where she discovers a mad former console cowboy named Wigan who believes he has found God. She also finds that a massive semirobotic entity dwelling in the wreckage of the Tessier-Ashpool cores is assembling the boxes. Marly becomes aware that Virek has been seeking the boxes in order to gain personal immortality and escape from his prison of flesh.

Bobby and Jackie use the net to try to contact Jaylene Slide in Los Angeles to tell her that Conroy has had her lover killed. Slide responds by destroying Conroy, but Bobby and Jackie accidentally plunge through Virek's security, and Jackie is killed. Bobby is about to be destroyed as well when Baron Samedi, the voodoo deity of death, enters the hallucinatory construct and destroys Virek in the net, leading to his physical death. Angie and Bobby go with Beauvoir to the Projects, where Angie will be protected and will learn to use her exceptional powers. Turner simply walks away from the action; seven years later, he is raising a son he had with Rudy's lover. Angie, with Bobby as her companion, in an understudy for the simstim star Tally Ashram.

In *Mona Lisa Overdrive*, Kumiko is sent by her father, a crime overlord, from Chiba City to London and into the protection of Swain and Petal. She is accompanied by Colin, a ROM device that generates a speaking image of a young Englishman to advise her. In London, Kumiko is befriended by Sally Shears (formerly Molly from the first book), who introduces her to Tick. Sally commissions Tick to discover who is controlling Swain and, indirectly, herself. It emerges that Swain and Sally are being forced to participate in the kidnapping of Angie Marshall, now a simstim star, and to substitute another body in her place.

Sally steals Kumiko away to the Sprawl, where Sally talks to the Finn, who now exists as a construct voice at an alleyway shrine. They talk of 3Jane being the mover behind the plots under way. Kumiko is taken back to London but escapes to Tick to get help; she tries to warn Sally that she will also be a victim of the plot. While attempting to warn Sally in cyberspace, they get caught up in a generated reality created by 3Jane (who appears as Kumiko's dead mother), but Colin intervenes to save them. Finally, Petal arrives: Swain has been destroyed by Kumiko's father, and Kumiko is free to return home.

Meanwhile, the former convict Slick Henry inhabits the Factory, a vast industrial ruin in a pollution field called Dog Solitude. There, he uses scrap materials to create large, radio-controlled figures such as the Judge—products of his imagination, which has been twisted by the chemical-psychological punishments he experienced in prison. Henry lives in uneasy peace with Gentry, who spends his time trying to understand the shape of the matrix. Kid Afrika brings Cherry-Lee Chesterfield and the comatose Bobby Newmark to Dog Solitude in order to hide Newmark. Newmark is connected to something called the "LF," and Gentry insists on jacking into it as well.

The "LF" turns out to be the "aleph," a vast biosoft that contains an abstract of cyberspace. Gentry is knocked out by his experience of it. The group rigs a way for Slick Henry to enter the aleph, where he meets with the illusion of Bobby, Count Zero, who cautions him that they must connect the aleph to the matrix if enemies come. Those enemies do arrive en masse, and Slick and Gentry reenter the aleph; they are briefly trapped by 3Jane in Straylight before the Count pulls them out. Sally-Molly arrives with Angie and Mona. Gentry and Slick Henry hold off and destroy their attackers with cyber help from Bobby (Count Zero), but Bobby's body dies, leaving him "alive" in cyberspace.

Angie Marshall has become a world-famous simstim star. She is recovering from drug addiction and is still haunted through her modified brain by voodoo gods, particularly one called Mamman Brigitte. Brigitte cautions her that those around her are plotting against her. Angie moves from Malibu to the Sprawl, responding evasively to Hilton Swift, the network's agent, and making use of Continuity, an AI who answers her questions and guides her. She investigates the history of the Tessier-Ashpools. On her arrival in the Sprawl, she is kidnapped by Sally-Molly, who is attempting to short-circuit 3Jane's plan. Sally-Molly takes Angie to the Factory, where Angie is reunited with Bobby's body and dies physically in order to enter cyberspace with him.

Meanwhile, Mona Lisa, a prostitute and drug addict, is taken from her pimp-lover by Prior, who arranges for her to have surgeries that make her an approximate double for Angie. Prior, Lanier, and Swain are acting under the distant direction of Lady 3Jane. They plan to kidnap Angie and leave Mona's body in her place. However, before they can execute their plan, Molly-Sally intervenes and takes both women to the Factory. After the struggles in the Factory, Molly leaves with the aleph; Mona plans to replace Angie as a media star, and Bobby, Angie, and Continuity exist only in cyberspace.

Critical Evaluation:

When *Neuromancer* was published in 1984, it was immediately recognized as a major breakthrough in science fiction. It won the three major science-fiction novel awards, the Hugo Award (1985), the Nebula Award (1984), and the Philip K. Dick Award (1984). The succeeding volumes of the Neuromancer Trilogy, also called the Sprawl trilogy, were also nominated for Hugo and Nebula awards. William Gibson had succeeded in creating a whole new framework for science fiction that was quickly labeled "cyberpunk." Its originality lay in the combination of a vision of a world radically altered by computer technology and other scientific developments and a vision of violence frequently perpetrated in the name of transnational commercial groupings. Thus, Gibson's new subgenre combined "cyber"—derived from cybernetics, the science of control typified by computing—and "punk"—a term used to designate both street violence and a music-based antiestablishment counterculture—while adding a surreal twist to the mixture.

Gibson's style features a dizzying array of invention and projection of the present into a richly textured world three hundred years in the future. Driven at a terrific narrative pace, a reader is whipped through this violent future without explanation or rationalization. Things simply "are," as the narratives are driven by chases, mysteries, and revelations.

Gibson coined the word "cyberspace" to describe a shared hallucination of the contents of all networked electronic media. In cyberspace, all data are represented in graphic form as virtual buildings or constellations. "Entering" this space using their computer talents, data thieves such as Case and the Count are future criminals addicted to their own skills. At the end of *Neuromancer*, there is a brief flash of an idea that beings actually can exist in the net—that it is a space after all, and not merely a hallucinatory representation of a nonspatial data structure. In the two succeeding novels, voodoo gods appear to exist in cyberspace, and then a number of the human characters who jack into cyberspace appear to be able to exist there, within their own illusory environments.

The texture of Gibson's writing has been likened to that of surrealism because he often takes real phenomena from the present world and twists them in order to represent their future shapes. For example, the housing projects near New York in *Mona Lisa Overdrive* are called "mincomes," a term derived from the minimal incomes of their residents. These mincomes are vast, and they suffer from an inner decay that leads to entire floors being devoted to the growing of marijuana.

Gibson creates several new fictional technologies of the future, many of which integrate humans and science in ways that alter or question identity. Simstim, for example, is a futuristic entertainment form in which participants exist in the consciousness of a human moderator, sharing all of the moderator's senses. Biosofts are biologically engineered memory structures that take advantage of the almost infinite coding possibilities of DNA.

Gibson's vision of violence is often exotic. Molly, for example, has scalpel blades hidden beneath her fingernails, and her senses have been modified so that she perceives regular movement in slow motion, allowing her to respond with amazing speed. No brief account of the inventiveness of these novels can suffice because every page is laden with newly imagined ideas. Most science fiction represents as-yet-unrealized devices, societies, or realities, but Gibson absolutely floods his texts with such inventions, creating a stunning surface along which a reader skims and that demands repeated readings to fully absorb myriad details.

A number of thought-provoking parallels are deployed in the novels. The continued existence in cyberspace of characters who have physically died evokes a vision of a technological afterlife that has no relationship to morality. The two AIs who unite in *Neuromancer* represent the two halves of the human self: the romantic and creative ego and the logical and mechanically reasoning ego.

Gibson presents an original, intense, and exciting world through driving action and mystery plots. Beyond the excitements of the world and its narratives, however, lie several hard truths about the imagined future that reflect upon humankind's present condition. Governments are hardly mentioned in the trilogy. Almost all power lies in the hands of amoral and rapacious multinational corporations that employ mercenaries to commit acts of physical and computer violence. The corporations and their mercenaries are only occasionally threatened by criminal elements.

Gibson's novels portray the struggles of characters who are very much pawns in this world of techno-capitalist determinism. The narratives may be exciting, but they present a very pessimistic vision. Moreover, as this vision represents an extrapolation of contemporary society, it is an implicit critique of today's world.

Special attention should be paid to the endings of the novels. In *Neuromancer*, many of the principals are dead, Case and Molly are paid off, and Molly ends the relationship they seem to be developing in order to follow her violent craft. The AIs, one of whom controlled the action, have achieved their unity and become an electronic creature capable of reaching out to the further universe. This ending just "is": It is not a human triumph or even a triumph for the specialized personnel who have survived the struggle. At the end of *Count Zero*, Turner escapes from the mercenary world to raise a family and Marly answers the question about the constructs. Angie, with Bobby the Count at her side, drifts off to become a simstim star. *Mona Lisa Overdrive* concludes with some of the principals having entered cyberspace as new types of beings after overcoming Lady 3Jane's mad and violent manipulations.

The novels are not about heroism, and they are not about success. No matter what their talents, individuals in Gibson's world are simply flung about by a reality where centralized power is augmented by the dominating cyber tool, computing. Gibson's achievement in the trilogy is even more impressive when readers consider that his imagining of cyberspace took place at a time when many computers were still command-line driven and e-mail was a wholly original

idea. He leapt forward imaginatively into worlds of new technologies rich with cyber-swashbuckling romantic action.

Peter Brigg

Further Reading

Bukatman, Scott. *Terminal Identity: The Virtual Subject in Postmodern Science Fiction.* Durham, N.C.: Duke University Press, 1993. Examines the representation of computer-human hybrids, electronic identity, cyberspace, and other forms of virtual and technologically altered subjectivity in science fiction.

Cavallaro, Dani. *Cyberpunk and Cyberculture: Science Fiction and the Work of William Gibson.* London: Athlone Press, 2000. Exhaustive study of cyberpunk and Gibson, giving consideration to virtuality, technology, emerging mythologies of the body, sexuality, commodification of the self, and the city in the shadow of cybernetic transformation.

McCaffery, Larry, ed. *Storming the Reality Studio.* Durham, N.C.: Duke University Press, 1992. An authoritative reader of excerpts from cyberpunk fiction; includes two excellent and wide-ranging introductory essays, as well as an excellent interview with Gibson.

Olsen, Lance. *William Gibson.* San Bernardino, Calif.: Borgo Press, 1992. A very good introductory study of Gibson and his work up to 1992; chapters 3, 4, and 5 are devoted to the three novels of the Neuromancer Trilogy. A good earlier section discusses Gibson's writing style.

Yoke, Carl. B., and Carol Robinson, eds. *The Cultural Influences of William Gibson, the "Father" of Cyberpunk Science Fiction.* Lewiston, N.Y.: Edwin Mellen Press, 2007. Collects sixteen essays on Gibson's achievements, six of which deal exclusively with the Sprawl trilogy. Dwells on the quality and nature of Gibson's vision and his influence on science fiction.

Never Cry Wolf

Author: Farley Mowat (1921-   )
First published: 1963
Type of work: Nature writing and memoir

Never Cry Wolf is a narrative, first-person account of conservationist-writer Farley Mowat's two summers and one winter on the Arctic tundra as a researcher for the Canadian government. In his 2008 memoir, *Otherwise,* Mowat writes of the years 1937 to 1948, hinting that the events in *Never Cry Wolf* may not be sequential. Also, in the added 1973 preface to *Never Cry Wolf,* Mowat admits changing names and locations and reworking his stories to add humor; he denies, however, that the work is fiction. He says that he never allows "facts to interfere with the truth" and denies altering the basic information. Indeed, libraries classify the book as nonfiction.

In *Never Cry Wolf,* Mowat traces the beginning of his interest in nature to age five. In a somewhat humorous tale, he says that he had captured some catfish, brought them into his grandmother's home, and placed them in the commode to keep them alive. His grandmother found the fish on a night visit to the bathroom and flushed them down the toilet.

In the book, Mowat employs the stylistic device of anthropomorphism. He assigns human characteristics, feelings, emotions, and behaviors to animals—especially wolves. Some scientists, however, consider anthropomorphism to be folk theory and misleading to readers. By contrast, Charles Darwin and other scientists have noted only one difference in degree between people and certain other animals.

In 1958-1959, Mowat had accepted an assignment from Canada's Dominion Wildlife Service (DWS) to survey the barren lands area in the Arctic area of north-central Canada. For the DWS, Mowat conducted a census of the wolves, caribou, and fauna in the area; he observed the actions of the animals, gathered appropriate statistical and analytical data, and led a somewhat solitary existence. Mowat's assignment came as a result of complaints made to the Canadian Department of Energy, Mines, and Resources. Gun and hunting clubs had bemoaned fewer deer kills, and they blamed wolf hordes for fewer deer. The hunters argued that wolves were regularly wreaking carnage on the deer population.

Mowat had begun his assignment by air force transport, but the plane's motor failed, forcing the plane to land in Churchill, Canada. After several days, Mowat and his pilot secured a 1938 bi-motor plane and continued their trip to wolf country. However, running low on fuel, the pilot had to set the plane down in an isolated area; Mowat was about three hundred miles north of Churchill. He remained at this isolated location to conduct his studies until the government sent someone to retrieve him.

Mowat had few provisions, which included a radio with a battery that would last six hours, half a canoe, and cases of Moose beer. He soon found that he was not completely isolated from people: He had met Mike, a trapper. For the use of Mike's rough cabin and his assistance—as needed—during the next three months, Mowat had given Mike an IOU for ten dollars.

Mowat soon found a family of four wolf pups. He named their mother Angeline, their father George, and an older wolf, who assisted in care and hunting, Albert. The wolves were nonaggressive—even oblivious—to Mowat, Mike, and Ootek, Mike's native cousin, who acted as a translator for Mowat. The wolves began to respect Mowat's "property lines" after he marked his territory with urine.

Mowat analyzed wolf scats, recorded the animals and vegetation he saw, and observed the wolf family. Among his findings are that wolves cannot outrun even a young caribou—instead, they separate the sick, infirm, and diseased animals from the rest of the herd and use these available deer as their prey. One wolf leaps to the shoulder of an impaired deer, knocks it off balance, seizes it by the neck, and brings it down to a swift kill. There is no evidence of "hamstringing," a method of disabling an animal that many legends attribute to wolves. Mowat also found that the wolf family killed only one deer at time, ate what they could of its carcass, and stored the rest. With wolves, there are no massive slaughters, contrary to the hunters' claims.

After the summer migration of the caribou to the North, the wolf's diet becomes mainly mice and lemmings. To verify that such a diet is nutritionally complete, Mowat subsisted off the mice alone, as had the wolves. He cooked the mice whole—except for the hair—and supplemented this diet with no other food.

Controversially, Mowat also found that one village had killed 112,000 caribou during one season. He had witnessed the hunters' slaughter of caribou, which had been shot from airplanes. Hunters, for the price of one thousand dollars per hunt from a plane, came to the area with a promise of a prime caribou head. Mowat had found that these hunts from a plane left decaying carcasses across the land. Mowat concluded in his report to the DWS that people—not wolves—had been depleting the deer herds.

To lend credibility to his field work and to convince readers of the false claims made against wolves, Mowat quotes from the numbers and statistics he collected during his time in wolf country. He had found only one wolf per six square miles; subtracting the area covered by water, there was only one wolf per two square miles. This sparse wolf population, he argues in the book, seemed insufficient to account for the diminishing supply of caribou. Mowat adds in a 1984 reprint of *Never Cry Wolf* that the caribou population of close to 5 million in 1930 had dropped to 170,000 in 1963.

Furthermore, fur trappers had told Mowat that they had been working hard to harvest wolves for bounties. One trapper reported killing up to two hundred wolves each year for the reward. Mowat determined that there were eighteen hundred trappers pursuing bounties in the Saskatchewan, Manitoba, and southern Keewatin areas alone. Mowat had estimated, even using the most conservative figures, that more than 100,000 wolves were killed by trappers in a given year.

Never Cry Wolf seems to have changed the treatment of wolves in Canada. In his added 1973 preface, Mowat reports that the government of the province of Ontario had repealed its bounty on wolves, and that Minnesota, in the United States, had been modifying its extermination plans.

Anita Price Davis

Further Reading

King, James. *Farley: The Life of Farley Mowat.* South Royalton, Vt.: Steerforth Press, 2002. Mowat contributed most of the photographs for this biography. King, his biographer, quotes from *Never Cry Wolf* and describes Mowat as having been a blundering young man when he took the assignment with the Dominion Wildlife Service. Also addresses the question of whether *Never Cry Wolf* is fiction or nonfiction, suggesting that facts are important only to transmit truth.

Mowat, Farley. *Born Naked: The Early Adventures of the Author of "Never Cry Wolf."* New York: Houghton Mifflin, 1993. Mowat centers this autobiography on his life in Canada from 1933 to 1937. He discusses his early experiences with nature and his first efforts as a writer. Helps readers understand the evolution of *Never Cry Wolf.*

_____. *Otherwise.* Toronto, Ont.: McClelland & Stewart, 2008. Excluding some of his war experiences, Mowat draws from his own life from 1937 to 1948 in this memoir. Some parts of these earlier experiences—especially his encounters with wolves—duplicate those outlined in *Never Cry Wolf.*

Underwood, Lamar, ed. *The Greatest Survival Stories Ever Told.* Guilford, Conn.: Lyons Press, 2001. Underwood reminds readers that death often lurks north of the Arctic Circle. This area, though, is home to a vast array of the living, including the Ihalmiut (inland Eskimos), wolves, and caribou. Includes a section from Mowat's short story "The Snow Walker" (1975) in his collection of great survival tales.

New Atlantis

Author: Francis Bacon (1561-1626)
First published: 1627
Type of work: Philosophy
Type of plot: Fable
Time of plot: Early seventeenth century
Locale: Bensalem, South Sea

Principal characters:
THE NARRATOR, a visitor to Bensalem
THE GOVERNOR OF THE HOUSE OF STRANGERS
JOABIN, a Jew in Bensalem
A FATHER, from Salomon's House

The Story:

An unidentified narrator, who is a member of a crew of 150 men sailing to China and Japan from Peru, records the events that transpire when their ship is blown off course. After some months at sea, they arrive at the port of a large island in an uncharted part of the South Sea. Eight people from the island approach the ship in a small boat and deliver a scroll whose message is repeated in Hebrew, Greek, Latin, and Spanish. The ship, the scroll says, can remain in port for sixteen days. It also extends the islanders' offer to bring whatever supplies are requested and admonishes against landing on the island. Three hours after the supplies are requested, another dignitary approaches the ship and asks if those on board are Christian. Upon an affirmative answer, some of the crew are given permission to land. Six members of the crew are brought to the House of Strangers. Those who are sick aboard the ship are given orange-scarlet fruit to resist infection and small whitish-gray pills to help them sleep.

After three days at the House of Strangers, the six visitors meet the Governor of that house. This man, by vocation a priest, welcomes the whole crew to stay for six weeks. Indicating that the island is called Bensalem, he explains that although its existence is relatively unknown, the Bensalemites know about the rest of the world. Offering to answer any questions, he is first queried about the presence of Christianity on Bensalem. According to the Governor, twenty years after the ascension of Christ, a mysterious pillar of light appeared off the east coast of the island. After the pillar was acknowledged as a miracle by a wise man from Salomon's House, the light disappeared, leaving a small cedar chest floating on the water. Inside the ark were the canonical and apocalyptic books of the Old and New Testaments and a letter from Bartholomew, who committed the ark and its contents to water by command of an angel. Similar to the miracle of the preaching at Pentecost, the books and letter were able to be read by all the people of Bensalem, despite the variety of native languages there.

On the next day, the Governor recounts the history of the island. Three thousand years before, Atlantis (identified as America), Mexico, and Peru were mighty kingdoms, and there was greater navigation throughout the world. Atlantis was destroyed by a flood, and, as a result of wars and other factors, navigation had also declined in other kingdoms. The existence of Bensalem was forgotten. The Governor then describes Salamona, the island's famous lawgiver of nineteen hundred years before. This king was renowned for establishing Salomon's House, or the "College of the Six Days Works," which was "dedicated to the Study of the Works and Creatures of God." Although visitors to the island were prohibited during his reign and Bensalemites were prevented from visiting other countries, every twelve years six Fellows from Salomon's House were sent abroad to gather information concerning sciences, arts, and inventions in other countries. A week later, the narrator learns more about the island's culture from Joabin, a Jew. The Jews of Bensalem descended from another son of Abraham, Nachoran. Unlike Jews elsewhere, they held the Christian Savior in high regard. Joabin, describing the sexual customs in Bensalem, explained there

was no polygamy, prostitution, or homosexuality. The spirit of chastity prevailed, and marriage and family were held in highest honor.

Their discussion is interrupted by news of the arrival of one of the Fathers of Salomon's House. Three days later, the entire crew is admitted into the Father's presence, but a private conference is granted to one member chosen among themselves, the narrator. The Father then discourses about the area known as Salomon's House. There were caves, high towers, lakes, orchards, and gardens—all for a variety of experiments and for observation. There were parks with birds and beasts as well as pools of fish, which were used for observation and for scientific purposes. There was a large number of structures and facilities for demonstration of and experimentation with sounds, light, colors, smells, tastes, weather conditions, machines, weapons, foods and beverages, and medicines.

The Father then detailed the variety of offices of the Fellows of Salomon's House. The Merchants of Light sailed to foreign countries and returned with books, reports, and experiments. Each of the following seven offices had three representatives. Depredators collected experiments from books. Mystery Men collected the experiments in mechanical arts and liberal sciences. Pioneers (Miners) tried the new experiments. Dowry-men (Benefactors) devised useful and practical applications from the experiments. Lamps hypothesized new experiments. Innoculators executed the new experiments devised by the Lamps. Interpreters of Nature translated the discoveries from the experiments into general principles and axioms. All of these men took an oath of secrecy and concealed or revealed their discoveries and inventions, both from the government and from the people, as they saw fit. The Father ends by briefly describing two houses called galleries, one for inventions and one for statues of inventors. The narrator then kneels before the Father—who places his right hand on the narrator's head and blesses him—and is given permission to publish the account related by the Father.

Critical Evaluation:

This unfinished utopian novel, written between 1610 and 1624, was published within a year of Francis Bacon's death by William Rawley, Bacon's chaplain and first biographer. Unlike the other visions of an ideal society to which Bacon indirectly refers (Plato's myth of Atlantis and Thomas More's *De Optimo Reipublicae Statu, deque Nova Insula Utopia*, 1516; *Utopia*, 1551), Bacon's vision does not emphasize new governmental and social institutions. There is only indirect mention, without explanation, of an existing government in Bensalem. The elite ruling class of the peaceful and tolerant Bensalemites consists of a society of scholars and scientists, laboring together and living by the rules of science.

The depiction of this ideal society occurs almost exclusively through monologues or dialogues between the unidentified narrator and the other three main characters (Governor, Joabin, Father). There is very little action in the story. The narrator does not tour the island or visit Salomon's House. There is, likewise, very little description of any of the characters. Apart from the rich costumes worn by the Bensalemites, Bacon offers no physical or psychological details about them. This kind of narrative approach results in flat characters who remain undeveloped and whose only role in the story is to narrate details about Bensalem and its scientific community.

Bacon adds verisimilitude in his narration in a number of ways that are traditional in utopian or science-fiction stories. The use of known departure and arrival points on the journey lends credibility to the existence of an unknown island in the South Sea, especially for a seventeenth century audience that was still aware that the earth had many as-yet-uncharted areas. The Bensalemites have alternate, exotic names for countries: Tyrambel (Mexico) and Coya (Peru). Bacon occasionally describes Bensalemite rituals (the Feast of the Family, which honors fathers of thirty or more living descendants) and cultural customs (the slight lifting of a cane when a command is given). He offers plausible explanations—although chiefly miraculous—for the presence of Christianity on the island and for the absence of language barriers for the narrator.

As the only fictive work in his vast body of writing, Bacon's *New Atlantis* is related to the rest of his work primarily in an ideological way. As early as 1592, Bacon outlined in a letter to Lord Burleigh, his uncle, his chief interest and desire: "I have taken all knowledge to be my province . . . [and hope to] bring in industrious observations, grounded conclusions, and profitable inventions and discoveries." Interested in reforming the state of human knowledge, Bacon opposed the Aristotelian approach of relying on authority and tradition and of basing its arguments from principles to particulars; he proposed, instead, reliance on observation and experiment as well as reasoning from particulars to general principles. In *The Advancement of Learning* (1605), Bacon surveyed the state of human knowledge in all realms of secular learning, calling attention to the lack of verified and verifiable knowledge. In his *Novum Organum* (1620; English translation, 1802), Bacon warns against the four categories of the idols of the mind, which can block a mind from arriving at truth. He also presents his new methodology, the in-

ductive method, for philosophical investigation. According to Bacon, those who wish "to examine and dissect the nature of this very world itself . . . must go to the facts themselves for everything."

New Atlantis, then, embodies Bacon's theories of scientific methodology outlined in his other writings. As the Father tells the narrator, the goal of Salomon's House is "knowledge of Causes and secret motions of things; and the enlarging of the bounds of Human Empire." What Bacon desired—with respect to the reformation of knowledge, the observation of nature and experimentation, and the improvement of conditions in human life—was a reality in Salomon's House. Bacon has been called the founder of modern science. Although he did not invent the inductive method, he was the first to emphasize its use and its application in acquiring truth and enlarging the domain of knowledge. The fictive, idealistic scientific society outlined in *New Atlantis*, however, was not an empty dream. Rawley said in the preface that this "fable" was written "to exhibit therein a model or description of a College instituted for the interpreting of nature." Bacon's ideas have generally been acknowledged to have been a major factor in prompting the foundation of a "college of philosophy" in 1645, which later grew into the Royal Society of London for Improving Natural Knowledge in 1660. Bacon's highly original vision of scientific research as a collaborative effort has become a reality in modern times.

Marsha Daigle-Williamson

Further Reading

Albanese, Denise. "*The New Atlantis* and the Uses of Utopia." In *New Science, New World.* Durham, N.C.: Duke University Press, 1996. Albanese uses modern literary theories to interpret *New Atlantis* and other seventeenth century works in which the novelty of science was expressed through the depiction of the new colonial world.

Briggs, John C. *Francis Bacon and the Rhetoric of Nature.* Cambridge, Mass.: Harvard University Press, 1989. Briggs's examination of *New Atlantis* focuses on the relationship between Bacon's scientific reform and his concepts of rhetoric, nature, and religion.

Coquillette, Daniel R. *Francis Bacon.* Stanford, Calif.: Stanford University Press, 1992. A systematic approach to Bacon's legal philosophy with analysis of the inductive method as applied to lawmaking. *New Atlantis* is analyzed from the juristic viewpoint.

Leary, John E., Jr. *Francis Bacon and the Politics of Science.* Ames: Iowa State University Press, 1994. A study of the relationship between Bacon's conservative political ideology and his scheme for organizing science as a collective, collaborative enterprise, organized hierarchically. Most of chapter 6 is devoted to political analysis of Salomon's House. Includes selected bibliography.

McKnight, Stephen A. *The Religious Foundations of Francis Bacon's Thought*. Columbia: University of Missouri Press, 2006. McKnight analyzes eight of Bacon's texts to examine his views on religion. His exploration begins with a discussion of *New Atlantis* because McKnight argues that all of Bacon's theological ideas are expressed in this work.

Martin, Julian. *Francis Bacon, the State, and the Reform of Natural Philosophy*. New York: Cambridge University Press, 1992. An analysis of the interplay between Bacon's legal and political career and the development of his natural philosophy. Chapter 5 includes discussion of Salomon's House as part of Bacon's vision of an imperial state.

Price, Bronwen, ed. *Francis Bacon's "The New Atlantis": New Interdisciplinary Essays*. New York: Manchester University Press, 2002. Eight essays provide various interpretations of the book, including discussions of its narrative content and Bacon's ideas about ethics, politics, natural knowledge, gender, and sexual difference.

Weinberger, Jerry. *Science, Faith, and Politics: Francis Bacon and the Utopian Roots of the Modern Age*. Ithaca, N.Y.: Cornell University Press, 1985. A detailed comparison of Bensalem and Plato's republic.

New Grub Street

Author: George Gissing (1857-1903)
First published: 1891
Type of work: Novel
Type of plot: Psychological realism and naturalism
Time of plot: 1880's
Locale: London

Principal characters:
EDWIN REARDON, a failed novelist
AMY REARDON, his increasingly dissatisfied wife
JASPER MILVAIN, an ambitious journalist
ALFRED YULE, an embittered man of letters
MARIAN YULE, his daughter
HAROLD BIFFEN, a dedicated and starving novelist

The Story:

Jasper Milvain is an ambitious young writer trying to establish himself as a journalist in London. During a stay with his mother and sisters in the country, he meets Alfred Yule, an experienced and disappointed man of letters, and his daughter, Marian, to whom Milvain finds himself troublingly attracted—troublingly because she is poor and because Milvain has already decided he must marry a woman who can help him in his career. With engaging frankness, Milvain explains to her his ideas about the importance of money in a literary life: It can buy the all-important first success as well as influential friends.

London novelist Edwin Reardon has won modest success with his fourth novel. At this hopeful stage of his life, he also meets Amy Yule, a cousin of Marian, and falls in love with her. Under the impression that he will become a novelist of some distinction, Amy accepts his proposal of marriage. Now, the painfully scrupulous Edwin, who disdains the literary marketplace, finds that he can no longer write work with which he is satisfied; he also comes to realize that

he suffers agony even in his attempt to produce marketable copy.

The Reardons are running short of money. The burgeoning reputation of Milvain, a friend of the family, points up the contrast between his energy and cheerful cynicism on one hand, and Reardon's ineffectual weakness and self-pity on the other.

Alfred Yule has experienced literary struggles at well. As a writer, he has been sincere, and he is by no means untalented, but his old-fashioned ideas about literature, combined with his awkward integrity and lack of tact, have hindered his advance. He is noticeably ashamed of his marriage to a woman from the working class who displays uneducated speech and manners, so he avoids entertaining publishers and critics. Alfred's frustration vents itself in occasional harshness that disturbs the family's peace.

Meanwhile, Reardon continues to find himself unable to produce anything but paltry work, of which he is ashamed. One Sunday, he is visited by his friend Harold Biffen, whose ambition is to write an utterly faithful account of "the igno-bly decent life" of lower-class Londoners, a necessarily bor-ing book that will eschew melodramatic or tragic incident. To this work Biffen is fiercely committed. He makes a poor living by private tutoring, but is often short of food and must sometimes pawn his clothes. Despite the dire conditions of their lives, the two men discuss meter in Greek drama with disinterested enthusiasm.

Reality intrudes on Reardon's life again when his pub-lishers offer very modest terms for the novel he has finally—in anguish—completed. His next novel is rejected outright. He decides he must act in a firm and manly way. He gets back his old job as a clerk but insists that he and his wife take less fashionable lodgings, which alienates Amy. Unable to accept this public fall in status, she moves back to the house of her mother and brother, taking her and Edwin's little son, Willie, with her.

Marian inherits a legacy of five thousand pounds at the death of an uncle, and Milvain, although he would have pre-ferred a larger sum, feels he can now give in to his feelings for Marian. He proposes marriage. Attracted by his energy and hopefulness, Marian has fallen in love with him and accepts his proposal, but her legacy fails to materialize because of the failure of the firm that was to have paid it. She is desolated at the consequent tepidness of her suitor, who furthermore ma-neuvers her into choosing between him and her parents, now dependent upon her because of Alfred's failing eyesight. Al-fred, who wrongly suspects Milvain of having written a caus-tic review of his latest book, will not accept charity from his wife.

Humiliated, Marian ends the engagement. Marian's cousin Amy has received a legacy of ten thousand pounds from the same uncle, but Reardon refuses to accept any part of it, as he considers that he has lost Amy's love. He catches a cold when visiting Amy and Willie, who is ill with diphtheria. Reardon falls ill with serious congestion of the lungs and dies, shortly after his son's death and a tearful reconciliation with his wife.

Milvain, now free, writes an article, "The Novels of Edwin Reardon," the proofs of which he does not fail to send to Amy. She responds with a warm letter of thanks, and their relationship blossoms. Amy has long found Milvain's atti-tude to literary London more congenial than that of Reardon. The clear-eyed Milvain is able to make an advantageous mar-riage to a rich and beautiful widow. Soon afterwards, he suc-ceeds to an editorship.

Critical Evaluation:

In the course of a twenty-seven-year career of ferocious literary labor, George Gissing published twenty-two novels;

volumes of literary criticism, travel writing, and fictional-ized autobiography; and 115 short stories. Although the fame, sales, and wealth he would have so much appreciated and deserved eluded him to the end, in the last years of his life he was widely acknowledged as one of the three leading En-glish novelists of the day, along with George Meredith and Thomas Hardy.

After his death, Gissing's reputation declined somewhat, but starting in the 1960's, a Gissing revival took place. Led by French scholar Pierre Coustillas, students of Gissing's work in Great Britain, continental Europe, North America, and Japan have published biographical and critical articles and books, edited editions of Gissing's novels, and contrib-uted to a thriving quarterly, *The Gissing Journal* (formerly *The Gissing Newsletter*).

Despite the vicissitudes of Gissing's reputation, *New Grub Street* has almost invariably been regarded as a master-piece. Gissing himself was pleased with the book, writing to his brother as he went through the proofs that "I am aston-ished to find how well it reads. There are savage truths in it." John Goode, editor of the World's Classics edition (1993), calls the work "the most eminent nineteenth-century novel dealing directly with the position of writing in the social con-text of its time" and compares Gissing's work with William Makepeace Thackeray's *The History of Pendennis: His For-tunes and Misfortunes, His Friends, and His Greatest Enemy* (1848-1850, serial; 1849, 1850, book) and Charles Dickens's *David Copperfield* (1849-1850, serial; 1850, book). These two novels have writers—a journalist and a novelist in the first case and a novelist in the second—as eponymous central characters around whose lives a varied autobiographical/biographical plot is arranged. However, Gissing uses a differ-ent technique, choosing rather to present a dramatic micro-cosm of failed, would-be, or successful writers in a world that is almost exclusively literary and almost exclusively London.

In the tradition of the boarders of the historical Grub Street, three people—Alfred Yule, Edwin Reardon, and Har-old Biffen—arrive in London honestly aspiring to win liter-ary fame and fortune. All of them fail, however. The embit-tered Alfred is exiled from London when he begins to lose his sight, and Reardon's slender talent is insufficient to with-stand the merciless demands of the literary marketplace. Biffen completes his magnum opus, but it is, of course, a crit-ical and commercial failure.

Behind these three primary characters is a collection of minor writers who are fascinating in their variety of shabby mediocrity or eccentricity. There is Alfred's lower-middle-class clique, lesser lights than himself whom he meets occa-sionally by chance in the British Museum's reading room or who gather once or twice a year in Alfred's (significantly) rented house for literary gossip. Three of these men—Hinks, Gorbutt, and Christopherson—are held back by unpresentable wives. Indeed, one of the themes of the novel, an ironic counterpoint to Milvain's careerist search for a moneyed female springboard, is the difficulty that intellectual men of little or no reliable income experience in finding suitable mates. Readers also meet Sykes, once found drunk and disorderly on Oxford Street, who is writing his autobiography (*Through the Wilds of Literary London*) in installments for a provincial newspaper.

It is perhaps the successful men who provide the strongest condemnation of late-Victorian literary London. Milvain, whose name would seem to be a version of "villain," sees clearly the commodification of literature in a world where, like everything else, literature is judged in utilitarian and monetary terms. Although not without geniality and generosity, his one aim is financial success. Another failed novelist in the story becomes a literary adviser, reading and correcting manuscripts and suggesting possible publishers to aspiring writers. In one manuscript, he changes the name, and style, of "chat" into "chit chat," even the former making too high a demand on its readers.

M. D. Allen

Further Reading

Arata, Stephen, ed. *"New Grub Street": George Gissing.* Peterborough, Ont.: Broadview, 2008. This edition includes textual footnotes, a preface with explanatory matter, and four appendixes, including "Gissing on Writing" and "Grub Street Old and New."

Coustillas, Pierre, and Colin Partridge, eds. *George Gissing: The Critical Heritage.* 1972. Reprint. New York: Routledge, 1995. Contains reviews of Gissing's novels by British and American critics of his time. Includes a generous selection of reviews of *New Grub Street* that offer insight into why Gissing did not achieve popular success.

Halperin, John. *Gissing: A Life in Books.* New York: Oxford University Press, 1982. A biography with many references to *New Grub Street*, including a discussion of its reflections of Gissing's own hardships.

James, Simon J. *Unsettled Accounts: Money and Narrative in the Novels of George Gissing.* London: Anthem Press, 2003. Examines Gissing's preoccupation with money as reflected in *New Grub Street* and his other novels, placing his work within the context of nineteenth century economic theory and the work of other English novelists. Concludes that Gissing's work expresses an "unhappy accommodation with money's underwriting of human existence and culture."

Liggins, Emma. *George Gissing, the Working Woman, and Urban Culture.* Burlington, Vt.: Ashgate, 2006. Examines *New Grub Street* and other works by Gissing to analyze how they realistically depict London culture and changing class and gender identities, particularly for working women.

Michaux, Jean-Pierre, ed. *George Gissing: Critical Essays.* New York: Barnes & Noble, 1981. One-half of this book is devoted to essays about *New Grub Street*, including selections by such prominent authors as Angus Wilson, John Middleton Murray, and Gissing's great admirer and champion, George Orwell. Also includes an influential essay by Q. D. Leavis, who praised Gissing's portrayal of the miseries of the Victorian world.

Ryle, Martin, and Jenny Bourne Taylor, eds. *George Gissing: Voices of the Unclassed.* Burlington, Vt.: Ashgate, 2005. Collection of essays that analyze *New Grub Street*, Gissing's representation of working women, his work in the context of the "cultural politics of food," and his place in twentieth century English literature.

Selig, Robert L. *George Gissing.* Rev. ed. New York: Twayne, 1995. An excellent introductory biography, with chapters on Gissing's major works and his career as a man of letters. Contains half a chapter on *New Grub Street*. Includes a chronology, notes, and an annotated bibliography.

The New Héloïse

Author: Jean-Jacques Rousseau (1712-1778)
First published: Julie: Ou, La Nouvelle Héloïse, 1761
    (English translation, 1761)
Type of work: Novel
Type of plot: Philosophical
Time of plot: Early eighteenth century
Locale: Switzerland

Principal characters:
JULIE D'ÉTANGE, a beautiful and virtuous young woman
BARON D'ÉTANGE, her father
SAINT-PREUX, her tutor
CLAIRE, her cousin
LORD EDWARD BOMSTON, Saint-Preux's patron and
    benefactor
MONSIEUR DE WOLMAR, Julie's husband

The Story:

Saint-Preux, a young Swiss man with unusual talents and sensibilities, is accepted by Madame d'Étange as a tutor for her daughter Julie and Julie's cousin Claire. For a year under Saint-Preux's instruction, the women make excellent progress, until Claire goes away to visit her own family. During her absence, Saint-Preux reveals his love for Julie. After some solicitation, Julie admits that she, too, is hopelessly in love. The young people view their situation as desperate, for the Baron d'Étange, Julie's father, has promised to marry her to his friend, de Wolmar. In addition, the baron is a lineage-proud man who would never hear of his daughter's marriage to a commoner such as Saint-Preux, regardless of the latter's abilities.

Julie fears that she may fall victim to her love for Saint-Preux; she writes to Claire and asks her to return as a protector. She writes to her cousin because she is afraid that, if her mother suspected the truth, she would immediately send the young man away. Claire returns, and for a time the romance continues to blossom. At last, Claire and Julie decide that Saint-Preux ought to leave until the baron returns from an absence that has kept him from home for well over a year. The women fear that the baron may dismiss Saint-Preux unless steps are taken to pave the way for the young man to continue as their tutor. Saint-Preux leaves. The women show themselves off to the baron when he returns, and he is so pleased with the progress of their education that he has Saint-Preux recalled.

Once again, the love between Saint-Preux and Julie grows. In spite of her virtue, however, Julie falls victim to Saint-Preux's pleas and becomes his mistress. A short time later, Saint-Preux is dismissed to facilitate Julie's marriage to de Wolmar. The shock of seeing her lover depart and the news from her father that her marriage day is not far off make Julie very ill. Only a visit from Saint-Preux, smuggled into the sickroom by Claire, saves the young woman's life.

After Julie recovers, there follow more than a year of surreptitious meetings between the lovers. As her passion waxes, Julie's fear of her father grows less, until she even has Saint-Preux stay with her through the night. Neither of the young people believes that they are committing sin, for they honestly feel that they are already married in the eyes of heaven and that only the baron's attitude keeps them from living together publicly and with outward virtue.

In the meantime, both Julie and Saint-Preux have met Lord Edward Bomston, a British peer living in Switzerland. Saint-Preux and Lord Bomston become friends, even though Lord Bomston is himself seeking Julie's hand in marriage. Bomston fails in his suit. One night, while he and Saint-Preux are drinking, Bomston charges that someone has already found Julie's favor. Saint-Preux challenges Lord Bomston to a duel, but Julie, mindful of her reputation, sends a letter to Lord Bomston, telling him about Saint-Preux and herself and warning him that her fate and Saint-Preux's rest in his hands. She knows that Saint-Preux would be killed if the duel were to go forward and that the duel would provoke enough scandal to ruin her and drive her to suicide. Lord Bomston is moved by her plea, calls off the duel, and publicly apologizes to Saint-Preux. Again, the two men become the firmest of friends.

Shortly afterward, Lord Bomston, interceding on Saint-Preux's behalf with Baron d'Étange, urges the baron to permit a marriage between Julie and Saint-Preux. The baron refuses, vowing that he will never break his promise to de Wolmar and that, in any case, he will never permit Julie to marry an adventurer. Lord Bomston therefore proposes that Julie and Saint-Preux elope to England and spend the rest of their lives as his pensioners on his estate in Oxfordshire. Julie, however, absolutely refuses to leave her home without her father's consent.

In the meantime, Claire has married a man friendly with

both Lord Bomston and Saint-Preux. The tutor is forced to leave Julie's vicinity after her father refuses to permit their marriage. Through Claire's husband, however, the two lovers manage to maintain a correspondence.

Saint-Preux, after spending some months in France and England, returns to Switzerland to find that Julie is about to marry de Wolmar. He is so overcome that Lord Bomston spirits him away to England and arranges for him to embark with an expedition leaving from England to travel around the world. Meanwhile, Julie reconciles herself to her father's will. Her mother, who might have permitted a marriage to Saint-Preux, has recently died.

Four years pass before Saint-Preux returns to Europe. By that time, Julie and her husband have two children and are settled into domestic tranquillity. De Wolmar, eager to see his wife happy, invites Saint-Preux to visit their home. During the visit, it becomes obvious that the two former lovers have become more or less reconciled to their situation. Both seem so filled with virtue that de Wolmar requests Saint-Preux to remain as tutor to his children. Saint-Preux, anxious to please everyone and to be near Julie, agrees to take on the responsibility, providing that Lord Bomston does not need his services elsewhere. Saint-Preux feels that he can never adequately repay the Englishman for keeping him from crime, madness, and possible death at the time of Julie's marriage.

It turns out that Lord Bomston does need Saint-Preux's aid for a short time. The Englishman is traveling to Italy, where he has hopes of marrying a marchioness, and he wishes Saint-Preux's aid in the affair. Saint-Preux, however, shows Lord Bomston that the woman is vicious and prevents the marriage; he also prevents a second attempt at marriage between the Englishman and a woman of doubtful reputation.

During Saint-Preux's absence, Julie discovers that Claire, who was widowed some time before, is in love with Saint-Preux. Hoping to help both Claire and Saint-Preux find happiness, Julie writes to the tutor and tells him of Claire's love. Saint-Preux replies that although he esteems Claire, he cannot marry her, for he still loves Julie. Julie still hopes to arrange the match upon Saint-Preux's return from Italy.

Before his return, however, an accident occurrs. One day, while Julie and her family are walking alongside a lake, Julie's little boy falls in the water. In saving him from death, Julie suffers severe shock and exhaustion. The results are fatal to her. Before dying, however, she writes a letter to Saint-Preux and asks him to take over the education of her children and of Claire's children. Her cousin, writes Julie, will take her own place in making Saint-Preux's life complete.

Critical Evaluation:

The New Héloïse, which Jean-Jacques Rousseau published in 1761, became the model for and the best example of the sentimental novel, depicting bourgeois life and mores. This type of novel became exceptionally popular during the second half of the eighteenth century, and its popularity was due in no small part to the enormous success of Rousseau's novel. In his portrayal of Clarens and of the life lived there by Julie, her husband M. de Wolmar, and their children, Rousseau depicts the well-ordered, tranquil life of the bourgeoisie, in which virtue and reasonableness are the guiding principles. M. de Wolmar is a man utterly controlled by his reason. Emotion never takes precedence over reasonableness for him. Julie, as his wife, conducts her life according to the dictates of reason and virtue. Moderation and calm reign throughout Clarens.

To depict this idealized bourgeois lifestyle, Rousseau creates characters who are embodiments of certain qualities and comes very close to writing an allegorical novel. M. de Wolmar is the good, wise father of the family, Julie is the perfect mother, devoted to her husband, children, and home. However, Rousseau's novel is more than a fictional tale of the virtuous life of a segment of society. The novel addresses one of the key philosophical concerns of the century and takes as its theme the conflict between reason and passion. Through his fiction, Rousseau confronts reason (M. de Wolmar and life at Clarens) with passion (Saint-Preux).

Consequently, the novel has two major themes: that of the idyllic life of the virtuous and reasonable bourgeoisie and that of the conflict between reason and passion, two contrary aspects of human nature. The novel is thus two novels in one, mirroring a split in its title character. Julie is not just Julie; she is both Julie d'Etange and Julie de Wolmar. The first part of the novel deals with Julie d'Etange, her cousin Claire, and their tutor Saint-Preux. The second part of the novel is the story of Julie de Wolmar. Rousseau brings the two stories together with the introduction of Saint-Preux into Clarens, as passion is invited into reason's realm. With complete confidence in reason, M. de Wolmar believes that he can cure Saint-Preux of his passion. This belief is fatal for life at Clarens. In the presence of Saint-Preux, Julie's duality becomes ever stronger. Rousseau has created the eternal triangle of woman, husband, and lover. The three cannot exist in tranquil happiness in the idyllic atmosphere of Clarens.

Rousseau, who was adamant in his writings about the absolute importance of chastity and fidelity, especially marital fidelity, could not make Julie unfaithful to M. de Wolmar, nor could he—with his belief in the union of souls—make Julie unfaithful to Saint-Preux. Julie d'Etange is never unfaithful to Saint-Preux, for at the moment of her marriage to M. de Wolmar, Julie is transformed into another woman. She is no longer Julie d'Etange; she is Julie de Wolmar. The two Julies simply cannot exist at the same time. Using the solution typical of the century's fiction, Rousseau brings about Julie's death. In death, the union of Julie d'Etange and Saint-Preux is preserved, as is the marriage of Julie de Wolmar and M. de Wolmar. Julie's death solves the dual problem of fidelity.

However, the ending also recognizes the dangerous and fatalistic power of passion and its ability to triumph over reason. In the latter part of the novel, Julie becomes increasingly aware that she cannot maintain her fidelity to M. de Wolmar as long as Saint-Preux is at Clarens. She even tries to arrange a marriage between Claire and Saint-Preux. Julie and Claire, as cousins, have always had a very close relationship, so close in fact that Claire is almost another Julie. Thus, through Claire, Julie could perhaps unite Julie d'Etange and Saint-Preux. Neither Claire nor Saint-Preux will agree to such an arrangement, and they do not understand why Julie wishes it. Although Julie's death is conceived by Rousseau, readers may have the sense that Julie herself has somehow brought it about.

As the title indicates, the novel is the story of Julie. Rousseau structures the novel in a series of circles around Julie. She is always at the center of the intrigue. Life at Clarens revolves around her. Even as her death approaches, Julie continues to control the lives of the other characters. As a result of her decision, M. de Wolmar, Claire, and Saint-Preux are to live at Clarens and care for the children.

Rousseau did not produce a theory of the novel, and he usually condemned the novel as a corrupting influence, especially upon young girls. Despite this, *The New Héloïse* is a significant work in the development of the novel as a genre. In it, Rousseau achieved the two goals of eighteenth century novelists: to produce a work characterized by realism and moral instruction. With its extensive descriptions of the virtuous, reasonable life at Clarens, the novel is definitely moral and instructive. Its moral tone and idyllic portrayal of Clarens seem to make the novel lack realism. However, the realist portrayal of Julie's early life at her father's home, her father's intransigent exercise of his authority, and her arranged marriage create a realist reflection of eighteenth century mores. The destruction of the reason-based utopia of Clarens by Saint-Preux's presence further anchors the novel in reality.

Rousseau's text is in many ways exemplary of French eighteenth century novels: It is written in the epistolary form. It portrays a love affair in relation to the social mores of the time. The society in which the characters live has an impor-

tant influence on their lives. A marriage between Julie and her tutor is unacceptable. She instead marries a man chosen by her father. However, the society Rousseau depicts is that of the virtuous bourgeoisie rather than that of the corrupt aristocracy. By depicting this lifestyle, Rousseau's novel was instrumental in enlarging the subject matter treated in novels generally and in creating the sentimental novel, a new type of novel, which contrasted sharply with the libertine novel of its predecessors.

"Critical Evaluation" by Shawncey Webb

Further Reading

Arico, Santo L. *Rousseau's Art of Persuasion in "La Nouvelle Héloïse."* Lanham, Md.: University Press of America, 1994. A study of the novel based upon its rhetorical devices.

Babbitt, Irving. *Rousseau and Romanticism.* New York: Meridian, 1955. This famous attack on Romantic art and attitudes regards Rousseau as their originator.

Coleman, Patrick. *Reparative Realism: Mourning and Modernity in the French Novel, 1730-1830.* Geneva: Librairie Droz, 1998. Examines *The New Héloïse* and novels by Abbé Prévost, Benjamin Constant, Madame de Stäel, and Honoré de Balzac to describe how issues of grief and bereavement were handled in eighteenth and nineteenth century French fiction.

Damrosch, Leo. *Jean-Jacques Rousseau: Restless Genius.* Boston: Houghton Mifflin, 2005. This one-volume biography is a useful addition to Rousseau scholarship, providing an incisive, accessible account of Rousseau's life and contributions to philosophy and literature. Includes illustrations, time line, bibliography, and index.

Ellis, M. B. *"Julie: Ou, La Nouvelle Héloïse": A Synthesis of Rousseau's Thought, 1749-1759.* Toronto, Ont.: University of Toronto Press, 1949. Compares themes in the novel with ideas appearing in other writings by Rousseau.

Howells, Robin. *Regressive Fictions: Graffigny, Rousseau, Bernardin.* London: Legenda, 2007. Analyzes *The New Héloïse* and works by two other writers to describe how the French novel changed in the mid-eighteenth century. Prior to that time, Howells maintains, novels reflected a worldly society, characterized by wit, social sophistication, and sexual experience; novels in the second half of the century were set in idealized, imaginary worlds characterized by originality, closeness to nature, and innocence.

Jones, James F., Jr. *"La Nouvelle Héloïse": Rousseau and Utopia.* Geneva: Librairie Droz, 1977. Concerned primarily with political implications of the novel; interesting for its Swiss perspective.

Miller, Ronald D. *The Beautiful Soul: A Study of Eighteenth-Century Idealism as Exemplified by Rousseau's "La Nouvelle Héloïse" and Goethe's "Die Leiden des Jungen Werthers."* Harrogate, England: Duchy Press, 1981. Compares two European novels of the eighteenth century, finding aspects of a common theme.

Pickering, Samuel, Jr. *The Moral Tradition in English Fiction, 1785-1850.* Hanover, N.H.: University Press of New England, 1976. Documents the opposition to Rousseau and his novel in England.

Riley, Patrick, ed. *The Cambridge Companion to Rousseau.* New York: Cambridge University Press, 2001. Includes an essay analyzing the images of authority in Rousseau's work, with an emphasis on *The New Héloïse*.

The New Life

Author: Dante (1265-1321)
First transcribed: La vita nuova, c. 1292 (English translation, 1861)
Type of work: Poetry

Dante's *The New Life*, a celebration in prose and poetry of the great poet's love for Beatrice Portinari, begins with the following words:

> In that part of the book of my mind before which there would be little to read is found a chapter heading which says: "Here begins the new life." It is my intention to copy into this little book the words I find written there; if not all of them, at least their essential doctrine.

Perhaps it is revealing to realize that this love was a poet's love; that is, Dante's love was not ordinary and practical, leading to forthright pursuit, engagement, marriage, and children. When Dante first saw Beatrice he was nine years and she was eight years old. He was so affected by the sight of her that his "vital spirit" trembled, his "animal spirit" was amazed, and his "natural spirit" wept. At least, this is how it was if readers accept *The New Life* literally.

Dante realized that, whatever a poet's passion, such early love could hardly be convincing to anyone save the victim. After a few more sentences of praise, *The New Life* describes an encounter nine years after the first, when Beatrice stood between two ladies and greeted Dante. It was the ninth hour of the day, and nine had already become a symbol of their love. Readers will not discover what Beatrice said, and it probably does not matter; the important thing is that her greeting inspired Dante's first poem of love for Beatrice. Readers are told that in a dream after being greeted by Beatrice, Dante had a vision of Love holding Beatrice in his

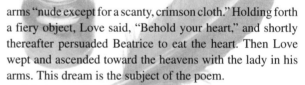

arms "nude except for a scanty, crimson cloth." Holding forth a fiery object, Love said, "Behold your heart," and shortly thereafter persuaded Beatrice to eat the heart. Then Love wept and ascended toward the heavens with the lady in his arms. This dream is the subject of the poem.

It is known from other sources that the poem, a sonnet, was sent to Guido Cavalcanti, who wrote a sonnet in return, initiating a strong friendship between the poets. In *The New Life*, Dante merely refers to "my first friend" and quotes the beginning of a sonnet by Cavalcanti.

Dante reports that love so weakened him that everyone noticed that he was not himself. When his glances at Beatrice were misinterpreted as being directed at another lady, Dante, seizing upon the opportunity to disguise the true object of his love, pretended that the other lady was his love, and he wrote several "trifles" for her. When the lady who served as his screen left Florence on a journey, Dante knew that he should pretend to be dismayed. In fact, he was, but not from love; he was upset because his lover's scheming had been frustrated. Despite the complications, the resultant sonnet satisfied Dante, and it is included in the collection. The beginning of the sonnet reads

> O voi che per la via d'Amor passate,
> Attendete e guardate
> S'elli e dolore alcun, quanto 'l mio, grave;
> E prego sol ch'audir mi sofferiate,
> E poi imaginate
> S'io son d'ogni tormento ostale e chiave.

A comparison of this first part of the sonnet with the translation by Mark Musa will give even those who do not read Italian a sense of Dante's poetic genius.

> O you who travel on the road of Love,
> Pause here and look about
> For any man whose grief surpasses mine.
> I ask this only; hear me out, then judge
> If I am not indeed
> Of every torment keeper and shade.

Despite the attraction of Dante's poetry, it would be a mistake to take *The New Life* as primarily a collection of poems, leaving the prose passages for those interested in biography and the poet's comments on style and intent. The prose passages are charming in themselves, and they reveal an intelligent, sensitive man who is always a poet. Perhaps it is truer to say that Beatrice was for the poems, rather than the poems were for Beatrice. Readers cannot say the same of the prose; it is not merely an instrument to provide a setting for the poetry, but together with the poetry it forms an organic work of art. Dante's account of his love is so clear and ingenuous in style that it is only the cold analysts looking back on what they have read who can say that the entire affair was largely a matter of the poet's imagination extravagantly at work. Although it may have been the imagination or the animal spirit that stirred Dante, the effect created convinces that the passion was genuine (as it probably was, however engendered) and under poetic control.

Upon observing the body of a young lady who had died and was being mourned by weeping ladies, Dante suddenly realized that he had seen her in the company of the lady whom he pretended to love to hide his love for Beatrice. Although this knowledge means that the departed lady is two times removed from Beatrice, Dante is moved to write two sonnets about death. The first begins, "If Love himself weep, shall not lovers weep,/ Hearing for what sad cause he pours his tears?" and the second begins, "Brute death, the enemy of tenderness,/ Timeless mother of grief . . . My tongue consumes itself with cursing you."

Since the lady who had served as Dante's screen had left the city, Dante imagined that Love directed him to another lady in order that, pretending to love her, he might hide his love for Beatrice. This device, celebrated in a sonnet, was so effective that Beatrice herself must have believed the stories concerning him—rumors that he himself initiated—and one day she refuses to greet him as he passes. In the middle of Dante's grief, described in long prose passages, Love again appears to him and tells him to write a poem explaining that it is Love's idea, not Dante's, that he pretend to love someone other than Beatrice.

Several poems that follow work out the implications of Beatrice's refusal to greet him. He explains in a sonnet that Love is both good and evil—the poet's way of saying that the lover, especially a poetic one like Dante, has difficulty in staying out of trouble.

A long *canzone*, directed to ladies "refined and sensitive in Love," contains some of Dante's most effective passages. Even Love says of Beatrice, "How can flesh drawn from clay,/ Achieve such purity?" and Dante adds, "She is the highest nature can achieve/ And by her mold all beauty tests itself."

After a *canzone* on the nature of Love ("Love and the gracious heart are but one thing . . ."), Dante includes a sonnet explaining that the power of Love is awakened by Beatrice. This comparatively pleasant and romantic interlude was interrupted by the death of Beatrice's father. Two sonnets recount, with fine poetic elaboration, how Dante wept for her sorrow; but it was only after these poetic tasks and after a serious illness during which Dante realized how frail his own existence was that he finally thought, "Some day the most gracious Beatrice will surely have to die." In his delirium he imagined that Beatrice had died and that he called upon Death to take him; then the ladies at his bedside woke him. The result is a long, dramatic *canzone* in which the events of the dream are told.

One of the most entertaining of the prose sections of *The New Life* is section 25, in which Dante defends his speaking of Love as if it were a thing in itself, a bodily substance. The defense is as charming as it is sophistical. He explains that as a poet writing in the vernacular, not in Latin, it is his duty to make what he writes understandable to ladies. Since the vernacular was invented to talk about love, poets using the vernacular to write about love enjoy the same privileges granted to the Latin poets. Also, because Latin poets often spoke of inanimate objects as if they were beings—and Dante gives examples from Vergil, Lucan, Horace, and Ovid—Dante, as a vernacular poet writing of love, has the same right to speak of Love as if it were a human being.

In subsequent poems and prose passages Dante celebrates Beatrice's capacity to delight all persons by her presence; he explains how a word from her revives his spirit when it is overcome by Love; and he argues that her power is such that even remembering her is enough to make one feel her influence.

In section 28, Dante reveals that Beatrice has died. He explains that it would not be proper in this book to discuss the *canzone* he was writing at the time, and he then devotes section 29 to a rather involved discussion of the significance of the number nine in connection with Beatrice. Scholars know that Beatrice—who in 1285 married Simone de' Bardi—died on June 8, 1290. How, then, can Dante read the number nine into the time of her death? He argues that, counting in the Arabian fashion, she departed "during the first hour of the ninth day of the month," and using the Syrian calendar which has a first month corresponding to the Western October, she departed in the ninth month. Other ingenious calculations are used to argue that Beatrice was a miracle since nine was her number and three is its root and the Trinity is the sole factor of all miracles.

A lengthy *canzone* tells of Dante's grief, after which he presents a sonnet cleverly devised to express a brother's sorrow in the first half—for Dante later sent the poem to Beatrice's brother—and the poet's own sorrow in the second half. As he explains in the remarks prefacing the sonnet, only a person examining the sonnet carefully can tell that the dramatic speaker changes.

Dante writes that he was observed while weeping and that the young woman who observed him did so with such compassion that he wrote a sonnet to her. The sonnet was followed by another, and the second by a third, the third a self-chastisement for taking such pleasure in writing poetry for the compassionate lady.

After a few more sonnets Dante decided that he had better cease writing about Beatrice until he could honor her in his writing as no other lady had ever been honored. Readers know that this hope was not mere sentiment or poetic falsehood, for Beatrice appears again as one of the most favored of Heaven, guiding Dante through paradise in *La divina commedia* (c. 1320; *The Divine Comedy*, 1802).

The New Life leaves the reader with an impression of Dante the poetic artist, constructing in his walks about Florence the ideas and lines so charmingly used in his book. Although one may be convinced that much of Dante's love was created by the artist for the sake of his poetry, there is so much skill and poetic grace in his work that the distinction between nonartist and artist is not important.

Further Reading

Dante. *Dante's Lyric Poetry*. Edited and translated by Kenelm Foster and Patrick Boyde. 2 vols. Oxford, England: Clarendon Press, 1967. Includes the poems, but not the prose, of *The New Life*, accurate English prose translations, and extensive commentary on grammatical, syntactical, thematic, and philosophical points in the poems.

_____. *Vita Nuova*. Translated by Mark Musa. Bloomington: Indiana University Press, 1973. Excellent translation. Musa's essay traces themes and patterns in *The New Life*. Discusses Dante's various roles as narrator, editor, and protagonist in the work.

Harrison, Robert Pogue. "Approaching the *Vita Nuova*." In *The Cambridge Companion to Dante*, edited by Rachel Jacoff. 2d ed. New York: Cambridge University Press, 2007. Provides an analysis of *The New Life*.

_____. *The Body of Beatrice*. Baltimore: Johns Hopkins University Press, 1988. Interprets *The New Life* without recourse to the narrative glosses and interpretive guidelines that Dante embedded in the prose portions of his work. Rejects Charles Singleton's theologized reading of *The New Life* for an approach focusing on the tensions inherent in the mixture of poetry and prose that constitutes Dante's work.

Mazzaro, Jerome. *The Figure of Dante: An Essay on the "Vita Nuova."* Princeton, N.J.: Princeton University Press, 1981. Focuses less on the literary content of *The New Life* and more on the degree to which Dante's poetry and prose reflect the poet's self-image and the changing society for which he wrote.

Scott, John A. *Understanding Dante*. Notre Dame, Ind.: University of Notre Dame Press, 2004. A critical overview of Dante's work. Chapter 1 analyzes *The New Life*, including a discussion of the poem's style, personification allegory, and vernacular love poetry and the character of Beatrice.

Singleton, Charles S. *An Essay on the "Vita Nuova."* Baltimore: Johns Hopkins University Press, 1977. The most influential American study of *The New Life* written in the twentieth century. Interprets Dante's work allegorically and as a prelude to his masterpiece, *The Divine Comedy*.

A New Way to Pay Old Debts

Author: Philip Massinger (1583-1640)
First produced: c. 1621-1622?; first published, 1633
Type of work: Drama
Type of plot: Comedy of manners
Time of plot: Early seventeenth century
Locale: England

Principal characters:
FRANK WELLBORN, a prodigal young man of good family
SIR GILES OVERREACH, Wellborn's uncle, a grasping miser
MARGARET OVERREACH, Sir Giles's beautiful daughter
LORD LOVELL, Margaret's suitor
LADY ALLWORTH, a rich young widow
TOM ALLWORTH, Lady Allworth's stepson and Lord Lovell's page
MARRALL, a hanger-on of Sir Giles

The Story:

Frank Wellborn, who by his prodigality had gone through a fortune and lost most of his friends, is now at a point where even the alehouses refuse to give him food or drink. One morning, as he is about to be thrown from an alehouse, he meets a young page whom he had once befriended. The boy, Allworth, offers to lend him money, but Wellborn refuses, knowing how little the boy has. Allworth confides to Wellborn that he is in love with Margaret, daughter of Sir Giles Overreach, who had despoiled young Wellborn in earlier days.

Later in the morning, Wellborn sees Allworth's widowed, wealthy young stepmother, Lady Allworth. When the lady promises to help him restore his reputation, his only request is that she receive him as a gentleman in her house. Meanwhile, Sir Giles Overreach is laying plans for his daughter's marriage, and for his own as well. After he marries Margaret to the rich Lord Lovell, he himself plans to marry Lady Allworth.

Overreach is angered to discover that Lady Allworth, who refuses to be at home to him, has entertained the prodigal Wellborn as if he were a suitor. His anger is somewhat dissipated, however, by Lord Lovell's visit. He realizes also that if Wellborn gets his hands on Lady Allworth's fortune, he, as the young man's uncle and creditor, might take it away.

Lovell, who had promised to visit Overreach's country place, knows of the love between Margaret and his page, Allworth, and he promises the page that he will do all he can to further the affair. Upon his arrival at the Overreach estate, he tells Margaret of his plans, and the two pretend to carry on a courtship to deceive her father.

During Lovell's visit, Lady Allworth, accompanied by Wellborn, arrives also. Overreach, who is not in love with Lady Allworth but only desires her money, is pleased by the prospect of marrying his daughter to a nobleman and getting

his hands on Lady Allworth's fortune through her possible marriage to his prodigal nephew. He even offers money to Wellborn, so that the latter can pay off his debts and appear once again as a respectable gentleman.

After the party leaves Overreach's estate, Lovell releases young Allworth from his position and tells of further plans to help the page's suit. He intends to send the young man, ostensibly as a letter carrier, every day to the young woman.

Overreach reveals his true character to Lovell by promising him anything if the nobleman would marry his daughter. The miser even offers lands belonging to Lady Allworth, who is highly esteemed by Lovell. When Overreach is told that those are not his to give, he explains to Lovell how he had acquired a fortune and would accumulate another. Lovell, indignant at what he hears, promises himself to right the many wrongs Overreach has done and decides to aid young Allworth's suit. Lovell tells Lady Allworth that he could never marry into the Overreach family. He adds that he had an honorable motive in the pretense she had seen.

Meanwhile, the suspected marriage between Lady Allworth and Wellborn, which has no basis in fact except that she treats him as a friend, causes Wellborn's debtors to drop their claims against him. Wellborn pays his debts, however, with the money his uncle lends on the strength of the supposed marriage.

One of Overreach's hangers-on, Marrall, promises to help Wellborn regain his lands, which his uncle had fraudulently taken from him for a fraction of their value. Marrall tells Wellborn to ask Overreach to present the deed.

At Overreach's house, young Allworth supposedly carries a letter to Margaret, which gives him a chance to talk with her. Overreach, reading the letter, learns that Lovell asks Margaret to marry him forthwith. Overjoyed, the miser sends a letter of command to his manor priest, telling the chaplain to marry Margaret to the gentleman who accompanies her with the letter. The young people leave and are immediately married, the letter acting as a means of getting the clergyman to perform the private ceremony.

Lady Allworth tells Lovell that she helped Wellborn regain his former position because Wellborn aided her dead husband in years gone by. With that action made clear, Lovell asks her to marry him. Lady Allworth consents. A short time later, Overreach appears, driving Marrall before him and questioning him about a document that had disappeared. Overreach is also hunting for his daughter, who failed to return home the night before. In his anger, Overreach asks for the thousand pounds he had lent to Wellborn. Wellborn, in turn, demands an accounting of his estates. Overreach takes his strongbox and removes a parchment that proves to be only a sealed paper with no writing on it. Marrall had removed the true deed.

Overreach realizes that he no longer has any legal right to Wellborn's lands. His daughter and young Allworth, married the day before, arrive to tell of their marriage, in which Overreach had unconsciously aided them by sending a letter to his clergyman.

Overreach, angered beyond measure, would have killed his daughter with his sword, had not Lovell stopped him. Lord Lovell then announces his intended marriage to Lady Allworth and promises to speed the unraveling of Overreach's affairs so that Wellborn could regain his estates, and Margaret and her husband could have their rightful portion of the miser's wealth.

Critical Evaluation:

Although a prolific and workmanlike playwright, Philip Massinger never achieved an outstanding individual style strong enough to distinguish him among his contemporaries or in theatrical history. After studying at Oxford, Massinger wrote plays in collaboration with Cyril Tourneur, John Fletcher, and Thomas Dekker; later he served for fifteen years as the principal playwright for William Shakespeare's old company, the King's Men. *A New Way to Pay Old Debts*, having remained popular over time, is his claim to enduring fame.

The plot, although not particularly original, is lively. The formula of the play, trickery to fool a criminal, was not a new one with Massinger, but he gave his theme dramatic interest and clever satire. The new way to pay old debts is credit, seen in the actions of Lady Allworth, which enables the prodigal Wellborn to establish himself once again in the respectable world after having been cozened by his uncle. The character of Sir Giles Overreach, a favorite with lead actors, was prob-

ably based on Sir Giles Mompessen (1584-1651), a famous extortioner of seventeenth century England who had commissions from James I for controlling licenses to innkeepers. His crimes were discovered, and he and his legal associate Francis Michel (Marrall in the play) were prosecuted and convicted a decade before the play appeared.

The themes of this comedy of manners are no more complicated than the plot, but they are valid and convincingly handled. Overreach represents the senseless desire to attain nobility, a desire that is paradoxical when accompanied by his disdain of the nobility's inability to fend successfully for itself in the mercantile world. Lovell is pitted against Sir Giles; birth and inherited riches are set against wealth won by individual industry. Overreach's complete lack of principle and scruples contrasts him with Lovell but also makes him a more interesting character. The scene between father and daughter is a clear presentation of the grasping man's willingness to make any means practicable for a determined end: "End me no ends," her father tells Margaret in act 5, scene 1, echoing his words in act 3, scene 2, "Virgin me no virgins!" Massinger neatly emphasizes the way in which Overreach—through the complicity of Greedy—sets about corrupting the law he professes, to suit his vicious purpose. The avarice at the heart of the action is a satirical reflection of the central motivation of contemporary society as Massinger views it.

Overreach is the main character, whose forceful personality dominates the stage even when he is not there. Scenes without him pale in dramatic interest by comparison; audiences wait for him to return, to outrage them again. His explanation to Margaret recalls Christopher Marlowe's Barabas (in *The Jew of Malta*, 1633): "Wasn't not to make thee great/ That I have now, and still pursue, those ways/ That hale down curses on me, which I mind not?" Margaret, however, is nothing more to her father than an object, a pawn he can move to his own will. Nobility of blood means nothing to her, but everything to him, who can never know it. He is so vulgar that he has no understanding even of the spiritual nobility Margaret strives to maintain in the face of his demands that she prostitute herself to Lovell: "Stand not on form," he tells her in an echo of Falstaff, "words are no substances."

Just as Greedy values only what he can taste, Overreach treasures only what he can touch and reach physically. His relationship with Marrall, as it unfolds, proves that there is not even honor among thieves in their world. His bombastic boorishness is reflected with perfect irony when, expecting Lovell, he asks of Marrall, "Is the loud music I gave order for/ Ready to receive him?" In his uncultured opinion, the louder the music is, the more impressive it is. His brazen, pompous overtures to Lovell in act 4 shock even jaded sensibilities; he and the nobleman are two entirely different kinds of people, and the audience may wonder uneasily who it is more like. The catharsis occurs shortly thereafter, when young Allworth manages to gull Sir Giles with one of his own characteristic legal tricks: "Good Master Allworth,/ This shall be the best night's work you ever made." The play continues with the pathetic spectacle of Overreach's fiscal and mental dissolution, until he is carried away in the outward shambles that finally correspond to his inner moral state.

Not nearly as interesting are the other characters, although Justice Greedy is unforgettably entertaining as a "compleat glutton." Self-styled "arch-president of the boil'd, the roast, the bak'd," he is epitomized by Furnace: "His stomach's as insatiate as the grave." It is one of the most delightful comic ironies of the play that Greedy cannot eat the dinner he prepares with such anxiety lest the fawn not be roasted with "a Norfolk dumpling in its belly." Revolving around Greedy are the uniformly sympathetic ordinary characters of Lady Allworth's cooks, butlers, and household attendants. By comparison with her servants, the lady herself is flat and uninteresting. Her advice to Allworth, in fact an uncannily accurate memory of her husband's dying advice to his son, makes her sound like a latter-day Polonius: "Beware ill company, for often men/ Are like to those with whom they do converse." She, like the nondescript Lovell, is as dramatically superficial as she is morally shallow; she is worried more about appearances than realities, the very opposite of Overreach. In her own subtle way she sells herself to Lovell as Overreach would have Margaret do.

Lady Allworth's son, too, is almost tiresomely virtuous, at his worst when he vows to his mother that he will serve Lovell loyally. She is all too right in calling him "like virgin parchment, capable of any/ Inscription," and one might wish that he were inscribed with more vivid ink. One of the great laughs of the play is Lovell's reaction to Allworth's simpering reception of his commission: "Nay, do not melt." Wellborn has at least a streak of the devil in him to make him interesting, although he does not have the dramatic force one would expect from the pivotal figure in the plot. His undisclosed whispering to Lady Allworth in act 1, scene 3, sets in motion the wheels that lead to the downfall of Overreach by his own trickery.

More successful is the character of Marrall, who has the virtue of being a thoroughly despicable parasite without the partially redeeming, intelligent self-irony of Ben Jonson's Mosca. Marrall is a low-class person out of his depth; this is portrayed riotously in Amble's report of his toasting the lady "in white broth" and humbly thanking "my worship" for serving him wine. Marrall ends up as an exaggerated carica-

ture of his own meanness as he offers to let Wellborn ride upon his own back and says, over-elaborately, "an it like your worship,/ I hope Jack Marrall shall not live so long/ To prove himself such an unmannerly beast . . ./ As to be cover'd/ When your worship's present." The audience has no more sympathy for him than Wellborn does and is delighted when Wellborn, having paid his own old debts with credit, cancels Marrall's credit rating as the knave deserves.

"Critical Evaluation" by Kenneth John Atchity

Further Reading

Ball, Robert Hamilton. *The Amazing Career of Sir Giles Overreach*. New York: Octagon Books, 1968. A detailed stage history. Offers a biography of Sir Giles Mompessen, on whom Overreach is based. Examines the play's production history in Great Britain and the United States.

Clark, Ira. "Massinger's Tragedies and Satiric Tragicomedies in Their Social and Family Settings." In *The Moral Art of Philip Massinger*. Cranbury, N.J.: Bucknell University Press, 1993. Opposes critics who see the play as a conservative attack on social mobility. Finds the play validates a social hierarchy based on gratitude, community service, and ability.

Lee, Huey-Ling. "The Devil or the Physician: The Politics of Cooking and the Gendering of Cooks in Jonson and Massinger." *English Literary Renaissance* 36, no. 2 (Spring, 2006): 250-277. Analyzes the depiction of cooks in *A New Way to Pay Old Debts* and Ben Jonson's *Bartholomew Fair*, describing how these characters reflect contemporary anxieties about the role of the cook, gender, and social class.

Leonard, Nancy S. "Overreach at Bay: Massinger's *A New Way to Pay Old Debts*." In *Philip Massinger: A Critical Reassessment*, edited by Douglas Howard. New York: Cambridge University Press, 1985. Characterizes the play as a revenge comedy, in which both Overreach and the nobility appeal to ideological positions to rationalize self-serving displays of power.

Neill, Michael. "Massinger's Patriarchy: The Social Vision of *A New Way to Pay Old Debts*." *Renaissance Drama*, n.s. 10 (1979): 185-213. Argues for a conservative reading of the play, which characterizes the patriarchal hierarchy as a supportive family. Overreach, a combination of biblical patriarch and Renaissance "new man," threatens this ideal by treating social relationships as financial transactions.

Sanders, Julie. *Caroline Drama: The Plays of Massinger, Ford, Shirley, and Brome*. Plymouth, England: Northcote

House/British Council, 1999. Analyzes plays written by Massinger and the three other dramatists for the public theater between 1625 and 1642, focusing on these plays' concerns with issues of community and hierarchy.

Zucker, Adam, and Alan B. Farmer, eds. *Localizing Caroline Drama: Politics and Economics of the Early Modern*

Stage, 1625-1642. New York: Palgrave Macmillan, 2006. Collection of essays about Caroline drama, including the work of Massinger. The numerous references to the playwright are listed in the index. In addition, one of the essays provides an analysis of Massinger's play *The Renegado*.

The New York Trilogy

Author: Paul Auster (1947-   )
First published: 1987; includes *City of Glass*, 1985; *Ghosts*, 1986; *The Locked Room*, 1986
Type of work: Novels
Type of plot: Detective and mystery
Time of plot: City of Glass, mid-1970's; *Ghosts*, February 3, 1947-August 10, 1948; *The Locked Room*, mid-1970's
Locale: New York City

Principal characters:
DANIEL QUINN, a mystery writer who writes under the pseudonym William Wilson
MAX WORK, the detective hero of Quinn's fiction
PAUL AUSTER THE DETECTIVE, an alleged detective whom Quinn impersonates
PETER STILLMAN, his client
PROFESSOR PETER STILLMAN, his client's father
VIRGINIA STILLMAN, his client's wife
PAUL AUSTER THE WRITER
BLUE, a detective
THE FUTURE MRS. BLUE, his fiancé
WHITE, his client
BLACK, the man Blue follows
UNNAMED NARRATOR
FANSHAWE, his childhood friend
SOPHIE FANSHAWE, Fanshawe's deserted wife

The Story:

In *City of Glass*, Daniel Quinn is a lonely mystery novelist who lives in New York City, where he writes one mystery novel per year, reads a great deal, and takes many walks. One night, he answers a wrong number and decides to impersonate the man being sought, Paul Auster the detective. He goes to meet his clients, the Stillmans.

Peter Stillman is a young man who has recently left a sanatorium after spending nine years of his childhood locked by himself in a dark room as part of an experiment conducted by his deranged father, Professor Peter Stillman. The Stillmans have sought Paul Auster to protect Peter from his father, who is himself scheduled to be released from a hospital for the criminally insane the next day. Virginia Stillman, the wife of the younger Stillman, pays Quinn with a five-hundred-dollar check in the name of Paul Auster and kisses him passionately before he leaves.

Quinn reads Professor Stillman's academic work, which

cites Henry Dark, who argued in the seventeenth century that a new Tower of Babel would be built in America in 1960, the year Stillman locked up his son. For the two weeks following Professor Stillman's release, Quinn follows him as Stillman walks about the city, picks up objects, and makes notes in a red notebook. Quinn keeps detailed notes of Stillman's route in a red notebook of his own and eventually realizes that Stillman's path is describing letters on the city streets. The first fifteen letters spell "The Tower of Babel."

Feeling emboldened by understanding Stillman's message, Quinn speaks with his quarry three times, using the personas of Quinn, Henry Dark, and finally Peter Stillman. Each time, Stillman responds with delight at the name Quinn uses, since "Quinn" rhymes with "twin," Henry Dark is a name Stillman invented in his research because it shared initials with Lewis Carroll's Humpty Dumpty, and Peter Stillman is his own name and that of his son.

Eventually, Quinn loses Stillman's trail and seeks Paul Auster the detective, hoping that the real detective will be able to help him protect the young Peter Stillman. Quinn finds only one Paul Auster in the New York City phone book, but when he goes to his apartment, he finds that it belongs to Paul Auster the writer, who knows nothing of detective work but tells Quinn of his current study of the print history of *Don Quixote de la Mancha* (1605, 1615).

After meeting with Auster, Quinn phones Virginia Stillman to tell her he has lost the trail, but her phone is constantly busy. Convinced that he must pursue the case nonetheless, Quinn stakes out the alley next to the Stillman home. He slowly reduces the amount of food and sleep he needs, taking shelter in a dumpster as necessary and always writing in his red notebook. He becomes an itinerant.

When Quinn runs out of money, he calls Auster, who had offered to cash the advance check Virginia Stillman had written to Quinn in Auster's name. Auster tells Quinn that the check bounced and that Professor Peter Stillman committed suicide two and a half months earlier. Quinn goes home to his apartment, only to find it occupied by a young woman who tells him she rented it after the the writer who used to live there disappeared.

Quinn returns to Peter Stillman's apartment and curls up in a small room. Trays of hot food appear regularly, and he lives alone and naked, writing in his red notebook and sleeping a great deal. Quinn's red notebook ends by asking what will happen when the red notebook is full.

An unnamed narrator addresses readers, claiming to have accompanied Paul Auster to the Stillman apartment and found Quinn's red notebook. The narrative, he claims, has been pieced together from Auster's recollections and the contents of the notebook.

In *Ghosts*, also narrated by an unnamed narrator, White hires Blue to watch Black, providing Blue with the key to the apartment across from Black's on Orange Street. White asks for weekly reports and pays a five-hundred-dollar advance with ten fifty-dollar bills.

Blue watches Black, who spends most of his time reading and writing, occasionally going out for groceries or a walk. With nothing to do but watch, Blue begins to turn inward for the first time in his life, and he invents stories about why he was hired. When it comes time to write his first weekly report, Blue realizes that he no longer believes that words and reality have a clear, transparent relationship, and he is tempted to include some of his speculations in his report. He eventually writes a terse report about Black's reading and writing habits, and he receives a money order by post a few days later.

This pattern continues for over a year with only a few minor interruptions. Once, Black and a woman meet for a lunch that ends in tears. Once, Blue bumps into the future Mrs. Blue, whom he has not contacted since taking the case, and she pounds his chest, yelling "You, You!" and breaks off their engagement. Another time, Blue watches the mailbox to which he sends his reports, only to see a man wearing a mask, whom he presumes to be White in disguise, picking up the report.

The boundaries of reality begin to break down for Blue, who wonders if White has also hired Black to live under Blue's gaze. Blue even wonders if there are several Blacks, each of whom performs for him and then returns to a normal life at the end of his workday.

Eventually, Blue arranges encounters with Black, adopting different personas. As Jimmy Rose, an elderly itinerant, he speaks to Black about nineteenth century American literature. Soon thereafter, Blue follows Black into Manhattan and sits down with him in a hotel bar, where each man orders a Black and White on the rocks. Black says he is a private detective and has been watching a man write a book for over a year. He assumes the man knows he is watching and needs him in order to feel alive.

Now certain that Black is in on the case, Blue disguises himself as a brush salesman and knocks on Black's door. Blue and Black discuss the merits of various brands of toothbrushes and hairbrushes, and Black purchases two brushes. Three nights later, Black leaves his apartment and Blue takes the opportunity to break in. He steals a stack of papers from Black's desk and finds them to be his own weekly reports.

Blue returns to his apartment in a state of depression and stays in, unshaved and unkempt, for several days. Finally, he decides to confront Black. He showers, shaves, and dresses in his best suit before crossing the street to Black's apartment. Black invites him in, wearing the same mask that Blue had seen on the man at the post office, suggesting that Black and White are the same person. Black and Blue fight, and Blue beats Black severely. Blue tries unsuccessfully to determine whether the other man is still alive; he thinks he hears Black's breathing, but it may be his own.

Blue takes the book that Black has been writing and returns to his apartment to read it. As Black told him, Blue knows the book by heart. Blue leaves his apartment. The narrator says that it is unknown what happened to Blue afterward, but perhaps he went to China.

In *The Locked Room*, the first-person narrator receives a letter from Sophie Fanshawe, the wife of his childhood friend. His friend Fanshawe has disappeared, and Sophie has hired the private detective Quinn to find him, to no avail.

Fanshawe, a writer, had named the narrator his literary executor. The narrator reads the Fanshawe manuscripts and, judging them to be brilliant, arranges for their publication over a period of several years. He takes Sophie out to celebrate, and the two fall in love.

All is well until the narrator receives an unsigned letter with a New York postmark. It is from Fanshawe, who thanks the narrator for taking care of his literary estate and family. He does not want to be found and threatens to kill the narrator should he be sought. The narrator does not tell Sophie about the letter. Eventually, he marries her and adopts Fanshawe's son. As the narrator works on Fanshawe's literary estate, people begin to wonder if the narrator and Fanshawe are the same person.

The narrator undertakes a biography of Fanshawe. He interviews Fanshawe's mother and ends up having violent sex with her. He travels to Paris, where he speaks with Fanshawe's acquaintances and sleeps with his former girlfriend. Unable to make progress and yet unable to go home, the narrator withdraws from the world, entering a blurry month of alcohol and sex with prostitutes. In reflecting on this time, the narrator explains that he is the author of *Ghosts* and *The Locked Room*, and that the three stories are versions of each other, representing his changing awareness of their meaning.

One night in a bar, the narrator sees a young man whom he calls "Fanshawe." The man corrects him, introducing himself as Peter Stillman. The narrator follows Stillman from the bar, and the two fight, with Stillman beating the narrator severely. The narrator is now ready to return to his family in New York.

Some time later, the narrator receives a final letter from Fanshawe asking him to come to a Boston address, where the two speak through the door of a locked room where Fanshawe now lives under the name Henry Dark. Fanshawe recounts his life since his disappearance, including an account of the few weeks he spent shadowing the narrator and his family. Fanshawe says he has taken poison and will soon die. He has, however, left a red notebook of his final writings under the stairs. At Fanshawe's request, the narrator leaves, taking the red notebook with him. In the train station, he reads the notebook, which is strangely constructed so that each sentence cancels out the one that came before. The narrator tears out the pages one by one, coming to the last page as his train arrives.

Critical Evaluation:

Paul Auster's creative output includes numerous novels, screenplays, and translations, as well as several collections of poetry and creative nonfiction. He is an American writer who lived for many years as a translator in Paris, where he developed a literary friendship with the absurdist writer Samuel Beckett. Auster's work has been seminal in the ways it has drawn together motifs from American literature and French philosophy, leading him to receive accolades on both sides of the Atlantic. *The New York Trilogy* is his most critically acclaimed work, and *City of Glass*, the first novel in the trilogy, was adapted in 1994 into a highly successful graphic novel.

The New York Trilogy's most prominent feature is its slipperiness, for it investigates slippages of meaning, genre, identity, and even fictionality. The three novels are easy to read but difficult to grasp; perhaps the only thing Auster scholars agree upon is that a coherent explanation of exactly what the novels mean would go against Auster's project.

The New York Trilogy demands intertextual readings, since all three novels are redolent with explicit and implicit references to other literary works, especially from nineteenth century American fiction. Indeed, the title *Ghosts* may refer to the haunting of postmodern writing by the literary luminaries of the American Renaissance, all of whom are mentioned by name in Auster's text. Herman Melville's *Benito Cereno* (1855, serial; revised, 1856) is mentioned, and Walt Whitman and Ralph Waldo Emerson appear in anecdotes told by Black to Blue. Henry David Thoreau's *Walden: Or, Life in the Woods* (1854) appears as a book that Blue watches Black read before reading it himself.

It is Nathaniel Hawthorne who features most prominently. In *Ghosts*, Black tells Blue the story of Wakefield, the title character of a Hawthorne short story who one day decides not to go home to his wife for reasons unknown even to himself and who lives nearby undetected for years before returning; the story ends as the door opens. Although "Wakefield" (1835) is most closely associated with Fanshawe, who leaves his own family in exactly the same way, it also adds depth to Blue's difficulty in contacting the future Mrs. Blue, something Blue cannot explain even to himself.

Hawthorne, whose first novel was titled *Fanshawe: A Tale* (1828), was known for having spent years in a virtual "locked room" learning how to write, which connects him to characters from all three novels: to Peter Stillman, whose childhood is spent in a locked room; to Quinn, who spends time in Stillman's locked room, writing; to Black and Blue, each in his locked room writing the story of the other; and to Fanshawe, who ends his life in the locked room in which he has filled his red notebook.

Edgar Allan Poe, often called the father of detective fiction, is also present in *The New York Trilogy*. Quinn mentions

Poe's *The Narrative of Arthur Gordon Pym* (1838) when trying to find meaning in Stillman's meanderings through the city. More subtle, Quinn's pseudonym is William Wilson, the title character of a Poe story about a man haunted by his double. "William Wilson" (1839) resonates most obviously with the relationships between Blue and Black and between Fanshawe and the unnamed narrator. The presence of William Wilson's name in *City of Glass* urges readers to seek Quinn's double, possibly the elder Peter Stillman, who also loves to wander the streets of New York and who carries a red notebook identical to Quinn's that Quinn thinks might contain the answers to the questions posed in his own red notebook. Quinn may have two doubles, though, as indicated by his tripartite understanding of his own identity as each of Daniel Quinn the man, William Wilson the writer, and Max Work the detective. Quinn's other double may be doubled or even tripled: It is Paul Auster the author of *The New York Trilogy* and Paul Auster the character, who is also doubled as the absent detective and the writer.

Paul Auster the writer is central in another major intertextual moment, when he tells Quinn that he is writing about the blurring of boundaries between the categories of reader, writer, and editor in Miguel de Cervantes' *Don Quixote de la Mancha*. This comment brings to mind Virginia Stillman's claim that Paul Auster the detective was recommended by the husand of Peter's nurse, Michael Saavedra, which is Cervantes' real name. Like Auster, then, Cervantes is also a character in the trilogy. The tearing of the fictional fabric caused by authors becoming fictional characters in novels about the intersections of detective work and writing invites astute readers to apply the fictional Paul Auster's argument about *Don Quixote de la Mancha* to the texts they are reading.

In an interview in his *The Red Notebook: True Stories* (2002), Auster characterizes *City of Glass* as a fictitious autobiography, suggesting that he could have become Quinn had he not met his wife. Subtle autobiographical details appear throughout the trilogy, including Auster and Quinn sharing an old address, Auster's birthday marking the opening date of *Ghosts*, and Auster and Fanshawe both having mentally ill sisters named Ellen. This autobiographical correspondence creates a metafictionality in the trilogy that relates to postmodern concerns around the unfixed nature of reality and fiction.

Like many postmodern texts, *The New York Trilogy* blurs genres. Although it appears to be a series of three detective stories, it can also be classified as antidetective or metaphysical detective fiction. The detective genre is ideal for exploring postmodern concerns, since it provides a familiar structure whose gradual dissolution highlights the unknowability

of not only the world but also the self. A classic detective narrative is set up as a game, providing readers the opportunity to match wits with the detective in uncovering clues and piecing them together to discover the truth. In Auster's trilogy, the mysteries under investigation not only do not seem to have solutions, but they also implicate the detective who finds himself rather than a criminal. Readers are thus thrown into a labyrinth of philosophical reflections and intertextual references that uncover nothing but the emptiness of meaning.

Pamela Bedore

Further Reading

Bernstein, Stephen. "'The Question Is the Story Itself': Postmodernism and Intertextuality in Auster's *New York Trilogy*." In *Detecting Texts: The Metaphysical Detective Story from Poe to Postmodernism*, edited by Patricia Merivale and Susan Elizabeth Sweeney. Philadelphia: University of Pennsylvania Press, 1999. Argues that reading through the intertextual clues in the trilogy allows readers to find a coherent message: that meaning is impossible to find.

Briggs, Robert. "Wrong Numbers: The Endless Fiction of Auster and Deleuze and Guattari and . . . ." *Critique: Studies in Contemporary Fiction* 44, no. 2 (2003): 213-224. Playful examination of *The New York Trilogy* alongside Auster's *The Red Notebook*, arguing that reading the two together creates an endless multiplicity of stories and interpretations of how authorship is portrayed throughout Auster's body of work.

Dimovitz, Scott A. "Public Personae and the Private I: Decompositional Ontology in Paul Auster's *The New York Trilogy*." *Modern Fiction Studies* 52, no. 3 (2006): 613-633. This compelling article suggests that the trilogy is neither postmodern nor poststructuralist in its inflections, arguing instead that it negates a postmodern worldview.

Morley, Catherine. "The Book of Allusions: Where Is Samuel Beckett in Paul Auster's *The New York Trilogy*?" In *Beckett's Literary Legacies*, edited by Matthew Feldman and Mark Nixon. Newcastle, England: Cambridge Scholars, 2007. Examines the intersections of Auster's trilogy and Beckett's trilogy of novels—*Molloy* (1951), *Malone Dies* (1951), and *The Unnameable* (1953)—paying attention to the themes of absurdity and futility.

Müller, Monika. "From Hard-Boiled Detective to Kaspar Hauser? Masculinity and Writing in Paul Auster's *The New York Trilogy*." In *Subverting Masculinity: Hegemonic and Alternative Versions of Masculinity in Con-*

temporary Culture, edited by Russell West and Frank Lay. Amsterdam: Rodopi, 2000. Argues that Auster's three novels can be seen as exploring the relationship of masculinity, writing, and domesticity; focuses on the trilogy's intertextuality with nineteenth century American writers.

Rubenstein, Roberta. "Doubling, Intertextuality, and the Postmodern Uncanny: Paul Auster's *New York Trilogy*." *LIT: Literature Interpretation Theory* 9, no. 3 (1998): 245-262. Lucid exploration of the Freudian uncanny as it appears repeatedly throughout Auster's trilogy.

Russell, Alison. "Deconstructing *The New York Trilogy*: Paul Auster's Anti-Detective Fiction." *Critique: Studies in Contemporary Fiction* 31, no. 2 (1990): 71-84. Derridean

reading of the trilogy that focuses on the multiple levels of linguistic recursiveness in the text.

Tish, Chris. "From One Mirror to Another: The Rhetoric of Disaffiliation in *City of Glass*." *Review of Contemporary Fiction* 14, no. 1 (1994): 46-52. This linguistically playful article argues that *City of Glass* challenges the authority of the father, thus questioning the stability of language, identity, and culture.

Zilcosky, John. "The Revenge of the Author: Paul Auster's Challenge to Theory." *Critique: Studies in Contemporary Fiction* 39, no. 3 (1998): 195-206. Argues that Auster's trilogy challenges Roland Barthes's theory that the author is dead, since the trilogy shows authorship as dispersed and complicated but very much alive.

The Newcomes
Memoirs of a Most Respectable Family

Author: William Makepeace Thackeray (1811-1863)
First published: 1853-1855, serial; 1855, book
Type of work: Novel
Type of plot: Social morality
Time of plot: Early nineteenth century
Locale: England

Principal characters:
COLONEL THOMAS NEWCOME, an Anglo-Indian soldier
CLIVE, his son
BRIAN and HOBSON, his half brothers
LADY ANN, Brian's wife
BARNES, Brian's son
ETHEL, Brian's daughter
LADY KEW, Lady Ann's mother
JAMES BINNIE, the colonel's friend
MRS. MACKENZIE, Binnie's half sister
ROSEY, Mrs. Mackenzie's daughter
LADY CLARA, Barnes's wife

The Story:

The elder Thomas Newcome marries his childhood sweetheart, who dies after giving birth to their son, who is named for him. Thomas remarries, and his second wife has two sons, Brian and Hobson. Young Thomas proves to be a trial to his stepmother and when he is old enough is sent to India, where he later becomes a colonel. He marries and has a son, Clive, whom he loves with a passion far beyond the normal devotion of a father. Having lost his mother, little Clive is sent to England to begin his education.

Brian and Hobson Newcome inherit their mother's wealthy banking house. Brian marries Lady Ann, who is well known in London for her lavish parties. After little Clive spends about seven years in England, his impatient father

crosses the ocean to join him. He expects to receive a warm welcome from his two half brothers, Brian and Hobson. Much to his bewilderment, the bankers receive him politely but coldly and pass on the responsibility of entertaining him to young Barnes, Brian's son, a social gadfly and a familiar figure in London's clubs.

Colonel Thomas Newcome's late wife has a sister and a brother. The sister, Miss Honeyman, runs a boardinghouse in Brighton, where little Alfred and Ethel go with their mother, Lady Ann, for a vacation; Colonel Newcome and Clive also arrive for a visit. The brother, Mr. Honeyman, also lives in Brighton, where the keeper's young son, John James Ridley, delights in drawing pictures from the storybooks that he finds in Mr. Honeyman's room. Clive, who aspires to be an artist, delights in Ridley's drawings; Ethel becomes extremely fond of the colonel and his unaffected manner. The colonel's great love for children causes him to be a favorite with all the Newcome youngsters, but it is fair-haired little Ethel who wins his heart with her simple, adoring ways and her sincerity.

Colonel Newcome buys a house in London, where he lives with Clive and Mr. James Binnie, the colonel's friend. Clive is given a tutor, but the young man neglects his studies to sketch. If the colonel is disappointed by Clive's choice of career, he says nothing and allows Clive to attend art school with his friend, Ridley. Clive is becoming a kind, generous, and considerate young man, and the colonel himself is satisfied that his son is growing up to be a fine man. He spends a considerable amount of money setting up a well-lighted studio for Clive in a house not far from his own. Meanwhile, Mr. Binnie fell from a horse and now is laid up in bed. Binnie's widowed half sister, Mrs. Mackenzie, and her daughter, Rosey, comes to stay with the bedridden Binnie in the colonel's house.

After a time, the colonel finds himself financially embarrassed. Realizing that he can no longer live on his income in London, he plans to return to India until he reaches a higher grade in the army. With a higher pension he will be able to afford to retire in London.

Ethel Newcome grows into a beautiful and charming young lady, and the colonel dreams of a match between Ethel and Clive; Lady Ann, however, places an early prohibition on such a match. She tells her brother-in-law that Ethel has been promised to Lord Kew, a relative of Lady Kew, Lady Ann's mother. The other Newcomes believe that Rosey Mackenzie would be a fine wife for Clive.

After Colonel Newcome returns to India, leaving Clive with a substantial income, Clive and Ridley, now a successful artist, travel to Baden. There, Clive meets Ethel and the other Newcome children, who are vacationing without the dampening presence of Lady Ann or her aristocratic mother. Ethel and Clive enjoy a short period of companionship and innocent pleasure, and Clive falls in love with his beautiful cousin. When Lady Ann and Lady Kew arrive, Clive is warned that he must not press his suit with Ethel any longer, for Ethel must marry in her own station of life. Clive is reminded that the family assumed that he had found a woman of his own social level in Miss Rosey Mackenzie. Clive bitterly takes his leave and goes to Italy with Ridley.

Ethel is beginning to rebel against the little niche that had been assigned to her in society, and she defies social custom and defends Clive against the charges her brother Barnes re-

peatedly brings against him. Finally, she breaks her engagement to young Lord Kew. When Clive hears of it, he returns to England to press his own suit once more.

In London, Clive has little time for his art, for he quickly becomes a favorite in London society, whose fashionable hosts think he is the only son of a wealthy officer in India. Against the wishes of her grandmother, Lady Kew, Ethel arranges frequent meetings with Clive. When Clive at last proposes marriage to her, she sadly explains to him that she will not inherit Lady Kew's fortune unless she marries properly. Ethel tells him that her younger brothers and sisters need the money, for after her father's death, Barnes Newcome had selfishly kept the family fortune for himself. Meanwhile, Lady Kew is wooing Lord Farintosh for Ethel.

After three years' absence, Colonel Newcome returns to London. During his absence, the colonel amassed a large fortune for his son. Armed with this wealth, Colonel Newcome goes to Barnes with a proposal of marriage between Ethel and Clive. Barnes is polite but noncommittal. Shortly afterward, Lady Kew announces Ethel's engagement to Lord Farintosh. Then, suddenly, Lady Kew dies, leaving her immense fortune to Ethel, whose only concern is that the money should go to her younger brothers and sisters.

Barnes's marriage to Lady Clara is not a happy one. Soon after they are married, he begins to mistreat his wife, who at last decides that she can no longer stand his bullying of her and runs off with a lover, leaving her small children behind. The shock of the scandal and the subsequent divorce opens Ethel's eyes to the dangers of loveless marriages. Realizing that she could never be happy with Lord Farintosh because she does not love him, she breaks her second engagement.

Ethel retires from her life in society to have children with Barnes. Clive, meanwhile, succumbs to the wishes of Mr. Binnie and his own father. Before the news of Ethel's broken engagement with Lord Farintosh reaches the colonel and his son, Clive marries sweet-faced Rosey Mackenzie. Clive's marriage is gentle but bare. The colonel is Rosey's chief protector and her greater admirer. Clive tries to be a good husband, but inwardly he longs for more companionship. He had admitted to his father that he still loves Ethel.

The colonel had been handling the family income very unwisely since returning from India. Shortly after the birth of Clive's son, Thomas, an Indian company in which the colonel had heavy investments failed, and he went bankrupt. Clive, Rosey, and colonel Newcome are now nearly penniless. Rosey's mother, Mrs. Mackenzie, descends upon them and begins ruling them with such tyranny that life becomes unbearable for the colonel. With the help of some friends, he retires to a poorhouse and lives separated from his beloved son. Clive, who faithfully stays with Rosey and his abusive mother-in-law, is able to make a meager living by selling his drawings.

When Ethel learned of the pitiful condition of the old colonel, whom she had always loved, and of Clive's distress, she contrived a plan whereby she was able to give them six thousand pounds without their knowing that it came from her. Rosey had been very ill. One night, Ethel visits Clive, and Mrs. Mackenzie raises such an indignant clamor that Rosey is seriously affected. She dies the following day. The colonel is broken in spirit and grows weaker by the day; soon afterward, he too dies.

Clive never lost his love for Ethel through all the years of his unfortunate marriage to Rosey. Many months after the death of his wife, he went once more to Baden with little Thomas. There it was said, by observers who knew the Newcomes, that Clive, Ethel, and little Tommy were often seen walking together through the woods.

Critical Evaluation:

"I am about a new story," William Makepeace Thackeray wrote an American friend shortly after his first visit to the United States (1852-1853), "but don't know as yet if it will be any good. It seems to me I am too old for story-telling." At the age of forty-three, with the success of *Vanity Fair* (1847-1848, serial; 1848, book), *The History of Pendennis* (1848-1850), and *The History of Henry Esmond, Esquire* (1852) behind him, Thackeray's strength was ebbing, and to his friends he had the physical appearance of an old man broken in health. Because, however, he needed money (his own estimate was the equivalent of thousands of dollars), he began writing *The Newcomes*. He wrote while living in various places in Italy, Germany, and Switzerland, and throughout the project he was often in ill health.

The novel was published serially between October, 1853, and August, 1855. Extensive even by Victorian standards, *The Newcomes* is a typical mid-nineteenth century family chronicle, replete with cogent observations of manners and morals. Despite its gentle comedy, it satirizes the human follies that Thackeray particularly scorned: snobbery, greed, and misguided romantic idealism.

The chronicle is narrated by Arthur Pendennis, an older friend of Clive Newcome, who purports to "edit" the memoirs of "a most respectable family." At first a mere spokesman for the author, Pendennis gradually becomes a character in his own right, participating in as well as commenting on the action. Prudish, smug, and whimsical, Pendennis provides ironical insight into the other characters. His admiration for Colonel Newcome ("so chivalrous, generous, good looking") is uncritical to the point that it becomes amusing. Moreover, his fulminations on folly, especially in the famous parody of moral anecdotes in chapter 1, ring hollow at last, in view of the narrator's own punctilious regard for class and status, his social snobbery, and his moralizing.

As is typical of Thackeray's fiction, the novel's heroes and heroines (Colonel Thomas Newcome, his son Clive, and Ethel and Rosey) are true-blue, the villains (Barnes Newcome, Lady Kew, and Mrs. Mackenzie) quite dastardly; yet even some of the unpleasant characters are redeemed, if not always completely successfully, by the author's pity. After Barnes Newcome, the colonel's longtime nemesis, is humiliated in the family election, he promises not to mistreat his wife any longer and finally comes to terms with Clive. The coldhearted Lady Kew leaves the bulk of her estate to Ethel. Ethel herself, psychologically the most interesting personality in the book, develops from a charming but calculating young lady to a woman capable of self-sacrifice and deep love. Unlike Rosey, who is simple, innocent, but vacuous, Ethel is sophisticated and clever. Her virtue is tested by life and consequently earned. She becomes a worthy mate for Clive, and the tender-hearted author promises his readers that the couple will be both happy and wealthy.

Clive, too, must earn the reader's approval. Spoiled by his doting father, he makes the most of his good looks, his modest talents as an artist, and the honorable reputation of his family. His young manhood, however, is spent in prodigality. Thwarted in his desire to marry Ethel, he chooses the sweet but dull Rosey Mackenzie and then chafes at the restraints of wedlock. Nevertheless, like Ethel, he is educated by life, learns his limitations, and grows in self-respect. In chapter 68, the emotional climax of the novel, Clive and his father come to regard each other as equals without recriminations and with mutual respect and affection. Clive comes into his own as a person of worth and a true gentleman.

The Newcomes is a social novel of manners that teaches the Victorian reader how to recognize and, if possible, become a true gentleman or gentlewoman. Colonel Newcome, the epitome of English gentility, is almost too perfect, that is to say, too proper, innocent, and augustly virtuous; his very rectitude becomes a subject for unconscious satire. Some of Thackeray's reviewers detected in the author's creation of the colonel an element of cynicism; one London critic went so far as to attack the book on the grounds of "morality and religion." Thackeray's avowed intention, however, was certainly not to satirize the true gentleman and his outmoded virtues but rather to expose the parvenu, the snob, and the ingrate. He ridicules the upstart middle-class, especially

Anglo-Indian, society by revealing it to be ill-bred, vulgarly assertive, and materialistic.

The thrust of Thackeray's satire is above all toward women. Barnes Newcome is a rascal, to be sure, but not a fool; Thackeray's obnoxious women, however, manipulate their men and lead them into folly, either through aggressiveness or their simpering, smiling domestic tyranny. "Theirs is a life of hypocrisy," concludes Pendennis, speaking for his author, and their chief wile is flattery. Even Ethel, the virtuous and clever heroine, does not wholly escape Thackeray's censure. When he criticizes her for prolonging her romance with Clive, he attributes her weakness to a fault of her gender rather than to a personal folly. Rosey, Clive's unfortunate wife, never transgresses the social prohibitions but is, like Amelia of *Vanity Fair*, a foolish innocent, to be protected and cherished like a pet. Her opposite is her mother, Mrs. Mackenzie, a mean and fearful woman.

The reader's final impression of *The Newcomes* is not one of abrasive social satire but rather one of reconciliation. At the end of the novel, Ethel and Clive are reunited and the good Colonel Newcome dies as nobly as he had lived in a scene that is touching in its restrained dignity. The reader is left hoping that the Newcome family, despite its human folly, will endure. To Thackeray, that hope—"Fable-land"—is the harmless anodyne to the pain of living.

"Critical Evaluation" by Leslie B. Mittleman

Further Reading

Clarke, Micael M. *Thackeray and Women*. DeKalb: Northern Illinois University Press, 1995. Examines Thackeray's life, novels, and other works from a feminist-sociological perspective to analyze his treatment of female characters, demonstrating how his writings critique the position of women in Western culture. Includes bibliographical references and an index.

Ferris, Ina. "The Way of the World: *The Newcomes*." In *William Makepeace Thackeray*, edited by Herbert Sussman. Boston: Twayne, 1983. Includes brief commentaries by Thackeray's contemporaries, as well as one by Thackeray himself. Discusses Thackeray's self-conscious realism and the way in which his fiction responded to the society in which he lived.

Fisher, Judith L. *Thackeray's Skeptical Narrative and the "Perilous Trade" of Authorship*. Burlington, Vt.: Ashgate, 2002. An analysis of Thackeray's narrative techniques,

describing how he sought to create a "kind of poised reading which enables his readers to integrate his fiction into their life."

Harden, Edgar F. *The Emergence of Thackeray's Serial Fiction*. Athens: University of Georgia Press, 1979. Discussion of the serial structure of five novels, including *The Newcomes*, with particular focus on Thackeray's manuscripts and his compositional process. Explains how the serial installments shaped the form of the novels.

_____. *Thackeray the Writer: From Journalism to "Vanity Fair."* New York: St. Martin's Press, 1998.

_____. *Thackeray the Writer: From "Pendennis" to "Denis Duval."* New York: Macmillan, 2000. Two-volume biography chronicling Thackeray's development as a writer, beginning with his experiences as a book reviewer and culminating in the creation of *Vanity Fair*. Traces how Thackeray became an increasingly perceptive social observer.

Hardy, Barbara. *The Exposure of Luxury: Radical Themes in Thackeray*. Pittsburgh, Pa.: University of Pittsburgh Press, 1972. Discusses aspects of Thackeray's social criticism and points out themes that illustrate his preoccupation with the surface manners of his society. Concludes that self-consciousness and lack of moral optimism are closely related as aspects of Thackeray's radical thinking.

Ray, Gordon. *The Buried Life: A Study of the Relation Between Thackeray's Fiction and His Personal History*. Cambridge, Mass.: Harvard University Press, 1952. Comprehensive biocritical study of Thackeray's state of mind while writing *The Newcomes*. An excellent resource for the serious researcher.

_____. "*The Newcomes*." In *Thackeray: A Collection of Critical Essays*, edited by Alexander Welsh. Englewood Cliffs, N.J.: Prentice-Hall, 1968. Discusses the structural importance of the novel's main themes, as well as how Thackeray reflects his disillusionment with his world.

Shillingsburg, Peter. *William Makepeace Thackeray: A Literary Life*. New York: Palgrave, 2001. An excellent introduction to the life of the novelist, thorough and scholarly, but accessible. Includes a chapter on reading *Vanity Fair*, notes, and index.

Taylor, D. J. *Thackeray: The Life of a Literary Man*. New York: Carroll and Graf, 2001. A lengthy biography that argues for Thackeray's preeminence among nineteenth century English novelists. A generally comprehensive study of Thackeray that sheds much light on his work.

News from Nowhere

Author: William Morris (1834-1896)
First published: 1890, as *New from Nowhere: Or, An Epoch of Rest, Being Some Chapters from a Utopian Romance*
Type of work: Novel
Type of plot: Utopian
Time of plot: Late nineteenth century and twenty-first century
Locale: London

Principal characters:
GUEST, the narrator
RICHARD "DICK" HAMMOND, a boatman
OLD HAMMOND, Dick's great-grandfather
CLARA, Dick's fiancé
ELLEN, a young woman whom Guest finds attractive

The Story:

One evening after a public meeting and political discussion, the narrator returns by train to his home in the London suburb of Hammersmith. When he wakes the next morning from a deep sleep and goes for swim in the Thames River, he is amazed to find that the industrial buildings have been transformed into a pastoral landscape. Encountering a boatman named Dick, who is dressed in simple but attractive fourteenth-century-style garb, he begins to question him and realizes that he has been transported to an England of the twenty-first century.

Dick takes the narrator, whom he calls Guest, to breakfast in the Guest House at Hammersmith, which resembles a medieval hall. There they meet Robert (Bob), the weaver, and Boffin, the dustman, who asks Guest many questions. A pleasant woman named Annie serves their food. After breakfast, Guest and Dick travel by horse carriage to visit Dick's great-grandfather, Old Hammond, who lives by the British Museum in the Bloomsbury district of London. As they ride through London, Guest marvels at the open-air markets, the attractive architecture, and the wooded areas and gardens that have replaced the tenements and industrial buildings of the nineteenth century.

Guest observes the playful children, and Dick tells him that they do not attend school but learn as their curiosity leads them. Guest and Dick stop at one of the small shops, and Guest receives an elaborately carved pipe from two polite children who are tending the shop. As when he had first tried to pay Dick, Guest finds that money is not exchanged because it is unnecessary in this society. Guest also discovers that there are no prisons, since everyone is honest and has an occupation.

When they arrive at the square in front of the British Museum, Dick escorts Guest to the living quarters of his great-grandfather, Old Hammond. A young woman named

Clara appears. She and Dick, who are obviously very much attracted to each other, retire to the upstairs room. Old Hammond explains to Guest that the couple had been married, had two children, and had grown apart, but that they are getting back together. In this new England, Nowhere, there is no such thing as divorce because the courts are unable to enforce "a contract of passion or sentiment."

Guest and Old Hammond talk for some time. Because of Old Hammond's advanced years, he can answer many of Guest's questions about the striking changes that have occurred in England since the late nineteenth century. He tells Guest about the freer and more equal relationships between men and women, the less structured education of children, and the fresh and new appearance of London and its environs after the "big murky places" that were "centres of manufacture" had been removed. Old Hammond explains to Guest how people left London for country villages that became peaceful, thriving communities.

Many of Guest's questions relate to the way government operates. Old Hammond tells him that formal governmental institutions no longer exist because the people live and work in harmony with nature and themselves. The two men also speak about labor, production, and trade. Old Hammond recalls how the new order came about after an uprising of the people overthrew the government.

In the evening, Dick and Clara drive Guest back to Hammersmith Guest House, where they have dinner and spend the night. The next morning, the three of them begin a journey by boat up the Thames River. Their destination is an area past Oxford where they plan to work at the hay harvest. As they travel, they observe the beautiful landscape with cottages and people working in the fields, orchards, and forests. They make several stops, first at Hampton Court, the former Tudor royal palace, which is preserved as a museum. The first evening they lodge at Runnymede with an old man who is nostalgic for past times, and his granddaughter, a beautiful, vivacious woman named Ellen.

After a second day observing the sights along the river, the trio spend the night with Walter Allen, one of Dick's friends, who regretfully reports that an unusual altercation between two men led to a murder. On the third day, they stop to look at a house being built of stone with sculptured reliefs. At Wallingford, where they eat lunch, they talk with an old man, Henry Morsom, about arts and handicrafts. As they leave again, Ellen catches up with them in a boat. Guest, who finds Ellen very attractive, joins Ellen in her boat, while Dick and Clara continue in theirs.

As the two couples continue up the Thames, Guest and Ellen have a chance to observe the beautiful June landscape. Ellen asks many questions about the state of things in the nineteenth century and about the history of the river. When they reach their destination on the upper Thames, the travelers are greeted by a crowd of haymakers. Ellen takes Guest to an old stone barn and together they explore the simple beauty of its architecture and sparse furnishings. Guest reflects on the contrasts between the past, present, and future. Ellen rejoices in her love for the earth, nature, and the seasons.

Ellen and Guest go to dinner with the haymakers in a church that is festively decorated with flowers. Suddenly, Guest realizes that he has become invisible to Dick, Clara, and Ellen. He walks down the road and encounters a decrepit old man. He himself seems to be enveloped in a black cloud, and when he wakes up he is back in his familiar house in his own century. He concludes that he had experienced a vision rather than a dream, and that he should continue to strive to communicate to others the ideals of Nowhere.

Critical Evaluation:

A utopian romance is an apt description for *News from Nowhere*. The novel combines a description of life in Nowhere—an ideal England at some future time—with some of the conventions of a medieval romance.

News from Nowhere can be considered an appropriate summation of William Morris's gifts and preoccupations. He was a prolific writer in Victorian England, whose verses, epics, and romances show the influence of medieval literature. He united his literary and design interests when he established Kelmscott Press with the goal of producing well-designed books. He was a staunch advocate of architectural preservation and opposed romantic restoration. Most of his income came from a design firm that produced stained glass, architectural ornaments, furniture, and textiles. Finally, he

was a socialist and became actively involved in politics during the later years of his life.

The common thread that joined Morris's diverse activities was his idealism. He believed in good design principles, which he thought were being undermined by mass production and the use of machines. His socialist political views protested the degrading working conditions brought by industrialization. He believed in the personal integrity and fulfillment of good craftsmanship. What attracted him to the Middle Ages was his perception that his aesthetic, individual, and communal ideals were embodied in that culture. Morris expressed his convictions in all of the many forms in which he worked.

In *News from Nowhere*, the narrator, who receives the name of Guest, is a thinly disguised self-portrait. When the narrator is asked his name at breakfast at the Guest House at Hammersmith, he replies that he should be called William Guest. The reader first encounters him leaving a political meeting where a socialist agenda had been under discussion. As he returns home he makes a point of noting his distaste for the grimy late nineteenth century surroundings in which he lives.

Guest's utopian dream vision weaves together four main elements of Morris's interests: his socialist politics, his aesthetic sensibilities, his medievalism, and his feeling for the natural environment. He envisions a society where people live in harmony with one another and are free from governmental restrictions. Individuals can pursue occupations that are related to their own interests and talents at the same time that they benefit the larger community.

Throughout the book, detailed and vividly drawn descriptions of architecture, clothing, decor, and objects such as Guest's new pipe reveal Morris's admiration for fine design and craftsmanship. The aesthetic models are based on Morris's concept of the Middle Ages, particularly the late medieval period, which began to show the use of natural ornament to enliven the construction of buildings and to decorate furnishings, fabrics, and books. Morris's delight in the natural environment is most fully depicted in the journey along the Thames River. In his descriptions of the city and the countryside, he contrasts the unspoiled beauty of nature with the environmental degradation found in Victorian England.

Critics have pointed out that in *News from Nowhere*, Morris fails to clarify many aspects of his utopian community and that he focuses on an idealized reverence for the past instead of on innovative ideas for the future. For example, Morris extols the value of human industry and craftsmanship but embraces machine technology where convenient, as in the system of locks that facilitates boat traffic along the Thames.

Judging the work by literary criteria, critics have noted that some chapters create abrupt juxtapositions, probably because the work was originally published in serial form in the journal *Commonweal*. The political discussion that occupies much of the first half has a static quality to it, while the description of the journey along the Thames resembles a travelogue.

These drawbacks notwithstanding, *News from Nowhere* remains an eloquent summation of Morris's beliefs and ideals. His utopian vision is not accompanied by completely realized solutions, but he affirms the value and integrity of human endeavor. His respect for nature, which takes the form of evocatively beautiful descriptions, reveals an understanding of the ecological balance between human needs and those of the environment. These qualities give *News from Nowhere* a timeless and universal theme.

Karen Gould

Further Reading

Clutton-Brock Arthur. *William Morris*. New York: Parkstone Press, 2007. A biography chronicling Morris's multifaceted career, including his work as a prose writer and poet and as a proponent of good design, craftsmanship, and architecture.

Faulkner, Peter. *Against the Age: An Introduction to William Morris*. Boston: Allen & Unwin, 1980. A concise discussion of Morris's wide-ranging interests and works. Places *News from Nowhere* in the context of Morris's other writings and activities.

Kirchhoff, Frederick. *William Morris*. Boston: Twayne, 1979. A study of Morris that concentrates on his literary works. *News from Nowhere* is discussed within the context of his socialist political views.

Latham, David, ed. *Writing on the Image: Reading William Morris*. Buffalo, N.Y.: University of Toronto Press, 2007. Several of this book's essays analyze *News from Nowhere*. Includes "*News from Nowhere* as Autoethnography: A Future History of 'Home Colonization'" and "To Live in the Present: *News from Nowhere* and the Representation of the Present in Late Victorian Utopian Fiction."

Le Bourgeois, John Y. *Art and Forbidden Fruit: Hidden Passion in the Life of William Morris*. Cambridge, England: Lutterworth Press, 2006. An analysis of Morris's life and poetry, describing his attachment to his sister, Emma, who was a source of inspiration for his work.

Silver, Carole. *The Romance of William Morris*. Athens: Ohio University Press, 1982. A study of Morris's prose romances, with a chapter on *News from Nowhere*.

The Nibelungenlied

Author: Unknown
First transcribed: c. 1200 (English translation, 1848)
Type of work: Poetry
Type of plot: Epic
Time of plot: c. 437
Locale: North-central Europe

Principal characters:
SIEGFRIED, the son of Siegmund and Sieglind
KRIEMHILD, a Burgundian princess and Siegfried's wife
GUNTHER,
GERNOT, and
GISELHER, the brothers of Kriemhild
HAGEN, their retainer
BRUNHILD, the wife of Gunther
ETZEL (ATTILA), Kriemhild's second husband
DANKWART, Hagen's brother

The Poem:

In Burgundy there lives a noble family that numbers three brothers and a sister. The sons are Gunther, who wears the crown, Gernot, and Giselher. The daughter is Kriemhild. About them is a splendid court of powerful and righteous knights, including Hagen of Trony, his brother Dankwart, and mighty Hunold. Kriemhild dreams one night that she rears a falcon that then is slain by two eagles. When she tells her dream to Queen Uta, her mother's interpretation is that Kriemhild should have a noble husband but that unless God's protection follows him he might soon die. Siegfried is born in

Niderland, the son of King Siegmund and Queen Sieglind. In his young manhood he hears of the beautiful Kriemhild, and, although he has never seen her, he determines to have her for his wife. Undeterred by reports of her fierce and warlike kinsmen, he makes his armor ready for his venture. Friends come from all parts of the country to bid him farewell, and many of them accompany him as retainers into King Gunther's land. When he arrives at Gunther's court, Hagen, who knows his fame, tells the brothers the story of Siegfried's first success, relating how Siegfried killed great heroes and won the hoard of the Nibelung, a treasure of so much gold and jewels that five score wagons cannot carry all of it. He also tells how Siegfried won the cloak of invisibility from the dwarf Albric and how Siegfried became invulnerable from having bathed in the blood of a dragon he slew. Gunther and his brothers admit Siegfried to their hall after they hear of his exploits, and the hero stays with them a year. In all that time, however, he does not once see Kriemhild.

The Saxons, led by King Ludger, threaten to overcome the kingdom of the Burgundians. Siegfried pledges to use his forces in overcoming the Saxons, and in the battle he leads his knights and Gunther's troops to a great victory. In the following days there are great celebrations at which Queen Uta and her daughter Kriemhild appear in public. On one of these occasions Siegfried and Kriemhild meet and become betrothed. King Gunther, wanting to marry Brunhild, Wotan's daughter, tells Siegfried that if he will help him win Brunhild, then he might wed Kriemhild. Gunther sets out at the head of a great expedition, all of his knights decked in costly garments in order to impress Brunhild. Her preference for a husband, however, is not a well-dressed prince but a hero. She declares that the man who will win her must surpass her in feats of skill and strength. With Siegfried's aid Gunther overcomes Brunhild, and she agrees to go with Gunther as his wife.

Siegfried is sent on ahead to announce a great celebration in honor of the coming marriage of Gunther to Brunhild. A double ceremony takes place, with Kriemhild becoming the bride of Siegfried at the same time. At the wedding feast Brunhild bursts into tears at the sight of Kriemhild and Siegfried together. Gunther tries to explain away her unhappiness, but once more, Gunther needs Siegfried's aid, for Brunhild determines never to let Gunther share her bed. Siegfried goes to her chamber and there overpowers her. Thinking she is overcome by Gunther, she is thus subdued. Brunhild gives birth to a son who is named for Siegfried. As time passes she wishes once more to see Siegfried, who returned with Kriemhild to his own country. Therefore, she instructs Gunther to plan a great hunting party to which Siegfried and Kriemhild should be invited.

At the meeting of the two royal families, there is great rivalry between Brunhild and Kriemhild. They vie with each other by overdressing their attendants and then argue as to the place each should have in the royal procession. Finally, Kriemhild takes revenge when she tells Brunhild the true story of Brunhild's wedding night. Accusing Brunhild of acting the part of a harlot, she says that Brunhild slept first with Siegfried, then with her husband, Gunther. For proof, she displays Brunhild's ring and girdle, both of which Siegfried won from Brunhild the night he overcame her. Brunhild, furious and desirous of revenge, seeks out her husband and confronts him with the story of her humiliation and betrayal. Gunther and Siegfried soon settle to their own satisfaction the quarrel between the two women, but Hagen, the crafty one, stirs up trouble among Gunther's brothers with his claim that Siegfried stained the honor of their house. They plot to trap Siegfried and to destroy him. When it is reported that the Saxons are to attack Gunther's knights, Kriemhild unwittingly reveals Siegfried's one vulnerable spot. While bathing in the dragon's blood, he failed to protect a portion of his body the size of a linden leaf because a leaf fell down between his shoulders. The villainous Hagen asks her to sew a token on the spot so that he can protect Siegfried during the fighting. Hagen sends men to say that the Saxons gave up the attack. Then, the fear of battle over, Gunther rides out to hunt with all of his knights. There, deep in the forest, as Siegfried is bending over a spring to drink, he is struck in the fatal spot by an arrow from Hagen's bow. Before he dies, Siegfried curses the Burgundians and their tribe forever. Indifferent to the dying man's curse, Hagen carries home the body of the dead hero.

He places Siegfried's body in the path where Kriemhild will see it on her way to church, but a chamberlain discovers the body before she passes. Kriemhild knows instinctively whose hand did the deed. A thousand knights headed by Siegmund, his father, mourn the dead hero, and everyone claims vengeance. The widow gives vast sums of money to the poor in honor of Siegfried. When Siegmund prepares to leave for Niderland, he asks Kriemhild to go with him. She refuses but allows him to take Siegfried's son with him. She is determined to stay with the Burgundians. Queen Brunhild, however, offers no compassion. The Nibelungen hoard is given to Kriemhild because it is her wedding gift. By order of Hagen, who plans to get possession of the treasure, all of it is dropped to the bottom of the Rhine. In the years that follow Kriemhild remains in mourning for Siegfried.

At last the mighty Etzel, king of the Huns, seeks to marry Kriemhild. After a long courtship he wins Kriemhild and takes her to his land to be his wife. Etzel is rich and strong, and after her long years of mourning, Kriemhild again occupies a position of power and honor. Now she begins to consider how she might avenge herself for the death of Siegfried. Hoping to get Hagen in her power, she sends a messenger to her brothers, saying that she longs to see all of them again. When they receive her message, the brothers and Hagen set out. Old Queen Uta tells them that in a dream she saw a vision of dire foreboding, but the Burgundians refuse to heed her warning. Hagen receives a token from some mermaids, who say none of the knights will return from Hunland. He disregards the prediction. Then a quarrel breaks out among the Burgundians, and Dankwart slays Gelfrat. Three evil omens now attend the coming journey, but still the brothers refuse to turn back. At last the Burgundians come to Etzel's castle. Gunther and his brothers are put into separate apartments. Dankwart and Hagen are sent to other quarters. Warned by Sir Dietrich that Kriemhild still plots vengeance for Siegfried's death, Hagen urges them all to take precautions. When Kriemhild asks them to give her their weapons, Hagen replies that it could not be. The Burgundians decide to post a guard to prevent a surprise attack while they sleep. The court goes to mass. At the services the Huns are displeased to see that Gunther and his party jostle Queen Kriemhild.

In honor of the Burgundians, a great tournament is held for all the knights. The feeling between the Burgundians and the Huns is so bad that King Etzel is forced to intervene in order to keep the peace. To appease the brothers, Etzel gives them Kriemhild's small son, Ortlieb, as a hostage. Sir Bloedel, however, presses into Dankwart's quarters demanding justice for Kriemhild. In a few minutes he arouses the anger of Dankwart, who rises from his table and kills Bloedel. For this deed the angered Huns killed Dankwart's retainers. Dankwart, at bay, runs to Hagen for help. Hagen, knowing that he will not live to seek his vengeance on Kriemhild later, slaughters the little prince, Ortlieb. Then a mighty battle follows in which Hagen and Gunther manage to kill most of their adversaries.

Kriemhild now urges her heroes to kill Hagen. The first to take up the challenge is Iring. After he wounds Hagen, he rushes back to Kriemhild for praise. Hagen recovers quickly and seeks Iring to kill him. The battle continues, and many knights from both sides fall in the bloody combat. Outnumbered, the Burgundians fall one by one. Kriemhild herself slays Hagen, the last of the Burgundians to survive. He dies without revealing the location of the treasure.

King Etzel grieves to see so many brave knights killed. At a sign from him, Hildebrand, one of his retainers, lifts his sword and ends the life of Kriemhild as well. In this way dies the secret of the new hiding place of the Nibelungen treasure.

Critical Evaluation:

The material that forms the subject matter of the Germanic heroic epics is derived from historical events that became part of an oral tradition and were passed down, sometimes for centuries, in the form of sagas, before being established in written form. The historical events that lie behind the Nibelung saga are to be found in the fifth and sixth centuries, the period of the tribal wanderings at the end of the Roman Empire. The Burgundians, under King Gundahari, whose capital was at Worms, were in fact destroyed by the Huns in 437. The Siegfried figure is probably of Merovingian origin and may derive from an intermarriage between the Burgundian and Frankish royal houses. The record of these events, mingled with purely legendary elements, is preserved in a number of works: Besides *The Nibelungenlied*, the Scandinavian *Poetic Edda* (ninth to twelfth centuries) is important. It was upon this latter source rather than the Germanic version that Richard Wagner based his four-part music drama, *The Ring of the Nibelung* (1876). There are four main themes in the work that reflect the saga tradition: the adventures of the young Siegfried, Siegfried's death, the destruction of the Burgundians, and the death of Etzel. These elements occurred as separate works in the early stages of composition. In the present version of the saga, composed by an anonymous German author around the year 1200, the various elements are woven together into a unified plot, linking the death of Siegfried with the destruction of the Burgundians through the motive of revenge. Traces of the older separate versions are evident, however, in such inner inconsistencies as the transformation of the character of Kriemhild, who appears initially as a model courtly figure but becomes the bloodthirsty avenger of her husband's death in the second part. It is a mark of the artistic talent of the anonymous author that he fuses the core episodes with such care and achieves a plausible and aesthetically satisfying work.

The Nibelungenlied is the product of a brilliant period of the Hohenstaufen dynasty of the Holy Roman Empire, a time when the courtly culture of Germany was at its height. The poet was probably of Austrian origin. The importance of the splendid court at Vienna and the noble figure of Bishop Pilgrim of Passau indicate that the poet may have enjoyed the patronage of these courts. That the poet remains anonymous is a tradition of the heroic epic form, evolving from the anonymous court singer of the wandering Germanic tribes. Whereas the writers of Arthurian epics and religious epics name themselves and often discuss their work in a prologue, the composer of the heroic epic remains outside his work, presenting his material more as history and without the self-conscious comments and digressions found in works such as *Parzival* (c. 1200-1210) or *Tristan and Isolde* (c. 1210), both of whose poets name themselves and go into some detail regarding their intentions and artistic conceptions. *The Nibelungenlied*, written in four-line stanzas, bears the signs of its history of oral presentation—frequent repetition of rhyme words, the use of formulaic descriptions and filler lines, and general looseness of composition. The poem was not conceived as a written work. It represents a written record of an oral performance tradition. Even after assuming written form, for centuries the work was read aloud to audiences, books being a scarce and expensive commodity during the Middle Ages.

The purpose of the work, like that of courtly poetry in general, is to mirror courtly society in its splendor, color, and activity. It presents images of an idealized world in which larger-than-life figures act out the social rituals of the time and provide for the audience models of courtly behavior. The work instructs in codes of honor, fortitude, and noble bearing under stress. Repeatedly in the work one observes long passages devoted to description of the court festivities—banquets, tournaments, processions—all filled with details of clothing and jewelry, splendid utensils, and weapons. Questions of etiquette and precedence provide some of the central conflicts of the work, while the lyrical episodes of the love between Siegfried and Kriemhild may be seen as an embodiment of the idealized conception of love. Although the grim events of the old dramatic saga material at times conflict with the more cultivated ideal of the thirteenth century, the poet succeeds even here in transforming the traditional material. Elements related to fairy-tale tradition—the stories of Siegfried's youth, the battle with the dragon, the magic aura surrounding Brunhild on her island—are largely suppressed.

Idealizing elements are, on the other hand, strongly developed. In the first part, Siegfried and Kriemhild stand out against the menacing forces of the Burgundian court, especially Hagen. In the second part, despite the atmosphere of betrayal and carnage, the high points are moments of fortitude and courage and the preservation of ethical integrity. Rudiger, who finds himself torn between feudal loyalty to King Etzel and his loyalty and friendship for the Burgundians, to one of whom his daughter is engaged, is one of the noblest figures. The episode in which he finds himself obliged to fight against the Burgundian Gernot, to whom he gives the sword that now will kill him, is one of the most poignant scenes in the work.

The chain of crime and revenge finds resolution only in the lament for the fallen warriors, and it is in this tragic sense of the inevitable suffering that follows joy that the work pre-

serves its links to the ancient Germanic heroic outlook, establishing its individuality against the more generally optimistic outlook of the Arthurian sagas. Here the fatalistic confrontation with destructive forces is opposed to the affirmation of order and the delight of life. This is typical of much literature of the Hohenstaufen period. The tension between these two attitudes provides much of the power of the work and lifts it into the realm of universal validity.

"Critical Evaluation" by Steven C. Schaber

Further Reading

Bekker, Hugo. *"The Nibelungenlied": A Literary Analysis.* Toronto, Ont.: University of Toronto Press, 1971. Deals at length with the four main characters and with numerous parallelisms in the epic. Bekker's main point is that Brunhild is offended not because Siegfried overpowers her in bed but because he breaches the rules of kingship by not consummating the sexual act.

Gibbs, Marion E., and Sidney M. Johnson. *"Nibelungenlied,* the *Klage* (and *Kudrun*)."* In *Medieval German Literature: A Companion.* New York: Routledge, 2001. This chapter provides an overview of the epic, including a discussion of its origins, dating, author, form, and the poem itself. It also describes the epic's impact after the Middle Ages.

Haymes, Edward R. *"The Nibelungenlied": History and Interpretation.* Champaign: University of Illinois Press, 1986. Discusses how the epic would have been received around the year 1200, when it was written. Haymes interprets the work as an argument for the stability of the old feudal structure and against new elements from chivalric literature.

McConnell, Winder. *The Nibelungenlied.* Boston: Twayne, 1984. An excellent discussion of the epic, with strong historical and cultural background and an interesting overview of the reception of the work in Germany. McConnell provides well-organized interpretations of the major characters, and she emphasizes the anonymous author's style of presenting the events without passing judgment.

Mowatt, D. G., and Hugh Sacker. *"The Nibelungenlied": An Interpretative Commentary.* Toronto, Ont.: University of Toronto Press, 1967. A good general introduction followed by more than one hundred pages of commentary that closely follow the original text. Most useful in conjunction with an English translation that retains the stanza numbers. Includes maps and a genealogical diagram.

Müller, Jan-Dirk. *Rules for the Endgame: The World of "The Nibelungenlied."* Translated by William T. Whobrey.

Baltimore: Johns Hopkins University Press, 2007. Müller argues that modern methods of interpretation, with their expectations of coherence, are not useful to understanding the epic, and he offers another means of analyzing the work's themes and structure.

The Nibelungenlied. Translated by A. T. Hatto. New York: Penguin Books, 1969. In addition to the translation, Hatto provides more than one hundred pages of information on the epic. He points out many discrepancies in the work. Includes a useful glossary of the characters' names.

Poor, Sara S., and Jana K. Schulman, eds. *Women and Medieval Epic: Gender, Genre, and the Limits of Epic Masculinity.* New York: Palgrave Macmillan, 2007. This collection of essays about the representation of gender in medieval epics includes two discussions of *The Nibelungenlied*: "Monstrous Mates: The Leading Ladies of *The Nibelungenlied* and *Völsunga Saga*" by Kaaren Grimstad and Ray M. Wakefield and "The Politics of Emotion in *The Nibelungenlied*" by Kathryn Starkey.

Nicholas Nickleby

Author: Charles Dickens (1812-1870)
First published: 1838-1839
Type of work: Novel
Type of plot: Social realism
Time of plot: Early nineteenth century
Locale: England

Principal characters:
NICHOLAS NICKLEBY, a young Englishman with no money
KATE NICKLEBY, his sister
MRS. NICKLEBY, his mother
RALPH NICKLEBY, his miserly uncle
WACKFORD SQUEERS, a vicious schoolmaster
SMIKE, a young boy befriended by Nicholas
THE CHEERYBLE BROTHERS, Nicholas's benefactors
FRANK CHEERYBLE, their nephew
MADELINE BRAY, their protégée

The Story:

When Nicholas Nickleby was nineteen years old, his father died, bankrupt. A short time after their bereavement, Nicholas, his sister Kate, and their mother set out for London. While there, they hope that the late Mr. Nickleby's brother, Ralph, might be willing to do something for them. Ralph Nickleby, a miserly moneylender, grudgingly allows his sister-in-law and Kate to move into empty lodgings he owns, and he secures a position for Nicholas as assistant to Wackford Squeers, who operates a boys' boarding school in Yorkshire.

Nicholas, leaving his mother and sister in Ralph's care, travels to the school and finds it a terrible place where the boys are starved and mistreated almost beyond human imagination. Nicholas is forced to endure the situation, for his uncle had warned him that any help given to his sister and mother depends upon his remaining where he had been placed. A crisis arises, however, when Wackford Squeers unjustly and unmercifully beats an older boy named Smike. Nicholas intervenes, wresting the whip from Squeers and beating the schoolmaster with it instead. Immediately after-

ward, Smike and Nicholas leave the school and start walking toward London.

In London, meanwhile, Ralph Nickleby tries to use Kate to attract young Lord Verisopht into borrowing money at high rates. He also finds work for Kate in a dressmaking establishment, where there is a great deal of labor and almost no pay. Kate does not mind the work, but she is deeply distressed at the leers she has to endure when invited to her uncle's home to dine with Lord Verisopht and Sir Mulberry Hawk. Not long afterward, the dressmaker goes bankrupt, and Kate becomes a companion to a wealthy but selfish and neurotic woman.

When Nicholas arrives in London, he seeks out Newman Noggs, his uncle's clerk, who had promised to help him if it were ever in his power. Newman Noggs helps Nicholas clear himself of the false charges of being a thief that had been brought against him by Squeers and Ralph Nickleby.

With some notion of becoming sailors, Nicholas and Smike decide to go to Bristol. On the way, they meet Vincent Crummles, a theatrical producer, whose troupe they join.

Both Smike and Nicholas are successful as actors. In addition, Nicholas adapts plays for the company to produce. After some weeks, however, Nicholas receives a letter from Newman Noggs warning him that his presence is urgently required in London. Nicholas leaves hurriedly and arrives in London late that night. Not wishing to disturb his family, Nicholas stays at an inn, where he encounters Sir Mulberry Hawk and Lord Verisopht and overhears them speaking in derogatory terms of Kate. Nicholas remonstrates with them and demands to know their names. In the altercation, Sir Mulberry's horse bolts and the baronet is thrown from his carriage and severely injured.

Newman asks Nicholas to return because Kate, exposed to the insulting attentions of Sir Mulberry and Lord Verisopht, is increasingly miserable. Both Mrs. Nickleby and the woman to whom Kate is a companion fail to see past the men's titles and are flattered at the acquaintance, and Kate is forced to be often in their company. For Sir Mulberry it is a point of honor to seduce her.

After Nicholas accidentally learns of the situation, he removes his mother and sister to new and friendlier lodgings, and all intercourse with Ralph Nickleby ceases. However, the future seems quite bleak, for Nicholas is long unsuccessful finding work in London. At an employment agency to which he applies, he becomes acquainted with a kindly gentleman, one of the philanthropic Cheeryble brothers. Hearing that the young man is destitute and believing him to be deserving, the brothers give Nicholas a job in their countinghouse at a decent salary and make a cottage available to him for himself, Kate, and their mother.

One day, a beautiful young woman visits the Cheeryble brothers, and Nicholas falls in love with her at first sight. Kate gradually falls in love with the Cheeryble brothers' nephew, Frank. Only Smike seems unhappy, for he has fallen in love with Kate, yet realizes his limitations more than ever before now that he is in cultivated surroundings. Once Wackford Squeers and Ralph Nickleby see that Nicholas has given a good home to Smike, they begin to conspire to kidnap Smike. Apart from the wish for revenge, Squeers is motivated by the fact that Smike has been an immensely valuable, unpaid drudge at the school. Smike is caught twice but escapes, and Nicholas is successful in keeping him out of Squeers's clutches, but the boy's happiness is short-lived. He dies of tuberculosis a few months later.

By then, Nicholas has discovered that the young woman with whom he has fallen in love, Madeline Bray, is the daughter of a bankrupt ne'er-do-well who lives off the little income she makes by sewing and painting. Unknown to Nicholas, Ralph Nickleby and a fellow miser, Arthur Gride, are planning to force Madeline into a marriage with Gride, who is seventy years old. Fortunately, Madeline's father dies an hour before he is to hand his daughter over to the old miser. Nicholas arrives on the scene and takes the young woman to his home, where she is cared for by Kate and his mother.

Meanwhile, Gride's old housekeeper leaves in a fit of jealousy and steals some of her employer's papers. One of the documents is a will that, if known, would make Madeline Bray a rich woman. Ralph learns of the will and persuades Squeers to steal it. When he does, however, Frank Cheeryble and Newman Noggs catch him and turn him over to the police. The prisoner confesses his part in the plot and also tells about the conspiracy between Ralph and Gride to get Madeline's fortune. An old employee of Ralph appears and reveals to the Cheeryble brothers that Smike is Ralph's son; years ago, as a way of revenging himself on his employer, he had told Ralph that his son had died in infancy. Ralph, when given the news, returns home and hangs himself.

Thinking that Frank Cheeryble is in love with Madeline, Nicholas asks the Cheeryble brothers that she be taken care of elsewhere. The Cheeryble brothers, in their good-hearted way, take the situation under observation and make it possible for both pairs of lovers, Nicholas and Madeline, as well as Frank and Kate, to be married shortly thereafter.

Years pass, and both couples prosper. Nicholas invests his wife's fortune in the Cheeryble brothers' firm and later becomes a partner in the house along with Frank Cheeryble. Newman Noggs, who had helped Nicholas so many times, is restored to respectability; he had been a wealthy gentleman before he had fallen into Ralph Nickleby's hands. Old Gride, who had tried to marry Madeline for her money, is murdered by robbers; Lord Verisopht is killed in a duel with his false friend Sir Mulberry Hawk, who subsequently also comes to a violent end.

Critical Evaluation:

Although Thomas Arnold, headmaster of Rugby, objected to *Nicholas Nickleby* on the grounds that the novel was insufficiently edifying, most Victorian readers—including Charles Dickens's rival, William Makepeace Thackeray—admired it; from its initial sale of fifty thousand copies, the book was one of Dickens's triumphs. The first of his novels in which the love story is the main subject, *Nicholas Nickleby* still retains many picaresque elements that appear in *The Pickwick Papers* (1836-1837) and *Oliver Twist* (1837-1838).

Dickens's greatest strength in *Nicholas Nickleby* lies in the marvelous descriptions of people and places. The characters still tend to be eccentrics dominated by a single passion (almost in the manner of Ben Jonson's "humors" characters, although lacking Jonson's theory of the psychology of humors); the minor characters in particular seem to be grotesques. However, there is a vitality in the farcical elements of the novel that is delightful. The influence of Tobias Smollett, both in the comedy and the tendency to realistic detail, is still strong in this early novel. The influence of melodramas also still colors the plot, but Dickens breathes new life into old stock situations.

Even if the melodramatic and episodic structure of *Nicholas Nickleby* is unoriginal, confusing, and improbable, the comedy and vitality of the book are the result of genius. Readers feel the tremendous force of life, of the changing times, of youth and growth, on every page. Tales develop within tales, and countless life stories crowd the chapters. It is a young man's creation, indignant, farcical, and romantic in turn, and it is filled with vivid scenes. At this stage of his career, Dickens was still attempting to provide something for everybody.

Because of his complicated, melodramatic plot, however, Dickens was not wholly successful in working out the psychology of the novel. As critic Douglas Bush has observed, the characters of Dickens's early fiction are given over to self-dramatization. Mrs. Nickleby, in particular, evades the responsibilities of her troubled life by withdrawing into her blissful vision of the past. She sees herself as a romantic heroine, although her admirer is only a lunatic neighbor who throws cucumbers over the wall. Like many other characters of the book—among them Vincent Crummles, Smike, and Nicholas himself—she is isolated in her own imagination, locked in an often inimical world. Her eccentricity, like that of most of the minor characters, is an outward symbol of estrangement from the hostile social mechanisms of convention, order, and mysterious power. Nicholas succeeds in love and fortune, not so much by his own resources but through chance—good luck with the Cheeryble brothers, for example—and through his own amiable disposition.

At this point in his development as a novelist, Dickens was unable to create—as he eventually would in David Copperfield, Pip, and other protagonists—a hero who is fully aware of his isolation and confronts his sense of guilt. The reader must accept Nicholas on the level of the author's uncomplicated psychology: as a genial, deserving fellow whose good luck, good friends, and honest nature reward him with happiness, affection, and prosperity.

Late criticism has focused on the importance of *Nicholas Nickleby* in Dickens's canon of work. For Dickens's art it represents a true advance over his methods in his first novel, *The Pickwick Papers*. *Nicholas Nickleby* features the characteristic array of malevolent characters trying to work their ruin on the hero. However, for the first time, Dickens deepens the psychology of one of his villains, recounting the unhappy upbringing of Ralph Nickleby.

The distinguished writer G. K Chesterton was one of the most astute early critics of the novel, praising it for its characterizations. The novel is suffused with what would be the major themes of Dickens's later fiction—love and money—and the loss and acquisition of both. *Nicholas Nickleby* is replete as well with Dickens's favorite plot feature: the abandoned child who is eventually reconnected to his or her true relatives, although in this novel with sad consequences. *Nicholas Nickleby* is double-layered, revolving around the adventures of both Nicholas and his long-suffering sister, Kate. The theatricality of the novel has been much noted, certainly a major reason for its frequent dramatization on stage and in film.

Revised by Howard Bromberg

Further Reading

Adrian, Arthur A. *Dickens and the Parent-Child Relationship*. Athens: Ohio University Press, 1984. Discusses the status of children in working-class Victorian England and Dickens's own experience as a son and a father. Includes drawings of children at work in a variety of occupations.

Bloom, Harold, ed. *Charles Dickens*. New York: Chelsea House, 1987. A collection of essays on various aspects of Dickens's art. Raymond Williams's contribution is especially illuminating with regard to Dickens's portrayal of urban life in *Nicholas Nickleby*.

Flint, Kate. *Dickens*. Atlantic Highlands, N.J.: Humanities Press International, 1986. Discusses Dickens's works in the context of a newly industrialized society. Flint also calls attention to Dickens's portrayal of women and actors.

Giddings, Robert, ed. *The Changing World of Charles Dickens*. London: Vision Press, 1983. A collection of essays on Dickens's style, generally and in specific works. Loralee MacPike discusses Dickens's influence on Fyodor Dostoevski; David Edgar and Mike Poole discuss stage and film productions of particular novels, including *Nicholas Nickleby*.

Hardy, Barbara. *Dickens and Creativity*. London: Continuum, 2008. Focuses on the workings of Dickens's creativity and imagination, which Hardy argues is at the heart of his self-awareness, subject matter, and narrative. *Nicholas Nickleby* is discussed in chapter 5, "Talkative Men and Women in *Pickwick Papers*, *Nicholas Nickleby*, *Martin Chuzzlewit*, and *Little Dorrit*."

Jordan, John O., ed. *The Cambridge Companion to Charles*

Dickens. New York: Cambridge University Press, 2001. Collection of essays with information about Dickens's life and times, analyses of his novels, and discussions of Dickens and language, gender, family, domestic ideology, the form of the novel, illustration, theater, and film.

Nelson, Harland. *Charles Dickens*. Boston: Twayne, 1981. Explores Dickens's philosophy of writing and his serial publications. Discusses the structure and narrative of seven of his novels.

Parker, David. *The Doughty Street Novels: "Pickwick Papers," "Oliver Twist," "Nicholas Nickleby," "Barnaby Rudge."* New York: AMS Press, 2002. Parker, the long-time curator of the Dickens House, traces Dickens's work on four early novels during the period when the writer lived on Doughty Street in London.

Paroissien, David, ed. *A Companion to Charles Dickens*. Malden, Mass.: Blackwell, 2008. Collection of essays providing information about Dickens's life and work, including Dickens as a reformer, Christian, and journalist and Dickens and gender, technology, America, and the uses of history. Also includes the essay *"Nicholas Nickleby"* by Stanley Friedman.

Nick of the Woods
Or, The Jibbenainosay, a Tale of Kentucky

Author: Robert Montgomery Bird (1806-1854)
First published: 1837
Type of work: Novel
Type of plot: Adventure
Time of plot: 1782
Locale: Kentucky

Principal characters:
CAPTAIN ROLAND FORRESTER, a veteran of the Revolutionary War
EDITH FORRESTER, his cousin
COLONEL BRUCE, the commander of Bruce's Station
TOM BRUCE, his son
NATHAN SLAUGHTER, a Quaker trapper
ROARING RALPH STACKPOLE, a frontier braggart and horse thief
PARDON DODGE, a pioneer
ABEL DOE, a renegade white man
TELIE DOE, his daughter
RICHARD BRAXLEY, a Virginia lawyer
WENONGA, a Shawnee chief

The Story:

The sun is still high on a sultry August afternoon in 1782, when a train of emigrants emerges from the gloom of the forest and rides slowly toward Bruce's Station, one of the principal forts in the district of Kentucky. The travelers, consisting of free and enslaved men, women, children, are accompanied by cattle and loaded packhorses, the whole group giving the appearance of a village on the march. In the position of responsibility rides a young man whose five years in the camps and battles of the American Revolution show in his military bearing and in the mature gravity of his features. The beautiful young woman at his side is sufficiently like him in appearance to suggest their kinship.

Captain Roland Forrester and his cousin, Edith, are on

their way to the Falls of the Ohio. The orphaned children of twin brothers who had died early in the Revolution, they had been reared as wards of their stern, wealthy uncle, Major Roland Forrester. A staunch Tory, the Major had never forgiven his younger brothers for supporting the cause of the American patriots, and to keep them from inheriting his estate—for he was unmarried—he had executed a will in favor of an illegitimate daughter. About the time that his brothers fell in battle, the child burned to death in the home of her foster mother. The Major then adopted his nephew and niece and repeatedly declared his intention of making them his heirs. Young Roland Forrester forfeited his share of the inheritance, however, when he enlisted in a troop of Virginia horsemen. Shortly after the Battle of Yorktown, he returned to find his cousin destitute. On her uncle's death, no will making her his heir could be found. Richard Braxley, the Major's lawyer and agent, had produced the original will and taken possession of the estate in the name of the Major's daughter, who was, he claimed, still alive and soon to appear and claim her heritage. Having no funds to contest the will, Roland decided to move to Kentucky, his plan being to place Edith in the care of a distant pioneer relative at the Falls while he carved from the wilderness a fortune that would allow him to marry his lovely cousin.

Colonel Bruce, the commander of the station, welcomes the emigrants, greeting the Forresters with special warmth and insisting that they share his cabin. Having served under Major Forrester in earlier Indian wars, he tells many stories of those border campaigns. Mrs. Bruce, equally voluble, bustles about giving orders to her daughters and telling them to be as circumspect as Telie Doe, who remains quietly at her loom after a startled glance up from her work when she hears the name of Roland Forrester mentioned. When the others escort Edith into the cabin, she remains on the porch, where Roland is explaining his intention of pushing on toward the Falls the next day. The Colonel, while deploring his guest's haste, says that there is no danger from Indians on the trace. At last, the Colonel notices Telie and orders her into the house. She is, he says, the daughter of a white renegade named Abel Doe. Out of pity, the Bruces had taken her into their own home.

At that moment Tom Bruce, the Colonel's oldest son, appears with news that the Jibbenainosay has been active again; some hunters had found an Indian with a split skull and a slashed cross on his breast. The Jibbenainosay, whom the settlers also call Nick of the Woods, was a mysterious avenger who had killed many Indians and marked them thus. The Shawnees, believing that he was either a ghost or a devil, had given him his name, which means Spirit-that-walks.

The news of the Jibbenainosay's latest killing was brought to the station by Roaring Ralph Stackpole, a swaggering braggart. When he challenges anyone in the settlement to a trial of strength, the rough frontiersmen decides to match him with Nathan Slaughter, a Quaker trapper nicknamed Bloody Nathan because of his peaceful ways and gentle speech. Much to the surprise of the crowd, he lifts Roaring Ralph and throws him to the ground. Ralph, admitting that he had been fairly beaten, asks to borrow a horse so he can continue his journey to Logan's Station. The Quaker trapper tells the settlers that the Miami Indians are gathering, but when the others refuse to take his news seriously, he exchanges his furs for lead and powder and leaves the station.

That night, Telie Doe begs Edith to let her go with the emigrants as a servant. When Edith refuses, the girl creeps away. Roland sleeps with Bruce's sons on the porch of the cabin. Aroused from sleep during the night, he hears a whispering voice telling him he is to cross Salt River. He decides that he is still dreaming.

The next morning, there is great confusion at the station. Roaring Ralph had sneaked back into the settlement and stolen Roland's horse. Knowing that the fugitive could not get far on the tired animal, Bruce's sons ride in pursuit. While the emigrant train starts on ahead, Roland, Edith, and one of the slaves stays at the station to await the return of the horse. The animal is found, wandering along the trail, and is brought back by one of the boys. He says that the others are tracking the thief, intending to make him an object of frontier justice. As the travelers are about to set out to overtake the emigrant party, a horseman arrives with word that Indians had attacked Bryant's Station. The need to muster every fighting man in the settlement leaves Roland and his cousin without an escort; nevertheless, they start out with only one surly frontiersman to guide them. On the way, their guide deserts them to return and join in the fighting. The travelers are relieved from their predicament when Telie Doe appears and offers to act as their guide.

When they arrive at the branch to the two fords, Roland insists on following the road to the upper ford, in spite of Telie Doe's pleadings. On the way, they find Roaring Ralph, his arms bound and a noose around his neck, astride a horse in such fashion that one movement of the animal would hang the rider from a limb overhead. Left to perish in that manner after the pursuers from Bruce's Station had overtaken him, he is grateful to his rescuers and offers to devote his life to Edith's service. Roland curtly sends the braggart and thief on his way.

Not far from the upper ford, they meet a fleeing settler named Pardon Dodge, who tells them that Indians on the warpath are blocking the road ahead. In their attempt to reach the lower ford, the travelers become lost. They then find a dead Indian with a cross gashed on his breast. While they wait for the dread Jibbenainosay to appear, they see harmless Nathan Slaughter, his faithful hound at his heels, coming through the forest. Hearing that Indians are close, the Quaker becomes terrified. He promises to guide the party only if he is not called upon to fight.

The travelers take refuge in a ruined cabin near the flooded river. Indians attack the cabin during the night, but they are repulsed. During the lull, it is agreed that Nathan should try to evade the warriors and bring help to the besieged. Shortly before daylight, Roaring Ralph comes down the river in a small dugout canoe. The group desperately decides to send Edith, Telie, and Ralph across the flooded stream in the canoe, while Roland, Dodge, and the slave try to follow on horseback. When Dodge's horse comes ashore without his rider, the others decide that Dodge has drowned.

Later that morning, the fugitives encounter another band of Indians. Edith is captured. Roaring Ralph escapes by rolling down the bank to the river; the slave is killed. Roland, knocked unconscious during the fight, awakes to find himself wounded and tightly bound. While he is wondering what had happened to Edith, a band of Kentuckians, led by young Tom Bruce, appears and engages the Indians. When Roaring Ralph climbs the bank and joins in the fight, the Kentuckians, believing that they are seeing the ghost of the man they had hanged, scatter in confusion. Roaring Ralph, throwing wounded Tom Bruce over the saddle, rides away on Roland's horse. The victorious Indians proceed to divide the spoils of victory under the direction of an old chief, whom Roland thought was of mixed Indian and white blood. He learns the man's identity when Telie runs up to protest the enslavement of Roland to a Piankeshaw warrior. The light-skinned warrior is Abel Doe, the renegade.

His arms bound, Roland is tethered to the Piankeshaw's saddle and forced to make a long, wearying march. Unable to sleep that night, he is startled to hear an explosion close at hand. Horrified when a dead Piankeshaw falls across his prostrate body, Roland loses consciousness. He revives to find Nathan Slaughter bending over him. Another dead Piankeshaw is nearby.

The Quaker overhears the renegade and another white man discuss the price to be paid for the capture of Roland and Edith. Convinced by Nathan's account that his cousin had fallen into Braxley's hands, Roland wishes to start at once to the main Indian village after the Quaker tells him that the old chief must have been Wenonga, a Shawnee chieftain notorious for his brutality. On their way to the Shawnee camp, Roland and the Quaker find five Indians with a white prisoner bound to a tree. While they struggle with the natives, the prisoner, Roaring Ralph, breaks his bonds and aids them in killing the warriors.

When they reach the Indian village, the Quaker daubs himself like a brave and moves stealthily among the houses to find Edith. Peering through the chinks in one cabin, he sees Braxley and Abel Doe, and, from the conversation, learns that Braxley has in his possession Major Forrester's second will. Having disposed of Roland, the lawyer is now planning to marry Edith and get her wealth. While he searches for Edith's place of imprisonment, Nathan finds old Chief Wenonga lying drunk in the grass. He is about to plunge his

knife into the old man's breast when he hears Edith's voice nearby. Leaving the chief, he goes to a skin tent and finds Braxley and his prisoner. Taking the other man by surprise, the Quaker seizes and binds him. With the will safe on his own person, Nathan is carrying Edith to safety when a clamor breaks out in the Indian encampment.

Roaring Ralph, ordered to steal four horses for Edith's and her rescuers' escape, attempts to drive off the whole herd, and the stampeding horses run through the village, arousing the warriors. Unable to escape, the party is captured. Roland and Roaring Ralph are bound and taken to separate wigwams. Nathan, dragged before the drunken old chief, defies Wenonga, which causes the Quaker to have an epileptic fit. The spasm, together with his fantastic disguise, convinces the Shawnee that his white prisoner is a great medicine man.

Doe and Braxley have yet to reach an agreement over the renegade's pay. What Braxley does not know is that Doe had taken the will when he had searched the Quaker after his capture. The next day, the renegade goes to Roland and offers him his freedom and the estate if he consents to marry Telie. Roland refuses, but offers Doe half the estate if he saves Edith. The man leaves sullenly.

That night, old Wenonga has the Quaker brought before him. After bragging of the white women and children he had killed and the scalps he had taken, the chief offers the prisoner his freedom if he will use his powers as a medicine man to put the Jibbenainosay in the power of the Shawnee. Nathan promises to do so if his bonds are cut. Freed, he reveals himself as the Jibbenainosay, a friendly settler whose wife and children Wenonga had treacherously killed years previously.

Seizing the chief's ax, he sinks it into Wenonga's head. Then, after cutting away Wenonga's scalp lock and gashing the dead man's chest, the Quaker retrieves the scalps of his children and with a triumphant cry disappears into the night.

The next morning, finding the Jibbenainosay's mark on their dead chief, the Shawnees are roused to wild fury. Roland and Roaring Ralph are tied to a stake, timber heaped about them. The fires are lighted, but before the flames can reach them, gunfire echoes above the yells, and a band of Kentuckians rides through the smoke to set the prisoners free. Braxley rides away with Edith. The resistance ends when Nathan, with Wenonga's scalp at his belt, appears striking right and left with his steel ax. The Indians scatter and run, but the rejoicing of the Kentuckians is dimmed by the death of heroic Tom Bruce.

During the confusion, Pardon Dodge rides up with Edith on the saddle before him. He had survived the flooded river and joined the rescue party, saving Edith from Braxley. Doe, mortally wounded, gives Roland the missing will, and the young Virginian promises to look after Telie with a brother's care. Roland and Edith, preparing to return to Virginia to claim her inheritance, assure Nathan that they owe life as well as fortune to his bravery and daring. Although they beg him to return with them, he refuses. The work of the Jibbenainosay is done and, after a time, the Quaker disappears into the woods.

Critical Evaluation:

In the tradition of Charles Brockden Brown's *Edgar Huntly* (1799) and James Fenimore Cooper's *Leatherstocking Tales* (1823-1841), Robert Montgomery Bird's *Nick of the Woods* serves as an early milepost in the distinctively American genre of frontier literature. As a number of critics have asserted, Bird reinforces the narrative pattern established by his two literary predecessors: A group of white people ventures into a wilderness setting occupied by Indian antagonists; the virtue of at least one white woman is threatened by some Indian predator or villainous white man; and ultimate tragedy is averted by the intervention of a frontier hero, savvy in the ways of the woods.

During a period of time when Indian warfare was far from a distant memory, Bird used as the subject of his adventure the turning point in the Western colonization of what would eventually become the state of Kentucky: the invasion of Shawnee territory by a citizen army led by George Rogers Clark. Thus, the author's fictional narrative is set against a historical event with which Bird was familiar both as an amateur historian and as a traveler who himself visited the scenes of his novel four years before its publication.

In addition to its place in the canon of wilderness novels, *Nick of the Woods* can be appreciated for its dramatic mode. Much of the novel's exciting, propulsive plot is essentially a direct consequence of Bird's earlier experience as a dramatist. His play, *The Gladiator* (1831), for instance, was one of the most popular dramas in nineteenth century America, and *Nick of the Woods* itself was successfully adapted for the stage at various times by a number of authors in both America and Britain.

As is characteristic of melodrama, the plot of the novel is developed by circumstance and not by character motivation. After seeking shelter in the ruined cabin of a settler family slaughtered by Indians, for example, the Forresters and their companions discover that their Indian foes are also using the spot as a camp. Vigorously besieged and at the point of desperation, the group is offered an escape route by the sudden appearance of Roaring Ralph Stackpole in a canoe. Thus, narrative respites are complicated and difficult situations are temporarily resolved by unexpected and improbable plot twists.

Setting is also used for dramatic effect. As Captain Roland Forrester, for instance, contemplates his predicament at the fort with Indians in front of him and the river behind, the scene is described almost in terms of scenic design. There are "frowning banks," "swollen waters," and "growling thunder." Bird uses setting to underscore incident and to appeal to the emotions of his readers. Repeatedly in the novel, Bird gives indications that he regards the scenes of his novel as stage sets; Wenonga's village, for example, the setting for the last ten chapters, is described as the "theatre in which was to be acted the last scene in the drama of their enterprise."

Besides plot and setting, some of the novel's major characters can be seen as little more than stock figures of the popular stage. Roland Forrester is the romantic and courageous, if not always effectual, gentleman-hero; Edith is the golden-haired damsel in distress; and Braxley is the villain and would-be seducer whose "evil-genius" has been kindled by a lust for possession.

What saves the novel from being largely a product of simple convention, however, is Bird's ability to create a few truly individual characters that play against type. Indeed, the novel's omniscient narrator asserts that frontier life breeds the "strangest contrasts" and the "strangest characters." Thus, the reader is introduced to the joyously larcenous horse thief Ralph Stackpole, the reluctant renegade Abel Doe, and above all, the schizophrenic Nathan Slaughter.

Nathan, the docile Quaker by day and ferocious Indian hater by night, is the character upon whom most modern critics of the novel focus their attention. It has been pointed out that since Bird himself trained as a physician, this literary use of abnormal psychology is not surprising. Slaughter suffers from a significant post-traumatic stress syndrome; in Pennsylvania, after he had surrendered his arms to neighboring Indians as a man of peace, he not only was forced to stand helpless while his wife, mother, and five children were murdered before his eyes but also was himself scalped and left for dead.

Some critics believe that Slaughter's personal conflict between the doctrine of Christian pacifism and the requirements of survival in a world of very real evil is a microcosm of the novel's larger thematic issue: the confrontation between the settled, agriculture-based economy of the European American and the nomadic hunter-gatherer society of the Native American. Both ways of life vied for possession of the virgin forests of North America. On the frontier, many a farmer became, of necessity, a fighter; in Bird's novel, many a peaceful settler is forced to become a "wicked Kentucky fighting-man" because of threats posed against him.

In this context, any discussion of Nathan Slaughter would be incomplete without reference to another fictional Nathaniel, the great woodsman created by Bird's contemporary, James Fenimore Cooper. In five novels, Natty Bumppo is forced farther and farther west to possess the space and freedom to follow his forest lifestyle. Bumppo and his Indian companion Chingachgook are displaced by the advance of civilization; their combined story is a valedictory of the life led according to the rhythms of nature and the precepts of natural law.

Bird, on the other hand, regarded the hunter lifestyle and the concept of the noble savage as the fantasies of "poets and sentimentalists"; to him, the progress of colonization in the "deserts of the West" was welcome, and the Indians' loss of their land inevitable. To prevent any thematic ambiguity, he demonizes the settlers' Indian adversaries. However, no matter how unflattering a picture of Native Americans Bird tries to paint, the Christian settlers, as exemplified by Nathan Slaughter and his satanic sobriquet, Nick of the Woods, are themselves touched by the evil they try to vanquish.

"Critical Evaluation" by S. Thomas Mack

Further Reading

Bellin, Joshua David. "Taking the Indian Cure: Thoreau, Indian Medicine, and the Performance of American Culture." *New England Quarterly* 79, no. 1 (March, 2006): 3-36. Bellin examines how the popularity of Indian medicine influenced American art and culture in the nineteenth century. Although he focuses on the works of Henry Tufts and Henry David Thoreau, he also mentions the representation of Indian medicine in *Nick of the Woods*.

Bryant, James C. "The Fallen World in *Nick of the Woods*." *American Literature* 38 (November, 1966): 352-364. Analyzes the novel's plot as being a struggle between de-monic barbarians and civilized Christians, emphasizing that, in an imperfect world, even the "children of light" are flawed. Discusses three major interpretations for Nathan Slaughter's dual personality.

Cowie, Alexander. *The Rise of the American Novel*. New York: American Book, 1948. A good introductory appraisal of Bird's career. Discusses the author's fictional works in the context of other significant contemporaries and followers of James Fenimore Cooper.

Crane, Gregg. "The Historical Romance." In *The Cambridge Introduction to the Nineteenth-Century American Novel*. New York: Cambridge University Press, 2007. *Nick of the Woods* is included in this discussion of the nineteenth century historical romance.

Dahl, Curtis. *Robert Montgomery Bird*. New York: Twayne, 1963. Comprehensive book-length study of Bird's literary canon—poetry, plays, novels, and prose works. Discusses *Nick of the Woods* within the context of the author's other "novels of outlaws and Indians." Includes a selective bibliography.

Hall, Joan Joffe. "*Nick of the Woods*: An Interpretation of the American Wilderness." *American Literature* 35 (May, 1963): 173-182. Focuses on the character of Nathan Slaughter and his internal moral conflict. Places *Nick of the Woods* in the context of wilderness novels by James Fenimore Cooper and Herman Melville.

Hoppenstand, Gary. "Justified Bloodshed: Robert Montgomery Bird's *Nick of the Woods* and the Origins of the Vigilante Hero in American Literature and Culture." *Journal of American Culture* 15, no. 2 (Summer, 1992): 51-61. Traces the evolution of the American vigilante hero from Bird's Nathan Slaughter to Clint Eastwood's Dirty Harry. Argues that Bird's negative depiction of the American Indian can be justified in literary terms since a revenge narrative requires that there be villainy to sanction retributive violence.

Nicomachean Ethics

Author: Aristotle (384-322 B.C.E.)
First transcribed: Ethika Nikomacheia c. 335-323 B.C.E.
  (English translation, 1797)
Type of work: Philosophy

The *Nicomachean Ethics*, frequently referred to as the *Ethics* or Aristotle's *Ethics*, is Aristotle's best-known work on ethics and is one of the most influential works in Western moral theory. The *Nicomachean Ethics* fits within the tradition of moral inquiry known as virtue ethics because of its emphasis on the importance of developing moral or character virtues in order to be good and achieve happiness. Aristotelian virtue ethics remains one of the three principal forms of moral inquiry, along with duty or rule-based ethics, exemplified in the works of Immanuel Kant (1724-1804), and utilitarian ethics, exemplified in the works of Jeremy Bentham (1748-1832) and John Stuart Mill (1806-1873).

Starting from the premise that every action and discipline is oriented toward some goal or good, Aristotle tries in book 1 of the *Nicomachean Ethics* to determine the goals toward which human life is oriented. In order to find the answer to this question, Aristotle first considers the nature of goals themselves and how an action or discipline is oriented toward a specific goal (for example, the goal of the medical discipline is health). He determines that some disciplines and some goals are more fundamental than others. For instance, the art of bridle-making is subordinate to the art of riding because bridles are made so that horses can be ridden. The highest goal of human life, Aristotle argues, must be that goal to which all other disciplines and goals are subordinated. Based on the common understanding of all people, Aristotle states, this highest good of human life is called *eudaimonia*, which is usually translated as "happiness" but sometimes as "human flourishing" or "excellence" to capture the original Greek term's reference to a state of living and being and not to a subjective feeling. Politics, in turn, is the highest discipline because it aims at happiness; and, Aristotle claims, all other disciplines are subject to it.

Happiness, according to Aristotle, is not something that merely happens. It is stable, objective, and universal. That happiness is stable means that it is not connected to transient feelings and that it is probably impossible to determine whether someone has achieved happiness while he or she is living. That happiness is objective means that people can be wrong when they believe that they have achieved happiness.

That happiness is universal means that it is basically the same sort of thing for all people.

Politics is of central importance to Aristotle because humans are, by nature and not merely by convenience or convention, social animals. Certain schools of philosophy, particularly in modern philosophy, suppose that humans are autonomous creatures with individual rights who come together in community largely to allow for the better defense of those individual rights. Aristotle would have found this emphasis on autonomy and individual rights at odds with humanity's basically social nature. Government is not, for Aristotle, merely a tool for the protection of rights that must be guarded against lest it move beyond its basic peacekeeping function. Government, rather, is a necessary component of the possibility of leading a fully human, and therefore social, life.

Throughout the *Nicomachean Ethics*, Aristotle indicates that the pursuit of happiness should be viewed as a discipline. Medicine, for instance, has both a goal (health) and specific virtues and skills that are necessary for medicine to function properly. Similarly, Aristotle maintains, human life has a goal (happiness) as well as specific virtues that are necessary to the fulfillment of that goal. Aristotle divides the human virtues into moral or character-related virtues (in books 2-5) and intellectual or thinking-related virtues (in book 6). Human virtues, like the skills in any discipline, are achieved and developed through practice—that is, by repeating their corresponding actions (in this case, by repeating virtuous acts). Developing the habit of acting virtuously tends to result in taking pleasure in virtuous acts, which is a sign that the person has acquired the relevant virtue. Since habit provides such a critical part of acting virtuously, the development of moral habits in children is particularly important. Aristotle even indicates that a person will not be able to achieve happiness if he or she has not developed the proper moral habits during childhood. Aristotle also seems to say that people generally will not be able to be virtuous if they have insufficient material resources or lack friends.

While Aristotle points out the importance of moral education and material prosperity, he does not state that good habits, wealth, and friendship are sufficient to achieve happiness. Good habits are sufficient for children, but adults must also have practical wisdom, which is the intellectual virtue associated with knowledge of how to achieve the goals of human life. It is practical wisdom that makes it possible for an individual to determine what is a virtuous act and what are the vices of excess and of defects associated with the virtue. For instance, the moral virtue of courage is the mean between cowardice and rashness, and it is in the exercise of practical wisdom that an individual can know whether a specific action is courageous, cowardly, or rash. This system means that it is generally impossible to determine precisely whether any specific type of act will be virtuous or vicious because, in most situations, the value of the act will depend on the circumstances. However, just as in medicine there are some actions that are always against health and therefore wrong, in life there are some actions that are always against human excellence and therefore wrong.

After considering human virtues in some depth, Aristotle moves to discussions of lack of self-control (book 7), friendship (books 8-9), and pleasure (books 7 and 10), before returning to some final remarks on the nature of happiness (book 10). Scholars remain divided over how to interpret Aristotle's conclusion regarding the nature of happiness. Aristotle mentions various elements, including pleasure or the enjoyment of material goods, the exercise of practical wisdom in political life, and the exercise of theoretical wisdom in contemplation. It is possible to interpret the *Nicomachean Ethics* to mean that the life of contemplation is the way to happiness and the lives of pleasure or politics are deficient. On the other hand, it is possible that the various elements are all intended to be part of every life, but that contemplation is simply the highest of the three elements and the one toward which the enjoyment of material goods and the exercise of practical wisdom should be oriented.

For introductory readers, the *Nicomachean Ethics* poses various challenges, some of which relate to its subject matter and some of which relate to its form and coherence. In regard to form, there are two issues that are particularly worth noting. First, the *Nicomachean Ethics* is a collection of lecture notes. It is not clear who took these notes, nor is it clear precisely what role Aristotle may have had in compiling them. The *Nicomachean Ethics* may be notes that Aristotle wrote or dictated, or they may be notes taken by someone listening to his lectures. Second, it is not clear whether the *Nicomachean Ethics* is actually one work or perhaps a combination of certain notes on ethics that have been consolidated with a portion of another of Aristotle's ethical works, the *Eudemean Ethics*. Scholars do not know which work came first, but they share certain sections in common. These issues regarding the coherence of the text should not be ignored, but they also should not be overly emphasized to introductory readers. There is a remarkable degree of unity in the *Nicomachean Ethics*, and most, even if not all, apparent inconsistencies and ambiguities in Aristotle's meaning can be clarified by a closer reading of the text and, when appropriate, a review of some of the secondary literature.

Joshua A. Skinner

Further Reading

Adler, Mortimer J. *Aristotle for Everybody: Difficult Thought Made Easy.* New York: Macmillan, 1978. Adler is probably the best-known modern popularizer of Aristotle's works. While Adler's book necessarily sacrifices some of the complexity in Aristotle's works, *Aristotle for Everybody* provides a helpful introduction and overview to Aristotle's philosophy.

Englard, Izhak. *Corrective and Distributive Justice: From Aristotle to Modern Times.* New York: Oxford University Press, 2009. This history of ethical thought begins and ends with Aritotle's *Nicomachean Ethics*, which it portrays as the most important work not only in the history of ethics but also for reinventing ethics in the twenty-first century.

Gottlieb, Paula. *The Virtue of Aristotle's Ethics.* New York: Cambridge University Press, 2009. Detailed analysis of Aristotle's moral philosophy focusing on its virtue-oriented nature and on the specific virtues valorized by Aristotle.

Pakaluk, Michael. *Aristotle's "Nicomachean Ethics": An Introduction.* New York: Cambridge University Press, 2005. Probably one of the best full-length introductions to the *Nichomachean Ethics*. The remarkable clarity of the work is undoubtedly assisted by Pakaluk's years of teaching experience. Each chapter provides citations to additional reading material on the topic addressed.

The Nigger of the Narcissus
A Tale of the Sea

Author: Joseph Conrad (1857-1924)
First published: 1897
Type of work: Novel
Type of plot: Symbolic realism
Time of plot: Late nineteenth century
Locale: At sea, between Bombay and London

Principal characters:
JAMES WAIT, a black sailor on the *Narcissus*
DONKIN, a fellow sailor
SINGLETON, another sailor
MR. BAKER, the first mate
CAPTAIN ALLISTOUN, the ship's godlike leader

The Story:

The British freighter *Narcissus* sits in Bombay harbor on a hot, sticky tropical night in the 1890's. Already loaded, it is to sail the next morning on its homeward voyage. The last crew member to come aboard is a huge black man, James Wait. Wait has a severe cough and asks his shipmates to help him in stowing his gear. A little later, the men are in their bunks, and the only sound is snoring, interrupted at times by Wait's fits of coughing.

At daylight, the *Narcissus* sails. That evening, as the sailors gather in little groups about the deck, the laughter and yarn spinning ceases at the sound of a weak rattle in Wait's bunk. It ends with a moan. Wait climbs up on deck, looks about, and makes the men miserable by berating them for making so much noise that he, a dying man, could have no rest. It seems, after a few days, that Wait looks upon his approaching death as a friend. He parades his trouble to everyone, railing bitterly at the salt meat, biscuits, and tea at mealtime.

All the men in the forecastle are touched by the dying man and his fits of coughing. There is nothing that they would not do for him, even stealing pie for him from the officers' mess. Even Donkin, a Cockney who thought that no one was ever right but him, catered to Wait. Wait did no work after they were a week at sea. The first mate finally orders him below to his bunk, and the captain upholds the mate's order. Each morning, the men carry Wait up on deck. Finally, he is put in one of the deckhouse berths. He never lets anyone doubt that his death is imminent. He fascinates the officers and taints the lives of the superstitious sailors, even those who grumble that his illness is a fraud.

As the *Narcissus* approaches the Cape of Good Hope, heavier sails are set, the hatches are checked, and everything loose on deck is securely lashed in place in preparation for the winds that are sure to come. On the thirty-second day out of Bombay, the ship begins to put its nose into the heavy waves, instead of riding over. Gear blows loose, and the men are tossed about the deck. At sunset, all sails are shortened in preparation for a terrific gale. That entire night, nothing seems left in the universe except darkness and the fury of the storm. In the gray morning, half the crew goes below to rest. The remainder of them and the officers of the ship stay on deck. Suddenly, a great wall of water looms out of the mist. The ship rises with it, as a gust of wind lays the vessel on its side. The watch below decks rushes out of the forecastle and crawls aft on hands and knees to join their comrades already on deck. The ship lays on its side for hours, while the men huddle against the various projections on the deck to which they had lashed themselves. At last, someone asks about Wait. Another man shouts that he was trapped in the deckhouse, now half under water, and had drowned, because the heavy wave had jammed the door.

With five volunteers, the boatswain inches forward along the deck to see if Wait might still be alive. Once above the side of the deckhouse, they let go and slide down to it as the backwash of the heavy seas foams around them. They crawl into the carpenter's shop next to the deckhouse cabin. One of the sailors drums on the bulkhead with a piece of iron. When he stops, they hear someone banging on the opposite side. Wait is still alive. He screams for help. Someone on deck finds a crowbar and passes it below. The men in the tiny carpenter's shop batter at the planks until there is a hole in the bulkhead. Wait's head appears in the hole and interrupts the work. Finally, on threat of being brained with the crowbar, he gets out of the way. In another minute or two, the men make a hole large enough to pull him out. With great difficulty, they carry him aft and lash him tight. When he recovers his breath and begins to lose his fear, he berates his rescuers for not being more prompt. The men both hate and pity him.

The day passes into night. The ship still is afloat but with half its deck under water. An icy wind from the Antarctic begins to numb the men who had lain in the open for twenty-four hours without food. At dawn, the captain prepares to bring some order to the ship, for the wind is subsiding. Slowly, the ship begins to turn and gather way, with the decks still half under. At every lurch, the crew expects the ship to slide out from under them and sink to the bottom of the sea; but when the wind is directly aft, the ship rises and is no longer at the mercy of wind and pounding seas.

The sailors are put to work, tired though they are, to make sail, to pump out the bilges, and to make the vessel shipshape once again. Down below, they find the forecastle a ruin. Most of their gear had floated away.

A fair wind pushes the ship northward up the Atlantic under a blue sky and a dancing sea. Wait is again established in the deckhouse. Once more, the doubt that he is really dying pervades the ship, although no one dares say so. The captain interviews him to be sure. The crew is in an ugly mood. The captain is certain the man is dying and refuses to let him go back to work; the crew, however, is convinced that Wait is well enough to share in their labors, and they threaten mutiny. Sure that Wait would die, the captain wants to let him die in peace. He persuades the men that Wait is dying, and their mutterings end.

As the ship sails northward, Wait seems to fade. His cheeks fall in, and his skull loses its flesh; his appearance hypnotizes the crew. Once again pitying him in his dying, they humor his whims. He is always in their talk and their thoughts. The ship seems too small to everyone; they cannot escape death.

As the ship approaches the Flores islands, Wait seems better. The older sailors, however, shake their heads; it is common superstition that dying men on shipboard wait until they are in sight of land to breathe their last. Wait dies as the Flores islands come over the horizon, and he is buried at sea. As the board on which his body lay is lifted to let the corpse slide into the sea, something catches. The men lifting the board hold their breath. Everyone seems in a trance until the corpse slides slowly downward and then plunges over the rail. The ship suddenly seems lighter, as though relieved of the burden of Death itself.

Critical Evaluation:

With *The Nigger of the Narcissus*, Joseph Conrad has constructed a tale that is at once a realistic and a symbolic, even mythic, representation of human life. The sailing ship *Narcissus* serves as a microcosm of society, with its crew forming an isolated cross section of humanity. In this relatively brief novel, Conrad establishes a surprisingly large number of individual characters with fully established personalities that represent the range of human possibilities. Conrad's description of the vessel as "a fragment detached from the earth" accurately summarizes his thematic purpose. The novel implies: These are the basic facts of human existence, and these are the ways in which people respond to their trials and difficulties.

The characters, clearly defined individuals, are also archetypes of personalities and philosophies. Captain Allistoun, the figure at the apex of this narrowly confined nautical society, is described in almost godlike fashion. He appears to see, hear, or notice nothing, but actually he is keenly aware of everything that takes place on the *Narcissus* and, except for the workings of the inexplicable and unmanageable powers of nature, is responsible for everything that takes place aboard his ship. As is often the case with the divine, the captain is sometimes ambiguous in his purpose and intent, and often apparently absent from the action. Throughout most of the voyage, for example, he fails to resolve the dilemma of Wait, refusing to either confirm that the man is dying or condemn him as a malingerer.

Others in the crew play their own particular roles, which often have ironic overtones. Donkin, the master of using language to fool, mislead, and control others, is a lackluster sailor, ultimately despised by his shipmates, but on land he becomes a success among a certain class of society. In contrast, the older man Singleton, an outstanding sailor whose long years of knowledge of the sea have made him almost silent but whose few words are epitomes of wisdom, becomes a sot when ashore.

The most symbolic figure is that of James Wait, the mysterious black sailor who is the last to board the *Narcissus* and who spends the entire voyage lying in his bunk, awaiting and avoiding death. Wait represents the common fate of humanity; all human lives are a wait, while on a journey, for death. In Conrad's fiction, however, meanings are more ambiguous and expansive. Wait's name is a pun upon his allegorical role. As he waits for death, he is a weight upon the *Narcissus* and its crew. His presence imposes a multiple burden on his shipmates. If he is lying about his illness and is merely a malingerer, then they have become his dupes, tricked into humoring a fraud. Should he actually be dying, however, then their doubts are cynical, undeserved accusations against a suffering fellow human being. The crew's inability to resolve its conflicting feelings about Wait generates much internal tension and gives the novel an additional level of suspense.

Wait is more than a bodiless symbol, and much of his mysterious power over the crew stems from Conrad's creation of him as such a realistic and believable individual. This is accomplished most notably with Conrad's careful selection of relevant details in his description of Wait and in his ability to provide Wait with a unique, highly distinctive voice. It is largely through the power of Wait's voice that Wait establishes and holds sway over the crew of the *Narcis-*

sus. Through much of the novel, as Wait lies unseen, his presence is established and his influence felt through voice alone.

Although a relatively early work (published in 1897), *The Nigger of the Narcissus* shows Conrad already possessing considerable artistic abilities, especially in his handling of action and events. The centerpiece of the novel is the dramatic storm scene. The scene flows into the equally compelling rescue of Wait from the wrecked deckhouse. Conrad's sentences, in their syntax and vocabulary, mimic the surging motion and even the sounds of the wind's fierce gusts and the waves' rising and crashing on the *Narcissus*.

This unity of language, action, and theme extends through the novel. At the end, when the *Narcissus* docks in London and the paid-off crew leaves, Conrad describes the ship as "dying," the life ebbing out of it with the departure of the men. The imagery, word choice, and sentence structure combine to present an increasing sense of heaviness, slowness, and, finally, stillness. This progression of the prose mimics and emphasizes the slide of the *Narcissus* into its kind of nautical death.

The most famous part of *The Nigger of the Narcissus*, and the one that has had the greatest critical impact, is Conrad's noted preface to the original edition. Originally, Conrad had intended to place this section at the end of the novel, where it would serve as a sort of epilogue, explaining the general meaning and aim of the book. Upon reflection, however, Conrad seems to have concluded that it should prepare the reader for the story that follows.

In his preface, Conrad calls for a community of readers with whom the writer can communicate, and with whom the author can share some understanding of the "sense of mystery surrounding our lives." To accomplish this, Conrad states, requires the writer to be honestly dedicated to achieving, through hard work, the purest possible creation. A work of art, Conrad insists, "should carry its justification in every line." That is the exacting requirement that Conrad imposed upon himself for *The Nigger of the Narcissus*, and the artistic success of the novel is proof that he achieved that goal.

"Critical Evaluation" by Michael Witkoski

Further Reading

Bloom, Harold, ed. *Joseph Conrad*. New York: Chelsea House, 1986. A selection of critical essays that help place *The Nigger of the Narcissus* within the framework of Conrad's fiction.

Kaplan, Carola M., Peter Mallios, and Andrea White, eds. *Conrad in the Twenty-first Century: Contemporary Approaches and Perspectives*. New York: Routledge, 2005. Collection of essays that analyze Conrad's depiction of postcolonialism, empire, imperialism, and modernism. *The Nigger of the Narcissus* is analyzed in Brian Richardson's essays "Conrad and Posthuman Narration: Fabricating Class and Consciousness on Board the *Narcissus*."

Karl, Frederick R. *A Reader's Guide to Joseph Conrad*. Rev. ed. New York: Syracuse University Press, 1997. An introductory volume, especially helpful in guiding the reader through the actions and activities of the novel and relating them to Conrad's thematic and artistic concerns.

North, Michael. "The *Nigger of the Narcissus* as a Preface to Modernism." In *The Dialect of Modernism: Race, Language, and Twentieth-Century Literature*. New York: Oxford University Press, 1994. This discussion of the novel as a precursor to literary modernism is included in North's study of the role of "racial masquerade" and "linguistic imitation" in the modernist writings.

Peters, John G. *The Cambridge Introduction to Joseph Conrad*. New York: Cambridge University Press, 2006. An introductory overview of Conrad, with information on his life, all of his works, and his critical reception.

Robert, Andrew Michael. *Conrad and Masculinity*. New York: St. Martin's Press, 2000. Uses modern theories about masculinity to analyze Conrad's work and explore the relationship of masculinity to imperialism and modernity. *The Nigger of the Narcissus* is discussed in the chapter entitled "Imperialism and Male Bonds: 'Karain,' *The Nigger of the Narcissus, Lord Jim*."

Schwarz, Daniel R. *Conrad: "Almayer's Folly" to "Under Western Eyes."* Ithaca, N.Y.: Cornell University Press, 1980. Views *The Nigger of the Narcissus* in terms of Conrad's developing style and point of view as an author, relating this growth to his own psychological state.

Winner, Anthony. *Culture and Irony: A Study in Conrad's Major Novels*. Charlottesville: University Press of Virginia, 1988. Although the contrast between East and West is not strongly represented in *The Nigger of the Narcissus*, the dichotomy between the land-based and sea-based views of life gives Conrad ample material in this novel.

Night

Author: Elie Wiesel (1928-   )
First published: Un di Velt hot geshvign, 1956 (English
    translation, 1960)
Type of work: Novel
Type of plot: Historical
Time of plot: 1941-1945
Locale: Eastern Europe

Principal characters:
ELIEZER, a teenage Jewish boy
FATHER of Eliezer
MOSHE THE BEADLE, Eliezer's tutor

The Story:

Eliezer lives with his parents and his three sisters in the village of Sighet in Transylvania. He studies the Talmud, the Jewish holy book, under the tutelage of Moshe the Beadle. Late in 1941, the Hungarian police expel all foreign Jews, including Moshe, from Sighet in cattle cars. Several months later, Moshe returns and informs Eliezer that the deported Jews had been turned over to the German Gestapo and executed in a forest in Poland. Moshe had managed to escape. He had returned to Sighet to warn the Jewish community of what would happen to all Jews if they remained in the area.

Moshe's warning is ignored, and the Jews of Sighet continue with their daily routines. During the Passover celebration of 1944, however, German soldiers arrive in Sighet, arrest Jewish leaders, confiscate the valuables of Jewish townspeople, and force all Jews to live in a restricted section of town. A short time later, all of Sighet's Jews are forced into cattle cars and transported to Auschwitz, the site of a Nazi concentration camp in Poland. On the train ride to Auschwitz, one woman goes mad; in her delirium, she has visions of a huge furnace spewing flames, a foreshadowing of the crematories that would take the lives of many concentration camp inmates.

When they arrive at Auschwitz, Eliezer and his father are separated from his mother and sisters. Many children are led directly toward a crematory, where they are immediately executed. All the men have their heads shaved and a number tattooed on their arms. Eliezer and his fellow captives are forced to live in squalid barracks; they are fed only bread, water, and tasteless broth. Although many of the inmates pray for strength to survive their horrific ordeal, Eliezer ceases to pray, and he begins to doubt God's sense of justice.

A short time later, Eliezer, his father, and hundreds of others are marched to another concentration camp, Buna, where conditions are no better. Eliezer is assigned to work in a warehouse, and he is sometimes beaten by his supervisor. Eliezer's gold-crowned tooth, an article of value to his captors, is removed with a rusty spoon by a concentration camp

dentist. Eliezer is whipped after being caught watching his supervisor having sex with a young Polish girl. During Eliezer's stay at Buna, four inmates are hanged for breaking concentration camp rules. At various times, weak and sick inmates are selected for execution in the crematories.

Eliezer loses his faith. He accuses God of creating the concentration camps and of running its crematories. He refuses to fast on Yom Kippur, the Jewish holy day. Other inmates share Eliezer's sense of despair. One inmate selected for extermination asks his friends to say the Kaddish, the Jewish prayer for the dead, for him, but no one recites the prayer when the man is executed. Eliezer's faith can not sustain him; he survives mainly because of his love and concern for his father, who is weakening with each passing week.

When the Russian army moves toward Buna, Eliezer and his fellow inmates are ordered on a forced march through the snow-covered Polish countryside. The weaker captives who cannot maintain the rapid pace fall by the roadside and die or are shot by the German guards. During one rest stop, dozens of inmates fall dead from exhaustion.

After a long trek, the captives arrive at Gleiwitz, another concentration camp. Eliezer meets Juliek, a boy whom Eliezer had first seen at Auschwitz. Juliek plays the violin, and he had managed to keep the instrument in his possession during his stay in the camps. During Eliezer's first evening at Gleiwitz, Juliek plays Beethoven's Violin Concerto, which moves Eliezer. The next morning, Eliezer sees Juliek's corpse lying on the barracks floor.

A few days later, Eliezer, his father, and hundreds of other inmates are packed into open cattle cars and transported to Buchenwald, another concentration camp. En route, many captives die and are unceremoniously thrown from the train cars; their naked corpses are left unburied in open fields. As the train passes through towns, people throw bread into the open cars, then watch as the prisoners beat and kill each other for food.

By the time the train reaches Buchenwald, Eliezer's father is seriously ill with dysentery. Eliezer keeps a vigil at his father's bedside. A guard hits Eliezer's father in the head when he asks for water. The next day, when Eliezer awakes, his father is gone; he had been taken to the crematory and put to death.

Eliezer lives for about three months at Buchenwald. In April, 1945, as the war nears its end, an evacuation of Buchenwald is announced. An air raid postpones the planned evacuation. Several days later, members of a resistance movement in the camp decide to act. After a brief battle, the German guards depart, leaving the camp in the hands of the resistance leaders. Later that day, an American tank approaches the gates of Buchenwald and liberates the camp.

Three days after the liberation of Buchenwald, Eliezer is hospitalized with food poisoning. In the hospital, he looks at a mirror and sees the face of a corpse staring back at him.

Critical Evaluation:

Night, the first novel of Elie Wiesel's trilogy on Holocaust concentration camp survivors, is an autobiographical novel that records the author's own long night of captivity in the Nazi death camps during World War II. Like Eliezer, the novel's narrator, Wiesel was forced from his own village into Auschwitz, became separated from his mother and sisters, witnessed his father's slow decline and death, and was eventually liberated at the end of the war.

Although the powerful tale told in *Night* is deeply personal, Eliezer's narrative can also be viewed as the story of all European Jews who suffered during the reign of Adolf Hitler. When Eliezer admonishes the Jews of Sighet for their refusal to heed the warnings of Moshe the Beadle, when he questions why his fellow Jewish citizens passively follow the orders of their German captors, when he asks why God lets thousands of Jews be put to death Eliezer becomes a Jewish Everyman struggling in anguish to understand the most troubling chapter in his people's history.

The process by which Eliezer begins to doubt God and eventually lose his faith reflects the experience of many Jews during and after the Holocaust. Seeing three concentration camp inmates hanging from a gallows, Eliezer reasons that God, too, has been hanged. During a Rosh Hashanah prayer ceremony, Eliezer asks why he should bless God: "Because He had had thousands of children burned in His pits? Because He kept six crematories working night and day, on Sundays and feast days? Because in his great might He had created Auschwitz?"

Eliezer's story is a cruel reversal of Exodus, the Old Testament epic of liberation and triumph. It is during the feast of Passover, when Jews celebrate the passing of the Angel of Death over their homes and their subsequent liberation from Egypt, that German soldiers begin arresting the Jewish leaders of Sighet. Exodus records the journey of God's chosen people toward a promised land provided by God; *Night* depicts the journey of a people selected for extermination entering into an oppressive captivity in the Nazi death camps. In the face of their trials, the chosen people of Exodus had united; on the other hand, the Jews depicted in *Night* often turn on one another, fighting, and even killing for food. To Wiesel, Hitler's Holocaust nullifies the triumph of Exodus. The Jews of Wiesel's time are faithless, despairing survivors of a long night of captivity; they are not fulfilled travelers who have reached their promised land.

Eliezer's camp is liberated at the end of *Night*, but he does not believe that freedom has been provided by the God of Exodus. Buchenwald is freed only when the camp's resistance movement takes up arms against its Nazi captors. The symbol of freedom is an American tank arriving at Buchenwald's gates. Eliezer is no longer a captive at the end of the novel, but Wiesel offers no hint of any physical or spiritual rebirth. The novel's final image is of Eliezer looking into a mirror and seeing a corpse stare back at him. *Night* is the tale of painful death, not of liberation and rebirth.

The narrating of this harrowing tale presented problems for its author. Wiesel, indeed any writer who tries to depict the horrors of the Holocaust, has to put into words a sequence of terrible events that can never be adequately rendered in language. No description of the Nazi death camps, no matter how skillfully and realistically narrated, can fully depict the terrors that millions of people experienced during World War II. Wiesel and other Holocaust survivors nevertheless felt compelled to record their stories for their contemporaries and for history, and in its plot, characterization, and prose strategies *Night* is a literary work of the highest order.

Wiesel narrates the events of his captivity in a series of vignettes suited to the story of separation, annihilation, and loss. Few of Wiesel's characters are substantially developed; Eliezer and his father are the novel's only well-rounded characters. This strategy is, however, well suited for a book that deals with the marginalization, suppression, and elimination of individuals. Wiesel's prose style is terse and often understated. Eliezer rarely editorializes in *Night*; he prefers to tell his story in lean, taut prose, allowing the events of the novel to speak for themselves.

Wiesel continued to explore the lives of Holocaust survivors in *L'Aube* (1960; *Dawn*, 1961) and *Le Jour* (1961; *The Accident*, 1962), the next two novels in the trilogy begun with *Night*, and in more than a dozen subsequent novels, nonfiction works, and plays. With *Night*, Wiesel became a spokesperson for all those who suffered during Hitler's reign. He was one of the first Holocaust survivors to record his experiences, and he made the rest of the world aware of the horrors that had been perpetrated by Hitler in his campaign to exterminate European Jewry. In 1986, Wiesel received the Nobel Peace Prize for serving as a "messenger to mankind" and as "one of our most important spiritual leaders and guides."

James Tackach

Further Reading

Bloom, Harold, ed. *Elie Wiesel's "Night."* Philadelphia: Chelsea House, 2001. Collection of critical essays, several by Holocaust scholars, interpreting Wiesel's depiction of this event.

Cargas, Harry James. *Conversations with Elie Wiesel.* South Bend, Ind.: Justice Books, 1992. A collection of interviews with the author that cover his life, politics, and literary works. Wiesel speaks frankly and extensively about his childhood in Sighet and his time in the concentration camps—events that formed the basis for *Night.*

Estess, Ted L. *Elie Wiesel.* New York: Frederick Ungar, 1980. An analysis of Wiesel's key literary works, including *Night, Dawn,* and *The Accident. Night* receives extended discussion in chapter 2.

Fine, Ellen S. *Legacy of Night: The Literary Universe of Elie Wiesel.* Albany: State University of New York Press, 1982. A critical study of *Night* and Wiesel's other Holocaust works.

Horowitz, Rosemary, ed. *Elie Wiesel and the Art of Storytelling.* Jefferson, N.C.: McFarland, 2006. Examines the form and content of Wiesel's storytelling and how he uses his stories as a form of activism. Analyzes his roots in the Jewish storytelling tradition and the other influences upon his works. The references to *Night* are listed in the index.

Rittner, Carol, ed. *Elie Wiesel: Between Memory and Hope.* New York: New York University Press, 1990. A collection of seventeen essays on Wiesel's life and literary works. *Night* receives an extended discussion in three essays and is mentioned in several others.

Rosen, Alan, ed. *Approaches to Teaching Wiesel's "Night."* New York: Modern Language Association of America, 2007. Contains essays providing numerous interpretations of *Night* that can be used to teach students about the book and the Holocaust. Includes discussions of the work's Jewish background, the book in its original Yiddish text and context, a comparison of *Night* with Holocaust literature by Hungarian writer Imre Kertész, *Night* and spiritual autobiography, and a close reading of chapter 1.

Walker, Graham B., Jr. *Elie Wiesel: A Challenge to Theology.* Jefferson, N.C.: McFarland, 1988. Focuses on Wiesel's religious dilemmas as they are reflected in his major literary works.

Night Flight

Author: Antoine de Saint-Exupéry (1900-1944)
First published: Vol de nuit, 1931 (English translation, 1932)
Type of work: Novel
Type of plot: Psychological realism
Time of plot: Early 1930's
Locale: South America

Principal characters:
RIVIÈRE, director of the airmail service
ROBINEAU, the inspector
FABIEN, the lost pilot
MADAME FABIEN, his wife
PELLERIN, a pilot
ROBLET, a former pilot
THE WIRELESS OPERATOR

The Story:

Fabien, along with his wireless operator, is flying at sunset, bringing the mail from Patagonia to Buenos Aires. Two other mail planes, one from Chile and one from Paraguay, are also headed for Buenos Aires, where another plane was to take off, at about two in the morning, with a cargo of South American mail intended for Europe. Fabien's wireless operator, hearing reports of storms ahead, urges Fabien to land in San Julian for the night; but Fabien, looking at the clear sky and the first stars, refuses and heads for Buenos Aires.

At Buenos Aires, Rivière, the head of the mail service, is

pacing the airport. Worried about the safety of his three planes, he is pleased when the plane from Chile lands safely early in the evening. Pellerin, the pilot of the plane from Chile, tells of flying through a great storm in the Andes. Although Pellerin had not experienced great difficulty, he is still shaken by his experience. Both men seem certain, at this point, that the storm would not cross the Andes. Robineau, the inspector at Buenos Aires, somewhat resentful of Rivière's severity and unwillingness to relax discipline, reveals more pity for Pellerin's experience than Rivière had shown. Robineau goes out to dinner with Pellerin, a meal over which they chat about women and domestic concerns, away from the tension of the airfield.

When Robineau returns to the field, Rivière criticizes him for making a friend of Pellerin. Rivière points out that supervisors, who had to order men to what might be their deaths, could not become friendly with the men under them; the supervisors had to maintain discipline and impersonality, because the success of the project, the conquest of space at night, depends on firm and immediate control. Rivière, although mastering the pain in his own side only with great difficulty, maintains severe discipline on the airfield at all times. He deprives pilots of bonuses if planes are not on time, no matter what the reason; he disciplines old Roblet severely for any minor infraction, even though Roblet had been the first man in Argentina to assemble a plane; he fires an electrician for some faulty wiring in a plane.

The wife of the pilot who was to fly from Buenos Aires to Europe receives a phone call. She awakens her husband, and he prepares for the flight. She is aware, as he is dressing, that he is already part of another world, that he has already lost interest in home, domesticity, herself. He then reports to Rivière, who reprimands him for turning back on a previous flight. Rivière is severe, although he silently admires the man's skill.

Meanwhile, the plane from Patagonia, piloted by Fabien, enters a violent storm. As the storm becomes more serious, Fabien tries to find a place to land, for he can see nothing; but all the airfields nearby are completely closed down by the storm. Rivière gets more and more concerned. Unable to contact Fabien by radio, he alerts police and emergency services throughout the country. Fabien's wife of only six weeks, accustomed to having him arrive for dinner by a certain hour, telephones the airfield. Rivière, feeling strong emotion, tries to reassure her that all will be well, but knows he cannot honestly say so.

When Fabien, in deep distress and thinking he might try a crash landing, throws out his only landing flare, he finds that he has been blown off course by the storm and is now over the ocean. He turns sharply west. After a time, he notices a clearing above and climbs to it. The storm is still solid beneath him, however, and he cannot find an airfield open for a landing. He has gas for only thirty minutes of flight. Buenos Aires informs him that the storm covers the whole interior of the country and that no airfield within thirty minutes' flying time is open. Rivière, realizing that Fabien cannot fly to safety, can only hope for a lucky crash landing through the storm.

Madame Fabien, distraught, arrives at the airfield. Rivière, knowing that he cannot comfort her, is too wise to try, but he sympathizes with her distress as he tries to explain the enormous effort it takes to conquer the skies. He does not speak melodramatically to her; rather, he is matter-of-fact, and they understand each other.

At last, they receive a blurred message from Fabien reporting that he is coming down and entering the rain clouds. They do not know whether the fuel has already run out or he is attempting to glide the plane through the storm to some safe spot.

In the meantime, the plane from Paraguay arrives safely, just skirting the edge of the storm. Robineau watches Rivière closely enough to realize that Rivière is enormously concerned, that his sense of discipline is not callousness but a dedicated sense of the purpose in his mission. Robineau comes into Rivière's office with some papers and, for a moment, there is a sense of understanding, of communion, between the two men.

As time passes, everyone realizes that Fabien is lost. Although some sign of him might still turn up the next day, there is nothing to do now and little hope that he and his wireless operator will be found alive. The pilot of the plane from Paraguay passes the pilot of the plane going to Europe. They exchange a few words about Fabien, but there is no sentimentality, for the pilots realize the necessity of carrying on with a minimum of expressed emotion. Rivière feels that this loss might be used as evidence to encourage the government to curtail nighttime flying operations. At the same time, he believes strongly that these operations must continue, that humanity must, in spite of disaster, carry on. He orders the next plane to take off on schedule.

Critical Evaluation:

Antoine de Saint-Exupéry's *Night Flight* achieved considerable critical praise when it was first published in 1931. The preface by André Gide gave Saint-Exupéry's work the imprimatur of the Parisian literary establishment. Critical reviews of the work were overwhelmingly positive, and Saint-Exupéry was awarded one of France's premier literary awards, the Fémina Prize, for this novel.

Night Flight is Saint-Exupéry's second novel (*Courrier sud* was published in 1929; *Southern Mail*, 1933), and is the author's most completely realized work of fiction, although, as with all of his writings, there are strong autobiographical elements. It is brief in scope, covering just a few hours in time, and brief in length, less than 150 pages in the original French edition. The author's style and literary technique combine poetic elements, particularly Fabien's struggles in the storm and in the starry skies above the clouds, with a lean, crisp narrative. The story is told in brief chapters that successfully move the narrative along by focusing on the protagonists one at a time and by including flashbacks, brief conversational dialogues, interior monologues, and the use of radio reports and telegrams. The Argentina locale is almost irrelevant; the events could have occurred anywhere.

What Gide admired in *Night Flight* was the heroism exhibited by Fabien and his fellow pilots in the line of duty. Flying was both dangerous and glamorous in the early twentieth century. America's Charles Lindbergh captured the world's attention in 1927 when he flew nonstop from New York to Paris. Saint-Exupéry himself was famous for his exploits in aviation in Africa and South America. The pilots in *Night Flight* rise to what Gide called "superhuman heights of valor." The novel was highly praised in part because of its assertion that humanity could strive to overcome not only nature's challenges in the form of mountains, seas, and storms, but also the weaknesses of human nature, not the least of which are fear and doubt. Fabien could have safely set down in advance of the worst of the storm, but he chose to continue his flight. Civilization in general, and France in particular, had succumbed to cynicism and apathy in the aftermath of the losses—physical, intellectual, and emotional—resulting from World War I. Saint-Exupéry's novel was a reassertion of human nobility.

For all of the pilots' bravery, however, at the center of *Night Flight* is Rivière, the chief operator. Modeled on Saint-Exupéry's first airmail flight supervisor, Didier Daurat, Rivière is the will behind the act. It is he who sends Fabien and the others into the night skies and it is he who keeps them there. He is the one who brings out the superhuman qualities noted by Gide. Fifty years of age and worried about his health, Rivière is the opposite of the clichéd version of the young and handsome hero, but he dominates this novel of heroism.

In brief conversations and in extended internal musings, Rivière ruminates about himself, his power, his responsibilities, and his duty. "For him," the novel relates, "a man was a mere lump of wax to be kneaded into shape. . . . Not that his aim was to make slaves of his men; his aim was to raise them above themselves." He loves his men, both pilots and ground staff, but he dares not show that love, or even pity. He questions whether he is too demanding, too critical, but the harder he is, the fewer accidents they have. Rivière's qualities of vision and leadership are brilliantly contrasted with the limitations and inadequacies of Robineau, the self-pitying inspector, who, Rivière claims, lacks even the capacity to think.

Night Flight also poses philosophical questions, most notably why human beings like Fabien must die for a cause, such as proving that flying at night is not only feasible but necessary. The two women in the work, Fabien's wife and the wife of the unnamed pilot who is supposed to continue to carry the mail to Europe, represent the reverse of superhuman striving. Intimate love, personal happiness, and comforting domestic life and values are placed in opposition to the qualities of duty, will, and challenge presented by night flying. Rivière finds it difficult even to meet with Fabien's wife; the gulf between their two realities is too wide. He admits that the ideals she represents might be of equal value to the ones he does, but contends that love and domestic tranquillity are not enough, that there is something higher than individual human life, noting the Incas of Peru who left their monuments of stone as testimony to a vanished world.

It is not even the goal, however, that ultimately matters. It is the progress toward that end, the striving itself, that means the most. Fabien's plane crashes, but the other two planes arrive safely and the European mail is dispatched on time. Because of Rivière's will, death and defeat are overcome, the human spirit is victorious. A momentary transcendence has been achieved.

By the end of the 1930's, Saint-Exupéry's emphasis upon the power of will and the obligations of duty had been perversely achieved in fascism, and to some readers *Night Flight* prefigured those fascist qualities. Today, the antihero has become the norm, and traditional heroic qualities have become suspect. In the early 1930's, however, during the height of the Great Depression and in the aftermath of the Great War, qualities of will and duty did not belong only to the fascists but also to democratic leaders such as Franklin D. Roosevelt, who claimed that the only thing to be feared was fear itself, that great deeds could be achieved through the combination of will and action.

Saint-Exupéry's *Night Flight* can be compared to other literary works. Charles Lindbergh's *The Spirit of St. Louis* (1953) concerns Lindbergh's nonstop flight across the Atlantic Ocean. Tom Wolfe's *The Right Stuff* (1979) chronicles the early days of space flight. However, the most apt comparison to *Night Flight* might be with Ernest Hemingway's *The Old*

Man and the Sea (1952). Both novels magnificently evoke natural elements, and, in both, the apparent defeat—the loss of the great fish, the death of Fabien—ends in humanity's triumph.

"Critical Evaluation" by Eugene Larson

Further Reading

Cate, Curtis. *Antoine de Saint-Exupéry: His Life and Times.* New York: G. P. Putnam's Sons, 1970. Born in France and educated in England and America, Cate wrote the first major biography of Saint-Exupéry in English. The author comments extensively on the airman's literary works.

DeRamus, Barnett. *From Juby to Arras: Engagement in Saint-Exupéry.* Lanham, Md.: University Press of America, 1990. Examines four of Saint-Exupéry's works, including *Night Flight*, focusing on his views of engagement, or commitment, to the major themes of nature, the desert, flight, and the enemy. Discusses the influence of World War I on Saint-Exupéry's postwar writing and analyzes the role of airplanes and flight in the literature of the 1920's and 1930's.

Des Vallieres, Nathalie. *Saint-Exupéry: Art, Writing, and Musings.* New York: Rizzoli International, 2004. Des Vallieres, Saint-Exupéry's great-niece, compiled this collection of Saint-Exupéry's photographs, letters, drawings, and private notebooks, which recount the writer's life in both words and images.

Migeo, Marcel. *Saint-Exupéry.* Translated by Herma Briffault. New York: McGraw-Hill, 1960. Shortly after the end of World War II, in the course of researching the life of Saint-Exupéry, the author interviewed Didier Daurat, the inspiration for Rivière.

Robinson, Joy D. Marie. *Antoine de Saint-Exupéry.* Boston: Twayne, 1984. Explores the philosophies and themes that underlie all Saint-Exupéry's works. The study is enriched by the extensive use of biographical material. Includes a chronology and a selected bibliography of English and French sources. Essential for any literary discussion of Saint-Exupéry.

Rumbold, Richard, and Lady Margaret Stewart. *The Winged Life: A Portrait of Antoine de Saint-Exupéry, Poet and Airman.* New York: David McKay, 1953. Written by a World War II Royal Air Force pilot and the daughter of a former secretary of air in the British cabinet, the work is a sympathetic study of the famous French pilot.

Schiff, Stacy. *Saint-Exupéry: A Biography.* New York: Knopf, 1994. This well-written biography explores the connection between Saint-Exupéry the pilot and Saint-Exupéry the writer. It includes a comprehensive discussion of the circumstances and influences surrounding *Night Flight*.

Smith, Maxwell A. *Knight of the Air.* London: Cassell, 1959. The author of this work concentrates not only on Saint-Exupéry's life but also, more specifically, on his literary works, including an excellent analysis of *Night Flight*.